Lecture Notes in Computer Science 9995

Formal Methods

Subline of Lectures Notes in Computer Science

More information about this series at http://www.springer.com/series/7408

John Fitzgerald · Constance Heitmeyer
Stefania Gnesi · Anna Philippou (Eds.)

FM 2016: Formal Methods

21st International Symposium
Limassol, Cyprus, November 9–11, 2016
Proceedings

Editors
John Fitzgerald
Newcastle University
Newcastle upon Tyne
UK

Stefania Gnesi
ISTI-CNR
Pisa
Italy

Constance Heitmeyer
US Naval Research Laboratory
Washington, DC
USA

Anna Philippou
University of Cyprus
Nicosia
Cyprus

ISSN 0302-9743 ISSN 1611-3349 (electronic)
Lecture Notes in Computer Science
ISBN 978-3-319-48988-9 ISBN 978-3-319-48989-6 (eBook)
DOI 10.1007/978-3-319-48989-6

Library of Congress Control Number: 2016956000

LNCS Sublibrary: SL2 – Programming and Software Engineering

Printed on acid-free paper

This Springer imprint is published by Springer Nature
The registered company is Springer International Publishing AG
The registered company address is: Gewerbestrasse 11, 6330 Cham, Switzerland

Preface

Over nearly three decades since its foundation in 1987, the "FM" Symposium has become a central part of the intellectual and social life of the Formal Methods community. We are therefore delighted to present the proceedings of FM 2016, the 21st symposium in the series, held in Limassol, Cyprus, during November 9–11, 2016. Throughout these years, Springer has supported the symposium through its *Lecture Notes in Computer Science* (LNCS) series. It is therefore with particular pleasure that we present this year's proceedings as the first volume in the new LNCS subline on Formal Methods. The creation of this subline reflects the maturity and growing significance of the discipline.

The 2016 symposium received 162 submissions to the main track – the largest number of contributions to a regular symposium in the FM series to date. Review of each submission by at least three Program Committee members followed by a discussion phase led to the selection of 43 papers – an acceptance rate of 0.265. These proceedings also contain six papers selected by the Program Committee of the Industry Track chaired by Georgia Kapitsaki (University of Cyprus), Tiziana Margaria (University of Limerick and Lero, Ireland), and Marcel Verhoef (European Space Agency, The Netherlands).

We were honored that three of the most creative and respected members of our community – Manfred Broy (Technical University of Munich), Peter O'Hearn (University College London, and Facebook), and Jan Peleska (University of Bremen and Verified Software International) – accepted our invitation to give keynote presentations at the symposium. Also scheduled during FM 2016 were four workshops selected by the Workshop Chairs, Nearchos Paspallis (University of Central Lancashire in Cyprus) and Martin Steffen (University of Oslo), eight tutorials selected by the Tutorial Chairs, Dimitrios Kouzapas (Glasgow University) and Oleg Sokolsky (University of Pennsylvania), and eight papers to be presented at a Doctoral Symposium organized by Andrew Butterfield (Trinity College Dublin) and Matteo Rossi (Politecnico di Milano). The resulting FM 2016 program reflects the breadth and vibrancy of both research and practice in formal methods today.

As in previous years, FM 2016 attracted submissions from all over the world: 299 authors from 22 European countries, 126 authors from eight Asian countries, 64 authors from North America, 24 authors from five countries in South America, 16 authors from Australia and New Zealand, and five authors from two African countries, Algeria and Tunisia. The largest number of authors from a single country were from China (58), the second largest number of authors came from France (56), the third largest number of authors were from the UK (53), and the fourth largest number of authors were from the USA (45).

Last year, the FM community mourned the passing of Prof. Peter Lucas, a former chair of the FME Association and a founding figure of the formal methods discipline.

This year, as a symposium highlight, we celebrated Peter's achievements by presenting the first Lucas Award for a highly influential paper in formal methods.

We are grateful to all involved in FM 2016, particularly the Program Committee members, subreviewers, and other committee chairs. The excellent local organization and publicity groups, chaired by Yannis Dimopoulos, Chryssis Georgiou, and George Papadopoulos (University of Cyprus), deserve special thanks.

Much of the symposium's activity would be impossible without the support of our sponsors. We gratefully acknowledge the support of: Springer, the Cyprus Tourism Organization, the University of Cyprus, and DiffBlue.

September 2016

John S. Fitzgerald
Stefania Gnesi
Constance Heitmeyer
Program Co-chairs

Anna Philippou
General Chair

Organization

Program Committee

Erika Abraham	RWTH Aachen University, Germany
Bernhard K. Aichernig	TU Graz, Austria
Myla Archer	Naval Research Laboratory, USA
Gilles Barthe	IMDEA Software Institute, Spain
Nikolaj Bjorner	Microsoft Research, USA
Michael Butler	University of Southampton, UK
Andrew Butterfield	Trinity College, University of Dublin, Ireland
Ana Cavalcanti	University of York, UK
David Clark	UCL, UK
Frank De Boer	CWI, The Netherlands
Ewen Denney	SGT/NASA Ames, USA
Jin Song Dong	National University of Singapore, Singapore
Javier Esparza	Technical University of Munich, Germany
John Fitzgerald	Newcastle University, UK
Vijay Ganesh	University of Waterloo, Canada
Diego Garbervetsky	Universidad de Buenos Aires, Argentina
Dimitra Giannakopoulou	NASA Ames, USA
Stefania Gnesi	ISTI-CNR, Italy
Wolfgang Grieskamp	Google, USA
Arie Gurfinkel	University of Waterloo, Canada
Anne E. Haxthausen	Technical University of Denmark, Denmark
Ian Hayes	University of Queensland, Australia
Constance Heitmeyer	Naval Research Laboratory, USA
Thai-Son Hoang	University of Southampton, UK
Jozef Hooman	TNO-ESI and Radboud University Nijmegen, The Netherlands
Laura Humphrey	Air Force Research Laboratory, USA
Ralf Huuck	UNSW/SYNOPSYS, Australia
Fuyuki Ishikawa	National Institute of Informatics, Japan
Einar Broch Johnsen	University of Oslo, Norway
Cliff Jones	Newcastle University, UK
Georgia Kapitsaki	University of Cyprus, Cyprus
Joost-Pieter Katoen	RWTH Aachen University, Germany
Gerwin Klein	NICTA and UNSW, Australia
Laura Kovacs	Vienna University of Technology, Austria
Thomas Kropf	Bosch, Germany
Peter Gorm Larsen	Aarhus University, Denmark

Thierry Lecomte	ClearSy, France
Yves Ledru	Université Grenoble Alpes, France
Rustan Leino	Microsoft Research, USA
Elizabeth Leonard	Naval Research Laboratory, USA
Martin Leucker	University of Lübeck, Germany
Michael Leuschel	University of Düsseldorf, Germany
Zhiming Liu	Southwest University, China
Tiziana Margaria	University of Limerick and Lero, Ireland
Mieke Massink	CNR-ISTI, Italy
Annabelle McIver	Macquarie University, Australia
Dominique Mery	Université de Lorraine, LORIA, France
Peter Müller	ETH Zürich, Switzerland
Tobias Nipkow	TU München, Germany
Jose Oliveira	Universidade do Minho, Portugal
Olaf Owe	University of Oslo, Norway
Sam Owre	SRI International, USA
Anna Philippou	University of Cyprus, Cyprus
Nico Plat	Thanos and West IT Solutions, The Netherlands
Elvinia Riccobene	University of Milan, Italy
Judi Romijn	Movares, The Netherlands
Grigore Rosu	University of Illinois at Urbana-Champaign, USA
Andreas Roth	SAP Research, Germany
Augusto Sampaio	Federal University of Pernambuco, Brazil
Gerardo Schneider	Chalmers University of Gothenburg, Sweden
Natasha Sharygina	University of Lugano, Switzerland
Marjan Sirjani	Reykjavik University, Iceland
Ana Sokolova	University of Salzburg, Austria
Jun Sun	Singapore University of Technology and Design, Singapore
Kenji Taguchi	AIST, Japan
Stefano Tonetta	FBK-irst, Italy
Marcel Verhoef	European Space Agency, The Netherlands
Aneta Vulgarakis	Ericsson, Sweden
Alan Wassyng	McMaster University, Canada
Heike Wehrheim	University of Paderborn, Germany
Michael Whalen	University of Minnesota, USA
Jim Woodcock	University of York, UK
Fatiha Zaidi	University of Paris-Sud, France
Gianluigi Zavattaro	University of Bologna, Italy
Jian Zhang	Chinese Academy of Sciences, China
Lijun Zhang	Chinese Academy of Sciences, China

Additional Reviewers

Aestasuain, Fernando
Aguirre, Nazareno
Ait Ameur, Yamine
Almeida, José Bacelar
Alt, Leonardo
Ambrona, Miguel
Andronick, June
Antignac, Thibaud
Arcaini, Paolo
Arming, Sebastian
Asadi, Sepideh
Azadbakht, Keyvan
Bagheri, Maryam
Bai, Guangdong
Bak, Stanley
Bandur, Victor
Bartocci, Ezio
Basile, Davide
Bertrand, Nathalie
Berzish, Murphy
Bonacina, Maria Paola
Bornat, Richard
Bourke, Timothy
Braghin, Chiara
Bravetti, Mario
Bright, Curtis
Bubel, Richard
Calinescu, Radu
Carvalho, Gustavo
Cassez, Franck
Castaño, Rodrigo
Chawdhary, Aziem
Chen, Xiaohong
Chen, Xin
Ciancia, Vincenzo
Ciriani, Valentina
Colom, José Manuel
Colvin, Robert
Cremers, Cas
Dalvandi, Mohammadsadegh
Dang, Thao
Decker, Normann
Dehnert, Christian
Delzanno, Giorgio
Demasi, Ramiro
Dghaym, Dana
Dimovski, Aleksandar S.
Dobrikov, Ivaylo
Dodds, Mike
Donat-Bouillud, Pierre
Dong, Naipeng
Dutertre, Bruno
Díaz, Gregorio
Engelmann, Björn
Fantechi, Alessandro
Fedyukovich, Grigory
Fokkink, Wan
Foster, Simon
Fox, Anthony
Freitas, Leo
Ghassabani, Elaheh
Habli, Ibrahim
Herbelin, Hugo
Heunen, Chris
Holzer, Andreas
Huisman, Marieke
Hyvärinen, Antti
Höfner, Peter
Immler, Fabian
Inoue, Jun
Jacob, Jeremy
Jafari, Ali
Jakobs, Marie-Christine
Jansen, Nils
Jegoure, Cyrille
Johansen, Christian
Junges, Sebastian
Katis, Andreas
Khamespanah, Ehsan
Kotelnikov, Evgenii
Kremer, Gereon
Kretinsky, Jan
Krämer, Julia Désirée
Kumar, Ramana
Laarman, Alfons
Lallali, Mounir

Lanese, Ivan
Laporte, Vincent
Li, Qin
Li, Xiaoshan
Li, Ximeng
Lienhardt, Michael
Lochau, Malte
Luttenberger, Michael
Ma, Feifei
Macedo, Hugo Daniel
Macedo, Nuno
Mallouli, Wissam
Marescotti, Matteo
Markin, Grigory
Martinelli, Fernan
Matheja, Christoph
Matichuk, Daniel
Mattarei, Cristian
Melgratti, Hernan
Melquiond, Guillaume
Menéndez, Héctor
Mohaqeqi, Morteza
Mori, Akira
Mota, Alexandre
Mu, Chunyan
Mu, Kedian
Nakata, Akio
Nejati, Saeed
Nguyen, Huu Nghia
Nogueira, Sidney C.
Núñez, Manuel
Olmedo, Federico
Park, Daejun
Pavese, Esteban
Perez, Gervasio
Petke, Justyna
Plat, Nico
Popescu, Andrei
Prabhakar, Pavithra
Proenca, Jose
Rabehaja, Tahiry
Radoi, Cosmin
Rakamaric, Zvonimir
Ratschan, Stefan
Ray, Sayak
Rezazadeh, Abdolbaghi
Ritter, Eike
Rizkallah, Christine
Robillard, Simon
Sangnier, Arnaud
Savicks, Vitaly
Scheffel, Torben
Schoepe, Daniel
Schumi, Richard
Schupp, Stefan
Serbanuta, Traian Florin
Sharifi, Zeinab
Shaver, Chris
Shi, Ling
Silva, Alexandra
Singh, Neeraj
Smetsers, Rick
Smith, Graeme
Snook, Colin
Spagnolo, Giorgio Oronzo
Spoletini, Paola
Stefanescu, Andrei
Steffen, Martin
Steinhorst, Sebastian
Strub, Pierre-Yves
Subramanyan, Pramod
Suda, Martin
Summers, Alexander J.
Sun, Meng
T. Vasconcelos, Vasco
Tan, Tian Huat
Tappler, Martin
Teixeira, Leopoldo
Ter Beek, Maurice H.
Thoma, Daniel
Thüm, Thomas
Timm, Nils
Tiwari, Ashish
Toews, Manuel
Travkin, Oleg
Urban, Caterina
Vafeiadis, Viktor
Van Eijck, Jan
Varshosaz, Mahsa
Velykis, Andrius
Voelzer, Hagen
Voisin, Frederic

Volk, Matthias
Wilkinson, Toby
Wimmer, Ralf
Winter, Kirsten
Wolff, Burkhart
Wong, Peter
Wu, Xi
Wu, Zhilin
Yadav, Maneesh
Yamagata, Yoriyuki
Yatapanage, Nisansala
Yovine, Sergio
Yu, Ingrid Chieh
Zeyda, Frank
Zhao, Hengjun
Zhao, Liang
Zoppi, Edgardo
Zulkoski, Ed

Abstracts of Invited Talks

A Logical Approach to Systems Engineering Artifacts: Semantic Relationships and Dependencies beyond Traceability - From Requirements to Functional and Architectural Views

Manfred Broy

Institut für Informatik, Technische Universität München, 80290 Munich, Germany

Abstract. Not only system assurance drives a need for semantically richer relationships across various artifacts, work products, and items of information than are implied in the terms "trace and traceability" as used in current standards and textbooks. This paper deals with the task of working out artifacts in software and system development, their representation, and the analysis and documentation of the relationships between their logical contents - herein referred to as tracing and traceability; this is a richer meaning of traceability than in standards like IEEE STD 830. Among others, key tasks in system development are as follows: capturing, analyzing, and documenting system level requirements, the step to functional system specifications, the step to architectures given by the decomposition of systems into subsystems with their connections and behavioral interactions. Each of these steps produces artifacts for documenting the development, as a basis for a specification and a design rationale, for documentation, for verification, and impact analysis of change requests. Crucial questions are how to represent and formalize the content of these artifacts and how to relate their content to support, in particular, system assurance. When designing multifunctional systems, key artifacts are system level requirements, functional specifications, and architectures in terms of their subsystem specifications. Links and traces between these artifacts are introduced to relate their contents. Traceability has the goal to relate artifacts. It is required for instance in standards for functional system safety such as the ISO 26262. An approach to specify semantic relationships is shown, such that the activity of creating and using (navigating through) these relationships can be supported with automation.

Moving Fast with Program Verification Technology

Peter W. O'Hearn

Facebook

Abstract. Catching bugs early in the development process improves software quality and saves developer time. At Facebook, we are building Infer (fbinfer.com), an open-source static analyzer for Android, iOS, and C++ code which has its roots in program verification research. In this talk, I will discuss the challenges we have faced in developing techniques that can cope with Facebook's scale and velocity, the challenges of different modes of deployment, and some lessons we have learned that might be relevant to formal methods research. Most importantly, adapting to Facebook's fast-paced engineering culture – illustrated by the "Move Fast and Break Things" and similar posters adorning its office walls – has taught us that if verification technology can move fast, in tune with programmers' workow, then it will fix more things.

Industrial-Strength Model-Based Testing of Safety-Critical Systems

Jan Peleska[1,2(✉)] and Wen-ling Huang[2]

[1] Verified Systems International GmbH, Bremen, Germany
[2] Department of Mathematics and Computer Science, University of Bremen, Bremen, Germany
{jp,huang}@cs.uni-bremen.de

Abstract. In this article we present an industrial-strength approach to automated model-based testing. This approach is applied by Verified Systems International GmbH in safety-critical verification and validation projects in the avionic, railway, and automotive domains. The SysML modelling formalism is used for creating test models. Associating SysML with a formal behavioural semantics allows for full automation of the whole work flow, as soon as the model including SysML requirements tracing information has been elaborated. The presentation highlights how certain aspects of formal methods are key enablers for achieving the degree of automation that is needed for effectively testing today's safety critical systems with acceptable effort and the degree of comprehensiveness required by the applicable standards. It is also explained which requirements from the industry and from certification authorities have to be considered when designing test automation tools fit for integration into the verification and validation work flow set up for complex system developments. From the collection of scientific challenges the following questions are addressed. (1) What is the formal equivalent to traceable requirements and associated test cases? (2) How can requirements based, property-based, and model-based testing be effectively automated? (3) Which test strategies provide guaranteed test strength, independent on the syntactic representation of the model?

Contents

Invited Presentations

Research Track

Industry Track

Invited Presentations

Industrial-Strength Model-Based Testing of Safety-Critical Systems

Jan Peleska[1,2(✉)] and Wen-ling Huang[2]

[1] Verified Systems International GmbH, Bremen, Germany
[2] Department of Mathematics and Computer Science, University of Bremen, Bremen, Germany
{jp,huang}@cs.uni-bremen.de

Abstract. In this article we present an industrial-strength approach to automated model-based testing. This approach is applied by Verified Systems International GmbH in safety-critical verification and validation projects in the avionic, railway, and automotive domains. The SysML modelling formalism is used for creating test models. Associating SysML with a formal behavioural semantics allows for full automation of the whole work flow, as soon as the model including SysML requirements tracing information has been elaborated. The presentation highlights how certain aspects of formal methods are key enablers for achieving the degree of automation that is needed for effectively testing today's safety critical systems with acceptable effort and the degree of comprehensiveness required by the applicable standards. It is also explained which requirements from the industry and from certification authorities have to be considered when designing test automation tools fit for integration into the verification and validation work flow set up for complex system developments. From the collection of scientific challenges the following questions are addressed. (1) What is the formal equivalent to traceable requirements and associated test cases? (2) How can requirements based, property-based, and model-based testing be effectively automated? (3) Which test strategies provide guaranteed test strength, independent on the syntactic representation of the model?

Keywords: Model-based testing · Equivalence class partition testing · Complete testing theories

1 Introduction

Model-Based Testing. Model-based testing (MBT) can be implemented using different approaches; this is also expressed in the current definition of MBT presented in Wikipedia[1].

> *Model-based testing is an application of model-based design for designing and optionally also executing artifacts to perform software testing or system testing. Models can be used to represent the desired behaviour of a*

[1] https://en.wikipedia.org/wiki/Model-based_testing, 2016-07-11.

J. Fitzgerald et al. (Eds.): FM 2016, LNCS 9995, pp. 3–22, 2016.
DOI: 10.1007/978-3-319-48989-6_1

System Under Test (SUT), or to represent testing strategies and a test environment.

In this paper, we follow the variant where formal models represent the desired behaviour of the SUT, because this promises the maximal return of investment for the effort to be spent on test model development.

- Test cases can be automatically identified in the model.
- If the model contains links to the original requirements (this is systematically supported, for example, by the SysML modelling language [19]), test cases can be automatically traced back to the requirements they help to verify.
- Since the model is associated with a formal semantics, test cases can be represented by means of logical formulas representing reachability goals, and concrete test data can be calculated by means of constraint solvers.
- Using model-to-text transformations, executable test procedures, including test oracles, can be generated in an automated way.
- Comprehensive traceability data linking test results, procedures, test cases, and requirements can be automatically compiled.

Objectives. This paper is about model-based functional testing of safety-critical embedded systems. The test approach discussed here is black box, as typically performed during HW/SW integration testing or system testing. The main message of this contribution is twofold.

- Effective automated model-based testing is possible and ready for application in an industrial context, when specialising on particular domains like safety-critical embedded systems. Here "effective" means both "high test strength" and "can be realised with acceptable effort".
- The considerable test strength that can be achieved using MBT-based testing strategies can only be exploited when full automation is available. The underlying algorithms are too complex and the number of test cases is too high to be handled in a manual way.

The methods described in this paper have been implemented in the model-based testing component of Verified Systems' test automation tool RT-Tester [21]. They are applied in testing campaigns for customers from the avionic, railway, and automotive domains. As of today, the applicable standards [5,14,36] do not yet elaborate on how MBT should be integrated into the workflow of development, validation, and verification campaigns for safety-critical systems. The description in this paper, however, is consistent with the general test-related requirements that can be found in these standards.

Overview. In Sect. 2, the workflow of typical testing campaigns in industry is compared to the extended workflow required for using MBT in practise. In Sect. 3, the development of test models with SysML is described, and a simple example is presented. In Sect. 4, we outline the underlying formal concepts enabling the automated test case identification and compilation of traceability data linking test cases to requirements. The question of test strength is discussed in Sect. 5, and the underlying theory that has been implemented in RT-Tester is described. In Sect. 6, three different perspectives for approaching MBT are described. Conclusions are presented in Sect. 7.

References to related work are given throughout the text. Notable overview material on MBT can be found in [1,29,34].

2 Conventional Testing Workflow vs. MBT Workflow

The workflow of conventional industrial test campaigns is shown in Fig. 1. All standards related to safety-critical systems verification emphasise that requirements-based testing should be the main focus of each campaign. Requirements are typically specified in natural language, but preferably as "atomic" statements that do not need to be decomposed into further sub-requirements. All of our customers use requirements managements systems, where dependencies among requirements can be recorded. Optionally, links to further development and V&V artefacts, such as design documents, source code, and test cases and results can be established. Due to the informal nature of requirements, there is no possibility to generate test cases directly from requirements.

As a first step of the test campaign, test cases are developed, so that each requirement is verified by at least one test case. Test cases and requirements are in $n : m$-relationship: one test case can help to test several requirements, and one requirement may need more than one test case to check it thoroughly. The relationship between requirements and test cases is documented in a traceability matrix.

Test cases are usually specified first in an abstract way, that is, the logical conditions to be fulfilled for each test step are described, but the concrete sequence of input vectors and the associated output sequences to be expected from the SUT are not yet identified. Therefore a further step is required to compute the concrete test data to be used or checked against when executing a concrete test case in a test procedure.

Next, test procedures are programmed, each procedure executing one or more concrete test cases. The procedures are executed against the SUT, and the results are documented and evaluated. Finally, the traceability matrix is extended to record the relationships between test cases and implementing procedures and the results obtained in the procedure executions.

According to the current state of practise, test execution, documentation, and compilation of traceability data are typically automated steps, but the initial steps from test case identification to test procedure programming (and frequently debugging ...) need to be performed manually.

A coverage analysis checks the code portions that have been covered by the requirements-based test cases so far. If uncovered code still exists, either the code has to be removed because it does not contribute to the functionality of the SUT, or requirements have to be added, specifying the SUT behaviour implemented by the code uncovered so far. This leads to additional test cases to be executed.

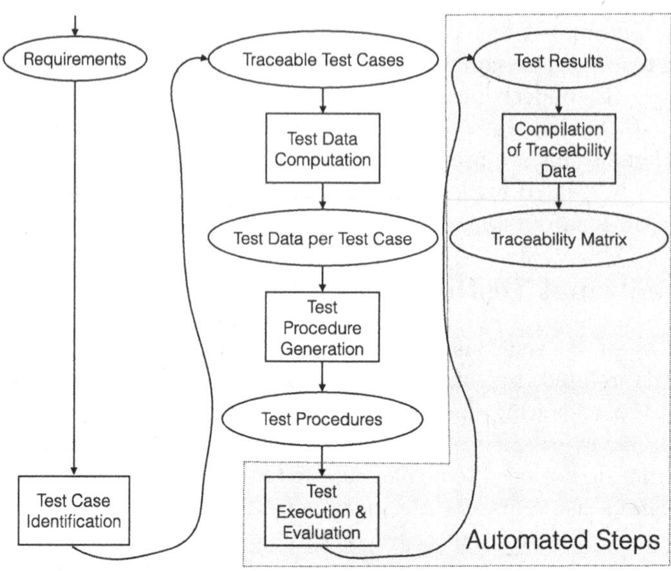

Fig. 1. Conventional testing workflow.

The MBT workflow is shown in Fig. 2. In comparison to conventional test campaigns, two new activities are introduced: during (1) test model development, a formal model specifying the expected behaviour of the SUT, as visible at the test interfaces, is created. In step (2) requirements tracing, the model elements are linked to the requirements they help to "implement". Again, these links need a formal interpretation. As a result of these steps, a formal behavioural model of the SUT is available, and each requirement can be traced to the model portions reflecting the requirement in a formal way.

As a "return of investment" to be gained from these two additional steps, the whole activity chain from test case identification to the completion of traceability data can be fully automated. In the sections to follow, we explain the steps involved and describe how automation support is enabled by various approaches from the field of formal methods.

3 SysML Test Models

The test model describes the interface between SUT and testing environment and specifies the SUT behaviour as far as visible on this interface. An essential feature of the functional model – regardless of the concrete modelling formalism used – is the possibility to perform top-down decompositions and express the overall SUT functionality by a set of concurrent sub-components with internal communication. Since the "real" internal SUT components and their internal communication are not monitored during black-box testing, the concurrent composition in the test model is purely functional and need not reflect the internal

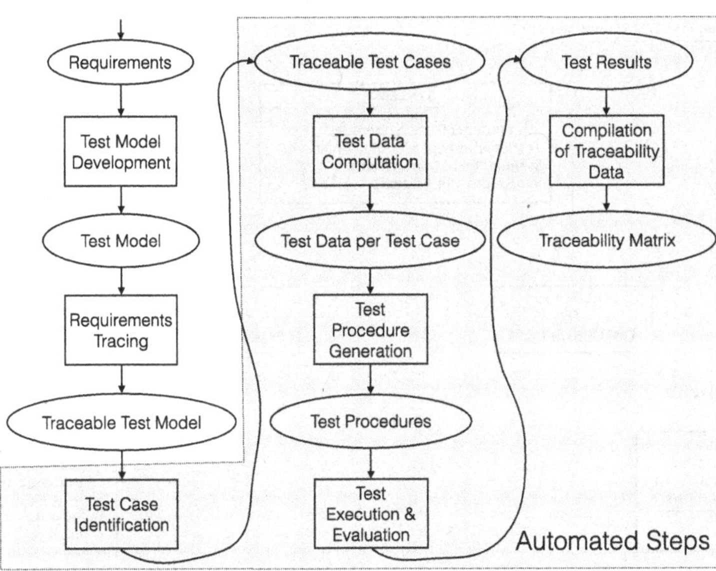

Fig. 2. MBT workflow.

SUT design. The functional composition, however, is helpful to facilitate the understanding of the observable SUT behaviour and the association between requirements and model elements.

To associate the test model with a formal behavioural semantics, the model state space is expressed by a vector of state components representing time, interface states, model variables, and control modes. Rather than labelled transition systems, we use Kripke structures as the underlying behavioural model, and follow the typical encoding recipes that are used in property checking [7] and bounded model checking [3]. This decision is based on the observation that many interfaces occurring in the embedded systems world follow the shared variable paradigm (e.g. dual ported RAM, reflective memories, memory mapped I/O, and data sampling interfaces), so that the concepts of atomic events and synchronous communication are considered as optional higher-level abstractions. The model semantics is then represented by the *model computations*, that is, the set of state sequences starting from an initial model state, such that each pair of consecutive states is a member of the transition relation. To support timed formalisms, delay transitions are distinguished from discrete transitions. The former allow for time to pass and admit input updates only, while the latter are performed in zero time and only change the valuations of internal state and outputs. The possible transitions between states are specified by means of a transition relation in propositional form, relating each model state to its post-states. The propositional representation guarantees that also infinite state systems can be represented without having first to abstract the model. A detailed description

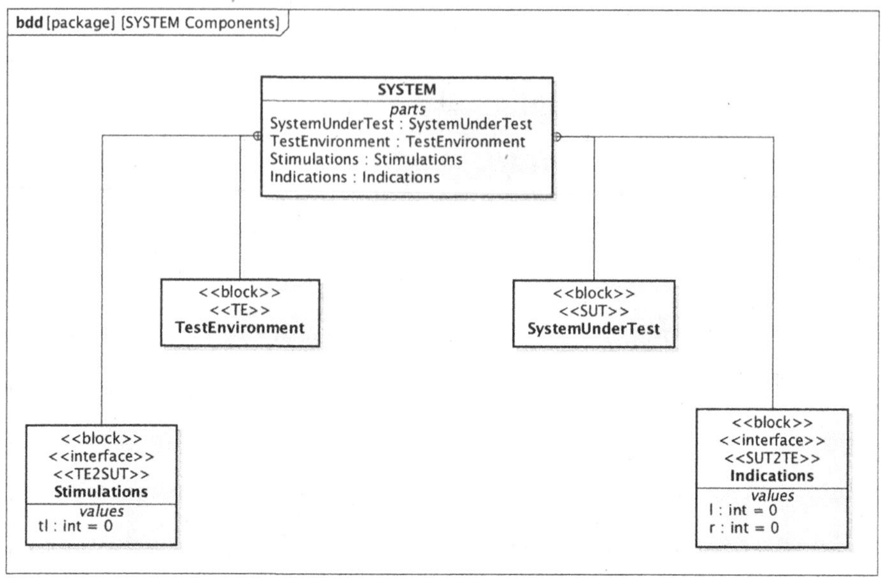

Fig. 3. SysML model of the test configuration.

explaining how to calculated the transition relation from SysML models can be found in [12, Chap. 11].

In the subsequent sections we will refer to a simple test model of a vehicle turn indication controller. In Fig. 3, the basic configuration of a SysML test model (called SYSTEM) for this controller is shown. The configuration consists of the TestEnvironment and the SystemUnderTest. Interface Stimulations specifies the input variables to the SUT which can be set by the test environment. In this example, variable tl specifies the position of the turn indication lever which is 0 for the neutral position, 1 for position 'left' and 2 for position 'right'. Interface Indications specifies the SUT outputs as far as they are observable by the testing environment. In the example, output variable l has value 1 if indication lights on the left-hand side are switched on, otherwise l is 0. Output variable r has value 1 if indication lights on the right-hand side are switched on.

The SUT sub-model is further decomposed as shown in Fig. 4. It consists of a single block representing the sequential turn indication controller. Its behaviour is modelled by a hierarchic state machine depicted in Fig. 5 and Fig. 6. When in simple state IDLE, the outputs are set to 0, so the indication lamps are switched off. As soon as the turn indication lever is switched to the left or right position ($\mathsf{tl} > 0$), the state machines changes to hierarchic state FLASHING. When entering this state, the left-hand side lights are switched on if the turn indication lever is in position 'left' (assignment `l = (tl == 1)`), and the right-hand side lamps are switched on if the lever is in position right. While in state FLASHING, the controller's behaviour is as specified by the sub-machine shown in Fig. 6. The activated indication lights stay on until 340 ms have passed. Then a transition into state OFF is performed, and the lights are switched off (`l = 0; r = 0;`). After 320 ms, the lights are switched back on according to the position of the turn indication lever memorised in auxiliary variable tl0.

Apart from "ordinary" flashing on the left-hand or right-hand side, the controller also realises the tip flashing functionality: when the turn indication lever is set back into neutral position (tl $= 0$), before 3 on-off flashing periods have been performed, the minimum number of 3 periods will be executed before the lights are switched off again. This requirement is reflected in the model by means of the auxiliary variables tl0 and c and the associated assignments.

Two requirements of the turn indication controller already introduced above will be discussed in more detail below; they are depicted in a SysML requirements diagram shown in Fig. 7. Requirement REQ-001 states that flashing shall be performed with 340 ms on and 320 ms off periods. Requirement REQ-002 states the tip flashing functionality.

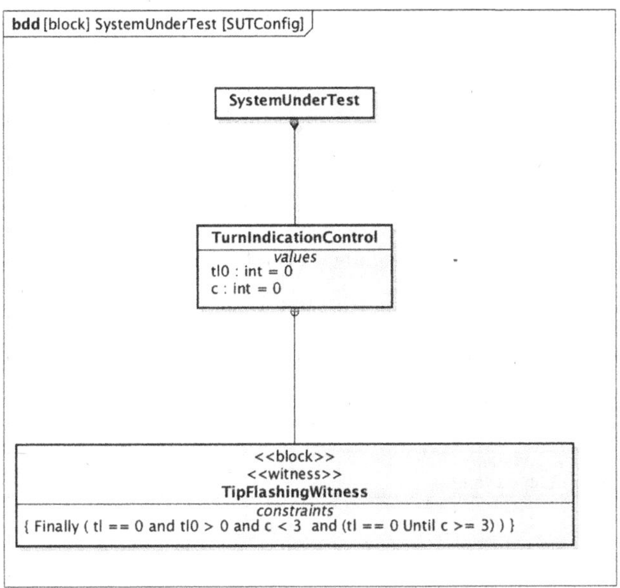

Fig. 4. System under test decomposition and witness specification.

The example introduced here is quite simple and only serves for illustration purposes of the concepts discussed below. A real-world model of such a controller has been made publicly available under www.mbt-benchmarls.org and described in [22].

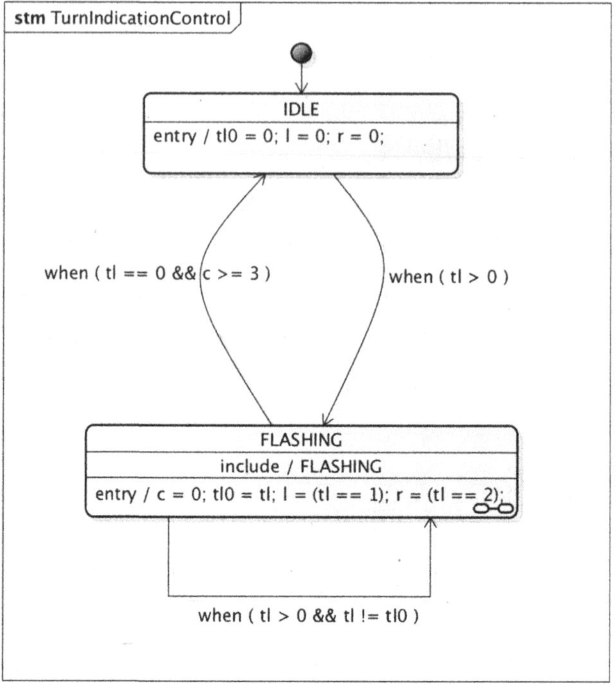

Fig. 5. Top-level state machine of the turn indication controller.

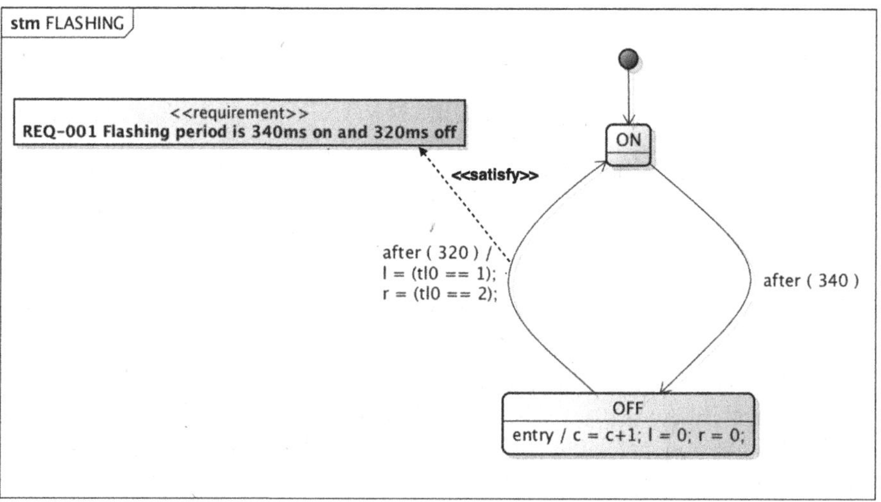

Fig. 6. Lower-level state machine of the turn indication controller.

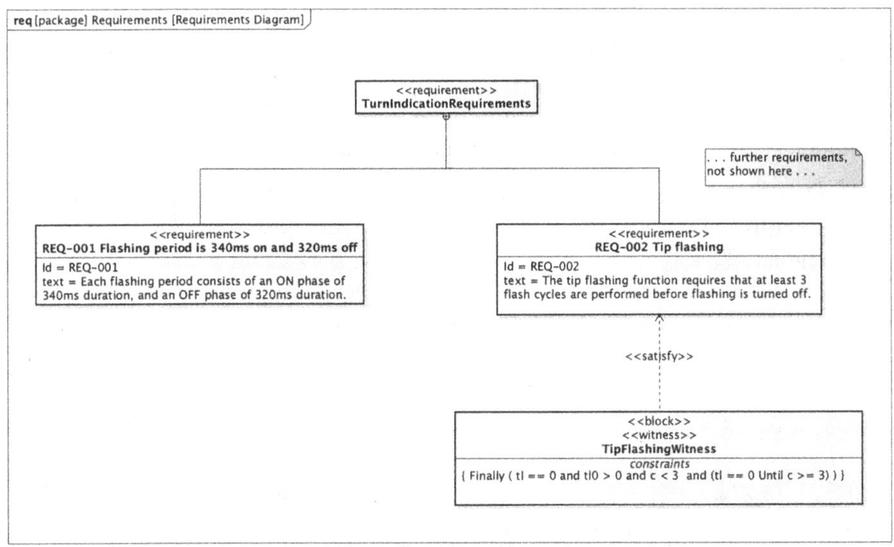

Fig. 7. Requirements model and usage of witness block.

4 Requirements Tracing

Requirements as Model Properties. Requirements are reflected by model properties. Properties are (typically infinite) sets of computations. For the Kripke structure semantics we have associated with SysML models as described in the previous section, computations are infinite paths $\pi = s_0.s_1.s_2\ldots$ of model states s_i, such that each pair $s_i.s_{i+1}$ is related by the transition relation of the underlying Kripke structure. In the context of testing, we are only interested in *safety properties*, because these are characterised by the fact that every property *violation* can already be detected on a finite prefix of some computation, that is, it can be detected by a terminating test run.

Temporal logic – we use LTL for this purpose – can be used to characterise property sets by finite expressions. The LTL formulas expressing safety properties can be inductively generated [31, Theorem 3.1]: (1) every atomic proposition is a safety formula, and (2) if ϕ, ψ are safety formulas, then the same holds for $\phi \wedge \psi$, $\phi \vee \psi$, $\mathbf{X}\phi$, $\phi\mathbf{W}\psi$, and $\mathbf{G}\phi$. Here $\mathbf{X}$ denotes the next operator: $\mathbf{X}\psi$ holds on a computation path $\pi = s_0.s_1.s_2\ldots$ if and only if ψ holds on $\pi^1 = s_1.s_2.\ldots$, the path starting with $\pi's$ second element. $\mathbf{W}$ denotes the weak until operator: $\phi\mathbf{W}\psi$ holds on π if and only if either (1) ϕ holds globally, that is, in every state of π, or (2) ψ holds finally on some segment π^i starting with the $(i+1)^{th}$ element of π, and until then, that is, on segments $\pi = \pi^0, \pi^1, \ldots, \pi^{(i-1)}$, formula ϕ holds. If case (2) applies and ψ already holds on $\pi = \pi^0$, then ϕ does not need to become true anywhere on the computation path. Other temporal operators can be defined as syntactic abbreviations, using $\mathbf{X}$ and $\mathbf{W}$. So $\mathbf{G}\phi$ is short for

$\phi\mathbf{W}\mathtt{false}$ ("ϕ holds globally on π"), $\mathbf{F}\phi$ is short for $\neg\mathbf{G}\neg\phi$ ("finally ϕ holds on π"), and $\phi\mathbf{U}\psi$ is short for $\phi\mathbf{W}\psi \wedge \mathbf{F}\psi$ (this is the "normal" until operator which guarantees that finally ψ will hold).

Summarising, every testable requirement corresponds to a safety property of the model, and it can be formally specified by means of a *Safety LTL formula.*

Black-Box Requirements Specification vs. Model-Based Requirements Specification. There is a fundamental distinction between application of temporal logic as black-box specifications on the one hand, and for specification of model properties on the other hand. In the former case, there does not exist a behavioural model, but just a black-box with a declaration of input and output variables. Requirements REQ are then typically specified by LTL formulas structured like

$$\psi_{\text{REQ}} \equiv \mathbf{G}(\psi_1 \Rightarrow \psi_2)$$

with the informal meaning that "*in every sequence of interface observations, an observation state fulfilling the pre-condition ψ_1 shall also fulfil the required reaction ψ_2*". The computations where the effect of ψ_{REQ} can be observed are the ones fulfilling $\mathbf{F}\psi_1$. In the latter case, the existence of a model allows for referring to both interfaces and internal state variables. Moreover, the required reactions are already encoded in the model. As a consequence, the model property containing all computations witnessing ψ_{REQ} can be specified much simpler by

$$\psi'_{\text{REQ}} \equiv \mathbf{F}\psi'_1$$

with the implicit assumption, that only model computations are considered. Here ψ'_1 is an equivalent to ψ_1, so that the restriction of model computations satisfying ψ'_1 to interface observations results in observation sequences satisfying ψ_1.[2] If requirement REQ has been modelled correctly, every computation satisfying $\mathbf{F}\psi'_1$, when restricted to interface observations, will also satisfy $(\mathbf{F}\psi_1)\wedge(\mathbf{G}(\psi_1 \Rightarrow \psi_2))$.

Model Coverage. The intuitive meaning of computations *covering* certain portions of a model can be formalised; this is achieved in the most effective way by defining coverage for the different syntactic elements occurring in the concrete modelling formalism.

(1) A control mode, such as the simple state OFF in the SysML state machine shown in Fig. 6, is covered by every computation containing a model state whose valuation indicates that this simple state is active. If, for example, a Boolean encoding of simple states is used, $s_i(\mathsf{OFF}) = \mathtt{true}$ indicates that simple state OFF is active in model state s_i. (2) A state machine transition, such as OFF $\longrightarrow$ ON in Fig. 6, is covered by computations containing a state s_i covering the source state, and where the transition's guard condition evaluates to true, such that the action associated with the transition contributes to the effect of the model

[2] If ψ_1 is stuttering invariant, we have $\psi'_1 = \psi_1$.

state transition $s_i \longrightarrow s_{i+1}$. In the example from Fig. 6 the condition for the transition to fire in state s_i is[3]

$$s_i(\mathsf{OFF}) \wedge (\hat{t} - t \geq 320).$$

Here the SysML time event after(320) ("after having stayed in OFF for 320 ms") is internally encoded by the actual model execution time $\hat{t}$ and the auxiliary variable t storing the execution time when state OFF had been entered. (3) An action is covered by computations containing model state transitions $s_i \longrightarrow s_{i+1}$ where the action contributes to the state changes involved when transiting from s_i to s_{i+1}. The state machine transition considered in (2), for example, covers action `l = (tl0 == 1); r = (tl0 == 2);`. When the associated transition is triggered in state s_i, the action's effect is visible in s_{i+1} as

$$s_{i+1}(\mathsf{ON}) \wedge s_{i+1}(\mathrm{l}) = (s_i(\mathrm{tl0}) = 1) \wedge s_{i+1}(\mathrm{r}) = (s_i(\mathrm{tl0}) = 2)$$

(4) An interface is covered by computations containing model state transitions changing the valuation of the interface variables involved. (5) A structural component – such as a block in SysML – is covered by computations stimulating its associated behaviours (state machines, operations, activities, ...).

These examples show that model coverage goals can also be regarded as model properties: the property contains all computations covering a given element or a set of elements. In the example above, the property "transition OFF $\longrightarrow$ ON is covered" can be specified using LTL by

$$\mathbf{F}(\mathsf{OFF} \wedge \mathbf{X}\mathsf{ON}).$$

Formalisation of SysML Requirements Tracing. The considerations above result in a mechanisable formalisation of the SysML requirements tracing concept. As indicated in Fig. 6, for example, behavioural model elements like control modes and transitions can be linked in SysML to requirements by using the «satisfy» relationship. The intuitive meaning of this example is that the transition OFF $\rightarrow$ ON contributes to the realisation of requirement REQ-001.

The graphical notation using the «satisfy» relationship is adequate for requirements whose witnesses can be specified by formulas

$$(\mathbf{F}\psi_1) \vee \cdots \vee (\mathbf{F}\psi_n),$$

meaning *"all computations associated with the requirement finally fulfil at least one of sub-properties* $\psi_1, \ldots, \psi_n$". Investigations performed in cooperation with a customer from the automotive domain showed that in typical test models 80 % of the requirements can be identified by simple sub-property disjunctions of this kind. For 20 % more complex requirements, more complex LTL formulas are required, and these are not representable by simple «satisfy» annotations

[3] Note that this simple condition only applies for deterministic state machines; the encoding is more complex for the nondeterministic case.

linking elements to requirements. These situations not only arise when model elements have to be covered in a specific sequence, but also when requirements are reflected by certain model variable valuations instead of graphical elements like state machine transitions or simple states.

Consider, for example, the requirement REQ-002 about the tip flashing functionality explained in Sect. 3. The computations witnessing this requirement need to visit a model state where flashing is active (this can be specified by $\mathsf{tl0} > 0$), the turn indication lever is back in neutral position ($\mathsf{tl} = 0$), but less than three flash cycles have been performed ($c < 3$). Moreover, we need to continue observing this computation until $c = 3$, so that it can be checked that the indication is switched off after the last mandatory cycle. Summarising this in an LTL formula, the computations witnessing REQ-002 are specified by

$$\mathbf{F}(\mathsf{tl} = 0 \land \mathsf{tl0} > 0 \land c < 3 \land (\mathsf{tl} = 0 \;\mathbf{U}\; c \geq 3)).$$

For defining such a witness specification in a SysML model, the RT-Tester profile introduces blocks stereotyped as «witness». These blocks are introduced in the SUT decomposition (see Fig. 4), so that interface variables and local SUT variables are in the scope of the formula to be specified. The LTL formula is inserted into the block's constraint compartment. Then the witness specification is linked to the associated requirement using again the «satisfy» relation (see requirements diagram in Fig. 7). Requirements without witness blocks are linked directly to other model elements as shown above for REQ-001.

It should be noted that we cannot use the existing UML/SysML concepts of constraints and constraint blocks to specify witnesses for requirements: constraints and constraint blocks are used to restrict the admissible behaviour specified in other model portions. In contrast to this, we only wish to identify the subset of computations contributing to a given requirement; all other executions implied by the model are legal as well. Note further that we expect to change the syntax for specifying witnesses with LTL in the future, as soon as LTL has been integrated into the Object Constraint Language OCL which seems to become the accepted standard for specifying constraints in UML and SysML [18, 32].

Automated Requirements-Based Test Case Identification. In requirements-driven testing, test cases are witnesses for the model properties ψ representing requirements as discussed above, such that a property violation can be detected within a maximal number of k steps. This can be specified by propositions of the type

$$tc \equiv \text{path}(s_0, k) \land G(s_0, \ldots, s_k) \tag{1}$$

with

$$\text{path}(s_0, k) \equiv \mathcal{I}(s_0) \land \bigwedge_{i=1}^{k} \Phi(s_{i-1}, s_i) \tag{2}$$

Proposition $\mathcal{I}(s_0)$ specifies admissible initial model states, Φ is the model's transition relation in propositional form. Proposition $\text{path}(s_0, k)$ states that state sequence $s_0, \ldots, s_k$ is a prefix of a model computation: each pair of states is contained in the transition relation. The proper test case tc specifies that we are looking for a model computation prefix fulfilling additional property $G(s_0, \ldots, s_k)$. Obviously G is the propositional logic equivalent to the LTL property ψ reflecting the requirement in the model, or for a more specific variant ϕ satisfying $\phi \Rightarrow \psi$. In any case, only witnesses are considered that make G become true within k steps. We use the *finite encoding* of LTL formulas described in [3] to transform ϕ into propositional form G. The finite encoding of $\phi \equiv \mathbf{F}(\mathsf{OFF} \wedge \hat{t} - t \geq 320)$, for example, is

$$G_\phi^k \equiv \bigvee_{i=0}^{k} \left(s_i(\mathsf{OFF}) \wedge s_i(\hat{t}) - s_i(t) \geq 320\right)$$

Automated Test Data Generation. Test case representations of the kind described above are still *abstract* (or *symbolic*), since they do not show the concrete test data that should be taken during a test execution. We use an SMT solver to solve constraints of the type $tc \equiv \text{path}(s_0, k) \wedge G(s_0, \ldots, s_k)$. The solver SONOLAR handles integer, bit vector, and floating point arithmetic and supports a theory for handling arrays [25]. The solution of tc contains a sequence of input vectors to the SUT plus associated time stamps indicating how much time should pass between two consecutive inputs, so that specific timing conditions derived from the model are met.

In [21] it is shown how test oracles are generated automatically from test models.

5 MBT Strategies with Guaranteed Test Strength

5.1 Problem Statement

Just switching from conventional testing to model-based testing will make the testing process more efficient, but it will not necessarily increase the strength – that is, the error detection capabilities – of the test suites produced by following the MBT paradigm. In particular, the test strength of well-known model coverage criteria like transition coverage or MC/DC coverage for state machines depends on the syntactic representation of the model. This means that semantically equivalent models will lead to test suites of different strength when applying these strategies, just because their syntactic representation differs. This is because these strategies generate test cases just by traversing the abstract syntax tree, without investigating the model semantics [23].

Even if a test case generation strategy is independent on the syntactic model representation, this does not automatically imply that it is clear which types of errors will be uncovered by the test suites generated according to this strategy.

5.2 Failure Models and Complete Testing Strategies

The second problem described above has been effectively tackled by introducing *failure models*. When slightly abstracting the original notions introduced in

[4,17,27] in the context of testing against finite state machine (FSM) models, a failure model $\mathcal{F} = (\mathcal{S}, \leq, \mathcal{D})$ consists of a reference model $\mathcal{S}$, a conformance relation $\leq$ between models, and a failure domain specifying a set of models $\mathcal{S}'$ that may or may not conform to $\mathcal{S}$.[4]

A test strategy is *complete* if, given a failure model $\mathcal{F}$, it produces complete test suites. The latter are complete if every SUT whose true behaviour is captured by a model $\mathcal{S}'$ in the failure domain $\mathcal{D}$, passes every test case in the suite, if and only if $\mathcal{S}' \leq \mathcal{S}$ holds. For behaviours corresponding to models outside the failure domain, no guarantees are made. This cannot be avoided in the context black box testing, because the internal SUT state cannot be monitored during tests. Therefore hidden "time bombs" – for example, counters that trigger non-conforming behaviour after a certain value has been reached – cannot be detected.

The conformance relations of interest in the context of this paper are *I/O-equivalence* (reference model and SUT can perform exactly the same input output traces) and *reduction* (the observable I/O-behaviour of the SUT is a subset of the behaviours that can be performed by the reference model).

The first complete test strategies have been elaborated for deterministic FSMs, see, for example, [6,35]. This has been extended to nondeterministic FSMs [9,16,26,28], extended finite state machines, and process algebras [8,20,33]. The failure domain for FSM testing contains FSMs M' with the same input/output alphabets as the reference FSM M, such that the observable minimal state machine (the so-called *prime machine*) associated with M has n states, and the prime machine associated with M' has at most $n + m$ states for some $m \geq 0$.

Due to their completeness properties, the number of test cases produced by these strategies is only manageable for input alphabets, state domains, and m-values of moderate size. To handle at least control systems with infinite input domains (but still finite internal domains for internal states and outputs), we have developed a complete input equivalence class testing strategy in the context of deterministic Kripke structures with input, output, and internal state variables [11] (in [10] it has been shown that the strategy can be extended to nondeterministic models). The essential observation for this strategy is that Kripke structures of this kind can be abstracted to deterministic FSMs, such that the input equivalence classes represent the input alphabets of these FSMs. Then it can be shown that complete test suites on FSM level can be translated to test suites on Kripke structure level, and this translation preserves the completeness property.

The failure domain now contains Kripke structures $\mathcal{S}'$ whose abstraction to observable minimal FSMs does not contain more than m additional states when compared to the prime machine abstracted from the reference model $\mathcal{S}$. Moreover, the input equivalence class partition $\mathcal{I}$ derived from the reference model also has to be a suitable partition for the SUT model $\mathcal{S}'$. Since the SUT

[4] In [30], a finer distinction between fault models, failure models, and defect models is made. Our approach described in this paper is focused on failure models.

model is unknown in the context of black box testing, these assumptions cannot be verified in general. However, by increasing m and by refining $\mathcal{I}$, the size of the failure domain is increased. The size of the test suite, however, grows exponentially with the size of m and the number of refinements performed on $\mathcal{I}$.

To avoid this exponential growth it has been shown experimentally, that the strength of this equivalence class strategy is very high for SUT behaviours *outside* the fault domain, if random and boundary value selections are performed each time a representative of an input class is needed. This has been shown by means of case studies from different domains [13,24].

5.3 Transformation-Independent Equivalence Classes

To overcome the first problem stated above, an algorithm has been designed that starts with any syntactic representation of the reference model and calculates a preliminary input equivalence partition $\mathcal{I}$ and its associated FSM M which is first made observable and minimised. This FSM is then analysed with respect to different inputs X_i, X_j leading to the same post states q' and produce the same outputs $b(q)$ for all pairs of transitions $q \xrightarrow{X_i/b(q)} q'$, $q \xrightarrow{X_j/b(q)} q'$ emanating from the same state q. Since the FSM inputs represent input equivalence classes, these pairs X_i, X_j can be aggregated to a single input equivalence class $X_i \cup X_j$. It can be shown that the resulting classes are invariant under syntactic model transformations, as long as they do not change the behavioural semantics.

More details about this algorithm and the underlying model-independent testing theory have been presented in [23].

5.4 Output Equivalence Class Testing

In practical testing, it is often suggested to combine input equivalence classes with output equivalence classes [15]: the output domains of the SUT are partitioned such that the SUT can be assumed to compute members of the same output class in the same way. Then input partitions are constructed such that members of the same input class will produce SUT outputs from the same output class.

It is noteworthy to point out that implicitly, the notion of output equivalence classes has already been covered by the theory above, at least for the systems with infinite inputs and finite internal states and outputs we are dealing with in this paper. In practise, simple model transformations allow for output equivalence class testing with the same methods – and therefore also with the same failure detection guarantees – as input equivalence class testing.

To see this, consider an SUT model with inputs $\boldsymbol{x}$ from an infinite domain, and internal state variables $\boldsymbol{m}$ and outputs $\boldsymbol{y}$ from finite domains, as shown in Fig. 8. Assume that $(k+1)$ output equivalence classes have been specified by means of propositions $\Psi_i(\boldsymbol{y}), i = 0, \ldots, k$: the predicate $\Psi_i(\boldsymbol{y})$ evaluates to `true` for a given output tuple $\boldsymbol{y}$, if and only if $\boldsymbol{y}$ is a member of class i. Now transform the model in the following (mechanisable) way.

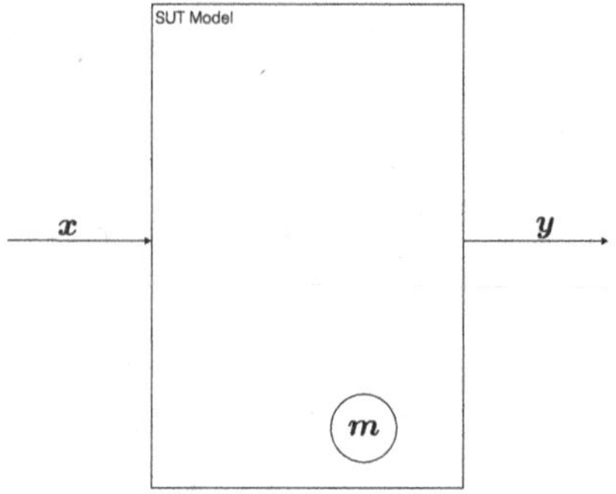

Fig. 8. Initial SUT model.

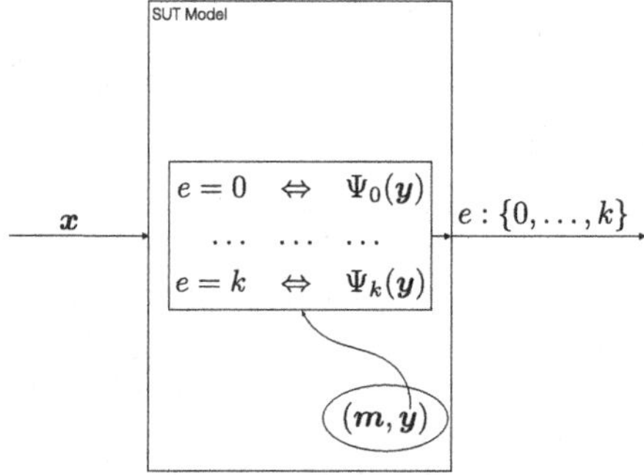

Fig. 9. Transformed SUT model with output equivalence class abstraction.

1. Re-declare the tuple of output variables $\boldsymbol{y}$ as internal model variables, extending the internal model state $\boldsymbol{m}$ to $(\boldsymbol{m}, \boldsymbol{y})$.
2. Introduce a new output variable e ranging over the output equivalence class identifications $0, \dots, k$.
3. Introduce a new block into the model which inputs $\boldsymbol{y}$ and sets output e to $i \in \{0, \dots, k\}$, if and only if $\Psi_i(\boldsymbol{y})$ evaluates to `true`.

The resulting model is depicted in Fig. 9.

6 Requirements-Driven, Model-Driven, and Property-Driven Testing

Model-based testing can be approached from three different perspectives. In *requirements-driven testing*, the objective is to cover all requirements defined as quickly and comprehensively as possible. As described Sect. 4, requirements can be automatically associated with test cases, and these can be automatically associated with concrete test data and executed in procedures.

In *model-driven testing*, the main objective is to check the SUT's conformance to the behaviour of the reference model. It has been shown in the previous section how this can be achieved, even with guaranteed failure detection capabilities. If I/O-equivalence is used as conformance relation, the model-driven approach automatically checks that also the requirements linked to the model have been correctly implemented. It is verified by the associated complete test suites whether the SUT shows only I/O-behaviour that is accepted by the reference model; as a consequence, I/O-traces performed by the SUT and violating a requirement would be detected by some test cases. Moreover, I/O-equivalence guarantees that the witness traces for each requirement – as far as observable at the SUT interface – can also be performed by the SUT, so no requirement has been forgotten in the implementation (note that this would not be guaranteed when testing for language inclusion).

In *property-driven testing*, a desired system property φ is specified – this corresponds to verifying a single requirement while "not caring" about the others that should also be fulfilled by the SUT. Of course, φ can be specified using LTL. In theory, the property-driven test perspective differs considerably from the other two, because it could be handled as follows.

- Generate the most nondeterministic model $\mathcal{S}_\varphi$ satisfying just φ (and of course all of its implications). This model can be created automatically from φ, since LTL formulas can be represented by Büchi automata [2].
- Calculate the input equivalence partitioning $\mathcal{I}$ for $\mathcal{S}_\varphi$, as described in the previous section – this is necessary as soon as φ refers to variables with infinite domains.
- Make an estimate for a refined input partitioning $\overline{\mathcal{I}}$ that is adequate for the SUT.
- Make an estimate m how many additional states the prime machine associated with the true SUT behaviour has, when compared to the prime machine associated with $\mathcal{S}_\varphi$.
- Create a test suite which is complete for failure model $\mathcal{F} = (\mathcal{S}_\varphi, \preceq, \mathcal{D})$, where the failure domain $\mathcal{D}$ contains all models $\mathcal{S}'$ for which $\overline{\mathcal{I}}$ is a valid input equivalence class partitioning and whose associated prime machines have at most m more states, when compared to the prime machine of $\mathcal{S}_\varphi$.

The property-driven test approach appears very attractive, since the reference model can be generated automatically from the property specification. There are, however, still several open research-related questions preventing the direct practical application. The most critical problem is that test suites derived from $\mathcal{S}_\varphi$ will frequently have to deal with quite large values of m, and the size of the test suite increases exponentially with this value. From our perspective it seems promising to refine $\mathcal{S}_\varphi$ with asserted knowledge about the SUT (e.g. further properties that have already been proven or with an additional model restricting the possible behaviours of the SUT), in order to reduce the size of the test suite.

7 Conclusion

We have described an approach to model-based testing that is currently practically applied by Verified Systems International for safety-related tests in the avionic, railway, and automotive domains. The methods described here have been implemented in the MBT component of Verified's test automation tool RT-Tester. Licences need to be obtained for this tool's commercial application, but it is freely available for research purposes. While considerable expertise is required to develop effective test models, skilled testing teams usually obtain a significant return of investment even in new testing campaigns where the test model has to be created from scratch: from projects performed at Verified Systems we estimate that MBT campaigns performed with MBT experts require at least 30 % less effort in comparison to conventional testing campaigns, just because test case identification, test data calculation and test procedure programming is automated. The efficiency is increased further in regression testing campaigns, where only small changes of the test model are required.

Acknowledgements. The authors would like to thank the members of the FM 2016 program committee for the invitation to present this paper.

We are also very grateful to our collaborators at the University of Bremen and Verified Systems International who contributed to the development of RT-Tester's MBT component; in particular we would like to thank Felix Hübner, Uwe Schulze, and Jörg Brauer.

The work presented in this paper has been elaborated within project *ITTCPS – Implementable Testing Theory for Cyber-physical Systems* (see http://www.informatik.uni-bremen.de/agbs/projects/ittcps/index.html) which has been granted by the University of Bremen in the context of the German Universities Excellence Initiative (see http://en.wikipedia.org/wiki/German_Universities_Excellence_Initiative).

References

1. Anand, S., Burke, E.K., Chen, T.Y., Clark, J.A., Cohen, M.B., Grieskamp, W., Harman, M., Harrold, M.J., McMinn, P.: An orchestrated survey of methodologies for automated software test case generation. J. Syst. Softw. **86**(8), 1978–2001 (2013)
2. Baier, C., Katoen, J.: Principles of Model Checking. MIT Press, Cambridge (2008)
3. Biere, A., Heljanko, K., Junttila, T., Latvala, T., Schuppan, V.: Linear encodings of bounded LTL model checking. Logical Methods Comput. Sci. **2**(5), 1–64 (2006). arXiv:cs/0611029
4. von Bochmann, G., Das, A., Dssouli, R., Dubuc, M., Ghedamsi, A., Luo, G.: Fault models in testing. In: Kroon, J., Heijink, R.J., Brinksma, E. (eds.) Proceedings of the IFIP TC6/WG6.1 Fourth International Workshop on Protocol Test Systems IV, 15–17 October 1991, Leidschendam, The Netherlands, pp. 17–30. North-Holland (1991). IFIP Transactions, vol. C-3
5. CENELEC: EN 50128: 2011 Railway applications - Communication, signalling and processing systems - Software for railway control and protection systems (2011)
6. Chow, T.S.: Testing software design modeled by finite-state machines. IEEE Trans. Softw. Eng. SE **4**(3), 178–186 (1978)

7. Clarke, E.M., Grumberg, O., Peled, D.A.: Model Checking. The MIT Press, Cambridge (1999)
8. Hennessy, M.: Algebraic Theory of Processes. MIT Press, Cambridge (1988)
9. Hierons, R.M.: Testing from a nondeterministic finite state machine using adaptive state counting. IEEE Trans. Comput. **53**(10), 1330–1342 (2004). http://doi.ieeecomputersociety.org/10.1109/TC.2004.85
10. Huang, W., Peleska, J.: Complete model-based equivalence class testing for nondeterministic systems. Formal Aspects of Computing Under review
11. Huang, W., Peleska, J.: Complete model-based equivalence class testing. STTT **18**(3), 265–283 (2016). http://dx.doi.org/10.1007/s10009-014-0356-8
12. Huang, W.l., Peleska, J., Schulze, U.: Test automation support. Technical report D34.1, COMPASS Comprehensive Modelling for Advanced Systems of Systems (2013). http://www.compass-research.eu/deliverables.html
13. Hübner, F., Huang, W., Peleska, J.: Experimental evaluation of a novel equivalence class partition testing strategy. In: Blanchette, J.C., Kosmatov, N. (eds.) TAP 2015. LNCS, vol. 9154, pp. 155–172. Springer, Heidelberg (2015). doi:10.1007/978-3-319-21215-9_10
14. ISO, DIS 26262-4: Road vehicles - functional safety - part 4: Product development: system level. Technical report, International Organization for Standardization (2009)
15. ISO, IEC, IEEE DIS 29119–4.2: Software and systems engineering - software testing - part: 4 test techniques, February 2014
16. Luo, G., von Bochmann, G., Petrenko, A.: Test selection based on communicating nondeterministic finite-state machines using a generalized WP-method. IEEE Trans. Softw. Eng. **20**(2), 149–162 (1994). http://doi.ieeecomputersociety.org/10.1109/32.265636
17. Morell, L.J.: A theory of fault-based testing. IEEE Trans. Softw. Eng. **16**(8), 844–857 (1990). http://dx.doi.org/10.1109/32.57623
18. Object Management Group: Object Constraint Language, Version 2.4. Technical report, Object Management Group (2014). http://www.omg.org/spec/OCL/2.4/
19. Object Management Group: OMG Systems Modeling Language (OMG SysML), Version 1.4. Technical report, Object Management Group (2015). http://www.omg.org/spec/SysML/1.4
20. Peleska, J.: Formal methods and the development of dependable systems. No. 9612, Christian-Albrechts-Universität Kiel, Institut fr Informatik und Praktische Mathematik , Habilitationsschrift, December 1996
21. Peleska, J.: Industrial-strength model-based testing-state of the art and current challenges. In: Petrenko, A.K., Schlingloff, H. (eds.) Proceedings Eighth Workshop on Model-Based Testing. Electronic Proceedings in Theoretical Computer Science, 17th March 2013, Rome, Italy, vol. 111, pp. 3–28. Open Publishing Association (2013)
22. Peleska, J., Honisch, A., Lapschies, F., Löding, H., Schmid, H., Smuda, P., Vorobev, E., Zahlten, C.: A real-world benchmark model for testing concurrent real-time systems in the automotive domain. In: Wolff, B., Zaïdi, F. (eds.) ICTSS 2011. LNCS, vol. 7019, pp. 146–161. Springer, Heidelberg (2011). doi:10.1007/978-3-642-24580-0_11
23. Peleska, J., Huang, W.: Model-based testing strategies and their (in)dependence on syntactic model representations. In: Beek, M.H., Gnesi, S., Knapp, A. (eds.) FMICS/AVoCS -2016. LNCS, vol. 9933, pp. 3–21. Springer, Heidelberg (2016). doi:10.1007/978-3-319-45943-1_1

24. Peleska, J., Huang, W., Hübner, F.: A novel approach to HW/SW integration testing of route-based interlocking system controllers. In: Lecomte, T., Pinger, R., Romanovsky, A. (eds.) RSSRail 2016. LNCS, vol. 9707, pp. 32–49. Springer, Heidelberg (2016). doi:10.1007/978-3-319-33951-1_3
25. Peleska, J., Vorobev, E., Lapschies, F.: Automated test case generation with SMT-solving and abstract interpretation. In: Bobaru, M., Havelund, K., Holzmann, G.J., Joshi, R. (eds.) NFM 2011. LNCS, vol. 6617, pp. 298–312. Springer, Heidelberg (2011). doi:10.1007/978-3-642-20398-5_22
26. Petrenko, A., Yevtushenko, N.: Adaptive testing of deterministic implementations specified by nondeterministic FSMs. In: Wolff, B., Zaïdi, F. (eds.) ICTSS 2011. LNCS, vol. 7019, pp. 162–178. Springer, Heidelberg (2011). doi:10.1007/978-3-642-24580-0_12
27. Petrenko, A., Yevtushenko, N., Bochmann, G.v.: Fault models for testing in context. In: Gotzhein, R., Bredereke, J. (eds.) Formal Description Techniques IX - Theory, Application and Tools, pp. 163–177. Chapman & Hall (1996)
28. Petrenko, A., Yevtushenko, N., Bochmann, G.V.: Testing deterministic implementations from nondeterministic FSM specifications. In: IFIP TC6 9th International Workshop on Testing of Communicating Systems, pp. 125–141. Chapman and Hall (1996)
29. Petrenko, A., Simao, A., Maldonado, J.C.: Model-based testing of software and systems: recent advances and challenges. Int. J. Softw. Tools Technol. Transf. **14**(4), 383–386 (2012). http://dx.doi.org/10.1007/s10009-012-0240-3
30. Pretschner, A.: Defect-based testing. In: Irlbeck, M., Peled, D.A., Pretschner, A. (eds.) Dependable Software Systems Engineering, NATO Science for Peace and Security Series, D: Information and Communication Security, vol. 40, pp. 224–245. IOS Press (2015). http://dx.doi.org/10.3233/978-1-61499-495-4-224
31. Sistla, A.P.: Safety, liveness and fairness in temporal logic. Formal Asp. Comput. **6**(5), 495–512 (1994). http://dx.doi.org/10.1007/BF01211865
32. Soden, M., Eichler, H.: Temporal extensions of OCL revisited. In: Paige, R.F., Hartman, A., Rensink, A. (eds.) ECMDA-FA 2009. LNCS, vol. 5562, pp. 190–205. Springer, Heidelberg (2009). doi:10.1007/978-3-642-02674-4_14
33. Tretmans, J.: Conformance testing with labelled transition systems: implementation relations and test generation. Comput. Netw. ISDN Syst. **29**(1), 49–79 (1996)
34. Utting, M., Pretschner, A., Legeard, B.: A taxonomy of model-based testing approaches. Softw. Test. Verif. Reliab. **22**(5), 297–312 (2012). http://dx.doi.org/10.1002/stvr.456
35. Vasilevskii, M.P.: Failure diagnosis of automata. Kibernetika (Transl.) **4**, 98–108 (1973)
36. WG-71, R.S.E.: Software Considerations in Airborne Systems and Equipment Certification. Technical report RTCA/DO-178C, RTCA Inc., 1140 Connecticut Avenue, N.W., Suite 1020, Washington, D.C. 20036, December 2011

Research Track

Counter-Example Guided Program Verification

Parosh Aziz Abdulla, Mohamed Faouzi Atig, and Bui Phi Diep(✉)

Uppsala University, Uppsala, Sweden
{parosh,mohamed_faouzi.atig,bui.phi-diep}@it.uu.se

Abstract. This paper presents a novel counter-example guided abstraction refinement algorithm for the automatic verification of concurrent programs. Our algorithm proceeds in different steps. It first constructs an abstraction of the original program by slicing away a given subset of variables. Then, it uses an external model checker as a backend tool to analyze the correctness of the abstract program. If the model checker returns that the abstract program is safe then we conclude that the original one is also safe. If the abstract program is unsafe, we extract an "abstract" counter-example. In order to check if the abstract counter-example can lead to a real counter-example of the original program, we add back to the abstract counter-example all the omitted variables (that have been sliced away) to obtain a new program. Then, we call recursively our algorithm on the new obtained program. If the recursive call of our algorithm returns that the new program is unsafe, then we can conclude that the original program is also unsafe and our algorithm terminates. Otherwise, we refine the abstract program by removing the abstract counter-example from its set of possible runs. Finally, we repeat the procedure with the refined abstract program. We have implemented our algorithm, and run it successfully on the concurrency benchmarks in SV-COMP15. Our experimental results show that our algorithm significantly improves the performance of the backend tool.

1 Introduction

Leveraging concurrency effectively has become key to enhancing the performance of software, to the degree that concurrent programs have become crucial parts of many applications. At the same time, concurrency gives rise to enormously complicated behaviors, making the task of producing correct concurrent programs more and more difficult. The main reason for this is the large number of possible computations caused by many possible thread (or process) interleavings. Unexpected interference among threads often results in Heisenbugs that are difficult to reproduce and eliminate. Extensive efforts have been devoted to address this problem by the development of testing and verification techniques. Model checking addresses the problem by systematically exploring the state space of a given program and verifying that each reachable state satisfies a given property. Applying model checking to realistic programs is problematic, due to the state explosion problem. The reason is that we need (1) to exhaustively explore the

J. Fitzgerald et al. (Eds.): FM 2016, LNCS 9995, pp. 25–42, 2016.
DOI: 10.1007/978-3-319-48989-6_2

entire reachable state space in all possible interleavings, and (2) to capture and store a large number of global states.

Counter-Example Guided Abstraction Refinement (CEGAR) (e.g., [4,5,11, 15,17]) approach is one of the successful techniques for verifying programs. This approach consists in four basic steps:

- *Abstraction step:* Construct a finite-state program as an abstraction of the original program using predicate abstraction (with a set of predicates) and go to the *Verification step.*
- *Verification step:* Use a model checker to check if the constructed finite state program satisfies the desired property. If it is the case, then the original program satisfies also the property and the verification algorithm terminates; otherwise extract a counter-example and go to the *Analysis step.*
- *Analysis Step:* Check if the retuned counter example is spurious or not. If it is not, then we have a real bug in the original program and the verification algorithm terminates; otherwise go to the *Refinement step.*
- *Refinement Step:* If the counter-example is spurious, refine the set of used predicates in the *Abstraction step* to eliminate the counter example. Return to the *Abstraction step* with this new refined set of predicates.

The CEGAR approach has been successfully implemented in tools, such as SLAM [4], BLAST [5], MAGIC [8] and CPAChecker [6]. However, CEGAR may also suffer from the state-space exploring problem in the case of concurrent programs due to the large number of possible interleavings.

In this paper we present a variant of the CEGAR algorithm (called Counter-Example Guided Program Verification (CEGPV)) that addresses the state-space explosion problem encountered in the verification of concurrent programs. The work-flow of our CEGPV algorithm is given in Fig. 1. The algorithm consists of four main modules, the *abstraction*, the *counter-example mapping*, the *reconstruction* and the *refinement.* It also uses an external model checker tool.

The *abstraction* module takes as input a concurrent program $\mathcal{P}$ and a subset V_0 of its shared variables. It then constructs an over-approximation of the program $\mathcal{P}$, called $\mathcal{P}'$, as follows. First, it keeps variables in the set V_0 and slices away all other variables of the program $\mathcal{P}$. Occurrences of the sliced variables are replaced by non-deterministic values. Second, some instructions, where the sliced variables occur, in the program $\mathcal{P}$ can be removed. Then, the *model checker* takes as input $\mathcal{P}'$, and checks whether it is safe or not. If the *model checker* returns that $\mathcal{P}'$ is safe, then $\mathcal{P}$ is also safe, and our algorithm terminates. If $\mathcal{P}'$ is unsafe, then the *model checker* returns a counter-example π'.

The *counter-example mapping* module takes the counter-example π' as its input. It transforms the run π' to a run π of the program resulting of the *abstraction* module (using V_0 as its set of shared variables).

The *reconstruction* module takes as input the counter-example π of $\mathcal{P}'$. It checks whether π can lead to a real counter-example of $\mathcal{P}$. In particular, if $\mathcal{P}'$ is identical to $\mathcal{P}$, then the algorithm concludes that $\mathcal{P}$ is unsafe, and terminates. Otherwise, the *reconstruction* adds back all omitted variables and lines of codes

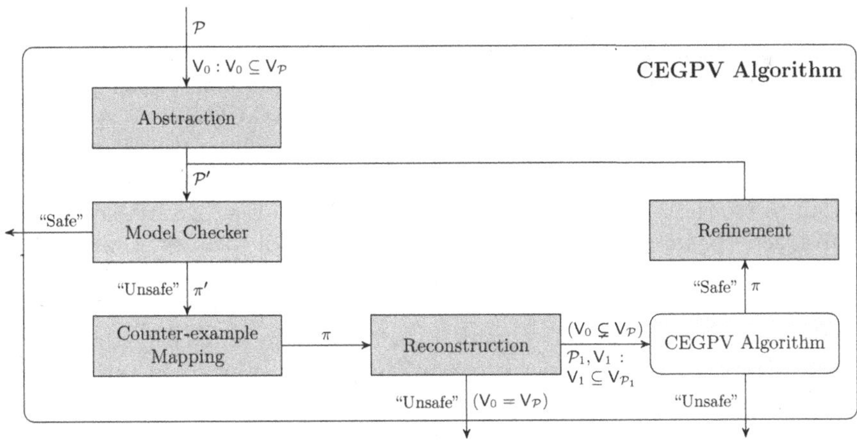

Fig. 1. An overview of the CEGPV algorithm.

to create a program $\mathcal{P}_1$ while respecting the flow of the instructions in π and the valuation of the variables in V_0. Hence, $\mathcal{P}_1$ has as its set of variables only the omitted ones. Then, CEGPV algorithm then recursively calls itself to check $\mathcal{P}_1$ in its next iteration. If the iteration returns that $\mathcal{P}_1$ is unsafe, then the run π leads to a counter-example of the program $\mathcal{P}$. The algorithm concludes that $\mathcal{P}$ is unsafe and terminates. Otherwise, the run π cannot lead to a counter-example of $\mathcal{P}$. Then the algorithm needs to discard the run π from $\mathcal{P}'$.

The *refinement* adds π to the set of spurious counter-examples of $\mathcal{P}'$. It then refines $\mathcal{P}'$ by removing all these spurious counter-examples from the set of runs of $\mathcal{P}'$. The new resulting program is then given back to the *model checker* tool.

Our CEGPV algorithm has two advantages. First, it reduces the number of variables in the model-checked programs to prevent the state-space explosion problem. Second, all modules are implemented using code-to-code translations.

In order to evaluate the efficiency of our CEGPV algorithm, we have implemented it as a part of an open source tool, called CEGPV, for the verification of C/pthreads programs. We used CBMC version 5.1 as the backend tool [10]. We then evaluated CEGPV on the benchmark set from the Concurrency category of the TACAS Software Verification Competition (SV-COMP15) [2]. Our experimental results show that CEGPV significantly improve the performance of CBMC, showing the potential of our approach.

Related Work. CEGAR is one of the successful techniques used in program verification. Our CEGPV algorithm can be seen as a new instance of the CEGAR algorithm that can be implemented on the top of any verification tool. In contrast with the classical CEGAR algorithms (e.g., [5,9,11,12,18]) where the programs are abstracted using a set of predicates, our CEGPV algorithm uses variable slicing techniques to obtain the abstract program.

Variable slicing is also one of the verification guided approaches to address the state-space exposing problem. In [18], an analysis tool for detecting memory leaks is presented based on slicing some of the program variables. Each generated abstract program is then checked by a backend tool. RankChecker [7] is a testing tool based on an assumption that most concurrency bugs have a small number of variables involved. To reduce the search space, it forces processes in a concurrent program to interleave at certain points that access a subset of variables. Corral [15] abstracts the input program by only keeping track of a subset of variables. If the counter-example of the abstract program is spurious, Corral then refines the abstraction by decreasing the set of omitted variables. The algorithm terminates once the counter-example corresponds to a run of the original program. Our CEGPV algorithm also abstract programs by slicing away some variables (as it is also done by the localization reduction techniques [13,14]). However, our CEGPV algorithm has the feature to recursively call itself in order to check if the counter-example can lead to a real one while trying to keep the number of variables of the model-checked programs as small as possible.

2 Motivating Example

In this section, we informally illustrate the main concepts of our algorithm.

Figure 2a is a simplified version of a program in the concurrent C benchmark in SVCOMP [2]. The program $\mathcal{P}$ has two processes, called P and Q, running in parallel. Processes communicate through five shared variables which are x, y, z, t1 and t2, ranging over the set of integers. All variables are initialized to 0. The behavior of a process is defined by a list of C-like instructions. Each instruction is composed of a unique label and a statement. For example, in process P, the instruction p1: x = y ? z ? 0 : 1 : 1 has p1 as a label, and x = y ? z ? 0 : 1 : 1 as a statement. That statement is a ternary assignment in which it assigns 0 to x if both y and z are equal to 1, and assigns 1 to x otherwise. The assertion labeled by p5 holds if the expression t1 + t2 is different from 1, and in that case the program is declared to be safe. Otherwise, the program is unsafe.

```
x = y = z = t1 = t2 = 0
process P:                    process Q:
p1: x = y?z?0:1:1;            q1: x = y?0:z?0:1;
p2: y = z;                    q2: y = !z;
p3: z = 0;                    q3: z = 1;
p4: t1 = x;                   q4: t2 = x;
p5: assert t1+t2 != 1;
```

(a) A simple program $\mathcal{P}$

```
x = y = z = 0
process P:                    process Q:
p1: x = *;                    q1: x = *;
p2: y = z;                    q2: y = !z;
p3: z = 0;                    q3: z = 1;
p4: t1 = x;                   q4: t2 = x;
p5: assert t1+t2 != 1;
```

(b) Abstract program $\mathcal{P}_1$

Fig. 2. A toy example and its abstraction

In order to apply our algorithm, we first need to determine a subset of program variables that will be sliced away. To that aim, we construct a dependency graph between variables. The dependency graph consists of a number of vertices and directed edges. Each vertex corresponds to a variable of the program. The edges describe the flow dependency between these variables. The dependency graph of the program $\mathcal{P}$ is given in Fig. 3. For instance, x depends on both y and z due to the two assignments labeled by p1 and q1. Similarly, the assignment labeled by p2 creates a dependency between the variables y and z. We use the dependency graph to decide the first set of variables to be sliced away. In general, we keep variables that influence the safety of the program. In the settings of the example, the variables t1 and t2 are used in the assertion at p5 and therefore we keep track of the variables t1 and t2. Furthermore, we keep also track of x since t1 and t2 are dependent on x.

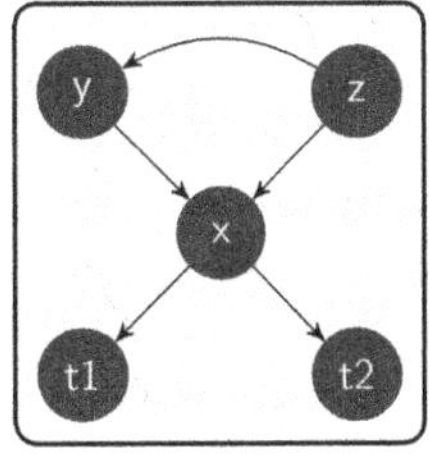

Fig. 3. Dependency graph of $\mathcal{P}$.

Once we have the subset of variables {t1, t2, x} to be preserved, we need to slice away the variables {y, z}. To do that, we abstract the program by replacing occurrences of the variables y and z by a non-deterministic value *. Assignments labeled by p1 and q1 are transformed to x = * ? * : 0 ? 1 ? 1 and x = * ? 0 : * ? 0 ? 1, respectively. We make a further optimization to transform these assignments to x = *. Since we are not anymore keeping track of the variables y and z, instructions which are assignments to these variables can be removed. In this case, we remove the instructions labeled by p2, p3, q2 and q3 from the abstract program. All the other instructions remain the same. Resulting abstract program, called $\mathcal{P}_1$, is given in Fig. 2b. $\mathcal{P}_1$ has only three variables t1, t2 and x, and five instructions.

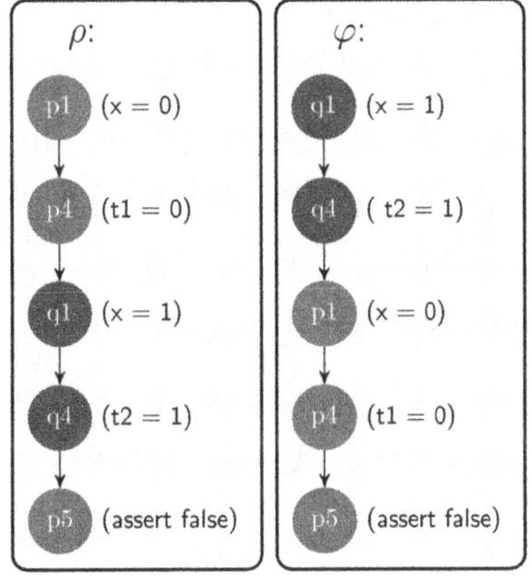

Fig. 4. Counter-examples of $\mathcal{P}_1$

The next step of our algorithm is to feed the abstract program to a model checker. The model checker checks whether the program is safe or not. If the program is unsafe, the model checker returns a counter-example. In our case, since $\mathcal{P}_1$ is unsafe, we assume the model checker returns a counter-example, called ρ, given in Fig. 4. In the obtained counter-example ρ, the process P executes the instruction labeled by p1. At that instruction, the non-deterministic symbol * returns the value 0, and therefore x is assigned to 0. Then the process P executes the instruction labeled by p4 and sets the value of t1 to 0. The control then switches to the process Q which executes the instructions labeled by q1 and q4. They evaluate both x and t1 to 1. Then, the assertion in the instruction labeled by p5 is checked. The expression in the assertion, t1 + t2 != 1, is evaluated to false, so the program is unsafe.

Although ρ is the counter-example of $\mathcal{P}_1$, ρ is not identified to be a counter-example of $\mathcal{P}$ since $\mathcal{P}_1$ is an abstraction of $\mathcal{P}$. In order to check whether ρ can lead to a counter-example of $\mathcal{P}$, we need to add back some of the omitted variables and lines of codes. Adding back this information to ρ will result in a new program, called $\mathcal{S}_\rho$. In this case, we add y and z to ρ.

The program $\mathcal{S}_\rho$ is given in Fig. 5. When adding back variables, several instructions are restored such as the instructions labeled by p2, p3, q2 and q3. Variables, which appear in the counter-example, can be discarded since their values are known. For example, x at p1 in ρ is 0. We replace the occurrence of x in q1 by 1. We also transform the assignment in the instruction labeled by p1 to an assumption to check whether the value of x is equal to the value of right hand side of assignment, i.e. assume 0 == y ? z ? 0 : 1 : 1. The assumption blocks the execution until the expression in the assumption is evaluated to true. Similarly, the instruction labeled by p4 is transformed to assume 0 == 0. Then, we remove assumptions that are trivially true such as assume 0 == 0. Since $\mathcal{S}_\rho$ needs to respect the order of instructions in ρ, the instruction labeled by p1 is only executed after the instruction labeled by q3.

```
y = z = 0
process P:                          process Q:
p1: assume 0 == y?z?0:1:1;
p2: y = z;                          q1: assume 1 == y?0:z?0:1;
p3: z = 0;                          q2: y = !z;
p4: assume 0 == 0                   q3: z = 1;
p5: assert false;                   q4: assume 1 == 1;
```

Fig. 5. The program $\mathcal{S}_\rho$

The model checker checks $\mathcal{S}_\rho$ and returns that $\mathcal{S}_\rho$ is safe. This means ρ can not lead to a counter-example of $\mathcal{P}$. We then need to refine $\mathcal{P}_1$ to exclude ρ from its set of runs. Therefore, we create a refinement of $\mathcal{P}_1$, called $\mathcal{P}_2$ and given in Fig. 6, as follows. We use an observer to check whether the actual run is identical to the run ρ. Two runs are identical if (1) their orders of executed instructions are the same, and (2) valuations of variables after each instruction are the same in both runs.

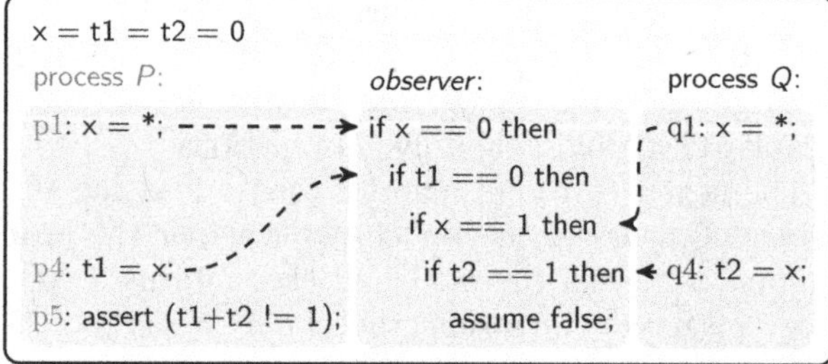
x = t1 = t2 = 0
process P:
observer:
process Q:
p1: x = *;
if x == 0 then
q1: x = *;
if t1 == 0 then
if x == 1 then
p4: t1 = x;
if t2 == 1 then
q4: t2 = x;
p5: assert (t1+t2 != 1);
assume false;

Fig. 6. The refined program $\mathcal{P}_2$

If the actual run is identical to the run ρ, then that run is safe. For the sake of simplicity, we model the observer as a sequence of conditional statements. After each instruction in the run ρ, except the assertion at the end of ρ, we create a conditional statement to re-evaluate values of variables. For instance, if x == 0 follows the assignment x = * at p1, where 0 is the value of x at instruction labeled by p1 in ρ. If if x == 0 is passed, then the execution can check if t1 == 0 after running assignment t1 = x at p4. Otherwise, the execution is no longer followed by the observer. If an execution passes all conditional statements of the observer, then the actual run is identical to ρ. The assumption assume false at the end of observer is to prevent the execution of the assertion at p5. Hence, $\mathcal{P}_2$ excludes ρ from its runs.

The model checker checks $\mathcal{P}_2$. It returns a counter-example, called φ, as given in Fig. 4. In φ, the instructions of the process Q, which are labeled by q1 and q4, are issued first. After that, the instructions of P, which are labeled by p1, p4 and p5, are performed. Similar to the way we verify ρ, we add y and z back to φ and construct a new program to simulate φ, called $\mathcal{S}_\varphi$. $\mathcal{S}_\varphi$ is presented in Fig. 7. In the counter-example $\mathcal{S}_\varphi$, the variables x, t1 and t2 are replaced by their values in φ. Then, instructions labeled by p4 and q4 are removed due to the optimization. We also force $\mathcal{S}_\varphi$ to respect the flow of the counter-example φ. For instance, the instruction labeled by p1 only runs after the instruction labeled by q3.

```
y = z = 0
process P:                          process Q:
p1: assume 1 == y?z?0:1:1;   <      q1: assume 0 == y?0:z?0:1;
p2: y = z;                          q2: y = ! z;
p3: z = 0;                          q3: z = 1;
p4: assume 1 == 1;                  q4: assume 1 == 1;
p5: assert false;
```

Fig. 7. The program $\mathcal{S}_\varphi$

The model checker checks $\mathcal{S}_\varphi$. It then concludes that $\mathcal{S}_\varphi$ is unsafe with a proof by a counter-example, called π, given in Fig. 8. We need to verify whether π can lead to a counter-example of $\mathcal{P}$ by adding more variables and lines of codes, and then constructing a new program that respects the flow of instructions in π. However, all variables of the program $\mathcal{P}$ are used, so π is a counter-example of $\mathcal{P}$. Thus, $\mathcal{P}$ is unsafe and the algorithm stops.

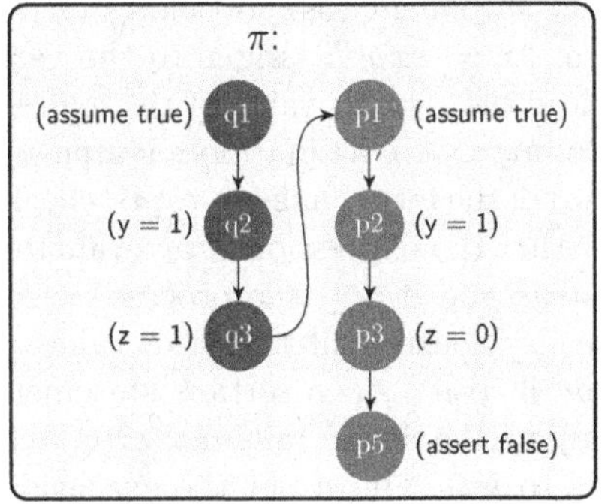

Fig. 8. Counter-example of $\mathcal{S}_\varphi$

3 Concurrent Programs

In this section, we describe the syntax and semantics of programs we consider but before that we will introduce some notations and definitions.

For A a finite set, we use $|A|$ to denote its size. Let A and B be two sets, we use $f : A \mapsto B$ to denote that f is a function that maps any element of A to an element of B. For $b \in B$, we use $b \in f$ to denote that there is an $a \in A$ such that $f(a) = b$. For $a \in A$ and $b \in B$, we use $f[a \hookleftarrow b]$ to denote the function f' where $f'(a) = b$ and $f'(a') = f(a')$ for all $a' \neq a$.

Syntax. Figure 9 gives the grammar for a C-like programming language that we use for defining concurrent programs. A concurrent program $\mathcal{P}$ starts by defining a set of shared variables. Each shared variable is defined by the command `var` followed by a unique identifier. We assume that the variable ranges over some (potentially infinite) domain $\mathbb{D}$. Then the program $\mathcal{P}$ defines a set of processes (or threads). Each process has a unique identifier p and its code is a sequence consists of instructions (which is placed between `begin` and `end`). An instruction ins is of the form "loc:stmt", where loc is a label (or control location), and stmt is a statement. We use $label(\mathsf{ins})$ to denote the label loc of the instruction ins and $stmt(\mathsf{loc})$ to denote the statement stmt. We use $\mathsf{V}_{\mathcal{P}}$ to denote the set of variables, $\mathsf{Proc}_{\mathcal{P}}$ to denote the set of processes of the program $\mathcal{P}$. For a process $P \in \mathsf{Proc}_{\mathcal{P}}$, let $\mathbb{I}_P$ be the set of instructions in the code of P and $\mathbb{Q}_P$ be the set of labels appearing in its code. We assume w.l.o.g. that each instruction has a unique label. Let $\mathbb{I}_{\mathcal{P}} := \cup_{P \in \mathsf{Proc}_{\mathcal{P}}} \mathbb{I}_P$, and $\mathbb{Q}_{\mathcal{P}} := \cup_{P \in \mathsf{Proc}_{\mathcal{P}}} \mathbb{Q}_P$. We assume that we dispose of a function $init : \mathsf{Proc} \mapsto \mathbb{Q}_{\mathcal{P}}$ that returns the label of the first instruction to be executed by each process.

A skip statement corresponds to the empty statement that leaves the program state unchanged. A goto statement of the form "`goto` $\mathsf{loc}_1, \ldots \mathsf{loc}_n$" jumps nondeterministically to an instruction labeled by loc_t for some $t \in \{1, \ldots, n\}$. An assignment statement (asg for short) of the form "$x := expr$" assigns to the variable x the current value of the expression $expr$. An assumption statement (asp) of the form "`assume` $expr$" checks whether the expression $expr$ evaluates to $true$ and if not, the process execution is blocked till that the value of $expr$ is $true$. An assertion statement (asr) of the form "`assert` $expr$" checks whether the expression $expr$ evaluates to $true$, and if not the execution of the program is aborted. A conditional statement (cnd) of the form "`if` $\langle expr \rangle$ `then` $inst_1$ `else` $inst_2$ `fi`" executes the instruction $inst_1$, if the expression $expr$ evaluates to $true$. Otherwise, it executes the instruction $inst_2$. We assume w.l.o.g. that the label of $inst_1$ is different from the label of $inst_2$. We assume a language of expressions $expr$ interpreted over $\mathbb{D}$. Furthermore, in order to allow nondeterminism, $expr$ can receive the

```
⟨c-prog⟩ ::= ⟨var⟩+ ⟨process⟩+
   ⟨var⟩ ::= var x ;
⟨process⟩ ::= process p begin ⟨inst⟩* end
  ⟨inst⟩ ::= loc:⟨stmt⟩;
  ⟨stmt⟩ ::= skip
           | x := ⟨expr⟩
           | goto loc1,... locn
           | assume ⟨expr⟩
           | assert ⟨expr⟩
           | if ⟨expr⟩
             then ⟨inst⟩else ⟨inst⟩ fi
  ⟨expr⟩ ::= ⟨expr⟩|*
```

Fig. 9. Syntax of concurrent programs

non-deterministic value $*$. We use Expr to denote the set of all expressions in $\mathcal{P}$. Let $\mathsf{Var}_{expr} : \mathsf{Expr} \mapsto 2^{\mathsf{V}_{\mathcal{P}}}$ be a function that returns the set of variables appearing in a given expression (e.g., $\mathsf{Var}_{expr}(\mathsf{y} + \mathsf{z} + 1) = \{\mathrm{y}, \mathrm{z}\}$).

Semantics. We describe the semantics informally and progressively. Let us first consider the case of a (sequential) program $\mathcal{P}_s$ that has only one process P (i.e., $\mathsf{Proc}_{\mathcal{P}_s}=\{P\}$). A sequential configuration c is then defined by a pair $(\mathsf{loc}, \mathsf{state})$ where $\mathsf{loc} \in \mathbb{Q}_P$ is the label of the next instruction to be executed by the process P, and $state : \mathsf{V}_{\mathcal{P}} \mapsto \mathbb{D}$ is a function that defines the valuation of each shared variable. The initial sequential configuration $c_{init}(\mathcal{P}_s)$ is defined by $(init(P), state_{init})$ where $state_{init}(x) = 0$ for all $x \in \mathsf{V}_{\mathcal{P}_s}$. In other words, at the beginning of the program, all variables have value 0 and the process P will execute the first instruction in its code. The transition relation $\rightarrow_{\mathcal{P}_s}$ on sequential configurations is defined as usual: For two sequential configurations c, c', we write $c \rightarrow_{\mathcal{P}_s} c'$ to denote that the program $\mathcal{P}_s$ can move from c to c'.

Now, we consider the case of the concurrent program $\mathcal{P}$ that has at least two processes (i.e., $|\mathsf{Proc}_{\mathcal{P}}| \geq 2$). For every $P \in \mathsf{Proc}_{\mathcal{P}}$, let $\mathcal{P}_P$ be the sequential program constructed from $\mathcal{P}$ by deleting the code of any process $P' \neq P$ (i.e., $\mathcal{P}_P$ contains only the instructions of the process P). We define a function *label definition* $\bar{q} : \mathsf{Proc}_{\mathcal{P}} \mapsto \mathbb{Q}_{\mathcal{P}}$ that associates for each process $P \in \mathsf{Proc}_{\mathcal{P}}$, the label $\bar{q}(P) \in \mathbb{Q}_P$ of the next instruction to be executed by P. A concurrent configuration (or simply configuration) c is a pair $(\bar{q}, state)$ where $\bar{q}$ is a label definition, and *state* is a memory state. We use $\mathsf{LabelOf}(c)$, $\mathsf{StateOf}(c)$ to denote $\bar{q}$ and *state* respectively. The initial configuration $c_{init}(\mathcal{P})$ is defined by $(\bar{q}_{init}, state_{init})$ where $\bar{q}_{init}(P) = init(P)$ for all $P \in \mathsf{Proc}_{\mathcal{P}}$, and $state_{init}(x) = 0$ for all $x \in \mathsf{V}_{\mathcal{P}}$. In other words, at the beginning, each process starts at the initial label, and all variables have value 0. We use $C(\mathcal{P})$ to denote the set of all configurations of the program $\mathcal{P}$. Then, the transition relation between configurations is defined as follows: For two given configurations $c = (\bar{q}, state)$ and $c' = (\bar{q}', state')$ and a label $\mathsf{loc} \in \mathbb{Q}_P$ of some process P, we write $c \xrightarrow{\mathsf{loc}}_{\mathcal{P}} c'$ to denote that program $\mathcal{P}$ can move from the configuration c to the configuration c' by executing the instruction labeled by loc of the process P. Formally, we have $c \xrightarrow{\mathsf{loc}}_{\mathcal{P}} c'$ iff $(\bar{q}(P), state) \rightarrow_{\mathcal{P}_P} (\bar{q}'(P), state')$, $\bar{q}(P) = \mathsf{loc}$, and for every $P' \in (\mathsf{Proc}_{\mathcal{P}} \setminus \{P\})$, we have $\bar{q}(P') = \bar{q}'(P')$.

A run π of $\mathcal{P}$ is a finite sequence of the form $c_0 \cdot \mathsf{loc}_1 \cdot c_1 \cdot \mathsf{loc}_2 \cdots \mathsf{loc}_m \cdot c_m$, for some $m \geq 0$ such that: (1) $c_0 = c_{init}(\mathcal{P})$ and (2) $c_i \xrightarrow{\mathsf{loc}_{i+1}}_{\mathcal{P}} c_{i+1}$ for all $i \in \{0, \ldots, m-1\}$. In this case, we say that π is labeled by the sequence $\mathsf{loc}_1 \mathsf{loc}_2 \ldots \mathsf{loc}_m$ and that the configuration c_m is reachable by $\mathcal{P}$. We use $\mathsf{Trace}(\pi)$ and $Target(\pi)$ to denote the sequence $\mathsf{loc}_1 \cdot \mathsf{loc}_2 \ldots \mathsf{loc}_m$ in π and the configuration c_m, respectively. We use $\Pi_{\mathcal{P}}$ to denote the set of all runs of the program $\mathcal{P}$. The program $\mathcal{P}$ is said to be safe if there is no run π reaching a configuration $c = (\bar{q}, state)$ (i.e., $Target(\pi) = c$) such that $\bar{q}(P)$, for some process $P \in \mathsf{Proc}_{\mathcal{P}}$, is the label of an assertion statement of the form "`assert` *expr*" where the expression *expr* can be evaluated to *false* at the configuration c.

4 Counter-Example Guided Program Verification

In this section, we present our Counter-Example Guided Program Verification (CEGPV) algorithm. The CEGPV algorithm takes a program $\mathcal{P}$ as its input and returns whether $\mathcal{P}$ is safe or not. The work-flow of the algorithm is given in Fig. 1. The algorithm consists of four modules, the *abstraction*, the *counter-example mapping*, the *reconstruction* and the *refinement*. It also uses an external *model checker* as a back-end tool. Recall that $\mathsf{V}_{\mathcal{P}}$ denotes the set of variables of the program $\mathcal{P}$. The algorithm starts by selecting a subset of variables $\mathsf{V}_0 \subseteq \mathsf{V}_{\mathcal{P}}$ using a dependency graph (not shown in Fig. 1 for sake of simplicity).

The *abstraction* takes $\mathcal{P}$ and V_0 as its input. It then constructs an over-approximation of $\mathcal{P}$, called $\mathcal{P}'$, as follows. First, it keeps variables in V_0 and slices away all other variables of $\mathcal{P}$. Occurrences of the sliced variables are replaced by a non-deterministic value. Second, some instructions, where the sliced variables occur, in $\mathcal{P}$ can be discarded. After that, $\mathcal{P}'$ is given to a *model checker*. Observe that $\mathcal{P}'$ has V_0 as its set of shared variables.

Then, the *model checker* takes as input $\mathcal{P}'$, generated by the *abstraction* module or the *refinement* module, and checks whether it is safe or not. If the *model checker* returns that the program is safe, then $\mathcal{P}$ is also safe, and our algorithm terminates. If the program is unsafe, then the *model checker* returns a counter-example π' of the form $c_0 \cdot \mathsf{loc}_1 \cdot c_1 \cdot \mathsf{loc}_2 \cdots \mathsf{loc}_m \cdot c_m$.

The *counter-example mapping* takes the counter-example π' as its input. It transforms the run π' to a run of the program resulting of the *abstraction* module.

The *reconstruction* takes always as input a counter-example π of $\mathcal{P}'$ (which results from the application of the *abstraction* module to the program $\mathcal{P}$). It then checks whether π can lead to a real counter-example of $\mathcal{P}$. In particular, if $\mathsf{V}_0 = \mathsf{V}_{\mathcal{P}}$, i.e. no variable was sliced away from $\mathcal{P}$, then $\mathcal{P}'$ is identical to $\mathcal{P}$. Therefore, π is also a counter-example of $\mathcal{P}$. The algorithm concludes that $\mathcal{P}$ is unsafe, and then terminates. Otherwise, the *reconstruction* adds back all omitted variables (i.e., $V_{\mathcal{P}} \setminus V_0$) and lines of codes to create a program $\mathcal{P}_1$. The program $\mathcal{P}_1$ also needs to respect the flow of the instructions in π. In other words, the instruction labeled by loc_i, for some $i \in \{1, \ldots, m\}$, in $\mathcal{P}_1$ can only be executed after executing all the instructions labeled by loc_j for all $j \in \{1, \ldots, i-1\}$. For each run of the program $\mathcal{P}_1$, let c_i' be the configuration after executing the instruction labeled by loc_i. The configuration c_i' needs to satisfy $\mathsf{StateOf}(c_i')(x) = \mathsf{StateOf}(c_i)(x)$ for all $x \in \mathsf{V}_0$, i.e. each value of variable in the set V_0 at the configuration c_i' is equal to its value in the configuration c_i.

Then CEGPV recursively calls itself to check $\mathcal{P}_1$ in its next iteration. Inputs of the next iteration are $\mathcal{P}_1$, and a subset of variables $\mathsf{V}_1 \subseteq \mathsf{V}_{\mathcal{P}_1} = (V_{\mathcal{P}} \setminus V_0)$, which is selected using the dependency graph. If the iteration returns that $\mathcal{P}_1$ is unsafe, then the run π leads to a counter-example of $\mathcal{P}$. The algorithm concludes that $\mathcal{P}$ is unsafe and terminates. Otherwise, π cannot lead to a counter-example of $\mathcal{P}$. Then the algorithm needs to discard π from the set of runs of $\mathcal{P}'$.

The *refinement* adds π to the set of spurious counter-examples of $\mathcal{P}'$ (resulting from the application of the *abstraction* module to $\mathcal{P}$). It then refines $\mathcal{P}'$ by removing all these spurious counter-examples from the set of runs of $\mathcal{P}'$. The new resulting program is then given back to the *model checker.*

In the following, we explain in more details each module of our CEGPV algorithm. The *counter-example mapping* module is described at the end of the subsection dedicated to the explanation of the *refinement* module (Sect. 4.3).

4.1 The Abstraction

The abstraction transforms $\mathcal{P}$ into a new program $\mathcal{P}'$ by slicing away all variables in $\mathsf{V}_{\mathcal{P}} \setminus \mathsf{V}_0$ and some lines of codes. In particular, we define a map function $\llbracket . \rrbracket_{ab}$ that rewrites $\mathcal{P}$ into $\mathcal{P}'$. The formal definition of the map $\llbracket . \rrbracket_{ab}$ is given in Fig. 10. In the following, we informally explain $\llbracket . \rrbracket_{ab}$.

The map $\llbracket . \rrbracket_{ab}$ keeps only the variables in V_0 and removes all other variables of $\mathcal{P}$. The map $\llbracket . \rrbracket_{ab}$ also keeps the same number of processes as in $\mathcal{P}$, and transforms the code of each process of $\mathcal{P}$ to a corresponding process in $\mathcal{P}'$.

For each instruction in a process, the map $\llbracket . \rrbracket_{ab}$ keeps the label and transforms the statement in that instruction. The map $\llbracket . \rrbracket_{ab}$ replaces occurrences of sliced variables in the statement by the non-deterministic value $*$. First, the skip and goto statements remain the same since they do not make use of any variable. Second, for an assignment statement of the form "x := *expr*", if the variable x is not in V_0, then that statement is transformed to the skip statement. If at least one discarded variable occurs in the expression *expr*, then the assignment is transformed to "$x := *$". Otherwise, the assignment remains the same. Third, for both an assumption statement of the form "`assume` *expr*" and an assertion of the form "`assert` *expr*", the map $\llbracket . \rrbracket_{ab}$ replaces the expression *expr* by the nondeterministic value $*$, if at least one discarded variable occurs in *expr*. Otherwise, the assumption and assertion remain the same. For a conditional statement, the map $\llbracket . \rrbracket_{ab}$ transforms its guard to be non-deterministic if it makes use of one of the discarded variables. The consequent instruction and alternative instruction are also transformed in a similar manner by the map $\llbracket . \rrbracket_{ab}$. Finally, we remove any instruction that *trivially* does not affect the behaviors of $\llbracket \mathcal{P} \rrbracket_{ab}$.

$$
\begin{aligned}
\llbracket \langle c\text{-}prog \rangle \rrbracket_{ab} &\stackrel{\text{def}}{=} \llbracket \langle \texttt{var}\ x \rangle \rrbracket_{ab}^{+} \llbracket \langle process \rangle \rrbracket_{ab}^{+} \\
\llbracket \langle \texttt{var}\ x \rangle \rrbracket_{ab} &\stackrel{\text{def}}{=} \begin{cases} \texttt{var}\ x;\ \text{if } x \in \mathsf{V}_0 \\ \cancel{\texttt{var}\ x;}\ \text{otherwise} \end{cases} \\
\llbracket \langle process \rangle \rrbracket_{ab} &\stackrel{\text{def}}{=} \texttt{process p begin } \llbracket \langle inst \rangle \rrbracket_{ab}^{*} \texttt{ end} \\
\llbracket \langle inst \rangle \rrbracket_{ab} &\stackrel{\text{def}}{=} \mathsf{loc}\text{:}\quad \llbracket \langle stmt \rangle \rrbracket_{ab}; \\
\llbracket \texttt{skip} \rrbracket_{ab} &\stackrel{\text{def}}{=} \texttt{skip} \\
\llbracket \texttt{goto}\ \mathsf{loc}_1, \ldots, \mathsf{loc}_n \rrbracket_{ab} &\stackrel{\text{def}}{=} \texttt{goto}\ \mathsf{loc}_1, \ldots, \mathsf{loc}_n \\
\llbracket \langle x := \langle expr \rangle \rrbracket_{ab} &\stackrel{\text{def}}{=} \begin{cases} \texttt{skip} & \text{if } x \notin \mathsf{V}_0 \\ x := \llbracket \langle expr \rangle \rrbracket_{ab} & \text{otherwise} \end{cases} \\
\llbracket \texttt{assume}\langle expr \rangle \rrbracket_{ab} &\stackrel{\text{def}}{=} \texttt{assume}\ \llbracket \langle expr \rangle \rrbracket_{ab} \\
\llbracket \texttt{assert}\langle expr \rangle \rrbracket_{ab} &\stackrel{\text{def}}{=} \texttt{assert}\ \llbracket \langle expr \rangle \rrbracket_{ab} \\
\llbracket \texttt{if}\ \langle expr \rangle\ \texttt{then}\ \langle inst_1 \rangle\ \texttt{else}\ \langle inst_2 \rangle\ \texttt{fi} \rrbracket_{ab} &\stackrel{\text{def}}{=} \texttt{if}\ \llbracket \langle expr \rangle \rrbracket_{ab}\ \texttt{then}\ \llbracket \langle inst_1 \rangle \rrbracket_{ab}\ \texttt{else}\ \llbracket \langle inst_2 \rangle \rrbracket_{ab}\ \texttt{fi} \\
\llbracket \langle expr \rangle \rrbracket_{ab} &\stackrel{\text{def}}{=} \begin{cases} *\ \text{if } \mathsf{Var}_{expr}(expr) \cap (\mathsf{V}_{\mathcal{P}_0} \setminus \mathsf{V}_0) \neq \varnothing \\ expr\ \text{otherwise} \end{cases}
\end{aligned}
$$

Fig. 10. Translation map $\llbracket . \rrbracket_{ab}$

Lemma 1. *If* $\llbracket \mathcal{P} \rrbracket_{ab}$ *is safe, then* $\mathcal{P}$ *is safe.*

4.2 The Reconstruction

Let π be a counter-example of the program $[\![\mathcal{P}]\!]_{ab}$ of the form $c_0 \cdot \mathsf{loc}_1 \cdot c_1 \cdot \mathsf{loc}_2 \cdots \mathsf{loc}_m \cdot c_m$. The reconstruction transforms $\mathcal{P}$ to a new program $\mathcal{P}_1$ by forcing $\mathcal{P}$ to respect the sequence of configurations and labels in π. In particular, we define a map function $[\![.]\!]_{co}$ to rewrite the program $\mathcal{P}$ into the program $\mathcal{P}_1$. The formal definition of the map $[\![.]\!]_{co}$ is given in Fig. 11. For a label loc, let $\mathsf{IndexOf}(\mathsf{loc}) = \{i \in \{1, \ldots, m\} \mid \mathsf{loc}_i = \mathsf{loc}\}$ be the set of positions where the label loc occurs in the run π. Let newloc be a function that returns a fresh label that has not used so far. The map $[\![.]\!]_{co}$ starts by adding a new variable cnt. The variable cnt is used to keep track of the execution order of the instructions in π. All variables in V_0 are removed by the map $[\![.]\!]_{co}$ since their values is determined by π. The map $[\![.]\!]_{co}$ also keeps the same number of processes as in the program $\mathcal{P}$, and transforms the code of each process.

$$
\begin{aligned}
[\![\langle c\text{-}prog\rangle]\!]_{co} &\stackrel{\text{def}}{=} \mathtt{var}\ cnt;\ [\![\langle \mathtt{var}\ x\rangle]\!]^{+}_{co}[\![\langle process\rangle]\!]^{+}_{co} \\
[\![\langle \mathtt{var}\ x\rangle]\!]_{co} &\stackrel{\text{def}}{=} \begin{cases} \mathtt{var}\ x; & \text{if } x \notin \mathsf{V}_0 \\ \xcancel{\mathtt{var}\ x;} & \text{otherwise} \end{cases} \\
[\![\langle process\rangle]\!]_{co} &\stackrel{\text{def}}{=} \mathtt{process}\ \mathrm{p}\ \mathtt{begin}\ [\![\langle inst\rangle]\!]_{co}\ \mathtt{end} \\
[\![\langle inst\rangle]\!]_{co} &\stackrel{\text{def}}{=} \begin{cases} [\![\mathsf{loc} : \langle stmt\rangle]\!]_{co,ab} & \text{if } \mathsf{loc} \in \mathbb{I}_{[\![\mathcal{P}]\!]_{ab}} \\ [\![\mathsf{loc} : \langle stmt\rangle]\!]_{co,oth}; & \text{otherwise} \end{cases} \\
[\![\mathsf{loc} : \langle stmt\rangle]\!]_{co,oth} &\stackrel{\text{def}}{=} \begin{cases} \mathsf{loc}\text{: } \mathtt{if}\ (cnt == 0)\ \mathtt{then}\ [\![\langle stmt\rangle]\!]^{0}_{co,oth};\ \mathtt{else} \\ \quad \ldots \\ \quad \mathtt{if}\ (cnt == m)\ \mathtt{then}\ [\![\langle stmt\rangle]\!]^{m}_{co,oth}; \\ \quad \mathtt{else\ skip;\ fi;} \ldots \mathtt{fi;} \end{cases} \\
[\![\mathsf{loc} : \langle stmt\rangle]\!]_{co,ab} &\stackrel{\text{def}}{=} \begin{cases} \mathsf{loc}\text{: } \mathtt{if}\ (cnt + 1 \in \mathsf{IndexOf}(\mathsf{loc}) \wedge cnt == 0)\ \mathtt{then} \\ \quad [\![\langle stmt\rangle]\!]^{0}_{co,ab};\ \mathtt{else} \\ \quad \ldots \\ \quad \mathtt{if}\ (cnt + 1 \in \mathsf{IndexOf}(\mathsf{loc}) \wedge cnt == m-1)\ \mathtt{then} \\ \quad [\![\langle stmt\rangle]\!]^{m-1}_{co,ab};\ \mathtt{else\ assume\ false;\ fi;} \ldots \mathtt{fi;} \\ \mathsf{newloc} : cnt := cnt + 1; \end{cases} \\
[\![\mathtt{skip}]\!]^{i}_{co,-} &\stackrel{\text{def}}{=} \mathtt{skip}\ \text{where } - \in \{ab, oth\} \\
[\![\mathtt{goto}\ \mathsf{loc}_1, \ldots, \mathsf{loc}_n]\!]^{i}_{co,-} &\stackrel{\text{def}}{=} \mathtt{goto}\ \mathsf{loc}_1, \ldots, \mathsf{loc}_n\ \text{where } - \in \{ab, oth\} \\
[\![\mathtt{assume}\ \langle expr\rangle]\!]^{i}_{co,-} &\stackrel{\text{def}}{=} \mathtt{assume}\ [\![\langle expr\rangle]\!]^{c}_{co}\ \text{where } - \in \{ab, oth\} \\
[\![\mathtt{assert}\ \langle expr\rangle]\!]^{i}_{co,-} &\stackrel{\text{def}}{=} \mathtt{assert}\ [\![\langle expr\rangle]\!]^{c}_{co}\ \text{where } - \in \{ab, oth\} \\
[\![x := \langle expr\rangle]\!]^{i}_{co,ab} &\stackrel{\text{def}}{=} \mathtt{assume}\ \mathsf{StateOf}(c_{i+1})(\mathrm{x}) == [\![\langle expr\rangle]\!]^{i}_{co} \\
[\![x := \langle expr\rangle]\!]^{i}_{co,oth} &\stackrel{\text{def}}{=} x := [\![\langle expr\rangle]\!]^{i}_{co} \\
\begin{matrix}[\![\mathtt{if}\ \langle expr\rangle\ \mathtt{then}\ \langle inst_1\rangle \\ \mathtt{else}\ \langle inst_2\rangle\ \mathtt{fi}]\!]^{i}_{co,ab}\end{matrix} &\stackrel{\text{def}}{=} \begin{cases} \mathtt{assume}\ [\![\langle expr\rangle]\!]^{i}_{co} == \mathtt{true};\ [\![\langle inst_1\rangle]\!]_{co} & \text{if } label(inst_1) \in \mathsf{LabelOf}(c_{i+1}) \\ \mathtt{assume}\ [\![\langle expr\rangle]\!]^{i}_{co} == \mathtt{false};\ [\![\langle inst_2\rangle]\!]_{co} & \text{otherwise} \end{cases} \\
\begin{matrix}[\![\mathtt{if}\ \langle expr\rangle\ \mathtt{then}\ \langle inst_1\rangle \\ \mathtt{else}\ \langle inst_2\rangle\ \mathtt{fi}]\!]^{i}_{co,oth}\end{matrix} &\stackrel{\text{def}}{=} \begin{matrix}\mathtt{if}\ [\![\langle expr\rangle]\!]^{i}_{co}\ \mathtt{then}\ [\![\langle inst_1\rangle]\!]_{co} \\ \mathtt{else}\ [\![\langle inst_2\rangle]\!]_{co}\ \mathtt{fi}\end{matrix} \\
[\![\langle expr\rangle]\!]^{i}_{co} &\stackrel{\text{def}}{=} \langle expr\rangle[\forall x \in \mathsf{V}_0 : x \hookleftarrow \mathsf{StateOf}(c_i)(x)]
\end{aligned}
$$

Fig. 11. Translation map $[\![.]\!]_{co}$

The map $[\![.]\!]_{co}$ transforms instructions in each process as follows. Instructions that occur in $[\![\mathcal{P}]\!]_{ab}$, are transformed by the map $[\![.]\!]_{co,ab}$, while other instructions are transformed by the map $[\![.]\!]_{co,oth}$. For an instruction of the form "loc: *stmt*", the map $[\![.]\!]_{co,oth}$ keeps the label loc and creates $m+1$ copies of the statement *stmt*. The i-th copy of *stmt*, with $i \in \{0, \ldots, m\}$, is executed after reaching the configuration c_i in the run π. Therefore, the i-th copy only can be only executed under the condition "$cnt == i$". Then, the statement $stmt$ is transformed based on the configuration c_i in the run π, denoted by $[\![.]\!]^i_{co,oth}$. Similarly, the map $[\![\cdot]\!]_{co,ab}$ keeps the label loc and creates m copies of the statement $stmt$ (which corresponds to number of instructions in the run π). The i-th copy of $stmt$, with $i \in \{1, \ldots, m\}$, is executed if the label loc appears at position i in the run π. Therefore, the i-th copy can be executed under the condition "$cnt + 1 \in \mathsf{IndexOf(loc)}$" (i.e., the label loc appears at the position $cnt + 1$) and that $cnt = i - 1$ (i.e., after reaching the configuration c_{i-1}). Then, the map $[\![.]\!]_{co,ab}$ transforms the statement $stmt$ based on the configurations c_{cnt-1} and c_{cnt} (i.e., the configurations before and after executing the instruction labeled by loc) in the run π, denoted by $[\![.]\!]^{cnt}_{co,ab}$. The variable cnt is then increased by one to denote that one more instruction in the run π has been executed.

In general, the map $[\![.]\!]^i_{co,ab}$, for some $i \in \{0, \ldots, m-1\}$ rewrites all expressions in statements. The skip and goto statement remain the same. For both an assertion of the form "`assert` $expr$" and assumption "`assume` $expr$", $[\![.]\!]^c_{co,ab}$ transforms their expressions $expr$. For an assignment of the form "$x := expr$", it rewrites that assignment by an assumption checking that, the value of x in the configuration c_{i+1} is equal to the value of $expr$ at the configuration c_i. For a conditional statement of the form `if` $\langle expr \rangle$ `then` $inst_1$ `else` $inst_2$ `fi`", $[\![.]\!]^c_{co,ab}$, we first check which branch has been taken in the run π. To do that, we check the labels appearing in the configuration c_{i+1}. After that, we add an assumption to check whether the branch has been correctly selected in the counter-example. if $expr$ is evaluated to `true` at the configuration c_i and the label of $inst_1$ appears at the configuration c_{i+1}, then it executes the instruction $[\![inst_1]\!]^i_{co,ab}$. Otherwise, it executes the instruction $[\![inst_2]\!]^i_{co,ab}$. Finally, all occurrences of variables in V_0 in any expressions $expr$ are replaced by their values in the configuration c_i.

The map $[\![.]\!]^i_{co,oth}$, for some $i \in \{0, \ldots, m\}$, transforms statements as follows. The skip and goto statement remain the same. For assignment, assumption, and assertion, $[\![.]\!]^i_{co,oth}$ rewrites expressions in these statements. For a conditional statement, it also rewrites the guards, the consequent instruction and the alternative instruction. The expression is transformed by replacing occurrences of variables in V_0 in that expression by their values in the configuration c_i.

Lemma 2. *If $[\![\mathcal{P}]\!]_{co}$ is unsafe, then $\mathcal{P}$ is unsafe.*

4.3 The Refinement

Given a set of runs R of $[\![\mathcal{P}]\!]_{ab}$, the *refinement* module constructs a program $\mathcal{P}'$ from $[\![\mathcal{P}]\!]_{ab}$ by discarding the set of runs in R from the set of runs of $[\![\mathcal{P}]\!]_{ab}$. Before giving the details of this module, we introduce some notations and definitions.

For a run π of the form $c_0 \cdot \mathsf{loc}_1 \cdot c_1 \ldots \mathsf{loc}_m \cdot c_m$, let $\mathsf{Loc}(\pi) = \{\mathsf{loc}_1, \ldots, \mathsf{loc}_m\}$ be the set of all labels occurring in π, and $\mathsf{Con}(\pi) = \{c_0, c_1, \ldots, c_m\}$ be the set of all configurations in π. Let $\mathsf{R}_{loc} = \bigcup_{\pi \in \mathsf{R}} \mathsf{Loc}(\pi)$ and $\mathsf{R}_{con} = \bigcup_{\pi \in \mathsf{R}} \mathsf{Con}(\pi)$. Let $\mathsf{Prefix}(\pi) = \{c_0 \cdot \mathsf{loc}_1 \cdot c_1 \ldots \mathsf{loc}_i \cdot c_i | i \in \{0, \ldots, m-1\}\}$ be the set of prefixes of π and $\mathsf{R}_{prefix} = \bigcup_{\pi \in \mathsf{R}} \mathsf{Prefix}(\pi)$ be the set of all prefixes of all runs in R.

Then, we construct a graph (or a tree) G_R to represent in concise manner the set of runs in R. The graph $G_R = (V, E)$ consists of a number of vertices V and directed edges E where $V = \mathsf{R}_{prefix}$ and $E = \{(v, v') | \exists \mathsf{loc} \in \mathsf{R}_{loc}, c \in \mathsf{R}_{con}$ and $v' = v \cdot \mathsf{loc} \cdot c\}$. In other words, each vertex corresponds to a prefix in R_{prefix}, and each edge describes the transition from one prefix to another one.

Let $v \in V$, $P \in \mathsf{Proc}_{[\![\mathcal{P}]\!]_{ab}}$, and $\mathsf{loc} \in \mathbb{Q}_P$. Let $\mathsf{Next}(v, \mathsf{loc}) = \{c | c \in \mathsf{R}_{con} : v \cdot \mathsf{loc} \cdot c \in (V \cup \mathsf{R})\}$ be the function that returns the set of configurations which can be reached from v through executing the instruction labeled by loc. Let $\mathsf{Reach}(v, P) = \{\mathsf{loc} | \mathsf{loc} \in \mathbb{Q}_P, \exists c \in C([\![\mathcal{P}]\!]_{ab})$ and $\exists v' \in \Pi([\![\mathcal{P}]\!]_{ab}) : (v' = v \cdot \mathsf{LabelOf}(\mathit{Target}(v))(P) \cdot c) \wedge (v' \notin (V \cup \mathsf{R})) \wedge (\mathsf{loc} = \mathsf{LabelOf}(c)(P))\}$ be the function that returns the set of all possible labels loc of the process P that can be reached by a run $v' \notin \mathsf{R} \cup V$ which is an extension of the prefix v by executing an instruction of the process P. In order to force the execution of $[\![\mathcal{P}]\!]_{ab}$ to perform a different run than the ones in R, we make sure that $[\![\mathcal{P}]\!]_{ab}$ follows the prefix $v \in \mathsf{R}_{prefix}$, and then performs the instruction of the process P that leads to a new prefix p' which was not part of R_{prefix} or R. Then, we create the output program $\mathcal{P}'$ of the *refinement* module from $[\![\mathcal{P}]\!]_{ab}$ by adding (1) an *observer* process to simulate the execution of the prefix v', and (2) a *controller* per process to continue execution of each process from the reached location after executing the prefix v'. We add a new variable, called *label*, used by the *observer* to communicate to each *controller* where the execution will resume for each process after leaving the *observer*.

We construct an *observer* as given in Fig. 12. The *observer* is executed before any processes in $[\![\mathcal{P}]\!]_{ab}$. It starts by non-deterministically jumping to a node v_i (representing a prefix of a run in R), where v_i represents a vertex of G_R. At the node v_i, values of variables are updated to the valuation at $\mathit{Target}(v_i)$. Then, the observer decides, in non-deterministic manner, to execute an instruction of a process $P_j \in [\![\mathcal{P}]\!]_{ab}$. If the execution of an instruction of P_j, from the prefix v_i, does not lead a new prefix which is not in $\mathsf{R} \cup \mathsf{R}_{prefix}$ (i.e., $\mathsf{Reach}(v, P_j)$ is empty), then the execution of the *observer* terminates (and so of the program $\mathcal{P}'$). If $\mathsf{Reach}(v, P_j)$ is not empty, we first distinguish the case where the next instruction to be executed by P_j is a non-deterministic assignment to some variable x. Then, the observer ensures

```
start: goto  v1, v2, ..., vn;
...
vi:    for all x ∈ V0: x := StateOf(Target(vi))(x);
       goto (vi, P1), ..., (vi, Pm);
       ...
       (vi, Pj): if Reach(vi, Pj) ≠ ∅ then
         loc := LabelOf(Target(vi))(Pj);
         if stmt(loc) of the form "x := *" then
           x := *;
           assume x ∉ {StateOf(c)(x) | c ∈ Next(vi, loc)};
         else assume false ; fi;
         label := *;
         assume label ∈ Reach(vi, Pj);
         flag := 1;
         for all P ∈ Proc_[[P]]ab \ {Pj}
           label := LabelOf(Target(vi)) (P);
       fi;
       assume false ;
       ...
...
```

Fig. 12. Pseudocode of observer with $V = \{v_1, \ldots, v_n\}$ and $\mathsf{Proc}_{[\![\mathcal{P}]\!]_{ab}} = \{P_1, \ldots, P_m\}$

that the new value assigned to x is different from its value in any configuration which can be reached from v_i through executing this non-deterministic assignment by P_j. After that, the *observer* communicates the new label of P_j by setting the variable *label* to it. Finally, it sets the variable *flag* to one to enable the execution of other processes and communicates to them their starting instruction by setting the variable *label*.

Each process P in $[\![\mathcal{P}]\!]_{ab}$ is controlled by a controller, given in Fig. 13. The controller is placed at the top of the code of P. The controller then checks if the label stored in the variable *label* is in indeed belongs to P, if it is the case, it jumps to that label. Otherwise, P needs to wait until one of its label is written.

```
assume flag == 1;
if label ∈ ℚ_P then goto label;
else assume false ;
...
```

Fig. 13. Pseudocode of controller of the process P

Finally, we can easily define a mapping *map* that maps any run of $\mathcal{P}'$ to a run of $[\![\mathcal{P}]\!]_{ab}$. This mapping *map* is used in the *Counter-example mapping* module. We can also extend the definition of the mapping *map* to sets of runs in the straightforward manner.

Lemma 3. $map(\Pi(\mathcal{P}')) = \Pi([\![\mathcal{P}]\!]_{ab}) \setminus R$.

5 Optimizations

In this section, we present two optimizations of our CEGPV algorithm. The first optimization concerns the reduction of the number of iterations of our GEGPV algorithm by considering several counter-examples instead of one at each iteration. The second optimization concerns an efficient implementation of the *reconstruction* and *refinement* modules when considering SMT/SAT based model-checkers such as CBMC [10].

Combining Counter-Examples. Our *reconstruction* module takes as input a counter-example π of the form $c_0 \cdot \mathsf{loc}_1 \cdot c_1 \cdot \mathsf{loc}_2 \cdots \mathsf{loc}_m \cdot c_m$ of the program $[\![\mathcal{P}]\!]_{ab}$, and construct the program $\mathcal{P}_1$ which needs to respect the flow of the instructions in π and also the evaluation of the set of shared variables in V_0. To do so efficiently, we drop the constraint that the program $\mathcal{P}_1$ should follow the valuations of the shared variables in V_0 in our code-code translation $[\![.]\!]_{co}$. This means that the constructed program $\mathcal{P}_1$ should only make sure to execute the instruction labeled by loc_i, for some $i \in \{1, \ldots, m\}$, after executing all the instructions labeled by loc_j for all $j \in \{1, \ldots, i-1\}$. We also modify the *refinement* module to discard all the runs π' in the set of runs of $[\![\mathcal{P}]\!]_{ab}$ such that $\mathsf{Trace}(\pi') = \mathsf{Trace}(\pi)$ in case that the program $\mathcal{P}_1$ is declared safe by *model-checker*.

We can furthermore optimize our CEGPV algorithm by not imposing any order on the execution of two instructions labeled by loc_i and loc_j if they can be declared to be independent (as done in stateless model-checking techniques [3]).

SMT Based Optimization. The CEGPV algorithm can be integrated into SMT/SAT based model-checkers such as CBMC [10]. Recall that in Sect. 4.2, we force a program running in a specific order of instructions, and in Sect. 4.3, we forbid that order of instructions in a program. These operations can be easily done performed using clock variables [16]. Indeed, for each label loc in the program, we associate to a clock variable $\mathsf{clock}_{\mathsf{loc}}$ ranging over the naturals. The clock variable $\mathsf{clock}_{\mathsf{loc}}$ is assigned 0 if the instruction labeled by loc is not executed. Given labels loc_1 and loc_2, in order to force the execution of the instruction labeled by loc_1 before the execution of the instruction labeled by loc_2, we need only to make sure that $0 < \mathsf{clock}_{\mathsf{loc}_1}$ and $\mathsf{clock}_{\mathsf{loc}_1} < \mathsf{clock}_{\mathsf{loc}_2}$. In the similar way, we can write a formula to force the SMT/SAT based model checker to return a counter-example different from the already encountered ones.

Table 1. Performance of CEGPV in comparison to CBMC on benchmarks of the SV-COMP15 *Concurrency category* [2]. Each row corresponds to a sub-category of the SV-COMP15 benchmarks, where we report the number of checked programs. The column *pass* gives the number of correct answers retuned by each tool. An answer is considered to be correct for a (un)safe program if the tool return "(un)safe". The columns *fail* report the number of unsuccessful analyses performed by each tool. An unsuccessful analysis includes crashes, timeouts. The columns *time* gives the total running time in seconds for the verification of each benchmark. Observe that we do not count, in the total time, the time spent by a tool when the verification fails.

		CBMC 5.1			CEGPV		
sub-catergory	#programs	pass	fail	time	pass	fail	time
pthread-wmm-mix-unsafe	466	466	0	40301	466	0	1076
pthread-wmm-podwr-unsafe	16	16	0	286	16	0	21
pthread-wmm-rfi-unsafe	76	76	0	958	76	0	141
pthread-wmm-safe-unsafe	200	200	0	12578	200	0	917
pthread-wmm-thin-unsafe	12	12	0	252	12	0	15
pthread-unsafe	17	12	5	441	17	0	302
pthead-atomic-unsafe	2	2	0	2	2	0	2
pthread-ext-unsafe	8	4	4	7	8	0	7
pthread-lit-unsafe	3	2	1	3	2	1	2
pthread-wmm-rfi-safe	12	12	0	3154	12	0	138
pthread-wmm-safe-safe	104	102	2	352	104	0	114
pthread-wmm-thin-safe	12	12	0	28	12	0	12
pthread-safe	14	7	7	124	13	1	63
pthead-atomic-safe	8	7	1	76	8	0	10
pthread-ext-safe	45	19	26	938	31	14	569
pthread-lit-safe	8	3	5	8	3	5	5

6 Experiment Results

In order to evaluate the efficiency of our CEGPV algorithm, we have implemented it as a part of an open source tool, called CEGPV [1], for the verification of C/pthreads programs. We used CBMC version 5.1 as a backend tool [10]. We then evaluated CEGPV on the benchmark set from the Concurrency category of the TACAS Software Verification Competition (SV-COMP15) [2]. The set consists of 1003 C programs. We have performed all experiments on an Intel Core i7 3.5 Ghz machine with 16 GB of RAM. We have used a 10 GB as memory limit and a 800 s as timeout parameter for the verification of each program.

In the following, we present two sets of results. The first part concerns the unsafe programs and the second part concerns safe ones. In both parts, we compare CEGPV results to the ones obtained using CBMC 5.1 tool [10]. To ensure a faire comparison between the two tools, we use the same loop-unwinding and thread duplication bounds for each program. Table 1 shows that CEGPV is highly competitive. We observe that, for unsafe programs, CEGPV significantly outperforms CBMC. CEGPV is more than 10 times faster (on average) than CBMC, except for few small programs. CEGPV also manages to verify almost all the unsafe benchmarks (except one) while CBMC fails in the verification of 10 programs due to timeout. For safe benchmarks, CEGPV still outperforms CBMC in the running time. In many programs, CEGPV succeeds to prove the safety of several programs (except 20 programs), while CBMC fails to prove the safety of 41 programs. Finally, we observe that, for the benchmark $pthread-lit$, the results of both tools are almost the same. The reason is that the programs in that benchmark only use few variables. Therefore, CEGPV does not slice away variables in these programs.

References

1. CEGPV. https://github.com/diepbp/SlicingCBMC
2. SV-COMP home page. http://sv-comp.sosy-lab.org/2015/
3. Abdulla, P.A., Aronis, S., Jonsson, B., Sagonas, K.F.: Optimal dynamic partial order reduction. In: POPL, pp. 373–384. ACM (2014)
4. Ball, T., Rajamani, S.K.: The SLAM project: debugging system software via static analysis. In: POPL, pp. 1–3. ACM (2002)
5. Beyer, D., Henzinger, T.A., Jhala, R., Majumdar, R.: The software model checker blast. STTT **9**(5–6), 505–525 (2007)
6. Beyer, D., Keremoglu, M.E.: CPAchecker: a tool for configurable software verification. In: Gopalakrishnan, G., Qadeer, S. (eds.) CAV 2011. LNCS, vol. 6806, pp. 184–190. Springer, Heidelberg (2011). doi:10.1007/978-3-642-22110-1_16
7. Bindal, S., Bansal, S., Lal, A.: Variable and thread bounding for systematic testing of multithreaded programs. In: ISSTA, pp. 145–155. ACM (2013)
8. Chaki, S., Clarke, E.M., Groce, A., Jha, S., Veith, H.: Modular verification of software components in C. IEEE Trans. Softw. Eng. **30**(6), 388–402 (2004)
9. Clarke, E.M., Grumberg, O., Jha, S., Lu, Y., Veith, H.: Counterexample-guided abstraction refinement for symbolic model checking. J. ACM **50**(5), 752–794 (2003)

10. Clarke, E., Kroening, D., Lerda, F.: A tool for checking ANSI-C programs. In: Jensen, K., Podelski, A. (eds.) TACAS 2004. LNCS, vol. 2988, pp. 168–176. Springer, Heidelberg (2004). doi:10.1007/978-3-540-24730-2_15
11. Henzinger, T.A., Jhala, R., Majumdar, R., Sutre, G.: Lazy abstraction. In: POPL, pp. 58–70. ACM (2002)
12. Komuravelli, A., Gurfinkel, A., Chaki, S., Clarke, E.M.: Automatic abstraction in SMT-based unbounded software model checking. In: Sharygina, N., Veith, H. (eds.) CAV 2013. LNCS, vol. 8044, pp. 846–862. Springer, Heidelberg (2013). doi:10.1007/978-3-642-39799-8_59
13. Kurshan, R.P.: Computer-Aided Verification of Coordinating Processes: The Automata-Theoretic Approach. Princeton University Press, Princeton (1994)
14. Kurshan, R.P.: Program verification. Not. AMS **47**(5), 534–545 (2000)
15. Lal, A., Qadeer, S., Lahiri, S.K.: A solver for reachability modulo theories. In: Madhusudan, P., Seshia, S.A. (eds.) CAV 2012. LNCS, vol. 7358, pp. 427–443. Springer, Heidelberg (2012). doi:10.1007/978-3-642-31424-7_32
16. Lamport, L.: Time, clocks, and the ordering of events in a distributed system. Commun. ACM **21**(7), 558–565 (1978)
17. Saïdi, H.: Model checking guided abstraction and analysis. In: Palsberg, J. (ed.) SAS 2000. LNCS, vol. 1824, pp. 377–396. Springer, Heidelberg (2000). doi:10.1007/978-3-540-45099-3_20
18. Valdiviezo, M., Cifuentes, C., Krishnan, P.: A method for scalable and precise bug finding using program analysis and model checking. In: Garrigue, J. (ed.) APLAS 2014. LNCS, vol. 8858, pp. 196–215. Springer, Heidelberg (2014). doi:10.1007/978-3-319-12736-1_11

Tighter Reachability Criteria for Deadlock-Freedom Analysis

Pedro Antonino(✉), Thomas Gibson-Robinson, and A.W. Roscoe

Department of Computer Science, University of Oxford, Oxford, UK
{pedro.antonino,thomas.gibson-robinson,bill.roscoe}@cs.ox.ac.uk

Abstract. We combine a prior incomplete deadlock-freedom-checking approach with two new reachability techniques to create a more precise deadlock-freedom-checking framework for concurrent systems. The reachability techniques that we propose are based on the analysis of individual components of the system; we use static analysis to summarise the behaviour that might lead components to this system state, and we analyse this summary to assess whether components can cooperate to reach a given system state. We implement this new framework on a tool called DeadlOx. This implementation encodes the proposed deadlock-freedom analysis as a satisfiability problem that is later checker by a SAT solver. We demonstrate by a series of practical experiments that this tool is more accurate than (and as efficient as) similar incomplete techniques for deadlock-freedom analysis.

1 Introduction

Deadlock-checking techniques seek to establish whether a finite-state concurrent system can reach a blocked state. Complete approaches construct and search a system's state space for blocked states, and thus, they either show that a system is deadlock free or they find a deadlock, namely, a *snapshot* of the system that is both reachable and blocked. A snapshot is a tuple containing a component state per component of the concurrent system, i.e. a possible state of the system. These techniques, however, tend not to be scalable: deadlock-freedom checking quickly becomes intractable as systems grow in size.

To cope with this lack of scalability, a number of incomplete deadlock-freedom-checking techniques have been proposed [2,3,5,6,12,13,16]. These techniques imprecisely characterise a deadlock using *local analysis*, that is, they analyse only small parts of the system (for instance, individual components or pairs of them) to establish, conservatively, whether a system can deadlock. This imprecise characterisation makes these techniques scalable at the expense of making them incomplete, namely, they either guarantee deadlock freedom or are inconclusive. In the latter case, the system might deadlock or not.

In [2], we presented an incomplete deadlock-checking technique that significantly improves on previous frameworks that use local analysis. It attempts to use purely local analysis to show that no blocked snapshot is reachable. While this works well for many classes of systems, it does not work in cases where the

J. Fitzgerald et al. (Eds.): FM 2016, LNCS 9995, pp. 43–59, 2016.
DOI: 10.1007/978-3-319-48989-6_3

interactions of the system maintain some global invariant that prevents deadlocks too subtle to identify with our original methods. This inability is a consequence of characterising snapshots reachability using pure local analysis.

In this paper, we propose two complementary reachability criteria, based on two common sorts of global invariant, that are combined with the pure-local-analysis technique in [2] to create a more precise deadlock-freedom technique. This new deadlock-freedom technique is implemented in the DeadlOx tool, which makes use of SAT checkers and FDR3's capabilities [9]. As in [2], using the capabilities of SAT checkers means we can be ambitious in the properties of snapshots that we seek to establish.

Outline. Sect. 2 briefly introduces CSP's operational semantics, which is the formalism upon which our strategy is based. However, this paper can be understood purely in terms of communicating systems of LTSs, and knowledge of CSP is not a prerequisite. Section 3 presents some related incomplete deadlock-freedom-checking techniques. In Sect. 4, we introduce our reachability criteria. Section 5 presents our new framework for imprecise deadlock-freedom checking. Section 6 presents an experiment conducted to assess the accuracy and efficiency of our DeadlOx tool. Finally, in Sect. 7, we present our concluding remarks.

2 Background

Communicating Sequential Processes (CSP) [11,19] is a notation used to model concurrent systems where processes interact, exchanging messages. Here we describe some structures used by the refinement checker FDR3 [9] in implementing CSP's operational semantics. As this paper does not depend on the details of CSP, we do not describe the details of the language or its semantics. These can be found in [19].

CSP's operational semantics interpret language terms as a *labelled transition system* (LTS).

Definition 1. *A labelled transition system is a 4-tuple* $(S, \Sigma, \Delta, \hat{s})$ *where* S *is a set of states,* Σ *is the alphabet,* $\Delta \subseteq S \times \Sigma \times S$ *is a transition relation, and* $\hat{s} \in S$ *is the starting state.*

FDR3 represents concurrent systems as *supercombinator machines.* A supercombinator machine consists of a set of component LTSs along with a set of rules that describe how components transitions should be combined. We restrict FDR3's usual definition to systems with pairwise communication, as per [2,13].

Definition 2. *A supercombinator machine is a pair* $(\mathcal{L}, \mathcal{R})$ *where:*

- $\mathcal{L} = \langle L_1, \ldots, L_n \rangle$ *is a sequence of component LTSs;*
- $\mathcal{R}$ *is a set of rules of the form* (i, e, a) *where:*
    - $i \in \mathbb{N}$ *is a unique identifier for the rule;*
    - $e \in (\Sigma \cup \{-\})^n$ *specifies the event that each component must perform, where* $-$ *indicates that the component performs no event; e must also be triple-disjoint, that is, at most two components must be involved in a rule.*

* $triple\_disjoint(e) \mathrel{\widehat{=}} \forall i, j, k \in \{1 \dots n\} \mid i \neq j \land j \neq k \land i \neq k \bullet$
$e_i = - \lor e_j = - \lor e_k = -$
- *$a \in \Sigma$ is the event the machine performs.*

The *participants* of a rule are the components required to perform an event. Given a supercombinator machine, a corresponding LTS can be constructed.

Definition 3. *Let $\mathcal{S} = (\langle L_1, \dots, L_n \rangle, \mathcal{R})$ be a supercombinator machine where $L_i = (S_i, \Sigma_i, \Delta_i, \hat{s}_i)$. The LTS induced by $\mathcal{S}$ is the tuple $(S, \Sigma, \Delta, \hat{s})$ such that:*

- $S = S_1 \times \dots \times S_n$;
- $\Sigma = \{i \mid \exists (i, e, a) \in \mathcal{R}\}$;
- $\Delta = \{((s_1, \dots, s_n), j, (s'_1, \dots, s'_n)) \mid \exists (j, (e_1, \dots, e_n), a) \in \mathcal{R} \bullet \forall i \in \{1 \dots n\} \bullet$
$(e_i = - \land s_i = s'_i) \lor (e_i \neq - \land (s_i, e_i, s'_i) \in \Delta_i)\}$;
- $\hat{s} = (\hat{s}_1, \dots, \hat{s}_n)$.

We slightly change the common definition of an induced LTS to focus on rule occurrences instead of system-event performances. Usually, a rule application is seen as an synchronisation between components that results in a system event. However, for our analyses, we are interested in the identifier of the rule used rather than the system event it produces.

We write $s \xrightarrow{r} s'$ if $(s, r, s') \in \Delta$. There is a path from s to s' with the sequence of rule identifiers $\langle r_1, \dots, r_n \rangle \in \Sigma^*$, represented by $s \xrightarrow{\langle r_1, \dots, r_n \rangle} s'$, if there exist $s_0, \dots, s_n$ such that $s_0 \xrightarrow{r_1} s_1 \dots s_{n-1} \xrightarrow{r_n} s_n$, $s_0 = s$ and $s_n = s'$. A trace is a path starting from the initial state. For our analyses, we will be mainly interested in the rule-identifier traces of induced LTSs.

Definition 4. *A LTS $(S, \Sigma, \Delta, \hat{s})$ deadlocks in a snapshot s if and only if the predicate $deadlocked(s)$ holds, where:*

- $deadlocked(s) \mathrel{\widehat{=}} reachable(s) \land blocked(s)$
- $reachable(s) \mathrel{\widehat{=}} \exists\, tr \in \Sigma^* \bullet \hat{s} \xrightarrow{tr} s$
- $blocked(s) \mathrel{\widehat{=}} \neg \exists\, s' \in S\, ;\, r \in \Sigma \bullet s \xrightarrow{r} s'$

3 Related Work

The *SDD* (State Dependency Digraph), developed by Martin in [13], is the basis of an incomplete technique that attempts to prove deadlock-freedom for triple-disjoint systems. It uses local analysis to construct the dependency digraph of a system. This framework relies on the fact that every deadlock produces a cycle in the system's dependency digraph. So, a cycle-free dependency digraph shows that a system is deadlock free. This characterisation can be efficiently checked by algorithms that detect cycles in a digraph. However, this cycle-of-dependencies characterisation for a deadlock can be rather imprecise.

In [2], we proposed *Pair*, an improved incomplete technique that checks deadlock-freedom for triple-disjoint systems. As per [13], it characterises a deadlock by analysing how pairs of components interact.

Definition 5. *Let* $\mathcal{S} = (\langle L_1, \ldots, L_n \rangle, \mathcal{R})$ *be a supercombinator machine. The* pairwise projection $\mathcal{S}_{i,j}$ *of the machine* $\mathcal{S}$ *on components* i *and* j *is given by:*

$$\mathcal{S}_{i,j} = (\langle L_i, L_j \rangle, \{(k, (e_i, e_j), a) \mid \exists (k, (e_1, \ldots, e_n), a) \in \mathcal{R} \bullet (e_i \neq - \vee e_j \neq -)\})$$

Instead of looking for cycles of dependencies, Pair characterises a deadlock as a snapshot of the system that is fully consistent with local reachability and blocking information. We call it a *Pair candidate.* As we use local analysis to its full extent, we end up with a framework that is strictly better than the SDD.

Definition 6. *Let* $\mathcal{S} = (\langle L_1, \ldots, L_n \rangle, \mathcal{R})$ *be a supercombinator machine, and* $(S, \Sigma, \Delta, \hat{s})$ *its induced LTS. A state* $s = (s_1, \ldots, s_n) \in S$ *is a* Pair candidate *iff* $pair\_candidate(s)$ *holds, where:*

- $pair\_candidate(s) \mathrel{\widehat{=}} pairwise\_reachable(s) \wedge blocked(s)$
- $pairwise\_reachable(s) \mathrel{\widehat{=}} \forall i, j \in \{1 \ldots n\} \mid i \neq j \bullet reachable_{i,j}((s_i, s_j))$

$reachable_{i,j}$ *is the reachable predicate for the pairwise projection* $\mathcal{S}_{i,j}$.

The analysis of pairs of components can be used to exactly characterise whether a snapshot is blocked; Pair does that. The reachability of a snapshot, however, cannot be exactly captured by this sort of local analysis. Thus, despite using pairwise-analysis to its full extent, Pair can only conservatively approximates reachability with the predicate $pairwise\_reachable(s)$. This limitation makes such techniques unable to, in particular, show that a snapshot is unreachable if that is due to some global property of the system's behaviour. For example:

Running Example 1 (From [19]*).* Let $\mathcal{S} = (\langle L_0, L_1, L_2 \rangle, \mathcal{R})$ be the supercombinator machine with L_0, L_1 and L_2 defined in Fig. 1 and $\mathcal{R}$ the set of rules that require components to synchronise on shared events; for instance, for event $ring_1$, we have rule $(n, (ring_1, ring_1, -), ring_1)$ where n can be any unique identifier. For the sake of presentation, we use the name of an event to refer to the rule that requires its synchronisation. As τ is not synchronised, there are three rules τ_0, τ_1, τ_2, such that τ_i allows component i to perform a τ. Components can receive messages either from another component, via event $ring_i$, or from its user, via event in_i. If it holds a message, it can pass the message along, via event $ring_{i \oplus 1}$, or output the message to its user, via out_i. The τ transitions represent an internal (non-deterministic) decision of the component. The Pair candidate (s_6, s_6, s_6) is not a deadlock; this snapshot is unreachable and yet pairwise reachable. □

Running Example 2. Let $\mathcal{S} = (\langle L_0, L_1, L_2 \rangle, \mathcal{R})$ be the supercombinator machine with L_0, L_1 and L_2 defined in Fig. 2 and $\mathcal{R}$ the set of rules that require components to synchronise on shared events. For the sake of presentation, we use the name of an event to identify the rule requiring its synchronisation. This system implements a token ring where process L_0 has the token initially and the events tk_i represents the passage of a token from $L_{i \ominus 1}$ to L_i, where $\ominus$ is subtraction modulo 3. The Pair candidate (s_1, s_2, s_2) is not a deadlock; this snapshot is pairwise reachable but it is not reachable. □

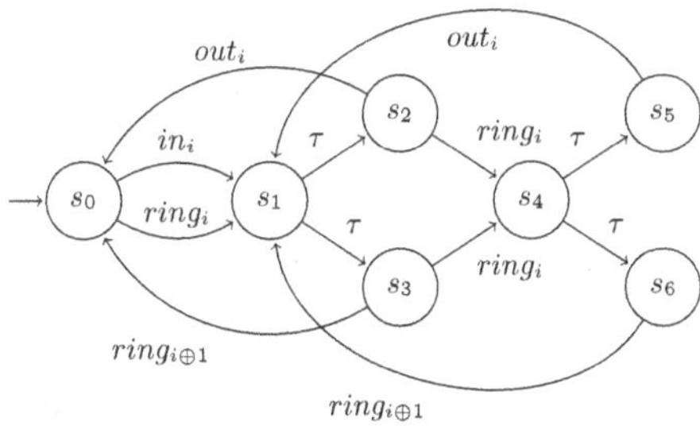

Fig. 1. LTS of component L_i where $\oplus$ represents addition modulo 3.

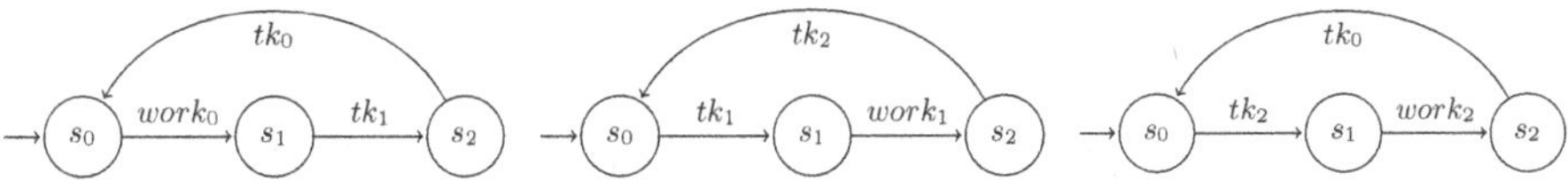

Fig. 2. LTSs of components L_0, L_1, and L_2, respectively.

To cope with this pure-local-analysis inadequacy, Martin proposed two extensions of the SDD: the *CSDD* (Coloured State Dependency Digraph) and *FSDD* (Flashing State Dependency Digraph) [13]. These extend the SDD by adding extra reachability information to a dependency, which in turn, leads to more precise cycle-of-dependencies characterisations for a deadlock. They can, in particular, prove that the previous two examples are deadlock free. As for the SDD, the characterisations proposed by these frameworks discard some local-analysis information, which could be used to increase precision, so they obtain efficiency.

4 Imprecise Reachability Using Local Static Analysis

In this section, we propose two techniques to decide whether a snapshot is reachable. The techniques make use of two global invariants of our concurrent systems: to reach a snapshot, components have to agree on the order in which they synchronise on rules, and they must agree on the number of times they perform shared rules. Informally, our techniques try to show that, for a given snapshot, components cannot satisfy these invariants, so the snapshot must be unreachable. If, however, components can meet these invariants, they might be able to cooperate to reach the snapshot, and so, we conservatively assume that the snapshot is reachable. The use of these global invariants make these techniques able to prove unreachability for snapshots that are beyond the capabilities of techniques using only pure local analysis.

To check whether these global invariants are met, both techniques analyse a *component projection* that depicts the component's behaviour in terms of the system rules in which it participates rather than its own local events.

Definition 7. *Let $\mathcal{S} = (\langle L_1, \ldots, L_n \rangle, \mathcal{R})$ be a supercombinator machine, where $L_i = (S_i, \Sigma_i, \Delta_i, \hat{s}_i)$, and $(S, \Sigma, \Delta, \hat{s})$ its induced LTS. The projection of $\mathcal{S}$ over component i is given by following supercombinator machine:*

$$\mathcal{S}_i = (\langle L_i \rangle, \{(j, (e_i), a) \mid \exists (j, (e_1, \ldots, e_n), a) \in \mathcal{R} \bullet e_i \neq -\})$$

4.1 Ordering of Rules Occurrences Consistency

In the first technique, we try to show that a snapshot is unreachable by showing that components cannot agree on the order in which they cooperate to reach this snapshot. We present our technique with the help of Running Example 1.

First of all, we analyse the traces that lead each component projection to its corresponding state in the snapshot. Note that there might be infinitely many traces leading such a projection to one of its states; this happens, for instance, if there exists a trace reaching the target state that passes by a loop in the component projection's induced LTS. We summarise this set of traces with a suffix that is common to all such traces. We adapt the general framework for static analysis presented in [15] to systematically calculate $SF_{i,j}$: the longest common suffix for the traces leading component i's projection to state s_j. We call $SF_{i,j}$ an *invariant suffix* of state s_j of component i.

Definition 8. *Let $\mathcal{S} = (\langle L_1, \ldots, L_n \rangle, \mathcal{R})$ be a supercombinator machine, $(S, \Sigma, \Delta, \hat{s})$ its induced LTS, $\mathcal{S}_i$ the projection of $\mathcal{S}$ over component i, and $L_i = (\{s_0, \ldots, s_\mathrm{m}\}, \Sigma_i, \Delta_i, s_0)$ its induced LTS. When applied to L_i, the following static analysis framework computes a collection $\mathbf{SF_i}$ with $\mathbf{m}+1$ elements, where $SF_{i,j} \in (\Sigma^* \cup \{\bot\})$ ($\mathbf{SF_i}$'s j-th element) is a sequence of rule identifiers that we call an* invariant suffix of state s_j of component i.

- *$Init = \langle\rangle$*
- *$D = (\{\bot\} \cup \Sigma^\mathbf{m}, \sqsubseteq)$, where $a \sqsubseteq b$ holds if b is a suffix of a and $\bot$ is the least element.*
- *$F_r(\bot) \mathrel{\widehat{=}} \bot$ and $F_r(d) \mathrel{\widehat{=}} d \frown \langle r \rangle$.*

Given these three elements and $\sqcup$, the join operator induced by the lattice D, the collection $\mathbf{SF_i}$ is the least fixed point for the following set of equations:

- *$SF_{i,0} = Init \sqcup SF_{i,0}$*
- *$SF_{i,j'} = F_r(SF_{i,j}) \sqcup SF_{i,j'}$, for each $(s_j, r, s_{j'}) \in \Delta_i$*

To see how these component suffixes translate to the participation of components on the system's behaviour, we can derive an *occurrence suffix* from them. An occurrence suffix translates a sequence of rule identifiers to a sequence of global (or system-wide) rule occurrences; i.e. they represent synchronisations a component must engage on to reach the associated state.

Definition 9. *Let $\mathcal{S} = (\langle L_1, \ldots, L_n \rangle, \mathcal{R})$ be a supercombinator machine, and $(S, \Sigma, \Delta, \hat{s})$ its induced LTS. An occurrence variable O_r^i denotes the i-th most recent occurrence of rule r, and $Rct(\bot) = \bot$ or $Rct(SF)$, where $SF \in \Sigma^*$, gives the sequence of occurrence variables that is obtained by replacing the i-th most recent occurrence of rule r in SF by O_r^i. We use $SFO_{i,j}$ to denote $Rct(SF_{i,j})$.*

Running Example 1. For the component states in the pair candidate analysed, we have the following invariant suffixes and occurrence suffixes: $SF_{0,6} = \langle \tau_0, ring_0, \tau_0 \rangle$, $SF_{1,6} = \langle \tau_1, ring_1, \tau_1 \rangle$, $SF_{2,6} = \langle \tau_2, ring_2, \tau_2 \rangle$, $SFO_{0,6} = \langle O^1_{\tau_0}, O^0_{ring_0}, O^0_{\tau_0} \rangle$, $SFO_{1,6} = \langle O^1_{\tau_1}, O^0_{ring_1}, O^0_{\tau_1} \rangle$, and $SFO_{2,6} = \langle O^1_{\tau_2}, O^0_{ring_2}, O^0_{\tau_2} \rangle$. □

Next, we present a predicate that formalises our technique. Roughly speaking, we use the clock variables clk^i_r, where clk^i_r marks the instant at which the occurrence O^i_r happened, to find a system synchronisation ordering that respects the occurrence suffixes of component states in the snapshot under analysis.

Definition 10. *Let $\mathcal{S} = (\langle L_1, \ldots, L_n \rangle, \mathcal{R})$ be a supercombinator machine, $(S, \Sigma, \Delta, \hat{s})$ its induced LTS, and $clk(O^i_r) \mathrel{\hat{=}} clk^i_r$. For $s = (s_{j(1)}, \ldots, s_{j(n)}) \in S$ and $occurs = \{O^a_b, \ldots, O^y_z\}$:*

$$reachable_{\mathcal{S}}(s) \mathrel{\hat{=}} \exists\, clk^a_b, \ldots, clk^y_z \in \mathbb{N} \bullet \bigwedge_{i \in \{1 \ldots n\}} HBC(i, j(i))$$

where:

- $HBC(i, j(i)) \mathrel{\hat{=}} \begin{cases} False & if\ SFO_{i,j(i)} = \bot \\ True & if\ SFO_{i,j(i)} = \langle\rangle \\ TC(i, j(i)) \wedge BC(i, j(i)) & otherwise \end{cases}$
- $TC(i, j(i)) \mathrel{\hat{=}} \bigwedge_{(O,O') \in adj(SFO_{i,j(i)})} clk(O) < clk(O')$
  - *The trace constraint (TC) enforces that a system synchronisation respects the order in which rule occurrences appear in $SFO_{i,j(i)}$.*
- $BC(i, j(i)) \mathrel{\hat{=}} \bigwedge_{O \in dif_i(SFO_{i,j(i)})} clk(O) < clk(head(SFO_{i,j(i)}))$
  - *A rule occurrence that requires the participation of component i but is not in $SFO_{i,j(i)}$ must have happened before the occurrences in $SFO_{i,j(i)}$; the before constraint (BC) enforces that a system synchronisation respects this principle.*
- $occurs \mathrel{\hat{=}} \bigcup\{\boldsymbol{SET}(SFO_{i,j(i)}) \mid i \in \{1 \ldots n\}\}$
  - *This represents the universal set of occurrences for the component states in the snapshot under analysis.*
- $adj(SFO) \mathrel{\hat{=}} \{(O, O') \mid \langle O, O' \rangle$ ***is a subsequence of*** $SFO\}$
  - *This set contains the pairs of adjacent elements in the sequence SFO, where the elements in these pairs are ordered by their order in SFO.*
- $dif_i(SFO) \mathrel{\hat{=}} \{O^l_r \mid O^l_r \in occurs \wedge i \in pts(r) \wedge O^l_r \notin \boldsymbol{SET}(SFO)\}$;
  - *This set contains the occurrences of rules that component i participates in but are not present on SFO.*
- $pts(r) \mathrel{\hat{=}} \{i \mid i \in \{1 \ldots n\} \wedge \exists (r, e, a) \in \mathcal{R} \bullet e_i \neq -\}$, *gives the participants of rule r.*

If this predicate holds, these HBCs (Happen-Before Constraints) are consistent and components can agree on an ordering in which they participate on these occurrences. Hence, the snapshot might be reachable. On the other hand, if the predicate is false, these constraints are inconsistent: either a component state is trivially unreachable within its own projection (for which $SF_{i,j} = \bot$), or there is an inconsistency between components happens-before orderings. Either way, components are unable to cooperate to reach the snapshot.

Running Example 1. For this example's pair candidate, we get the following happens-before constraints:

1. $HBC(0,6) = clk^1_{\tau_0} < clk^0_{ring_0} \wedge clk^0_{ring_0} < clk^0_{\tau_0} \wedge clk^0_{ring_1} < clk^1_{\tau_0}$;
2. $HBC(1,6) = clk^1_{\tau_1} < clk^0_{ring_1} \wedge clk^0_{ring_1} < clk^0_{\tau_1} \wedge clk^0_{ring_2} < clk^1_{\tau_1}$;
3. $HBC(2,6) = clk^1_{\tau_2} < clk^0_{ring_2} \wedge clk^0_{ring_2} < clk^0_{\tau_2} \wedge clk^0_{ring_0} < clk^1_{\tau_2}$.

From 1, 2 and 3, we can deduce that $clk^0_{ring_0} < clk^0_{ring_2} < clk^0_{ring_1} < clk^0_{ring_0}$, this contradiction shows that $reachable((s_6, s_6, s_6))$ is false and that components cannot agree on the order in which they participate on these rule occurrences. Note that this predicate could show the pair candidate unreachable for any such system with 3 or more components. □

Given that components must synchronise on shared rules to reach snapshots, for any reachable snapshot, components must be able to, in particular, agree on the occurrences suffixes leading to this snapshot. So[1]:

Theorem 1. *Let* $\mathcal{S} = (\langle L_1, \dots, L_n \rangle, \mathcal{R})$ *be a supercombinator machine with* $(S, \Sigma, \Delta, \hat{s})$ *its induced LTS. For a snapshot* $s \in S$, $reachable(s) \Rightarrow reachable_{\mathcal{S}}(s)$.

Hence, this predicate over-approximates reachability, and as a consequence, it can be soundly used for deadlock-freedom analysis.

4.2 Number of Rules Occurrences Consistency

In the second technique, we try to show that a snapshot is unreachable by showing that components cannot agree on the number of times they need to cooperate to reach the snapshot. We use Running Example 2 to introduce this technique.

In this technique, we summarise the traces leading component i's projection to its state s_j by an *invariant relation* $\oplus^{k,l}_{i,j}$ that relates the number of times that rules k and l have been applied in any of these traces. We can systematically calculate such a relation as follows.

Firstly, we use static analysis to compute $DS^{k,l}_{i,j}$: a set of integers in which the difference $t \downarrow k - t \downarrow l$ lies for all traces t leading component i's projection to its state s_j ($t \downarrow l$ counts the number of times rule l occurred in the trace t).

Definition 11. *Let* $\mathcal{S} = (\langle L_1, \dots, L_n \rangle, \mathcal{R})$ *be a supercombinator machine,* $(S, \Sigma, \Delta, \hat{s})$ *its induced LTS,* S_i *the projection of* $\mathcal{S}$ *over component* i, *and* $L_i = (\{s_0, \dots, s_{\mathbf{m}}\}, \Sigma_i, \Delta_i, s_0)$ *its induced LTS. When applied to* L_i *and parametrised by rules* k *and* l, *the following static analysis framework computes a collection* $\mathbf{DS^{k,l}_i}$ *with* $\mathbf{m}+1$ *elements, where* $DS^{k,l}_{i,j} \in (\{\emptyset, \mathbb{Z}\} \cup \{\{a\} \mid a \in \mathbb{Z}\})$ *(*$\mathbf{DS^{k,l}_i}$*'s* j*-th element) is a set of integers called an* invariant difference set *for rules* k *and* l *and state* s_j *of component* i.

[1] Formal proofs for all theorems in this work can be found in [4].

- $Init = \{0\}$;
- $D = (\{\emptyset, \mathbb{Z}\} \cup \{\{a\} \mid a \in \mathbb{Z}\}, \subseteq)$ *the flat integer domain where* $\subseteq$ *is the usual order on sets;*
- $F_r(\{d\}) \mathrel{\widehat{=}} \begin{cases} \{d+1\} & \textbf{\textit{if}}\ r = k \\ \{d-1\} & \textbf{\textit{if}}\ r = l \\ \{d\} & otherwise \end{cases}$, $F_r(\emptyset) \mathrel{\widehat{=}} \emptyset$ *and* $F_r(\mathbb{Z}) \mathrel{\widehat{=}} \mathbb{Z}$.

Given these three elements and $\sqcup$*, the join operator induced by the lattice* D*, the collection* $\mathbf{DS_i^{k,l}}$ *is the least fixed point for the following set of equations:*

- $DS_{i,0}^{k,l} = Init \sqcup DS_{i,0}^{k,l}$
- $DS_{i,j'}^{k,l} = F_r(DS_{i,j}^{k,l}) \sqcup DS_{i,j'}^{k,l}$, *for each* $(s_j, r, s_{j'}) \in \Delta_i$

From this difference set, we can obtain $\oplus_{i,j}^{k,l}$ as follows.

Definition 12. *We define* $\oplus_{i,j}^{k,l} = Rel(DS_{i,j}^{k,l})$*, where* $Rel(DS)$ *for* $DS \in (\{\emptyset, \mathbb{Z}\} \cup \{\{d\} \mid d \in \mathbb{Z}\})$ *is:*

- $<$ *if* $DS \subseteq \{d \mid d < 0\} \wedge DS \neq \emptyset$,
- $>$ *if* $DS \subseteq \{d \mid d > 0\} \wedge DS \neq \emptyset$,
- $=$ *if* $DS = \{0\}$,
- $\bot$ *if* $DS = \emptyset$,
- $\top$ *if* $DS = \mathbb{Z}$;

and $\bot$ *and* $\top$ *stand for the empty and the universal relation on* $\mathbb{N}$*, respectively.*

Running Example 2. For the sake of brevity, we only present the invariant difference sets and relations that are relevant to prove the pair candidate unreachable. So, $DS_{0,1}^{tk_0,tk_1} = \{0\}$, $DS_{1,2}^{tk_1,tk_2} = \{1\}$, $DS_{2,2}^{tk_2,tk_0} = \{1\}$, $\oplus_{0,1}^{tk_0,tk_1}$ is $=$, $\oplus_{1,2}^{tk_1,tk_2}$ is $>$, and $\oplus_{2,2}^{tk_2,tk_0}$ is $>$. □

We formalise this technique as follows. Simply put, we find values N_i, where N_i represents the value agreed by components as the number of times they applied rule i, such that they respect the relations we calculate for components.

Definition 13. *Let* $\mathcal{S} = (\langle L_1, \ldots, L_n \rangle, \mathcal{R})$ *be a supercombinator machine,* $(S, \Sigma, \Delta, \hat{s})$ *its induced LTS. For* $s = (s_{j(1)}, \ldots, s_{j(n)}) \in S$*:*

$$reachable_N(s) \mathrel{\widehat{=}} \exists N_1, \ldots, N_{|\Sigma|} \in \mathbb{N} \bullet \bigwedge_{i \in \{1 \ldots n\}} RC(i, j(i))$$

where:

- $RC(i, j(i)) \mathrel{\widehat{=}} \bigwedge_{\substack{k,l \in \Sigma \wedge \\ i \in pts(k) \cap pts(l)}} \begin{cases} True & if\ \oplus_{i,j(i)}^{k,l} = \top \\ False & if\ \oplus_{i,j(i)}^{k,l} = \bot \\ N_k \oplus_{i,j(i)}^{k,l} N_l & otherwise \end{cases}$

This predicate is false if either one the component states is trivially unreachable in its own component projection, for which $\oplus^{k,l}_{i,j(i)} = \bot$, or if all component states are trivially reachable but there exists an inconsistency on the RCs (Relation Constraints) calculated that shows that components cannot agree on the number of times they performed some rules. Either way, the snapshot must be unreachable.

Running Example 2. Given the relations calculated, from $RC(0,1)$ we derive that $N_{tk_0} = N_{tk_1}$, from $RC(1,2)$ that $N_{tk_1} > N_{tk_2}$, and from $RC(2,2)$ that $N_{tk_2} > N_{tk_0}$. So, we can deduce that $N_{tk_0} = N_{tk_1}$ and $N_{tk_0} > N_{tk_1}$, a contradiction that shows that components cannot agree on the number of times they perform these rules and that $reachable_N((s_1, s_2, s_2))$ does not hold. Note this technique can show that the blocked state is unreachable for any such system with M ($M > 1$) components of which m ($M > m > 0$) hold initially a token. □

Given that components must synchronise on shared rules to reach snapshots, for any reachable snapshot, components must be able to, in particular, agree on the number of times they perform shared rules. So:

Theorem 2. *Let $\mathcal{S} = (\langle L_1, \ldots, L_n\rangle, \mathcal{R})$ be a supercombinator machine with $(S, \Sigma, \Delta, \hat{s})$ its induced LTS. For $s \in S$, $reachable(s) \Rightarrow reachable_N(s)$.*

Thus, this predicate conservatively over-approximates reachability, and as such, it can be soundly used for deadlock-freedom analysis.

4.3 Abstraction

We can extend and improve these techniques by carrying out some abstractions. Firstly, observe that single-participant rules are irrelevant in our reachability analysis, as our techniques are based on the search of an inconsistency in the way components collaborate to reach a snapshot.

Secondly, we can achieve a sort of data abstraction for our techniques as follows. Intuitively, the application of a rule can be seen as a communication taking place between participants in this rule, whereas a set of rules involving the same exact participants might be seen as a set of possible values that they can communicate. With this view in mind, if we identify rules with the same participants, we are abstracting away these values and focusing on the fact a communication occurred between these participants. Our concrete framework and this abstract one can be seamlessly and uniformly integrated in our techniques by using the following partitioning and slightly modified component projection.

Definition 14. *Let $\mathcal{S} = (\langle L_1, \ldots, L_n\rangle, \mathcal{R})$ be a supercombinator machine and $(S, \Sigma, \Delta, \hat{s})$ its induced LTS. For a given rule identifier $i \in \Sigma$, we have the following partitions:*

- *Concrete:* $[i]_C \mathrel{\widehat{=}} i$
- *Abstract:* $[i]_A \mathrel{\widehat{=}} \boldsymbol{min}(\{j \mid j \in \Sigma \wedge\!\bullet\, pts(i) = pts(j)\})$ *(where* **min** *returns the smallest integer in a non-empty finite set)*

We analyse slightly different component projections, depending on the level of abstraction we want.

Definition 15. *Let $\mathcal{S} = (\langle L_1, \ldots, L_n\rangle, \mathcal{R})$ be a supercombinator machine, where $L_i = (S_i, \Sigma_i, \Delta_i, \hat{s}_i)$, and $(S, \Sigma, \Delta, \hat{s})$ its induced LTS, and $x \in \{A, C\}$ a level of abstraction. The projection of $\mathcal{S}$ over component i is given by the supercombinator machine $\mathcal{S}_i = (\langle L_i\rangle, \{([j]_x, (e_i), a) \mid \exists (j, (e_1, \ldots, e_n), a) \in \mathcal{R} \bullet e_i \neq -\})$.*

So, we end up with two different predicates for each technique: $reachable^C_N(s)$ and $reachable^C_S(s)$ represent our original predicates, while $reachable^A_N(s)$ and $reachable^A_S(s)$ their abstract counterparts.

4.4 Discussion

Our frameworks are intended to automate some common methods for proving that a snapshot is unreachable. Some methods use the recent behaviour of components to show that they cannot cooperate to reach a system's snapshot [12,13], while other methods rely on relational invariants to characterise states and prove snapshots unreachable [8,17]. As both of our running examples show, we provide a fully systematic framework to carry out these specific sorts of reasoning.

Our reachability tests were inspired by Martins's CSDD and FSDD, which were in turn inspired by proof rules from [17]. We have, however, removed some of FSDD and CSDD's limitations. In particular, we propose reachability criteria that are completely independent of the safety property that is being checked, while both the CSDD and FSDD are centred on deadlock analysis.

5 Combining Reachability Tests with Local Analysis

In this section we combine the Pair characterisation, proposed in [2], with the new reachability tests presented in Sect. 4. In this new framework, a potential deadlock is a pair candidate that meets our new reachability tests.

Definition 16. *Let S be a supercombinator machine and $(S, \Sigma, \Delta, \hat{s})$ its induced LTS. A snapshot $s \in S$ is a* deadlock candidate *iff the following predicate holds:*

$$deadlock\_candidate(s) \mathrel{\widehat{=}} pair\_candidate(s) \wedge reachable^C_N(s) \wedge reachable^C_S(s) \\ \wedge reachable^A_N(s) \wedge reachable^A_S(s)$$

Given that our reachability tests over-approximate reachability and that every deadlock is also a pair candidate [2], every deadlock must also be a deadlock candidate. So, a system free of deadlock candidates has to be deadlock free.

Theorem 3. *If a supercombinator machine is deadlock-candidate free, then it must also be deadlock free.*

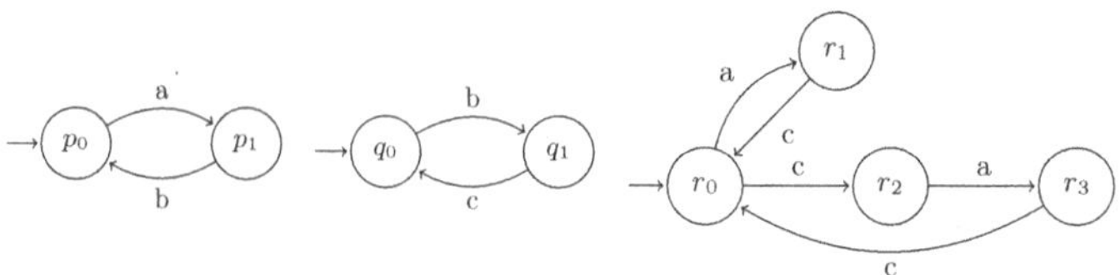

Fig. 3. LTSs of components L_1, L_2 and L_3, respectively.

Our new characterisation is clearly more precise than the Pair one, but it remains imprecise: a blocked snapshot can be unreachable and yet meet all the imprecise reachability tests proposed. Nevertheless, by conjoining these new tests, we tighten the snapshot space analysed. Observe that it only takes one failed reachability test, out of the four proposed, to consider a snapshot unreachable. The incompleteness of our method is illustrated by the following example.

Example 1. Let $\mathcal{S} = (\langle L_1, L_2, L_3 \rangle, \mathcal{R})$ be the supercombinator machine such that L_1, L_2 and L_3 are described in Fig. 3 and $\mathcal{R}$ requires components to synchronise on shared events. The snapshot (p_0, q_0, r_3) is blocked and it meets all reachability tests, but it is not reachable. Thus, it constitutes a deadlock candidate but not a deadlock. Neither local analysis nor the underlying proof methods in our reachability tests are strong enough to prove this snapshot unreachable. □

5.1 Implementation

We built upon [2] to create an efficient implementation for our framework. So, we encode the search for a deadlock candidate as a satisfiability problem to be later checked by a SAT solver. For the remainder of this section, let $\mathcal{S} = (\langle L_1, \ldots, L_n \rangle, \mathcal{R})$ be a supercombinator machine, $(S, \Sigma, \Delta, \hat{s})$ its induced LTS, $\mathcal{S}_i$ the projection of $\mathcal{S}$ on component i, and $(S_i, \Sigma_i, \Delta_i, \hat{s}_i)$ its induced LTS.

In our propositional encoding, $s_{i,j}$ is the boolean variable representing the state s_j of component i, and $\mathcal{U}$ represents the disjoint union of all S_i sets. The assignment $s_{i,j} = true$ indicates this component state belongs to a deadlock candidate, whereas $s_{i,j} = false$ means it does not. Our formula $\mathcal{F} \mathrel{\widehat{=}} PC \wedge Reach_N^C \wedge Reach_S^C \wedge Reach_N^A \wedge Reach_S^A$ is a conjunction of five sub-formulas, each of them captures a predicate of our deadlock characterisation. The combination of component states assigned to true in a satisfying assignment of $\mathcal{F}$ forms a deadlock candidate.

The first sub-formula PC captures the pair-candidate characterisation; we reuse the propositional formula that is presented in [2]. The component states assigned to true in a satisfying assignment for PC form a pair-candidate snapshot.

Next, we present a way to encode our newly proposed reachability tests. First, we present how to encode the predicates $reachable_N^x$ for $x \in \{A, C\}$.

$$Reach_N^x \mathrel{\widehat{=}} \bigwedge_{s_{i,j} \in \mathcal{U}} s_{i,j} \Rightarrow RC(i, j)$$

We encode the variables $N_1, \ldots, N_{|\Sigma|}$ as bit-vectors of size $\lceil \log_2 |\Sigma| \rceil$, as we need $|\Sigma|$ distinct values to find a model for such a constraint[2]. We encode $<$, $=$ and $>$ as the corresponding operations on bit-vectors.

As follows, we present how to encode the predicates $reachable^x_S$ for $x \in \{A, C\}$. Let $occurs = \{P^a_b, \ldots, P^y_z\}$ with $occurs \mathrel{\widehat{=}} \bigcup\{\mathbf{SET}(SFO_{i,j}) \mid s_{i,j} \in \mathcal{U}\}$.

$$Reach^x_S \mathrel{\widehat{=}} \bigwedge_{s_{i,j} \in \mathcal{U}} s_{i,j} \Rightarrow HBC(i,j)$$

We encode the variables $clk^a_b, \ldots, clk^y_z$ as bit-vectors of size $\lceil \log_2 |occurs| \rceil$, again we only need $|occurs|$ distinct values to satisfy this formula (see Footnote 2). We encode $<$ as the corresponding operation on bit-vectors.

The rationale behind these two last sub-formulas is as follows. If the component state is assigned to true in a satisfying assignment, we make sure, by the implication, that the associated reachability constraint is also met. So, any satisfying-assignment snapshot has to meet our reachability tests.

6 Practical Evaluation

We here evaluate our new framework. FDR3's ability to analyse CSP and generate supercombinator machines is exploited in generating our SAT encoding, which is then checked by the Glucose 4.0 solver [7]. We call this new tool *DeadlOx*. A prototype of our DeadlOx and the models used in this section are available at [1]. For this experiment, we checked deadlock freedom for some CSP benchmark problems. The experiment was conducted on a dedicated machine with a quad-core Intel Core i5-4300U CPU @ 1.90 GHz, and 8 GB of RAM. We compare our prototype against: SDD, CSDD and FSDD (which are implemented in Martin's Deadlock Checker tool [14]); Pair technique [2]; FDR3's built-in deadlock freedom assertion [9], and its combination with partial order reduction (FDRp) [10] or compression techniques (FDRc) [18].

We analyse 13 systems that are deadlock free and triple disjoint. Out of these systems, 12 can be proved deadlock free by DeadlOx, 6 can be proved by CSDD, and 5 can be proved by FSDD. The latter two frameworks combine to prove 7 of the 13 systems deadlock free. Pair proves 6 of them deadlock-free, and SDD only 4 of them. The systems that we evaluated are: the alternating bit protocol (ABP), the butler solution to the dining philosophers (Butler), a distributed database (DDB), a matrix multiplication system (Matmul), the asymmetric solution to the dining philosophers (Phils), a ring network (Ring), the mad postman routing algorithm (Rout), the sliding window protocol (SWP), Milner's scheduler (Scheduler), a telephone switch system (Tel), a token ring system with a single token (Token Ring), a token ring system with $N/2$ tokens (Token Ring HF) and a train track system. These problems are discussed in detail in [19]. Table 1 presents the results that we obtain for 12 of the 13 systems; the train track system is not presented in this table as none of the incomplete techniques

[2] The cases where $|\Sigma| = 1$ or $|occurs| = 1$ are trivially possibly-reachable.

Table 1. Benchmark efficiency comparison. N is a parameter that is used to alter the size of the system. We measure in seconds the time taken to check deadlock freedom for each system. * means that the method took longer than 300 sec. - means that the method is unable to prove deadlock freedom. + means that no efficient compression technique could be found.

		Incomplete					Complete		
Example	N	**DeadlOx**	SDD	Pair	CSDD	FSDD	FDR3c	FDR3p	FDR3
ABP	50	**0.06**	0.27	0.06	0.28	0.29	+	0.13	0.17
	100	**0.07**	0.71	0.07	0.62	0.75	+	0.23	0.39
	200	**0.12**	1.89	0.12	1.95	1.97	+	0.60	1.29
Butler	5	**0.06**	-	0.06	-	-	0.10	0.07	0.07
	10	**0.36**	-	0.37	-	-	0.46	1.36	116.93
	12	**1.75**	-	1.72	-	-	1.30	12.78	*
	15	**19.57**	-	22.10	-	-	13.79	*	*
DDB	5	**0.15**	-	-	-	-	0.31	0.41	0.13
	10	**1.61**	-	-	-	-	*	*	*
	20	**56.39**	-	-	-	-	*	*	*
Matmul	5	**0.20**	-	-	0.11	-	0.16	0.07	*
	10	**3.66**	-	-	0.16	-	15.27	0.32	*
	20	**48.08**	-	-	0.59	-	*	22.18	*
	30	*	-	-	1.97	-	*	*	*
Phils	20	**0.07**	0.16	0.07	0.16	0.16	0.27	0.14	*
	50	**0.11**	0.23	0.13	0.23	0.23	1.42	0.75	*
	100	**0.18**	0.35	0.30	0.36	0.35	13.20	5.50	*
	500	**1.72**	2.78	5.42	2.80	2.80	*	*	*
Ring	50	**0.10**	-	-	-	0.13	0.29	*	*
	100	**0.15**	-	-	-	0.16	0.60	*	*
	200	**0.27**	-	-	-	0.28	1.41	*	*
	500	**0.81**	-	-	-	0.83	5.87	*	*
Rout	5	**0.10**	0.13	0.12	0.15	0.15	0.19	*	*
	10	**0.28**	0.30	0.99	0.32	0.31	0.68	*	*
	20	**2.05**	1.1	14.06	1.31	1.19	4.14	*	*
	50	**24.45**	21.5	*	23.05	22.30	115.36	*	*
SWP	3	**0.15**	0.91	0.14	0.93	0.90	0.24	0.21	2.9
	5	**3.52**	*	3.20	*	*	4.58	41.9	41.81
	7	**107.69**	*	105.69	*	*	136.64	*	*
Scheduler	100	**0.13**	-	-	0.15	-	0.29	0.43	*
	500	**0.57**	-	-	0.40	-	2.32	106.26	*
	1000	**1.36**	-	-	0.86	-	8.14	*	*
	1500	**2.43**	-	-	1.32	-	23.47	*	*
Tel	3	**0.06**	-	0.06	-	-	2.05	*	*
	5	**0.32**	-	0.32	-	-	*	*	*
	8	**2.88**	-	31.69	-	-	*	*	*
	10	**38.73**	-	*	-	-	*	*	*
Token Ring	15	**2.42**	-	-	-	-	+	5.62	0.34
	20	**11.95**	-	-	-	-	+	38.45	1.07
	25	**48.94**	-	-	-	-	+	171.52	2.97
Token Ring HF	15	**2.14**	-	-	-	-	+	*	*
	20	**11.63**	-	-	-	-	+	*	*
	25	**45.16**	-	-	-	-	+	*	*

evaluated here can prove it deadlock free. DeadlOx fails on this example because neither of the additional reachability arguments are sufficient for this system; it seems to require invariants based explicitly on the number of tokens (i.e. trains), and the movement of the tokens is too unpredictable to capture using our rules.

For the benchmark problems analysed, DeadlOx is significantly more accurate than the other incomplete techniques (i.e. SDD, Pair, CSDD, and FSDD) while faring similarly in terms of analysis time. Comparing to the complete approaches (i.e. FDR3, FDR3c, FDR3p), DeadlOx is consistently faster than the best complete approach, which is the combination of FDR3's deadlock assertion with compression techniques, while being able to prove deadlock freedom for all the benchmark problems except for the train track example. We point out, however, that the effective use of compression techniques requires a careful and skilful application of those, whereas our method is fully automatic.

7 Conclusion

We combine the Pair imprecise characterisation given in [2] with two newly proposed reachability techniques to create a new framework for deadlock-freedom analysis. These new reachability techniques combine information extracted from static analysis of components with a global property of the system to show that components cannot cooperate to reach the snapshot under analysis. Our new framework is strictly more accurate than the Pair framework. Particularly, while Pair is unable to show that a snapshot is unreachable if that depends on a global aspect of the system, our new reachability tests can show that with respect to two specific global invariants of the system, namely, components have to agree on the order of cooperation and on the number of time they cooperate. Note, we only restrict this work to pairwise-communicating systems so we can re-use Pair's efficient strategy to encode the *blocked* predicate; our reachability tests and their encodings can be applied to systems with multiway communication. Moreover, the ideas in this paper should transfer easily to any formalism where systems are described by interacting LTSs.

We have implemented this new framework in the DeadlOx tool. This implementation shows that for the assessed benchmark systems, DeadlOx is substantially more accurate than similar incomplete techniques, whilst taking a similar amount of time to analyse systems. Also, as it seems to be consistently more efficient than complete techniques, it could be used as a preliminary step in deadlock-freedom checking. If it fails to prove deadlock freedom, then a complete method should be used. Note DeadlOx uses FDR3 to obtain supercombinator machines from systems described using CSP, but a tool analogous to DeadlOx could be created for other notations by replacing its use of FDR3 to generate such machines.

We plan to extend this work in two directions. Firstly, we would like to see how we could reuse (a part of) this framework to check other safety properties. In particular, we plan to reuse it to check trace-refinement properties and a notion of freedom from permanently blocked subsystems. Secondly, we plan to create additional imprecise tests for reachability, so we can have an even more accurate framework. Note, for instance, that our techniques are not strong enough to prove deadlock-freedom for one of the benchmark systems evaluated. We are particularly interested in the application of SAT solvers to infer system invariants.

Acknowledgements. The first author is a CAPES Foundation scholarship holder (Process no: 13201/13-1). The second and third authors are partially sponsored by DARPA under agreement number FA8750-12-2-0247. We thank the anonymous reviewers for their valuable comments.

References

1. Antonino, P., Gibson-Robinson, T., Roscoe, A.W.: Experiment package (2016). http://www.cs.ox.ac.uk/people/pedro.antonino/pkg.zip
2. Antonino, P., Gibson-Robinson, T., Roscoe, A.W.: Efficient Deadlock-Freedom Checking Using Local Analysis and SAT Solving. In: Ábrahám, E., Huisman, M. (eds.) IFM 2016. LNCS, vol. 9681, pp. 345–360. Springer, Heidelberg (2016). doi:10.1007/978-3-319-33693-0_22
3. Antonino, P.R.G., Oliveira, M.M., Sampaio, A.C.A., Kristensen, K.E., Bryans, J.W.: Leadership election: an industrial SoS application of compositional deadlock verification. In: Badger, J.M., Rozier, K.Y. (eds.) NFM 2014. LNCS, vol. 8430, pp. 31–45. Springer, Heidelberg (2014). doi:10.1007/978-3-319-06200-6_3
4. Antonino, P., Roscoe, A.W., Gibson-Robinson, T.: Tighter reachability criteria for deadlock-freedom analysis. Technical report, University of Oxford (2016). http://www.cs.ox.ac.uk/people/pedro.antonino/reach_techreport.pdf
5. Antonino, P., Sampaio, A., Woodcock, J.: A refinement based strategy for local deadlock analysis of networks of CSP processes. In: Jones, C., Pihlajasaari, P., Sun, J. (eds.) FM 2014. LNCS, vol. 8442, pp. 62–77. Springer, Heidelberg (2014). doi:10.1007/978-3-319-06410-9_5
6. Attie, P.C., Bensalem, S., Bozga, M., Jaber, M., Sifakis, J., Zaraket, F.A.: An abstract framework for deadlock prevention in BIP. In: Beyer, D., Boreale, M. (eds.) FMOODS/FORTE-2013. LNCS, vol. 7892, pp. 161–177. Springer, Heidelberg (2013). doi:10.1007/978-3-642-38592-6_12
7. Audemard, G., Simon, L.: Predicting learnt clauses quality in modern SAT solvers. In: IJCAI 2009, San Francisco, CA, USA, pp. 399–404 (2009)
8. Dathi, N.: Deadlock and deadlock freedom. Ph.D. thesis, University of Oxford (1989)
9. Gibson-Robinson, T., Armstrong, P., Boulgakov, A., Roscoe, A.W.: FDR3—a modern refinement checker for CSP. In: Ábrahám, E., Havelund, K. (eds.) TACAS 2014. LNCS, vol. 8413, pp. 187–201. Springer, Heidelberg (2014). doi:10.1007/978-3-642-54862-8_13
10. Gibson-Robinson, T., Hansen, H., Roscoe, A.W., Wang, X.: Practical partial order reduction for CSP. In: Havelund, K., Holzmann, G., Joshi, R. (eds.) NFM 2015. LNCS, vol. 9058, pp. 188–203. Springer, Heidelberg (2015). doi:10.1007/978-3-319-17524-9_14
11. Hoare, C.A.R.: Communicating Sequential Processes. Prentice-Hall, Upper Saddle River (1985)

12. Lambertz, C., Majster-Cederbaum, M.: Analyzing component-based systems on the basis of architectural constraints. In: Arbab, F., Sirjani, M. (eds.) FSEN 2011. LNCS, vol. 7141, pp. 64–79. Springer, Heidelberg (2012). doi:10.1007/978-3-642-29320-7_5
13. Martin, J.M.R.: The design and construction of deadlock-free concurrent systems. Ph.D. thesis, University of Buckingham (1996)
14. Martin, J.M.R., Jassim, S.A.: An efficient technique for deadlock analysis of large scale process networks. In: Fitzgerald, J., Jones, C.B., Lucas, P. (eds.) FME 1997. LNCS, vol. 1313, pp. 418–441. Springer, Heidelberg (1997). doi:10.1007/3-540-63533-5_22
15. Nielson, F., Nielson, H.R., Hankin, C.: Principles of Program Analysis. Springer, Secaucus (1999)
16. Oliveira, M.V.M., Antonino, P., Ramos, R., Sampaio, A., Mota, A., Roscoe, A.W.: Rigorous development of component-based systems using component metadata and patterns. Formal Aspects Comput. **28**, 1–68 (2016)
17. Roscoe, A.W., Dathi, N.: The pursuit of deadlock freedom. Inf. Comput. **75**(3), 289–327 (1987)
18. Roscoe, A.W., Gardiner, P.H.B., Goldsmith, M.H., Hulance, J.R., Jackson, D.M., Scattergood, J.B.: Hierarchical compression for model-checking CSP or how to check 10^{20} dining philosophers for deadlock. In: Brinksma, E., Cleaveland, W.R., Larsen, K.G., Margaria, T., Steffen, B. (eds.) TACAS 1995. LNCS, vol. 1019, pp. 133–152. Springer, Heidelberg (1995). doi:10.1007/3-540-60630-0_7
19. Roscoe, A.W.: Understanding Concurrent Systems. Springer, Heidelberg (2010)

Compositional Parameter Synthesis

Lacramioara Aştefănoaei[1(✉)], Saddek Bensalem[2], Marius Bozga[2], Chih-Hong Cheng[1], and Harald Ruess[1]

[1] fortiss - An-Institut Technische Universität München, Munich, Germany
astefanoaei@fortiss.org
[2] Univ. Grenoble Alpes, VERIMAG, 38000 Grenoble, France

Abstract. We address the problem of parameter synthesis for parametric timed systems (PTS). The motivation comes from industrial configuration problems for production lines. Our method consists in compositionally generating over-approximations for the individual components of the input systems, which are translated, together with global properties, to ∃∀SMT problems. Our translation forms the basis for optimised and robust parameter synthesis for slightly richer models than PTS.

1 Introduction

Synthesis for parametric timed automata (PTA) has drawn considerable attention [1–3,7,10,12–15,17–21,25,26]. These approaches explore the *global* state space of all interacting components. In contrast, our method is compositional, consequently, in this regard, it scales well to large systems.

Our motivation comes from parameter configuration problems for production lines such as the ones from the food sector described in [8]. Seeing the constituting machines as interacting PTAs, configuration problems fit well the class of systems we study. Concretely, our contribution is to show how, given (1) a *parametric timed system* $\mathcal{S}$ with unknown parameters p, (2) constraints ϕ_p on p, and (3) a safety property ϕ_{safe} for $\mathcal{S}$, we automatically generate, in a compositional manner and by means of an ∃∀SMT solver, valuations for p such that the desired safety property holds. In particular, we reduce the parameter synthesis problem to solving formulae of the type:

$$\exists p \in \phi_p . \forall v . (\psi_{\mathcal{S}}(p, v) \rightarrow \phi_{safe}) \quad (1)$$

where v represents all other variables (clocks, locations) except p and $\psi_{\mathcal{S}}(p, v)$ is an over-approximation of the behaviour of $\mathcal{S}$. A PTS is composed of components (PTAs) interacting by multi-party interactions. Given n components C_i and interactions γ, $\|_\gamma C_i$ denotes the corresponding PTS. To compute $\psi_{\mathcal{S}}$ for $\mathcal{S} \triangleq \|_\gamma C_i$ we adapt and extend the methodology from [4] to the parametric setup. We first equip each component C_i with history clocks. Let C_i^h be the results. We then compute three types of invariants: (1) interaction invariant

Work supported by the European projects BEinCPPS, CPSE-labs and OpenMOS.

J. Fitzgerald et al. (Eds.): FM 2016, LNCS 9995, pp. 60–68, 2016.
DOI: 10.1007/978-3-319-48989-6_4

from γ; (2) component invariants from the parametric zones of C_i^h; and (3) relations between history clocks. In [4], history clocks were used to derive relations between clocks in different components. In the parametric case, history clocks are used to also derive relations on parameters. This helps synthesise parameters which, for instance, do not introduce deadlock in the system.

2 Parametric Timed Systems and Properties

A valuation $\mathbf{v}$ is a function that assigns a real value $\mathbf{v}(x)$ to each variable x. A linear inequality has the form $\sum_{i=1}^{n} \alpha_i x_i \# \beta$ with x_i being variables, $\alpha_i, \beta \in \mathbb{Z}$, $\# \in \{<, \leq, =, \geq, >\}$. A convex linear constraint is a finite conjunction of linear inequalities. The set of convex linear constraints over a set of variables $\mathcal{V}$ is denoted by $\mathcal{L}(\mathcal{V})$.

Definition 1. *A component is a PTA* $(L, l_0, \mathcal{X}, \mathcal{P}, A, T, \mathsf{tpc})$ *where:* l_0 *is an initial location;* $L, \mathcal{X}, \mathcal{P}, A, T$ *are finite sets of locations, clock variables, parameters (variables whose values do not change over time), actions, and transitions. Transitions* $l \xrightarrow{a,g,\mu} l'$ *consist of a source* $l \in L$ *and a target location* $l' \in L$*, an action* $a \in A$*, a guard condition* g *in* $\mathcal{L}(\mathcal{X} \cup \mathcal{P})$*, and a jump relation* $\mu \in \mathcal{L}(\mathcal{X} \cup \mathcal{X}')$ *with* $\mathcal{X}'$ *denoting the clocks at* l'. $\mathsf{tpc} : L \rightarrow \mathcal{L}(\mathcal{X} \cup \mathcal{P})$ *assigns convex linear clock constraints to locations.*

For a parameter valuation $\mathbf{v}$ and a component C, the concrete semantics of C under $\mathbf{v}$, $C(\mathbf{v})$, is that of a timed automaton. Since this semantics yields an infinite state space, we work with *parametric zone graphs* as finite symbolic representations. The symbolic states in a parametric zone graph are pairs (l, ζ) of a location l and a convex linear constraint ζ over clocks and parameters which can be represented by convex polyhedra [20]. For $C \triangleq (L, l_0, \mathcal{X}, \mathcal{P}, A, T, \mathsf{tpc})$ the parametric zone graph is computed from T starting from an initial symbolic state $(l_0, \mathbf{v}_0)$, with $\mathbf{v}_0(x) = 0$ for all $x \in \mathcal{X}$, and using the successor operator. For a transition t, the successor operator of (l, ζ) is defined as $\mathsf{succ}(t, (l, \zeta)) \triangleq \mathsf{time\_succ}(\mathsf{disc\_succ}(t, (l, \zeta)))$ where $\mathsf{disc\_succ}$. resp. $\mathsf{time\_succ}$ are the discrete, resp. the time successor. We recall their definitions from [21]. The operation $\mathsf{time\_succ}$ for letting time progress within a symbolic state is defined as $\mathsf{time\_succ}((l, \zeta)) \triangleq (l, \zeta^{\nearrow})$ where $^{\nearrow}$ is the time-elapse operator. The successor with respect to a transition $t \triangleq (l, (\_, g, \mu), l')$ is defined as $\mathsf{disc\_succ}(t, (l, \zeta)) \triangleq (l', \zeta')$ where $\mathbf{v}' \in \zeta'$ iff $\exists \mathbf{v} \in \zeta \cap \mathsf{tpc}(l) \cap g.(\mathbf{v}, \mathbf{v}') \in \mu \wedge \mathbf{v}' \in \mathsf{tpc}(l')$.

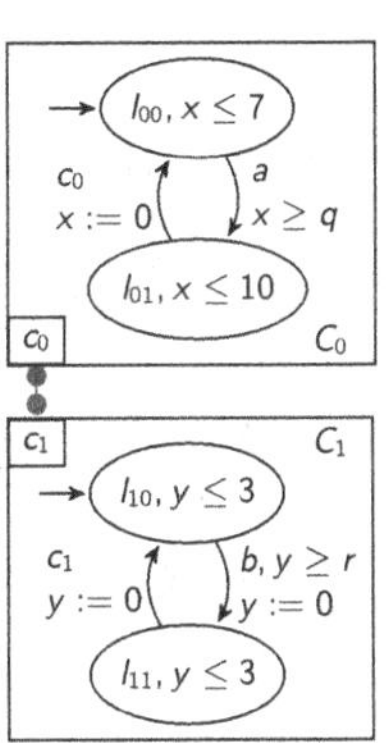

Fig. 1. A PTS

Given disjoint actions A_i, an interaction is a subset of actions $\alpha \subseteq \bigcup_i A_i$ containing at most one action per component. Given a set of interactions $\gamma \subseteq 2^{\bigcup_i A_i}$, $Act(\gamma)$ denotes the actions in γ, that is, $Act(\gamma) \triangleq \bigcup_{\alpha \in \gamma} \alpha$. A PTS $\|_\gamma C_i$ is the composition of components C_i for the interaction set γ such that $Act(\gamma) \triangleq$

$\bigcup_i A_i$. For n components $C_i \triangleq (L_i, l_0^i, \mathcal{X}_i, \mathcal{P}_i, A_i, T_i, \mathsf{tpc}_i, \mathcal{D}_i)$ with $L_i \cap L_j = \emptyset$, $A_i \cap A_j = \emptyset$, $\mathcal{X}_i \cap \mathcal{X}_j = \emptyset$, for any $i \neq j$, the *composition* $\|_\gamma C_i$ with respect to γ is defined by $(L, \bar{l}_0, \mathcal{X}, \mathcal{P}, \gamma, T_\gamma, \mathsf{tpc})$ where $\bar{l}_0$ is $(l_0^1, \dots, l_0^n)$, $\mathcal{X}, \mathcal{P}, L, \mathsf{tpc}(\bar{l})$ are respectively $\bigcup_i \mathcal{X}_i$, $\bigcup_i \mathcal{P}_i$, $\times_i L_i$, $\bigcap_i \mathsf{tpc}_i(l_i)$, and T_γ is such that for $\alpha \triangleq \{a_i\}_{i \in I}$, $\bar{l} \xrightarrow{\alpha, g, \mu} \bar{l}'$ where $\bar{l}$ is $(l_1, \dots, l_n)$, $g \triangleq \bigcap_{i \in I} g_i$, $\mu \triangleq \bigcap_{i \in I} \mu_i$, and $\bar{l}'(i)$ is l_i if $(i \notin I)$ else l_i' for $l_i \xrightarrow{a_i, g_i, \mu_i} l_i'$.

Figure 1 illustrates a system of 2 PTAs C_0, C_1 interacting on $\{c_0, c_1\}$. Initially, both C_0 and C_1 execute locally a, resp. b in either way. This is followed by a synchronisation on c_0 and c_1. We note that because y is reset on each transition, $y \leq x$ is a global property of the system. We also note that if $q = 7$ the system is deadlocked for any value of r: we have that $r \leq 3$ by the invariant of l_{10}, and because C_1 cannot stay in l_{11} for more than 3 units of time, it is impossible for the action a to be executed. This is a simple illustration showing that local parameter bounds might need to be tightened in the composed system in order to not introduce deadlocks.

Definition 2 (Parameter Synthesis Problem). *Given a system $\mathcal{S}$, parameter constraints*[1] *ϕ_p, and a safety property ϕ_{safe}, a parameter synthesis problem is to find an assignment $\mathbf{v}$ for $\mathcal{P}$ such that $\mathbf{v}$ satisfies ϕ_p and $\mathcal{S}(\mathbf{v})$ satisfies ϕ_{safe}, $\mathcal{S}(\mathbf{v}) \models \phi_{safe}$. A satisfying assignment $\mathbf{v}$ is called a* solution.

3 Compositional Parameter Synthesis

We show how the method from [4] can be adapted to compute $\psi_{\mathcal{S}}$ in Formula (1). There are three steps to generate: (1) interaction invariants from γ; (2) component invariants from components with history clocks; (3) relations on history clocks.

Interaction Invariants. Interaction invariants are over-approximations of global locations. As their computation depends only on γ, it does not change in the parametric setup. Consequently, we omit its definition (to be found in [5,22]) and instead illustrate it by means of our running example. We recall that $\gamma \triangleq \{a, b, \{c_0, c_1\}\}$. If a happens from l_{00} and l_{10}, C_0 reaches l_{01} while C_1 remains in l_{10}. If $\{c_0, c_1\}$ happens from l_{01} and l_{11}, l_{00} and l_{10} are reached. Continuing this reasoning for all combinations, we obtain as interaction invariant $\mathcal{I}(\gamma)$ the formula $(l_{00} \wedge l_{10}) \vee (l_{00} \wedge l_{11}) \vee (l_{01} \wedge l_{10}) \vee (l_{01} \wedge l_{11})$.

Component Invariants. Component invariants characterise the reachable states of components when considered alone. Given a component C with locations L, we assume that the symbolic states resulting from the computation of its parametric zone graph are $\{s_i\}_I$ with s_i being (l_j, ζ_j). We consider the following formula:

$$\mathcal{I}(C) \triangleq \bigwedge_{i \in I} (s_i \rightarrow (l_j \wedge \zeta_j)) \wedge \bigwedge_{l \in L} (l \rightarrow \bigvee_{l \in s} s). \tag{2}$$

[1] Parameter constraints are conjunctions of inequalities on $\mathcal{P}$ and $\mathbb{R}$ such as $q \in [0, 6]$.

By abuse of notation, l_j is used to denote the predicate that holds whenever C is at location l_j and $l \in s$ holds if $s = (l, \zeta)$.

The parametric zone graph of C_0 for our running example (Fig. 1), as computed with Imitator [2], is in Fig. 2. By Eq. (2), $\mathcal{I}(C_0)$ is as follows:

$$\begin{aligned}\mathcal{I}(C_0) = & s_0 \rightarrow (l_{00} \wedge x \leq 7) \wedge \\ & s_1 \rightarrow (l_{01} \wedge q \leq x \leq 10 \wedge q \leq 7) \wedge \\ & s_2 \rightarrow (l_{00} \wedge x \leq 7 \wedge q \leq 7) \wedge \\ & l_{00} \rightarrow (s_0 \vee s_2) \;\wedge\; l_{01} \rightarrow s_1\end{aligned}$$

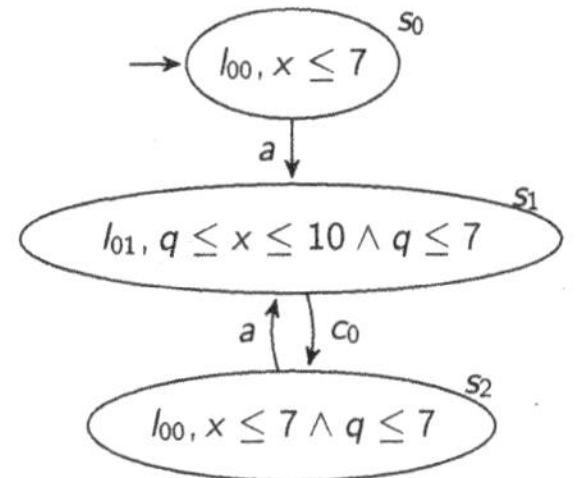

Fig. 2. The zone graph for C_0

The formula in Eq. (2) is more precise than the one in [4]. There, the choice was to take the disjunction of $l_j \wedge \zeta_j$ as an invariant. In a parametric setup, such an encoding is not enough: since $s_0 \vee s_2$ reduces to $l_{00} \wedge x \leq 7$, the relation $q \geq 7$ is lost.

More importantly, the formula in Eq. (2) is not necessarily an invariant. For instance, for the valuation $\mathbf{v} \triangleq \{q = 8\}$, $CI(C_0)(\mathbf{v})$ reduces to false. $\mathcal{I}(C)$ is an invariant only under the parameter valuations which satisfy the parameter constraints in it. Let us denote by $K_p(C)$ the parameter constraints in Eq. (2). $K_p(C)$ is obtained from $\mathcal{I}(C)$ by a similar approach as in [2], that is, by seeing clocks as existential variables and doing quantifier elimination. For instance, $K_p(C_0)$ is $q \leq 7$.

Proposition 1. *For a component C with parameter constraints K_p, $\mathcal{I}(C)(\mathbf{v})$ is an invariant of $C(\mathbf{v})$ for any $\mathbf{v}$ such that $\mathbf{v} \models K_p$.*

History Clocks and Auxiliary Constraints. In general, component and the interaction invariants are not enough to prove global properties, especially when such properties involve relations between clocks in different components. In the case of $\exists\forall$ solving, a weak invariant leads to no solution: there is not enough information to synthesise parameters such that the global property holds. For instance, in our toy example, we cannot find parameters such that $y \leq x$ holds by only having at hand the invariants for components and interactions: there are no relations relating both x and y. By means of *history clocks* we are able to derive new global constraints from the simultaneity of interactions and the synchrony of time progress. These new constraints make it possible to successfully find parameter valuations such that global properties hold.

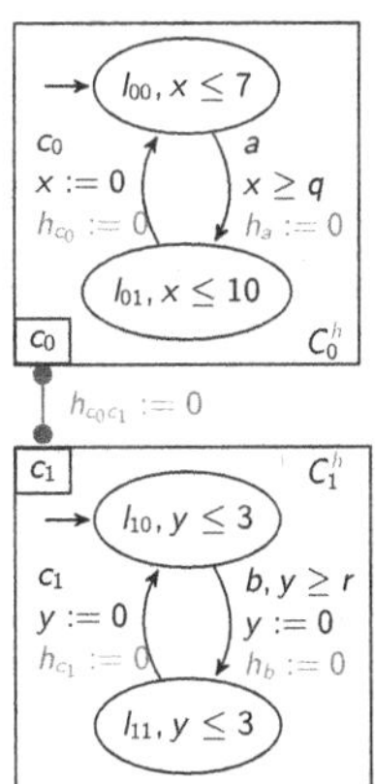

Fig. 3. A PTS with history clocks

Adding History Clocks. History clocks are associated with actions and interactions. For a component C we use C^h to denote its extension with history clocks. The extension of the system is obtained from the extensions of the components alone together with the history clocks for interactions. As an illustration, Fig. 3 shows the extension of the system in Fig. 1.

The intuition behind history clocks is as follows. When interaction α takes place, the history clocks h_α and h_a associated to α and to any action $a \in \alpha$ are reset. Thus they measure the time passed from the last occurrence of α, respectively of a. Since there is no timing constraint involving history clocks, the behaviour of the components is not changed by the addition of history clocks.

For timed automata, the zone graph is finite, consequently so is the computation of $\mathcal{I}(C)$ and $\mathcal{I}(C^h)$ as in Eq. (2). This is no longer the case in the parametric setup. For instance, the parametric zone graph of the component C in Fig. 4 has two symbolic states $l_0 \wedge x \leq 5$ and $l_1 \wedge x \leq 3 \wedge r \leq 5$ while the one of C^h contains infinitely many symbolic states such as $l_1 \wedge x \leq 3 \wedge r \leq 5 \wedge y = h_c \geq h_a \wedge y + 3k \geq h_a$ for $k \in \mathbf{N}$. We note that, though one could find particular solutions depending on the systems in cause, since the reachability problem is undecidable for parametric timed automata [1], one cannot hope for general solutions.

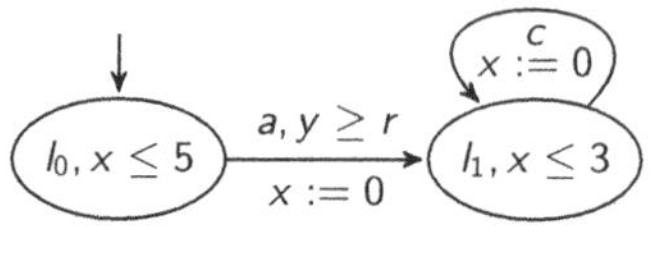

$l_0, x \leq 5$ —($a, y \geq r$ / $x := 0$)→ $l_1, x \leq 3$; self-loop on l_1: c, $x := 0$

Fig. 4. A PTA with an infinite zone graph

Generating Interaction Equalities from History Clocks. The basic underlying observation is that a history clock h_a for an action a from a last executed interaction α is necessarily *less* than any h_β with β another interaction containing a. This is because the clocks of the actions in α are the last ones being reset. Consequently, given a common action a of $\alpha_0, \alpha_2, \dots, \alpha_p$, h_a is the minimum of h_{α_i}, $h_a \triangleq \min_{0 \leq i \leq p} h_{\alpha_i}$. The invariant for a given interaction set γ is denoted as $\epsilon(\gamma)$ and defined as follows:

$$\epsilon(\gamma) \triangleq \bigwedge_{a \in Act(\gamma)} h_a = \min_{\alpha \in \gamma, a \in \alpha} h_\alpha.$$

For our running example, $\epsilon(\{c_0, c_1\})$ is simply $h_{c_0} = h_{c_1}$.

Generating Inequalities from Conflicting Interactions. Without conflicts, that is, when interactions do not share any action, $\epsilon(\gamma)$ is quite tight in the sense that it is essentially a conjunction of equalities. However, $\epsilon(\gamma)$ is weaker in the presence of conflicts because any action in conflict can be used in different interactions. The disjunctions (implicit in the definition of min) in $\epsilon(\gamma)$ reflect precisely this uncertainty. History clocks on interactions are introduced to capture the time lapses between conflicting interactions. The basic information exploited in [4] is that when two conflicting interactions compete for the same action a, no matter which one is first, the other one must wait until the component which owns a is again able to execute a. This has been referred to as a "separation constraint" for conflicting interactions and was defined as the following invariant:

$$\sigma(\gamma) \triangleq \bigwedge_{a \in Act(\gamma)} \bigwedge_{\substack{\alpha \neq \beta \in \gamma \\ a \in \alpha \cap \beta}} |h_\alpha - h_\beta| \geq k_a$$

where $|x|$ denotes the absolute value of x and k_a represents the minimum elapsed time between two consecutive executions of a. In the case of timed automata, the computation of such minimum elapses follows the classical [11] which consists in finding a shortest path in a weighted graph built from the zone graph associated to a timed automaton. The extension to PTAs follows the same construction.

A more practical solution is to construct an observer. To compute the delay between two consecutive executions of a in C, we can check if $C\|_a\mathcal{O}^a \models \psi^a_{obs}$ is not true, where $\mathcal{O}^a$ is the automaton in Fig. 5 and ψ^a_{obs} is $\Box\neg l_2$.

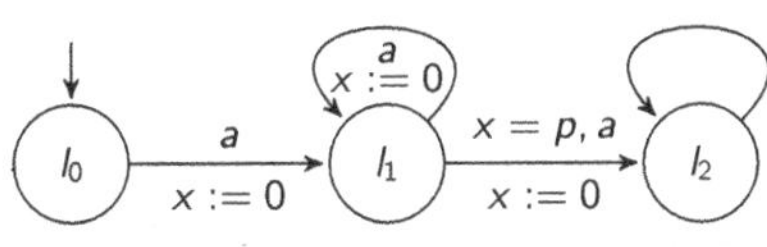

Fig. 5. An observer for computing k_a

In our running example, there are no conflicting interactions. If there were another component with action c_2 interacting with C_0 by means of interaction $\{c_0, c_2\}$ then $\{c_0, c_2\}$ is in conflict with $\{c_0, c_1\}$. The separation between them is given by the time elapse between two consecutive c_0 which in this particular case is simply q.

The formulae computed throughout this section are invariants. Together, they form the over-approximation $\psi_\mathcal{S}$ in the $\exists\forall$ Formula from (1).

Proposition 2. *Given $\mathcal{S} \triangleq \|_\gamma C_i$, let $K_p(C_i)$ be the parameter constraints for C_i and let $\psi_\mathcal{S}$ denote the formula $\bigwedge_i \mathcal{I}(C_i^h) \wedge \mathcal{I}(\gamma) \wedge \epsilon(\gamma) \wedge \sigma(\gamma)$ after the elimination of history clocks. We have that for any $\mathbf{v}$ such that $\mathbf{v} \models \wedge_i K_p(C_i)$, $\psi_\mathcal{S}(\mathbf{v})$ is an invariant of $\mathcal{S}$.*

Finding Satisfying Instances for $\exists\forall$ Formulae. We recall that we reduce our synthesis problem to solving the $\exists\forall$ formulae in (1). For illustration, we show how the formula looks like for our running example. We have the following formulae:

$$\begin{aligned}
\mathcal{I}(C_0^h) = & s_0 \rightarrow (l_{00} \wedge x \leq 7 \wedge x = h_a = h_{c_0}) \wedge \\
& s_1 \rightarrow (l_{01} \wedge q + h_a \leq x \leq min(10, h_a + 7) \wedge x = h_{c_0}) \wedge \\
& s_2 \rightarrow (l_{00} \wedge x \leq 7 \wedge q + h_a - 10 \leq x \leq min(7, h_a) \wedge x = h_{c_0}) \wedge \\
& l_{00} \rightarrow (s_0 \vee s_2) \ \wedge \ l_{01} \rightarrow s_1 \\
\mathcal{I}(C_1^h) = & s_0' \rightarrow (l_{10} \wedge y \leq 3 \wedge y = h_b = h_{c_1}) \wedge \\
& s_1' \rightarrow (l_{11} \wedge r + y \leq h_{c_1} \leq y + 3 \wedge y = h_b) \wedge \\
& s_2' \rightarrow (l_{10} \wedge y \leq 3 \wedge y \leq h_b \leq y + 3 \wedge y = h_{c_1}) \wedge \\
& l_{10} \rightarrow (s_0' \vee s_2') \ \wedge \ l_{11} \rightarrow s_1'
\end{aligned}$$

By inspecting $\mathcal{I}(C_0^h)$ and $\mathcal{I}(C_1^h)$, we can derive that $K_p(C_0^h)$ is $q \leq 7$ and that $K_p(C_1^h)$ is $r \leq 3$. Assuming ϕ_{safe} is $y \leq x$, the $\exists\forall$ Formula (1) is:

$$\exists q, r. q \leq 7 \wedge r \leq 3. \forall l \in L, s \in S, x, y. \mathcal{I}(\gamma) \wedge qe(\mathcal{I}(C_0^h) \wedge \mathcal{I}(C_1^h) \wedge h_{c_0} = h_{c_1}) \rightarrow y \leq x$$

where L denotes $\{l_{00}, l_{01}, l_{10}, l_{11}\}$, S denotes $\{s_0, s_1, s_2, s'_0, s'_1, s'_2\}$, and qe denotes the result of eliminating the history clocks. Since both $x = h_{c_0}$ and $y \leq h_{c_1}$ are invariants, together with $h_{c_0} = h_{c_1}$, it can be derived that $y \leq x$. Consequently, for any $r \leq 3$ and $q \leq 7$, the system satisfies $y \leq x$.

We also note that for an interaction property expressing that a happens before b to hold, q must be smaller or equal than 3, though the upper bound in the local constraint is 7. This is because s_1 must be reached while still at s'_0 where $y = h_{c_1} \leq 3$. Since $q \leq x$ and $x = h_{c_0}$ we have that $q \leq 3$ by using $h_{c_0} = h_{c_1}$. This shows that history clocks forbid parameter valuations which satisfy local parameter constraints but which could introduce deadlocks in the system.

When the ∃∀SMT solver returns `unsat`, there are two interpretations: (1) either ϕ_{safe} does not hold or (2) ψ_S is too coarse. To check (1), one might apply the method from [4] and feed $\psi_S \wedge \phi_{safe}$ to an SMT solver. If the result is `unsat`, then ϕ_{safe} is not a property of the system. For instance, if for our running example we take $x < y$ as ϕ_{safe}, the ∃∀SMT solver returns `unsat` for Formula (1). Since $\psi_S \wedge x < y$ returns `unsat` as well, we know that $x < y$ is not valid.

We conclude the section by stating the correctness of our approach which follows from the fact that $\psi_S(\mathbf{v})$ is an over-approximation (Proposition 2).

Proposition 3. *Given $\mathcal{S} \triangleq \|_\gamma C_i$ let $K_p(C_i)$ denote the parameter constraints for C_i. If $\mathbf{v}$ is such that it satisfies Formula (1) together with $\bigwedge_i Kp(C_i)$ then $\mathbf{v}$ is a solution to the parameter synthesis problem, i.e., $\mathbf{v} \in \phi_p$ and $\mathcal{S}(\mathbf{v}) \models \phi_{safe}$.*

4 Experiments and Extensions

We have implemented a prototype[2] to experiment with our approach. The prototype takes as input components as PTAs in Imitator [2], a file describing the interactions, the constraints over parameters and a safety property. It uses EFSMT [9] and Z3 [23] to return either `unsat` or a parameter assignment under which the safety property holds. We have also connected our prototype with the one in [4] such that, in case the result is `unsat`, we check if the global property given as input is not actually false. With respect to performance, our prototype returns an answer within a second for variations on toy benchmarks such as the train gate controller or the temperature controller with as many as 16 trains, respectively rods. As final notes, we make two observations: (1) our experiments with invariants without history clocks show that these invariants are clearly weaker in the sense that the solver does not find any parameter valuations; (2) on the negative side, even for minimal models of production lines with filling and packaging machines, the computation of the set of reachable states does not terminate.

Due to our encoding of the parameter synthesis problem as ∃∀SMT formulae, we can readily solve the following extensions of parameter synthesis for PTS.

Beyond PTA. Using the expressiveness of decidable ∃∀-constraints, one can encode guards such as $t_1 + 3\,t_4 \geq 10$ and also non-linear arithmetic constraints, as obtained from some richer classes of hybrid automata.

[2] The source code and examples can be found at github.com/astefano/efsmt_coverts.

Quantitative Synthesis. Our method does not generate optimised parameter values, since this would require an additional quantifier alternation [9]. However, EFSMT can be modified for optimisation by using a MaxSMT solver (e.g. νZ [6]) instead of an SMT solver for formulae of existential polarity (the so-called E-solver).

Robustness Synthesis. The imprecision of systems may be modelled by means of universally quantified, bounded variables. For example, one may model the imprecision for a guard $t_1 > 2$ by $t_1 > 2 + \delta$, for $\delta \in [-0.05, 0.05]$ by simply adding $\forall \delta \in [-0.05, 0.05]$ in the $\exists\forall$SMT formula.

Interaction Properties in LTL. Interaction properties such as "eventually interaction a will happen before b", can effectively be transformed into safety properties based on the encodings of a corresponding Büchi automata along the lines proposed for bounded synthesis [16] or for bounded model checking [24].

Acknowlegdement. We warmly thank Étienne André for suggesting us the construction of the observer to compute the separations in Sect. 3.

References

1. Alur, R., Henzinger, T.A., Vardi, M.Y.: Parametric real-time reasoning. In: ACM, pp. 592–601 (1993)
2. André, É.: IMITATOR II: a tool for solving the good parameters problem in timed automata. In: INFINITY (2010)
3. André, É., Soulat, R.: Synthesis of timing parameters satisfying safety properties. In: Reachability Problems (2011)
4. Aştefănoaei, L., Rayana, S., Bensalem, S., Bozga, M., Combaz, J.: Compositional invariant generation for timed systems. In: Ábrahám, E., Havelund, K. (eds.) TACAS 2014. LNCS, vol. 8413, pp. 263–278. Springer, Heidelberg (2014). doi:10.1007/978-3-642-54862-8_18
5. Bensalem, S., Bozga, M., Sifakis, J., Nguyen, T.-H.: Compositional verification for component-based systems and application. In: Cha, S.S., Choi, J.-Y., Kim, M., Lee, I., Viswanathan, M. (eds.) ATVA 2008. LNCS, vol. 5311, pp. 64–79. Springer, Heidelberg (2008). doi:10.1007/978-3-540-88387-6_7
6. Bjørner, N., Phan, A.-D., Fleckenstein, L.: νZ - an optimizing SMT solver. In: Baier, C., Tinelli, C. (eds.) TACAS 2015. LNCS, vol. 9035, pp. 194–199. Springer, Heidelberg (2015). doi:10.1007/978-3-662-46681-0_14
7. Bruttomesso, R., Carioni, A., Ghilardi, S., Ranise, S.: Automated analysis of parametric timing-based mutual exclusion algorithms. In: Goodloe, A.E., Person, S. (eds.) NFM 2012. LNCS, vol. 7226, pp. 279–294. Springer, Heidelberg (2012). doi:10.1007/978-3-642-28891-3_28
8. Cheng, C., Guelfirat, T., Messinger, C., Schmitt, J.O., Schnelte, M., Weber, P.: Semantic degrees for industrie 4.0. CoRR, abs/1505.05625 (2015)
9. Cheng, C., Shankar, N., Ruess, H., Bensalem, S.: EFSMT: a logical framework for cyber-physical systems. CoRR, abs/1306.3456 (2013)
10. Cimatti, A., Griggio, A., Mover, S., Tonetta, S.: Parameter synthesis with IC3. In: FMCAD, pp. 165–168. IEEE (2013)
11. Courcoubetis, C., Yannakakis, M.: Minimum and maximum delay problems in real-time systems. Formal Methods Syst. Des. **1**, 385 (1992)

12. Damm, W., Ihlemann, C., Sofronie-Stokkermans, V.: Ptime parametric verification of safety properties for reasonable linear hybrid automata. Math. Comput. Sci. **5**(4), 469 (2011)
13. Dang, T., Dreossi, T., Piazza, C.: Parameter synthesis through temporal logic specifications. In: Bjørner, N., de Boer, F. (eds.) FM 2015. LNCS, vol. 9109, pp. 213–230. Springer, Heidelberg (2015). doi:10.1007/978-3-319-19249-9_14
14. Donzé, A.: Breach, a toolbox for verification and parameter synthesis of hybrid systems. In: Touili, T., Cook, B., Jackson, P. (eds.) CAV 2010. LNCS, vol. 6174, pp. 167–170. Springer, Heidelberg (2010). doi:10.1007/978-3-642-14295-6_17
15. Faber, J., Ihlemann, C., Jacobs, S., Sofronie-Stokkermans, V.: Automatic verification of parametric specifications with complex topologies. In: Méry, D., Merz, S. (eds.) IFM 2010. LNCS, vol. 6396, pp. 152–167. Springer, Heidelberg (2010). doi:10.1007/978-3-642-16265-7_12
16. Finkbeiner, B., Schewe, S.: Bounded synthesis. STTT **15**(5–6), 519–539 (2013)
17. Frehse, G., Jha, S.K., Krogh, B.H.: A counterexample-guided approach to parameter synthesis for linear hybrid automata. In: Egerstedt, M., Mishra, B. (eds.) HSCC 2008. LNCS, vol. 4981, pp. 187–200. Springer, Heidelberg (2008). doi:10.1007/978-3-540-78929-1_14
18. Fribourg, L., Kühne, U.: Parametric verification and test coverage for hybrid automata using the inverse method. Int. J. Found. Comput. Sci. **24**, 233 (2013)
19. Henzinger, T.A., Wong-Toi, H.: Using HyTech to synthesize control parameters for a steam boiler. In: FMIA (1995)
20. Hune, T., Romijn, J., Stoelinga, M., Vaandrager, F.W.: Linear parametric model checking of timed automata. J. Log. Algebr. Program. **52**, 183 (2002)
21. Jovanović, A., Lime, D., Roux, O.H.: Integer parameter synthesis for timed automata. In: Piterman, N., Smolka, S.A. (eds.) TACAS 2013. LNCS, vol. 7795, pp. 401–415. Springer, Heidelberg (2013). doi:10.1007/978-3-642-36742-7_28
22. Legay, A., Bensalem, S., Boyer, B., Bozga, M.: Incremental generation of linear invariants for component-based systems. In: ACSD (2013)
23. Moura, L., Bjørner, N.: Efficient e-matching for SMT solvers. In: Pfenning, F. (ed.) CADE 2007. LNCS (LNAI), vol. 4603, pp. 183–198. Springer, Heidelberg (2007). doi:10.1007/978-3-540-73595-3_13
24. Moura, L., Rueß, H., Sorea, M.: Lazy theorem proving for bounded model checking over infinite domains. In: Voronkov, A. (ed.) CADE 2002. LNCS (LNAI), vol. 2392, pp. 438–455. Springer, Heidelberg (2002). doi:10.1007/3-540-45620-1_35
25. Sofronie-Stokkermans, V.: Hierarchical reasoning for the verification of parametric systems. In: Giesl, J., Hähnle, R. (eds.) IJCAR 2010. LNCS (LNAI), vol. 6173, pp. 171–187. Springer, Heidelberg (2010). doi:10.1007/978-3-642-14203-1_15
26. Wang, F.: Symbolic parametric safety analysis of linear hybrid systems with BDD-like data-structures. In: Alur, R., Peled, D.A. (eds.) CAV 2004. LNCS, vol. 3114, pp. 295–307. Springer, Heidelberg (2004). doi:10.1007/978-3-540-27813-9_23

Combining Mechanized Proofs and Model-Based Testing in the Formal Analysis of a Hypervisor

Hanno Becker, Juan Manuel Crespo, Jacek Galowicz, Ulrich Hensel, Yoichi Hirai, César Kunz, Keiko Nakata, Jorge Luis Sacchini, Hendrik Tews(✉), and Thomas Tuerk

Dresden, Germany
uv@lists.askra.de

Abstract. Virtualization engines play a critical role in many modern software products. In an effort to gain definitive confidence on critical components, our company has invested on the formal verification of the NOVA micro hypervisor, following recent advances in similar academic and industrial operating-system verification projects. There are inherent difficulties in applying formal methods to low-level implementations, and even more under specific constraints arising in commercial software development. In order to deal with these, the chosen approach consists in the splitting of the verification effort by combining the definition of an abstract model of NOVA, the verification of fundamental security properties over this model, and testing the conformance of the model w.r.t. the NOVA implementation. This article reports on our experiences in applying formal methods to verify a hypervisor for commercial purposes. It describes the verification approach, and the security properties under consideration, and reports the results obtained.

1 Introduction

Virtualization is prominent in many recent software products. It is used commercially inside cloud services as well as privately for sandboxing or running incompatible legacy applications. Virtualization provides the basis for high-security products that separate applications in disjoint operating-system instances as well as for certain cyber-security products.

The trustworthiness of all these virtualization applications relies fundamentally on the correctness of the hypervisor that implements virtual machine instances on top of the hardware. Encouraged by the success in formal verification applied to large-scale systems in academia [10,12] and, more recently, also in industrial contexts [6,17], a number of companies are investing now into formally-verified hypervisors. The authors of this paper worked in a large team together with kernel developers to build a formally verified virtualization solution based on an improved version of the NOVA [23] micro-hypervisor targeting one of the previously mentioned application domains.

Our company wants to remain anonymous.

J. Fitzgerald et al. (Eds.): FM 2016, LNCS 9995, pp. 69–84, 2016.
DOI: 10.1007/978-3-319-48989-6_5

A notable case study in formal verification applied to the domain of operating systems is the seL4 project [10]. One could argue that it even constitutes a roadmap or methodology for the verification of low-level large-scale software systems, such as the one we are tackling. However, while the seL4 project was carried out in an academic context, we have to accommodate certain requirements that stem from working in a commercial software development environment.

Challenges. There are some challenges that are specific to the commercial software development context around our targetted hypervisor.

1. The further development of NOVA is driven by feature requests and performance concerns. While the development team is very eager to hear the opinion of the formal methods team, ease of formal verification is not the highest priority when it comes to choice during the development.
2. Release dates are determined according to potential product value and the Company's go-to market strategy. Therefore, it is very likely that the first release will take place before the source code is formally verified. We need to adapt our workflow to these release dates and choose a verification process that permits the release of intermediate results that already provide substantial value to the customer and that can be extended in subsequent releases.
3. We are currently verifying a moving target. Because NOVA lies at the bottom of a stack of components whose design is in constant evolution, the feature set of our version of NOVA changes often and in significant ways. This requires us to adapt the proofs and the correctness and security arguments promptly.
4. NOVA is developed in C++. While there has been work on formalizing aspects of C++ semantics [18,19]—to the best of our knowledge—there are no mechanized semantics for C++11 as specified by ISO/IEC 14882:2011, which is the flavor pervasively used in the source code.

In order to accommodate to these requirements and restrictions, we have decoupled the high-level properties and their proofs from the low level C++ implementation details. Moreover, we focused on sequential execution NOVA, running on a single core. To this end, we formally prove security properties on an abstract model of the system (written in Coq), and check the correlation between that model and the implementation by model-based testing (which we call conformance testing).

Results. The main objective of our project is to increase the trustworthiness of our virtualization engine using formal methods. In this respect, since the hypervisor is a main building block of the virtualization architecture, the obtained security proofs of the model of the hypervisor are essential to obtain a high-level security property of the whole trusted computing base (TCB).

The number of bugs found and their severeness is considered by the company's management as an important impact indicator of our work. Using our methodology we have discovered at least a couple of dozen of bugs in the hypervisor component, including a few security-critical bugs, and provided the developers with valuable feedback since the earliest stages of development.

Our methodology also impacts the C++ design quality through all its stages: formal modeling (in cooperation with the C++ developers) drives high quality code reviews in early stages, formal proofs yield the discovery of hard to find corner cases, and the conformance testing provides effective regression testing and excellent test coverage.

Contributions. The main contribution of the paper is to report our experience in applying formal methods in a commercial software-development context. We evaluate advantages and drawbacks of our approach as well as describe our methodology, we discuss possible alternatives and current project status in more technical depth.

Structure of the Paper. In Sect. 2 we describe in detail the verification methodology used. In Sect. 3 we provide some background on the NOVA hypervisor. Section 4 describes our Coq formalization. Section 5 presents the high-level security properties that we establish on the model. In Sect. 6 we present our conformance-testing infrastructure. We review related work in Sect. 7 and we present future work and conclusions in Sect. 8.

2 Overview of the Methodology

Developing an abstract model of some real-world system is a common formal verification approach. In our setting, the *real system* is the hypervisor written in C++ and executing in hardware, while the *model* is a formalization within the logic of the Coq proof assistant intended to represent the real system. By their different nature, regardless of the level of detail of the model in question, only empirical evidence can be provided for the adequacy of the representation, and the process of providing this evidence we call *conformance testing.*

There are three main strategies for building the real system and the model:

- Generating the model from the system's source code.
- Generating the system's source code from the model.
- Developing the model and the real system independently.

One benefit of generating the model from the source code, or vice versa, is that one can rely on (or verify) the correctness of the generation mechanism. However, these two strategies pose serious challenges in our setting.

Generating the model from the hypervisor source code is problematic since there is no formalization of the various new features of C++ that are used, and building one is out of scope. Indeed, formal verification is not one of the main objectives of the engineering team developing the C++ implementation of the hypervisor, therefore their design decisions might not always be optimal for verification purposes. Building an ad hoc generator just for our purposes might be possible, but certainly time consuming, and the output model would be very detailed and thus hard to reason about.

Generating source code from a model leads to similar challenges. One would need to generate source code that executes on bare metal and is aware of special hardware features of various architectures. Moreover this source code has to satisfy also non-verification related objectives like efficiency. Generating such source code from Coq can be too convoluted and, even if we successfully managed to solve these challenges, it would be time consuming to leverage the expert knowledge of the hypervisor developers. Moreover, this approach would also result on a very detailed model.

The chosen approach, an independent development of the model and the real system, provides more flexibility in the design, and the necessary freedom for the C++ source code to address hardware specific issues as well as non verification related objectives, while the model is abstract enough to be easily understandable and easy to reason about. Moreover, this decoupling means that small, low level changes in the C++ source code do not even need to be reflected in the model and thereby grants the model and our proofs much greater stability. However, there is a price to pay: due to the decoupling it is possible that the model and the real system do not agree with each other. In order to overcome this issue, we use model-based testing to provide evidence of the agreement between the implementation and the model, hinting that the properties that we prove in the latter, with a high level of certainty, also hold in the former.

Our starting point is a Coq model of our version of the NOVA hypervisor, based on its design documents. The main components of the Coq model are the hypervisor state and the hypervisor system calls (called *hypercalls* in the rest of the article). The state is an abstraction of the concrete state of the implementation of the hypervisor and comprises all necessary information required to faithfully simulate the behavior of a hypervisor execution. We establish a security property that shows confinement of the resources accessed by a potentially malicious component running on top of the hypervisor on any given execution.

We rely on the Coq extraction mechanism to obtain an executable OCaml version of the model. Around this automatically generated software component, we build a scaffold for running tests in order to empirically assess conformance between the model and the implementation. Additionally, this also constitutes an effective framework to perform fuzzing on the implementation, using our model as an oracle for expected behavior.

3 A Primer on the NOVA Micro Hypervisor

This section provides a brief overview of our improved version of NOVA (referred to simply as hypervisor below) and its high-level design. It also introduces some concepts that are used in the reminder of the paper.

The NOVA micro hypervisor [23] runs directly on the hardware, and it is constructed according to micro-kernel design principles [13] in the tradition of the L4 family [7]. In traditional designs, the *Virtual Machine Monitor* (VMM) is often integrated into the hypervisor for performance reasons. In contrast, in a micro-kernel design, the hypervisor is the sole component running in the most

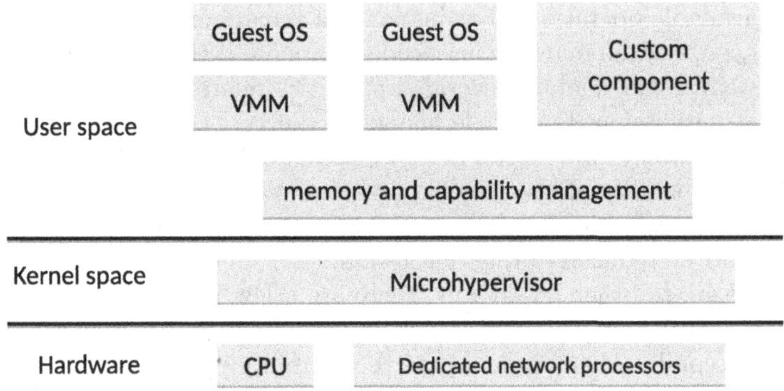

Fig. 1. Potential NOVA based application architecture

privileged mode of the hardware (host mode ring 0 on x86). The VMM runs as a separate module in unprivileged mode (host mode ring 3 on x86). The hypervisor contains exclusively the functionality that cannot be implemented in unprivileged mode because of performance requirements or hardware restrictions. This design permits to potentially have isolated VMM instances for different guest operating systems as well as to run most device drivers as user applications in unprivileged mode, see Fig. 1 for illustration.

Resource separation is an important design objective that the TCB needs to provide. For instance, guest OSs or applications therein must not be able to arbitrarily modify the main memory of other components. Our virtualization architecture relies on the TCB to correctly enforce resource separation, so that potentially malicious guest OSs cannot escape their virtualized environment. The verification of the hypervisor and the correct behavior of its hypercall interface marks our first step towards ensuring the separation property of the whole TCB.

To provide access control, NOVA uses a capability model that is inspired by the take-grant model [14] as well as the EROS capability model [22]. A *capability* is a reference to a resource together with access permissions. NOVA uses three classes of capabilities: memory capabilities (referencing physical memory tiles), object capabilities (referencing *kernel objects*, see below) and I/O capabilities (referencing hardware I/O ports). The access permissions depend on the capability class. For example, permissions in memory capabilities refer directly to the hardware permission bits in the page table entries, while access permissions of kernel objects enable certain hypercalls.

For memory and I/O port capabilities, the capability selectors have a special meaning. For memory, the capability selector denotes the virtual page index at which the referenced memory tile is available in virtual memory. For I/O ports, the selector number is the I/O port number. Therefore, NOVA enforces that I/O port capabilities can only be delegated to identical capability selectors.

Unprivileged programs can reference capabilities via process specific *capability selectors* but cannot directly modify capabilities. The access permissions govern the available operations. For instance, a semaphore capability only permits the down operation on the referenced semaphore if the dn permission bit is set. The system might contain several capabilities referencing the same object with different permissions to provide fine-grained access control to different programs. Every capability owner can delegate a capability to a different process if he possesses a capability of the target that permits delegation. Thereby, delegation grants the target process access to the referenced kernel object. The access permissions can be reduced during delegation.

In comparison to other L4 designs, there are a few interesting differences in our version of NOVA. Firstly, delegation is decoupled from inter-process communication. Secondly, there is no recursive capability revocation, one can only delegate empty capabilities to overwrite the contents of certain capability selectors inside a certain process.[1]

3.1 Kernel Objects

The hypervisor provides hypercalls for creation and manipulation of kernel objects. There are five categories of kernel objects.

Processes: processes provide a mechanism for spatial isolation. A process is a collection of capabilities to memory, kernel objects, and I/O ports.[2]

Threads: a thread is a piece of a program that can be independently scheduled. A thread is permanently bound to a process at creation time. Threads can run in *host mode* or *guest mode*. The latter is used to execute a guest OS. Each thread possesses a *user thread-control block* (UTCB) that is used during inter-process communication and which is allocated at thread creation time from the kernel memory pool.

Portals: a portal is a communication endpoint bound to a service-providing thread.

Scheduling objects: scheduling objects provide priorities and execution time. The hypervisor provides a fixed-priority, round-robin scheduler that schedules the threads that possess scheduling objects.

Semaphores: the hypervisor provides counting semaphore objects for thread synchronization.

Kernel objects are allocated in kernel-space memory and are not accessible from unprivilied (user-level) processes (they can only be indirectly referenced through selectors). UTCBs are a special case: for efficiency reasons, they are allocated in kernel memory, but a user-level thread has direct access to its UTCB through a memory selector.

[1] In order to enforce resource revocation from untrusted components in our NOVA version, one needs a trusted component that performs all delegations and tracks them similarly to the mapping database that is part of many L4 implementations.

[2] The NOVA documentation uses *protection domain* instead of *process* and *execution context* instead of *thread* but we stick to traditional terminology here.

3.2 Hypercalls

The hypercalls provide user processes with mechanisms that can be categorized as follows:

Communication: start and terminate inter-process communication calls. Calls always reference a portal and will establish a handshake with the thread that the portal points to. A reply terminates a call and signals the availability of the thread for the next call. For data exchange, the hypervisor appropriately copies the contents of the UTCB from the caller to the callee and back.

Object creation: create kernel objects with a certain set of permissions, and associate them with capability selectors.

Capability delegation: delegation of capabilities to the own or other processes, restricting capability permissions, and deleting capabilities (by delegating empty capabilities).

Object modification: permit modification of relevant aspects of kernel objects (e.g. change the value of a semaphore).

Device management: there is one hypercall to configure direct memory access (DMA) devices and one for associating interrupts to semaphores. Internally both configure the I/O MMU. These device management hypercalls are not relevant for this paper.

There are some interesting aspects of how hardware events are handled in the hypervisor. Firstly, device interrupts are mapped to semaphore-up operations. A thread that wants to wait for an interrupt must perform a down operation on the right semaphore. Secondly, CPU exceptions (e.g., page-fault or divide-by-zero), virtual machine intercepts or exits (VM exits), are mapped to inter-process communication. On behalf of the faulting thread, the hypervisor sets up a call to a portal that depends on the exception or intercept, and fills the UTCB with data describing the exception or intercept as well as the content of the CPU registers of the faulting thread.

4 Coq Model

The Coq abstract model of the hypervisor is essentially defined as a transition system. The states are abstract representations of the hypervisor internal state while the transitions correspond to events performed by (a sequential execution of) the hypervisor. These events can be roughly divided between external events (e.g. a thread issuing a hypercall), and internal events (e.g. the hypervisor resumes a blocked thread).

Structurally, the abstract model is divided in the following components: basic infrastructure, hypervisor state, and semantics. The basic infrastructure component defines the core data structures and lemmas used in the entire development. It contains the definition of the libraries used in the hypervisor semantics, and a large collection of lemmas and tactics for proof automation.

We describe the hypervisor state and semantics in the rest of this section. In Sect. 5 we describe the security properties we prove for this semantics.

4.1 Hypervisor State

The hypervisor state type $\mathcal{K}$ represents the hypervisor internal state. It is defined as a record containing:

- a collection of kernel objects, defined as a partial map from *pointers* (non-negative numbers) to typed kernel objects;
- the addresses of UTCBs to track which parts of the kernel memory might be accesses from unprivileged mode
- architecture-specific state: interrupt mapping, device status, etc.;

Kernel objects refer to each other using pointers (e.g. a thread contains a pointer to the process it belongs to). Accessing an object through a pointer may fail if the pointer is not in the partial map, or the mapped object has the wrong type. Therefore, functions to access objects are defined in the error monad (see Sect. 4.2).

Each type of kernel object is defined as a record. Processes are represented as collections of capabilities of a specific type:

- memory capabilities are represented as a map from memory capability selectors (virtual addresses) to physical addresses and permissions;
- object capabilities are represented by a map from object capability selectors to kernel-object pointers;
- I/O capabilities are represented by the set of I/O ports that the process is allowed to access.

Threads contain a stack pointer, a UTCB pointer, a pointer to the associated process, and a status value. The status value is taken from an enumeration type that indicates if the thread is running, available for execution, blocked in a semaphore, etc. The status is not explicitly implemented in the hypervisor, but it is a useful abstraction to have in the model.

Semaphores contain a counter value and a queue of pointers to blocked threads.

Portals and scheduling objects are similarly represented with records, but their contents are not relevant to this paper.

4.2 Semantics

The semantics of the hypervisor is specified as a transition system on the set of kernel states whose transitions are steps that the hypervisor may perform. Steps are divided in categories as follows.

Hypercalls: these are executed by a thread to require a hypervisor service.

Hypervisor events: these are internal to the hypervisor in the sense that they change the state, but are not directly visible for user processes. For example, a semaphore timeout may cause a blocked thread to become unblocked.

Exceptions: this class includes events such as interrupts, DMA access steps, exceptions, etc. Depending on the type of event, they may cause a switch to kernel mode.

Concretely, we define the transition system as a function

$$\mathsf{stepRun} : \mathcal{K} \rightarrow \mathcal{S} \rightarrow \mathcal{M}(\mathcal{R}, \mathcal{K})$$

where $\mathcal{S}$ is the type representing the hypervisor steps, $\mathcal{R}$ is the result of executing the step, and $\mathcal{M}$ is a non-determinism error monad. This function is extracted to an executable program in OCaml, which we use for conformance testing (see Sect. 6).

The error monad is used to model successful executions as well as failures. Executing a step may fail for several reasons, most typically, when accessing a non-existent object in memory (but we proved an invariant about the absence of certain failures, see Sect. 5 below).

The stepRun function proceeds by first checking *feasibility* of the step to be executed. Feasibility is defined as an over-approximation of the valid steps in a given kernel state. For example, in the case of a hypercall step executed by a thread pointer p, feasibility means that p points to a valid thread object whose status allows execution (i.e. it is not blocked on a semaphore). This notion of feasibility is naturally extended to traces.

If the step is not feasible, execution fails. Otherwise, the function stepRun proceeds to execute the step. Let us illustrate the semantics with the implementation of the create_thread hypercall. We simplify some details that are not relevant for this level of detail. The create_thread hypercall takes four parameters:

$$\mathsf{create\_thread}(\mathit{proc\_sel}, \mathit{th\_sel}, \mathit{utcb\_sel}, \mathit{data})$$

where *proc_sel* is a capability selector referencing the process that shall contain the new thread, *th_sel* is the selector that shall contain the new capability referencing the newly created thread, *utcb_sel* is a memory capability selector describing where the UTCB of the new thread shall be accessible in user virtual memory, and *data* contains other parameters not relevant here (e.g. stack pointer).

We model the create_thread hypercall as a function

$$\mathsf{create\_thread} : \mathcal{K} \rightarrow \mathsf{ptr} \rightarrow \mathsf{sel} \rightarrow \mathsf{sel} \rightarrow \mathsf{sel} \rightarrow \mathsf{data} \rightarrow \mathcal{M}(\mathcal{R}, \mathcal{K})$$

where the first argument is the kernel state where the hypercall is being executed and the second argument is a pointer in the kernel state to the thread executing the hypercall. In Coq, it is defined as follows:

```
create_thread ks t proc_sel th_sel utcb_sel data :=
  p ← get_process ks t;
  if has_ct_perm ks p proc_sel
    then
      ks1, utcb ← allocate_utcb ks proc_sel utcb_sel;
      ks2, th ← new_thread ks1 utcb data;
      ks3 ← map_selector ks2 proc_sel th_sel th;
      return (Success, ks3)
    else
      return (BadPermission, ks)
```

Here we use Coq notations to write monadic-style code: $v \leftarrow f$; *body* is a shorthand for $(\lambda v\,.\,body) f$, that is, evaluate *body* with v bound to the result of f. The function proceeds as follows: first, get the process corresponding to the executing thread (t) in the current state (ks). This can fail if t does not point to a valid thread. Then, check that the process referenced by *proc_sel* has permission to create threads. If not, return without modifying the kernel state. Otherwise, allocate a new UTCB (using allocate_utcb), create the new thread object (using new_thread), and finally map a reference to the newly-created thread (using map_selector) at the selector given by the user (*th_sel*).

5 Security Properties

The main security properties we prove for our model are *authority confinement* and *memory confinement*. Authority confinement states that a process cannot gain access to a capability unless it was explicitly delegated to it. In other words, a process cannot "trick" the hypervisor into gaining capabilities by executing a sequence of steps. Memory confinement states that a thread cannot access kernel memory except when it represents a UTCB.

In order to establish these properties on the model, we need to first show a consistency invariant on the semantics. We divide this proof as a conjunction of 10 individual invariants. Most of these invariants refer to internal consistency of our data structures and consistency of the kernel state. For example, memory confinement is proved as an invariant of the state (see below).

Two important examples of invariants proved are *no-dangling pointers* and *semaphore consistency*. No-dangling pointers state that all pointers in a kernel object point to valid objects of the right type. For example, a thread has a valid pointer to its corresponding process; a semaphore's blocked-queue contains pointers to valid threads.

Semaphore consistency refers to the internal consistency of the semaphore structure in a kernel state. It is defined as the conjunction of the following three properties:

- the blocked-queue in any semaphore contains no duplicates and any thread in any semaphore's blocked-queue has a status field indicating it is blocked by a semaphore;
- if a thread status indicates it is blocked by a semaphore, then there exists a semaphore that contains a pointer to the thread in its blocked-queue;
- for any pair of semaphores, their blocked-queues are disjoint.

5.1 Authority Confinement

Consider a partitioning of the processes into two sets that we call *trusted* and *untrusted*. Consider further an initial state k, a kernel event trace $\overline{s}$ and a capability c. Our authority confinement property states that the untrusted processes can never gain access to c as long as the following three conditions are fulfilled.

Firstly, c must not be present in any untrusted process in state k. Secondly, if c is created in $\overline{s}$, it must be created inside a trusted process. Finally, c is never delegated from a trusted to an untrusted process.

This property shows that one can effectively prevent any (untrusted) set of processes $\mathcal{S}$ from gaining access to a certain resource c: one only needs to restrict delegation into $\mathcal{S}$ and the rights of $\mathcal{S}$ to create capabilities by creating new kernel objects. Then, regardless of the actions that are performed inside $\mathcal{S}$, no process inside $\mathcal{S}$ will ever gain access to c.

Authority confinement is proved by a simple induction on the kernel event trace $\overline{s}$, showing that c can only appear inside the untrusted processes if it is either delegated to one of the untrusted processes or created by one of them.

5.2 Memory Confinement

Consider a kernel state k. We say that k satisfies the memory confinement property if for every process p and memory capability m, such that p holds m in k, one of the following holds:

- m does not point in kernel memory, or
- m points to a UTCB.

Memory confinement is proved as an invariant of the semantics. It is an essential security property of the hypervisor: if a process can access kernel memory, then it could potentially access any resource.

6 Conformance Testing

We use conformance testing to provide evidence about the correct implementation of the NOVA hypervisor w.r.t. our abstract model. In turn, this indicates that the properties that we proved for the abstract model hold for running instances of our NOVA version.

For conformance testing we run a kernel event trace (consisting of hypercalls, hypervisor events, and exceptions) both in the hypervisor and in the abstract model, see Fig. 2. Running an input trace in the hypervisor or the abstract model produces a final kernel state and an output trace of the kernel events that were actually performed together with hypercall status results. We compare the output traces and the final kernel states and check that the output traces correspond to the input trace. Any mismatch in the comparison indicates a difference in the executions of the abstract model and the hypervisor that needs investigation.

Running a kernel event trace on the hypervisor requires booting the hypervisor together with our test interpreter process, which can execute an arbitrary kernel event trace. The whole testing currently requires certain changes in the hypervisor. They are needed for generating the output trace and the final kernel state. We try to minimize the changes made to the hypervisor in order to ensure that we do not affect the hypervisor semantics.

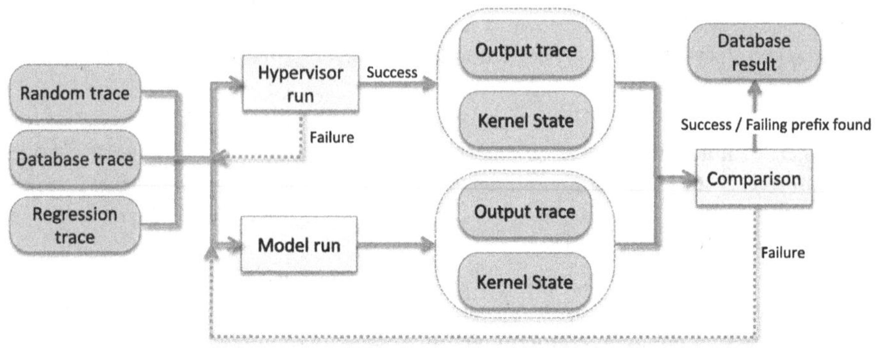

Fig. 2. Scheme of the testing process.

For running the traces in the abstract model, we use the Coq code-extraction facilities to generate OCaml code from the abstract model. We trust the correctness of the Coq extraction mechanisms and assume that the generated code allows evaluating a trace in OCaml according to the Coq model.

Efficiency of the extracted code is an important requirement. For our workload, we found that some data structures in the Coq standard library are not efficient. Concretely, this applies to the standard set library. We proposed a relaxed interface for this library and implemented instances that better fit our workload (see [24]).

Our conformance testing framework provides additional features to ease debugging of failing test cases and simplify our development process. For failing test cases, our framework automatically searches the first step in the input event trace that exhibits a difference in the behavior of the abstract model and the hypervisor. Test data and especially failing test cases can be conveniently investigated via an web front-end.

Traces for running conformance testing come from three different sources: randomly generated, handwritten, and previously-executed traces.

The most important source of traces is our random generator. Simple random trace generation would produce a huge amount of unfeasible steps and almost all hypercalls would fail because of invalid arguments. We therefore use the abstract model to guide the random step generation. Starting from a kernel state, we collect feasible events from the abstract model and randomly chose one of them. For hypercalls we also extract correct arguments and chose with a certain probability only from these arguments. Once a step has been generated, it is run in the abstract model to continue the trace generation with the next kernel state.

The second source of traces for conformance is a set of about 16,000 short handwritten traces that we use for regression testing during the development process. For defining this set, we only require basic coverage of the model and the hypervisor.

Finally, the testing framework supports rerunning traces that were generated in the past. We use this feature for validating whether bugs in the hypervisor or in the model have been fixed.

At the time of writing we have about 12 million executed conformance tests in our data base, of which slightly less than 5 % fail for various known bugs in the abstract model or the hypervisor. All these bugs will be addressed in due time before the product release.

7 Related Work

The most relevant to our work is arguably the seL4 project. Initially, Klein et al. established functional correctness of the low-level implementation with respect to a Haskell reference implementation [10]. This correctness proof was extended in several directions, to ensure security properties: integrity [20] and information flow [16]. These properties are proved directly at the implementation level. As we discussed in Sect. 1, we have different challenges: seL4 was developed with the main goal of being verified, whereas our targetted hypervisor is developed as a bedrock for several products in an industrial environment.

The CertiKOS project carried out at Yale University [9] is focused on developing the necessary program logics and infrastructure for the verification of low-level features such as self-modifying code [5] or hardware interrupts and preemptive threads [8], to mention a few. In recent work, Shao [21] proposes redesigning the underlying programming language in which OS kernels are programmed and how it interacts with theorem provers and program logics.

More recently, Liu et al. [15] perform a security analysis of the Goldfish android kernel. In their work, they use the Goanna static analyzer to search for potential vulnerabilities with security implications. They aim at ensuring absence of common coding errors rather than functional correctness.

Our work has strong connections with theorem prover-based testing [4], an instance of model-based testing in which the model is developed in a theorem prover, enabling the proof of properties on top of the model.

Recently, Kosmatov et al. [11] have also combined proofs and testing in the context of hypervisor verification. Concretely, they targeted the virtual memory system of the Axagoros hypervisor. They applied Hoare-style reasoning directly on source code using the Frama-C toolset. When automatic provers fail to discharge proof obligations, they split and isolate the unproven parts and perform all-path testing.

There has also been some work on establishing isolation properties in the context of virtualization [1]. The properties are established in an idealized model with no specific target and therefore, without connection with any particular implementation.

Other work on the verification of large scale systems includes the CompCert C compiler [12] and work carried out by Cousot et al. [2] in the application of static analyses to synchronous control/command in the context of aerospace software. Other recent work targeting this domain includes [3,25].

Finally, it is worth mentioning that there has been increasing interest in applying formal methods in the high-tech industry: Facebook has been applying static analysis on their mobile applications [6] and Amazon has been using TLA+ to prove properties of concurrent systems at the design level [17].

8 Conclusions

In this paper we have described the challenges we faced when applying formal methods in an industrial context—under a different set of constraints than in most academic work—and the methodology we applied to accommodate to this context. We believe that the lessons we have learned and shared in this paper can be useful when undertaking large-scale verification projects under a similar context.

The work presented in this paper required approximately 3 person-years, which roughly break down into 25 % spent in model construction, 35 % spent in developing Coq proofs, 15 % spent in developing the conformance testing infrastructure (including trace generation), and 25 % spent in analyzing conformance testing results.

Throughout the project, approximately a couple of dozen bugs were found in the hypervisor source code. Half of them have been found via code review during model construction and proof. The rest are found via investigation of discrepancies between the model and hypervisor during conformance testing. For most of these bugs, the test cases that trigger them do not crash the hypervisor and do not break any immediate assertion. Therefore, comparing the internal hypervisor state with an expected value (given by the model) is an effective way to show the existence of a bug.

The model is essential during conformance testing as it acts as a executable specification.

We should also point out that we found as many bugs in our model (including the Coq model and conformance testing infrastructure), which showed up as false positives during conformance testing.

Testing-related results appeared to be the most efficient way to communicate to the developer teams: we are using metrics like model-based coverage, number of tests and number of reported bugs to convey the impact on increased quality through our work.

The abstract model and its proven security properties demonstrate that there is no security vulnerability in the design of the hypervisor. Millions of conformance tests and the associated coverage provide a convincing argument that design and implementation correlate. Together, our results establish a very high degree of customer confidence in the quality and security of hypervisor-based products.

Future Work. There are essentially four dimensions to extend our work. First, we are interested in exploring stronger security properties that can be built on top of our current authority confinement property. Second, we would like to provide stronger evidence of the connection between the model and the source code. Work is already underway in applying program refinement to construct a chain of increasingly precise models, all the way down to the source code. Third, we aim at extending the verification target to components that run above the hypervisor and that play a crucial role from a security standpoint. In particular, some work has been started on establishing correctness properties at the source level of library code which contains critical data-structures pervasively used in a majority of modules of the system to track notions of ownership and access permission. Finally, the abstract model, the proven properties and conformance testing needs to be extended to parallel execution.

References

1. Barthe, G., Betarte, G., Campo, J.D., Luna, C.: Formally verifying isolation and availability in an idealized model of virtualization. In: Butler, M., Schulte, W. (eds.) FM 2011. LNCS, vol. 6664, pp. 231–245. Springer, Heidelberg (2011). doi:10.1007/978-3-642-21437-0_19
2. Bertrane, J., Cousot, P., Cousot, R., Feret, J., Mauborgne, L., Miné, A., Rival, X.: Static analysis and verification of aerospace software by abstract interpretation. Found. Trends Program. Lang. **2**(2–3), 71–190 (2015)
3. Brat, G., Bushnell, D., Davies, M., Giannakopoulou, D., Howar, F., Kahsai, T.: Verifying the safety of a flight-critical system. In: Bjørner, N., de Boer, F. (eds.) FM 2015. LNCS, vol. 9109, pp. 308–324. Springer, Heidelberg (2015). doi:10.1007/978-3-319-19249-9_20
4. Brucker, A.D., Wolff, B.: On theorem prover-based testing. Formal Aspects Comput. **25**(5), 683–721 (2013)
5. Cai, H., Shao, Z., Vaynberg, A.: Certified self-modifying code. In: Proceedings of the ACM SIGPLAN 2007 Conference on Programming Language Design and Implementation, San Diego, California, USA, June 10–13, 2007, pp. 66–77 (2007)
6. Calcagno, C., et al.: Moving fast with software verification. In: Havelund, K., Holzmann, G., Joshi, R. (eds.) NFM 2015. LNCS, vol. 9058, pp. 3–11. Springer, Heidelberg (2015). doi:10.1007/978-3-319-17524-9_1
7. Elphinstone, K., Heiser, G.: From L3 to seL4 - what have we learnt in 20 years of L4 microkernels? In: Proceedings of the Twenty-Fourth ACM Symposium on Operating Systems Principles, SOSP 2013, pp. 133–150. ACM, New York (2013)
8. Feng, X., Shao, Z., Dong, Y., Guo, Y.: Certifying low-level programs with hardware interrupts and preemptive threads. In: Proceedings of the ACM SIGPLAN 2008 Conference on Programming Language Design and Implementation, Tucson, AZ, USA, June 7–13, 2008, pp. 170–182 (2008)
9. Gu, L., Vaynberg, A., Ford, B., Shao, Z., Costanzo, D.: Certikos: a certified kernel for secure cloud computing. In: APSys 2011 Asia Pacific Workshop on Systems, Shanghai, China, July 11-12, 2011, p. 3 (2011)
10. Klein, G., Elphinstone, K., Heiser, G., Andronick, J., Cock, D., Derrin, P., Elkaduwe, D., Engelhardt, K., Kolanski, R., Norrish, M., Sewell, T., Tuch, H., Winwood, S.: sel4: formal verification of an OS kernel. In: Proceedings of the 22nd ACM Symposium on Operating Systems Principles 2009, SOSP 2009, Big Sky, Montana, USA, October 11–14, 2009, pp. 207–220 (2009)

11. Kosmatov, N., Lemerre, M., Alec, C.: A case study on verification of a cloud hypervisor by proof and structural testing. In: Seidl, M., Tillmann, N. (eds.) TAP 2014. LNCS, vol. 8570, pp. 158–164. Springer, Heidelberg (2014). doi:10.1007/978-3-319-09099-3_12
12. Leroy, X.: A formally verified compiler back-end. J. Autom. Reasoning **43**(4), 363–446 (2009)
13. Liedtke, J.: Toward real μ-kernels. Commun. ACM **39**(9), 70–77 (1996)
14. Lipton, R.J., Snyder, L.: A linear time algorithm for deciding subject security. J. ACM **24**(3), 455–464 (1977)
15. Liu, T., Huuck, R.: Case study: static security analysis of the android goldfish kernel. In: Bjørner, N., de Boer, F. (eds.) FM 2015. LNCS, vol. 9109, pp. 589–592. Springer, Heidelberg (2015). doi:10.1007/978-3-319-19249-9_39
16. Murray, T.C., Matichuk, D., Brassil, M., Gammie, P., Bourke, T., Seefried, S., Lewis, C., Gao, X., Klein, G.: sel4: from general purpose to a proof of information flow enforcement. In: 2013 IEEE Symposium on Security and Privacy, SP 2013, Berkeley, CA, USA, May 19–22, 2013, pp. 415–429 (2013)
17. Newcombe, C., Rath, T., Zhang, F., Munteanu, B., Brooker, M., Deardeuff, M.: How amazon web services uses formal methods. Commun. ACM **58**(4), 66–73 (2015)
18. Ramananandro, T., Reis, G.D., Leroy, X.: Formal verification of object layout for c++ multiple inheritance. In: Proceedings of the 38th ACM SIGPLAN-SIGACT Symposium on Principles of Programming Languages, POPL 2011, Austin, TX, USA, January 26–28, 2011, pp. 67–80 (2011)
19. Ramananandro, T., Reis, G.D., Leroy, X.: A mechanized semantics for C++ object construction and destruction, with applications to resource management. In: Proceedings of the 39th ACM SIGPLAN-SIGACT Symposium on Principles of Programming Languages, POPL 2012, Philadelphia, Pennsylvania, USA, January 22–28, 2012, pp. 521–532 (2012)
20. Sewell, T., Winwood, S., Gammie, P., Murray, T., Andronick, J., Klein, G.: seL4 enforces integrity. In: Eekelen, M., Geuvers, H., Schmaltz, J., Wiedijk, F. (eds.) ITP 2011. LNCS, vol. 6898, pp. 325–340. Springer, Heidelberg (2011). doi:10.1007/978-3-642-22863-6_24
21. Shao, Z.: Clean-slate development of certified OS kernels. In: Proceedings of the 2015 Conference on Certified Programs and Proofs, Cp. 2015, Mumbai, India, January 15–17, 2015, pp. 95–96 (2015)
22. Shapiro, J.S., Weber, S.: Verifying the eros confinement mechanism. In: Proceedings of the 2000 IEEE Symposium on Security and Privacy, SP 2000, p. 166. IEEE Computer Society, Washington, DC (2000)
23. Steinberg, U., Kauer, B.: Nova: a microhypervisor-based secure virtualization architecture. In: Proceedings of the 5th European Conference on Computer Systems, EuroSys 2010, pp. 209–222. ACM, New York (2010)
24. FireEye Formal Methods Team. Efficiently executable sets used by FireEye. Presented at the 8th Coq Workshop (2016). https://github.com/fireeye/MSetsExtra
25. Zhao, H., Yang, M., Zhan, N., Gu, B., Zou, L., Chen, Y.: Formal verification of a descent guidance control program of a lunar lander. In: Jones, C., Pihlajasaari, P., Sun, J. (eds.) FM 2014. LNCS, vol. 8442, pp. 733–748. Springer, Heidelberg (2014). doi:10.1007/978-3-319-06410-9_49

A Model Checking Approach to Discrete Bifurcation Analysis

Nikola Beneš(✉), Luboš Brim, Martin Demko, Samuel Pastva, and David Šafránek

Systems Biology Laboratory, Faculty of Informatics, Masaryk University, Botanická 68a, 602 00 Brno, Czech Republic
{xbenes3,brim,xdemko,xpastva,xsafran1}@fi.muni.cz

Abstract. Bifurcation analysis is a central task of the analysis of parameterised high-dimensional dynamical systems that undergo transitions as parameters are changed. The classical numerical and analytical methods are typically limited to a small number of system parameters. In this paper we propose a novel approach to bifurcation analysis that is based on a suitable discrete abstraction of the system and employs model checking for discovering critical parameter values, referred to as bifurcation points, for which various kinds of behaviour (equilibrium, cycling) appear or disappear. To describe such behaviour patterns, called phase portraits, we use a hybrid version of a CTL logic augmented with direction formulae. We demonstrate the method on a case study taken from systems biology.

1 Introduction

Continuous dynamical systems mostly contain certain kinds of parameters. It can happen that a slight variation in a parameter has a significant impact on the system flow dynamics. It is obvious that insight into the qualitative structure of flow fields is of great importance and appears as the ultimate aim of flow research. A prominent classical example is the sudden transition from laminar to turbulent flow which takes place in a circular pipe (Poiseuille flow) when the speed in the centre of the pipe exceeds a critical value. Central issues when studying these flows are the characterisation of the range of parameters values over which particular flows exist and the mechanisms of transition between different flow patterns.

To tackle flow transition problems, numerical models are essential. Starting from a certain initial condition and given model parameters, the model is integrated forward in time and the long-time behaviour of quantities of interest is studied. To determine transition behaviour and critical conditions, parameters are subsequently changed and the transient and asymptotic behaviour of the model solutions is studied. In this way, transitions between different types of equilibrium behaviour (steady or time-dependent) are found.

This work has been supported by the Czech Science Foundation grant GA15-11089S.

J. Fitzgerald et al. (Eds.): FM 2016, LNCS 9995, pp. 85–101, 2016.
DOI: 10.1007/978-3-319-48989-6_6

Since the primary interest is in the changes in asymptotic behaviour when parameters change, another class of numerical methods can be used that focuses directly on the computation of the asymptotic flow states in the models. These may be steady states, periodic orbits, quasi-periodic orbits or more complicated states, usually referred to as attractors of the model. The issue of finding critical conditions for transitions is then rephrased in terms of dynamical systems theory to that of finding the parameter values at which bifurcations exist. The methods for the numerical bifurcation analysis, in particular continuation techniques, consist of efficient numerical schemes to determine attractors as a function of parameters. A disadvantage of these methods is that they are more complicated, especially in their need for sophisticated numerical linear algebra and, as a result, their application in flow analysis is limited. It is important to note that a comprehensive understanding of the mechanisms leading a system to exhibit turbulent behaviour is one of the grand challenges of physical and mathematical sciences.

The goal of *bifurcation analysis* is to produce parameter space maps or bifurcation diagrams that divide the parameter space into regions where parameters do not qualitatively affect the behaviour patterns, called *phase portraits*. Bifurcations occur at points that do not lie in the interior of one of these regions.

When applying numerical methods to continuous dynamical systems we often approximate the phase-space by a discrete state-transition system. This opens the door for the application of formal methods as known from computer science. In this paper we propose a novel approach to bifurcation analysis that is based on model checking. Model checking is widely accepted as a universal tool for exploration of complex dynamical systems under parameter uncertainty, especially in the domain of systems biology [3,4,15,17,18].

We suppose the system under consideration is abstracted into a discrete (often finite state) non-deterministic state-transition system in which transitions are annotated by directions (of flow). In such a system a run follows an orbit (trajectory) that changes directions in individual states. In such a way orbits in the original continuous system are abstracted into discrete orbits (runs), hence phase portraits are represented as their discrete counterparts. *Discrete phase portraits* can be characterised logically by temporal logic formulae that take into account changes in directions.

It is important to notice that the phase portraits do not show the time dependence of the orbits, but several important properties of the system dynamics can be obtained from them. Moreover, the phase portraits can be determined also for non-linear systems, for which the analytic solution is not available.

To capture most of the interesting phase portraits we employ a hybrid extension of the UCTL logic [5]. The need for extending branching logics and the related emphasis on global analysis have been already considered in [2,20] for non-parameterised setting. Especially, in [2] the authors employ hybrid CTL to express complex phenomena that are also relevant for bifurcation analysis. To keep the efficiency of the model checking procedure we intentionally do not consider a richer framework of spatio-temporal or topological logics.

The main contribution of the paper is in adaptation and application of formal methods, model-checking in particular, to an area that has been traditionally governed by numerical methods. The model checking approach can handle a richer set of bifurcations occurring in high-dimensional dynamical systems with reasonable efficiency. We demonstrate the approach on a case study taken from the highly interdisciplinary area of systems biology.

Related Work. Traditional bifurcation analysis techniques typically target continuous-time dynamical systems and employ numerical continuation based on Newton's method to detect bifurcation points [16]. Most of the techniques start with computing equilibria as a function of parameters. The existing tools are capable of detecting several kinds of equilibria bifurcation as well as bifurcations of cycles and connecting orbits. However, the limitation is the number of parameters – the so-called co-dimensionality. Numerical methods perform well up to two parameters but for higher co-dimension there is no universal solution [7]. In general, numerical techniques are not fully automatised and require fine-tuning of the methods settings. Regarding the systems dimensionality and co-dimensionality, their performance is limited [14].

Techniques based on model checking provide an alternative way to bifurcation analysis. The advantages include fully automated exhaustive exploration of systems dynamics under parameter uncertainty, identification of attraction basins by reachability analysis, and good scalability for higher co-dimension. However, the expressiveness in terms of types of bifurcations that can be detected relies on the precision of the systems phase-space discretisation. In [8] we have addressed bifurcations of single-state phase portraits in piecewise affine systems with rectangular abstraction of the dynamics. The major drawback of the method was the insufficient expressiveness of dCTL (CTL logic extended with direction propositions), notably, the impossibility to express complex phase portraits of systems dynamics. In this paper, we employ hybrid temporal logics that significantly strengthen the expressiveness. Moreover, we demonstrate the applicability of the method to a broader class of dynamical systems as in the case study we employ discretisation of piecewise multi-affine systems. This class of systems sufficiently covers systems with positive and negative feedback [4,17].

2 Preliminaries

As a motivation we suppose an n-dimensional rectangular abstraction of a given dynamical system, like the one defined in [22] and further adapted in [3,8,17] (see [12] for overview). In such a kind of abstraction the states are arranged in an n-dimensional space with neighbouring states being placed axis-parallel. Every transition between two states has a *direction*. A 2D example is shown in Fig. 1.

We base our framework on an extension of Kripke structures that allows to use labels on transitions. Such a framework is a special case of the so-called doubly labelled transition systems [13]. Doubly labelled transition systems are very similar to the so-called labelled Kripke structures [10] or Kripke transition systems [21] defined as an extension of Kripke structures with transition labels.

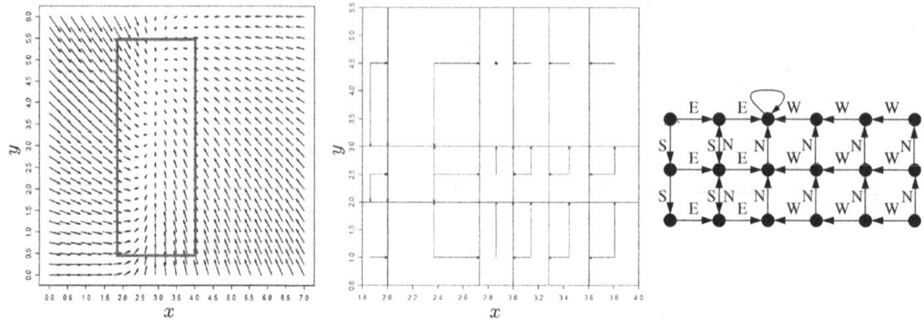

Fig. 1. A vector field (left) and a discretisation of the emphasised region (middle). Thresholds determining the rectangles were obtained by the algorithm in [17]. Arrows in the rectangles show the directions of transitions abstracting the systems dynamics in the particular rectangle. The states and transitions of the labelled transition system corresponding to the discretisation (right). The system is two-dimensional, therefore cardinal directions are employed to naturally label the transitions.

We do not suppose the above-mentioned rectangular structure on the state space in this section as the suggested approach is general; however, the intended meaning of transition labels in our framework is a *direction* in which the transition changes the state. We will consider a particular application in Sect. 5. Furthermore, we consider families of such systems indexed by a set of parameters. Let's start with the non-parameterised case.

Definition 1. *A* direction transition system *(DTS) is a tuple* (S, Dir, T, AP, L), *where:*

- S *is a set of states;*
- Dir *is a finite non-empty set of* directions*;*
- $T \subseteq S \times Dir \times S$ *is the transition relation satisfying the following conditions:*
  - T *is* total, *i.e. for each* s *there are* s' *and* d *such that* $(s, d, s') \in T$,
  - T *is* past-total, *i.e. for each* s *there are* s' *and* d *such that* $(s', d, s) \in T$,
  - *for each* $s \neq s'$ *there is at most one* d *such that* $(s, d, s') \in T$,
  - *for each* s *either there is no* d *such that* $(s, d, s) \in T$ *or for all* $d \in Dir$: $(s, d, s) \in T$;

  instead of $(s, d, s') \in T$ *we also write* $s \xrightarrow{d} s'$;
- AP *is a set of atomic propositions;*
- $L : S \to 2^{AP}$ *is a labelling function that associates a subset of* AP *to each state.*

Definition 2 (runs). *Let* (S, Dir, T, AP, L) *be a DTS and let* $s_0 \in S$ *be its state. A* future run *of* s *is an infinite sequence* $s_0, d_1, s_1, d_2, s_2, \ldots$, *where* $(s_i, d_{i+1}, s_{i+1}) \in T$ *for all* i. *A* past run *of* s *is an infinite sequence* $s_0, d_1, s_1, d_2, s_2, \ldots$, *where* $(s_{i+1}, d_{i+1}, s_i) \in T$ *for all* i. *For a (past or future) run* $\pi = s_0, d_1, s_1, d_2, s_2, \ldots$, *we further define the* ith *state of* π *as* $\pi(i) = s_i$ *and the* ith *action of* π *as* $\alpha(\pi, i) = d_i$. *We denote by* $fruns(s)$ *the set of all future runs of* s *and by* $pruns(s)$ *the set of all past runs of* s.

Note that due to the requirement of the DTS to be past-total and due to the lack of a single initial state, we assume that the past runs are neither finite nor initialised. This is in contrast to other works that deal with past temporal logics, such as [19]. Also note that the sets of future and past runs are always nonempty for each state and every outgoing or incoming path of each state may be always extended into a future or past run.

To formulate properties of runs over a DTS we use a hybrid extension [1] of the temporal logic UCTL [5]. UCTL is a UML-oriented branching-time temporal logic that is able to express state predicates over system states, event predicates over single-step system evolutions, and combine these with temporal and Boolean operators in the style of CTL. The hybrid extension allows the use of *state variables* that can be fixed in certain parts of the formula as well as quantified. We also include the possibility to express properties of past as well as future. We call the resulting logic hybrid UCTL with past (HUCTL$_P$ for short).

Note that there are two possible ways of defining the semantics of CTL and its extension. The models of the formulae can be either defined as (infinite) trees or as graphs (Kripke structures). Although in the case of standard CTL the two semantics coincide (every Kripke structure is equivalent to its unwinding, which is an infinite tree), this makes difference with respect to the past operators and the hybrid extension. In the past operator case, the semantics used here is known as the *branching past* semantics [19]. As for the hybrid extension, the state variables are going to be bound to the states of the Kripke structures, not the tree nodes in its unwinding.

Also note that instead of past temporal operators, we use an equivalent definition (w.r.t. the branching past) that uses past path quantifiers here.

Definition 3 (direction formulae). *Let Dir be a set of directions. Then the language of direction formulas on Dir is defined as follows:*

$$\chi ::= \mathit{true} \mid d \mid \neg\chi \mid \chi \wedge \chi$$

where d ranges over Dir.

Definition 4 (semantics of direction formulae). *The satisfaction relation $\models$ is defined for directions $\hat{d}$ as follows:*

$$\begin{aligned} &\hat{d} \models \mathit{true} && \\ &\hat{d} \models d && \iff \hat{d} = d \\ &\hat{d} \models \neg\chi && \iff \hat{d} \not\models \chi \\ &\hat{d} \models \chi_1 \wedge \chi_2 && \iff \hat{d} \models \chi_1 \text{ and } \hat{d} \models \chi_2 \end{aligned}$$

In the following, we sometimes use the notion of a χ-*transition* to denote a transition (s, d, s') such that $d \models \chi$. We then also call s' a χ-*successor* of s.

Definition 5 (HUCTL$_P$ formulae). *Let AP be a set of atomic propositions, let Dir be a set of directions, and let Var be a set of state variables. The language of CTL formulae is defined as follows:*

$$\varphi ::= true \mid p \mid \neg\varphi \mid \varphi \wedge \varphi \mid \boldsymbol{E}\psi \mid \mathbf{A}\psi \mid \hat{\mathbf{E}}\,\psi \mid \hat{\mathbf{A}}\,\psi \mid x \mid \downarrow x.\varphi \mid @x.\varphi \mid \exists x.\varphi$$
$$\psi ::= \mathbf{X}_\chi\varphi \mid \varphi\,{}_\chi\mathbf{U}\,\varphi \mid \varphi\,{}_\chi\mathbf{U}_\chi\,\varphi \mid \varphi\,{}_\chi\mathbf{W}\,\varphi \mid \varphi\,{}_\chi\mathbf{W}_\chi\,\varphi$$

where p ranges over AP, χ are direction formulae over Dir, and x ranges over Var. We call the formulae defined by φ above state formulae *and the formulae defined by ψ above* path formulae.

To define the semantics of HUCTL$_\text{P}$, we need to extend the model with a valuation of the state variables $h : Var \to S$. In the following, we shall use $h[x \mapsto s]$ to denote a valuation that maps the variable x to state s and is otherwise defined as the valuation h. Formally, $h[x \mapsto s](x) = s$, $h[x \mapsto s](y) = h(y)$ for all $y \neq x$.

Definition 6. *Let M be a DTS and $h : Var \to S$ be a valuation of state variables. The satisfaction relation for states and runs of M w.r.t. HUCTL$_P$ formulae is defined as follows:*

$$\begin{aligned}
&(M, h, s) \models true && \\
&(M, h, s) \models p && \iff p \in L(s)\\
&(M, h, s) \models \neg\varphi && \iff (M, h, s) \not\models \varphi\\
&(M, h, s) \models \varphi_1 \wedge \varphi_2 && \iff (M, h, s) \models \varphi_1 \textit{ and } (M, h, s) \models \varphi_2\\
&(M, h, s) \models \boldsymbol{E}\psi && \iff \exists \pi \in \textit{fruns}(s) : (M, h, \pi) \models \psi\\
&(M, h, s) \models \mathbf{A}\psi && \iff \forall \pi \in \textit{fruns}(s) : (M, h, \pi) \models \psi\\
&(M, h, s) \models \hat{\mathbf{E}}\,\psi && \iff \exists \pi \in \textit{pruns}(s) : (M, h, \pi) \models \psi\\
&(M, h, s) \models \hat{\mathbf{A}}\,\psi && \iff \forall \pi \in \textit{pruns}(s) : (M, h, \pi) \models \psi\\
&(M, h, s) \models x && \iff h(x) = s\\
&(M, h, s) \models \downarrow x.\varphi && \iff (M, h[x \mapsto s], s) \models \varphi\\
&(M, h, s) \models @x.\varphi && \iff (M, h, h(x)) \models \varphi\\
&(M, h, s) \models \exists x.\varphi && \iff \exists s' \in S : (M, h[x \mapsto s'], s) \models \varphi\\
&(M, h, \pi) \models \mathbf{X}_\chi\varphi && \iff \alpha(\pi, 1) \models \chi \textit{ and } \pi(1) \models \varphi\\
&(M, h, \pi) \models \varphi_1\,{}_\chi\mathbf{U}\,\varphi_2 && \iff \exists i : \pi(i) \models \varphi_2\\
& && \qquad \textit{and } \forall j < i : \pi(j) \models \varphi_1 \textit{ and } \alpha(\pi, j+1) \models \chi\\
&(M, h, \pi) \models \varphi_1\,{}_\chi\mathbf{U}_\xi\,\varphi_2 && \iff \exists i > 0 : \pi(i) \models \varphi_2, \alpha(\pi, i) \models \xi, \pi(i-1) \models \varphi_1,\\
& && \qquad \textit{and } \forall j < i-1 : \pi(j) \models \varphi_1 \textit{ and } \alpha(\pi, j+1) \models \chi\\
&(M, h, \pi) \models \varphi_1\,{}_\chi\mathbf{W}\,\varphi_2 && \iff (M, h, \pi) \models \varphi_1\,{}_\chi\mathbf{U}\,\varphi_2\\
& && \qquad \textit{or } \forall i : \alpha(\pi, i+1) \models \chi \textit{ and } \pi(i) \models \varphi_1\\
&(M, h, \pi) \models \varphi_1\,{}_\chi\mathbf{W}_\xi\,\varphi_2 && \iff (M, h, \pi) \models \varphi_1\,{}_\chi\mathbf{U}_\xi\,\varphi_2\\
& && \qquad \textit{or } \forall i : \alpha(\pi, i+1) \models \chi \textit{ and } \pi(i) \models \varphi_1
\end{aligned}$$

We are usually interested in formulae without free variables. In such a case, we write $(M, s) \models \varphi$ instead of $(M, h, s) \models \varphi$ as the choice of h is irrelevant.

We allow universal quantification over state variables by defining the formula $\forall x.\varphi$ to mean $\neg\exists x.\neg\varphi$. We also define several derived path operators as follows:

$$\varphi_1 \, \mathbf{U} \, \varphi_2 \equiv \varphi_1 \, {}_{true}\mathbf{U} \, \varphi_2 \qquad \varphi_1 \, \mathbf{W} \, \varphi_2 \equiv \varphi_1 \, {}_{true}\mathbf{W} \, \varphi_2$$

$$_\chi\mathbf{F} \, \varphi \equiv true \, {}_\chi\mathbf{U} \, \varphi \qquad {}_\chi\mathbf{G} \, \varphi \equiv \varphi \, {}_\chi\mathbf{W} \, \mathit{false}$$

$$\mathbf{F}\varphi \equiv {}_{true}\mathbf{F} \, \varphi \qquad \mathbf{G}\varphi \equiv {}_{true}\mathbf{G} \, \varphi$$

$$\widetilde{\mathbf{X}}_\chi \, \varphi \equiv \neg \mathbf{X}_\chi \neg\varphi \qquad {}_\chi\widetilde{\mathbf{F}} \, \varphi \equiv \neg \, {}_\chi\mathbf{G} \, \neg\varphi$$

The operators $\mathbf{U}$ (until), $\mathbf{W}$ (weak until), $\mathbf{F}$ (future/eventually), and $\mathbf{G}$ (globally/always) are the standard CTL operators. The operators ${}_\chi\mathbf{F}$ and ${}_\chi\mathbf{G}$ are UCTL extensions of $\mathbf{F}$ and $\mathbf{G}$; the intuitive meaning of ${}_\chi\mathbf{F} \, \varphi$ is "eventually a state satisfying φ is found after χ-transitions only" and the intuitive meaning of ${}_\chi\mathbf{G} \, \varphi$ is "the run only consists of χ-transitions and all its states satisfy φ".

Note that although in the standard CTL, the operators $\mathbf{F}$ and $\mathbf{G}$ are dual (one can be defined in terms of the other using negations), the UCTL extensions are not. Indeed, the intuitive semantics of $\neg \, {}_\chi\mathbf{G} \, \neg\varphi$ is "if the run only consists of χ-transitions, eventually a state satisfying φ is found". Similarly, $\mathbf{X}_\chi$ is not self-dual, as the meaning of $\neg\mathbf{X}_\chi\neg\varphi$ is "if the first transition is a χ-transition, the next state satisfies φ". For this reason, we have included the two operators $\widetilde{\mathbf{X}}_\chi$ and ${}_\chi\widetilde{\mathbf{F}}$ in our list of derived operators. The operators can be particularly useful in combination with the $\mathbf{A}$ quantifier, as the formula $\mathbf{A}\widetilde{\mathbf{X}}_\chi \, \varphi$ (equivalent to $\neg \, \mathbf{E}\mathbf{X}_\chi \, \neg\varphi$) means "all χ-successors of the current state satisfy φ" and the formula $\mathbf{A}_\chi\widetilde{\mathbf{F}} \, \varphi$ (equivalent to $\neg \, \mathbf{E}_\chi\mathbf{G} \, \neg\varphi$) means "on all future runs of the current state consisting of χ-transitions only, φ holds eventually".

Bifurcation analysis requires the systems to be parameterised. To this end we consider parameterised DTSs. This notion encapsulates a family of DTSs with the same state space but with different transitions. The existence of transitions is governed by parameter valuations.

Definition 7. *Let AP be a set of atomic propositions. A* parameterised direction transition system *(PDTS for short) is a tuple* $\mathcal{K} = (\mathcal{P}, S, \mathit{Dir}, \widehat{T}, AP, L)$, *where* $\mathcal{P}$ *is a finite set of parameter valuations,* $\widehat{T} = \{T_p \mid p \in \mathcal{P}, T_p \subseteq S \times \mathit{Dir} \times S\}$, *and for each* $p \in \mathcal{P}$ *the tuple* $\mathcal{K}_p = (S, \mathit{Dir}, T_p, AP, L)$ *is a DTS.*

Fixing a concrete parameter valuation $p \in \mathcal{P}$ thus reduces the parameterised direction transition system $\mathcal{K}$ to a DTS. We use the notation $\mathcal{P}(s,t,d) = \{p \in \mathcal{P} \mid s \xrightarrow{d}_p t\}$ to denote the set of all parameter valuations that enable the transition from s to t in direction d.

3 Parameter Synthesis Algorithm

The parameter synthesis problem is defined in the following way. Suppose we are given a parameterised direction transition system $\mathcal{K} = (\mathcal{P}, S, \mathit{Dir}, \widehat{T}, AP, L)$ and a HUCTLP formula φ without free state variables. The *parameter synthesis problem* for $\mathcal{K}$ and φ is to compute the function $\mathcal{F}^{\mathcal{K}}_{\varphi} : S \to 2^{\mathcal{P}}$ such that $\mathcal{F}^{\mathcal{K}}_{\varphi}(s) = \{p \in \mathcal{P} \mid (\mathcal{K}_p, s) \models \varphi\}$.

To solve the parameter synthesis problem, we extend the coloured model checking approach [9], originally devised for parameter synthesis with standard (state-based) CTL. The general idea of the algorithm is similar to that of standard CTL model checking [11], in which the states are iteratively labelled (using a bottom-up approach) by subformulae that are satisfied in them. Our algorithm here needs to deal with three orthogonal extensions to the algorithm: the use of directions (UCTL), the use of past quantifiers, and the hybrid extension (state variables). We start by describing the way we deal with the UCTL part.

The approach of [6,9] uses three algorithms to deal with formulae using the **EX**, **EU**, and **AU** operators. In the UCTL extension, we deal with the $\mathbf{EX}_\chi$, $\mathbf{AX}_\chi$, $\mathbf{E}_\chi\mathbf{U}$, $\mathbf{A}_\chi\mathbf{U}$, and $\mathbf{A}_\chi\widetilde{\mathbf{F}}$ operators. The ${}_\chi\mathbf{W}$ operators are dealt with using the following equivalences:

$$\mathbf{A}[\varphi_1 \,{}_\chi\mathbf{W}\, \varphi_2] \equiv \neg\mathbf{E}[\neg\varphi_2 \,\mathbf{U} (\neg\varphi_2 \wedge (\neg\varphi_1 \vee \mathbf{EX}_{\neg\chi}\, true))]$$

$$\mathbf{E}[\varphi_1 \,{}_\chi\mathbf{W}\, \varphi_2] \equiv \mathbf{E}[\varphi_1 \,{}_\chi\mathbf{U}\, \varphi_2] \vee \neg\, \mathbf{A}_\chi\widetilde{\mathbf{F}}\, \neg\varphi_1$$

We omit the ${}_\chi\mathbf{U}_\xi$ and ${}_\chi\mathbf{W}_\xi$ operators here. They can be dealt with similarly.

The $\mathbf{EX}_\chi\varphi$ formula holds in all states s and under all parameter valuations p such that there is a transition $s \xrightarrow{d}_p s'$ with $d \models \chi$ and $s' \models \varphi$. Similarly, the $\mathbf{AX}_\chi\varphi$ formula holds in states s under parameter valuations p such that all d, s' with $s \xrightarrow{d}_p s'$ satisfy $d \models \chi$ and $s' \models \varphi$.

To deal with $\mathbf{E}[\varphi_1 \,{}_\chi\mathbf{U}\, \varphi_2]$ we use the fact that this formula is the least fixpoint of the equation $Z = \varphi_2 \vee (\varphi_1 \wedge \mathbf{EX}_\chi Z)$. We thus mark each state satisfying φ_2 under given parameter valuation and then iteratively mark all states satisfying φ_1 and having an outgoing χ-transition to a marked state.

The formulae $\mathbf{A}[\varphi_1 \,{}_\chi\mathbf{U}\, \varphi_2]$ and $\mathbf{A}_\chi\widetilde{\mathbf{F}}\,\varphi$ are dealt with similarly, as they are the least fixpoints of the equations: $Z = \varphi_2 \vee (\varphi_1 \wedge \mathbf{AX}_\chi Z)$ and $Z = \varphi \vee \widetilde{\mathbf{AX}}_\chi\, Z$, respectively.

Extending the algorithms to past quantifiers is straightforward. As noted in [19], we can simply use the algorithms for future quantifiers with the transitions reversed.

We now describe the way we deal with the state variables and the various operators used in the hybrid extension. We say that a variable x is bound in a formula φ if each of its occurrences in φ is inside a subformula of the form $\exists x.\varphi'$ or $\downarrow x.\varphi'$; otherwise we say that x is free in φ. Dealing with subformulae with no free variables is not different from the above algorithm. However, when a subformula does contain free variables, we need to expand the state space. For a subformula with k free variables, the state space is going to be S^{k+1} where S is the original set of states. The extra information in the states represents the possible values of the variables. We write $(s, s_x, s_y, \ldots)$ for the elements of S^{k+1}, where s_x represents the value of $h(x)$ etc. The four kinds of subformulae we need to deal with are x, $@x.\varphi$, $\downarrow x.\varphi$, and $\exists x.\varphi$.

- Considering the formula x, we mark all states $(s, s_x, s_y, \ldots)$ such that $s = s_x$. Clearly, the formula is satisfied in exactly those states.
- Considering the formula $@x.\varphi$, every state $(s, s_x, s_y, \ldots)$ gets the same satisfaction information regardless of s: the satisfaction of the subformula φ in the state $(s_x, s_x, s_y, \ldots)$.
- Considering the satisfaction of the formula $\downarrow x.\varphi$ on the state $(s, s_y, \ldots)$ (note that there is no s_x here, as this formula does not have free x), we mark the state if $(s, s_x = s, s_y, \ldots)$ satisfies φ.
- Considering the formula $\exists x.\varphi$, we mark each state $(s, s_y, \ldots)$ if there exists at least one state s' such that $(s, s_x = s', s_y, \ldots)$ satisfies φ, otherwise we mark no states at all.

4 Discrete Bifurcation Analysis

In this section we apply the framework to *discrete bifurcation analysis* of parameterised discrete non-deterministic transition systems with directions. Our approach is based on a suitable discrete abstraction of the given, typically continuous, dynamical system that allows to employ the parameter synthesis algorithm for discovering critical parameter values, referred to as *bifurcation points*, for which various kinds of systems behaviour (equilibria, cycling) appear or disappear. A particular kind of such an abstraction will be mentioned in Sect. 5.

We suppose a DTS M. Runs of M have various properties. Here we are primarily interested in "geometric" shapes of runs, but other properties are not excluded. The simplest such property is a *self loop* (fixed point, equilibrium). A state $s \in M$ is called a *fixed point* if $s \xrightarrow{d} s$ for some $d \in D$. A system in a fixed point has the possibility of remaining there forever. Thus, fixed points represent the simplest mode of behaviour of the system. Another relatively simple type of run is a cycle. A *cycle* is a periodic run, namely a non-fixed-point run $s_0, d_1, s_1, d_2, s_2, \ldots, s_n$ where $s_i \xrightarrow{d_{i+1}} s_{i+1}$, $s_i \neq s_{i+1}$ for all $i : 0 \leq i < n$ and $s_0 = s_n$. The number n is called the *period* of the cycle. If a system starts its evolution at a point s on the cycle, it has the possibility to return exactly to this point after every n units of time. The system as such then exhibits *periodic oscillations.*

We can roughly classify all possible runs in discrete dynamical systems into fixed points, cycles, and "all others".

A *phase portrait* of a dynamical system is a partitioning of the state space according to properties of runs. The individual parts of the phase portrait are called *portrait elements* or *patterns.* The phase portrait contains a lot of information on the behaviour of a dynamical system. By looking at the phase portrait, we can for example determine the number and types of asymptotic states like fixed points or cycles. Of course, it is impossible to draw all runs in a figure. In practice, only several key runs are depicted in the diagrams to present phase portraits schematically.

It is important to note that we consider *discrete-time* systems here. In continuous-time dynamical systems a phase portrait captures both the position and

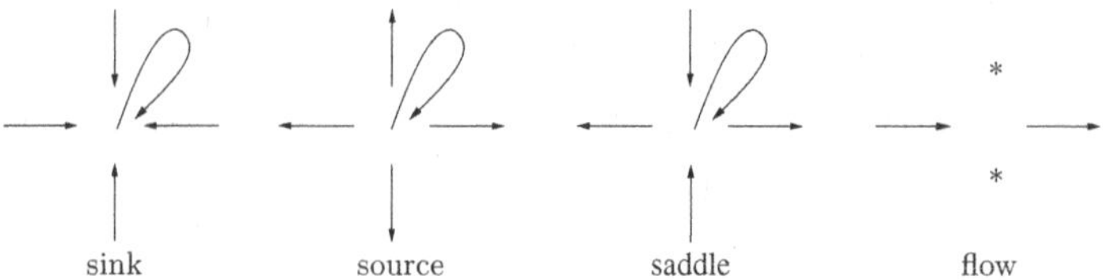

Fig. 2. Some single-state portrait patterns. The asterisk symbol denotes either situation: incoming only, outgoing only, both or none. Note that saddle and flow can be rotated along a particular axis, which gives additional examples. We can also consider "partial" patterns like a sink without any edges in some direction(s).

the momentum of a continuous-time system described by a system of ordinary differential equations. These momentum variables set up the "field" that gives structure to the phase portrait. In a discrete-time system, we generally do not have the same kind of momentum. In our approach we therefore simplify the velocity vectors that are put together to make a phase portrait of the continuous-time system by "vectors" all having the same size. The interpretation of the bifurcation analysis is thus relative to the way the original system has been abstracted into a DTS in case the original system is not given directly as a DTS.

In the following we therefore consider *discrete phase portraits* only. To further classify elements of a phase portrait, in particular, other possible asymptotic states of the system covered by "all other" above, the following definition is useful. An *invariant set* of a dynamical system is a nontrivial strongly connected component (SCC). A system placed in an arbitrary state of an invariant set either cannot escape from the set (strong invariancy, the SCC is final) or may stay in the set forever (weak invariancy). A fixed point is thus a special case of an invariant set.

Studying phase portraits, unlike individual runs, gives a more global view on the system's behaviour. As we have already seen above, the elements of phase portraits can have many shapes (patterns). Some other typical patterns that can appear in a 2-dimensional case (like the one shown at the beginning of Sect. 2) are the single-state patterns in Fig. 2.

The patterns are characterised by properties of runs and the properties of runs can be formalised as formulae of $\mathrm{HUCTL_P}$. We will distinguish several types of formulae. The first group are formulae that define single-state patterns. Here are some examples.

Single-state patterns

- sink (stable steady state): $\downarrow s.\mathbf{AX}s$
- self-loop existence (unstable steady state): $\downarrow s.\mathbf{EX}s$
- source (only self-loops, no other incoming): $\downarrow s.\,\hat{\mathbf{A}}\mathbf{X}\,s$
- 2d-saddle: $\mathbf{AX}_{N\vee S}\mathit{true} \wedge \mathbf{EX}_N\mathit{true} \wedge \mathbf{EX}_S\mathit{true} \wedge \hat{\mathbf{A}}\mathbf{X}_{E\vee W}\ \mathit{true} \wedge \hat{\mathbf{E}}\mathbf{X}_E\ \mathit{true} \wedge \hat{\mathbf{E}}\mathbf{X}_W\ \mathit{true}$ (north-south outgoing, west-east incoming)
- membership in a cycle: $\downarrow s.\mathbf{EX}\,\mathbf{EF}\,s$

Another kind of general multi-state patterns are invariant sets like periodic runs or limit cycles. Here are some examples.

Invariant sets (multi-state patterns)

- state in a nontrivial SCC: $\downarrow s.\mathbf{EX}\,\mathbf{EF}\,s$
- state in a final SCC (generalised sink): $\downarrow s.\,\mathbf{AG}\,\mathbf{EF}\,s$
- state in an initial SCC (generalised source): $\downarrow s.\,\hat{\mathbf{A}}\mathbf{G}\,\hat{\mathbf{E}}\mathbf{F}\,s$
- non-north flow in the whole system: $\forall s.\,@s.\mathbf{AX}_{\neg N}\,\mathit{true}$

Using HUCTL$_P$ formulae we can also describe relations among elements (patterns) of phase portraits. Here are some examples.

Relations among patterns

- at least two sinks in the whole system: $\exists s.\exists t.(@s.\neg t \wedge \mathbf{AX}s) \wedge (@t.\mathbf{AX}t)$
- at least two final SCCs in the whole system: $\exists s.\exists t.(@s.\,\mathbf{AG}\,\neg t \wedge \mathbf{AG}\,\mathbf{EF}\,s) \wedge (@t.\,\mathbf{AG}\,\mathbf{EF}\,t)$ (similarly for initial SCCs)
- formula that is true in states that have two outgoing paths to two different sinks: $\exists s.\exists t.(@s.\neg t \wedge \mathbf{AX}s) \wedge (@t.\mathbf{AX}t) \wedge \mathbf{EF}\,s \wedge \mathbf{EF}\,t$ (intersection of basins of attraction of two different sinks)
- formula that is true in states that satisfy φ_1 and can reach a state satisfying φ_2 without ever going north: $\varphi_1 \wedge \exists s.(@s.\varphi_2) \wedge \mathbf{E}_{\neg N}\mathbf{F}\,s$

We now turn our attention to the *bifurcation analysis* workflow. In bifurcation analysis we are interested in the question of how the phase portrait changes when parameters change. We therefore suppose a *parameterised* n-dimensional DTS. The parameters are taken from a finite set $\mathcal{P}$. For the purpose of the discrete bifurcation analysis we assume $\mathcal{P}$ to be a partially ordered set. For two points $x, y \in \mathcal{P}$ we say that y covers x, if $x < y$ and there is no $z \in \mathcal{P}$ with $x < z < y$. For a subset $X \subseteq \mathcal{P}$ we define its *boundary points* to be all the points $x \in X$ with the property that either x covers or is covered by a point not in X.

Bifurcation analysis allows to characterise *qualitative (structural)* changes in phase portraits only. To capture such changes in our approach, we will identify a phase portrait with a *finite set* of HUCTL$_P$ formulae – the so-called *phase portrait specification.* The set defines in an obvious way a division of the state space into elements according to the validity of individual formulae (the structure of the phase portrait) as exemplified in Fig. 3. Practically, the phase portrait specification is supposed to describe various patterns appearing in the phase portrait and their mutual relationship. As an example consider two formulae, one expressing the reachability of a sink state ($\varphi_1 \stackrel{\text{df}}{=} \mathbf{EF}(\downarrow s.\mathbf{AX}s)$) and the other one expressing the backward reachability of a source state ($\varphi_2 \stackrel{\text{df}}{=} \hat{\mathbf{E}}\mathbf{F}(\downarrow s.\,\hat{\mathbf{A}}\mathbf{X}\,s)$). The state space is in general divided into four parts. The situation is shown in Fig. 3 (left).

Any change in parameters may change the transition relation and thus may result in a change of truth value of any particular formula in the portrait specification. If a change in parameters results in non-satisfiability of one of the

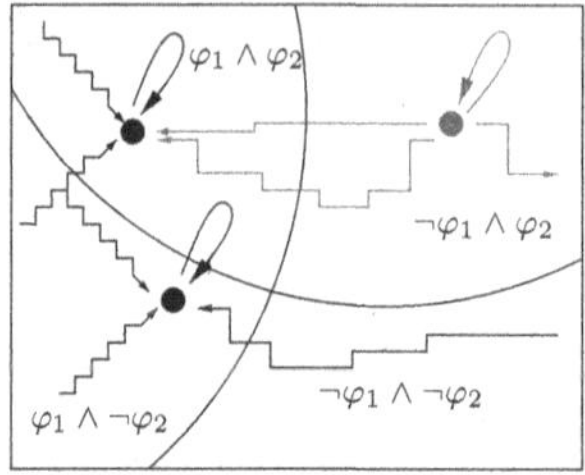

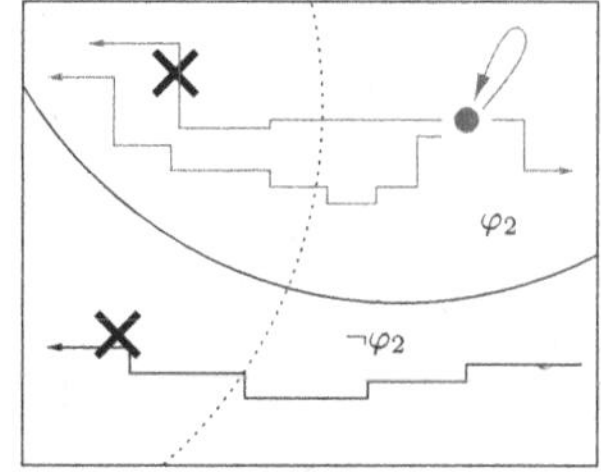

Fig. 3. An example of a characterisation of a phase portrait by formulae.

formulae (or its negation) in the specification, we consider this as a *structural change* in the phase portrait – a *bifurcation*. For the example above, if the parameter changes in such a way that the formula φ_1 does not hold in any state, the four part "structure" collapses into two parts, as shown in Fig. 3 (right). The set of all parameters for which the structure of the phase portrait does not change is called a *stratum*. A boundary point of a stratum is called a *bifurcation point*. Taking all strata in the parameter space with respect to a given phase portrait specification, we obtain the *parametric portrait* of the system. The parametric portrait together with its characteristic phase portraits constitute a *bifurcation diagram*. The set of phase portraits that are characteristic for a given parametric portrait is called *phase portrait pattern*.

Let $\mathbb{I}(m)$ denote the set of indices $\{1, ..., m\}$. Formally, we define the *phase portrait specification* $\Phi = \{\varphi_1, ..., \varphi_m\}$ as a finite set of HUCTL$_\text{P}$ formulae. The *phase portrait pattern* is then defined as the set of formulae $ptr(\Phi)$ generated from Φ in the following way:

$$ptr(\Phi) = \{\Phi_J \mid \Phi_J = \bigwedge_{j \in J} \varphi_j \wedge \bigwedge_{j \in \mathbb{I}(m) \setminus J} \neg\varphi_j, J \subseteq \mathbb{I}(m)\}.$$

An example of a phase portrait pattern can be seen in Fig. 3 (left).

Let $\mathcal{K} = (\mathcal{P}, S, Dir, \widehat{T}, AP, L)$ be a PDTS. For every $\Phi_J \in ptr(\Phi)$, the set of valid parameter values satisfying Φ_J, denoted by $\mathcal{P}(\Phi_J)$, is defined as $\mathcal{P}(\Phi_J) = \bigcup_{s \in S} \mathcal{F}_\varphi^\mathcal{K}(s)$. We understand a stratum to be characterised by a particular subset of formulae in the phase portrait pattern. More specifically, we define *stratum* as a set of parameter values satisfying all formulae in $X \subseteq ptr(\Phi)$ where X is some non-empty subset of formulae in the phase portrait pattern. Formally, the set of all *strata* of the PDTS $\mathcal{K}$ *with respect to the portrait specification* Φ, denoted as $\Gamma_\Phi^\mathcal{K}$, is defined as follows:

$$\Gamma_\Phi^\mathcal{K} = \{\gamma_I \mid \gamma_I = \bigcap_{J \in I} \mathcal{P}(\Phi_J), I \subseteq 2^{\mathbb{I}(m)}, I \neq \emptyset, \gamma_I \neq \emptyset\}.$$

The *set of bifurcation points* is defined as $\bigcup_{\gamma \in \Gamma_\Phi^\mathcal{K}} bdp(\gamma)$ where $bdp(\gamma)$ denotes the set of all boundary points of γ.

The goal of the discrete bifurcation analysis is to compute the parametric portrait for a given PDTS $\mathcal{K}$ and a given portrait specification Φ. The procedure is the following. The set $\Gamma_{\Phi}^{\mathcal{K}}$ is computed by post-processing of the results obtained from applying the parameter synthesis algorithm presented in Sect. 3 to $\mathcal{K}$ and every formula in $ptr(\Phi)$.

Note that bifurcation analysis is typically done in several stages. At the beginning we often do not have enough information about the structure of the phase portrait. As the knowledge deepens we can add more or refine existing formulae defining the current state of the phase portrait.

5 Application to Biological Case

To demonstrate our workflow, we conduct a bifurcation analysis of a dynamical system modelling dynamics of a two-gene regulatory network presented in [23]. The model describes interaction of the tumour suppressor protein pRB and the central transcription factor $E2F1$ (see Fig. 4 (left)). This system represents an important mechanism of a *biological switch* governing the transition from G_1 to S phase in the mammalian cell cycle. In the G_1-phase the cell makes an important decision. In high concentration levels, $E2F1$ activates the phase transition. In low concentration of $E2F1$, transition to S-phase is rejected provided that the cell avoids division. We consider the model to be parameterised by the parameter α_{pRB}. The parameter space $\mathcal{P}$ is determined as an interval $\alpha_{pRB} \in [0.001, 0.5]$ representing the biologically-admissible range.

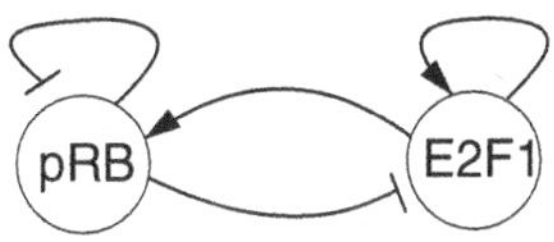

$$\frac{d[pRB]}{dt} = k_1 \frac{[E2F1]}{K_{m1}+[E2F1]} \frac{J_{11}}{J_{11}+[pRB]} - \alpha_{pRB}[pRB]$$

$$\frac{d[E2F1]}{dt} = k_p + k_2 \frac{a^2+[E2F1]^2}{K_{m2}^2+[E2F1]^2} \frac{J_{12}}{J_{12}+[pRB]} - \alpha_{E2F1}[E2F1]$$

$a = 0.04$, $k_1 = 1$, $k_2 = 1.6$, $k_p = 0.05$, $\alpha_{E2F1} = 0.1$
$J_{11} = 0.5$, $J_{12} = 5$, $K_{m1} = 0.5$, $K_{m2} = 4$

Fig. 4. G_1/S transition regulatory network and the respective dynamical system taken from [23]. Value of the parameter α_{pRB} is considered in the range $[0.001, 0.5]$.

In order to prepare the model for our discrete bifurcation analysis, we first construct the piecewise multi-affine approximation (PMA) of the original non-linear continuous model that is then further translated into a finite state Kripke structure. To this end, we subsequently apply the approximation and abstraction procedures introduced in [4,17]. In particular, we approximate each non-linear function appearing in the right-hand side of the model equations with a sum of piecewise affine ramp functions making an optimal sequence well-fitting the original function. As a result, we obtain a finite PDTS that exactly over-approximates the PMA. Details on abstracting this particular model into a parameterised Kripke structure can be found in [3].

The main principle of the abstraction is shown in Fig. 1. The labelling of the transitions is obtained naturally by using cardinal directions. To turn our model into a PDTS, we consider transition increasing/decreasing the variable $E2F1$ as north/south and for pRB we consider west/east directions.

An important property of the employed abstraction is the fact that it partitions the system phase space into finitely many rectangles. The parameter space is also adequately partitioned into finitely many regions. Every region represents a class of (continuous) parameter values that give qualitatively equivalent vector field in the boundaries (facets) of all rectangles. In consequence, all parameters in the class have an isomorphic DTS.

We conduct the bifurcation analysis with respect to the parameter α_{pRB}. The biological switch is known to be bistable, i.e. two different stable states can exist in the systems dynamics. In this particular case, bistability is known to be sensitive to change in α_{pRB}. To this end, we formulate the portrait specification including the following formulae:

- $\varphi_1 := \exists s.\exists t.(@s.\,\mathbf{AG}\,\mathbf{EF}\,s) \wedge (@t.\neg\,\mathbf{EF}\,s \wedge \mathbf{AG}\,\mathbf{EF}\,t) \wedge \mathbf{E}_{\neg N}\mathbf{F}\,s \wedge \mathbf{E}_{\neg S}\mathbf{F}\,t$
  There are at least two final SCCs (generalised stable states). The formula is true in all states that have a non-north path (i.e. path using only south, east, and west directions) to one of the final SCCs and a non-south path to the other final SCC.
- $\varphi_2 := \neg\varphi_1 \wedge \downarrow s.\,\mathbf{AG}\,\mathbf{EF}\,s \wedge E2F1 < 4$
  There is exactly one final SCC and it is **below** $E2F1$ *value* 4. *It is true in states that are included in the final SCC.*
- $\varphi_3 := \neg\varphi_1 \wedge \downarrow s.\,\mathbf{AG}\,\mathbf{EF}\,s \wedge E2F1 > 4$
  There is exactly one final SCC and it is **above** $E2F1$ *value* 4.

Due to relations among the three formulae and the previous knowledge about the systems dynamics, we do not compute the entire parametric portrait. We rather focus directly on mutual bifurcations between the portraits characterised by the individual formulae. The results obtained with our prototype implementation are the following: φ_1 holds for $\alpha_{pRB} \in [0.011, 0.0136]$, φ_2 for $\alpha_{pRB} \in [0.002, 0, 011]$ and φ_3 for $\alpha_{pRB} \in [0.0136, 0.5]$. In consequence, values 0.011 and 0.0136 represent bifurcation points. For $\alpha_{pRB} = 0.011$ the portrait changes between φ_2 and φ_1 and for $\alpha_{pRB} = 0.0136$ it changes between φ_1 and φ_3. In Fig. 5, there are depicted vector fields and corresponding abstractions for three sampled values of α_{pRB} each one belonging to one of the computed intervals. The states satisfying particular formulae are shown in emphasised rectangles.

Additionally, we have explored a variant of formula φ_1 where we also claim that the states satisfying the formula are not sources (and thus are actually saddle states): $\varphi_1' := \varphi_1 \wedge \neg(\downarrow s.\,\hat{\mathbf{A}}\mathbf{X}\,s)$. We have obtained the results showing that this formula also holds for $\alpha_{pRB} \in [0.011, 0.0136]$.

Note that the obtained results are affected by precision of the approximation and abstraction of the original continuous model. The computed intervals of α_{pRB} are compliant with the numerical bifurcation analysis presented in [23].

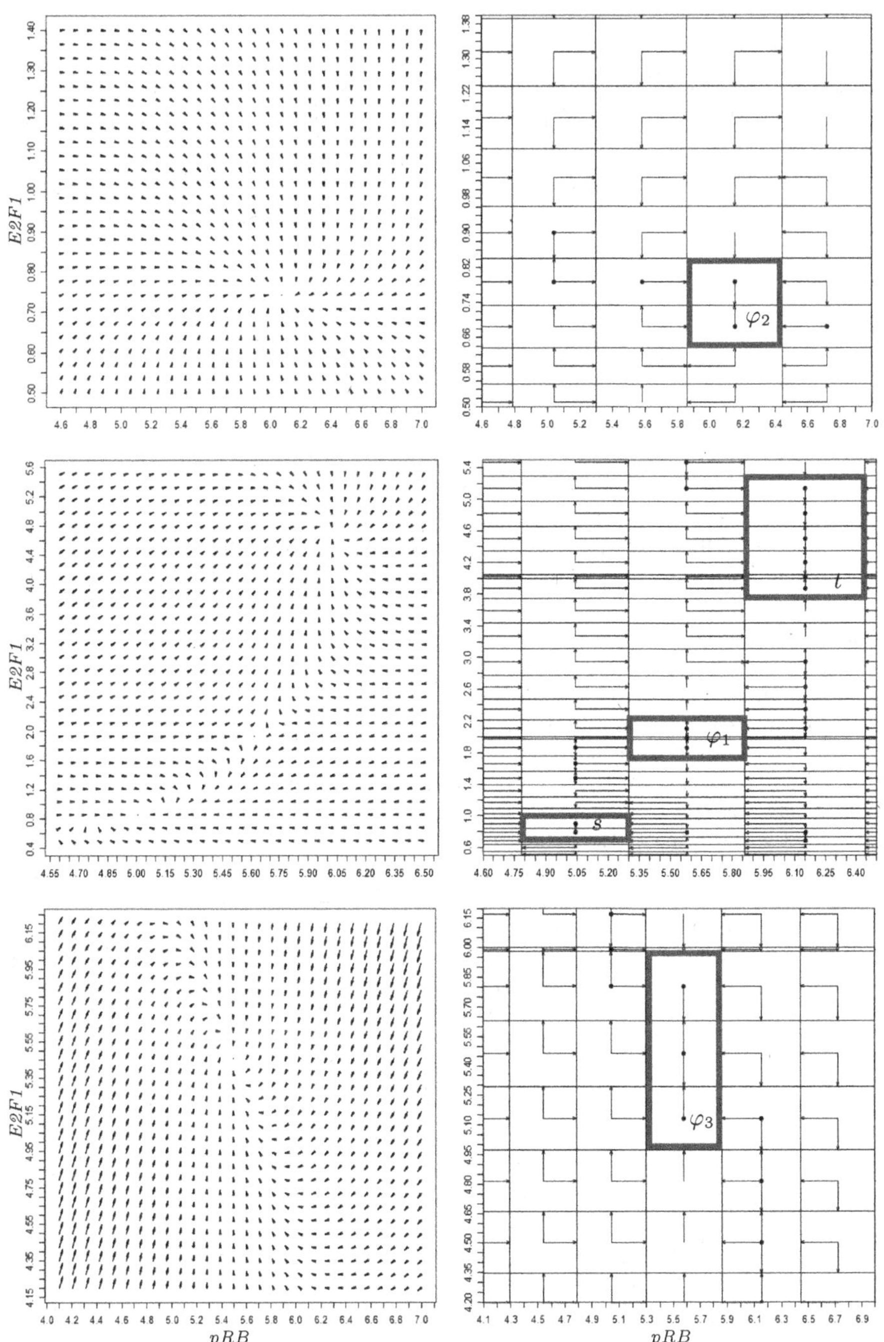

Fig. 5. Vector fields (left) and corresponding abstractions (right) obtained for three different values of α_{pRB}: 0.0075 (top), 0.0115 (middle) and 0.014 (bottom). The states satisfying the respective formula are emphasised in bold rectangles. The rectangles marked s and t denote the states matching the corresponding variables in φ_1.

6 Conclusion

Bifurcation analysis allows to classify in a very condensed way all possible modes of behaviour of the system and transitions between them (bifurcations) under parameter variations. In this paper we have proposed an alternative approach to classical numerical methods as used in bifurcation analysis with the aim to achieve a scalable efficiency. Our preliminary experiments show promising results as demonstrated on the case study. The answers obtained by our method comply with those given by numerical analysis.

In the future we would like to look in more detail on some specific bifurcations and also apply the method to other kind of parameter-dependent systems like Boolean networks.

References

1. Areces, C., ten Cate, B.: Hybrid logics. In: Blackburn, P., van Benthem, J., Wolter, F. (eds.) Handbook of Modal Logic. Elsevier, Amsterdam (2007)
2. Arellano, G., Argil, J., Azpeitia, E., Benítez, M., Carrillo, M., Góngora, P., Rosenblueth, D.A., Alvarez-Buylla, E.R.: "Antelope": a hybrid-logic model checker for branching-time Boolean GRN analysis. BMC Bioinform. **12**(1), 1–15 (2011). http://dx.doi.org/10.1186/1471-2105-12-490
3. Barnat, J., Brim, L., Krejci, A., Streck, A., Safranek, D., Vejnar, M., Vejpustek, T.: On parameter synthesis by parallel model checking. IEEE/ACM Trans. Computat. Biol. Bioinform. **9**(3), 693–705 (2012)
4. Batt, G., Belta, C., Weiss, R.: Model checking liveness properties of genetic regulatory networks. In: Grumberg, O., Huth, M. (eds.) TACAS 2007. LNCS, vol. 4424, pp. 323–338. Springer, Heidelberg (2007). doi:10.1007/978-3-540-71209-1_25
5. ter Beek, M.H., Fantechi, A., Gnesi, S., Mazzanti, F.: A state/event-based model-checking approach for the analysis of abstract system properties. Sci. Comput. Program. **76**, 119–135 (2011)
6. Beneš, N., Brim, L., Demko, M., Pastva, S., Šafránek, D.: Parallel SMT-based parameter synthesis with application to piecewise multi-affine systems. In: Artho, C., Legay, A., Peled, D. (eds.) ATVA 2016. LNCS, vol. 9938, pp. 192–208. Springer, Heidelberg (2016). doi:10.1007/978-3-319-46520-3_13
7. Beyn, W.J.: The numerical computation of connecting orbits in dynamical systems. IMA J. Num. Anal. **10**(3), 379–405 (1990)
8. Brim, L., Demko, M., Pastva, S., Šafránek, D.: High-performance discrete bifurcation analysis for piecewise-affine dynamical systems. In: Abate, A., Šafránek, D. (eds.) HSB 2015. LNCS, vol. 9271, pp. 58–74. Springer, Heidelberg (2015). doi:10.1007/978-3-319-26916-0_4
9. Brim, L., Češka, M., Demko, M., Pastva, S., Šafránek, D.: Parameter synthesis by parallel coloured CTL model checking. In: Roux, O., Bourdon, J. (eds.) CMSB 2015. LNCS, vol. 9308, pp. 251–263. Springer, Heidelberg (2015). doi:10.1007/978-3-319-23401-4_21
10. Chaki, S., Clarke, E., Ouaknine, J., Sharygina, N., Sinha, N.: Concurrent software verification with states, events, and deadlocks. Formal Aspects Comput. **17**(4), 461–483 (2005). http://dx.doi.org/10.1007/s00165-005-0071-z

11. Clarke, E.M., Grumberg, O., Peled, D.A.: Model Checking. MIT Press, Cambridge (2001). http://books.google.de/books?id=Nmc4wEaLXFEC
12. Collins, P., Habets, L.C., van Schuppen, J.H., Černá, I., Fabriková, J., Šafránek, D.: Abstraction of biochemical reaction systems on polytopes. In: IFAC World Congress, pp. 14869–14875. IFAC (2011)
13. De Nicola, R., Vaandrager, F.: Three logics for branching bisimulation. J. ACM **42**(2), 458–487 (1995). http://doi.acm.org/10.1145/201019.201032
14. Detroux, T., Renson, L., Masset, L., Kerschen, G.: The harmonic balance method for bifurcation analysis of large-scale nonlinear mechanical systems. Comput. Methods Appl. Mech. Eng. **296**, 18–38 (2015)
15. Gallet, E., Manceny, M., Le Gall, P., Ballarini, P.: Adapting LTL model checking for inferring biological parameters. In: Proceedings of the Approches Formelles dans l'Assistance au Développement de Logiciels (AFADL), pp. 46–60 (2014)
16. Govaerts, W.: Numerical bifurcation analysis for ODEs. J. Comput. Appl. Math. **125**(12), 57–68 (2000). (numerical Analysis 2000. Vol. VI: Ordinary Differential Equations and Integral Equations)
17. Grosu, R., Batt, G., Fenton, F.H., Glimm, J., Guernic, C., Smolka, S.A., Bartocci, E.: From cardiac cells to genetic regulatory networks. In: Gopalakrishnan, G., Qadeer, S. (eds.) CAV 2011. LNCS, vol. 6806, pp. 396–411. Springer, Heidelberg (2011). doi:10.1007/978-3-642-22110-1_31
18. Khalis, Z., Comet, J.P., Richard, A., Bernot, G.: The SMBioNet method for discovering models of gene regulatory networks. Genes Genomes Genomics **3**(1), 15–22 (2009)
19. Kupferman, O., Pnueli, A., Vardi, M.Y.: Once and for all. J. Comput. Syst. Sci. **78**(3), 981–996 (2012). http://dx.doi.org/10.1016/j.jcss.2011.08.006
20. Mateescu, R., Monteiro, P.T., Dumas, E., Jong, H.: Computation tree regular logic for genetic regulatory networks. In: Cha, S.S., Choi, J.-Y., Kim, M., Lee, I., Viswanathan, M. (eds.) ATVA 2008. LNCS, vol. 5311, pp. 48–63. Springer, Heidelberg (2008). doi:10.1007/978-3-540-88387-6_6
21. Müller-Olm, M., Schmidt, D., Steffen, B.: Model-checking: a tutorial introduction. In: Cortesi, A., Filé, G. (eds.) SAS 1999. LNCS, vol. 1694, pp. 330–354. Springer, Heidelberg (1999). doi:10.1007/3-540-48294-6_22
22. Rizk, A., Batt, G., Fages, F., Soliman, S.: A general computational method for robustness analysis with applications to synthetic gene networks. Bioinformatics **25**(12), i169–i17 (2009)
23. Swat, M., Kel, A., Herzel, H.: Bifurcation analysis of the regulatory modules of the mammalian G1/S transition. Bioinformatics **20**(10), 1506–1511 (2004)

State-Space Reduction of Non-deterministically Synchronizing Systems Applicable to Deadlock Detection in MPI

Stanislav Böhm[1(✉)], Ondřej Meca[1,2], and Petr Jančar[2]

[1] IT4Innovations, VŠB Technical University of Ostrava, Ostrava, Czech Republic
stanislav.bohm@vsb.cz

[2] Department of Computer Science, FEECS VŠB Technical University of Ostrava, Ostrava, Czech Republic

Abstract. The paper is motivated by non-deterministic synchronizations in MPI (Message Passing Interface), where some send operations and collective operations may or may not synchronize; a correctly written MPI program should count with both options. Here we focus on the deadlock detection in such systems and propose the following reduction of the explored state space. The system is first analyzed without forcing the respective synchronizations, by applying standard partial-order reduction methods. Then a suggested algorithm is used that searches for potentially missed deadlocks caused by synchronization. In practical examples this approach leads to major reductions of the explored state-space in comparison to encoding the synchronization options into the state-space search directly. The algorithm is presented as a stand-alone abstract framework that can be also applied to the future versions of MPI as well as to other related problem domains.

Keywords: Verification · State-space reduction · Partial-order methods · MPI · Deadlock

1 Introduction

MPI (Message Passing Interface) [1] is standardized message-passing system for distributed memory computation in the area of High Performance Computing. A usual MPI application is a computational non-interactive program that runs with a fixed number of processes, on a given input.

We are motivated by verification (searching of bugs independently on their probability of occurrence) of MPI programs. In our context we use dynamic state-space analysis for fixed input and cover all non-deterministic behaviors of an analysed program. In this paper we are focusing on one specific property of MPI: *nondeterministic synchronization* (ndsync). MPI standard defines that some send and collective operations may or may not synchronize; a correctly written MPI program should count with both options.

J. Fitzgerald et al. (Eds.): FM 2016, LNCS 9995, pp. 102–118, 2016.
DOI: 10.1007/978-3-319-48989-6_7

MPI offers several variants of send operations with different conditions when they are completed. A *synchronous* send is completed after matching with a receiving operation in a different process. A *buffered* send is completed when the message is copied into a local buffer and with no necessity of a matching operation. In the case of *standard* send, the implementation may nondeterministically decide between "rendezvous" and "eager" mode, i.e. if it waits for a matching request (as a synchronous send) or is completed independently on the remote site (as a buffered send). This decision made by MPI implementation cannot be tested by the user code. The reason for such a nondeterministic behavior is to give a sufficient freedom for an MPI implementation to achieve the best performance. Nevertheless, it transfers more responsibility to the programmer, since it is easy to create an invalid program while the error is manifested in the dependence on a particular behavior of the used MPI implementation.

A classic example is shown in Fig. 1(left) containing two standard sends. If both sends synchronize (rendezvous mode) then the deadlock occurs. The example in Fig. 1(right) disproves a simple idea that for observing all deadlocks it is sufficient to consider only rendezvous mode of standard sends. When all standard sends choose the rendezvous mode or all choose the eager mode, then no deadlock occurs. However, when the first send in process 1 chooses the eager mode and the rest of them the rendezvous mode, then the deadlock may occur.

Process 0	Process 1
`Send(to=1)`	`Send(to=0)`
`Recv(from=1)`	`Recv(from=0)`

Process 0	Process 1	Process 2
`Send(to=2)`	`Send(to=0)`	`Recv(from=*)`
`Recv(from=1)`	`Send(to=2)`	`Send(to=0)`
`Recv(from=2)`		`Recv(from=*)`

Fig. 1. (left) Simple deadlock situation of standard sends. (right) Deadlock may occur only when all sends synchronize except the first one in the process 1.

A similar problem as with sends is related to collective operations – operations where more processes are involved (e.g. broadcast, reduce, scatter). All processes in a particular communicator (a group of processes) have to call the operation to finish it correctly; however, a collective operation (except `MPI_Barrier`) may or may not have a synchronization effect. In other words, a collective call in a process may choose to wait until all other processes also enter the operation. As in the previous case, it is not sufficient to examine only the most synchronizing variant. The example is shown in Fig. 2, where a deadlock may occur only when the second broadcast behaves as a barrier and the first one has a minimal synchronization effect (in the case of the broadcast, the only dependency is that all non-root processes have to wait for the root process that sends the data).

As already said, we are motivated by a dynamic verification of an application by a systematical exploration of the application state-space. A naive exploration is usually infeasible due to the state explosion. Various techniques

Process 0	Process 1	Process 2
`Bsend(to=1)`	`Recv(to=*)`	`Bcast(root=2)`
`Bcast(root=2)`	`Bcast(root=2)`	`Bsend(to=1)`
`Bcast(root=2)`	`Recv(from=2)`	`Bcast(root=2)`
	`Bcast(root=2)`	`Bsend(to=1)`
	`Recv(from=*)`	

Fig. 2. Deadlock occurs when the second broadcast operation synchronizes, the first one not, and the first receive in Process 1 matches with the first send operation from Process 2. (`Bsend` is "buffered send", i.e. non-synchronizing send)

have been introduced to deal with this problem. Binary decision diagrams [2] or unfolding [6] represent the compression approach where symbolic representations for sets of states are used. The techniques based on partial-order reduction (POR) [9,16,22] construct the state space directly; however, the full state space is pruned in a way that preserves all "interesting" properties.

In this paper, we propose a new reduction method for a state space analysis of systems (that are possibly reduced by POR), in the presence of the described ndsync, i.e. the situation where some operation may decide to synchronize, but the application cannot directly test this decision. We have the MPI environment in mind, but we handle the problem on an abstract level as a formal framework. This allows us to present the basic ideas without dealing with semantics of a particular MPI operations. This also gives a flexibility to apply the ideas to the future version of MPI standard, or to different systems with similar properties.

A straightforward approach to deal with the described problem is to explicitly encode both rendezvous and eager mode into the state-space and prune it by POR. However, decisions between rendezvous/eager mode is irreducible by standard POR methods, since this decision creates two dependent actions.

The basic idea of the reduction is based on the following observation. Since the application cannot directly test if a ndsync operation synchronizes, such decision cannot introduce "new" behaviors, it may only restrict some of them. This leads us to considering the state space only for the *eager system* – the system where we assume that ndsync operations have no synchronization effect; i.e. the ndsync choices are removed from the system. This system preserves all local process states. Hence, it suffices to construct such a system to detect errors like invalid memory access or invalid arguments to MPI calls. However, the eager system does not preserve deadlocks of the original system. To fix this, we present an algorithm detecting deadlocks in the original system by taking the eager system as the input while we allow that the provided system is already reduced by a POR method. The correctness of the algorithm is the core of this paper.

Idea Summarization. We propose the two step analysis for systems containing ndsync: First, a system is explored considering only eager behavior (i.e. there are not ndsync decisions). We allow that this phase may use an arbitrary POR method as far as it satisfies some standard properties. On this system a full analysis of local state may be executed.

The second phase is a new post-processing algorithm on the output from the first phase that detects deadlocks introduced by ndsync that may be missed in the first phase.

This approach is more efficient than explicitly considering ndsync decisions during analysis, because a system containing only eager behavior is usually significantly smaller than system containing ndsync decisions. This property is also demonstrated in Sect. 5 on MPI benchmarks.

Remark: We present the second phase as a post-processing in the whole paper for the sake of simplicity of the ideas exposition; however, there is no obstacle to apply it as an on-the-fly method.

Contribution. This paper introduces abstract framework for reducing system with ndsync. When the ideas were implemented into a tool for MPI verification, we obtain $3\times - 15\times$ faster verification process on our testing programs based on real applications.

Related Work. In the MPI world, there exist many tools for checking correctness of the MPI applications. MUST [10], IMC [5], and MPI-CHECK [13] can be named as tools focus on runtime detection of errors in MPI programs. These tools do not guarantee revealing of all deadlocks.

MPI-Spin [19] and Kaira [14] are tools providing verification of MPI application through models. Hence, they are not able to verify generic MPI applications. The paper [12] shows verification of MPI protocols. In [15], a variant of POR was proposed to determine which sends and receives can match in MPI programs, that is useful for a state-less analysis. TASS [20] and MPISE [8] offer symbolic verification, but support only synchronizing MPI operations. Tools ISP [21] and DAMPI [23] provide dynamic state-less analysis for MPI programs.

In the context of this paper, we look closer to deadlock detection approaches. The And-Or graph approach was proposed in [11] for detecting MPI deadlock at runtime. This was later extended by [10] to support more MPI functions. The overall idea is to build a graph describing waiting dependencies between processes and the existence of a knot in the graph indicates a deadlock situation. Since the approach was designed for the runtime approach, it is not evident if we can apply the method in state space analysis on a reduced system and preserve completeness w.r.t. all deadlocks.

In [18] Siegel proposes modelling of MPI applications as state machines and argues that it suffices to explore the state space while considering all ndsync operation as synchronized operations for wild-card free programs (programs that exclude receive operations with MPI_ANY_SOURCE or MPI_ANY_TAG and some other operations).

Later a generalized model including wild-card receives was introduced in [17]. This approach encodes decisions of ndsync operations directly into the state space and proposes a particular reduction for it. The method is tightly connected to semantics of MPI operations. We use it as a base point for comparison in Sect. 5.

ISP is able to detect deadlocks, but ndsync is analyzed only in two corner cases, when everything or nothing synchronize. Hence, it misses deadlocks like the second example in Fig. 1. MOPPER [7] uses encoding traces of ISP to SAT to provide more efficient deadlock detection. However, it is limited only to the programs where no control flow affects process communication and it considers only two cases of ndsync as ISP. DAMPI detects deadlocks by timeout of computation of an analyzed interleaving.

Organization of the Paper. Section 2 explains the main theoretical core underpinning our verification algorithm; Sect. 3 adds some remarks on its efficient implementation. Section 4 describes an actual usage of the algorithm in MPI and Sect. 5 shows experiments with the algorithm on MPI programs.

2 Explanation of the Main Algorithm in a Formal Context

We first recall some standard definitions, including a variant of independence relations on the set of system actions that is naturally suitable for our application domain. Then we describe the novel ideas how a (reduced) eager system (that imposes no potential synchronization constraints) can be efficiently analysed with the aim to discover implicit deadlocks that could be caused by applying *some* of the potential synchronization constraints.

By $\mathbb{N} = \{0, 1, 2, \dots\}$ we denote the set of nonnegative integers. For $i, j \in \mathbb{N}$, by $[i, j]$ we denote the set $\{i, i{+}1, \dots, j\}$. For a set A, by A^* we denote the set of *words over* A, i.e., the set of finite sequences of elements of A; we reserve ε for denoting the empty word.

Labeled Transition Systems, Paths, Runs. We define a *labeled transition system* (LTS) as a tuple $\mathcal{T} = (S, A, (\xrightarrow{a})_{a \in A}, s_0)$ where S is the set of *states*, A is the set of *actions*, $\xrightarrow{a} \subseteq S \times S$ is the set of a-transitions, for each $a \in A$, and s_0 is the *initial state*. As usual, we write $s \xrightarrow{a} s'$ instead of $(s, s') \in \xrightarrow{a}$, and we extend the relations $\xrightarrow{a}$ to $\xrightarrow{u} \subseteq S \times S$ for all $u \in A^*$ inductively: $s \xrightarrow{\varepsilon} s$; if $s \xrightarrow{a} s'$ and $s' \xrightarrow{u} s''$, then $s \xrightarrow{au} s''$.

The set $\mathsf{enact}(s)$ consists of the *actions enabled in* s, i.e., $\mathsf{enact}(s) = \{a \in A \mid s \xrightarrow{a} s' \text{ for some } s'\}$; by writing $s \xrightarrow{u}$ we denote that $s \xrightarrow{u} s'$ for some s', and by writing $s \not\xrightarrow{u}$ we denote that $s \xrightarrow{u}$ does not hold. A *state* s is *terminal* if $\mathsf{enact}(s) = \emptyset$; we often use the notation s_{T} for terminal states.

By a *path from* s *to* s' we mean a sequence $s \xrightarrow{a_1} s_1 \xrightarrow{a_2} s_2 \cdots \xrightarrow{a_\ell} s_\ell = s'$, or also just s (a zero-length path) if $s = s'$; a *run from* s is a path from s to some terminal state s_{T}.

For our aims it suffices to restrict the attention to the LTSs that are

- *finite*: both S and A are finite,
- *deterministic*: for any $s \in S$ and $a \in A$ there is at most one s' such that $s \xrightarrow{a} s'$, and
- *weakly terminating*: from each state a terminal state is reachable, i.e., for each $s \in S$ there is $u \in A^*$ and $s_T \in S$ where $s \xrightarrow{u} s_T$ and $\mathsf{enact}(s_T) = \emptyset$.

We further refer to a fixed such LTS $\mathcal{T} = (S, A, (\xrightarrow{a})_{a \in A}, s_0)$ if not said otherwise.

Remark. The above mentioned properties of LTSs follow naturally from our problem domain. As discussed in the introduction, we concentrate on the post-processing algorithm, which assumes such an LTS as an input. Weak termination is a natural property of computational programs; the first processing phase verifies also this property (before the post-processing algorithm starts).

Independence Relations, and Mazurkiewicz Traces. Now we define a standard variant of independence relations $\mathbf{I}$ on the set A of actions. We often write $a\mathbf{I}b$ instead of $(a, b) \in \mathbf{I}$ (a, b are independent), and $a \, \mathbf{D} \, b$ (a, b are dependent) instead of $(a, b) \notin \mathbf{I}$. A relation $\mathbf{I} \subseteq A \times A$ is an *independence relation for the LTS* $\mathcal{T}$ if the following conditions hold:

1. $\mathbf{I}$ is irreflexive ($a \, \mathbf{D} \, a$ for each $a \in A$) and symmetric ($a\mathbf{I}b$ implies $b\mathbf{I}a$).
2. If $s \xrightarrow{a} s_1$ and $s \xrightarrow{b} s_2$ where $a\mathbf{I}b$, then there is s' such that $s_1 \xrightarrow{b} s'$ and $s_2 \xrightarrow{a} s'$ (hence $s \xrightarrow{ab} s'$ and $s \xrightarrow{ba} s'$).
3. If $s \xrightarrow{a} s_1$ and $s \stackrel{b}{\not\rightarrow}$ where $a\mathbf{I}b$, then $s_1 \stackrel{b}{\not\rightarrow}$.

By $\mathbf{I}$ we further refer to an independence relation on the LTS $\mathcal{T}$.

For $u \in A^*$ we put $\mathsf{act}(u) = \{a \in A \mid a$ occurs in u, i.e. $u = u_1 a u_2$ for some $u_1, u_2 \in A^*\}$, and we note the following standard fact:

Proposition 1. *If $s \xrightarrow{a} s_1$ and $s \xrightarrow{u} s_2$ where $a\mathbf{I}b$ for all $b \in \mathsf{act}(u)$, then there is s' such that $s_1 \xrightarrow{u} s'$ and $s_2 \xrightarrow{a} s'$ (hence $s \xrightarrow{au} s'$ and $s \xrightarrow{ua} s'$).*

It is also standard to define the equivalence $\equiv_\mathbf{I}$ on A^*: it is the least congruence w.r.t. word concatenation that satisfies $ab \equiv_\mathbf{I} ba$ for all $a\mathbf{I}b$. (Hence $u \equiv_\mathbf{I} v$ iff we can get v from u by a series of replacing ab with ba where $a\mathbf{I}b$.) By $[u]_\mathbf{I}$ we denote the equivalence class $\{v \mid v \equiv_\mathbf{I} u\}$; such a class is also called a *Mazurkiewicz trace*, or an *M-trace* for short.

We note that each *path* π of the form $s \xrightarrow{a_1} s_1 \xrightarrow{a_2} s_2 \dots \xrightarrow{a_\ell} s_\ell$ has the *associated M-trace* $\mathrm{MT}(\pi) = [a_1 a_2 \dots a_\ell]_\mathbf{I}$.

Reduced LTSs (Keeping Mazurkiewicz Traces of Runs). For the relations $\xrightarrow{a}$ in our fixed LTS $\mathcal{T} = (S, A, (\xrightarrow{a})_{a \in A}, s_0)$ we will also use the notation $\xrightarrow{a}_\mathcal{T}$. We will also refer to $\mathcal{T}$ as to the *full LTS*. A reduced LTS $\mathcal{R}$ will arise from $\mathcal{T}$ by replacing each $\xrightarrow{a}_\mathcal{T}$ with a subset $\xrightarrow{a}_\mathcal{R} \subseteq \xrightarrow{a}_\mathcal{T}$, i.e., $\mathcal{R}$ arises from $\mathcal{T}$ by (possibly) removing some transitions $s \xrightarrow{a} s'$. We now formalize when such a reduction is consistent with a fixed independence relation $\mathbf{I} \subseteq A \times A$.

By a $(\mathcal{T}, \mathbf{I})$*-reduced system* we mean any LTS $\mathcal{R} = (S, A, (\xrightarrow{a}_\mathcal{R})_{a \in A}, s_0)$ satisfying the following conditions:

1. For each $a \in A$ we have $\xrightarrow{a}_{\mathcal{R}} \subseteq \xrightarrow{a}_{\mathcal{T}}$; hence $s \xrightarrow{a}_{\mathcal{R}} s'$ entails $s \xrightarrow{a}_{\mathcal{T}} s'$.
2. If $\mathsf{enact}_{\mathcal{T}}(s) \neq \emptyset$, then $\mathsf{enact}_{\mathcal{R}}(s) \neq \emptyset$. (Reducing cannot turn a non-terminal state into a terminal state.)
3. If $s \xrightarrow{a_1 a_2 \ldots a_n}_{\mathcal{T}}$ and a_n is dependent on some $b \in \mathsf{enact}_{\mathcal{R}}(s)$ (hence $s \xrightarrow{b}_{\mathcal{R}}$ and $a_n \, \mathbf{D} \, b$, i.e. $(a_n, b) \notin \mathbf{I}$), then $s \xrightarrow{a_i}_{\mathcal{R}}$ for some $i \in [1, n]$.

The point 3 (starting in s, performing any sequence from X^* in $\mathcal{T}$, where $X = \{a \mid a\mathbf{I}b \text{ for all } b \in \mathsf{enact}_{\mathcal{R}}(s)\}$, cannot enable an action $c \in A \smallsetminus (\mathsf{enact}_{\mathcal{R}}(s) \cup X)$), is crucial for guaranteeing that though the runs of a $(\mathcal{T}, \mathbf{I})$-reduced $\mathcal{R}$ constitute a subset of the set of runs of $\mathcal{T}$, for any state $s \in S$ we have that *the set of M-traces of runs from s in $\mathcal{T}$ is the same as the set of M-traces of runs from s in $\mathcal{R}$*. This is also captured by the next standard proposition (see, e.g., [9]).

Proposition 2. *Let $\mathcal{R} = (S, A, (\xrightarrow{a}_{\mathcal{R}})_{a \in A}, s_0)$ be a $(\mathcal{T}, \mathbf{I})$-reduced system. Then the following conditions are satisfied:*

1. *If $s \xrightarrow{u}_{\mathcal{T}} s'$ (in particular if $s \xrightarrow{u}_{\mathcal{R}} s'$) then $\forall u' \in [u]_{\mathbf{I}} : s \xrightarrow{u'}_{\mathcal{T}} s'$.*
2. *If $s \xrightarrow{u}_{\mathcal{T}} s_{\mathrm{T}}$ where s_{T} is a terminal state, then $\exists u' \in [u]_{\mathbf{I}} : s \xrightarrow{u'}_{\mathcal{R}} s_{\mathrm{T}}$.*

The next proposition can be easily derived by using Propositions 1 and 2. (By $\mathcal{R}$ we always refer to a $(\mathcal{T}, \mathbf{I})$-reduced LTS.)

Proposition 3. *Let $u = vaw \in A^*$ and $b\mathbf{I}a$ for all $b \in \mathsf{act}(v)$. Let $s \xrightarrow{u}_{\mathcal{T}} s_{\mathrm{T}}$, where s_{T} is a terminal state, and $s \xrightarrow{a}_{\mathcal{R}} s'$. Then there is $u' \in A^*$ such that $s' \xrightarrow{u'}_{\mathcal{R}} s_{\mathrm{T}}$ (hence $s \xrightarrow{au'}_{\mathcal{R}} s_{\mathrm{T}}$) and $[au']_{\mathbf{I}} = [u]_{\mathbf{I}}$.*

Synchronization-Constraint Candidates, Synch-deadlock. We refer to a fixed LTS $\mathcal{T} = (S, A, (\xrightarrow{a})_{a \in A}, s_0)$. By a set of *synchronization-constraint candidates*, or just of *candidates* for short, we mean a set $\textsc{Cand} \subseteq A \times 2^A$. If the synchronization related to a candidate (a, D) is indeed forced, then this is reflected in the LTS $\mathcal{T}$ so that any path $s_0 \xrightarrow{ua}$ where $\mathsf{act}(u) \cap D = \emptyset$ is invalid (i.e., performing a must be preceded by performing an action from D).

Formally, for $\mathcal{C} \subseteq A \times 2^A$ a *path* π of the form $s_0 \xrightarrow{a_1} s_1 \xrightarrow{a_2} s_2 \cdots \xrightarrow{a_\ell} s_\ell$ is *$\mathcal{C}$-valid* if for each $i \in [1, \ell]$ and each $(a_i, D) \in \mathcal{C}$ we have that $\mathsf{act}(a_1 a_2 \ldots a_{i-1}) \cap D \neq \emptyset$. Such a $\mathcal{C}$-valid path π is a *$\mathcal{C}$-valid run* if there is no $\mathcal{C}$-valid prolongation of π, i.e.: either s_ℓ is terminal (in which case π is a run in $\mathcal{T}$), or for each $a \in \mathsf{enact}(s_\ell)$ there is $(a, D) \in \mathcal{C}$ such that $\mathsf{act}(a_1 a_2 \ldots a_\ell) \cap D = \emptyset$.

We say that $\mathcal{T}$ *has a synch-deadlock w.r.t.* $\textsc{Cand} \subseteq A \times 2^A$ if there is $\mathcal{C} \subseteq \textsc{Cand}$ and a $\mathcal{C}$-valid run that is no run in $\mathcal{T}$. E.g., on the left in Fig. 3 s_0 is a (zero-length) $\mathcal{C}_3$-valid run that is no run in $\mathcal{T}$; on the other hand, each $\mathcal{C}_1$-valid run (i.e. just $s_0 \xrightarrow{ba}$) is a run in $\mathcal{T}$. On the right each $\mathcal{C}_3$-valid run (just $s_0 \xrightarrow{c}$) is a run in $\mathcal{T}$ but $s_0 \xrightarrow{a}$ is a $\mathcal{C}_2$-valid run that is no run in $\mathcal{T}$ (which also entails that $\mathcal{T}$ has a synch-deadlock w.r.t. $\textsc{Cand} = \mathcal{C}_3$, since $\mathcal{C}_2 \subseteq \mathcal{C}_3$).

Full-Witness (of Synch-deadlock). Consider the (full) LTS $\mathcal{T}$ and a set $\textsc{Cand}$ of candidates. We now define a witness of synch-deadlock in a way that will be technically convenient for the later algorithm.

$C_1 = \{(a, \{b\})\}$
$C_2 = \{(b, \{a\})\}$
$C_3 = C_1 \cup C_2$

$C_1 = \{(a, \{c\})\}$
$C_2 = \{(b, \{c\})\}$
$C_3 = C_1 \cup C_2$

Fig. 3. Examples of simple synchronization constraints

For $A' \subseteq A$, by an *A'-full-witness* (of synch-deadlock w.r.t. CAND) we mean a run $s_0 \xrightarrow{u} s_T$ where u can be written $u = wav$ so that we have the following:

1. $w \in (A \setminus A')^*$ and $a \in A'$;
2. for each $b \in A'$ there is at least one $(b, D) \in$ CAND such that $\mathsf{act}(w) \cap D = \emptyset$;
3. for $s_0 \xrightarrow{w} s$ we have $\mathsf{enact}(s) \subseteq A'$ (and $\mathsf{enact}(s) \neq \emptyset$ since $s_0 \xrightarrow{wa}$).

Proposition 4. *LTS $\mathcal{T}$ has a synch-deadlock w.r.t.* CAND *iff there is an A'-full-witness for some $A' \subseteq A$.*

Proof. If there is an A'-full-witness (as above), then $s_0 \xrightarrow{w} s$ is a $\mathcal{C}$-valid run where $\mathcal{C}$ consists of the candidates (b, D) where $b \in A'$ and $\mathsf{act}(w) \cap D = \emptyset$ (since $\mathsf{enact}(s) \subseteq A'$, there is no $\mathcal{C}$-valid path $s_0 \xrightarrow{w} s \xrightarrow{b}$). Since $s_0 \xrightarrow{w} s$ is no run in $\mathcal{T}$ (s is not terminal), there is indeed a synch-deadlock in $\mathcal{T}$.

On the other hand, if we have a $\mathcal{C}$-valid run $s_0 \xrightarrow{w} s$ that is no run in $\mathcal{T}$, we make a prolongation $s_0 \xrightarrow{w} s \xrightarrow{av} s_T$ to some terminal state s_T, and note that this is an A'-full-witness for $A' = \mathsf{enact}(s)$. □

Remark. Such a full-witness could be found by breadth-first (or depth-first) search in the (full) LTS $\mathcal{T}$; the information sufficient from the prefix that has been read is the set of actions that have already occurred; doing this, we can also "release" candidates in CAND: we declare a candidate (a, D) as released when we have read some action $x \in D$. But our problem will be to find a witness of synch-deadlock in $\mathcal{T}$ by scanning the reduced LTS $\mathcal{R}$ only.

Dotting Procedure, and A'-witnesses in the Reduced LTS $\mathcal{R}$. Informally speaking, we look for an "image" of an A'-full-witness when scanning $\mathcal{R}$, by a depth-first search traversal, say. Given a run

$$s_0 \xrightarrow{a_1}_{\mathcal{R}} s_1 \xrightarrow{a_2}_{\mathcal{R}} s_2 \cdots \xrightarrow{a_\ell}_{\mathcal{R}} s_\ell \qquad (1)$$

of $\mathcal{R}$ (where s_ℓ is terminal), we mark all "events" in the M-trace $[a_1 a_2 \ldots a_\ell]_{\mathbf{I}}$ that are "causally dependent" on A' as follows:

1. start with all positions $i \in [1, \ell]$ as *clean*, i.e. with no dots;
2. make an initial distribution of *a-dots* for $a \in A'$: to each *position* $i \in [1, \ell]$ such that $a_i \in A'$ add an a_i-dot;
3. iterate the following step (until no dots can be added):
   if $i < j$, a_i has an a-dot, and $a_i \mathbf{D} a_j$ (i.e. $(a_i, a_j) \notin \mathbf{I}$), then the position j gets an a-dot.

After this dotting is completed (some positions might have got a-dots for several actions $a \in A'$), by the *clean word* we mean $w = a_{i_1} a_{i_2} \dots a_{i_k}$ where $i_1 < i_2 < \cdots < i_k$ and $\{i_1, i_2, \dots, i_k\}$ is the set of all clean (i.e. non-dotted) positions in $[1, \ell]$. By the *dotted word* we mean $a_{j_1} a_{j_2} \dots a_{j_{k'}}$ where $j_1 < j_2 < \cdots < j_{k'}$ and $\{j_1, j_2, \dots, j_{k'}\}$ is the set of all dotted positions in $[1, \ell]$.

We now inspect the *offshoots* (alternative transitions) of dotted positions, i.e.: for each dotted $j \in [1, \ell]$ (i.e., $j \in \{j_1, j_2, \dots, j_{k'}\}$) we consider all alternatives (in $\mathcal{R}$) to the action a_j, i.e., all a such that $s_{j-1} \xrightarrow{a}_{\mathcal{R}}$ (besides $s_{j-1} \xrightarrow{a_j}_{\mathcal{R}} s_j$). Such an offshoot $s_{j-1} \xrightarrow{a}_{\mathcal{R}}$ gets dotted if $a \in A'$ or there is $i < j$ where i has a dot (i.e., is not clean) and $a_i \, \mathbf{D} \, a$; otherwise the offshoot stays clean.

A run (1) is an A'*-witness* (which is a different term than A'-full-witness) if the following conditions hold after the dotting procedure has been performed:

1. at least one $a \in A'$ occurs in $a_1 a_2 \dots a_\ell$ (which entails that at least one position $i \in [1, \ell]$ has got dotted);
2. all offshoots (of dotted positions) have got dotted;
3. for each $a \in A'$ there is at least one $(a, D) \in \text{CAND}$ such that $\mathsf{act}(w) \cap D = \emptyset$ where w is the clean word $a_{i_1} a_{i_2} \dots a_{i_k}$.

Proposition 5. *If a run $s_0 \xrightarrow{u}_{\mathcal{R}} s_{\text{T}}$ (in $\mathcal{R}$) is an A'-witness, w is the respective clean word, and av is the (nonempty) dotted word, then the run $s_0 \xrightarrow{wav} s_{\text{T}}$ is an A'-full-witness in $\mathcal{T}$ (w.r.t. the fixed set* CAND*).*

Proof. Suppose $s_0 \xrightarrow{u}_{\mathcal{R}} s_{\text{T}}$ is an A'-witness, in the form (1), i.e., $s_0 \xrightarrow{a_1}_{\mathcal{R}} s_1 \xrightarrow{a_2}_{\mathcal{R}} s_2 \cdots \xrightarrow{a_\ell}_{\mathcal{R}} s_\ell$. Let $w = a_{i_1} a_{i_2} \dots a_{i_k}$ be the clean word and $av = a_{j_1} a_{j_2} \dots a_{j_{k'}}$ be the dotted word; our dotting procedure guarantees that $wav \in [u]_{\mathbf{I}}$ (all "clean positions" can "bubble" to the left since they are independent with the preceding "dotted positions"). By Proposition 2(1), $s_0 \xrightarrow{wav}_{\mathcal{T}} s_{\text{T}}$ (where $s_{\text{T}} = s_\ell$) is a run in $\mathcal{T}$; we suppose that it is no A'-full-witness, for the sake of contradiction.

We have $s_0 \xrightarrow{w}_{\mathcal{T}} s \xrightarrow{av}_{\mathcal{T}} s_{\text{T}}$ for some s. Since $a \in A'$, $\mathsf{act}(w) \cap A' = \emptyset$, and for each $x \in A'$ there is $(x, D) \in \text{CAND}$ such that $\mathsf{act}(w) \cap D = \emptyset$, we must have $\mathsf{enact}(s) \not\subseteq A'$ (otherwise $s_0 \xrightarrow{wav}_{\mathcal{T}} s_{\text{T}}$ would be an A'-full-witness); hence there is $f \in A \smallsetminus A'$ for which $s_0 \xrightarrow{w}_{\mathcal{T}} s \xrightarrow{f}_{\mathcal{T}}$.

Let now $j \in [1, \ell]$ be the maximum such that we have

1. $s_0 \xrightarrow{a_1 a_2 \cdots a_j}_{\mathcal{R}} s_j \xrightarrow{a_{i_{j'}} a_{i_{j'+1}} \cdots a_{i_k} f}_{\mathcal{T}}$,
2. j' is the least such that $j < i_{j'}$; if none exists, $a_{i_{j'}} a_{i_{j'+1}} \cdots a_{i_k}$ is empty,
3. $a_i \mathbf{I} f$ for each dotted position i in $[1, j]$.

There must be such maximum j since $j = 0$ clearly satisfies the conditions. Necessarily $j < \ell$, since we cannot have $s_\ell \xrightarrow{f}_{\mathcal{T}}$ (recall that $s_\ell = s_{\text{T}}$ is terminal).

We must have $j{+}1 < i_{j'}$ (otherwise j was not maximum); hence $j{+}1$ is dotted. We have $a_{j+1} \mathbf{I} a_{i_{j'}}$, $a_{j+1} \mathbf{I} a_{i_{j'+1}}$, ..., $a_{j+1} \mathbf{I} a_{i_k}$ due to our dotting procedure; but we must have $a_{j+1} \, \mathbf{D} \, f$, since otherwise j was not maximum (recall Proposition 1). By the condition 3 imposed on $(\mathcal{T}, \mathbf{I})$-reduced systems we thus have that one of the actions $a_{i_{j'}}, a_{i_{j'+1}}, \ldots a_{i_k}, f$ is enabled in s_j in the reduced system $\mathcal{R}$. But then this offshoot of the dotted position $j+1$ is not dotted, which contradicts with the assumption that $s_0 \xrightarrow{u}_{\mathcal{R}} s_{\mathrm{T}}$ is an A'-witness. □

Algorithm ALG **(Searching an A'-witness in $\mathcal{R}$).** We describe the crux of the algorithm, ignoring some obvious optimizations that would technically complicate the description. The next section describes how to implement the algorithm without analyzing each path separately.

The algorithm ALG gets a reduced system $\mathcal{R}$, a relation $\mathbf{I}$ and a set CAND as the input. It performs depth-search of $\mathcal{R}$ from s_0, considering also runs with possible cycles ($\mathcal{R}$ is only guaranteed to be weakly terminating); nevertheless the inclusion of cycles is carefully restricted (so that it just suffices for finding a possible synch-deadlock). For each examined run $s_0 \xrightarrow{u}_{\mathcal{R}} s_{\mathrm{T}}$ ALG performs the following procedure:

Put $A' := A$
while $A' \cap \mathsf{act}(u) \neq \emptyset$ **do**
Perform the dotting procedure, and check the conditions 2 (dotted offshoots) and 3 (for each $a \in A'$ the clean word does not release at least one candidate) put on A'-witnesses; if this succeeds, an A'-witness is found (and a synch-deadlock in $\mathcal{T}$ is demonstrated), otherwise continue.

1. If the clean word releases all (a, D) for some $a \in A'$ ($\mathsf{act}(w) \cap D \neq \emptyset$), then put $A' := A' \setminus \{a\}$ and start the next execution of the while loop. (This a cannot belong to $A'' \subseteq A'$ for which the run $s_0 \xrightarrow{u}_{\mathcal{R}} s_{\mathrm{T}}$ is an A''-, since the set of clean positions gets only bigger when A' gets smaller.)
2. Otherwise there is a clean offshoot a'_i of a dotted a_i; say that the position i has an a-dot (among its dots); hence as long as $a \in A'$, the offshoot-condition fails. So we can safely put $A' := A' \setminus \{a\}$ (and start the next execution of the while loop).

The completeness of our algorithm is captured by the next proposition.

Proposition 6. *If (the full LTS) $\mathcal{T}$ has a synch-deadlock w.r.t.* CAND, *then the algorithm* ALG *finds an A'-witness for some $A' \subseteq A$ and some run from s_0 in (the reduced LTS) $\mathcal{R}$.*

Proof. Let us fix an A_0-full-witness $s_0 \xrightarrow{w'}_{\mathcal{T}} s \xrightarrow{av}_{\mathcal{T}} s_{\mathrm{T}}$ in $\mathcal{T}$. (We use A_0 since we reserve A' for denoting the ALG-variable A', and w' for not mixing with the clean word w below.) Hence $w' \in (A \setminus A_0)^*$, $a \in A_0$, $\mathsf{enact}(s) \subseteq A_0$, and for each $b \in A_0$ there is at least one $(b, D) \in$ CAND such that $\mathsf{act}(w') \cap D = \emptyset$.

The set $Lin = \{u \in A^* \mid u \in [w'av]_{\mathbf{I}}, s_0 \xrightarrow{u}_{\mathcal{R}} s_{\mathrm{T}}\}$ is nonempty, by Proposition 2(2). Imagine that we perform the dotting procedure (with no offshoot considering) for each $u \in Lin$, w.r.t. A_0. In each case we get some clean word $w = a_{i_1} a_{i_2} \cdots a_{i_k}$; it is easy to verify that $w \in [w']_{\mathbf{I}}$. (Dotting $w'av$ w.r.t. A_0 leaves w' clean, and the rest av gets dotted, since otherwise our conditions on

$\mathbf{I}$ would entail that some $f \in A \smallsetminus A_0$ [clean in av] is enabled in s. We also observe that switching two positions with independent actions b_1, b_2, together with their dots in the dotting result on $v_1 b_1 b_2 v_2$, corresponds to the dotting result on $v_1 b_2 b_1 v_2$.)

We now fix a run $s_0 \xrightarrow{u}_{\mathcal{R}} s_{\mathrm{T}}$ in $\mathcal{R}$, where $u \in \mathit{Lin}$, such that the vector $(i_1, i_2, \ldots, i_k)$ corresponding to the clean word is *lexicographically minimal.* (We have $(i_1, i_2, \ldots, i_k) \prec (i'_1, i'_2, \ldots, i'_k)$ if $i_m < i'_m$ for the least m for which i_m, i'_m differ). We show that ALG finds a witness when processing this run $s_0 \xrightarrow{u}_{\mathcal{R}} s_{\mathrm{T}}$.

As long as $A' \supseteq A_0$, during the while-loop in ALG no $a \in A_0$ can be removed from A' by the first (candidate releasing) condition: $\mathsf{act}(w')$ does not release all candidates for any $a \in A_0$, and our above discussion entails that $\mathsf{act}(w) \subseteq \mathsf{act}(w')$ where w is the clean word resulting from dotting u w.r.t. $A' \supseteq A_0$.

Suppose that $A' \supseteq A_0$, and some $a \in A_0$ should be removed from A' due to the "clean-offshoot-condition". Then also the dotting result for u w.r.t. A_0 must have a clean offshoot (of a dotted position) in $s_0 \xrightarrow{u}_{\mathcal{R}} s_{\mathrm{T}}$. We now contradict this, by which the proof will be finished (ALG finds an A'-witness for some $A' \supseteq A_0$).

We write the run $s_0 \xrightarrow{u}_{\mathcal{R}} s_{\mathrm{T}}$ in more detail as $s_0 \xrightarrow{a_1}_{\mathcal{R}} s_1 \xrightarrow{a_2}_{\mathcal{R}} s_2 \cdots \xrightarrow{a_\ell}_{\mathcal{R}} s_\ell$, and let $j \in [1, \ell]$ be the least such that the position $j{+}1$ is dotted (in the dotting result w.r.t. A_0) and there is a clean offshoot $s_j \xrightarrow{f}_{\mathcal{R}}$ (of $s_j \xrightarrow{a_{j+1}}_{\mathcal{R}} s_{j+1}$); necessarily $f \notin A_0$. Let $w = a_{i_1} a_{i_2} \cdots a_{i_k}$ be the clean word, and j' the least such that $j{+}1 < i_{j'}$ if $j{+}1 < i_k$. We perform the following case analysis.

1. $f = a_{i_m}$ for some $i_m > j{+}1$ and f is independent on all $a_{i_{j'}}, a_{i_{j'+1}}, \ldots, a_{i_{m-1}}$; f is thus independent on all a_n where $n \in [j{+}1, i_m{-}1]$. We apply Proposition 3: we have $s_j \xrightarrow{a_{j+1} \ldots a_{i_m -1} f v'}_{\mathcal{R}} s_{\mathrm{T}}$ and $s_j \xrightarrow{f}_{\mathcal{R}}$; hence there is u' such that $s_j \xrightarrow{fu'}_{\mathcal{R}} s_{\mathrm{T}}$ and $[fu']_{\mathbf{I}} = [a_{j+1} \ldots a_{i_m -1} f v']_{\mathbf{I}}$, and our $u = a_1 a_2 \ldots a_\ell$ thus was not lexicographically minimal.
2. Suppose f in independent on all a_{i_m} where $j{+}1 < i_m$ (there might be none). Let u_1 be the dotted (scattered) subword of $a_1 a_2 \ldots a_j$ (f must be independent on all elements of u_1 since it is a clean offshoot), and let u_2 be the clean subword of $a_1 a_2 \ldots a_j$. Let v_1 be the clean subword of $a_{j+1} a_{j+2} \ldots a_\ell$ (f is independent on all elements of v_1 by our assumption), and let v_2 be the dotted subword of $a_{j+1} a_{j+2} \ldots a_\ell$. Since $u_2 v_1 u_1 v_2$ (all clean first and all dotted next) belongs to $[u]_{\mathbf{I}}$, we have $s_0 \xrightarrow{u_2 v_1 u_1 v_2}_{\mathcal{T}} s_{\mathrm{T}}$ and also $s_0 \xrightarrow{u_2 v_1}_{\mathcal{T}} s \xrightarrow{f}_{\mathcal{T}}$ (by the fact $u_2 v_1 \in [w']_{\mathbf{I}}$ and the conditions assumed for $\mathbf{I}$) and $s_0 \xrightarrow{u_2 v_1}_{\mathcal{T}} s$. The fact that $f \in \mathsf{enact}(s) \smallsetminus A_0$ contradicts with the assumptions on our starting A_0-full-witness.
3. It remains to explore the case when there is the least m such that $j{+}1 < i_m$ and $f\,\mathbf{D}\,a_{i_m}$ where, moreover, $f \neq a_{i_m}$ (since $f = a_{i_m}$ belongs to 1). The word $a_{i_{j'}} a_{i_{j'+1}}, \ldots a_{i_m}$ is enabled in s_j in $\mathcal{T}$, and it contains a first action that is dependent on some $x \in \mathsf{enact}_{\mathcal{R}}(s_j)$ (since $a_{i_m}\,\mathbf{D}\,f$); hence there must be the least $n \in [j', m]$ such that $s_j \xrightarrow{a_{i_n}}_{\mathcal{R}}$ (by the condition 3 for $(\mathcal{T}, \mathbf{I})$-reduced systems). The action a_{i_n} is independent on the previous $a_{i_{j'}}, a_{i_{j'+1}}, \ldots a_{i_{n-1}}$ since otherwise some of them would be again dependent on some $x \in \mathsf{enact}_{\mathcal{R}}(s_j)$

(namely on a_{i_n}) and n was not the least. Here we again invoke Proposition 3, and we find that our u was not lexicographically minimal. □

3 Optimization Ideas

The previous section shows an algorithm that checks every run in the reduced system and, moreover, each run is evaluated repeatedly (if no witness is found). Here we present a few observations regarding to an efficient implementation.

The first observation is that we do not need repeatedly compute what actions are clean when A' is shrinking. We can go through a path only once while remembering:

- already processed non-clean actions and what candidates causes it
- dependencies between candidate (forcing that a candidate has to be removed when an another candidate is removed). These dependencies are generated by offshoots.

This information remembered when a path is traversed is named as *NI* (*ndsync information*). When we see that a candidate has to be removed from A', we can just update NI without recomputing the whole path. After processing a path, NI is sufficient for a decision if a path is witness or not.

Since we process the path from the beginning to the end (and current NI depends on previous action and not on the rest of the path), we do not need to inspect each path separately, but we can traverse reduced system by depth-first or bread-first search while collecting NI.

Another observation concerns the confluence of paths in the reduced system. During traversing the reduced system, we can arrive to a state from different paths and having more different NIs. The following observations enables to explore continuations for only some of NIs. Assume that we have arrived into a state from two paths that generated two different NIs. We can continue with search from this state considering only one of NIs if:

- they differ only by removed candidates and this difference contains only actions that cannot occur in the rest of the path.
- or if there exists bijections $f : \textsc{Cand} \rightarrow \textsc{Cand}$ such that: $\forall (a, D) \in \textsc{Cand} : f((a, D)) = (a', D') \implies [D = D' \wedge \forall a'' \in A : (a, a'') \in \mathbf{I} \iff (a', a'') \in \mathbf{I}]$ and if we rename candidates in the first NI we obtain the second one.

The idea is the following: there is a deadlock-witnessing continuation from the state and one of NI iff the there is a deadlock continuation while using the second NI. Both observations have this property and are actually useful in MPI verification. In practice, it leads to exploration of only one NI for each state of reduced system. It is demonstrated in Sect. 5.

4 Usage of the Reduction in MPI

To demonstrate a usage of the abstract framework in MPI, we describe its implementation in tool Aislinn. Aislinn[1] is a dynamic verifying tool for MPI applica-

[1] http://verif.cs.vsb.cz/aislinn.

tions that covers nondeterministic behavior introduced by parallel execution and MPI (for a fixed input). Aislinn is mainly focused on detecting memory and MPI related errors, and deadlocks. The tool has been created by one of the authors and is released under an open source license.

Aislinn builds the partial-order reduced state of eager system while checking correctness of memory accesses in each process and validity of MPI calls. The example of the state space built by Aislinn is available online[2]. When a state with no successors and without properly terminated processes is found, then a deadlock (not involving ndsync) is found. When all processes are terminated then the state is checked for resource leaks.

When no error is so far found, the state space graph is passed to the algorithm presented in this paper to find ndsync deadlocks. An example of such a graph is in Fig. 4. The graph contains MPI events on arcs and states contains only a list of outgoing arcs without additional information. The full description of state is dropped when all relevant successors are searched during the previous step of the analysis; only hashes of states remain to detect already searched states. In the example, r_i represents an MPI request object connected to the operation (Aislinn internally creates requests even for blocking ones); $\overline{r_i}$ denotes a completed request. Action *Matching* represents a pairing between sending and receiving operations and completes the latter one. Action *continue* represents resuming a process from a blocking operation, its argument is a completed request that causes process unblocking.

The independence relation (**I**) is not given explicitly, but it directly follows from MPI semantics and can be derived by the following rules: Two operations are dependent when they have the same process number, or there is a request that occurs in both of them. In the example, [b] and [c] are dependent since they are executed on the same process, and [c] and [d] since both involve request r_4. Moreover, Matching(r_i, r_j) and Matching($r_{i'}$, $r_{j'}$) are dependent if Matching(r_i, $r_{j'}$) (resp. Matching($r_{i'}$, r_j)) is a valid matching and r_j and $r_{j'}$ (resp. r_i and $r_{i'}$) where created by the same process; this assures non-overtaking property of the messages. In other cases, two operations are independent.

The synchronization candidates (Cand) are also given implicitly. Assume that a creates a request r_i in a process p. If a is a standard send then we put (a, D) into Cand where D are all matchings involving r_i. If a is a collective operation on communicator c, then we put $(a, \{a'\})$ into Cand for each corresponding collective operation a' in a process of communicator c other than p.

Aislinn implements 80 MPI functions, that covers the majority of the commonly used MPI functions. Almost all MPI-2 functions related to point-to-point communication, collective communication, the group and communicator management, data types, user-defined operations, and keyvals; from MPI-3, nonblocking collective operations are implemented.

[2] http://verif.cs.vsb.cz/aislinn/doc/sspace.html.

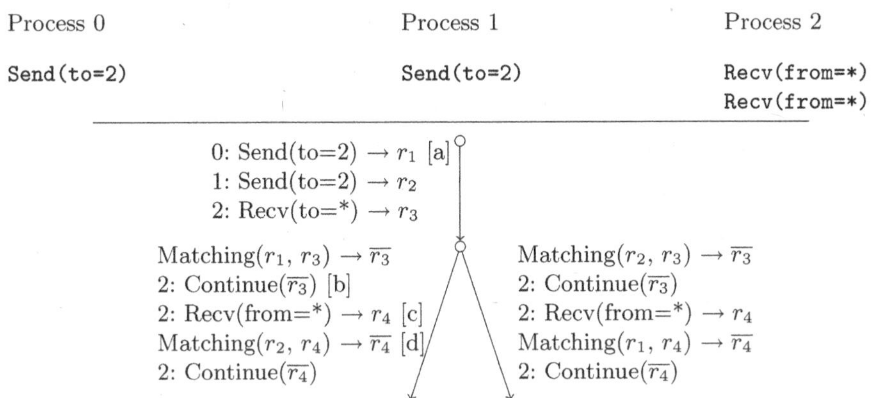

Fig. 4. The example of a graph for an MPI that serves as an input for ndsync deadlock analysis in Aislinn. (The first number in an action is the process id; the square brackets are used only for the references in the text)

5 Experimental Evaluation

The experiments are performed in Aislinn on MPI programs containing standard sends. Each program was analyzed under three analyses:

- **E** ("eager") – all operations with nondeterministic synchronization are considered having a minimal synchronization effect.
- **N** ("encoding") – synchronization choices of standard sends are directly encoded into the state space.
- **P** ("eager + post-processing algorithm") – it starts as **E**, but the presented post-processing algorithm is performed at the end.

Let us note that **N** encodes nondeterministic synchronizations only for standard sends and not for collective operations, while **P** considers also both synchronizations. It would be possible enrich **N** in this way; however, it would lead to even bigger state spaces for **N**; **P** outperforms **N** already in this settings. The results of benchmarks are in Table 1. The number of states is presented in a compressed form – when there is sequence of actions, where POR allowed to explore only one continuation, the intermediate states are not counted (as in Fig. 4).

In all cases, POR is employed. The implemented algorithm is a particular implementation of algorithm 10.5.2 for queues in [4], where *pre* and *dep* are straightforwardly derived from MPI semantics. It can also be seen as generalization of "Lazy matching" in [8]. **N** also contains a reduction based on method from [17] to reduce branching of synchronization by standard sends.

An arc between two states may contain more MPI events as is shown in the example in the previous section; therefore, there are significantly more MPI calls than states in the state space.

Table 1. Results of benchmarks

Name	N	Sz E	Sz N	Sz P	Calls	Sends	E tm	N tm	P tm	ISP tm
petsc/ksp/ex18	4	249	4181	249	32088	882	17s	53s	17s	X
–	5	1744	68966	1744	120424	5464	57s	856s	60s	X
petsc/ksp/ex23	4	250	4182	250	25908	906	13s	45s	14s	X
–	5	1762	68984	1762	112456	5752	50s	772s	53s	X
petsc/ts/ex2	3	862	1313	862	179476	6588	82s	85s	82s	X
workers/8 jobs	4	1369	8682	1369	9114	3477	8s	52s	8s	2287s
–	5	6873	54274	6873	51652	18091	44s	401s	46s	>7200s
monte (0.002)	3	2378	18596	2378	19550	5794	19s	115s	20s	4337s

N = The number of MPI processes in the analyzed application; Sz E = Size of the state space for E; Sz N = Size of the state space for N; Sz P = The number of states visited in post-processing; Calls = The number of MPI calls analyzed in E state space; Sends = The number of standard sends in the E state space; E/N/P tm = The total running time of Aislinn in case of E/N/P; ISP tm = Verification time in tool ISP (X = execution ends by an error; reported to authors, but not solved).

First three benchmarks are examples for PETSc [3] (Portable, Extensible Toolkit for Scientific Computation). It is a complex framework for solving physics engineering and scientific problems. PETSc examples are taken from "PETSc Hands On Exercise"[3]. The tests themselves are relatively short (hundreds lines of code), but they call a complex library using MPI underneath that is also a part of the analysis. PETSc examples contain also collective communication.

Benchmark *Monte* computes π using Monte Carlo method and was obtained from the web page of ISP. Benchmark *Workers* is an implementation of a simple master-workers load-balancing algorithm; the used instance balances eight jobs.

Aislinn implements all optimizations mentioned in Sect. 3. In all cases "Sz P" is equal to "Sz E"; this means that each state is explored exactly with one NI in **P**.

All results are obtained by tool Aislinn except the last one. The last column are execution times of tool ISP. Only the state space of **E** were explored, because ISP does not support a precise analysis of ndsync; however, even for this case it slower by an order of the magnitude. Despite our efforts, we were not able to analyze these programs in other MPI verification tools.

Acknowledgements. We thank anonymous reviewers for helpful comments. This work was supported by The Ministry of Education, Youth and Sports from the National Programme of Sustainability (NPU II) project "IT4Innovations excellence in science - LQ1602" and from the Large Infrastructures for Research, Experimental Development and Innovations project "IT4Innovations National Supercomputing Center – LM2015070", and partially by Grant SGS No. SP2016/118, FEECS VŠB - TU of Ostrava, Czech Republic.

[3] http://www.mcs.anl.gov/petsc/petsc-current/src/ksp/ksp/examples/tutorials/index.html.

References

1. Message Passing Interface Forum. http://www.mpi-forum.org/
2. Akers, S.B.: Binary decision diagrams. IEEE Trans. Comput. **C–27**(6), 509–516 (1978)
3. Balay, S., Abhyankar, S., Adams, M.F., Brown, J., Brune, P., Buschelman, K., Eijkhout, V., Gropp, W.D., Kaushik, D., Knepley, M.G., McInnes, L.C., Rupp, K., Smith, B.F., Zhang, H.: PETSc users manual. Technical report ANL-95/11 - Revision 3.5, Argonne National Laboratory (2014). http://www.mcs.anl.gov/petsc
4. Clarke Jr., E.M., Grumberg, O., Peled, D.A.: Model Checking. MIT Press, Cambridge (1999)
5. DeSouza, J., Kuhn, B., de Supinski, B.R., Samofalov, V., Zheltov, S., Bratanov, S.: Automated, scalable debugging of MPI programs with Intel message checker. In: Proceedings of the Second International Workshop on Software Engineering for High Performance Computing System Applications, SE-HPCS 2005, pp. 78–82. ACM, New York (2005)
6. Esparza, J., Heljanko, K.: Unfoldings - A Partial-Order Approach to Model Checking. Monographs in Theoretical Computer Science. An EATCS Series. Springer, Heidelberg (2008)
7. Forejt, V., Kroening, D., Narayanaswamy, G., Sharma, S.: Precise predictive analysis for discovering communication deadlocks in MPI programs. In: Jones, C., Pihlajasaari, P., Sun, J. (eds.) FM 2014. LNCS, vol. 8442, pp. 263–278. Springer, Heidelberg (2014). doi:10.1007/978-3-319-06410-9_19
8. Fu, X., Chen, Z., Zhang, Y., Huang, C., Wang, J.: MPISE: symbolic execution of MPI programs (2014). http://arxiv.org/abs/1403.4813
9. Godefroid, P.: Partial-Order Methods for the Verification of Concurrent Systems: An Approach to the State-Explosion Problem. Springer-Verlag New York Inc., Secaucus (1996)
10. Hilbrich, T., Protze, J., Schulz, M., de Supinski, B.R., Müller, M.S.: MPI runtime error detection with MUST: advances in deadlock detection. In: Proceedings of the International Conference on High Performance Computing, Networking, Storage and Analysis, SC 2012, pp. 30:1–30:11. IEEE Computer Society Press, Los Alamitos (2012). http://dl.acm.org/citation.cfm?id=2388996.2389037
11. Hilbrich, T., de Supinski, B.R., Schulz, M., Müller, M.S.: A graph based approach for MPI deadlock detection. In: Proceedings of the 23rd International Conference on Supercomputing, ICS 2009, pp. 296–305. ACM, New York (2009). http://doi.acm.org/10.1145/1542275.1542319
12. López, H.A., Marques, E.R.B., Martins, F., Ng, N., Santos, C., Vasconcelos, V.T., Yoshida, N.: Protocol-based verification of message-passing parallel programs. In: OOPSLA 2015, pp. 280–298. ACM (2015)
13. Luecke, G.R., Chen, H., Coyle, J., Hoekstra, J., Kraeva, M., Zou, Y.: MPI-CHECK: a tool for checking fortran 90 MPI programs. Concurrency Comput. Pract. Exper. **15**(2), 93–100 (2003)
14. Meca, O., Böhm, S., Běhálek, M., Jančar, P.: An approach to verification of MPI applications defined in a high-level model. In: 16th International Conference on Application of Concurrency to System Design, pp. 55–64. IEEE Computer Society (2016)

15. Palmer, R., Gopalakrishnan, G., Kirby, R.M.: Semantics driven dynamic partial-order reduction of MPI-based parallel programs. In: Proceedings of the 2007 ACM Workshop on Parallel and Distributed Systems: Testing and Debugging, PADTAD 2007, pp. 43–53. ACM, New York (2007). http://doi.acm.org/10.1145/1273647.1273657
16. Peled, D.: All from one, one for all: on model checking using representatives. In: Courcoubetis, C. (ed.) CAV 1993. LNCS, vol. 697, pp. 409–423. Springer, Heidelberg (1993). doi:10.1007/3-540-56922-7_34
17. Siegel, S.F.: Efficient verification of halting properties for MPI programs with wildcard receives. In: Cousot, R. (ed.) VMCAI 2005. LNCS, vol. 3385, pp. 413–429. Springer, Heidelberg (2005). doi:10.1007/978-3-540-30579-8_27
18. Siegel, S.F., Avrunin, G.S.: Modeling wildcard-free MPI programs for verification. In: Proceedings of the Tenth ACM SIGPLAN Symposium on Principles and Practice of Parallel Programming, PPoPP 2005, pp. 95–106. ACM, New York (2005). http://doi.acm.org/10.1145/1065944.1065957
19. Siegel, S.F., Avrunin, G.S.: Verification of halting properties for MPI programs using nonblocking operations. In: Cappello, F., Herault, T., Dongarra, J. (eds.) EuroPVM/MPI 2007. LNCS, vol. 4757, pp. 326–334. Springer, Heidelberg (2007). doi:10.1007/978-3-540-75416-9_44
20. Siegel, S., Zirkel, T.: TASS: the toolkit for accurate scientific software. Math. Comput. Sci. **5**(4), 395–426 (2011)
21. Vakkalanka, S.S., Sharma, S., Gopalakrishnan, G., Kirby, R.M.: ISP: a tool for model checking MPI programs. In: Proceedings of the 13th ACM SIGPLAN Symposium on Principles and practice of parallel programming, PPoPP 2008, pp. 285–286. ACM, New York (2008). http://doi.acm.org/10.1145/1345206.1345258
22. Valmari, A.: Stubborn sets for reduced state space generation. In: Rozenberg, G. (ed.) ICATPN 1989. LNCS, vol. 483, pp. 491–515. Springer, Heidelberg (1991). doi:10.1007/3-540-53863-1_36
23. Vo, A., Aananthakrishnan, S., Gopalakrishnan, G., Supinski, B.R.d., Schulz, M., Bronevetsky, G.: A scalable and distributed dynamic formal verifier for MPI programs. In: Proceedings of the 2010 ACM/IEEE International Conference for High Performance Computing, Networking, Storage and Analysis, SC 2010, pp. 1–10. IEEE Computer Society, Washington (2010). http://dx.doi.org/10.1109/SC.2010.7

Formal Verification of Multi-Paxos for Distributed Consensus

Saksham Chand(✉), Yanhong A. Liu, and Scott D. Stoller

Computer Science Department, Stony Brook University, Stony Brook, NY 11794, USA
{schand,liu,stoller}@cs.stonybrook.edu

Abstract. This paper describes formal specification and verification of Lamport's Multi-Paxos algorithm for distributed consensus. The specification is written in TLA+, Lamport's Temporal Logic of Actions. The proof is written and checked using TLAPS, a proof system for TLA+. Building on Lamport, Merz, and Doligez's specification and proof for Basic Paxos, we aim to facilitate the understanding of Multi-Paxos and its proof by minimizing the difference from those for Basic Paxos, and to demonstrate a general way of proving other variants of Paxos and other sophisticated distributed algorithms. We also discuss our general strategies for proving properties about sets and tuples that helped the proof check succeed in significantly reduced time.

1 Introduction

Distributed consensus is a fundamental problem in distributed computing. It requires that a set of processes agree on some value or values. Consensus is essential when distributed services are replicated for fault-tolerance, because non-faulty replicas must agree. Unfortunately, consensus is difficult when the processes or communication channels may fail.

Paxos [16] is an important algorithm, developed by Lamport, for solving distributed consensus. Basic Paxos is for agreeing on a one-shot value, such as whether to commit a database transaction. Multi-Paxos is for agreeing on an infinite sequence of values, for example, a stream of commands to execute. Multi-Paxos has been used in many important distributed services, e.g., Google's Chubby [1,3] and Microsoft's Autopilot [13]. There are other Paxos variants, e.g., that reduce a message delay [19] or add preemption [17], but Multi-Paxos is the most important in making Paxos practical for distributed services that must perform a continual sequence of operations.

Paxos handles processes that run concurrently without shared memory, where processes may crash and may later recover, and messages may be delayed indefinitely or lost. In Basic Paxos, each process may repeatedly attempt to be the

This work was supported in part by NSF grants CCF-1414078, CCF-1248184, and CNS-1421893, ONR grant N000141512208, and AFOSR grant FA9550-14-1-0261. Any opinions, findings, and conclusions or recommendations expressed in this material are those of the authors and do not necessarily reflect the views of these agencies.

J. Fitzgerald et al. (Eds.): FM 2016, LNCS 9995, pp. 119–136, 2016.
DOI: 10.1007/978-3-319-48989-6_8

leader and propose some value, and wait for appropriate replies from appropriate subsets of the processes while also replying appropriately to other processes; consensus is reached eventually if enough processes and channels are non-faulty to elect a leader. In Multi-Paxos, many more different attempts, proposals, and replies may happen in overlapping fashions to reach consensus on values in different slots in the continual sequence.

Paxos has often been difficult to understand, even though it was created almost three decades ago [21]. Lamport later wrote a much simpler description of the phases of the algorithm but only for Basic Paxos [17]. Lamport, Merz, and Doligez [22] wrote a formal specification and proof of Basic Paxos in TLA+ [18] and TLAPS [26]. Many efforts, especially in recent years, have been spent on formal specification and verification of Multi-Paxos, but they use more restricted or less direct language models, some mixed in large systems with many unrelated functionalities, or handle other variants of Paxos than Multi-Paxos, as discussed in Sect. 7. What is lacking is formal specification and proof of the exact phases of Multi-Paxos, in a most direct and general language like TLA+ [18], with a complete proof that is mechanically checked, and a general method for doing such specifications and proofs in a more feasible way.

This paper addresses this challenge. We describe a formal specification of Multi-Paxos written in TLA+, and a complete proof written and automatically checked using TLAPS. Building on Lamport, Merz, and Doligez's specification and proof for Basic Paxos, we aim to facilitate the understanding of multi-Paxos and its proof by minimizing the difference from those for Basic Paxos. The key change in the specification is to replace operations involving two numbers with those involving a set of 3-tuples, for each of a set of processes, exactly capturing the minimum conceptual difference between Basic Paxos and Multi-Paxos. However, the proof becomes significantly more difficult because of the handling of sets and tuples in place of two numbers.

This work also aims to show the minimum-change approach as a general way of specifying and verifying other variants of Paxos, and more generally of specifying and verifying other sophisticated algorithms by starting from the basics. We demonstrate this by further showing the extension of the specification and proof of Multi-Paxos to add preemption—letting processes abandon proposals that are already preempted by other proposals [17,29]. We also extended the specification and proof of Basic Paxos with preemption, which is even easier.

Finally, we discuss a general method we attempted to follow to tackle tedious and difficult proof obligations involving sets and tuples, a well-known significant complication in general. For difficult properties involving sets, we use induction and direct the prover to focus on the changes in the set values. For properties involving tuples, we change the ways of accessing and testing the elements to yield significantly reduced proof-checking time. Overall, we were able to keep the specification minimally changed, and keep the proof-checking time to about 2 min or less while the prover checks the proofs for over 900 obligations for both Multi-Paoxs and Multi-Paxos with Preemption.

Our full TLA+ specification and TLAPS-checked proof of Multi-Paxos with Preemption are included in the Appendix of the full version [2].

2 Distributed Consensus and Paxos

A system is a set of processes that can process values individually and communicate with each other by sending and receiving messages. The processes may crash and may later recover. The messages may be delayed indefinitely or lost.

Distributed consensus. The basic consensus problem, called single-value consensus or single-decree consensus, is to ensure that a single value is chosen from among the values proposed by the processes. The safety requirements for basic consensus are [17]:

- Only a value that has been proposed may be chosen.
- Only a single value is chosen.
- A process never learns that a value has been chosen unless it actually has been chosen.

Formally this is defined as

$$Consistency_{basic} \triangleq \forall\, v_1, v_2 \in \mathcal{V} \,:\, \phi(v_1) \wedge \phi(v_2) \Rightarrow v_1 = v_2 \qquad (1)$$

where $\mathcal{V}$ is the set of possible proposed values, and ϕ is a predicate that given a value v evaluates to true iff v was chosen by the algorithm. The specification of ϕ is part of the algorithm.

The more general consensus problem, called multi-value consensus or multi-decree consensus, is to choose a sequence of values, instead of a single value. Here we have

$$Consistency_{multi} \triangleq \forall\, v_1, v_2 \in \mathcal{V}, s \in \mathcal{S} \,:\, \phi(v_1, s) \wedge \phi(v_2, s) \Rightarrow v_1 = v_2 \qquad (2)$$

where $\mathcal{V}$ is as above, $\mathcal{S}$ is a set of *slots* used to index the sequence of decisions, and ϕ is a predicate that given a value v and a slot s evaluates to true iff v was chosen for s by the algorithm.

Basic Paxos and Multi-Paxos. Paxos solves the problem of consensus. Two main roles of the algorithm are performed by two kinds of processes:

- $\mathcal{P}$ is the set of proposers. These processes propose values that can be chosen.
- $\mathcal{A}$ is the set of acceptors. These processes vote for proposed values. A value is chosen when there are enough votes for it.

A set $\mathcal{Q}$ of subsets of the acceptors, i.e., $\mathcal{Q} \subseteq 2^{\mathcal{A}}$, is used as a quorum system. It must satisfy the following properties:

- $\mathcal{Q}$ is a set cover for $\mathcal{A}$, i.e., $\bigcup_{Q \in \mathcal{Q}} Q = \mathcal{A}$.
- Any two quorums overlap, i.e., $\forall Q_1, Q_2 \in \mathcal{Q} \,:\, Q_1 \cap Q_2 \neq \emptyset$.

The most commonly used quorum system $\mathcal{Q}$ takes any majority of acceptors as an element in $\mathcal{Q}$.

Basic Paxos solves single-value consensus. It defines predicate ϕ as

$$\phi(v) \triangleq \exists Q \in \mathcal{Q} : \forall a \in Q : \exists b \in \mathcal{B} : sent(\text{"2b"}, b, v, a) \tag{3}$$

where $\mathcal{B}$ is the set of proposal numbers, also called ballots, which is any set that can be strictly totally ordered. $sent(\text{"2b"}, b, v, a)$ means that a message of type "2b" with ballot b and value v was sent by acceptor a (to some set of processes). An acceptor votes by sending such a message.

Multi-Paxos solves the problem of multi-value consensus. It trivially extends predicate ϕ to decide a value for each slot s in $\mathcal{S}$:

$$\phi(v, s) \triangleq \exists Q \in \mathcal{Q} : \forall a \in Q : \exists b \in \mathcal{B} : sent(\text{"2b"}, b, v, a, s) \tag{4}$$

To satisfy the safety requirements, $\mathcal{S}$ need not have any relations defined on it. In practice, $\mathcal{S}$ is usually the natural numbers.

Putting the actions of the proposer and acceptor together, we see that the algorithm operates in the following two phases.

Phase 1. (a) A proposer selects a proposal number n and sends a *prepare* request with number n to a majority of acceptors.
(b) If an acceptor receives a *prepare* request with number n greater than that of any *prepare* request to which it has already responded, then it responds to the request with a promise not to accept any more proposals numbered less than n and with the highest-numbered proposal (if any) that it has accepted.

Phase 2. (a) If the proposer receives a response to its *prepare* requests (numbered n) from a majority of acceptors, then it sends an *accept* request to each of those acceptors for a proposal numbered n with a value v, where v is the value of the highest-numbered proposal among the responses, or is any value if the responses reported no proposals.
(b) If an acceptor receives an *accept* request for a proposal numbered n, it accepts the proposal unless it has already responded to a *prepare* request having a number greater than n.

A proposer can make multiple proposals, so long as it follows the algorithm for each one. ... It is probably a good idea to abandon a proposal if some proposer has begun trying to issue a high-numbered one. Therefore, if an acceptor ignores a *prepare* or *accept* request because it has already received a *prepare* request with a higher number, then it should probably inform the proposer, who should then abandon its proposal. This is a performance optimization that does not affect correctness.

To learn that a value has been chosen, a learner must find out that a proposal has been accepted by a majority of acceptors. The obvious algorithm is to have each acceptor, whenever it accepts a proposal, respond to all learners, sending them the proposal. ...

Fig. 1. Lamport's description of Basic Paxos in English [17].

Figure 1 shows Lamport's description of Basic Paxos [17]. It uses any majority of acceptors as a quorum. In Phase 2a, it instructs the *accept* request be sent to each acceptor that replied with the proposer's ballot n, but it is sufficient for safety to send *accept* to any subset of $\mathcal{A}$. However, because the proposer is waiting for a quorum, the set of receivers should contain at least one quorum, which again is allowed to be different from the quorum that responded to n.

Multi-Paxos can be built from Basic Paxos by carefully adding slots. In Basic Paxos, acceptors cache the value they have accepted with the highest ballot. With slots, we have a sequence of these values indexed by slot. Therefore,

- In Phase 1b, the acceptor now replies with a mapping in $\mathcal{S} \to \mathcal{B} \times \mathcal{V}$ as opposed to just one pair in $\mathcal{B} \times \mathcal{V}$.
- The same change is needed in Phase 2b.
- Upon receiving such a mapping as a reply, in Phase 2a, a proposer proposes a mapping in $\mathcal{S} \to \mathcal{V}$ instead of just one value in $\mathcal{V}$. In the same way that v was chosen in Basic Paxos, by picking the value backed by the highest received ballot, in Multi-Paxos, the proposer does this calculation for each slot in the received mapping.
- Phase 1a is unchanged.
- Learning, as described in the last part of Fig. 1, is also unchanged, except to consider different slots separately—a process learns that a value is chosen for a slot if a quorum of acceptors accepted it for that slot.

Note that the size of messages replied by the acceptors grows as $\mathcal{S}$ increases, which is a common abstraction before applying optimizations [16,29].

3 Specification of Multi-Paxos

We give a formal specification of Multi-Paxos by minimally extending that of Basic Paxos by Lamport et al. [22].

Variables. The specification of Multi-Paxos has four global variables.

msgs—the set of messages that have been sent. Processes read from or add to this set. This is the same as in the specification of Basic Paxos.

accVoted—per acceptor, a set of triples in $\mathcal{B} \times \mathcal{S} \times \mathcal{V}$, capturing a mapping in $\mathcal{S} \to \mathcal{B} \times \mathcal{V}$, that the acceptor has voted for. This contrasts two numbers per acceptor, in two variables, *maxVBal* and *maxVal*, in Basic Paxos.

accMaxBal—per acceptor, the highest ballot seen by the acceptor. This is named *maxBal* in the specification of Basic Paxos.

proBallot—per proposer, the ballot of the current ballot being run by the proposer. This is not in the specification of Basic Paxos; it is added to support preemption and is only updated during preemption.

Basic Paxos	Multi-Paxos
$Phase1a(b \in \mathcal{B}) \triangleq$ $\land \nexists\, m \in msgs : (m.type = \text{“1a”}) \land$ $(m.bal = b)$ $\land Send([type \mapsto \text{“1a”},$ $bal \mapsto b)$ $\land$UNCHANGED $\langle maxVBal, maxBal,$ $maxVal \rangle$	$Phase1a(p \in \mathcal{P}) \triangleq$ $\land \nexists\, m \in msgs : (m.type = \text{“1a”}) \land$ $(m.bal = proBallot[p])$ $\land Send([type \mapsto \text{“1a”},$ $bal \mapsto proBallot[p], from \mapsto p])$ $\land$UNCHANGED $\langle accVoted, accMaxBal,$ $proBallot \rangle$

Fig. 2. Phase 1a of Basic Paxos and Multi-Paxos

Basic Paxos	Multi-Paxos
$Phase1b(a \in \mathcal{A}) \triangleq$ $\exists\, m \in msgs :$ $\land m.type = \text{“1a”}$ $\land m.bal > maxBal[a]$ $\land Send([type \mapsto \text{“1b”},$ $bal \mapsto m.bal,$ $maxVBal \mapsto maxVBal[a],$ $maxVal \mapsto maxVal[a],$ $acc \mapsto a])$ $\land maxBal' =$ $[maxBal$ EXCEPT $![a] = m.bal]$ $\land$UNCHANGED $\langle maxVBal, maxVal \rangle$	$Phase1b(a \in \mathcal{A}) \triangleq$ $\exists\, m \in msgs :$ $\land m.type = \text{“1a”}$ $\land m.bal > accMaxBal[a]$ $\land Send([type \mapsto \text{“1b”},$ $bal \mapsto m.bal,$ $voted \mapsto accVoted[a],$ $from \mapsto a])$ $\land accMaxBal' =$ $[accMaxBal$ EXCEPT $![a] = m.bal]$ $\land$UNCHANGED $\langle accVoted, proBallot \rangle$

Fig. 3. Phase 1b of Basic Paxos and Multi-Paxos

Note that in *accVoted*, we maintain a set of pairs in $\mathcal{B} \times \mathcal{V}$, not just the pair with the maximum ballot. This is an abstraction that simplifies the specification and allows possible generalization of Paxos [29].

Algorithm Steps. The algorithm consists of repeatedly executing two phases.

Phase 1a. Figure 2 shows the specifications of Phase 1a for Basic Paxos and Multi-Paxos, which are in essence the same. Parameter ballot b, in Basic Paxos is replaced with proposer p executing this phase in Multi-Paxos, to allow extensions such as preemption that need to know the proposer of a ballot; uses of b are changed to $proBallot[p]$; and $from \mapsto p$ is added in *Send*. *Send* is a macro that adds its argument to *msgs*, i.e., $Send(m) \triangleq msgs' = msgs \cup \{m\}$. In this specification, 1a messages do not have a receiver, making them accessible to all processes. However, this is not required. It is enough to send this message to any subset of $\mathcal{A}$ that contains a quorum.

Basic Paxos	Multi-Paxos
$Phase2a(b \in \mathcal{B}) \triangleq$ $\land \nexists m \in msgs : (m.type = \text{"2a"}) \land$ $(m.bal = b)$ $\land \exists v \in \mathcal{V} :$ $\land \exists\, Q \in \mathcal{Q} : \exists S \in \text{SUBSET}\ \{m \in msgs :$ $(m.type = \text{"1b"}) \land$ $(m.bal = b)\} :$ $\land \forall a \in Q : \exists m \in S : m.acc = a$ $\land \lor \forall m \in S : m.maxVBal = -1$ $\lor \exists c \in 0..(b-1) :$ $\land \forall m \in S : m.maxVBal =< c$ $\land \exists m \in S : (m.maxVBal = c)$ $\land m.maxVal = v$ $\land Send([type \mapsto \text{"2a"}, bal \mapsto b, val \mapsto v])$ $\land \text{UNCHANGED}\ \langle maxBal, maxVBal,$ $maxVal \rangle$	$Phase2a(p \in \mathcal{P}) \triangleq$ $\land \nexists m \in msgs : (m.type = \text{"2a"}) \land$ $(m.bal = proBallot[p])$ $\land \exists\, Q \in \mathcal{Q}, S \in \text{SUBSET}\ \{m \in msgs :$ $(m.type = \text{"1b"}) \land$ $(m.bal = proBallot[p])\} :$ $\land \forall a \in Q : \exists m \in S : m.from = a$ $\land Send([type \mapsto \text{"2a"},$ $bal \mapsto proBallot[p],$ $decrees \mapsto ProposeDecrees(\text{UNION}$ $\{m.voted : m \in S\}),$ $from \mapsto p])$ $\land \text{UNCHANGED}\ \langle accMaxBal, accVoted,$ $proBallot \rangle$ $Bmax(T) \triangleq$ $\{[slot \mapsto t.slot, val \mapsto t.val] : t \in$ $\{t \in T : \forall t2 \in T : t2.slot = t.slot$ $\Rightarrow t2.bal =< t.bal\}\}$ $FreeSlots(T) \triangleq$ $\{s \in \mathcal{S} : \nexists t \in T : t.slot = s\}$ $NewProposals(T) \triangleq$ $\text{CHOOSE}\ D \in (\text{SUBSET}\ [slot :$ $FreeSlots(T), val : \mathcal{V}]) \setminus \{\} :$ $\forall d1, d2 \in D : d1.slot = d2.slot \Rightarrow$ $d1 = d2$ $ProposeDecrees(T) \triangleq$ $Bmax(T) \cup NewProposals(T)$

Fig. 4. Phase 2a of Basic Paxos and Multi-Paxos

Phase 1b. Figure 3 shows the specifications of Phase 1b. Parameter acceptor a executes this phase. The only key difference between the specifications is the set $accVoted[a]$ of triples in *Send* of Multi-Paxos vs. the two numbers $maxVBal[a]$ and $maxVal[a]$ in Basic Paxos.

Phase 2a. Figure 4 shows Phase 2a. The key difference is, in *Send*, the bloating of a single value v in $\mathcal{V}$ in Basic Paxos to a set of pairs given by *ProposeDecrees* capturing a mapping in $\mathcal{S} \rightarrow \mathcal{V}$ in Multi-Paxos. The operation of finding the value with the highest ballot in Basic Paxos is performed for each slot by *Bmax* in Multi-Paxos; *Bmax* takes a set T of triples capturing a mapping in $\mathcal{S} \rightarrow \mathcal{B} \times \mathcal{V}$ and returns a set of pairs capturing a mapping in $\mathcal{S} \rightarrow \mathcal{V}$. *NewProposals* generates a set of pairs capturing a mapping in

$\mathcal{S} \to \mathcal{V}$ where values are proposed for slots not in *Bmax*. Note that this is significantly more sophisticated than running Basic Paxos for each slot, because the ballots are shared and changing for all slots, and slots are paired with values dynamically where slots that failed to reach consensus values earlier are also detected and reused.

Phase 2b. Figure 5 shows Phase 2b. In Basic Paxos, the acceptor updates its voted pair *maxVBal*[*a*] and *maxVal*[*a*] upon receipt of a 2a message of the highest ballot. In Multi-Paxos, this is performed for each slot. The acceptor updates *accVoted* to have all decrees in the received 2a message and all previous values in *accVoted* for slots not mentioned in that message.

Basic Paxos	Multi-Paxos
$Phase2b(a \in \mathcal{A}) \triangleq$ $\exists\, m \in msgs$: $\quad \land m.type =$ "2a" $\quad \land m.bal >= maxBal[a]$ $\quad \land Send([type \mapsto$ "2b", $\qquad bal \mapsto m.bal,$ $\qquad val \mapsto m.val,$ $\qquad acc \mapsto a])$ $\quad \land maxBal' =$ $\qquad [maxBal$ EXCEPT $![a] = m.bal]$ $\quad \land maxVBal' =$ $\qquad [maxBal$ EXCEPT $![a] = m.bal]$ $\quad \land maxVal' =$ $\qquad [maxVal$ EXCEPT $![a] = m.val]$	$Phase2b(a \in \mathcal{A}) \triangleq$ $\exists\, m \in msgs$: $\quad \land m.type =$ "2a" $\quad \land m.bal >= accMaxBal[a]$ $\quad \land Send([type \mapsto$ "2b", $\qquad bal \mapsto m.bal,$ $\qquad decrees \mapsto m.decrees,$ $\qquad from \mapsto a)$ $\quad \land accMaxBal' =$ $\qquad [accMaxBal$ EXCEPT $![a] = m.bal]$ $\quad \land accVoted' = [accVoted$ EXCEPT $![a] =$ $\qquad \cup\{[bal \mapsto m.bal, slot \mapsto d.slot,$ $\qquad\quad val \mapsto d.val] : d \in m.decrees\}]$ $\qquad \cup\{e \in accVoted[a]$: $\qquad\quad \nexists\, r \in m.decrees : e.slot = r.slot\}$ $\quad \land$UNCHANGED $\langle proBallot \rangle$

Fig. 5. Phase 2b of Basic Paxos and Multi-Paxos

Complete Algorithm Specification. To complete the algorithm specification, we define *vars*, *Init*, *Next*, and *Spec*, typical TLA+ macro names for the set of variables, the initial state, possible actions leading to the next state, and the system specification, respectively:

$$
\begin{aligned}
vars &\triangleq \langle msgs, accVoted, accMaxBal, proBallot \rangle \\
Init &\triangleq msgs = \{\} \land accVoted = [a \in \mathcal{A} \mapsto \{\}] \land \\
&\qquad accMaxBal = [a \in \mathcal{A} \mapsto -1] \land proBallot = [p \in \mathcal{P} \mapsto 0] \\
Next &\triangleq \lor \exists\, p \in \mathcal{P} : Phase1a(p) \lor Phase2a(p) \\
&\qquad \lor \exists\, a \in \mathcal{A} : Phase1b(a) \lor Phase2b(a) \\
Spec &\triangleq Init \land \Box[Next]_{vars}
\end{aligned}
\tag{5}
$$

4 Verification of Multi-Paxos

We first define the auxiliary predicates and invariants used, by extending those for the proof of Basic Paxos with slots, and then describe our proof strategy which proves *Consistency* of Multi-Paxos.

Auxiliary Predicates. These predicates are used throughout the proof. We define the predicate ϕ in (4) by $\phi(v, s) \equiv Chosen(v, s)$, where:

$$\begin{aligned}
&VotedForIn(a \in \mathcal{A}, v \in \mathcal{V}, b \in \mathcal{B}, s \in \mathcal{S}) \triangleq \\
&\quad \exists\, m \in msgs : \\
&\quad\quad m.type = \text{“2b”} \wedge m.bal = b \wedge m.from = a \wedge \\
&\quad\quad \exists\, d \in m.decrees : d.slot = s \wedge d.val = v \\
&ChosenIn(v \in \mathcal{V}, b \in \mathcal{B}, s \in \mathcal{S}) \triangleq \\
&\quad \exists\, Q \in \mathcal{Q} : \forall\, a \in Q : VotedForIn(a, v, b, s) \\
&Chosen(v \in \mathcal{V}, s \in \mathcal{S}) \triangleq \\
&\quad \exists\, b \in \mathcal{B} : ChosenIn(v, b, s)
\end{aligned} \tag{6}$$

Predicate $MaxVotedBallotInSlot(D \in \text{SUBSET}\,[slot : \mathcal{S}, bal : \mathcal{B}], s \in \mathcal{S})$ returns the highest ballot among all pairs in set D with slot s.

$$\begin{aligned}
&Maximum(B) \triangleq \\
&\quad \text{CHOOSE } b \in B : \forall\, b2 \in B : b >= b2 \\
&MaxVotedBallotInSlot(D \in \text{SUBSET}\,[slot : \mathcal{S}, bal : \mathcal{B}], s \in \mathcal{S}) \triangleq \\
&\quad \text{LET } B \triangleq \{d.bal : d \in \{d \in D : d.slot = s\}\} \\
&\quad \text{IN } \quad \text{IF } \{d \in D : d.slot = s\} = \{\} \text{ THEN } -1 \\
&\quad\quad\quad\quad\quad\quad\quad\quad\quad\quad\quad\quad\quad\quad \text{ELSE } Maximum(B)
\end{aligned} \tag{7}$$

Type Invariants. Type invariants are captured by *TypeOK*.

$$\begin{aligned}
&Messages \triangleq \\
&\quad \cup\, [type : \{\text{“1a”}\}, bal : \mathcal{B}, from : \mathcal{P}] \\
&\quad \cup\, [type : \{\text{“1b”}\}, bal : \mathcal{B}, voted : \text{SUBSET}\,[bal : \mathcal{B}, slot : \mathcal{S}, val : \mathcal{V}], from : \mathcal{A}] \\
&\quad \cup\, [type : \{\text{“2a”}\}, bal : \mathcal{B}, decrees : \text{SUBSET}\,[slot : \mathcal{S}, val : \mathcal{V}], from : \mathcal{P}] \\
&\quad \cup\, [type : \{\text{“2b”}\}, bal : \mathcal{B}, from : \mathcal{A}, decrees : \text{SUBSET}\,[slot : \mathcal{S}, val : \mathcal{V}]] \\
&\quad \cup\, [type : \{\text{“preempt”}\}, bal : \mathcal{B}, to : \mathcal{P}, maxBal : \mathcal{B}] \\
&TypeOK \triangleq \\
&\quad \wedge\, msgs \in \text{SUBSET } Messages \\
&\quad \wedge\, accVoted \in [\mathcal{A} \rightarrow \text{SUBSET}\,[bal : \mathcal{B}, slot : \mathcal{S}, val : \mathcal{V}]] \\
&\quad \wedge\, accMaxBal \in [\mathcal{A} \rightarrow \mathcal{B} \cup \{-1\}] \\
&\quad \wedge\, proBallot \in [\mathcal{P} \rightarrow \mathcal{B}] \\
&\quad \wedge\, \forall\, a \in \mathcal{A} : \forall\, t \in accVoted[a] : accMaxBal[a] >= t.bal
\end{aligned} \tag{8}$$

Invariants About Messages. The following invariant is for 1b messages. The first conjunct establishes that the ballot is at most the highest ballot seen by the sending acceptor. The second conjunct states that the decrees contained within the message body have been voted for by the sending acceptor. The last conjunct asserts that for each slot, relative to the timeline established by ballots, since the last time this acceptor voted in the slot to the time this message was sent, no voting occurred on the slot by this acceptor.

$$
\begin{aligned}
&\mathit{MsgInv1b} \triangleq \\
&\quad \forall\, m \in \mathit{msgs} : (m.\mathit{type} = \text{"1b"}) \Rightarrow \\
&\qquad \land\, m.\mathit{bal} =< \mathit{accMaxBal}[m.\mathit{from}] \\
&\qquad \land\, \forall\, t \in m.\mathit{voted} : \mathit{VotedForIn}(m.\mathit{from}, t.\mathit{val}, t.\mathit{bal}, t.\mathit{slot}) \\
&\qquad \land\, \forall\, b2 \in \mathcal{B}, s \in \mathcal{S}, v \in \mathcal{V} : b2 \in (\mathit{MaxVotedBallotInSlot}(m.\mathit{voted}, s), m.\mathit{bal}) \\
&\qquad\quad \Rightarrow \neg\, \mathit{VotedForIn}(m.\mathit{from}, v, b2, s)
\end{aligned} \tag{9}
$$

Proof Strategy. The proof is developed following a standard hierarchical structure and uses proof by induction and contradiction.

$$
\begin{aligned}
&\mathit{MsgInv} \triangleq \mathit{MsgInv1b} \land \mathit{MsgInv2a} \land \mathit{MsgInv2b} \\
&\mathit{Inv} \triangleq \mathit{TypeOK} \land \mathit{AccInv} \land \mathit{MsgInv} \\
&\mathit{Consistency} \triangleq \forall\, v_1, v_2 \in \mathcal{V}, s \in \mathcal{S} : \mathit{Chosen}(v_1, s) \land \mathit{Chosen}(v_2, s) \Rightarrow v_1 = v_2 \\
&\text{THEOREM } \mathit{Consistent} \triangleq \mathit{Spec} \Rightarrow \Box\, \mathit{Consistency}
\end{aligned} \tag{10}
$$

where *AccInv* is an invariant about acceptors, and *MsgInv*2*a* and *MsgInv*2*b* are invariants for 2a and 2b messages, respectively, and these three invariants are defined in the Appendix of the full version [2].

The main theorem to prove is *Consistent* as defined in Eq. (10). For this, we define *Inv* and first prove $\mathit{Inv} \Rightarrow \mathit{Consistency}$. Then, we prove $\mathit{Spec} \Rightarrow \Box \mathit{Inv}$ which by temporal logic, concludes $\mathit{Spec} \Rightarrow \Box \mathit{Consistency}$. To prove $\mathit{Spec} \Rightarrow \Box \mathit{Inv}$, we employ a systematic proof strategy that works very well for algorithms described in the event driven paradigm, including message-passing distributed algorithms. We demonstrate the strategy for some invariants in *Inv*.

First, consider invariant *TypeOK*. The goal is $\mathit{Spec} \Rightarrow \Box\, \mathit{TypeOK}$. Recall $\mathit{Spec} \triangleq \mathit{Init} \land \Box[\mathit{Next}]_{\mathit{vars}}$. The induction basis, $\mathit{Init} \Rightarrow \mathit{TypeOK}$, is trivial, and TLAPS handles it automatically. Next, we want to prove $\mathit{TypeOK} \land [\mathit{Next}]_{\mathit{vars}} \Rightarrow \mathit{TypeOK}'$, where the left side is the induction hypothesis, and right side is the goal to be proved. $[\mathit{Next}]_{\mathit{vars}}$ is a disjunction of phases, as for any algorithm, and TypeOK' is a conjunction of smaller invariants, as for many invariants. Now, the basis can be stripped down to each disjunct separately, and each smaller goal needs to be proved from all smaller disjuncts. This process is mechanical, and TLAPS provides a feature for precisely this expansion into smaller proof obligations. This breakdown is the first step in our proof strategy. For *TypeOK*, this expands to 5 smaller assertions; with 5 phases in *Next*, we obtain 25 small proofs done by the prover with no manual intervention.

MsgInv and *AccInv* are more involved. We proceed like we did for *TypeOK* and create a proof tree, each branch of which aims to prove an invariant for some disjunct in *Next*. To explain the rest of our strategy, we show one combination: *MsgInv* and *Phase*1*b*. Equation (11) gives the skeleton of the proof; the full proof is in the Appendix of the full version [2]. Goal for the prover is step $\langle 4 \rangle 2$ which states that *MsgInv*′ holds if an acceptor, a, executes *Phase*1*b*. m is any message in the new set of messages, $msgs'$. Substeps $\langle 5 \rangle 1, 2, 3$ focus on *MsgInv*1*b*, *MsgInv*2*a*, *MsgInv*2*b*, respectively.

*Phase*1*b* generates a 1*b* message. $\langle 5 \rangle 3$ is easy for the prover as it argues about 2*b* messages. Intuitively, $\langle 5 \rangle 2$ should be easy for the prover too since, like $\langle 5 \rangle 3$, it involves a message type that is not what *Phase*1*b* generates. However, this is not the case because of predicate *SafeAt*, which is used in *MsgInv*2*a* and expresses whether it is safe to accept a given value for a given ballot for a given slot (the formal definition is in the Appendix of the full version [2]). At this point the prover needs a continuity lemma.

We define a *continuity lemma* as a lemma which asserts that a predicate continues to hold (or not hold) as the system goes from one state to the next in a single step. For example, the continuity lemma for *SafeAt* states that *SafeAt* continues to hold for any disjunct in *Next*, which includes *Phase*1*b*(a). The characteristic property of such lemmas is their reuse. In our proof of Multi-Paxos, we defined 5 continuity lemmas which are asserted in 24 places.

Lastly, we need to prove $\langle 5 \rangle 1$. Since $\langle 5 \rangle 1$ asserts about 1*b* messages and *Phase*1*b* generates such messages, the proof is more complicated and the prover needs manual intervention. Here we split the set of messages in the new state into two: $\langle 6 \rangle 1$ for the old messages, and $\langle 6 \rangle 2$ for the increment created in this step. For the old messages, we need continuity lemmas. The most challenging is the increment. To deal with the increment, we focus on the cause of the increment—the definition of *Phase*1*b*—and treat each goal conjunct separately in $\langle 7 \rangle 1, 2, 3$. The prover proves $\langle 7 \rangle 1$ by just the definition of *Phase*1*b* and the fact that it is the increment. For $\langle 7 \rangle 2$, along with the definition of *Phase*1*b*, the prover also needs a continuity lemma for *VotedForIn*. $\langle 7 \rangle 3$ required, along with the definition of *Phase*1*b* and continuity lemmas, some problem-specific manual intervention. In this case, we helped the prover understand the change in limits of the set $MaxVotedBallotInSlot(m.voted, s) + 1..m.bal - 1$.

$$
\begin{array}{l}
\langle 4\rangle 2.\text{ASSUME NEW } a \in \mathcal{A}, \text{NEW } m \in \mathit{msgs}', \mathit{Phase1b}(a) \text{ PROVE } \mathit{MsgInv}' \\
\quad \langle 5\rangle 1.((m.\mathit{type} = \text{"1b"}) \Rightarrow \ (*\ \mathit{MsgInv1b}'\ *) \\
\qquad \wedge\, m.\mathit{bal} \leq \mathit{acceptorMaxBal}[m.\mathit{from}] \\
\qquad \wedge\, \forall\, r \in m.\mathit{voted} : \mathit{VotedForIn}(m.\mathit{from}, r.\mathit{val}, r.\mathit{bal}, r.\mathit{slot}) \\
\qquad \wedge\, \forall\, s \in \mathcal{S}, v \in \mathcal{V}, c \in \mathcal{B} : \\
\qquad\quad c \in \mathit{MaxVotedBallotInSlot}(m.\mathit{voted}, s) + 1..m.\mathit{bal} - 1 \Rightarrow \\
\qquad\quad \neg\, \mathit{VotedForIn}(m.\mathit{from}, v, c, s))' \\
\qquad\quad \langle 6\rangle 1.\text{CASE } m \in \mathit{msgs}\ \ldots \\
\qquad\quad \langle 6\rangle 2.\text{CASE } m \in \mathit{msgs}' \setminus \mathit{msgs} \\
\qquad\qquad \langle 7\rangle 1.(m.\mathit{bal} \leq \mathit{acceptorMaxBal}[m.\mathit{from}])' \\
\qquad\qquad \langle 7\rangle 2.(\forall\, r \in m.\mathit{voted} : \mathit{VotedForIn}(m.\mathit{from}, r.\mathit{val}, r.\mathit{bal}, r.\mathit{slot}))'\ \ldots \\
\qquad\qquad \langle 7\rangle 3.(\forall\, s \in \mathcal{S}, v \in \mathcal{V}, c \in \mathcal{B} : \\
\qquad\qquad\quad c \in \mathit{MaxVotedBallotInSlot}(m.\mathit{voted}, s) + 1..m.\mathit{bal} - 1 \Rightarrow \\
\qquad\qquad\quad \neg\, \mathit{VotedForIn}(m.\mathit{from}, v, c, s))'\ \ldots \\
\quad \langle 5\rangle 2.((m.\mathit{type} = \text{"2a"}) \Rightarrow \ (*\ \mathit{MsgInv2a}'\ *) \\
\qquad \wedge\, \forall\, d \in m.\mathit{decrees} : \mathit{SafeAt}(d.\mathit{val}, m.\mathit{bal}, d.\mathit{slot}) \\
\qquad \wedge\, \forall\, d1, d2 \in m.\mathit{decrees} : d1.\mathit{slot} = d2.\mathit{slot} \Rightarrow d1 = d2 \\
\qquad \wedge\, \forall\, \mathit{ma} \in \mathit{msgs} : (\mathit{ma}.\mathit{type} = \text{"2a"}) \wedge (\mathit{ma}.\mathit{bal} = m.\mathit{bal}) \Rightarrow (\mathit{ma} = m))'\ \ldots \\
\quad \langle 5\rangle 3.((m.\mathit{type} = \text{"2b"}) \Rightarrow \ (*\ \mathit{MsgInv2b}'\ *) \\
\qquad \wedge\, \exists\, \mathit{ma} \in \mathit{msgs} : \mathit{ma}.\mathit{type} = \text{"2a"} \wedge \mathit{ma}.\mathit{bal} = m.\mathit{bal} \wedge \mathit{ma}.\mathit{decrees} = m.\mathit{decrees} \\
\qquad \wedge\, m.\mathit{bal} \leq \mathit{acceptorMaxBal}[m.\mathit{from}])'
\end{array}
\tag{11}
$$

Induction for properties over sets, and ways of accessing elements of tuples. After developing the proof using the above strategy, we were still faced with certain assertions which were difficult to prove. One of the main difficulties lay in proving properties about tuples and sets of tuples for each of a set of processes in Multi-Paxos, as opposed to scalars for each of a set of processes in Basic Paxos. It may appear that, in many places, this requires simply adding an extra parameter for the slot, but the proof became significantly more difficult: even in places where an explicit inductive proof is not needed, auxiliary facts had to be added to help TLAPS succeed or proceed faster.

For example, adding slots to the proof of THEOREM *Consistent* for Basic Paxos caused the prover to take about 90 s to check it. To aid the proof, we added $\exists\, a \in \mathcal{A} : \mathit{VotedForIn}(a, v_1, b_1, s) \wedge \mathit{VotedForIn}(a, v_2, b_1, s)$ as an intermediary fact derivable from $\mathit{ChosenIn}(v_1, b_1, s) \wedge \mathit{ChosenIn}(v_2, b_2, s) \wedge b_1 = b_2$. Following this, the prover asserted the conclusion $v_1 = v_2$ in a few milliseconds.

Tuples have only a fixed number of components and therefore do not require separate inductive proofs, but they often turn out to be tricky and require special care in choosing the ways to access and test their elements, to reduce TLAPS's proof-checking time. For example, consider the definition of *VotedForIn* in Eq. (6). Originally a test $[\mathit{slot} \mapsto s, \mathit{val} \mapsto v] \in m.\mathit{decrees}$ was written, because it was natural, but it had to be changed to $\exists\, d \in m.\mathit{decrees} : d.\mathit{slot} = s \wedge d.\mathit{val} = v$, because the prover found the latter more helpful. With the original version, the proof did not carry through after 1 or 2 min. After the change, the proof

$$
\begin{aligned}
&NewBallot(bb \in \mathcal{B}) \triangleq \text{CHOOSE } b \in \mathcal{B} : \\
&\qquad \land b > bb \\
&\qquad \land \nexists\, m \in msgs : m.type = \text{"1a"} \land m.bal = b \\
&Preempt(p \in \mathcal{P}) \triangleq \exists\, m \in msgs : \\
&\qquad \land m.type = \text{"preempt"} \\
&\qquad \land m.to = p \\
&\qquad \land m.bal > proBallot[p] \\
&\qquad \land proBallot' = [proBallot \text{ EXCEPT } ![p] = NewBallot(m.bal)] \\
&\qquad \land \text{UNCHANGED } \langle msgs, accVoted, accMaxBal \rangle
\end{aligned}
$$

Phase 1b without Preemption	Phase 1b with Preemption
$Phase1b(a \in \mathcal{A}) \triangleq$ $\exists\, m \in msgs$: $\land m.type =$ "1a" $\land m.bal > accMaxBal[a]$ $\land Send([type \mapsto$ "1b", $bal \mapsto m.bal,$ $voted \mapsto accVoted[a],$ $from \mapsto a])$ $\land accMaxBal' =$ $[accMaxBal$ EXCEPT $![a] = m.bal]$ $\land$UNCHANGED $\langle accVoted, proBallot\rangle$	$Phase1b(a \in \mathcal{A}) \triangleq$ $\exists\, m \in msgs$: $\land m.type =$ "1a" $\land$IF $m.bal > accMaxBal[a]$ THEN $\land Send([type \mapsto$ "1b", $bal \mapsto m.bal,$ $voted \mapsto accVoted[a],$ $from \mapsto a])$ $\land accMaxBal' =$ $[accMaxBal$ EXCEPT $![a] = m.bal]$ $\land$UNCHANGED $\langle accVoted, proBallot\rangle$ ELSE $\land Send([type \mapsto$ "preempt", $to \mapsto m.from,$ $bal \mapsto acceptorMaxBal[a]])$ $\land$UNCHANGED $\langle accVoted, accMaxBal,$ $proBallot\rangle$

Fig. 6. Extension of Multi-Paxos to Multi-Paxos with Preemption

proceeded quickly. One minute of waiting for such simple, small tests felt very long, making it uncertain whether the proof would carry through, even if it would in a longer time. With dozens of places like this, one also cannot afford to wait for this long at each such place.

5 Multi-Paxos with Preemption

Preemption is described informally in Lamport's description of Basic Paxos in Fig. 1, in the paragraph about abandoning a proposal. Preemption has an acceptor reply to a proposer, in both Phases 1b and 2b, if the proposer's ballot is stale i.e., the acceptor has seen a higher ballot than the one just received from the proposer. This reply is a hint to the proposer to increase its ballot.

To specify preemption, each of Phases 1b and 2b adds a new case for when the acceptor receives a lower ballot than some ballot it has seen before. We also define predicate *Preempt* that specifies how proposers update *proBallot* upon receiving a preemption message. Figure 6 shows Phase 1b with and without the modifications to add preemption. Modifications to Phase 2b are similar and are omitted for brevity.

Preemption adds a new phase in the variable *Next*, modifies definitions of existing phases, and adds a new type of message. This meant increasing the width of the proof tree for the new phase. This new branch of the proof was proven by asserting continuity lemmas already established earlier. The whole task of adding the new specification and proof took less than an hour.

6 Results of TLAPS-checked Proof

Figure 7 summarizes the results from our specification and proof.

The specification size grew by only 18 lines (16 %), from 115 lines for Basic Paxos to 133 lines for Multi-Paxos; another 23 lines are added for Preemption.

The proof size increased significantly by 763 lines (180 %), from 423 for Basic Paxos to 1106 for Multi-Paxos, due to the complex interaction between slots and ballots; only 30 more lines are added for Preemption, thanks to the reuse of all lemmas, especially continuity lemmas.

The maximum level of proof tree nodes increased from 7 to 11 going from Basic Paxos to Multi-Paxos but remained 11 after adding Preemption; this contrast is even stronger for the maximum degree of proof tree nodes, consistent with challenge of going to Multi-Paxos.

The increase in number of lemmas is due to the change from *Maximum* in Basic Paxos to *MaxVotedBallotInSlot* in Multi-Paxos, defined in Eq. (7). Five lemmas were needed for this predicate alone to aid the prover, as we moved from scalars to a set of tuples for each acceptor.

No proof by induction on set increment is used for Basic Paxos. Four such proofs are used for Multi-Paxos and for Multi-Paxos with Preemption.

Proof by contradiction is used once in the proof of Basic Paxos, and we extended it with slots in the proof of Multi-Paxos and Multi-Paxos with Premption.

The number of proof obligations to the prover increased most significantly, by 679 (284 %), from 239 for Basic Paxos to 918 for Multi-Paxos. Only another 41 proof obligations were added for Multi-Paxos with Preemption.

The proof-checking time increased significantly, by 104 s, from 24 for Basic Paxos to 128 for Multi-Paxos, despite our continuous efforts to help the prover reduce it, because of the greatly increased size and complexity of the inductions used, leading to significantly more obligations to the prover. Going to Multi-Paxos with Preemption, however, the proof-checking time decreased by about 25 %. This was initially surprising, but our understanding of Paxos and experience with proofs help support it: (1) adding the preemption cases to the original Phases 1b and 2b helps make the obligations in these cases more specialized and the remaining steps for proving consistency (which carry on longer in these cases before) easier; (2) adding preemption with Phases 1a and 2a increases the number of proof obligations, but the new obligations are easy, because they let the proposer start over (and thus there are no remaining steps in these cases). We are investigating further to confirm these.

Metric	Basic Paxos	Multi-Paxos	Multi-Paxos w/ Preemption
Size of specification (lines)	115	133	158
Size of proof (lines)	423	1106	1136
Max level of proof tree nodes	7	11	11
Max degree of proof tree nodes	3	17	17
# lemmas	4	11	12
# continuity lemmas	1	5	6
# uses of continuity lemmas	8	27	29
# proofs by induction on set increment	0	4	4
# proofs by contradiction	1	1	1
# obligations in TLAPS	239	918	959
Time to check by TLAPS (seconds)	24	128	94

Fig. 7. Summary of results. An obligation is a condition that TLAPS checks. The time to check is on an Intel i7-4720HQ 2.6 GHz CPU with 16 GB of memory, running Windows 10 and TLAPS version 1.5.2.

7 Related Work and Conclusion

We discuss closest related results on verification of Paxos, categorized by the verification technique.

Model checking. Model checking automatically explores the state space of systems [6]. Lamport wrote TLA+ specifications for Basic Paxos and its variants, e.g., Fast Paxos [19], and checked them using the TLA+ model checker TLC [25], but he has not done this for Multi-Paxos or its variants; a number of MS students at our university have also done this in course projects, including for Multi-Paxos. Delano et al. [8] modeled Basic Paxos in Promela and checked it using the Spin model checker [31]. To reduce the state space, they use counting guards to track majority, reset local variables after state operations, and use sorted *send* instead of FIFO *send* (with random *receive*, to model non-FIFO channels). They checked Basic Paxos for pairs of numbers of proposers and acceptors up to (2,8), (3,5), (4,4), (5,3), and (8,2). Yabandeh et al. [35] checked a C++ implementation of Basic Paxos using CrystalBall, a tool built on Mace [15], which includes a model checker. Yang et al. [36] used their model checker MoDist to check a Multi-Paxos-based service system developed by a Microsoft product team [24]. With dynamic partial-order reduction [10], they found 13 bugs including 2 bugs in the Paxos implementation, with as few as 3 replicas and a few slots. In all cases, existing work in model checking either does not check Multi-Paxos or can check it for only a very small number of slots and processes.

Deductive verification. Kellomaki [14] formally specified and verified Basic Paxos using PVS [32]. Charron-Bost and Schiper [5] expressed Basic Paxos in the Heard-Of model, and Charron-Bost and Merz [4] verified it formally using Isabelle/HOL [33]. Drăgoi et al. [9] specified and verified a version of Basic Paxos in PSync, which is based on the Heard-Of model, so the specification and proof are similar to [4,5]. Lamport et al. [22] give a formal specification of Basic Paxos in TLA+ and a TLAPS-checked proof of its correctness. Lamport [20] wrote a TLA+ specification of Byzantine Paxos, a variant of Basic Paxos that tolerates arbitrary failures, and a TLAPS-checked proof that it refines Basic Paxos. With IronFleet, Hawblitzel et al. [11] verified a state machine replication system that uses Multi-Paxos at its core. Their specification mimics TLA+ models but is written in Dafny [23], which has no direct concurrency support but has more automated proof support than TLAPS. This work is superior to its peers by proving not only safety but also liveness properties. Schiper et al. [30] used EventML [28] to specify Multi-Paxos and used NuPRL [7] to verify safety. Using the Verdi framework, Wilcox et al. [34] expressed Raft [27], an algorithm similar to Multi-Paxos, in OCAML and verified it using Coq [12]. All these works either do not handle Multi-Paxos or handle it using more restricted or less direct language models than TLA+, some mixed in large systems, making the essence of the algorithm's proof harder to find and understand.

In contrast, our work is the first to specify the exact phases of Multi-Paxos in a most direct and general language model, TLA+, with a complete correctness proof automatically checked using TLAPS. Building on Lamport, Merz, and Doligez's specification and proof for Basic Paxos [22], we aim to facilitate the understanding of Multi-Paxos and its proof by minimizing the difference from those for basic Paxos. We also show this as a general way for specifying and proving variants of Multi-Paxos, by doing so for Multi-Paxos extended with preemption. We also discuss the significantly more complex but necessary subproofs by induction. Future work may automate inductive proofs and support the verification of variants that improve and extend Multi-Paxos, by extending specifications of variants of Paxos, e.g., Fast Paxos [19] and Byzantine Paxos [20], to Multi-Paxos and verifying these variants of Multi-Paxos as well as Raft [27].

References

1. Burrows, M.: The Chubby lock service for loosely-coupled distributed systems. In: Proceedings of the 7th USENIX Symposium on Operating Systems Design and Implementation, pp. 335–350. USENIX Association (2006)
2. Chand, S., Liu, Y.A., Stoller, S.D.: Formal Verification of Multi-Paxos for Distributed Consensus. arXiv preprint arXiv:1606.01387 (2016)
3. Chandra, T.D., Griesemer, R., Redstone, J.: Paxos made live–An engineering perspective. In: Proceedings of the 26th Annual ACM Symposium on Principles of Distributed Computing, pp. 398–407 (2007)
4. Charron-Bost, B., Merz, S.: Formal verification of a consensus algorithm in the Heard-Of model. Int. J. Softw. Inform. **3**(2–3), 273–303 (2009)
5. Charron-Bost, B., Schiper, A.: The Heard-Of model: computing in distributed systems with benign faults. Distrib. Comput. **22**(1), 49–71 (2009)
6. Clarke Jr., E.M., Grumberg, O., Peled, D.A.: Model Checking. MIT Press, Cambridge (1999)

7. Constable, R.L., Allen, S.F., Bromley, H.M., Cleaveland, W.R., Cremer, J.F., Harper, R.W., Howe, D.J., Knoblock, T.B., Mendler, N.P., Panangaden, P., Sasaki, J.T., Smith, S.F.: Implementing Mathematics with the Nuprl Proof Development System. Prentice-Hall, Upper Saddle River (1986)
8. Delzanno, G., Tatarek, M., Traverso, R.: Model checking Paxos in Spin. In: Proceedings of the 5th International Symposium on Games, Automata, Logics and Formal Verification, pp. 131–146 (2014)
9. Drăgoi, C., Henzinger, T.A., Zufferey, D.: Psync: A partially synchronous language for fault-tolerant distributed algorithms. In: Proceedings of the 43rd Annual ACM SIGPLAN-SIGACT Symposium on Principles of Programming Languages, pp. 400–415 (2016)
10. Flanagan, C., Godefroid, P.: Dynamic partial-order reduction for model checking software. In: Proceedings of the 32nd ACM SIGPLAN-SIGACT Symposium on Principles of Programming Languages, pp. 110–121 (2005)
11. Hawblitzel, C., Howell, J., Kapritsos, M., Lorch, J.R., Parno, B., Roberts, M.L., Setty, S., Zill, B.: IronFleet: proving practical distributed systems correct. In: Proceedings of the 25th Symposium on Operating Systems Principles, pp. 1–17 (2015)
12. INRIA: The Coq Proof Assistant. http://coq.inria.fr/. (Last released January 2016)
13. Isard, M.: Autopilot: Automatic data center management. ACM SIGOPS Oper. Syst. Rev. **41**(2), 60–67 (2007)
14. Kellomäki, P.: An annotated specification of the consensus protocol of Paxos using superposition in PVS. Report 36, Institute of Software Systems, Tampere University of Technology (2004)
15. Killian, C.E., Anderson, J.W., Braud, R., Jhala, R., Vahdat, A.M.: Mace: language support for building distributed systems. In: Proceedings of the 28th ACM SIGPLAN Conference on Programming Language Design and Implementation, pp. 179–188 (2007)
16. Lamport, L.: The part-time parliament. ACM Trans. Comput. Syst. **16**(2), 133–169 (1998)
17. Lamport, L.: Paxos made simple. SIGACT News (Distrib. Comput. Column) **32**(4), 51–58 (2001)
18. Lamport, L.: Specifying Systems: The TLA+ Language and Tools for Hardware and Software Engineers. Addison-Wesley, Amsterdam (2002)
19. Lamport, L.: Fast Paxos. Distrib. Comput. **19**(2), 79–103 (2006). http://research.microsoft.com/pubs/64624/tr-2005-112.pdf
20. Lamport, L.: Byzantizing paxos by refinement. In: Peleg, D. (ed.) DISC 2011. LNCS, vol. 6950, pp. 211–224. Springer, Heidelberg (2011). doi:10.1007/978-3-642-24100-0_22
21. Lamport, L.: My writings. http://research.microsoft.com/en-us/um/people/lamport/pubs/pubs.html#lamport-paxos. Accessed 24 Jan 2016. Lamport's history of paper [16]
22. Lamport, L., Merz, S., Doligez, D.: A TLA spefication of the Paxos Consensus algorithm described in Paxos Made Simple and a TLAPS-checked proof of its correctness. file /tlapm/examples/paxos/Paxos.tla in TLAPS distribution, November 2012. http://tla.msr-inria.inria.fr/tlaps/dist/current/tlaps-1.4.3.tar.gz. Accessed 28 Nov 2014
23. Leino, K.R.M.: Dafny: an automatic program verifier for functional correctness. In: Clarke, E.M., Voronkov, A. (eds.) LPAR 2010. LNCS (LNAI), vol. 6355, pp. 348–370. Springer, Heidelberg (2010). doi:10.1007/978-3-642-17511-4_20

24. Liu, X., Guo, Z., Wang, X., Chen, F., Lian, X., Tang, J., Wu, M., Kaashoek, M.F., Zhang, Z.: D3S: debugging deployed distributed systems. In: Proceedings of the 5th USENIX Symposium on Networked Systems Design and Implementation, pp. 423–437. USENIX Association (2008)
25. Microsoft Research: The TLA Toolbox. http://research.microsoft.com/en-us/um/people/lamport/tla/toolbox.html. Accessed 4 Jan 2016
26. Microsoft Research-Inria Joint Center: TLA+ Proof System (TLAPS). http://tla.msr-inria.inria.fr/tlaps/. (Last released June 2015)
27. Ongaro, D., Ousterhout, J.: In search of an understandable consensus algorithm. In: 2014 USENIX Annual Technical Conference (USENIX ATC 14), pp. 305–319. USENIX Association (2014). http://www.usenix.org/conference/atc14/technical-sessions/presentation/ongaro
28. PRL Project: EventML. http://www.nuprl.org/software/#WhatisEventML. Accessed 21 Sep 2012
29. van Renesse, R., Altinbuken, D.: Paxos made moderately complex. ACM Comput. Surv. **47**(3), 1–36 (2015)
30. Schiper, N., Rahli, V., van Renesse, R., Bickford, M., Constable, R.L.: Developing correctly replicated databases using formal tools. In: Proceedings of the 44th Annual IEEE/IFIP International Conference on Dependable Systems and Networks, pp. 395–406. IEEE CS Press (2014)
31. Spin Community: Verifying Multi-threaded Software with Spin. http://spinroot.com/spin/whatispin.html. (Last released January 1, 2016)
32. SRI: PVS Specification and Verification System. http://pvs.csl.sri.com/. (Last released February 11, 2013)
33. University of Cambridge: Isabelle (a generic proof assistant). http://isabelle.in.tum.de/. (Last released May 25, 2015)
34. Wilcox, J.R., Woos, D., Panchekha, P., Tatlock, Z., Wang, X., Ernst, M.D., Anderson, T.: Verdi: A framework for implementing and formally verifying distributed systems. In: Proceedings of the 36th ACM SIGPLAN Conference on Programming Language Design and Implementation, pp. 357–368 (2015)
35. Yabandeh, M., Knezevic, N., Kostic, D., Kuncak, V.: CrystalBall: predicting and preventing inconsistencies in deployed distributed systems. In: Proceedings of the 6th USENIX Symposium on Networked Systems Design and Implementation, pp. 229–244. USENIX Association (2009)
36. Yang, J., Chen, T., Wu, M., Xu, Z., Liu, X., Lin, H., Yang, M., Long, F., Zhang, L., Zhou, L.: MoDist: transparent model checking of unmodified distributed systems. In: Proceedings of the 6th USENIX Symposium on Networked Systems Design and Implementation, pp. 213–228. USENIX Association (2009)

Validated Simulation-Based Verification of Delayed Differential Dynamics

Mingshuai Chen[1], Martin Fränzle[2], Yangjia Li[1(✉)], Peter N. Mosaad[2], and Naijun Zhan[1]

[1] State Key Laboratory of Computer Science, Institute of Software, CAS, Beijing, China
{chenms,yangjia,znj}@ios.ac.cn

[2] Department of Computing Science, C. v. Ossietzky Universität Oldenburg, Oldenburg, Germany
{fraenzle,peter.nazier.mosaad}@informatik.uni-oldenburg.de

Abstract. Verification by simulation, based on covering the set of time-bounded trajectories of a dynamical system evolving from the initial state set by means of a finite sample of initial states plus a sensitivity argument, has recently attracted interest due to the availability of powerful simulators for rich classes of dynamical systems. System models addressed by such techniques involve ordinary differential equations (ODEs) and can readily be extended to delay differential equations (DDEs). In doing so, the lack of validated solvers for DDEs, however, enforces the use of numeric approximations such that the resulting verification procedures would have to resort to (rather strong) assumptions on numerical accuracy of the underlying simulators, which lack formal validation or proof. In this paper, we pursue a closer integration of the numeric solving and the sensitivity-related state bloating algorithms underlying verification by simulation, together yielding a safe enclosure algorithm for DDEs suitable for use in automated formal verification. The key ingredient is an on-the-fly computation of piecewise linear, local error bounds by nonlinear optimization, with the error bounds uniformly covering sensitivity information concerning initial states as well as integration error.

1 Introduction

Delayed coupling between state variables of dynamic systems occurs in many domains. Prominent examples include population dynamics, where birth rate follows changes in population size with a delay related to reproductive age,

The first, third and fifth authors are supported partly by "973 Program" under grant No. 2014CB340701, by NSFC under grants 91418204 and 61502467, by CDZ project CAP (GZ 1023), and by the CAS/SAFEA International Partnership Program for Creative Research Teams. The second and fourth authors are supported partly by Deutsche Forschungsgemeinschaft within the Research Training Group "SCARE - System Correctness under Adverse Conditions" (DFG GRK 1765).

J. Fitzgerald et al. (Eds.): FM 2016, LNCS 9995, pp. 137–154, 2016.
DOI: 10.1007/978-3-319-48989-6_9

spreading of infectious diseases, where delay is induced by the incubation period, exhaust gas control in internal combustion engines, where relevant sensors, like the λ probe, are located downstream the exhaust system such that gas transport induces a delay between the controlled combustion processes and sensing their effect, or networked control systems with their associated transport delays when forwarding data through the communication network, to name just a few. Most examples feature feedback dynamics and it should be obvious that the presence of feedback delays reduces controllability due to the impossibility of immediate reaction and enhances likelihood of transient overshoot or even oscillation in the feedback system. In fact, the introduction of delays into a feedback system may reduce stabilization rates of or even destabilize an otherwise stable system, it may provoke overshoot and drive the system to otherwise unreachable states, it is likely to stretch dwell times, and it may induce residual error that never cancels. As this implies that safety or stability certificates obtained on idealized, delay-free models of systems prone to delayed coupling may be erratic, automated methods for system verification ought to address models of system dynamics reflecting delays, rendering verification tools only addressing ordinary differential equations (ODE) and their derived models, like hybrid automata, vastly insufficient. It can well be argued that such tools should better address delay differential equations (DDE), as introduced in [2].

Generalizing techniques developed for ODE to DDE is not as straightforward as it may seem at first glance. The reason is that the future evolution of a DDE is no longer governed by the current state instant only, but depends on a chunk of its past trajectory, such that introducing a delay immediately renders a system with finite-dimensional state into an infinite-dimensional dynamical system. Consequently, approximate numerical methods for solving DDEs as well as methods for stability analysis have well been developed in the field of control, while in automatic verification, hitherto only few approaches address the effects of delays due to the immediate impact of delays on the structure of the state spaces to be traversed by state-exploratory methods.

In this paper, we address this problem by suitably adapting the paradigm of verification by simulation to delay differential equations. Verification by simulation provides bounded-time verification of dynamical systems based on covering the full set of time-bounded trajectories of a dynamical system evolving from the initial state set by means of a finite sample of initial states plus a sensitivity argument. To achieve this, a sufficiently dense sample of initial states is drawn from the set of all possible initial states, numeric simulation is then used for obtaining the trajectories originating from the sample points, and finally a quantitative sensitivity argument permits to pessimistically over-approximate the "tube" of trajectories originating from arbitrary start states by means of "bloating" the individual simulated trajectories into a neighborhood of the radius given by the bound on sensitivity on the start state, see e.g. [8,9,15,20]. If a validated numerical solver is used for the simulations, the above procedure will immediately yield a safe over-approximation of the set of possible trajectories; else, more aggressive bloating additionally covering the possible inaccuracies of numeric integration of differential equations has to be employed to obtain a sound, validated method.

The class of systems we approach features delayed differential dynamics governed by DDE of the following form:

$$\begin{cases} \dot{\mathbf{x}}(t) = \boldsymbol{f}(\mathbf{x}(t), \mathbf{x}(t-r_1), \ldots, \mathbf{x}(t-r_k)), & t \in [0, \infty) \\ \mathbf{x}(t) = \boldsymbol{g}(t), \quad t \in [-r_{\max}, 0] \end{cases} \tag{1}$$

It thus involves a combination of ODE and DDE with multiple constant delays $r_i > 0, i = 1, \ldots, k$. Here, $r_{\max} = \max\{r_1, \ldots, r_k\}$ is the maximal delay, $\mathbf{x} : \mathbb{R}_{\geq -r_{\max}} \mapsto \mathbb{R}^n$ is a trajectory, $\boldsymbol{f} : (\mathbb{R}^n)^{k+1} \mapsto \mathbb{R}^n$ a vector field, and $\boldsymbol{g} : [-r_{\max}, 0] \mapsto \mathbb{R}^n$ is a continuous function providing the initial condition. This form of equations has been successfully used to model various real world systems in the fields of, e.g., biology, control theory, and economics.

Generally speaking, formal verification of temporally unbounded reachability properties of system dynamics governed by Eq. (1) inherits undecidability from similar properties for ODE. Therefore, and also due to our wish to use simulation as an underlying mechanism of system analysis, we restrict ourselves to time-bounded reachability problems. Such a time-bounded reachability problem for a given model of the form (1) is parameterized by a temporal horizon (i.e., a time bound) set by the user, a set of initial states which in the case of DDE generalizes to constant functions over the time frame $[-r_{\max}, 0]$ immediately preceding system start, and a set of unsafe states that system dynamics is expected to avoid. The proof obligation is to determine whether there exists a *trajectory* of the model starting in some initial state which reaches any unsafe state within the time bound. In our approach, we first trigger a set of numerical approximations of the behaviours from a finite sampling of the initial states. Such a simulation does not yield a trajectory, but rather a timed trace, i.e., a sequence of time-stamp value pairs. Along each simulation run, we bloat each snapshot, i.e., each time-stamp value pair by a distance determined via an *error bound* computed automatically on-the-fly, where the error bound incorporates coverage and sensitivity information concerning the sampled start states as well as the integration error incurred by numerical solving. The union of these bloatings covers all time-bounded trajectories possibly evolving from all initial states, and thus yields an over-approximation of the states reachable from the initial set within the time bound. If this over-approximation proves safety in the sense that the cover of the reachable states is disjoint from the unsafe states, or conversely if the simulation produces a valid counter-example in the sense that it can prove that a trajectory inevitably hits the unsafe states, then the algorithm generates the corresponding verdict. Otherwise, it refines the sample drawn from the initial states, thus requiring less aggressive bloating of simulation runs, and computes a more precise over-approximation.

Our approach is distinguished from competing approaches by providing a validated verification-by-simulation paradigm for DDE. Given that validated methods for DDE enclosure are not readily available, it achieves this by pursuing a closer than traditional integration of the numeric solving and the sensitivity-related state bloating algorithms underlying verification by simulation, together yielding a safe enclosure algorithm for DDE guaranteed to contain the true solution. The key ingredient is an on-the-fly computation of piecewise linear, local error bounds by nonlinear optimization, which provides an alternative to established methods computing discrepancy bounds from Lipschitz constants and Jacobians, as employed in [13]. Some experimental results obtained on several benchmark systems involving delayed differential dynamics are further demonstrated. Due to lack of space, the detailed proofs of theorems are available in [5].

Related Work. Zou *et al.* proposed in [27] a procedure for generating stability and safety certificates for the simplest class of DDEs of the form $\dot{\mathbf{x}}(t) = \boldsymbol{f}(\mathbf{x}(t-r))$. This is achieved by iterating interval-based Taylor over-approximations of the time-wise segments of the solution to a DDE, which depends essentially on the fact that the interval coefficients of the solution over the time interval $(n, n+1]$ can be represented as a function of those of the solution over $(n-1, n]$. Extracting the operator mapping coefficients at one time frame to those of the next, one obtains a time-invariant discrete-time dynamical system. Thus, stability analysis and safety verification of the original DDE is reduced to appropriate counterparts encoding these properties on the resulting time-invariant discrete-time dynamical system. This approach does not immediately generalize to mixed ODE-DDE forms as in Eq. (1), as the delayed parts of the dynamics would there function as inputs to an ODE with input, rendering the above operator time-variant. Though this is doable in principle, we have herein opted for the more immediate approach of verification by simulation.

In [22], Pola *et al.* proposed an approach abstracting incrementally input-to-state stable (δ-ISS) nonlinear control systems with constant and known delays to finite-state symbolic models, and establish approximate bisimilarity between them. In [21], they extended the work in [22] to incrementally-input-delay-to-state stable (δ-IDSS) nonlinear control systems with time-varying and unknown delays, and proved that the original δ-IDSS nonlinear control systems and the corresponding symbolic models are alternating approximately bisimilar. The crucial differences between their work and ours lie in, firstly, their approach being confined to δ-ISS nonlinear control systems, while our approach being applicable to any kind of nonlinear control systems with constant and known time delays. So, our method relaxes a problematic applicability condition. Second, their approach can do unbounded verification of time-delay systems, while our approach currently can only conduct bounded verification. Third, their approach can be applied to δ-IDSS nonlinear control systems with time-varying and unknown delays, while our approach cannot yet. It is a crucial aspect of our future work to extend our approach to nonlinear control systems with time-varying and unknown delays, without sacrificing its applicability beyond δ-IDSS systems.

Verifying delayless dynamical systems, in particular ODE, using numerical simulations has well been studied, e.g., in [8,9,15,20], where similar concepts based on sensitivity information provided by discrepancy functions or simulation functions, respectively, have been presented to bloat the traces obtained from simulations to "trajectory tubes" over-approximating time-bounded reach sets.

While the first settings resorted to user-supplied sensitivity information, Fan and Mitra in [13] proposed an algorithm for automatically computing piecewise exponential discrepancy functions. This algorithm pessimistically estimates the sensitivity of the ODE on its initial value, but also takes assumed error bounds of the numerical simulation, which in that case is Matlab's `ode45` solver, into account. This, however, renders the soundness of this algorithm dependent on the assumption that Matlab's built-in ODE solver can always guarantee those numerical error bounds, while it is possible to find extremely stiff ODEs as follows for which the solver returns very inaccurate results.

$$\dot{x}(t) = 1 + \delta_a(x - \sqrt{2}), \text{ with } \delta_a(y) = \frac{1}{a\sqrt{\pi}} \mathrm{e}^{-y^2/a^2} \tag{2}$$

$\delta_a(y)$ approximates the *Dirac δ function* [7] modelling a tall narrow spike around $y = 0$, where the spike shrinks as $a \to 0$. When Eq. (2) is simulated with $a = 10^{-3}$ by Matlab's ODE solver `ode45`, results show that the solver can detect the sharp increment of the derivative with a user-specified `MaxStep` as 0.01, while not the case with 0.1. Furthermore, adjusting the simulation step width could not essentially cure the problem, yet just shifts it to a smaller a for which the solver fails to identify the leaping trajectory and instead follows straight-line dynamics. This motivates us to address the issue of numerical errors in discrepancy computation. Moreover, the method in [13] requires computations of a global Lipschitz constant as well as a bound on the eigenvalues of the Jacobians within a region, which may not be feasible in some dynamical systems.

2 Problem Formulation

Notations. For a vector $\mathbf{x} \in \mathbb{R}^n$, x_i refers to its ith component, and $\|\mathbf{x}\|$ denotes the ℓ^2-norm. The notation $\|\cdot\|$ extends to an $n \times n$ real matrix $A \in \mathbb{R}^{n\times n}$ with $\|A\| = \sqrt{\lambda_{\max}(A^{\mathrm{T}}A)}$, where $\lambda_{\max}(A)$ is the largest eigenvalue of A. For $\mathbf{x}, \mathbf{x}' \in \mathbb{R}^n$, $\|\mathbf{x}' - \mathbf{x}\|$ is the Euclidean distance between the points, and we define for $\delta \geq 0$, $\mathcal{B}_\delta(\mathbf{x}) = \{\mathbf{x}' \in \mathbb{R}^n \,|\, \|\mathbf{x}' - \mathbf{x}\| \leq \delta\}$ as the closed ball of radius δ centered at $\mathbf{x}$. For a set $S \subseteq \mathbb{R}^n$, $\mathcal{B}_\delta(S) = \cup_{\mathbf{x}\in S}\mathcal{B}_\delta(\mathbf{x})$. The diameter of a compact set S is $dia(S) = \sup_{\mathbf{x},\mathbf{x}'\in S} \|\mathbf{x} - \mathbf{x}'\|$, and a δ-*cover* of S is a finite collection of points $\mathcal{X}$ such that $S \subseteq \cup_{\mathbf{x}\in\mathcal{X}}\mathcal{B}_\delta(\mathbf{x})$. For a set $S \subseteq \mathbb{R}^n$, its convex hull is denoted as $conv(S)$.

Delayed Dynamical Systems. We consider a timed-bounded delayed dynamical system of the form

$$\begin{cases} \dot{\mathbf{x}}(t) = \boldsymbol{f}(\mathbf{x}(t), \mathbf{x}(t - r_1), \ldots, \mathbf{x}(t - r_k)), & t \in [0, \infty) \\ \mathbf{x}(t) \equiv \mathbf{x}_0 \in \Theta, \quad t \in [-r_k, 0], \end{cases} \tag{3}$$

[1]where $\mathbf{x}$ is the time-dependent *state* vector in $\mathbb{R}^n$, $\dot{\mathbf{x}}$ denotes its temporal derivative $\mathrm{d}\mathbf{x}/\mathrm{d}t$, and t is a real variable modelling time. The discrete delays are assumed to be ordered as $r_k > \ldots > r_1 > 0$, and the initial states are generalized to a constant function over $[-r_k, 0]$ taking values from a compact set Θ.

Let the vector-valued function $\boldsymbol{f} : (\mathbb{R}^n)^{k+1} \mapsto \mathbb{R}^n$ be continuous and continuously differentiable in the first argument, which implies that the system has a unique maximal *solution* (or *trajectory*) from each constant initial condition valued $\mathbf{x}_0 \in \mathbb{R}^n$, denoted as $\xi_{\mathbf{x}_0}(t) : [-r_k, \ell) \mapsto \mathbb{R}^n$, where $\ell = \infty$ holds if $\boldsymbol{f}$ is Lipschitz.

Example 1 (Gene Regulation [12,24]*).* The control of gene expression in cells is often modelled with time delays in equations of the form

$$\begin{cases} \dot{x_1}(t) = g(x_n(t - r_n)) - \alpha_1 x_1(t) \\ \dot{x_j}(t) = g(x_{j-1}(t - r_{j-1})) - \alpha_j x_j(t), 1 < j \leq n, \end{cases} \tag{4}$$

where the gene is transcribed producing mRNA (x_1), which is translated into enzyme x_2 that turn produces another enzyme x_3 and so on. The end product x_n acts to repress the transcription of the gene by $\dot{g} < 0$. Time delays are introduced to account for time involved in transcription, translation, and transport. The $\alpha_j > 0$ represent decay rates of the species. The dynamic described in Eq. (4) falls exactly into the scope of systems considered in this paper, and in fact, it instantiates a more general family of systems known as monotone cyclic feedback systems (MCFS) [19], which includes neural networks, testosterone control, and many other effects in systems biology.

Safety Verification Problem. Given a set $\mathcal{U} \subseteq \mathbb{R}^n$ of unsafe or otherwise bad states, a delayed dynamical system of shape (3) is said to be (time-bounded) *safe* iff all the trajectories originating from any $\mathbf{x}_0 \in \Theta$ do not intersect with $\mathcal{U}$ (within the given time bound T), otherwise it is called *unsafe*.

3 Verification of Delayed Dynamical Systems via Simulation

Generating formal guarantees for DDEs of the form (3) tends to be challenging due to unavailability of guaranteed for solving them. We are trying to alleviate that problem by adopting approximate numeric methods, enhancing them with methods for rigorous error tracking, thus rendering them validated numerical methods, and adding sensitivity information for being able to cover sets of initial states based on simulating and bloating the trajectories originating from finitely many samples. This approach has been inspired by similar approaches for ODE, in particular the discrepancy functions of [13].

[1] In general, the initial condition is represented by $\mathbf{x}(t) = \xi_0(t)$, for $t \in [-r_k, 0]$, where $\xi_0 \in \mathcal{X} \subseteq C^0([-r_k, 0], \mathbb{R}^n)$, $C^0([-r_k, 0], \mathbb{R}^n)$ stands for all continuous functions mapping from $[-r_k, 0]$ to $\mathbb{R}^n$, $\mathcal{X}$ is compact and bounded. So, we can let $\Theta = \cup_{\xi \in \mathcal{X}} \xi([-r_k, 0])$. Clearly, Θ is compact and bounded.

We will now expose in detail the overall procedure of simulation by verification, which hinges on the validated simulation of DDE that we will turn to in Sect. 4. For the sake of simplifying the exposition, we first consider the special case of delayed dynamical systems featuring a single delay, as in

$$\begin{cases} \dot{\mathbf{x}}(t) = \boldsymbol{f}(\mathbf{x}(t), \mathbf{x}(t-r)), & t \in [0, \infty) \\ \mathbf{x}(t) \equiv \mathbf{x}_0 \in \Theta, & t \in [-r, 0]. \end{cases} \tag{5}$$

In this case, the differential dynamics is a function $\boldsymbol{f}(\mathbf{x}, \mathbf{u})$ of two states, namely the current state $\mathbf{x}$ and the past state $\mathbf{u}$.

The basic idea of simulation-based verification of a DDE (5), as implemented by Algorithm 1, can be sketched as follows:
First, we build on a validated simulation procedure Simulation, whose design is shown in Sect. 4. Given a delayed dynamical system as above, a subset $\mathcal{X}_0 \subset \Theta$ of the initial states, and a time bound T, Simulation yields a *simulation trace* $(t_0, \mathbf{y}_0), \ldots, (t_n, \mathbf{y}_n)$ consisting of pairs of time stamps $t_i \in [0, T]$ and states $\mathbf{y}_i \in \mathbb{R}^n$ with $\mathbf{y}_0 = \mathbf{x}_0$, as well as a sequence of *local error bounds* $d_0, d_1, \ldots, d_n \geq 0$ providing a *validation* of this trace observing the following two properties:

- P1: $0 = t_0 < t_1 < \ldots < t_n = T$, i.e., the time stamps in the trace are ascending and cover the temporal horizon of interest.
- P2: For each of the trajectories $\xi_{\mathbf{x}_0}(t)$ of (5) starting from any point $\mathbf{x}_0 \in \mathcal{X}_0$, the validation property

$$(\xi_{\mathbf{x}_0}(t), t) \in conv\left((\mathcal{B}_{\mathbf{d}_i}(\mathbf{y}_i) \times \{t_i\}) \cup (\mathcal{B}_{\mathbf{d}_{i+1}}(\mathbf{y}_{i+1}) \times \{t_{i+1}\}) \right) \tag{6}$$

  holds for each $t \in [t_i, t_{i+1}]$, $i = 0, 1, \ldots, n-1$. I.e., the reported error bounds $\mathbf{d}_i$ span a piecewise linear tube around the points $(\mathbf{y}_i, t_i)$ in the simulation trace such that $\xi_{\mathbf{x}_0}(t)$ is properly enclosed for any $\mathbf{x}_0 \in \mathcal{X}_0$ and any $t \in [0, T]$.

Then, time-bounded safety verification of system (5) can be obtained as follows:

1. At the beginning, we cover the given initial set $\mathcal{X}_0$ by a finite set of balls of radius δ; so, δ-Partition($\mathcal{X}_0$) in line 2 of Algorithm 1 returns a finite δ-cover of the compact set $\mathcal{X}_0$. We then call Simulation to each of these balls. For each ball B, we collect all states contained in the bloating of the N-step simulation trace $\mathbf{y}$ as $\mathcal{B}_{\mathbf{d}}(\mathbf{y}) = \bigcup_{n=0}^{N-1} conv(\mathcal{B}_{\mathbf{d}_n}(\mathbf{y}_n) \cup \mathcal{B}_{\mathbf{d}_{n+1}}(\mathbf{y}_{n+1}))$, cf. line 8. This yields an over-approximation of the states reachable from B following (5) within time up to T.
2. If the over-approximation of the reachable set thus obtained is disjoint to the unsafe set (line 9), then (5) is *safe* when starting in B; otherwise, if there exists a sampling point in the simulation which has its full bloating with the corresponding local error bound being contained in the unsafe set (line 11), then (5) is definitely *unsafe*. If none of these two conditions applies, we compute a finer partition of B (line 14), and we repeat the above procedure until the granularity of the partition becomes finer than the given threshold. In this case, we cannot give an answer whether or not (5) is safe and terminate with the inconclusive result *unknown*.

Algorithm 1. Simulation-based Verification for Delayed Dynamical Systems

input : The dynamics $\boldsymbol{f}(\mathbf{x}, \mathbf{u})$, delay term r, initial set $\mathcal{X}_0$, unsafe set $\mathcal{U}$, time bound T, precision ϵ.
/* initialization */
$\mathcal{R} \leftarrow \emptyset$; $\delta \leftarrow dia(\mathcal{X}_0)/2$; $\tau \leftarrow \tau_0$;
$\mathcal{X} \leftarrow \delta$-Partition$(\mathcal{X}_0)$;
while $\mathcal{X} \neq \emptyset$ **do**
    if $\delta < \epsilon$ **then**
        return (UNKNOWN, $\mathcal{R}$);
    for $\mathcal{B}_\delta(\mathbf{x}_0) \in \mathcal{X}$ **do**
        $\langle \mathbf{t}, \mathbf{y}, \mathbf{d} \rangle \leftarrow$ Simulation$(\mathcal{B}_\delta(\mathbf{x}_0), \boldsymbol{f}(\mathbf{x}, \mathbf{u}), r, \tau, T)$;
        $\mathcal{T} \leftarrow \bigcup_{n=0}^{N-1} conv(\mathcal{B}_{\mathbf{d}_n}(\mathbf{y}_n) \cup \mathcal{B}_{\mathbf{d}_{n+1}}(\mathbf{y}_{n+1}))$;
        if $\mathcal{T} \cap \mathcal{U} = \emptyset$ **then**
            $\mathcal{X} \leftarrow \mathcal{X} \backslash \mathcal{B}_\delta(\mathbf{x}_0)$; $\mathcal{R} \leftarrow \mathcal{R} \cup \mathcal{T}$;
        else if $\exists i.\ \mathcal{B}_{\mathbf{d}_i}(\mathbf{y}_i) \subseteq \mathcal{U}$ **then**
            return (UNSAFE, $\mathcal{T}$);
        else
            $\mathcal{X} \leftarrow \mathcal{X} \backslash \mathcal{B}_\delta(\mathbf{x}_0)$; $\mathcal{X} \leftarrow \mathcal{X} \cup \frac{\delta}{2}$-Partition$(\mathcal{B}_\delta(\mathbf{x}_0))$;
    $\delta \leftarrow \delta/2$;
return (SAFE, $\mathcal{R}$);

Obviously, our approach is different from existing approaches providing simulation-based verification for dynamical systems modeled by ordinary differential equations, like [8,9]. In our approach, the simulation procedure provides a rigorous validation of the above property P2, rather than relying on assumptions concerning numerical accuracy of the underlying simulator. Second, our approach covers rigorous simulation-based formal verification of DDE rather than just ODE. The correctness of the resulting algorithm is captured by the following theorem:

Theorem 1 (Correctness). *If* Simulation *satisfies above properties* P1 *and* P2 *(which will be verified in the next section), then Algorithm 1 terminates and its outputs are guaranteed to satisfy the following soundness properties:*

- *it reports (*SAFE,$\mathcal{R}$*) only if the system is safe.*
- *it reports (*UNSAFE, $\mathcal{T}$*) only if the system is unsafe and $\mathcal{T}$ is a counter-example.*

The general case of multiple different delays in Eq. (3) can be dealt with analogously to the case (5) of a single delay: we only need to allow **u** to have more components, meanwhile, we need to revise Algorithm 2 accordingly by introducing multiple different m_i as $m_1 \leftarrow r_1/\tau, \ldots, m_k \leftarrow r_k/\tau$. Thus, the delayed states y_{n-m_i}s can be exactly located when computing y_{n+1} by $\boldsymbol{f}(y_n, y_{n-m_1}, \ldots, y_{n-m_k})$ (line 6 in Algorithm 2) as well as when finding the minimal e (line 7 in Algorithm 2).

4 Validated Simulation

In this section, we elaborate on simulation and on computation of rigorous local error bounds to guarantee the *enclosure property* P2. Instead of directly computing the error bounds $d_0, \ldots, d_n$ accompanying the simulation trace $(t_0, \mathbf{y}_0), \ldots, (t_n, \mathbf{y}_n)$, we compute an initial error bound d_0 and a sequence $e_1, \ldots, e_n$ of error slopes recursively defining error bounds $E(t)$ for each $t \in [0, T]$ — and thus not only for time stamps in the simulated trace — as follows:

$$E(t) = \begin{cases} d_0, & \text{if } t = 0, \\ E(t_i) + (t - t_i)e_{i+1}, & \text{if } t \in [t_i, t_{i+1}]. \end{cases} \tag{7}$$

The validation property (P2) can thus be rewritten as

P2': For each of the trajectories $\xi_{\mathbf{x}_0}(t)$ of system (5) starting from any point $\mathbf{x}_0 \in \mathcal{X}_0$, the validation property

$$\xi_{\mathbf{x}_0}(t) \in \mathcal{B}_{E(t)}\left(\frac{(t - t_i)\mathbf{y}_i + (t_{i+1} - t)\mathbf{y}_{i+1}}{t_{i+1} - t_i}\right) \tag{8}$$

holds for each $t \in [t_i, t_{i+1}]$.

I.e., the e_i's provide the slopes of piecewise conic enclosures around the linear interpolations between the points $(t_i, \mathbf{y}_i)$ in the simulation trace.

The Simulation Algorithm. Inferring formal proofs from simulations essentially attributes to a validated numerical solver which can produce rigorous error bounds on the generated sampling points. We present in Algorithm 2 a procedure[2] Simulation that provides a trace of sampling points bundled with their local error bounds thus giving an over-approximation of the reachable set in terms of an initial state space.

The algorithm is provided with an initial ball $\mathcal{B}_\delta(\mathbf{x}_0)$ and it proceeds with a discrete simulation starting from $\mathbf{x}_0$ paced by a fixed stepsize τ. Three *list* structures (denoted as $[\![\cdot]\!]$) with the same length are introduced respectively as (1) $\mathbf{t}$: storing a sequence of time stamps on which the approximations are computed, (2) $\mathbf{y}$: keeping a sequence of sampling points that approximates the trajectory starting from $\mathbf{x}_0$, and (3) $\mathbf{d}$: capturing the corresponding sequence of local error bounds. Due to the nature of DDEs where the evolving of states may refer to those ahead of time $t_0 = 0$, we index the lists beginning from -1 and assume that all the evaluations of $\mathbf{y}$ and $\mathbf{d}$ with a negative index return the element at -1, namely $\mathbf{y}_{<0} = \mathbf{y}_{-1}$[3], and analogously for $\mathbf{d}$.

At $t_0 = 0$, the corresponding local error is initialized with the radius of the initial set $d_0 = \delta$ (line 1). An offest m is computed in line 2 such that $\mathbf{y}_{n-m}$ locates the delayed approximation at $t_n - r$. In each iteration of the simulation loop, the state is extrapolated in line 6 using the well-known *forward Euler method*, which computes y_{n+1} explicitly from previous points y_n and y_{n-m}. Higher-order

[2] For ease of presentation, we demonstrate the approach on DDEs with one single delay, and it readily extends to that with multiple delays as discussed in Sect. 3.

[3] For a general initial condition $\boldsymbol{g}(t)$, $\mathbf{y}$ is initialized as $\mathbf{y} \leftarrow [\![\boldsymbol{g}(-r), \boldsymbol{g}(-r + \tau), \ldots, \boldsymbol{g}(0)]\!]$.

Algorithm 2. Simulation: a validated DDE solver producing rigorous bounds

input : The initial set $\mathcal{B}_{\delta}(\mathbf{x}_0)$, dynamics $\boldsymbol{f}(\mathbf{x}, \mathbf{u})$, delay term r, stepsize τ, time bound T.
output: A triple $\langle \mathbf{t}, \mathbf{y}, \mathbf{d} \rangle$, where the components represent lists, with the same length, respectively for the time points, numerical approximations (possibly multi-dimensional), and the rigorous local error bounds.

/* initializing the lists, whose indices start from -1 */
1 $\mathbf{t} \leftarrow [\![-\tau, 0]\!]$; $\mathbf{y} \leftarrow [\![\mathbf{x}_0, \mathbf{x}_0]\!]$; $\mathbf{d} \leftarrow [\![0, \delta]\!]$;
/* r has to be divisible by τ (in FP numbers) */
2 $n \leftarrow 0$; $m \leftarrow r/\tau$;
3 **while** $\mathbf{t}_n < T$ **do**
4 $\quad t_{n+1} \leftarrow \mathbf{t}_n + \tau$;
$\quad$ /* approximating y_{n+1} using *forward Euler method* */
5 $\quad y_{n+1} \leftarrow \mathbf{y}_n + \boldsymbol{f}(\mathbf{y}_n, \mathbf{y}_{n-m}) * \tau$;
$\quad$ /* computing error slope by constrained optimization, where σ is a positive slack constant */
6 $\quad e_n \leftarrow$ **Find** minimum e s.t.

$$\begin{cases} \|\boldsymbol{f}(\mathbf{x} + t * \mathbf{f}, \mathbf{u} + t * \mathbf{g}) - \boldsymbol{f}(\mathbf{y}_n, \mathbf{y}_{n-m})\| \leq e - \sigma, \text{ for} \\ \forall t \in [0, \tau] \\ \forall \mathbf{x} \in \mathcal{B}_{\mathbf{d}_n}(\mathbf{y}_n) \\ \forall \mathbf{u} \in \mathcal{B}_{\mathbf{d}_{n-m}}(\mathbf{y}_{n-m}) \\ \forall \mathbf{f} \in \mathcal{B}_e(\boldsymbol{f}(\mathbf{y}_n, \mathbf{y}_{n-m})) \\ \forall \mathbf{g} \in \mathcal{B}_{e_{n-m}}(\boldsymbol{f}(\mathbf{y}_{n-m}, \mathbf{y}_{n-2m})); \end{cases} \tag{9}$$

7 $\quad d_{n+1} \leftarrow \mathbf{d}_n + \tau e_n$;
$\quad$ /* updating the lists by appending the extrapolation */
8 $\quad \mathbf{t} \leftarrow [\![\mathbf{t}, t_{n+1}]\!]$; $\mathbf{y} \leftarrow [\![\mathbf{y}, y_{n+1}]\!]$; $\mathbf{d} \leftarrow [\![\mathbf{d}, d_{n+1}]\!]$;
9 $\quad n \leftarrow n + 1$;
10 **return** $\langle \mathbf{t}, \mathbf{y}, \mathbf{d} \rangle$;

Runge-Kutta methods [1] could be employed here to obtain more precise approximations. Line 7 derives a local error bound d_{n+1} based on the local error slope e_n satisfying the enclosure property (P2'). The computation of e_n is reduced to a constrained optimization problem (line 6).

Correctness of Simulation. Note that the constrained optimization problem (9) need not have a finite solution, in which case our algorithm fails to provide a useful enclosure. Straightforward continuity arguments do, however, show that for small enough stepsize τ, it will always have a solution, which motivated us to implement stepsize control, as discussed below. When being able to compute useful, i.e., finite error slopes, the simulation delivers a safe enclosure satisfying (P2):

Theorem 2 (Correctness). *Suppose the maximum index of the lists generated by Algorithm 2 is N, then $\forall t \in [0, T]$ and $\forall \mathbf{x} \in \mathcal{B}_{\delta}(\mathbf{x}_0)$,*

$$\xi_{\mathbf{x}}(t) \subseteq \bigcup_{n=0}^{N-1} conv(\mathcal{B}_{\mathbf{d}_n}(\mathbf{y}_n) \cup \mathcal{B}_{\mathbf{d}_{n+1}}(\mathbf{y}_{n+1})).$$

The completeness result can be formally stated as follows:

Theorem 3 (Completeness). *Suppose the function $\boldsymbol{f}$ in Eq. (5) is continuously differentiable in both arguments and the dynamical system is solvable for time interval $[0, T]$, then for any $\varepsilon > 0$, there exists δ, τ and σ such that the optimization problem (9) has a solution e_n for all $n \leq \frac{T}{\tau}$, and moreover $\mathbf{d}_n \leq \varepsilon$.*

Algorithm 3. Simulation: a simulation procedure with local stepsize control

input : $\mathcal{B}_\delta(\mathbf{x}_0)$, $\boldsymbol{f}(\mathbf{x}, \mathbf{u})$, r, τ_0, T.
output: $\langle \mathbf{t}, \mathbf{y}, \mathbf{d} \rangle$
1 $\mathbf{t} \leftarrow [\![-\tau_0, 0]\!]$; $\mathbf{y} \leftarrow [\![\mathbf{x}_0, \mathbf{x}_0]\!]$; $\mathbf{d} \leftarrow [\![0, \delta]\!]$;
2 $n \leftarrow 0$;
3 **while** $\mathbf{t}_n < T$ **do**
4 $\quad \tau \leftarrow \tau_0$; $m \leftarrow r/\tau$;
$\quad$ /* relocating the bias m by a backward search */
5 $\quad$ **for** $j \leftarrow$ Length($\mathbf{t}$); $j \geq 1$; $j - -$ **do**
6 $\quad\quad$ **if** $\mathbf{t}_n - r \in (\mathbf{t}_{j-1}, \mathbf{t}_j]$ **then**
7 $\quad\quad\quad m \leftarrow n - j$;
8 $\quad\quad\quad$ Break;
9 $\quad$ **while** True **do**
10 $\quad\quad t_{n+1} \leftarrow \mathbf{t}_n + \tau$; $y_{n+1} \leftarrow \mathbf{y}_n + \boldsymbol{f}(\mathbf{y}_n, \mathbf{y}_{n-m}) * \tau$;
11 $\quad\quad$ **if** minimal e satisfying Eq. (10) under the constraints of (9) is found **then**
12 $\quad\quad\quad e_n \leftarrow e$; $d_{n+1} \leftarrow \mathbf{d}_n + \tau e_n$;
13 $\quad\quad\quad$ Break;
14 $\quad\quad$ **else**
15 $\quad\quad\quad \tau \leftarrow \tau/2$;
$\quad\quad$ /* Smaller e, tighter the bloating. */
16 $\quad \mathbf{t} \leftarrow [\![\mathbf{t}, t_{n+1}]\!]$; $\mathbf{y} \leftarrow [\![\mathbf{y}, y_{n+1}]\!]$; $\mathbf{d} \leftarrow [\![\mathbf{d}, d_{n+1}]\!]$;
17 $\quad n \leftarrow n + 1$;
18 **return** $\langle \mathbf{t}, \mathbf{y}, \mathbf{d} \rangle$;

Extension to Variable Stepsize. Local stepsize control reducing the current stepsize whenever Eq. (9) has no finite solution seems natural. An improved simulation procedure with flexible stepsize control is presented in Algorithm 3, where in each step of simulation, the procedure first tries to find a finite upper bound e satisfying Eq. (9) with an initial stepsize τ_0. If it fails, the current interval is split into two (line 15) and the above operations repeat. Termination of refining the stepsize is guaranteed by the continuous differentiability of $\boldsymbol{f}$ in both of its arguments. Along with variation of τ, the bias locating the delayed state within the list of sampling points need to be recomputed in each step by a backward search (line 8). This may generate extra error, as the nearest sampling point $\mathbf{y}_{n-m}$ may not feature exactly the desired delay. This additional error is accounted for by modifying the first line of the constrained optimization (9) into

$$\|(\mathbf{x} + t_1 * \mathbf{f}, \mathbf{u} + t_2 * \mathbf{g}) - \boldsymbol{f}(\mathbf{y}_n, \mathbf{y}_{n-m})\| \leq e - \sigma \tag{10}$$

for any $t_1, t_2 \in [0, \tau]$. The correctness and completeness arguments for Algorithm 3 are akin to Theorem 2.

5 Implementation and Experimental Results

To evaluate the approach of verification along simulations, we have implemented the proposed algorithms with local stepsize control as a prototype[4] in Matlab. It takes a time-bounded safety verification problem of delayed dynamical systems

[4] Available from http://lcs.ios.ac.cn/~chenms/tools/DDEChecker_v1.0.tar.bz2.

as input, and it terminates with one of the three results SAFE, UNSAFE, or UNKNOWN, reflecting the fact that a fine enough over-approximation has been found to prove the system safe or unsafe, respectively, or that the maximum permitted density of covering the initial set was insufficient for obtaining a definite answer.

As our algorithm relies on solving the constrained optimization problems (9) or (10), resp., for determining validated bounds, we have tried different solvers for discharging that optimization problem, namely the numerical (and thus devoid of formal guarantees concerning completeness and soundness) procedure `fmincon` provided by Matlab and the optimization-modulo-theory procedure offered by the nonlinear SAT-modulo theory solver `HySAT II`[5] [16]. The constrained optimization problems (9) and (10) involve a universally quantified constraint of the shape

$$\text{find } \min\{e \geq 0 \mid \forall x : \phi(x, e) \implies \psi(x, e)\}, \tag{11}$$

which is outside the scope of the above solving procedures, as these handle existential constraints only. We therefore have substituted (11) by the existentially constrained optimization problem

$$\text{find } \max\{e \geq 0 \mid \exists x : \phi(x, e) \wedge \neg\psi(x, e)\}. \tag{12}$$

Due to the linear ordering on $\mathbb{R}_{\geq 0}$, problem (12) is guaranteed to yield an upper bound on the solution of (11), which is safe in our context. Both `fmincon` and `HySAT II` proved to be able to efficiently solve (9) and (10) in the formulation (12), with `HySAT II` being able to provide a validated solution due to global search based on a combination of interval constraint propagation with optimization-modulo-theory solving.

`HySAT II` [16] is a sat-modulo-theory (SMT) solver accepting formulas containing arbitrary boolean combinations of theory atoms involving linear, polynomial and transcendental functions. It internally rewrites these formulae into an equi-satisfiable conjunctive normal form by means of a definitional translation introducing auxiliary propositional and numeric variables representing the truth values of sub-formulae and the numeric values of subexpressions, resp., thus generalizing the well-known Tseitin transformation [25]. `HySAT II` then solves the resulting CNF through a tight integration of the Davis-Putnam-Logemann-Loveland (DPLL) algorithm [6] in its conflict-driven clause learning (CDCL) variant with interval constraint propagation (ICP) [3]. Details of the algorithm, which operates on interval valuations for both the Boolean and the numeric variables and alternates between choice steps splitting such intervals and deduction steps narrowing them based on logical deductions computed through ICP or Boolean constraint propagation (BCP), can be found in [14]. Implementing a branch-and-prune search in interval lattices and conflict-driven learning of clauses comprising irreducible atoms in those lattices, it can be classified as an early implementation of abstract conflict-driven clause learning (ACDCL) [4].

By this ACDCL proof search, `HySAT II` will successively construct a cover of the actual solution set of the constraint problem by tiny interval boxes, a

[5] Available from https://www.uni-oldenburg.de/en/hysat/.

sequence of so-called candidate solution boxes together enclosing all solutions. Optimization then is based on a branch-and-prune search over the candidate solution boxes, which is straightforward to integrate into the ACDCL proof search by biasing the ACDCL splitting rule to better values when splitting along the variable representing the optimization criterion, plus learning bounds that impose blocking on any solutions worse than the best value up-to-now found.

The soundness of this procedure for solving the optimization problems (9) or (10) in the formulation (12) follows immediately from the soundness properties of ICP, which narrows the search space by chopping off regions not containing any solution, but will never remove solutions [3]. It consequently is an invariant of the iSAT algorithm's proof search, as implemented in `HySAT II`, that its residual search space internally represented by interval boxes plus the already reported solution boxes together safely over-approximate the actual solution space [14]. This in turn implies that the maximum found by `HySAT II` always is a safe upper bound of the actual maximum, irrespective of possible non-convexity of the optimization problem at hand. We can conclude that solving the optimization problems (9) or (10) in the formulation (12) with `HySAT II` will provide a safe upper bound on the actual optimal value of (12), which in turn is an upper bound on (9) or (10), resp., in the original form (11). As any upper bound renders the enclosure in Algorithms 2 or 3, resp., correct, we can conclude that `HySAT II`'s optimization procedure guarantees soundness of the overall algorithm. The possible failure of `HySAT II`'s optimization procedure in determining a sharp over-approximation of the optimal value will at most impact performance, as it may enforce an unnecessarily dense cover by simulation traces due to overly pessimistic bloating of the original traces.

In the following, we demonstrate our approach by verification of some quintessential DDEs.

Delayed Logistic Equation. In 1948, G. Hutchinson [17] introduced the delayed logistic equation

$$\dot{n}(t) = a[1 - n(t-T)/K]n(t)$$

to model a single population whose percapita rate of growth at time t

$$\dot{n}(t)/n(t) = a[1 - n(t-T)/K]$$

depends on the population size T times units in the past. This would be a reasonable model for a population that features a significant minimum reproductive age or depends on a resource, like food, needing time to grow and those to recover its availability. If we let $N(t) = n(t)/K$ and rescale time, then we get the discrete-delay logistic equation

$$\dot{N}(t) = N(t)[1 - N(t-r)], t \geq 0. \tag{13}$$

Arguments in [24] established that for any initial function $N_0 > 0$, there exists a unique non-negative solution $N(\phi, t)$ defined for all $t > 0$. Wright's conjecture [26], still unsolved, is that if $r \leq \pi/2$ then $N(\phi, t) \to 1$ as $t \to \infty$ for all solutions of Eq. (13) satisfying $N_0 > 0$.

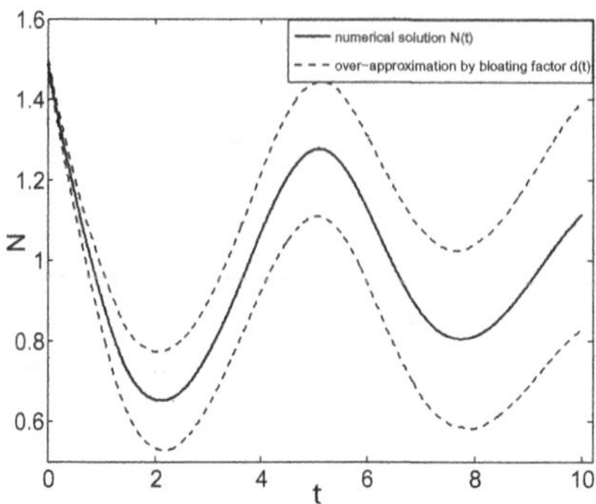

Fig. 1. Over-approximation of the solutions of Eq. (13) originating from region $\mathcal{B}_{0.01}(1.49)$ under delay $r = 1.3$. Initial stepsize $\tau_0 = 0.01$, time bound $T = 10\,\text{s}$.

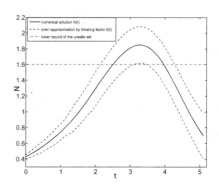

Fig. 2. Over-approximation rigorously proving Eq. (13) unsafe, with $r = 1.7$, $\mathcal{X}_0 = \mathcal{B}_{0.025}(0.425)$, $\tau_0 = 0.1$, $T = 5\,\text{s}$ and $\mathcal{U} = \{N | N > 1.6\}$.

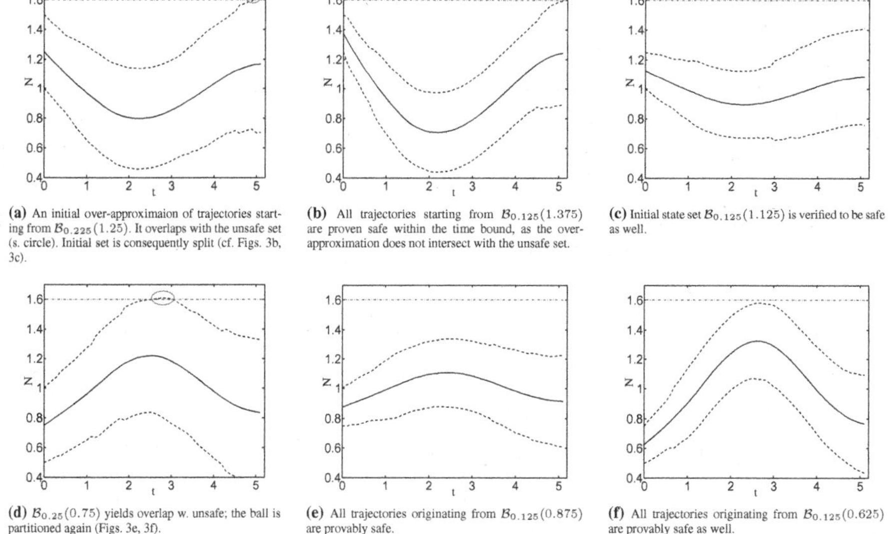

(**a**) An initial over-approximaion of trajectories starting from $\mathcal{B}_{0.225}(1.25)$. It overlaps with the unsafe set (s. circle). Initial set is consequently split (cf. Figs. 3b, 3c).

(**b**) All trajectories starting from $\mathcal{B}_{0.125}(1.375)$ are proven safe within the time bound, as the over-approximation does not intersect with the unsafe set.

(**c**) Initial state set $\mathcal{B}_{0.125}(1.125)$ is verified to be safe as well.

(**d**) $\mathcal{B}_{0.25}(0.75)$ yields overlap w. unsafe; the ball is partitioned again (Figs. 3e, 3f).

(**e**) All trajectories originating from $\mathcal{B}_{0.125}(0.875)$ are provably safe.

(**f**) All trajectories originating from $\mathcal{B}_{0.125}(0.625)$ are provably safe as well.

Fig. 3. The logistic system (13) is proven safe through 6 rounds of simulation with base stepsize $\tau_0 = 0.1$. Delay $r = 1.3$, initial state set $\mathcal{X}_0 = \{N | N \in [0.5, 1.5]\}$, time bound $T = 5\,\text{s}$, unsafe set $\{N | N > 1.6\}$.

Figure 1 illustrates an over-approximation of trajectories of Eq. (13) in terms of a specific initial set. It provides an intuitive description of our simulation approach equipped with computation of on-the-fly linear local error bounds. To investigate Wright's conjecture, we further explore the safety verification framework based upon validated simulations with a delay $r = 1.3 < \pi/2$, for which the trajectories are expected to converge within a time interval. The detailed verification process is elaborated in Fig. 3. Meanwhile, we also successfully falsified an unsafe case with $r = 1.7$ where the over-approximation of a diverging trajectory can be rigorously shown to violate the safety property (see Fig. 2).

Delayed Microbial Growth. Ellermeyer *et al.* [10,11] introduced a delay in the standard bacterial growth model in a chemostat which, after scaling time and the dependent variables, can be written as

$$\begin{aligned} \dot{S}(t) &= 1 - S(t) - f(S(t))x(t)\,, \\ \dot{x}(t) &= \mathrm{e}^{-r} f(S(t-r))x(t-r) - x(t)\,, \end{aligned} \tag{14}$$

where $f(S) = \alpha S/(\beta + S)$, and $S(t)$ denotes the substrate (food for bacteria) concentration, while $x(t)$ is the biomass concentration of bacteria. The delay r reflects the assumption that whereas cellular absorption of substrate is assumed to be an instantaneous process, a resulting increase in microbial biomass reflecting assimilation is assumed to lag by a fixed amount of time r. A specific verification problem of Eq. (14) is shown in Fig. 4, where different rounds of simulation are depicted together in the phase space of S and x, and for a clear presentation, we only sketch the over-approximations around those numerically computed sampling points.

Gene Regulation. To further investigate the scalability of our approach to high dimensions, we recall an instantiation of Example 1 by setting $n = 5$, namely with 5 state components $\mathbf{x} = (x_1; x_2; \ldots; x_5)$ and 5 delay terms $\mathbf{r} = (r_1; r_2; \ldots; r_5)$ involved. This essentially yields, in each step of simulation, an optimization procedure of the form (10) with 23 scalar variables, i.e., e, t_1, t_2 and $\mathbf{x}, \mathbf{u}, \mathbf{f}, \mathbf{g} \in \mathbb{R}^5$. By further setting $\mathbf{r} = (0.1; 0.2; 0.4; 0.8; 1.6)$, $\mathcal{X}_0 = \mathcal{B}_{0.2}((1;1;1;1;1))$, $\mathcal{U} = \{\mathbf{x} | x_1 < 0\}$, and $T = 2\,\mathrm{s}$, the system of Eq. (4) is

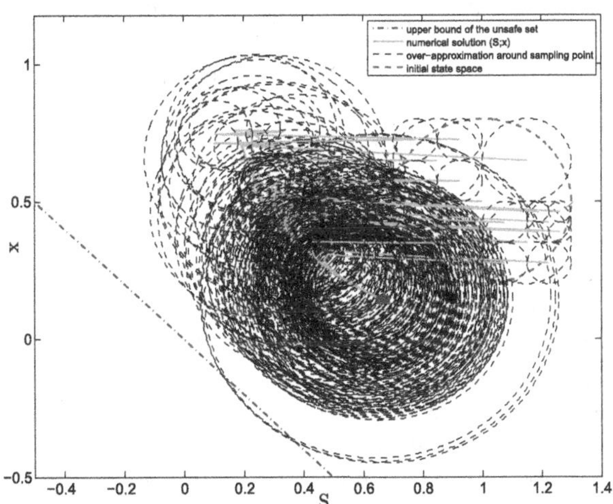

Fig. 4. Equation (14) is proven safe by 17 rounds of simulation w. $\tau_0 = 0.45$. The simulated trajectories start from within a cover of $\mathcal{X}_0$ (the red dashed circle on the right) and converge eventually to a *basin of attraction* (marked by a small blue rectangle). Here, $\alpha = 2\mathrm{e}$, $\beta = 1$, $r = 0.9$, $\mathcal{X}_0 = \mathcal{B}_{0.3}((1;0.5))$, $\mathcal{U} = \{(S;x) | S + x < 0\}$, $T = 8\,\mathrm{s}$. (Colour figure online)

rigorously proven unsafe, which means that the dosage of mRNA might degrade to negative in this hypothetical setting.

As an intuitive observation, the verification time consumed by our prototype is fairly sensitive to the specific setting of the verification problem, including the initial set $\mathcal{X}_0$, the delays $\mathbf{r}$, the unsafe set $\mathcal{U}$, and the time bound T as well. However, the optimization routine proved well scalable to high dimensions, and particularly, verifications of the above benchmark systems all completed successfully in a handful of minutes.

6 Conclusion and Future Work

We have exposed an approach for automated formal verification of time-bounded reachability properties of a class of systems that feature delayed differential dynamics governed by delay differential equations (DDEs) with multiple different delays (including 0, i.e., direct feedback). This class of system models has successfully been used to model various real-world systems in the field of biology, control theory, economics, and other domains. Our approach is based on adapting the paradigm of verification-by-simulation to DDEs. It provides bounded-time verification by covering the full set of time-bounded trajectories of a dynamical system evolving from the initial state set by means of investigating a finite sample of initial states plus generalization via a sensitivity argument. Initially, it triggers a finite set of numerically approximate simulations of the dynamic behaviors, thereby generating a finite set of approximate simulation traces originating from a finite sample of the initial states. As the sample does not cover all initial states, and as simulation is only approximate, we bloat each time-stamp value pair returned from the simulation by a distance determined via an error bound computed automatically on-the-fly during simulation. This error bound incorporates both sensitivity information concerning start states and rigorous bounds on integration error incurred by numerical solving. Hence, the union of the state sets reached by all the individual bloated trajectories provides a safe over-approximation of the states actually reachable from the initial set within the time bound. If this over-approximation proves safety in the sense that the reachable states do not intersect the unsafe states, or conversely if the simulation produces a valid counter-example in the sense that it can prove that a trajectory hits the unsafe states, then the algorithm generates the corresponding verdict. Otherwise, our algorithm refines its sample of initial states and repeats the previous steps to compute a more precise over-approximation.

Based on that approach, we have implemented a prototype of a validated solver for DDE. Using it, we have successfully demonstrated the method on several benchmark systems involving delayed differential dynamics.

As a future work, we plan to replace Euler's direct method by high-order Runge-Kutta methods [1] in order to obtain more precise approximations. Furthermore, the method of Zou *et al.* [27] can be extended to provide a safe enclosure algorithm for the class of systems (3) suitable for use in unbounded formal verification, based on the fact that the iSAT constraint solver [14] used therein supports unbounded verification by means of Craig interpolation. In addition, it could be quite interesting to investigate how to combine the technique of conformance testing for hybrid systems [18,23] with our approach. The potential merits of such combination is twofold: on the one hand, it can extend the conformance testing technique to deal with hybrid systems with delays; on the other hand, it may improve the efficiency of the conformance testing technique by using simulation-based approach to over-approximate the reachable set instead of directly computing.

References

1. Bellen, A., Zennaro, M.: Numerical Methods for Delay Differential Equations. Numerical Mathematics and Scientific Computation. Clarendon Press, Oxford (2003)
2. Bellman, R.E., Cooke, K.L.: Differential-difference equations. Technical report R-374-PR, RAND Corporation, Santa Monica, California, January 1963
3. Benhamou, F., Granvilliers, L.: Continuous and interval constraints. In: Rossi, F., van Beek, P., Walsh, T. (eds.) Handbook of Constraint Programming, Foundations of Artificial Intelligence, Chap. 16, pp. 571–603. Elsevier, Amsterdam (2006)
4. Brain, M., D'Silva, V., Griggio, A., Haller, L., Kroening, D.: Interpolation-based verification of floating-point programs with abstract CDCL. In: Logozzo, F., Fähndrich, M. (eds.) SAS 2013. LNCS, vol. 7935, pp. 412–432. Springer, Heidelberg (2013). doi:10.1007/978-3-642-38856-9_22
5. Chen, M., Fränzle, M., Li, Y., Mosaad, P.N., Zhan, N.: Validated simulation-based verification of delayed differential dynamics (full version). http://lcs.ios.ac.cn/chenms/papers/FM2016_FULL.pdf
6. Davis, M., Logemann, G., Loveland, D.: A machine program for theorem proving. Commun. ACM **5**, 394–397 (1962)
7. Dirac, P.A.M.: The Principles of Quantum Mechanics. Clarendon Press, Oxford (1981)
8. Donzé, A., Maler, O.: Systematic simulation using sensitivity analysis. In: Bemporad, A., Bicchi, A., Buttazzo, G. (eds.) HSCC 2007. LNCS, vol. 4416, pp. 174–189. Springer, Heidelberg (2007). doi:10.1007/978-3-540-71493-4_16
9. Duggirala, P.S., Mitra, S., Viswanathan, M.: Verification of annotated models from executions. In: Proceedings of the Eleventh ACM International Conference on Embedded Software, p. 26. IEEE Press (2013)
10. Ellermeyer, S.F.: Competition in the chemostat: global asymptotic behavior of a model with delayed response in growth. SIAM J. Appl. Math. **54**(2), 456–465 (1994)
11. Ellermeyer, S.F., Hendrix, J., Ghoochan, N.: A theoretical and empirical investigation of delayed growth response in the continuous culture of bacteria. J. Theoret. Biol. **222**(4), 485–494 (2003)
12. Fall, C.P., Marland, E.S., Wagner, J.M., Tyson, J.J. (eds.): Computational Cell Biology, vol. 20. Springer, New York (2002)
13. Fan, C., Mitra, S.: Bounded verification with on-the-fly discrepancy computation. In: Finkbeiner, B., Pu, G., Zhang, L. (eds.) ATVA 2015. LNCS, vol. 9364, pp. 446–463. Springer, Heidelberg (2015). doi:10.1007/978-3-319-24953-7_32

14. Fränzle, M., Herde, C., Ratschan, S., Schubert, T., Teige, T.: Efficient solving of large non-linear arithmetic constraint systems with complex Boolean structure. J. Satisfiability Boolean Model. Comput. **1**, 209–236 (2007)
15. Girard, A., Pappas, G.J.: Approximate bisimulation: a bridge between computer science and control theory. Eur. J. Control **17**(5–6), 568–578 (2011)
16. Herde, C.: Efficient Solving of Large Arithmetic Constraint Systems with Complex Boolean Structure. Vieweg+Teubner, Wiesbaden (2011)
17. Hutchinson, G.E.: Circular causal systems in ecology. Ann. NY Acad. Sci. **50**(4), 221–246 (1948)
18. Khakpour, N., Mousavi, M.R.: Notions of conformance testing for cyber-physical systems: overview and roadmap (invited paper). In: CONCUR 2015. LIPIcs, vol. 42, pp. 18–40 (2015)
19. Mallet-Paret, J., Sell, R.: The poincaré-bendixson theorem for monotone cyclic feedback systems with delay. J. Diff. Eq. **125**, 441–489 (1996)
20. Nahhal, T., Dang, T.: Test coverage for continuous and hybrid systems. In: Damm, W., Hermanns, H. (eds.) CAV 2007. LNCS, vol. 4590, pp. 449–462. Springer, Heidelberg (2007). doi:10.1007/978-3-540-73368-3_47
21. Pola, G., Pepe, P., Di Benedetto, M.D.: Symbolic models for time-varying time-delay systems via alternating approximate bisimulation. Int. J. Robust Nonlinear Control **25**, 2328–2347 (2015)
22. Pola, G., Pepe, P., Di Benedetto, M.D., Tabuada, P.: Symbolic models for nonlinear time-delay systems using approximate bisimulations. Syst. Contr. Lett. **59**(6), 365–373 (2010)
23. Roehm, H., Oehlerking, J., Woehrle, M., Althoff, M.: Reachset conformance testing of hybrid automata. In: HSCC 2016, pp. 277–286 (2016)
24. Sagirow, P.: Introduction. In: Sagirow, P. (ed.) Stochastic Methods in the Dynamics of Satellites. ICMS, vol. 57, pp. 5–7. Springer, Heidelberg (1970)
25. Tseitin, G.S.: On the complexity of derivations in propositional calculus. In: Slisenko, A. (ed.) Studies in Constructive Mathematics and Mathematical Logics (1968)
26. Wright, E.M.: A non-linear difference-differential equation. J. Reine Angew. Math. **194**, 66–87 (1955)
27. Zou, L., Fränzle, M., Zhan, N., Mosaad, P.N.: Automatic verification of stability and safety for delay differential equations. In: Kroening, D., Păsăreanu, C.S. (eds.) CAV 2015. LNCS, vol. 9207, pp. 338–355. Springer, Heidelberg (2015). doi:10.1007/978-3-319-21668-3_20

Towards Learning and Verifying Invariants of Cyber-Physical Systems by Code Mutation

Yuqi Chen(✉), Christopher M. Poskitt, and Jun Sun

Singapore University of Technology and Design, Singapore, Singapore
yuqi_chen@mymail.sutd.edu.sg

Abstract. Cyber-physical systems (CPS), which integrate algorithmic control with physical processes, often consist of physically distributed components communicating over a network. A malfunctioning or compromised component in such a CPS can lead to costly consequences, especially in the context of public infrastructure. In this short paper, we argue for the importance of constructing invariants (or models) of the physical behaviour exhibited by CPS, motivated by their applications to the control, monitoring, and attestation of components. To achieve this despite the inherent complexity of CPS, we propose a new technique for learning invariants that combines machine learning with ideas from mutation testing. We present a preliminary study on a water treatment system that suggests the efficacy of this approach, propose strategies for establishing confidence in the correctness of invariants, then summarise some research questions and the steps we are taking to investigate them.

1 Introduction

Cyber-physical systems (CPS), characterised by their tight integration of algorithmic control and physical processes, are prevalent across engineering domains as diverse as aerospace, autonomous vehicles, and medical monitoring; they are also used to control critical public infrastructure such as smart grids and water treatment plants [16,18]. In such contexts, CPS often consist of distributed software components (the "cyber" part) that communicate over a network and interact with their local environments via sensors and actuators (the "physical" part). A component that exhibits faulty behaviour—or worse still, becomes compromised [7]—can lead to costly and damaging consequences, motivating research into approaches for ensuring their correctness, safety, and security.

Reasoning about a CPS as a whole, however, is very challenging, given that models must capture both discrete behaviour in the cyber part as well as continuous behaviour in the physical part [30]. With source code for the former and ordinary differential equations (ODEs) for the latter, it becomes possible to model the CPS as a hybrid system and apply a variety of techniques (e.g. model checking [11], SMT solving [12], non-standard analysis [13], concolic testing [17], or theorem proving [23,24]). Yet CPS are inherently complex, and even with domain-specific expertise, it can be difficult to determine ODEs that are accurate enough in practice: there might always remain some discrepancy between

J. Fitzgerald et al. (Eds.): FM 2016, LNCS 9995, pp. 155–163, 2016.
DOI: 10.1007/978-3-319-48989-6_10

the verified model and the behaviour of the actual CPS, emphasising the importance of techniques that can be applied at runtime [20].

Our Approach. As an alternative to the endeavour of manual modelling, we pursue in this paper a more systematic approach. We propose to apply machine learning (ML) to the sensor data of CPS to construct models in the form of *invariants*—conditions that must hold in all states amongst the physical processes controlled by the CPS—and to make those invariants checkable at runtime. To achieve this, the learner must be trained on traces of sensor data representing "normal" runs (the positive case, satisfying the invariant), and also on traces representing incorrect behaviour (the negative case); the former being easy to obtain, but the latter requiring more ingenuity. We obtain our negative traces by the novel application of code mutation (*à la* mutation testing [14]) to the software components of CPS. Besides characterising the CPS, the learnt invariants have some important applications in controlling, monitoring, and attesting the software components [25]. It is thus important to ascertain that the learnt invariants *actually* are invariants of the CPS: to address this, we propose to verify them using statistical model checking and symbolic execution.

Our Contributions. This short paper describes a novel approach for generating invariants (or models) of CPS, based on the application of machine learning to traces of sensor data obtained under mutated software components. We present the results of a preliminary experiment on (a simulator of) Secure Water Treatment (SWaT) [1], a water purification testbed, which suggest the efficacy of the approach and motivate the need for further research. Furthermore, we propose the use of statistical model checking and symbolic execution for establishing confidence in the correctness of the learnt invariants, and highlight some important open research questions which we are investigating in ongoing work. For the formal methods community, this paper represents the start of a line of work to model and verify—"warts and all"—a complex, real-world CPS. For the CPS community, it describes a systematic approach for constructing invariants that can be applied in controlling, monitoring, and attesting software components. For the ML community, it presents a new application of learning arising from a novel combination of ideas from CPS and mutation testing.

2 SWaT Testbed and Cyber-Physical System Invariants

SWaT. We are currently investigating our approach in the context of a particular CPS: the SWaT testbed [1]. SWaT, built for cyber-security research at the Singapore University of Technology and Design, is a scaled-down but fully operational water treatment plant, capable of producing five gallons of safe drinking water per minute. Water is treated in six distinct, co-operating stages, under which it undergoes chemical processes such as ultrafiltration, de-chlorination, and reverse osmosis. Each stage is controlled by an independent programmable logic controller (PLC), which receives sensor data such as water flow rates and tank levels, and then computes signals to send to actuators including pumps and motorised valves. This communication all takes place over a network. Sensor data is also available to a Supervisory Control and Data Acquisition (SCADA) system, and is recorded by a historian to facilitate offline analyses.

Control is expressed in the programs that PLCs repeatedly cycle through. These are structurally very simple, essentially boiling down to big (nested) if-statements. The programs use only the simplest constructs: loops, for example, are completely absent. Furthermore, the source code can easily be viewed, modified, and re-deployed to the PLCs using Rockwell's RSLogix 5000, an industrial-standard software suite. While the cyber part of SWaT is thus relatively simple, the same is not true of the physical part: runs of the system are governed by laws concerning the dynamics of water flow, the evolution of pH values, and the chemical processes associated with the six water treatment stages.

To complement the SWaT testbed, we also have access to a simulator implemented in Python (relying on some of its scientific libraries). The cyber part is simulated faithfully as the PLC code was translated to Python directly. Since the actual ODEs governing the physical part of SWaT are unknown, the simulator is not as accurate in this regard. The ODEs it does implement, however, have been improved over time by cross-validating data from the simulator with real SWaT data collected by the historian.

CPS Invariants. The safety of water treatment plants is of paramount importance, as breaches or malfunctioning components can lead to costly consequences. In SWaT, for example, there is a risk of damaging the mechanics of the system if the water levels in certain tanks become too high or too low [15]. One way to detect when runs of a system are diverging into such territory is to monitor invariants—conditions that must hold in all states amongst the physical processes controlled by the CPS—and raise an alarm when they are no longer satisfied. This approach has been applied to a number of CPS [9,22], including for stages of SWaT itself [3,4]. Typically, however, the invariants are *manually* derived using the laws of physics and domain-specific knowledge. Moreover, they are derived for specific, expected physical relationships, and may not capture other important patterns hiding in the sensor data.

Beyond providing a characterisation of CPS and their important applications in monitoring for safety, invariants can also be seen as facilitating a form of code attestation. That is to say, if the actual behaviour of a CPS does not satisfy our mathematical model of the physical world under its control (i.e. the invariant), then it is possible that the cyber part has been compromised and that ill-intended manipulations are occurring. This form of attestation is known as *physical attestation* [25,27], and while weaker than typical software- and hardware-based attestation schemes (e.g. [5,6,8,26]), it is much more lightweight—neither the firmware nor the hardware of the PLCs require modification.

3 Learning with Mutants

Learning SWaT Invariants. Rather than deriving further invariants for SWaT manually, we propose to learn them systematically by applying ML—initially,

Support Vector Machines (SVM)—to traces of SWaT sensor data, taking the *classifiers* they learn as our invariants. To learn such a classifier, SVM must be provided with traces that should be classified as positive (i.e. correct behaviour) and traces that should be classified as negative. The data available from the SWaT historian can be seen as representing correct (and thus positive) behaviour of the system as a whole: the SWaT PLCs and actual (unknown) ODEs together. In contrast, we propose to collect negative traces by running the system under small manipulations. Since we cannot change the ODEs (we cannot yet bend the laws of physics!), we propose to manipulate the part of SWaT that we can: the programs running on the PLCs.

As previously discussed, it is straightforward to change the PLC programs of SWaT and collect some negative traces, but it is more challenging to do so in a systematic way that ensures the strength of the invariant and precision of the classifier. The solution we propose is directly inspired by mutation testing [14], a fault-based testing technique that deliberately seeds errors—small, syntactic changes called *mutations*—into multiple copies of a program, which are executed to assess the quality of a test suite (good ones should detect the mutants). Rather than using mutations to improve the completeness of a test suite, we are using them to generate a more comprehensive set of negative traces for training on. By training on traces resulting from small syntactic changes, we hope to learn a classifier as close to the boundary between correct and suspicious behaviour as possible. Our rationale is that smaller changes are more likely to reveal negative traces that are relevant in practice, corresponding, for example, to isolated PLCs or sensors failing, or an attacker attempting to keep their changes undetected.

Using mutations for learning is also attractive because of the structural simplicity of the PLC programs. Were we assessing a test suite on them, we could do so efficiently and without redundancy by using the five basic (arithmetic, relational, and logical) mutation operators identified by Offutt et al. [21]. We hypothesise that (and are investigating whether) this result has an analogue for learning that could help us in minimising the number of redundant traces. Even if so, there remain some additional challenges to overcome. For example, if mutations are not executed, this must be detected, and thus the traces rejected as negative samples. Even if a mutant is executed, it may not lead to a physical effect immediately (or ever) and thus could generate traces indistinguishable from positive ones. Other issues include how many mutations to use in each copy, and how to handle valid modes of operation in SWaT that are rarely entered.

Preliminary Evaluation. As a very first step towards evaluating the outlined approach, we undertook an experiment to ascertain the effectiveness of a classifier learnt from traces produced by the SWaT simulator under a number of manually applied mutations. Note that we used the simulator to facilitate a quick proof-of-concept without the resource costs of the real system (e.g. water usage, human monitoring); this ML approach can be applied to traces collected from the real system in the same way.

First, we manually launched the SWaT simulator in three different initial states (i.e. assignments of variables modelling sensors), collecting three traces of correct behaviour each spanning 30 min. Following this, we made 20 copies of the PLC code and manually applied a different (random) mutation to each. Of these 20 mutants, 14 of them generated traces equivalent to correct behaviour and were manually rejected. Seven mutants generated different traces, although one mutant was rejected for generating a trace too similar to another. The six remaining mutants were selected to generate our negative traces; three of the mutations each modified an assignment, whereas the other three modified an arithmetic expression in a conditional guard. We generated traces for each mutant using the same three initial states as before.

We proceeded to apply SVM to learn six classifiers for the six mutants respectively, each against the correct code. We selected 10 features: the first five representing the water levels of the five tanks, and the next five representing the same levels after 250 ms. For training the classifiers and evaluating their accuracy, we applied k-fold cross-validation to the traces with $k = 5$. On average, the classifiers achieved an accuracy of 99 %.

Finally, we applied SVM to all the traces from all six mutants to learn a single classifier, i.e. to determine whether a trace represents correct behaviour or the behaviour caused by any one of the mutations. We found that this combined classifier maintained a similar level of accuracy to the individual ones: 98.41 %. We extracted the learnt invariant from this classifier, which, albeit complicated, expresses a linear relationship between water tank levels (mm) at one time point $(v_1, \dots v_5)$ and 250 ms after it $(v_1', \dots v_5')$. For simplicity of presentation, the coefficients are given below to three decimal places. The full model and training data are all available online (see [2]).

$$
\begin{aligned}
&-0.349v_1 + 9.789v_2 - 10.192v_3 + 0.803v_4 - 5.561v_5 \\
&-0.630v_1' - 10.455v_2' + 10.333v_3' + 0.803v_4' + 3.928v_5' \; < -786.416
\end{aligned}
$$

This experiment has shown that it is possible to apply SVM to learn an accurate classifier for traces of sensor data, using the negative samples generated under a small number of mutated PLC programs. It is, of course, too limited in its present scope to allow for more general conclusions; a much more extensive evaluation of the outlined approach is needed, and is underway. It does however suggest the feasibility of the basic idea, and has highlighted a number of important challenges. For instance, the process should be more automatic: mutation operators should be applied automatically, as should the detection of unexercised mutations, as well as the comparison of the generated traces against the positive ones. Furthermore, to ensure as strong an invariant and precise a classifier as possible, a number of questions must be answered empirically, regarding, e.g. the number of mutations (and the possibility of multiple mutations per copy), the sufficiency of mutation operators, and the length of traces.

Our experiment also highlighted the role that a simulator can play in mutation "screening" before applying them to the real SWaT system and collecting negative traces that are based on the actual ODEs. This helps to avoid wasting time and resources otherwise lost by applying the mutations to the real PLCs first. Note that while the ML technique can be applied to SWaT data in exactly the same way as for the simulator, a human technician must be present while collecting the data itself to ensure that the mutations do not lead the system into a state that causes damage. This raises another research question: whether one can determine a class of "safe" mutations for SWaT that still facilitate a precise classifier but avoid entirely the possibility of causing damage.

4 Correctness of Invariants

Our preliminary experiment has allowed us to learn a new invariant for SWaT (or rather, at least to begin with, its simulator). But is it *actually* an invariant? It is not particularly intuitive to reason about. And even if it were, to argue for its correctness, we would need some expertise in the physics of water treatment plants; a requirement we wanted to avoid in the first place. As alternatives to manual, ad hoc proofs, we propose two contrasting approaches for establishing confidence in the correctness of invariants, and highlight their well-suitedness to CPS like SWaT.

First, we will apply statistical model checking (SMC) to SWaT, a standard technique for analysing and verifying CPS [10]. In SMC, executions of the system (i.e. traces of sensor data) are observed, and hypothesis testing or statistical estimation techniques are applied to determine whether or not the executions provide statistical evidence of the invariant holding. SMC estimates the probability of correctness, rather than guaranteeing it outright, but is simple to apply to SWaT (and its simulator) since it only requires the system to be executable. Furthermore, should the ODEs of the SWaT simulator become more accurate in the future, then our mutation-based learning approach could take place entirely on that; SMC could then determine whether or not the learnt invariants are also invariants of the real system, without having to apply any mutations to it.

Second, we will investigate the use of symbolic execution for analysing SWaT with respect to a learnt invariant. In the PLC programs, symbolic values will be used to abstract away from concrete sensor inputs. The technique will then build, along the different paths of the PLC code, path constraints over the symbolic values (i.e. path conditions in conjunction with an assertion based on the learnt invariant). The PLC programs have a simple structure that is well-suited to this task: they are free of loops, and the paths through the programs are short (maximal depth of three; maximal branching of 28). Our invariants, however, are based upon sensor readings at two different time points, so we cannot analyse them with respect to the cyber part of SWaT alone: a model of the physical processes is needed too, for reasoning about the effects that signals will have. As we have discussed, we cannot expect to manually derive a completely accurate one, but we could nonetheless use approximate models (e.g. as defined in the simulator), or even models of SWaT that were automatically constructed using different approaches to ours (e.g. the probabilistic model of [29]).

It should be emphasised that while neither technique can fully guarantee correctness, they differ in where precision is lost, and so should complement each other in helping to establish confidence in the learnt invariants. SMC, for example, estimates a probability of correctness based only on the executions it is provided with (leading to challenges such as handling rare events); yet by working with actual system executions, its results are based on the actual physical processes. Symbolic execution, in contrast, must work with an approximate physical model, but performs an analysis on the actual source code in the cyber part (and not just on a subset of the possible system executions).

5 Conclusion and Next Steps

This short paper has proposed a novel approach for learning invariants of CPS that trains a ML technique such as SVM on positive and negative traces of sensor data, with the latter obtained by applying mutation operators to copies of the programs in the cyber part—the part of the CPS that we can most easily control. We presented a preliminary study on SWaT, a raw water treatment plant, that suggested the effectiveness of constructing invariants this way. We furthermore outlined the use of SMC and symbolic execution for establishing confidence in the correctness of learnt invariants, and discussed their use in CPS applications such as physical attestation.

Much work remains to be done to truly ascertain the effectiveness of our approach for CPS. First, we will automate—as much as possible—our experiment on the SWaT simulator, to allow for classifiers to be trained on several additional mutants and initial states more easily, and to automatically detect those mutants that do not cause the system to exhibit different physical behaviour. Then, within this framework, we will begin investigating the challenges raised in Sect. 3 and the verification approaches outlined in Sect. 4, before shifting our experimentation to traces obtained from the real SWaT system. We will investigate the use of ML systems other than SVM, and compare our supervised model learning approach against proposed unsupervised ones for CPS (e.g. [19,28]). Finally, we will investigate the application of learnt invariants to code attestation, by instigating cyber-attacks on the SWaT system and evaluating whether or not our classifiers are effective in detecting them.

Acknowledgements. We thank Pingfan Kong for assisting us with the SWaT simulator, and the anonymous referees for their helpful comments and criticisms. This work was supported by NRF Award No. NRF2014NCR-NCR001-40.

References

1. Secure Water Treatment (SWaT). http://itrust.sutd.edu.sg/research/testbeds/secure-water-treatment-swat/. Accessed Sep 2016
2. Supplementary material. http://sav.sutd.edu.sg/?page_id=3258
3. Adepu, S., Mathur, A.: Distributed detection of single-stage multipoint cyber attacks in a water treatment plant. In: Proceedings of ACM Asia Conference on Computer and Communications Security (AsiaCCS 2016), pp. 449–460. ACM (2016)

4. Adepu, S., Mathur, A.: Using process invariants to detect cyber attacks on a water treatment system. In: Hoepman, J.-H., Katzenbeisser, S. (eds.) Proceedings of International Conference on ICT Systems Security and Privacy Protection (SEC 2016). IFIP AICT, vol. 471, pp. 91–104. Springer, New York (2016)
5. Alves, T., Felton, D.: TrustZone: integrated hardware and software security. ARM white paper (2004)
6. Anati, I., Gueron, S., Johnson, S.P., Scarlata, V.R.: Innovative technology for CPU based attestation and sealing. Intel white paper (2013)
7. Cárdenas, A.A., Amin, S., Sastry, S.: Research challenges for the security of control systems. In: Proceedings of USENIX Workshop on Hot Topics in Security (HotSec 2008). USENIX Association (2008)
8. Castelluccia, C., Francillon, A., Perito, D., Soriente, C.: On the difficulty of software-based attestation of embedded devices. In: Proceedings of ACM Conference on Computer and Communications Security (CCS 2009), pp. 400–409. ACM (2009)
9. Choudhari, A., Ramaprasad, H., Paul, T., Kimball, J.W., Zawodniok, M.J., McMillin, B.M., Chellappan, S.: Stability of a cyber-physical smart grid system using cooperating invariants. In: Proceedings of IEEE Computer Software and Applications Conference (COMPSAC 2013), pp. 760–769. IEEE (2013)
10. Clarke, E.M., Zuliani, P.: Statistical model checking for cyber-physical systems. In: Bultan, T., Hsiung, P.-A. (eds.) ATVA 2011. LNCS, vol. 6996, pp. 1–12. Springer, Heidelberg (2011). doi:10.1007/978-3-642-24372-1_1
11. Frehse, G., Guernic, C., Donzé, A., Cotton, S., Ray, R., Lebeltel, O., Ripado, R., Girard, A., Dang, T., Maler, O.: SpaceEx: scalable verification of hybrid systems. In: Gopalakrishnan, G., Qadeer, S. (eds.) CAV 2011. LNCS, vol. 6806, pp. 379–395. Springer, Heidelberg (2011). doi:10.1007/978-3-642-22110-1_30
12. Gao, S., Kong, S., Clarke, E.M.: dReal: An SMT solver for nonlinear theories over the reals. In: Bonacina, M.P. (ed.) CADE 2013. LNCS (LNAI), vol. 7898, pp. 208–214. Springer, Heidelberg (2013). doi:10.1007/978-3-642-38574-2_14
13. Hasuo, I., Suenaga, K.: Exercises in *nonstandard static analysis* of hybrid systems. In: Madhusudan, P., Seshia, S.A. (eds.) CAV 2012. LNCS, vol. 7358, pp. 462–478. Springer, Heidelberg (2012). doi:10.1007/978-3-642-31424-7_34
14. Jia, Y., Harman, M.: An analysis and survey of the development of mutation testing. IEEE Trans. Softw. Eng. **37**(5), 649–678 (2011)
15. Kang, E., Adepu, S., Jackson, D., Mathur, A.P.: Model-based security analysis of a water treatment system. In: Proceedings of International Workshop on Software Engineering for Smart Cyber-Physical Systems (SEsCPS 2016), pp. 22–28. ACM (2016)
16. Khaitan, S.K., McCalley, J.D.: Design techniques and applications of cyberphysical systems: a survey. IEEE Syst. J. **9**(2), 350–365 (2015)
17. Kong, P., Li, Y., Chen, X., Sun, J., Sun, M., Wang, J.: Towards concolic testing for hybrid systems. In: Fitzgerald, J., et al. (eds.) FM 2016. LNCS-FM, vol. 9995, pp. 460–478. Springer, Heidelberg (2016)
18. Lee, E.A.: Cyber physical systems: design challenges. In: Proceedings of International Symposium on Object-Oriented Real-Time Distributed Computing (ISORC 2008), pp. 363–369. IEEE (2008)
19. Maier, A.: Online passive learning of timed automata for cyber-physical production systems. In: Proceedings of IEEE International Conference on Industrial Informatics (INDIN 2014), pp. 60–66. IEEE (2014)

20. Mitsch, S., Platzer, A.: ModelPlex: verified runtime validation of verified cyber-physical system models. In: Bonakdarpour, B., Smolka, S.A. (eds.) RV 2014. LNCS, vol. 8734, pp. 199–214. Springer, Heidelberg (2014). doi:10.1007/978-3-319-11164-3_17
21. Offutt, A.J., Lee, A., Rothermel, G., Untch, R.H., Zapf, C.: An experimental determination of sufficient mutant operators. ACM Trans. Softw. Eng. Methodol. (TOSEM) **5**(2), 99–118 (1996)
22. Paul, T., Kimball, J.W., Zawodniok, M.J., Roth, T.P., McMillin, B.M., Chellappan, S.: Unified invariants for cyber-physical switched system stability. IEEE Trans. Smart Grid **5**(1), 112–120 (2014)
23. Platzer, A., Quesel, J.-D.: KeYmaera: a hybrid theorem prover for hybrid systems (system description). In: Armando, A., Baumgartner, P., Dowek, G. (eds.) IJCAR 2008. LNCS (LNAI), vol. 5195, pp. 171–178. Springer, Heidelberg (2008). doi:10.1007/978-3-540-71070-7_15
24. Quesel, J., Mitsch, S., Loos, S.M., Arechiga, N., Platzer, A.: How to model and prove hybrid systems with KeYmaera: a tutorial on safety. Int. J. Softw. Tools Technol. Transf. **18**(1), 67–91 (2016)
25. Roth, T., McMillin, B.: Physical attestation of cyber processes in the smart grid. In: Luiijf, E., Hartel, P. (eds.) CRITIS 2013. LNCS, vol. 8328, pp. 96–107. Springer, Heidelberg (2013). doi:10.1007/978-3-319-03964-0_9
26. Seshadri, A., Perrig, A., van Doorn, L., Khosla, P.K.: SWATT: software-based ATTestation for embedded devices. In: Proceedings of IEEE Symposium on Security and Privacy (S&P 2004), p. 272. IEEE (2004)
27. Valente, J., Barreto, C., Cárdenas, A.A.: Cyber-physical systems attestation. In: Proceedings of IEEE International Conference on Distributed Computing in Sensor Systems (DCOSS 2014), pp. 354–357. IEEE (2014)
28. Vodencarevic, A., Kleine Büning, H., Niggemann, O., Maier, A.: Identifying behavior models for process plants. In: Proceedings of IEEE Conference on Emerging Technologies & Factory Automation (ETFA 2011), pp. 1–8. IEEE (2011)
29. Wang, J., Sun, J., Yuan, Q., Pang, J.: Should we learn probabilistic models for model checking? a new approach and an empirical study. CoRR abs/1605.08278 (2016). http://arxiv.org/abs/1605.08278
30. Zheng, X., Julien, C., Kim, M., Khurshid, S.: Perceptions on the state of the art in verification and validation in cyber-physical systems. IEEE Syst. J. **PP**(99), 1–14 (2015)

From Electrical Switched Networks to Hybrid Automata

Alessandro Cimatti[1], Sergio Mover[2], and Mirko Sessa[1,3(✉)]

[1] Fondazione Bruno Kessler, Trento, Italy
{cimatti,sessa}@fbk.eu
[2] University of Colorado Boulder, Boulder, USA
sergio.mover@colorado.edu
[3] University of Trento, Trento, Italy

Abstract. In this paper, we propose a novel symbolic approach to automatically synthesize a Hybrid Automaton (HA) from a switched electrical network. The input network consists of a set of physical components interconnected according to some reconfigurable network topology. The underlying model defines a local dynamics for each component in terms of a Differential-Algebraic Equation (DAE), and a set of network topologies by means of discrete switches. Each switch configuration induces a different topology, where the behavior of the system is a Hybrid Differential-Algebraic Equations.

Two relevant problems for these networks are validation and reformulation. The first consists of determining if the network admits an Ordinary Differential Equations (ODE) that describes its dynamics; the second consists of obtaining such ODE from the initial DAE. This step is a key enabler to use existing formal verification tools that can cope with ODEs but not with DAEs.

Since the number of network topologies is exponential in the number of switches, first, we propose a technique based on Satisfiability Modulo Theories (SMT) that can solve the validation problem symbolically, avoiding the explicit enumeration of the topologies. Then, we show an SMT-based algorithm that reformulates the network into a symbolic HA. The algorithm avoids to explicitly enumerate the topologies clustering them by equivalent continuous dynamics.

We implemented the approach with several optimizations and we compared it with the explicit enumeration of configurations. The results demonstrate the scalability of our technique.

1 Introduction

Many practical systems feature emerging behaviors from the complex interactions of physical components, that are interconnected according to some reconfigurable topology. Typical examples include hydraulics [25] and electrical power supply networks [23]. The components interact by exchanging energy along the network branches, in a bidirectional fashion, that results in a relational, global model, that depends on the specific system configuration (or mode).

J. Fitzgerald et al. (Eds.): FM 2016, LNCS 9995, pp. 164–181, 2016.
DOI: 10.1007/978-3-319-48989-6_11

Kirchhoff Networks [14] are a well-known and powerful framework for component-based physical modeling, that allows to cover power-conserving network rules. Dedicated analysis methods, devised for "single-mode" networks, support the validation of some basic sanity properties (e.g. absence of VC-loops, or IL cutsets [24]). Following the Electronic-Hydraulic analogy [2], it is also possible to analyze interesting classes of hydraulic circuits, such as the WBS in Fig. 1.

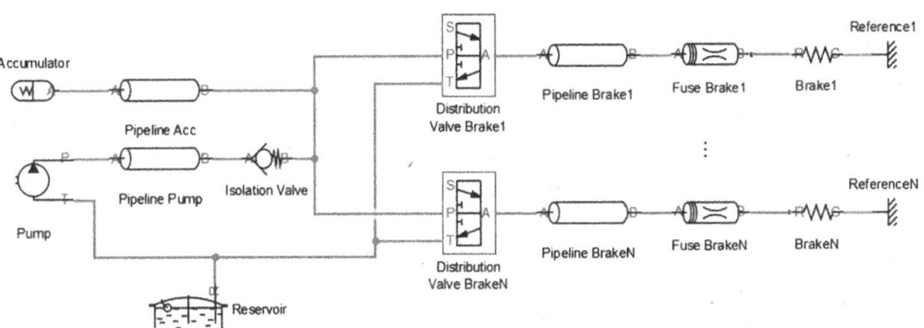

Fig. 1. Wheel Braking Systems (WBS) with N braking lines.

Unfortunately, dynamic reconfiguration yields networks that are associated with a potentially exponential number of modes. Consider, for example, the simple electrical circuit in Fig. 2: depending on the status of the switches and fuses, sixteen configurations are possible, each of which is associated with a suitable set of differential equations. Similar considerations apply, on a larger scale, to the hydraulic circuit from [25] in Fig. 1. In this paper, we tackle two key problems. The *network validation* problem consists of showing that the dynamics of the network can be expressible in form of an ODE (in order for it to be amenable to formal verification), and that all the output variables (i.e. variables that should be functionally represented by the state of the network) can be uniquely determined. The *network reformulation* problem consists of converting the network into an equivalent hybrid automaton, in order to enable functional verification of the network. The challenge lies in the fact that, for each discrete configuration, the dynamics of the network is defined by a Differential-Algebraic Equation (DAE). However, the available tools expect an Ordinary Differential Equation (ODE). Although solving the problem for a fixed configuration is rather simple, given a configuration of the switches, the number of configurations is exponential in the number of switches. Thus, an enumerative approach is hardly feasible: one would have to analyze all the possible modes, to rule out the ones that are deemed unfeasible and build a suitable equational model for each of the remaining modes. In practice, such an approach is not feasible, for two main reasons. First, a manual approach is an extremely tedious and error prone task. Second, an enumerative approach may results in an enormous model, that is hardly manageable for verification tools. Such an enumerative approach is in fact applied in [22], to the modeling of a few two-switches circuit.

In this work, we discuss how to automatically reformulate a Linear Electrical Kirchhoff Network into the corresponding Hybrid Automaton with ODE continuous dynamics. We propose a symbolic approach to the network validation problem, and a symbolic algorithm for the reformulation problem. The idea is to aggregate the discrete modes that share the same dynamics, with different variants in the computation. This results in a more efficient reformulation, and a more compact Hybrid Automaton.

The approach is experimentally evaluated on several electrical and hydraulic benchmarks, where we carry out the validation, and compare (the variants of) the proposed symbolic reformulation approach with its enumerative counterpart. The results demonstrate a much greater scalability of the symbolic approach. We also discuss the application of the proposed approach to some benchmarks in the literature [16,22].

The paper is organized as follows: In Sect. 2 we describe some background. In Sect. 3 we formally define the problem at hand. In Sect. 4 we describe the validation routine, and in Sect. 5 we describe the reformulation methods. In Sect. 6 we describe the related work, and in Sect. 7 we experimentally evaluate the proposed approach. In Sect. 8 we draw some conclusions and promising research directions. In [6] we work out a motivating example, report the proofs of the theorems, and present some additional experimental results.

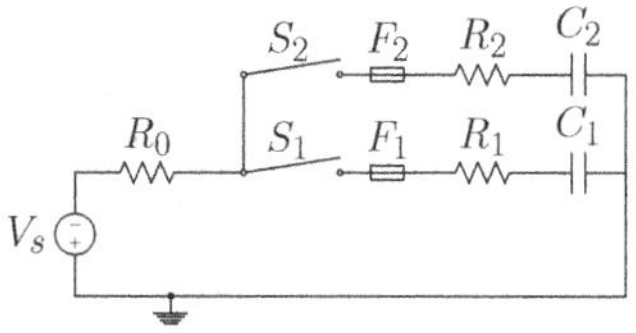

Fig. 2. Switched RC Network.

2 Background

Notation. We use the standard notions of theory, satisfiability, validity, and logical consequence. We restrict to formulas interpreted with the Theory of Linear Real Arithmetic (LRA) [4].

Given a formula in first-order logic ψ and a set of variables X, we write $\psi(X)$ to denote that X is the set of free variables in ψ. We write $\varphi \models_{\mathcal{T}} \psi$ to denote that the formula ψ is a logical consequence of φ in the theory $\mathcal{T}$; when clear from context, we omit $\mathcal{T}$ and simply write $\varphi \models \psi$. An assignment μ for a set of variables X is the set $\{x \mapsto c \mid x \in X \text{ and } c \text{ is a constant}\}$, $\mu_{|X}$ is the projection of all the assignments in μ only to variables contained in X, and $\mu(x)$ is the value assigned to x in μ. We denote with $|X|$ the cardinality of the set X. Given a set of real variables X, we will use the the notation $\boldsymbol{X}$ to refer to the vector that contains all the variables in X ordered in a lexicographic order. If X is a set of variables, then X' and $\dot{X}$ are the sets obtained by replacing each element x with its primed and dotted version respectively.

Hybrid Automata. *Hybrid automata* (HA) [13] represent a system with continuous and discrete dynamics. We use a symbolic representation of hybrid automata, where the discrete locations and transitions are represented symbolically [9].

A *Hybrid automaton* is a tuple $H = \langle D, R, Init, Invar, Trans, Flow\rangle$ where (1) D is the set of discrete variables; (2) R is the set of continuous variables; (3) $Init(D, R)$ represents the set of initial states; (4)$Invar(D, R)$ represents the set of invariant states; (5)$Trans(D, R, D', R')$ represents the set of discrete transitions; (6)$Flow(D, \dot{R}, R)$ represents the flow condition. We assume that all the formulas $Init$, $Invar$, $Trans$ and $Flow$ are quantifier-free and linear. We assume $Invar$ to be of the form $\psi(D) \rightarrow \bigwedge_{p\in P} p(R)$, where $p \in P$ is a predicate, to ensure the convexity of the invariants. We assume $Flow$ to be of the form $\psi(D) \rightarrow \bigwedge_{p\in P} p(R, \dot{R})$, where $p \in P$ is an equality.

In the above definition, $Flow$ may either define a system of Differential-Algebraic Equations (DAEs) or Ordinary Differential Equations (ODEs). We say that the automaton has an *ODE dynamics* if, for each assignment μ to D, the conjunct of $\psi(D) \rightarrow \bigwedge_{p\in P} p(R, \dot{R})$ that holds for μ is a system of ODEs. Otherwise, the automaton has a *DAE dynamics*.

A *state* of a hybrid automaton H is an assignment s to the variables $D \cup R$. Informally, a *run* of the automaton is a sequence of states such that the first state is in the initial states, every state belongs to the invariant states, and each pair of consecutive states either satisfies a discrete transition or follows the solution of the differential equations described in the flow condition. The semantics of the HA is provided in terms of the runs that it accepts.

Electrical Networks. An (non-switched) electrical network is formed by the connection of a set of (continuous) components. Without loss of generality, we consider only components with two terminals. A *continuous component* e_i defines two quantities, the voltage (difference of potential) across the two terminals of the component, and the current that flows through the component. We denote with $i_i(t)$ and $v_i(t)$ the current and the voltage of e_i. $v_i(t)$ and $i_i(t)$ change continuously in time according to a *constitutive relation*, ψ_i, a Differential-Algebraic Equation among $v_i(t)$, $i_i(t)$, and their derivatives $\dot{v}_i, \dot{i}_i$. Furthermore, for each component e_i we consider the variables v_i^- and v_i^+, that represent the value of the potential at the two terminals of e_i. These variables are connected to v_i through the *voltage equation* $v_i = v_i^+ - v_i^-$.

We denote with V_i the set of variables of e_i. We further partition V_i into the following subsets: (1) $X_i := \{x \mid \dot{x} \textit{ appears in } \psi_i\}$ is the set of *state* variables (their derivatives appear in the constitutive relation of e_i); (2) U_i is the set of *input* variables, which depends on the component type; (3) Y_i is the set of *output* variables, which depends on the component type. The sets X_i, U_i, Y_i are disjoint, and $V_i = X_i \cup U_i \cup Y_i$. $\dot{X}_i$ is the set of first derivatives of X_i. In Table 1 we report the constitutive relations for the electrical components considered in this paper and their sets of variables. Furthermore, we say that a component is *active* if it has at least a state or input variable, and *passive* otherwise.

The connection of components terminals is represented by a directed graph: an oriented edge represents a component and a node represents the connection of components terminals. As usual, the orientation of the edges is chosen arbitrarily assuming a reference direction for the current.

Table 1. Constitutive relations and variables of continuous components.

Component	Constitutive relation	X_i	U_i	Y_i	Constants
Voltage source	$v_i = V_s$	$\emptyset$	$\{v_i\}$	$\{i_i, v_i^+, v_i^-\}$	V_s
Current source	$i_i = I_s$	$\emptyset$	$\{i_i\}$	$\{v_i, v_i^+, v_i^-\}$	I_s
Resistor	$v_i = R\, i_i$	$\emptyset$	$\emptyset$	$\{i_i, v_i, v_i^+, v_i^-\}$	R
Capacitor	$i_i = C\, \dot{v}_i$	$\{v_i\}$	$\emptyset$	$\{i_i, v_i^+, v_i^-\}$	C
Inductor	$v_i = L\, \dot{i}_i$	$\{i_i\}$	$\emptyset$	$\{v_i, v_i^+, v_i^-\}$	L
Ground	$v_i^+ = 0$	$\emptyset$	$\emptyset$	$\{i_i, v_i^+\}$	

Definition 1 (Electrical network). *An* electrical network *[5, 24] is a directed graph $G = \langle N, E, \eta \rangle$, where (1) N is a set of nodes; (2) E is a set of components; (3) $\eta : E \mapsto N \times N$ defines the directed edges between nodes.*

Let $E_n^{in} = \{e \mid e \in E \text{ and } (n_1, n) = \eta(e)\}$ and $E_n^{out} = \{e \mid e \in E \text{ and } (n, n_1) = \eta(e)\}$ be the sets of incoming and outgoing edges of the node n. Additionally, let $P_n = \bigcup_{e_i \in E_n^{in}} v_i^+ \cup \bigcup_{e_i \in E_n^{out}} v_i^-$ denote the set of all the potentials of the components incident on the node n, considering also the direction sign imposed by the edge orientation. The connection of the components is described by the *Kirchhoff Current Law* (KCL) and the *Kirchhoff Voltage Law* (KVL):

$$KCL_G := \bigcup_{n \in N} \left(\sum_{c_i \in E_n^{in}} i_i - \sum_{c_i \in E_n^{out}} i_i = 0 \right) \quad KVL_G := \bigcup_{n \in N} \bigcup_{p_1, p_2 \in P_n} (p_1 = p_2)$$

Definition 2 (Differential-Algebraic Equation of a network). *Given a network $G = \langle N, E, \eta \rangle$, its associated DAE, called DAE_G, is defined by the set of constitutive equations $\{\psi_i \mid e_i \in E\}$, the set of voltage equations $v_i = v_i^+ - v_i^-$, and the sets of algebraic equations KCL_G and KVL_G.*

While there exist several equivalent DAE systems to represent an electrical network, we basically use the one obtained applying the Node Tableau Analysis (NTA) [24].

We extend the notation used to specify the component's variables and their partitions to a network G. Hence, we have the sets $V_G := \bigcup_{e_i \in E} V_i$, $X_G := \bigcup_{e_i \in E} X_i$, $U_G := \bigcup_{e_i \in E} U_i$, $Y_G := \bigcup_{e_i \in E} Y_i$. A *state* of the network is given by an assignment μ to all the variables V_G. A state μ is a *consistent initial value* for DAE_G if DAE_G has a solution for μ (i.e. if replacing all the variables with the assigned constants in μ the resulting system of algebraic equations has a solution). A variable $y \in Y_G$ is *underdetermined* if there exist two solutions μ' and μ'' of DAE_G such that $\mu'_{|V_G \setminus \{y\}} = \mu''_{|V_G \setminus \{y\}}$ and $\mu'(y) \neq \mu''(y)$.

Definition 3 (Electrical network semantics). *The semantics of the network is defined by its associated DAE_G. We say that there exists a trajectory from a* *state μ to a state μ' if μ is a consistent initial value and there exists a continuously differentiable function $f : (0,t] \to V_G$ such that: $f(0) = \mu$, $f(t) = \mu'$, and for all $\delta \in (0,t]$, $\frac{df}{dt}(\delta)$ and $f(\delta)$ are a solution of DAE_G.*

Structural Analysis for Electrical Network. Structural analysis for (non-switched) electrical networks is a standard technique used to determine if it is possible to *reformulate* the DAE into a system of *Ordinary Differential Equations* (ODEs). In the following, we will reuse established results from structural analysis. We use the standard definition of loops and cutset for a graph G. A sequence $n_0, e_0, \ldots, n_{k+1} \in N \times (E \times N)^k$ of nodes and edges is a *loop* if there exists a path from n_0 to n_{k+1} (for $i \in [0,k]$, either $\eta(e_i) = (n_i, n_{i+1})$ or $\eta(e_i) = (n_{i+1}, n_i)$), and all the nodes are different, apart from n_0 and n_{k+1} (for $i \in [0,k]$, $n_i \neq n_{i+1}$ and $n_0 = n_{k+1}$). The definition of loop ignores the edges orientation. We use the standard notion of subgraph, connected graph and connected component of a graph. If $G = \langle N, E, \eta \rangle$ is a connected graph, $K \subseteq E$ is a *cutset* of G if removing K from E results in a disconnected graph, and K is minimal (i.e. removing a proper subset of K does not disconnect G). A loop is a V-loop (resp. VC-loop) if the only components on the edges are voltage sources (resp. voltage sources and capacitors). A cutset is an I-cutset (resp. IL-cutset) if the only components in the cutset are current sources (resp. current sources and inductors).

Theorem 1 (Existence of an ODE reformulation (Theorem 6.3 from [24])). *Given a connected electrical network G, the network has neither VC-loops nor IL-cutsets if and only if its associated DAE_G can be reformulated into the ODE model:*

$$\dot{X_G} = AX_G + BU_G \qquad\qquad Y_G = CX_G + DU_G \tag{1}$$

where $A \in \mathbb{R}^{|X_G| \times |X_G|}$, $B \in \mathbb{R}^{|X_G| \times |U_G|}$, $C \in \mathbb{R}^{|Y_G| \times |X_G|}$, $D \in \mathbb{R}^{|Y_G| \times |U_G|}$.

The goal of the reformulation is to get the ODE, instead of a DAE, which are more amenable for simulation and verification.

The reformulation of DAE_G as an ODE can be performed applying the *Superposition Theorem* [26]. The theorem tells that the response (the voltage and the current) of a component of a linear circuit is equal to the sum of the responses caused by each source acting alone (with all the other sources off). Turning on/off a voltage source means setting its voltage to 1/0 (the value for *on* must be different from 0), while turning on/off a current source means setting its current to 1/0. Capacitors and inductors are considered sources (of voltage and current respectively). The reformulation works by determining the contribution of each source (including inductors and capacitors) on the response (current or voltage) of each other component. Formally, for a component e_i with a reformulated variable w, the reformulation works determining the coefficients $a_{w,z}$ such that:

$$w = \textstyle\sum_{z \in (X_G \cup U_G)} a_{w,z} z \tag{2}$$

where a coefficient $a_{w,z} \in \mathbb{R}$ represents the effect of the source variable z on the reformulated variable w. $a_{w,z}$ is obtained considering only the effect of z, while disregarding the effects of the other sources. In practice, $a_{w,z}$ is the assignment to the variable w in the system DAE_G constrained by adding the constraints $z = 1$ and $l = 0$, for all the $l \in X_G \cup U_G \setminus \{z\}$.

Switched Electrical Networks. A *switch* e_i is a component with two discrete states, *open* and *closed.* The state of the switch is represented with the Boolean variable m_i (i.e. m_i is true iff the switch is open). Let $M_i := \{m_i\}$ be the set of discrete variables, $C_i := X_i \cup U_i \cup Y_i$ the set of continuous variables and $V_i = M_i \cup C_i$ the set of all the variables of a switch. The constitutive relation of a switch is $\psi_i := \begin{cases} i_i = 0 & \text{if } m_i \\ v_i = 0 & \text{otherwise} \end{cases}$ (i.e. the switch disconnects or connects its terminals when it is open or closed). The switching behavior is defined by an invariant and a guard condition, $invar_i : 2^{M_i} \rightarrow \phi(C_i)$ and $guard_i : 2^{M_i} \rightarrow \phi(C_i)$. $invar_i$ defines the invariant condition of the switch that must hold in each discrete state, while $guard_i$ defines the condition that must hold in a discrete state to allow the transition to the other state.

Definition 4 (Switched Electrical Network). *A* switched electrical network *$G = \langle N, E, \eta \rangle$ is an electrical network where E may include also switches.*

We extend the set of variables defined for a component to the switched network in the obvious way. Also, let $E_m \subseteq E$ be the subset of all the switches components in E. We refer to each possible (complete) assignment μ to the discrete variables M_G as a *discrete configuration* of the network, and we denote with 2^{M_G} the set of all the possible discrete configurations. Notice that, every different discrete configuration of the switches induces a (non-switched) electrical network. In the following, given a discrete configuration μ, we refer to $DAE_G(\mu)$ as the DAE associated to the (non-switched) electrical network induced by μ.

Definition 5 (Valid switched electrical network). *We say that a switched electrical network G is* valid, *if, for all possible discrete configurations $\mu \in 2^{M_G}$, $DAE_G(\mu)$ can be reformulated into an ODE.*

In other words, a switched electrical network G is *valid*, if, for all possible discrete configurations $\mu \in 2^{M_G}$:

(i) $DAE_G(\mu)$ has neither VC-loops nor IL-cutsets.
(iI) All the output variables Y_G in $DAE_G(\mu)$ are not underdetermined.

Definition 6 (Valid switched electrical network semantics). *We define the semantics of a valid switched electrical network $G = \langle N, E, \eta \rangle$ as the hybrid automaton $H_G = \langle D, R, Init, Invar, Trans, Flow \rangle$ where (1) $D := M_G$; (2) $R := C_G$; (3) $Init(D, R) := True$; (4) $Invar(D, R) := \bigwedge_{e_i \in E_m} (m_i \rightarrow invar_i(\{m_i\})) \wedge (\neg m_i \rightarrow invar_i(\emptyset))$; (5) $Trans(D, R, D', R') := (\bigvee_{e_i \in E_m} (m_i \wedge \neg m_i' \wedge guard_i(\{m_i\})) \vee (\neg m_i \wedge m_i' \wedge guard_i(\emptyset)) \wedge (\bigwedge_{x \in X_G} x' = x)$; (6) $Flow(D, \dot{R}, R) := DAE_G$;*

Notice that the flow conditions of the automaton that defines the semantic of the network still define a Differential-Algebraic Equation (DAE) and not an Ordinary Differential Equation (ODE).

3 Problem Definition

In this paper, we address the following problems.

Definition 7 (Network validation problem). *The network validation problem consists of determining if a switched electrical network is valid. Additionally, if it is not the case, the problem also consists of finding the set of the discrete configurations that are not valid.*

A valid network can be encoded into a symbolic hybrid automaton where *Flow* defines a system of ODEs for each configuration.

The hybrid automaton H_G that defines the semantics of the network G (see Definition 6) is a concise representation of the network. However, no model checking tools are able to analyze this kind of input (the combined symbolic representation and DAE). Thus, the problem that must be solved to enable the verification of a switched electrical network is the reformulation of the electrical switched network G into a hybrid automaton with an ODE dynamics. Note that this problem extends the reformulation problem in Theorem 1 from a single DAE to a set of DAEs, one for each discrete configuration in 2^{M_G}.

Definition 8 (Hybrid Automata reformulation). *Given a valid switched electrical network G, the reformulation problem consists of encoding G into a symbolic hybrid automaton with ODE dynamics.*

4 Network Validation

We show how to reduce the validation conditions to a series of SMT checks.

SMT encoding. Given a switched network $G = \langle N, E, \eta \rangle$, we encode the Differential-Algebraic Equation DAE_G defined by the network as a quantifier free-formula in LRA. This formula will be used both for the validation and the reformulation steps.

The encoding formula predicates over the same variables of the network. We reuse the same notation for the different sets of variables used for the network G. In the encoding, we interpret each variable in M_G as a Boolean variable and each variable in $X_G \cup U_G \cup Y_G$ as a Real variable. The encoding also predicates over the first-order derivatives of X_G, $\dot{X}_G$. We interpret each variable in $\dot{X}_G$ as a Real (the semantics should be clear from the context). The main reason is that both the validation and the reformulation just consider the algebraic relations defined by the equations, and not how the variables change as a function of time.

The formula ψ_{DAE_G} connects the constitutive relation and voltage equation for each component e_i through the KCL and KVL conditions:

$$\psi_{DAE_G} := \bigwedge_{e_i \in E \setminus E_{sources}} (\psi_i) \wedge \bigwedge_{e_i \in E} (v_i = v_i^+ - v_i^-) \wedge \psi_{KCL} \wedge \psi_{KVL}$$

$$\psi_{KCL} := \bigwedge_{n \in N} \Big(\sum_{e_i \in E_n^{in}} i_i - \sum_{e_i \in E_n^{out}} i_i = 0 \Big) \quad \psi_{KVL} := \bigwedge_{n \in N} \Big(\bigwedge_{p_1 \in P_n} \Big(\bigwedge_{p_2 \in P_n} p_1 = p_2 \Big) \Big)$$

Existence of VC-loops or IL-cutsets. As stated in Theorem 1, the DAE of a single configuration can be reformulated into an ODE if the network G does not have any *VC-loops* or any *IL-cutsets* and if the network is connected. We encode these conditions in the following formulas.

$$val_z := \exists C_G, \dot{X}_G . (\psi_{DAE_G} \wedge z = 1 \wedge \textstyle\bigwedge_{l \in X_G \cup U_G \setminus \{z\}} l = 0)$$
$$val := \textstyle\bigwedge_{Z \in X_G \cup U_G} val_z$$

The formula val_z sets to 1 the state or input variable z of an active component (i.e. voltage sources, current sources, capacitors and inductors), while it keeps all the other state and input variables to 0. If val_z is unsatisfiable for some discrete configuration in 2^{M_G}, we have either a *VC-loop* or an *IL-cutset* involving z. This is due to the KVL and the KCL conditions. The first ensures that the sum of the voltages in a loop must be equal to 0. The latter ensures that the sum of the currents on the components in a cutset must be 0. For example, consider a configuration μ with a *VC-loop* that contains the voltage source e_i. The sum of the KVL equations for the loop only contains variables from X_G and U_G, and in particular the input variable v_i of e_i. In the formula val_{v_i} we have that $v_i = 1$, while all the other state and input variables are equal to zero. Thus, the KVL equation of the loop reduces to $1 = 0$, and hence val_{v_i} is unsatisfiable for μ. An analogous reasoning can be done for an *IL-cutset* and the KCL conditions.

Lemma 1. *The formula val_{v_i} (resp. val_{i_i}) is satisfiable for all configurations $\mu \in 2^{M_G}$ if and only if the switched electrical network G does not have any VC-loops (resp. IL-cutsets) involving v_i (resp. i_i).*

For lack of space, we provide the proofs in [6]. As a corollary of Lemma 1, we have that the formula *val* represents the set of all the configurations that do not have any *VC-loop* or *IL-cutset*. By Theorem 1, each configuration of the network admits a reformulation if there are no *VC-loops* or *IL-cutsets* and the network is connected.

Existence of underdetermined output variables. In a switched network, a configuration on a switch may induce a topology of the network that is not connected, but is formed by several connected components (of the graph of the network). The Theorem 1 can still be applied on each discrete configuration and on each connected component. In fact, for a network with neither *VC-loops* nor *IL-cutsets*, the theorem still guarantees the existence of the reformulation in terms of the state and input variables for each connected component of the graph containing at least an active component. We encode a sufficient condition for the connectedness of the network in the following formula:

$$und := \exists C_G, \dot{X}_G.(\psi_{DAE_G} \wedge \bigwedge_{z \in X_G \cup U_G}(z = 0) \wedge \bigvee_{y \in Y_G}(y \neq 0)) \qquad (3)$$

We consider the fact that all the output variables of a graph component are uniquely determined (i.e. are not underdetermined) by the input and state variables contained in such component if and only if the component is connected and does not show *degenerate* configurations such as *VC-loops* or *IL-cutsets*. The formula encodes that there exists a $y \in Y_G$ that can have a value different from 0 when all the input and state variables are 0. If the formula is satisfiable for some configuration μ, then y is underdetermined in that configuration.

Lemma 2. *The formula und is satisfiable for some configuration* $\mu \in 2^{M_G}$ *if and only if there exists a variable* $y \in Y_G$ *that is underdetermined.*

As a corollary of Lemma 2, we have that *und* represents the set of all the configurations that contain some underdetermined variable.

5 Network Reformulation to Hybrid Automaton

5.1 Reformulation Algorithm

Given a network $G = \langle N, E, \eta \rangle$, $H_G^r = \langle D^r, R^r, Init^r, Invar^r, Trans^r, Flow^r \rangle$ is the reformulated hybrid automaton. H_G^r is defined as the hybrid automaton H_G in the Definition 6, except for $Invar^r$ and $Flow^r$. The invariant condition $Invar^r$ is given by $Invar^r := Invar \wedge Invar_Y^{ref}$, where $Invar$ is the invariant condition of H_G, and $Invar_Y^{ref}$ represents the reformulation of the output variables Y_G (see Eq. 2). $Flow^r$ represents the ODE dynamics in terms of $\dot{X}_G$, X_G, and U_G. The goal of the reformulation process is to synthesize both the $Flow^r$ and $Invar_Y^{ref}$ formulas.

In the following algorithms, we use a standard stack-based interface of an SMT solver (*push*, *assert*, *isSat*, *pop*, *reset* primitives). This allows us, after asserting a formula γ, to set a backtrack point (*push*), assert another formula β (*assert*), check the satisfiability of the conjunction of the asserted formulas (*isSat*), and restore the state of the solver (i.e. asserted formulas and learned clauses) at the backtrack point (*pop*). This way, the satisfiability problem is solved keeping several learned clauses. Additionally, we assume to have the primitive *getModel*, to get a complete satisfying assignment to the free variables of the formula in the stack, and *quantify*, to eliminate the quantifiers present in the formula.

We describe a symbolic approach that groups together the discrete configurations that share the same ODE system. The algorithm REFORMULATE in Fig. 3 reformulates only a subset of variables $W \subseteq \dot{X}_G \cup Y_G$. The algorithm can be used to reformulate all the dotted and output variables of the system by setting

$W = \dot{X}_G \cup Y_G$. However, we will show how the modularity of REFORMULATE can be used to obtain different, and usually coarser, partitionings of the discrete configurations.

REFORMULATE takes as input the encoding of the network ψ_{DAE_G}, the sets of state and input variables X_G, U_G, and a set of variables W to be reformulated. The main loop (line 3) of the algorithm enumerates all the discrete configurations of the network. Initially, the solver picks a random discrete configuration μ (line 4), and then symbolically applies the superposition theorem (on the network induced by μ) calling the function GETCOEFFICIENTS (line 5). The output of GETCOEFFICIENTS is a map of coefficients F: for a $w \in W$ and a $z \in X_G \cup U_G$, $F(w)(z) \in \mathbb{R}$ is the coefficient that was obtained by observing the effect of the source z on the variable w. Then, at line 6, the function GETEQMODES computes the set of all the *equivalent* discrete configurations β. GETEQMODES guarantees that $\mu' \in \beta$ if and only if GETCOEFFICIENTS finds the same coefficients when called on μ and on μ' with the same parameters ψ_{DAE_G}, X_G, U_G and W. Then, at line 7, the algorithm *blocks* all the discrete configurations represented in β; this is a key step in the algorithm that prunes a set of discrete configurations from the search, avoiding their explicit enumeration. Finally, from line 8 to the end of the loop, REFORMULATE constructs the flow and invariant conditions.

REFORMULATE ($\psi_{DAE_G}, X_G, U_G, W$):
1. $(Flow_W, Invar_W) := (True, True)$
 # Tautology over the variables M_G
2. solver.assert($\bigwedge_{m \in M_G} m \vee \neg m$)
3. **while** solver.isSat():
    # Get a configuration where $Flow_W$ is not defined
4. μ := solver.getModel()
    # Get the coefficients that contribute to each $w \in W$
5. F := GETCOEFFICIENTS ($\psi_{DAE_G}, X_G, U_G, W, \mu$)
    # Get the modes that have the same dynamic for W
6. β := GETEQMODES ($\psi_{DAE_G}, X_G, U_G, W, F$)
    # Block the equivalent modes
7. solver.assert($\neg\beta$)
8. $(ref_{\dot{X}_G}, ref_{Y_G})$:= GETREF (X_G, U_G, W, F)
9. $(Flow_W, Invar_W) := (Flow_W \wedge (\beta \rightarrow ref_{\dot{X}_G}), Invar_W \wedge (\beta \rightarrow ref_{Y_G}))$
10. **return** $(Flow_W, Invar_W)$

Fig. 3. Reformulate a set of variables W.

The functions GETCOEFFICIENTS in Fig. 6 implements the reformulation by the superposition theorem. Each execution of the loop at line 3, computes the effect of a state and input variable on all the variables in W.

The function GETEQMODES, shown in Fig. 5, computes the set of configurations equivalent to μ in terms of reformulation. For each state and input variable, the function re-encodes the superposition conditions (line 4) and additionally encodes the coefficient constraints for the current discrete configurations μ (line 6). Then, the formula β (line 9) encodes all the discrete configurations that have exactly the same reformulation of μ. We also consider an alternative implementation of GETEQMODES, GETEQMODESMODULAR, that computes the existential quantification independently for each single conjunct of the formula γ, instead of the whole formula γ.

5.2 All and Single Variables Partitioning

The REFORMULATE algorithm allows us to reformulate sets of variables (i.e. subsets of $\dot{X}_G \cup Y_G$) instead of all the variables $\dot{X}_G \cup Y_G$. Thus, it allows us to obtain different kinds of partitioning of the discrete configurations and the ordinary differential equations. We define two reformulation algorithms that obtain different partitioning. The ALLREF algorithm, shown at the top of Fig. 7, first reformulates all the controlled variables X_G. Thus, in this case we obtain sets of discrete configurations that share the same system of ODEs (a system of equations of the form $\dot{\boldsymbol{X}}_{\boldsymbol{G}} = A\boldsymbol{X}_{\boldsymbol{G}} + B\boldsymbol{U}_{\boldsymbol{G}}$). Then, ALLREF reformulates all the output variables Y_G independently.

The other algorithm, SINGLEREF (shown in the bottom of Fig. 7), instead reformulates all the variables independently.

```
GETREF (X_G, U_G, W, F):
(ref_{Ẋ_G}, ref_{Y_G}) := (True, True)
for each w ∈ W:
    rhs_w := 0
    for each z ∈ X_G ∪ U_G:
        rhs_w := rhs_w + F(w)(z) * z
    if w ∈ Ẋ_G :
        ref_{Ẋ_G} := ref_{Ẋ_G} ∧ w = rhs_w
    else:
        ref_{Y_G} := ref_{Y_G} ∧ w = rhs_w
return (ref_{Ẋ_G}, ref_{Y_G})
```

Fig. 4. Construction of the reformulation formulas.

```
GETEQMODES (ψ_{DAE_G}, X_G, U_G, W, F):
1. eqSolver.reset()
2. γ := True
3. for each z ∈ X_G ∪ U_G:
4.     sup_z := z = 1 ∧ ⋀_{l∈(X_G∪U_G)\{z}} l = 0
5.     γ_F := True
6.     for each w ∈ W:
7.         γ_F := γ_F ∧ w = F(w)(z)
8.     γ := γ ∧ ∃C_G, Ẋ_G.(ψ_{DAE_G} ∧ γ_F ∧ sup_z)
9. β := eqSolver.quantify(γ)
10. return β
```

Fig. 5. Find the discrete configurations with an equivalent dynamics for a set of variables W.

```
GETCOEFFICIENTS (ψ_{DAE_G}, X_G, U_G, W, μ):
# F maps vars in W and X_G ∪ U_G to real values
F : W → (X_G ∪ U_G) → ℝ
coeffSolver.assert(ψ_{DAE_G} ∧ μ)
for each z ∈ X_G ∪ U_G:
    coeffSolver.push()
    sup_z := z = 1 ∧ ⋀_{l∈(X_G∪U_G)\{z}} l = 0
    coeffSolver.assert(sup_z)
    μ' := coeffSolver.getModel()
    for each w ∈ W:
        # μ'(w) represents the effect of z on w
        F(w)(z) := μ'(w)
    coeffSolver.pop()
return F
```

Fig. 6. Computes the superposition coefficients for a set of variables W.

```
ALLREF (ψ_{DAE_G}, X_G, U_G):
1. (Flow^r, Invar_Y^{ref}) := REFORMULATE (ψ_{DAE_G}, X_G, U_G, Ẋ_G)
2. for each w ∈ Y_G:
3.     (Flow_w, Invar_w) := REFORMULATE (ψ_{DAE_G}, X_G, U_G, {w})
4.     (Flow^r, Invar_Y^{ref}) := (Flow^r ∧ Flow_w, Invar_Y^{ref} ∧ Invar_w)
5. return (Flow^r, Invar_Y^{ref})

SINGLEREF (ψ_{DAE_G}, X_G, U_G):
1. (Flow^r, Invar_Y^{ref}) := (True, True)
2. for each w ∈ Ẋ_G ∪ Y_G:
3.     (Flow_w, Invar_w) := REFORMULATE (ψ_{DAE_G}, X_G, U_G, {w})
4.     (Flow^r, Invar_Y^{ref}) := (Flow^r ∧ Flow_w, Invar_Y^{ref} ∧ Invar_w)
5. return (Flow^r, Invar_Y^{ref})
```

Fig. 7. Reformulation algorithms with different reformulation strategies.

As a further observation, in practice we do not need to reformulate all the output variables Y_G. In fact, we need to reformulate only those variables needed to define the dynamics of the system (e.g. they may be used in the invariant $invar_i$ and $guard_i$ conditions of a switch) or the variables that we want to observe.

6 Related Work

The solutions to the validation and reformulation problems for electrical networks (without switches) are well known [5,24]. We differ from these works since we focus on networks with discrete switches, where the main issue is to cope with the exponential explosion in the number of discrete configurations. Then, we reuse several techniques from structural analysis, as the superposition principle [26], but we re-interpret them in a symbolic setting.

Other works consider also networks with discrete switches. Several approaches [19] do not consider ideal switches, but model the switch introducing parasitic resistances. A drawback of this approach is that it requires to determine a priori a set of parameters (e.g. the resistance of the resistor); then, these parameters have the effect to change the dynamics of the systems, producing as a result an approximation of the intended behavior. Ideal switches have been mainly considered in context of simulation, for example in [18]. While the focus is often on non-linear dynamics, the problem solved in these works is to produce a single simulation of the network. In this context, they reformulate the DAE into an ODE every time the simulator performs a discrete switch. Thus, these works do not solve the validation and the reformulation problem, since they focus on a single execution of the system.

Several works focus on the translation from Stateflow/Simulink models to hybrid automata [1,17,20]. We point out that the Simulink modeling is based on a functional representation of a system where every block is seen as an unidirectional Input-Output function, thus it is not suitable for a component-based physical modeling that is intrinsically bidirectional. There are several works [29] on the formal verification of Analog-Mixed-Signal (AMS) circuits. Most works focus on non-switched circuits [10,11,16] and try to solve a reachability problem. They start from the network representation but they manually encode it as a hybrid automaton. A different approach is considered in [30], where a non-linear circuit is automatically abstracted and encoded using SMT. We remark that none of these works solves the validation and reformulation problem for a switched electrical network.

Finally, our reformulation approach produces a symbolic hybrid automata model that can be analyzed by model checkers tools like HybridSAL [27] and HyComp[7], using relational abstraction [21,28], or dReach [3,15].

7 Experimental Evaluation

The approach was implemented in pySMT [12], a library for SMT formulae manipulation and solving, using MathSat5 [8] for Quantifier Elimination. We evaluated the effectiveness and the scalability of the symbolic approach in the validation and reformulation problems. The experimental evaluation was run on a 64 bit system with an Intel Xeon E3-1246 processor at 3.5 GHz and 16 GB RAM. The tool and the benchmarks used in the experiments are available at https://es.fbk.eu/people/sessa/attachment/FM2016/fm16.tar.bz2.

Benchmarks. We consider several classes of benchmarks. The following (Buck, Boost, Buck-Boost) *DC-DC converters* are taken from [22].

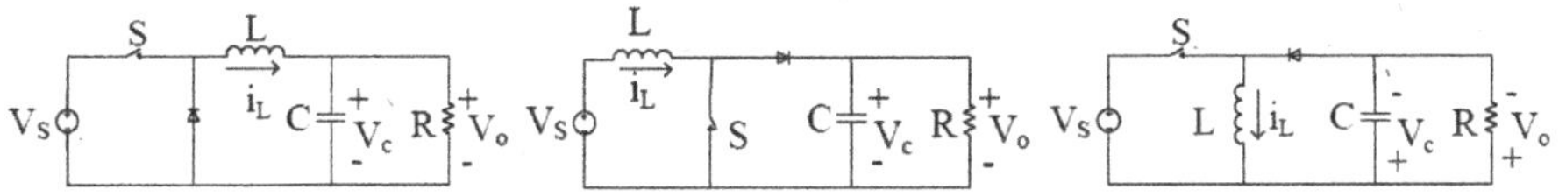

The *Switched RC Network* SRCN_N is a scalable benchmark obtained from the circuit of Fig. 2 by parameterizing the number of (up to 8) capacitive branches.

The *Non Linear Transmission Line (NLTL)* depicted below represents a well-known phenomenon (discretization of propagation) along a transmission line [16]. We parameterize the benchmark NLTL_N on the number N of (up to 10) pairs of stages.

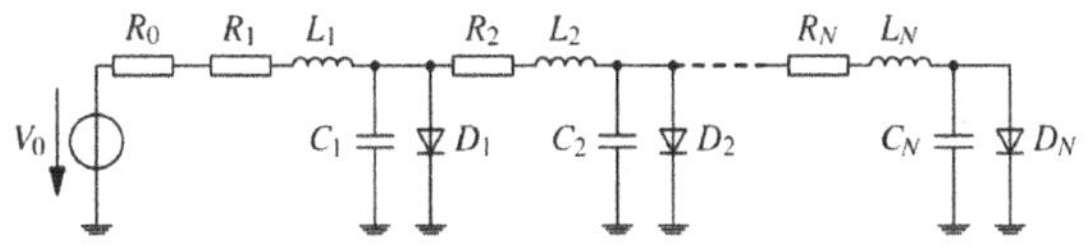

The *Wheel Braking System* benchmarks follow the description in the SAE Standard AIR6110 [25] (see Fig. 1). We consider the WBS_N benchmarks, parameterized on the number of (up to 6) braking lines. The WBS consists of a pressure supply line made of a pump, an accumulator, pipelines and an isolation valve, connected to replicas of a braking line made of pipelines, distribution valves, fuses and brakes. Following the Electronic-Hydraulic analogy, the pump is modeled as an ideal constant voltage source, the pipes as resistors, the accumulator and the brakes as capacitors, the distribution valves and the fuses as ideal switches, and the isolation valve as a diode.

For each of the scalable benchmarks, the number of discrete configurations grows exponentially with the problem size, reaching a million of system configurations for the NLTL_{10}. Additional information are available in the in [6].

Validation. We first consider the results of the validation. For the scalable benchmarks, we report the comparison of three different strategies: the baseline *Enum* strategy, explicitly enumerates the system configurations and for each of them validates the induced DAE; the *SyGlo* and *SyMod* strategies apply quantifier elimination (QE) over two different SMT encoding of the validation problem. The former tries to minimize the number of QEs encoding the validation problem into a global SMT formula, the latter tries to reduce the complexity of the global QE decomposing the global encoding into a modular sequence of simpler formulas. From the results (SRCN, NLTL, WBS from the left) we see that the symbolic approaches outperform the enumerative approach at least of one order of magnitude in all the benchmarks. While the two symbolic approaches show similar performance on the SRCN, for the WBS and NLTL *SyMod* accomplishes the task while *SyGlo* times out. In general, *SyMod* performs much better than *SyGlo*.

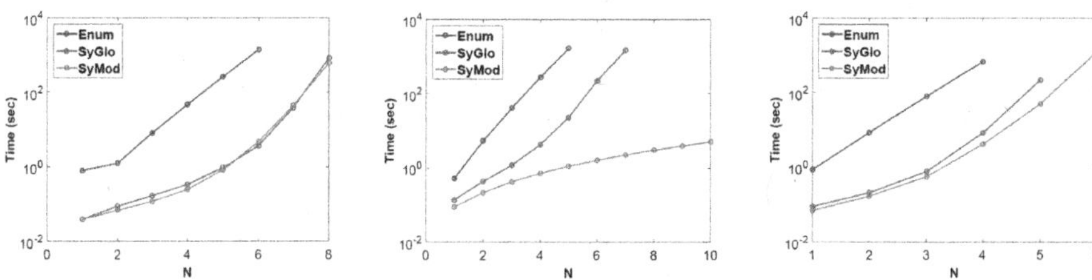

The non-scalable benchmarks are validated all within one second, but provide interesting insights. Specifically, the models of the DC-DC converters result in four discrete configurations, given by the switch S and diode D. The hybrid automata provided in [22] only contain the two discrete modes $S = open, D = closed$ and $S = closed, D = open$. In fact, the validation phase detects (for each converter) two non valid configurations, corresponding to $S = open, D = open$ and $S = closed, D = closed$, that induce an IL-cutset and a VC-loop, respectively. These two modes are exactly those excluded in the manual modeling phase leading to the hybrid automata provided in [22].

Reformulation. In the reformulation phase, for each model, we reformulate all the *derivative* variables and only the *output* variables contained in the invariant and guard formulas of the system components (e.g. the voltage and current of a diode).

Applying the reformulation phase to the DC-DC converters restricted to only the two valid configurations $S = open, D = closed$ and $S = closed, D = open$, we get two distinct ODEs whose coefficients agree with the dynamics of the converters provided in [22]. We refer the reader to the [6] for further details on the output of the converters reformulation.

For each scalable benchmark, the following plots (SRCN, NLTL, WBS from the left) show the reformulation time for five different approaches that mix the *Enum* and *Symbolic* strategies with different *reformulation strategies. Enum-Flat* represents the naive approach that enumerates the system configurations and reformulates the derivative and output variables as a unique set of variables; the *SyGlo-All* and the *SyMod-All* approaches apply the AllRef reformulation algorithm; the *SyGlo-Single* and the *SyMod-Single* approaches apply the SingleRef algorithm. In general, the two symbolic approaches outperform the enumerative approach and exhibit similar performance, with the exception of the *SyMod-Single* reformulation, that has significant advantage over the others in the NLTL benchmarks due to its favorable topology. The choice of the strategy (*All* vs *Single*) in the symbolic reformulation affects the amount of discovered equivalence classes, that is directly correlate with the reformulation time. Additional details are reported in [6].

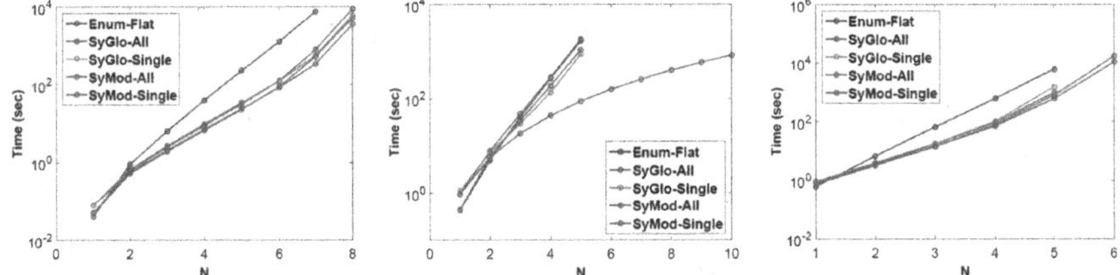

8 Conclusion

In this paper we presented a novel, symbolic approach to the validation and reformulation problem of a switched electrical network. The method is able to analyze the validity conditions of the network, where the dynamics are expressed as Differential-Algebraic Equations, and to reformulate them in form of a (symbolically represented) Hybrid Automaton. The proposed approach scales much better than an naive approach based on the enumerative analysis of the individual configurations, and produces significantly more compact HA due to the clustering of the equivalent configurations.

In the future, we will explore, amongst other research directions, how the approach can be generalized to other physical domains (e.g. mechanical) where the conditions needed for the network validation are different, and to deal with partially underdetermined networks.

References

1. Agrawal, A., Simon, G., Karsai, G.: Semantic translation of simulink/stateflow models to hybrid automata using graph transformations. Electron. Notes Theoret. Comput. Sci. **109**, 43–56 (2004). Proceedings of the Workshop on Graph Transformation and Visual Modelling Techniques (GT-VMT2004). http://www.sciencedirect.com/science/article/pii/S1571066104052089
2. Akers, A., Gassman, M., Smith, R.: Hydraulic Power System Analysis. Fluid Power and Control. CRC Press, Boca Raton (2006). https://books.google.it/books?id=Uo9gpXeUoKAC
3. Bae, K., Kong, S., Gao, S.: SMT encoding of hybrid systems in dReal. In: Frehse, G., Althoff, M. (eds.) 1st and 2nd International Workshop on Applied verification for Continuous and Hybrid Systems, ARCH14 2015. EPiC Series in Computing, vol. 34, pp. 188–195. EasyChair, Manchester (2015)
4. Barrett, C.W., Sebastiani, R., Seshia, S.A., Tinelli, C.: Satisfiability modulo theories. In: Handbook of Satisfiability, pp. 825–885 (2009). http://dx.doi.org/10.3233/978-1-58603-929-5-825
5. Benner, P.: Large-scale Networks in Engineering and Life Sciences. Springer, New York (2014)
6. Cimatti, A., Mover, S., Sessa, M.: From electrical switched networks to hybrid automata (extended version). In: Fitzgerald, J., et al. (eds.) FM 2016. LNCS, vol. 9995, pp. 164–181. Springer, Heidelberg (2016). http://es.fbk.eu/people/sessa/paper/FM2016/main.pdf
7. Cimatti, A., Griggio, A., Mover, S., Tonetta, S.: HyComp: an SMT-based model checker for hybrid systems. In: Baier, C., Tinelli, C. (eds.) TACAS 2015. LNCS, vol. 9035, pp. 52–67. Springer, Heidelberg (2015). doi:10.1007/978-3-662-46681-0_4
8. Cimatti, A., Griggio, A., Schaafsma, B.J., Sebastiani, R.: ETAPS 2013, pp. 93–107. Springer, Heidelberg (2013). doi:10.1007/978-3-642-36742-7_7
9. Cimatti, A., Mover, S., Tonetta, S.: A quantifier-free SMT encoding of non-linear hybrid automata. In: FMCAD, pp. 187–195 (2012). http://ieeexplore.ieee.org/xpl/articleDetails.jsp?arnumber=6462573
10. Dang, T., Donzé, A., Maler, O.: Verification of analog and mixed-signal circuits using hybrid system techniques. In: Hu, A.J., Martin, A.K. (eds.) FMCAD 2004. LNCS, vol. 3312, pp. 21–36. Springer, Heidelberg (2004). doi:10.1007/978-3-540-30494-4_3
11. Frehse, G., Krogh, B.H., Rutenbar, R.A., Maler, O.: Time domain verification of oscillator circuit properties. Electron. Notes Theoret. Comput. Sci. **153**(3), 9–22 (2006). doi:10.1016/j.entcs.2006.02.019
12. Gario, M., Micheli, A.: pysmt: a solver-agnostic library for fast prototyping of smt-based algorithms. In: SMT Workshop (2015)
13. Henzinger, T.A.: The theory of hybrid automata. In: Proceedings of 11th Annual IEEE Symposium on Logic in Computer Science, New Brunswick, New Jersey, USA, 27–30 July 1996, pp. 278–292 (1996). http://dx.doi.org/10.1109/LICS.1996.561342
14. Janschek, K.: Mechatronic Systems Design: Methods, Models, Concepts. Springer Science & Business Media, Berlin (2011)
15. Kong, S., Gao, S., Chen, W., Clarke, E.: dReach: δ-reachability analysis for hybrid systems. In: Baier, C., Tinelli, C. (eds.) TACAS 2015. LNCS, vol. 9035, pp. 200–205. Springer, Heidelberg (2015). doi:10.1007/978-3-662-46681-0_15

16. Lee, H.L., Althoff, M., Hoelldampf, S., Olbrich, M., Barke, E.: Automated generation of hybrid system models for reachability analysis of nonlinear analog circuits. In: The 20th Asia and South Pacific Design Automation Conference, ASP-DAC 2015, Chiba, Japan, 19–22 January 2015, pp. 725–730 (2015). http://dx.doi.org/10.1109/ASPDAC.2015.7059096
17. Manamcheri, K., Mitra, S., Bak, S., Caccamo, M.: A step towards verification and synthesis from simulink/stateflow models. In: Proceedings of the 14th ACM International Conference on Hybrid Systems: Computation and Control, HSCC 2011, Chicago, IL, USA, 12–14 April 2011, pp. 317–318 (2011). http://doi.acm.org/10.1145/1967701.1967749
18. Massarini, A., Reggiani, U., Kazimierczuk, M.K.: Analysis of networks with ideal switches by state equations. IEEE Trans. Circ. Syst. I: Fundam. Theory Appl. **44**(8), 692–697 (1997)
19. Mathworks, T.: Simscape power systems. http://it.mathworks.com/help/physmod/sps/index.html
20. Minopoli, S., Frehse, G.: SL2SX translator: from simulink to spaceex models. In: Proceedings of the 19th International Conference on Hybrid Systems: Computation and Control, HSCC 2016, Vienna, Austria, 12–14 April 2016, pp. 93–98 (2016). http://doi.acm.org/10.1145/2883817.2883826
21. Mover, S., Cimatti, A., Tiwari, A., Tonetta, S.: Time-aware relational abstractions for hybrid systems. In: EMSOFT, pp. 14:1–14:10 (2013). http://dx.doi.org/10.1109/EMSOFT.2013.6658592
22. Nguyen, L.V., Johnson, T.T.: Benchmark: DC-to-DC switched-mode power converters (buck converters, boost converters, and buck-boost converters). In: Frehse, G., Althoff, M. (eds.) ARCH14 2015, 1st and 2nd International Workshop on Applied Verification for Continuous and Hybrid Systems. EPiC Series in Computing, vol. 34, pp. 19–24. EasyChair (2015)
23. Nuzzo, P., Xu, M., Ozay, N., Finn, J.B., Sangiovanni-Vincentelli, A., Murray, R., Donze, A., Seshia, S.: A contract-based methodology for aircraft electric power system design. IEEE Access. http://icyphy.org/pubs/35.html
24. Riaza, R.: Differential-Algebraic Systems: Analytical Aspects and Circuit Applications. World Scientific, Singapore (2008)
25. SAE International: AIR 6110 - Contiguous Aircraft/System Development Process Example (2011)
26. Skaar, D.L.: Using the superposition method to formulate the state variable matrix for linear networks. IEEE Trans. Educ. **44**(4), 311–314 (2001)
27. Tiwari, A.: HybridSAL relational abstracter. In: Madhusudan, P., Seshia, S.A. (eds.) CAV 2012. LNCS, vol. 7358, pp. 725–731. Springer, Heidelberg (2012). doi:10.1007/978-3-642-31424-7_56
28. Tiwari, A.: Time-aware abstractions in HybridSal. In: Kroening, D., Păsăreanu, C.S. (eds.) CAV 2015. LNCS, vol. 9206, pp. 504–510. Springer, Heidelberg (2015). doi:10.1007/978-3-319-21690-4_34
29. Zaki, M.H., Tahar, S., Bois, G.: Formal verification of analog and mixed signal designs: survey and comparison. In: 2006 IEEE North-East Workshop on Circuits and Systems, pp. 281–284, June 2006
30. Zhang, Y., Sankaranarayanan, S., Somenzi, F.: Piecewise linear modeling of nonlinear devices for formal verification of analog circuits. In: FMCAD, pp. 196–203 (2012). http://ieeexplore.ieee.org/xpl/articleDetails.jsp?arnumber=6462574

Danger Invariants

Cristina David[1], Pascal Kesseli[1(✉)], Daniel Kroening[1], and Matt Lewis[1,2]

[1] University of Oxford, Oxford, UK
pascal.kesseli@cs.ox.ac.uk
[2] Improbable, London, UK

Abstract. Static analysers search for overapproximating proofs of safety commonly known as *safety invariants*. Conversely, static bug finders (e.g. Bounded Model Checking) give evidence for the failure of an assertion in the form of a *counterexample trace*. As opposed to safety invariants, the size of a counterexample is dependent on the *depth of the bug*, i.e., the length of the execution trace prior to the error state, which also determines the computational effort required to find them. We propose a way of expressing danger proofs that is independent of the depth of bugs. Essentially, such danger proofs constitute a compact representation of a counterexample trace, which we call a *danger invariant*. Danger invariants summarise sets of traces that are guaranteed to be able to reach an error state. Our conjecture is that such danger proofs will enable the design of bug finding analyses for which the computational effort is independent of the depth of bugs, and thus find deep bugs more efficiently. As an exemplar of an analysis that uses danger invariants, we design a bug finding technique based on a synthesis engine. We implemented this technique and compute danger invariants for intricate programs taken from SV-COMP 2016.

1 Introduction

Safety analysers search for proofs of safety commonly known as *safety invariants* by overapproximating the set of program states reached during all program executions. Fundamentally, they summarise traces into abstract states, thus trading the ability to distinguish traces for computational tractability [1].

Conversely, static bug finders that use techniques such as Bounded Model Checking (BMC) search for proofs that safety can be violated. Dually to safety proofs, we will call these *danger proofs*. Traditionally, a danger proof is represented by a concrete counterexample trace leading to an error state [2].

For illustration, we examine the safe and unsafe programs in Fig. 1. The program in Fig. 1a is safe as witnessed by the safety invariant $Inv(x) = x \neq y$, which holds in the initial state (where $x{=}0$ and $y{=}1$), is inductive with respect to the body of the loop ($x \neq y \Rightarrow (x{+}1) \neq (y{+}1)$) and, on exit from the loop, makes the assertion hold. Now, if we replace the guard by `x<1000000`, the program remains safe as witnessed by the same safety invariant.

This research was supported by ERC project 280053 (CPROVER).

J. Fitzgerald et al. (Eds.): FM 2016, LNCS 9995, pp. 182–198, 2016.
DOI: 10.1007/978-3-319-48989-6_12

```
x = 0; y = 1;
// while (x<1000000)
while (x<10){
    x++;
    y++;
}

assert ( x != y );
```

(a)

```
x = 0; y = 1;
// while (x<1000000)
while (x<10){
    x++;
    if(*) y++;
}

assert ( x != y );
```

(b)

Fig. 1. Safe and unsafe example programs

On the other hand, the program in Fig. 1b is unsafe as, depending on a nondeterministic choice (denoted by "*"), y may not be incremented in each iteration. A possible danger proof for this example is given by the concrete counterexample trace: $(x{=}0, y{=}1)$, $(x{=}1, y{=}1)$, $(x{=}2, y{=}2)$, $(x{=}3, y{=}3)$, $(x{=}4, y{=}4)$, $(x{=}5, y{=}5)$, $(x{=}6, y{=}6)$, $(x{=}7, y{=}7)$, $(x{=}8, y{=}8)$, $(x{=}9, y{=}9)$, $(x{=}10, y{=}10)$.

Similarly to what we did for the program in Fig. 1a, let the guard in Fig. 1b now be replaced by `x<1000000`. However, as opposed to the program in Fig. 1a, now we cannot use the same danger proof we computed for the original program (instead a possible danger proof for the modified program is $(x{=}0, y{=}1)$, $(x{=}1, y{=}1)$, $(x{=}2, y{=}2)$, $(x{=}3, y{=}3)$, $\cdots$ $(x{=}1000000, y{=}1000000)$). The cause for this is that, as opposed to safety invariants, the size of a counterexample trace is dependent on the *depth of the bug*, i.e., the length of the execution trace prior to the error state. The bug in the original program in Fig. 1b manifests in execution traces of length 10, whereas for the modified program we need execution traces of length 1000000 to expose the bug. We will refer to bugs that only manifest in long execution traces as *deep bugs*.

The size of the counterexample also impacts the computational effort required to find them. For instance, bounded model checkers compute counterexample traces by progressively unwinding the transition relation. Consequently, the computational effort required to discover an assertion violation typically grows exponentially with the depth of the bug. Notably, the scalability problem is not limited to procedures that implement BMC. Approaches based on a combination of over- and underapproximations such as predicate abstraction [3] and lazy abstraction with interpolants (LAwI) [4] are not optimised for finding deep bugs either. The reason for this is that they can only detect counterexamples with deep loops after the repeated refutation of increasingly longer spurious counterexamples. The analyser first considers a potential error trace with one loop iteration, only to discover that this trace is infeasible. Consequently, the analyser increases the search depth, usually by considering one further loop iteration. This repeated search suffers from the same exponential blow-up as BMC.

In this paper we propose a way of expressing danger proofs that is independent of the depth of the bug. Essentially, such a danger proof constitutes a compact representation of a counterexample trace, which we call a *danger invariant*. Similarly to safety invariants, danger invariants are based on summarisation. Our conjecture is that such danger proofs will enable the design of bug finding analyses for which the computational effort is also independent of the depth of bugs, and thus have the potential to find deep bugs more efficiently.

As an exemplar of an analysis that uses the newly introduced notion of danger invariants, we design a bug finding technique based on a synthesis engine.

Contributions:

- We introduce the notion of danger invariant, which, similarly to safety invariants, uses summarisation to compactly represent counterexamples. We discuss danger invariants both in the context of total and partial correctness.
- We present a procedure for inferring such danger invariants based on program synthesis. Our program synthesiser is specifically tailored for danger invariants, being able to efficiently synthesise multiple programs.
- We implemented our analysis and applied it to intricate programs taken from the Competition on Software Verification SV-COMP 2016 [5]. The focus of our experimental evaluation are danger invariants for code with deep bugs. Our experimental results show that our technique outperforms other tools when the bugs require many iterations of a loop in order to manifest. This suggests that it has strengths complementary to those of other techniques and could be used in combination with them (e.g., a compositional analysis based on may/must analysis and danger invariants).

2 Illustration

To illustrate some of the pitfalls involved in proving that a program has a bug, we direct the reader's attention to Fig. 2a. This program is unsafe (the assertion can be violated), but this fact is hard to prove for traditional bug finders (based on random testing, BMC or concolic execution). We found that SMACK 1.5.1 [6] and CBMC 5.5 [7] timed out on this example, Seahorn 2.6 [8] returned "unknown" and CPAChecker 1.4 [9] (incorrectly) says "safe". This program is difficult for bug finders to analyse for the following reasons:

- The program is nondeterministic and the vast majority of the paths through the program do not trigger the bug.
- Many of the initial values of the program variables do not lead to the bug.
- The assertion violation does not occur until a very large number of loop iterations have executed.

Despite these features and the difficulty that automated tools have with this program, it is quite easy to convince a human that the program is unsafe using an argument something like the following:

1. In the second loop, if we ever reach a state with $i = j$, we can maintain that $i = j$ by taking the "if" branch and incrementing j.
2. If we are in the second loop with $i < j$, we can reduce the gap between i and j by *not* taking the "if" branch, so i will be incremented but j will not. If $j - i \leq 1000000$ then we can eventually have i "catch up" with j by repeatedly taking the "else" branch.

```
int i, j, k;

for (k = 0; k < 100; k++) {
  if (*) j++;
}
for (i = 0; i < 1000000; i++) {
  if (*) j++;
}
assert(i != j);
```

(a)

```
x = 0; y = 1;
while (x < 10) {
  y++;
}
assert(x < 10);
```

(b)

Fig. 2. Illustrative examples

3. Therefore, if we begin the second loop with $0 \leq j \leq 1000000$, we can eventually reach a state with $i = j$ and from there eventually exit the loop with $i = j$, at which point the assertion will be violated.
4. We can enter the second loop with $0 \leq j \leq 1000000$ quite easily. For example, if $0 \leq j \leq 999900$ then any path through the first loop will land us at the start of the second loop in such a state.
5. There are several valid initial states with $0 \leq j \leq 999900$, and so the assertion can certainly be violated.

This argument is quite unlike the argument that an existing automated bug finder would use. We have not provided a concrete error trace, or even a concrete initial input, but we have still been able to prove that there is definitely an error in the program. It is worth noting that this proof is *much* shorter than a full error trace (which would be at least 1000100 steps long), it is much easier for a human to understand than the full, explicit error trace and indeed it is *much easier to find.*

The proof outlined above makes use of several techniques usually associated with safety proving: abstraction (we described sets of states symbolically), induction (e.g., we argued by induction that the state $i = j$ could be maintained once reached) and compositional reasoning (we proved a lemma about each loop separately, then combined these lemmas into a proof that the program as a whole had a bug). At the same time, such a proof does not admit false alarms.

In the remainder of this paper, we will show how this intuitive notion of symbolically proving the existence of a bug without providing an explicit error trace can be made precise by introducing the concept of a danger invariant. Our definition is presented abstractly, so that any method of symbolic reasoning or invariant generation (including manual annotation by a verification engineer) can be used to generate and verify danger invariants. We will also show how the constraints defining a danger invariant can be solved using program synthesis.

3 Danger Invariants

In this section, we formalise the notion of a danger invariant. We represent a program P as a transition system with state space X and transition relation

$T \subseteq X \times X$. For a state $x \in X$ with $T(x, x')$, x' is said to be a successor of x under T. We denote initial states by I and error states by E. We start by defining some background notions.

Definition 1 (Execution Trace). *An execution trace $\langle x_0 \dots x_n \rangle$ is a (potentially infinite) sequence of states such that any two successive states are related by the program's transition relation T, i.e. $\forall 0 \leq i < n . T(x_i, x_{i+1})$.*

Definition 2 (Counterexample Trace). *A finite execution trace $\langle x_0 \dots x_n \rangle$ is a counterexample iff x_0 is an initial state, $x_0 \in I$, and x_n is an error state, $x_n \in E$.*

A counterexample trace is a proof of the existence of a reachable error state (i.e., a state where some safety assertion is violated).

The question we try to answer in this paper is whether we can derive a compact representation of a danger proof that does not require us to explicitly write down every intermediate state. For a loop $L(I, G, T, A)$ (I denotes the initial states, G is the guard, T is the transition relation and A is the assertion immediately after the loop), this is captured by the notion of *danger invariant*, defined next.

Definition 3 (Danger Invariant). *A predicate D is a danger invariant for the loop $L(I, G, T, A)$ iff it satisfies the following criteria:*

$$\exists x_0 . I(x_0) \wedge D(x_0) \tag{1}$$

$$\forall x . D(x) \wedge G(x) \rightarrow \exists x' . T(x, x') \wedge D(x') \tag{2}$$

$$\forall x . D(x) \wedge \neg G(x) \rightarrow \neg A(x) \tag{3}$$

A danger invariant is a dual of a safety invariant that captures the fact that there is some trace containing an error state starting from an initial state: (1) captures the fact that D is reachable from an initial state x_0, (2) shows that there exists some transition with respect to which D is inductive and (3) checks that the assertion is violated on exit from the loop.

The existential quantifier for x' in (2) is important for nondeterministic programs, where it is enough for the danger invariant to capture the existence of some error trace for only one nondeterministic choice. We make this explicit by introducing a Skolem function S that chooses the successor x':

$$\exists S . \forall x . D(x) \wedge G(x) \rightarrow T(x, S(x)) \wedge D(S(x)) \tag{4}$$

Our definition of an execution trace (Definition 1) includes infinite traces. Thus, the trace containing the error may be infinite and the error state will not be reachable at all. For example, consider Fig. 2b. A danger invariant is '`true`', which meets all of the criteria (1), (2) and (3).

However, we can actually prove partial correctness of the program – the program contains no terminating traces and so the assertion is never even reached. To ensure that the error traces are finite, we will introduce a *ranking function*, which will serve as a proof of termination. Below we recall the definition of a ranking function:

Definition 4 (Ranking function). *A function $R : X \to Y$ is a* ranking function *for the transition relation T if Y is a well-founded set with order $>$ and R is injective and monotonically decreasing with respect to T.*

We assume that programs have unbounded but countable nondeterminism, and so require that our ranking functions' co-domains are recursive ordinals. In particular, we will consider ranking functions with co-domain ω^n, i.e., n-tuples of natural numbers ordered lexicographically. This is the final piece we need to define a partial danger invariant:

Definition 5 (Partial Danger Invariant). *A predicate D_p is a danger invariant for the loop $L(I, G, T, A)$ in the context of partial correctness iff it satisfies the following criteria:*

$$\exists x_0 . I(x_0) \wedge D_p(x_0) \tag{5}$$

$$\exists R, S . \forall x . D_p(x) \wedge G(x) \to R(x) > 0 \wedge T(x, S(x)) \wedge \\ D_p(S(x)) \wedge R(S(x)) < R(x) \tag{6}$$

$$\forall x . D_p(x) \wedge \neg G(x) \to \neg A(x) \tag{7}$$

Note that the ranking function R does not guarantee the termination of all possible executions, but only the termination of some erroneous one. It is also important to notice that D_p is *not an underapproximation* of the reachable program states – there may well be D_p-states that are unreachable, and there may well be D_p-states that do not violate the assertion. However, every $(D_p \wedge \neg G)$-state does violate the assertion, and it is certainly the case that at least one such state is reachable.

Example 1. *With Definition 5, for the example in Fig. 2b there exists no danger invariant.*

For the program in Fig. 1b a danger invariant is $D_p(x, y) = y = (x < 1?1 : x)$ and ranking function $R(x, y) = 10-x$. Essentially, this invariant says that y must not be incremented for the first iteration of the loop (until x reaches the value 1), and from that point, for the remaining iterations, y gets always incremented such that $x = y$. For this case, D_p is a compact and elegant representation of a feasible counterexample trace. The witness Skolem function that we get is $S_y(x, y) = (x < 1?y : y + 1)$.

In Sect. 1, we have seen that the counterexample trace for the modified version of the program in Fig. 1b (the one with a larger guard) was much longer than that for the original version of the program. However, both the original and the modified programs have the same danger invariant $D_p(x, y) = y = (x < 1?1 : x)$ and the same Skolem function. This supports our conjecture that danger invariants are independent on the depth of bugs. A ranking function for the modified program in Fig. 1b is $R(x, y) = 1000000 - x$, which is also a valid ranking function for the original one.

Danger Invariants for Total Correctness. While Definition 5 defines a danger invariant for partial correctness, we argue that the danger invariant in Definition 3 proves the existence of an erroneous trace in the context of total correctness. This trace may either be an error trace leading to an assertion violation, or a recurrence set denoting an infinite execution trace. We can differentiate between the two scenarios by checking whether the loop guard G holds for all the states in D, i.e. $\forall x.D(x) \Rightarrow G(x)$. If this is true, then Formula 3 is always vacuously true and D is a proof of the existence of a recurrence set. Otherwise, D is a proof of the existence of an assertion violation.

Example 2. *With Definition 3, a possible danger invariant for the example in Fig. 2b is* $D(x) = x<10$. *As the guard of the loop holds for all the D-states, this is a recurrence set.*

4 Generating Second-Order Verification Conditions

In this section, we present an algorithm for generating second-order constraints describing the existence of a danger proof for a program with potentially nested loops. We only give the algorithm for partial correctness as it is the more complex one (the corresponding procedure for total correctness does not have to generate the constraints for the ranking functions). We define the notion of a danger proof with respect to two assertions A and B:

Definition 6. *A danger proof of a triple* (A, P, B) *shows the existence of a finite path through the program* P *from a state* x *to a state* x' *such that* $A(x)$ *and* $\neg B(x')$.

The generation of the verifications conditions is performed by Algorithm 1. This algorithm allows danger invariants for pieces of a program to be composed together into a danger proof for the whole program. We discuss solving these constraints in the next section.

Algorithm 1 is split into two procedures. The ExistsDangerPath procedure generates the constraints showing the existence of some erroneous execution trace that might not be reachable from the initial states (it overapproximates the initial states). Overapproximating invariants are easier to compose than underapproximating ones, which enables us to construct a modular constraint generation technique for arbitrary programs and only add the reachability constraints at the outer level in the DangerConstraints procedure.

Proposition 1. *The constraints generated by a call to the function* ExistsDangerPath(A, P, B) *are satisfiable iff there is a finite path through the program* P *from a state* x *to a state* x' *such that* $A(x)$ *and* $\neg B(x')$.

The high-level strategy for the ExistsDangerPath procedure is the following. Given a program P, introduce fresh function symbols denoting Skolem functions for the n nondeterministic assignments, as well as to the danger invariants and ranking functions required by each of the loops.

The most interesting branch of the algorithm is the one for a loop with guard G and transition relation T. In this case, we need to emit the constraints necessary for a danger invariant. As previously stated, at this point we do not check that the danger invariant is reachable from the initial states. Instead, the first emitted constraint captures the fact that the danger invariant D_p is an over-approximation of the initial states A. The second constraint captures the fact that the negation of the post-state B must hold on exit from the loop and the third constraint captures the fact that the ranking function R is bounded from below. The inductiveness and the ranking function's monotonicity are proven through the recursive call to ExistsDangerPath, where the pre-state denotes the LHS of the inductiveness proof and the post-state represents the RHS plus the monotonicity of the ranking function. Note that the negation in the post-state ensures the fact that the generated verification conditions correspond to the situation where the inductiveness and monotonicity hold. The additional fresh variables $\underline{\mathbf{v}}^f$ are needed to express the (relational) monotonicity condition for the ranking function.

Procedure DangerConstraints adds the necessary constraints such that the danger proof is reachable from an initial state $\underline{\mathbf{v_0}}$.

The end result of Algorithm 1 is a set of second-order constraints, where the freshly introduced second-order variables (for the Skolem functions, danger invariants and ranking functions) are existentially quantified. If the resulting system of second-order constraints is satisfiable, then the solution (i.e., an assignment to the uninterpreted function symbols) is a danger proof for the full program. In other words, the second-order constraints generated are satisfiable iff the program contains a finite error trace.

Example 3. *In Fig. 3 we illustrate how Algorithm 1 works by using it to generate a danger proof for the nondeterministic program at the level 0 call to* DangerConstraints *with the generic pre- and post-states being* A *and* B*, respectively. The explicit levels in the figure denote the call stack together with the constraints generated for each of them. Additionally, when going from level 3 to level 4, we omit the recursive call for the sequential composition and simply apply the weakest precondition for the whole code, resulting in the following VC:*

$$D_p(i) \wedge i{\leq}10 \Rightarrow wp((\texttt{i}^f\texttt{=i; if(*)i=i+1}), D_p(i) \wedge R(i^f){>}R(i))$$

The overall verification condition is the conjunction of the constraints generated at each level, where the second-order entities D_p*,* R*,* S *and* C *are existentially quantified. The existential quantifier over* i_0 *ranges over all the emitted VCs. If we consider* $A(i) = true$ *and* $B(i) = (i{=}10)$*, then a satisfying assignment for these constraints is:*

$$i_0 \mapsto 0, \quad D_p(i) \mapsto i{\leq}11, \quad R(i) \mapsto 12{-}i, \quad S(i) \mapsto true, \quad C(i) \mapsto i{\leq}11$$

The recursive constraint generation technique given in Algorithm 1 makes it easy to generate verification conditions for nested loops in a modular manner. One example with nested loops is given the extended version of the paper [10].

Initial call to DANGERCONSTRAINTS:
DANGERCONSTRAINTS(
A,
```
while (i ≤ 10) {
  if (*) i := i+1;
},
```
B)

(**Level 0**)

Emitted VCs:

$$\exists i_0 . A(i_0)$$

Initial call to EXISTSDANGERPATH:
EXISTSDANGERPATH(
$\langle i \rangle, true,$
```
i = i0;
while (i ≤ 10) {
  if (*) i := i+1;
},
```
B)

(**Level 1**)

Recursive calls:
EXISTSDANGERPATH(
$\langle i \rangle, true,$
```
i = i0,
```
$\neg C$)
EXISTSDANGERPATH(
$\langle i \rangle, C,$
```
while (i ≤ 10) {
  if (*) i := i+1;
},
```
B)

(**Level 2**)

Emitted VCs:

$$\begin{aligned} &\forall i. true \Rightarrow C(i_0) \wedge \\ &\quad C(i) \Rightarrow D_p(i) \wedge \\ &\quad D_p(i) \wedge i{>}10 \Rightarrow \neg B(i) \wedge \\ &\quad D_p(i) \wedge i{\leq}10 \Rightarrow R(i){>}0 \end{aligned}$$

Recursive call:
EXISTSDANGERPATH(
$\langle i, i^f \rangle, D(i) \wedge i{\leq}10,$
```
i^f = i;
if (*) i := i+1,
```
$\neg(D(i) \wedge R(i^f){>}R(i)))$

(**Level 3**)

Emitted VCs:

$$\forall i. D_p(i) \wedge i{\leq}10 \Rightarrow (S(i) \wedge D_p(i{+}1) \wedge R(i){>}R(i{+}1)) \ \vee (\neg S(i) \wedge D_p(i) \wedge R(i){>}R(i))$$

(**Level 4**)

Fig. 3. Generating verification conditions for a program with nondeterminism

Algorithm 1. Generate VCs for the triple (A, P, B) over program variables $\underline{\mathbf{v}}$

```
procedure ExistsDangerPath(v, A, P, B))
    switch P do
        case while(G) do T end
            D_p ← Fresh
            R ← Fresh
            v^f ← FreshCopy(v)
            Emit(∀v.A(v) ⇒ D_p(v))
            Emit(∀v.D_p(v) ∧ ¬G(v) ⇒ ¬B(v))
            Emit(∀v.D_p(v) ∧ G(v) ⇒ R(v) > 0)
            ExistsDangerPath(v + v^f,
                D_p(v) ∧ G(v),
                v^f := v; T,
                ¬(D_p(v) ∧ R(v^f) > R(v)))
        case x := *
            S ← Fresh
            ExistsDangerPath(v, A, x := S(v), B)
        case P_1; P_2
            C ← Fresh
            ExistsDangerPath(v, A(v), P_1, ¬C(v))
            ExistsDangerPath(v, C(v), P_2, B(v))
        case default
            Emit(∀v.A(v) ⇒ wp(¬B, P)(v))

procedure DangerConstraints(A, P, B)
    v ← fv(P)
    v_0 ← FreshCopy(v)
    Emit(∃v_0.A(v_0))
    ExistsDangerPath( v, ⊤, v := v_0; P, B(v))
```

5 Generating Danger Invariants Using Synthesis

Since the programs we are analysing are either safe or unsafe, and assuming that a proof is expressible in our logic, a program either accepts a safety invariant SI or a danger invariant D_p. For a loop $L(I, G, T, A)$, we model this as a disjunction as stated in Definition 7. The generalised safety formula is a theorem of second-order logic, and our decision procedure will always be able to find witnesses SI, D_p, S, R, y_0 demonstrating its truth, provided such a witness is expressible in our logic. The synthesised predicate SI is a purported safety invariant and the D_p, N, R, y_0 constitute a purported danger invariant (Fig. 4).

If SI is really a safety invariant, the program is safe, otherwise D_p (with witnesses to the existence of an error trace with Skolem function S, initial state y_0 and ranking function R) will be a danger invariant and the program is unsafe. Exactly one of these proofs will be valid, i.e., either SI will satisfy the criteria for a safety invariant, or D_p, S, R, y_0 will satisfy the criteria for a danger invariant. We can simply check both cases and discard whichever "proof" is incorrect. We omit the algorithm for generating safety verification conditions for a whole program as this is well covered in the literature [11].

Definition 7 (Generalised Safety Formula)

$$\exists SI, D_p, S, R, y_0. \forall x, x', y. \begin{pmatrix} I(x) \rightarrow SI(x) \land \\ SI(x) \land G(x) \land T(x, x') \rightarrow SI(x') \land \\ SI(x) \land \neg G(x) \rightarrow A(x) \end{pmatrix} \lor$$
$$\begin{pmatrix} I(y_0) \land D_p(y_0) \land \\ D_p(y) \land G(y) \rightarrow R(y) > 0 \land T(y, S(y)) \land D(S(y)) \\ \qquad \land R(y) > R(S(y)) \land \\ D_p(y) \land \neg G(y) \rightarrow \neg A(y) \end{pmatrix}$$

Fig. 4. General second-order safety formula

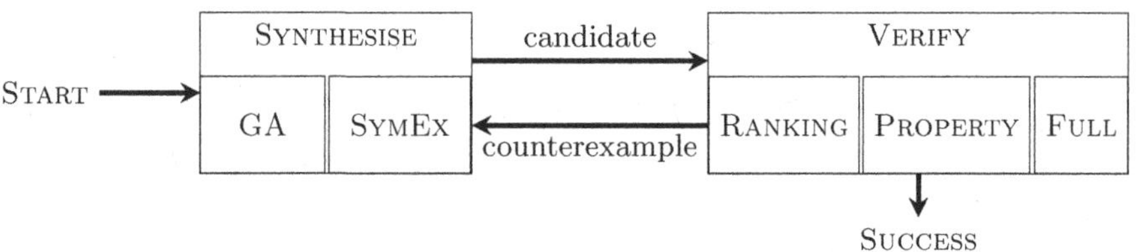

Fig. 5. Synthesis loop with multiple backends

Synthesis Engine. We employ Counterexample-Guided Inductive Synthesis (CEGIS) to synthesise programs for SI, D_p, S, R. The processes is graphically illustrated in Fig. 5. Our synthesis engine conjectures solution programs based on a limited set of counterexamples C. These solutions are guaranteed to satisfy all known counterexamples $c_i \in C$ and are refined with each new c_i. Each conjecture is verified by a verifier component, which terminates the process if the constraint holds (SUCCESS). Otherwise the resulting c_j is added to C and provided to the synthesiser for further refinement. As mentioned earlier, for our particular use case the synthesiser must always find a solution (although in practice this might take a very long time as discussed in the experimental section).

In order to efficiently synthesise SI, D_p, S, R simultaneously, our algorithm implements concurrent backends in both the synthesis and verification stage. In the synthesis stage, a symbolic execution (SYMEX) as well as a genetic algorithm (GA) backend concurrently search for new candidates satisfying C. *GA* is an alternative way to traverse the space of possible solutions, simulating an evolutionary process using selection, mutation and crossover operators. It maintains a large population of programs which are paired using crossover operation, combining successful program features into new solutions. In order to avoid local minima, the mutation operator replaces instructions by random values at a comparatively low probability. The backends share information about synthesised candidates and pass a complying solution on to the verification component.

Synthesis components use different instruction sets for SI, D_p, S, R optimised for their clause in the full danger constraint.

To facilitate concurrent synthesis of multiple programs, the verification component searches for different counterexamples in the same iteration. It restricts the full danger constraint to either find a c_i witnessing an inconsistent ranking (RANKING) or a violation of the user property for which we are proving danger (PROPERTY). Furthermore, the engine provides one counterexample over the full, unrestricted danger constraint (FULL). This ensures that the synthesis component receives sufficient information at each iteration to refine all synthesised programs SI, D_p, S, R. The GA synthesis backend considers these counterexamples in its selection and crossover operators. Candidates that solve distinct sets of counterexamples have a higher probability of selection as crossover partners in order to produce solutions that satisfy all types of counterexamples and hence implement SI, D_p, S, R correctly. This is preferable over fitness values based on solved counterexamples only, since it avoids local minima where candidates may solve a multitude of counterexamples of one particular kind.

6 Experimental Results

6.1 Experimental Setup

To evaluate our algorithm, we have implemented the DANGERZONE module for the bounded model checker CBMC 5.5.[1] It generates a danger specification from a given C program and implements a second-order SAT solver as discussed in [12] to obtain a proof. We ran the resulting prover on 50 programs from the loop acceleration category in SV-COMP 2016 [5]. We picked this specific category as it has benchmarks with deep bugs and we were interested in challenging our hypothesis that danger invariants are well-suited to expose deep bugs and can complement the capabilities of existing approaches such as BMC. Unfortunately we had to exclude programs that make use of arrays, since these are not yet supported by the synthesiser. In addition to this, we also introduced altered versions of the selected SV-COMP 2016 benchmarks with extended loop guards to create deeper bugs, challenging our hypothesis even further.

For each benchmark we try to synthesise both a partial danger invariant (i.e. a danger invariant, a ranking function, an initial state and Skolem functions witnessing the nondeterminism corresponding to partial correctness in Definition 5) and a total danger invariant (i.e. a danger invariant, an initial state and Skolem functions corresponding to total correctness in Definition 3). To provide a comparison point, we also ran two state-of-the-art bounded model checking (BMC) tools, CBMC 5.5 [7] and SMACK+CORRAL 1.5.1 [6] on the same benchmarks. In addition to this, we ran the benchmarks against CPAchecker 1.4 [9], the overall winner of SV-COMP 2015, and Seahorn 2.6 [8], the second-placed

[1] https://github.com/diffblue/cbmc/archive/bbae05d8faecfec18a42724e72336d8f8c4e3d8d.zip.

tool in the loops category after CPAchecker. We reproduced each tool's SV-COMP 2015 configuration, with small alterations to account for the benchmarks where we increased loop guards. Finally, we manually translated the benchmarks to be compatible with Microsoft's Static Driver Verifier Research Platform (SDVRP [13]) with the Yogi 2.0 [14] back end. Yogi's main algorithms are Synergy, Dash, Smash and Bolt.

We say that a benchmark contains a deep bug if it is only reachable after at least 1'000'000 unwindings. Each tool was given a time limit of 300 s, and was run on a 12-core 2.40 GHz Intel Xeon E5-2440 with 96 GB of RAM. The full result table of these experiments is given in the extended version of the paper [10].

6.2 Discussion of Results

The results demonstrate that the DANGERZONE module outperforms all other tools on programs with deep bugs. It solves 37 (partial) and 38 (total) out of the 50 benchmarks in standalone mode, and 46 when used with CBMC. By itself, CBMC only finds 27, SMACK+CORRAL 24, CPAchecker 26 and Seahorn 31 bugs. This result can be explained by the fact that the complexity of finding a danger invariant is orthogonal to the number of unwindings necessary to reach it. DANGERZONE's success is not determined by how deep the bug is, but by the complexity of the invariant describing it. As a result, we perform comparably on both deep and shallow bugs and are able to expose 18 out of the 20 deep bugs in the benchmark set. This supports our hypothesis that danger invariants are well-suited for this category of errors.

Danger invariants and BMC complement each other perfectly in our experiments and together solve 46 out of the 50 problems. We consider this further evidence for our hypothesis that danger invariants extend existing model checkers' capabilities to expose deep bugs.

6.3 Manually Solving a Danger Constraint

As a case study we also tried using danger invariants to analyse a bug in Sendmail that has been proposed as a challenge for verification tools [15]. This program makes use of arrays, which our program synthesiser does not support. We decided that it would be interesting to see whether danger invariants could be used to semi-automatically prove the existence of such a difficult bug, and so wrote the danger invariant by hand. We then used CBMC to verify that the danger invariant we had written did indeed satisfy all of the criteria for a danger invariant as given in Definition 5, thereby proving the existence of the bug. This process was successful, with the verification step taking 0.23 s. We therefore believe that danger invariants could be used in semi-automatic tools to aid humans in finding complex bugs without the need for full blown automatic tools.

7 Related Work

Compositional may/must Analysis. Compositional approaches to property checking such as [16] involve decomposing the whole-program analysis into

$$I \xrightarrow{must^-} \phi_2 \qquad\qquad \phi_1 \xrightarrow{must^+} \neg A$$

Check that $\phi_2 \cap \neg A$ is non-empty. Check that $\phi_1 \cap I$ is non-empty.

Fig. 6. Danger proofs using must$^-$ and must$^+$ analyses.

several sub-analyses and summarising the results of these sub-analyses for later uses. The summaries are either may or must summaries.

The must summaries used in [16] (denoted $\phi_1 \xrightarrow{must} \phi_2$) are proofs that for every state $y \in \phi_2$, there exists a state $x \in \phi_1$ such that there is an execution trace from x to y. In the terminology of [17], this is a must$^-$ summary. The underapproximating nature of such summaries allows checking for bugs by inspecting the intersection between the must$^-$ set (the states reachable from the initial states via must$^-$ transitions) and the error states. Any state in this intersection must be reachable from an initial state, and therefore is a true bug. By contrast, Danger Invariants can be seen as a form of must$^+$ analysis, where we prove facts of the form $\phi_1 \xrightarrow{must^+} \phi_2$, which means that every $x \in \phi_1$ can reach a state $y \in \phi_2$. The two styles of must analysis are compared in Fig. 6: to prove that an assertion A can be violated starting from initial states I, you can either use a must$^-$ analysis to find an underapproximation of the reachable states and show that these intersect with the error states, or you can use a must$^+$ analysis to find a non-empty underapproximation of the initial states that can reach an error state.

In [16], the authors use automated random testing techniques (DART) [18] to compute the must$^-$ summaries (required to show the existence of bugs). DART is based on single-path execution, which means that deep loops will cause the exploration of a large number of paths (corresponding to executing the loop once, twice, etc.), which may cause an exponential blow-up. As opposed to this approach, danger invariants are must$^+$ summaries which may encompass multiple paths through a loop, which can avoid exponential blow-up in many cases. Thus, the two approaches could be complementary.

Temporal Logic. With respect to the verification of temporal properties, a danger invariant for a loop with an assertion A essentially proves the CTL property $\models \mathbf{EF}\neg A$ over the loop. While there exist CTL verifiers based on a reduction to exist-forall quantified Horn clauses [19,20], we specialise the concept for finding deep bugs and describe a modular constraint generation technique over arbitrary programs, rather than for transition systems.

Underapproximate Acceleration. Another successful technique for finding deep bugs without false alarms is loop acceleration [21,22]. This approach works by taking a single path at a time through a loop, computing a symbolic representation of the exact transitive closure of the path (an accelerator) and adding it back into the program before using an off-the-shelf bug finder such as a bounded model checker. Loop acceleration requires that each accelerated path can be represented in closed-form by a polynomial over the program variables, which is not always possible. In contrast, danger invariants are complete – a program has a corresponding danger invariant iff it has a bug.

Constraint Solving. There is a lot of work on the generation of linear invariants of the form $c_1x_1 + \ldots + c_nd_n + d \leq 0$ [23,24]. The main idea behind these techniques is to treat the coefficients $c_1, \ldots, c_n, d$ as unknowns and generate constraints on them such that any solution corresponds to a safety invariant. In [24], Colon et al. present a method based on Farkas' Lemma, which synthesises linear invariants by extracting non-linear constraints on the coefficients of a target invariant from a program. In a different work, Sharma and Aiken use randomised search to find the coefficients [24]. It would be interesting to investigate how these methods can be adapted for generating constraints on the coefficients $c_1, \ldots, c_n, d$ such that solutions correspond to linear danger invariants.

Doomed Program Locations. The term "doomed program point" was introduced in [25] and denotes a program location that will inevitably lead to an error regardless of the state in which it is reached. The notion is more restrictive than a danger invariant D. Our experiments revealed multiple unsafe benchmarks for which we could synthesise a danger proof, but no doomed program location exists.[2]

Error Invariants. The concept of error invariant [26] was introduced in order to localize the cause of an error in an error trace. An error invariant is an invariant for a position in an error trace that only captures states that will still produce the error. As opposed to an error invariant, a danger invariant is inductive and may describe multiple traces through the program.

Program Synthesis. Counterexample-Guided Inductive Synthesis (CEGIS) relies on inductive conjectures and refinement through counterexample information. This learning pattern is used in a multitude of learning applications, including Angluin's classic DFA learning algorithm L^* [27]. Syntax-Guided Synthesis (SyGuS) by Alur et al. is based on the same principle [28]. They employ a CEGIS loop with a grammar to restrict the space of possible programs. Our implementation focuses on concurrent synthesis of multiple danger constraint programs.

8 Conclusions

In this paper, we introduced the concept of *danger invariants* – the dual to safety invariants. Danger invariants summarise sets of traces that are guaranteed to reach an error state. As the size of a danger invariant is independent of the depth of its corresponding bug, it can enable bug finding techniques for which the computational effort is also independent of the depth of bugs, and thus have the potential to find deep bugs more efficiently. As an exemplar of an analysis using danger invariants, we presented a bug finding technique based on a synthesis engine.

[2] More details in the extended version [10].

References

1. Cousot, P., Cousot, R.: Abstract interpretation: a unified lattice model for static analysis of programs by construction or approximation of fixpoints. In: POPL, pp. 238–252 (1977)
2. Clarke, E.M., Biere, A., Raimi, R., Zhu, Y.: Bounded model checking using satisfiability solving. Formal Methods Syst. Des. **19**(1), 7–34 (2001)
3. Clarke, E.M., Grumberg, O., Long, D.E.: Model checking and abstraction. ACM Trans. Program. Lang. Syst. **16**, 1512–1542 (1994)
4. McMillan, K.L.: Lazy abstraction with interpolants. In: Ball, T., Jones, R.B. (eds.) CAV 2006. LNCS, vol. 4144, pp. 123–136. Springer, Heidelberg (2006). doi:10.1007/11817963_14
5. SV-COMP (2016). http://sv-comp.sosy-lab.org/2016/
6. Haran, A., Carter, M., Emmi, M., Lal, A., Qadeer, S., Rakamarić, Z.: SMACK+Corral: a modular verifier. In: Baier, C., Tinelli, C. (eds.) TACAS 2015. LNCS, vol. 9035, pp. 451–454. Springer, Heidelberg (2015). doi:10.1007/978-3-662-46681-0_42
7. Clarke, E., Kroening, D., Lerda, F.: A tool for checking ANSI-C programs. In: Jensen, K., Podelski, A. (eds.) TACAS 2004. LNCS, vol. 2988, pp. 168–176. Springer, Heidelberg (2004). doi:10.1007/978-3-540-24730-2_15
8. Gurfinkel, A., Kahsai, T., Navas, J.A.: SeaHorn: a framework for verifying C programs (competition contribution). In: Baier, C., Tinelli, C. (eds.) TACAS 2015. LNCS, vol. 9035, pp. 447–450. Springer, Heidelberg (2015). doi:10.1007/978-3-662-46681-0_41
9. Beyer, D., Keremoglu, M.E.: CPAchecker: a tool for configurable software verification. In: Gopalakrishnan, G., Qadeer, S. (eds.) CAV 2011. LNCS, vol. 6806, pp. 184–190. Springer, Heidelberg (2011). doi:10.1007/978-3-642-22110-1_16
10. David, C., Kesseli, P., Kroening, D., Lewis, M.: Danger invariants (extended version). https://www.cs.ox.ac.uk/files/8323/danger-paper-extended.pdf
11. Gulwani, S., Srivastava, S., Venkatesan, R.: Program analysis as constraint solving. In: Proceedings of Programming Language Design and Implementation (PLDI), pp. 281–292 (2008)
12. David, C., Kroening, D., Lewis, M.: Using program synthesis for program analysis. In: Davis, M., Fehnker, A., McIver, A., Voronkov, A. (eds.) LPAR 2015. LNCS, vol. 9450, pp. 483–498. Springer, Heidelberg (2015). doi:10.1007/978-3-662-48899-7_34
13. Ball, T., Bounimova, E., Levin, V., Kumar, R., Lichtenberg, J.: The static driver verifier research platform. In: Touili, T., Cook, B., Jackson, P. (eds.) CAV 2010. LNCS, vol. 6174, pp. 119–122. Springer, Heidelberg (2010). doi:10.1007/978-3-642-14295-6_11
14. Nori, A.V., Rajamani, S.K.: An empirical study of optimizations in Yogi. In: International Conference on Software Engineering (ICSE). Association for Computing Machinery Inc., May 2010
15. Dullien, T.: Exploitation and state machines. In: Proceedings of Infiltrate (2011)
16. Godefroid, P., Nori, A.V., Rajamani, S.K., Tetali, S.: Compositional may-must program analysis: unleashing the power of alternation. In: Proceedings of Principles of Programming Languages, POPL, pp. 43–56 (2010)
17. Ball, T., Kupferman, O., Yorsh, G.: Abstraction for falsification. In: Etessami, K., Rajamani, S.K. (eds.) CAV 2005. LNCS, vol. 3576, pp. 67–81. Springer, Heidelberg (2005). doi:10.1007/11513988_8

18. Godefroid, P., Klarlund, N., Sen, K.: DART: directed automated random testing. In: Proceedings of Programming Language Design and Implementation, PLDI, pp. 213–223 (2005)
19. Beyene, T.A., Popeea, C., Rybalchenko, A.: Solving existentially quantified Horn clauses. In: Sharygina, N., Veith, H. (eds.) CAV 2013. LNCS, vol. 8044, pp. 869–882. Springer, Heidelberg (2013). doi:10.1007/978-3-642-39799-8_61
20. Beyene, T.A., Brockschmidt, M., Rybalchenko, A.: CTL+FO verification as constraint solving. In: Proceedings of 2014 International Symposium on Model Checking of Software, SPIN 2014, San Jose, CA, USA, 21–23 July 2014, pp. 101–104 (2014)
21. Kroening, D., Lewis, M., Weissenbacher, G.: Under-approximating loops in C programs for fast counterexample detection. In: Sharygina, N., Veith, H. (eds.) CAV 2013. LNCS, vol. 8044, pp. 381–396. Springer, Heidelberg (2013). doi:10.1007/978-3-642-39799-8_26
22. Kroening, D., Lewis, M., Weissenbacher, G.: Proving safety with trace automata and bounded model checking. In: Bjørner, N., de Boer, F. (eds.) FM 2015. LNCS, vol. 9109, pp. 325–341. Springer, Heidelberg (2015). doi:10.1007/978-3-319-19249-9_21
23. Colón, M.A., Sankaranarayanan, S., Sipma, H.B.: Linear invariant generation using non-linear constraint solving. In: Hunt, W.A., Somenzi, F. (eds.) CAV 2003. LNCS, vol. 2725, pp. 420–432. Springer, Heidelberg (2003). doi:10.1007/978-3-540-45069-6_39
24. Sharma, R., Aiken, A.: From invariant checking to invariant inference using randomized search. In: Biere, A., Bloem, R. (eds.) CAV 2014. LNCS, vol. 8559, pp. 88–105. Springer, Heidelberg (2014). doi:10.1007/978-3-319-08867-9_6
25. Hoenicke, J., Leino, K.R.M., Podelski, A., Schäf, M., Wies, T.: It's doomed; we can prove it. In: Cavalcanti, A., Dams, D.R. (eds.) FM 2009. LNCS, vol. 5850, pp. 338–353. Springer, Heidelberg (2009). doi:10.1007/978-3-642-05089-3_22
26. Ermis, E., Schäf, M., Wies, T.: Error invariants. In: Giannakopoulou, D., Méry, D. (eds.) FM 2012. LNCS, vol. 7436, pp. 187–201. Springer, Heidelberg (2012). doi:10.1007/978-3-642-32759-9_17
27. Angluin, D.: Learning regular sets from queries and counterexamples. Inf. Comput. **75**(2), 87–106 (1987)
28. Alur, R., Bodík, R., Juniwal, G., Martin, M.M.K., Raghothaman, M., Seshia, S.A., Singh, R., Solar-Lezama, A., Torlak, E., Udupa, A.: Syntax-guided synthesis. In: Formal Methods in Computer-Aided Design, FMCAD 2013, Portland 20–23 October 2013, pp. 1–8 (2013). http://ieeexplore.ieee.org/xpl/freeabs_all.jsp?arnumber=6679385

Local Planning of Multiparty Interactions with Bounded Horizons

Mahieddine Dellabani[1,2(✉)], Jacques Combaz[1,2(✉)], Marius Bozga[1,2(✉)], and Saddek Bensalem[1,2(✉)]

[1] University Grenoble Alpes, VERIMAG, 38000 Grenoble, France
{mahieddine.dellabani,jacques.combaz,marius.bozga, saddek.bensalem}@imag.fr

[2] CNRS, VERIMAG, 38000 Grenoble, France
http://www.verimag.fr/rsd

Abstract. Dynamic scheduling of distributed real-time systems with multiparty interactions is acknowledged to be a very hard task. For such systems, multiple schedulers are used to coordinate the parallel activities of remotely running components. In order to ensure global consistency and timing constraints satisfaction, these schedulers must cope with significant communication delays while moreover, use only point-to-point message passing as communication primitive on the platform.

In this paper, we investigate a formal model for such systems as compositions of timed automata subject to multiparty interactions, and we propose a distributed implementation method aiming to overcome the communication delays problem through planning ahead interactions. Moreover, we identify static conditions allowing to make the planning decisions local to different schedulers, and thus to decrease the overall coordination overhead. The method has been implemented and we report preliminary results on benchmarks.

Keywords: Distributed real-time systems · Timed automata · Knowledge

1 Introduction

Over the past few decades, real-time systems have undergone a shift from the use of single processor based hardware platforms, to large sets of interconnected and distributed computing nodes. Such evolution stems from an increase in complexity of real-time software embedded on such platforms (e.g. electronic control in avionics and automotive domains [1]), and the need to integrate formerly isolated systems [2] so that they can cooperate as well as share resources, improving functionality and reducing costs.

The design and the implementation of distributed systems is acknowledged to be a very difficult task. A central question is how to efficiently coordinate parallel activities in a distributed system by means of primary communication primitives

J. Fitzgerald et al. (Eds.): FM 2016, LNCS 9995, pp. 199–216, 2016.
DOI: 10.1007/978-3-319-48989-6_13

offered by the platform, such as point-to-point messages or broadcast. Considering real-time constraints brings additional complexity since any scheduling or control decision may not only impact system performance, but may also affect the satisfaction of timing constraints. To deal with such complexity, the community of safety critical systems often restricts its scope to predictable systems, which are represented with domain specific models (e.g. periodic tasks, synchronous systems, time-deterministic systems) for which the range of possible executions is small enough to be easily analyzed, allowing the precomputation of optimal control strategies. For non-critical systems, the standard practice is not to rely on models for precomputing scenarios but rather to design systems dynamically adapting at runtime to the actual context of execution. Such approaches do not offer any formal guarantee of timeliness. The lack of a priori knowledge on system behavior leaves also little room for static optimization.

In our framework, systems consist of components represented as timed automata that may synchronize on particular actions to coordinate their activities. Timed automata are strictly more expressive [3] than time-deterministic systems considered in time-triggered approaches [4–7]. Our framework also differs from the one proposed in [8,9] by considering not only binary, but also multiparty (n-ary) synchronizations, a.k.a. *interactions*, expressing the fact that a subset of components may jointly (and atomically) switch their states if given preconditions are fulfilled. Such high level coordination means are rarely part of the built-in primitives offered by distributed platforms, and thus need to be implemented using simpler ones, e.g. exchange of messages. This has been extensively studied in the untimed context [10–17] but to the best of our knowledge, it has been solved for timed systems only under the assumption of non-decreasing deadlines in [18,19].

We contribute to this research field by proposing methods for scheduling interactions with bounded horizons, which aims to reduce the impact of communication delays on systems execution. In particular, *(i)* we define a semantics for *planning* interactions with bounded horizons, *(ii)* we provide sufficient conditions for this semantics to be correct, and *(iii)* we present an operational method to check those conditions using system knowledge.

The rest of the paper is organized as follows. In Sect. 2, we provide a formal definition of composition of timed automata with respect to multiparty interactions. We also present a semantics for planning interactions with bounded horizons. In Sect. 3, we study sufficient conditions for a safe planning of interactions. Thereafter, we use global knowledge of the system to refine the latest conditions for more precise results and in order to avoid unnecessary verification (Sect. 4). Finally, the application of previous results on various examples is presented in Sect. 5. Note that all the proofs can be found in the technical report [20].

2 Timed Systems and Properties

2.1 Global State Semantics

In the framework of the present paper, components are timed automata and systems are compositions of timed automata with respect to multiparty interactions.

The timed automata we use are essentially the ones from [21], however, slightly adapted to embrace a uniform notation throughout the paper.

Definition 1 (Component). *A* component *is a tuple* $(\mathcal{L}, \ell_0, A, T, \mathcal{X}, tpc)$ *where* $\mathcal{L}$ *is a finite set of* locations, $\ell_0 \in \mathcal{L}$ *is an* initial *location,* A *a finite set of* actions, $\mathcal{X}$ *is a finite set of* clocks, $T \subseteq \mathcal{L} \times (A \times \mathcal{C} \times 2^{\mathcal{X}}) \times \mathcal{L}$ *is a set of* transitions *labeled with an action, a guard, and a set of clocks to be reset, and* $tpc : \mathcal{L} \to \mathcal{C}$ *assigns a* time progress condition, tpc_ℓ, *to each location, where* $\mathcal{C}$ *is the set of* clock constraints *defined by the following grammar:*

$$C := true \mid x \sim ct \mid x - y \sim ct \mid C \wedge C \mid false,$$

with $x, y \in \mathcal{X}$, $\sim \in \{<, \leq, =, \geq, >\}$ *and* $ct \in \mathbb{R}_{\geq 0}$. *Time progress conditions are restricted to conjunctions of constraints of the form* $x \leq ct$.

Throughout the paper, we consider that components are deterministic timed automata, that is, at a given location ℓ and for a given action a, there is at most one outgoing transition from ℓ labeled by a. Given a timed automaton $(\mathcal{L}, \ell_0, A, T, \mathcal{X}, tpc)$, we write $\ell \xrightarrow{a,g,r} \ell'$ if there exists a transition $\tau = (\ell, (a, g, r), \ell') \in T$. We also write:

$$guard(a, \ell) = \begin{cases} g, & \text{if } \exists \tau = (\ell, (a, g, r), \ell') \in T \\ false, & \text{otherwise} \end{cases}$$

Let $\mathcal{V}$ be the set of all clock valuation functions $v : \mathcal{X} \to \mathbb{R}_{\geq 0}$. For a clock constraint C, $C(v)$ is a boolean value corresponding to the evaluation of C on v. For a valuation $v \in \mathcal{V}$, $v + \delta$ is the valuation satisfying $(v + \delta)(x) = v(x) + \delta$, while for a subset of clocks r, $v[r]$ is the valuation obtained from v by resetting clocks of r, i.e. $v[r](x) = 0$ for $x \in r$, $v[r](x) = v(x)$ otherwise. We also denote by $C + \delta$ the clock constraint C shifted by δ, i.e. such that $C(v + \delta)$ iff $C(v)$.

Definition 2 (Semantics). *A component* $B = (\mathcal{L}, \ell_0, A, T, \mathcal{X}, tpc)$ *defines the labeled transition system (LTS)* $(Q, A \cup \mathbb{R}_{>0}, \to)$ *where* $Q \subseteq \mathcal{L} \times \mathcal{V}(\mathcal{X})$ *denotes the* states *of* B *and* $\to \subseteq Q \times (A \cup \mathbb{R}_{>0}) \times Q$ *denotes the set of transitions between states according to the rules:*

- $(\ell, v) \xrightarrow{a} (\ell', v[r])$ *if* $\ell \xrightarrow{a,g,r} \ell'$, *and* $g(v)$ *is true (action step).*
- $(\ell, v) \xrightarrow{\delta} (\ell, v + \delta)$ *if* $tpc_\ell(v + \delta)$ *(time progress).*

We define the predicate $urg(tpc_\ell)$ characterizing the urgency of a time progress condition $tpc_\ell = \bigwedge_{i=1}^{m} x_i \leq ct_i$ at a state (ℓ, v) as follows:

$$urg(tpc_\ell) = \bigvee_{i=1}^{m} (x_i = ct_i),$$

An *execution sequence* of B from a state (ℓ, v) is a path in the LTS starting at (ℓ, v) and that alternates action steps and time steps (time progress), that is:

$$(\ell_1, v_1) \xrightarrow{\sigma_1} \dots \xrightarrow{\sigma_i} (\ell_n, v_n), n \in \mathbb{Z}_{\geq 0}, \sigma \in A \cup \mathbb{R}_{>0}$$

In this paper, we always assume components with *well formed guards* meaning that transitions $\ell \xrightarrow{a,g,r} \ell'$ satisfy $g(v) \Rightarrow tpc_\ell(v) \wedge tpc_{\ell'}(v[r])$ for any $v \in \mathcal{V}$. We say that a state (ℓ, v) is *reachable* if there is an execution sequence from the initial configuration (ℓ_0, v_0) leading to (ℓ, v), where v_0 assigns 0 to all clocks. Notice that the set of reachable states is in general infinite, but it can be partitioned into a finite number of symbolic states [22–24]. A symbolic state is defined by a pair (ℓ, ζ) where, ℓ is a location of B, and ζ is a zone, i.e. a set of clock valuations defined by a clock constraint (as defined in Definition 1). Efficient algorithms for computing symbolic states and operations on zones are fully described in [23]. Given symbolic states $\{(\ell_j, \zeta_j)\}_{j \in J}$ of B, the predicate $Reach(B)$ characterizing the reachable states can be formulated as:

$$Reach(B) = \bigvee_{j \in J} \mathsf{at}(\ell_j) \wedge \zeta_j,$$

where $\mathsf{at}(\ell_j)$ is true on states whose location is ℓ_j, and clock constraint ζ_j is straightforwardly applied to clock valuation functions of states.

We also define the predicate $Enabled(a)$ characterizing states (ℓ, v) at which an action a is enabled, i.e. such that $(\ell, v) \xrightarrow{a} (\ell', v')$. It can be written:

$$Enabled(a) = \bigvee_{(\ell,a,g,r,\ell') \in T} \mathsf{at}(\ell) \wedge guard(a, \ell)$$

Definition 3 (Deadlock). *We say that a state (ℓ, v) of a component B deadlocks, if neither action steps nor time steps can be done from this state. The following equation characterizes those states:*

$$\forall a \in A.\ \neg Enabled(a)\ \wedge\ urg(tpc_\ell)$$

In our framework, components communicate by means of *multiparty interactions*. A multiparty interaction is a rendez-vous synchronization between actions of a fixed subset of components. It takes place only if all the participants agree to execute the corresponding actions. Given n components B_i, $i = 1, \ldots, n$, with disjoint sets of actions A_i, an interaction is a subset of actions $\alpha \subseteq \cup_{1 \leq i \leq n} A_i$ containing at most one action per component, i.e. $\alpha \cap A_i$ is either empty or a singleton $\{a_i\}$. That is, an interaction α can be put in the form $\{a_i\}_{i \in I}$ with $I \subseteq \{1, \ldots, n\}$ and $a_i \in A_i$ for all $i \in I$.

Definition 4 (Composition). *For n components $B_i = (\mathcal{L}_i, \ell_0^i, A_i, T_i, \mathcal{X}_i, tpc_i)$, with $\mathcal{L}_j \cap \mathcal{L}_j = \emptyset$, $A_i \cap A_j = \emptyset$, and $\mathcal{X}_i \cap \mathcal{X}_j = \emptyset$ for any $i \neq j$, the* composition *$\gamma(B_1, \ldots, B_n)$ w.r.t. a set of interactions γ is defined by a timed automaton $S = (\mathcal{L}, \ell_0, \gamma, T_\gamma, \mathcal{X}, tpc)$ where $\ell_0 = (\ell_0^1, \ldots, \ell_0^n)$, $\mathcal{X} = \mathcal{X}_1 \cup \ldots \cup \mathcal{X}_n$, $\mathcal{L} = \mathcal{L}_1 \times \ldots \times \mathcal{L}_n$, $tpc = tpc_1 \wedge \ldots \wedge tpc_n$ for $\ell = (\ell_1, \ldots, \ell_n)$, and T_γ is such that $\ell \xrightarrow{\alpha,g,r} \ell'$ for $\alpha = \{a_i\}_{i \in I}$, $\ell = (\ell_1, \ldots, \ell_n)$, and $\ell' = (\ell'_1, \ldots, \ell'_n)$, if for $i \notin I$ we have $\ell'_i = \ell_i$, and for $i \in I$ we have $\ell_i \xrightarrow{a_i,g_i,r_i} \ell'_i$, and $g_\alpha = \bigwedge_{i \in I} g_i$ and $r = \bigcup_{i \in I} r_i$.*

In practice we do not explicitly build compositions of components as presented in Definition 4. We rather interpret their semantics at runtime by evaluating enabled interactions based on current states of components. In a composition of n components $B_{i\in\{1,\cdots,n\}}$, denoted by $\gamma(B_1,\ldots,B_n)$, an action a_i can execute only as part of an interaction α such that $a_i \in \alpha$, that is, along with the execution of all other actions $a_j \in \alpha$, which corresponds to the usual notion of multiparty interaction.

Property 1 (Semantics of a Composition). Given a set of components $\{B_1,\cdots,B_n\}$ and an interaction set γ. The semantics of the composite component $S = (\mathcal{L}, \ell_0, \gamma, T_\gamma, \mathcal{X}, tpc)$ w.r.t the set of interaction γ, is the LTS $(\mathrm{Q}_g, \gamma \cup \mathbb{R}_{>0}, \rightarrow_\gamma)$ where:

- $\mathrm{Q}_g = \mathcal{L} \times \mathcal{V}(\mathcal{X})$ is the set of global states, where $\mathcal{L} = \mathcal{L}_1 \times \cdots \times \mathcal{L}_n$ and $\mathcal{X} = \bigcup_{i=1}^{n} \mathcal{X}_i$. We write a state $q = (\ell, v)$ where $\ell = (\ell_1, \cdots, \ell_n) \in \mathcal{L}$ is a global location and $v = (v_1, \cdots, v_n) \in \mathcal{V}(\mathcal{X})$ is a global clocks valuations.
- γ is the set of interactions
- $\rightarrow_\gamma$ is the set of labeled transitions defined by the rules:
  - Action steps:

$$\frac{\alpha = \{a_i\}_{i\in I} \in \gamma, \quad \forall i \in I.(\ell_i, v_i) \xrightarrow{a_i} (\ell'_i, v'_i), \quad \forall i \notin I.(\ell_i, v_i) = (\ell'_i, v'_i)}{(\ell, v) \xrightarrow{\alpha}_\gamma (\ell', v')}$$

  - Time steps:

$$\frac{\delta \in \mathbb{R}_{>0} \quad \forall i \in \{1, \cdots, n\} \quad tpc_i(v_i + \delta)}{(\ell, v) \xrightarrow{\delta}_\gamma (\ell, v + \delta)}$$

In what follows, we consider only deadlock-free systems w.r.t the presented semantics. By abuse of notation, predicates $\mathsf{at}(\ell_i)$ of individual components B_i are interpreted on states of S, being true for (ℓ, v) iff B_i is at location ℓ_i in ℓ, i.e. iff $\ell \in \mathcal{L}_1 \times \ldots \times \mathcal{L}_{i-1} \times \{\ell_i\} \times \mathcal{L}_{i+1} \times \ldots \times \mathcal{L}_n$. Similarly, clock constraints of components B_i are applied to clock valuation functions v of the composition $S = (\mathcal{L}, \ell_0, \gamma, T_\gamma, \mathcal{X}, tpc)$ by restricting v to clocks $\mathcal{X}_i$ of B_i. Given an interaction $\alpha \in \gamma$, these notations allow us to write $Enabled(\alpha)$ as:

$$\begin{aligned}
Enabled(\alpha) &= \bigvee_{\ell=(\ell_1,\cdots,\ell_n)\in\mathcal{L}_\alpha} \mathsf{at}(\ell) \wedge guard(\alpha, \ell), \\
&= \bigvee_{(\ell_1,\cdots,\ell_n)\in\mathcal{L}_\alpha} \mathsf{at}(\ell) \wedge \bigwedge_{a_i\in\alpha} guard(a_i, \ell_i), \\
&= \bigvee_{(\ell_1,\cdots,\ell_n)\in\mathcal{L}_\alpha} \bigwedge_{i=1}^{n} \mathsf{at}(\ell_i) \wedge \bigwedge_{a_i\in\alpha} guard(a_i, \ell_i), \\
&= \bigwedge_{a_i\in\alpha} Enabled(a_i),
\end{aligned}$$

where $\mathcal{L}_\alpha = \{\ell \in \mathcal{L} | \ell \xrightarrow{\alpha,g,r} \ell'\}$.

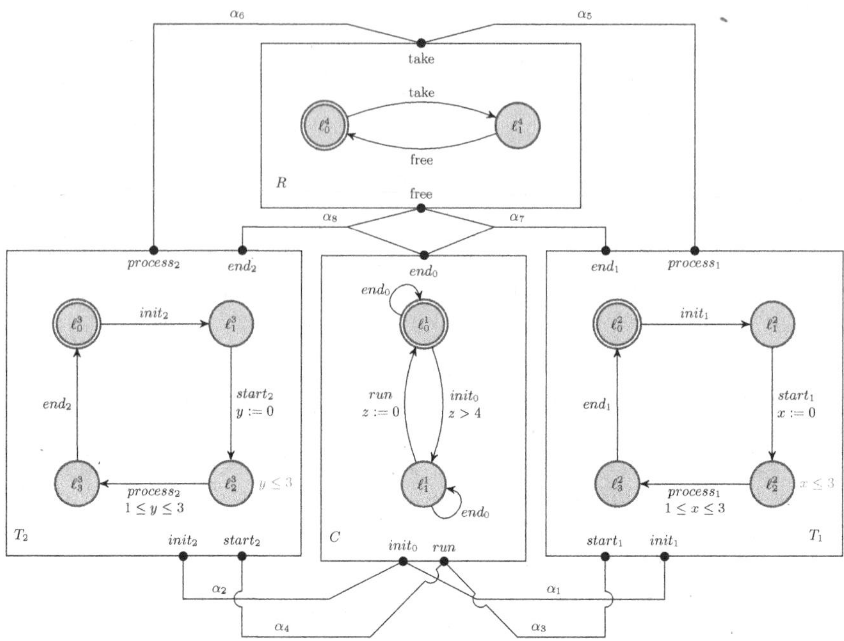

Fig. 1. Task Manager

Example 1 (Running Example). Let us consider as a running example the composition of four components C, T_1, T_2, and R of Fig. 1. Component C represents a controller that initializes, releases, and ends tasks T_1 and T_2. Tasks use the shared resource R during their execution. To implement such behavior, we consider the following interactions between C, R, and T_1: $\alpha_1 = \{init_0, init_1\}$, $\alpha_3 = \{run, start_1\}$, $\alpha_5 = \{take, process_1\}$, $\alpha_7 = \{end_0, free, end_1\}$, and similar interactions α_2, α_4, α_6, α_8 for task T_2, as shown by connections on Fig. 1. The controller is responsible for firing the execution of each task. First, it nondeterministically initializes one of the two tasks, i.e. executes α_1 or α_2, and then releases it through interaction α_3 or α_4. Tasks perform their processing independently of the controller, after being granted an access to the shared resource (α_5 or α_6). When ended by the controller, a task releases the resource (interactions α_7 or α_8) and go back to its initial location. An example of execution sequence of the system of Fig. 1 is given below, in which valuations v of clocks x, y, and z are represented as a tuples $(v(x), v(y), v(z))$:

$$((\ell_0^1, \ell_0^2, \ell_0^3, \ell_0^4), (0,0,0)) \xrightarrow{5}_\gamma ((\ell_0^1, \ell_0^2, \ell_0^3, \ell_0^4), (5,5,5)) \xrightarrow{\alpha_1}_\gamma ((\ell_1^1, \ell_1^2, \ell_0^3, \ell_0^4), (5,5,5))$$
$$\xrightarrow{\alpha_3}_\gamma ((\ell_0^1, \ell_2^2, \ell_0^3, \ell_0^4), (0,5,0)) \xrightarrow{2}_\gamma ((\ell_0^1, \ell_2^2, \ell_0^3, \ell_0^4), (2,7,2)) \xrightarrow{\alpha_5}_\gamma ((\ell_0^1, \ell_3^2, \ell_0^3, \ell_1^4), (2,7,2))$$
$$\xrightarrow{3}_\gamma ((\ell_0^1, \ell_3^2, \ell_0^3, \ell_1^4), (5,10,5)) \xrightarrow{\alpha_2}_\gamma ((\ell_1^1, \ell_3^2, \ell_1^3, \ell_1^4), (5,10,5))$$

2.2 Weak Planning Semantics

The presented semantics is based on a global state operational semantics, that is, the operational semantics rules and the computation of possible interactions between timed components is achieved through global states. Considering a distributed context, components are intrinsically concurrent and their execution is asynchronous. This means that even if states of components participating in an interaction α are known, α cannot be executed in the global state semantics until the states of all components are known, which breaks the principle of distribution. Usually, components are mapped at different areas on the distributed platform in a way that better suits their interactions. In other terms, components that synchronize their actions are more likely to be next to each others. However, there are cases where several components participate in the same interaction but are mapped far from each other, which adds on communication delays to the interaction corresponding to the exchange of messages.

In order to reach an efficient scheduling, able of taking decisions ahead and using only partial (local) information, we define a different semantics based on a local planning of interactions. It aims to alleviate the problem of communication delays through an early decision making mechanism while preserving deadlock freedom property of the system. This is achieved by planning each interaction ahead, which means to choose an execution time within a certain horizon for each interaction, based only on the states of components involved in that interaction. Consequently, components are notified ahead through communication primitive, and will wait until the chosen execution time to perform their corresponding actions. Our approach is to define for each interaction its earliest planning date, which correspond to the maximum horizon value that ensure a safe planning of the considered interaction.

Preliminaries. We define the predicate $\mathit{Enabled}^{\nearrow^\delta}(\alpha)$ characterizing all states from which α is *enabled* if time progresses by δ units of time, that is:

$$\mathit{Enabled}^{\nearrow^\delta}(\alpha) = \bigvee_{\ell \in \mathcal{L}_\alpha} \big(\mathsf{at}(\ell) \wedge \bigwedge_{a_i \in \alpha} (\mathit{guard}(a_i, \ell_i) + \delta)\big), \tag{1}$$

Property 2. Let (ℓ, v) be a state of the composition S. For any interaction $\beta \in \gamma$ such that, $\text{part}(\alpha) \cap \text{part}(\beta) = \emptyset$ and $(\ell, v) \xrightarrow{\beta}_\gamma (\ell', v')$, where $\text{part}(\alpha)$ (resp. $\text{part}(\beta)$) represents components participating in interaction α (resp. β), if $\mathit{Enabled}^{\nearrow^\delta}(\alpha)$ holds at state (ℓ, v) then it still holds at state (ℓ', v').

This property derives from the fact that executing interactions with disjoint set of components than α does not change the states of components participating in α, that is, for $a_i \in \alpha$ we have $\ell_i = \ell'_i$ and $v_i = v'_i$.

Property 3. Let (ℓ, v) and $(\ell, v + \delta')$, with $\delta' \in \mathbb{R}_{>0}$ be two states of the composition S. If $\mathit{Enabled}^{\nearrow^\delta}(\alpha)$ is *true* at state (ℓ, v) then $\mathit{Enabled}^{\nearrow^{\delta-\delta'}}(\alpha)$ is true at state $(\ell, v + \delta')$ for $\delta' \leq \delta$.

This property can be found directly by writing Eq. 1 on state $(\ell, v + \delta')$.

Let $\delta_{\max}$ be a partial function $\delta_{\max} : \gamma \rightarrow \mathbb{R}_{\geq 0}$ that defines for each interaction a maximum horizon to be planned with. We define the predicate $Enabled^{\nearrow[0,\delta_{\max}(\alpha)]}(\alpha)$ characterizing all states from which α can be planned with a $\delta_{\max}(\alpha)$-horizon as follows:

$$Enabled^{\nearrow[0,\delta_{\max}(\alpha)]}(\alpha) = \bigvee_{\ell \in \mathcal{L}_\alpha} (\mathsf{at}(\ell) \wedge \swarrow^{\delta_{\max}(\alpha)} (\bigwedge_{a_i \in \alpha} guard(a_i, \ell_i))),$$

with $\swarrow^{\delta_{\max}(\alpha)}$ represents an adaptation of the backward operators [22] that satisfies:

$$\swarrow^{\delta_{\max}(\alpha)} g(x) \Leftrightarrow \exists \delta \leq \delta_{\max}(\alpha).g(x+\delta),$$

Property 4. If the predicate $Enabled^{\nearrow^{\delta}}(\alpha)$ is *true* at a state (ℓ, v), then the predicate $Enabled^{\nearrow[0,\delta_{\max}(\alpha)]}(\alpha)$ is also *true* for $\delta \leq \delta_{\max}(\alpha)$.

Definition 5 (Plan). *We say that two interactions α and β, $\alpha \neq \beta$,* conflicts *if* $\mathrm{part}(\alpha) \cap \mathrm{part}(\beta) \neq \emptyset$*, and we write $\alpha \# \beta$. A plan π is a partial function $\pi : \gamma \rightarrow \mathbb{R}_{\geq 0}$ defining relative times for executing a subset of non conflicting interactions, i.e.:*

$$\alpha \neq \alpha', \pi(\alpha) \neq \perp, \pi(\alpha') \neq \perp \implies \neg(\alpha \# \alpha').$$

We also denote by $conf(\pi)$ the set of interactions conflicting with the plan π, i.e. $conf(\pi) = \{\alpha \mid \exists \beta \# \alpha \ . \ \pi(\beta) \neq \perp\}$, and $\mathrm{part}(\pi)$ *the set of components involved in interactions planned by π, i.e.* $\mathrm{part}(\pi) = \{B_i \mid \exists \alpha \ . \ \pi(\alpha) \neq \perp \wedge B_i \in \mathrm{part}(\alpha)\}$.

We denote by $\min \pi$ the closest relative execution time of interactions in the plan π, i.e. $\min \pi = \min \{\pi(\alpha) \mid \alpha \in \gamma \wedge \pi(\alpha) \neq \perp\} \cup \{+\infty\}$. Notice that since π stores relative times, whenever time progresses by δ the value $\pi(\alpha)$ assigned by π to an interaction α should be decreased by δ, until it reaches 0 which means that α have to execute. We write $\pi - \delta$ describing the progress of time over the plan, that is, $(\pi - \delta)(\alpha) = \pi(\alpha) - \delta$ for interactions α such that $\pi(\alpha) \neq \perp$. We also write $\pi - \alpha$ to denote the removal of interaction α from the plan π, i.e. $(\pi - \alpha)(\beta) = \pi(\beta)$ for any interaction $\beta \neq \alpha$, $(\pi - \alpha)(\alpha) = \perp$. Similarly, $\pi \cup \{\alpha \mapsto \delta\}$ assigns relative time δ to α, $\alpha \notin conf(\pi)$, into existing plan π, i.e. $(\pi \cup \{\alpha \mapsto \delta\})(\beta) = \delta$ for $\beta = \alpha$, $(\pi \cup \{\alpha \mapsto \delta\})(\beta) = \pi(\alpha)$ otherwise. Finally, the plan π such that $\pi(\alpha) = \perp$ for all interactions $\alpha \in \gamma$ is denoted by $\emptyset$.

We define below the semantics for planning each interaction $\alpha \in \gamma$ with $\delta_{\max}(\alpha)$-horizon.

Definition 6 (Weak Planning Semantics). *Given a set of components $\{B_1, \cdots, B_n\}$ and an interaction set γ, we define the weak planning semantics of the composite component $S = (\mathcal{L}, \ell_0, \gamma, T_\gamma, \mathcal{X}, tpc)$, as the labeled transition system $S_p = (\mathrm{Q}_\pi, \gamma \cup \mathbb{R}_{>0} \cup \{$**plan**$\}, \rightsquigarrow)$ where:*

- $\mathrm{Q}_\pi = \mathcal{L} \times \mathcal{V}(\mathcal{X}) \times \Pi$*, where $\mathcal{L}$ is the set of global location, $\mathcal{V}(\mathcal{X})$ is the set of global clocks valuations, and Π is the set of plans.*

- **plan** *defines the action of planning interactions*
- $\rightsquigarrow$ *is the set of labeled transitions defined by the rules:*
  - *Plan:*

$$\frac{\delta \leq \delta_{\max}(\alpha), \alpha \in \gamma, \text{part}(\alpha) \cap \text{part}(\pi) = \emptyset \quad Enabled^{\nearrow^{\delta}}(\alpha)}{(\ell, v, \pi) \overset{\textbf{plan}(\alpha,\delta)}{\rightsquigarrow} (\ell, v, \pi \cup \{\alpha \mapsto \delta\}).}$$

  - *Exec:*

$$\frac{\pi(\alpha) = 0}{(\ell, v, \pi) \overset{\alpha}{\rightsquigarrow} (\ell', v', \pi - \alpha)\}}$$

  - *Time Progress:* $\delta \in \mathbb{R}_{>0}$

$$\frac{\delta \leq min\ \pi \wedge tpc_i(v_i + \delta)_{i \in \{1,\cdots,n\}}}{(\ell, v, \pi) \overset{\delta}{\rightsquigarrow} (\ell, v + \delta, \pi - \delta)}$$

Example 2. Let us consider the following execution sequence for the example of Fig. 1 under the weak planning semantics rules and for a value $\delta_{\max} = 5$ for all interactions except α_5 and α_6 that will be assigned a $\delta_{\max} = 3$:

$$((\ell_0^1, \ell_0^2, \ell_0^3, \ell_0^4), (0,0,0), \emptyset) \overset{\textbf{plan}(\alpha_1,5)}{\rightsquigarrow} ((\ell_0^1, \ell_0^2, \ell_0^3, \ell_0^4), (0,0,0), \{\alpha_1 \mapsto 5\}) \overset{5}{\rightsquigarrow}$$
$$((\ell_0^1, \ell_0^2, \ell_0^3, \ell_0^4), (5,5,5), \{\alpha_1 \mapsto 0\}) \overset{\alpha_1}{\rightsquigarrow} ((\ell_1^1, \ell_1^2, \ell_0^3, \ell_0^4), (5,5,5), \emptyset) \overset{\textbf{plan}(\alpha_3,2)}{\rightsquigarrow}$$
$$((\ell_1^1, \ell_1^2, \ell_0^3, \ell_0^4), (5,5,5), \{\alpha_3 \mapsto 2\}) \overset{2}{\rightsquigarrow} ((\ell_1^1, \ell_1^2, \ell_0^3, \ell_0^4), (7,7,7), \{\alpha_3 \mapsto 0\}) \overset{\alpha_3}{\rightsquigarrow}$$
$$((\ell_0^1, \ell_2^2, \ell_0^3, \ell_0^4), (0,7,0), \emptyset) \overset{\textbf{plan}(\alpha_5,2)}{\rightsquigarrow} ((\ell_0^1, \ell_2^2, \ell_0^3, \ell_0^4), (0,7,0), \{\alpha_5 \mapsto 2\}) \overset{2}{\rightsquigarrow}$$
$$((\ell_0^1, \ell_2^2, \ell_0^3, \ell_0^4), (2,9,2), \{\alpha_5 \mapsto 0\}) \overset{\alpha_5}{\rightsquigarrow} ((\ell_0^1, \ell_3^2, \ell_0^3, \ell_1^4), (2,9,2), \emptyset) \overset{\textbf{plan}(\alpha_2,3)}{\rightsquigarrow}$$
$$((\ell_0^1, \ell_3^2, \ell_0^3, \ell_1^4), (2,9,2), \{\alpha_2 \mapsto 3\}) \overset{3}{\rightsquigarrow} ((\ell_0^1, \ell_3^2, \ell_0^3, \ell_1^4), (5,12,5), \{\alpha_2 \mapsto 0\}) \overset{\alpha_2}{\rightsquigarrow}$$
$$((\ell_1^1, \ell_3^2, \ell_1^3, \ell_1^4), (5,12,5), \emptyset) \overset{\textbf{plan}(\alpha_4,0)}{\rightsquigarrow} ((\ell_1^1, \ell_3^2, \ell_1^3, \ell_1^4), (5,12,5)\{\alpha_4 \mapsto 0\}) \overset{\alpha_4}{\rightsquigarrow}$$
$$((\ell_0^1, \ell_3^2, \ell_2^3, \ell_1^4), (5,0,0), \emptyset) \overset{\textbf{plan}(\alpha_7,4)}{\rightsquigarrow} ((\ell_0^1, \ell_3^2, \ell_2^3, \ell_1^4), (5,0,0), \{\alpha_7 \mapsto 4\}) \overset{3}{\rightsquigarrow}$$
$$((\ell_0^1, \ell_3^2, \ell_2^3, \ell_1^4), (8,3,3), \{\alpha_7 \mapsto 1\})$$

This execution sequence represents a path that alternates plan actions, time steps and execution of some interactions. We can see that for interaction α_7 which is planned 4 units of time ahead, the system cannot reach the state from which it can be executed since there is a time progress expiration in component T_2 after 3 time units from planning this interaction. This means that local planning of interactions doesn't always allow the progress of time and may thus, introduce deadlocks even if the system under the global semantics rules is deadlock-free.

2.3 Relation Between Global and Weak Planning Semantics

We use weak simulation to compare the model under the global semantics rules and the one under the weak planning semantics rules by considering **plan**-transitions unobservable. As explained in Example 2, the weak planning semantics does not preserve the deadlock property of our system. Nevertheless, the following proves weak simulation relations between the two semantics.

Theorem 1. *For all the reachable states (ℓ, v, π) of the weak planning semantics, and $\forall \alpha \in \pi$, the predicate $Enabled^{\nearrow \pi(\alpha)}(\alpha)$ is true.*

Let $S_g = (Q_g, \gamma \cup \mathbb{R}_{>0}, \rightarrow_\gamma)$ (resp. $S_p = (Q_p, \gamma \cup \mathbb{R}_{>0} \cup \{\mathbf{plan}\}, \rightsquigarrow)$) the labeled transition system characterizing the global (resp. weak planning) semantics.

Proposition 1

Relation 1 $\forall \delta \in \mathbb{R}_{>0}.(\ell, v, \pi) \overset{\delta}{\rightsquigarrow} (\ell', v', \pi') \Rightarrow (\ell, v) \xrightarrow{\delta}_\gamma (\ell', v')$
Relation 2 $\forall \alpha \in \gamma.(\ell, v, \pi) \overset{\alpha}{\rightsquigarrow} (\ell', v', \pi') \Rightarrow (\ell, v) \xrightarrow{\alpha}_\gamma (\ell', v')$

It is straightforward that Relation 1 is a consequence of the definition of time progress in the weak planning semantics. For Relation 2, using Definition 6, we can deduce that:

$$(\ell, v, \pi) \overset{\alpha}{\rightsquigarrow} (\ell', v', \pi') \Rightarrow \pi(\alpha) = 0$$

By Theorem 1, this implies that $Enabled^{\nearrow 0}(\alpha)$ is *true* at state (ℓ, v, π), meaning that $Enabled(\alpha)$ is also *true*, which allows to infer Relation 2.

Corollary 1. *If a state $(\ell, v, \pi) \in Reach(S_p)$, then $(\ell, v) \in Reach(S_g)$.*

Definition 7 (Weak Simulation). *A weak simulation over $A = (Q_A, \sum \cup \{\beta\}, \rightarrow_A)$ and $B = (Q_B, \sum \cup \{\beta\}, \rightarrow_B)$ is a relation $R \subseteq Q_A \times Q_B$ such that we have: $\forall (q, r) \in R, a \in \sum . q \xrightarrow{a}_A q' \implies \exists r' : (q', r') \in R \wedge r \xrightarrow{\beta^* a \beta^*}_B r'$ and $\forall (q, r) \in R : q \xrightarrow{\beta}_A q' \implies \exists r' : (q', r') \in R \wedge r \xrightarrow{\beta^*} r'$. B simulates A, denoted by $A \sqsubseteq_R B$, means that B can do everything A does.*

The definition of weak simulation is based on the unobservability of $\beta-$transitions. In our case, $\beta-$transitions corresponds to **plan**$-$transitions.

Corollary 2. *$S_p \sqsubseteq_{R_1} S_g$ with $R_1 = \{(q, \pi); q) \in Q_p \times Q_g\}$.*

Corollary 2 corresponds to a notion of correctness of the weak planning semantics: any execution in weak planning semantics corresponds to an execution in the global state semantics.

Theorem 2. *$S_g \sqsubseteq_{R_2} S_p$ with $R_2 = \{(q; (q, \pi)) \in Q_g \times Q_p | \pi = \emptyset\}$.*

Theorem 2 states that the weak planning semantics preserves all execution sequences of the global state semantics. They are obtained using immediate planning, i.e. plans π such that $\pi(\alpha) = 0$ or $\pi(\alpha) = \bot$. The weak planning semantics aims to reduces the impact of communication delays in the system through planning interactions execution ahead, and by considering only the state of components involved in the planned interaction, which is more suitable for distributed real-time systems than the global state semantics. It does not restrict the behavior of the global state semantics (see Theorem 2), and it executes only sequences allowed by the global state semantics (see Corollary 2). However, it may introduce deadlocks as shown by the scenario presented in Example 2. In the following, we present sufficient conditions for deadlock-free planning of interactions.

3 Deadlock-Free Planning

As explained in Example 2, local planning of interactions can introduce deadlocks in the system since it does not consider time progress conditions of components not participating in the planned interactions. Effectively, the weak planning semantics ensures that time can progress until the chosen execution date only w.r.t timing constraints of participating components, but such progress may be disallowed by the rest of the system leading to deadlock states. In this section, we provide sufficient conditions for having deadlock-free planning.

Planning an interaction α implies not only blocking components participating in α until α executes, but also preventing the system from planning interactions involving these components, that is, interactions of $conf(\alpha)$. Consequently, the subset of interactions $\gamma' \subseteq \gamma$ that can be planned at a given state (ℓ, v, π) depends on the content of the plan π. It satisfies $\gamma' = \{\gamma \setminus \pi \cup conf(\pi)\}$.

By Corollary 1, a (reachable) deadlock state (ℓ, v, π) of the weak planning semantics S_p is such that (ℓ, v) is a reachable state of the global state semantics S_g. Since we assume that S_g is deadlock-free, (ℓ, v) is not a deadlock in S_g. A deadlock state (ℓ, v, π) of S_p is caused by the plan π which is restricting the execution in S_p w.r.t. S_g: interactions α of π cannot execute before $\pi(\alpha)$ time units, and interactions $\alpha \in conf(\pi)$ are blocked for (at least) $\max \{\pi(\beta) \mid \beta \# \alpha\}$. Notice that due to well-formed guards, in a deadlock state (ℓ, v, π) we have necessarily $\mathsf{at}(\ell_i) \wedge urg(tpc_{\ell_i})$ for a location ℓ_i of a component $B_i \notin \mathrm{part}(\pi)$.

Theorem 3. *If a state $(\ell, v, \pi) \in Reach(S_p)$ deadlocks, the following equation is satisfied:*

$$\begin{aligned} &\underbrace{\bigwedge_{\alpha \in \pi} Enabled^{\nearrow \pi(\alpha)}(\alpha)}_{A} \;\wedge\; \underbrace{\bigvee_{B_i \in S \setminus \mathrm{part}(\pi)} \bigvee_{\ell_i \in \mathcal{L}_i} \ell_i \wedge urg(tpc_{\ell_i})}_{B} \\ &\wedge \underbrace{\bigwedge_{\alpha \in \pi} \pi(\alpha) \neq 0 \wedge \Big(\bigvee_{\alpha \in \pi} (Enabled(\alpha) \vee \bigvee_{\alpha \in conf(\pi)} Enabled(\alpha)\Big)}_{C} \end{aligned} \tag{2}$$

From Theorem 1, Term A of Eq. 2 represents an invariant of the system. On the other hand, terms B and C characterize the deadlock: Term B expresses the urgency of time progress condition in components not involved in the planned interactions, whereas, term C specifies the origin of the deadlock: it characterizes states (ℓ, v, π) of S_p for which π restricts the execution of an interaction α whereas it can be executed at (ℓ, v) in S_g. As explained above, such an interaction satisfies $\pi(\alpha) > 0$ or $\alpha \in conf(\pi)$.

It is clear that Eq. 2 depends on the reachable states of the planning semantics since it explicitly depends on plans π. The following gives weaker conditions for deadlocks which are independent of the plan.

Theorem 4. *Let $\Phi(\alpha)$ be the following predicate:*

$$\widetilde{Enabled^{\nearrow[0,\delta_{\max}(\alpha)]}}(\alpha) \;\wedge \bigvee_{B_i \in S \setminus \mathtt{part}(\alpha)} \bigvee_{\ell_i \in \mathcal{L}_i} \mathtt{at}(\ell_i) \wedge urg(tpc_{\ell_i}) \wedge \bigvee_{\beta \in \alpha \cup conf(\alpha)} Enabled(\beta) \tag{3}$$

where $\widetilde{Enabled^{\nearrow[0,\delta_{\max}(\alpha)]}}(\alpha)$ is the result of transforming all the timing constraints of the form $x \le ct$ by $x < ct$ in $\nearrow^{\delta_{\max}(\alpha)}\ (\bigwedge_{a_i \in \alpha} guard(a_i, \ell_i))$ of $Enabled^{\nearrow[0,\delta_{\max}(\alpha)]}(\alpha)$.

If a reachable state of the system (ℓ, v, π) deadlocks then the following is satisfied:

$$\exists \alpha \in \gamma, \Phi(\alpha) \wedge \delta_{\max}(\alpha) \neq 0 \tag{4}$$

Let $schedule(\alpha, \delta_{\max}(\alpha))$ be the following predicate:

$$schedule(\alpha, \delta_{\max}(\alpha)) = \neg\Phi(\alpha) \vee (\delta_{\max}(\alpha) = 0)$$

Using Theorem 4 and Corollary 1, we can conclude that for all interactions $\alpha \in \gamma$ and for all reachable states of the global state semantics S_g, if the predicate $schedule(\alpha, \delta_{\max}(\alpha))$ is satisfied, then the weak planning semantics is deadlock-free. Notice that given an interaction $\alpha \in \gamma$ the satisfaction of $schedule(\alpha, \delta_{\max}(\alpha))$ on $Reach(S_g)$ depends only on $\delta_{\max}(\alpha)$. Moreover, it is monotonic, that is, if it holds for $\delta_{\max}(\alpha)$ then it holds for any $\delta_{\max}(\alpha)' < \delta_{\max}(\alpha)$. This provides means for building implementations that plan interactions as soon as possible by taking for $\delta_{\max}(\alpha)$ the maximal value of δ such that $schedule(\alpha, \delta)$ holds on $Reach(S_g)$.

4 Using Knowledge to Enhance Deadlock-Free Planning

In Sect. 3, we presented sufficient conditions that ensure a deadlock-free planning of interactions. Effectively, we use an SMT solver to check the satisfiability of those conditions on the reachable states of the planning semantics. As explained in Sect. 3 to prove deadlock-freedom of weak planning semantics it is sufficient to prove that for all interactions $\alpha \in \gamma$ the following formula:

$$Reach(S_g) \wedge \neg schedule(\alpha, \delta_{\max}(\alpha))$$

is unsatisfiable. In practice, we do not calculate $Reach(S_g)$ to avoid the combinatorial explosion problem inherent to composition of timed automata. Instead, we use over-approximations of the latter which enable us to build stronger conditions of deadlock freedom. As explained in more detail below, these over-approximations take the form of invariants I (i.e. such that $Reach(S_g) \Rightarrow I$) that are used to establish deadlock freedom by checking the unsatisfiability of:

$$I \wedge \neg schedule(\alpha, \delta_{\max}(\alpha))$$

Timed Invariants. Our approach consists in leveraging global knowledge of the system in the form of invariants that will be used to approximate $Reach(S_g)$. Locations reachable in a composition $S = \gamma(B_1, \dots, B_n)$ are necessary combinations of reachable locations of individual components B_i, i.e., $Reach(S_g) \Rightarrow \bigwedge_{i=1}^{n} Reach(B_i)$. However, in general not all combinations are reachable since components are not fully independent as they synchronize through interaction set γ. Moreover, individual reachable states of components do not express the fact that time progresses the same way in all components.

For example, a global location may be not reachable because component locations having disjoint time progress conditions, or an interaction may be not enabled from a state because of an empty timing constraint. Such properties require additional relationships relating clocks of different components that are not available in $Reach(B_i)$ as it is is restricted to clocks of a single component.

We follow the approach of [25–27] for reinforcing individual reachable states of components with global invariants on clocks. They are induced by simultaneity of transitions execution when executing an interaction and the synchrony of time progress. To compute such invariants, additional *history* clocks are first introduced in components. History clocks are associated to actions of components and to interactions, and reset upon their execution. They do not modify the behavior since they are not involved in timing constraints. They only reveal local timing of components, relevant to the interaction layer, which allows to infer further properties referred as *history clocks inequalities* in [25], expressing the fact that the history clock of an interaction is necessary equal to history clocks of its actions after its execution and until the execution of another interaction involving these actions. By combining history clocks inequalities $\mathcal{E}(S)$ and symbolic states of components, we have:

$$Reach(S_g) \Rightarrow \bigwedge_{i=1}^{n} Reach(B_i) \wedge \quad \mathcal{E}(S_g) \tag{5}$$

Notice that for such systems with multiparty interactions, other types of invariants could be used, like those of [28] that corresponds to the notion of *S-invariants* in the Petri net community [29]. Even if they are time abstracted, it is proved that they are appropriate for verifying non coverage of subsets of individual locations.

Example 3. We illustrate the application of (5) for a safe planning of interactions by considering again example of Fig. 1. It can be shown that locations

configuration including location ℓ_2^3 (resp. ℓ_2^2) does not satisfy the predicate *schedule*$(\alpha, \delta_{\max}(\alpha))$ for interaction α_5 (resp. α_6). In the following, we prove how such configurations can be excluded using history clocks inequalities.
Since action *run* of C is synchronized with either $start_1$ of T_1 or $start_2$ of T_2, and since history clocks h_a of an action a is reset whenever a is executed, by [25] the history clock inequalities for *run* are:

$$(h_{run} = h_{start_1} < h_{start_2} - 4) \lor (h_{run} = h_{start_2} < h_{start_1} - 4). \qquad (6)$$

Equation (6) states that h_{run} is equal to the history clock corresponding to the last synchronization, i.e. either h_{start_1} or h_{start_2}, and is lower than history clocks of previous synchronizations. Value 4 in (6) is obtained considering *separation constraints* computed from symbolic states of components [25]: two occurrences of *run* are separated by at least 4 time units because of timing constraints of C, and so do occurrences of $start_1$ or $start_2$ which can only execute jointly with *run*. To relate history clocks with components clocks, we simply include history clocks when computing symbolic states of components (i.e. *Reach*(B_i) for components), which is used to establish here that $x = h_{start_1}$ and $y = h_{start_2}$. That is, combined with (6) we obtain $x < y - 4$ or $y < x - 4$.

By definition of *Enabled* we have *Enabled*$(\alpha_6) = \mathsf{at}(\ell_2^3) \land (1 \leq x \leq 3)$. Similarly, *Enabled*$(\alpha_6) = \mathsf{at}(\ell_2^3) \land (1 \leq y \leq 3)$. This proves that components T_1 and T_2 can never be at locations ℓ_2^3 and ℓ_2^2 at the same time. Thus, while checking for interaction α_5 (resp. α_6) that $\bigwedge_{i=1}^n Reach(B_i) \land \mathcal{E}(S_g) \land \neg schedule(\alpha, \delta_{\max}(\alpha))$ is unsatisfiable, this case will be excluded using history clock inequalities.

5 Implementation and Experiments

The presented method has been implemented as a middleend filter of the BIP compiler. BIP [30] is a highly expressive, component-based framework with rigorous semantics that allows the construction of complex, hierarchically structured models from single components characterized by their behavior. The method input consists of real-time BIP model and a file containing an approximation of the reachable states of components combined with history clock inequalities as explained in Sect. 4. The latter is generated using the RTD-Finder tool, a verification tool for real-time component based systems modeled in the RT-BIP language. Our filter generates for each interaction of the input model a Yices [31] file containing system invariants together with the condition for planning the considered interaction, that is, $\neg schedule(\alpha, \delta_{\max}(\alpha))$. Thereafter, Yices checks the satisfiability of $\bigwedge_{i=1}^n Reach(B_i) \land \mathcal{E}(S_g) \land \neg schedule(\alpha, \delta_{\max}(\alpha))$. We also define $\delta_{\max}(\alpha)$ as free variable. If this condition is unsatisfiable, then planning interactions α is safe and unbounded that is, $\delta_{\max} = +\infty$. Otherwise, Yices generates a counter-example. Due to the monotony of the condition, this counter-example can be used to find the maximal value of $\delta_{\max}(\alpha)$ satisfying the above condition using a binary search algorithm. Together, the determined values of the bounds $\delta_{\max}$ for each interaction will affect the dynamic of the hole system: for an interaction α the greater $\delta_{\max}(\alpha)$ is, the more flexible the scheduling of α will be.

Table 1. Detailed results of the Task Manager experiments

Interaction	Conflicting interactions	*tpc*	$\delta_{\max}(\alpha)$
α_1	$\alpha_2, \alpha_4, \alpha_8$	ℓ_2^3	∞
α_3	$\alpha_2, \alpha_4, \alpha_8$	ℓ_2^3	∞
α_5	α_6, α_8	ℓ_2^3	∞
α_7	α_2, α_4	ℓ_2^3	0

Table 2. Results of experiments

Model	Number of interactions		
	$\delta_{\max} = 0$	$\delta_{\max} = \infty$	total
Task Manager	2	6	8
Pacemaker	0	6	6
Gear	0	17	17
Fischer	0	10	10

We ran our experiments on three other models besides of the model presented in Fig. 1: Pacemaker [32], Fischer [33], and Gear controller [34]. We developed an implementation of these models in RT-BIP. The following tables show the result of our experiments. Table 1 gives a detailed result of the experiments ran on the Task Manager model Fig. 1. It summarizes, for each interaction, its *conflicting interactions* and the potential locations for which a time progress condition may expire while planning it (column *tpc*). The last column, $\delta_{\max}(\alpha)$, details the maximum horizon for planning interaction α. Notice that the symmetry of the model allows to perform the verification on interactions $\alpha_1, \alpha_3, \alpha_5$, and α_7 and deduce the results for the other interactions. Table 2 depicts the results of our experiments on different models. For each model, it summarizes the number of interactions that can be safely planned with an unbounded horizon ($\delta_{\max} = \infty$). It also gives the number of interactions that cannot be planned in advance, and thus, need to be executed immediately after being planned ($\delta_{\max} = 0$).

6 Conclusion and Future Work

We presented a method for scheduling real-time systems in a distributed context considering models including multiparty interactions. The proposed approach defines sufficient conditions ensuring a deadlock-free local planning of interactions with certain horizons. Moreover, it is proved that those conditions are interaction dependent, in other terms, this means that changing the planning horizon of an interaction does not affect the planning of other interactions. A key innovative idea is the use of global knowledge in addition to local components informations to enhance the local scheduling of interactions. The computed knowledge captures not only the way components synchronize through interactions, but it also consider the history clock inequalities between those interactions and express explicitly the synchrony of time progress.

There are many open problems to be investigated such as: *(i)* when planning an interaction, identifying conditions based on the state of components involved in this interaction, and *(ii)* defining a lower bound for planning interaction. The latter represents an important point meaning that, if planning interactions can be ensured for a lower bound, that effectively represents the communication delays of the target platform, then all the problems induced by those delays, such as global consistency and performance dropping will be solved.

References

1. Charette, R.N.: This car runs on code. IEEE Spectrum (2009)
2. Kopetz, H.: An integrated architecture for dependable embedded systems. In: Proceedings of the 23rd IEEE International Symposium on Reliable Distributed Systems, SRDS 2004, pp. 160–161. IEEE Computer Society, Washington, DC (2004)
3. Abdellatif, T., Combaz, J., Sifakis, J.: Model-based implementation of real-time applications. In: EMSOFT (2010)
4. Kopetz, H.: Time-triggered real-time computing. Ann. Rev. Control **27**(1), 3–13 (2003)
5. Chabrol, D., David, V., Aussaguès, C., Louise, S., Daumas, F.: Deterministic distributed safety-critical real-time systems within the oasis approach. In: International Conference on Parallel and Distributed Computing Systems, PDCS, 14–16 November 2005, Phoenix, AZ, USA, pp. 260–268 (2005)
6. Ghosal, A., Henzinger, T.A., Kirsch, C.M., Sanvido, M.A.A.: Event-driven programming with logical execution times. In: Alur, R., Pappas, G.J. (eds.) HSCC 2004. LNCS, vol. 2993, pp. 357–371. Springer, Heidelberg (2004). doi:10.1007/978-3-540-24743-2_24
7. Henzinger, T.A., Kirsch, C.M., Matic, S.: Composable code generation for distributed giotto. In: Proceedings of the 2005 ACM SIGPLAN/SIGBED Conference on Languages, Compilers, and Tools for Embedded Systems (LCTES 2005), 15–17 June 2005 Chicago, Illinois, USA, pp. 21–30 (2005)
8. Behrmann, G., David, A., Guldstrand Larsen, K., Håkansson, J., Pettersson, P., Yi, W., Hendriks, M.: UPPAAL 4.0. In: QEST (2006)
9. Zhao, Y., Liu, J., Lee, E.A.: A programming model for time-synchronized distributed real-time systems. In: Proceedings of the 13th IEEE Real-Time and Embedded Technology and Applications Symposium, RTAS, 3–6 April 2007, Bellevue, Washington, USA, pp. 259–268 (2007)
10. Bagrodia, R.: Process synchronization: design and performance evaluation of distributed algorithms. IEEE Trans. Softw. Eng. **15**(9), 1053–1065 (1989)
11. Bagrodia, R.: A distributed algorithm to implement n-party rendevouz. In: Proceedings Foundations of Software Technology and Theoretical Computer Science, Seventh Conference, Pune, India, 17–19 December 1987, pp. 138–152 (1987)
12. Mani Chandy, K., Misra, J.: Parallel Program Design: A Foundation. Addison-Wesley Longman Publishing Co., Inc., Boston (1988)
13. Mani Chandy, K., Misra, J.: The drinking philosopher's problem. ACM Trans. Program. Lang. Syst. **6**(4), 632–646 (1984)

14. Pérez, J.A., Corchuelo, R., Ruiz, D., Toro, M.: An order-based, distributed algorithm for implementing multiparty interactions. In: Arbab, F., Talcott, C. (eds.) COORDINATION 2002. LNCS, vol. 2315, pp. 250–257. Springer, Heidelberg (2002). doi:10.1007/3-540-46000-4_24
15. Parrow, J., Sjödin, P.: Multiway synchronizaton verified with coupled simulation. In: Proceedings of CONCUR '92, Third International Conference on Concurrency Theory, 24–27 August 1992, Stony Brook, NY, USA, pp. 518–533 (1992)
16. Bensalem, S., Bozga, M., Graf, S., Peled, D., Quinton, S.: Methods for knowledge based controlling of distributed systems. In: Bouajjani, A., Chin, W.-N. (eds.) ATVA 2010. LNCS, vol. 6252, pp. 52–66. Springer, Heidelberg (2010). doi:10.1007/978-3-642-15643-4_6
17. Bensalem, S., Bozga, M., Quilbeuf, J., Sifakis, J.: Knowledge-based distributed conflict resolution for multiparty interactions and priorities. In: Giese, H., Rosu, G. (eds.) FMOODS/FORTE -2012. LNCS, vol. 7273, pp. 118–134. Springer, Heidelberg (2012). doi:10.1007/978-3-642-30793-5_8
18. Bensalem, S., Bozga, M., Combaz, J., Triki, A.: Rigorous system design flow for autonomous systems. In: Margaria, T., Steffen, B. (eds.) ISoLA 2014. LNCS, vol. 8802, pp. 184–198. Springer, Heidelberg (2014). doi:10.1007/978-3-662-45234-9_13
19. Triki, A.: Distributed Implementation of Timed Component-based Systems. Ph.D. thesis, UJF (2015)
20. Saddek Bensalem Marius Bozga Mahieddine Dellabani, Jacques Combaz. Local planning of multiparty interactions with bounded horizon. Technical Report TR-2016-05, Verimag Research Report, 2016
21. Alur, R., Dill, D.L.: A theory of timed automata. Theor. Comput. Sci. **126**, 183–235 (1994)
22. Tripakis, S.: The analysis of timed systems in practice. Ph.D. thesis, Joseph Fourier University (1998)
23. Bengtsson, J., Yi, W.: On clock difference constraints and termination in reachability analysis of timed automata. In: Dong, J.S., Woodcock, J. (eds.) ICFEM 2003. LNCS, vol. 2885, pp. 491–503. Springer, Heidelberg (2003). doi:10.1007/978-3-540-39893-6_28
24. Henzinger, T.A., Nicollin, X., Sifakis, J., Yovine, S.: Symbolic model checking for real-time systems. Inf. Comput. **11**, 193–244 (1994)
25. Aştefănoaei, L., Rayana, S., Bensalem, S., Bozga, M., Combaz, J.: Compositional invariant generation for timed systems. In: Ábrahám, E., Havelund, K. (eds.) TACAS 2014. LNCS, vol. 8413, pp. 263–278. Springer, Heidelberg (2014). doi:10.1007/978-3-642-54862-8_18
26. Ben Rayana, S., Astefanoaei, L., Bensalem, S., Bozga, M., Combaz, J.: Compositional verification for timed systems based on automatic invariant generation. CoRR, abs/1506.04879 (2015)
27. Bensalem, M.B.S., Boyer, B., Legay, A.: Compositional invariant generation for timed systems. Technical report TR-2012-15, Verimag Research Report (2012)
28. Bensalem, S., Bozga, M., Boyer, B., Legay, A.: Incremental generation of linear invariants for component-based systems. In: 13th International Conference on Application of Concurrency to System Design (ACSD), pp. 80–89, July 2013
29. Murata, T.: Petri nets: properties, analysis and applications. Proc. IEEE **77**(4), 541–580 (1989)
30. Basu, A., Bozga, M., Sifakis, J.: Modeling heterogeneous real-time components in bip. In: Proceedings of the Fourth IEEE International Conference on Software Engineering and Formal Methods, SEFM 2006, Washington, DC, USA, pp. 3–12, IEEE Computer Society (2006)

31. Dutertre, B., de Moura, L.: The yices SMT solver. Technical report, SRI International (2006)
32. Jiang, Z., Pajic, M., Moarref, S., Alur, R., Mangharam, R.: Modeling and verification of a dual chamber implantable pacemaker. In: Flanagan, C., König, B. (eds.) TACAS 2012. LNCS, vol. 7214, pp. 188–203. Springer, Heidelberg (2012). doi:10.1007/978-3-642-28756-5_14
33. Lamport, L.: A fast mutual exclusion algorithm. ACM Trans. Comput. Syst. **5**(1), 1–11 (1987)
34. Lindahl, M., Pettersson, P., Yi, W.: Formal design and analysis of a gearbox controller. Springer Int. J. Softw. Tools Technol. Transf. (STTT) **3**(3), 353–368 (2001)

Finding Suitable Variability Abstractions for Family-Based Analysis

Aleksandar S. Dimovski(✉), Claus Brabrand, and Andrzej Wąsowski

IT University of Copenhagen, Copenhagen, Denmark
adim@itu.dk

Abstract. For program families (Software Product Lines), specially designed *variability-aware* static (dataflow) analyses allow analyzing all variants (products) of the family, simultaneously, in a single run without generating any of the variants explicitly. They are also known as *lifted* or *family-based* analyses. The variability-aware analyses may be too costly or even infeasible for families with a large number of variants. In order to make them computationally cheaper, we can apply variability abstractions which aim to tame the combinatorial explosion of the number of variants (configurations) and reduce it to something more tractable. However, the number of possible abstractions is still intractably large to search naively, with most abstractions being too imprecise or too costly.

In this work, we propose a technique to efficiently find suitable variability abstractions from a large family of abstractions for a variability-aware static analysis. The idea is to use a *pre-analysis* to estimate the impact of variability-specific parts of the program family on the analysis's precision. Then we use the pre-analysis results to find out when and where the analysis should turn off or on its variability-awareness. We demonstrate the practicality of this approach on several Java benchmarks.

1 Introduction

Software Product Lines (SPLs) [7] appear in many application areas and for many reasons. They use features to control presence and absence of software functionality in a product family. Different family members, called *variants*, are derived by switching features on and off, while reuse of the common code is maximized. SPLs are commonly seen in development of embedded software (e.g., cars and phones), system level software (e.g., the Linux kernel), etc. While there are many implementation strategies, many popular industrial SPLs are implemented using annotative approaches such as conditional compilation.

One challenge in development of SPLs is their formal analysis and verification [26]. *Variability-aware* (lifted, family-based) dataflow analysis takes as input only the common code base, which encodes all variants of a program family (SPL),

Supported by The Danish Council for Independent Research under a Sapere Aude project, VARIETE.

J. Fitzgerald et al. (Eds.): FM 2016, LNCS 9995, pp. 217–234, 2016.
DOI: 10.1007/978-3-319-48989-6_14

and produces precise analysis results corresponding to all variants. Variability-aware analysis can be significantly faster than the naive "brute-force" approach, which generates and analyzes all variants one by one [3]. However, the computational cost of the variability-aware analysis still depends on the number of variants, which is in the worst case exponential in the number of features. To speed-up variability-aware analysis, a range of abstractions at the variability level can be introduced [14]. They aim to abstract the configuration space (number of variants) of the given family. Each *variability abstraction* expresses a compromise between precision and speed in the induced abstract variability-aware analysis. Thus, we obtain a range of (abstract) variability-aware analysis *parameterized* by the choice of abstraction we use. The abstractions are chosen from a large family (calculus) that allows abstracting different variability-specific parts (features, variants, and preprocessor `#ifdef` statements) of a family with varying precision. This poses a hard search problem in practice. The number of possible abstractions is intractably large to search naively, with most abstractions being too imprecise or too costly to show the analysis's ultimate goal.

In this paper, we propose an efficient method to address the above search problem. We present a method for performing selective (abstract) variability-aware analysis, which uses variability-awareness only when and where doing so is likely to improve the analysis precision. The method consists of two phases. The first phase is a *pre-analysis* which aims only to estimate the impact of variability on the main analysis. Hence, it aggressively abstracts the semantic aspects of the analysis that are not relevant for its ultimate goal. The second phase is the main analysis with selective variability-awareness, i.e. the abstract variability-aware analysis, which uses the results of pre-analysis, selects influential features and variants for precision, and selectively applies variability-awareness only to those features and variants. The pre-analysis represents an over-approximation of the main analysis. However, it uses very simple abstract domain and transfer functions, so it can be efficiently run even with full variability-awareness. The pre-analysis and the resulting abstract variability-aware main analysis are different: the pre-analysis is more precise in terms of variability-awareness, but it is worse in tracking non-variability specific parts (i.e. language specific parts that operate on the program state) of the program family. We aim to use the pre-analysis results in order to construct an abstraction which is effective at slicing away (discarding) variability-specific program details (features and variants) that are irrelevant for showing the analysis's goal. The experiments show that the constructed abstract variability-aware analysis achieves competitive cost-precision tradeoffs when applied to Java SPL benchmarks.

In this work, we make the following contributions: (1) We show how to design and use a pre-analysis that estimates the impact of variability on a client (main) analysis; (2) We present a method for constructing a suitable abstract variability-aware analysis that receives guidance from the pre-analysis; (3) We experimentally show the effectiveness of our method using Java program families.

2 Motivating Example

We illustrate our approach using the interval analysis and the program family P:

```
1 x := 0;                          3 #if (B) y := y+2 #endif;
2 #if (A) x := x+2 #endif;         4 #if (¬A) x := x-2 #endif
```

The set of (Boolean) features in the above program family P is $\mathbb{F} = \{A, B\}$, and we assume the set of valid configurations is $\mathbb{K} = \{A \wedge B, A \wedge \neg B, \neg A \wedge B, \neg A \wedge \neg B\}$. Note that the variable y is (deliberately) uninitialized in P. For each configuration a different variant (single program) can be generated by appropriately resolving `#if` statements. For example, the variant corresponding to the configuration $A \wedge B$ will have both features A and B enabled (set to true), thus yielding the single program: `x := 0; x := x+2; y := y+2`. The variant for $\neg A \wedge \neg B$ is: `x := 0; x := x-2`. The *interval analysis* computes for every variable a lower and an upper bound for its possible values at each program point. The basic properties are of the form: $[l, h]$, where $l \in \mathbb{Z} \cup \{-\infty\}$, $h \in \mathbb{Z} \cup \{+\infty\}$, and $l \leq h$. The coarsest property is $\top = [-\infty, +\infty]$. We want to check the following two *queries* on P: "find all configurations for which x and y are non-negative at the end of P, and determine *accurately* the corresponding intervals".

Full variability-aware analysis. Full variability-aware (lifted) analysis operates on lifted stores, $\overline{a}$, that contain one component for every valid configuration from $\mathbb{K}$. For the "`#if` (θ) s" statement, lifted analysis checks for each configuration $k \in \mathbb{K}$ whether the feature constraint θ is satisfied by k and, if so, it updates the corresponding component of the lifted store by the effect of analyzing s. Otherwise, the corresponding component of the lifted store is not updated. We assume that the initial lifted store consists of uninitialized x and y, i.e. they have the initial property $\top$. We use a convention here that the first component of the lifted store corresponds to configuration $A \wedge B$, the second to $A \wedge \neg B$, the third to $\neg A \wedge B$, and the fourth to $\neg A \wedge \neg B$. We write $\overline{a} \overset{\mathtt{stm}\ n}{\longmapsto} \overline{a'}$ when the lifted store $\overline{a'}$ is the result of analyzing the statement "n" at the input lifted store $\overline{a}$.

$$([\mathrm{x} \mapsto \top, \mathrm{y} \mapsto \top], [\mathrm{x} \mapsto \top, \mathrm{y} \mapsto \top], [\mathrm{x} \mapsto \top, \mathrm{y} \mapsto \top], [\mathrm{x} \mapsto \top, \mathrm{y} \mapsto \top])$$

$$\overset{\mathtt{stm}\ 1}{\longmapsto} ([\mathrm{x} \mapsto [0,0], \mathrm{y} \mapsto \top], [\mathrm{x} \mapsto [0,0], \mathrm{y} \mapsto \top], [\mathrm{x} \mapsto [0,0], \mathrm{y} \mapsto \top], [\mathrm{x} \mapsto [0,0], \mathrm{y} \mapsto \top])$$

$$\overset{\mathtt{stm}\ 2}{\longmapsto} ([\mathrm{x} \mapsto [2,2], \mathrm{y} \mapsto \top], [\mathrm{x} \mapsto [2,2], \mathrm{y} \mapsto \top], [\mathrm{x} \mapsto [0,0], \mathrm{y} \mapsto \top], [\mathrm{x} \mapsto [0,0], \mathrm{y} \mapsto \top])$$

$$\overset{\mathtt{stm}\ 3}{\longmapsto} ([\mathrm{x} \mapsto [2,2], \mathrm{y} \mapsto \top], [\mathrm{x} \mapsto [2,2], \mathrm{y} \mapsto \top], [\mathrm{x} \mapsto [0,0], \mathrm{y} \mapsto \top], [\mathrm{x} \mapsto [0,0], \mathrm{y} \mapsto \top])$$

$$\overset{\mathtt{stm}\ 4}{\longmapsto} ([\mathrm{x} \mapsto [2,2], \mathrm{y} \mapsto \top], [\mathrm{x} \mapsto [2,2], \mathrm{y} \mapsto \top], [\mathrm{x} \mapsto [-2,-2], \mathrm{y} \mapsto \top], [\mathrm{x} \mapsto [-2,-2], \mathrm{y} \mapsto \top])$$

As the result of analysis, we can deduce that at the end of P, x is non-negative (the exact interval is $[2, 2]$) for configurations that satisfy A (that is, $A \wedge B$ and $A \wedge \neg B$), whereas x is negative for configurations that satisfy $\neg A$ (that is, $\neg A \wedge B$ and $\neg A \wedge \neg B$). But, y is always $\top$ so we cannot prove any query for it.

Need for abstraction. However, using full variability-aware analysis is not always the best solution. It is often too expensive to run such an analysis with large number of configurations. More importantly, in many cases, full variability-awareness does not help, i.e. either it does not improve some analysis results or the full precision is not useful for establishing some facts. For example, full variability-awareness is not helpful to establish the interval of `y`. Also, we can ignore variants that satisfy $\neg A$ (the last two components) if we only want to establish the exact interval when `x` is non-negative. Moreover, we can see that analyzing the feature B is unnecessary for establishing the interval of `x`.

A family of abstractions. We consider a range of variability abstractions [14] which aim to reduce the size of configuration space. In effect, we obtain computationally cheaper but less precise abstract variability-aware analyses. The three basic abstractions are: (1) to confound (join) all valid variants into one single program with over-approximated control-flow, denoted $\boldsymbol{\alpha}^{\mathrm{join}}$; (2) to project (divide-and-conquer) the configuration space onto a certain subset of variants that satisfy some constraint ϕ, denoted $\boldsymbol{\alpha}^{\mathrm{proj}}_{\phi}$; (3) to ignore a feature, $A \in \mathbb{F}$, deemed as not relevant for the current problem, denoted $\boldsymbol{\alpha}^{\mathrm{fignore}}_{A}$. We also use sequential composition, denoted $\circ$, and product, denoted $\otimes$. Any abstraction α induces an abstract variability-aware analysis, denoted $\overline{\mathcal{A}}_{\alpha}$, which is derived in [14]. Since variability abstractions affect only the variability-specific aspect of the variability-aware analysis (i.e. the transfer function of `#if` statement), it was shown in [14] that they can be also defined as source-to-source transformations. More specifically, for each program family P and abstraction α, we can define an abstract program $\alpha(P)$ such that $\overline{\mathcal{A}}_{\alpha}[\![P]\!] = \overline{\mathcal{A}}[\![\alpha(P)]\!]$, where $\overline{\mathcal{A}}$ represents (unabstracted) variability-aware analysis.

The coarsest abstraction. If we apply the coarsest abstraction $\boldsymbol{\alpha}^{\mathrm{join}}$, which confounds control-flow of all valid configurations into a single program with over-approximated control-flow, we will obtain the following program $\boldsymbol{\alpha}^{\mathrm{join}}(P)$:

```
x = 0;
if (*) then x:=x+2 else skip;
if (*) then y:=y+2 else skip;
if (*) then x:=x-2 else skip
```

where $*$ models an arbitrary integer. Note that $\boldsymbol{\alpha}^{\mathrm{join}}(P)$ is a single program with no variability in it. When $\boldsymbol{\alpha}^{\mathrm{join}}(P)$ is analyzed using the standard (single-program) interval analysis we obtain the same analysis results as analyzing P with abstract lifted analysis $\overline{\mathcal{A}}_{\boldsymbol{\alpha}^{\mathrm{join}}}$. As result of the above analysis, at the end of P we obtain the output store: $([\mathtt{x} \mapsto [-2,+2], \mathtt{y} \mapsto \top])$. These estimations are not strong enough to show any of our queries for `x` and `y`.

Finding suitable abstractions. The abstract variability-aware analysis aims at analyzing families with only needed variability-awareness. It takes into account only those features and configurations that are likely to improve the precision of the analysis. For the family P, our method should predict that increasing variability-awareness is likely to help answer the first query about the non-negative interval of `x`, but the second query about the non-negative interval of y will not benefit. Next, our method should find out that we can bring the full benefit of variability-awareness for the first query by taking into account only variants that satisfy A. This abstraction is denoted $\boldsymbol{\alpha}^{\text{proj}}_{(A \wedge B) \vee (A \wedge \neg B)}$, or $\boldsymbol{\alpha}^{\text{proj}}_{A}$ for short. Also, the feature B does not influence the final value of x so we can ignore it obtaining the abstraction $\boldsymbol{\alpha}^{\text{fignore}}_{B} \circ \boldsymbol{\alpha}^{\text{proj}}_{A}$. The abstract program $\boldsymbol{\alpha}^{\text{fignore}}_{B} \circ \boldsymbol{\alpha}^{\text{proj}}_{A}(P)$ is:

```
1 x := 0;
2 x := x+2;
3 if (*) then y := y+2 else skip;
4 skip
```

The single-program interval analysis of the above program produces the store: $([\mathtt{x} \mapsto [2,2], \mathtt{y} \mapsto \top])$. In this way, we can successfully prove that the first query holds for all configurations that satisfy A since the analysis always analyzes the statement "2", and skips the statement "4".

Pre-analysis. The key idea is to use a pre-analysis and estimate the impact of variability on the most precise main analysis. The pre-analysis uses a simple abstract domain and simple transfer functions, and can be run efficiently even with full variability-awareness. For example, we approximate the interval analysis using a pre-analysis with the abstract domain: $\mathit{Var} \to \{\bigstar, \top\}$, where $\bigstar$ means a non-negative interval, i.e. $[0, +\infty]$. This simple abstract domain of the pre-analysis is chosen because we are interested in showing queries that some variables are non-negative. We run this pre-analysis under full variability-awareness for P:

$$
\begin{aligned}
&([\mathtt{x} \mapsto \top, \mathtt{y} \mapsto \top], [\mathtt{x} \mapsto \top, \mathtt{y} \mapsto \top], [\mathtt{x} \mapsto \top, \mathtt{y} \mapsto \top], [\mathtt{x} \mapsto \top, \mathtt{y} \mapsto \top]) \\
&\overset{\text{stm 1}}{\longmapsto} ([\mathtt{x} \mapsto \bigstar, \mathtt{y} \mapsto \top], [\mathtt{x} \mapsto \bigstar, \mathtt{y} \mapsto \top], [\mathtt{x} \mapsto \bigstar, \mathtt{y} \mapsto \top], [\mathtt{x} \mapsto \bigstar, \mathtt{y} \mapsto \top]) \\
&\overset{\text{stm 2}}{\longmapsto} ([\mathtt{x} \mapsto \bigstar, \mathtt{y} \mapsto \top], [\mathtt{x} \mapsto \bigstar, \mathtt{y} \mapsto \top], [\mathtt{x} \mapsto \bigstar, \mathtt{y} \mapsto \top], [\mathtt{x} \mapsto \bigstar, \mathtt{y} \mapsto \top]) \\
&\overset{\text{stm 3}}{\longmapsto} ([\mathtt{x} \mapsto \bigstar, \mathtt{y} \mapsto \top], [\mathtt{x} \mapsto \bigstar, \mathtt{y} \mapsto \top], [\mathtt{x} \mapsto \bigstar, \mathtt{y} \mapsto \top], [\mathtt{x} \mapsto \bigstar, \mathtt{y} \mapsto \top]) \\
&\overset{\text{stm 4}}{\longmapsto} ([\mathtt{x} \mapsto \bigstar, \mathtt{y} \mapsto \top], [\mathtt{x} \mapsto \bigstar, \mathtt{y} \mapsto \top], [\mathtt{x} \mapsto \top, \mathtt{y} \mapsto \top], [\mathtt{x} \mapsto \top, \mathtt{y} \mapsto \top])
\end{aligned}
$$

The pre-analysis in this case precisely estimates the impact of variability: it identifies where the interval analysis accurately tracks the possible (non-negative) values of x. In general, our pre-analysis might lose precision and use $\top$ more often than in the ideal case. However, it does so only in a sound manner.

Constructing an abstraction out of pre-analysis. From the pre-analysis results, we can select those features and configurations that help improve precision regarding given queries. We first identify queries whose variables are assigned with $\bigstar$ in the pre-analysis run. Then, for each query that is judged promising, we find variability-specific parts of the program family that contribute to the query. In our example, pre-analysis assigns $\bigstar$ to x in two valid configurations, $A \wedge B$ and $A \wedge \neg B$, which is a good indication that fully variability-aware interval analysis is likely to answer the first query accurately. We keep precision with respect to these two configurations by calculating the abstraction $\boldsymbol{\alpha}^{\text{proj}}_{(A\wedge B)\vee(A\wedge\neg B)}$. We can also see that the feature B does not affect the possible values of `x` at all. Thus, we can ignore the feature B obtaining $\boldsymbol{\alpha}^{\text{fignore}}_{B} \circ \boldsymbol{\alpha}^{\text{proj}}_{(A\wedge B)\vee(A\wedge\neg B)}$. For the second query that `y` is non-negative, we obtain that `y` is $\top$ for all configurations. This is indication that we cannot prove this query even with full variability-aware analysis. Our method guarantees that if the pre-analysis calculates $\bigstar$ for a variable, then the constructed abstract variability-aware analysis will compute an accurate non-negative interval for that variable. However, it is possible that the pre-analysis returns $\top$ for a query due to its own over-approximation, and not because the main analysis cannot prove the query. In this case, our approach will miss the possibility to use variability-awareness to improve the analysis precision.

3 A Language for Program Families

A finite set of Boolean variables $\mathbb{F} = \{A_1, \ldots, A_n\}$ describes the set of available *features* in the family. Each feature may be *enabled* or *disabled* in a particular variant. A *configuration* k is a truth assignment or a valuation which gives a truth value to each feature, i.e. k is a mapping from $\mathbb{F}$ to $\{\text{true}, \text{false}\}$. If a feature $A \in \mathbb{F}$ is enabled for the configuration k then $k(A) = \text{true}$, otherwise $k(A) = \text{false}$. Any configuration k can also be encoded as a conjunction of literals: $k(A_1) \cdot A_1 \wedge \cdots \wedge k(A_n) \cdot A_n$, where $\text{true} \cdot A = A$ and $\text{false} \cdot A = \neg A$. We write $\mathbb{K}$ for the set of all *valid* configurations defined over $\mathbb{F}$ for a family. Note that $|\mathbb{K}| \leq 2^{|\mathbb{F}|}$, since in general not every combination of features yields a valid configuration. We define *feature expressions*, denoted *FeatExp*, as the set of well-formed propositional logic formulas over $\mathbb{F}$ generated using the grammar: $\phi ::= \text{true} \mid A \in \mathbb{F} \mid \neg\phi \mid \phi_1 \wedge \phi_2$.

We use the language $\overline{\text{IMP}}$ for writing program families. $\overline{\text{IMP}}$ is an extension of the imperative language IMP [22] often used in semantic studies. $\overline{\text{IMP}}$ adds a compile-time conditional statement for encoding multiple variants of a program. The new statement "`#if` (θ) s" contains a feature expression $\theta \in \textit{FeatExp}$ as a presence condition, such that only if θ is satisfied by a configuration $k \in \mathbb{K}$ then the statement s will be included in the variant corresponding to k. The syntax is:

$$s ::= \texttt{skip} \mid \texttt{x:=}e \mid s;s \mid \texttt{if}\,(e)\,\texttt{then}\,s\,\texttt{else}\,s \mid \texttt{while}\,(e)\,\texttt{do}\,s \mid \texttt{\#if}\,(\theta)\,s, \quad e ::= n \mid \texttt{x} \mid e \oplus e$$

where n ranges over integers, `x` ranges over variable names *Var*, and $\oplus$ over binary arithmetic operators. The set of all generated statements s is denoted by *Stm*, whereas the set of all expressions e is denoted by *Exp*. Notice that $\overline{\text{IMP}}$ is only used for presentation purposes as a well established minimal language. The introduced methodology is not limited to $\overline{\text{IMP}}$ or its features.

The semantics of $\overline{\text{IMP}}$ has two stages: first, given a configuration $k \in \mathbb{K}$ compute an IMP single program without `#if`-s; second, evaluate the obtained variant using the standard IMP semantics [22]. The first stage is a simple *preprocessor* which takes as input an $\overline{\text{IMP}}$ program and a configuration $k \in \mathbb{K}$, and outputs a variant corresponding to k. The preprocessor copies all basic statements of $\overline{\text{IMP}}$ that are also in IMP, and recursively pre-processes all sub-statements of compound statements. The interesting case is the "`#if` (θ) s" statement, where the statement s is included in the resulting variant iff $k \models \theta$ (means: k entails θ), otherwise the statement s is removed.

4 Parametric (Abstract) Variability-Aware Analysis

Variability-aware (lifted) analyses are designed by *lifting* existing single-program analyses to work on program families, rather than on individual programs. In this section, we first briefly explain the process of "lifting" introduced in [21]. Then, we recall the calculus of variability abstractions defined in [14] for reducing the configuration space. Finally, we present the induced abstract variability-aware (lifted) analysis [14], whose transfer functions are parametric in the choice of abstraction.

Lifting Single-program Analysis. Suppose that we have a monotone dataflow analysis for IMP phrased in the abstract interpretation framework [9,22]. Such an analysis is specified by the following data. A complete lattice $\langle \mathbb{P}, \sqsubseteq_{\mathbb{P}} \rangle$ for describing the *properties* of the analysis. A domain $\mathbb{A} = Var \to \mathbb{P}$ of abstract stores, ranged over by a, which associates properties from $\mathbb{P}$ to the program variables Var. The *analysis domain* is $\langle \mathbb{A}, \sqsubseteq, \sqcup, \sqcap, \bot, \top \rangle$, which inherits the lattice structure from $\mathbb{P}$ in a point-wise manner. There are also *transfer functions* for expressions $\mathcal{A}'[\![e]\!] : \mathbb{A} \to \mathbb{P}$ and for statements $\mathcal{A}[\![s]\!] : \mathbb{A} \to \mathbb{A}$, which describe the effect of analyzing expressions and statements in an abstract store.

By using variational abstract interpretation [21], we can lift any single-program analysis defined as above to the corresponding *variability-aware (lifted) analysis* for $\overline{\text{IMP}}$, which is specified as follows. Given a set of valid configurations $\mathbb{K}$, the *lifted analysis domain* is $\langle \mathbb{A}^{\mathbb{K}}, \dot{\sqsubseteq}, \dot{\sqcup}, \dot{\sqcap}, \dot{\bot}, \dot{\top} \rangle$, which inherits the lattice structure of $\mathbb{A}$ in a configuration-wise manner. Here $\mathbb{A}^{\mathbb{K}}$ is shorthand for the $|\mathbb{K}|$-fold product $\prod_{k\in\mathbb{K}} \mathbb{A}$, and so in the lifted domain there is one separate copy of $\mathbb{A}$ for each configuration of $\mathbb{K}$. For $\overline{a}, \overline{a}' \in \mathbb{A}^{\mathbb{K}}$, the lifted ordering $\dot{\sqsubseteq}$ is defined as: $\overline{a} \dot{\sqsubseteq} \overline{a}'$ iff $\pi_k(\overline{a}) \sqsubseteq \pi_k(\overline{a}')$ for all $k \in \mathbb{K}$. The projection π_k selects the kth component of a tuple. Similarly, all other elements of the lattice $\mathbb{A}$ are lifted, thus obtaining $\dot{\sqcup}, \dot{\sqcap}, \dot{\bot}, \dot{\top}$. As an example, $\dot{\top} = \prod_{k\in\mathbb{K}} \top = (\top, \ldots, \top)$, where $\top \in \mathbb{A}$.

The lifted transfer function for statements $\overline{\mathcal{A}}[\![s]\!]$ (resp., for expressions $\overline{\mathcal{A}'}[\![e]\!]$) is a function from $\mathbb{A}^{\mathbb{K}}$ to $\mathbb{A}^{\mathbb{K}}$ (resp., from $\mathbb{A}^{\mathbb{K}}$ to $\mathbb{P}^{\mathbb{K}}$). However in practice, using a tuple of $|\mathbb{K}|$ independent simple functions of type $\mathbb{A} \to \mathbb{A}$ (resp., $\mathbb{A} \to \mathbb{P}$) is sufficient, since lifting corresponds to running $|\mathbb{K}|$ independent analyses in parallel. Therefore, the *lifted transfer functions* are given by the functions $\overline{\mathcal{A}}[\![s]\!] : (\mathbb{A} \to \mathbb{A})^{\mathbb{K}}$ and $\overline{\mathcal{A}'}[\![e]\!] : (\mathbb{A} \to \mathbb{P})^{\mathbb{K}}$. The k-th component of the above functions defines the analysis corresponding to the configuration $k \in \mathbb{K}$.

Interval analysis. In the following, we will use the interval analysis to demonstrate this method. The interval analysis is based on the property domain

$\langle Interval, \sqsubseteq_I \rangle$: $Interval = \{\bot_I\} \cup \{[l,h] \mid l \in \mathbb{Z} \cup \{-\infty\}, h \in \mathbb{Z} \cup \{+\infty\}, l \leq h\}$, where $\bot_I$ denotes the empty interval, and $\top_I = [-\infty, +\infty]$. The partial ordering $\sqsubseteq_I$ is: $[l_1, h_1] \sqsubseteq_I [l_2, h_2]$ iff $l_2 \leq l_1 \wedge h_1 \leq h_2$. The partial ordering $\sqsubseteq_I$ induces the definitions for $\sqcup_I$ and $\sqcap_I$. For each arithmetic operator $\oplus$, we have the corresponding $\widehat{\oplus}$ defined on properties from *Interval* [9]:

$$[l_1, h_1]\widehat{\oplus}[l_2, h_2] = [\min_{x \in [l_1, h_1],\, y \in [l_2, h_2]} \{x \oplus y\}, \max_{x \in [l_1, h_1],\, y \in [l_2, h_2]} \{x \oplus y\}] \quad (1)$$

Thus, we have: $[l_1, h_1] \widehat{+} [l_2, h_2] = [l_1 + l_2, h_1 + h_2]$ and $[l_1, h_1] \widehat{-} [l_2, h_2] = [l_1 - h_2, h_1 - l_2]$. For example, $[2,2] \widehat{+} [1,2] = [3,4]$ and $[2,2] \widehat{-} [1,2] = [0,1]$.

The *single-program transfer function* for constants is: $\mathcal{A}'[\![\mathtt{n}]\!] = \lambda a.abst_{\mathbb{Z}}(\mathtt{n})$, where $a \in \mathbb{A} = Var \to Interval$, and $abst_{\mathbb{Z}} : \mathbb{Z} \to Interval$ is a function for turning values to properties defined as: $abst_{\mathbb{Z}}(n) = [n, n]$. The corresponding *lifted transfer function* becomes $\overline{\mathcal{A}'}[\![\mathtt{n}]\!] = \lambda \overline{a}. \prod_{k \in \mathbb{K}} abst_{\mathbb{Z}}(\mathtt{n})$, where $\overline{a} \in \mathbb{A}^{\mathbb{K}}$. The complete list of definitions is given in Fig. 1, where for full variability-aware analysis the parameter α is instantiated with the identity abstraction $\boldsymbol{\alpha}^{\text{id}}$. Note that for simplicity, here we overload the λ-abstraction notation, so creating a tuple of functions looks like a function on tuples: we write $\lambda \overline{a}. \prod_{k \in \mathbb{K}} f_k(\pi_k(\overline{a}))$ to mean $\prod_{k \in \mathbb{K}} \lambda a_k.f_k(a_k)$. Similarly, if $\overline{f} : (\mathbb{A} \to \mathbb{A})^{\mathbb{K}}$ and $\overline{a} \in \mathbb{A}^{\mathbb{K}}$, then we write $\overline{f}(\overline{a})$ to mean $\prod_{k \in \mathbb{K}} \pi_k(\overline{f})(\pi_k(\overline{a}))$.

Variability Abstractions. We now introduce abstractions for reducing the lifted analysis domain $\mathbb{A}^{\mathbb{K}}$. The set *Abs* of abstractions is given by [14]:

$$\alpha ::= \boldsymbol{\alpha}^{\text{id}} \mid \boldsymbol{\alpha}^{\text{join}} \mid \boldsymbol{\alpha}^{\text{proj}}_{\phi} \mid \boldsymbol{\alpha}^{\text{fignore}}_{A} \mid \alpha \circ \alpha \mid \alpha \otimes \alpha$$

where $\phi \in FeatExp$, and $A \in \mathbb{F}$. For each abstraction α, we define the effect of applying α on sets of configurations $\mathbb{K}$, and on domain elements $\overline{a} \in \mathbb{A}^{\mathbb{K}}$. Note that, the set of features is fixed, i.e. we have $\alpha(\mathbb{F}) = \mathbb{F}$ for any α.

The $\boldsymbol{\alpha}^{\text{id}}$ is an identity on $\mathbb{K}$ and $\overline{a} \in \mathbb{A}^{\mathbb{K}}$. So, $\boldsymbol{\alpha}^{\text{id}}(\mathbb{K}) = \mathbb{K}$ and the abstraction and concretization functions: $\boldsymbol{\alpha}^{\text{id}}(\overline{a}) = \overline{a}$, $\boldsymbol{\gamma}^{\text{id}}(\overline{a}) = \overline{a}$, form a Galois connection[1].

The *join* abstraction, $\boldsymbol{\alpha}^{\text{join}}$, gathers (joins) the information about all configurations $k \in \mathbb{K}$ into one (over-approximated) value of $\mathbb{A}$. We have $\boldsymbol{\alpha}^{\text{join}}(\mathbb{K}) = \{\bigvee_{k \in \mathbb{K}} k\}$, i.e. after abstraction we obtain a single valid configuration denoted by the compound formula $\bigvee_{k \in \mathbb{K}} k$. The abstraction and concretization functions between $\mathbb{A}^{\mathbb{K}}$ and $\mathbb{A}^{\{\bigvee_{k \in \mathbb{K}} k\}} \equiv \mathbb{A}^1$, which form a Galois connection [14], are: $\boldsymbol{\alpha}^{\text{join}}(\overline{a}) = \left(\bigsqcup_{k \in \mathbb{K}} \pi_k(\overline{a})\right)$, and $\boldsymbol{\gamma}^{\text{join}}(a) = \prod_{k \in \mathbb{K}} a$.

The *projection* abstraction, $\boldsymbol{\alpha}^{\text{proj}}_{\phi}$, preserves only the values corresponding to configurations from $\mathbb{K}$ that satisfy $\phi \in FeatExp$. The information about configurations violating ϕ is disregarded. We have $\boldsymbol{\alpha}^{\text{proj}}_{\phi}(\mathbb{K}) = \{k \in \mathbb{K} \mid k \models \phi\}$, and the Galois connection [14] between $\mathbb{A}^{\mathbb{K}}$ and $\mathbb{A}^{\{k \in \mathbb{K} \mid k \models \phi\}}$ is defined as: $\boldsymbol{\alpha}^{\text{proj}}_{\phi}(\overline{a}) = \prod_{k \in \mathbb{K}, k \models \phi} \pi_k(\overline{a})$, and $\boldsymbol{\gamma}^{\text{proj}}_{\phi}(\overline{a}') = \prod_{k \in \mathbb{K}} \begin{cases} \pi_k(\overline{a}') & \text{if } k \models \phi \\ \top & \text{if } k \not\models \phi \end{cases}$.

[1] $\langle L, \leq_L \rangle \overset{\gamma}{\underset{\alpha}{\leftrightarrows}} \langle M, \leq_M \rangle$ is a *Galois connection* between lattices L and M iff α and γ are total functions that satisfy: $\alpha(l) \leq_M m \iff l \leq_L \gamma(m)$ for all $l \in L, m \in M$.

The abstraction $\boldsymbol{\alpha}_A^{\text{fignore}}$ ignores a single feature $A \in \mathbb{F}$ that is not directly relevant for the current analysis. It merges configurations that only differ with regard to A, and are identical with regard to remaining features, $\mathbb{F}\backslash\{A\}$. Given $\phi \in FeatExp$, we write $\phi\backslash_A$ for a formula obtained by eliminating the feature A from ϕ (see [14] for details). For each formula $k' \equiv k\backslash_A$ where $k \in \mathbb{K}$, there will be one configuration in $\boldsymbol{\alpha}_A^{\text{fignore}}(\mathbb{K})$ determined by the formula $\bigvee_{k\in\mathbb{K},k\backslash_A\equiv k'} k$. Therefore, we have $\boldsymbol{\alpha}_A^{\text{fignore}}(\mathbb{K}) = \{\bigvee_{k\in\mathbb{K},k\backslash_A\equiv k'} k \mid k' \in \{k\backslash_A \mid k \in \mathbb{K}\}\}$. The Galois connection [14] between $\mathbb{A}^{\mathbb{K}}$ and $\mathbb{A}^{\boldsymbol{\alpha}_A^{\text{fignore}}(\mathbb{K})}$ is defined as: $\boldsymbol{\alpha}_A^{\text{fignore}}(\overline{a}) = \prod_{k'\in\boldsymbol{\alpha}_A^{\text{fignore}}(\mathbb{K})} \bigsqcup_{k\in\mathbb{K},k\models k'} \pi_k(\overline{a})$, and $\boldsymbol{\gamma}_A^{\text{fignore}}(\overline{a}') = \prod_{k\in\mathbb{K}} \pi_{k'}(\overline{a}')$ if $k \models k'$.

We also have two compositional operators: *sequential composition* $\alpha_2 \circ \alpha_1$, which will run two abstractions α_1 and α_2 in sequence; and *product* $\alpha_1 \otimes \alpha_2$, which will run both abstractions α_1 and α_2 in parallel ("side-by-side"). For precise definitions of $\alpha_2 \circ \alpha_1$ and $\alpha_1 \otimes \alpha_2$, the reader is referred to [14]. In the following, we will simply write $(\alpha, \gamma) \in Abs$ for any $\langle \mathbb{A}^{\mathbb{K}}, \dot{\sqsubseteq}\rangle \underset{\alpha}{\overset{\gamma}{\longleftrightarrow}} \langle \mathbb{A}^{\alpha(\mathbb{K})}, \dot{\sqsubseteq}\rangle$, which is constructed using the operators presented in this section.

Example 1. Consider the lifted interval analysis and $\overline{a} = ([\mathtt{x} \mapsto [2,2]], [\mathtt{x} \mapsto [2,2]], [\mathtt{x}\mapsto[0,0]], [\mathtt{x}\mapsto[\text{-}2,\text{-}2]])$, where $\mathbb{K} = \{A \wedge B, A \wedge \neg B, \neg A \wedge B, \neg A \wedge \neg B\}$.

We have $\boldsymbol{\alpha}^{\text{join}}(\overline{a}) = (\pi_{A\wedge B}(\overline{a}) \sqcup \pi_{A\wedge\neg B}(\overline{a}) \sqcup \pi_{\neg A\wedge B}(\overline{a}) \sqcup \pi_{\neg A\wedge\neg B}(\overline{a})) = ([\mathtt{x}\mapsto [\text{-}2,2]])$. Thus, the state is significantly decreased to only one component, but the abstraction $\boldsymbol{\alpha}^{\text{join}}$ loses precision by saying that $\mathtt{x}$ can have any value between -2 and 2. Then, we have $\boldsymbol{\alpha}_A^{\text{proj}}(\overline{a}) = (\pi_{A\wedge B}(\overline{a}), \pi_{A\wedge\neg B}(\overline{a})) = ([\mathtt{x} \mapsto [2,2]], [\mathtt{x} \mapsto [2,2]])$. Now the state is decreased to two components that satisfy A. Also, $\boldsymbol{\alpha}^{\text{join}} \circ \boldsymbol{\alpha}_A^{\text{proj}}(\overline{a}) = (\pi_{A\wedge B}(\overline{a}) \sqcup \pi_{A\wedge\neg B}(\overline{a})) = ([\mathtt{x}\mapsto [2,2]])$. We have $\boldsymbol{\alpha}_A^{\text{fignore}}(\mathbb{K}) = \{(A\wedge B)\vee(\neg A\wedge B) \equiv B, (A\wedge\neg B)\vee(\neg A\wedge\neg B) \equiv \neg B\}$, and so $\boldsymbol{\alpha}_A^{\text{fignore}}(\overline{a}) = (\pi_{A\wedge B}(\overline{a}) \sqcup \pi_{\neg A\wedge B}(\overline{a}), \pi_{A\wedge\neg B}(\overline{a}) \sqcup \pi_{\neg A\wedge\neg B}(\overline{a})) = ([\mathtt{x}\mapsto [0,2]], [\mathtt{x}\mapsto [\text{-}2,2]])$. □

Induced Abstract Lifted Analysis. Recall that any analysis phrased in the abstract interpretation framework can be lifted to the corresponding variability-aware analysis [21], which is specified by the domain $\langle \mathbb{A}^{\mathbb{K}}, \dot{\sqsubseteq}\rangle$, and lifted transfer functions $\overline{\mathcal{A}}[\![s]\!] : (\mathbb{A} \to \mathbb{A})^{\mathbb{K}}$ and $\overline{\mathcal{A}'}[\![e]\!] : (\mathbb{A} \to \mathbb{P})^{\mathbb{K}}$. Given a Galois connection $(\alpha, \gamma) \in Abs$, the abstract lifted analyses induced by (α, γ) has been derived algorithmically in [14]. The derivation finds an over-approximation of $\alpha \circ \overline{\mathcal{A}}[\![s]\!] \circ \gamma$ obtaining a new abstract statement transfer function $\overline{\mathcal{A}}_\alpha[\![s]\!] : (\mathbb{A} \to \mathbb{A})^{\alpha(\mathbb{K})}$. Also, a new abstract expression transfer function $\overline{\mathcal{A}'}_\alpha[\![e]\!] : (\mathbb{A} \to \mathbb{P})^{\alpha(\mathbb{K})}$ is derived, which over-approximates $\alpha \circ \overline{\mathcal{A}'}[\![e]\!] \circ \gamma$. Note that full variability-aware analysis $\overline{\mathcal{A}'}[\![e]\!]$ and $\overline{\mathcal{A}}[\![s]\!]$ are included as a special case, i.e. they coincide with $\overline{\mathcal{A}'}_{\boldsymbol{\alpha}^{\text{id}}}[\![e]\!]$ and $\overline{\mathcal{A}}_{\boldsymbol{\alpha}^{\text{id}}}[\![s]\!]$. The derivation of $\overline{\mathcal{A}'}_\alpha[\![e]\!]$ and $\overline{\mathcal{A}}_\alpha[\![s]\!]$ is based on the calculational approach to abstract interpretation [8], which advocates simple algebraic manipulation to obtain a *direct expression* for the abstract transfer functions.

The definitions of $\overline{\mathcal{A}}_\alpha[\![s]\!]$ and $\overline{\mathcal{A}'}_\alpha[\![e]\!]$ are given in Fig. 1. The function $\overline{\mathcal{A}}_\alpha[\![s]\!]$ (resp. $\overline{\mathcal{A}'}_\alpha[\![e]\!]$) captures the effect of analysing the statement s (resp., expression e) in a lifted store $\overline{a} \in \mathbb{A}^{\alpha(\mathbb{K})}$ by computing an output lifted store $\overline{a'} \in \mathbb{A}^{\alpha(\mathbb{K})}$ (resp, property $\overline{p} \in \mathbb{P}^{\alpha(\mathbb{K})}$). For "$\mathtt{x}$:= e", the value of $\mathtt{x}$ is updated in every

$$\overline{\mathcal{A}}_\alpha[\![\texttt{skip}]\!] = \lambda\overline{a}.\,\overline{a}, \qquad \overline{\mathcal{A}}_\alpha[\![\texttt{x := } e]\!] = \lambda\overline{a}.\prod_{k'\in\alpha(\mathbb{K})} \pi_{k'}(\overline{a})[\texttt{x} \mapsto \pi_{k'}(\overline{\mathcal{A}'}_\alpha[\![e]\!]\overline{a})]$$

$$\overline{\mathcal{A}}_\alpha[\![s_0\ \texttt{;}\ s_1]\!] = \overline{\mathcal{A}}_\alpha[\![s_1]\!] \circ \overline{\mathcal{A}}_\alpha[\![s_0]\!], \qquad \overline{\mathcal{A}}_\alpha[\![\texttt{while}\ e\ \texttt{do}\ s]\!] = \mathrm{lfp}\lambda\overline{\Phi}.\,\lambda\overline{a}.\,\overline{a} \mathbin{\dot\sqcup} \overline{\Phi}(\overline{\mathcal{A}}_\alpha[\![s]\!]\,\overline{a})$$

$$\overline{\mathcal{A}}_\alpha[\![\texttt{if}\ e\ \texttt{then}\ s_0\ \texttt{else}\ s_1]\!] = \lambda\overline{a}.\,\overline{\mathcal{A}}_\alpha[\![s_0]\!]\overline{a} \mathbin{\dot\sqcup} \overline{\mathcal{A}}_\alpha[\![s_1]\!]\overline{a}$$

$$\overline{\mathcal{A}}_\alpha[\![\texttt{\#if}\,(\theta)s]\!] = \lambda\overline{a}.\prod_{k'\in\alpha(\mathbb{K})}\begin{cases}\pi_{k'}(\overline{\mathcal{A}}_\alpha[\![s]\!]\overline{a}) & \text{if } k' \models \theta\\ \pi_{k'}(\overline{a}) & \text{if } k' \models \neg\theta\\ \pi_{k'}(\overline{a}) \sqcup \pi_{k'}(\overline{\mathcal{A}}_\alpha[\![s]\!]\overline{a}) & \text{if } \mathrm{sat}(k'\wedge\theta)\wedge\mathrm{sat}(k'\wedge\neg\theta)\end{cases}$$

$$\overline{\mathcal{A}'}_\alpha[\![n]\!] = \lambda\overline{a}.\prod_{k'\in\alpha(\mathbb{K})} abst_{\mathbb{Z}}(\texttt{n}), \qquad \overline{\mathcal{A}'}_\alpha[\![\texttt{x}]\!] = \lambda\overline{a}.\prod_{k'\in\alpha(\mathbb{K})} \pi_{k'}(\overline{a})(\texttt{x})$$

$$\overline{\mathcal{A}'}_\alpha[\![e_0 \oplus e_1]\!] = \lambda\overline{a}.\prod_{k'\in\alpha(\mathbb{K})} \pi_{k'}(\overline{\mathcal{A}'}_\alpha[\![e_0]\!]\overline{a}) \mathbin{\widehat{\oplus}} \pi_{k'}(\overline{\mathcal{A}'}_\alpha[\![e_1]\!]\overline{a})$$

Fig. 1. Definitions of $\overline{\mathcal{A}}_\alpha[\![\overline{s}]\!] : (\mathbb{A} \to \mathbb{A})^{\alpha(\mathbb{K})}$ and $\overline{\mathcal{A}'}_\alpha[\![\overline{e}]\!] : (\mathbb{A} \to \mathbb{P})^{\alpha(\mathbb{K})}$.

component of the input lifted store $\overline{a}$ by the value of the expression e evaluated in the corresponding component of $\overline{a}$. The most interesting case is the analysis of "**#if** (θ) s", which checks the relation between each abstract configuration $k' \in \alpha(\mathbb{K})$ and the presence condition θ. Since k' can be any compound formula, not only a valuation formula as in $\mathbb{K}$, there are three possible cases: (1) if $k' \models \theta$, the corresponding component of the input store is updated by the effect of evaluating the statement s; (2) if $k' \models \neg\theta$, the corresponding component of the store is not updated; (3) if $(k' \wedge \theta)$ and $(k' \wedge \neg\theta)$ are both satisfiable, then the component is updated by the least upper bound of its initial value and the effect of s. For example, when $k' = A$, we obtain: the case (1) if $\theta = A$, the case (2) if $\theta = \neg A$, and the case (3) if $\theta = B$. Note that for $\boldsymbol{\alpha}^{\mathrm{id}}$, since all configurations k in $\mathbb{K}$ are valuation formulas (i.e. either $k \models \theta$ or $k \models \neg\theta$), only the first two cases are possible. Note that, only definitions for constants n and binary operators $\oplus$ are analysis-dependent. So our approach is general and applicable to any static dataflow analysis chosen as a client. The monotonicity and the soundness (i.e., $\alpha \circ \overline{\mathcal{A}'}[\![e]\!] \circ \gamma \mathrel{\dot\sqsubseteq} \overline{\mathcal{A}'}_\alpha[\![e]\!]$ and $\alpha \circ \overline{\mathcal{A}}[\![s]\!] \circ \gamma \mathrel{\dot\sqsubseteq} \overline{\mathcal{A}}_\alpha[\![s]\!]$) of the abstract lifted analysis follows by construction as shown in [14].

5 Pre-analysis for Finding α

Given a program family and a set of queries, we want to find a good abstraction α for a variability-aware (main) analysis defined by: the domain $\langle \mathbb{A}^{\mathbb{K}}, \dot\sqsubseteq \rangle$, where $\mathbb{A} = Var \to \mathbb{P}$, and the transfer functions $\overline{\mathcal{A}'}[\![e]\!] : (\mathbb{A} \to \mathbb{P})^{\mathbb{K}}$, $\overline{\mathcal{A}}[\![s]\!] : (\mathbb{A} \to \mathbb{A})^{\mathbb{K}}$. In this section, we first present how to design a pre-analysis, then we describe how we can construct an appropriate abstraction α for the main analysis based on the pre-analysis results.

Definition of Pre-Analysis. We replace the property domain $\langle \mathbb{P}, \sqsubseteq_{\mathbb{P}} \rangle$ from the main analysis with a suitable abstract property domain $\langle \mathbb{P}^{\#}, \sqsubseteq_{\mathbb{P}^{\#}} \rangle$, from which the pre-analysis is induced. The pre-analysis is fully variability-aware and is specified by the following domains: $\langle \mathbb{A}^{\#} = Var \to \mathbb{P}^{\#}, \sqsubseteq \rangle$, $\langle \mathbb{A}^{\#\mathbb{K}}, \dot{\sqsubseteq} \rangle$; and transfer functions: $\overline{\mathcal{A}'^{\#}}[\![e]\!] : (\mathbb{A}^{\#} \to \mathbb{P}^{\#})^{\mathbb{K}}$, $\overline{\mathcal{A}^{\#}}[\![s]\!] : (\mathbb{A}^{\#} \to \mathbb{A}^{\#})^{\mathbb{K}}$. Any designed pre-analysis should fulfill two conditions: *soundness* and *computational efficiency.*

Soundness. We design the pre-analysis which runs with full variability-awareness but with a simpler abstract domain and simpler abstract transfer functions than those of the main analysis.

First, there should be a pair of abstraction $\widehat{\alpha}^{\#} : \mathbb{P} \to \mathbb{P}^{\#}$ and concretization functions $\widehat{\gamma}^{\#} : \mathbb{P}^{\#} \to \mathbb{P}$ forming a Galois connection $\langle \mathbb{P}, \sqsubseteq_{\mathbb{P}} \rangle \underset{\widehat{\alpha}^{\#}}{\overset{\widehat{\gamma}^{\#}}{\longleftrightarrow}} \langle \mathbb{P}^{\#}, \sqsubseteq_{\mathbb{P}^{\#}} \rangle$. These functions formalize the fact that an abstract property from $\mathbb{P}^{\#}$ in the pre-analysis means a set of properties from $\mathbb{P}$ in the main analysis. By point-wise lifting we obtain the Galois connection $\langle \mathbb{A}, \sqsubseteq \rangle \underset{\alpha^{\#}}{\overset{\gamma^{\#}}{\longleftrightarrow}} \langle \mathbb{A}^{\#}, \sqsubseteq \rangle$ by taking: $\alpha^{\#}(a) = \lambda x.\widehat{\alpha}^{\#}(a(x))$ and $\gamma^{\#}(a^{\#}) = \lambda x.\widehat{\gamma}^{\#}(a^{\#}(x))$. By configuration-wise lifting we obtain the Galois connection $\langle \mathbb{A}^{\mathbb{K}}, \dot{\sqsubseteq} \rangle \underset{\overline{\alpha}^{\#}}{\overset{\overline{\gamma}^{\#}}{\longleftrightarrow}} \langle \mathbb{A}^{\#\mathbb{K}}, \dot{\sqsubseteq} \rangle$ by: $\overline{\alpha}^{\#}(\overline{a}) = \prod_{k \in \mathbb{K}} \alpha^{\#}(\pi_k(\overline{a}))$ and $\overline{\gamma}^{\#}(\overline{a^{\#}}) = \prod_{k \in \mathbb{K}} \gamma^{\#}(\pi_k(\overline{a^{\#}}))$. Similarly, by configuration-wise lifting we can construct the Galois connection $\langle \mathbb{P}^{\mathbb{K}}, \dot{\sqsubseteq} \rangle \underset{\overline{\widehat{\alpha}}^{\#}}{\overset{\overline{\widehat{\gamma}}^{\#}}{\longleftrightarrow}} \langle \mathbb{P}^{\#\mathbb{K}}, \dot{\sqsubseteq} \rangle$.

Second, the transfer functions $\overline{\mathcal{A}'^{\#}}[\![e]\!]$ and $\overline{\mathcal{A}^{\#}}[\![s]\!]$ of the pre-analysis should be *sound* with respect to those of the variability-aware main analysis: $\overline{\widehat{\alpha}}^{\#} \circ \overline{\mathcal{A}'}[\![e]\!] \circ \overline{\gamma}^{\#} \dot{\sqsubseteq} \overline{\mathcal{A}'^{\#}}[\![e]\!]$, and $\overline{\alpha}^{\#} \circ \overline{\mathcal{A}}[\![s]\!] \circ \overline{\gamma}^{\#} \dot{\sqsubseteq} \overline{\mathcal{A}^{\#}}[\![s]\!]$, for any $e \in Exp, s \in Stm$. In this way, we ensure that pre-analysis over-approximates variability-aware main analysis.

Computational efficiency. We define a query, q, to be of the form: $(s, P, \mathtt{x}) \in Stm \times \mathcal{P}(\mathbb{P}) \times Var$, which represents an assertion that after the statement s the variable $\mathtt{x}$ should always have a property value from the set $P \subseteq \mathbb{P}$. We want to design a pre-analysis, which although estimates computationally expensive main analysis, still remains computable. We achieve *computational efficiency* of the pre-analysis by choosing very simple property domain $\mathbb{P}^{\#}$. Let $\mathbb{P}^{\#} = \{\bigstar, \top_{\mathbb{P}^{\#}}\}$ be a complete lattice with $\bigstar \sqsubset \top_{\mathbb{P}^{\#}}$. Given the query $q = (s, P, \mathtt{x})$, the functions $\widehat{\alpha}^{\#} : \mathbb{P} \to \mathbb{P}^{\#}$ and $\widehat{\gamma}^{\#} : \mathbb{P}^{\#} \to \mathbb{P}$ are defined as:

$$\widehat{\alpha}^{\#}(p) = \begin{cases} \bigstar & \text{if } p \in P \\ \top_{\mathbb{P}^{\#}} & \text{otherwise} \end{cases} \qquad \widehat{\gamma}^{\#}(\bigstar) = \bigsqcup P,\ \widehat{\gamma}^{\#}(\top_{\mathbb{P}^{\#}}) = \top_{\mathbb{P}}$$

The only non-trivial case is $\bigstar$ denoting at least the properties from the set $P \subseteq \mathbb{P}$ that the given query q wants to establish after analyzing some program code. From now on, we omit to write subscripts $\mathbb{P}$ and $\mathbb{P}^{\#}$ in lattice operators whenever they are clear from the context.

The variability-aware pre-analysis with simple property domain (e.g. $\mathbb{P}^\# = \{\bigstar, \top\}$) can be computed by an efficient algorithm based on *sharing representation* [3], where sets of configurations with equivalent analysis information are compactly represented as bit vectors or formulae. For example, the pre-analysis with sharing for the variational program P of Sect. 2 runs as: $([\![\text{true}]\!] \mapsto [\mathtt{x} \mapsto \top, \mathtt{y} \mapsto \top]) \ldots \overset{\text{stm 3}}{\longmapsto} ([\![\text{true}]\!] \mapsto [\mathtt{x} \mapsto \bigstar, \mathtt{y} \mapsto \top]) \overset{\text{stm 4}}{\longmapsto} ([\![A]\!] \mapsto [\mathtt{x} \mapsto \bigstar, \mathtt{y} \mapsto \top], [\![\neg A]\!] \mapsto [\mathtt{x} \mapsto \top, \mathtt{y} \mapsto \top])$, where $[\![true]\!] = \{A \wedge B, A \wedge \neg B, \neg A \wedge B, \neg A \wedge \neg B\}$, $[\![A]\!] = \{A \wedge B, A \wedge \neg B\}$, and $[\![\neg A]\!] = \{\neg A \wedge B, \neg A \wedge \neg B\}$. Since the abstract domain $\mathbb{P}^\#$ of our pre-analysis is very small (has only 2 values), the possibilities for sharing (i.e. configurations with equivalent analysis results) are very promising.

Interval pre-analysis. We now design a pre-analysis for the interval analysis example with respect to queries that require non-negative intervals for variables. The pre-analysis aims at predicting which variables get assigned non-negative values when the program family is analyzed by the variability-aware interval analysis. Suppose that $Interval^\# = \{\bigstar, \top\}$, where $\bigstar \sqsubseteq \top$. We define $\widehat{\gamma}^\#(\bigstar) = [0, +\infty]$, and $\widehat{\gamma}^\#(\top) = [-\infty, +\infty]$. That is, $\bigstar$ denotes all non-negative intervals. Then, we have $\mathbb{A}^\# : Var \to Interval^\#$, and $\mathbb{A}^{\#\mathbb{K}} = \prod_{k \in \mathbb{K}} \mathbb{A}^\#$. We can calculate the transfer functions for expressions by following the soundness condition: $\overline{\mathcal{A}'^\#}[\![e]\!] \mathrel{\dot{\sqsupseteq}} \overline{\widehat{\alpha}}^\# \circ \overline{\mathcal{A}'}[\![e]\!] \circ \overline{\gamma}^\#$. The resulting functions can be computed effectively (in constant time) for constants and all binary operators as follows: $\overline{\mathcal{A}'^\#}[\![n]\!] = \lambda\overline{a^\#}.(\texttt{if } n \geq 0 \texttt{ then } \overline{\bigstar} \texttt{ else } \overline{\top})$, $\overline{\mathcal{A}'^\#}[\![e_1 - e_2]\!] = \lambda\overline{a^\#}.\overline{\top}$, and $\overline{\mathcal{A}'^\#}[\![e_1 + e_2]\!] = \lambda\overline{a^\#}.\prod_{k \in \mathbb{K}} \pi_k(\overline{\mathcal{A}'^\#}[\![e_1]\!]\overline{a^\#}) \sqcup \pi_k(\overline{\mathcal{A}'^\#}[\![e_2]\!]\overline{a^\#})$, where $\overline{\bigstar} = (\bigstar, \ldots, \bigstar), \overline{\top} = (\top, \ldots, \top) \in Interval^{\#\mathbb{K}}$. The analysis approximately tracks integer constants n, i.e. non-negative values get abstracted to $\bigstar$, whereas negative values to $\top$. Note that the addition "+" operator (similarly "*" and "/") is interpreted as the least upper bound $\sqcup$, so that for a configuration $k \in \mathbb{K}$, $e_1 + e_2$ evaluates to $\bigstar$ only when both e_1 and e_2 are $\bigstar$. For the subtraction "−" operator, the analysis always produces $\top$, thus losing precision. Also note that since the pre-analysis works on a lattice with finite height ($Interval^\#$) there is no need of defining widening operators to compute the fixed point of `while` loops. In contrast, the (main) interval analysis works on a lattice with infinite ascending chains ($Interval$) so it needs widening operators for handling loops.

Constructing Abstractions. We can use the results obtained during the pre-analysis to: (1) find queries that are likely to benefit from increased variability-awareness of the main analysis; (2) find configurations and features that are worth being distinguished during the main analysis. The found *configurations* and *features* are used to construct an abstraction α, which instructs how much variability-awareness the main analysis should use.

First, we find whether a query can benefit from increased variability-awareness. For simplicity, we assume that there is only one query $q = (s, P, \mathtt{x}) \in Stm \times \mathcal{P}(\mathbb{P}) \times Var$. The analysis should prove the query $q = (s, P, \mathtt{x})$ by computing a lifted store $\overline{a}$ after analyzing the statement s, and checking for which $k \in \mathbb{K}$ it holds: $\pi_k(\overline{a})(\mathtt{x}) \sqsubseteq_{\mathbb{P}} \sqcup P$. To find whether the given query will benefit from increased variability-awareness, we run the variability-aware pre-analysis. Let $\overline{\mathcal{A}^{\#}}[\![s]\!]\overline{a_0^{\#}}$ be the result of the pre-analysis, where $\overline{a_0^{\#}}$ denotes the initial abstract lifted store with all variables set to $\top_{\mathbb{P}^{\#}}$. Using this result, we check if there is some $k \in \mathbb{K}$ such that: $\pi_k(\overline{\mathcal{A}^{\#}}[\![s]\!]\overline{a_0^{\#}}(\mathtt{x})) = \bigstar$. Let $\mathbb{K}_{promise} \subseteq \mathbb{K}$ be the set of all *promising configurations* k that satisfy the above equation for a selected query.

We now compute the set $\mathbb{F}_{good} \subseteq \mathbb{F}$ of *necessary features* for a given query via dependency analysis, which is simultaneously done with the pre-analysis as follows. Let $\mathbb{P}'^{\#} = \mathbb{P}^{\#} \times \mathcal{P}(\mathbb{F})$. The idea is to over-approximate the set of features involved in analyzing each variable in the second component of $\mathbb{P}'^{\#}$. The abstract domain is $\mathbb{A}^{\#} = Var \to \mathbb{P}'^{\#}$. For lifted abstract store $\overline{a^{\#}} \in \mathbb{A}^{\#\mathbb{K}}$, we define $\pi_k(\overline{a^{\#}}(x))|_1 \in \mathbb{P}^{\#}$ as the property associated with the variable x in the component of $\overline{a^{\#}}$ corresponding to $k \in \mathbb{K}$; and $\pi_k(\overline{a^{\#}}(x))|_2 \in \mathcal{P}(\mathbb{F})$ as the set of features involved in producing the analysis result for x in the component of $\overline{a^{\#}}$ corresponding to $k \in \mathbb{K}$. The abstract semantics $\overline{\mathcal{A}'^{\#}}[\![e]\!]^F$ and $\overline{\mathcal{A}^{\#}}[\![s]\!]^F$ are the same as before except that they also maintain the set of involved features $F \subseteq \mathbb{F}$. The parameter $F \subseteq \mathbb{F}$ is propagated for all sub-statements of statements. For example: $\overline{\mathcal{A}^{\#}}[\![\mathtt{\#if}\ (\theta)\ s]\!]^F = \lambda\overline{a^{\#}}.\prod_{k\in\mathbb{K}} \begin{cases} \pi_k(\overline{\mathcal{A}^{\#}}[\![s]\!]^{F\cup FV(\theta)}\overline{a^{\#}}) & \text{if } k \models \theta \\ \pi_k(\overline{a^{\#}}) & \text{if } k \not\models \theta \end{cases}$, where $FV(\theta)$ denotes the set of features occurring in θ. For the `#if` statement, we also propagate the set of features in θ for each configuration k that satisfies θ, since the analysis result for those configurations will depend on features in θ. For "`x := `e", we record in the analysis which features have contributed for calculating the given property of `x`. We compute $\mathbb{F}_{good}$ as the union of all S, such that for some $k \in \mathbb{K}_{promise}$ we obtain: $\pi_k(\overline{\mathcal{A}^{\#}}[\![s]\!]^{\emptyset}\overline{a^{\#}}(\mathtt{x})) = (\bigstar, S)$. Then, we set $\mathbb{F}_{ignore} = \mathbb{F}\backslash\mathbb{F}_{good}$. The final constructed abstraction is: $\boldsymbol{\alpha}^{\text{fignore}}_{\mathbb{F}_{ignore}} \circ \boldsymbol{\alpha}^{\text{proj}}_{\bigvee_{k\in\mathbb{K}_{promise}}k}$.

Example 2. If we calculate $\overline{\mathcal{A}^{\#}}[\![P]\!]^{\emptyset}\overline{a_0^{\#}}$, where P is our example from Sect. 2 and $\overline{a_0^{\#}} = \prod_{k\in\mathbb{K}}(\lambda x.(\top, \emptyset))$ is the initial store, we obtain the final store: $([\mathtt{x}\mapsto(\bigstar,\{A\}),\mathtt{y}\mapsto(\top,\{B\})],[\mathtt{x}\mapsto(\bigstar,\{A\}),\mathtt{y}\mapsto(\top,\{B\})],[\mathtt{x}\mapsto(\top,\{A\}),\mathtt{y}\mapsto(\top,\{B\})],[\mathtt{x}\mapsto(\top,\{A\}),\mathtt{y}\mapsto(\top,\{B\})])$.

Therefore, we select the first query that asks for non-negative values of `x` as promising with $\mathbb{K}_{promise} = \{A \wedge B, A \wedge \neg B\}$ (which contains all configurations where `x` is mapped to $\bigstar$), $\mathbb{F}_{good} = \{A\}$, and $\mathbb{F}_{ignore} = \{B\}$. The abstraction regarding the first query is: $\boldsymbol{\alpha}^{\text{fignore}}_{B} \circ \boldsymbol{\alpha}^{\text{proj}}_{(A\wedge B)\vee(A\wedge\neg B)}$. But the second query that asks for non-negative values of `y` is rejected, since `y` is always mapped to $\top$. □

Finally, by using the soundness of pre-analysis, and suitability of the pre-analysis for the given query (definitions of $\mathbb{K}_{promise}$ and $\mathbb{F}_{ignore}$), we can show:

Theorem 1 (Promising Preservation). *Let $\mathbb{F}_{ignore}$ and $\mathbb{K}_{promise}$ be the sets of ignored features and promising configurations for a query (s, P, x) defined by the result of our pre-analysis $\overline{\mathcal{A}^{\#}}[\![s]\!]^{\emptyset}\overline{a_0^{\#}}$. Let $\alpha = \boldsymbol{\alpha}^{\text{fignore}}_{\mathbb{F}_{ignore}} \circ \boldsymbol{\alpha}^{\text{proj}}_{\bigvee_{k\in\mathbb{K}_{promise}}k}$ and*

$\gamma = \gamma^{\text{proj}}_{\vee_{k \in \mathbb{K}_{promise}} k} \circ \gamma^{\text{fignore}}_{\mathbb{F}_{ignore}}$. *Then:* $\gamma(\overline{\mathcal{A}}_\alpha [\![s]\!] \overline{a_0}(\boldsymbol{x})) \mathrel{\dot{\sqsubseteq}} \overline{\gamma}^\#(\overline{\mathcal{A}^\#}[\![s]\!]\overline{a_0^\#}(\boldsymbol{x}))$, *where* $\overline{a_0} \in \mathbb{A}^{\alpha(\mathbb{K})}$ *and* $\overline{a_0^\#} \in \mathbb{A}^{\# \mathbb{K}}$ *are the initial (uninitialized) lifted stores.*

6 Evaluation

We now evaluate our pre-analysis guided approach for finding suitable variability abstractions for lifted analysis. For our experiments, we use SOOT's intra-procedural dataflow analysis framework [27] for analyzing Java programs and an existing SOOT extension for lifted dataflow analyses of Java program families [3]. The lifted dataflow analysis framework uses CIDE (Colored IDE) [17], which is an Eclipse plug-in, to annotate statements using background colors rather than `#ifdef` directives. Every feature in a program family is thus associated with a unique color. We consider optimized lifted intra-procedural analyses with improved representation via sharing of analysis equivalent configurations using a high-performance bit vector library [15]. Note that our pre-analysis guided approach for lifted analysis is orthogonal to the particular analysis chosen as a client, since it depends only on variability-specific constructs of the language.

First, we have implemented interval pre-analysis and interval analysis in the SOOT framework. For interval analysis, the delayed widening is implemented using the *flowThrough* method of *ForwardFlowAnalysis* class by counting the times a node was visited and applying a widening operator once a threshold has been reached. Then, on top of a lifted dataflow analyzer [3], we have implemented variability-aware versions of interval pre-analysis and interval analysis described in Sects. 4 and 5, respectively. The pre-analysis reports a set of promising configurations and a set of features that should be ignored. This information is used to construct an abstraction, which is passed as parameter to the subsequent variability-aware interval analysis. The implemented analysis tracks the range of possible values for all integer (*int* and *long*) variables.

For our experiment, we use three Java benchmarks from the CIDE project [17]. Graph PL (GPL) is a small desktop application with intensive feature usage. It contains about 1,35 kLOC, 18 features, and 19 methods with integer variables. Prevayler is a slightly larger product line with low feature usage, which contains 8 kLOC, 5 features, and 174 methods with integer variables. BerkeleyDB is a larger database library with moderate feature usage, containing about 84 kLOC, 42 features, and 2654 methods with integer variables.

All experiments are executed on a 64-bit Intel®Core^{TM} i5 CPU with 8 GB memory. All times are reported as averages over ten runs with the highest and lowest number removed. We report only the times needed for actual intra-procedural analyses to be performed. In experiments, to illustrate our approach we consider *queries* which ask for the exact non-negative possible values of local integer variables at the end (final nodes) of their methods.

Table 1 compares the performance of our approach based on pre-analysis followed by the corresponding abstract variability-aware interval analysis (table below) with full variability-aware interval analysis which is used as a baseline

Table 1. Performance results for unabstract variability-aware analysis which is used as a baseline (table above) vs. our pre-analysis guided approach which consists of running a pre-analysis followed by a subsequent abstract variability-aware analysis (table below). All times are in ms (milliseconds).

Benchmark	*Unabstract variability-aware analysis*				
	analysis results				Time
	var []	con []	var ⊤	con ⊤	
`GPL`	33	216	18	26	73.1
`Prevayler`	56	58	166	168	83.2
`BerkeleyDB`	1144	3197	2139	4189	2908

Benchmark	*Pre-analysis guided approach*						
	full precision				prec. loss		Time
	var []	con []	var ⊤	con ⊤	var⊤	con⊤	
`GPL`	33	216	18	26	0	0	33.4
`Prevayler`	56	58	166	168	0	0	62.3
`BerkeleyDB`	1141	3154	2137	4232	3	43	1933

(table above). We measured the analysis precision by the number of integer variables for which our approach accurately calculates their analysis information (see full precision column, table below), which can be a non-negative interval (var []) or the ⊤ value (var ⊤), such that the same analysis results are obtained with the full variability-aware interval analysis (analysis results column, table above). We report the number of configurations (con [] and con ⊤) in which those precisely tracked variables occur. We also measured the number of variables and corresponding configurations where there is a precision loss (see precision loss column, table below), i.e. our approach produces the ⊤ value but the full variability-aware interval analysis can establish that their intervals are non-negative. For each of the benchmarks, we only analyze the methods that contain integer variables. We report the sum of analysis times for all such methods in a benchmark. We can see that for GPL and Prevayler there is no precision loss with our approach, but we obtain speed-ups in running times. For GPL we observe 2.2 times speed-up, whereas for Prevayler we have 1.3 times speed-up (pre-analysis+abstract vs. unabstract variability-aware analysis). For BerkeleyDB, we have precision loss for 3 variables found in 43 valid configurations (out of 7386 configurations where integer variables occur) which represents 0.58 % precision loss in total, but we still keep precision for all the other $7386 - 43 = 7343$ cases (configurations). Yet, we achieve 1.5 times speed-up with our approach for BerkeleyDB.

7 Related Work and Conclusion

Using pre-analysis to adjust the main analysis precision was first introduced in [23, 24]. They design pre-analysis for finding various precision parameters, such as: context sensitivity, flow sensitivity, and relational constraints between variables. In this work, we adapt this idea to the setting of variability-aware analysis for program families. In [20], machine learning is used to find a minimal abstraction that is sufficient to prove all queries provable by the most precise abstraction. The technique presented in [28] finds the optimum abstraction that proves a given query, but it is applicable only to disjunctive analysis.

The work in [3] lifts a dataflow analysis from the monotone framework, resulting in a variability-aware dataflow analysis that works on the level of families. Another efficient implementation of the lifted dataflow analysis formulated within the IFDS framework [25] was proposed in SPL^{LIFT} [2]. However, this technique is limited to work only for analyses phrased within the IFDS framework [25], and many dataflow analyses, including interval, cannot be encoded in IFDS. Other approaches for lifting existing analysis techniques to work on the level of families are: lifted syntax checking [19], lifted type checking [4,18], lifted model checking in the settings of transition systems [1,5,6,12,13] and game semantics [10,11], lifted testing [16]. All these lifted techniques could benefit from using variability abstractions and from the present approach on finding a good abstraction.

To conclude, in this work we presented a technique for automatically finding abstractions that enable effective abstract variability-aware analysis. The suitable abstraction parameters are calculated by a pre-analysis. We demonstrate the effectiveness of our approach with experiments.

References

1. Apel, S., von Rhein, A., Wendler, P., Größlinger, A., Beyer, D.: Strategies for product-line verification: case studies and experiments. In: 35th International Conference on Software Engineering, ICSE 2013, pp. 482–491 (2013)
2. Bodden, E., Tolêdo, T., Ribeiro, M., Brabrand, C., Borba, P., Mezini, M.: Spl^{lift}: statically analyzing software product lines in minutes instead of years. In: ACM SIGPLAN Conference on PLDI 2013, pp. 355–364 (2013)
3. Brabrand, C., Ribeiro, M., Tolêdo, T., Winther, J., Borba, P.: Intraprocedural dataflow analysis for software product lines. In: Leavens, G.T., Chiba, S., Tanter, É. (eds.) Transactions on Aspect-Oriented Software Development X. LNCS, vol. 7800, pp. 73–108. Springer, Heidelberg (2013). doi:10.1007/978-3-642-36964-3_3
4. Chen, S., Erwig, M., Walkingshaw, E.: An error-tolerant type system for variational lambda calculus. In: ACM SIGPLAN International Conference on Functional Programming, ICFP 2012, pp. 29–40 (2012)
5. Classen, A., Cordy, M., Heymans, P., Legay, A., Schobbens, P.-Y.: Model checking software product lines with SNIP. STTT **14**(5), 589–612 (2012)
6. Classen, A., Heymans, P., Schobbens, P.-Y., Legay, A., Raskin, J.-F.: Model checking lots of systems: efficient verification of temporal properties in software product lines. In: Proceedings of the 32nd ACM/IEEE International Conference on Software Engineering, ICSE 2010, vol. 1, pp. 335–344 (2010)
7. Clements, P., Northrop, L., Lines, S.P.: Practices and Patterns. Addison-Wesley, Reading (2001)
8. Cousot, P.: The calculational design of a generic abstract interpreter. In: Broy, M., Steinbrüggen, R. (eds.) Calculational System Design. NATO ASI Series. F. IOS Press, Amsterdam (1999)

9. Cousot, P., Cousot, R., Abstract interpretation: a unified lattice model for static analysis of programs by construction or approximation of fixpoints. In: Sethi, R. (ed.) POPL 1977, Los Angeles, California, pp. 238–252, January 1977
10. Dimovski, A.S.: Program verification using symbolic game semantics. Theor. Comput. Sci. **560**, 364–379 (2014)
11. Dimovski, A.S.: Symbolic game semantics for model checking program families. In: Bošnački, D., Wijs, A. (eds.) SPIN 2016. LNCS, vol. 9641, pp. 19–37. Springer, Heidelberg (2016). doi:10.1007/978-3-319-32582-8_2
12. Dimovski, A.S., Al-Sibahi, A.S., Brabrand, C., Wąsowski, A.: Family-based model checking without a family-based model checker. In: Fischer, B., Geldenhuys, J. (eds.) SPIN 2015. LNCS, vol. 9232, pp. 282–299. Springer, Heidelberg (2015). doi:10.1007/978-3-319-23404-5_18
13. Dimovski, A.S., Al-Sibahi, A.S., Brabrand, C., Wasowski, A.: Efficient family-based model checking via variability abstractions. STTT (2016). doi:10.1007/s10009-016-0425-2
14. Dimovski, A.S., Brabrand, C., Wasowski, A.: Variability abstractions: trading precision for speed in family-based analyses. In: 29th European Conference on Object-Oriented Programming, ECOOP 2015. LIPIcs, vol. 37, pp. 247–270. Schloss Dagstuhl - Leibniz-Zentrum fuer Informatik (2015)
15. CERN: European Organization for Nuclear Research: The colt project: open source libraries for high performance scientific and technical computing in Java. In: CERN (1999)
16. Iosif-Lazar, A.F., Al-Sibahi, A.S., Dimovski, A.S., Savolainen, J.E., Sierszecki, K., Wasowski, A.: Experiences from designing and validating a software modernization transformation (E). In: 30th IEEE/ACM International Conference on Automated Software Engineering, ASE 2015, pp. 597–607 (2015)
17. Kästner, C.: Virtual Separation of Concerns: toward Preprocessors 2.0. Ph.D. thesis, University of Magdeburg, Germany, May 2010
18. Kästner, C., Apel, S., Thüm, T., Saake, G.: Type checking annotation-based product lines. ACM Trans. Softw. Eng. Methodol. **21**(3), 14 (2012)
19. Kästner, C., Giarrusso, P.G., Rendel, T., Erdweg, S., Ostermann, K., Berger, T.: Variability-aware parsing in the presence of lexical macros and conditional compilation. In: Proceedings of the 26th Annual ACM SIGPLAN Conference on Object-Oriented Programming, Systems, Languages, and Applications, OOPSLA 2011, part of SPLASH 2011, pp. 805–824 (2011)
20. Liang, P., Tripp, O., Naik, M.: Learning minimal abstractions. In: Proceedings of the 38th ACM SIGPLAN-SIGACT Symposium on Principles of Programming Languages, POPL 2011, pp. 31–42 (2011)
21. Midtgaard, J., Dimovski, A.S., Brabrand, C., Wasowski, A.: Systematic derivation of correct variability-aware program analyses. Sci. Comput. Program. **105**, 145–170 (2015)
22. Nielson, F., Nielson, H.R., Hankin, C.: Principles of Program Analysis. Springer, Secaucus (1999)
23. Oh, H., Lee, W., Heo, K., Yang, H., Yi, K.: Selective context-sensitivity guided by impact pre-analysis. In: ACM SIGPLAN Conference on Programming Language Design and Implementation, PLDI 2014, p. 49 (2014)
24. Hakjoo, O., Lee, W., Heo, K., Yang, H., Yi, K.: Selective x-sensitive analysis guided by impact pre-analysis. ACM Trans. Program. Lang. Syst. **38**(2), 6 (2016)
25. Reps, T., Horwitz, S., Sagiv, M.: Precise interprocedural dataflow analysis via graph reachability. In: Proceedings of the 22nd ACM SIGPLAN-SIGACT Symposium on Principles of Programming Languages, POPL 1995, pp. 49–61 (1995)

26. Thüm, T., Apel, S., Kästner, C., Schaefer, I., Saake, G.: A classification and survey of analysis strategies for software product lines. ACM Comput. Surv. **47**(1), 6 (2014)
27. Vallée-Rai, R., Co, P., Gagnon, E., Hendren, L., Lam, P., Sundaresan, V.: Soot - a Java bytecode optimization framework. In: Proceedings of the 1999 Conference of the Centre for Advanced Studies on Collaborative Research (CASCON 1999), p. 13. IBM Press (1999)
28. Zhang, X., Naik, M., Yang, H.: Finding optimum abstractions in parametric dataflow analysis. In: ACM SIGPLAN Conference on Programming Language Design and Implementation, PLDI 2013, pp. 365–376 (2013)

Recovering High-Level Conditions from Binary Programs

Adel Djoudi[1(✉)], Sébastien Bardin[1], and Éric Goubault[2]

[1] CEA, LIST, Université Paris-Saclay, Gif-sur-Yvette, France
{adel.djoudi,sebastien.bardin}@cea.fr
[2] Lix, École Polytechnique, CNRS, Université Paris-Saclay, 91128 Palaiseau, France
eric.goubault@polytechnique.edu

Abstract. The need to get confidence in binary programs without access to their source code has pushed efforts forward to directly analyze executable programs. However, low-level programs lack high-level structures (such as types, control-flow graph, etc.), preventing the straightforward application of source-code analysis techniques. Especially, conditional jumps rely on low-level flag predicates, whereas they often encode high-level "natural" conditions on program variables. Most static analyzers are unable to infer any interesting information from these low-level conditions, leading to serious precision loss compared with source-level analysis. In this paper, we propose *template-based recovery*, an automatic approach for retrieving high-level predicates from their low-level flag versions. Especially, the technique is sound, efficient, platform-independent and it achieves very high ratio of recovery. This method allows more precise analyses and helps to understand machine encoding of conditionals rather than relying on error-prone human interpretation or (syntactic) pattern-based reasoning.

1 Introduction

Context. Static analysis [28] offers techniques for computing safe approximations of the set of values or behaviors arising at run-time when executing a program. Since the early 2000's, many successful source-code analysis techniques and tools have been proposed to check safety and security properties of industrial software [2,17,23].

Yet, there are many important situations *where the program must be analyzed directly at the level of executable code*, for example mobile code, off-the-shelf components, malware, etc. [2,13]. Such binary-level static analysis is highly challenging. Even on *managed code* (executable coming from standard high-level language such as C and compiled in a standard way), it is very hard to match the precision of an analysis performed at source-level mainly due to the lack of high-level information, such as types, variables, control-flow information or

Work partially funded by ANR, grant 12-INSE-0002.

J. Fitzgerald et al. (Eds.): FM 2016, LNCS 9995, pp. 235–253, 2016.
DOI: 10.1007/978-3-319-48989-6_15

high-level conditions. The last decade has seen significant progress in binary-level static analysis, including precise control-flow graph recovery [7,14,22,24], formal intermediate representations (IR) [6,8,18,31], type and variables identification [5,26], or dedicated abstract domains [9,10,12,29,31]. Yet, the field remains highly challenging.

Problem and Challenges. We focus in this paper on *high-level condition recovery* from low-level flag conditions. Indeed, on most modern architectures, high-level conditions from the original program are translated at binary-level into low-level predicates operating on *flags*, i.e. boolean registers recording either high-level relationships between registers ($==$, $\leq$) or low-level facts such as occurrences of signed/unsigned overflows. High-level constructs such as `if`, `while`, `for`, etc. are no longer available. Hence, unless tracking relational information between program instructions, guard transfer functions of simple static analyzers will fail to refine propagated abstract states, because conditional jumps depend on flag values and not directly on registers and/or memory locations that set the corresponding flags.

Several solutions have been proposed in [11,13,25,31] to address low-level condition issues, yet they are either unsound and/or architecture dependent (patterns [13]), or intermediate-representation dependent (virtual flags [31]), or not generic enough (logic-based recovery [11,25,27,31]). We are looking for a solution which is both *sound*, *generic* (i.e. achieve a high recovery ratio in practice) and *independent from a given architecture or IR-encoding.*

Contributions. Our main contributions are the followings

- We present *template-based condition recovery* (Sect. 4), a new approach to high-level predicate recovery enjoying all the above desired properties: automatic, sound, architecture- / IR- independent, efficient and achieving a high recovery ratio in practice. The approach extends the logic-based method [11,25,27,31] and yields to significantly better recovery ratio. Compared to pattern-based methods [13], the technique is architecture independent and can infer high-level conditions from "non-regular" patterns – for example, optimized patterns introduced by compilers, cf. Sect. 7. Moreover, both template-based and pattern-based recovery can be fruitfully combined.
- We also address two questions closely related to the problem of high-level condition recovery and precise static analysis: the issue of ubiquitous data transfer between registers and memory, and the detection and positioning of widening points. We describe in Sect. 5 the two problems and present our solutions, namely a lightweight domain dedicated to equality propagation (on arbitrary *lhs* of the program) and a smart widening point positioning heuristic.
- The approach has been implemented in the new BinSec/va static analysis module of the BinSec platform [19]. We detail the implementation (Sect. 6), and we describe several experimental evaluations (Sect. 7) assessing the recovery ability, efficiency and practical utility of our technique. Especially, template-based recovery yields only a small overhead and achieves a very high ratio of high-level condition recovery (between 89 % to 95 % in average). We also sketch potential applications to value analysis and deobfuscation.

Impact. Template-based recovery can help to adapt any formal analysis from source-level analysis to binary-level analysis, as illustrated in Sect. 7. It can also be useful for example for computer-aided reverse engineering, where it may help the reverser to quickly understand the real semantic of unusual flag manipulations, introduced either for optimization or obfuscation purposes (Sect. 7).

2 Motivation

2.1 The Issue of Low-Level Conditions in Binary-Level Program Analysis

The following example illustrates the problem of (low-level) flag encoding.

Example 1. Let us consider the following x86 instructions: `cmp x 100; je addr` encoding the high level condition `if (x = 100) then...`. According to Intel documentation [21], this sequence reads as follows: instruction `cmp x 100` evaluates if equality `x = 100` holds and stores the (boolean) result into the specific flag `ZF` (other flags are updated, but they are not relevant here), then instruction `je` branches to address `addr` if `ZF` contains 1, to the next address otherwise. This can be expressed in the more abstract formalism of DBA (cf. Sect. 3) as follows (right column), where `ZF` is a 1-bit variable:

```
1: ZF := (x = 100);              // x ↦ ⊤
2: if (ZF) then goto addr;       // x, ZF ↦ ⊤, [0, 1]
...                              ...
addr: ...                        // x, ZF ↦ ⊤, [1, 1]
```

Let us now consider a standard interval analysis starting from $x \in \top$ at address `1`. The analysis will derive $ZF \in [0,1]$ after the first instruction, then $ZF \in [1,1]$ if the true branch is taken.

However, nothing is derived for x (i.e. $x \in \top$) while it is straightforward that $x \in [100, 100]$. ⊠

Note that while this sort of low-level encoding can be found in C code, the situation is much problematic on binary code where low-level condition encoding is the norm.

Our goal is precisely to obtain source-level like propagation on binary code thanks to the recovery of high-level conditions.

2.2 Standard Solutions and Drawbacks

Logic-based solution. Several authors have independently proposed a similar solution to high-level condition recovery [11,25,31], that we call here *logic-based recovery.* The basic idea is to record relations into flag variables, to propagate these relations (taking operand updates into account) and to use them for refining the current state of the analysis once the flag value becomes 1 or 0. On the above example, flag propagation infers that `ZF` $\mapsto [x == 100]$ at line `addr`. Since

ZF $\mapsto$ $[1,1]$, predicate `x==100` is also inferred, refining the abstract domain with x $\mapsto$ $[100,100]$, *which is exactly the result we are looking for.*

Yet, logic-based recovery is not always sufficient. The following example illustrates another conditional jump in x86 architecture where logic-based recovery fails.

Example 2. Let us consider the following x86 code sequence `cmp x y; jg addr`, encoding `if (x > y) then goto addr`. Internally, `jg` checks a combination of three flags updated by `cmp`, namely `ZF`, `OF` (overflow) and `SF` (sign).

```
OF := (x{31,31}=y{31,31})& (x{31,31}=(x-y){31,31});
SF := (x - y < 0);
ZF := (x - y = 0);
if (¬ZF ∧ (OF = SF)) then goto addr;
```

Here, relation propagation does not help, as the recovered low-level condition (below) is far from the *natural* high-level condition `x > y`. *Logic-based recovery is not able to identify most of high-level conditions coming from x86 flag encodings.*

```
if (¬(x-y = 0) ∧ ((x{31,31}=y{31,31}) &(x{31,31}=(x-y){31,31})) = (x-y<0)) then goto addr;
```

Pattern based solution. Balakrishnan *et al.* [13] suggests to pattern match the successions of comparisons and conditional jumps for deducing the corresponding high-level comparison. Standard x86 patterns are depicted in Table 1. *While precise on common cases, this approach is very architecture-specific. Hence, supporting several architectures is time-consuming. Moreover, it is very fragile w.r.t. non standard uses of flags and conditional branches, as found in optimization or obfuscation (cf. Sect. 7).* Note that ensuring soundness requires some care, e.g. taking properly into account flag/operand updates between the comparison and the conditional branch.

Table 1. High-level predicates for x86 conditional jumps [13]

	cmp x y / sub x y flag predicate[a]	cmp x y predicate[b]	sub x y predicate[b]	test x y flag predicate[c]	predicate[b]
ja, jnbe	$\neg CF \wedge \neg ZF$	$x >_u y$	$x' \neq 0$	$\neg ZF$	$x\&y \neq 0$
jae, jnb, jnc	$\neg CF$	$x \geq_u y$	true	true	true
jb, jnae, jc	CF	$x <_u y$	$x' \neq 0$	false	false
jbe, jna	$CF \vee ZF$	$x \leq_u y$	true	ZF	$x\&y = 0$
je, jz	ZF	$x = y$	$x' = 0$	ZF	$x\&y = 0$
jne, jnz	$\neg ZF$	$x \neq y$	$x' \neq 0$	$\neg ZF$	$x\&y \neq 0$
jg, jnle	$\neg ZF \wedge (OF = SF)$	$x > y$	$x' > 0$	$\neg ZF \wedge \neg SF$	$(x\&y \neq 0) \wedge (x > 0 \vee y > 0)$
jge, jnl	$(OF = SF)$	$x \geq y$	true	$\neg SF$	$(x \geq 0 \vee y \geq 0)$
jl, jnge	$(OF \neq SF)$	$x < y$	$x' < 0$	SF	$(x < 0 \wedge y < 0)$
jle, jng	$ZF \vee (OF \neq SF)$	$x \leq y$	*true*	$ZF \vee SF$	$(x\&y = 0) \vee (x < 0 \wedge y < 0)$

[a]: flag-level condition checked by the instruction. [b]: expected corresponding high-level condition
[c]: the same as [a], taking into account that test sets OF and CF to 0. (x' is defined by $x - y$)

Approach	archi. independent	IR encoding independent	Sound	Complete enough [1] standard [1]	non-standard [1]
Patterns	×	✓	✓/×[2]	✓	×
Virtual flags	✓	×	✓/×[3]	✓	×
Logic-based	✓	✓	✓	×	×
Template-based	✓	✓	✓	✓	✓

[1]: does the technique achieve a large ratio of condition recovery in practice? We distinguish between standard flag encodings and non-standard ones (cf Section 7).
[2]: need to ensure that no flag / operand update happens between comparison and branching
[3]: need to ensure at each program step the coherence between virtual flags and concrete flags

Fig. 1. Comparison of high-level predicate recovery approaches

Virtual flags. Sepp *et al.* [31] proposed to tackle the problem while translating machine instructions into their own Intermediate Representation RREIL. Flag calculations are translated, if possible, into arithmetic instructions. Typically a comparison between operands is assigned into a *virtual flag*. If a virtual flag is used later on, relational information between operands may be recovered and conveyed to numeric domains.

Example 3. The succession of the two x86 instructions `cmp x y; jg addr;` seen in previous example is translated in RREIL as depicted on the right, with virtual flags `CForZF`, `SFxorOF` and `SFxorOForZF` representing combinations of concrete flags. At conditional branch, the test matching the flag is applied. Yet, the approach requires to add many virtual flags (updated at each instruction) dedicated to the targeted architecture and to ensure their consistency with the concrete flags, which can be tricky.

```
sub      t0:32, y:32, x:32
cmpltu   CF:1, y:32, x:32
cmpleu   CForZF:1, y:32, x:32
cmplts   SFxorOF:1, y:32, x:32
cmples   SFxorOForZF:1, y:32, x:32
cmpeq    ZF:1, y:32, x:32
cmplts   SF:1, t0:32, 0:32
xor      OF:1, SFxorOF:1, SF:1
brc      SFxorOF:1, addr:32
```

Summary. State of the art solutions are summarized in Fig. 1, together with the template-based recovery method described latter in Sect. 4. *Our approach extends the logic-based method with more powerful recovery ability, while still being architecture and IR-encoding independent. Moreover, virtual flags and patterns, if available and soundly implemented, can complement template-based recovery in a fruitful way.*

3 Background

Our approach is based on abstract interpretation [15,16], a theory explaining how to link a very precise (but generally uncomputable) *concrete semantics* to

Instructions	Expressions
- `lhs := rhs, goto addr`	- `e{i .. j}`, $\texttt{ext}_{u,s}\texttt{(e,n)}$, `e :: e`
- `goto addr`	- `@(e)`
- `goto e`	- `e` $\{+, -, \times, /_{u,s}, \%_{u,s}\}$ `e`
- `ite(cond)? goto addr : goto addr'`	- `e` $\{<_{u,s}, \leq_{u,s}, =, \neq, \geq_{u,s}, >_{u,s}\}$ `e`
- `stop`	- `e` $\{\wedge, \vee, \oplus, <<, >>_{u,s}\}$ `e`, `!e`

Fig. 2. DBA instructions

its *sound approximation*, referred to as *abstract semantics*. This section first defines the syntax and concrete semantics of our Intermediate Representation, then a few notations of abstract interpretation.

DBA and concrete semantics. Automatic analysis of executables requires tools to abstract from the instruction set of each individual architecture by using an intermediate representation (IR). We rely on Dynamic Bit-vector Automata (DBA) [6], a generic, side-effect free and concise formal model for low-level programs, whose **syntax** is presented in Fig. 2. DBA program manipulates a finite set of global variables ranging over fixed-size bit-vectors (registers) and an array of bit-vectors of size 8 (memory). All bit-vector sizes are statically known. Conditions are bit-vectors of size 1. *Instructions* mostly include assignments and (static/conditional/dynamic) jumps, while *expressions* are built on standard bit-vector operators (bit-wise logical operations, shift, size restriction `e{i..j}` and extension `ext(e,n)`, concatenation `::`, (un-)signed machine arithmetic – unsigned operators are denoted with $\_u$) and memory accesses `@(e)`. A DBA program is a map from (code) addresses (i.e. bit-vectors of size `addr_size`) to DBA instructions, together with an initial address. In the following, the set of variables (resp. expressions) is denoted `Var` (resp. `Expr`).

DBA are given a standard imperative **semantic**. A *concrete state* (or environment) of a program is a map $\rho \in \mathbb{BV}^{var^+}$ assigning a bit-vector value from the set $\mathbb{BV}$ to each variable and memory location (denoted var^+). Expressions evaluate over bit-vectors. The semantics of an expression e in the concrete state ρ is denoted by $eval(e)_\rho$. In case an expression has no variable nor memory access, its semantic is given by $eval(e)_\emptyset$, simply denoted $eval(e)$. Assignments and conditions are given the standard semantic. A static jump `goto addr` branches to (the instruction at) address `addr`, while a dynamic jump `goto e` branches to address $eval(e)_\rho$.

From a modeling point of view, a single machine instruction is decoded into a block of DBA instructions - including intermediate computations and temporary variables. Floating-point arithmetic, multi-thread and self-modification are currently out of scope of DBA.

Abstract interpretation. Abstract interpretation-based analyses [15,16] rely on an abstract domain D, whose computable elements model a set of concrete states at a given program point. Such abstract domains must provide the abstract counterparts of the concrete (set) operations over $(\mathcal{P}(\mathbb{BV}^{var^+}))^{\mathbb{N}}$: a partial order

$\sqsubseteq_D$ over abstract states; a monotone concretization function γ_D from D to $\mathcal{P}(\mathbb{BV}^{var^+})$; greatest and smallest elements $\top_D$ and $\bot_D$, s.t. $\gamma_D(\top_D) = \mathbb{BV}^{var^+}$ and $\gamma_D(\bot_D) = \emptyset$; sound *over-approximations* join $\sqcup_D$ and meet $\sqcap_D$ of the union and intersection of concrete states, i.e. $\gamma_D(d_1) \cup \gamma_D(d_1) \subseteq \gamma_D(d_1 \sqcup_D d_2)$ and $\gamma_D(d_1) \cap \gamma_D(d_1) \subseteq \gamma_D(d_1 \sqcap_D d_2)$; sound abstract transfer functions $[\![i]\!]^{\#}_D$ from D to D that *over-approximate* the concrete semantics, i.e. $[\![i]\!](\gamma_D(d)) \subseteq \gamma_D([\![i]\!]^{\#}_D(d))$. The key property in abstract interpretation-based software verification is *soundness*, which ensures that each step in the abstract overapproximates all corresponding possible concrete steps.

4 Template-Based Recovery

4.1 Principles

We start from the idea of logic-based recovery and flag propagation. The issue here is that the high-level conditional expression may be too complex to be dealt with by basic non relational abstract domains, and that brute substitution of predicates in a non-trivial flag predicate often results in a complex low-level predicate, possibly hiding a simple predicate (cf. Example 2). *Template-based recovery* complements logic-based recovery with a *normalization* step for simplifying the current flag expression into a high-level form. It relies on **two key ideas**:

- first, there is only a finite set of high-level condition patterns we are interested in – built on $>_u, >, <_u, <, \geq_u, \geq, \leq_u, \leq, =, \neq$, with only two operands – since we consider on three-address instruction sets;
- second, equivalence between a high-level condition candidate and a given low-level condition can be checked by a SMT solver (in the theory of bit-vectors and arrays) – the check should be very efficient as the formula is expected to be very small.

Our approach works as follows. We first retrieve a set of potential operands from the low-level condition under analysis. A potential operand x must be either a variable, a memory access, or a restriction of a variable or memory access, i.e.

$$\texttt{x} \in \{\texttt{v},\ \texttt{@[e]},\ \texttt{v}_{\{i,j\}},\ \texttt{@[e]}_{\{i,j\}},\ \texttt{c} \mid \texttt{v} \in \texttt{Var},\ \texttt{e} \in \texttt{Expr},\ \texttt{c} \in \mathbb{BV},\ \texttt{j>i}\}$$

Given a low-level condition cond, once the potential operands x and y are selected, we try to assert the equivalence of cond with the following high-level candidates:

$\texttt{cond} \Leftrightarrow \texttt{x} >_u \texttt{y}$	$\texttt{cond} \Leftrightarrow \texttt{x} <_u \texttt{y}$	$\texttt{cond} \Leftrightarrow \texttt{x} \geq_u \texttt{y}$	$\texttt{cond} \Leftrightarrow \texttt{x} \leq_u \texttt{y}$
$\texttt{cond} \Leftrightarrow \texttt{x} > \texttt{y}$	$\texttt{cond} \Leftrightarrow \texttt{x} < \texttt{y}$	$\texttt{cond} \Leftrightarrow \texttt{x} \geq \texttt{y}$	$\texttt{cond} \Leftrightarrow \texttt{x} \leq \texttt{y}$
$\texttt{cond} \Leftrightarrow \texttt{x} = \texttt{y}$	$\texttt{cond} \Leftrightarrow \texttt{x} \neq \texttt{y}$	s.t. $\texttt{x, y} \in_{syntax} \texttt{cond}$	

If an equivalence is found with candidate cond′, then cond′ is used instead of cond during the abstract fixpoint computation. Otherwise, recovery fails and the abstract computation goes on with cond, following the logic-based approach.

4.2 Formalization

We consider an abstract interpretation framework with an abstract domain $F^\#$ associating to each flag an expression (elements $\mathtt{f}$: $Flag \rightarrow Expr$), alongside a numerical non-relational abstract domain $A^\#$ lifted to program variables and memory locations $D^\#$ (elements $\mathtt{d}$: $var^+ \rightarrow A^\#$), with its evaluation operator $(\!|.|\!) : Expr \rightarrow D^\# \rightarrow A^\#$ and condition propagation $assume : D^\# \rightarrow Expr \rightarrow D^\#$.

Our full abstract transfer function is the relation $. \rightarrow^\# . : (D^\# \times F^\# \times \mathbb{A}ddress) \rightarrow (D^\# \times F^\# \times \mathbb{A}ddress)$, from abstract states to new abstract states, described in Figure 3, where $\mathtt{f} \in F^\#$, $\mathtt{d} \in D^\#$ and $\mathtt{l} \in \mathbb{A}ddress$. The syntax s$[\cdot \mapsto \cdot]$ denotes the state obtained by updating part of state s with a new abstract value. The flag abstract state (second component of an abstract state) is updated only at assignments, used at conditional jumps and merely propagated through other instructions. If any operand of the flag expression $\mathtt{f}$(flag) is potentially affected by

$$\frac{[\![flag := e; l']\!]}{\left(\mathtt{d}, \mathtt{f}, l\right) \rightarrow^\# \left(\mathtt{d}[flag \mapsto (\!|e|\!)(\mathtt{d})],\ \mathtt{f}[flag \mapsto e], l'\right)}$$

$$\frac{[\![v := e; l']\!] \quad v \preceq \mathtt{f}(flag_1) \quad \dots \quad v \preceq \mathtt{f}(flag_n)}{\left(\mathtt{d}, \mathtt{f}, l\right) \rightarrow^\# \left(\mathtt{d}[v \mapsto (\!|e|\!)(\mathtt{d})],\ \mathtt{f}[flag_1, \dots, flag_n \mapsto \top, \dots, \top], l'\right)}$$

$$\frac{[\![@(e_1, c) := e_2; l']\!] \quad @(e_1, c) \simeq \mathtt{f}(flag_1) \quad \dots \quad @(e_1, c) \simeq \mathtt{f}(flag_n)}{\left(\mathtt{d}, \mathtt{f}, l\right) \rightarrow^\# \left(\mathtt{d}[((\!|e_1|\!)(\mathtt{d}), c) \mapsto (\!|e_2|\!)(\mathtt{d})],\ \mathtt{f}[flag_1, \dots, flag_n \mapsto \top, \dots, \top], l'\right)}$$

$$\frac{[\![ite(e)?\, l_1 : l_2]\!] \quad e' = \text{normalize}(e)(\mathtt{f}) \quad \gamma((\!|e'|\!)(\mathtt{d})) \neq \{0\}}{\left(\mathtt{d}, \mathtt{f}, l\right) \rightarrow^\# \left(assume(\mathtt{d})(e'),\ \mathtt{f},\ l_1\right)}$$

$$\frac{[\![ite(e)?\, l_1 : l_2]\!] \quad e' = \text{normalize}(e)(\mathtt{f}) \quad 0 \in \gamma((\!|e'|\!)(\mathtt{d}))}{\left(\mathtt{d}, \mathtt{f}, l\right) \rightarrow^\# \left(assume(\mathtt{d})(!e'),\ \mathtt{f},\ l_2\right)}$$

$$\text{normalize}(e)(\mathtt{f}) \triangleq \begin{cases} t_1 \odot t_2 & \text{if } \phi(t_1, t_2) \Leftrightarrow t_1 \odot t_2 \\ & \text{s.t. } \phi(t_1, t_2) = e[\mathtt{f}(flag_1)/flag_1, \dots; \mathtt{f}(flag_2)/flag_2], \\ & t_1, t_2 \preceq e[\mathtt{f}(flag_1)/flag_1, \dots; \mathtt{f}(flag_2)/flag_2] \\ e & \text{otherwise} \end{cases}$$

$$x \preceq e \triangleq \begin{cases} true & \text{if } e \in \{x,\ x\{i, j\}\} \\ x \preceq e' & \text{if } e \in \{@(e', c),\ e'\{i, j\},\ !e',\ ext_{u,s}(e', n)\} \\ x \preceq e_1 \vee x \preceq e_2 & \text{if } e \in \{e_1 \odot e_2 \mid \odot \text{ is a binary operator}\} \end{cases}$$

$$x \simeq e \triangleq \begin{cases} (\!|e_1 + [0, c_1]|\!)(\mathtt{d}) \sqcap^\#_{\mathtt{d}} & \\ (\!|e_2 + [0, c_2]|\!)(\mathtt{d}) \neq \bot_{\mathtt{d}} & \text{if } (x = @(e_1, c_1) \wedge y = @(e_2, c_2)) \\ x \simeq e' & \text{if } e \in \{@(e', c),\ e'\{i, j\},\ !e',\ ext_{u,s}(e', n)\} \\ x \simeq e_1 \vee x \simeq e_2 & \text{if } e \in \{e_1 \odot e_2 \mid \odot \text{ is a binary operator}\} \\ false & \text{otherwise} \end{cases}$$

$$\mathtt{f}_1 \sqcup^\#_{\mathtt{f}} \mathtt{f}_2 = \mathtt{f} \quad \text{s.t. foreach } flag \text{ in } \mathtt{f}, \begin{cases} \mathtt{f}(flag) = e & \text{if } \mathtt{f}_1(flag) = \mathtt{f}_2(flag) = e \\ \mathtt{f}(flag) = \top & \text{if } \mathtt{f}_1(flag) \neq \mathtt{f}_2(flag) \end{cases}$$

Fig. 3. Abstract propagation of flags abstract domain

an assignment, either because one of its subterm is directly modified or because of potential memory aliasing, then f(flag) is reset to $\top$. $\preceq$ denotes syntactic subterm, $\simeq$ denotes potential memory aliasing. Function normalize : $Expr \rightarrow F^{\#} \rightarrow Expr$ tries to recover a high-level condition from an expression e. If high-level condition recovery fails, e is left unchanged. When control flow recombines after a conditional block or loop, abstract states are joined.

Theorem 1 (soundness). *The template based solution is sound i.e. if $\phi(t_1, t_2)$ is a flag predicate involving at least two terms t_1 and t_2 at address a, s.t. the template based solution asserts that $\phi(t_1, t_2) \Leftrightarrow t_1 \odot t_2$, then for each execution trace of the program the assertion holds at address a.*

4.3 Optimizations

Repeated calls to the SMT solver may raise efficiency issues. We propose two optimizations in order to mitigate this problem.

Optimization 1: Normalization cache. Each time a flag conditional is met at address a, the low-level condition is saved in the cache at address a together with the retrieved high-level condition. If the same condition at the same address a is met later in the analysis, then the saved high-level condition can be safely reused.

Optimization 2: Templates filtering. The order in which the templates are checked directly affects the efficiency of high-level predicate recovery. The problem is all the more important that the number of checked templates is higher. If the number of potential templates is reduced to one or two, the issue will be largely mitigated.

The idea behind *template filtering* is that many templates can be cheaply discarded by comparing the evaluation of the low-level condition to the template evaluation on a set of well-chosen values.

We denote by cond[x/t] the condition cond where each occurrence of syntactic term t is replaced by another syntactic term x. If $\mathtt{op}_1$ and $\mathtt{op}_2$ are non-constant operands syntactically appearing in condition cond, we can generate conditions $\mathtt{cond}_1$, $\mathtt{cond}_2$, $\mathtt{cond}_3$ and $\mathtt{cond}_4$:

$$\mathtt{cond}_1 \triangleq \mathtt{cond[0/op_1][0/op_2]}$$
$$\mathtt{cond}_2 \triangleq \mathtt{cond[0/op_1][1/op_2]}$$
$$\mathtt{cond}_3 \triangleq \mathtt{cond[1/op_1][0/op_2]}$$
$$\mathtt{cond}_4 \triangleq \mathtt{cond[0/op_1][max_u/op_2]}$$

The resulting four conditions will be evaluated in order to discard irrelevant templates. The intuition behind this set of values is that we need to distinguish between symmetric and antisymmetric operators $((0, 0))$, between the direction for antisymmetric operators $((0, 1))$, between signed and unsigned comparisons $((0, max_u))$, and finally we have to distinguish between a strict comparison and a disequality $((1, 0)$ together with $(0, 1))$.

Discarding templates according to conditions evaluation is given by the following consecutive tests. $\mathtt{cond}_3$ is a special case requested when $eval(\mathtt{cond}_2) = true$. Here: if $eval(\mathtt{cond}_2) = eval(\mathtt{cond}_3)$ then keep only template $\neq$, else remove $\neq$.

If $eval(\mathtt{cond}_1) = false$ then templates ($\mathtt{op}_1$ $\{=, \leq_u, \geq_u, \leq, \geq\}$ $\mathtt{op}_2$) are discarded
else templates ($\mathtt{op}_1$ $\{\neq, <_u, >_u, <, >\}$ $\mathtt{op}_2$) are discarded
If $eval(\mathtt{cond}_2) = false$ then templates ($\mathtt{op}_1$ $\{<, <_u, \leq, \leq_u, \neq\}$ $\mathtt{op}_2$) are discarded
else templates ($\mathtt{op}_1$ $\{>, >_u, \geq, \geq_u, =\}$ $\mathtt{op}_2$) are discarded
If $eval(\mathtt{cond}_4) = false$ then templates ($\mathtt{op}_1$ $\{>, <_u, \geq, \leq_u, \neq\}$ $\mathtt{op}_2$) are discarded
else templates ($\mathtt{op}_1$ $\{<, >_u, \leq, \geq_u, =\}$ $\mathtt{op}_2$) are discarded

Whatever the low-level condition is, with only four tests we can eliminate all template candidates but one, which is then passed to the solver.

Example 4. Let us consider an arbitrary low-level condition $\mathtt{cond}$, with two operands $\mathtt{x}$ and $\mathtt{y}$. We compute cond_1 to cond_4 as defined before. Let us imagine that: $\mathrm{cond}_1 = 0$, $\mathrm{cond}_2 = 1$, $\mathrm{cond}_3 = 0$, $\mathrm{cond}_4 = 1$. Then the only remaining possible template is $\mathtt{x} <_u \mathtt{y}$.

$eval(\mathtt{cond}_1) = false$ then templates ($\mathtt{x}$ $\{=, \leq_u, \geq_u, \leq, \geq\}$ $\mathtt{y}$) are discarded
$eval(\mathtt{cond}_2) = true$ then templates ($\mathtt{x}$ $\{>, >_u\}$ $\mathtt{y}$) are discarded
$eval(\mathtt{cond}_3) = false$ then template ($\mathtt{x}$ $\{\neq\}$ $\mathtt{y}$) is discarded
$eval(\mathtt{cond}_4) = true$ then template ($\mathtt{x}$ $\{<\}$ $\mathtt{y}$) is discarded ⊠

Similarly, if $\mathtt{op}_1$ is already a constant value c then $\mathtt{cond}_1$, $\mathtt{cond}_2$, $\mathtt{cond}_3$ and $\mathtt{cond}_4$ are defined as follows:

$$\mathtt{cond}_1 \triangleq \mathtt{cond[c/op_2]}$$

$$\mathtt{cond}_2 \triangleq \begin{cases} \mathtt{cond[max_s/op_2]} & \text{if } c <_u \max_s \\ \mathtt{cond[max_u/op_2]} & \text{if } c >_u \max_s \end{cases}$$

$$\mathtt{cond}_3 \triangleq \begin{cases} \mathtt{cond[0/op_2]} & \text{if } 0 < c <_u \max_s \\ \mathtt{cond[max_s/op_2]} & \text{if } c >_u \max_s \end{cases}$$

$$\mathtt{cond}_4 \triangleq \begin{cases} \mathtt{cond[max_u/op_2]} & \text{if } c <_u \max_s \\ \neg\mathtt{cond[max_s/op_2]} & \text{if } c >_u \max_s \end{cases}$$

5 Other Issues Related to the Precise Handling of Conditions

We describe two situations closely related to low-level conditions that may yield to significant precision loss, even in the presence of high-level condition recovery, together with possible mitigation.

5.1 Ubiquitous Data Moves Between Memory and Registers

Problem. Architecture-specific constraints may blur the encoding of high-level constructs. Typically, like the majority of x86 instructions, the `cmp` instruction allows at most one memory operand. So, in order to compare contents of two memory locations, we need first to load at least one of them into a register, then perform the comparison. Hence ubiquitous data move from memory (stack) to registers. Example 5 illustrates that a low-level analysis unable to track relational information through data manipulation will infer domain reduction on the compared registers (*which do not matter*), but not on the memory contents themselves (*which matter*).

Example 5. This example shows that even when a natural high level condition is available, a standard analysis may still miss obvious information.

```
1: eax := @[100];                       // @[100] ↦ [0, 130]

2: if (eax < 4) then goto addr;         // eax, @[100] ↦ [0,130],[0,130]

...                                     ...

addr: ...                               // eax, @[100] ↦ [0,3],[0,130]
```

Starting from `@[100]` $\in [0, 130]$, a static analysis with non-relation abstract domain will infer that both `eax` and `@[100]` range over the interval $[0, 130]$ after the first instruction. Yet, at address **addr**, the computed abstract state will only express that `@[100]` $\in [0, 130]$, while actually `@[100]` $\in [0, 3]$. ⊠

Solution. We propose to enrich the propagated abstract state with a *lightweight relational abstract domain* keeping track of *equalities between arbitrary lhs* (expressions of the form x or $@[e]$) syntactically present in the program. We propose to use an abstract domain of the form $\mathcal{P}^{\#} \triangleq \{\mathcal{C}(x) \mid x \in Lhs\}$ that builds a set of equivalence classes $\mathcal{C}(x) \triangleq \{y \in Lhs \mid x = y\}$. The two key points are (1) the trade-off between efficiency and precision (actually, we lose information in an aggressive manner, keeping only obvious equalities), and (2) the ability to refine the non-relational domains of all *lhs* of an equivalence class when one is refined by a comparison (here, we attach a domain to each class, refined each time a variable of the class is refined, and queried when a variable of the class is evaluated). On Example 5, the technique infers that `@[100] == eax` holds at the beginning of line 2, allowing to refine `@[100]` to $[0, 3]$ at line **addr**.

Our implementation relies on a combination of union-find structure and maps, allowing efficient join and widening in $\mathcal{O}(n.ln(n))$ time, with n the number of *lhs*.

5.2 Widening Point Positioning

Problem. *Widening* [15] is the standard approach to ensure termination of loop treatment. Basically, widening is a kind of join operation satisfying the *non-ascending chain* property. Termination is ensured if each loop contains a widening point. In high-level programs, such widening points are easily deduced from the loop structure. However, binary programs lack such information. While we need to ensure that every cycle in the program control flow contains at least one widening point, there may have several positionings, all ensuring termination but with significant difference in precision, as illustrated in Example 6. Finding an optimal set of widening points is NP-complete [1].

Example 6. This example illustrates the effect of the widening point position on the precision of the final invariant, with widening points ∇_1 and ∇_2.

Program	abstract states (with ∇_1)	abstract states (with ∇_2)
`0: eax:= 0`	`0: eax` $\mapsto [0,0]$	`0: eax` $\mapsto [0,0]$
`1: eax:= eax + 1`	`1: eax` $\mapsto [min, max]$	`1: eax` $\mapsto [0,99]$
`2: ebx:= @[eax](4)`	`2: eax` $\mapsto [min, max]$	`2: eax` $\mapsto [0,100]$
`3: if(eax<100) goto 1`	`3: eax` $\mapsto [min, max]$	`3: eax` $\mapsto [0, max]$
`4:`	`4: eax` $\mapsto [100, max]$	`4: eax` $\mapsto [100, max]$

⊠

Solution. We rely on a depth-first numbering of the CFG nodes for the identification of widening points. Actually, the set of back edges of the depth-first search tree is an admissible set of widening points, as it ensures that each loop in the CFG features at least one widening point. Yet, considering precision, it remains an important decision to make: given a *back* edge $\mathsf{a} \to \mathsf{b}$, which node should be taken at widening point? *Our solution is that a widening point should be positioned at the beginning of a conditional jump (∇_2 here), so that the guarded transfer function can refine the widened abstract state.*

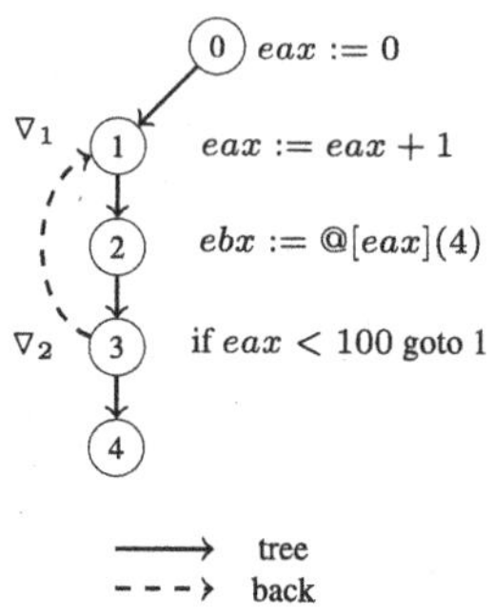

6 Implementation

We have implemented the approaches described so far in BinSec [19,20]. The platform is based on DBA [6,19] and is composed of the following main modules: loading and decoding (ELF and PE, x86 architecture), disassembly and heavy simplification of the resulting IR [19], DBA simulation, dynamic symbolic execution [20], and an ongoing static analysis module BinSec/VA. BinSec is implemented in OCaml. We describe here the static analysis module BinSec/VA. It will be available in open-source at http://binsec.gforge.inria.fr/tools.html.

BinSec/VA provides a generic fixpoint computation for abstract domains given as lattices, allowing one to quickly prototype binary-level analyzers. The main features are the following. **Value domain:** Since overflow and wrapping (between signed and unsigned representations) must be taken into account at binary-level, we keep track of both signed and unsigned values of each lhs, abstracted as a pair of intervals. Then, each component is reduced according to the other one. This *dual interval representation* is very simple (w.r.t. wrapped intervals [29]), and yet it still prevents the most common cases of precision loss. Typically, considering the following dual representation $d^\# \triangleq ([254, 255]_u, [-2, -1]_s)$, then $d^\# + 1$ evaluates to $([0, 255]_u, [-1, 0]_s)$: here the unsigned part loses all precision, while the signed part remains precise. **Memory domain:** Value domains are lifted to byte-precise memory domains in a standard way, following for example [23] (in a simpler manner). **Other**

domains: The analysis also provides flag propagation with template-based recovery and an equality domain as described in Sects. 4 and 5.1.

Trading efficiency for precision. Since binary-level static analysis is very challenging, we give the user several levers for tuning trade-offs between precision and scalability, namely: k-callstring context sensitivity, loop unrolling, and different flavors of widening, such as delayed widening or widening with threshold.

CFG recovery. Precise Control-flow Graph (CFG) recovery is a major issue of binary-level static analysis [7] in presence of dynamic jumps, i.e. jump statements whose target is computed at runtime (like `jmp eax`). In our case, the imprecision due to the use of intervals may lead to significant loss of precision on dynamic jumps. We combine ideas from [3,14] in order to get precise dynamic target evaluation: on a jump instruction, we compute a symbolic representation of the k-predecessors of the instruction, then pass this information enriched with our own forward abstract computation to a SMT solver and query all possible jump targets. Experiments on benchmarks from [14] confirm that the approach is precise and practical.

Precision recovery and degraded mode. In case the address of a `load` or `store` evaluates to $\top$, the user can ask the engine to *refine* the address value with a mechanism similar to that of our CFG recovery. In case refinement fails, the analysis can still enter a *degraded mode* (inspired from [22]), keeping when possible the former (non-$\top$) address value for propagation. Soundness will be lost, yet the analysis can go forward and (hopefully) discover interesting information.

7 Experiments

We want to assess the practical merits of the approach described so far. We are interested in the three following Research Questions: **RQ1:** What is the ability of template-based recovery to effectively recover high-level conditions, especially w.r.t. standard approaches? **RQ2:** What is the overhead of template-based recovery? **RQ3:** Does template-based recovery yield practical benefits to program analysis?

Practical concerns. We consider 66 programs taken from the JULIET/Samate benchmark from NIST [30] and 400 functions taken from 10 standard programs, such as `firefox` or `coreutils`. All programs are 32bit x86 executables for Linux (ELF format). Analysis have been performed with a limited bound on the calldepth (functions are stubbed once the bound is reached). Experiments have been performed on a Intel Core i5 CPU equipped with 8 GB of RAM, and we rely on the Z3 SMT solver with a time-out of 1 s (no time-out was encountered). For the sake of comparison, we have implemented pattern-based recovery and logic-based recovery in BinSec/va.

7.1 Recovery Ability (RQ1) and Efficiency (RQ2)

We compare the three condition recovery approaches on all our benchmark functions. Results are presented in Table 2 (template-based approach) and Table 4 (summary).

The template-based approach performs very well (cf. Table 2), successfully recovering 89 % of all conditions. A manual check on the 218 cases of failure indicates that most of them are actually not high-level conditions (columns DF, PF, x&y=0, CF_*add* in Table 2 – only column opt truly corresponds to unrecovered high-level conditions). The approach recovers in average 95 % of high-level conditions (min: 92 %, max: 100 %).

Moreover, template-based recovery performs significantly better than logic-based and pattern-based approaches, which recover respectively 31 % and 68 % of the total number of conditions (Table 4). A more detailed analysis shows that template-based recovery is strictly better than logic-based recovery (*that was expected*), but also that template-based recovery and pattern-based recovery are not comparable, in the sense that they both recover some conditions not recovered by the other method. *This latter result was unexpected*, as patterns of Table 1 should represent all legitimate uses of flags.

Typically, the pattern-based method was able to recover tests to x&y==0, while template-based recovery typically beats patterns on optimized comparisons introduced by compilers, such as `or eax 0; je ...` for checking `eax = 0` (cf. Table 3).

We can fruitfully combine patterns and templates in the following way: template recovery is used only when no pattern is found. This combination is faster, since patterns are significantly cheaper than templates, and it discovers more

Table 2. Template-based high-level condition recovery

progs	# fun	#loc†	#conds‡	#succ*		#fail						#smt	#cache	time	time$_{all}$
						DF	PF	x&y=0	CF$_{add}$	opt	all			(s)	(s)
firefox	40	21488	150 **(137)**	**134**	89% **(98%)**	2	0	11	0	3	16	234	902	1.40	55.91
cat	40	6490	132 **(125)**	**116**	88% **(92%)**	3	0	4	0	9	16	154	508	1.08	259.24
chmod	40	8954	183 **(172)**	**159**	87% **(92%)**	3	0	8	0	13	24	203	750	1.44	313.17
cp	40	67199	174 **(162)**	**152**	87% **(94%)**	0	0	12	0	10	22	533	4287	4.79	346.84
cut	40	7358	148 **(138)**	**132**	89% **(96%)**	3	0	7	0	6	16	176	527	1.16	211.73
dir	40	9732	137 **(126)**	**118**	86% **(94%)**	5	0	6	0	8	19	159	967	1.26	201.67
echo	40	8016	190 **(182)**	**168**	88% **(92%)**	3	0	5	0	14	22	203	816	1.43	274.60
kill	40	6911	142 **(133)**	**125**	88% **(94%)**	5	0	4	0	8	17	163	520	1.17	209.79
ln	40	88837	203 **(185)**	**177**	87% **(96%)**	3	0	16	0	7	26	558	6565	4.88	531.58
mkdir	40	6347	125 **(117)**	**109**	87% **(93%)**	3	0	5	0	8	16	147	505	1.01	235.80
Verisec	66	11552	394 **(370)**	**370**	87% **(100%)**	0	8	0	16	0	24	463	735	3.31	34.48
total	466	242884	1978 **(1847)**	**1760**	89% **(95%)**	30	8	78	16	86	218	2993	17082	22.93	2674.81

†: number of analyzed instructions only.

‡: total number of conditions (resp. high-level conditions). DF, PF, CF$_{add}$ and $x\&y = 0$ are not considered high-level.

*: total number of successfully recovered conditions, ratio w.r.t. total number of conditions (resp. high-level conditions)

#smt: number of calls to the smt solver – #cache: number of calls to the cache

time: time for recovery alone (s) – time$_{all}$: time for the whole analysis (s)

DF: check on direction flag – PF: check on parity flag – CF$_{add}$: low-level tricks on CF – x&y=0: encoded via `test`

opt: high-level conditions with operand update

Table 3. High-level conditions recovered by templates, not by patterns

Example	Discussion
`or eax, 0 je ...`	The conditional jump is equivalent to `if (eax = 0) then goto ....`
`cmp eax, 0 jns ...`	Because the second operand of `cmp` is zero, checking the sign flag SF is sufficient to check if eax is greater that or equals zero i.e. (eax >= 0). Note that the pattern based method may miss this case if it expects a `jge` or a `jnl` instruction instead of `jns`. Note also that the folklore method may succeed to retrieve the high-level comparison if SF is encoded in DBA as `(eax < 0)` instead of `eax{31, 31}`.
`sar ebp, 1je ...`	Although this case seems to be complicated at first glance, the corresponding high-level predicate is merely equivalent to `if (ebp = 0) then goto ...`, where **ebp** holds its shifted value.
`dec ecx jg ...`	In addition to tracking assignments to flags as symbolic expressions, the template based solution also tracks assignments to operands mentioned in expressions of tracked flags. Hence it is able to infer the following high-level conditional jump `if (ecx` $\geq$ `0) then goto ...`

Table 4. Summary: high-level condition recovery

method	#loc	#conds	#succ[a]	#fail	time	$time_{all}$
templates	242884	1978	**1760 (89 %)**	218	**22.93**	2674.81
logic	247894	2260	**694 (31 %)**	1566	0.003	2561.64
patterns	229255	1987	**1357 (68 %)**	630	0.014	2373.33
templates + patterns	242884	1978	**1838 (92 %)**	140	**9.17**	2659.95
templates **w/o cache**	242884	1978	**1760 (89 %)**	218	29.76	2697.67
templates **w/o filtering**	242884	1978	**1760 (89 %)**	218	51.13	2726.45
templates **w/o cache, w/o filtering)**	242884	1978	**1760 (89 %)**	218	**66.52**	2752.73

[a]: ratio computed w.r.t. the total number of conditions

conditions than templates or patterns alone (especially, tests to x&y==0 are recovered). Results in Table 4 demonstrate a slight improvement in recovery and a 2x speedup.

Performance. Results in Tables 2 and 4 demonstrate that the approach has a low overhead, 1 % in average (column time vs $time_{all}$). Hence, while template-based recovery is indeed much more expensive than the two other methods (Table 4), the extra-cost is clearly affordable. Finally, optimizations allow to win a factor 3x on average, up to 20x.

Conclusion. The template-based recovery approach is able to recover a large part of high-level conditions (**RQ1**), achieving significantly better results than related approaches. Especially, it can recover optimized comparisons introduced at compile-time, while they are beyond the scope of the pattern approach, and it can also sometimes synthesizes high-level conditions from low-level conditions with a priori no high-level counter-part in the source code. Concerning efficiency (**RQ2**), the method is very cheap, in the sense that its overhead w.r.t. the whole analysis cost is negligible. Moreover, templates can be fruitfully combined with patterns.

7.2 Practical Impact (RQ3)

We consider two potential applications of this work: precision of static analysis and deobfuscation.

Application to value analysis. We are interested here in evaluating the gain of precision brought by better high-level condition recovery to a standard forward value propagation. We compare several versions of BINSEC/VA, based on templates, patterns and logic. Results are presented in Table 5. Here, template-based recovery leads to the computation of abstract memory states which are strictly more precise than those computed with logic-based recovery (on 41 % of analyzed locations, up to 64 %) and than those computed with pattern-based recovery (on 18 % of analyzed locations, up to 38 %). Moreover, template-based

Table 5. Precision comparison between different condition recovery methods

progs	#loc[a]	# fail	# fail	# fail	$\#loc_{\sqsubset}$	$\#loc_{\sqsubset}$
		templ.	logic	patterns	logic vs templ.	pattern vs templ.
firefox	15099	242	433	400	8852 (59 %)	5725 (38 %)
cat	4192	136	143	145	1171 (28 %)	604 (14 %)
chmod	5768	188	201	202	1252 (22 %)	652 (11 %)
cp	5605	152	161	152	3237 (58 %)	545 (10 %)
cut	4870	148	232	156	1686 (35 %)	605 (12 %)
dir	5022	144	147	148	1442 (29 %)	700 (14 %)
echo	5570	176	185	186	2616 (47 %)	1009 (18 %)
kill	4626	150	157	158	1245 (27 %)	625 (14 %)
ln	8091	243	248	293	5166 (64 %)	815 (10 %)
mkdir	4062	134	141	142	1139 (28 %)	589 (15 %)
Verisec	8334	28	137	153	1474 (18 %)	1075 (13 %)
total	71239	1741	2185	2135	29280 (41 %)	12944 (18 %)

[a]: number of instructions analyzed by all three analyzers (instr. missed by at least one analyzer are discarded).

#fail: number of failures in the analysis due to a load/store index or jump expression evaluating to $\top$

$\#loc_{\sqsubset}$: number of locations for which the abstract state computed by template-recovery is strictly more precise than the one computed with logic (resp. pattern) recovery

recovery does allow us to reduce the number of analysis failures in a tangible way (−18 % in average, up to −80 % on Verisec and −40 % on firefox).

Application to deobfuscation. Obfuscation techniques aim at tricking reversers (either humans or tools) for preventing them to understand how a piece of code works. While it is legitimately used for IP protection, it is also massively used for malware protection, hence the need for automatic binary-level analysis of obfuscated programs. The code snippet `cmp eax ebx ; cmc ; jae` illustrates an obfuscation technique (reported in [32]) aiming at luring the reverser on the real semantic of a conditional jump. The standard `cmp eax ebx ; jae` pattern is usually read as branching on $eax \geq_u ebx$. But `jae` actually reads the carry flag `cf` (see Table 1), which is inverted by the `cmc` instruction. Hence, here, the true semantic of `jae` will be to branch on condition $eax <_u ebx$. *Template-based recovery succeeds to recover the true semantic of the jump, while pattern-based recovery and logic-based recovery fail.*

8 Related Works

Logic-based [11,25,27,31], pattern-based [13] and virtual flag [31] solutions have already been lengthy discussed in Sect. 2. Basically our approach extends the logic-based method, and it is orthogonal to pattern in terms of recovery ability (yet, templates recover significantly more conditions than patterns). Templates can also be fruitfully combined with virtual flags and patterns, if available. Especially, very specific conditions such as `x&y==0` can be recovered this way. Finally, note that many syntactic disassembly techniques use patterns in an unsound way, for example not taking operand or flag updates into account.

Other more general proposed solution consists in tracing the bit-level calculation of flags. In this case, SAT solving is used to reason about values of variables. However, using SAT solving to perform static analysis faces scalability problems as soon as non-trivial loops are analyzed, even when combining SAT solving with abstraction to numeric ranges [10]. Interestingly, binary-level underapproximated techniques such as DSE [4] do not face this issue, and can rely on SAT solving and low-level flag encoding w/o any serious penalty.

9 Conclusion

We have presented template-based recovery, a sound and generic technique for recovering high-level conditions from binary codes. The method performs significantly better than state-of-the-art approaches, and it can also be combined with some of them. Template-based recovery can help to adapt any formal analysis from source-level analysis to binary-level analysis, and it can also be useful for reverse engineering.

References

1. Bourdoncle, F.: Efficient chaotic iteration strategies with widenings. In: Bjørner, D., Broy, M., Pottosin, I.V. (eds.) Formal Methods in Programming and Their Applications, vol. 735, pp. 128–141. Springer, Heidelberg (1993)
2. Ball, T., Cook, B., Levin, V., Rajamani, S.K.: SLAM and static driver verifier: technology transfer of formal methods inside Microsoft. In: Boiten, E.A., Derrick, J., Smith, G. (eds.) IFM 2004. LNCS, vol. 2999, pp. 1–20. Springer, Heidelberg (2004). doi:10.1007/978-3-540-24756-2_1
3. Bardin, S., Delahaye, M., David, R., Kosmatov, N., Papadakis, M., Traon, Y.L., Marion, J.: Sound and quasi-complete detection of infeasible test requirements. In: ICST 2015, pp. 1–10. IEEE, Graz (2015)
4. Bardin, S., Herrmann, P.: Structural testing of executables. In: ICST 2008. IEEE, Los Alamitos (2013)
5. Balakrishnan, G., Reps, T.: DIVINE: DIscovering variables IN executables. In: Cook, B., Podelski, A. (eds.) VMCAI 2007. LNCS, vol. 4349, pp. 1–28. Springer, Heidelberg (2007). doi:10.1007/978-3-540-69738-1_1
6. Bardin, S., Herrmann, P., Leroux, J., Ly, O., Tabary, R., Vincent, A.: The BINCOA framework for binary code analysis. In: Gopalakrishnan, G., Qadeer, S. (eds.) CAV 2011. LNCS, vol. 6806, pp. 165–170. Springer, Heidelberg (2011). doi:10.1007/978-3-642-22110-1_13
7. Bardin, S., Herrmann, P., Védrine, F.: Refinement-based CFG reconstruction from unstructured programs. In: Jhala, R., Schmidt, D. (eds.) VMCAI 2011. LNCS, vol. 6538, pp. 54–69. Springer, Heidelberg (2011). doi:10.1007/978-3-642-18275-4_6
8. Brumley, D., Jager, I., Avgerinos, T., Schwartz, E.J.: BAP: a binary analysis platform. In: Gopalakrishnan, G., Qadeer, S. (eds.) CAV 2011. LNCS, vol. 6806, pp. 463–469. Springer, Heidelberg (2011). doi:10.1007/978-3-642-22110-1_37
9. Brauer, J., King, A.: Transfer function synthesis without quantifier elimination. In: Barthe, G. (ed.) ESOP 2011. LNCS, vol. 6602, pp. 97–115. Springer, Heidelberg (2011). doi:10.1007/978-3-642-19718-5_6
10. Brauer, J., King, A.: Automatic abstraction for intervals using boolean formulae. In: Cousot, R., Martel, M. (eds.) SAS 2010. LNCS, vol. 6337, pp. 167–183. Springer, Heidelberg (2010). doi:10.1007/978-3-642-15769-1_11
11. Blazy, S., Laporte, V., Pichardie, D.: Verified abstract interpretation techniques for disassembling low-level self-modifying code. In: Klein, G., Gamboa, R. (eds.) ITP 2014. LNCS, vol. 8558, pp. 128–143. Springer, Heidelberg (2014). doi:10.1007/978-3-319-08970-6_9
12. Balakrishnan, G., Reps, T.: Analyzing memory accesses in x86 executables. In: Duesterwald, E. (ed.) CC 2004. LNCS, vol. 2985, pp. 5–23. Springer, Heidelberg (2004). doi:10.1007/978-3-540-24723-4_2
13. Balakrishnan, G., Reps, T.W.: WYSINWYX: what you see is not what you eXecute. ACM Trans. Program. Lang. Syst. **36**, 23:1–23:84 (2010)
14. Reinbacher, T., Brauer, J.: Precise control flow reconstruction using boolean logic. In: EMSOFT 2011. ACM (2011)
15. Cousot, P., Cousot, R.: Abstract interpretation: a unified lattice model for static analysis of programs by construction or approximation of fixpoints. In: ACM Symposium on Principles of Programming Languages, POPL, pp. 238–252. ACM (1977)
16. Cousot, P., Cousot, R.: Abstract interpretation frameworks. J. Logic Comput. **2**, 511–547 (1992)

17. Cousot, P., Cousot, R., Feret, J., Mauborgne, L., Miné, A., Monniaux, D., Rival, X.: The ASTREÉ analyzer. In: Sagiv, M. (ed.) ESOP 2005. LNCS, vol. 3444, pp. 21–30. Springer, Heidelberg (2005). doi:10.1007/978-3-540-31987-0_3
18. Dullien, T., Porst, S.: REIL: a platform-independent intermediate representation of disassembled code for static code analysis. In: CanSecWest (2009). http://www.zynamics.com/downloads/csw09.pdf
19. Djoudi, A., Bardin, S.: BINSEC: binary code analysis with low-level regions. In: Baier, C., Tinelli, C. (eds.) TACAS 2015. LNCS, vol. 9035, pp. 212–217. Springer, Heidelberg (2015). doi:10.1007/978-3-662-46681-0_17
20. David, R., Bardin, S., Ta, T.D., Feist, J., Mounier, L., Potet, M., Marion, J.: BINSEC/SE: a dynamic symbolic execution toolkit for binary-level analysis. In: SANER (2016)
21. Intel® 64 and IA-32 Architectures Software Developer's Manual. Order Number: 32546
22. Kinder, J., Kravchenko, D.: Alternating control flow reconstruction. In: Kuncak, V., Rybalchenko, A. (eds.) VMCAI 2012. LNCS, vol. 7148, pp. 267–282. Springer, Heidelberg (2012). doi:10.1007/978-3-642-27940-9_18
23. Kirchner, F., Kosmatov, N., Prevosto, V., Signoles, J., Yakobowski, B.: Frama-C: a software analysis perspective. Formal Asp. Comput. **27**, 573–609 (2015)
24. Kinder, J., Zuleger, F., Veith, H.: An abstract interpretation-based framework for control flow reconstruction from binaries. In: Jones, N.D., Müller-Olm, M. (eds.) VMCAI 2009. LNCS, vol. 5403, pp. 214–228. Springer, Heidelberg (2008). doi:10.1007/978-3-540-93900-9_19
25. Logozzo, F., Fähndrich, M.: On the relative completeness of bytecode analysis versus source code analysis. In: Hendren, L. (ed.) CC 2008. LNCS, vol. 4959, pp. 197–212. Springer, Heidelberg (2008). doi:10.1007/978-3-540-78791-4_14
26. Mycroft, A.: Type-based decompilation (or program reconstruction via type reconstruction). In: Swierstra, S.D. (ed.) ESOP 1999. LNCS, vol. 1576, pp. 208–223. Springer, Heidelberg (1999). doi:10.1007/3-540-49099-X_14
27. Miné, A.: Symbolic methods to enhance the precision of numerical abstract domains. In: Emerson, E.A., Namjoshi, K.S. (eds.) VMCAI 2006. LNCS, vol. 3855, pp. 348–363. Springer, Heidelberg (2005). doi:10.1007/11609773_23
28. Nielson, F., Nielson, H.R., Hankin, C.: Principles of Program Analysis. Springer-Verlag New York, Inc., New York (1999)
29. Navas, J.A., Schachte, P., Søndergaard, H., Stuckey, P.J.: Signedness-agnostic program analysis: precise integer bounds for low-level code. In: Jhala, R., Igarashi, A. (eds.) APLAS 2012. LNCS, vol. 7705, pp. 115–130. Springer, Heidelberg (2012). doi:10.1007/978-3-642-35182-2_9
30. https://samate.nist.gov/SARD/testsuite.php
31. Sepp, A., Mihaila, B., Simon, A.: Precise static analysis of binaries by extracting relational information. In: WCRE 2011. IEEE, Los Alamitos (2011)
32. Yadegari, B., Johannesmeyer, B., Whitely, B., Debray, S.: A generic approach to automatic deobfuscation of executable code. In: SP 2015. IEEE (2015)

Upper and Lower Amortized Cost Bounds of Programs Expressed as Cost Relations

Antonio Flores-Montoya(✉)

Department of Computer Science, TU Darmstadt, Darmstadt, Germany
aeflores@cs.tu-darmstadt.de

Abstract. Resource analysis aims at statically obtaining bounds on the resource consumption of programs in terms of input parameters. A well known approach to resource analysis is based on transforming the target program into a set of cost relations, then solving these into a closed-form bound. In this paper we develop a new analysis for computing *upper and lower cost bounds* of programs expressed as cost relations. The analysis is *compositional*: it computes the cost of each loop or function separately and composes the obtained expressions to obtain the total cost. Despite being modular, the analysis can obtain precise upper and lower bounds of programs with *amortized* cost. The key is to obtain bounds that depend on the values of the variables at the beginning and *at the end* of each program part. In addition we use a novel cost representation called *cost structure*. It allows to reduce the inference of complex polynomial expressions to a set of linear problems that can be solved efficiently. We implemented our method and performed an extensive experimental evaluation that demonstrates its power.

Keywords: Cost analysis · Cost relations · Amortized cost · Lower bounds

1 Introduction

Cost or resource analysis aims at statically obtaining bounds on the resource consumption (such as time or memory consumption) of programs in terms of their input parameters. Such bounds constitute useful feedback for developers and help detect performance bugs. This is particularly relevant in the context of cloud applications where one pays according to the amount of resources used.

One common approach for computing both upper and lower bounds is based on *cost relations* (CRs) which are similar to recurrence equations annotated with linear constraints [2]. In this approach, the cost analysis is carried out in two phases: (1) given a program, for the given resource we want to measure (time, memory, etc.), we generate a set of recursive *cost relations* (CRs) that represent the cost of the program for the given resource; and (2) the CRs are then analyzed and a closed-form upper (or lower) bound expression is computed. Here CRs act as a language-independent intermediate representation. The second phase

J. Fitzgerald et al. (Eds.): FM 2016, LNCS 9995, pp. 254–273, 2016.
DOI: 10.1007/978-3-319-48989-6_16

Program 1

```
1 {x > 0, y > 0, z > 0}
2 void p1(int x,y,z){
3   while(x>0) {
4     x--;
5     y++;
6     while(y>0 && *)
7       y--;//tick(2);
8   }
9   while(y>0){
10    y--;
11    int i=0;
12    while(i<z)
13      i++;//tick(1);
14 }}
```

Cost relations:

1: $p1(x,y,z) = wh3(x,y,x_o,y_o) + wh9(y_o,z)$	$\{x > 0, y > 0, z > 0\}$
2: $wh3(x,y,x_o,y_o) = 0$	$\{x = x_o = 0, y_o = y\}$
3: $wh3(x,y,x_o,y_o) = wh6(y_1,y_2) + wh3(x',y',x_o,y_o)$	$\{x > 0, x' = x - 1, y_1 = y + 1, y' = y_2\}$
4: $wh6(y,y_o) = 0$	$\{y = y_o\}$
5: $wh6(y,y_o) = 2 + wh6(y',y_o)$	$\{y \geq 1, y' = y - 1\}$
6: $wh9(y,z) = 0$	$\{y \leq 0\}$
7: $wh9(y,z) = wh12(0,z) + wh9(y',z)$	$\{y \geq 1, y' = y - 1, z > 0\}$
8: $wh12(i,z) = 0$	$\{i \geq z\}$
9: $wh12(i,z) = 1 + wh12(i',z)$	$\{i < z, i' = i + 1\}$

Upper bound $= max(2,z) * (x + y)$
Lower bound $= min(2,z) * (x + y)$

Fig. 1. Program 1 and its cost relations

of the analysis can be reused to solve CRs generated from programs written in different source languages (e.g., Java bytecode [4], ABS [1,17], Llvm IR [18]) and to measure different kinds of resources such as time or memory. Our work focuses on that second part of the analysis. Given a set of CRs, we present an analysis that obtains closed-form upper and lower bounds of its cost.

Example 1. Consider program 1 in Fig. 1. We use $tick(c)$ annotations to indicate that c resource units are consumed (or released if c is negative) at an execution point. The term $*$ (in line 6) represents an unknown value. Assuming the initial values of x, y and z are positive, the upper and lower cost bounds of function p1 are $max(2,z) * (x + y)$ and $min(2,z) * (x + y)$, respectively.

In the CR representation, we have 5 cost relations: $p1$, $wh3$, $wh6$, $wh9$ and $wh12$: one for the function p1 and one for each while loop located at lines 3, 6, 9 and 12. Each cost relation is composed of a set of cost equations. Each cost equation (CE) corresponds to a path of a loop or function and defines its cost. Each CE is annotated with set of linear constraints that model the conditions for its applicability and its behavior.

Consider CE 8 that represents the case where the loop condition is unsatisfied. Its cost is 0 and its constraint set is $\{i \geq z\}$. Conversely, CE 9 represents the case where $i < z$ and the loop body is executed. CE 9 defines the cost of $wh12(i,z)$ as the cost of one iteration plus the cost of the remaining loop $wh12(i',z)$, where i' represents the value of i after one iteration $i' = i + 1$. In loop $wh12$ the cost of one iteration is 2 and the final value of y (i.e., y_o) is included in the abstraction. Observe that at the base case of $wh6$ in CE 4 the initial and final values of y are equal: $y = y_o$. The inclusion of final variable values in loops such as $wh6$ and $wh3$ is essential to compute precise bounds. Note that $wh6$ is non-deterministic, because the constraints of CE 4 and 5 are not mutually exclusive (due to the unknown value $*$).

Cost relations have several advantages over other abstract representations: They support recursive programs naturally. In fact, loops are modelled as recursive definitions and that allows us to analyze loops and recursive functions in a uniform manner. In contrast, difference constraints do not support recursion [26] and integer rewrite systems need to be extended [9]. More importantly, CRs have a modular structure. Each loop or function is abstracted into a separate cost relation. This enables a compositional approach to compute the cost of a program by combining the costs of its parts.

In our example, we first compute the cost of entering the inner loop $wh6$, then use it to compute the cost of the outer loop $wh3$. Similarly for loops $wh12$ and $wh9$. Finally, we combine the cost of loop $wh3$ with that of loop $wh9$ to obtain the total cost of the program. Each relation is computed only once.

Besides being compositional, we want our analysis to be precise. This is challenging for program 1, because it presents *amortized* cost: taken individually, the cost of entering loop $wh6$ once is at most $2 * (x + y)$ (in terms of $p1$'s input parameters). But the loop can be entered x times and still its total cost is at most $2 * (x + y)$ and not $2 * (x + y) * x$ as one might expect. This is even more relevant for lower bounds. Considered individually, the cost of $wh3$ can be 0 (if no iterations of the inner loop $wh6$ are executed) and the cost of $wh9$ can also be 0 (if the inner loop $wh6$ iterates until y reaches 0). However, the lower cost bound of $wh3$ followed by $wh9$ is $min(2, z) * (x + y)$. We know of no other cost analysis method that can infer a precise lower bound of program 1.

As noted in [8], a key aspect to obtain precise bounds for programs with amortized cost is to take the final variable values into account. In our example, if we infer that the cost of $wh3$ and $wh9$ is $2*(x+y-y_0)$ and $z*(y_0)$, respectively (in the context of CE 1), we can cancel the positive and negative y_0 summand and obtain the upper and lower bounds reported in Fig. 1. Unfortunately, the approach of [8] is computationally expensive and does not scale to larger programs. We propose instead to represent cost by a combination of simple expressions and constraints (cost structures), where the inference of complex resource bounds is reduced to the solution of (relatively) small linear programming problems.

The contributions are: (1) A new cost representation (cost structure) that can represent complex polynomial upper and lower bounds (Sect. 3); and (2) techniques to infer cost structures of cost relations in terms of the initial and final values of the variables and compose them precisely (obtaining amortized cost) and efficiently (Sects. 4 and 5); (3) the implementation of the analysis as part of an open source cost analysis tool CoFloCo[1]; (4) an extensive experimental evaluation for both upper and lower bounds comparing our tool with other cost analysis tools: KoAT [9], Loopus [26], C4B [10] and the previous version of CoFloCo [15] for upper bounds and PUBS [5] for lower bounds (Sect. 7).

[1] https://github.com/aeflores/CoFloCo.

2 Preliminaries

In this section, we formally define the concepts and conventions used in the rest of the paper. The symbol $\overline{x}$ represents a sequence of variables $x_1, x_2, \cdots, x_n$ of any length. We represent the concatenation of $\overline{x}$ and $\overline{y}$ as $\overline{xy}$. A variable assignment $\alpha : V \mapsto D$ maps variables from the set of variables V to elements of a domain D. Let t be a term, $\alpha(t)$ denotes the replacement of all the variables x in t by $\alpha(x)$. The variable assignment $\alpha|_V$ is the restriction of α to the domain V. A *linear expression* has the form $l(\overline{x}) := q_0 + q_1 * x_1 + \cdots + q_n * x_n$ where $q_i \in \mathbb{Q}$ and $x_1, x_2, \cdots, x_n$ are variables. A *linear constraint* over $\overline{x}$ is $lc(\overline{x}) := l(\overline{x}) \geq 0$ where $l(\overline{x})$ is a linear expression. For readability we often express linear constraints as $l_1 \leq l_2$, $l_1 = l_2$ or $l_1 \geq l_2$. These can be easily transformed to the form above. A *constraint set* $\varphi(\overline{x})$ is a conjunction of linear constraints $lc_1(\overline{x}) \wedge lc_2(\overline{x}) \wedge \cdots \wedge lc_n(\overline{x})$. A constraint set $\varphi(\overline{x})$ is *satisfiable* if there exists an assignment $\alpha : V \mapsto \mathbb{Q}$ such that $\varphi(\overline{\alpha(x)})$ is valid (α satisfies $\varphi(\overline{x})$). We say that $\varphi(\overline{x}) \Rightarrow \varphi'(\overline{x})$ if every assignment that satisfies $\varphi(\overline{x})$ satisfies $\varphi'(\overline{x})$ as well. Next, we define cost relations which are our abstract representation of programs:

Definition 1 (Cost relation). *A* cost relation C *is a set of* cost equations $c := \langle C(\overline{x}) = q + \sum_{i=1}^{n} D_i(\overline{y_i}), \varphi(\overline{xy})\rangle$, *where $q \in \mathbb{Q}$; C and D_i are cost relation symbols; and $\varphi(\overline{xy})$ is a constraint set that relates the variables on the left side $C(\overline{x})$ and those in the $D_i(\overline{y_i})$ where $\overline{y} = \overline{y_1 y_2 \cdots y_n}$.*

A cost equation (CE) $\langle C(\overline{x}) = q + \sum_{i=1}^{n} D_i(\overline{y_i}), \varphi(\overline{xy})\rangle$ states that the cost of $C(\overline{x})$ is q plus the sum of the costs of each $D_i(\overline{y_i})$. The constraint set $\varphi(\overline{xy})$ serves two purposes: it restricts the applicability of the equation with respect to the input variables $\overline{x}$ and it relates the variables $\overline{x}$ with each $\overline{y_i}$. One can view a CR C as a non-deterministic function that executes a cost equation in C. Given a cost equation $\langle C(\overline{x}) = q + \sum_{i=1}^{n} D_i(\overline{y_i}), \varphi(\overline{xy})\rangle$, C consumes q resources and calls the functions $D_1, D_2, \ldots, D_n$.

2.1 Cost Relation Refinement

In this work, we do not consider arbitrary CRs but instead CRs that are the result of a control-flow refinement presented in [15]. This refinement produces a set of execution patterns (called chains and denoted *ch*) for each CR. These execution patterns are regular expressions of CE identifiers and represent all possible executions of the CR. The formal definition of chains is as follows:

Definition 2 (Phase, Chain). *Let C be a cost relation. A* phase *(ph) can be: (1) one or more recursive CEs executed a positive number of times $(c_1 \vee \cdots \vee c_n)^+$ with $c_i \in C$; or (2) a single (non-recursive) CE executed once (c_i).*

A chain *(ch) is a sequence of phases $ch := [ph_1 \cdot ph_2 \cdots ph_n]$ in C. A chain can represent a terminating execution if ph_n contains a single non-recursive CE (c_i) or a non-terminating execution if ph_n has the form $(c_1 \vee \cdots \vee c_n)^+$.*

1.1:	$p1(x,y,z) = wh3[(3.1 \vee 3.2)^{+}2](x,y,x_o,y_o) + wh9[6](y_o,z)$ $\{x>0, y>0, z>0, \mathbf{x_o = 0, y_o \leq 0}\}$
1.2:	$p1(x,y,z) = wh3[(3.1 \vee 3.2)^{+}2](x,y,x_o,y_o) + wh9[7.1^{+}6](y_o,z)$ $\{x>0, y>0, z>0, \mathbf{x_o = 0, y_o > 0, x + y \geq y_o}\}$
3.1:	$wh3(x,y,x_o,y_o) = wh6[4](y_1,y_2) + wh3(x',y',x_o,y_o)$ $\{x>0, x'=x-1, y_1=y+1, y'=y_2, \mathbf{y_2 = y_1}\}$
3.2:	$wh3(x,y,x_o,y_o) = wh6[5^{+}4](y_1,y_2) + wh3(x',y',x_o,y_o)$ $\{x>0, x'=x-1, y_1=y+1, y'=y_2, \mathbf{y_2 < y_1}\}$
7.1:	$wh9(y,z) = wh12[9^{+}8](0,z) + wh9(y',z)$ $\{y \geq 1, y'=y-1, z>0\}$

Fig. 2. Refined cost equations from Program 1

For instance, the CR $wh6$ contains two phases $(5)^{+}$ and (4) (where a number n refers to CE n in Fig. 1). From these phases, we can have two chains '[4]' and '$[5^{+}4]$' that represent the case where the loop body is not executed '[4]' and the case when it is executed a finite number of times '$[5^{+}4]$'. In principle, we could also have a non-terminating chain '$[5^{+}]$' but the refinement in [15] discards non-terminating chains that can be proved terminating. Any external reference to a CR C_1 from another CR C_2 is annotated with a chain: C_1ch that determines which CEs will be applied and in which order. In this manner, the cost equations are refined. CE 3 from Fig. 1 becomes CE 3.1 and 3.2 in Fig. 2 which contain annotated references to $wh6$ with the corresponding chains $wh6[4](y_1,y_2)$ and $wh6[5^{+}4](y_1,y_2)$. Similarly, CE 1 becomes 1.1 and 1.2 in Fig. 2 and CE 7 becomes 7.1. The constraint sets of the refined equations also contain a summary of the behavior of these references (the bold constraints in Fig. 2). Note that the refinement discards unfeasible references. For example, CR $wh9$ does not have a reference to $wh12[8]$ because z is guaranteed to be positive.

The refined CRs can be ordered in a sequence $\langle C_1, C_2 \dots C_n\rangle$ in which a cost equation of C_i can contain at most one recursive reference to C_i and any number of references to C_j $j > i$ annotated with chains of C_j. Its general form is: $\langle C_i(\overline{x}) = q + \sum_{i=1}^{n} Dch_i(\overline{y_i}) + C_i(\overline{x'}), \varphi(\overline{xx'y})\rangle$ where $D \in \{C_{i+1} \dots C_n\}$ if it is recursive or without the summand $+C_i(\overline{x'})$ if it is non-recursive.

Most programs can be expressed as refined CRs [15]. The only current limitation of this approach is the analysis of CRs with multiple recursion (when a CE contains more than one recursive reference).

2.2 Refined Cost Relation Semantics

Cost relations can be evaluated to a cost with respect to a variable assignment $\alpha : V \mapsto \mathbb{Q}$. We define the evaluation relation $\Downarrow$ for refined CRs. This relation is not meant to be executed but rather to serve as a formal definition of the cost of CRs. Figure 3 contains the rules for evaluating chains, phases and CEs.

We write a non-recursive CE $\langle C(\overline{x}) = k_0 + \sum_{i=1}^{n} Dch_i(\overline{y_i}), \varphi(\overline{xx'y})\rangle$ as $nrc(\overline{x})$. Rule (Non-recursive CE) extends the assignment α to α' such that it is defined for $\overline{y}$ and the constraint set of the CE is valid $\varphi(\alpha'(\overline{xy}))$.

$$\text{(NON-RECURSIVE CE)}\quad \frac{\alpha = \alpha'|_{\overline{x}} \quad \varphi(\alpha'(\overline{xy})) \quad \bigwedge_{i=1}^{n} (\langle \alpha'|_{\overline{y_i}}, ch_i(\overline{y_i})\rangle \Downarrow k_i)}{\langle \alpha, nrc(\overline{x})\rangle \Downarrow k_0 + \sum_{i=1}^{n} k_i}$$

$$\text{(RECURSIVE CE)}\quad \frac{\alpha = \alpha'|_{\overline{xx'}} \quad \varphi(\alpha'(\overline{xx'y})) \quad \bigwedge_{i=1}^{n} (\langle \alpha'|_{\overline{y_i}}, ch_i(\overline{y_i})\rangle \Downarrow k_i)}{\langle \alpha, rc(\overline{xx'})\rangle \Downarrow k_0 + \sum_{i=1}^{n} k_i}$$

$$\text{(BASE PHASE)}\quad \frac{\langle \alpha, c_i(\overline{xx_f})\rangle \Downarrow k}{\langle \alpha, (c_1 \vee \cdots \vee c_n)^+(\overline{xx_f})\rangle \Downarrow k}$$

$$\text{(REC PHASE)}\quad \frac{\alpha = \alpha'|_{\overline{xx_f}} \quad \langle \alpha'|_{\overline{xx'}}, c_i(\overline{xx'})\rangle \Downarrow k_1 \quad \langle \alpha'|_{\overline{x'x_f}}, (c_1 \vee \cdots \vee c_n)^+(\overline{x'x_f})\rangle \Downarrow k_2}{\langle \alpha, (c_1 \vee \cdots \vee c_n)^+(\overline{xx_f})\rangle \Downarrow k_1 + k_2}$$

$$\text{(CHAIN)}\quad \frac{\alpha = \alpha'|_{\overline{x}} \quad \bigwedge_{i=1}^{n} (\langle \alpha'|_{\overline{x_i x_{i+1}}}, ph_i(\overline{x_i x_{i+1}})\rangle \Downarrow k_i)}{\langle \alpha, [ph_1 \cdots ph_n](\overline{x})\rangle \Downarrow \sum_{i=1}^{n} k_i}$$

Fig. 3. Semantics for the evaluation of chains, phases and cost equations

The cost of $nrc(\overline{x})$ with variable assignment α is the sum of the costs of the evaluations of the chains referenced by $nrc(\overline{x})$ plus k_0. A recursive CE $\langle C(\overline{x}) = k_0 + \sum_{i=1}^{n} Dch_i(\overline{y_i}) + C(\overline{x'}), \varphi(\overline{xx'y})\rangle$ is written $rc(\overline{xx'})$. Because a recursive CE always appears within a recursive phase $(c_1 \vee \cdots \vee c_n)^+$, we will not include the recursive reference during its evaluation. That is, (RECURSIVE CE) does not add the cost of the recursive reference. That will be instead considered in the evaluation of the *phase*. Hence, (RECURSIVE CE) and (NON-RECURSIVE CE) are almost identical, but we include the variables $\overline{x'}$ of the recursive reference in the former so they can be matched with the initial variables of the next CE in the phase. Rules (REC PHASE) and (BASE PHASE) define the recursive evaluation of a phase. As before we include the variables of the last recursive reference $\overline{x_f}$ in the phase representation $(c_1 \vee \cdots \vee c_n)^+(\overline{xx_f})$ so they can be matched with the initial variables of the next phase in the chain. Finally, the evaluation of a chain is the sum of the evaluations of its phases. If the chain is terminating, ph_n will be $(nrc(\overline{x}))$ and the sequence of variables $\overline{x_{n+1}}$ will be empty. If the chain is non-terminating, ph_n will be $(c_1 \vee \cdots \vee c_n)^+$ and $\overline{x_{n+1}}$ will be undefined.

We follow the same evaluation structure to compute bounds. We also compute bounds that depend on the variables of the recursive references for CEs $(\overline{x'})$ and for phases $(\overline{x_f})$. This might seem unnecessary at first, but it allows us to compute precise bounds in a modular way. Consider the chain '$[5^+4]$' of CR $wh6$. We want to obtain the precise (upper and lower) bound $2(y - y_0)$ but when we consider the phase $(5)^+$, we do not have any information about how y_0 relates to y (which is contained in CE 4). Instead, we infer the cost of $(5)^+$ as $2(y - y_f)$, where y_f is the value of y in the last recursive reference of $(5)^+$. Later we combine this bound with the information of CE 4 $\{y = y_o\}$ to obtain $2(y - y_0)$.

3 Cost Structures

In order to obtain upper and lower bounds, we developed a symbolic cost representation that can represent the costs of chains, phases or CEs. We call this cost representation *cost structure.*

We define cost structures as combinations of linear expressions in such a way that they can be inferred and composed by merely solving problems over sets of linear constraints. Instead of a single complex expression, we use simple linear cost expressions E over *intermediate variables* (iv) and constraints that bind the intermediate variables to the variables of the CRs. We distinguish two kinds of constraints. *non-final* constraints IC that relate intermediate variables among each other and *final* constraints $FC(\overline{x})$ that relate intermediate variables with the variables of the CRs ($\overline{x}$). The formal definition of cost structures is as follows:

Definition 3 (Cost Structure). *A* cost structure *is a tuple* $\langle E, IC, FC(\overline{x})\rangle$.

- *E is the main cost expression and is a linear expression $l(\overline{iv})$ over intermediate variables. Intermediate variables always represent positive numbers.*
- *Let $\bowtie$ be $\leq$ or $\geq$. IC is a set of* non-final *constraints of the form $\sum_{k=1}^{m} iv_k \bowtie SE$ where SE can be $SE := l(\overline{iv}) \mid iv_i * iv_j \mid max(\overline{iv}) \mid min(\overline{iv})$.*
- *$FC(\overline{x})$ is a set of* final *constraints of the form $\sum_{k=1}^{m} iv_k \bowtie |l(\overline{x})|$ where $|l(\overline{x})| := max(l(\overline{x}), 0)$ and $l(\overline{x})$ is a linear expression over the CR variables.*

Even though the constraints in IC and $FC(\overline{x})$ are relatively simple, we can express complex polynomial expressions by combining them. In Fig. 4 we have some of the cost structures of program 1 that will be obtained in the following sections ($a = b$ stands for $a \leq b$ and $a \geq b$). Thanks to the constraints we can represent both upper and lower bounds with a single cost structure. Moreover, we can have several constraints that bind the same intermediate variables and thus represent multiple bound candidates. Finally, having multiple iv on the left side of the constraints can represent a disjunction or choice. This is the case for $iv_6 + iv_3 = |y + x|$ of chain [1.2]. The bigger iv_6 is, the smaller iv_3 becomes. This capability is key to obtain a non-trivial lower bound for program 1.

We infer cost structures incrementally. In a sequence of CRs $\langle C_1, C_2 \dots C_n\rangle$, we start with C_n and proceed backwards until C_1. For each C_i we compute the

Chain/Phase/CE(Variables): Cost Structure

$[1.2](x, y, z) : \langle iv_2 + 2iv_6, \{iv_2 = iv_3 * iv_4\}, \{iv_3 + iv_6 = |y + x|, iv_4 = |z|\}\rangle$
- $[(3.1 \vee 3.2)^+ 2](x, y, x_o, y_o) : \langle 2iv_6, \emptyset, \{iv_6 = |y - y_o + x|\}\rangle$
  - $(3.1 \vee 3.2)^+(x_s, y_s, x_{os}, y_{os}, x_f, y_f, x_{of}, y_{of}) : \langle 2iv_6, \emptyset, \{iv_6 = |y_s + x_s - y_f - x_f|\}\rangle$
    - $3.2(x, y, x_o, y_o, x', y', x'_o, y'_o) : \langle 2iv_5, \emptyset, \{iv_5 = |y - y' + 1|\}\rangle$
- $[7.1^+ 6](y, z) : \langle iv_2, \{iv_2 = iv_3 * iv_4\}, \{iv_3 = |y|, iv_4 = |z|\}\rangle$
  - $(7.1)^+(y_s, z_s, y_f, z_f) : \langle iv_2, \{iv_2 = iv_3 * iv_4\}, \{iv_3 = |y_s - y_f|, iv_4 = |z_s|\}\rangle$
    - $7.1(y, z, y', z') : \langle iv_1, \emptyset, \{iv_1 = |z|\}\rangle$

Fig. 4. Some of the cost structures of Program 1

cost structures of the CEs first (Sect. 4), then of the phases (Sect. 5) and finally of the chains (Sect. 4). This way, at each step, the cost structures of all the components have already been computed and it suffices to compose them.

Example 2. The sequence of CRs in Program 1 is $\langle p1, wh3, wh6, wh9, wh12\rangle$. We start computing cost structures for $wh12$ and finish by computing cost structures for $p1$. For each CR, we compute cost structures for the CEs, the phases and the chains. Consider CR $wh9$ for instance. We compute the cost of CEs 7.1 and 6 first. These are $\langle iv_1, \emptyset, \{iv_1 = |z|\}\rangle$ which originates from its reference to $wh12[9^+8]$ (See Fig. 2) and $\langle 0, \emptyset, \emptyset\rangle$ (See CE 6 in Fig. 1). Then, we compute the cost of phase 7.1^+. In phase 7.1^+ CE 7.1 is evaluated a number of times and each time it has a cost $\langle iv_1, \emptyset, \{iv_1 = |z|\}\rangle$. The cost of 7.1^+ is the sum of all these costs. In particular iv_2 corresponds to the sum of all the copies of iv_1 of all the evaluations of CE 7.1. The variables iv_3 and iv_4 have an auxiliary role. They maintain the two parts of the cost separated $|y_s - y_f|$ and $|z_s|$ and, together with the non-final constraint, represent a non-linear bound. Finally, the cost of $[7.1^+6]$ is the sum of the costs of 7.1^+ and 6 but expressed only in terms of the initial variable values y and z. The process is similar for other CRs. In CR $wh3$, we compute the costs for CEs 3.1 and 3.2 and 2, we combine the ones from 3.1 and 3.2 to obtain the cost of $(3.1 \vee 3.2)^+$ which in turn we combine with the cost of 2 to obtain the cost of $[(3.1 \vee 3.2)^+2]$. Here, iv_6 represents the sum of all iv_5 of all the evaluations of CE 3.2 in phase $(3.1 \vee 3.2)^+$.

Definition 4 (Valid Cost Structure). *Let $T(\overline{x})$ be a chain, phase or CE. The cost structure $\langle E, IC, FC(\overline{x})\rangle$ is* valid *for T if for every $\langle \alpha, T(\overline{x})\rangle \Downarrow k$, there exists an extension of α denoted α' ($\alpha'|_{\overline{x}} = \alpha$) that assigns all the intermediate variables such that $\alpha'(IC \wedge FC(\overline{x}))$ is valid and $\alpha'(E) = k$.*

A valid cost structure of $T(\overline{x})$ can be evaluated to any cost k s.t. $\langle \alpha, T(\overline{x})\rangle \Downarrow k$. Given a valid cost structure $\langle E, IC, FC(\overline{x})\rangle$, we can easily obtain closed-form upper/lower bounds such as the ones given in Fig. 1 by maximizing/minimizing the main cost expression E according to the constraints IC and $FC(\overline{x})$. This is done by incrementally substituting intermediate variables in E for their upper/lower bounds defined in the constraints until E does not contain any intermediate variable. The details on how this process is implemented can be found in [14].

Example 3. The lower bound of chain [1.2] is computed as follows: We start from the main cost expression $iv_2 + 2iv_6$ and we minimize each iv using the constraints: (1) $iv_2 \geq iv_3 * iv_4$ (2) $iv_4 \geq |z|$ and (3) $iv_3 + iv_6 \geq y + x$: $iv_2 + 2iv_6 \geq^{(1)} iv_3 * iv_4 + 2iv_6 \geq^{(2)} iv_3 * |z| + 2iv_6 \geq^{(3)} min((|y+x| * |z|) + 0,\ 0 + 2|y+x|) = min(|z|, 2) * |y+x|$.

4 Cost Structures of Cost Equations and Chains

We want to obtain a valid cost structure of a recursive CE $rc(\overline{xx'}) := \langle C(\overline{x}) = k_0 + \sum_{i=1}^{n} Dch_i(\overline{y_i}) + C(\overline{x'}), \varphi(\overline{xx'y})\rangle$ (the non-recursive case is analogous).

Let k_i be the cost of $ch_i(\overline{y_i})$, the cost of $rc(\overline{xx'})$ is $k_0 + \sum_{i=1}^{n} k_i$ (See Fig. 3). Similarly, we can obtain a valid cost structure for $rc(\overline{xx'})$ by composing the cost structures of each $ch_i(\overline{y_i})$.

Remark 1. Let $\langle E_{ch_i}, IC_{ch_i}, FC_{ch_i}(\overline{y_i})\rangle$ be a valid cost structure of $ch_i(\overline{y_i})$, the following cost structure is valid for $rc(\overline{xx'})$:

$$\langle k_0 + \sum_{i=1}^{n} E_{ch_i}, \bigcup_{i=1}^{n}(IC_{ch_i}), \bigcup_{i=1}^{n}(FC_{ch_i}(\overline{y_i}))\rangle$$

We add the main cost expressions E_{ch_i} plus k_0 and join the constraint sets IC_{ch_i} and $FC_{ch_i}(\overline{y_i})$. Note that in the base case (i.e. when $n = 0$), the resulting cost structure is simply $\langle k_0, \emptyset, \emptyset\rangle$. Unfortunately, the final constraints in $\bigcup_{i=1}^{n}(FC_{ch_i}(\overline{y_i}))$ contain variables other than $\overline{xx'}$ and have to be transformed to obtain a cost structure that only contains CR variables in $\overline{xx'}$.

Transformation of final constraints. We perform this transformation with the help of the CE's constraint set $\varphi(\overline{xx'y})$. Recall that final constraints are of an almost linear form $(\sum_{k=1}^{m} iv_k \bowtie |l(\overline{y})|)$. If we guarantee that $l(\overline{y})$ is non-negative $(\varphi(\overline{xx'y}) \Rightarrow l(\overline{y}) \geq 0)$, we can simply use the linear constraint $\sum_{k=1}^{m} iv_k \bowtie l(\overline{y})$. Let FC^+ be the set of all constraints obtained thus from $\bigcup_{i=1}^{n} FC_{ch_i}(\overline{y_i})$. We perform (Fourier-Motzkin) quantifier elimination on $\exists\overline{y}.(FC^+ \wedge \varphi(\overline{xx'y}))$ and obtain a constraint set that relates directly the intermediate variables of FC^+ with $\overline{xx'}$. We can then extract syntactically from the resulting constraint set new final constraints in terms of $\overline{xx'}$.

Example 4. We combine the cost of chains $[(3.1 \vee 3.2)^+ 2]$ and $[7.1^+ 6]$ from Fig. 4 into that of CE 1.2, instantiated according to CE 1.2 with variables (x, y, x_o, y_o) and (y_o, z), respectively. The resulting expression is: $\langle iv_2 + 2iv_6, \{iv_2 = iv_3 * iv_4\}, \{iv_6 = |y - y_o + x|, iv_3 = |y_o|, iv_4 = |z|\}\rangle$. This is the cost structure of [1.2] in Fig. 4 except for the final constraints which need to be transformed. The constraint set of CE 1.2 from Fig. 2 ($\varphi_{1.2}$) guarantees that $y - y_o + x$, y_o and z are non-negative. Therefore, we generate a constraint set $FC^+ = \{iv_6 = y - y_o + x, iv_3 = y_o, iv_4 = z\}$ and perform quantifier elimination over $\exists x_o, y_o.(FC^+ \wedge \varphi_{1.2})$. This results in $\{iv_6 + iv_3 = y + x, iv_4 = z, x > 0, y > 0, z > 0\}$ from which we syntactically extract the constraints $iv_3 + iv_6 = |y + x|$ and $iv_4 = |z|$. This procedure allows us to find dependencies among constraints ($iv_6 = y - y_o + x$ and $iv_3 = y_0$) and merge them precisely (into $iv_3 + iv_6 = |y + x|$).

We transform the rest of the final constraints, i.e. the ones that cannot be guaranteed to be positive, one by one. Let $\sum_{k=1}^{m} iv_k \bowtie |l(\overline{y})|$ be a constraint, if we find $l'(\overline{xx'})$ such that $\varphi(\overline{xx'y}) \Rightarrow l(\overline{y}) \bowtie l'(\overline{xx'})$, then we have that $\sum_{k=1}^{m} iv_k \bowtie |l'(\overline{xx'})|$ holds as well.[2] We find $l'(\overline{xx'})$ by creating a linear template of $l'(\overline{xx'})$ and finding coefficients that satisfy $\varphi(\overline{xx'y}) \Rightarrow l(\overline{y}) \bowtie l'(\overline{xx'})$ using Farkas' Lemma.

[2] This can be easily seen by distinguishing cases ($l(\overline{y}) \geq 0$ and $l(\overline{y}) \leq 0$).

Chains. The case of computing a cost structure $\langle E_{ch}, IC_{ch}, FC_{ch}(\overline{x})\rangle$ of a chain $ch = [ph_1 \cdot ph_2 \cdots ph_n]$ is analogous. Let $\langle E_{ph_i}, IC_{ph_i}, FC_{ph_i}(\overline{x_i x_{i+1}})\rangle$ be the cost structure of $ph_i(\overline{x_i x_{i+1}})$, we add the main cost expressions and join the constraint sets to obtain: $\langle \sum_{i=1}^{n} E_{ph_i}, \bigcup_{i=1}^{n}(IC_{ph_i}), \bigcup_{i=1}^{n}(FC_{ph_i}(\overline{x_i x_{i+1}}))\rangle$. We transform the final constraints $FC_{ph_i}(\overline{x_i x_{i+1}})$ to express them in terms of the initial variables $\overline{x}$ as above. But this time we perform the transformation incrementally. We transform first $FC_{ph_n}(\overline{x_n})$ and $FC_{ph_{n-1}}(\overline{x_{n-1}x_n})$ in terms of $\overline{x_{n-1}}$. Then, we transform the result together with $FC_{ph_{n-2}}(\overline{x_{n-2}})$ in terms of $\overline{x_{n-2}}$ and so on until we reach the first phase of the chain. In each step the constraint set used is $\varphi_{ph_i}(\overline{x_i x_{i+1}})$ which is a summary of the behaviors of $ph_i, \cdots, ph_n$.

5 Cost Structures of Phases

Let $ph = (c_1 \vee \cdots \vee c_n)^+$ be a phase. Our objective is to compute a valid cost structure $\langle E_{ph}, IC_{ph}, FC_{ph}(\overline{x_s x_f})\rangle$ for the phase ph. Such a cost structure must be expressed in terms of initial values of the variables ($\overline{x_s}$) and the values of the variables in the last recursive call of the phase ($\overline{x_f}$) and must represent the sum of all the evaluations of $c_i \in ph$ (according to the semantics Fig. 3). For each evaluation of c_i, we can define an instantiation of its cost structure.

Definition 5 (Cost Structure Instances). *Let $\langle E_{c_i}, IC_{c_i}, FC_{c_i}(\overline{xx'})\rangle$ be a valid cost structure of c_i and let $\#c_i$ be the number of times c_i is evaluated in ph. $\langle E_{c_ij}, IC_{c_ij}, FC_{c_ij}(\overline{x_{c_ij}x'_{c_ij}})\rangle$ represents the cost structure instance of the j-th CE evaluation of c_i for $1 \leq j \leq \#c_i$. That is, the cost structure of c_i instantiated with the variables corresponding to the j-th CE evaluation of c_i: $\overline{x_{c_ij}x'_{c_ij}}$.*

Remark 2. The total cost of a phase is the sum of all the cost structure instances for $1 \leq j \leq \#c_i$ and for all $c_i \in ph$:

$$\langle \sum_{i=1}^{n}\sum_{j=1}^{\#c_i} E_{c_ij}, \bigcup_{i=1}^{n}\bigcup_{j=1}^{\#c_i}(IC_{c_ij}), \bigcup_{i=1}^{n}\bigcup_{j=1}^{\#c_i}(FC_{c_ij}(\overline{x_{c_ij}x'_{c_ij}}))\rangle$$

Based on this, we generate a cost structure $\langle E_{ph}, IC_{ph}, FC_{ph}(\overline{x_s x_f})\rangle$ in three steps: (1) we transform the expression $\sum_{i=1}^{n}\sum_{j=1}^{\#c_i} E_{c_ij}$ into a valid main cost expression E_{ph}; (2) we generate non-final constraints IC_{ph} using the CEs' non-final constraints IC_{c_i} (in Sect. 5.1); and (3) we generate final constraints $FC_{ph}(\overline{x_s x_f})$ using the CEs' final constraints $FC_{c_i}(\overline{x_{c_i}x'_{c_i}})$ and the CE definitions (in Sect. 5.2).

In order to transform $\sum_{i=1}^{n}\sum_{j=1}^{\#c_i} E_{c_ij}$ into a valid cost expression E_{ph}, we have to remove the sums over the unknowns $\#c_i$. For this purpose, we define the following new intermediate variables:

Definition 6 (Sum intermediate variables). *Let iv be an intermediate variable in $\langle E_{c_i}, IC_{c_i}, FC_{c_i}(\overline{xx'})\rangle$. The intermediate variable $smiv := \sum_{j=1}^{\#c_i} iv_j$ is the sum of all instances of iv in the different evaluations of c_i in the phase.*

Now, we can reformulate each $\sum_{j=1}^{\#c_i} E_{c_ij}$ into a linear expression in terms of *smiv*. Let $E_{c_i} := q_0 + q_1 * iv_1 + \cdots + q_m * iv_m$, we have that $\sum_{j=1}^{\#c_i} E_{c_ij} = q_0 * \#c_i + q_1 * smiv_1 + \cdots + q_m * smiv_m$ (where $\#c_i$ is also an intermediate variable). If we do this transformation for each i in $\sum_{i=1}^{n}\sum_{j=1}^{\#c_i} E_{c_ij}$, we obtain a valid cost expression for the phase E_{ph}.

Example 5. Consider phase $(3.1 \vee 3.2)^+$. Let $E_{3.1} = 0$ and $E_{3.2} = 2iv_5$. The main cost expression of the phase is $E_{(3.1\vee 3.2)^+} = \sum_{j=1}^{\#c_{3.1}} 0 + \sum_{j=1}^{\#c_{3.2}} 2iv_{5j} = 2smiv_5$ (where $smiv_5$ corresponds to iv_6 in Fig. 4).

5.1 Transforming Non-final Constraints

In this section we want to generate a new set of non-final constraints IC_{ph} that bind the new intermediate variables (*smiv*) that appear in our main cost expression E_{ph}.

We iterate over the non-final constraints of each IC_{c_i} for $c_i \in ph$. For each constraint $\sum_{k=1}^{m} iv_k \bowtie SE \in IC_{c_i}$, we sum up all its instances $\sum_{j=1}^{\#c_i}\sum_{k=1}^{m} iv_{kj} \bowtie \sum_{j=1}^{\#c_i} SE_j$ and reformulate the constraint using *smiv* variables. We reformulate the left-hand side directly: $\sum_{j=1}^{\#c_i}\sum_{k=1}^{m} iv_{kj} = \sum_{k=1}^{m} smiv_k$ However, the right-hand side of the constraints might contain sums over non-linear expressions. These sums cannot be reformulated only in terms of Sum variables. Therefore, we introduce a new kind of intermediate variable:

Definition 7 (Max/Min intermediate variables). *The variables* $\lceil iv \rceil := \max_{1\leq j\leq \#c_i}(iv_j)$ *and* $\lfloor iv \rfloor := \min_{1\leq j\leq \#c_i}(iv_j)$ *are the maximum and minimum value that an instance* iv_j *of* iv *can take in a evaluation of* c_i *in* ph.

With the help of this new kind of variables we can reformulate the right hand side of the expression: $\sum_{j=1}^{\#c_i} SE_j$. We distinguish cases for each possible SE:

- $SE := q_0 + q_1 * iv_1 + \cdots + q_m * iv_m$:
  We have that $\sum_{j=1}^{\#c_i} SE_j = q_0 * \#c_i + q_1 * smiv_1 + \cdots + q_m * smiv_m$.
- $SE := iv_k * iv_p$: We approximate $\sum_{j=1}^{\#c_i} SE_j$ with the help of $\lfloor iv \rfloor_p$ or $\lceil iv \rceil_p$ depending on whether $\bowtie$ is $\leq$ or $\geq$:
  $\sum_{j=1}^{\#c_i} SE_j \leq smiv_k * \lceil iv \rceil_p$ and $\sum_{j=1}^{\#c_i} SE_j \geq smiv_k * \lfloor iv \rfloor_p$.[3]
- $SE := max(\overline{iv})$ or $min(\overline{iv})$: We reduce this to the previous case. We reformulate SE as $1 * SE$ and substitute each factor by a fresh intermediate variable: $iv_k * iv_p$. Then, we add the constraints $iv_k \bowtie 1$ and $iv_p \bowtie SE$ to IC_{c_i} so they are later transformed. This way, $smiv_p$ is not generated ($\lceil iv \rceil_p$ or $\lfloor iv \rfloor_p$ will be generated instead) and we do not have to compute $\sum_{j=1}^{\#c_i} SE_j$.

[3] We could also approximate to $\lfloor iv \rfloor_k * smiv_p$ and $\lceil iv \rceil_k * smiv_p$ but in general the chosen approximation works better. The variable iv_k usually represents an outer loop and iv_p and inner loop (See basic product strategy in Sect. 5.2).

In the generated constraints new variables of the form $\lfloor iv \rfloor$ and $\lceil iv \rceil$ might have been introduced that also need to be bound. We iterate over the constraints in IC_{c_i} from $c_i \in ph$ again to generate constraints over $\lfloor iv \rfloor$ and $\lceil iv \rceil$ variables. Let $iv \leq SE \in IC_{c_i}$ (the $\geq$ case is symmetric). We distinguish cases for SE:[4]

- $SE := q_0 + q_1 * iv_1 + \cdots + q_m * iv_m$: Let $V_k := \lceil iv \rceil_k$ if $q_k \geq 0$ or $V_k := \lfloor iv \rfloor_k$ if $q_k < 0$. We generate $\lceil iv \rceil \leq q_0 + q_1 * V_1 + \cdots + q_m * V_m$.
- $SE := iv_k * iv_p$: We generate $\lceil iv \rceil \leq \lceil iv \rceil_k * \lceil iv \rceil_p$.
- $SE := max(iv_1 \cdots iv_n)$: We generate $\lceil iv \rceil \leq max(\lceil iv \rceil_1 \cdots \lceil iv \rceil_n)$.
- $SE := min(iv_1 \cdots iv_n)$: We generate $\lceil iv \rceil \leq \lceil iv \rceil_k$ (for $1 \leq k \leq n$).

All these newly generated constraints form the non-final constraint set IC_{ph}.

5.2 Transforming Final Constraints

Previously, we computed a main cost expression E_{ph} and a set of non-final constraints IC_{ph} for a phase $ph = (c_1 \vee \cdots \vee c_n)^+$. We complete the phase's cost structure with a set of final constraints $FC_{ph}(x_s x_f)$ (and possibly additional non-final constraints) that bind the intermediate variables of E_{ph} and IC_{ph}. We propose the following algorithm:

Algorithm initialization. For each c_i with cost structure $\langle E_{c_i}, IC_{c_i}, FC_{c_i}(\overline{xx'})\rangle$ the algorithm maintains two sets of *pending* constraints:

(1) $Psums^{c_i}$ is initialized with the constraints $\sum_{k=1}^{m} iv_k \bowtie |l(\overline{xx'})| \in FC_{c_i}(xx')$ such that some $smiv_k$ appear in our phase cost structure (in E_{ph} or IC_{ph}) and $iv_{it_i} \leq 1$ and $iv_{it_i} \geq 1$ if $\#c_i$ appears in our phase cost structure. The variable iv_{it_i} represents the number of times c_i is evaluated and $smiv_{it_i} = \#c_i$.
(2) Pms^{c_i} is initialized with the constraints $iv \bowtie |l(\overline{xx'})| \in FC_{c_i}(xx')$ such that $\lceil iv \rceil$ or $\lfloor iv \rfloor$ appear in our phase cost structure.

Algorithm. At each step, the algorithm removes one constraint from one of the pending sets and applies one or several strategies to the removed constraint. A strategy generates new constraints (final or non-final) for the phase's cost structure: they are added to the sets IC_{ph} or $FC_{ph}(x_s x_f)$. A strategy can also add additional pending constraints to the sets $Psums^{c_i}$ or Pms^{c_i} to be processed later. The algorithm repeats the process until $Psums^{c_i}$ and Pms^{c_i} are empty or all the intermediate variables in E_{ph} and IC_{ph} are bound by constraints.

In principle, the algorithm can finish without generating constraints for all intermediate variables. For instance, if the cost of the phase is actually infinite. It can also not terminate if new constraints keep being added to the pending sets indefinitely. This does not happen often in practice and we can always stop the computation after a number of steps. We propose the following strategies:

[4] This transformation is not valid for constraints with multiple variables on the left side. The constraints with $\leq$ can be split ($\sum_{k=1}^{m} iv_k \leq SE$ implies $iv_k \leq SE$ for $1 \leq k \leq m$). But this is not the case for the constraints with $\geq$.

Inductive Sum Strategy. Let $\sum_{k=1}^{m} iv_k \bowtie |l(\overline{xx'})| \in Psums^{c_i}$, the strategy will try to find a linear expression that approximates the sum $\sum_{j=1}^{\#c_i} |l(\overline{x_{c_ij}x'_{c_ij}})|$ in terms of the initial and final variables of the phase $(\overline{x_s x_f})$.

Let us consider first the simple case where c_i is the only CE in the phase. The strategy uses the CE's constraint set $\varphi_i(\overline{xx'y})$ and Farkas' Lemma to generate a candidate linear expression $cd(\overline{x})$ such that $\varphi_i(\overline{xx'y}) \Rightarrow (|l(\overline{xx'})| \bowtie cd(\overline{x}) - cd(\overline{x'}) \geq 0)$. If a candidate $cd(\overline{x})$ is found, we have:

$$\sum_{j=1}^{\#c_i} |l(\overline{x_{c_ij}x'_{c_ij}})| \bowtie \sum_{j=1}^{\#c_i} (cd(\overline{x_{c_ij}}) - cd(\overline{x'_{c_ij}})) = cd(\overline{x_s}) - cd(\overline{x_f})$$

This is because each intermediate $-cd(\overline{x'_{c_ij}})$ and $cd(\overline{x_{c_ij+1}})$ cancel each other $(cd(\overline{x'_{c_ij}}) = cd(\overline{x_{c_ij+1}}))$. Therefore, the constraint $\sum_{k=1}^{m} smiv_k \bowtie |cd(\overline{x_s}) - cd(\overline{x_f})|$ is valid and can be added to $FC_{ph}(x_s x_f)$.

Example 6. This is the case of phase $9^+(i_s, z_s, i_f, z_f)$ with $Psums^9 = \{iv_{it_9} \leq 1, iv_{it_9} \geq 1\}$. The strategy generates the candidate $-i$ and the final constraints $smiv_{it_9} \leq |i_f - i_s|$ and $smiv_{it_9} \geq |i_f - i_s|$. Later $|i_f - i_s|$ will become $|z - i|$ in $[9^+8]$ and $|z|$ in CE 7.1. The variable $smiv_{it_9}$ corresponds to iv_1 in Fig. 4.

If the phase contains other CEs c_e $(e \neq i)$, we have to take their behavior into account. E.g. suppose that we have another c_e $(e \neq i)$ that increments our candidate by two $(\varphi_e(\overline{xx'y}) \Rightarrow cd(\overline{x'}) = cd(\overline{x}) + 2)$. Let $\#c_e$ be the number of evaluations of c_e, the sum is $\sum_{j=1}^{\#c_i} cd(\overline{x_{c_ij}}) - cd(\overline{x'_{c_ij}}) = cd(\overline{x_s}) - cd(\overline{x_f}) + 2 * \#c_e$. That is, the sum computed for the simple case $cd(\overline{x_s}) - cd(\overline{x_f})$ plus the sum of all the increments to the candidate $2 * \#c_e$ effected by CE c_e.

In the general case, the strategy generates a candidate (using c_i constraint set $\varphi_i(\overline{xx'y})$ and Farkas' Lemma as before); it classifies the CEs of the phase $c_e \in ph$ (including c_i) according to their effect on the candidate; and it uses this classification to generate constraints that take these effects into account.

Cost Equation Classification. Each class has a condition and it defines a (linear) term (See Fig. 5). In order to classify a CE c_e into a class, its condition has to be implied by the corresponding CE's constraint set $\varphi_e(\overline{xx'y})$. This implication can be verified and the unknown linear expressions $dc_e(\overline{xx'})$ $ic_e(\overline{xx'})$ or $rst_e(\overline{xx'})$ (For the classes *Dc*, *Ic* and *Rst* respectively) can be inferred using Farkas' Lemma. The considered classes in this strategy are[5]:

	Condition when $\bowtie$ is $\leq$	Condition when $\bowtie$ is $\geq$	Defines
Cnt	$(\sum_{k=1}^{m} iv_k \bowtie \lvert l'(\overline{xx'})\rvert) \in Psums^{c_e}$ $\wedge$	$\lvert l'(\overline{xx'})\rvert \bowtie cd(\overline{x}) - cd(\overline{x'}) \geq 0$	$cnt_e = \sum_{k=1}^{m} smiv_k$
Dc	$0 \leq dc_e(\overline{xx'}) \leq cd(\overline{x}) - cd(\overline{x'})$	$dc_e(\overline{xx'}) \geq cd(\overline{x}) - cd(\overline{x'})$	$iv_{dc_e} = \lvert dc_e(\overline{xx'})\rvert$
Ic	$ic_e(\overline{xx'}) \geq cd(\overline{x'}) - cd(\overline{x})$	$0 \leq ic_e(\overline{xx'}) \leq cd(\overline{x'}) - cd(\overline{x})$	$iv_{ic_e} = \lvert ic_e(\overline{xx'})\rvert$
Rst	$cd(\overline{x'}) \bowtie \lvert rst(\overline{x})\rvert$		$iv_{rst_e} = \lvert rst_e(\overline{x})\rvert$

Fig. 5. Classes of CE c_e w.r.t a candidate $cd(\overline{x})$, their condition and defined term

[5] The class *Rst* will be used and explained in the *Max-Min* strategy.

- *Cnt*: $c_e \in Cnt$ if there is a constraint $\sum_{k=1}^{m} iv_k \bowtie |l'(\overline{xx'})| \in Psums^{c_e}$ that can also be bound by the candidate: $|l'(\overline{xx'})| \bowtie cd(\overline{x}) - cd(\overline{x'})$. We can incorporate $\sum_{k=1}^{m} smiv_k$ to the left hand side of our constraint. We define $cnt_e := \sum_{k=1}^{m} smiv_k$ as a shorthand. Note that c_i, whose constraint was used to generate the candidate, trivially satisfies the condition and thus $c_i \in Cnt$.
- *Dc*: $c_e \in Dc$ if in each evaluation of c_e the candidate is decremented by at least $dc_e(\overline{xx'})$ (or at most $dc_e(\overline{xx'})$ if $\bowtie$ is $\geq$). We assign a fresh intermediate variable to this amount $iv_{dc_e} := |dc_e(\overline{xx'})|$. To generate a valid constraint, we will subtract the sum of all those decrements i.e. $smiv_{dc_e}$.
- *Ic*: $c_e \in Ic$ if in each evaluation of c_e the candidate is incremented by at most $ic_e(\overline{xx'})$ (or at least $ic_e(\overline{xx'})$ if $\bowtie$ is $\geq$). As before, we assign a fresh intermediate variable to that amount $iv_{ic_e} := |ic_e(\overline{xx'})|$. To generate a valid constraint, we will add the sum of all those increments i.e. $smiv_{ic_e}$.

Lemma 1. *Let* $!\bowtie$ *be the reverse of* $\bowtie$ *(e.g.* $\geq$ *if* $\bowtie = \leq$*). If we classify every* $c_e \in ph$ *into Cnt, Ic or Dc w.r.t.* $cd(\overline{x})$*, the following constraints are valid:*

$$\sum_{c_e \in Cnt} cnt_e \bowtie iv_{cd+} - iv_{cd-} + \sum_{c_e \in Ic} smiv_{ic_e} - \sum_{c_e \in Dc} smiv_{dc_e},$$
$$iv_{cd+} \bowtie |cd(\overline{x_s}) - cd(\overline{x_f})|, \quad iv_{cd-} ! \bowtie | - cd(\overline{x_s}) + cd(\overline{x_f})|$$

These are the constraints generated by the *Inductive Sum* strategy. Note that iv_{cd+} and $-iv_{cd-}$ represent the positive and negative part of $cd(\overline{x_s}) - cd(\overline{x_f})$. The constraints bind the sum of all *smiv* in cnt_e (for each $c_e \in Cnt$) to $cd(\overline{x_s}) - cd(\overline{x_f})$ plus all the increments $\sum_{c_e \in Ic} smiv_{ic_e}$ minus all the decrements $\sum_{c_e \in Dc} smiv_{dc_e}$. If Ic is empty, $cd(\overline{x_s}) - cd(\overline{x_f})$ is guaranteed to be positive (the candidate is never incremented) and we can eliminate the summand $-iv_{cd-}$ (and its corresponding constraint $iv_{cd-} ! \bowtie | - cd(\overline{x_s}) + cd(\overline{x_f})|$).

Finally, the strategy adds constraints for the new intermediate variables iv_{ic_e} and iv_{dc_e} to the pending sets so their sums $smiv_{ic_e}$ and $smiv_{dc_e}$ are bound afterwards: $iv_{ic_e} \bowtie |ic(\overline{xx'})|$ is added to $Psums^{c_e}$ for each $c_e \in Ic$, and $iv_{dc_e} ! \bowtie |dc(\overline{xx'})|$ is added to $Psums^{c_e}$ for each $c_e \in Dc$.

Example 7. In phase $(3.1 \vee 3.2)^+$ we have $iv_5 \leq |y - y' + 1| \in Psums^{3.2}$. A valid candidate is $y + x$. The CEs are classified as follows: CE 3.2 $\in Cnt$ because it has generated the candidate ($cnt_{3.2} := smiv_5$); and CE 3.1 $\in Dc$ because $y + x$ decreases in CE 3.1 by $dc_{3.1} = 0$. The generated constraints are: $smiv_5 \leq iv_{cd+} - iv_{cd-} - smiv_{dc}$, $iv_{cd+} \leq |(y_s + x_s) - (y_f + x_f)|$ and $iv_{cd+} \leq | - (y_s + x_s) + (y_f + x_f)|$. However, given that Ic is empty and $dc_{3.1} = 0$, we can simplify them to a single constraint: $smiv_5 \leq |(y_s + x_s) - (y_f + x_f)|$ (where $smiv_5$ is iv_6 in Fig. 4).

Example 8. The class *Cnt* allows us to bind Sum variables of different c_i under a single constraint. For instance, if we had[6] $iv_{it_{3.1}} \geq 1 \in Psums^{3.1}$ and $iv_{it_{3.2}} \geq 1 \in Psums^{3.2}$, the expression x would be a valid candidate with the classification $Cnt = \{3.1, 3.2\}$ with $cnt_{3.1} := smiv_{it_{3.1}}$ and $cnt_{3.2} := smiv_{it_{3.2}}$. The strategy

6 $smiv_{it_{3.1}}$ and $smiv_{it_{3.2}}$ are actually not needed for computing the cost of the program in this case. Therefore, these constraints are never added to the pending sets.

would generate the (simplified) constraint $smiv_{it_{3.1}} + smiv_{it_{3.2}} \geq |x_s - x_f|$ which is equivalent to $\#c_{3.1} + \#c_{3.2} \geq |x_s - x_f|$ and represents that $wh3$ iterates at least $|x_s - x_f|$ times. Without *Cnt*, we would fail to obtain a non-trivial lower bound for $\#c_{3.1}$ or $\#c_{3.2}$ as they can both be 0 (if considered individually).

Basic Product Strategy. Often, given a constraint $\sum_{k=1}^{m} iv_k \bowtie |l(\overline{xx'})| \in Psums^{c_i}$, it is impossible to infer a linear expression representing $\sum_{j=1}^{\#c_i} |l(\overline{x_j x'_j})|$.

Example 9. Consider the cost computation of phase 7.1^+. We have a constraint $iv_1 \leq |z| \in Psums^{7.1}$. The variable z does not change in CE 7.1 and $\#c_{7.1}$ is at most y so $\sum_{j=1}^{\#c_7} |z| = |y| * |z|$ which is not linear. We can obtain this result by rewriting the constraint $iv_1 \leq |z|$ as $iv_1 \leq 1*|z|$. Then, we generate the constraint $smiv_1 \leq smiv_{it_{7.1}} * \lceil iv \rceil_{mz}$ (that corresponds to $iv_2 \leq iv_3 * iv_4$ in Fig. 4) and add $iv_{it_{7.1}} \leq 1$ to $Psums^{7.1}$ and $iv_{mz} \leq |z|$ to $Pms^{7.1}$. These constraints will be later processed by the strategies *Inductive Sum* and *Max-Min* respectively.

In general, given a $\sum_{k=1}^{m} iv_k \leq |l(\overline{xx'})| \in Psums^{c_i}$ where $l(\overline{xx'})$ is not a constant, the *Basic Product* strategy generates $\sum_{k=1}^{m} smiv_k \leq smiv_{it_i} * \lceil iv \rceil_p$ and adds the pending constraints $iv_{it_i} \leq 1$ to $Psums^{c_i}$ and $iv_p \leq |l(\overline{xx'})|$ to Pms^{c_i}. This way, the strategy reduces a complex sum into a simpler sum and a max/minimization. The strategy proceeds analogously for constraints with $\geq$.

Max-Min Strategy. This strategy deals with constraints $iv \bowtie |l(\overline{xx'})| \in Pms^{c_i}$ and its role is to generate constraints for Max $\lceil iv \rceil$ and Min $\lfloor iv \rfloor$ variables.

Similarly to the *Inductive Sum* strategy, it generates a candidate $cd(\overline{x})$ using the CE's constraint set $\varphi_i(\overline{xx'y})$ and then it classifies the CEs in the phase according to their effect on the candidate. However, the condition used to generate the candidate is different since we want to bind a single instance of $l(\overline{xx'})$ instead of the sum of all its instances. Additionally, this strategy considers the class *Rst* for the classification but not the class *Cnt* (See Fig. 5). If $c_e \in Rst$ the candidate is reset to a value of at most $|rst_e(\overline{x})|$ (or at least $|rst_e(\overline{x})|$ if $\bowtie$ is $\geq$). A fresh intermediate variable is assigned to such reset value $iv_{rst_e} := |rst_e(\overline{x})|$.

Lemma 2. *Let* $iv \leq |l(\overline{xx'})| \in Pms^{c_i}$ *and let* $cd(\overline{x})$ *be a candidate such that* $\varphi_i(\overline{xx'y}) \Rightarrow l(\overline{xx'}) \leq cd(\overline{x})$*. If we classify every* $c_e \in ph$ *into Dc, Ic and Rst with respect to* $cd(\overline{x})$*, the following constraints are valid:*

$$\lceil iv \rceil \leq iv_{max} + \sum_{c_e \in Ic} smiv_{ic_e}, \quad iv_{max} \leq \max_{c_e \in Rst}(\lceil iv \rceil_{rst_e}, iv_{cd}), \quad iv_{cd} \leq |cd(\overline{x_s})|$$

These are the constraints generated by the *Max-Min* strategy. They bind $\lceil iv \rceil$ to the sum of all the increments $smiv_{ic_e}$ for $c_e \in Ic$ plus the maximum of all the maximum values that the resets can take $\lceil iv \rceil_{rst_e}$. This maximum also includes the candidate $cd(\overline{x_s})$ in case it is never reset.

Finally, the strategy adds the constraints $iv_{ic_e} \leq |ic_e(\overline{xx'})|$ to $Psums^{c_i}$ and $iv_{rst_e} \leq |rst_e(\overline{x})|$ to Pms^{c_i} so $smiv_{ic_e}$ and $\lceil iv \rceil_{rst_e}$ are bound later. The strategy proceeds analogously for constraints with $\geq$ but it subtracts the decrements instead of adding the increments and takes the minimum of the resets $\lfloor iv \rfloor_{rst_e}$.

Example 10. In Example 9 we added $iv_{mz} \leq |z|$ to $Pms^{7.1}$ during the computation of the cost of 7.1^+. Using the *Max-Min* strategy, we generate a candidate z and classify CE 7.1 in Dc with $dc_{7.1} := 0$ (z is not modified in CE 7.1).The resulting (simplified) constraint is $\lceil iv \rceil_{mz} \leq |z_s|$ (which corresponds to $iv_4 \leq |z_s|$ in Fig. 4).

To summarize, we transform the complex problem of obtaining a cost structure for a phase into a set of simpler problems: computation of sums, maximization, minimization of simple constraints. These smaller problems are solved incrementally through strategies that collaborate with each other by adding new constraints to the pending sets. The inference problems in the strategies can be solved efficiently using Farkas' Lemma as they only use the constraint set of one CE at a time. We provide two extra strategies in [14] to obtain upper bounds defined only in terms of $\overline{x_s}$ and to obtain better bounds for sums of expressions whose value varies in each iteration.

6 Soundness

Theorem 1. *Let $T(\overline{x})$ be a chain, a phase or a CE. Then the cost structure $\langle E_T, IC_T, FC_T(\overline{x})\rangle$ obtained following the algorithms of Sects. 4 and 5 is valid.*

Proof sketch. The cost structures in Remarks 1 and 2 result from applying the semantics rules to the cost structures of the components. The latter transformation of E_{ph} is syntactic and the constraints generated in Sects. 4, 5.1 and 5.2 are implied (logical consequence) by the ones in Remarks 1 and 2 and the CEs' constraint sets. Therefore, they can be added to the cost structures without compromising their validity. This implication for the constraints in Sect. 5.2 (Lemmas 1 and 2) is proved by induction on the number of CEs evaluations in [14].

7 Related Work and Experiments

This work constitutes a significant improvement over previous techniques based on cost relations [3,5,7,15]. It builds on the refinement in [15] but presents a new approach for obtaining bounds that is much more powerful. We define a new cost structure representation that has more expressive power than the cost structures in [15] (it can represent lower bounds) and yet it can be inferred by applying simple rules to its constraints (See Sects. 5.1 and 5.2). In [15], ranking functions are used to bind the sums of constant expressions but the rest of the sums are obtained using (a variant of) the *Basic Product* strategy. Therefore, the system in [15] fails to obtain amortized costs except for simple cases. In particular, it fails to infer a linear upper bound for $wh3$. In the work [7] Farkas' Lemma is used to obtain sums of linear expressions. However, it cannot infer bounds for expressions that are incremented or reset. Also, their generated bounds do not depend on the final variables of the phase and thus they are unable to obtain amortized cost. Finally, neither [7] nor [15] can obtain lower bounds.

Other approaches include KoAt [9] which obtains complexity bounds of integer programs by alternating size and bound analysis. Loopus [25,26] follows a similar schema using in a representation based on difference constraints and can compute amortized bounds. These ideas are present in how the cost is computed in this work. Instead of sizes and bounds there is a similar interplay between the the computation of constraints for *smiv* and $\lceil iv \rceil / \lfloor iv \rfloor$ variables in Sect. 5. None of the mentioned work can compute lower bounds. It is worth to mention the SPEED project [19–21,28] where different cost analyses are proposed based on counter instrumentation [20], control flow refinement and progress invariants [19], proof rules [21] and the *size-change* abstraction [28]. These approaches are not publicly available so we cannot perform an experimental comparison. However, our experimental evaluation includes all examples from these papers.

Another active line of research is about amortized cost analysis based on the potential method [10,22,23]. The authors of [22] present a type inference system that is able to obtain polynomial cost upper bounds for functional programs with data structures such as lists or trees. The key advantage of this analysis is its ability to reduce the polynomial cost inference to a linear programming problem (using type inference). In [23], they extend this analysis to deal with natural numbers. The system C4B [10] (to which we compare) adapts this approach for C programs with integers, but it can only infer linear bounds at the moment.

Based on the pioneering work of [27], several cost analyses based on recurrence relations were developed [11,12,24]. The authors of [5] present an analysis which extracts recurrence relations that approximate the cost of CRs and can later be solved by an external solver. Some of these approaches can also compute lower bounds but are unable to find cost bounds for loops with increments or resets or for programs that present amortized cost (such as program 1). Finally, the technique presented in [16] infers "worst" lower bounds (a lower bound on the derivation height) which are not comparable to our "best" lower bounds.

UB	1	n	n^2	n^3	$> n^3$	F	T
CoFloCo	3	62	33	2	1	20	1.19
Old	3	55	32	1	1	29	2.11
Loopus	2	56	27	0	2	34	0.03
KoAT	3	45	40	8	4	21	5.12
C4B	1	42	-	-	-	78	1.24

LB	1	n	n^2	n^3	$> n^3$	F	T
CoFloCo	48	85	23	2	0	2	1.89
PUBS	95	38	9	4	0	14	7.58

CoFloCo	KoAT	Loopus	Old	C4B	Pubs(LB)
better	28	20	12	59	60
worse	5	3	1	1	2

Fig. 6. Experimental results: The number of examples with a given complexity order or (F)ailed for upper (UB) and lower (LB) bounds. (T) is the average time per example in secs. On the right bottom, a comparison between CoFloCo and the other tools.

We perform one experimental evaluation for upper bounds and one for lower bounds. The results of these experiments are summarized in Fig. 6. In all evaluations, the tools are run with a timeout of 60 s per example. In the first evaluation we analyze a total of 121 challenging programs written in C mainly extracted from [6,10]. We compare our approach with Loopus [26], the previous version of CoFloCo (called "Old" in the table) [15], KoAt [9], and C4B [10]. We use the tool llvm2kittel [13] to transform the llvm-IR programs into integer rewrite systems (for KoAT) which are translated to cost relations by a dedicated script. These CRs are used by our tool, and "Old". On Fig. 6, we can see for each tool how many examples are reported in each complexity category and the average time in seconds needed per program for each of the tools. The times of CoFloCo and Old include the refinement process of [15]. On the right-bottom, we report for how many programs CoFloCo computes a better or worse asymptotic bound that the other tools. For instance, CoFloCo computes a better bound than KoAt in 28 examples and Loopus computes a better bound than CoFloCo in 3 examples. It can be seen that CoFloCo computes better bounds for a higher number of examples than any other tool. The second evaluation compares CoFloCo and PUBS [5] for computing lower bounds. We analyze a total of 160 examples. The 121 examples from the first evaluation plus the examples of PUBS's evaluation. CoFloCo obtains a better result (a higher complexity order) in 60 examples. In contrast PUBS obtains better bounds in 2 examples. A detailed experimental report is online: http://cofloco.se.informatik.tu-darmstadt.de/experiments.

Acknowledgements. Research partly funded by the EU project FP7-610582 ENVISAGE: Engineering Virtualized Services. I thank the anonymous reviewers, R. Hähnle, F. Zuleger, M. Sinn and S. Genaim for their careful reading.

References

1. Albert, E., Arenas, P., Genaim, S., Gómez-Zamalloa, M., Puebla, G., COSTABS: a cost and termination analyzer for ABS. In: Kiselyov,O., Thompson, S., (eds.) Proceedings of the 2012 ACM SIGPLAN Workshop on Partial Evaluation and Program Manipulation, PEPM 2012, 23–24 January 2012, Philadelphia, Pennsylvania, USA, pp. 151–154. ACM Press (2012)
2. Albert, E., Arenas, P., Genaim, S., Puebla, G.: Cost relation systems: a language-independent target language for cost analysis. In: Spanish Conference on Programming and Computer Languages (PROLE 2008). Electronic Notes in Theoretical Computer Science, vol. 248, pp. 31–46. Elsevier (2009)
3. Albert, E., Arenas, P., Genaim, S., Puebla, G.: Closed-form upper bounds in static cost analysis. J. Autom. Reasoning **46**(2), 161–203 (2011)
4. Albert, E., Arenas, P., Genaim, S., Puebla, G., Zanardini, D., COSTA: a cost and termination analyzer for Java Bytecode. In: Proceedings of the Workshop on Bytecode Semantics, Verification, Analysis and Transformation (Bytecode). Electronic Notes in Theoretical Computer Science, Budapest, Hungary. Elsevier, April 2008
5. Albert, E., Genaim, S., Masud, A.N.: On the inference of resource usage upper, lower bounds. ACM Trans. Comput. Logic **14**(3), 1–35 (2013)

6. Alias, C., Darte, A., Feautrier, P., Gonnord, L.: Multi-dimensional rankings, program termination, and complexity bounds of flowchart programs. In: Cousot, R., Martel, M. (eds.) SAS 2010. LNCS, vol. 6337, pp. 117–133. Springer, Heidelberg (2010). doi:10.1007/978-3-642-15769-1_8
7. Alonso-Blas, D.E., Arenas, P., Genaim, S.: Precise cost analysis via local reasoning. In: Hung, D., Ogawa, M. (eds.) ATVA 2013. LNCS, vol. 8172, pp. 319–333. Springer, Heidelberg (2013). doi:10.1007/978-3-319-02444-8_23
8. Alonso-Blas, D.E., Genaim, S.: On the limits of the classical approach to cost analysis. In: Miné, A., Schmidt, D. (eds.) SAS 2012. LNCS, vol. 7460, pp. 405–421. Springer, Heidelberg (2012). doi:10.1007/978-3-642-33125-1_27
9. Brockschmidt, M., Emmes, F., Falke, S., Fuhs, C., Giesl, J.: Alternating runtime and size complexity analysis of integer programs. In: Ábrahám, E., Havelund, K. (eds.) TACAS 2014. LNCS, vol. 8413, pp. 140–155. Springer, Heidelberg (2014). doi:10.1007/978-3-642-54862-8_10
10. Carbonneaux, Q., Hoffmann, J., Shao, Z.: Compositional certified resource bounds. In: Proceedings of the 36th ACM SIGPLAN Conference on Programming Language Design and Implementation, PLDI 2015, pp. 467–478. ACM, New York (2015)
11. Debray, S.K., Lin, N.W.: Cost analysis of logic programs. ACM Trans. Program. Lang. Syst. **15**(5), 826–875 (1993)
12. Debray, S.K., López-García, P., Hermenegildo, M., Lin, N.-W.: Lower bound cost estimation for logic programs. In: 1997 International Logic Programming Symposium, pp. 291–305. MIT Press, Cambridge, October 1997
13. Falke, S., Kapur, D., Sinz, C.: Termination analysis of C programs using compiler intermediate languages. In: Schmidt-Schauß, M. (ed.) RTA 2011. Leibniz International Proceedings in Informatics (LIPIcs), vol. 10, pp. 41–50. Schloss Dagstuhl-Leibniz-Zentrum fuer Informatik, Dagstuhl, Germany (2011)
14. Flores-Montoya, A.: Upper and lower amortized cost bounds of programs expressed as cost relations. Technical report, Technische Universität Darmstadt, September 2016. http://www.informatik.tu-darmstadt.de/fileadmin/user_upload/Group_SE/Publications/FM2016_extended.pdf
15. Flores-Montoya, A., Hähnle, R.: Resource analysis of complex programs with cost equations. In: Garrigue, J. (ed.) APLAS 2014. LNCS, vol. 8858, pp. 275–295. Springer, Heidelberg (2014). doi:10.1007/978-3-319-12736-1_15
16. Frohn, F., Naaf, M., Hensel, J., Brockschmidt, M., Giesl, J.: Lower runtime bounds for integer programs. In: Olivetti, N., Tiwari, A. (eds.) IJCAR 2016. LNCS (LNAI), vol. 9706, pp. 550–567. Springer, Heidelberg (2016). doi:10.1007/978-3-319-40229-1_37
17. Garcia, A., Laneve, C., Lienhardt, M.: Static analysis of cloud elasticity. In: Proceedings of the 17th International Symposium on Principles and Practice of Declarative Programming, 14–16 July 2015, Siena, Italy, pp. 125–136. ACM (2015)
18. Grech, N., Georgiou, K., Pallister, J., Kerrison, S., Morse, J., Eder, K.: Static analysis of energy consumption for LLVM IR programs. In Proceedings of the 18th International Workshop on Software and Compilers for Embedded Systems, SCOPES 2015, pp. 12–21. ACM, New York (2015)
19. Gulwani, S., Jain, S., Koskinen, E.: Control-flow refinement and progress invariants for bound analysis. In: PLDI (2009)
20. Gulwani, S., Mehra, K.K., Chilimbi, T.: Speed: precise and efficient static estimation of program computational complexity. In: POPL, pp. 127–139. ACM, New York (2009)
21. Gulwani, S., Zuleger, F.: The reachability-bound problem. In: PLDI 2010, pp. 292–304. ACM, New York (2010)

22. Hoffmann, J., Aehlig, K., Hofmann, M.: Multivariate amortized resource analysis. SIGPLAN Not. **46**(1), 357–370 (2011)
23. Hoffmann, J., Shao, Z.: Type-based amortized resource analysis with integers and arrays. In: Codish, M., Sumii, E. (eds.) FLOPS 2014. LNCS, vol. 8475, pp. 152–168. Springer, Heidelberg (2014). doi:10.1007/978-3-319-07151-0_10
24. Serrano, A., López-García, P., Hermenegildo, M.V.: Resource usage analysis of logic programs via abstract interpretation using sized types. TPLP **14**(4–5), 739–754 (2014)
25. Sinn, M., Zuleger, F., Veith, H.: A simple and scalable static analysis for bound analysis and amortized complexity analysis. In: Biere, A., Bloem, R. (eds.) CAV 2014. LNCS, vol. 8559, pp. 745–761. Springer, Heidelberg (2014). doi:10.1007/978-3-319-08867-9_50
26. Sinn, M., Zuleger, F., Veith, H.: Difference constraints: an adequate abstraction for complexity analysis of imperative programs. In: Formal Methods in Computer-Aided Design, FMCAD 2015, 27–30 September 2015, Austin, Texas, USA, pp. 144–151 (2015)
27. Wegbreit, B.: Mechanical program analysis. Commun. ACM **18**(9), 528–539 (1975)
28. Zuleger, F., Gulwani, S., Sinn, M., Veith, H.: Bound analysis of imperative programs with the size-change abstraction. In: Yahav, E. (ed.) SAS 2011. LNCS, vol. 6887, pp. 280–297. Springer, Heidelberg (2011). doi:10.1007/978-3-642-23702-7_22

Exploring Model Quality for ACAS X

Dimitra Giannakopoulou[1], Dennis Guck[2(✉)], and Johann Schumann[1]

[1] NASA Ames Research Center, Moffett Field, CA, USA
[2] Formal Methods and Tools, University of Twente, Enschede, The Netherlands
d.guck@utwente.nl

Abstract. The next generation airborne collision avoidance system, ACAS X, aims to provide robustness through a probabilistic model that represents sources of uncertainty. From this model, dynamic programming produces a look-up table that is used to give advisories to the pilot in real time. The model is not present in the final system and is therefore not included in the standard certification processes. Rather, the model is checked indirectly, by ensuring that ACAS X performs as well as, or better than, the state-of-the-art, TCAS. We claim that to build confidence in such systems, it is important to target model quality directly. We investigate this issue of model quality as part of our research on informing certification standards for autonomy. Using ACAS X as our driving example, we study the relationship between the probabilistic model and the real world, in an attempt to characterize the quality of the model for the purpose of building ACAS X. This paper presents model conformance metrics, their application to ACAS X, and the results that we obtained from our study.

1 Introduction

Advanced algorithms for decision-making often rely on the use of models, i.e., abstract representations of knowledge that the algorithms need in order to operate correctly. Such algorithms appear increasingly in safety critical systems with the introduction of autonomy, and the need to make decisions, initiate mitigation actions, and adapt to changing environments and unanticipated situations.

Our encounter with such algorithms has been in the context of ACAS X, the next generation Airborne Collision Avoidance System [7,8]. The current collision avoidance standard, TCAS [9], is required on all large passenger and cargo aircraft worldwide, and has been successful in preventing mid-air collisions. However, its deterministic logic limits robustness in the presence of unanticipated circumstances.

To increase robustness, ACAS X uses a probabilistic model to represent uncertainty. Simulation studies with recorded radar data have confirmed that this novel approach leads to a significant improvement in safety and operational performance. ACAS X has also been the target of several formal verification efforts [6,15,16]. The FAA has formed a team of organizations to mature

D. Guck—Author performed this work while employed by SGT, Inc. as an intern at the NASA Ames Research Center.

J. Fitzgerald et al. (Eds.): FM 2016, LNCS 9995, pp. 274–290, 2016.
DOI: 10.1007/978-3-319-48989-6_17

ACAS X into a new international standard for collision avoidance for manned and unmanned aircraft.

In this work, we focus on the problem of identifying quality metrics for models used in decision-making. In particular, since a model is an abstraction of information, how can we determine whether this model is satisfactory? In the context of ACAS X, the ultimate goal is to avoid aircraft collisions. However, to establish trust in such a safety-critical system, we claim that one must additionally show that each decision is supported by accurate model information.

To address these questions, our research aims at establishing criteria for model quality. These criteria should be measurable, and should be helpful in developing certification standards for algorithms that use models. Moreover, model quality should be directly associated with overall system quality. In other words, poor model quality should indicate or predict violations of system requirements.

The work presented in this paper focuses on ACAS X and defines relations between the probabilistic model and the real world. We discuss model conformance relations that we developed and the (sometimes unanticipated) results of their application to ACAS X. Moreover, we have developed techniques that stress-test ACAS X by generating test cases that may exhibit poor model quality with respect to our defined relations.

The rest of the paper is organized as follows. Section 2 describes the ACAS X system and motivates this work, while Sect. 3 discusses the probabilistic model used by ACAS X in more detail. Section 4 discusses the relations that we have defined for evaluating model quality. The application of these relations to ACAS X is presented in Sect. 5. In Sect. 6 we focus on the generation of data for stress-testing ACAS X, and present the results of our analysis. Section 7 lists related work and Sect. 8 closes the paper with conclusions and future work.

2 Background and Motivation

The aim of aircraft collision avoidance systems is to reliably prevent midair collisions while minimizing unnecessary pilot alerting and evasive maneuvers. Uncertainties such as sensor noise or errors, aircraft intent, and pilot behavior make it challenging to design such systems.

In the context of collision avoidance algorithms, we use the term loss of horizontal separation (LHS) to describe the situation where two aircraft are within 500 ft from each other if their altitude difference is ignored. A Near Mid-Air Collision (NMAC) occurs when the altitude difference between the two aircraft is at most 100 ft when LHS occurs. We refer to the aircraft equipped with a collision avoidance system as the *ownship*, and the other aircraft as the *intruder*.

The current collision avoidance standard, TCAS [9], uses several sources to estimate the current state of the aircraft on which it is deployed and other aircraft in its vicinity. If another aircraft is a potential threat, then TCAS issues a traffic advisory, which gives the pilots of the ownship an audio announcement "Traffic, Traffic" and highlights the intruder on a traffic display. This serves as a warning to raise the pilot's awareness for the potential need to maneuver.

If a maneuver becomes necessary the system will issue a resolution advisory (RA) instructing the pilot to climb or descend in order to maintain a safe distance. After the encounter is resolved, TCAS issues a "Clear of Conflict" (`COC`). Only advisories for vertical maneuvers (climb, descend, and maintain altitude) are given, together with the target rate. For example, advisory `DES1500` stands for descend with rate 150 ft/min. Preventive advisories to avoid climbing or descending may also be provided, as described in [7].

The TCAS system has been implemented as a traditional piece of software with conditional branches that model all the different situations. Several years of research have resulted in the development of the ACAS X system. Although the interface of ACAS X to the pilot is the same as TCAS, the underlying collision avoidance algorithm is dramatically different [7,8].

In ACAS X, a probabilistic Markov Decision Process (MDP) model provides a coarse abstraction of how an encounter between two aircraft progresses as a result of applying resolution advisories and of time passing. Based on a reward function and this MDP, dynamic programming generates a look-up table (LUT), which associates each encounter state in the MDP with a cost for each possible ACAS X advisory. The LUT is deployed onboard the aircraft. Every second, ACAS X uses sensors and other information to compute a probability distribution of the states in which an encounter may be at the current time t. ACAS X interpolates the state estimate within the discrete states of the LUT, and calculates the advisory that bears the lowest cost.

In essence, the cost of an advisory computed by dynamic programming is based on how the MDP expects an encounter to evolve from the current state. Therefore, there is a trade-off between the MDP model being accurate enough for the advisories to be appropriate for collision avoidance in reality, but also abstract enough for enabling a compact LUT that can be deployed onboard the aircraft. The ACAS X system is based on a relatively simple dynamic model of how aircraft behave. As explained in [7], a simple model is easier to understand and validate, makes the dynamic programming problem more tractable, and results in a smaller controller, which is easier to fit into memory onboard an aircraft. How can we establish that this simple model is acceptable for ACAS X? Even though the resulting system is tested extensively with independent high fidelity simulations and flight data, it is hard to establish whether the behavior of such optimization algorithms is as expected.

The aim of our work is therefore to develop measurable criteria that directly address model quality. The approaches that we present in this paper are all based on establishing relationships between the evolution of encounters (1) as expected by the MDP model and (2) as recorded by high fidelity simulations and actual flight data.

3 The ACAS X Model

The formulation of the collision avoidance problem used for ACAS X consists of two aircraft, the ownship and the intruder, on a collision course.[1] The ACAS X

[1] ACAS X handles cases with multiple aircraft but this paper focuses on scenarios involving two aircraft.

model keeps record of the altitude of the intruder relative to the ownship, the aircraft climb rates, the produced advisory and the pilot response.

To keep the model tractable, ranges are set for each variable. The MDP discretizes each state variable with a resolution that depends on the proximity between the aircraft. Previous work [16] has shown that the discretization resolution constitutes an important trade-off between accuracy and the size of the LUT, which is important for implementation on-board the aircraft.

For a state variable x, we denote its discretized value by $\hat{x}$. The discretized MDP model state $\hat{s} = \langle \hat{\mathrm{z}}_{\mathrm{rel}}, \widehat{\mathrm{dz}}_{\mathrm{o}}, \widehat{\mathrm{dz}}_{\mathrm{i}}, \mathrm{sRA} \rangle$ encodes

1. $\mathrm{z}_{\mathrm{rel}} \in [-1000, 1000]$ ft, the altitude difference between the two aircraft;
2. $\mathrm{dz}_{\mathrm{o}} \in [-2500, 2500]$ ft/min, the ownship's climb rate;
3. $\mathrm{dz}_{\mathrm{i}} \in [-2500, 2500]$ ft/min, the intruder's climb rate;
4. sRA, encoding the ACAS X advisory produced one second earlier and the advisory the pilot is following, thus modeling pilot delay.

Given a discrete state $\hat{s} = \langle \hat{\mathrm{z}}_{\mathrm{rel}}, \widehat{\mathrm{dz}}_{\mathrm{o}}, \widehat{\mathrm{dz}}_{\mathrm{i}}, \mathrm{sRA} \rangle$ and an advisory adv, the MDP provides probabilistic state transitions into new states $\hat{s}'$, i.e., MDP : $(\hat{s}, \mathsf{adv}) \xrightarrow{p} \hat{s}'$ with state transition probability p.

In order to obtain an optimal controller, the individual advisories are associated with a cost. For example, a clear-of-conflict (COC) carries a reward, whereas alerting the pilot through climb and descend advisories carry a small cost to avoid unnecessary pilot alerting. An NMAC situation has an extremely high cost.

Although the MDP in itself is not aware of timing throughout the encounter, the ACAS X system uses a temporal distribution (τ-distribution) to model the temporal sequence of the encounter and avoidance strategy, since it is expected to operate when NMAC situations may occur within the next 40–50 s.

Figure 1 shows the overall architecture of the ACAS X system and its development process. The top of the panel shows the development of the probabilistic

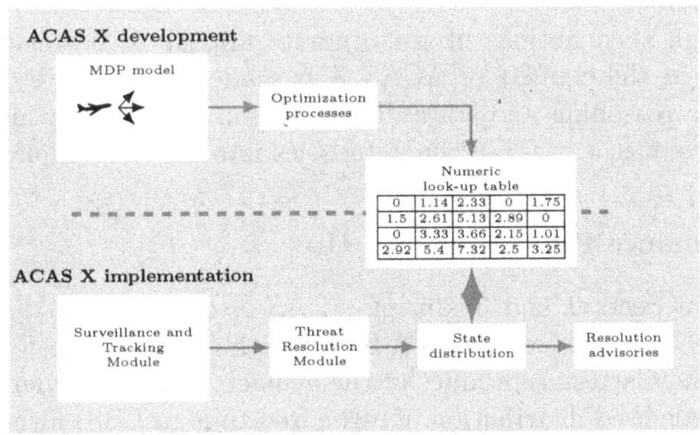

Fig. 1. Principled architecture of the ACAS X modeling process (top) and on-board software architecture (bottom).

MDP model and the generation of the look-up table using dynamic programming. This LUT comprises the core of the ACAS X software that is running on-board the aircraft (bottom part of Fig. 1). During each 1-second update, new estimates of the aircraft involved and uncertainties are calculated based upon sensor measurements and transponder responses. This information is then used to update the aircraft state and τ distribution, and the look-up table is consulted to come up with an appropriate advisory. In addition to the LUT costs discussed previously, on-line corrections are also taken into account in selecting advisories (see [7] for details).

4 Model Conformance

As discussed, the MDP model used by ACAS X captures the expected evolution of flight encounters as a result of time passing and of the application of resolution advisories. To ensure safe operation, the model and the actual system behavior must in some way "match up". In other words, we need to be able to justify that the model is appropriate for the decision making that it is used for.

To this aim, we introduce several notions of *conformance* to characterize model quality. All of these notions capture desired relations between the behavior or states of a model $\mathcal{M}$ and the actual system $\mathcal{A}$ that uses this model. In ACAS X for example, conformance might require that whenever an encounter results in an NMAC in the actual ACAS X system, then the model of this encounter also results in an NMAC. Or when the actual system $\mathcal{A}$ produces an advisory adv, then the model will produce an identical or compatible advisory.

Similarly, one might expect that all situations that occur in practice in the system will be reflected in the model (within the bounds of the model abstraction). This notion is related to over-approximation in formal methods. Imagine, for example, that during flight, an encounter reaches a state s' from a state s, a transition that the model does not anticipate (i.e., in the model s cannot directly transition to s'). ACAS X may still work appropriately or may produce wrong or unsafe results.

Even though such notions of conformance appear to be relatively simple, defining them in the context of ACAS X is made non-trivial by the presence of probabilistic reasoning and state discretization. In the following sections we describe how we factor in these characteristics into our model quality criteria.

4.1 Conformance Framework Set Up

As discussed in Sects. 2 and 3, during ACAS X deployment, the (geometric) state of an encounter is represented by a weighted distribution of states. At each second, the Cartesian product of the geometric state estimate with the τ-distribution (weighted distribution of estimated time to LHS) forms the current state estimate. This state estimate is then interpolated within the discrete states of the LUT in order to calculate a resolution advisory.

To establish model conformance in this context, our framework needs to set up the model and the actual system appropriately. The model $\mathcal{M}$ is ACAS X as deployed within the MDP model.[2] This means that the geometric state distribution is provided by the transitions of the MDP model, as opposed to sensor information. The actual system $\mathcal{A}$ is ACAS X as deployed and using the LUT within a real flight environment or within a high fidelity simulator. To then establish model conformance we set up a common initial state for $\mathcal{M}$ and $\mathcal{A}$ and compare their evolutions according to conformance criteria. More specifically, the initial state of $\mathcal{M}$ is set to the initial state of $\mathcal{A}$ for each encounter $\mathcal{E}$ to be analyzed for conformance.

There are two options for comparing the evolution of encounters. One is a *stepwise* synchronization, which means that we re-synchronize the state of $\mathcal{M}$ and $\mathcal{A}$ once every second, namely every time ACAS X is invoked. The second is an *initial-state* synchronization, where we start from the same state but then let the two systems evolve independently.

For $\mathcal{A}$, state and τ distributions are obtained by the state estimation components, as discussed in earlier sections. For $\mathcal{M}$, the time to LHS decreases by one with every invocation of ACAS X, which is the way it is also updated for the purpose of calculating the LUT. The state distributions are obtained as follows. Let us assume that at some point in encounter $\mathcal{E}$, the MDP moves from state set $\hat{S}_{\mathcal{M}}$ to state set $\hat{S}'_{\mathcal{M}}$. Then the probability $p_{\mathcal{M}}(s')$ of each state $s' \in \hat{S}'_{\mathcal{M}}$ is obtained as follows. For each $s \in \hat{S}_{\mathcal{M}}$ let $p_{\mathcal{M}}(s, s')$ denote the probability associated with the transition from s to s' in the MDP ($p_{\mathcal{M}}(s, s') = 0$ means that s cannot transition to s' in a single step). Then $p_{\mathcal{M}}(s') = \sum_{s \in \hat{S}_{\mathcal{M}}} p(s, s')$.

Decision making is based on the LUT. The LUT used by $\mathcal{M}$ is identical to that used by $\mathcal{A}$ for ACAS X deployment. For this reason, we compare states of $\mathcal{M}$ and $\mathcal{A}$ in terms of their interpolated states within the LUT. Figure 2 illustrates an example of a stepwise synchronization between $\mathcal{M}$ and $\mathcal{A}$. $\mathcal{M}$ and $\mathcal{A}$ start at the same set $\hat{S}_{\mathcal{A}}$ of geometric states, which has been estimated during operation of $\mathcal{A}$. Note that we only illustrate the possible states in which the system may be, without including the probabilities associated with those states. At the next ACAS X cycle, one second later, the grey state set $\hat{S}'_{\mathcal{M}}$ is computed based on MDP transitions starting from $\hat{S}_{\mathcal{A}}$, whereas the blue set of states $\hat{S}'_{\mathcal{A}}$ is computed based on sensor and transponder information.

4.2 Conformance Relations

Based on the above setup, we can define expectations for model and actual system behavior. If $\mathcal{M}(\mathcal{E})$ is the behavior of the model $\mathcal{M}$ on encounter $\mathcal{E}$, and $\mathcal{A}(\mathcal{E})$ the behavior of ACAS X on $\mathcal{E}$, conformance establishes an expected relation $\mathcal{C}$ between the two behaviors: $\mathcal{C}(\mathcal{M}(\mathcal{E}), \mathcal{A}(\mathcal{E}))$. For the ACAS X system, conformance can be defined at three distinct levels: NMAC conformance, advisory conformance, and state conformance.

[2] We use the MDP rather than its corresponding continuous version for aircraft dynamics, because the generation of the LUT is based on the MDP model.

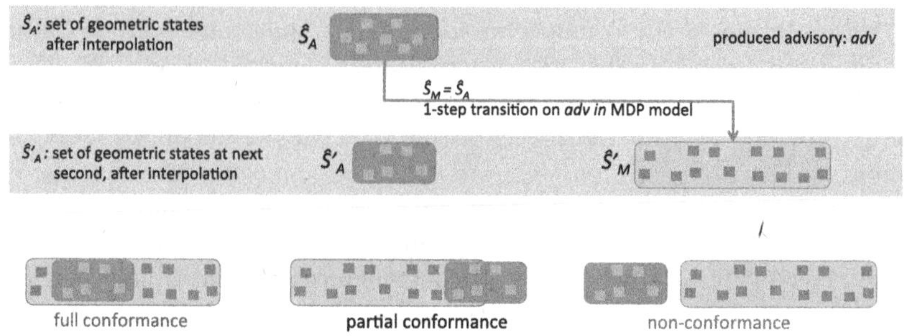

Fig. 2. State conformance between ACAS X and the MDP.

The NMAC conformance metric is the coarsest one and just focuses on the dangerous NMAC state: whenever $\mathcal{A}(\mathcal{E})$ encounters an NMAC, $\mathcal{M}(\mathcal{E})$ has to encounter an NMAC, and vice versa.

At the next level of detail, we focus on the interactions of ACAS X with the outside world, namely the sequence of advisories. Model and implementation are in conformance if the sequence of advisories issued are the same or compatible, where the notion of compatibility has to be specified. For example, we may tolerate small deviations in the time at which an advisory is issued.

A state conformance requires that, at each point in time, the state of $\mathcal{M}$ and $\mathcal{A}$ are compatible, where compatibility may take into account state distributions. For simplicity, we first consider the geometric states of $\mathcal{M}$ and $\mathcal{A}$, without taking into account their associated probabilities, as illustrated in Fig. 2. Each state can be viewed as a point in a high-dimensional state space, where each dimension corresponds to one of the state variables in the geometric state.

One measure of conformance is to expect that the system states are fully contained in the model states, which we name *full state conformance* (Fig. 2).

Intuitively, this means that the model anticipates all the possible evolutions of the encounter in a single step. Whereas full conformance represents the ideal situation, a partial overlap might also be acceptable, leading to a notion of *partial state conformance*. For this particular case, and given that states are weighted, partial conformance relations may also take these weights into account in order to evaluate the significance of the overlap.

Finally, if the model and system states are disjoint, we have an undesirable *no state conformance* situation. Decision making in ACAS X is based on how the MDP expects encounters to evolve. Such an extreme mismatch between the MDP and the actual system may result in providing advisories that will not prevent an NMAC from occurring. Figure 2 illustrates these three types of conformance.

Note that "no state conformance" need not directly result in a violation of ACAS X requirements for the encounter that is being studied; it is possible that NMAC just happens to be avoided. However, detecting non-conformance in a tested encounter is still valuable since it indicates a mismatch that may result in dangerous behavior in other encounters that are not included in the testing.

As such, conformance relations might be useful for predictive runtime analysis of systems.

5 Analyzing Conformance Issues

We applied a variety of conformance metrics to ACAS X test data that we obtained from the ACAS X team as part of the ACAS X Run 13 distribution. We ran both initial-state and stepwise variants of these metrics. Overall, we observed several conformance issues that need to be studied more carefully to determine their significance. For example, Fig. 3B illustrates three bars of advisories at the bottom. The first bar is for the actual system, the second for the interpolated system states (i.e., ACAS X without on-line advisory corrections) and the third one for the model with a stepwise synchronization of the MDP and the system. We can observe that the same advisories are produced but in the third case the descend advisory is issued much earlier.

Among all the observations we made through our experiments, the cases that we believe need the most immediate investigation are cases of stepwise non-conformance. In fact, we did not anticipate that such mismatches between model and system might be possible within a single step. In this section, we analyze one of the cases of non-conformance.

Let us consider as an example encounter 86 within the official ACAS X distribution referred to as Run 13. Figure 3A shows a 3D representation of the flight path for each of the involved aircraft. The encounter starts when the two aircraft are still safely apart (locations marked by small circles). As soon as the ACAS X system on the ownship detects a potentially dangerous development (at $t = 19\,\mathrm{s}$) into the encounter, an alarm “Descend, Descend!” is annunciated in the cockpit and an advisory to descend with 1500 ft/min (`DES1500`) is issued (Fig. 3B, red line). After a short delay, the pilot reacts and follows that advisory and the vertical velocity of the ownship becomes negative. The vertical speed of both aircraft are shown in Fig. 3B, middle panel. At time $t = 29\,\mathrm{s}$, ACAS X advises the pilot to not climb (`DNC`, Fig. 3B, green line) and the pilot levels off. As soon as the danger of an NMAC has been averted, a `COC` advisory is given ($t = 45\,\mathrm{s}$) and the encounter ends successfully.

We checked state conformance on this encounter. We remind the reader that state conformance synchronizes the geometric model state to that of the system at each step, and then compares the geometric states of the system and model in the next step. Given that the value of sRA is always the same in this encounter, we focus on the remaining 3 state variables: $\mathrm{z_{rel}}$, $\mathrm{dz_o}$, and $\mathrm{dz_i}$.

Figure 3D–F illustrates model/system states as gray/blue clouds respectively, at different points in the encounter. Each cloud contains the projection of states on these 3 variables. Due to uncertainties in movement of the intruder and pilot reactions, size and shape of the overlapping parts of the blue and gray clouds vary during the encounter. Figure 3F, however, illustrates a non-conformance situation. The red plane in the figure clearly separates the two clouds.

To analyze non-conformance situations such as the one illustrated in Fig. 3F, it is sometimes helpful to analyze the conformance with respect to individual

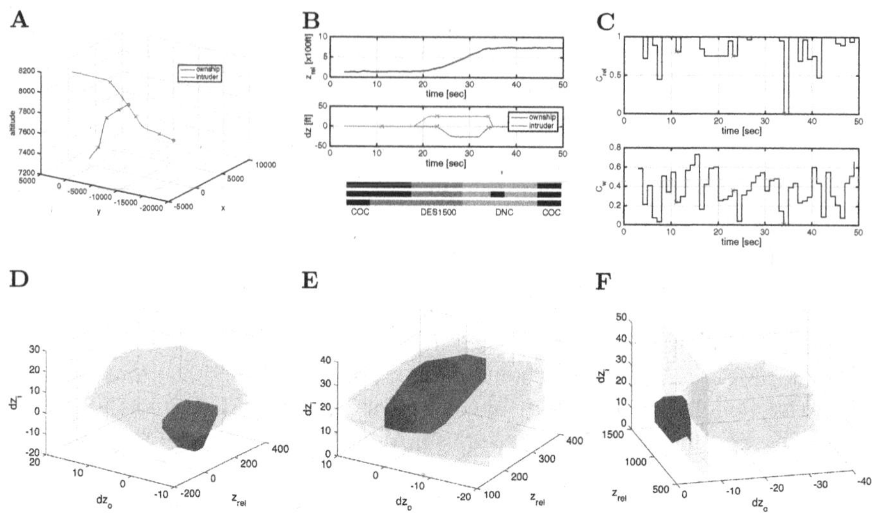

Fig. 3. Visualization of non-conformance encounter. **A:** trajectories of ownship (blue) and intruder (red). Circles mark the starting-points. **B:** ACAS X data showing (top to bottom) relative altitude z_{rel} over time, vertical velocities (dz_o and dz_i) and sequence of produced advisories by ACAS X, interpolated system states, stepwise synchronized MDP. **C:** Conformance metrics C_{rel} (top) and C_w (bottom). Small red x signs indicate time points $t = 11$ s, 23 s, 34 s, associated with panels D–F. **D–F:** 3D projections of $\hat{S}'_{\mathcal{M}}$ (gray) and $\hat{S}'_{\mathcal{A}}$ (blue) at $t = 11$ s, 23 s, 34 s. (Color figure online)

variables of the state. The reason is that non-conformance may be due to the way a particular variable is modeled, which enables us to give precise and helpful information to developers. For example, the non-conformance situation of Fig. 3 is due to variable dz_o. Note that this does not necessarily occur in all non-conformance situations. It may be that variables are covered individually, but their combination is not.

We define a metric of relative state conformance w.r.t. $\hat{S}'_{\mathcal{M}}$ and $\hat{S}'_{\mathcal{A}}$ as follows:

$$C_{\mathrm{rel}} = \frac{|\hat{S}'_{\mathcal{M}} \cap \hat{S}'_{\mathcal{A}}|}{|\hat{S}'_{\mathcal{A}}|}.$$

Hence, $C_{\mathrm{rel}} \in [0, 1]$ where $C_{\mathrm{rel}} = 0$ describes a non-conformance situation and $C_{\mathrm{rel}} = 1$ full conformance. Figure 3C (top) shows C_{rel} for the example shown in Fig. 3. The non-conformance at $t = 34$ s is clearly visible.

In order to study more accurately cases of partial conformance i.e., $0 < C_{\mathrm{rel}} < 1$, we want to consider additional information perusing the fact that $\hat{S}'_{\mathcal{A}}$ and $\hat{S}'_{\mathcal{M}}$ are distributions. Informally speaking, the higher $p_{\mathcal{A}}(s)$ of some $s \in \hat{S}'_{\mathcal{A}}$, the more weight it carries for decision making. If those important states are well represented in the MDP (with a high $p_{\mathcal{M}}$) then conformance is very good and the metric should be high. In other words, we wish to measure the similarity between the MDP and actual system information. In an ideal situation, the model and the system will contain the exact same pairs of states and corresponding weights.

Let us assume that we are comparing $\hat{S}'_{\mathcal{M}}$ and $\hat{S}'_{\mathcal{A}}$ for state conformance, where each state $s_{\mathcal{M}} \in \hat{S}'_{\mathcal{M}}$ and $s_{\mathcal{A}} \in \hat{S}'_{\mathcal{A}}$ is associated with probability $p_{\mathcal{M}}(s)$ and $p_{\mathcal{A}}(s)$, respectively. We then define a weighted state conformance metric $C_w = 1 - C_{\text{diff}}$ in terms of the sum of the absolute differences between the probabilities of the states in $\hat{S}'_{\mathcal{A}}$ and $\hat{S}'_{\mathcal{M}}$:

$$C_{\text{diff}} = \frac{1}{2} \sum_{s \in (\hat{S}'_{\mathcal{A}} \cup \hat{S}'_{\mathcal{M}})} |p_{\mathcal{A}}(s) - p_{\mathcal{M}}(s)|$$

The sum is divided by 2, which represents the maximum possible divergence between the sets. Indeed, in the presence of non-conformance, the probability differences will add up to 1 for the model, and 1 for the system, for a total of 2. Note that when a state does not belong to a set of states, we represent it as its probability being 0 for that set. $C_w = 1$ corresponds to $C_{\text{diff}} = 0$, i.e., the sets have the same states with the same associated probabilities. Full conformance situations only have a high value of C_w if the probability mass of the model lies mostly within the subset that is covered by the actual system, and if the states in that subset are weighted similarly to their corresponding ones in the actual system. Figure 3C (bottom) shows C_w for our example encounter.

Since the case of non-conformance is the most urgent to report to the ACAS X team, the rest of the paper focuses on our study of non-conformance cases aiming at providing useful information for the developers to examine the issue. Since non-conformance is very rare in the test data that we received as part of the ACAS X release, we decided to focus on generating additional encounters exhibiting non-conformance, using machine learning.

6 Automatic Generation of Non-conformance Encounters

The complexity of the ACAS X input domain makes it hard to explore it systematically. We therefore based our initial experiments on test encounters prepared by the developers of ACAS X that were included with the ACAS X distribution. When measuring state conformance on those, we encountered only a handful of situations where non-conformance exists. However, those situations are a hint that there are discrepancies between the real world evolution based on ACAS X and the corresponding MDP model. For a more thorough analysis of this phenomenon a much larger data set is required.

In this section, we propose techniques for the automated generation of non-conformance scenarios. In addition to generating such scenarios, we want to be able to provide constraints that further filter the encounters to the most interesting and safety-critical cases. For example, we wish to focus on situations where an actual advisory is issued because of the close proximity of the aircraft.

6.1 The Scenario Generation Environment

Our approach extends the RLESCAS (Reinforcement Learning Encounter Simulator for Collision Avoidance Systems) package for adaptive stress testing of airborne collision avoidance systems [10]. RLESCAS uses Monte Carlo Tree Search (MCTS) to automatically generate two-aircraft NMAC encounters.

Figure 4 illustrates how our framework extends RLESCAS for the case where a single aircraft is equipped with ACAS X. Our framework implements two main changes to the original framework. First, it introduces the MDP in order to compute information needed for the conformance relations. Second, it modifies the reward function to favor the generation of low-conformance encounters.

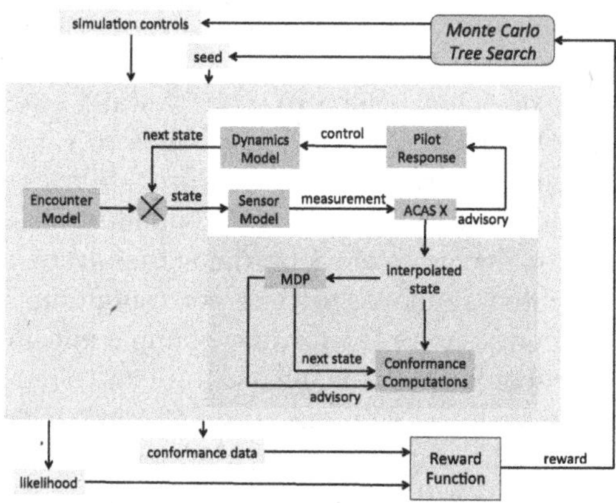

Fig. 4. Encounter generation framework. The white box at the top is RLESCAS for one aircraft equipped with ACAS X, and the orange box is our extension. (Color figure online)

The original framework relies on a simulator for aircraft encounters; in our case one of the aircraft is equipped with ACAS X. Inputs to this simulation environment are basic simulator controls, like initialize, and a seed. These are the only variables that the framework is able to manipulate in order to target specific types of encounters.

Our extension intercepts the operation of the ACAS X component within the simulation to obtain interpolated states that can be fed to the MDP. Then the MDP and the LUT are used as described in the previous sections to calculate conformance data. The output of the framework is the likelihood of the current transition, a variable describing the conformance of the current state, and the weighted conformance metric. The outputs are subjected to our modified reward function used by the MCTS algorithm. The result of the MCTS is in turn used to choose the seed and control inputs for the simulator. A detailed description of the original RLESCAS and the MCTS algorithm can be found in [10].

6.2 The Reward Function

The encounter generation framework aims at maximizing the reward function. Therefore, our reward function $\mathcal{R}$ must be designed to reward the occurrence of non-conformance, but it must also be able to provide guidance on how to evaluate the current situation.

We start with the reward function given in [10] and gradually modify it to serve the purposes of our framework. The objective of the function in [10] is to find high probability encounters that contain NMAC events:

$$\mathcal{R}(s_t, s_{t+1}) = \begin{cases} 0 & \text{if } s_t \in \text{NMAC}, \\ -\infty & \text{if } s_t \notin \text{NMAC}, t \geq T, \\ log(P(s_{t+1} \mid s_t)) & \text{if } s_t \notin \text{NMAC}, t < T. \end{cases} \tag{1}$$

The reward for going from a state s_t to s_{t+1} depends on two main events: (1) if an NMAC occurs ($s_t \in$ NMAC), and (2) if the maximum simulation time has been reached ($t \geq T$). T is set to the time horizon of ACAS X, which is 50 s in the RLESCAS framework. Reaching T therefore indicates a terminal state in our framework; all NMAC situations, if any, have to occur by that time.

The first two conditions of $\mathcal{R}$ represent the NMAC occurrence constraint. If an NMAC occurs a maximal reward is issued, whereas if the time horizon T has been reached and no NMAC has occurred, an infinite penalty is issued. In all other cases a reward based on the probability to be in the current state is issued to maximize the likelihood of the encounter. Note that this function assigns negative rewards, in other words, penalizes undesirable situations to a higher or lower degree, and assigns 0 to the desired outcome.

To adapt the reward function for the generation of non-conformance encounters we investigate variations of Eq. (1). As a first attempt, our objective is similar to that of the original reward function, but for non-conformance (NC) instead of NMAC events. Our reward function then infinitely penalizes the learner when no non-conformance event is encountered.

However, we introduce a change for the evaluation of intermediate situations, because we want to generally encourage mismatches between the system and the MDP. We do so by rewarding small intersections between system and model states, i.e., partial conformance (the smaller the intersection the better):

$$\mathcal{R}(s_t, s_{t+1}) = \begin{cases} nc & \text{if } s_t \in \mathsf{NC}, \\ 0 & \text{if } s_t \notin \mathsf{NC}, t \geq T, \\ (1 - C_{\text{rel}}) \cdot pc & \text{if } s_t \notin \mathsf{NC}, t < T. \end{cases} \tag{2}$$

Hence, $\mathcal{R}$ is geared towards finding encounters with a non-conformance event (NC) and with a low conformance metric throughout the encounter. Note that instead of using negative rewards as in Eq. (1) this function uses positive rewards. We define two positive reward parameters nc and pc representing the reward for non-conformance events and partial conformance events, respectively. We parameterize the reward function in this fashion in order to be able to experiment with different levels of relative importance to the two aspects of the targeted encounters. Parameter pc is weighted by $(1 - C_{\text{rel}})$, which represents the ratio of system states that are not covered by the model. If no non-conformance event occurred, a reward of 0 is issued.

Applying the reward function given in Eq. (2) in the MCTS algorithm enables us to generate non-conformance encounters. However, we observed that in many cases, the altitude difference between the two aircraft remained high, so ACAS X never issued any advisories other than COC. Such encounters are not very interesting for our study.

The natural next step is then to find a reward function that combines objectives from Eqs. (1) and (2). The objective of our new reward function is to trigger non-conformance, involve low conformance, and minimize the altitude difference between the aircraft at the time of closest approach.

$$\mathcal{R}(s_t, s_{t+1}) = \begin{cases} nc & \text{if } s_t \in \mathsf{NC}, \\ fc & \text{if } s_t \in \mathsf{FC}, \\ (1 - C_w) \cdot pc & \text{if } s_t \in \mathsf{PC}, t < T, \\ -\mathrm{z}_{\text{rel}} & \text{if } s_t \notin \text{NMAC}, t \geq T. \end{cases} \tag{3}$$

Like before, nc and pc are positive parameters, and we introduce parameter fc, which is negative or 0. Function $\mathcal{R}$ now includes both positive and negative rewards. It penalizes encounters with no NMAC with the relative distance, whereas positively rewards partial and non-conformance. Partial conformance (PC) is weighted by $(1 - C_w)$ to encourage a low probability match between the model and system states. Full conformance (FC) receives a negative or 0 reward. Note that, in order to increase the likelihood of such encounters, one could add to the reward the probability to be in the current state, similarly to Eq. (1).

Table 1. Subset of generated non-conformance encounters, including conformance information per state variable.

EC #	Time point	$C_{\text{rel}\,\vert\,\mathrm{z}_{\text{rel}}}$	$C_{\text{rel}\,\vert\,\mathrm{dz_o}}$	$C_{\text{rel}\,\vert\,\mathrm{dz_i}}$	$C_{\text{rel}\,\vert\,\mathrm{sRA}}$
1	24	16/16	16/16	0/16	16/16
	49	26/30	30/30	0/30	30/30
6	19	10/12	12/12	0/12	12/12
	33	24/28	28/28	0/28	28/28
	35	28/28	28/28	4/28	28/28
	45	20/20	20/20	0/20	20/20
9995	35	40/40	40/40	0/40	40/40
	40	24/28	28/28	0/28	28/28
	42	24/24	12/24	4/24	24/24

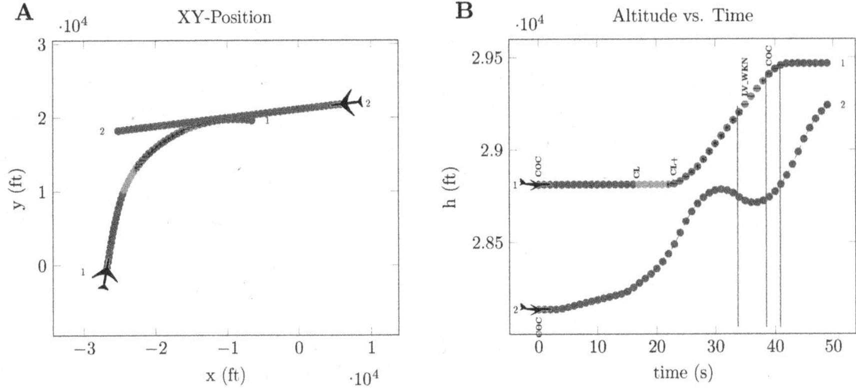

Fig. 5. Encounter 9995 generated with reward function from Eq. (3). Thin red lines indicate non-conformance at $t = 35$ s, 40 s, 42 s. (Color figure online)

6.3 Analysis of Generated Non-conformance Encounters

We used reward function (3) in our framework to generate 18 encounters with a total of 33 non-conformance events. Table 1 displays three of these encounters and decomposes non-conformance events into conformance of individual state variables, to identify whether mismatches are associated with particular variables, as discussed in Sect. 5.

We use $\mathcal{P}_{\mathrm{z_{rel}}}(\mathcal{S})$, $\mathcal{P}_{\mathrm{dz_o}}(\mathcal{S})$, $\mathcal{P}_{\mathrm{dz_i}}(\mathcal{S})$ and $\mathcal{P}_{\mathrm{sRA}}(\mathcal{S})$, to denote the sets obtained by projecting each state $s \in \mathcal{S}$ onto its variable $\mathrm{z_{rel}}$, $\mathrm{dz_o}$, $\mathrm{dz_i}$, and sRA, respectively. Then for system state $\hat{S}_{\mathcal{A}}$ and model state $\hat{S}_{\mathcal{M}}$, conformance relative to each state variable x is defined as:

$$C_{\mathrm{rel}\,|x} = \frac{|\mathcal{P}_x(\hat{S}_{\mathcal{M}}) \cap \mathcal{P}_x(\hat{S}_{\mathcal{A}})|}{|\mathcal{P}_x(\hat{S}_{\mathcal{A}})|}$$

Table 1 indicates that for the wide majority of non-conformance events, the states deviate in variable $\mathrm{dz_i}$. We further analyzed some of these encounters to gain intuition of the types of characteristics that may be causing non-conformance. Consider Fig. 5B visualizing the encounter of two aircraft w.r.t. their altitude over time, for example. The corresponding non-conformance time points of this encounter are at 35, 40 and 42 s into the encounter. Inspecting the altitude changes of the intruder in the interval of [35, 42] reveals a sudden change from descend to a relatively strong climb. This sudden and steep altitude change is not reflected in the MDP.

Even though in such encounters the behavior of ACAS X appears reasonable, it is important to study non-conformance occurrences closely, in case they trigger problematic decision-making under potentially rare circumstances. We are currently in the process of examining these results together with the ACAS X team in order to determine whether model fine-tuning may be beneficial, and whether the root cause is in the continuous model or its discretization.

7 Related Work

Essen and Giannakopoulou developed the Verica tool and applied probabilistic verification and synthesis to an early version of ACAS X [15,16]. Their aim was to study the impact of design issues such as model discretization and the selection of costs for the dynamic programming.

Jeannin et al. [6] analyzed ACAS X using hybrid approaches. They performed analysis on hybrid models of the system. They then used the KeYmaera tool to compute safe regions for restricted types of encounters and for a single advisory. Safe regions characterize the types of advisories that are safe for the corresponding encounter. ACAS X advisories for specific encounters can then be compared against their corresponding safe regions. The advantage of taking a hybrid approach is that it does not require discretization. However, the entire hybrid model for ACAS X is prohibitively large, which forced the authors to work with a restricted number of scenarios.

Researchers [2,3,11–14] have investigated hybrid techniques and theorem proving for other collision avoidance systems. Some researchers have developed testing frameworks for automated air-traffic control [1,4,5]. In order to evaluate the performance of ACAS X, the ACAS X team heavily relies on the simulation of a large number of encounters including recorded flight data.

More broadly, our work is related to several disciplines, such as model-based design, runtime monitoring, abstraction, and model validation. Model-based design uses models to describe, analyze, and generate code for a software system. In our work, models are abstractions of the real-world that software algorithms use for decision-making. Our conformance relations can be viewed as requirements that can be monitored at runtime, and be used for predictive analysis. These requirements are aimed particularly at establishing model quality. With respect to abstraction and model validation, our work develops metrics for validation of an abstraction in the context of its use for decision making. In other words, our conformance relations set application-specific requirements for an abstraction.

8 Conclusions

Autonomy requires models for decision making, adaptation and self-healing. For safety-critical autonomous systems, it is imperative that we develop new methods for establishing trust in these models.

In this paper, we explored and applied several model conformance criteria in the context of the ACAS X collision avoidance system, and discovered rare cases of non-conformance. We used machine learning to automatically generate additional encounters that exhibit non-conformance, and were able to identify potential causes for this issue.

In the future, we will work with the ACAS X team on developing approaches that help them prioritize the issues that our techniques report. We will also experiment with additional reward functions for encounter generation. Finally, we plan to use statistical learning techniques for the analysis of conformance issues in order to help developers with debugging their models.

Acknowledgements. We thank Ritchie Lee for his help with RLECAS, Ryan Gardner for helping us interpret the MDP, and Ryan Gardner, Mykel Kochenderfer, Ritchie Lee, and Josh Silbermann for useful discussions and for proof-reading the paper. This work was performed under the Safe Autonomous Systems Operations (SASO) project of the NASA AOSP program.

References

1. Dimjasevic, M., Giannakopoulou, D.: Test-case generation for runtime analysis, vice versa: verification of aircraft separation assurance. In: Proceedings of the 2015 International Symposium on Software Testing and Analysis, ISSTA 2015, Baltimore, 12–17 July 2015, pp. 282–292 (2015)
2. Galdino, A.L., Muñoz, C., Ayala-Rincón, M.: Formal verification of an optimal air traffic conflict resolution and recovery algorithm. In: Leivant, D., Queiroz, R. (eds.) WoLLIC 2007. LNCS, vol. 4576, pp. 177–188. Springer, Heidelberg (2007). doi:10.1007/978-3-540-73445-1_13
3. Ghorbal, K., Jeannin, J., Zawadzki, E., Platzer, A., Gordon, G.J., Capell, P.: Hybrid theorem proving of aerospace systems: applications and challenges. J. Aerospace Inf. Sys. **11**(10), 702–713 (2014)
4. Giannakopoulou, D., Bushnell, D.H., Schumann, J., Erzberger, H., Heere, K.: Formal testing for separation assurance. Ann. Math. Artif. Intell. **63**(1), 5–30 (2011)
5. Giannakopoulou, D., Howar, F., Isberner, M., Lauderdale, T., Rakamaric, Z., Raman, V.: Taming test inputs for separation assurance. In: ACM/IEEE International Conference on Automated Software Engineering, ASE 2014, Vasteras, 15–19 September 2014, pp. 373–384 (2014)
6. Jeannin, J.-B., Ghorbal, K., Kouskoulas, Y., Gardner, R., Schmidt, A., Zawadzki, E., Platzer, A.: A formally verified hybrid system for the next-generation airborne collision avoidance system. In: Baier, C., Tinelli, C. (eds.) TACAS 2015. LNCS, vol. 9035, pp. 21–36. Springer, Heidelberg (2015). doi:10.1007/978-3-662-46681-0_2
7. Kochenderfer, M.J.: Decision Making Under Uncertainty: Theory and Application. MIT Press, Cambridge (2015)
8. Kochenderfer, M.J., Chryssanthacopoulos, J.P. : Robust airborne collision avoidance through dynamic programming. Project Report ATC-371, Massachusetts Institute of Technology, Lincoln Laboratory (2011)
9. Kuchar, J., Drumm, A.C.: The traffic alert and collision avoidance system. Linc. Lab. J. **16**(2), 277 (2007)
10. Lee, R., Kochenderfer, M.J., Mengshoel, O.J., Brat, G.P., Owen, M.P.: Adaptive stress testing of airborne collision avoidance systems. In: 2015 IEEE/AIAA 34th Digital Avionics Systems Conference (DASC), p. 6C2-1. IEEE (2015)
11. Loos, S.M., Renshaw, D.W., Platzer, A.: Formal verification of distributed aircraft controllers. In: Proceedings of the 16th International Conference on Hybrid systems: Computation and Control, HSCC 2013, Philadelphia, 8–11 April 2013, pp. 125–130 (2013)
12. Lygeros, J., Lynch, N.: On the formal verification of the TCAS conflict resolution algorithms. In: 36th IEEE Conference on Decision and Control, pp. 1829–1834 (1997)

13. Platzer, A., Clarke, E.M.: Formal verification of curved flight collision avoidance maneuvers: a case study. In: Cavalcanti, A., Dams, D.R. (eds.) FM 2009. LNCS, vol. 5850, pp. 547–562. Springer, Heidelberg (2009). doi:10.1007/978-3-642-05089-3_35
14. Tomlin, C., Pappas, G.J., Sastry, S.: Conflict resolution for air traffic management: a study in multiagent hybrid systems. IEEE Trans. Autom. Control **43**(4), 509–521 (1998)
15. Essen, C., Giannakopoulou, D.: Analyzing the next generation airborne collision avoidance system. In: Ábrahám, E., Havelund, K. (eds.) TACAS 2014. LNCS, vol. 8413, pp. 620–635. Springer, Heidelberg (2014). doi:10.1007/978-3-642-54862-8_54
16. von Essen, C., Giannakopoulou, D.: Probabilistic verification and synthesis of the next generation airborne collision avoidance system. STTT **18**(2), 227–243 (2016)

Learning Moore Machines from Input-Output Traces

Georgios Giantamidis[1(✉)] and Stavros Tripakis[1,2(✉)]

[1] Aalto University, Espoo, Finland
{georgios.giantamidis,stavros.tripakis}@aalto.fi
[2] University of California, Berkeley, Berkeley, USA

Abstract. The problem of learning automata from example traces (but no equivalence or membership queries) is fundamental in automata learning theory and practice. In this paper we study this problem for finite state machines with inputs and outputs, and in particular for Moore machines. We develop three algorithms for solving this problem: (1) the PTAP algorithm, which transforms a set of input-output traces into an incomplete Moore machine and then completes the machine with self-loops; (2) the PRPNI algorithm, which uses the well-known RPNI algorithm for automata learning to learn a product of automata encoding a Moore machine; and (3) the MooreMI algorithm, which directly learns a Moore machine using PTAP extended with state merging. We prove that MooreMI has the fundamental *identification in the limit* property. We also compare the algorithms experimentally in terms of the size of the learned machine and several notions of accuracy, introduced in this paper. Finally, we compare with OSTIA, an algorithm that learns a more general class of transducers, and find that OSTIA generally does not learn a Moore machine, even when fed with a *characteristic sample*.

1 Introduction

An abundance of data from the internet and from other sources (e.g., sensors) is revolutionizing many sectors of science, technology, and ultimately our society. At the heart of this revolution lies *machine learning*, a broad spectrum of techniques to derive information from data. Traditionally, objects studied by machine learning include classifiers, decision trees, and neural networks, with applications to fields as diverse as artificial intelligence, marketing, finance, or medicine [37].

In the context of system design, an important problem, with numerous applications, is automatically generating models from data. There are many variants of this problem, depending on what types of models and data are considered, as well as other assumptions or restrictions. Examples include, but are by no means limited to, the classic field of system identification [34], as well as more

This work was partially supported by the Academy of Finland and the U.S. National Science Foundation (awards #1329759 and #1139138). An extended version of this paper is available as [17].

J. Fitzgerald et al. (Eds.): FM 2016, LNCS 9995, pp. 291–309, 2016.
DOI: 10.1007/978-3-319-48989-6_18

recent works on synthesizing programs, controllers, or other artifacts from examples [5,21,40,41,43].

In this paper we consider a basic problem, that of learning a Moore machine from a set of input-output traces. A Moore machine is a type of finite-state machine (FSM) with inputs and outputs, where the output always depends on the current state, but not on the current input [30]. Moore machines are typically *deterministic* and *complete*, meaning that for given state and input, the next state is always defined and is unique; and for given state, the output is also always uniquely defined. Such machines are useful in many applications, for instance, for representing digital circuits or controllers. In this paper we are interested in learning deterministic and complete Moore machines.

We want to learn a Moore machine from a given set of *input-output traces*. One such trace is a sequence of inputs, ρ_{in}, and the corresponding sequence of outputs, ρ_{out}, that the machine must produce when fed with ρ_{in}. As in standard machine learning methods, we call the set of traces given to the learning algorithm the *training* set. Obviously, we would like the learned machine M to be *consistent* w.r.t. the training set R, meaning that for every pair $(\rho_{in}, \rho_{out}) \in R$, M must output ρ_{out} when fed with ρ_{in}. But in addition to consistency, we would like M to behave well w.r.t. several *performance* criteria, including complexity of the learning algorithm, size of the learned machine M (its number of states), and *accuracy* of M, which captures how well M performs on a *testing* set of traces, different from the training set.

Even though this is a basic problem, it appears not to have received much attention in the literature. In fact, to the best of our knowledge, this is the first paper which formalizes and studies this problem. This is despite a large body of research on *grammatical inference* [14] which has studied similar, but not exactly the same problems, such as learning deterministic finite automata (DFA), which are special cases of Moore machines with a binary output, or subsequential transducers, which are more general than Moore machines.

Our contributions are the following:

1. We define formally the LMoMIO problem (learning Moore machines from input-output traces). Apart from the correctness criterion of *consistency* (that the learned machine be consistent with the given traces) we also introduce several *performance* criteria including size and accuracy of the learned machine, and computational complexity of the learning algorithm.
2. We adapt the notion of *characteristic sample*, which is known for DFA [14], to the case of Moore machines. Intuitively, a characteristic sample of a machine M is a set of traces which contains enough information to "reconstruct" M. The *characteristic sample requirement* (CSR) states that, when given as input a characteristic sample, the learning algorithm must produce a machine equivalent to the one that produced the sample. CSR is important, as it ensures *identification in the limit*: this is a key concept in automata learning theory which ensures that the learning algorithm will eventually learn the right machine when provided with a sufficiently large set of examples [18].

3. We develop three algorithms to solve the LMoMIO problem, and analyze them in terms of computational complexity and other properties. We show that although all three algorithms guarantee consistency, only the most advanced among them, called *MooreMI*, satisfies the characteristic sample requirement. We also show that MooreMI achieves identification in the limit.
4. We report on a prototype implementation of all three algorithms and experimental results. The experiments show that MooreMI outperforms the other two algorithms not only in theory, but also in practice.
5. We show that the well-known transducer-learning algorithm OSTIA [39] cannot generally learn a Moore machine, even in the case where the training set is a characteristic sample of a Moore machine. This implies that an algorithm to learn a more general machine (e.g., a transducer) is not necessarily good at learning a more special machine, and therefore further justifies the study of specialized learning algorithms for Moore machines.

2 Related Work

There is a large body of research on learning automata and state machines, which can be divided into two broad categories: learning with (examples and) queries (*active* learning), and learning only from examples (*passive* learning). A seminal work in the first category is Angluin's work on learning DFAs with membership and equivalence queries [7]. This work has been subsequently extended to other types of machines, such as Mealy machines [42], symbolic/extended Mealy machines [11,28], I/O automata [2], register automata [1,26], or hybrid automata [35]. These works are not directly applicable to the problem studied in this paper, as we explicitly forbid both membership and equivalence queries. In practice, performing queries (especially complete equivalence queries) is often infeasible.

In the domain of passive learning, a seminal work is Gold's study of learning DFAs from sets of positive and negative examples [18,19]. In this line of work we must distinguish algorithms that solve the *exact identification* problem, which is to find a *smallest* (in terms of number of states) automaton consistent with the given examples, from those that learn not necessarily a smallest automaton[1] (let us call them *heuristic* approaches). Gold showed that exact identification is NP-hard for DFAs [19]. Several works solve the exact identification problem by reducing it into boolean satisfiability [25,47].

Heuristic approaches are dominated by state-merging algorithms like Gold's algorithm for DFAs [19], RPNI [38] (also for DFAs), for which an incremental version also exists [16], and derivatives, like EDSM [31] (which also learns DFAs, but unlike RPNI does not guarantee identification in the limit) and OSTIA [39]

[1] The term *smallest* automaton is used in the exact identification problem, instead of the more well-known term *minimal* automaton. Among equivalent machines, one with the fewest states is called *minimal*. Among machines which are all consistent with a set of traces but not necessarily equivalent, one with the fewest states is called *smallest*.

(which learns subsequential transducers). This line of work also includes gravitational search algorithms [44], genetic algorithms [4], ant colony optimization [10], rewriting [36], as well as state splitting algorithms [48]. Spichakova [44] learns Moore machines, but unlike our work does not guarantee identification in the limit. [4,10,36,48] all learn Mealy machines.

All algorithms developed in this paper belong in the heuristic category in the sense that we do not attempt to find a *smallest* machine. However, we would still like to learn a *small* machine. Thus, size is an important *performance* criterion, as explained in Sect. 5.1. Like RPNI and other algorithms, MooreMI is also a state-merging algorithm.

Takahashi et al. [45] is close to our work, but the algorithm described there does not always yield a deterministic Moore machine, while our algorithms do. This is important because we want to learn systems like digital circuits, embedded controllers (e.g. modeled in Simulink), etc., and such systems are typically deterministic. The k-tails algorithm for finite state machine inference [9] may also result in non-deterministic machines. Moreover, this algorithm does not generally yield smallest machines, since the initial partition of the input words into equivalence classes (which then become the states of the learned machine) can be overly conservative (see [17] for details).

The work in [29] deals with learning finite state machine abstractions of non-linear analog circuits. The algorithm described in [29] is very different from ours, and uses the circuit's number of inputs to determine a subset of the states in the learned abstraction. Also, identification in the limit is not considered in [29].

Learning from "inexperienced teachers", i.e. by using either (1) only equivalence queries or (2) equivalence plus membership queries that may be answered inconclusively, has been studied in [20].

Related but different from our work are approaches which synthesize state machines from *scenarios and requirements*. Scenarios can be provided in various forms, e.g. message sequence charts [5], event sequence charts [24], or simply, input-output examples [46]. Requirements can be temporal logic formulas as in [5,46], or other types of constraints such as the *scenario constraints* used in [24]. In this paper we have examples, but no requirements.

Also related but different from ours is work in the areas of *invariant generation* and *specification mining*, which extract properties of a program or system model, such as invariants [13,22,23], temporal logic formulas [27,33] or non-deterministic finite automata [6].

FSM learning is related to FSM testing [32]. In particular, notions similar to the *nucleus* of an FSM and to *distinguishing suffixes* of states, which are used to define characteristic samples, are also used in [12,15]. The connection between conformance testing and regular inference is made explicit in [8] and [32] describes how an active learning algorithm can be used for fault detection.

Finally, let us point out the similarity of Moore and Mealy machines: a Moore machine is a special case of a Mealy machine where the output depends only on the state but not on the input; and a Mealy machine can be transformed into a Moore machine by delaying the output by one step. This similarity naturally raises the question to what extent methods to learn Mealy machines can be used to learn Moore machines (and vice versa). Answering this question is beyond the scope of the current paper. However, note that an algorithm that learns a Mealy machine cannot be used as a *black box* to learn Moore machines, for two reasons: first, the input-output traces for a Moore machine are not directly compatible with Mealy machines, and therefore need to be transformed somehow; second, the learned Mealy machine must also be transformed into a Moore machine. The exact form of such transformations and their correctness remain to be demonstrated. Such transformations may also incur performance penalties which make a learning method especially designed for Moore machines more attractive in practice.

3 Preliminaries

3.1 Finite State Machines and Automata

A *finite state machine* (FSM) is a tuple M of the form $M = (I, O, Q, q_0, \delta, \lambda)$, where: I is a finite set of *input symbols*; O is a finite set of *output symbols*; Q is a finite set of *states*; $q_0 \in Q$ is the *initial state*; $\delta : Q \times I \rightarrow Q$ is the *transition function*; and λ is the *output function*, which can be of two types: $\lambda : Q \rightarrow O$, in which case the FSM is a *Moore machine*, or $\lambda : Q \times I \rightarrow O$, in which case the FSM is a *Mealy machine*.

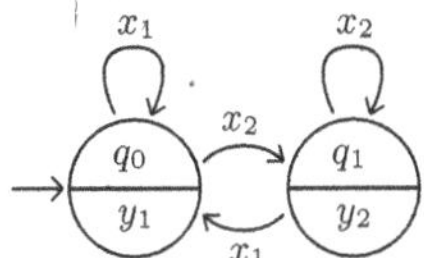

(a) Moore machine M_1 on input-output sets $I = \{x_1, x_2\}$ and $O = \{y_1, y_2\}$.

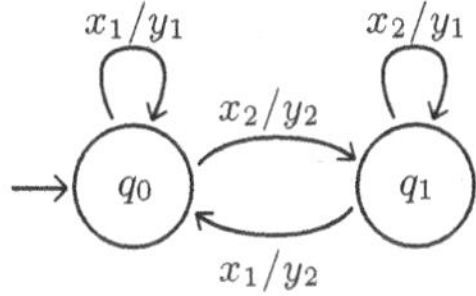

(b) Mealy machine M_2 on input-output sets $I = \{x_1, x_2\}$ and $O = \{y_1, y_2\}$.

Fig. 1. Examples of finite state machines.

If both δ and λ are total functions, we say that the FSM is *complete*. If any of δ and λ is a partial function, we say that the FSM is *incomplete*. Examples of a Moore and a Mealy machine are given in Fig. 1. Both FSMs are complete.

We also define $\delta^* : Q \times I^* \rightarrow Q$ as follows (X^* denotes the set of all finite sequences over some set X; $\epsilon \in X^*$ denotes the empty sequence over X; $w \cdot w'$ denotes the concatenation of two sequences $w, w' \in X^*$): for $q \in Q$, $w \in I^*$, and $a \in I$: $\delta^*(q, \epsilon) = q$ and $\delta^*(q, w \cdot a) = \delta(\delta^*(q, w), a)$. We also define $\lambda^* : Q \times I^* \rightarrow O^*$. The rest of this paper focuses on Moore machines, thus we define λ^* only in the case where M is a Moore machine (the adaptation to a Mealy machine is straightforward): $\lambda^*(q, \epsilon) = \lambda(q)$ and $\lambda^*(q, w \cdot a) = \lambda^*(q, w) \cdot \lambda(\delta^*(q, w \cdot a))$.

Two Moore machines M_1, M_2, with $M_i = (I_i, O_i, Q_i, q_{0\_i}, \delta_i, \lambda_i)$, are said to be *equivalent* iff $I_1 = I_2$, $O_1 = O_2$, and $\forall w \in I_1^* : \lambda_1^*(q_{0\_1}, w) = \lambda_2^*(q_{0\_2}, w)$.

A Moore machine $M = (I, O, Q, q_0, \delta, \lambda)$ is *minimal* if for any other Moore machine $M' = (I', O', Q', q_0', \delta', \lambda')$ such that M and M' are equivalent, we have $|Q| \leq |Q'|$, where $|X|$ denotes the size of a set X.

A *deterministic finite automaton* (DFA) is a tuple $A = (\Sigma, Q, q_0, \delta, F)$, where: Σ (the *alphabet*) is a finite set of *letters*; Q is a finite set of *states*; $q_0 \in S$ is the *initial state*; $\delta : Q \times \Sigma \to Q$ is the *transition function*; $F \subseteq Q$ is the set of *accepting states.*

A DFA can be seen as a special case of a Moore machine, where the set of input symbols I is Σ, and the set of output symbols is binary, say $O = \{0, 1\}$, with 1 and 0 corresponding to accepting and non-accepting states, respectively. The concepts of *complete* and *incomplete* DFAs, as well as the definition of δ^*, are similar to the corresponding ones for FSMs. Elements of Σ^* are usually called *words.* A DFA $A = (\Sigma, Q, q_0, \delta, F)$ is said to accept a word w if $\delta^*(q_0, w) \in F$.

A *non-deterministic finite automaton* (NFA) is a tuple $A = (\Sigma, Q, Q_0, \Delta, F)$, where Σ, Q, and F are as in a DFA, and: $Q_0 \subseteq Q$ is the *set of initial states*; $\Delta \subseteq Q \times \Sigma \times Q$ is the *transition relation.* Examples of a DFA and an NFA are given in Fig. 2. Accepting states are drawn with double circles.

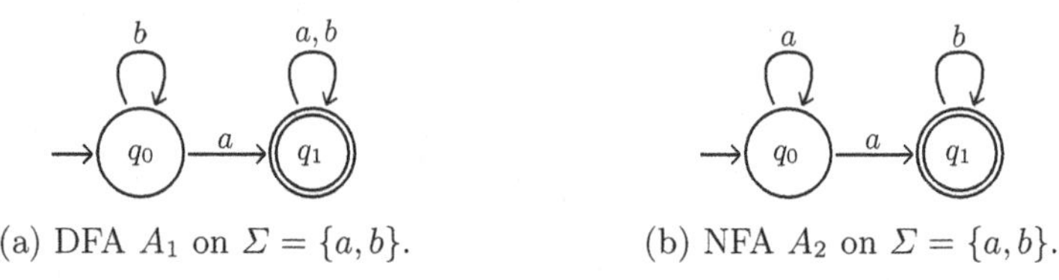

(a) DFA A_1 on $\Sigma = \{a, b\}$. (b) NFA A_2 on $\Sigma = \{a, b\}$.

Fig. 2. Examples of finite state automata.

Given two NFAs, $A_1 = (\Sigma, Q_1, Q_0^1, \Delta_1, F_1)$ and $A_2 = (\Sigma, Q_2, Q_0^2, \Delta_2, F_2)$, their *synchronous product* is the NFA $A = (\Sigma, Q_1 \times Q_2, Q_0^1 \times Q_0^2, \Delta, F_1 \times F_2)$, where $((q_1, q_2), a, (q_1', q_2')) \in \Delta$ iff $(q_1, a, q_1') \in \Delta_1$ and $(q_2, a, q_2') \in \Delta_2$. The synchronous product of automata is used in several algorithms presented in the sequel.

3.2 Input-Output Traces and Examples

Given sets of input and output symbols I and O, respectively, a *Moore* (I, O)-*trace* is a pair of finite sequences $(x_1 x_2 \cdots x_n,\ y_0 y_1 \cdots y_n)$, for some natural number $n \geq 0$, such that $x_i \in I$ and $y_i \in O$ for all $i \leq n$. That is, a Moore (I, O)-trace is a pair of a input sequence and an output sequence, such that the output sequence has length one more than the input sequence. Note that n may be 0, in which case the input sequence is empty (i.e., has length 0), and the output sequence contains just one output symbol.

Given a Moore (I,O)-trace $\rho = (x_1x_2\cdots x_n,\ y_0y_1\cdots y_n)$, and a Moore machine $M = (I,O,Q,q_0,\delta,\lambda)$, we say that ρ *is consistent with* M if $y_0 = \lambda(q_0)$ and for all $i = 1,...,n$, $y_i = \lambda(q_i)$, where $q_i = \delta(q_{i-1}, x_i)$.

Similarly to the concept of a Moore (I,O)-trace we define a *Moore* (I,O)-*example* as a pair of a finite input symbol sequence and an output symbol: $(x_1x_2\cdots x_n,\ y)$, where $x_i \in I$, for $i = 1,...,n$, and $y \in O$. We say that a Moore machine $M = (I,O,Q,q_0,\delta,\lambda)$ is consistent with a Moore (I,O)-example $\rho = (x_1x_2\cdots x_n,\ y)$ if $\lambda(\delta^*(q_0, x_1x_2\cdots x_n)) = y$.

Since a DFA can be seen as the special case of a Moore machine with a binary output alphabet, the concept of a Moore (I,O)-example is naturally carried over to DFAs, in the form of *positive and negative examples.* Specifically, a finite word w is a *positive* example for a DFA if it is accepted by the DFA, and a *negative* example if it is rejected. Viewing a DFA as a Moore machine with binary output, a positive example w corresponds to the Moore example $(w,1)$, while a negative example corresponds to the Moore example $(w,0)$.

3.3 Prefix Tree Acceptors and Prefix Tree Acceptor Products

Given a finite and non-empty set of positive examples over a given alphabet Σ, $S_+ \subseteq \Sigma^*$, we can construct, in a non-unique way, a tree-shaped, incomplete DFA, that accepts all words in S_+, and rejects all others. Such a DFA is called a *prefix tree acceptor* [14] (PTA) for S_+. For example, a PTA for $S_+ = \{b, aa, ab\}$ is shown in Fig. 3.

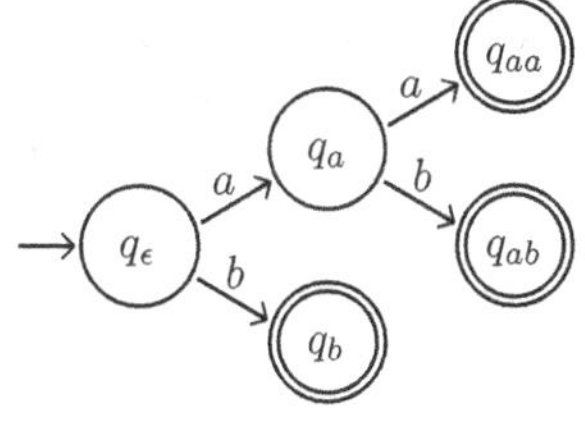

Fig. 3. A PTA for $S_+ = \{b, aa, ab\}$.

We extend the concept of PTA to Moore machines. Suppose that we have a set S_{IO} of Moore (I,O)-examples. Let $N = \lceil \log_2 |O| \rceil$ be the number of bits necessary to represent an element of O. Then, given a function f that maps elements of O to bit tuples of length N, we can map S_{IO} to N pairs of positive and negative example sets, $\{(S_{1+}, S_{1-}), (S_{2+}, S_{2-}), \cdots, (S_{N+}, S_{N-})\}$. In particular, for each pair $(w,y) \in S_{IO}$, if the i-th element of $f(y)$ is 1, then S_{i+} should contain w

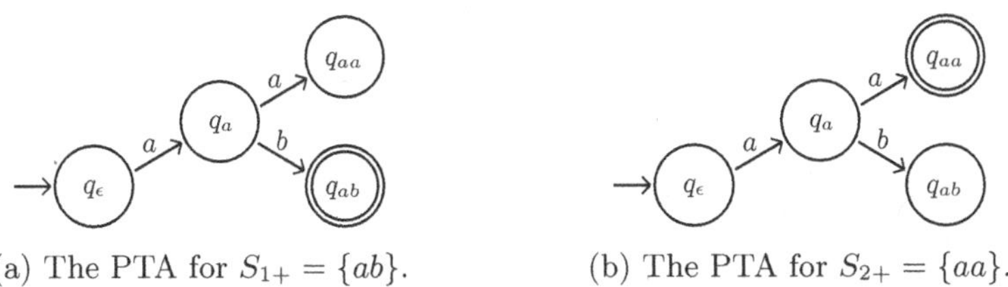

(a) The PTA for $S_{1+} = \{ab\}$. (b) The PTA for $S_{2+} = \{aa\}$.

Fig. 4. A PTAP for $S_{IO} = \{(b,0),(aa,1),(ab,2)\}$, with $I = \{a,b\}$, $O = \{0,1,2\}$, and $f = \{0 \mapsto (0,0), 1 \mapsto (0,1), 2 \mapsto (1,0)\}$. The positive and negative example sets are: $S_{1+} = \{ab\}$, $S_{1-} = \{b, aa\}$, $S_{2+} = \{aa\}$, $S_{2-} = \{b, ab\}$.

and S_{i-} should not. Similarly, if the i-th element of $f(y)$ is 0, then S_{i-} should contain w and S_{i+} should not.

We can subsequently construct a *prefix tree acceptor product* (PTAP), which is a collection of N PTAs, one for each positive example set, S_{i+}, for $i = 1, \cdots, N$. An example of a PTAP consisting of two PTAs is given in Fig. 4.

4 Characteristic Samples

An important concept in automata learning theory is that of a *characteristic sample* [14]. A characteristic sample for a DFA is a set of words that captures all information about that automaton's set of states and behavior. In this paper we extend the concept of characteristic sample to Moore machines.

4.1 Characteristic Samples for Moore Machines

Let $M = (I, O, Q, q_0, \delta, \lambda)$ be a minimal Moore machine. Let $<$ denote a total order on input words, i.e., on I^*, such that $w < w'$ iff either $|w| < |w'|$, or $|w| = |w'|$ but w comes before w' in lexicographic order ($|w|$ denotes the length of a word w). For example, $b < aa$ and $aaa < aba$.

Given a state $q \in Q$, we define the *shortest prefix* of q as the shortest input word which can be used to reach q:

$$S_P(q) = min_<\{w \in I^* \mid \delta^*(q_0, w) = q\}.$$

Notice that M is minimal, which implies that all its states are reachable (otherwise we could remove unreachable states). Therefore, $S_P(q)$ is well-defined for every state q of M.

Next, we define the set of *shortest prefixes of* M, denoted $S_P(M)$, as:

$$S_P(M) = \{S_P(q) \mid q \in Q\}$$

We can now define the *nucleus* of M which contains the empty word and all one-letter extensions of words in $S_P(M)$:

$$N_L(M) = \{\epsilon\} \cup \{w \cdot a \mid w \in S_P(M),\ a \in I\}.$$

We also define the *minimum distinguishing suffix* for two different states q_u and q_v of M, as follows:

$$M_D(q_u, q_v) = min_<\{w \in I^* \mid \lambda^*(q_u, w) \neq \lambda^*(q_v, w)\}.$$

$M_D(q_u, q_v)$ is guaranteed to exist for any two states q_u, q_v because M is minimal.

Let W be a set of input words, $W \subseteq I^*$. $Pref(W)$ denotes the set of all prefixes of all words in W:

$$Pref(W) = \{x \in I^* \mid \exists w \in W, y \in I^* : x \cdot y = w\}.$$

Definition 1. *Let S_{IO} be a set of Moore (I,O)-traces, and let S_I be the corresponding set of input words: $S_I = \{\rho_I \in I^* \mid (\rho_I, \rho_O) \in S_{IO}\}$. S_{IO} is a* characteristic sample *for a Moore machine M iff:*

1. $N_L(M) \subseteq Pref(S_I)$.
2. $\forall u \in S_P(M) : \forall v \in N_L(M) : \forall w \in I^* :$

$$\delta^*(q_0, u) \neq \delta^*(q_0, v) \wedge w = M_D(\delta^*(q_0, u), \delta^*(q_0, v)) \Rightarrow \{u \cdot w, v \cdot w\} \subseteq Pref(S_I).$$

For example, consider the Moore machine M_1 from Fig. 1. We have: $S_P(q_0) = \epsilon$, $S_P(q_1) = x_2$, $S_P(M_1) = \{\epsilon, x_2\}$, and $N_L(M_1) = \{\epsilon, x_1, x_2, x_2x_1, x_2x_2\}$. The following set is a characteristic sample for M_1:

$$S_{IO} = \{\ (x_1,\ y_1y_1),\ (x_2x_1,\ y_1y_2y_1),\ (x_2x_2,\ y_1y_2y_2)\ \}.$$

While it is intuitive that a characteristic sample should contain input words that in a sense *cover* all states and transitions of M (Condition 1 of Definition 1), it may not be obvious why Condition 2 of Definition 1 is necessary. This becomes clear if we look at machines having the same output on several states. For example, consider the Moore machine M in Fig. 5a. The set of (I, O)-traces $S_{IO}^1 = \{(aa, 020), (ba, 012), (bb, 012), (aba, 0222), (abb, 0222)\}$ satisfies Condition 1 but not Condition 2 (because $S_P(q_2) = a$, $ba \in N_L(M)$, $\delta^*(q_0, ba) = q_3$, $M_D(q_2, q_3) = a$, but no input word in S_{IO}^1 has baa as a prefix), and therefore is not a characteristic sample of the machine of Fig. 5a. If we use S_{IO}^1 to learn a Moore machine, we obtain the machine in Fig. 5b (this machine was produced by our MooreMI algorithm, described in Sect. 5.2). Clearly, the two machines of Fig. 5 are not equivalent. For instance, the input word baa results in different outputs when fed to the two machines. The reason why the learning algorithm produces the wrong machine is that the set S_{IO}^1 does not contain enough information to clearly distinguish between states q_2 and q_3.

Instead, consider the set $S_{IO}^2 = \{(aa, 020), (baa, 0122), (bba, 0122), (abaa, 02220), (abba, 02220)\}$. S_{IO}^2 satisfies both Conditions 1 and 2, and therefore is a characteristic sample. Given S_{IO}^2 as input, our MooreMI algorithm is able to learn the correct machine, i.e., the machine of Fig. 5a. In this case, the minimum distinguishing suffix of states q_2 and q_3 is simply the letter a, since $\delta(q_2, a) = q_0$, $\delta(q_3, a) = q_2$ and $\lambda(q_0) = 0 \neq 2 = \lambda(q_2)$. Notice that S_{IO}^2 can be constructed from S_{IO}^1 by extending with the letter a the input words of the latter that land on q_2 or q_3.

The intuition, then, behind Condition 2 is that states in M that have the same outputs cannot be distinguished by just those (outputs); additional suffixes that differentiate them are required.

4.2 Computation, Minimality, Size, and Other Properties of Characteristic Samples

It is easy to see that adding more traces to a characteristic sample preserves the characteristic sample property, i.e., if S_{IO} is a characteristic sample for a

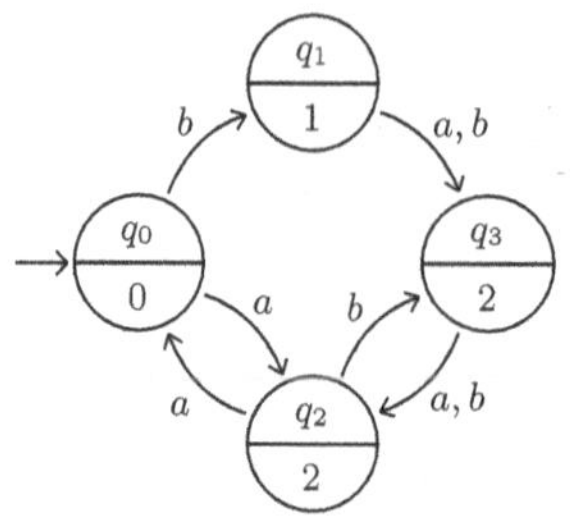

(a) Target minimal Moore machine.

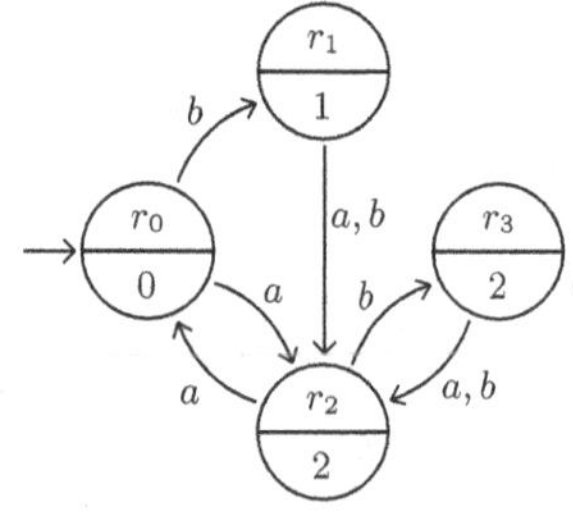

(b) Moore machine learned by our MooreMI algorithm if we use a set of traces that does not satisfy Condition 2 of Definition 1.

Fig. 5. Example illustrating the need for Condition 2 of Definition 1.

Moore machine M and $S'_{IO} \supseteq S_{IO}$, then S'_{IO} is also a characteristic sample for M. Also, arbitrarily extending the input word of an existing (I, O)-trace in S_{IO} and accordingly extending the corresponding output word, again yields a new characteristic sample for M. The questions are raised, then, whether there exist characteristic samples that are minimal in some sense, how many elements they consist of, what are the lengths of their elements, and how can we construct them.

In [17], we outline a simple procedure that, given a minimal Moore machine M, returns a characteristic sample S_{IO} that is minimal in the sense that removing any (I, O)-trace from it or dropping any number of letters at the end of an input word in it (and accordingly adjusting the corresponding output word) will result in a set that is not a characteristic sample. By doing so, we also constructively establish the existence of at least one characteristic sample for any minimal Moore machine M.

Space limitations prevent us from including the description of the procedure in this paper: it can be found in [17], together with an analysis of the procedure in order to determine the "size" of the characteristic sample S_{IO}. It seems reasonable to measure this size as the sum of the lengths of all elements in S_{IO}. As it turns out, this sum is $O(|Q|^4|I|)$.

5 Learning Moore Machines from Input-Output Traces

5.1 Problem Definition

The problem of learning Moore machines from input-output traces (LMoMIO) is defined as follows. Given an input alphabet I, an output alphabet O, and a set R_{train} of Moore (I, O)-traces, called the *training set*, we want to synthesize automatically a deterministic, complete Moore machine $M = (I, O, Q, q_0, \delta, \lambda)$, such that M is consistent with R_{train}, i.e., $\forall\ (\rho_I, \rho_O) \in R_{\mathsf{train}} : \lambda^*(\rho_I) = \rho_O$.

(R_{train} is assumed to be itself consistent, in the sense it does not contain two different pairs with the same input word.)

In addition to consistency, we would like to evaluate our learning technique w.r.t. various *performance* criteria, including:

- *Size* of M, in terms of number of states. Note that, contrary to the *exact identification* problem [19], we do *not require* M to be the smallest (in terms of number of states) machine consistent with R_{train}.
- *Accuracy* of M, which, informally speaking, is a measure of how well M performs on a set of traces, R_{test}, *different* from the training set. R_{test} is called the *test set.* Accuracy is a standard criterion in machine learning.
- *Complexity* (e.g., running time) of the learning algorithm itself.

In the rest of this paper, we present three learning algorithms which solve the LMoMIO problem, and evaluate them w.r.t. the above criteria. Complexity of the algorithm and size of the learned machine are standard notions. Accuracy is standard in machine learning topics such as classification, but not in automata learning. Thus, we elaborate on this concept next.

There are more than one ways to measure the accuracy of a learned Moore machine M against a test set R_{test}. We call an *accuracy evaluation policy* (AEP) any function that, given a Moore (I, O)-trace (ρ_I, ρ_O) and a Moore machine $M = (I, O, Q, q_0, \delta, \lambda)$, will return a real number in $[0, 1]$. We will call that number the accuracy of M on (ρ_I, ρ_O). In this paper, we use three AEPs which we call *strong*, *medium*, and *weak*, defined below. Let $(\rho_I, \rho_O) = (x_1x_2\cdots x_n,\ y_0y_1\cdots y_n)$ and $z_0z_1\cdots z_n = \lambda^*(q_0, \rho_I)$.

- *Strong*: if $\lambda^*(q_0, \rho_I) = \rho_O$ then 1 else 0.
- *Medium*: $\frac{1}{n+1} \cdot |\{i \mid y_0y_1\cdots y_i = z_0z_1\cdots z_i\}|$.
- *Weak*: $\frac{1}{n+1} \cdot |\{i \mid y_i = z_i\}|$.

The strong AEP says that the output of the learned machine M must be identical to the output in the test set. The medium AEP returns the proportion of the largest output prefix that matches. The weak AEP returns the number of output symbols that match. For example, if the correct output is 0012 and M returns 0022 then the strong accuracy is 0, the medium accuracy is $\frac{2}{4}$, and the weak accuracy is $\frac{3}{4}$. Ideally, we want the learned machine to achieve a high accuracy with respect to the strong AEP. However, the medium and weak AEPs are also useful, because they allow to distinguish, say, a machine which is "almost right" (i.e., outputs the right sequence except for a few symbols) from a machine which is always or almost always wrong.

Given an accuracy evaluation policy f and a test set R_{test}, we define the accuracy of M on R_{test} as the averaged accuracy of M over all traces in R_{test}, i.e.,

$$\frac{\sum_{(\rho_I, \rho_O) \in R_{\mathsf{test}}} f((\rho_I, \rho_O), M)}{|R_{\mathsf{test}}|}.$$

It is often the case that the test set R_{test} contains traces generated by a "black box", for which we are trying to learn a model. Suppose this black box corresponds to an unknown machine $M_?$. Then, ideally, we would like the learned machine M to be equivalent to $M_?$. In that case, no matter what test set is generated by $M_?$, the learned machine M will always achieve 100 % accuracy. Of course, achieving this ideal depends on the training set: if the latter is "poor" then it does not contain enough information to identify the original machine $M_?$. A standard requirement in automata learning theory states that when the training set is a characteristic sample of $M_?$, then the learning algorithm should be able to produce a machine which is equivalent to $M_?$. We call this the *characteristic sample requirement* (CSR). CSR is important, as it ensures *identification in the limit*, a key concept in automata learning theory [18]. In what follows, we show that among the algorithms that will be presented in Sect. 5.2, only MooreMI satisfies CSR.

Before proceeding, we remark that a given Moore (I, O)-trace $(\rho_I, \rho_O) = (x_1 x_2 \cdots x_n,\ y_0 y_1 \cdots y_n)$ can be represented as a set of $n+1$ Moore (I, O)-examples, specifically $\{(\epsilon, y_0), (x_1, y_1), (x_1 x_2, y_2), \cdots, (x_1 x_2 \cdots x_n, y_n)\}$. Because of this observation, in all approaches discussed below, there is a preprocessing step to convert the training set, first into an equivalent set of Moore (I, O)-examples, and second, into an equivalent set of N pairs of positive and negative example sets (the latter conversion was described in Sect. 3.3).

5.2 Algorithms to Solve the LMoMIO Problem

The PTAP Algorithm. This algorithm is a rather straightforward one. The set of Moore (I, O)-examples obtained after the preprocessing step described above is used to construct a PTAP, as described in Sect. 3.3. Recall that a PTAP is a collection of N PTAs having the same state-transition structure. The synchronous product of these N PTAs is then formed, *completed*, and returned as the result of the algorithm. Note that a PTA is a special case of an NFA: the PTA is deterministic, but it is generally incomplete. The synchronous product of PTAs is therefore the same as the synchronous product of NFAs. The product of PTAs is deterministic, but also generally incomplete, and therefore needs to be completed in order to yield a complete DFA. *Completion* in this case consists in adding self-loops to states that are missing outgoing transitions for some input symbols. The added self-loops are labeled with the missing input symbols.

Although the PTAP algorithm is relatively easy to implement and runs efficiently, it has several drawbacks. First, since no state minimization is attempted, the resulting Moore machine can be unnecessarily large. Second, and most importantly, the produced machines generally have poor accuracy since completion is done in a trivial manner.

The PRPNI Algorithm. Again, consider the N pairs of positive and negative example sets obtained after the preprocessing step. The PRPNI algorithm starts by executing the RPNI DFA learning algorithm [38] on each pair, thus obtaining N learned DFAs. Then, the synchronous product of these DFAs is formed, *completed*, and returned as the algorithm result. As in the case of the

PTAP algorithm, the synchronous product of the DFAs in the PRPNI algorithm is deterministic but generally not complete.

The completion step of the PRPNI algorithm is more intricate than the completion step of the PTAP algorithm. The reason is that the synchronous product of the learned DFAs may contain reachable states whose bit encoding does not correspond to any valid output in O. For example, suppose $O = \{0, 1, 2\}$, so that we need 2 bits to encode it, and thus $N = 2$ and we use RPNI to learn 2 DFAs. Suppose the encoding is $0 \mapsto 00, 1 \mapsto 01, 2 \mapsto 10$. This means that the code 11 does not correspond to any valid output in O. However, it can still be the case that in the product of the two DFAs there is a reachable state with the output 11, i.e., where both DFAs are in an accepting state. Note that this problem does not arise in the PTAP algorithm, because all PTAs there are guaranteed to have the same state-transition structure, which is also the structure of their synchronous product.

To solve this invalid-code problem, we assign all invalid codes to an arbitrary valid output. In our implementation, we use the lexicographic minimum. In the above example, the code 11 will be assigned to the output 0.

Compared to the PTAP algorithm, the PRPNI algorithm has the advantage of being able to learn a minimal Moore machine when provided with enough (I, O)-traces. However, it can also perform worse in terms of both running time and size (number of states) of the learned machine, due to potential state explosion while forming the DFA product. The PTAP algorithm does not have this problem because, as explained above, the structure, and therefore also the number of states, of the product is identical to those of the component PTAs.

The MooreMI Algorithm. As we saw above, both the PTAP and PRPNI algorithms have several drawbacks. In this section we propose a novel algorithm, called, MooreMI, which remedies these. Moreover, we shall prove that MooreMI satisfies CSR.

The MooreMI algorithm begins by building a PTAP represented as N PTAs, as in the PTAP algorithm. Then, a merging phase follows, where a merge operation is accepted only if all resulting DFAs are consistent with their respective negative example sets. In addition, a merge operation is either performed on all DFAs at once or not at all. Finally, the synchronous product of the N learned DFAs is formed, completed by adding self loops for any missing input symbols, as in the PTAP algorithm, and returned. The pseudocode for the MooreMI algorithm can be found in [17]. Space limitations prevent us from including it in this paper.

MooreMI is able to learn minimal Moore machines, while avoiding the state explosion and invalid code issues of PRPNI. To see this, notice first that, at every point of the algorithm, the N learned DFAs are identical in terms of states and transitions, modulo the marking of their states as final. Indeed, this invariant holds by construction for the N initial prefix tree acceptors, and the additional merge constraints make sure it is maintained throughout the algorithm. Therefore, the product formed at the end of the algorithm can be obtained by simply "overlaying" the N DFAs on top of one another, as in the PTAP approach, which implies no state explosion. The absence of invalid output codes is also easy to see. Invalid codes generally are results of problematic state tuples in the DFA product, that cannot appear in MooreMI due to the additional merge constraints. Indeed, if a state tuple occurs in the final product, it must also occur in the initial prefix tree acceptor product, and if it occurs there, its code cannot be invalid.

5.3 Properties of the Algorithms

All three algorithms described above satisfy consistency w.r.t. the input training set. For PTAP and PRPNI, this is a direct consequence of the properties of PTAs, of the basic RPNI algorithm, and of the synchronous product. The proof for MooreMI is somewhat more involved, therefore the result for MooreMI is stated as a theorem (proofs can be found in [17]):

Theorem 1 (Consistency). *The output of the MooreMI algorithm is a complete Moore machine, consistent with the training set. Formally, let S_{IO} be the set of Moore (I, O)-traces used as input for the algorithm, and let $M = (I, O, Q, q_0, \delta, \lambda)$ be the resulting Moore machine. Then, δ and λ are total functions and $\forall\ (\rho_I, \rho_O) \in S_{IO}\ :\ \lambda^*(q_0, \rho_I) = \rho_O$.*

We now show that MooreMI satisfies the characteristic sample requirement, i.e., if it is fed with a characteristic sample for a machine M, then it learns a machine equivalent to M. If M is minimal then the learned machine will in fact be isomorphic to M.

Theorem 2 (Characteristic Sample Requirement). *If the input to MooreMI is a characteristic sample of a minimal Moore machine M, then the algorithm returns a machine M_A that is isomorphic to M.*

Finally, we show that the MooreMI algorithm achieves identification in the limit.

Theorem 3 (Identification in the Limit). *Let $M = (I, O, Q, q_0, \delta, \lambda)$ be a minimal Moore machine. Let $(\rho_I^1, \rho_O^1), (\rho_I^2, \rho_O^2), \cdots$ be an infinite sequence of (I, O)-traces generated from M, such that $\forall \rho \in I^* : \exists i : \rho = \rho_I^i$ (i.e., every input word appears at least once in the sequence). Then there exists index k such that for all $n \geq k$, the MooreMI algorithm learns a machine equivalent to M when given as input the training set $\{(\rho_I^1, \rho_O^1), (\rho_I^2, \rho_O^2), \cdots, (\rho_I^n, \rho_O^n)\}$.*

5.4 Complexity Analysis

Let I and O be the input and output alphabets, and let S_{IO} be the set of Moore (I, O)-traces provided as input to the learning algorithms. Let $N = \lceil log_2(|O|) \rceil$ be the number of bits required to encode the symbols in O. Let $S_{1+}, S_{1-}, ..., S_{N+}, S_{N-}$ be the positive and negative example sets obtained by the preprocessing step at the beginning of each algorithm. Let $m_+ = \sum_{i=1}^{N} \sum_{w \in S_{i+}} |w|$, $m_- = \sum_{i=1}^{N} \sum_{w \in S_{i-}} |w|$, and $k = \sum_{(\rho_I, \rho_O) \in S_{IO}} |\rho_I|^2$.

The time required for the preprocessing step is $O(N \cdot k)$, and is the same for all three algorithms. The time required for the rest of the phases of each algorithm is $O((N + |I|) \cdot m_+)$ for PTAP, $O((N + |I|) \cdot m_+^N + N \cdot m_+^2 \cdot (m_+ + m_-))$ for PRPNI, and $O((N + |I|) \cdot m_+ + N \cdot m_+^2 \cdot (m_+ + m_-))$ for MooreMI. It can be seen that the complexity of MooreMI is no more than logarithmic in the number of output symbols, linear in the number of inputs, and cubic in the total length of training traces. This polynomial complexity does not contradict Gold's NP-hardness result [19], since the problem we solve is not the exact identification problem (c.f. also Sect. 2).

6 Implementation and Experiments

All three algorithms presented in Sect. 5.2 have been implemented in Python. The source code, including random Moore machine and characteristic sample generation, learning algorithms and testing, spans roughly 2000 lines of code. The code and experiments are available upon request.

6.1 Experimental Comparison

We randomly generated several minimal Moore machines of sizes 50 and 150 states, and input and alphabet sizes $|I| = |O| = 25$ (see [17] for details on the random generation method). From each such machine, we generated a characteristic sample, and ran each of the three algorithms on this characteristic sample, i.e., using it as the training set. Then we took the learned machines generated by the algorithms, and evaluated these machines in terms of size (# states) and accuracy. For accuracy, we used a test set of size double the size of the training set. The length of words in the test set was double the maximum training word length.

The results are shown in Table 1. "Algo 1, 2, 3" refers to PTAP, PRPNI, and MooreMI, respectively. "Time" refers to the average execution time of the learning algorithm, in seconds. "States" refers to the average number of states of the learned machines. For accuracy, we used the three AEPs, Strong, Medium, and Weak, defined in Sect. 5.1. The table is split into two tabs according to the size of the original machines mentioned above. Each row represents the average performance of an algorithm over training sets generated by 5 different Moore machines. The only exception is row 2 of the 50 states tab, where one of the 5 experiments timed out and the reported averages are over 4 experiments. "Timeout" means that the algorithm was unable to terminate within the given time limit (60 seconds) in any of the 5 experiments with 150 states.[2]

[2] Note, however, that our algorithms perform better in terms of execution time than approaches that solve exact identification problems. For example, [46] report experiments where learning a Mealy machine of 18 states requires more than 29 h. The majority of the execution time here is spent in proving that there exists no machine with fewer than 18 states which is also consistent with the examples. Since we don't require the smallest machine, our algorithms avoid this penalty.

Table 1. 50 (resp. 150) states tab: average training set size: 1305 (resp. 4540), average input word length in training set: 3.5 (resp. 4).

Algo	50 states					150 states				
	Time	States	Accuracy (%)			Time	States	Accuracy (%)		
			Strong	Medium	Weak			Strong	Medium	Weak
1	0.973	2113	0	32.44	35.39	8.329	7135	0	28.28	31.13
2	12.753	8925	0	33.82	36.57	60	Timeout	–	–	–
3	0.348	50	100	100	100	2.545	150	100	100	100

As expected, MooreMI always achieves 100 % accuracy, since the input is a characteristic sample (we verified that indeed the machines learned by MooreMI are in each case equivalent to the original machine that produced the training set). But as it can be seen from the table, neither PTAP nor PRPNI learn the correct machines, even though the training set is a characteristic sample.

The table also shows that PTAP and PRPNI generate much larger machines than the correct ones. This in turn explains why MooreMI performs better in terms of running time than the other two algorithms, which spend a lot of time completing the large number of generated states.

6.2 Comparison with OSTIA

OSTIA [39] is a well-known algorithm that learns *onward subsequential transducers*, a class of transducers more general than Moore and Mealy machines. Then, a question arising naturally is whether it is possible to use OSTIA for learning Moore machines. In particular, we would like to know what happens when the input to OSTIA is a set of Moore (I,O)-traces: will OSTIA learn a Moore machine?

The answer here is negative, as indicated by an experiment we performed. We constructed a characteristic sample for the Moore machine in Fig. 5a and ran the OSTIA algorithm on it (we used the open source implementation described in [3]). The resulting machine is depicted in Fig. 6. Notice that there are transitions whose corresponding outputs are words of length more than 1 (e.g., transition label $b/0122$), or even the empty word (output of initial state q_0). We conclude that in general OSTIA cannot learn Moore machines, even when the training set is a set of Moore traces, and is also a characteristic sample.

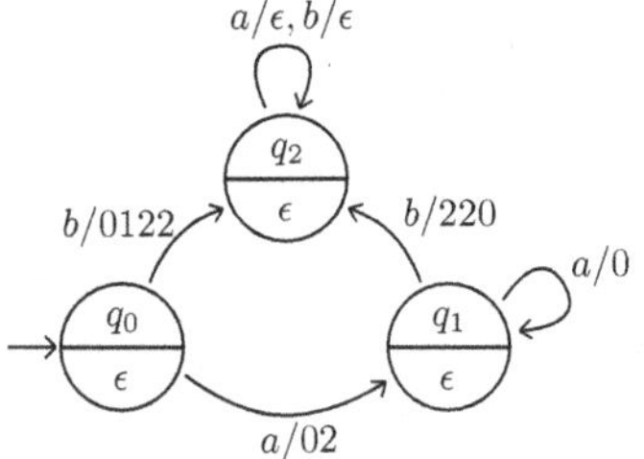

Fig. 6. The transducer learned by OSTIA given a characteristic sample for the Moore machine in Fig. 5a as input.

7 Conclusion and Future Work

We formalized the problem of learning Moore machines for input-output traces and developed three algorithms to solve this problem. We showed that the most advanced of these algorithms, MooreMI, has desirable theoretical properties: in particular it satisfies the characteristic sample requirement and achieves identification in the limit. We also compared the algorithms experimentally and showed that MooreMI is also superior in practice.

Future work includes: (1) studying learning for Mealy and other types of state machines; (2) developing incremental versions of the learning algorithms presented here; (3) further implementation and experimentation; and (4) application of the methods presented here for learning models of various types of black-box systems.

References

1. Aarts, F., Fiterau-Brostean, P., Kuppens, H., Vaandrager, F.: Learning register automata with fresh value generation. In: Leucker, M., Rueda, C., Valencia, F.D. (eds.) ICTAC 2015. LNCS, vol. 9399, pp. 165–183. Springer, Heidelberg (2015). doi:10.1007/978-3-319-25150-9_11
2. Aarts, F., Vaandrager, F.: Learning I/O automata. In: Gastin, P., Laroussinie, F. (eds.) CONCUR 2010. LNCS, vol. 6269, pp. 71–85. Springer, Heidelberg (2010). doi:10.1007/978-3-642-15375-4_6
3. Akram, H.I., Higuera, C., Xiao, H., Eckert, C.: Grammatical inference algorithms in MATLAB. In: Sempere, J.M., García, P. (eds.) ICGI 2010. LNCS (LNAI), vol. 6339, pp. 262–266. Springer, Heidelberg (2010). doi:10.1007/978-3-642-15488-1_22
4. Aleksandrov, A.V., Kazakov, S.V., Sergushichev, A.A., Tsarev, F.N., Shalyto, A.A.: The use of evolutionary programming based on training examples for the generation of finite state machines for controlling objects with complex behavior. J. Comput. Syst. Sci. Int. **52**(3), 410–425 (2013)
5. Alur, R., Martin, M., Raghothaman, M., Stergiou, C., Tripakis, S., Udupa, A.: Synthesizing finite-state protocols from scenarios and requirements. In: Yahav, E. (ed.) HVC 2014. LNCS, vol. 8855, pp. 75–91. Springer, Heidelberg (2014). doi:10.1007/978-3-319-13338-6_7
6. Ammons, G., Bodík, R., Larus, J.R.: Mining specifications. In: POPL 2002, pp. 4–16. ACM (2002)
7. Angluin, D.: Learning regular sets from queries and counterexamples. Inf. Comput. **75**(2), 87–106 (1987)
8. Berg, T., Grinchtein, O., Jonsson, B., Leucker, M., Raffelt, H., Steffen, B.: On the correspondence between conformance testing and regular inference. In: Cerioli, M. (ed.) FASE 2005. LNCS, vol. 3442, pp. 175–189. Springer, Heidelberg (2005). doi:10.1007/978-3-540-31984-9_14
9. Biermann, A.W., Feldman, J.A.: On the synthesis of finite-state machines from samples of their behavior. IEEE Trans. Comput. **21**(6), 592–597 (1972)
10. Buzhinsky, I.P., Ulyantsev, V.I., Chivilikhin, D.S., Shalyto, A.A.: Inducing finite state machines from training samples using ant colony optimization. J. Comput. Syst. Sci. Int. **53**(2), 256–266 (2014)

11. Cassel, S., Howar, F., Jonsson, B., Steffen, B.: Learning extended finite state machines. In: Giannakopoulou, D., Salaün, G. (eds.) SEFM 2014. LNCS, vol. 8702, pp. 250–264. Springer, Heidelberg (2014). doi:10.1007/978-3-319-10431-7_18
12. Chow, T.S.: Testing software design modeled by finite-state machines. IEEE Trans. Softw. Eng. **4**(3), 178–187 (1978)
13. Colón, M.A., Sankaranarayanan, S., Sipma, H.B.: Linear invariant generation using non-linear constraint solving. In: Hunt, W.A., Somenzi, F. (eds.) CAV 2003. LNCS, vol. 2725, pp. 420–432. Springer, Heidelberg (2003). doi:10.1007/978-3-540-45069-6_39
14. de la Higuera, C.: Grammatical Inference: Learning Automata and Grammars. CUP, Cambridge (2010)
15. Dorofeeva, R., El-Fakih, K., Maag, S., Cavalli, A.R., Yevtushenko, N.: FSM-based conformance testing methods: a survey annotated with experimental evaluation. Inf. Softw. Technol. **52**(12), 1286–1297 (2010)
16. Dupont, P.: Incremental regular inference. In: Miclet, L., Higuera, C. (eds.) ICGI 1996. LNCS, vol. 1147, pp. 222–237. Springer, Heidelberg (1996). doi:10.1007/BFb0033357
17. Giantamidis, G., Tripakis, S.: Learning Moore machines from input-output traces. ArXiv e-prints, v2, September 2016. http://arxiv.org/abs/1605.07805
18. Gold, E.M.: Language identification in the limit. Inf. Control **10**(5), 447–474 (1967)
19. Gold, E.M.: Complexity of automaton identification from given data. Inf. Control **37**(3), 302–320 (1978)
20. Grinchtein, O., Leucker, M.: Learning finite-state machines from inexperienced teachers. In: Sakakibara, Y., Kobayashi, S., Sato, K., Nishino, T., Tomita, E. (eds.) ICGI 2006. LNCS (LNAI), vol. 4201, pp. 344–345. Springer, Heidelberg (2006). doi:10.1007/11872436_30
21. Gulwani, S.: Automating string processing in spreadsheets using input-output examples. In: 38th POPL, pp. 317–330 (2011)
22. Gulwani, S., Srivastava, S., Venkatesan, R.: Program analysis as constraint solving. In: PLDI 2008, pp. 281–292. ACM (2008)
23. Gupta, A., Rybalchenko, A.: InvGen: an efficient invariant generator. In: Bouajjani, A., Maler, O. (eds.) CAV 2009. LNCS, vol. 5643, pp. 634–640. Springer, Heidelberg (2009). doi:10.1007/978-3-642-02658-4_48
24. Heitmeyer, C.L., Pickett, M., Leonard, E.I., Archer, M.M., Ray, I., Aha, D.W., Trafton, J.G.: Building high assurance human-centric decision systems. Autom. Softw. Eng. **22**(2), 159–197 (2015)
25. Heule, M.J., Verwer, S.: Software model synthesis using satisfiability solvers. Empir. Softw. Eng. **18**(4), 825–856 (2013)
26. Howar, F., Steffen, B., Jonsson, B., Cassel, S.: Inferring canonical register automata. In: Kuncak, V., Rybalchenko, A. (eds.) VMCAI 2012. LNCS, vol. 7148, pp. 251–266. Springer, Heidelberg (2012). doi:10.1007/978-3-642-27940-9_17
27. Jin, X., Donz, A., Deshmukh, J.V., Seshia, S.A.: Mining requirements from closed-loop control models. IEEE Trans. Comput. Aided Des. Integr. Circuits Syst. **34**(11), 1704–1717 (2015)
28. Jonsson, B.: Learning of automata models extended with data. In: Bernardo, M., Issarny, V. (eds.) SFM 2011. LNCS, vol. 6659, pp. 327–349. Springer, Heidelberg (2011). doi:10.1007/978-3-642-21455-4_10
29. Karthik, A.V., Ray, S., Nuzzo, P., Mishchenko, A., Brayton, R., Roychowdhury, J.: ABCD-NL: approximating continuous non-linear dynamical systems using purely Boolean models for analog/mixed-signal verification. In: ASP-DAC, pp. 250–255 (2014)

30. Kohavi, Z.: Switching and Finite Automata Theory, 2nd edn. McGraw-Hill, New York (1978)
31. Lang, K.J., Pearlmutter, B.A., Price, R.A.: Results of the Abbadingo one DFA learning competition and a new evidence-driven state merging algorithm. In: Honavar, V., Slutzki, G. (eds.) ICGI 1998. LNCS, vol. 1433, pp. 1–12. Springer, Heidelberg (1998). doi:10.1007/BFb0054059
32. Lee, D., Yannakakis, M.: Principles and methods of testing finite state machines-a survey. Proc. IEEE **84**(8), 1090–1123 (1996)
33. Lemieux, C., Park, D., Beschastnikh, I.: General LTL specification mining. In: Automated Software Engineering (ASE), pp. 81–92, November 2015
34. Ljung, L. (ed.): System Identification: Theory for the User, 2nd edn. Prentice Hall, Englewood Cliffs (1999)
35. Medhat, R., Ramesh, S., Bonakdarpour, B., Fischmeister, S.: A framework for mining hybrid automata from input/output traces. In: Embedded Software (EMSOFT), pp. 177–186 (2015)
36. Meinke, K.: CGE: a sequential learning algorithm for Mealy automata. In: Sempere, J.M., García, P. (eds.) ICGI 2010. LNCS (LNAI), vol. 6339, pp. 148–162. Springer, Heidelberg (2010). doi:10.1007/978-3-642-15488-1_13
37. Mitchell, T.M.: Machine Learning. McGraw-Hill, New York (1997)
38. Oncina, J., Garcia, P.: Identifying regular languages in polynomial time. In: Advances in Structural and Syntactic, Pattern Recognition, pp. 99–108 (1992)
39. Oncina, J., García, P., Vidal, E.: Learning subsequential transducers for pattern recognition interpretation tasks. IEEE Trans. Pattern Anal. Mach. Intell. **15**(5), 448–458 (1993)
40. Ray, B., Posnett, D., Filkov, V., Devanbu, P.: A large scale study of programming languages and code quality in github. In: ACM SIGSOFT, FSE 2014 (2014)
41. Seshia, S.A.: Sciduction: combining induction, deduction, and structure for verification and synthesis. In: DAC, pp. 356–365, June 2012
42. Shahbaz, M., Groz, R.: Inferring Mealy machines. In: Cavalcanti, A., Dams, D.R. (eds.) FM 2009. LNCS, vol. 5850, pp. 207–222. Springer, Heidelberg (2009). doi:10.1007/978-3-642-05089-3_14
43. Solar-Lezama, A.: Program sketching. STTT **15**(5–6), 475–495 (2013)
44. Spichakova, M.: An approach to inference of finite state machines based on gravitationally-inspired search algorithm. Proc. Estonian Acad. Sci. **62**(1), 39–46 (2013)
45. Takahashi, K., Fujiyoshi, A., Kasai, T.: A polynomial time algorithm to infer sequential machines. Syst. Comput. Jpn. **34**(1), 59–67 (2003)
46. Ulyantsev, V., Buzhinsky, I., Shalyto, A.: Exact finite-state machine identification from scenarios and temporal properties. CoRR, abs/1601.06945 (2016)
47. Ulyantsev, V., Zakirzyanov, I., Shalyto, A.: BFS-based symmetry breaking predicates for DFA identification. In: Dediu, A.-H., Formenti, E., Martín-Vide, C., Truthe, B. (eds.) LATA 2015. LNCS, vol. 8977, pp. 611–622. Springer, Heidelberg (2015). doi:10.1007/978-3-319-15579-1_48
48. Veelenturf, L.P.J.: Inference of sequential machines from sample computations. IEEE Trans. Comput. **27**(2), 167–170 (1978)

Modal Kleene Algebra Applied to Program Correctness

Victor B.F. Gomes[1(✉)] and Georg Struth[2(✉)]

[1] Computer Laboratory, University of Cambridge, Cambridge, UK
victor.gomes@cl.cam.ac.uk

[2] Department of Computer Science, University of Sheffield, Sheffield, UK
g.struth@sheffield.ac.uk

Abstract. Modal Kleene algebras are relatives of dynamic logics that support program construction and verification by equational reasoning. We describe their application in implementing versatile program correctness components in interactive theorem provers such as Isabelle/HOL. Starting from a weakest precondition based component with a simple relational store model, we show how variants for Hoare logic, strongest postconditions and program refinement can be built in a principled way. Modularity of the approach is demonstrated by variants that capture program termination and recursion, memory models for programs with pointers, and program trace semantics.

1 Introduction

Modal Kleene algebras (MKA) [9] are algebraic relatives of propositional dynamic logic (PDL) [14] in the tradition of the dynamic algebras proposed by Németi and Pratt [22,26] and Hollenberg's algebra of dynamic negation [15]. A particularity of MKA is that reasoning is equational, symmetries between modalities are captured by algebraic and order-theoretic dualities, and soundness and completeness results arise from properties of morphisms between algebras.

MKA has highly compact axioms. It expands Kleene algebra by two dual operations and three simple equational axioms for each of them. While the Kleene algebra operations capture the sequential composition, nondeterministic choice and finite iteration of programs, the additional ones model those states from which a program can be executed and in which it can terminate. Despite its simplicity, MKA has the expressive power of PDL: modal box and diamond operators, i.e. predicate transformers, can be defined; propositions and assertions can be modelled. This makes MKA an interesting tool for program correctness.

Over the last decade, the mathematics of MKA has been well investigated, models relevant to computing have been constructed, extensions and variations introduced, applications from game theory to termination analysis considered, and mathematical components for interactive theorem provers implemented. Nevertheless, the obvious potential of MKA for building construction and verification tools for imperative programs remains to be explored. The main goal of this article is to bridge this gap.

J. Fitzgerald et al. (Eds.): FM 2016, LNCS 9995, pp. 310–325, 2016.
DOI: 10.1007/978-3-319-48989-6_19

Our main contribution therefore consists in MKA-based program correctness components for Isabelle/HOL [24] in which imperative programs can be verified or constructed by stepwise refinement. Yet our design method is generic and applies beyond Isabelle. In a nutshell, it consists in deriving verification conditions for the control structure of programs by equational reasoning within MKA, in linking the algebra formally with denotational semantics of the store and data domain, and in adding data-level verification conditions, notably assignment laws, to the concrete semantics. Detailed contributions are as follows.

- We derive laws for calculating weakest (liberal) preconditions in MKA, most of them equational (Sect. 3), show how assignment statements and a weakest precondition rule for assignments can be obtained in the relational model of MKA (Sect. 4), and sketch how this development can be implemented as a simple verification (and dynamic logic) component in Isabelle (Sect. 5).
- We show how the opposition duality present in MKA yields verification components for strongest postconditions and a Floyd-style assignment rule in the style of [13] with minimal implementation effort (Sect. 6).
- We formally prove that MKA subsumes Kleene algebras with tests: all theorems of the latter setting hold in the former. This brings previous verification and refinement components based on Hoare logic [2] into scope (Sect. 7).
- We propose a new meta-equational while rule for weakest preconditions in the context of divergence Kleene algebras and formalise the relational model of these algebras in Isabelle, yielding a total correctness component (Sect. 8).
- We extend the MKA components for while programs to quantale-based ones for recursive procedures and provide new explicit definitions of modalities in this setting (Sect. 9).
- We further evidence the versatility of the approach by outlining a more abstract treatment of predicate transformer algebras in Isabelle and by demonstrating how other memory models and denotational program semantics can be integrated in modular ways (Sect. 10).

Many of the verification rules used in our components are well known, but have been derived in the algebra by simple equational reasoning (and automated theorem proving) in model-independent fashion. Similar store models have been used by the interactive theorem proving community, but our separation of data and control and their modular integration via a shallow embedding is new and yields components that are particularly simple, modular and reusable. Program verification can be performed directly in the concrete denotational semantics by using instances of the abstract algebraic rules and providing a minimal program syntax as a façade. For applications, grammars and semantic maps for suitable fragments of imperative programming languages should be provided, and facilities for code generation should be included. Integrating algebras and models also makes our components correct by construction: our formal soundness proofs make all axiomatic extensions consistent with Isabelle's small trustworthy core.

All results discussed in this article have been programmed in Isabelle and made accessible to readers in the Archive of Formal Proofs [12], including all verification components and a suite of verification examples.

2 Modal Kleene Algebra

Modal Kleene algebras are semirings expanded by two operations.

A *semiring* is a structure $(S,+,\cdot,0,1)$ such that $(S,+,0)$ is a commutative monoid and $(S,\cdot,1)$ a monoid. These interact via the distributivity laws $w(x+y)z = wxz + wyz$ and the annihilation laws $0x = 0 = x0$. Here and henceforth we drop the multiplication symbol. As in PDL, elements $x, y \in S$ represent programs; xy models sequential composition and $x + y$ nondeterministic choice. The programs 0 and 1 model abort and skip.

An *antidomain semiring* [9] is a semiring S expanded by an antidomain operation $a : S \to S$ that satisfies

$$(a\,x)x = 0, \qquad a\,x + a\,(a\,x) = 1, \qquad a\,(xy) + a\,(x(a\,(a\,y))) = a\,(x(a\,(a\,y))).$$

Intuitively, the antidomain ax of program x represents those states from which x cannot be executed, whereas the domain $d\,x = (a \circ a)x$ of x models those states from which it can be. The three antidomain axioms give rise to a rich structure with symmetries and dualities.

Firstly, antidomain semirings are ordered. Addition is idempotent, $x+x = x$ holds for all $x \in S$, which is essential for interpreting it as choice. Thus S is a *dioid* and $(S,+)$ a semilattice with order relation $x \leq y \leftrightarrow x + y = y$. Addition and multiplication are order preserving or isotone; 0 is the lest element with respect to $\leq$. The converse of $\leq$ is the refinement order on programs.

Secondly, $(a(S),+,\cdot,a,0,1)$, with $a(S)$ denoting the image of the set S under a, is a boolean subalgebra of S with $+$ as join, $\cdot$ as meet, a as complementation and 0 and 1 as least and greatest elements. The set $d(S) = a(S)$ is closed under the operations because $d \circ d = d$, which implies that x is in $a(S)$ iff $d\,x = x$. (Anti)domain elements in $a(S)$, for which we henceforth write p, q, r, can therefore be used as assertions or propositions. We also write $\bar{p}$ instead of $a\,p$ and encode conditionals à la PDL as **if** p **then** x **else** $y = px + \bar{p}y$.

Thirdly, the *opposite* of a dioid is a dioid. Opposition swaps the order of multiplication and runs programs backwards. Yet the class of antidomain semirings is not closed under this duality. In fact, the (anti)domain of a reverse program is the (anti)range of the original one: it represents the set of those states in which it can(not) end. The opposite of an antidomain semiring is thus an *antirange semiring* with dual axioms $x(ar\,x) = 0$, $ar\ \ x + r\ \ x = 1$ and $ar\,(x \cdot y) + ar\,(x(r\,y)) = ar\,(xr(y))$, where $r = ar \circ ar$.

Fourthly, forward modal operators can be defined in antidomain semirings,

$$|x\rangle p = d\ (xp), \qquad \text{and} \qquad |x]p = a\,(x(a\,p)),$$

whereas backward modalities are definable by opposition in antirange semirings as $[x|y = ar\,(x(ar\,y))$ and $\langle x|y = r\,(xy)$. This is justified by the PDL semantics of $|x\rangle p$, which yields those states (in a Kripke frame) from which executing x may lead into states where p holds, whereas $[x]p$ describes those states from which x must lead to states satisfying p. Note that, in antidomain semirings, px and xp model the domain and range restriction of x to states satisfying p.

A *modal semiring* [9] is an antidomain semiring S that is also an antirange semiring in which $d\,(r\,x) = r\,x$ and $r\,(d\,x) = d\,x$ hold for all $x \in S$, and consequently $a(S) = ar\,(S)$.

In this setting, boxes and diamonds satisfy a number of dualities: the De Morgan laws $|x]p = \overline{|x\rangle \bar{p}}$, $|x\rangle yp = \overline{|x]\bar{p}}$, $[x|p = \overline{\langle x|\bar{p}}$, and $\langle x|p = \overline{[x|\bar{p}}$, the conjugations $(|x\rangle p)q = 0 \leftrightarrow p(\langle x|q) = 0$ and $(|x]p)q = 0 \leftrightarrow p([x|q) = 0$, and, most importantly for our purposes, the Galois connections

$$\langle x|p \leq q \leftrightarrow p \leq |x]q \qquad \text{and} \qquad |x\rangle p \leq q \leftrightarrow p \leq [x|q.$$

Modal semirings are therefore boolean algebras with operators $\langle\_|$, $[\_|$, $|\_\rangle$ and $|\_]$ of type $S \to (a(S) \to a(S))$ in the sense of Jónsson and Tarski [16]. These operators are otherwise known as predicate transformers.

PDL allows encoding while programs without assignments. A notion of finite iteration of programs must be added to a dioid for that purpose. A *Kleene algebra* is a dioid K expanded by an operation $^* : K \to K$ that satisfies the star unfold and induction axioms

$$1 + xx^* \leq x^* \qquad \text{and} \qquad z + xy \leq y \to x^*z \leq y$$

as well as their opposites $1 + x^*x \leq x^*$ and $z + yx \leq y \to zx^* \leq y$. An *antidomain Kleene algebra* [9] is an antidomain semiring that is also a Kleene algebra and likewise for antirange Kleene algebras. A *modal Kleene algebra* is a modal semiring that is also a Kleene algebra. As in PDL one can now define **while** p **do** $x = (px)^*\bar{p}$.

Henceforth we write AKA for the class of antidomain Kleene algebras and MKA for the class of modal Kleene algebras.

3 Laws for Weakest Preconditions

Conjugations and Galois connections give theorems for free, but many additional properties hold in AKA and MKA. A comprehensive list can be found in the Isabelle formalisation in the Archive of Formal Proofs [11].

In addition to these, the following laws are helpful for program verification.

Lemma 1. *Let $S \in$ AKA. For all $p, q \in a(S)$ and $x, y \in S$,*

1. $p \leq q \to |x]p \leq |x]q$ *and* $x \leq y \to |y]p \leq |x]p$,
2. $\bar{p} + |x]q = |px]q$,
3. $|x\bar{p}]q = |x](p + q)$,
4. $|x]p \leq |x\bar{q}](p\bar{q})$,
5. $p|$**if** p **then** x **else** $y]q = p|x]q$ *and* $\bar{p}|$**if** p **then** x **else** $y]q = \bar{p}|y]q$,
6. $|$**while** p **do** $x]q = (p + q)(\bar{p} + |x]|$**while** p **do** $x]q)$,
7. $p|$**while** p **do** $x]q = p|x]|$**while** p **do** $x]q$ *and* $\bar{p}|$**while** p **do** $x]q \leq q$.

These facts can be used for deriving verification conditions for the control structure of programs. To this end we define a while loop annotated with a loop invariant: **while** p **inv** i **do** $x =$ **while** p **do** x.

Lemma 2. *Let $S \in \mathsf{AKA}$. For all $p, q, i, t \in a(S)$, $x, y \in S$,*

1. $|xy]q = |x]|y]q$,
2. $|\textbf{if } p \textbf{ then } x \textbf{ else } y]q = (\bar{p} + |x]q)(p + |y]q) = \textbf{if } p \textbf{ then } |x]q \textbf{ else } |y]q$,
3. $pq \leq |x]p \to p \leq |\textbf{while } q \textbf{ do } x](p\bar{q})$,
4. $p \leq i \wedge i\bar{t} \leq q \wedge it \leq |x]i \to p \leq |\textbf{while } t \textbf{ inv } i \textbf{ do } x]q$.

In PDL, $|x]q$ models the weakest (liberal) precondition of program x and postcondition q. The specification statement for partial correctness—if precondition p holds before executing program x and if x terminates, then postcondition q holds upon termination—is captured by $p \leq |x]q$. The formulas in Lemma 2 thus calculate weakest preconditions recursively from the structure of while programs. Equation (1) yields a rule for sequential composition, (2) yields rules for conditionals, (3) is a quasi-equation for loops, and (4) a quasi-equation for loops with invariants. All rules except those for loops are purely equational and therefore superior to those of Hoare logic in applications.

4 Relational Program Semantics

The standard PDL semantics uses a Kripke frame (S, h). A program x is interpreted as a binary relation $h\,x$ between states in S and a proposition p as a subset $h\,p$ of states in S. Diamond and box formulas are interpreted as $h\,|x\rangle p = \{s \mid \exists s'.\ (s, s') \in h\,x \wedge s' \in h\,p\}$ and $h\,|x]p = \{s \mid \forall s'.\ (s, s') \in h\,x \to s' \in h\,p\}$.

With MKA it is more convenient to interpret programs and assertions uniformly as binary relations over S by embedding subsets A of S into *subidentity relations* $\{(a, a) \mid a \in A\}$.

Proposition 1 ([9,11])**.** *Let $(2^{S\times S}, \cup, ;, a, \emptyset, Id, ^*)$ be the set of all binary relations over the set S with the following operations: set union $\cup$, relational composition $R; S = \{(s, s') \mid \exists s''.\ (s, s'') \in R \wedge (s'', s') \in S\}$, relational antidomain $a\,R = \{(s, s) \mid \neg\exists s'.\ (s, s') \in R\}$, the identity relation $Id = \{(s, s) \mid s \in S\}$, the empty relation $\emptyset$, and the reflexive-transitive closure $R^* = \bigcup_{i\in\mathbb{N}} R^i$ of R.*

1. *This structure forms an* AKA, *the* full relation AKA *over S.*
2. *Each of its subalgebras forms a* relation AKA.

This soundness result justifies our previous programming intuitions. The algebraic structure of AKA is reflected at the level of relations; the algebra of subidentities $(a(2^{S\times S}), \cup, ;, a, \emptyset, Id)$ is again a boolean subalgebra. The antidomain operation can be written as $a\,R = Id \cap -(R\top)$, where $-R$ denotes the complement of R in $2^{S\times S}$, whereas a is complementation on $a(2^{S\times S})$. The universal relation $\top$ is defined as $\{(s, s') \mid s, s' \in S\}$. The relational domain operation is defined accordingly as $d\,R = \{(s, s) \mid \exists s'.\ (s, s') \in R\}$. The boolean algebra of subidentities in $a(2^{S\times S})$, the boolean algebra of subsets of S and the boolean algebra of predicates as boolean-valued functions of type $S \to \mathbb{B}$ are of course isomorphic. More precisely, the coercion functions $\lceil P \rceil = \{(s, s) \mid P s\}$ from predicates to relations and $\lfloor R \rfloor = \{a \mid \exists b.\ (a, b) \in R\}$ from subidentity relations to predicates form a bijective pair that preserves joins/unions, meets/intersections and negations/complements. The Kripke semantics of relational boxes and diamonds is consistent with the algebraic one: $|R\rangle P = d\,(R; P)$ and $|R]P = a\,(R; a\,P)$.

The dual of Proposition 1 links, accordingly, relations with antirange operation $ar\,R = \{(s', s') \mid \neg\exists s.(s, s') \in R\}$ and antirange Kleene algebras. In combination, these results show that MKA has relational models.

The standard relational semantics of while programs—and that of first-order dynamic logic—considers the store as a function from variables in V to values in a set E, that is, $s : V \to E$ and S is the function space E^V.

Let the update $f[b/a]\,x$ of function $f : A \to B$ in argument $a \in A$ by value $b \in B$ be defined as b whenever $x = a$ and as fa otherwise. The relational semantics of an assignment statement is then given by

$$(v := e) \;=\; \{(s, s[(e\,s)/v]) \mid s \in E^V\},$$

where $e\ s$ denotes the value of expression e in store s. This definition allows calculating weakest preconditions of assignments.

Lemma 3. *In every relation* AKA, $|v := e]\lceil Q\rceil = \lceil \lambda s.\ Q(s[(e\,s)/v])\rceil$.

On the one hand, the formulas in Lemmas 2 and 3 give us all we need for verifying while programs. On the other hand, they yield a hybrid encoding of first-order dynamic logic, where the propositional part is captured algebraically and the first-order part modelled within the relational semantics. The following section transforms this approach into a verification component.

5 Verification Component Using Weakest Preconditions

The results from Sects. 3 and 4 suffice for implementing a simple component for dynamic logic, and primarily a verification component, quickly and easily in an interactive theorem prover; see [12] for details. Our Isabelle/HOL components use a shallow embedding; verification is performed on the concrete relational store semantics from Sect. 4. Relational instances of the algebraic weakest precondition laws (Sect. 3) are brought into scope by formalising Proposition 1. Data types for expressions, statements and while-programs and a semantic map into the relation AKA could be added easily. Instead we merely supply some syntactic sugar for relational programs. We now sketch this implementation.

Firstly, Isabelle provides axiomatic type classes and locales for formalising modular algebraic hierarchies and their models. Our verification component is based on comprehensive mathematical components for Kleene algebras [4] and AKA [11]. AKA, for instance, could have been formalised as follows.

```
class antidomain-kleene-algebra = kleene-algebra +
  fixes ad :: 'a ⇒ 'a (ad)
  assumes as1 [simp]: ad x · x = 0
  and as2 [simp]: ad (x · y) + ad (x · ad (ad y)) = ad (x · ad (ad y))
  and as3 [simp]: ad (ad x) + ad x = 1
```

This definition expands the type class of Kleene algebras to the class of AKA by adding the antidomain operation and the three antidomain axioms. The type of the antidomain operation indicates that AKAs are polymorphic and can be instantiated—for instance to the type of polymorphic binary relations or that of binary relations over a polymorphic store. Notions such as domain, boxes or diamonds can be defined within this class. Isabelle's simplifiers and integrated theorem provers can be used for proving facts about AKA, and, by the expansion, all facts proved about Kleene algebras are in scope as well.

Secondly, our Isabelle components provide soundness proofs for various models. That of relation AKA, for instance, can be formalised as follows.

interpretation *rel-aka*: *antidomain-kleene-algebra*
  Id $\{\}$ *op* $\cup$ *op* ; *op* $\subseteq$ *op* $\subset$ *rtrancl rel-ad*

The interpretation statement says that any relational structure specified as in Proposition 1 forms an AKA. Isabelle dictates its proof obligations. After discharging them, instances of all abstract properties proved about AKA are available in the concrete relational semantics; in particular those from Lemma 2. In addition, the soundness proof makes the axiomatic extension of AKA consistent with Isabelle's small trustworthy core. Our verification components thus become correct by construction relative to it.

The relations introduced in the soundness proof are again polymorphic. They can be instantiated further to relations over a polymorphic store, which is defined as **type-synonym** $'a$ *store* $=$ *string* $\Rightarrow$ $'a$. It can model data of arbitrary and heterogenous type. The assignment command and the corresponding weakest precondition rule can then be implemented as follows.

definition *gets* :: *string* $\Rightarrow$ ($'a$ *store* $\Rightarrow$ $'a$) $\Rightarrow$ $'a$ *store rel* (- ::= - [70, 65] 61) **where**
  v ::= e = $\{(s,s\ (v := e\ s))\ |s.\ True\}$
lemma *wp-assign* [*simp*]: *wp* (v ::= e) $\lceil Q \rceil = \lceil \lambda s.\ Q\ (s\ (v := e\ s)) \rceil$

Here, ::= is syntax for assignments, whereas := denotes Isabelle's built-in function update. After programming additional syntactic sugar for program specifications and syntax, one can start verifying while programs.

lemma *euclid*:
  PRE (λs::*nat store*. s ''x'' $= x \wedge s$ ''y'' $= y$)
  (*WHILE* (λs. s ''y'' $\neq 0$) *INV* (λs. *gcd* (s ''x'') (s ''y'') = *gcd* x y)
   DO
    (''z'' ::= (λs. s ''y''));
    (''y'' ::= (λs. s ''x'' *mod* s ''y''));
    (''x'' ::= (λs. s ''z''))
   OD)
  POST (λs. s ''x'' = *gcd* x y)
  by (*rule rel-antidomain-kleene-algebra.fbox-while*) (*auto simp*: *gcd-non-0-nat*)

In this simple example proof, a relational instance of the while rule from Lemma 2(4) is applied first. All proof obligations generated are then simplified. As all rules except the one for loops are pure equations, they can be added to Isabelle's simplifier. Here, in particular, the sequential composition rule from Lemma 2(1) and the assignment rule from Lemma 3 eliminate the entire control structure. Automated theorem proving can then finish off the remaining data-level proof. For straight-line programs, verification proofs are purely equational and the entire control structure of programs can usually be simplified away.

Several variables of heterogenous type are handled by instantiating the type $'a$ of the store by a sum type. Verifying a typical sorting algorithm, for instance, requires type $nat + 'a + 'a\ list$ with the natural number measuring the length of the input list and $'a$ being a linearly ordered type. Assignments of variables of a summand type can then be expressed by using projections and injections. Our Isabelle theories contain an example verification of insertion sort [12].

Verification condition generation can be automated further with tactics that apply the while rule recursively. These can be programmed elegantly in Isabelle's Eisbach proof method language [18]. Verifying simple programs thus reduces to calling an Eisbach method to eliminate the control structure and then using Isabelle's provers and simplifiers for the data level; see our online examples [12].

The Isabelle formalisation provides a template for developing external verification tools. This makes it desirable to generate proof obligations as far as possible within first-order logic, so that they can be tackled by automated theorem provers and SMT solvers. It is easy to tune verification condition generation accordingly. The weakest precondition operator can, for instance, be presented as $\lfloor wp\, X\, \lceil Q \rceil \rfloor = \lambda s.\ \forall s'.\ (s, s') \in X \rightarrow Q\, s'$, the loop rule allows deriving $\forall s.\ P\, s \rightarrow \lfloor wp\, (\mathsf{WHILE}\ T\ \mathsf{INV}\ I\ \mathsf{DO}\ X\ \mathsf{OD})\, \lceil Q \rceil \rfloor\, s$ from the assumptions $\forall s. P\, s \rightarrow I\, s$, $I\, s \wedge \neg\, T\, s \rightarrow Q\, s$ and $I\, s \wedge T\, s \rightarrow \lfloor wp\, X\, \lceil I \rceil \rfloor\, s)$, and the assignment rule can be written as $\lfloor wp(v ::= e)\, \lceil Q \rceil \rfloor = \lambda s.\ Q\, (s[(e\, s)/v])$.

6 Verification Component Using Strongest Postconditions

In an influential article, Gordon and Collavizza [13] contrast the backwards approach that uses weakest preconditions and Hoare's assignment law with the lesser known forward one with strongest postconditions and Floyd's assignment law. With MKA, the two approaches are related by opposition duality, the Galois connection between forward boxes and backward diamonds. As indicated in Sect. 2, the specification statement $p \leq |x]q$ is equivalent to $\langle x|p \leq q$, with $\langle x|p$ capturing the strongest postcondition of program x and precondition p.

We have formalised opposition duality between antidomain and antirange Kleene algebras in Isabelle and implemented MKA based on that duality [11]. As a consequence, all facts for forward modalities can be dualised by Isabelle rather effortlessly. Facts from Lemma 1 dualise, for instance, to $p\langle x|q = \langle xp|q$, $\langle x|(pt) = \langle tx|p$, $\langle x|p \leq \langle \bar{q}x|(p\bar{q})$. More importantly, we immediately obtain the following dual statements to those in Lemma 2.

Lemma 4. *Let $S \in \mathsf{MKA}$. For all $p, q, i, t \in a(S)$, $x, y \in S$,*

1. $\langle xy|p = \langle y|\langle x|p$,
2. $\textbf{if } p \textbf{ then } x \textbf{ else } y|q = \langle x|(pq) + \langle y|(\bar{p}q)$,
3. $\langle x|(pq) \leq p \rightarrow \langle \textbf{while } q \textbf{ do } x|p \leq (p\bar{q})$,
4. $p \leq i \wedge i\bar{t} \leq q \wedge \langle x|(t\bar{i}) \rightarrow \langle \textbf{while } t \textbf{ inv } i \textbf{ do } x|p \leq q$.

The lemmas listed in the following proof show how Isabelle picks up duality.

lemma *bdia-seq-var*: $\langle x|\ p \leq p' \Longrightarrow \langle y|\ p' \leq q \Longrightarrow \langle x \cdot y|\ p \leq q$
by (*metis ardual.ds.fd-subdist-1 ardual.ds.fdia-mult dual-order.trans* ...)

A forward assignment law is derivable in the relational store model.

lemma *bdia-assign* [*simp*]:
rel-aka.bdia $(v ::= e)\ \lceil P \rceil = \lceil \lambda s.\ \exists\, w.\ s\ v = e\ (s(v := w)) \wedge P\ (s(v{:=}w)) \rceil$

Here, *rel-aka.bdia* denotes the backward diamond operator of relation MKA. Once more, the rules in Lemma 4 and our variant of Floyd's assignment axiom suffice for program verification; the algebraic and the relational layer are linked seamlessly by the relational soundness proof for MKA. We found little difference in performance between the backward and the forward approach on simple examples. Beyond that, the forward approach offers potential for symbolic execution and static analysis [13].

7 Components for Hoare Logic and Refinement

We have previously developed program correctness components using Kleene algebras with tests (KAT) [1,2]: a verification component based on Hoare logic and a refinement component based on Morgan's specification statement [21].

Inspired by MKA we have implemented KAT as a Kleene algebra K expanded by an *antitest operation* $n : K \rightarrow K$ that satisfies

$$t\,1 = 1, \quad t\,((t\,x)(t\,y)) = (t\,x)(t\,y), \quad (n\,x)(t\,x) = 0, \quad (n\,x)(n\,y) = n\,(t\,x + t\,y),$$

where $t = n \circ n$ is the *test operation*. Similarly to MKA, $n(K) = t(K)$ forms a boolean subalgebra useful for modelling tests and assertions.

Propositional Hoare logic, that is, Hoare logic without assignment axioms, is subsumed by PDL [14]. Here we obtain the following correspondence.

Proposition 2 ([9]). *Every* AKA *and antirange Kleene algebra is a* KAT.

Formalising this fact in Isabelle brings the verification components for KAT into the scope of MKA. In KAT, Hoare triples are defined as

$$H\,p\,x\,q \leftrightarrow px \leq xq,$$

where x is a program and p, q are tests. In MKA, in turn, $p \leq |x]q \leftrightarrow px \leq xq \leftrightarrow \langle x|p \leq q$. Thus Hoare triples relate to the specification statements for weakest preconditions and strongest postconditions:

$$H\,p\,x\,q \leftrightarrow p \leq |x]q \leftrightarrow \langle x|p \leq q,$$

and this correspondence confirms that $|x]q$ is indeed the weakest precondition and $\langle x|q$ the strongest postcondition satisfying the Hoare triple. However, weakest preconditions or strongest postconditions cannot be expressed in KAT [28].

The standard rules for propositional Hoare logic are thus available in MKA and can once more be combined with Floyd and Hoare's assignment axioms. Hoare's axiom, for instance, is derivable because

$$\lceil \lambda s.\ P\,(s[(e\,s)/v]\rceil; (v := e) \;=\; (v := e); \lceil P \rceil.$$

KAT has been expanded to *refinement* KAT [2] by adding an operation $R : K \times K \to K$ and an axiom

$$H\,p\,x\,q \leftrightarrow x \leq R\,p\,q,$$

stating that Morgan's *specification statement* $R\,p\,q$ is the greatest program that satisfies the Hoare triple $H\,p\,x\,q$. MKA can be expanded to *refinement* MKA in the same way, but Galois connections

$$\langle x|p \leq q \leftrightarrow x \leq R\,p\,q \leftrightarrow p \leq [x|q$$

between the specification statements are now revealed. Once more, every refinement MKA is a refinement KAT, and the simple refinement component developed previously for KAT in Isabelle is automatically available for MKA.

8 A Meta-Equational while-Rule

A *divergence Kleene algebra* [8] is an AKA K expanded by a divergence operation $\nabla : K \to K$ that satisfies the unfold and coinduction axioms

$$\nabla\, x \leq |x\rangle \nabla\, x \qquad \text{and} \qquad p \leq |x\rangle p + q \to p \leq \nabla\, x + |x^*\rangle q.$$

Intuitively, ∇x models the set of those states from which program x need not terminate. We have formalised divergence Kleene algebras [11] and their relational models in Isabelle. In this setting, $\nabla\, R = \bigcup\{P.\ P \subseteq |R\rangle P\}$, and we have proved in Isabelle that $\nabla R = 0$ if and only if R is *noetherian* in the sense that there are no infinitely ascending R-chains. This is the case if and only if the converse of R is wellfounded. This condition is interesting for total program correctness because $\nabla\, x = 0$ relates to loop termination.

In [27], algebraic conditions for the existence of solutions in y of equations of the form $y = xy + z$ have been investigated in the context of Kleene algebras. It is well known that, by Arden's rule, a unique solution $y = x^*z$ exists in the regular language models of Kleene algebra if language x does not contain the empty word. In relational models this empty word property can be replaced by a noethericity assumption. This analogy motivates a new meta-equational while rule for predicate transformers.

Lemma 5. *In every divergence Kleene algebra, if* $\nabla x = 0$*, then*

1. $p = |x\rangle p + q \leftrightarrow p = |x^*\rangle q$,
2. $p = q|x]p \leftrightarrow p = |x^*]q$.

The second meta-equation can be derived from the first one. It specialises to while loops and weakest preconditions as follows.

Lemma 6. *In every divergence Kleene algebra, if* $\nabla (tx) = 0$*, then*

1. $p = (t+q)|tx]p \leftrightarrow p = |\mathbf{while}\ t\ \mathbf{do}\ x]q$,
2. $i = (t+q)|tx]i \leftrightarrow i = |\mathbf{while}\ t\ \mathbf{inv}\ i\ \mathbf{do}\ x]q$.

In these rules, $\nabla (tx) = 0$ prevents that the body x of the while loop can be executed forever from states where test t holds. This of course expresses loop termination. Dual rules for forward reasoning with strongest postconditions follow immediately from the Galois connections. Partial correctness reasoning now no longer hides the explicit assumption of program termination, whereas total correctness requires discharging this assumption. Our relational soundness proof for divergence Kleene algebras in Isabelle links the absence of divergence formally with wellfoundedness and brings Isabelle's tools for termination analysis into scope (e.g. [19]). A deeper investigation of total program correctness in applications remains beyond the scope of this article.

A second benefit of the rules in Lemma 6 is that they can simplify verification condition generation, as equations for calculating the weakest precondition of a loop can be simplified to equivalent equations involving only the body of the loop. In our Isabelle implementation, however, we found it so far difficult to make this rule cooperate with the simplifiers. See our Isabelle theories for examples [12].

9 Domain Quantales and Components for Recursion

A limitation of MKA is that recursion cannot be expressed. This requires the more expressive setting of quantales, which subsume MKA, and in which classical fixpoint theory, and thus recursion, can be developed. Antidomain and modal operators can be axiomatised as before, but we present a class of quantales consistent with the relational semantics, in which an antidomain operation can be defined explicitly. We restrict our attention to single recursive procedures; mutual recursion could be captured as well by using polyvariadic fixpoint combinators.

Formally a *quantale* (or *standard Kleene algebra* [7]) is a structure $(Q, \cdot, 1, \leq)$ such that $(Q, \cdot, 1, \leq)$ is a monoid, $(Q, \leq)$ a complete lattice, and the infinite distributivity laws $x(\bigsqcup_{i\in I} y_i)z = \bigsqcup_{i\in I} xy_iz$ hold, where $\bigsqcup X$ denotes the supremum of a set $X \subseteq Q$. A quantale is *boolean* if the underlying complete lattice is a complete boolean algebra. Thus the infinite distributivity laws $x \sqcap (\bigsqcup_{i\in I} y_i) = \bigsqcup_{i\in I}(x \sqcap y_i)$ and its lattice dual $x \sqcup (\bigsqcap_{i\in I} y_i) = \bigsqcap_{i\in I}(x \sqcup y_i)$ are required, where we write $\bigsqcap X$ for the infimum of $X \subseteq Q$.

Every quantale is a Kleene algebra with $x^* = \bigsqcup_{i\in \mathbb{N}} x^i$, and binary relations under the usual operations form boolean quantales. In every quantale, $x \sqcup y = \bigsqcup\{x, y\}$; the annihilation laws are special cases of distributivity and $\bigsqcup_{i\in\emptyset} x_i = \bot$.

Boolean quantales are similar to algebras of relations; only the operation of relational converse and the associated axioms are absent. The domain and antidomain of a relation can be defined explicitly in relation algebra as $d\,x = 1 \sqcap x\top$ and $a\,x = 1 \sqcap -(d\,x) = 1 \sqcap -(x\top)$. In boolean quantales this is impossible.

Lemma 7. *In some boolean quantale,* $(1 \sqcap x\top)x \neq x$ *and* $(1 \sqcap -(x\top))x \neq \bot$.

Proof. Consider the four-element boolean quantale with $Q = \{\bot, 1, \alpha, \top\}$ in which the order, infima, suprema and complements are defined by the fact that 1 and α are incomparable and multiplication is given by $\alpha\alpha = \bot$, $\alpha\top = \alpha = \top\alpha$ and $\top\top = \top$. Then $(1 \sqcap \alpha\top)\alpha = \bot \neq \alpha$ whereas $(1 \sqcap -(\alpha\top))\alpha = \alpha \neq \bot$. □

Though that does not rule out other explicit definitions, one can resort to axiomatising (anti)domain in quantales as in the case of MKA. As an alternative, we present a new explicit definition of antidomain for a class of boolean quantales that is consistent with binary relations.

Proposition 3. *Every boolean quantale S in which* $(z \sqcap x\top)y = zy \sqcap x\top$ *holds for all* $x, y, z \in S$ *is an* AKA *with* $a\,x = 1 \sqcap -(x\top)$.

In fact, the AKA axioms are already derivable in boolean monoids, i.e., boolean quantales where infinite infima and suprema need not exist. A dual result holds for antirange Kleene algebras satisfying $x(y \sqcap \top z) = xy \sqcap \top z$ and $ar\,x = 1 \sqcap \top x$. Boolean quantales satisfying both laws and $a(Q) = ar\,(Q)$ are thus MKAs.

We have already added test axioms, as described in Sect. 7, to quantales [2] and implemented a basic fixpoint calculus for quantales in Isabelle [3]. Two key ingredients are Knaster-Tarski's and Kleene's fixpoint theorems. A subsumption result similar to Proposition 2 can also be formalised in Isabelle.

Proposition 4. *Every antidomain and antirange quantale is a test quantale.*

Our previous components for test quantales are thus in the scope of domain quantales and can be combined with the rules for weakest preconditions and strongest postconditions from Sects. 3, 4, 5 and 6. The following recursion rule, for example, can be derived for every isotone endofunction f over a domain quantale:

$$(\forall x \in Q.\ p = |x]q \rightarrow p = |f\ x]q) \rightarrow p = |\mu f]q.$$

Examples showing this rule at work have already been published in the setting of test quantales [2] and are not worth repeating.

Finally, many of the concepts used so far can be defined explicitly in the modal quantale setting. In particular,

$$|x]q = \bigsqcup\{p \mid px \leq xq\}, \qquad \langle x|p = \bigsqcap\{q \mid px \leq xq\},$$

$$R\,p\,q = \bigsqcup\{x \mid px \leq xq\}, \qquad \nabla\,x = \bigsqcup\{p \mid p \leq |x\rangle p\},$$

where of course $px \leq xq \leftrightarrow H\,p\,x\,q$ and $|x\rangle p = \bigsqcap\{q \mid xp \leq qx\}$ by opposition duality. Hence every antidomain quantale is a modal refinement Kleene algebra in the sense of Sect. 7 and a divergence Kleene algebra in the sense of Sect. 8.

10 Extensions and Variations

Program Transformation and Optimisation. By contrast to PDL and similarly to KAT, MKA allows considering programs outside of modal formulas as first class citizens. This allows, for instance, the treatment of program transformations and optimisations, for example in the context of a compiler [2,17].

Predicate Transformer Algebras. The algebra of predicate transformers as functions $S \to (a(S) \to a(S))$ can be studied abstractly in the setting of MKA [20]. Consider transformers $|x] = \lambda p.|x]p$ under multiplication $|x]|y] = |x] \circ |y]$ as function composition, meet as $|x] \sqcap |y] = \lambda p.(|x]p)(|y]p)$, a multiplicative unit $|1] = \lambda p.d\,p$ and an additive unit $|0] = \lambda p.1$. Transformers over (left) antidomain Kleene algebras then form (left) Kleene algebras with meet as addition and $|x]^* = |x^*]$ [20]. Some laws from Lemma 2 can now be represented in point-free style. Equation (1), for instance, becomes $|xy] = |x] \circ |y]$; equation (2) becomes $|\textbf{if } p \textbf{ then } x \textbf{ else } y] = |d\,p] \circ |x] \sqcap |a\,p] \circ |y]$. The Kleene algebra structure simplifies proofs at this level, but unfortunately it seems impossible to implement the lifting result in Isabelle, though all laws needed for it can be derived.

Changing the Memory Model. The simple store from Sect. 5 can be replaced modularly, for instance, by one of type *string ⇒ ('a ref + ('a⇒ 'a ref))*, where *'a ref* is a polymorphic reference type for pointers and heaps provided by Nipkow [23]. Our approach is modular with respect to this new memory model for verifying pointer algorithms in the predicate transformer setting while using Nipkow's lemmas, for example for linked lists (see our Isabelle theories [12]), at the data level. A store in which variables of heterogeneous type are modelled by Isabelle records, which is another standard implementation (e.g. [2]), could also be added with little effort.

Changing the Program Semantics. One can also replace the relational program semantics modularly by other ones. As an example we have implemented a path semantics that considers non-empty finite paths $(s_1, \dots, s_n)$ of program stores generated by the actions of a program [4,5]. Paths $(s_1, \dots, s_m)$ and $(t_1, \dots, t_n)$ are composed by a fusion product that yields $(s_1, \dots, s_m, t_2, \dots t_n)$ if $s_m = t_1$ and is undefined otherwise. Sets of non-empty paths under the product $XY = \{p \mid \exists p' \in X, p'' \in Y.\ p = p'p''\}$, set union, the empty set, the set of all paths of length one and $X^* = \bigcup_{i \in \mathbb{N}} R^i$ form Kleene algebras [4], in fact AKAs with $a\,X = \{s \mid \neg(\exists p \in X.\, s = \mathsf{first}\,p)\}$. Then $(v := e) = \{(s, s[(e\,s)/v))] \mid s \in E^V\}$ models (the paths semantics of) assignments, predicates are lifted to paths by $\lceil P \rceil = \{s \mid P\,s\}$ and a path assignment rule $|(x := e)]\lceil Q \rceil = \lceil \lambda s.\ Q(s[(e\,s)/v]) \rceil$ can be derived in the path model. It can be combined with the path instances of our abstract algebraic rules for verifying programs in the path semantics.

11 Conclusion

Our program correctness components [12] are small. Relative to the previous mathematical components for MKA [11], the weakest precondition component outlined in Sect. 5 required proving about 30 facts, most of them by automated theorem proving within the algebra. Based on this, the strongest postconditions component needed about 10 facts, mainly to make the dual verification rules explicit. The verification and refinement components for KAT were brought into scope (Sect. 7) by proving three routine facts in the algebra. The development of the meta-equational while rule and the resulting total correctness component required again about 30 facts. Integrating the memory model for pointers and the path model needed once more just a handfull of proofs. Only the proofs linking divergence Kleene algebras with noethericity in the relational model required some more tedious background work.

The components for (modal) Kleene algebras in Isabelle [4,11] include axiomatic variants that can be used, for instance, for comparing programs and processes up to simulation and bisimulation equivalence and that are suitable, for instance, for analysing probabilistic programs. They also contain further models of computational interest. We expect that verification components for many of them can be developed as minor variations to the ones presented. To make such developments easy, we have usually expanded proofs in our Isabelle components to make them readable, easy to compile and robust to change.

In verification proofs we have obtained a high level of automation that compares with similar tools. Domain-specific data level proof support or techniques for inferring invariants seem crucial for enhancing automation further.

A modular extension of MKA to separation logic will be the subject of a successor article (cf. [10]); the integration of more advanced predicate transformer models with angelic and demonic nondeterminism, as described in Back and von Wright's book [6], seems equally possible. Finally, dynamic logic forms the basis of Platzer's approach to verifying hybrid and cyber-physical systems [25]. Developing MKA-based Isabelle components for it would require implementing a substantial amount of continuous mathematics in Isabelle, but might still be modular with respect to an algebraic control flow layer.

Acknowledgements. This work was partly supported by EPSRC Programme Grant *REMS: Rigorous Engineering for Mainstream Systems*, EP/K008528/1.

References

1. Armstrong, A., Gomes, V.B.F., Struth, G.: Kleene algebra with tests and demonic refinement algebras. In: Archive of Formal Proofs (2014)
2. Armstrong, A., Gomes, V.B.F., Struth, G.: Building program construction and verification tools from algebraic principles. Form. Asp. Comput. **28**(2), 265–293 (2016)
3. Armstrong, A., Struth, G.: Automated reasoning in higher-order regular algebra. In: Kahl, W., Griffin, T.G. (eds.) RAMICS 2012. LNCS, vol. 7560, pp. 66–81. Springer, Heidelberg (2012). doi:10.1007/978-3-642-33314-9_5
4. Armstrong, A., Struth, G., Weber, T.: Kleene algebra. In: Archive of Formal Proofs (2013)

5. Armstrong, A., Struth, G., Weber, T.: Programming, automating mathematics in the Tarski-Kleene hierarchy. J. Log. Algebraic Methods Program. **83**(2), 87–102 (2014)
6. Back, R., von Wright, J.: Refinement Calculus - A Systematic Introduction. Springer, New York (1998)
7. Conway, J.H.: Regular Algebra and Finite Machines. Chapman and Hall, London (1971)
8. Desharnais, J., Möller, B., Struth, G.: Algebraic notions of termination. Log. Methods Comput. Sci. **7**(1), 1–29 (2011)
9. Desharnais, J., Struth, G.: Internal axioms for domain semirings. Sci. Comput. Program. **76**(3), 181–203 (2011)
10. Gomes, V.B.F.: Algebraic principles for program correctness tools in Isabelle/HOL. PhD thesis, University of Sheffield (2015)
11. Gomes, V.B.F., Guttman, W., Höfner, P., Struth, G., Weber, T.: Kleene algebra with domain. In: Archive of Formal Proofs (2016)
12. Gomes, V.B.F., Struth, G.: Program construction and verification components based on Kleene algebra. In: Archive of Formal Proofs (2016)
13. Gordon, M., Collavizza, H.: Forward with Hoare. In: Roscoe, A.W., Jones, C.B., Wood, K.W. (eds.) Reflections on the Work of C.A.R. Hoare, pp. 101–121. Springer, London (2010). doi:10.1007/978-1-84882-912-1_5
14. Harel, D., Kozen, D., Tiuryn, J.: Dynamic Logic. MIT Press, Cambridge (2000)
15. Hollenberg, M.: An equational axiomatization of dynamic negation and relational composition. J. Log. Lang. Inf. **6**(4), 381–401 (1997)
16. Jónsson, B., Tarski, A.: Boolean algebras with operators, Part I. Am. J. Math. **73**(4), 207–215 (1951)
17. Kozen, D., Patron, M.-C.: Certification of compiler optimizations using Kleene algebra with tests. In: Lloyd, J., Dahl, V., Furbach, U., Kerber, M., Lau, K.-K., Palamidessi, C., Pereira, L.M., Sagiv, Y., Stuckey, P.J. (eds.) CL 2000. LNCS (LNAI), vol. 1861, pp. 568–582. Springer, Heidelberg (2000). doi:10.1007/3-540-44957-4_38
18. Matichuk, D., Murray, T.C., Wenzel, M.: Eisbach: a proof method language for Isabelle. J. Autom. Reason. **56**(3), 261–282 (2016)
19. Meng, J., Paulson, L.C., Klein, G.: A termination checker for Isabelle Hoare logic. In: International Verification Workshop (2007)
20. Möller, B., Struth, G.: Algebras of modal operators and partial correctness. Theór. Comput. Sci. **351**(2), 221–239 (2006)
21. Morgan, C.: Programming from Specifications, 2nd edn. Prentice Hall, London (1994)
22. Németi, I.: Dynamic algebras of programs. In: Gecseg, F. (ed.) FCT 1981. LNCS, vol. 117, pp. 281–290. Springer, Heidelberg (1981)
23. Nipkow, T., Klein, G.: Concrete Semantics-With Isabelle/HOL. Springer, Switzerland (2014)
24. Nipkow, T., Wenzel, M., Paulson, L.C.: Isabelle/HOL. LNCS, vol. 2283. Springer, Heidelberg (2002)
25. Platzer, A.: Logical analysis of hybrid systems. In: Kutrib, M., Moreira, N., Reis, R. (eds.) DCFS 2012. LNCS, vol. 7386, pp. 43–49. Springer, Heidelberg (2012). doi:10.1007/978-3-642-31623-4_3

26. Pratt, V.: Dynamic algebras as a well-behaved fragment of relation algebras. In: Bergman, C.H., Maddux, R.D., Pigozzi, D.L. (eds.) Algebraic Logic and Universal Algebra in Computer Science. LNCS, vol. 425, pp. 77–110. Springer, Heidelberg (1990). doi:10.1007/BFb0043079
27. Struth, G.: Left omega algebras and regular equations. J. Log. Algebraic Program. **81**(6), 705–717 (2012)
28. Struth, G.: On the expressive power of Kleene algebra with domain. Inf. Proces. Lett. **116**(4), 284–288 (2016)

Mechanised Verification Patterns for Dafny

Gudmund Grov(✉), Yuhui Lin, and Vytautas Tumas

Heriot-Watt University, Edinburgh, UK
{G.Grov,Y.Lin,vt50}@hw.ac.uk

Abstract. In Dafny, the program text is used to both specify and implement programs in the same language [24]. It then uses a fully automated theorem prover to verify that the implementation satisfies the specification. However, the prover often needs further guidance from the user, and another role of the language is to provide such necessary hints and guidance. In this paper, we present a set of *verification patterns* to support this process. In previous work, we have developed a *tactic language* for Dafny, where users can encode their verification patterns and re-apply them for several proof tasks [16]. We extend this language with new features, implement our patterns in this tactic language and show, through experiments, generality of the patterns, and applicability of the tactic language.

1 Introduction

Dafny [24] is a program verifier and programming language where the specification of desired properties is intertwined with their implementation in the program text. It uses an automated theorem prover to *prove* that the specification is satisfied by the program. A specification serves two purposes: (1) it *specifies* the properties to be proven and acts as a *documentation* of the program, which is desirable to include in the program text; (2) it is used to *guide the prover* if a property cannot be verified without help. This is a necessary evil, which is not desirable and may obfuscate the readability of the program text. We will call this type of specification elements for *proofs*.

The process of creating a proof typically involves changing, and in most cases adding, auxiliary annotations such as assertions and loop (in)variants, as well as manipulation of a *ghost state*: a state that can be updated and used as normal, but is only used for verification purposes and will not be compiled. In addition to increasing the size of the program text, the process of generating proofs can be very time consuming.

In this paper, we investigate and document a set of *verification patterns* that captures common proofs of Dafny programs (Sect. 3). We have previously developed *Tacny*, a *tactic language* for Dafny, which enable users to encode and apply verification patterns [16]. In Sect. 4 we extend this with new features, before we mechanise the patterns in Tacny and evaluate them on a set of examples (Sect. 5). We conclude and discuss relevant and future work in Sect. 6.

This work has been supported by EPSRC grants EP/M018407/1 and EP/N014758/1. Special thanks to Rustan Leino and his colleagues at MSR.

J. Fitzgerald et al. (Eds.): FM 2016, LNCS 9995, pp. 326–343, 2016.
DOI: 10.1007/978-3-319-48989-6_20

2 Background on Dafny and Tacny

Dafny combines imperative, object-oriented and functional programming language paradigms. It support features such as inductive [25], co-inductive [26] and higher-order [23] types. It uses familiar notations for assignment (x := e), declarations (**var** x := e;), conditionals (**if** and **if** −**else**) and loops (e.g. **while**). It also supports pattern matching (**match**) and a 'such as' operator, where x :| p means that x is assigned a value such that p holds.

Dafny has been designed for verification. Properties are specified by *contracts* for methods/functions in terms of preconditions (**requires**) and postconditions (**ensures**). To verify a program, Dafny translates it into an *intermediate verification language* called Boogie [4]. From Boogie a set of VCs is generated and sent to the Z3 SMT solver [28]. If it fails, then the failure is translated back to the Dafny code, via Boogie.

In the case of failure, a user must provide guidance in the program text in terms of proof details. The simplest form is to add assertions (**assert**) of true properties in the program text. In the case of loops, we might also provide loop invariants (**invariant**). Loops and recursion have to be shown to terminate and for advanced cases a user needs to provide a variant (**decreases**) to help Dafny prove this.

For more advanced verification tasks, one can make use of the *ghost state*. A ghost variable (**ghost var**) or ghost method can be introduced and used by the verifier. A lemma (**lemma**) is a type of ghost method that can be used to express richer properties, where assumptions are preconditions, and the conclusion becomes the postcondition. The proof is a method body that satisfies the postcondition, given the precondition. We will see examples of this below, but note that standard programming language elements are used in the body of the lemma, which illustrates the close correspondence between proofs and programs.

Tacny is a conservative extension of Dafny with features to implement verification patterns as *tactics* [16]. This tactic language is a *meta-language* for Dafny, where evaluation of a tactic works at the Dafny level: it takes a Dafny program with tactics and tactic applications, evaluates the applications and produces a new valid Dafny program, where tactic calls are replaced by Dafny constructs which tactics have generated.

A *tactic* is a special Dafny ghost method, recognised by the **tactic** keyword. It contains many features to talk *about* a program, and features to *generate* proofs in terms of Dafny by *transforming* the program. A crucial property is that neither the program, nor the actual (non-proof) specification, can be changed – which we call *contract-preserving transformations* [16].

The application of a tactic will transform a tactic call into the Dafny code generated. To illustrate, the following tactic

```
tactic nat_assert()
{ tactic var n :| n in variables();
  assert n ≥ 0; }
```

will first bind n to a local variable where it was called. This binding is in the tactic world. If there are more than one variables then a search branch will be created for each variable (and it will fail if there are none). The result of applying this tactic is that an assertion, which asserts that the variable is positive, replaces the tactic call. A tactic will either be evaluated until the tactic reach the end of the code, or a proof is found. The top-level tactic application (a tactic that is not applied by another tactic) will only succeed if a proof is found on termination. A formal evaluation semantics is given in [16][1].

A design goal for Tacny is to make Tacny intuitive for Dafny users. It therefore makes use of many Dafny constructs, and follows standard Dafny conventions otherwise. As far as possible, the language supports *declarative* (or *schematic*) tactics, i.e. a schematic representation of a proof patterns is given and Tacny is used to fill in the details. A more detailed account of the Tacny features is given in Sect. 4, where we describe the new features developed here. Next, we outline some more informal verification patterns that are independent of Tacny.

3 Verification Patterns for Dafny

Although Dafny relies on an automatic prover, Dafny proofs should not be seen as automatic. Instead they are called *auto-active* as the proof guidance is abstracted from the underlying prover to the program text. This has had positive usability effects on a *syntactic* level, as one do not need to learn an additional language to conduct proofs; and *conceptually*, as one can think of proofs in terms of programming, rather than the prover. The verification patterns introduced in this section capture proofs at the Dafny level. They are a result of analysing programs in the Dafny repository [1], analysing programs we have developed, and discussion with the developers of IronFleet [19], a large Dafny development consisting of $40K$ lines of proofs [18]. The source code and additional details of the examples can be found on a dedicated web-page [2].

3.1 Patterns as Macros

A very simple pattern is to capture repetitive code, possibly with slight variations. This can be seen as a *macro*, as found in some programming languages (e.g. C). In our sense, we see a macro as a named entity of some repetitive code, as illustrated by the following lemmas:

```
lemma minus_dist() ensures ∀ m, n • minus(add(m, n), n) =m;
{ assert ∀ m,n • add(Suc(m),n) =Suc(add(m,n));
  assert ∀ m, n • add(m, n) =add(n, m); }

lemma geq_dist() ensures ∀ m, n • geq(add(Suc(m),n),n) =True;
{ assert ∀ m,n • add(Suc(m),n) =Suc(add(m,n));
  assert ∀ m, n • add(m, n) =add(n, m); }
```

[1] The requirement that a tactic has to find a proof is a result of user feedback, and is not required in the semantics described in [16].

Here the proofs (i.e. body) of these lemmas are identical, and can thus be turned into a macro (see Sect. 5). Possible reasons for using macros is to hide details in code, or to reuse code across verifications tasks. Note that the macro pattern is common in the IronFleet proofs [19].

3.2 Proof by Cases and Induction

Two common and general proof patterns are *proof by cases* and *proof by induction*. We discuss these together as their representation are very similar in Dafny.

In its simplest form, a *proof by cases* step is achieved by an **if** statement, where the condition is the case to split on. For a proof by *natural induction*, the lemma being proven typically has a natural number n as an argument, and the condition is used to separate base from step cases (often n =0). In the step case, a recursive call is made to the lemma with n decremented. This will reveal the *induction hypothesis* (i.e. the postcondition of the lemma for n−1).

To illustrate, consider a mutually recursive definition of even and odd. The following lemma proves that all natural numbers are either even or odd:

```
lemma even_or_odd(n : nat)
  ensures even(n) ∨ odd(n)
{ if n = 0 ∨ n = 1{ }
  else{ even_or_odd(n−1); }}
```

Note that Dafny has a hard-coded tactic for this type of induction proofs [25]. It normally proves these simple cases where the step case only involves a call to itself. However, it did not work in this case, possibly due to the mutually recursive nature of even and odd. In cases where the step case needs more work, Dafny's induction tactic will not work (automatically), and more interaction is required (see e.g. [18] for examples). The pattern could also be written in different ways, such as:

```
if n = 0 { return; } ...                    if n ≠ 0 { ... }
```

The dots (...) represents the step case. A proof by cases is similar, but without the recursive call. Multiple cases can be achieved by multiple **if** statements.

Another type of induction is when each case is a constructor in an inductively defined data type. In that case, a **match** statement is used, which will also perform a suitable binding of the variables in the constructor. For constructors with recursive arguments, a recursive call to the same lemma is made. This is a proof technique called *structural induction* [7]. To illustrate, consider the following inductive data type:

```
datatype aexp = N(n: int) | V(x: vname) | Plus(0: aexp,1: aexp)
```

Here, the Plus constructor has two recursive arguments (i.e. they are of the same aexp type). Omitting irrelevant parts, a proof of a lemma by structural induction will then look as follows in Dafny:

```
lemma AsimpConst(a: aexp, s: state) ...
{ match a
```

```
    case N(n) ⇒
    case V(x) ⇒
    case Plus(a0,a1) ⇒ AsimpConst(a0,s); AsimpConst(a1,s);}
```

This is a very common proof technique when working with inductive data types. In fact, most interactive theorem provers will automatically generate an induction principle when defining inductive data types such as aexp. As shown in [16], a similar pattern can be applied for *co-induction* [26].

3.3 Proof by Contradiction

Another common proof pattern (for classical logics) is *proof by contradiction*. In order to prove a property P, this amounts to assuming $\neg P$ and derive *false* from it. Again, this technique is frequently used in [18]. To implement it in Dafny, the negated property $\neg P$ becomes the condition of an **if** statement, with **false** asserted at the of the body of the **if** statement. The following example illustrates this pattern:

```
lemma set_inter_empty_contr(A: set<int>, B: set<int>, x: int)
 requires x in A ∧ A * B = {}
 ensures ¬(x in B)
{ if x in B {
    assert x in A * B;
    set_eq_simple(A*B,{},x);
    assert x in {};
    assert false; }}
```

Here, set_eq_simple states that if x is in A*B (the intersection of A and B) then x is in {}. This (rather trivial) lemma application was required for the proof.

3.4 Loop Invariants

The discovery of sufficiently strong loop invariants is one of the most important parts of verifying imperative code. A substantial amount of work has been conducted to automate such discovery. Techniques include abstract interpretation [11], constraint-based techniques [10,17], inductive logic programming [13], symbol elimination [20] and predicate abstraction [29]. Dafny uses abstract interpretation (at the Boogie-level) [4]. Still, there are many cases where the user has to provide loop invariants manually in order to verify code. Below we outline three patterns for "manual" loop invariant discovery.

The Gries and van de Snepscheut Approach. In their systematic approaches to program development, Gries [15] and van de Snepscheut [32] developed several heuristics for verified program construction. Here, we adapt their heuristics for loop invariant discovery (assuming the actual code has been provided), resulting in the following patterns where an invariant is created by: (*i*) deleting a conjunction in a postcondition; (*ii*) replacing a constant of a postcondition with a local variable; and (*iii*) enlarging the range of a variable of a loop guard. The following example illustrates all of these loop patterns:

```
method FindMax(a: array<int>) returns (i: int)
   requires a ≠ null ∧ a . Length > 0
   ensures (0 ≤ i < a . Length)
   ensures (∀ k • 0 ≤k < a . Length ⟹ a[i] ≥a[k])
{  var idx, j, i := 0, 0, 0;
   while (idx < a . Length)
     invariant idx ≤a . Length //( iii )
     invariant 0 ≤ i < a . Length //(i)
     invariant ∀ k • 0 ≤k < idx ⟹a[i] ≥a[k] //( ii )
   { if (a[idx] > a [i]) { i := idx; }
     idx := idx + 1; }}
```

Use of Guards. Another pattern seen (albeit not as commonly) combines (negated) loop guards and guards of conditionals in the invariant. This is illustrated in the following example:

```
method Main() {
     var a,b,c,i := 0,−1,0,100;
     while a ≠ b
      invariant ¬(c < i) ⟹ ¬(a ≠ b)
      decreases i−c
     {    b, c := a, c + 1;
          if (c < i) {
           a := a + 1;}}}
```

Use of Recursive Functions. One may argue that it is easier to reason in the functional fragment of Dafny compared with imperative code. A pattern exploring this generates a recursive function that is defined in the same way as the loop, and proves that this function satisfies the desired postcondition (of the method). This is typically proven by induction. A loop invariant is required to relate the function to the loop body. To illustrate, the following code has a loop invariant that relates the code to a function called find_max_aux:

```
method find_max_idx (a : seq<int>) returns (x : int)
 requires a ≠ []
 ensures 0 ≤ x ≤|a| − 1
 ensures ∀ i • 0 ≤i ≤|a| − 1 ⟹ a[i] ≤a[x]
{ var x,y,N,A := 0,|a|−1,0,|a|−1;
  while (x ≠ y) ...
   invariant find_max_aux(a,x,y) = find_max_aux(a,N,A)
  { if (a[x] ≤ a[y]){x := x + 1;}
    else {y := y − 1;}}
  proof_find_max_aux(a, N, A);}
```

The function is defined as follows:

```
function find_max_aux(a: seq<int>, x: int , y: int): int ... {
  if |a[x .. y+1]| = 1 then x
  else if (a[x] ≤ a[y]) then find_max_aux(a, x + 1, y)
  else find_max_aux(a, x, y − 1) }
```

As can be seen, the code of find_max_aux captures the body of the **while** loop[2]. The proof_find_max_aux lemma relates the function to the postcondition:

```
lemma proof_find_max_aux(a: seq<int>,x: int,y: int) ...
 ensures ∀ i • x ≤i ≤y ⟹a[i] ≤ a[find_max_aux(a, x, y)]{}
```

4 Tactics for Dafny (Tacny)

To mechanise the verification patterns as Dafny tactics (Sect. 5), new features of the Tacny language [16] are required. Here we describe these features, and outline some existing important language properties used in the tactics of Sect. 5. It will be clear which parts are from [16] – the rest, which is summarised in Appendix A, should be considered as a contribution.

A design goal of Tacny is to make the language as familiar as possible to users by exploiting known Dafny constructs and conventions. As far as possible, we try to support *declarative* features in the tactics, where *schematic* representations of proof patterns are given as opposed to a set of procedures. Consequently, a tactic should look like Dafny code, which we believe will be more familiar and intuitive for users. This has been inspired by declarative tactic languages for interactive theorem provers (e.g. [3]).

A tactic is a ghost method, identified by the **tactic** keyword, for example:

```
tactic ex_tac(v : Element, t : Term, tac : Tactic)
  requires P
  ensures Q
{ ... }
```

Types. As this is a meta-level language, constructs to talk *about* a program are required. To achieve this, two new types were introduced in [16]: Element captures a named element of the Dafny program text, such as a variable, method or lemma; while Term refers to the term representation of a formula (which can then be manipulated). Here, we introduce a third type Tactic, which makes a tactic a first class value. A (fully instantiated) tactic application can be passed to another tactic and used therein. A limitation is that it has to be fully instantiated, meaning that proper higher-order programming, where tactics can take arguments, is not (yet) supported. We use the Tactic type extensively in Sect. 5.

[2] The generation of this function happens to be the inverse of the well-known *tail-recursion to loop* compiler optimisation [8].

Statements.[3] When used within Tacny, Dafny constructs have two different uses: in a declarative tactic they are part of an outline of code to be generated by Tacny, and we call this the *object-level*; they can also be used to control evaluation of tactics, and in this case they are at the *tactic-level.* It is a design decision if these should be separated syntactically, i.e. separate constructs for each level (meaning additional syntax) vs. the same constructs for both levels (meaning different semantics for the same syntax). We are using a combinations of these approaches.

Both **if** and **while** statements are used across the object-level and the tactic-level: they belong to the tactic-level if Tacny can evaluate the condition (to either **true** or **false**); and to the object-level if not[4]. The justification for this is that such constructs are familiar for users. Variable declarations, on the other hand, have been syntactically separated as the distinction is less clear. This is achieved by preceding a tactic-level declaration by **tactic**[5]:

```
tactic var x := e;
```

If **tactic** is omitted, then variable x will be in the object-level and thus part of the code to be generated. One can shorten **tactic var** and just write **tvar**.

In addition to assignment (x := e), the 'such as' operator (x : | p) is supported, albeit in a restricted form. Here, we need to be able to enumerate all possible values that x can have, and Tacny will generate a branch in its search space for each possibility. The Tacny statement, s || t, will either apply statement s, or statement t. Tactic calls are supported, which become normal method calls. To develop new tactics, a set of hard-coded and low-level *atomic tactics* are provided by the Tacny system, while expressions are extended with a set of *lookup functions* about the program. These are discussed next.

Atomic Tactics. The simplest atomic tactic involves (generating code for) a lemma or ghost method application. Following our declarative approach, this is represented exactly like a method call. For example, assume **tvar** m,a := lem,v, where lem is a lemma and v is a variable. The statement m(a+1); within a tactic will result in code containing the method call lem(v+1)[6]. Assertions, invariants and variants are handled using existing Dafny constructs, as can be seen below:

```
assert a = 1;        invariant a = 1;        decreases a;
```

Tacny will instantiate the tactic-level constructs (a) to the object-level counterpart (v). Note that if **invariant** or **decreases** is used in the body of a loop (or method for the latter), then they will be added to the loop invariant (or method

[3] All the statements, including the atomic tactics (modular some name changes) were introduced in [16].

[4] Meaning, code such as **while true** {...} cannot be generated.

[5] This naming convention is used for ghost variables in Dafny, which in certain cases needs to be declared as **ghost var**.

[6] If a sequence is given as argument for a method that does not expect a sequence, then Tacny will automatically unroll the sequence into multiple arguments.

declaration for variants) and not at the point of the tactic call as normally happens. They can also be called where the invariant/contract is stated.

The explore(m: Element,args: Seq<Element>) tactic generates all possible application of ghost method/lemma m with arguments taken from args. The proof of AsimpConst (Sect. 3.2) illustrated the use of the **match** statement to do a case analysis of all constructors for a variable v of an inductively defined type. The tactic **tactic match** v { ...} will generate such a match. Here, v is of type Element, and its body (...) contains tactics to be applied for each constructor. **tmatch** is a shorthand notation for **tactic match**[7].

Lookup Functions and Expression-Level Atomic Tactics. One often need properties of the program in tactics, and Tacny keeps track of a *context* that contains such information. Several "look-up" functions from the context are provided. lemmas(), methods() and functions () return the name of available lemmas, methods and functions as sequences of Elements (Seq<Element>). caller () returns the name (type Element) of the method/lemma/function in which the tactic call was made[8]. The functions below works on the original caller. They also accept an optional argument (omitted below), allowing users to look up these properties on other methods and lemmas. preconditions () and postconditions () return sequences of Terms holding all the preconditions or postconditions; args () and variables () return the local arguments and variables of the element (type Seq<Element>); if_guards () and loop_guards() return sequences of Terms, holding the guard of all conditionals and loops, respectively, while loop_guard() returns the loop guard of the loop where the tactic call is made (and fails otherwise).

The predicates is_inductive (v: Element) and is_nat (v: Element) check if the given elements are variables of an inductively defined type or a natural number, respectively; is_inductive can also be applied to a constructor to check if any of its arguments are recursive. eq_type(x: Expr,y: Expr) checks if two expressions are of the same type. When applied within the body of a **match** or **tmatch**, get_constructor () will return a pair of the constructor name (Element) and its arguments (Seq<Element>).

consts(t: Term) returns all constants of t (as a sequence of Terms); split (t: Term,sep: Term) splits all occurrences of sep in t into (a sequence of) separate terms[9]; replace(x: Element,y: Element,z: **seq**<Element>) replaces all occurrences of x with y in z; subst(t: Term,m: **map**<T,U>) applies the substitutions of map m in t. The map is overloaded: it allows T and U to be of types Term, Element or string, where the latter two are treated as named constants. Finally, explore can also be applied as an expression, and returns a term with a function application.

[7] In [16], explore was called perm and **tactic match** called cases.
[8] If this is a nested tactic call, then it refers to the name of the method/lemma/function that called the parent tactic.
[9] For example, split ($A \wedge B$, $\wedge$) will return [A,B].

Tactic Calls within Expressions. A limitation of [16] was that tactics could only be used within statements. Here, we extend the framework with tactic applications within expressions. These have the syntax[10]:

```
function tactic expr_tac(..) {..}
```

Note that a function tactic will not necessarily generate any code; it will return a Term which may generate code depending on where the call is made (and possible generate multiple search branches). E.g. it will not generate code on the r.h.s of a **tvar**, but it will when called in a Tacny tactic such as:

```
assert expr_tac(...);
```

Tactic-Level Contracts and Annotations. A new feature added is to support annotations/contracts at the tactic-level. These are interpreted dynamically, and are used to cut-off invalid branches as early as possible: e.g. if a tactic-level assertion or precondition fail (returns **false**), then the tactic will fail. We can write an assertion P as

```
tactic assert P;
```

or just tassert , while ex_tac illustrates the tactic contracts. This is used in Sect. 5.

Runtime Improvements. We have made improvements in the runtime and memory usage of tactics as a result of improved static checking, lazy evaluation and improved support for different search strategies. On our test data [31], an average speed-up of 44 % and memory usage reduction of 23 % was achieved (and these increased with the size and complexity of tactics). The details are omitted for space reasons – see Tumas' honours thesis for details [31].

5 Verification Patterns Implemented as Dafny Tactics

With the new extensions to the Tacny language, we can now implement the verification patterns from Sect. 3 as Dafny tactics, and apply them in the Tacny tool. The results from this application is summarised at the end of this section, while all the code is available from [2][11].

5.1 Tactics as Macro Expansions

In Sect. 3, we saw that a common pattern is to extract repeated code, possibly with slight variations, as a *macro*. It does not have to contain an underlying high-level pattern, so in many ways this is just syntactical. Instantiating macros is normally called *macro expansion*, and we therefore see tactic applications as macro expansions.

The proof of lemmas minus_dist and geq_dist are identical (see Sect. 3), so the macro becomes the code within their proofs:

[10] This syntax is inspired by the syntax for **function method** used in Dafny.

[11] The supported tool syntax has some minor limitations and thus deviates slightly.

```
tactic dist_macro()
{ assert ∀ m, n • add(Suc(m), n) = Suc(add(m,n));
  assert ∀ m, n • add(m, n) = add(n, m); }
```

The lemmas using this tactic will then only contain a tactic call:

```
lemma minus_dist() ensures ∀ m, n • minus(add(m, n), n) = m;
{ dist_macro(); }
lemma geq_dist() ensures ∀ m, n • geq(add(Suc(m), n), n) = True;
{ dist_macro(); }
```

When there are slight variations one can either provide the parts that varies as arguments, or introduce search into the tactic.

In Dafny, commonalities can often be captured as as a lemma or a method. However, due to modularity, they require that all assumptions are explicitly stated as preconditions, and that all the relevant outcomes are explicitly stated as postconditions. If the goal is to capture some repetitive code as a macro, then, in most cases, stating these assumptions and outcomes can be very tedious, making lemmas unsuitable for this task. As tactics replaces a call with the generated code, such explicit statements are not required, thus making it a more suitable representation.

5.2 Proof by Cases and Induction

As in Sect. 3, we treat induction and case-split together as the former needs a case-split first in Dafny. The following tactic is a generic tactic for *natural induction*:

```
tactic nat_ind(cond: Tactic, base: Tactic, step: Tactic)
{    if cond() {  base(); }
     else{ tactic var m := caller();
           tvar a :| a in args()
           tactic assert is_nat(a);
           m(a-1);
           step(); }}
```

The tactic takes three tactics as arguments: the first (cond) is used to generate the condition (e.g. n =0 when n is the inductive argument); the second (base) is used to handle the base case; and the third (step) is used for the step case. The first four lines of the step case will generate a recursive call to reveal the induction hypothesis. This is the only difference with proof by cases, where these four lines are omitted.

For the even_or_odd lemma, the condition is defined using a function tactic:

```
function tactic nat_ind_cond()
{ tvar a :| a in args() ∧ is_nat(a);
  a=0 ∨ a=1 }
```

The lemma can then be proved by the call: nat_ind(nat_ind_cond(), id(), id()).

For *structural induction*, a **match** statement is generated using our **tactic match** tactic, with recursive calls for the recursive constructors:

```
tactic struct_ind(v: Element, t: Tactic)
 requires is_inductive(v);
{ tactic match v {
    tvar c, cargs := get_constructor();
    if is_inductive(c) {
       tvar m, args := caller(), args();
       tvar i := 0;
       while i < |cargs|
       { if eq_type(v, cargs[i])
         { m(replace(v, cargs[i], args) }
         i := i + 1; }
    t(); }}
```

The tactic takes as arguments: a variable v of an inductively defined type (ensured by the precondition); and a tactic t to be applied to each case. For the recursive constructors, a recursive call to the caller is made for each (constructor) argument of the same type of v, with v replaced by this argument.

5.3 Proof by Contradiction

Proof by contradiction involves assuming the negation of the desired property and deriving false. For Dafny, the property is often (one of) the postcondition(s). The following contr tactic picks one postcondition, and shows, using an **if** condition, that its negation will result in a contradiction. The method takes a tactic as argument that is used to derive the contradiction:

```
tactic contr(tac : Tactic)
{  tactic var post :| post in postconditions();
   if ¬post {
    tac();
    assert false; }}
```

For our set_inter_empty_contr lemma, we can follow the macro expansion approach and give the code directly:

```
tactic tbody()
{    assert x in A * B;
     set_eq_simple(A*B,{},x);
     assert x in {}; }
```

The lemma is verified by the following call: cntr(tbody()).

5.4 Loop Patterns

The Gries & van de Snepscheut Approach. In Sect. 3.4, we described an approach that we called the 'Gries & van de Snepscheut approach'. It contains three patterns, and we implement each of them as a tactic:

```
tactic delete_conj_post ()
{ tvar post :| post in postconditions();
  tvar inv :| inv in split(post,∧);
  invariant inv; }

tactic const_to_var()
{ tvar post := postconditions();
  tvar inv0 :| inv in split(post,∧);
  tvar cons :| const in consts(post');
  tvar v :| v in variables();
  invariant subst(inv0, map[c := v]); }

tactic strengthen_guard()
{ invariant subst(loop_guard(),map["<":="≤", ">":="≥"]);}
```

A simple implementation of an overall pattern applies them one after another:

```
tactic GvdS_approach()
{ delete_conj_post(); const_to_var(); strengthen_guard(); }
```

Note that this rules out multiple application of one pattern and would fail if either of them fail. For space reasons we have omitted more generic and complex versions. This tactic is able to discover the invariants for the FindMax lemma and thus verify it.

Use of Guards. The second loop pattern is a combination of (possibly negated) guards:

```
tactic inv_guard()
{  tvar xx :| xx in if_guard() + loop_guards();
   tvar yy :| yy in if_guard() + loop_guards();
   tvar x :| x = xx ∨ x = ¬xx;
   tvar y :| y = yy ∨ y = ¬yy;
   invariant x ⟹ y; }
```

The inv_guard tactic projects all the guards from **if** and **while** statements. It then creates an invariant, which is an implication where both the antecedent and consequent is a guard or a negated guard. This tactic generates the invariant and proves the Main method of Sect. 3.4:

Use of Recursive Functions. Tacny only partly supports the 'use of recursive functions' pattern of Sect. 3.4. The pattern requires: generation of a function (from the loop body); generation of a lemma (to connect the function and postcondition); and a lemma call outside the loop body (i.e. on the loop exit). Currently, lemma and function generation is not (yet) supported. This is however planned future work (see Sect. 6). A limited version can be implemented if we assume the existence of such function, lemma and lemma call. Tacny can then generate the required loop invariant, which link the function with the loop body:

```
tactic rec_func (func: Element)
{ tvar args := variables() + args();
  tvar lhs := explore(func, args);
  tvar rhs := explore(func, args);
  invariant lhs = rhs; }
```

A tactic could have generated the lemma call too, however this requires the loop invariant to be generated within the loop, whilst the call has to be outside the loop body. Generated such code multiple places from a tactic is not currently supported and discussed further in Sect. 6.

5.5 Summary and Results

Figure 1 summarises the results from our experiments with the patterns as tactics. Further details and code can be found on a dedicated web-page [2]. The table on the l.h.s. shows the total number of pattern instances (**Inst**) and the number of different tactics implemented (**Tactics**). In order to get an idea of time and memory usage, the r.h.s. summarises the run-time (X-axis) and search space size in terms of the number of nodes/steps (Y-axis) using logarithmic scales. Many tactics were re-used across methods and programs, but in some cases slightly different implementations were required (e.g. multiple different macro expansions). In most cases, Tacny used less than 10 s to run on a standard laptop (Intel i7 with 8GB RAM). On average, Boogie accounted for around 95 % of the execution time, highlighting the importance of improving the integration with Boogie and Dafny. This is the reasons for the two outliers in Fig. 1 (right), which has a considerable larger search space and runtime compared with the other examples.

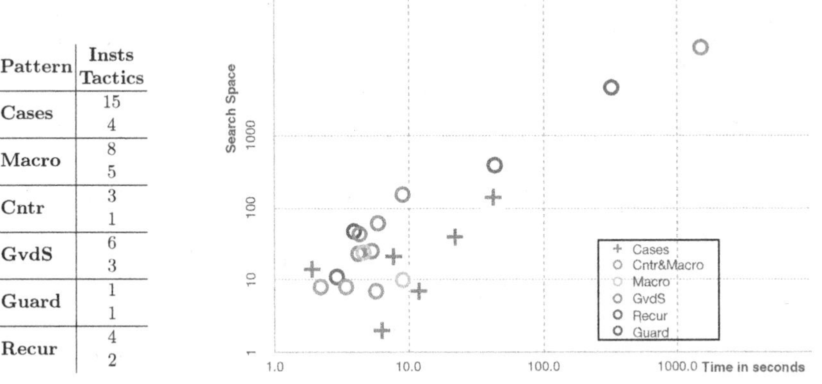

Pattern	Insts	Tactics
Cases	15	4
Macro	8	5
Cntr	3	1
GvdS	6	3
Guard	1	1
Recur	4	2

Fig. 1. Evaluation results

6 Related Work, Conclusion and Future Work

One contribution has been a set of (informal) *verification patterns*, extracted from various sources including [1,15,18,32], which we believe could support novices with their proofs. Surprisingly little work has been done in capturing and documenting verification patterns for mechanised systems[12]. Freitas and Whiteside [14] captures a set of proof patterns for formal methods conjectures in an interactive theorem proving (ITP) setting. Bundy's *proof plans* [5] is a more formal representation of proof patterns for meta-level reasoning, and includes work for algebraic equations in the PRESS system [30] and the rippling strategy for inductive proofs [6]. There is also a book by Joshi on proof patterns for mathematics [21], but this does not address mechanised proofs.

Although undocumented, patterns are still used within most theorem proving based system, implemented as heuristics or tactics in some cases. For example, Dafny has an "induction tactic" [25] to automate simple, yet common, cases of inductive proofs, while ITP systems such as Isabelle and Coq, will have a large collection of tactics to support users. These systems have also started to move the language where tactics are implemented from its implementation language (typically ML variants) to the proof language (e.g. LTac for Coq [12] and EisBach for Isabelle [27]). Autexier and Dietrich [3] has taken this even further and developed a *declarative tactic language* where tactics are written schematically. Inspired by declarative tactics, our work is analogous to [3,12,27], as users can encode proof patterns (tactics) in the program text of Dafny, as opposed to its implementation language (C#), as was the case in e.g. [25].

Building on our initial tactic language [16], our main contributions have been the encoding of the discovered proof patterns as Dafny tactics, together with the necessary extensions to the language. We have shown that the patterns and tactics are generic by applying them to multiple examples, with a reasonable running time. In addition to being an exercise in encoding Dafny tactics, we have shown feasibility and highlighted invaluable language features. Firstly, the language gives a tactic developer freedom to focus on encoding the patterns without concerns of soundness issues (which was the case in [25]), as the actual verification is still conducted by Dafny[13]. The ability to pass tactics as arguments has enabled us to develop more generic tactics. However, in many cases it would have been useful to improve tactic composition by supporting tactics *with arguments* to be passed between tactics. Dafny's type system now supports higher-order features [23]. A next step is to improve the type system in Tacny, and incorporating such features would be beneficial.

The code fragment `x :| x in P` is used extensive in our tactics and a shorthand notation for this will be useful[14]. We are also considering automatically binding variables that occurs frequently (as in [27]) to reduce the code that users have

[12] Klein's FM 2014 keynote also addressed this limitations and its importance.

[13] Under the proviso of *contract preservation* as discussed in Sect. 2 and formalised in [16].

[14] For example, Event-B has an operator $x :\in P$ to express this.

to write, e.g. vars (or Tacny.vars) for variables (). Instead of explicitly introduce branches through assigning a variable with : |, a similar notation could be used. For example, in cases where sequences are not expected, split (P $\wedge$ Q,$\wedge$) could automatically be bound to P in one branch and Q in another branch.

We would also like to include features to generate new lemmas and functions, and investigate how to encode tactics that generate code at different places in a method. This will help us to encode the full 'recursive function' loop pattern. Dafny's (experimental) refinement feature uses a '...' notation to step over code [22], which would serve as a starting point. Another limitation is that we need to hard-code functions, such as replace in the struct_ind tactic, which could have been implemented in Dafny directly (user-defined Dafny functions are not supported at the tactic-level). This will require us to write an interpreter, or possible utilise Dafny's existing compiler into C# (our implementation language).

Following from user feedback, we have improved the language of [16], and *user evaluations* will also play crucial role to ensure a user friendly language in the future. We are now in the process of developing a tighter integration with Dafny, Boogie and the Dafny IDE, where failure-handling and features for debugging tactics are high on our agenda; we believe that these are crucial for adaptation. This will hopefully help us addressing the Boogie bottleneck (see Sect. 5.5).

Some of our tactics can be found in ITP systems: e.g. proof by contradiction, natural induction and structural induction are common; while Dafny can already automate simple inductive lemmas. The explore tactic is a simple form of *term synthesis* at the Dafny level, as used in e.g. HipSpec for Haskell [9]. We plan to implement tactics for richer explorations, supporting more than single statements and conditionals. We have already discussed automated approaches for loop invariant discovery in Sect. 3.4. A key distinction from these techniques is that tactics follows a more *human-oriented* approach, where the developer's (mental) pattern is encoded as a tactic.

Other important challenges include the discovery of new patterns and their corresponding tactic implementations, and to address *scalability* of the approach. For example, a common pattern used in IronFleet is to first unfold universal quantification, set up a proof by contradiction and then apply some lemmas afterwards [19]. We support some of these components, but would like to complete the circle and see if we can develop a tactic for the complete pattern, which also handles the size of this program.

A Summary of New Tacny Features

This paper has extended and improved Tacny from the version presented in [16] as follows:

- A new type Tactic that makes a tactic a first class value is introduced.
- **function tactic** and tactic applications within expressions are now supported.
- Contracts for tactics, and tactic-level assertions have been added.

- Several new atomic tactics and lookup functions are supported, including: caller (); preconditions (); postconditions (); if_guards (); loop_guards(); is_inductive (v: Element); is_nat (v: Element); eq_type(x: Expr,y: Expr); get_constructor (); consts(t: Term); split (t: Term,sep: Term); replace(x: Element,y: Element,z: **seq**<Element>); subst(t: Term,m: **map**<T,U>); and explore as an expression.
- Considerable runtime improvements have been achieved.
- The syntax is improved to align with Dafny conventions and declarative tactics. For example: cases has become **tactic match** (or **tmatch**); tactic-level variable declarations have changed from **var** to **tactic var** (or **tvar**); Dafny-level variable declarations have changed from **fresh var** to **var**.

References

1. Dafny Website. research.microsoft.com/dafny
2. The Tacny project: FM 2016 information. https://sites.google.com/site/tacnyproject/fm-2016. Accessed 29 May 2016
3. Autexier, S., Dietrich, D.: A tactic language for declarative proofs. In: Kaufmann, M., Paulson, L.C. (eds.) ITP 2010. LNCS, vol. 6172, pp. 99–114. Springer, Heidelberg (2010). doi:10.1007/978-3-642-14052-5_9
4. Barnett, M., Chang, B.-Y.E., DeLine, R., Jacobs, B., Leino, K.R.M.: Boogie: a modular reusable verifier for object-oriented programs. In: Boer, F.S., Bonsangue, M.M., Graf, S., Roever, W.-P. (eds.) FMCO 2005. LNCS, vol. 4111, pp. 364–387. Springer, Heidelberg (2006). doi:10.1007/11804192_17
5. Bundy, A.: A science of reasoning. In: Lassez, J.L., Plotkin, G. (eds.) Computational Logic - Essays in Honor of Alan Robinson, pp. 178–198. MIT Press, Cambridge (1991)
6. Bundy, A., Basin, D., Hutter, D., Ireland, A.: Rippling: Meta-level Guidance for Mathematical Reasoning. Cambridge Tracts in Theoretical Computer Science, vol. 56. Cambridge University Press, Cambridge (2005)
7. Rod, M.: Burstall: proving properties of programs by structural induction. Comput. J. **12**(1), 41–48 (1969)
8. Burstall, R.M., Darlington, J.: A transformation system for developing recursive programs. J. ACM (JACM) **24**(1), 44–67 (1977)
9. Claessen, K., Johansson, M., Rosén, D., Smallbone, N.: Automating inductive proofs using theory exploration. In: Bonacina, M.P. (ed.) CADE 2013. LNCS (LNAI), vol. 7898, pp. 392–406. Springer, Heidelberg (2013). doi:10.1007/978-3-642-38574-2_27
10. Colón, M.A., Sankaranarayanan, S., Sipma, H.B.: Linear invariant generation using non-linear constraint solving. In: Hunt, W.A., Somenzi, F. (eds.) CAV 2003. LNCS, vol. 2725, pp. 420–432. Springer, Heidelberg (2003). doi:10.1007/978-3-540-45069-6_39
11. Cousot, P., Halbwachs, N.: Automatic discovery of linear restraints among variables of a program. In: Proceedings of the 5th ACM SIGACT-SIGPLAN Symposium on Principles of Programming Languages, pp. 84–96. ACM (1978)
12. Delahaye, D.: A tactic language for the system Coq. In: Parigot, M., Voronkov, A. (eds.) LPAR 2000. LNAI, vol. 1955, pp. 85–95. Springer, Heidelberg (2000). doi:10.1007/3-540-44404-1_7

13. Ernst, M.D., Perkins, J.H., Guo, P.J., McCamant, S., Pacheco, C., Tschantz, A.S., Xiao, C.: The Daikon system for dynamic detection of likely invariants. Sci. Comput. Program. **69**(1), 35–45 (2007)
14. Freitas, L., Whiteside, I.: Proof patterns for formal methods. In: Jones, C., Pihlajasaari, P., Sun, J. (eds.) FM 2014. LNCS, vol. 8442, pp. 279–295. Springer, Heidelberg (2014). doi:10.1007/978-3-319-06410-9_20
15. Gries, D.: The Science of Programming, 1st edn. Springer, New York (1987)
16. Grov, G., Tumas, V.: Tactics for the dafny program verifier. In: Chechik, M., Raskin, J.-F. (eds.) TACAS 2016. LNCS, vol. 9636, pp. 36–53. Springer, Heidelberg (2016). doi:10.1007/978-3-662-49674-9_3
17. Gupta, A., Rybalchenko, A.: InvGen: an efficient invariant generator. In: Bouajjani, A., Maler, O. (eds.) CAV 2009. LNCS, vol. 5643, pp. 634–640. Springer, Heidelberg (2009). doi:10.1007/978-3-642-02658-4_48
18. Hawblitzel, C., Howell, J., Kapritsos, M., Lorch, J.R., Parno, B., Roberts, M.L., Setty, S., Zill, B.: Ironfleet: proving practical distributed systems correct. In: Proceedings of the 25th Symposium on Operating Systems Principles, pp. 1–17. ACM (2015)
19. Hawblitzel, C., Lorch, J., Parno, B.: Personal discussions, December 2015
20. Hoder, K., Kovács, L., Voronkov, A.: Invariant generation in vampire. In: Abdulla, P.A., Leino, K.R.M. (eds.) TACAS 2011. LNCS, vol. 6605, pp. 60–64. Springer, Heidelberg (2011). doi:10.1007/978-3-642-19835-9_7
21. Joshi, M.: Proof Patterns. Springer, New York (2015)
22. Jason Koenig, K., Leino, R.M.: Programming language features for refinement (2015)
23. Leino, K.R.M.: Types in Dafny, 27 February 2015. http://research.microsoft.com/en-us/um/people/leino/papers/krml243.html. (Manuscript KRML 243)
24. Leino, K.R.M.: Dafny: an automatic program verifier for functional correctness. In: Clarke, E.M., Voronkov, A. (eds.) LPAR 2010. LNCS (LNAI), vol. 6355, pp. 348–370. Springer, Heidelberg (2010). doi:10.1007/978-3-642-17511-4_20
25. Leino, K.R.M.: Automating induction with an SMT solver. In: Kuncak, V., Rybalchenko, A. (eds.) VMCAI 2012. LNCS, vol. 7148, pp. 315–331. Springer, Heidelberg (2012). doi:10.1007/978-3-642-27940-9_21
26. Leino, K.R.M., Moskal, M.: Co-induction simply. In: Jones, C., Pihlajasaari, P., Sun, J. (eds.) FM 2014. LNCS, vol. 8442, pp. 382–398. Springer, Heidelberg (2014). doi:10.1007/978-3-319-06410-9_27
27. Matichuk, D., Wenzel, M., Murray, T.: An isabelle proof method language. In: Klein, G., Gamboa, R. (eds.) ITP 2014. LNCS, vol. 8558, pp. 390–405. Springer, Heidelberg (2014). doi:10.1007/978-3-319-08970-6_25
28. Moura, L., Bjørner, N.: Z3: an efficient SMT solver. In: Ramakrishnan, C.R., Rehof, J. (eds.) TACAS 2008. LNCS, vol. 4963, pp. 337–340. Springer, Heidelberg (2008). doi:10.1007/978-3-540-78800-3_24
29. Srivastava, S., Gulwani, S.: Program verification using templates over predicate abstraction. In: ACM Sigplan Notices, vol. 44, pp. 223–234. ACM (2009)
30. Sterling, L., Bundy, A., Byrd, L., O'Keefe, R., Silver, B.: Solving symbolic equations with press. In: Calmet, J. (ed.) EUROCAM 1982. LNCS, vol. 144, pp. 109–116. Springer, Heidelberg (1982). doi:10.1007/3-540-11607-9_13
31. Tumas, V.: Search space reduction for Tacny tactics. Honours thesis, Heriot-Watt University (2016). https://sites.google.com/site/tacnyproject/
32. van de Snepscheut, J.L.A.: What Computing is All About. Springer, New York (1993)

Formalising and Validating the Interface Description in the FMI Standard

Miran Hasanagić(✉), Peter W.V. Tran-Jørgensen, Kenneth Lausdahl, and Peter Gorm Larsen

Department of Engineering, Aarhus University,
Finlandsgade 22, 8200 Aarhus, Denmark
{miran.hasanagic,pvj,lausdahl,pgl}@eng.au.dk

Abstract. The Functional Mock-up Interface (FMI) aims to support the interoperability in an interdisciplinary formal methods setting by describing an interface between different formal models in a tool co-simulation setting. However, the FMI standard describes the requirements for the static limitations on the interfaces in an informal manner using tables and textual descriptions. In this short paper we demonstrate how this kind of static constraints can be formalised using the Vienna Development Method Specification Language, and how the formalisation can be examined and validated exhaustively. Afterwards we present how this can be transferred into code in order to develop a tool that can be used by anyone using the FMI standard enabling a more well-founded basis in such an interdisciplinary setting, by having a formal description of the FMI interface.

Keywords: VDM-SL · Functional Mock-up Interface · Co-simulation · Code generation · Combinatorial testing

1 Introduction

In an interdisciplinary setting individual models are typically described using different formalisms with separate tools supporting them. This is especially the case for Cyber-Physical Systems (CPSs) where the underlying mathematics have different roots [14]. In order to enable exchange between such semantically heterogeneous formal models the Functional Mock-up Interface (FMI) standard provides a computer-based language for describing the interface between constituent models [3]. Tools following this standard must have a capability for producing Functional Mock-up Units (FMUs) that either provide a stand-alone simulation or a model exchange capability of a constituent model. Afterwards, such FMUs can be combined by a co-simulation orchestration engine, acting as a master for co-simulation. Each FMU has inputs, outputs and parameters which are exposed according to the FMI standard and referred to as Scalar Variables (SVs). For these SVs the standard contains a number of tables and natural language explanations on the different static constraints for the SVs of the FMUs.

J. Fitzgerald et al. (Eds.): FM 2016, LNCS 9995, pp. 344–351, 2016.
DOI: 10.1007/978-3-319-48989-6_21

Describing the FMI static constrains informally may introduce ambiguity and misunderstanding between tool vendors. In order to formalise these static constraints we have used the Vienna Development Method Specification Language (VDM-SL) that has been standardised by ISO [7,8]. VDM is one of the most mature formal methods with a long history of developing computer-based systems [2,9]. The development of VDM was originally carried out at IBM in Vienna in the 1970s to support the development of a compiler for PL/1. Different tools support VDM-SL, and here we have used the open-source Overture tool [11] where different extensions of the language have been systematically performed [1], that are used for this work. One of the extensions has been the definition of traces which are used for test automation in VDM [12]. Furthermore, Overture supports automatic code generation to Java [10], and recently extensions of this work also support the use of the Java Modelling Language (JML) for contract-based aspects of VDM such as invariants, pre- and post-conditions [15]. Formalising the static semantics has revealed inconsistencies in FMUs generated by modelling tools, such as the commercial tool Dymola[1].

The rest of this paper is structured as follows: Sect. 2 explains how the static constraints of SVs in the FMI standard is modelled and validated in VDM-SL. Afterwards, Sect. 3 explains how the VDM-SL model is realised using code generation and incorporated as a part of larger tool[2] that support FMI based co-simulation. Finally, Sect. 4 provides concluding remarks including comments about how it was helpful in overcoming problems as well as considerations about future work.

2 Static Semantics and Validation Using VDM

VDM has a long history in the development of both static semantics as well as dynamic semantics for a long list of computer-based languages, which corresponds to type checking and run-time validation, respectively [4,5]. In this work we model the static semantics of the FMI standard. The purpose of a static semantics is to divide all syntactically correct descriptions into those that are semantically meaningful (i.e. those that have no semantic errors statically) and those that are violating one or more of the semantic constraints. Hence, at one level of abstraction the result of a static semantics is essentially just a boolean function. However, as a user it is not very helpful if one just gets told that the description has an error, without any kind of indication about what the problem might be. Thus, one can also define a static semantics at a more detailed level where a list of errors is presented to the user. In this work both of these

[1] See http://www.modelon.com/products/dymola/.
[2] See INTO-CPS App: http://into-cps.github.io/download/.

principles are used in the sense that the explicit parts of the functions produce a list of errors (possibly empty) whereas the associated post-condition simply captures the more abstract notion focusing on whether the description can be given a meaning.

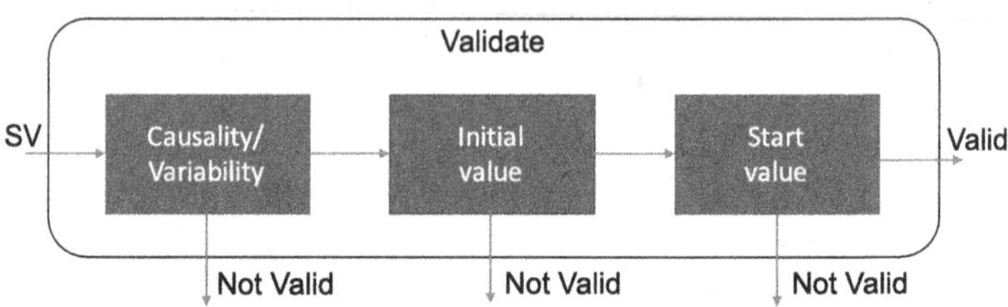

Fig. 1. Overview of standard conformance with the FMI standard of a scalar variable

The FMI standard defines a SV by four different properties: *`Causality`*, *`Variability`*, *`Initial`* and *`Type`*. Values of these properties define in combination the semantic validity of a SV. The top-level function `Validate` consists of sub-functions which model different aspects of the FMI standard separately, as shown by the grey boxes in Fig. 1, where the checking order it indicated by the arrows. This checking order is implied by the FMI standard, as described below. Each of these sub-functions models constraints described either by tables or natural language according to the FMI standard, which in combination define the validity of a scalar variable. Such an approach supports the detection of which part of a SV that is not consistent with the FMI standard. For each of these sub-functions pre- and post-conditions are modelled as well, where the pre-condition describes assumptions under which the function guarantees to return a result satisfying the post-condition. Hence this forms a contract for a function, and enables the testing of each sub-function separately. For example this captures that the "Initial value" sub-function in Fig. 1 requires that the *`Causality`* and *`Variability`* combination of a SV taken as input is valid, since a specific combination implies a specific constrain on the *`Initial`* property.

The general structure of the VDM-SL specification can be seen from a small extract of the top-level function called `Validate`, which highlights the sub-function `CausalityVariabilityOk` for checking the *`Causality`* and *`Variability`* combination, which also will be used as an example throughout the rest of this paper:

```
Validate : SV -> bool * seq of char
Validate(sv) ==
...
let mk_(cv_ok, cv_msg) = CausalityVariabilityOk(sv2.causality,
                                                 sv2.variability)
in
   if not cv_ok
   then mk_(false, cv_msg)
   else ...
post RESULT.#1 = let mk_SV(c,v,i,t) = sv
                 in
                   ...
                   cases c:
                     <input> ->
                       v in set {<discrete>, <continuous>} and
                       i = nil and
                       (v = <continuous> => t.type = <Real>) and
                       t.startValue <> nil
         ...
```

Here the first **bool** in the result pair indicates whether the input SV scalar variable is statically valid, and the second one is a string with an error message. The body of the function contains a let expression using pattern matching for such a pair. Note how the post-condition simply looks at the first element to determine if the result given meets the static constraints. The FMI standard prescribes a default value for a property if not set by the user. As a consequence sv and sv2 model a SV before and after possible default values are set. To capture this in the VDM-SL model the type of a scalar variables is defined as a record type SV, where the square brackets indicate an optional type, i.e. adding a special **nil** value to the type:

```
SV ::
  causality   : [Causality]
  variability : [Variability]
  initial     : [Initial]
  type        : Type;
```

The types used inside this record type are modelled as quotes (like enumerated types), as an example the types of *Causality* and *Variability*, in accordance with the options seen in Fig. 2, are specified as:

```
Causality   = <parameter> | <calculatedParameter> | <input>
              | <output> | <local> | <independent>;
Variability = <constant> | <fixed> | <tunable> | <discrete>
              | <continuous>;
```

The valid combination of the *Causality* and *Variability*, as described in the FMI standard, is indicated by numbers in Fig. 2. The following part of the model detects validation error (a) listed in Fig. 2:

```
CausalityVariabilityOk: Causality * Variability ->
                        bool * seq of char
CausalityVariabilityOk(c,v) ==
if c in set {<parameter>, <calculatedParameter>, <input>} and
   v = <constant>
then mk_(false, ErrorMsg(c,v))
...
else mk_(true, "Valid combination of Causality and Variability.")
post RESULT.#1 => ValidCV(c,v);
```

For each of the letters seen in Fig. 2, which indicates a combination that is not valid, a meaningful error message is created.

Since the allowed values yield a finite number of combination it is possible to exhaustively test the different definitions a number of traces. Essentially a trace can be considered as a regular expression that is used for expressing the different sequences of tests that one would like to conduct. Since we only deal with functions here the test sequencing aspects are not needed so essentially it is simply expressed with a choice from all the possible combinations and the tool support then automatically explore all of these:

```
T_CausalityVariabilityOk:
let mk_(c,v) in set allCV()
in
  CausalityVariabilityOk(c,v);
```

			causality					
			parameter	calculated Parameter	input	output	local	independent
variability	data	constant	-- (a)	-- (a)	-- (a)	(7)	(10)	-- (c)
		fixed	(1)	(3)	-- (d)	-- (e)	(11)	-- (c)
		tunable	(2)	(4)	-- (d)	-- (e)	(12)	-- (c)
	signals	discrete	-- (b)	-- (b)	(5)	(8)	(13)	-- (c)
		continuous	-- (b)	-- (b)	(6)	(9)	(14)	(15)

Fig. 2. Table taken from the FMI standard [3] indicating valid combination (numbers) and invalid combinations (letters)

For validating all possible combinations, the `allCV` function yields a set with the possible combinations:

```
allC: () -> set of Causality
allC() == {<parameter>,<calculatedParameter>,<input>,<output>,
           <local>,<independent>};

allV: () -> set of Variability
allV() == {<constant>,<discrete>,<fixed>,<tunable>,<continuous>};

allCV: () -> set of (Causality * Variability)
allCV() ==
{ mk_(c,v) | v in set allV(), c in set allC()};
```

These traces are applied both for the validating the top-level function `Validate` as well as each sub-function individually. Such traces are used to validate the VDM-SL specification, and here it is possible to test it with all possible combinations in a few minutes using the VDM interpreter in a way similar to the simplest form for model checking. For example these traces generate 3600 different test cases for the `Validate` function, while the trace for the function `CausalityVariabilityOk` generates 30 test cases. Additionally such traces can also be code generated (making use of JML) in order to speed up the execution and test the implementation.

3 Software Tool Integration

The VDM-SL specification of the static constraints of the FMI standard interface described above needs to be realised in a programming language in order for software tools to make use of it. Here we use automatic code generation to Java to realise the VDM-SL specification. The generated code can be used either in the development of a stand-alone tool that can be used to check that the FMUs generated by a tool satisfy the constraints by the FMI standard, or it can be used inside a larger tool suite such as that from the INTO-CPS project [6,13], which contains a simulation environment for FMUs. In our case it is integrated inside the INTO-CPS tool chain.

Validating that the generated code preserves the semantics of the VDM specification both unit-testing and using a contract-based implementation language such as JML can be utilised. Both approaches can been exploited with the VDM specification. In the latter approach the pre- and post-conditions are included as a part of the code using JML, and additionally the traces are generated for validating the code. Finally, consistency between the model traces and the code tests, which are based on the model traces, is validated [16].

When integrating the generated Java code within another tool, such as the INTO-CPS FMU co-simulation engine, it is necessary to provide glue code which enables the interoperability between the different system components. In this case it is required to ensure that the different data types are unified in the same format.

4 Concluding Remarks

The main contribution of this short paper addresses the following points (1) Tool support for an interdisciplinary framework. (2) Using VDM-SL in practice finding issues both with our own tools in INTO-CPS, as well as with other tools. (3) Tool integration and automation by supporting validation, and integrating it with the rest of the tool support in INTO-CPS. The tool produced based on the static semantics described in this paper found errors in the baseline modelling tools used in the INTO-CPS project as well as in the commercial tool Dymola. As part of the INTO-CPS project this supported the development of valid FMUs, by the INTO-CPS modelling tools. As an example Dymola exported a constant value generator with the causality `output` and variability `fixed`, which is not allowed according to the FMI standard, as seen in Fig. 2. These errors where found, when the INTO-CPS co-simulation engine loads an FMU, and it checks an FMUs validity by using the generated Java code from the VDM-SL specification.

Most of the static constrains from the FMI standard have been modelled in this work and as a consequence that is now supported inside the INTO-CPS tool chain. However, the remaining parts of the standard could also be included in the model. In addition it could potentially also make sense to use the generated code to build a stand-alone tool that would be useful for checking constraints on an individual FMU instead of relying on this check inside the INTO-CPS tool chain.

Acknowledgments. The work presented here is partially supported by the INTO-CPS project funded by the European Commission's Horizon 2020 programme under grant agreement number 664047.

References

1. Battle, N., Haxthausen, A., Hiroshi, S., Jørgensen, P.W.V., Plat, N., Sahara, S., Verhoef, M.: The overture approach to VDM language evolution. In: The Overture 2013 Workshop, August 2013
2. Bjørner, D., Jones, C.B. (eds.): The Vienna Development Method: The Meta-Language. LNCS, vol. 61. Springer, Heidelberg (1978)
3. Blochwitz, T.: Functional mock-up interface for model exchange and co-simulation, July 2014. https://www.fmi-standard.org/downloads
4. C.C.I.T.T.: The specification of chill. Technical report Recommendation Z200, International Telegraph and Telephone Consultative Committee, Geneva, Switzerland (1980)
5. Andrews, D.J., Garg, A., Lau, S.P.A., Pitchers, J.R.: The formal definition of modula-2 and its associated interpreter. In: Bloomfield, R.E., Marshall, L.S., Jones, R.B. (eds.) VDM 1988. LNCS, vol. 328, pp. 167–177. Springer, Heidelberg (1988). doi:10.1007/3-540-50214-9_15
6. Fitzgerald, J., Gamble, C., Larsen, P.G., Pierce, K., Woodcock, J.: Cyber-physical systems design: formal foundations, methods and integrated tool chains. In: FormaliSE: FME Workshop on Formal Methods in Software Engineering, ICSE 2015, Florence, Italy, May 2015

7. Fitzgerald, J., Larsen, P.G.: Modelling Systems - Practical Tools and Techniques in Software Development, 2nd edn. Cambridge University Press, Cambridge (2009). ISBN 0-521-62348-0
8. ISO: Information technology - Programming languages, their environments and system software interfaces - Vienna Development Method - Specification Language - Part 1: Base language, December 1996
9. Jones, C.B.: Systematic Software Development Using VDM, 2nd edn. Prentice-Hall International, Englewood Cliffs (1990). ISBN 0-13-880733-7
10. Jørgensen, P.W.V., Larsen, P.G.: Towards an overture code generator. In: The Overture 2013 workshop, August 2013
11. Larsen, P.G., Battle, N., Ferreira, M., Fitzgerald, J., Lausdahl, K., Verhoef, M.: The overture initiative - integrating tools for VDM. SIGSOFT Softw. Eng. Notes **35**(1), 1–6 (2010). http://doi.acm.org/10.1145/1668862.1668864
12. Larsen, P.G., Lausdahl, K., Battle, N.: Combinatorial testing for VDM. In: Proceedings of the 2010 8th IEEE International Conference on Software Engineering and Formal Methods, SEFM 2010, pp. 278–285. IEEE Computer Society, Washington, DC, September 2010. http://dx.doi.org/10.1109/SEFM.2010.32. ISBN 978-0-7695-4153-2
13. Larsen, P.G., Thule, C., Lausdahl, K., Bardur, V., Gamble, C., Pierce, K., Brosse, E., Sadovykh, A., Bagnato, A., Couto, L.D.: Integrated tool chain for model-based design of cyber-physical systems. In: Submitted for the 14th Overture Workshop, Cyprus, November 2016
14. Lee, E.: Cyber-physical systems - are computing foundations adequate? In: NSF Workshop On Cyber-Physical Systems: Research Motivation, Techniques and Roadmap, Austin, TX, October 2006
15. Tran-Jørgensen, P.W.V., Larsen, P.G., Leavens, G.T.: Automated translation of VDM to JML annotated Java (January 2016 Submitted to the International Journal on Software Tools for Technology Transfer (STTT))
16. Tran-Jørgesen, P.W., Larsen, P.G., Battle, N.: Using JML-based code generation to enhance the test automation for VDM models. Submitted for the 14th Overture Workshop, Cyprus, November 2016

An Algebra of Synchronous Atomic Steps

Ian J. Hayes[1(✉)], Robert J. Colvin[1], Larissa A. Meinicke[1], Kirsten Winter[1], and Andrius Velykis[2]

[1] School of Information Technology and Electrical Engineering, The University of Queensland, Brisbane, Australia
{Ian.Hayes,kirsten}@itee.uq.edu.au
[2] School of Computing Science, Newcastle University, Newcastle upon Tyne, UK

Abstract. This research started with an algebra for reasoning about rely/guarantee concurrency for a shared memory model. The approach taken led to a more *abstract algebra of atomic steps*, in which atomic steps synchronise (rather than interleave) when composed in parallel. The algebra of rely/guarantee concurrency then becomes an interpretation of the more abstract algebra. Many of the core properties needed for rely/guarantee reasoning can be shown to hold in the abstract algebra where their proofs are simpler and hence allow a higher degree of automation. Moreover, the realisation that the synchronisation mechanisms of standard process algebras, such as CSP and CCS/SCCS, can be interpreted in our abstract algebra gives evidence of its unifying power. The algebra has been encoded in Isabelle/HOL to provide a basis for tool support.

1 Introduction

Our goal is to provide better methods for deriving concurrent programs from abstract specifications, and to provide tool support for compositional reasoning about their correctness. The rely/guarantee approach of Jones [Jon81,Jon83] achieves compositionality by abstracting the interference a process can tolerate from and inflict on its environment. A *rely* condition r is a binary relation between states that represents an assumption bounding the interference that a process p can tolerate from its environment. If the environment fails to meet its obligation r, p may deviate from its specification and show erratic behaviour (i.e. abort). A *guarantee* condition g is the corresponding notion that bounds the interference inflicted on its environment by p. For a system of parallel processes to function correctly, each process's guarantee must imply the rely of every other parallel process. These concepts can be captured uniformly (and hence the manipulation of process terms kept simple) in a framework in which both the steps of a process and the steps of its environment are explicitly represented.

The semantic model for rely/guarantee reasoning suggested by Aczel is one such framework [Acz83,dR01]. In this model, parallel composition *synchronises*

This work is supported by Australian Research Council (ARC) Discovery Project DP130102901 and the UK EPSRC Taming Concurrency research grant.

J. Fitzgerald et al. (Eds.): FM 2016, LNCS 9995, pp. 352–369, 2016.
DOI: 10.1007/978-3-319-48989-6_22

a program step of one process with an environment step of another, to give a program step of their composition. Aczel's approach, of insisting each step of one process is synchronised with a step of the other process, differs from the commonly used approach of interleaving atomic steps of processes (except when they communicate), e.g. CCS [Mil89], CSP [Hoa85] and ACP [BK84,BK85]. Aczel's approach is closer to Milner's Synchronous CCS (SCCS) [Mil89, Sect. 9.3] and Meije (the calculus at the basis of the synchronous programming language Esterelle) [BC85].

Our methodology is to develop a refinement calculus for concurrent programs that lifts rely and guarantee conditions to commands[1] [JHC15,HJC14] (from parameters to the notion of correctness). That allows algebraic reasoning about concurrent programs in a rely/guarantee style. To this end we have designed a *Concurrent Refinement Algebra* (CRA) to support the rely/guarantee approach [Hay16]. In exploring the laws in CRA, we discovered that atomic steps have specific algebraic properties that can be captured in an *abstract algebra of atomic steps* which is embedded in CRA.

The abstract algebra of atomic steps delivers a range of useful properties for manipulating process terms. For example, based on the notion of atomic steps the parallel composition of processes can be simplified as follows

$$(a \,;\, c) \parallel (b \,;\, d) = (a \parallel b) \,;\, (c \parallel d), \tag{1}$$

where a and b are atomic steps and c and d are arbitrary processes. Note that the above equivalence does not hold if a and b are arbitrary processes. For an interleaving operator $|||$ the corresponding law is the more complicated:

$$(a \,;\, c) \,|||\, (b \,;\, d) = a \,;\, (c \,|||\, b \,;\, d) \sqcap b \,;\, (a \,;\, c \,|||\, d). \tag{2}$$

In (1), parallel composition of two atomic steps a and b gives an atomic step $a \parallel b$, where the interpretation of $a \parallel b$ depends on the particular model. As a consequence, the algebra can be applied to a range of models. For example, as well as allowing an Aczel-trace model to support shared variable concurrency, communication in process algebras such as CSP and CCS/SCCS can be interpreted in the abstract algebra and hence it provides a foundation for a range of concurrency models.

Kleene Algebra with Tests (KAT) by Kozen [Koz97] combines Kleene algebra (the algebra of regular expressions [Con71]) with a Boolean sub-algebra representing tests. KAT supports sequential programs with conditionals and finite iterations (partial correctness). The *Demonic Refinement Algebra* (DRA) of von Wright [vW04] generalises Kozen's work to support possibly infinite iteration and with that the concept of aborting behaviour. The approach used in this paper is based on that of von Wright in order to faithfully capture Jones' theory, in particular his rely condition.

Concurrent Kleene Algebra (CKA) [HMSW11] adds a parallel operator to Kleene algebra to support sequential and parallel programs. Prisacariu's

[1] We use the terms *command*, *program* and *process* synonymously.

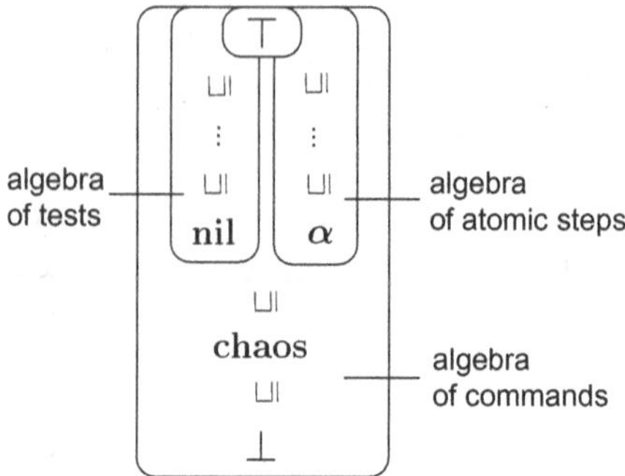

Fig. 1. The Concurrent Refinement Algebra and its sub-algebras

Synchronous Kleene Algebra (SKA) [Pri10] extends Kleene algebra with a synchronous parallel operator similar to that in Milner's SCCS [Mil89]. Like Milner he proposes a specific interpretation of the parallel composition of atomic steps. In contrast to both CKA and SKA, our *Concurrent Refinement Algebra* [Hay16], which we use as a basis for this work, adds a parallel operator to the sequential algebra DRA (rather than Kleene algebra).

The major contribution of this paper is an *algebra of atomic steps* which introduces a synchronous parallel operator for atomic steps. The interpretation of two atomic steps acting in parallel, however, is left open, hence allowing a range of different models (including those of Milner and Prisacariu). Further, atomic steps are treated as a Boolean sub-algebra (similar to the way in which tests are treated as a Boolean sub-algebra in KAT). Hence the Concurrent Refinement Algebra (CRA) contains both a sub-algebra of tests and a sub-algebra of atomic steps (as illustrated in Fig. 1 via their lattices). Separating out these sub-algebras enables one to prove properties that are specific to atomic steps using the full power of a Boolean algebra. This raises the level of support for reasoning about programs provided by our algebra, as well as the level of automation that is possible for the mechanised proof support by the theorem prover Isabelle.

To build the algebra, we start in Sect. 2 with CRA for reasoning about commands in general. Commands include a sub-lattice of tests (Sect. 3) as well as a second sub-lattice of atomic steps (Sect. 4), the novel contribution of this paper. Section 5 gives an interpretation of the abstract algebra based on Aczel's trace model. A simplified treatment of relies and guarantees is outlined in Sect. 6. Section 7 illustrates how the communication models of CCS, CSP and SCCS can be interpreted in our abstract algebra of atomic steps.

2 Concurrent Refinement Algebra

A Concurrent Refinement Algebra (CRA) is defined as the following structure

$$(\mathcal{C}, \sqcap, \sqcup, \ ; \ , \|, \bot, \top, \mathbf{nil}, \mathbf{skip})$$

where the carrier set $\mathcal{C}$ is the set of *commands*. Sequential composition (;) has higher precedence than parallel ($\|$), which has higher precedence than $\sqcap$ and $\sqcup$, which have equal precedence.

Commands form a complete distributive lattice $(\mathcal{C}, \sqcap, \sqcup, \bot, \top)$ with *nondeterministic choice* as the lattice meet ($c \sqcap d$), and *conjunction* of commands as the lattice join ($c \sqcup d$). The top of the lattice $\top$ is the infeasible command (called "magic" in the refinement calculus) and the bottom of the lattice $\bot$ is the command that aborts. The partial order defined on commands is the refinement relation $c \sqsubseteq d$ meaning c is refined (or implemented by) d. For any commands $c, d \in \mathcal{C}$, $c \sqsubseteq d \mathrel{\widehat{=}} (c \sqcap d) = c$, and hence $\bot \sqsubseteq c \sqsubseteq \top$. We refer to this as the *refinement lattice* (see Fig. 1). Note that since CRA is a *refinement* algebra it uses $\sqsubseteq$ as partial order instead of Kozen's $\geq$ and hence our lattice of commands is the dual of Kozen's lattice (i.e., $\sqcap$ in CRA matches $\sqcup$ in KAT, and $\sqcup$ in CRA matches $\sqcap$ in KAT). Given commands form a complete lattice, for any monotone function least/greatest fixed points are well defined. In particular, fixed points are used to define iteration operators below.

Sequential composition of commands $(c\,;\,d)$ is associative and has identity **nil**. As an abbreviation, the sequential composition operator may be elided. Sequential composition has both $\top$ and $\bot$ as left (but not right) annihilators[2], i.e. $\top\, c = \top$ and $\bot\, c = \bot$. It distributes over arbitrary choices on the right (3),

$$(\textstyle\bigsqcap C)\, d = \bigsqcap_{c \in C}(c\, d). \tag{3}$$

+The iteration of a command is inductively defined as $c^0 = \mathbf{nil}$ and $c^{i+1} = c\, c^i$. More general iteration operators are captured via greatest (ν) and least (μ) fixed points: $c^\star \mathrel{\widehat{=}} \nu x.\mathbf{nil} \sqcap c\, x$ for finite iteration zero or more times, and $c^\omega \mathrel{\widehat{=}} \mu\, x.\mathbf{nil} \sqcap c\, x$ for finite or possibly infinite iteration. Infinite iteration is defined as $c^\infty = c^\omega \top$. The unfolding laws (4) and (5) result from the fixed point definitions for iterations, and (6) follows from (4) and the definition of c^∞ which also justifies (8). Law (7) follows from (6) by induction.

$$c^\omega = \mathbf{nil} \sqcap c\, c^\omega \tag{4}$$

$$c^\star = \mathbf{nil} \sqcap c\, c^\star \tag{5}$$

$$c^\infty = c\, c^\infty \tag{6}$$

$$c^\infty = c^i\, c^\infty \tag{7}$$

$$c^\infty\, d = c^\infty \tag{8}$$

Some models also distribute sequential composition over non-empty choices on the left (9) (i.e., in refinement calculus terms the operator is conjunctive).

$$D \neq \{\} \Rightarrow c\,(\textstyle\bigsqcap D) = \bigsqcap_{d \in D}(c\, d) \tag{9}$$

This axiom is not assumed to generally hold in CCS and CSP but it holds for our relational model in Sect. 5 and is required to show laws (10) and (11). Laws (12) and (13) follow from (10), (8) and (6).

---

[2] Here our approach based on DRA differs from approaches based on Kleene algebra, like CKA and SKA, in which $\top$ is also a right annihilator.

$$c^{\omega} = c^{\star} \sqcap c^{\infty} \quad (10) \qquad c^{\omega}\, d = c^{\star}\, d \sqcap c^{\infty} \quad (12)$$

$$c^{\star} = \bigsqcap_{i \in \mathbb{N}} c^{i} \quad (11) \qquad c\, c^{\omega}\, d = c\, c^{\star}\, d \sqcap c^{\infty} \quad (13)$$

Parallel composition of commands is associative, commutative, has the identity **skip**. Parallel distributes over non-deterministic choice of any non-empty set of commands D, $c \parallel (\bigsqcap D) = \bigsqcap_{d \in D}(c \parallel d)$. Note the identities for sequential and parallel composition, **nil** and **skip** respectively, differ. However, they are related by $\mathbf{skip} \sqsubseteq \mathbf{nil}$ and $\mathbf{nil} \parallel \mathbf{nil} = \mathbf{nil}$.

3 The Boolean Sub-algebra of Tests

Tests are special commands that are used to model conditionals and loops and hence form an essential construct when reasoning about programs. Assume t is a test, $\neg\, t$ is its negation, and c and d are commands, an abstract algebraic representation of conditionals and while loops for sequential programs is given by

$$\mathbf{if}\ t\ \mathbf{then}\ c\ \mathbf{else}\ d \mathrel{\widehat{=}} t\, c \sqcap \neg\, t\, d \quad \text{and} \quad \mathbf{while}\ t\ \mathbf{do}\ c \mathrel{\widehat{=}} (t\, c)^{\omega}\ \neg\, t$$

Blikle [Bli78] used this style of representation of programs in a relational algebra and [GM93] and [vW04] in the refinement calculus. Kozen [Koz97] provided a more abstract *Kleene Algebra with Tests* (KAT) as a framework for reasoning about programs. Kleene algebra is the algebra of regular expressions, where for the interpretation as programs, alternation becomes non-deterministic choice with unit $\top$, concatenation becomes sequential composition with unit **nil**, and iteration becomes finite iteration of commands. Tests, in Kozen's approach, form a Boolean sub-algebra within the Kleene algebra.

We follow this construction for the Concurrent Refinement Algebra. That means in CRA tests form a subset of commands for which a negation operator $\neg$ is defined. This results in an extended algebra

$$(\mathcal{C}, \mathcal{B}, \sqcap, \sqcup, \ ;\ , \parallel, \bot, \top, \mathbf{nil}, \mathbf{skip}, \ \neg)$$

where the additional carrier set $\mathcal{B}$ is the set of *test commands* ($\mathcal{B} \subseteq \mathcal{C}$). As in Kozen's work, tests form a Boolean algebra $(\mathcal{B}, \sqcap, \sqcup, \ \neg\ , \top, \mathbf{nil})$ which is a *sub-lattice* of commands (see Fig. 1).

The sub-lattice of tests shares its top element (the false test) with the top of the lattice of commands, $\top$, but does not share its bottom element, the true test, that instead corresponds to the command **nil**, that has no effect and immediately terminates. Tests are closed under lattice meet and join, as well as sequential and parallel composition as both are defined via the join operator $\sqcup$ on commands. For any t and t' in $\mathcal{B}$,

$$t\, t' = t \sqcup t' \quad (14) \qquad t \parallel t' = t \sqcup t' \quad (15)$$

where the join of two test acts as logical conjunction. Property (15) can be generalised to the following interchange axiom. For any commands c and d in $\mathcal{C}$ and any tests t and t' in $\mathcal{B}$ the following hold.

$$(t\, c) \parallel (t\, d) = t\, (c \parallel d) \quad (16) \qquad (t\, c) \sqcup (t'\, d) = (t \sqcup t')\, (c \sqcup d) \quad (17)$$

A range of useful laws follow from this axiomatisation that help simplifying program terms involving tests.

Tests also give rise to the concept of *assertions* (preconditions) [vW04, Sol07]. The assertion corresponding to a test t is a command which terminates if the test holds and aborts if the test does not hold, i.e., $\mathbf{assert}\, t = t \sqcap \neg\, t\, \bot$.

4 Abstract Atomic Steps

This section gives an abstract algebra for the subset of commands that correspond to atomic steps. This algebra delivers core properties of atomic steps (that do not hold for commands in general) under only a few assumptions about the form of atomic steps. Atomic steps are closed under parallel composition but the parallel composition of atomic steps, $a \parallel b$, is left uninterpreted. Lifting these properties to the level of an abstract algebra results in simpler proofs and allows for their reuse in different interpretations. Section 5 forms an interpretation of the atomic step algebra that corresponds to Aczel's program and environment steps and defines parallel composition of atomic steps in detail. Section 7 on the other hand, uses the atomic step algebra to capture CCS-style as well as CSP-style communication of events, which resides in a very different domain.

In the same manner that tests form a sub-lattice of commands, the set of atomic steps, $\mathcal{A}$, forms a sub-lattice of commands which is a Boolean algebra and shares the lattice meet and join of commands (see Fig. 1). The top of the sub-lattice is the same as the top of the command lattice ($\top$) but the bottom of the sub-lattice is the new command $\boldsymbol{\alpha}$, that can be thought of as the non-deterministic choice between all possible atomic steps. In fact, tests and atomic steps share only one element ($\top$) and hence

$$\boldsymbol{\alpha} \sqcup \mathbf{nil} = \top. \tag{18}$$

The term *step* is used exclusively for an atomic step. Steps are closed under lattice meet and join as well as parallel composition (but not sequential composition). As for commands, the meet corresponds to non-deterministic choice, $a \sqcap b$, and can behave as either a or b. The join of two steps, $a \sqcup b$, can be thought of as a step that both a and b agree to do. (In Sect. 5 this corresponds to the intersection of the sets of primitive steps a and b can make.)

Because $\mathcal{A}$ forms a Boolean algebra, all of the laws of Boolean algebra are available to manipulate combinations of steps not involving sequential composition. The theorem prover Isabelle directly supports forming such an interpretation and hence the theory of Boolean algebra can be re-used for $\mathcal{A}$. This is a significant saving, as the laws of Boolean algebra do not need to be reproven.

In addition, atomic steps are assumed to have an *identity*, $\mathcal{E}$, of parallel composition, giving the following axiom.

$$a \parallel \mathcal{E} = a \tag{19}$$

Prefixing a command c with $\mathcal{E}$, i.e. $\mathcal{E}\ c$, allows the process to wait one step before behaving as c, and $\mathcal{E}^{\omega}\ c$ allows it to wait any number of steps (including 0). The step $\mathcal{E}$ can be interpreted as a placeholder for one step taken by its environment.

Besides laws for reasoning about atomic steps in isolation, one needs laws that allow reasoning about their interaction with non-atomic commands. A small set of additional axioms is used as the basis of these laws. The approach taken to handling parallel composition is not the usual interleaving of steps, rather each step of one process must synchronise with a step of the other process. If a and b cannot synchronise then $a \parallel b$ is infeasible ($\top$). For steps a and b, and any commands c and d, we assume the following axioms.

$$a\,c \parallel b\,d = (a \parallel b)\,(c \parallel d) \quad (20) \qquad\qquad a\,c \parallel \mathbf{nil} = \top \quad (22)$$

$$a\,c \sqcup b\,d = (a \sqcup b)\,(c \sqcup d) \quad (21) \qquad\qquad a\,c \sqcup \mathbf{nil} = \top \quad (23)$$

The interchange axioms (20) and (21) become refinements from left to right if a and b are allowed to be arbitrary commands (which corresponds to the weak interchange law in CKA [HMSW11]). The abstract algebra does not define the details of parallel composition of pairs of steps. (See the relational interpretation of the algebra in Sect. 5 for one example of defining parallel composition of atomic steps.) The command, **nil**, that terminates immediately without making any steps whatsoever cannot synchronise with a process that makes at least one step, i.e. (22) and (23).

The *negation* operator (!) for atomic steps satisfies the following axioms of a Boolean algebra. Steps a and $!\,a$ have no common behaviour (24) and $!\,a$ has all the step behaviours that a does not have (25).

$$a \sqcup !\,a = \top \quad (24) \qquad\qquad a \sqcap !\,a = \boldsymbol{\alpha} \quad (25)$$

Note that negation for tests ($\neg$) differs from negation for atomic steps (!) as we have $\neg\top = \mathbf{nil}$ but $!\top = \boldsymbol{\alpha}$. The inclusion of a negation operator on steps allows one to define an equivalent of an assertion for steps on the abstract level. For any step a define,

$$\mathbf{assume}\, a \mathrel{\widehat{=}} a \sqcap (!\,a)\,\bot. \qquad (26)$$

The command **assume** a behaves as a and terminates, or as $!\,a$ and aborts. It represents an assumption that step a occurs in the sense that any other step allows any behaviour to occur after that step. It provides the basis for rely conditions because they specify assumptions about the environment's behaviour (see Sect. 6).

4.1 Canonical Representation of Commands

If the primitive commands of our language are tests, atomic steps and $\bot$, and all other commands are built from these primitives using the operators of the language, then initially, a command may either terminate immediately, abort or perform some atomic step. That leads to the canonical representation theorem, in which c can terminate if some test t succeeds, abort if some test t' succeeds, or performs some step a_i followed by some command c_i, for some $i \in I$.

Theorem 1 (canonical-representation). *Any command c can be expressed in the following form*

$$c = t \sqcap t' \bot \sqcap \textstyle\bigsqcap_{i \in I} a_i \, c_i$$

where t and t' are tests, and for any i in some (possibly empty) index set I, a_i is an atomic step not equal to $\top$, and c_i is a command.

The proof is conducted by structural induction over commands. Note that if c cannot terminate immediately, t is $\top$. If c cannot abort, t' is $\top$. If c cannot perform any step, $I = \{\}$. A similar theorem can be found in [Pri10] for SKA.

Because $\mathcal{E}$ is the identity of parallel for a single step, $\mathcal{E}^\omega$ acts as the identity of any sequence of steps and hence $\mathcal{E}^\omega$ is the identity of parallel, i.e. **skip** $= \mathcal{E}^\omega$.

Lemma 1 (atomic-identity-iteration). $\mathcal{E}^\omega \parallel c = c$

The proof makes use of Theorem 1 to express c in canonical form (the proof is included in the appendix of [HCM+16]).

4.2 Properties of Iterations of Atomic Steps

In addition to defining programming statements such as while loops, iterators are used to build specifications from atomic steps. For instance commands corresponding to Jones' rely and guarantee concepts are constructed as iterations of relatively straightforward commands that make assumptions about the steps of the environment and constrain the steps of the program, respectively (see Sect. 6). Below we provide some useful properties of iterations of atomic steps.

Because **nil** performs no steps, if it is run in parallel with a (possibly) finite iteration, the composition cannot perform any steps but can terminate and hence equals **nil**. If **nil** is run in parallel with an infinite iteration, the combination cannot perform any steps but cannot terminate, and hence equals the infeasible command $\top$.

Lemma 2 (atomic-iteration-nil)

$$a^\star \parallel \mathbf{nil} = \mathbf{nil} \qquad a^\omega \parallel \mathbf{nil} = \mathbf{nil} \qquad a^\infty \parallel \mathbf{nil} = \top$$

Proof. The properties follow from axiom (22) using unfolding of the iterations (i.e. $a^\star = \mathbf{nil} \sqcap a\, a^\star$, $a^\omega = \mathbf{nil} \sqcap a\, a^\omega$ and $a^\infty = a\, a^\infty$). □

For the following lemmas, let a and b be atomic steps, and c and d any commands. Axiom (20) can be extended to iteration i times as given in the following lemma, which is proven by induction on i.

Lemma 3 (atomic-iteration-power). $a^i\, c \parallel b^i\, d \; = \; (a \parallel b)^i\, (c \parallel d)$

Choosing c and d to both be **nil** gives the corollary that $a^i \parallel b^i = (a \parallel b)^i$.

For all further lemmas in this sub-section, we assume that sequential composition is conjunctive (9) and hence that properties (10) and (11) hold. Two useful properties are the following.

$$a^\star \parallel b^\star = (a \parallel b)^\star \qquad (27) \qquad\qquad a^\infty \parallel b^\infty = (a \parallel b)^\infty \qquad (28)$$

Property (27) can be proven using the property that non-deterministic choice over an arbitrary set distributes over parallel. A proof of (28) would follow straightforwardly if the supremum over an arbitrary set (or even a chain) distributed over parallel, however, that distribution property does not hold in general. We take property (28) as an axiom because it does hold in our intended model. Whether this axiom is independent of the other axioms in our algebra is an open question.

Property (27) holds for atomic steps a and b but is only a refinement from left to right if a and b are replaced by arbitrary commands. Property (27) can be generalised to the following lemma where we take into account that the number of iterations of a and b might be the same, or there are more iterations of a than b (and hence the additional iterations of a are in parallel with the start of d), or the symmetric case when there are more occurrences of b than a.

Lemma 4 (atomic-iteration-finite)

$$a^\star\, c \parallel b^\star\, d = (a \parallel b)^\star\, ((c \parallel d) \sqcap (c \parallel b\, b^\star\, d) \sqcap (a\, a^\star\, c \parallel d))$$

Isabelle/HOL proofs of these lemmas have been completed. They may be also found in the appendix of [HCM+16]. Choosing c and d to both be **nil** gives (27) as a corollary.

An infinite iteration in parallel with an initial finite iteration matches the finite iteration as well as what follows it.

Lemma 5 (atomic-iteration-finite-infinite). $a^\star\, c \parallel b^\infty = (a \parallel b)^\star\, (c \parallel b^\infty)$

Lemma 4 can be extended to initial iterations that are either finite or infinite.

Lemma 6 (atomic-iteration-either)

$$a^\omega\, c \parallel b^\omega\, d = (a \parallel b)^\omega\, ((c \parallel d) \sqcap (c \parallel b\, b^\omega\, d) \sqcap (a\, a^\omega\, c \parallel d))$$

Choosing c and d to both be **nil** gives the corollary that $a^\omega \parallel b^\omega = (a \parallel b)^\omega$.

To see the relationship to an interleaving operator, for any step a, define an *action* as $\langle a \rangle = \mathcal{E}^\omega\, a\, \mathcal{E}^\omega$, then properties of $\langle a \rangle$ can be proven using properties of the abstract algebra. For example, one can derive the following lemma.

Lemma 7 (atomic-interleaving). $\langle a \rangle \parallel \langle b \rangle \;=\; \langle a \parallel b \rangle \sqcap \langle a \rangle \langle b \rangle \sqcap \langle b \rangle \langle a \rangle$

If a and b cannot synchronise (i.e. $a \parallel b = \top$) then $\langle a \rangle \parallel \langle b \rangle \;=\; \langle a \rangle \langle b \rangle \sqcap \langle b \rangle \langle a \rangle$ which echoes the following property of an interleaving operator: $a \mathbin{|||} b = a\, b \sqcap b\, a$. Hence by including an identity, $\mathcal{E}$, for parallel with an atomic step, one can represent interleaving properties in the synchronising algebra albeit in a more complex form. This approach was used by Milner in Synchronous CCS [Mil83] to allow the encoding of the better-known process algebra CCS. Our identity element takes on a similar role, although we lift it to a command as opposed to a transition event as in Milner's operational semantics. The advantage of the synchronising algebra is that one can represent both synchronising events and interleaving events in the one theory. By using separate program and environment events, such a theory supports the rely/guarantee approach of Jones for reasoning about concurrent programs.

5 Relational Atomic Steps

This section examines an interpretation of the abstract atomic step algebra $\mathcal{A}$ in terms of Aczel's program and environment state transitions.[3] The resulting *relational atomic steps* are used to define guarantees and relies in Sect. 6. This interpretation assumes that sequential composition is conjunctive (9).

Given a state space Σ and a binary relation $r \in \mathbb{P}(\Sigma \times \Sigma)$, the command $\boldsymbol{\pi}(r)$ can take an atomic *program* step from state σ to σ' for any pair of states (σ, σ') in r. Similarly, $\boldsymbol{\epsilon}(r)$ is a command that can perform any environment step from state σ to σ' whenever $(\sigma, \sigma') \in r$.

$$\boldsymbol{\pi} : \mathbb{P}(\Sigma \times \Sigma) \to \mathcal{A} \qquad\qquad \boldsymbol{\epsilon} : \mathbb{P}(\Sigma \times \Sigma) \to \mathcal{A}$$

The commands $\boldsymbol{\pi}(\varnothing)$ and $\boldsymbol{\epsilon}(\varnothing)$ are infeasible, i.e., $\boldsymbol{\pi}(\varnothing) = \boldsymbol{\epsilon}(\varnothing) = \top$. The images of $\boldsymbol{\pi}$ and $\boldsymbol{\epsilon}$ are disjoint except when the relation is empty, i.e. for all r_1 and r_2,

$$\boldsymbol{\pi}(r_1) \sqcup \boldsymbol{\epsilon}(r_2) = \top. \tag{29}$$

Together $\boldsymbol{\pi}$ and $\boldsymbol{\epsilon}$ form a sub-lattice of commands with two further sub-lattices: all the $\boldsymbol{\pi}(r)$ commands form a sub-lattice and all the $\boldsymbol{\epsilon}(r)$ commands form a sub-lattice.

The functions $\boldsymbol{\pi}$ and $\boldsymbol{\epsilon}$ are injective, i.e. different relations map to different commands, and union of relations maps to a non-deterministic choice between the mappings of the relations and intersection maps to the supremum in the command ordering.

$$r_1 = r_2 \Leftrightarrow \boldsymbol{\pi}(r_1) = \boldsymbol{\pi}(r_2) \tag{30}$$

$$\boldsymbol{\pi}(r_1 \cup r_2) = \boldsymbol{\pi}(r_1) \sqcap \boldsymbol{\pi}(r_2) \tag{31}$$

$$\boldsymbol{\pi}(r_1 \cap r_2) = \boldsymbol{\pi}(r_1) \sqcup \boldsymbol{\pi}(r_2) \tag{32}$$

If $r_1 \subseteq r_2$, then $\boldsymbol{\pi}(r_1) \sqcap \boldsymbol{\pi}(r_2) = \boldsymbol{\pi}(r_1 \cup r_2) = \boldsymbol{\pi}(r_2)$, and therefore $\boldsymbol{\pi}(r_2) \sqsubseteq \boldsymbol{\pi}(r_1)$. Similar laws hold for $\boldsymbol{\epsilon}$ steps.

In this interpretation one can instantiate the test command from Sect. 3 as $\tau(p)$ for $p \in \mathbb{P}\,\Sigma$, which succeeds and terminates immediately if p holds but is $\top$ otherwise, e.g. $\tau(\varnothing) = \top$ and $\tau(\Sigma) = \mathbf{nil}$. As in the refinement calculus, a precondition command $\{p\}$ can then be defined as **assert** $\tau(p)$, which equals $\tau(p) \sqcap \tau(\neg\, p)\,\bot$, and hence terminates immediately if p holds but aborts otherwise, e.g. $\{\varnothing\} = \bot$ and $\{\Sigma\} = \mathbf{nil}$.

[3] A semantic model for this interpretation may be found in [CHM16].

6 Relies and Guarantees

The rely/guarantee approach of Jones [CJ07] makes use of a rely condition, r, a binary relation on states that expresses an assumption that every step made by the environment of the process satisfies r between its before and after states. Complementing that, all processes in its environment have a guarantee condition, g, a binary relation on states that expresses that every program step made by the process satisfies g. For each process, its guarantee condition must imply the rely conditions of all the processes in its environment. This section encodes guarantees and relies using the abstract algebra of atomic steps.

6.1 The Guarantee Command

For a process to ensure a guarantee g, every atomic program ($\boldsymbol{\pi}$) step made by the program must satisfy g. A guarantee puts no constraints on the environment of the process. A guarantee command, **guar** g, is defined in terms of the iteration of a single step guarantee, (π-**restrict** g), defined as follows.

$$(\pi\text{-}\mathbf{restrict}\, g) \mathrel{\widehat{=}} \boldsymbol{\pi}(g) \sqcap \mathcal{E} \qquad\qquad \mathbf{guar}\, g \mathrel{\widehat{=}} (\pi\text{-}\mathbf{restrict}\, g)^{\omega}$$

A command c with a guarantee of g enforced on every program step could possibly be expressed as $(\mathbf{guar}\, g) \sqcup c$, but that turns out to be too strong a requirement because it masks any aborting behaviour of c because the guarantee never aborts, $(\mathbf{guar}\, g) \sqcup \bot = (\mathbf{guar}\, g)$. Instead, the weak conjunction operator is used.

Weak conjunction on commands, $\Cap$, behaves like $\sqcup$ unless one of its operands aborts in which case we have $c \Cap \bot = \bot$. The operator is associative, commutative and idempotent, and satisfies $c \Cap (\bigsqcap D) = (\bigsqcap_{d \in D} c \Cap d)$ for any non-empty set of commands D. For any commands c and d, steps a and b, and tests t and t' weak conjunction satisfies the following axioms. (Note the similarities between (36) and (21), (37) and (23) and (38) and (28).)

$$c \Cap \bot = \bot \quad (33) \qquad\qquad (a\, c) \Cap (b\, d) = (a \Cap b)\,(c \Cap d) \quad (36)$$

$$a \Cap b = a \sqcup b \quad (34) \qquad\qquad (a\, c) \Cap \mathbf{nil} = \top \quad (37)$$

$$t \Cap t' = t \sqcup t' \quad (35) \qquad\qquad a^{\infty} \Cap b^{\infty} = (a \Cap b)^{\infty} \quad (38)$$

Hence $a \Cap \boldsymbol{\alpha} = a \sqcup \boldsymbol{\alpha} = a$, i.e. $\boldsymbol{\alpha}$ is the atomic step identity of weak conjunction. More generally, **chaos** $\mathrel{\widehat{=}} \boldsymbol{\alpha}^{\omega}$ is the identity of weak conjunction for any sequence of atomic steps. The following lemma (and its proof) is similar to the corollary of Lemma 6.

Lemma 8 (atomic-iteration-conjunction). $a^{\omega} \Cap b^{\omega} = (a \Cap b)^{\omega}$

A command c with a guarantee g is represented by $(\mathbf{guar}\, g) \Cap c$. In the theory of Jones, a guarantee on a process may be strengthened. That is reflected by the fact that if $g_1 \subseteq g_2$, then $\boldsymbol{\pi}(g_2) \sqsubseteq \boldsymbol{\pi}(g_1)$ and hence $(\pi\text{-}\mathbf{restrict}\, g_2) \sqsubseteq (\pi\text{-}\mathbf{restrict}\, g_1)$.

A process that must satisfy both guarantee g_1 and guarantee g_2, must satisfy $g_1 \cap g_2$ because

$$
\begin{aligned}
& (\pi\textbf{-restrict}\, g_1) \Cap (\pi\textbf{-restrict}\, g_2) \\
=\; & (\boldsymbol{\pi}(g_1) \sqcap \mathcal{E}) \Cap (\boldsymbol{\pi}(g_1) \sqcap \mathcal{E}) \\
=\; & (\boldsymbol{\pi}(g_1) \Cap \boldsymbol{\pi}(g_2)) \sqcap (\boldsymbol{\pi}(g_1) \Cap \mathcal{E}) \sqcap (\mathcal{E} \Cap \boldsymbol{\pi}(g_2)) \sqcap (\mathcal{E} \Cap \mathcal{E}) \\
=\; & \boldsymbol{\pi}(g_1 \cap g_2) \sqcap \mathcal{E} \\
\doteq\; & (\pi\textbf{-restrict}(g_1 \cap g_2))
\end{aligned}
$$

The weak conjunction of a possibly infinite iteration of atomic steps distributes over the sequential composition of commands c and d.

Lemma 9 (atomic-infinite-distribution). $a^\omega \Cap (c\; d) \;=\; (a^\omega \Cap c)\,(a^\omega \Cap d)$

The proof uses the canonical representation of a command (Theorem 1) and can be found in the appendix of [HCM+16]. As a consequence guarantees distribute over a sequence of commands.

$$(\textbf{guar}\, g) \Cap (c\; d) = ((\textbf{guar}\, g) \Cap c)\,((\textbf{guar}\, g) \Cap d)$$

6.2 The Rely Command

A rely condition r represents an assumption about environment steps. If any environment step does not satisfy r, i.e. a step that refines $\boldsymbol{\epsilon}(\overline{r})$, the process may do anything, which can be represented by it aborting. Any other step is allowed. The rely command is defined in terms of a single step assumption, itself defined in terms of the abstract command **assume** (26) as follows.

$$
\begin{aligned}
(\epsilon\textbf{-assm}\, r) &\mathrel{\widehat=} \textbf{assume}(!\,\boldsymbol{\epsilon}(\overline{r})) \qquad = !\,\boldsymbol{\epsilon}(\overline{r}) \sqcap \boldsymbol{\epsilon}(\overline{r})\,\bot \\
\textbf{rely}\, r &\mathrel{\widehat=} (\epsilon\textbf{-assm}\, r)^\omega
\end{aligned}
$$

An environment assumption is placed on a command c by placing the assumption on every step of c, i.e. $(\textbf{rely}\, r) \Cap c$. A command c with rely r and guarantee g is expressed as $(\textbf{rely}\, r) \Cap (\textbf{guar}\, g) \Cap c$, for which every program step is required to satisfy g unless an environment step does not satisfy r, in which case it aborts. Here using weak conjunction ($\Cap$) rather than the lattice join ($\sqcup$) is essential to prevent the guarantee masking the possible aborting behaviour of the rely. Because $\textbf{assume}\, a \Cap \textbf{assume}\, b = \textbf{assume}(a \sqcup b)$, combining environment assumptions gives

$$
\begin{aligned}
(\epsilon\textbf{-assm}\, r_1) \Cap (\epsilon\textbf{-assm}\, r_2) &= \textbf{assume}(!\,\boldsymbol{\epsilon}(\overline{r_1}) \sqcup !\,\boldsymbol{\epsilon}(\overline{r_2})) \;=\; \textbf{assume}(!\,\boldsymbol{\epsilon}(\overline{r_1 \cap r_2})) \\
&= (\epsilon\textbf{-assm}(r_1 \cap r_2))\;.
\end{aligned}
$$

From Lemma 9 and Theorem 1, a rely can be distributed over a sequential composition (the proof is included in the appendix of [HCM+16]).

$$(\textbf{rely}\, r) \Cap (c\; d) = (\textbf{rely}\, r \Cap c)\,(\textbf{rely}\, r \Cap d)$$

6.3 Rely/Guarantee Logic

Rely/guarantee reasoning is traditionally formulated in terms of a quintuple $\{p, r\}c\{g, q\}$, which extends Hoare logic with the rely r and guarantee g to handle concurrency. The quintuple states that every step of c satifies g and that it terminates and establishes the postcondition q, provided it is executed from an initial state satisfying p and interference from the environment is bounded by r. This quintuple is interpreted in our logic as the following refinement.[4]

$$\{p\}\,((\mathbf{rely}\; r) \Cap (\mathbf{guar}\; g) \Cap [q]) \sqsubseteq c$$

This demonstrates the application of the algebra to reasoning about shared data. As well as being able to express any law presented in terms of quintuples, we are able to reason about the component commands separately, e.g., strengthening a guarantee g does not involve p, r and q.

7 Abstract Communication in Process Algebras

In the process algebra domain, processes communicate via a set of synchronisation events, in contrast to processes in a shared memory concurrency model which interleave operations on state. We may build a core process algebra from the basic operators, with the addition of a set of atomic program steps $\pi(a)$ that model a process engaging in the corresponding abstract event $a \in \mathit{Event}$, where Event includes at least the silent event ι. The basic properties of this language are those of the underlying algebra but we do not assume conjunctivity of sequential composition (9) in order to be consistent with CCS.

Similarly to notation introduced in Sect. 4.2 we define

$$\langle a \rangle \mathrel{\widehat{=}} \mathcal{E}^{\omega}\pi(a)\mathcal{E}^{\omega} \tag{39}$$

This models process engaging in event a (note that we drop the 'π' tag from the $\langle a \rangle$ notation) preceded and succeeded by steps of the environment, similar to *asynchronising* in Synchronous CCS [Mil83] (discussed in [Mil89]). This is the building block of event based languages: we interpret both prefixing in CCS ($a.p$) and CSP ($a \to p$) as ($\langle a \rangle\, p$). We extend the core algebra to give two types of abstract interprocess communication: CCS-style binary synchronisation (achieved by restricting the program) and CSP-style multi-way synchronisation (achieved in-part by restricting the environment).

7.1 Communication in CCS

The main point of difference with the rely-guarantee algebra is that program steps representing events can combine into a single program step (communication). Interactions with $\mathcal{E}$ remain the same as in the abstract algebra. In CCS

[4] We use the syntax of Morgan's specification command $[q]$ [Mor88] whose definition is omitted for space reasons. It represents any sequence of atomic steps that establishes q between its initial and final states. See [CHM16] for details.

each non-silent event a has a complementary event $\overline{a}$. A program step $\pi(a)$ and its corresponding complementary program step $\pi(\overline{a})$ may synchronise to become a silent step, $\pi(a) \parallel \pi(\overline{a}) = \pi(\iota)$, and hence using an instantiation of Lemma 7,

$$\langle a \rangle \parallel \langle \overline{a} \rangle \ = \ \langle \iota \rangle \sqcap \langle a \rangle \langle \overline{a} \rangle \sqcap \langle \overline{a} \rangle \langle a \rangle. \tag{40}$$

As such, events may synchronise *or* interleave. In CCS the restriction operator $p \backslash A$, where A is a set of *Events*, may be employed to exclude the final two interleaving options and hence force processes to synchronise and generate a silent step. It may be defined straightforwardly using join ($\sqcup$) to forbid events in A, where we use the abbreviation $\pi(A) \mathrel{\widehat{=}} \bigsqcap_{a \in A} \pi(a)$ and note that $!\,\pi(A) = \pi(\overline{A}) \sqcap \mathcal{E}$.

$$p \backslash A \mathrel{\widehat{=}} p \sqcup (!\,\pi(A))^{\omega} \tag{41}$$

Hence, by (40) and (41), $(\langle a \rangle \parallel \langle \overline{a} \rangle) \backslash \{a, \overline{a}\} \ = \ \langle \iota \rangle$.

7.2 Communication in CSP

To achieve CSP-style multi-way communication, a process p prevents its environment from communicating via an event in p's alphabet until p is ready. We introduce a step $\epsilon(a)$, where $\mathcal{E} \sqsubseteq \epsilon(a)$ for all $a \in \mathit{Event}$. Its interactions through the parallel operator are defined (in a different way to CCS) below; all other combinations of atomic steps result in $\top$.

$$\pi(a) \parallel \pi(a) \ = \ \pi(a) \quad \text{for } a \neq \iota \qquad \pi(a) \parallel \epsilon(a) \ = \ \pi(a) \qquad \epsilon(a) \parallel \epsilon(a) \ = \ \epsilon(a)$$

Fundamental to CSP is the notion of a process's *alphabet*, the set of events via which it may communicate and in particular upon which the environment may not independently synchronise. Here we explicitly associate an alphabet $A \subseteq \mathit{Event}$ with process p by the syntax $A{:}p$, defined by,

$$A{:}p \mathrel{\widehat{=}} p \sqcup (!\,\epsilon(A))^{\omega} \tag{42}$$

where analogously to program steps we define $\epsilon(A) \mathrel{\widehat{=}} \bigsqcap_{a \in A} \epsilon(a)$. Note the similarity to CCS's restriction operator (41) but here it is the environment that is restricted, rather than the program.

In an early formulation by Hoare [Hoa85] every process p implicitly has an alphabet A associated with it (A is sometimes syntactically deduced from p). In formulations such as Roscoe's [Ros98] the alphabets are not associated with processes but are instead made explicit on the parallel operator. We may define alphabetised parallel straightforwardly as $p_1 \underset{A}{\parallel} p_2 \mathrel{\widehat{=}} (A{:}p_1) \parallel (A{:}p_2)$. Each side of the parallel composition prevents the other from taking a unilateral program step on events in A by restricting its environment. Some of the basic communication properties from CSP follow from the above definitions and the atomic algebra, for instance, recalling that CSP's prefixing operator $a \rightarrow p \mathrel{\widehat{=}} \langle a \rangle\, p$, for any $a \in A$, $(a \rightarrow p_1 \underset{A}{\parallel} a \rightarrow p_2) = a \rightarrow (p_1 \underset{A}{\parallel} p_2)$.

The *hiding* operator of CSP, $p/_A$, affects program steps, renaming events in A to silent events. Hiding distributes over sequential and choice (but not parallel); its relationship with atomic steps follows.

$$b/_A = \begin{cases} \pi(\iota) & \text{if } b \text{ is of the form } \pi(a) \text{ and } a \in A \\ b & \text{otherwise} \end{cases}$$

7.3 Communication in SCCS

Synchronous CCS (SCCS) [Mil83, Mil89] is a process algebra designed to be as minimal as possible in terms of operators. It includes event prefix, disjunction (nondeterministic choice), composition (corresponding to our parallel), and restriction similar to that of CCS (41). SCCS events may be structured from a finite set of "particles", forming a commutative group $(Event, \mathbf{1}, \times, ^{-1})$. Every event is the product of particles: for instance, the step a is an event $(a^1 \times b^0 \times c^0 \times \ldots)$. The silent (or waiting) event $\mathbf{1}$ is event identity, and fulfils a similar role to that of $\mathcal{E}$ in our algebra. The complement of event a is simply a^{-1} and hence the product of an event and its complement, $a^1 \times a^{-1}$, naturally equals $\mathbf{1}$.

The key aspect of SCCS is its simple definition of parallel composition in terms of product: for atomic steps a and b, $a \parallel b = a \times b$. An event process $\langle a \rangle$ is defined as $\mathbf{1}^\omega\, a\, \mathbf{1}^\omega$, which has the effect of *asynchronising* the event, preserving Lemma 7. Milner shows that CCS can be encoded in SCCS through the addition of asynchronising actions defined through the operational semantics; in an algebraic setting the **1**s are made explicit in the processes. Note that in this model there is no distinction between silent steps and environment steps: in SCCS both are $\mathbf{1}$, whereas in CCS the former is $\pi(\iota)$.

8 Related Work

Our Concurrent Refinement Algebra (CRA) (Sect. 2) compares to Concurrent Kleene Algebra (CKA) [HMSW11] in that both extend a sequential algebra to allow for reasoning about parallel composition. Synchronous Kleene Algebra (SKA) [Pri10] is also based on Kleene Algebra but, unlike CKA, it adds tests and a synchronous parallel operator based on that of Milner's SCCS [Mil83]. Both CKA and SKA are based on Kleene algebra and hence only support finite iteration and partial correctness. In comparison, our CRA supports general fixed points and hence recursion and both finite and infinite iteration. The richer structure of DRA contains a sub-lattice of commands below **chaos** (see Fig. 1) that includes assertions (and hence preconditions in the relational interpretation) and assumptions (and hence rely commands), and allows the weak conjunction operator, $\Cap$, to be distinguished from strong conjunction, $\sqcup$. All these constructs are needed to faithfully represent rely/guarantee theory.

CKA is also applied to rely/guarantee rules [HMSW11] but they define a Jones-style 5-tuple (as in Sect. 6.3) in terms of two separate refinement conditions, whereas in our approach the existing (single) refinement relation can be used directly. In Jones' theory, a guarantee has to be satisfied only from initial states satisfying the precondition of the program, and further, if its rely condition is broken by the environment, the program can abort. However, in the CKA framework, the guarantee has to always be maintained by the program, irrespective of what the initial state is and how the environment is behaving; that over restricts the set of possible implementations. Our theory faithfully reflects Jones' approach.

Our algebra of atomic steps makes use of a synchronous parallel operator similar to that in SCCS [Mil89] and in SKA [Pri10] but it differs in two ways:

- instead of atomic actions being separate from commands (as in SCCS and SKA), they are treated as a sub-algebra within CRA and
- while both SCCS and SKA explicitly define composition of atomic steps (their $\times$ operator), our parallel operator is used directly on atomic steps (because they are commands) and its definition is left open.

9 Conclusion

This paper presents an abstract algebra of atomic steps for concurrent programs. It is a Boolean algebra that is embedded as a sub-lattice into our Concurrent Refinement Algebra in a similar way as tests are embedded in Kleene algebras. As for tests, a range of useful laws can be derived for atomic steps within this abstract algebra (e.g., on iteration and distributivity), despite the fact that the interpretation of the parallel composition of two atomic steps is left open.

This construction simplifies many essential laws and their proofs, as most supporting lemmas almost come for free on this abstract level. Accordingly, the mechanisation of the theory within the theorem prover Isabelle is lean and achieved a high degree of automation. As the Concurrent Refinement Algebra was conceived to support reasoning with relies and guarantees this simplification is of particular benefit in our laws for rely and guarantee commands.

A further gain of the generic shape of the abstract algebra lies in its potential for reuse. We have demonstrated this by instantiating our abstract algebra with two quite different styles of communication, a synchronous model (as in SKA [Pri10] and SCCS) versus an interleaving model (as in CCS and CSP). For both styles the abstract algebra of atomic steps proves to be suitable.

The concept of sub-algebras in our Concurrent Refinement Algebra is also applicable to assertions and assumptions. Assertions form a Boolean algebra with **nil** as top element and $\bot$ as bottom element whereas step assumptions form a Boolean algebra with top element $\boldsymbol{\alpha}$ and bottom $\boldsymbol{\alpha}\,\bot$. Both inherit the laws on Boolean algebras similarly to tests and atomic steps. Future work will investigate these structures and will extend our theories accordingly.

The relationship between CCS and CSP has been explored in several papers [Bro83, vG97] including augmenting the operational rules of CSP so that the failures-divergences model (FDR) is respected in CCS [HH10]. Future work is to apply a more algebraic approach to the relationships between well known process algebras (especially ACP [BK84]).

Acknowledgements. This work has benefited from input from Cliff Jones and Kim Solin.

References

[Acz83] Aczel, P.H.G.: On an inference rule for parallel composition, Private communication to Cliff Jones (1983). http://homepages.cs.ncl.ac.uk/cliff.jones/publications/MSs/PHGA-traces.pdf

[BC85] Berry, G., Cosserat, L.: The ESTEREL synchronous programming language and its mathematical semantics. In: Brookes, S.D., Roscoe, A.W., Winskel, G. (eds.) CONCURRENCY 1984. LNCS, vol. 197, pp. 389–448. Springer, Heidelberg (1985). doi:10.1007/3-540-15670-4_19

[BK84] Bergstra, J.A., Klop, J.W.: Process algebra for synchronous communication. Inf. Control **60**(1–3), 109–137 (1984)

[BK85] Bergstra, J.A., Klop, J.W.: Algebra of communicating processes with abstraction. Theor. Comput. Sci. **37**, 77–121 (1985)

[Bli78] Blikle, A.: Specified programming. In: Blum, E.K., Paul, M., Takasu, S. (eds.) Mathematical Studies of Information Processing. LNCS, vol. 75, pp. 228–251. Springer, Heidelberg (1979). doi:10.1007/3-540-09541-1_29

[Bro83] Brookes, S.D.: On the relationship of CCS and CSP. In: Diaz, J. (ed.) ICALP 1983. LNCS, vol. 154, pp. 83–96. Springer, Heidelberg (1983). doi:10.1007/BFb0036899

[CHM16] Colvin, R.J., Hayes, I.J., Meinicke, L.A.: Designing a semantic model for a wide-spectrum language with concurrency (2016). http://arxiv.org/abs/1609.00195

[CJ07] Coleman, J.W., Jones, C.B.: A structural proof of the soundness of rely/guarantee rules. Journal of Logic and Computation **17**(4), 807–841 (2007)

[Con71] Conway, J.H.: Regular Algebra and Finite Machines. Chapman & Hall, Boca Raton (1971)

[dR01] de Roever, W.-P., Verification, C.: Introduction to Compositional and Non-compositional Methods. Cambridge University Press, Cambridge (2001)

[GM93] Gardiner, P.H.B., Morgan, C.: A single complete rule for data refinement. Formal Aspects Comput. **5**, 367–382 (1993)

[Hay16] Hayes, I.J.: Generalised rely-guarantee concurrency: an algebraic foundation. Form. Asp. Comput. **28**(6), 1057–1078 (2016)

[HCM+16] Hayes, I.J., Colvin, R.J., Meinicke, L.A., Winter, K., Velykis, A.: An algebra of synchronous atomic steps (2016). http://arxiv.org/pdf/1609.00118v1.pdf

[HH10] He, J., Hoare, C.A.R.: CSP is a retract of CCS. Theor. Comput. Sci. **411**(11–13), 1311–1337 (2010)

[HJC14] Hayes, I.J., Jones, C.B., Colvin, R.J.: Laws and semantics for rely-guarantee refinement. Technical report CS-TR-1425, Newcastle University, July 2014

[HMSW11] Hoare, C.A.R., Möller, B., Struth, G., Wehrman, I.: Concurrent Kleene algebra and its foundations. J. Log. Algebr. Program. **80**(6), 266–296 (2011)

[Hoa85] Hoare, C.A.R.: Communicating Sequential Processes. Prentice-Hall, Upper Saddle River (1985)

[JHC15] Jones, C.B., Hayes, I.J., Colvin, R.J.: Balancing expressiveness in formal approaches to concurrency. Formal Aspects Comput. **27**(3), 475–497 (2015)

[Jon81] Development methods for computer programs including a notion of interference. Ph.D. thesis, Oxford University, June 1981: Oxford University Computing Laboratory (now Computer Science) Technical Monograph PRG-25

[Jon83] Jones, C.B.: Specification and design of (parallel) programs. In: Proceedings of IFIP 1983, pp. 321–332. North-Holland (1983)

[Koz97] Kozen, D.: Kleene algebra with tests. ACM Trans. Prog. Lang. Sys. **19**(3), 427–443 (1997)

[Mil83] Milner, R.: Calculi for synchrony and asynchrony. Theor. Comput. Sci. **25**(3), 267–310 (1983)

[Mil89] Milner, A.J.R.G.: Communication and Concurrency. Prentice-Hall, Upper Saddle River (1989)

[Mor88] Morgan, C.C.: The specification statement. ACM Trans. Prog. Lang. Sys. **10**(3), 403–419 (1988)

[Pri10] Prisacariu, C.: Synchronous Kleene algebra. J. Logic Algebraic Program. **79**(7), 608–635 (2010)

[Ros98] Roscoe, A.W.: The Theory and Practice of Concurrency. Prentice Hall, Upper Saddle River (1998)

[Sol07] Solin, K.: Abstract algebra of program refinement. Ph.D. thesis, Turku Centre for Computer Science (2007)

[vG97] van Glabbeek, R.J.: Notes on the methodology of CCS and CSP. Theor. Comput. Sci. **177**(2), 329–349 (1997)

[vW04] von Wright, J.: Towards a refinement algebra. Sci. Comput. Program. **51**, 23–45 (2004)

Error Invariants for Concurrent Traces

Andreas Holzer[1], Daniel Schwartz-Narbonne[2], Mitra Tabaei Befrouei[3(✉)], Georg Weissenbacher[3], and Thomas Wies[4]

[1] University of Toronto, Toronto, Canada
[2] Amazon, Seattle, USA
[3] TU Wien, Vienna, Austria
tabaei@forsyte.at
[4] New York University, New York, USA

Abstract. Error invariants are assertions that over-approximate the reachable program states at a given position in an error trace while only capturing states that will still lead to failure if execution of the trace is continued from that position. Such assertions reflect the effect of statements that are involved in the root cause of an error and its propagation, enabling slicing of statements that do not contribute to the error. Previous work on error invariants focused on sequential programs. We generalize error invariants to concurrent traces by augmenting them with additional information about hazards such as write-after-write events, which are often involved in race conditions and atomicity violations. By providing the option to include varying levels of details in error invariants—such as hazards and branching information—our approach allows the programmer to systematically analyze individual aspects of an error trace. We have implemented a hazard-sensitive slicing tool for concurrent traces based on error invariants and evaluated it on benchmarks covering a broad range of real-world concurrency bugs. Hazard-sensitive slicing significantly reduced the length of the considered traces and still maintained the root causes of the concurrency bugs.

1 Introduction

Debugging is notoriously time consuming. Once a program failure has been observed, the developer must identify a cause-effect chain of events that led to it. This task is complicated by the fact that the underlying failing execution trace can contain a large number of events that do not contribute to the failure.

A. Holzer—Funded by the Erwin Schrödinger Fellowship J3696-N26 of the Austrian Science Fund (FWF).
D. Schwartz-Narbonne—Research was performed at NYU.
M. Tabaei Befrouei and G. Weissenbacher—Supported by the Austrian National Research Network S11403-N23 (RiSE), the LogiCS doctoral program W1255-N23 of the Austrian Science Fund (FWF) and by the Vienna Science and Technology Fund (WWTF) through grant VRG11-005.
T. Wies—Funded in part by the National Science Foundation under grant CCF-1350574.

J. Fitzgerald et al. (Eds.): FM 2016, LNCS 9995, pp. 370–387, 2016.
DOI: 10.1007/978-3-319-48989-6_23

Code fragment-Deposit: T_1	Code fragment-Withdrawal: T_2
⋮	⋮
acquire ℓ;	acquire ℓ;
⋮	⋮
L_1: bal := **balance**;	L'_1: bal := **balance**;
release ℓ;	release ℓ;
if (bal+a[i]≤MAX)	if (bal-a[j]≥MIN)
bal = bal+a[i];	bal = bal-a[j];
acquire ℓ;	acquire ℓ;
L_2: **balance** := bal;	L'_2: **balance** := bal;
⋮	⋮
release ℓ;	release ℓ;
⋮	⋮

Fig. 1. Non-atomic update of bank account balance

Error invariants [2,6,22] are (automatically generated) annotations of a given failing execution trace that can support the developer in his endeavor to narrow down the statements involved in the failure. Error invariants provide, for each point in the trace, an over-approximation of the reachable states that will produce a failure if execution of the trace is continued from that point (cf. Definition 7). Consequently, two subsequent error invariants in an erroneous execution reflect the relevance of the interjacent statement to the observed failure. Statements that leave the error invariant unchanged do not contribute to the failure and can be safely ignored during the failure analysis [22].

Intuitively, failure analysis with error invariants can be understood as a variant of dynamic slicing [28] that takes the semantics of the failure into account. Existing dynamic slicing techniques are based on data- and control-flow dependencies and remove statements which can not impact the failing state via any chain of dependencies. However, compared to error invariants the precision of these syntax-based slicing techniques is limited by the fact that the semantics of the erroneous trace is not taken into account.

Error invariants have been successfully deployed for constructing semantics-aware slices in sequential software. The enabling techniques for the automated generation of error invariants and slicing are *unsatisfiable cores* and *interpolation*. An error trace translated into an unsatisfiable first-order logical formula yields a proof of unsatisfiability from which interpolants can be extracted. These interpolants which correspond to assertions representing the error invariants can be used to construct a slice of the error trace that abstracts from the irrelevant statements and explains the faulty behavior. This approach produces a slice of the original trace annotated with assertions (the obtained error invariants) showing the relevant values and variables to the failure.

Error Invariants for Concurrent Traces. While error invariants faithfully reflect sequential control- and data-flow, concurrency aspects are ignored entirely. Consequently, a naive application of error invariants to concurrent traces leads to undesirable slices.

Consider, for example, the code fragments in Fig. 1. At locations L_2 and L'_2, respectively, threads T_1 and T_2 update the balance of a bank account which is stored in the shared variable balance. The array a contains the sequence of 5 amounts to be transferred, partitioned into three deposits ($1 \leq i \leq 3$) and two withdrawals ($4 \leq j \leq 5$) executed by thread T_1 and T_2 in parallel, respectively. Figure 2 shows the suffix of a failing interleaved execution in which the third deposit is lost because of an atomicity violation. After three successful transactions (two deposits and one withdrawal) thread T_2 stores the current balance in a thread-local variable bal. At this point, T_1 interferes and updates the value of balance by performing the third deposit. Thread T_2, then, proceeds with the now stale value stored in bal and stores the result of the last withdrawal transaction in balance. Consequently, the execution results in a discrepancy of the expected and the actual balance on the account.

The problem is that the final value of balance depends on the sequence (or timing) of concurrently executed statements, i.e., the program contains a *data hazard*. As the statements are not executed in the order expected by the programmer, the hazard results in an erroneous state, which propagates to the end of the program where it surfaces as a failure. In this setting, the fault the programmer is looking for is the above-mentioned data hazard, in particular the write-after-write dependency between L_2 and L'_2.

The gray assertions in Fig. 2 represent error invariants computed using the approach we propose in this paper. The assertion after L'_1 states that the local variable bal reflects at most two deposits and one withdrawal. At this point, the fault has not been triggered yet. The last conjunct in the error invariant after the context switch indicates that the value of bal is unchanged. The error invariants produced by previous techniques [2,6,22] track only the state information captured by this final conjunct. Therefore they would slice away all the statements of thread T_1 since the error invariants before and after the context switch would be identical. Thus, the resulting slice would not reflect the data hazard and not even the relevant interleaving.

To address this shortcoming, we lift interpolation-based slicing techniques to a concurrency setting by taking into account control and data dependencies between threads. The second assertion in T_2 (after the context switch) already reflects this adaptation: the expression $\mathsf{hb}(L'_1, L_2) \wedge \mathsf{hb}(L_2, L'_2)$ indicates that the statement at L'_1 happened before the statement at L_2, which in turn happened before the one at L'_2. This specific order is crucial to the failure. A slicing algorithm taking this information into account cannot safely slice the statement at L_2 in thread T_1 anymore. Note that, unlike previous techniques, error invariants in our approach not only reflect a set of states but also the execution order of critical statements via the happens-before relation (cf. Sect. 3.2).

Inter-thread data dependencies enable us to isolate (among other bugs) race conditions and atomicity violations which constitute the predominant class of non-deadlock concurrency bugs [18]. Contrary to other concurrency debugging tools [5,8,9,23–25] which target specific kinds of bugs, we provide a general framework for concurrency bug explanation. We applied an implementation of

T_2	T_1
⋮	
L'_1: bal := **balance**	
release ℓ	
{bal $\leq a[1] + a[2] - a[4]$}	
	acquire ℓ
	L_1: bal := **balance**
	⋮
	bal = bal+a[3];
	L_2: **balance** := bal
	release ℓ
⋮	
{hb(L'_1, L_2) ∧ hb(L_2, L'_2) ∧ (bal $\leq a[1] + a[2] - a[4]$)}	
bal = bal-a[5];	
acquire ℓ	
L'_2: **balance** := bal	
{bal $\leq a[1] + a[2] - a[4] - a[5]$}	
⋮	

Fig. 2. Error trace with hazard-sensitive error invariants

our approach to error traces generated from concurrent C programs using the directed testing tool ConCrest [7]. We evaluate our approach on benchmarks that contain bugs found in real-world software such as Apache, GCC, and MySQL [17]. On average, our slices yield a significant reduction of the number of variables and the length of the considered traces while maintaining information that is crucial to understand the underlying concurrency bug.

2 Preliminaries

Syntax of Concurrent Programs. A concurrent program comprises multiple threads each represented by its control-flow graph (CFG) [21, Sect. 7].

Definition 1 (Control-Flow Graph). *A CFG $\langle N, E\rangle$ comprises nodes N and edges E. Each node $n \in N$ corresponds to a single programming construct from a simple imperative language comprising assignments* x:=e *and conditions R.*

Nodes representing conditional statements have two outgoing edges labeled `Y` *and* `N`*, respectively, corresponding to the positive and negative outcome of the condition. All other nodes – except the exit node, which has no successors – have out-degree one.*

If a node m is control dependent on a node n and n represents a condition, its outcome can determine whether m is reached:

Definition 2 (Dominators and Control Dependency). *A node m post-dominates a node n if all paths to the exit node starting at n must go through m. Node m is control dependent on n (where $n \neq m$) if m does not post-dominate n and there exists a path from n to m such that m post-dominates all nodes (other than n) on that path.*

Based on Definition 2, we introduce our notion of a scope:

Definition 3 (Scope). *A node m is in scope of the condition at node n if m is control dependent on n or in scope of a condition that is control dependent on n.*

A CFG is in Static Single Assignment (SSA) form [3] if each variable is assigned exactly once. The standard mechanism to translate CFGs into SSA form is to subscript each definition of a variable with a unique version number; consequently, each definition is uniquely identified by the corresponding SSA variable. Conflicting definitions at a control-flow merge point m in a CFG are resolved by introducing an arbiter node n (with sole successor m) to which we divert the incoming edges of m. The arbiter node n is annotated with a ϕ-function which switches between the definitions from different incoming paths (see Fig. 3). Algorithms to convert a program into SSA form are described in [3] and [21, Sect. 8.11].

Definition 4 (Program Path). *Let $\langle N_t, E_t\rangle$ be a CFG representing a thread t. A path P_t of thread t is a sequence $n_1, \langle n_1, n_2\rangle, n_2, \ldots, \langle n_{k-1}, n_k\rangle, n_k$ of nodes $n_i \in N_t$ and edges $\langle n_i, n_{i+1}\rangle \in E_t$. A program path $P \stackrel{\text{def}}{=} n_1, \langle n_1, n_2\rangle, n_2, \ldots, \langle n_{k-1}, n_k\rangle, n_k$ corresponds to an interleaving of paths of threads (starting at their respective initial nodes) such that for each i with $1 \leq i < k$ either $n_i, n_{i+1} \in N_t$ and $\langle n_i, n_{i+1}\rangle \in E_t$ for some thread t, or n_i and n_{i+1} belong to different threads and $\langle n_i, n_{i+1}\rangle$ is an inter-thread edge representing a context switch.*

Given a (program) path P, let $[n_i, n_j]$ denote the sub-path $n_i, \langle n_i, n_{i+1}\rangle, n_{i+1}, \ldots, n_{j-1}, \langle n_{j-1}, n_j\rangle, n_j$ of P including the nodes n_i and n_j and (n_i, n_j) the sub-path $\langle n_i, n_{i+1}\rangle, n_{i+1}, \ldots, n_{j-1}, \langle n_{j-1}, n_j\rangle$ excluding the nodes n_i and n_j. We use $P\downharpoonright_t$ to denote the projection of a program path P to thread t in which only nodes $n_i \in N_t$ and edges $\langle n_i, n_{i+1}\rangle \in E_t$ are retained and any sub-path (n_i, n_j) with $n_i, n_j \in N_t$ and $n_l \notin N_t$ for $i < l < j$ is replaced with the edge $\langle n_i, n_j\rangle$, i.e., $P\downharpoonright_t$ is a path of the thread t. Consequently, for each program path P, $P\downharpoonright_t$ is either empty (if P does not visit thread t) or a path of thread t starting at the initial node of t. Finally, $P\downharpoonright_N$ and $P\downharpoonright_E$ denote the projection of P to the sequence of nodes N and edges E in P, respectively.

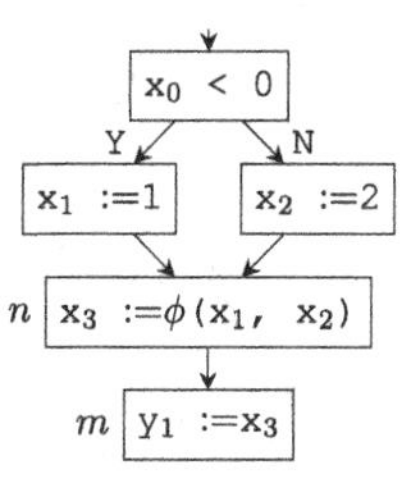

Fig. 3. SSA form of: `if (x < 0) then x := 1 else x := 2; y := x`

Semantics, Feasible Executions and Error Traces. The variables of a program are partitioned into *global* and *thread-local* variables. A state s maps each variable to a value, and $s(e)$ denotes the value of expression e in state s.

A program path P corresponds to a sequence of statements. We require that each statement refers to at most one global variable, and hence statements execute atomically.

Definition 5 (Execution). *An execution of a path P corresponds to an execution of the statements of P in order (starting in an initial state). We use*

$\mathsf{stmt}_P(n_i)$ *to denote the statement represented by node* n_i *in a path* P. *In particular, if node* n_i *represents the condition* R, *let* t *be such that* $n_i \in N_t$ *and let* $\langle n_i, n_j \rangle$ *be the first edge in* $P\downharpoonright_t$ *succeeding* n_i. *Then* $\mathsf{stmt}_P(n_i)$ *is* R *if* $\langle n_i, n_j \rangle$ *is labeled* `Y`, $\neg R$ *if the edge is labeled* `N`. *If* n_i *is the last node of a thread* t, *then* $\mathsf{stmt}_P(n_i) = \mathsf{true}$.

The execution of one statement in the current program state s *is defined as follows:*

- *If* $\mathsf{stmt}_P(n_i)$ *is the assignment* `x`$:=e$, *the successor state of* s *is updated such that* `x` *evaluates to* $s(e)$ *and all other variables are unchanged.*
- *If* n_i *is a conditional statement* R, *the execution proceeds iff* $s(\mathsf{stmt}_P(n_i))$ *is true.*

A path P is *feasible* if there exists an initial state s for which the execution of P is not blocked by a condition which is false. Given a path P, we use stmts_P to denote the sequence of statements represented by P. Abusing our notation, we sometimes call stmts_P a path and will use P and stmts_P interchangeably.

We use $\mathsf{stmts}_P[i]$ to denote the ith statement $\mathsf{stmt}_P(n_i)$ of a path P, and $\mathsf{stmts}_P[i,j]$ to denote the sub-path $\mathsf{stmts}_P[i]; \ldots; \mathsf{stmts}_P[j]$ ($[n_i, n_j]$, respectively). We drop the subscript P if it is clear from the context.

A state s_j is reachable from a state s_{i-1} via a sub-path $\mathsf{stmts}_P[i,j]$ if an execution of $\mathsf{stmts}_P[i,j]$ starting in s_{i-1} does not block and results in state s_j.

We assume that the correctness of a path is determined by an assertion ψ expected to hold after the execution of the path. Error traces which result in the violation of ψ are defined as:

Definition 6 (Error Trace). *A path* P *is an* error trace *for the assertion* ψ *if* P *is feasible and always results in a state* s *such that* $s(\psi)$ *is false.*

Intuitively, an error trace is an execution of a failing test case that does not satisfy the specification ψ. We assume (w.l.o.g.) that path P in Definition 6 reaches the end of the main thread, where ψ is asserted. Consequently, ψ is not in scope of any condition.

3 Error Explanation

In this section, we first recall the interpolation-based slicing approach presented in [2,6] for sequential software. We then explain how we extend it to concurrent executions.

3.1 Interpolation-Based Slicing for Sequential Traces

Ermis et al. [6] and Christ et al. [2] use *error invariants* to identify statements that do not contribute to the assertion violation in sequential traces.

Definition 7 (Error Invariant). *Given an error trace* P *of length* k *for assertion* ψ, *an error invariant for position* i *(with* $i \leq k$*) is a set of states* E *such that*

(a) *E contains (at least) all states reachable from an initial state via* $\mathsf{stmts}_P[1, i]$, *and*
(b) *every feasible execution of* $\mathsf{stmts}_P[i+1, k]$ *starting from a state in E results in a state in which* ψ *is false.*

An error invariant E is recurring[1] *for positions* $i \leq j$ *if E is an error invariant for* i *as well as for* j.

Intuitively, an error invariant E represents an over-approximation of the states that are reachable via the path $\mathsf{stmts}[1, i]$ such that $\mathsf{stmts}[i+1, k]$ if executed from a state in E still results in failure. According to [2,6], statements between a recurring error invariant are "not needed to reproduce the error."

Error invariants can be derived using Craig interpolation (defined below) and a symbolic encoding of a path P [2,6]. In the following, we derive a symbolic encoding $\mathsf{enc}(P)$ similar to the one in [6] from a straight-line program in SSA form, which represents the path P to be encoded. This straight-line program is obtained by traversing the CFG along P. If a node is visited repeatedly (via a cycle in one of the CFGs), a new version of the variable is introduced; for straight-line programs (which do not contain control-flow merge points) it suffices to increase the version number of a variable each time it is assigned and refer to the latest version of each variable in conditions and right-hand sides of assignments.

Given a path P in SSA form as described above, the formula $\mathsf{enc}(P)$ is a conjunction $\bigwedge_{i=1}^{k} \mathsf{enc}_P(n_i)$ of the encodings of the individual statements:

$$\mathsf{enc}_P(n_i) \stackrel{\text{def}}{=} \begin{cases} (\mathsf{x}_i = e) & \text{if } \mathsf{stmt}_P(n_i) \text{ is } \mathsf{x}_i := e \\ \mathsf{stmt}_P(n_i) & \text{if } \mathsf{stmt}_P(n_i) \text{ is a condition} \end{cases} \quad (1)$$

Variable assignments that satisfy formula $\mathsf{enc}(P)$ correspond to executions; note that if all variables in P are initialized before being used, $\mathsf{enc}(P)$ has only one unique satisfying assignment. In this context, interpolants (as defined in [19]) are a symbolic representation of sets of states. Let $\mathrm{Var}(A)$ be the set of (free) variables occurring in a formula A. An interpolant I is a predicate that encodes all states s for which $s(I)$ is true. We define $\mathsf{states}(I) \stackrel{\text{def}}{=} \{s \mid s(I) = \mathsf{true}\}$. The following definition is a generalization of interpolants as defined in [19] under the assumption that all non-logical symbols in A and B are interpreted:

Definition 8 (Inductive Interpolant Sequence). *Let* $A_1, \ldots, A_n$ *be a sequence of first-order formulas whose conjunction is unsatisfiable. Then* $I_0, \ldots I_n$ *is an inductive interpolant sequence if*

- $I_0 = \mathsf{true}$ *and* $I_n = \mathsf{false}$,
- *for all* $1 \leq i \leq n$, $I_{i-1} \wedge A_i \Rightarrow I_i$, *and*
- *for all* $1 \leq i < n$, $\mathrm{Var}(I_i) \in (\mathrm{Var}(A_1 \wedge \ldots \wedge A_i) \cap \mathrm{Var}(A_{i+1} \wedge \ldots \wedge A_n))$.

[1] To avoid confusion with inductive interpolant sequences (Definition 8), we replace the notion of *inductive error invariants* [2,6] with recurring error invariants.

Given a path $P \stackrel{\text{def}}{=} n_1, \langle n_1, n_2\rangle, n_2, \ldots, \langle n_{k-1}, n_k\rangle, n_k$ in SSA form, a sequence interpolant $I_0, \ldots, I_{k+1}$ derived from the formulas $\mathsf{enc}_P(n_1), \ldots, \mathsf{enc}_P(n_k)$, ψ is inductive in the sense that $\mathsf{states}(I_i)$ contains all states reachable from $\mathsf{states}(I_{i-1})$ via $\mathsf{stmt}(n_i)$ (and potentially more) [20, 22]. Moreover, $I_k \wedge \psi$ is not satisfiable, i.e., all states represented by I_k violate assertion ψ. If I_i represents an error invariant for positions i and j (i.e., $\mathsf{states}(I_i)$ is an error invariant for j and I_i implies I_j) then I_i is inductive with respect to the sub-path $\mathsf{stmts}_P[i+1, j]$. Accordingly, slicing $[n_{i+1}, n_j]$ away (i.e., replacing it with an edge $\langle n_{i+1}, n_j\rangle$) preserves the assertion violation.

A trace obtained by removing statements between recurring error invariants from P is sound in the sense of Definition 9 below:

Definition 9 (Sound Slice). *A slice of path P of length k is a path Q of length m with* $\mathsf{stmts}_Q[1] = \mathsf{stmts}_P[i_1]$, $\mathsf{stmts}_Q[2] = \mathsf{stmts}_P[i_2]$, $\ldots$, $\mathsf{stmts}_Q[m] = \mathsf{stmts}_P[i_m]$ *with $1 \le i_1 < i_2 < \ldots < i_m \le k$. Given an error trace P for ψ, a slice Q of P is* sound *if Q is also an error trace for ψ.*

3.2 Interpolation-Based Slicing for Concurrent Traces

In the following, we enhance and extend the interpolation-based slicing technique discussed in Sect. 3.1 to take control dependency as well as concurrency into account.

Control Dependencies. The following example shows that the encoding $\mathsf{enc}(\mathsf{stmts})$ fails to capture control dependence (Definition 2).

Example 1. Figure 4a shows the statements of a path P (in SSA form) and a corresponding interpolant sequence on the right. The example is a sequential variation of the bank account example which fails if the required minimum balance MIN is larger than zero. The resulting slice (indicated in bold) contains only the last assignment to bal and the assertion ψ. It does not reflect the fact that the Y-branch of the conditional statement has to be taken for the failure to occur.

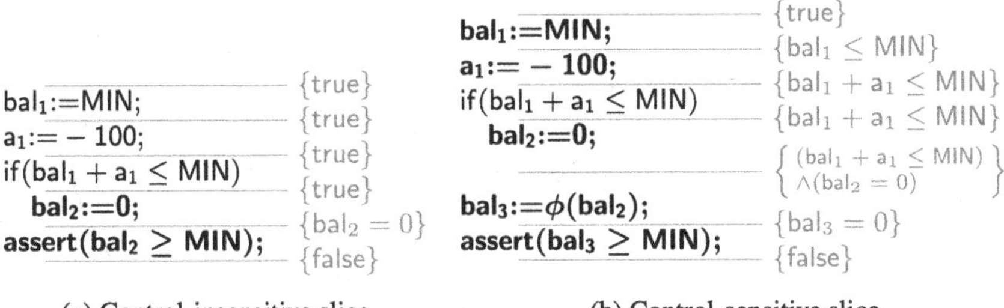

(a) Control-insensitive slice (b) Control-sensitive slice

Fig. 4. Slicing sequential trace with Error Invariants

We present a (modular) extension to the encoding defined in Sect. 3.1 that enables the inclusion of control dependencies. Unlike prior work [2], which addresses this problem using a custom-tailored control-sensitive encoding, our technique is based on the SSA representation. As in Sect. 3.1, the starting point of our approach is a straight-line representation of the error trace P. Unlike before, however, we include the ϕ-nodes from the SSA presentation of the program in P:

ϕ-functions at $n \in N_t$ for a variable x, take as parameters the subscripted variable versions representing definitions of x in thread t that reach n.

Consequently, when generating the straight-line presentation of P, we include all ϕ-nodes of the SSA presentation of the program that are traversed by P. As we are encoding a single path P, however, ϕ takes only one parameter, since only one definition of each variable x reaches n in P. Our extension csenc(stmts) of the encoding enc(stmts) is based on assignments $\mathsf{x}_i := \phi(\mathsf{x}_j)$, which make control dependencies in an error trace P explicit. In order for x_i to take the value of x_j, the outcomes of the conditional statements preceding the assignment of x_j in P have to permit the assignment to be executed.

Let $\mathsf{stmt}(n_j)$ be the statement assigning x_j, and note that control dependency coincides with our notion of a scope (as defined in Definition 3). We define

$$\mathsf{guard}(n_j) \stackrel{\text{def}}{=} \bigwedge \{\mathsf{enc}(n_i) \mid n_j \text{ is in scope of } n_i\} \ . \tag{2}$$

In order for the definition of x_j in n_j to be reachable along P, $\mathsf{guard}(n_j)$ needs to evaluate to true. Moreover, since trace P does not traverse alternative branches, the value of x_i is unknown if $\mathsf{guard}(n_j)$ does not hold. Based on this insight, we define a *control-sensitive* encoding $\mathsf{csenc}(P)$ as follows:

$$\mathsf{csenc}(n_i) \stackrel{\text{def}}{=} \begin{cases} \mathsf{guard}(n_j) \Rightarrow (\mathsf{x}_i = \mathsf{x}_j) & \text{if } \mathsf{stmt}(n_i) \text{ is } \mathsf{x}_i := \phi(\mathsf{x}_j) \\ & \quad \text{and } n_j \text{ assigns } \mathsf{x}_j \\ \mathsf{enc}(n_i) & \text{if } n_i \text{ is an assignment} \\ \mathsf{true} & \text{if } n_i \text{ is a condition} \end{cases} \tag{3}$$

An inductive error invariant for the encoding $\mathsf{csenc}(P)$ induces a control-sensitive slice (cf. Definition 4 of flow-sensitivity and Theorem 6 in [2]):

Definition 10 (Control-sensitive Slice). *Let P be an error trace for the assertion ψ. A (sound) slice Q is* control-sensitive *if for every statement* $\mathsf{stmts}_Q[k] = \mathsf{stmts}_P[i]$ *and every assumption* $\mathsf{stmts}_P[j]$ *such that* $\mathsf{stmts}_P[i]$ *is in scope of* $\mathsf{stmts}_P[j]$*, there is some prefix* $\mathsf{stmts}_Q[1,h]$ *of* $\mathsf{stmts}_Q[1,k]$ *(with $h < k$ such that* $\mathsf{stmts}_Q[h]$ *precedes and* $\mathsf{stmts}_Q[h+1]$ *succeeds or equals* $\mathsf{stmts}_P[j]$ *in P) such that* $\mathsf{stmts}_Q[1,h]$ *is an error trace for* $\neg(\mathsf{stmts}_P[j])$.

Intuitively, the definition requires that Q justifies that every branch containing a relevant statement will be taken.

Theorem 1. *Let P be a (concurrent) error trace for ψ of length k and let I_0, I_1, ..., I_{k-1}, I_{k+1} be error invariants (with $I_0 = \mathsf{true}$ and $I_{k+1} = \mathsf{false}$) obtained from an inductive sequence interpolant for* $\mathsf{csenc}(n_1), \ldots, \mathsf{csenc}(n_k), \psi$. *Let Q be the slice obtained from P by removing each sub-path $P[i, j]$ for which I_{i-1} is inductive. Then Q is a sound control-sensitive slice for P. (Proof in [11])*

Note that the interpolants in Theorem 1 may contain different versions of a variable x, since the encoding of ϕ-nodes may refer to conditions in the "past". This corresponds to *history* or *ghost* variables used in Hoare logic and does not affect soundness.

Example 2. Figure 4b shows the path P from Example 1 sliced using a control-sensitive encoding $\mathsf{csenc}(P)$ based on ϕ-nodes. Note that the statements initializing bal and amount, which guarantee that the Y-branch is taken, are included in the slice.

Synchronization. In the simple interleaving semantics deployed in this paper, locks can be modeled using an integer variables ℓ and atomicity constraints. Lock ℓ is available if its value is 0. Any other value t indicates that the lock ℓ is held by thread t. Let n be a node of thread t with a self-loop waiting for $(\ell = 0)$ to become true, and m its successor node assigning t to ℓ. By constraining the execution such that no thread other than t can execute between n and m, we guarantee that lock acquisition is performed atomically. Analogously, a lock ℓ held by the current thread (guaranteed by condition $\ell = t$) is released by the statement $\ell := 0$. Control-sensitive slices also take into account lock acquisition statements, as relevant statements executed in a locked region are in the scope of the corresponding condition $(\ell = 0)$.

Hazards. A trace contains a *data hazard* if its outcome depends on the sequence (or timing) of concurrently executed statements. As explained for the sub-trace in Fig. 2 discussed in Sect. 1, applying error invariants in their original form [6] to sequential paths results in slices that ignore important characteristics of concurrent traces. While $\mathsf{csenc}(P)$ reflects control-flow, it fails to capture *data dependencies*, which are constraints arising from the flow of data between statements [21]:

Read-after-write If statement $\mathsf{stmt}(n)$ writes a value read by statement $\mathsf{stmt}(m)$, then the two statements are *flow dependent.*

Write-after-read An *anti dependence* occurs when statement $\mathsf{stmt}(n)$ reads a value that is later updated (over-written) by $stmt(m)$.

Write-after-write An *output dependence* exists if $\mathsf{stmt}(n)$ as well as $\mathsf{stmt}(m)$ set the value of the same variable.

While this definition also applies to single threads, we concern ourselves exclusively with *inter-thread* data dependencies. In a path P, a data dependency between different threads can indicate a conflicting access (i.e., a *race condition* or *hazard*).

T_2	T_1
	L_2: **balance₁** := bal + a[3];
L'_2: **balance₂** := bal − a[5] **balance₃** := π(**balance₁**, **balance₂**); assert(**balance₃** = a[1] + a[2] + a[3] − a[4] − a[5]);	

Fig. 5. Part of a path with hazard and π-node

Unlike flow dependence (which is taken into account by $\mathsf{enc}(P)$ and $\mathsf{csenc}(P)$, since the SSA form represents use-definition pairs and therefore also flow dependence explicitly), anti and output dependencies are not explicit in the SSA-based encoding of P used in Sects. 3.1 and 3.2. Similar to merge points in sequential programs, inter-thread dependencies in P give rise to conflicting definitions of global variables. The Concurrent SSA (CSSA) form of paths presented in [26,29] introduces π-functions to resolve dependencies between accesses to global variables in different threads.

To convert an error trace into CSSA form, we introduce an arbiter node before every read access to a global variable x in an error trace P (analogously to the arbiter nodes for ϕ-functions in Sect. 2). The arbiter node is annotated with a π-function that selects from all definitions of the global variable x in P the most recent definition:

π-functions at $n \in N_t$ for a global variable x, take as parameters the subscripted variables representing definitions of x in all threads.[2]

Figure 5 shows a simplified suffix of the trace in Fig. 2. The simplified trace consists of two threads with a π-node (arbitrating between the definitions $\mathsf{balance}_1$ and $\mathsf{balance}_2$) inserted before an assertion ψ that states the expected outcome. Note that unlike the degenerate ϕ-functions used in Sect. 3.2, a π-function for x has as many parameters as there are definitions of x in P.

To encode WAR and WAW dependencies, we introduce an irreflexive, transitive, and anti-symmetric relation $\mathsf{hb}(n_i, n_j)$ which indicates that node n_i is executed before node n_j. This happens-before relation enables us to encode the edges of a program trace, reflecting the program order and the schedule.

In addition, $\mathsf{rd}(\mathsf{x}, n_i)$ and $\mathsf{wr}(\mathsf{x}, n_j)$ indicate that x is read at node n_i and written at node n_j. These primitives allow for an explicit encoding of data dependencies:

$$\begin{aligned} \mathsf{wr}(\mathsf{x}, n_i) \wedge \mathsf{hb}(n_i, n_j) \wedge \mathsf{rd}(\mathsf{x}, n_j) &\Leftrightarrow \mathsf{raw}_{\mathsf{x}}(n_i, n_j) \\ \mathsf{rd}(\mathsf{x}, n_i) \wedge \mathsf{hb}(n_i, n_j) \wedge \mathsf{wr}(\mathsf{x}, n_j) &\Leftrightarrow \mathsf{war}_{\mathsf{x}}(n_i, n_j) \\ \mathsf{wr}(\mathsf{x}, n_i) \wedge \mathsf{hb}(n_i, n_j) \wedge \mathsf{wr}(\mathsf{x}, n_j) &\Leftrightarrow \mathsf{waw}_{\mathsf{x}}(n_i, n_j) \end{aligned} \quad (4)$$

The hazard-sensitive encoding presented below incorporates data dependencies into the encoding of a trace. The encoding is derived directly from a program

[2] As an optimization, only the *last* definition of x in thread t before n is added.

path P, taking advantage of the information encoded in the edges. Assignments (without π-functions) are encoded as follows:

$$\mathsf{hsenc}(n_i) \quad \stackrel{\text{def}}{=} \quad \begin{cases} \mathsf{wr}(\mathsf{x}, n_i) \wedge \mathsf{enc}(n_i) & \text{if } n_i \text{ writes global var. } \mathsf{x} \\ \mathsf{rd}(\mathsf{x}, n_i) \wedge \mathsf{enc}(n_i) & \text{if } n_i \text{ reads global var. } \mathsf{x} \\ \mathsf{enc}(n_i) & \text{otherwise} \end{cases} \tag{5}$$

Nodes n_i with π-functions incorporate happens-before information. Let n_i be a π-node assigning x_i, let n_j be an assignment to x_j and the last node before n_i in P updating the global variable x. Then $\mathsf{hsenc}(n_i)$ is:

$$\mathsf{rd}(\mathsf{x}, n_i) \wedge (\mathrm{DEP}(n_i, n_j) \Rightarrow (\mathsf{x}_i = \mathsf{x}_j)) \tag{6}$$

where $\mathrm{DEP}(n_i, n_j)$ is the following condition:

$$\mathsf{raw}_\mathsf{x}(n_j, n_i) \wedge \bigwedge_{\substack{m \in \{n \in P \,|\, \mathsf{wr}(\mathsf{x}, n)\} \\ m \neq n_j}} (\mathsf{waw}_\mathsf{x}(m, n_j) \vee \mathsf{war}_\mathsf{x}(n_i, m)) \tag{7}$$

Intuitively, $\mathrm{DEP}(n_i, n_j)$ states that x_j is written before x_i is read, and no other definition of x interferes.

Finally, edges are encoded as happens-before relations:

$$\mathsf{hsenc}(\langle n_i, n_{i+1}\rangle) \stackrel{\text{def}}{=} \mathsf{hb}(n_i, n_{i+1}) \tag{8}$$

Given a path $P \stackrel{\text{def}}{=} n_1, \langle n_1, n_2\rangle, n_2, \ldots, \langle n_{k-1}, n_k\rangle, n_k$, applying sequence interpolation to the formulas $\mathsf{hsenc}(n_1)$, $\mathsf{hsenc}(\langle n_1, n_2\rangle)$, $\mathsf{hsenc}(n_2)$, $\ldots$, $\mathsf{hsenc}(\langle n_{k-1}, n_k\rangle)$, $\mathsf{hsenc}(n_k)$, ψ yields a sequence $\mathsf{in}_1, \mathsf{out}_1, \ldots, \mathsf{in}_k, \mathsf{out}_k$ of formulas such that

$$\mathsf{in}_i \wedge \mathsf{hsenc}(n_i) \Rightarrow \mathsf{out}_i \text{ and } \mathsf{out}_i \wedge \mathsf{hsenc}(\langle n_i, n_{i+1}\rangle) \Rightarrow \mathsf{in}_{i+1}\,.$$

Unlike before, in_i and out_i propagate facts about states as well as execution order. We can slice sub-path $[n_i, n_j]$ if $\mathsf{in}_i \Rightarrow \mathsf{out}_j$, sub-path (n_i, n_j) if $\mathsf{out}_i \Rightarrow \mathsf{in}_j$, sub-path $[n_i, n_j)$ if $\mathsf{in}_i \Rightarrow \mathsf{in}_j$, and sub-path $(n_i, n_j]$ if $\mathsf{out}_i \Rightarrow \mathsf{out}_j$. The resulting sliced path Q corresponds to a sequence of statements stmts_Q and a set of edges $Q\lfloor_E$ representing context switches and program order constraints relevant to the error.

Definition 11 (Hazard-sensitive slice). *Given an error trace P, a (sound) slice Q is* hazard-sensitive *if for every statement $\mathsf{stmts}_Q[k] = \mathsf{stmts}_P[j]$ and statement $\mathsf{stmts}_P[i]$ such that there is an inter-thread data dependency between $\mathsf{stmts}_P[i]$ and $\mathsf{stmts}_P[j]$, there is an h such that $\mathsf{stmts}_Q[h] = \mathsf{stmts}_P[j]$.*

Theorem 2. *Let P be a concurrent error trace and let Q be the slice obtained from P as explained above. Then Q is a sound hazard-sensitive slice of P. (Proof in [11])*

Example 3. Consider the path in Fig. 5. A hazard-insensitive slice would contain the statement at node L_2' but not the statement at node L_2' (as explained in Sect. 1) since L_2 has no influence on the state after L_2'. Encoding (6) and (7) of the π-node require the interpolant before the π-node to imply $\mathsf{waw}_{\mathsf{balance}}(L_2, L'_2)$, and consequently $\mathsf{wr}(\mathsf{balance}, L_2)$, $\mathsf{wr}(\mathsf{balance}, L'_2)$, and $\mathsf{hb}(L_2, L'_2)$ (as indicated in Fig. 2). Nodes L_2 and L'_2 as well as the edge $\langle L_2, L'_2\rangle$ are included in the resulting slice.

3.3 Fine-Tuning Explanations

The encodings presented in Sect. 3.2 can be combined in a straightforward manner, providing us with a choice of control WAR, and WAW dependencies reflected by the resulting explanation. Control-flow or hazard-sensitivity can be added (or removed) by (dis-)regarding π-nodes and ϕ-nodes in P. Control-flow dependency can be incorporated into π-nodes in Eq. (6) by prefixing the assignment $\mathsf{x}_i = \mathsf{x}_j$ with the guard of the definition of x_j at node n_j: $\mathsf{guard}(n_j) \Rightarrow (\mathrm{DEP}(n_i, n_j) \Rightarrow (\mathsf{x}_i = \mathsf{x}_j))$, similar to the guard in the definition of $\mathsf{csenc}(n_i)$ in Encoding (3). Moreover, Encoding (6) can be made insensitive to WAR dependencies by restricting m to predecessors of n_i and by dropping the disjunct $\mathsf{war}_{\mathsf{x}}(n_i, m)$ from (7) (and similarly for WAW dependencies). Note that flow dependency has a special role, since use-definition chains are explicit in the SSA representation.

The partial order given by the subset relation $\subseteq$ over the power-set of the remaining dependencies $\{\mathsf{cs}, \mathsf{war}, \mathsf{waw}\}$ reflects possible levels of detail of explanations, as illustrated by the Hasse diagram to the right. As indicated in the diagram, the configuration $\emptyset$ corresponds to the basic approach presented in [6,22], whereas $\{\mathsf{cs}\}$ represents control-flow sensitive approach.

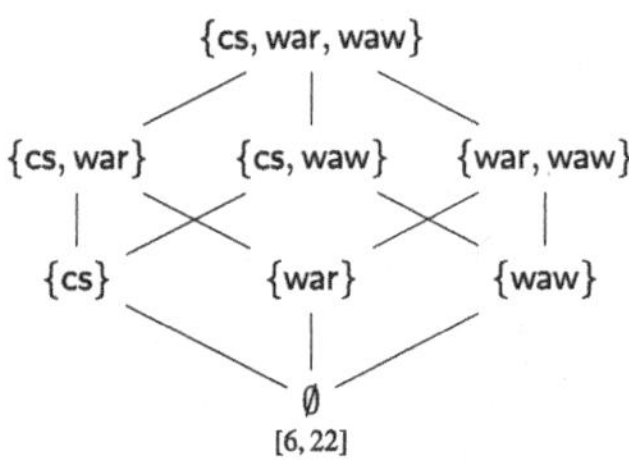

While we see interpolants as an inherent part of the explanation, the level of detail provided by these annotations cannot be related or formalized as easily as it is the case for dependencies: changing the underlying encoding typically has an unpredictable effect on the structure and strength of interpolants [4,20].

4 Experiments

We implemented our approach as an extension of the directed testing tool ConCrest [7]. We generate error traces of concurrent programs and then produce slices as described in Sect. 3. While all slices provided by our tool are sound in the sense of Definition 9, the level of detail might not be sufficient to reflect the underlying bug: for example, the hazard-sensitive slice for the account benchmark readily reveals the atomicity violation. Therefore, it is not necessary to compute a more detailed control-sensitive slice.

The results from Sect. 3.3 enable the developer to gradually increase the detail in an iterative manner until the bug can be understood. This section provides an empirical evaluation of the size and accuracy of slices with varying levels of detail.

Effectiveness of the Method. To evaluate our method, we applied it on a collection of faulty C programs to show how effective the different dependency encodings are at revealing different types of concurrency bugs. We used four different encodings to track data and control dependencies: **hs** refers to hazard-sensitive encoding for tracking inter-thread data dependencies, **cs** refers to control-sensitive encoding for tracking control dependencies, and **ds** denotes the basic encoding enc_P of Sect. 3. The symbol "+" indicates combinations of encodings.

Our definition of whether the bug was captured depends on the type of bug. For data race bugs, we required that the slice reflecting the bug contains both conflicting accesses. For atomicity violations, a slice reflecting the bug contains conflicting statements from another thread interrupting the desired atomic region. For order violations, a slice reflecting the bug contains conflicting statements in the problematic order.

Table 1 summarizes our empirical results. The benchmarks in this table are classified into two groups. The first group consists of 33 multithreaded C programs taken from [17].[3] These programs capture the essence of concurrency bugs reported in various versions of open source applications such as Mozilla, Apache, and GCC. The apache2 and bluetooth benchmarks in the second group are simplified versions of applications taken from [7]. The pool-simple-2 benchmark is a lock-free concurrent data structure with a linearizability bug. We discuss this benchmark in depth in [11]. The remaining two benchmarks in the second group are variants of the program discussed in Sect. 1. For each benchmark program, the name, the number of lines of code (LOC), the number of threads, and the type of bug are listed in Table 1. The number of error traces (#T) per benchmark varies due to specific assertions and ConCrest's ability to produce error traces. They do not reflect any preselection of traces. In total, ConCrest generated 90 error traces from the 38 programs all of which we considered in our evaluation.

We use ✓ to indicate that the explanations obtained using the corresponding encoding capture the bug, and – if the bug was not captured. By manually inspecting the slices we found that for all but two benchmarks, tracking all dependencies **ds+cs+hs** yields explanations that capture the corresponding concurrency bug. For most benchmarks there exists at least one additional encoding which provides smaller slices that still reveal the bug. This encoding is usually **hs** (68 %) or **cs** (50 %) depending on the nature of the bug and the assertions. Interestingly, our analysis revealed that boop, freebsd_auditarg and gcc-java-25530 from [17] contain sequential bugs already reflected in a **ds**-slice rather than concurrency bugs (even though in [17] they are classified as concurrency bugs).

In two of the three error traces of freebsd_auditarg the bug is triggered by non-interleaved executions of the threads. For these traces, any encoding yields an adequate explanation. In one error trace, however, the bug is triggered by an interference between two threads, which is only reflected by the encodings **ds+hs** and **ds+cs+hs**.

[3] ConCrest's search heuristic failed to generate an error trace for the fibbench_longer, a variant of fibbench with larger parameters. We emphasize that this failure is related to the generation of traces rather than slicing.

Table 1. Experimental comparison of sensitivity-configurations for slicing

Benchmark	#T	LOC	AIT	Threads	Bugs	ds+cs+hs					ds+hs					ds+cs					ds				
						S[%]		V[%]			S[%]		V[%]			S[%]		V[%]			S[%]		V[%]		
						μ	σ	μ	σ	RB	μ	σ	μ	σ	RB	μ	σ	μ	σ	RB	μ	σ	μ	σ	RB
account	3	43 (58)	51.7	4	AV	62	12	77	6	✓	42	10	68	6	✓	43	8	68	6	–	29	5	59	5	–
apache-21287	2	30 (79)	43	3	AV	72	0	87	0	✓	28	0	53	0	–	51	0	87	0	✓	9	0	40	0	–
apache-25520	1	88 (192)	34	3	AV	38	–	50	–	–	9	–	33	–	–	26	–	50	–	–	9	–	33	–	–
barrier_vf_false	12	57 (85)	27	4	AV	70	0	80	0	✓	19	0	40	0	–	67	0	80	0	✓	15	0	40	0	–
boop	1	58 (98)	40	3	SB	38	–	47	–	✓	30	–	40	–	✓	35	–	47	–	✓	28	–	40	–	✓
cherokee_01	1	88 (188)	28	3	AV	46	–	60	–	–	11	–	40	–	–	32	–	60	–	–	11	–	40	–	–
counter_seq	1	28 (41)	29	3	DR	72	–	90	–	✓	38	–	70	–	✓	52	–	80	–	–	31	–	60	–	–
fibbench	2	34 (47)	34	3	AV	94	3	97	3	✓	94	3	97	3	✓	88	3	97	3	✓	88	3	97	3	✓
freebsd_auditarg	3	52 (104)	37	4	SB	67	7	86	0	✓	32	5	64	0	✓	57	10	79	10	✓ (2/3)	30	8	57	10	✓ (2/3)
gcc-java-25530	2	36 (86)	17	3	SB	35	0	40	0	✓	35	0	40	0	✓	24	0	40	0	✓	24	0	40	0	✓
gcc-libstdc++-3584	1	40 (104)	37	3	AV	62	–	79	–	✓	35	–	64	–	✓	46	–	71	–	–	30	–	57	–	–
gcc-libstdc++-21334	1	36 (86)	27	3	OV	63	–	78	–	✓	22	–	33	–	✓	48	–	78	–	–	15	–	33	–	–
gcc-libstdc++-40518	2	40 (104)	23	3	AV	43	0	56	0	✓	30	0	56	0	–	39	0	56	0	✓	22	0	56	0	–
glib-512624_02	2	50 (94)	27.5	3	AV	84	2	100	0	✓	47	3	80	0	✓	60	4	85	5	–	38	5	65	5	–
hash_table	1	51 (114)	69	3	AV	41	–	61	–	✓	4	–	21	–	–	29	–	54	–	–	4	–	21	–	–
jetty-1187	1	24 (98)	26	3	AV	81	–	100	–	✓	35	–	78	–	✓	58	–	89	–	–	27	–	67	–	–
lazy01_false	2	39 (55)	23	4	OV	91	0	100	0	✓	65	0	100	0	✓	87	0	100	0	✓	61	0	100	0	✓
lineEq_2t_01	1	35 (58)	52	3	AV	69	–	81	–	✓	46	–	71	–	✓	52	–	76	–	✓	37	–	67	–	✓
linux-iio	1	54 (87)	55	3	DR	40	–	59	–	✓	20	–	50	–	✓	27	–	41	–	–	16	–	32	–	–
linux-tg3	1	93 (115)	167	3	DR	19	–	38	–	✓	13	–	36	–	✓	8	–	11	–	✓	2	–	9	–	–
list_seq	1	59 (122)	53	3	AV	58	–	95	–	✓	6	–	30	–	–	40	–	75	–	–	6	–	30	–	–
llvm-8441	2	149 (244)	32.5	3	AV	74	4	92	0	✓	18	0	33	0	✓	55	7	83	8	–	12	0	33	0	–
mozilla-61369	1	19 (68)	6	1	OV	67	–	100	–	✓	67	–	100	–	✓	67	–	100	–	✓	67	–	100	–	✓
ms_queue02	1	67 (97)	66	3	AV	44	–	52	–	✓	5	–	20	–	–	35	–	48	–	–	5	–	20	–	–
mysql5	1	21 (27)	28	3	AV	82	–	89	–	✓	46	–	67	–	✓	46	–	89	–	–	25	–	67	–	–
mysql-644	1	68 (165)	16	3	AV	38	–	33	–	✓	38	–	33	–	✓	25	–	33	–	–	25	–	33	–	–
mysql-3596	1	30 (83)	6	3	DR	100	–	100	–	✓	100	–	100	–	✓	67	–	100	–	✓	67	–	100	–	✓
mysql-12848	1	51 (142)	14	2	AV	71	–	67	–	✓	43	–	50	–	–	50	–	67	–	✓	29	–	50	–	–
read_write_false	1	78 (140)	58	5	AV	17	–	27	–	✓	17	–	27	–	✓	17	–	27	–	✓	17	–	27	–	✓
reorder2_false	8	50 (105)	10.5	5	AV	86	14	100	0	✓	86	14	100	0	✓	62	8	100	0	✓	62	8	100	0	✓
testconc02	1	15 (19)	9	2	AV	89	–	100	–	✓	89	–	100	–	✓	56	–	100	–	–	56	–	100	–	–
transmission-1.42	1	25 (78)	5	3	DR	100	–	100	–	✓	100	–	100	–	✓	80	–	100	–	✓	80	–	100	–	✓
VectPrime02	1	97 (183)	115	3	AV	25	–	68	–	✓	9	–	45	–	✓	18	–	59	–	–	7	–	36	–	–
apache2	8	719 (–)	235.5	3	AV	8	2	9	2	✓	1	0	1	0	–	7	2	9	2	✓	1	0	1	0	✓
bankaccount-lock-for-loop	5	103 (–)	247	3	AV	46	2	44	2	✓	12	1	30	2	✓	40	2	42	2	–	9	1	23	3	–
bankaccount-simple-lock	2	50 (–)	45	3	AV	71	0	80	0	✓	31	0	60	0	✓	62	0	73	0	–	24	0	53	0	–
bluetooth	5	87 (–)	35.8	3	AV	42	0	63	0	✓	14	0	31	0	–	36	0	63	0	✓	11	0	31	0	–
pool-simple-2	8	298 (–)	885.5	3	LV	30	1	58	2	✓	0	0	2	0	–	29	1	56	2	✓	0	0	2	0	–
Total	90					58.8		72		88	35		54		47	45		67.7		61	27		50.5		22

#T: No. of Traces in Benchmark **LOC**: Lines of Code[a] AIT: Average No. of Instructions in a Trace
ds: Basic Encoding **cs**: Control-Sensitive Encoding **hs**: Hazard-Sensitive Encoding
S: Slice Size / Trace Size V: No. of Variables in Slice / No. of Variables in Trace
μ: Average σ: Standard Deviation
RB: Reflects Concurrency Bug AV: Atomicity Violation SB: Sequential Bug
DR: Data Race OV: Order Violation LV: Linearizability Violation

[a] LOC excluding comments and blank lines; LOC in parentheses are as stated in [17].

Only the programs hash_table, ms_queue02, and list_seq, which contain bugs in intricate concurrent data structures, require the full **ds+cs+hs** encoding.

Only for the two benchmarks apache-25520 and cherokee_01 the slices produced by our method failed to reveal the bugs. The problem is that the root cause of the assertion violation is that a specific branch of a conditional statement is not taken during the execution. Slices of single error traces cannot reveal the non-occurrence of an event as the cause for failure. Therefore, we plan to analyze merged error traces in future work.

Running times. The generation of the slices takes an average of 2.43 s ($\sigma = 11.02\,s$) across all encodings with a maximum of 168.8 s. As expected, the running times increase with the amount of detail captured by the encoding. Generating a **ds** explanation takes 0.43 s on average ($\sigma = 0.18\,s$) whereas a **ds+cs+hs** explanation takes 7.3 s ($\sigma = 21.25\,s$).

Quantitative Evaluation. Table 1 shows the effect of tracking different dependencies on the size of the slices. μ refers to average percentage reduction as the quotient of the number of remaining and original instructions, so smaller numbers mean smaller slices. As expected, increasing the sensitivity of the algorithm by tracking more dependencies leads to smaller reductions. However, as we have seen previously, the hazard-sensitive explanations (**ds+hs**), which capture the concurrency bugs in 68 % of the benchmarks, on average contain 35 % of the original instructions and 54 % of the original variables. We gained the maximum reduction with the encoding (**ds**), however the resulting explanations reflected the concurrency bugs in only 23 % of the benchmarks. The amount of reduction differs across benchmarks with a maximum of 93 % for the apache2 benchmark program. Slices which are hazard- but not control-flow sensitive tend to be much smaller than slices which are control-flow sensitive, but not data-hazard sensitive.

5 Related Work

The original work on error invariants [2,6] is discussed in Sects. 2 and 3. Murali et al. [22] relate error invariants to unsatisfiable cores and consistency-based diagnosis. The latter is also implemented in ConcBugAssist [17], a repair tool for concurrent programs, and BugAssist [15] for the diagnosis of sequential bugs. Both BugAssist and ConcBugAssist take into account multiple traces simultaneously and can yield better accuracy in certain cases (e.g., benchmarks apache-25520 and cherokee_01 in Sect. 4). Neither [15,17] nor [22] report branch conditions (or statements explaining why they hold). On the benchmarks from [17], we found that ConcBugAssist yields similar reduction ratios as our tool using the **hs+ds** encoding. The dependency of ConcBugAssist on a bounded model checker for the constraint generation entails scalability issues: even on a simplified version of pool_simpl_2 for which we provided the minimal unwinding depth necessary to detect the bug, ConcBugAssist timed out after 45 min, while our approach generated a slice in 2.5 min for the non-simplified program.

Other static approaches for simplifying and summarizing concurrent error traces include [10,12,13,16]. In [10], an SMT solver and model enumeration is used to derive a symbolic representation of *all* reorderings of a given trace that violate a safety property, which is then used to explain the bug. Instead, we analyze a single failing trace, ensuring that our encoding explicitly captures which happens-before relations are relevant for the faulty behavior.

Tools that attempt to minimize the number of context switches, such as SimTrace [12] and Tinertia [13], are orthogonal to the approach presented in this paper.

Many techniques for detecting race conditions or atomicity/serializability violations are geared towards specific bug characteristics [9,18,30]. Similarly, dynamic techniques such as Falcon [24] and Unicorn [23] rely on bug patterns. Our approach encodes data-dependencies rather than relying on bug patterns or specific bug characteristics. Recent work [27] uses mining of failing and passing traces to isolate erroneous sequences of statements. Our technique only considers failing traces.

Afix [14] and ConcurrencySwapper [1] automatically fix concurrency-related errors. The latter uses error invariants to generalize a linear error trace to a partially ordered trace, which is then used to synthesize a fix. This approach may potentially benefit from our more fine-tuned trace encoding that enables error invariants to capture concurrent data dependencies.

6 Conclusion

We proposed to augment error invariants with information about inter-thread data dependency and hazards to capture a broad range of concurrency bugs. Our technique generates sound slices of concurrent error traces, enabling developers to quickly isolate and focus on the relevant aspects of error traces. We proved that the reported slices are sound and sufficient to trigger the failure. The experimental evaluation of our prototype implementation showed that the approach is effective and significantly reduces the amount of code that needs to be inspected.

References

1. Černý, P., Henzinger, T.A., Radhakrishna, A., Ryzhyk, L., Tarrach, T.: Efficient synthesis for concurrency by semantics-preserving transformations. In: Sharygina, N., Veith, H. (eds.) CAV 2013. LNCS, vol. 8044, pp. 951–967. Springer, Heidelberg (2013). doi:10.1007/978-3-642-39799-8_68
2. Christ, J., Ermis, E., Schäf, M., Wies, T.: Flow-sensitive fault localization. In: Giacobazzi, R., Berdine, J., Mastroeni, I. (eds.) VMCAI 2013. LNCS, vol. 7737, pp. 189–208. Springer, Heidelberg (2013). doi:10.1007/978-3-642-35873-9_13
3. Cytron, R., Ferrante, J., Rosen, B.K., Wegman, M.N., Kenneth-Zadeck, F.: Efficiently computing static single assignment form, the control dependence graph. ACM Trans. Program. Lang. Syst. (TOPLAS) **13**(4), 451–490 (1991)
4. D'Silva, V., Kroening, D., Purandare, M., Weissenbacher, G.: Interpolant strength. In: Barthe, G., Hermenegildo, M. (eds.) VMCAI 2010. LNCS, vol. 5944, pp. 129–145. Springer, Heidelberg (2010). doi:10.1007/978-3-642-11319-2_12
5. Engler, D.R., Ashcraft, K., RacerX: effective, static detection of race conditions and deadlocks. In: SOSP, pp. 237–252. ACM (2003)
6. Ermis, E., Schäf, M., Wies, T.: Error invariants. In: Giannakopoulou, D., Méry, D. (eds.) FM 2012. LNCS, vol. 7436, pp. 187–201. Springer, Heidelberg (2012). doi:10.1007/978-3-642-32759-9_17
7. Farzan, A., Holzer, A., Razavi, N., Veith, H.: Con2colic testing. In: Foundations of Software Engineering (FSE), pp. 37–47. ACM (2013)
8. Flanagan, C., Freund, S.N.: FastTrack: efficient and precise dynamic race detection. Commun. ACM **53**(11), 93–101 (2010)
9. Flanagan, C., Qadeer, S.: A type and effect system for atomicity. In: Programming Language Design and Implementation (PLDI), pp. 338–349. ACM (2003)
10. Gupta, A., Henzinger, T.A., Radhakrishna, A., Samanta, R., Tarrach, T.: Succinct representation of concurrent trace sets. In: POPL, pp. 433–444. ACM (2015)
11. Holzer, A., Schwartz-Narbonne, D., Tabaei Befrouei, M., Weissenbacher, G., Wies, T.: Error invariants for concurrent traces. ArXiv e-prints, abs/1608.08584, August 2016

12. Huang, J., Zhang, C.: An efficient static trace simplification technique for debugging concurrent programs. In: Yahav, E. (ed.) SAS 2011. LNCS, vol. 6887, pp. 163–179. Springer, Heidelberg (2011). doi:10.1007/978-3-642-23702-7_15
13. Jalbert, N., Sen, K.: A trace simplification technique for effective debugging of concurrent programs. In: Foundations of Software Engineering (FSE), pp. 57–66. ACM (2010)
14. Jin, G., Song, L., Zhang, W., Lu, S., Liblit, B.: Automated atomicity-violation fixing. In: Programming Language Design and Implementation (PLDI), pp. 389–400. ACM (2011)
15. Jose, M., Majumdar, R.: Cause clue clauses: error localization using maximum satisfiability. In: Programming Language Design and Implementation (PLDI) (2011)
16. Kashyap, S., Garg, V.K.: Producing short counterexamples using "Crucial Events". In: Gupta, A., Malik, S. (eds.) CAV 2008. LNCS, vol. 5123, pp. 491–503. Springer, Heidelberg (2008). doi:10.1007/978-3-540-70545-1_47
17. Khoshnood, S., Kusano, M., Wang, C., ConcBugAssist: constraint solving for diagnosis and repair of concurrency bugs. In: ISSTA, pp. 165–176. ACM (2015)
18. Shan, L., Park, S., Seo, E., Zhou, Y.: Learning from mistakes: a comprehensive study on real world concurrency bug characteristics. ACM SIGPLAN Not. **43**, 329–339 (2008)
19. McMillan, K.L.: An interpolating theorem prover. Theoret. Comput. Sci. **345**(1), 101–121 (2005)
20. McMillan, K.L.: Lazy abstraction with interpolants. In: Ball, T., Jones, R.B. (eds.) CAV 2006. LNCS, vol. 4144, pp. 123–136. Springer, Heidelberg (2006). doi:10.1007/11817963_14
21. Muchnick, S.S.: Advanced Compiler Design Implementation. Morgan Kaufmann, San Francisco (1997)
22. Murali, V., Sinha, N., Torlak, E., Chandra, S.: A hybrid algorithm for error trace explanation. In: VSTTE (2014)
23. Park, S., Vuduc, R., Harrold, M.J.: A unified approach for localizing non-deadlock concurrency bugs. In: Software Testing, Verification and Validation (ICST), pp. 51–60. IEEE (2012)
24. Park, S., Vuduc, R.W., Harrold, M.J.: Falcon: fault localization in concurrent programs. In: International Conference on Software Engineering (ICSE), pp. 245–254. ACM (2010)
25. Savage, S., Burrows, M., Nelson, G., Sobalvarro, P., Anderson, T.E.: Eraser: a dynamic data race detector for multithreaded programs. ACM Trans. Comput. Syst. **15**(4), 391–411 (1997)
26. Sinha, N., Wang, C.: On interference abstractions. In: Principles of Programming Languages (POPL), pp. 423–434. ACM (2011)
27. Tabaei Befrouei, M., Wang, C., Weissenbacher, G.: Abstraction and mining of traces to explain concurrency bugs. In: Bonakdarpour, B., Smolka, S.A. (eds.) RV 2014. LNCS, vol. 8734, pp. 162–177. Springer, Heidelberg (2014). doi:10.1007/978-3-319-11164-3_14
28. Tip, F.: A survey of program slicing techniques. J. Program. Lang. **3**, 121–189 (1995)
29. Wang, C., Kundu, S., Limaye, R., Ganai, M., Gupta, A.: Symbolic predictive analysis for concurrent programs. Formal Aspects Comput. **23**(6), 781–805 (2011)
30. Xu, M., Bodík, R., Hill, M.D.: A serializability violation detector for shared-memory server programs. In: Programming Language Design and Implementation (PLDI), pp. 1–14. ACM (2005)

An Executable Formalisation of the SPARCv8 Instruction Set Architecture: A Case Study for the LEON3 Processor

Zhe Hou[1(✉)], David Sanan[1], Alwen Tiu[1], Yang Liu[1], and Koh Chuen Hoa[2]

[1] School of Computer Science and Engineering, Nanyang Technological University, Singapore, Singapore
zhe.hou@ntu.edu.sg
[2] Singapore DSO, Singapore, Singapore

Abstract. The SPARCv8 instruction set architecture (ISA) has been used in various processors for workstations, embedded systems, and space missions. However, there are no publicly available formal models for the SPARCv8 ISA. In this work, we give the first formal model for the integer unit of SPARCv8 ISA in Isabelle/HOL. We capture the operational semantics of the instructions using monadic definitions. Our model is a detailed model, which covers many features specific to SPARC processors, such as delayed-write for control registers, windowed general registers, and more complex memory access. Our model is also general, as we retain an abstract layer of the model which allows it to be instantiated to support all SPARCv8 compliant processors. We extract executable code from our formalisation, giving us the first systematically verified executable semantics for the SPARCv8 ISA. We have tested our model extensively against a LEON3 simulation board, covering both single-step executions and sequential execution of programs. We prove some important properties for our formal model, including a non-interference property for the LEON3 processor.

1 Introduction

Formal models of instruction set architectures (ISAs) not only provide a rigorous understanding of the semantics for instructions, but also are useful in verifying low-level programs such as hardware drivers, virtual machines, compilers, etc. Defining an ISA model in a theorem prover opens up the possibility to reason about properties and semantics of the ISA and machine code. For an extensively developed application of an ARMv7 formal model, see Khakpour et al.'s work on verifying non-interference at the ISA level [20]. There have been various publicly available formal models for ISAs in the literature, e.g., for ARM6 [14], ARMv7 [17], x86 [25]. However, to the best of our knowledge, there are no formalisations of the SPARC family architectures.

The SPARC architecture has many important applications. For instance, SPARC was commonly used in Sun Oracle station in 2010 when it was acquired by Oracle. Oracle then launched many SPARC based servers, such as Sun Blade

J. Fitzgerald et al. (Eds.): FM 2016, LNCS 9995, pp. 388–405, 2016.
DOI: 10.1007/978-3-319-48989-6_24

Servers and Sun Netra Carried-Grade Servers [13]. SPARC is also used in supercomputers. Fujitsu's K computer [2], ranked NO.1 in TOP500 2011, combined 88,128 SPARC CPUs. Tianhe-2 [8], ranked NO.1 in TOP500 2014, has a number of components with SPARC based processors. Most importantly, SPARC is widely used in defense, aviation systems, and space missions. ESA chose to use SPARCv8, mainly because SPARC is one of the few fully open ISAs (other than RISC-V [5] etc.), and has significant support. ESA then started the LEON project to develop processors for space projects [1].

This work is a part of a research project called Security, which aims to verify an execution stack ranging from CPU, micro-kernel, libraries to applications. We use a multi-layer verification approach where we formalize each layer separately and use a refinement-based approach to show that important properties proved at the top level are preserved at the lower levels. One such property is a non-interference property between different partitions in a micro-kernel. We have recently completed a formalization of the high-level specification of a separation micro-kernel [27], and the idea is to show that the implementation of such a micro-kernel preserves the non-interference property, both at the software and the hardware level. As a concrete case study, we choose to formalize the XtratuM [9] micro-kernel that runs on top of the multi-core LEON3 processor; these formalization efforts are still on-going. The ISA formalisation described in this paper is a key component bridging these two formalizations. Our choice of XtratuM and LEON3 is mainly driven by the fact that they are open source and that our intended applications will be built on these platforms. Our model can be instantiated to LEON2 and LEON4, we do not use the latter because its source code is not available. Since our goal is to support the verification of XtratuM machine code, we currently focus on formalizing the integer unit (IU) of SPARCv8, which contains all the instructions used in XtratuM.

This paper presents the first detailed Isabelle/HOL model for the IU in the SPARCv8 ISA. Although there are formal models for other ISAs in the literature (e.g., [14,25]), the difference in architecture and several special features of SPARC make the adaptation of existing models to our work challenging. For example, the register model in SPARCv8 is not a flat 32-register model, but instead consists of a set of overlapping register windows arranged in a circular buffer. There are flags such as `annul` that may cause instructions to be skipped [13]. Memory access in SPARCv8 requires an additional parameter, i.e., the address space identifier (ASI), that specifies whether the processor is in supervisor or user mode, and whether the memory access is data access. Finally, the write control register instructions may be delayed, thus we have to devise a mechanism to perform delayed executions. A similar feature appears in the MIPS architecture, which is modeled in L3 [3].

Our model covers the following aspects of IU: control registers, system registers, and general registers; operations on registers (e.g., RDPSR, WRPSR, etc.); a strong consistency memory model with treatments for address spaces; a simple cache model with write-through policy; flags such as `annul`, signals such as `execute_mode` and `error_mode`; and a trap (exception and interruption) model with all the trap table assignments. We also model store barrier and flush. Except for hardware signals and interrupts, we have captured all the details of the IU defined in Appendix C of the SPARCv8 manual [7]. We also provide a memory management unit (MMU) model to support multi-core micro-kernel verification. Although our model does not cover the co-processor unit and the float-point unit, they can be added to our model using the same methodology.

Our main contributions are: (1) We give a formal model for the IU of SPARCv8 ISA. (2) Our model can be exported to OCaml code for both single step execution and sequential execution. (3) Our model has been extensively tested against a LEON3 simulation board through more than 100,000 instruction instances. (4) To demonstrate the applicability of our model, we first prove a correctness property which ensures that the execution of an instruction will not result in failure when the pre-state satisfies a well-formedness condition. We also show a security property: if the pre-state meets certain conditions, then the privilege will not be lifted during the execution. Finally, we show a non-interference property for the LEON3 processor: given two user-mode states which have the same low privilege resources, after a series of user-mode execution, the low privilege resources in the two resultant states are still equivalent. That is, the difference in high privilege data does not affect low privilege execution.

The complete source code of our formalization of SPARCv8 ISA and the simulator extracted from our formal model can be found at the Securify project website [6].

Related Work. Santoro et al. [24] gave an executable specification for the SPARCv9 architecture with Rapide. However, their model is not built in a theorem proving, thus it is not suitable for formal verification purposes. Fox studied verification of the ARM6 micro-architecture at the RTL level [14]. Fox and Myreen later gave more detailed models for ARM ISAs ranging from version 4 to version 7. Their model for ARMv7 uses monadic specifications and covers details from instruction decoding to operational semantics in the architecture [17]. Their ARMv7 model is the closest work to ours and it provides a good methodological direction for formalising an ISA and validating the model. Fox et al. then started a project to specify various ISAs using a specification language called L3 [3,15]. Fox recently developed a framework for formal verification of ISAs [16]. The framework consists of the L3 language for modelling ISAs, Standard ML for efficient emulation, and HOL4 for formal reasoning. On validation, we mainly test our model using randomly generated instructions. This is a standard method used in [11,17]. There are also formal models for the x86 architecture, such as Sarkar et al.'s work on the semantics of x86-CC machine code [25]. Another interesting work is the ACL2 ISA models [18]. Similarly to our work, the ACL2 ISA models define instruction semantic functions over states and provide functions for executing the model for one instruction or sequentially. A difference is that the ACL2 models are more general whereas our model is more specific and detailed for SPARCv8. The advantage of using ACL2 is that ACL2 naturally supports fast evaluation. The Compcert project gave a formally verified compiler for PowerPC, ARM, and IA32 processors [21,22]. A

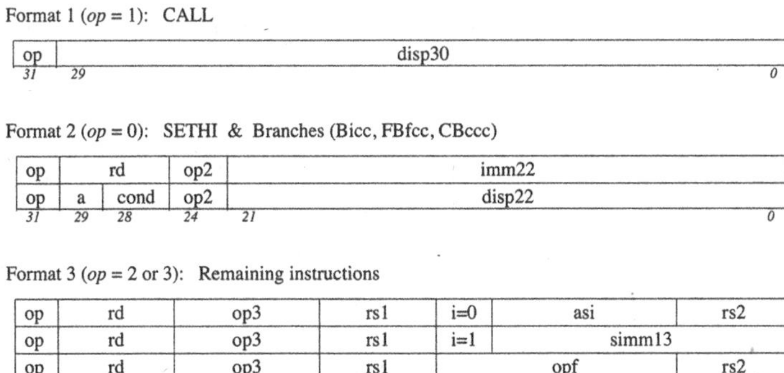

Fig. 1. The formats for SPARCv8 instructions. Source: [7].

remotely related work is Liu and Moore's executable JVM model M6 [23], which is written in a subset of Common Lisp and allows for analytical reasoning as well as simulation. Finally, the JVM specification given by Atkey [10] inspired us to define the model in a proof assistant which supports code export for execution.

2 Background

This section introduces the necessary background of the SPARCv8 architecture and the monadic modeling approach.

2.1 Overview of SPARCv8 ISA

The IU of SPARCv8 contains 40 to 520 general-purpose registers depending on the implementation. The IU also controls the overall operation of the processor, thus it is a major part of the processor. All SPARCv8 instructions are 32-bit wide. Instructions in the IU fall into four categories: (1) load/store; (2) arithmetic/logical/shift; (3) control transfer; (4) read/write control register. There are only three instruction formats, shown in Fig. 1. The load and store instructions are the only instructions that access memory. SPARC only has two addressing modes: a memory address is given by either two registers or a register and a signed 13-bit immediate value. Most instructions operate on two registers, and write the result in the third register. Traps are vectored through a table, and cause an allocation of a fresh register window in the register file. The main special features of SPARCv8 are highlighted below.

Windowed Registers. Unlike other architectures, the general purpose registers in SPARC are grouped in overlapping windows. This design allows for straightforward, high-performance compilers and a significant reduction in memory load/store instructions over other RISCs [7]. A *window* contains 8 *in* registers, 8 *local* registers, and 8 *out* registers. At a given time, an instruction can access 8 *global*

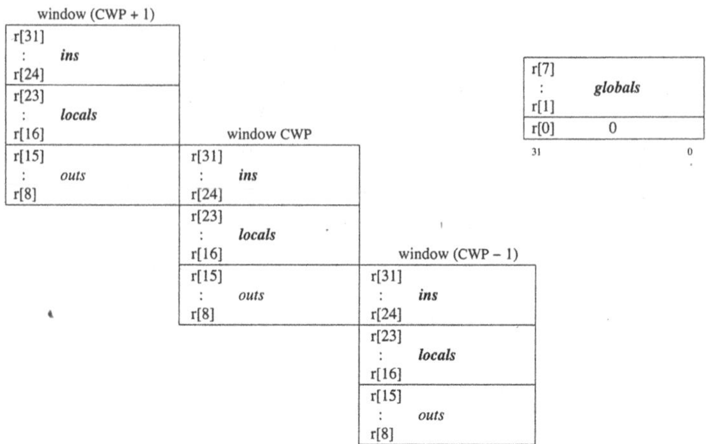

Fig. 2. Three overlapping windowed registers and the global registers. Source: [7].

registers and the 24 register in the current window. The *in* registers of the current window are the *out* registers of the next window; the *out* registers of the current window are the *in* registers of the previous window. This is visualised in Fig. 2. The windows are arranged in a circular buffer, where the last window's *out registers* overlaps with the first window's *in* registers. The current window of registers is determined by a segment in the processor state register (PSR). The Window Invalid Mask (WIM) register keeps a bit map that contains information about which windows are currently invalid.

Address Space Identifier. The memory model in SPARCv8 contains a linear 32-bit address space. When the IU accesses memory, it appends to the address an address space identifier (ASI), which encodes whether the processor is in supervisor or user mode and whether the access is to instruction memory or to data memory, among others. The ASI is also used to access device registers and perform certain operations on devices. The SPARC architecture defines 4 of the 256 address spaces: user instruction, user data, supervisor instruction, and supervisor data [7].

Delayed-write. Besides the general registers, there are also control registers such as the PSR. The write instructions for control registers are delayed-write instructions. That is, "they may take until completion of the third instruction following the write instruction to consummate their write operation. The number of delay instructions (0 to 3) is implementation-dependent" [7].

Signals. There are some signals either from instructions or from hardware that play important roles in the execution of instructions. For example, SPARC, like other RISC ISAs, features delayed control transfer instructions. When a delayed (conditional) jump instruction is executed, the jump is not effected immediately.

Rather, the next instruction (also referred to as the delay slot) will be executed before the control transfer to the jump location is done. However, the delayed control transfer instructions in SPARC may contain an annul bit that signals that the instruction in the delay slot is to be skipped. We thus need to keep track of such information in the state and use it to determine whether certain instructions are to be skipped or not.

2.2 Monads in Operational Semantics

As with the ARMv7 formalisation [17], we use sequential monads to define operations in the ISA. A monad is an abstract data type that represents computations. Our Isabelle monad library is a modified version of the one used in NICTA's seL4 project [12]. Instead of using non-deterministic monads in [12], here we use deterministic monads (cf. Sect. 4 for reasons) defined as below, where `M` is a shorthand for `det_monad`.

```
type_synonym ('s,'a) M ="'s ⇒ ('a ×'s) × bool"
```

which returns a pair `('a × 's)` of the result and the next state, and also a failure flag. A 'true' value in the failure flag denotes failure of execution, whereas a 'false' value denotes a successful execution. We use the following operations on monads:

```
return: 'a ⇒ ('s, 'a) M
fail: 'a ⇒ ('s, 'a) M
bind: ('s, 'a) M ⇒ ('a ⇒ ('s, 'b) M) ⇒ ('s, 'b) M
gets: ('s ⇒ 'a) ⇒ ('s, 'a) M
modify: ('s ⇒ 's) ⇒ ('s, unit) M
```

The operation `return` x does not fail, does not change the state, and returns x. The operation `fail` sets the failure flag to true. We often use semicolon in Isabelle code for `bind`, which composes computations. The `gets` operation applies a function to the current state and returns the result without changing the state. The `modify` operation changes the current state using the function passed in. The code segment for monad operations is in a `do` $\cdots$ `od` block.

3 Isabelle/HOL Specification for the SPARCv8 ISA

This section discusses the outline of our SPARCv8 ISA model. We first introduce our definition of a state, and discuss how various special features of SPARCv8 described in the previous section can be accommodated in the components of the state. We then give an example to show how an instruction is modelled. The official descriptions of SPARCv8 are sometimes semi-formal. Many details, such as memory access and cache flush, are not described at all. Thus we can only formalise those operations based on our understanding. In Sect. 5 we discuss how our formal model is validated against an actual implementation of SPARCv8, i.e., the LEON3 processor.

The core of a monadic specification is the notion of a state. Monad operations transform a state into another. The state in our SPARCv8 model is defined as:

```
record ('a) sparc_state =
cpu_reg:: cpu_context              user_reg:: "('a) user_context"
sys_reg:: sys_context              mem:: mem_context
mmu:: MMU_state                    cache:: cpu_cache
dwrite:: delayed_write_pool        state_var:: sparc_state_var
traps:: "Trap set"                 undef:: bool
```

In general, we deal with implementation-dependent aspects of the ISA by parameterising them as variables in the model. For example, the parameter 'a indicates the number of windows for general registers. The cpu_reg are the control registers; user_reg are general registers; sys_reg are implementation-dependent system registers; followed by memory, MMU, and cache. Delayed write pool is a list of delayed write control register instructions. The state also includes necessary signals and state variables in state_var, which contains the annul bit, indicators of execute_mode, reset_mode, error_mode of the processor, among others. The state also records a set of traps (exceptions and interrupts) that may occur during execution, although in SPARCv8, there should not be more than one trap at any given time. The last member of the state is a failure flag.

The type user_context models windowed registers and is defined as follows:

```
type_synonym window_context = "user_reg_type ⇒ reg_type"
type_synonym ('a) window_size = "'a word"
type_synonym ('a) user_context = "('a) window_size ⇒ window_
    context"
```

where user_reg_type is a 5-bit word, reg_type is a 32-bit word. Our model guarantees that the global register $r[0]$ is always 0; the content of *in* registers of window n is synchronised with the content of *out* registers of window $n+1$; and the content of *out* registers of window n is synchronised with the content of *in* registers of window $n-1$. In particular, let NWINDOWS be the maximum number of windows, the *in* registers of window NWINDOWS -1 are the same as *out* registers of window 0; *out* registers of window 0 are the same as *in* registers of window NWINDOWS -1.

The SPARCv8 manual does not specify how exactly memory access functions operate, it only provides interfaces for memory read and write, both of which require a memory address and an ASI as input. Accordingly, we define memory access as

```
type_synonym mem_context = "asi_type ⇒ phys_address ⇒ mem_val_
    type option"
```

where phys_address is a 36-bit word physical address and mem_val_type is an 8-bit word, the length of ASI is fixed in SPARCv8 as an 8-bit word. Our model is an extension of the traditional memory access method which is usually defined as a partial function from addresses to values.

The MMU_state contains all the MMU registers which are used when the MMU translates a 36-bit physical address to a 32-bit virtual address by looking up three levels of Page Table Descriptors. The MMU also decides whether a page is accessible in a state or not by checking the Page Table Entry flags against the ASI. If the MMU is turned off, the virtual address is simply translated by appending two 0s in the beginning. Our MMU model conforms with the SPARCv8 reference MMU model (Appendix H, [7]).

We do not give a detailed discussion of the cache model here because it does not play an important role at the ISA level. We model it only to give information about whether the caches are empty or not, which is useful in higher level verification such as reasoning about memory context switch.

To model the delayed-write instructions, we define the following list type:

```
type_synonym delayed_write_pool = "(int × reg_type × CPU_
    register) list"
```

where `int` is the delay, i.e., the number of instructions to wait. This number is reduced by 1 in every instruction execution. When the number becomes 0, the 32-bit word `reg_type` is written into the control register `CPU_register`. For a write control register instruction, we add a delayed-write in the `delayed_write_pool` list where the delay is implementation-dependent. If the delay is 0, the value is written to the control register immediately without modifying the pool.

We then define a `sparc_state_monad` as a pair of a `sparc_state` and the result `'e` of the monad:

```
type_synonym ('a,'e) sparc_state_monad = "(('a) sparc_state,'e)
    det_monad"
```

Our definition of instructions has the interface

```
"('b) instruction ⇒ ('a,unit) sparc_state_monad"
```

where `"('b) instruction"` is a data type consisting of the name of the instruction and all its parameters such as registers, immediates etc.

Example Specification. We show an example of one of the simplest instruction formalisations here. The SETHI instruction is defined in SPARCv8 manual as below [7]:

```
if (rd ≠ 0) then (r[rd]<31:10> ← imm22;r[rd]<9:0> ← 0)
```

Our corresponding formalisation is given below.

```
sethi_instr instr ≡
let op_list = snd instr;
  imm22 = get_operand_w22 (op_list!0);
  rd = get_operand_w5 (op_list!1) in
if rd ≠ 0 then do
  curr_win ← get_curr_win();
  write_reg (((ucast(imm22))::word32) << 10) curr_win rd;
  return () od
else return ()
```

We first get the parameter `imm22` for this instruction from `op_list`, which is obtained from the decoding of the instruction. To write a value into a general register, we need to get the current window, as is done by the function get_curr_win. In the SPARCv8 manual, imm22 is written to the bits 31 to 10 (inclusive) of rd, and the bits 9 to 0 are 0s. In our formalisation, we first convert the 22-bit word imm22 to a 32-bit word, then we shift the lower 22 bits to the left for 10 bits, leaving the lower 10 bits as 0s. Finally, this value is written to the register by the function write_reg, which is defined as:

```
write_reg w win ur ≡ do
  modify (λs.(user_reg_mod w win ur s));
  return () od
```

Note that the state is only changed by the modify operation. We omit details of other definitions such as user_reg_mod, which are available in the full formalization in [6].

4 Model Execution

When executing our model, we first need to instantiate it to a particular SPARCv8 compliant processor. The LEON3 processor core [4] is a synthesisable VHDL model of a 32-bit processor compliant with the SPARCv8 ISA [7]. Its full source code is available under the GNU GPL license. We use LEON3 as a running example for our SPARCv8 model. We discuss both the execution of a single instruction and sequential composition of multiple instructions.

Exporting formal models to executable code. Before we discuss the operational semantics of instruction execution, we discuss briefly how we export our formal model into the executable code so that one can simulate instruction execution more efficiently. There has been work on exporting a formal model into executable code, e.g., [10]. However, there are various restrictions in Isabelle's code export feature; much care is required to ensure that the code can be exported. For example, Isabelle2015 cannot export a function that returns a set of functions. Consider the following example:

```
definition f:: "int ⇒ (int ⇒ int) set" where "f i ≡ {λx. x}"
```

This is a legitimate definition, but the Isabelle command value "f 1", which exports the code to ML and executes it, gives an error. The original NICTA library for monad defines non-deterministic monads as below.

```
type_synonym ('s,'a) nondet_monad = "'s ⇒ ('a ×'s) set × bool"
```

When we use non-deterministic monad, instruction definitions return "('a,unit) sparc_state_monad", which is equal to "('a,'d) sparc_state ⇒ (unit × ('a,'d) sparc_state) set ×bool", which contains a set. The error occurs because sparc_state is a tuple containing functions with infinite domains. Since instruction semantics are deterministic and we do not model concurrent behaviours at the ISA level, we decide to modify the NICTA monad library to handle deterministic monads, which avoid the errors.

Single Step Execution. An execution cycle in our model includes the following operations (page 158 of [7]): (1) If there is a trap, execute the trap and skip the following. (2) Execute delayed-writes. (3) Fetch and decode instruction. (4) If the annul signal is false, dispatch and execute the instruction. Then, if the instruction is not a control transfer instruction, increment program counter (PC) and next program counter (nPC) by 4. (5) If the annul signal is true, make it false, and skip this instruction.

Recall that the failure flag True in our monad means failure and False means no failure. We define a next state function as below:

```
"NEXT s ≡ case execute_instruction() s of (_,True) ⇒ None
  | (s',False) ⇒ Some (snd s')"
```

We need to provide some implementation-dependent details that are not specified in the SPARCv8 model, such as the maximum number of register windows. For the LEON3 processor, we set `NWINDOWS = 8` and `DELAYNUM = 0`, and instantiate the parameter `('a)` in the definition of the state to a 5-bit word:

```
type_synonym leon3_state = "(word_length5) sparc_state"
```

Finally, we need to initialise the environment, which includes PC, nPC etc., certain general registers and memory addresses that will be used in the instruction. These details will not be elaborated here, but are available from [6].

Sequential Execution. We define sequential execution as follows:

```
function (sequential) SEQ:: "nat ⇒ ('a) sparc_state ⇒ ('a) sparc_
    state option" where "SEQ 0 s = Some s"
|"SEQ n s = (case SEQ (n-1) s of None ⇒ None | Some t ⇒ NEXT t)"
```

Preparing the environment for sequential execution requires initialising control registers and all the general registers and memory addresses involved in the sequence of instructions. We note that details such as updating PC and nPC make sequential execution easier to model and to simulate. A formal ISA model without these details may deviate from the official documentation when modeling sequential execution. Sequential execution can prove useful when analysing and validating programs.

To run large scale code such as the XtratuM hypervisor, we need to initialise the memory in our model to be consistent with real LEON3 hardware. XtratuM may assume certain values at specific memory addresses for peripheral devices etc. Performance-wise, we are able to execute an instruction in 0.005s on an Intel Xeon E5-1620 v2 CPU using a single core. Optimisation and execution of large code are left as future work.

5 Validation

To gain confidence that our formal model is correct, we validate our formal model against an actual implementation of SPARCv8 ISA, as described next. In the sequel, we use the OCaml version of our model extracted by the previous section. Isabelle can also generate other functional language code, but performance differences for other languages is beyond the scope of this paper.

5.1 Random Single Instruction Testing

Validating the formal model against real hardware by running single step instruction executions is a standard and systematic solution in the literature, cf. [17,25], to gain confidence that the formal model captures the behaviour of the actual hardware it intends to model. We use a Xilinx Virtex-7 FPGA VC707 Evaluation Kit to run the official LEON3 simulator. We use the LEON3/GRLIB source code to generate bitstream code for LEON3 single core, duo core, and quad code processors. We use GRMON 2 to test the execution of instructions on those LEON3 processors.[1]

We have developed a tool to generate random instructions with random input and pre-states for our model. We have also written a tool to prepare the same pre-state for the LEON3 simulator, run the tests on our model and on the LEON3 simulator, and compare the results. We describe the details below.

The randomly generated instruction is checked to make sure it is a valid encoding. We then analyse the instruction instance and determine which memory addresses are involved. Our generator ensures that the majority of memory addresses are well-aligned. To initialise the pre-state, we generate random 32-bit values for the general registers in the current window and random 8-bit values for the involved memory addresses. Furthermore, we generate random flags such as the icc bits of PSR. The value of PC is 0 x 40000000, the values of other control registers are 0s. Since one of the intended applications of our formalisation is to reason about security properties, we also generate various tests to test integer overflow and underflow which may lead to security vulnerabilities in applications. Such tests are important to make sure that our model does not abstract away integer operations to their ideal mathematical counterparts and would thus miss potential vulnerabilities caused by integer overflow/underflow.

We then generate the GRMON 2 commands for the LEON3 simulator. The GRMON 2 commands initialise the pre-state of the LEON3 simulator to be the same as the pre-state of our model. This includes the instruction to be executed.

Our validation tool executes both our model and the LEON3 simulator, and compares the post-state. Given an instruction instance, we only examine the registers and memory addresses involved in it. The other elements in the state are not important for the validation against LEON3. For example, `delayed_write_pool` is always empty. Trap set and `error_mode` etc. will cause exceptions and the result can be observed by the validator. The side effect of control transfer instructions (modifying the annul flag) can be checked by examining PC and nPC. The side effects of arithmetic instructions can be checked by examining PSR. Note that some of these cannot be examined in the official

[1] We thank Charles Zhang for his help with our experiment setup.

Table 1. Programs tested in sequential execution.

Program	Number of instructions	Time (in sec)
Addition	12	0.033
Multiplication	12	0.033
Swap two variables	14	0.041
Add the digits in a number	107	0.361
Reverse the digits in a number	116	0.339
Find the maximum number in an array	122	0.394
Greatest common divisor & least common multiple	122	0.238
Fibonacci series	141	0.468
Bubble sort	432	1.361

GRMON tool. The tested instructions should not have other side effects which may cause bugs in our model.

Our random testing has a large coverage. We test instructions in single core, duo core, and quad core LEON3 processors; and we test in both supervisor mode and user mode. Similarly to the validation of the ARMv7 model [17], we cannot fully test implementation-dependent system features. Our validation has tested more than 100k instruction instances, and still counting. We believe our validation has been thorough and efficient; this increases our confidence of the accuracy of our model.

5.2 Program Execution Testing

We choose C programs that range from toy examples to non-trivial functions, covering a wide range of operations that involve most of the instructions in the IU. The programs are cross-compiled to obtain SPARC executables, from which we extract the machine code for execution. As there may be loops in the programs and it is hard to anticipate how many steps to be executed, we run the machine code on our model until we have an `instruction_access_exception` trap, which indicates that the program is finished and the next instruction is not initialised.

The tested programs are given in Table 1. The second column of Table 1 shows the number of instructions executed, the third column gives the run time in our Isabelle model. The number of instructions executed may vary depending on the input. We run these programs with arrays of length 5 for illustration. When the execution of these programs is terminated, we examine the memory addresses for the variables and arrays. Our Isabelle model gives the same result as the LEON3 simulation board on all these programs for various input.

5.3 Limitations and Implementation-Dependent Specifications for LEON3

We summarize some lessons learned from our experiment on the LEON3 board here.

According to the GRMON 2 tool, LEON3 does not implement delay write for control register instructions. Instructions such as WRPSR, WRWIM, WRY, WRTBR write the value into the register immediately. LEON3 implements 8 windows for general registers, while our SPARCv8 model supports up to 32 windows.

We approximate the LEON3 memory access behaviours by testing memory access with various ASI values: 8 (user instruction), 9 (supervisor instruction), 10 (user data), and 11 (supervisor data) on the simulation board. We observe the following facts: (1) Writing value v to ASI 11 of address x, then reading from x in ASI 10 gives the same value v. (2) Writing v to ASI 11 of address x, then reading from x in ASI 8 gives a different value from v. (3) In both user mode and supervisor mode, reading memory with ASI 8,9,10 or 11 all work. (4) In user mode, writing to memory with ASI 11 raises a trap. (5) In user mode, writing to memory with ASI 10 will override the data at the same address in ASI 11. All the above tests assume that the MMU is turned off. If the MMU is turned on, then the accessibility depends on the MMU setup.

We noticed an unexpected behaviour: even in supervisor mode, writing to memory with ASI 8 or 9 does not seem to have any effect. The execution does not raise a trap, neither does it change the value at the involved addresses. This is possibly because the hardware defines the instruction memory space to be a segment of addresses we did not test. For this reason, we have only tested load/store instructions with ASI 10 and 11 in the random testing. We have enriched our SPARCv8 model with the above behaviours specific to the LEON3 processor for testing purposes. Hence our model gives the same result as the LEON3 simulation board when accessing memory in the above cases.

Due to hardware limitations, each SPARCv8 processor only accepts specific values for PSR, while our model is more general and it does not specify such details. Thus writing an arbitrary value into PSR may lead to different results in our model and in the LEON3 processor. This is not considered an error during testing. Another hardware limitation is that each board only supports a limited amount of memory, thus accessing random memory addresses may have different outcomes in our model and in the LEON3 simulator. As a result, we mainly test memory addresses ranging from 0 x 40000000 to 0 x 50000000.

The branching instructions sometimes give different results of PC and nPC when the instruction sets the "annul" bit to 1. Closer inspection reveals that the "step" command in GRMON2 may have skipped the annulled instruction, whereas our model pauses before the annulled instruction. In this case, manual checks against the SPARCv8 manual confirm that our model is correct.

6 Formal Verification of Security Properties

In this section we prove an important security property, namely non-interference for the LEON3 processor.

6.1 Single Step Theorem

We first show that when a state satisfies a condition called `good_context`, a single step execution from the state does not result in a failure. The execution of an instruction may generate traps, but not all traps are considered failure. A normal trap, i.e., exception or interruption, causes the CPU to run the trap handling functions, and is not considered a failure. A failure happens only in a special situation where a trap is raised and the CPU goes to `error_mode` and awaits to be reset. The rather involved condition `good_context` is crafted to avoid failure in execution. Interested readers are referred to the source code [6] for details. We then show a single step theorem as below:

```
theorem single_step:"good_context s ⟹ NEXT s =
  Some (snd (fst (execute_instruction() s)))"
```

The proof covers each instruction and shows that the monad never returns a failure if `good_context` holds; the latter is thus a good standard for verifying if a pre-state is "sensible" or not.

6.2 Privilege Safety Theorem

Next we show that a successful one step execution in user mode does not lift the privilege to supervisor mode.

```
theorem privilege_safety:
assumes "get_delayed_pool s = [] ∧ get_trap_set s = {} ∧
  snd (execute_instruction() s) = False ∧
  s' = snd (fst (execute_instruction() s)) ∧
  ((ucast (get_S (cpu_reg_val PSR s)))::word1) = 0"
shows "((ucast (get_S (cpu_regval PSR s')))::word1) = 0"
```

We assume that the delayed-write pool is empty since the LEON3 processor has no delayed write. We also assume that there are no traps to be executed. If there is a trap, the instruction will not be executed, the processor will go to supervisor mode and execute the trap instead. The third conjunct in the assumption says `execute_instruction` does not return a failure, the fourth conjunct says `s'` is the post-state, the last conjunct says the S bit in the pre-state `s` is 0 (i.e., `s` is in user mode). We show that the S bit in the post-state `s'` is also 0. This proof is a case analysis for each instruction and it checks that the execution mode is not modified.

6.3 Non-interference Theorem

Non-interference is an essential requirement for security. It allows user applications or virtual machines to co-exist without violating confidentiality, and it can save costly hardware which is otherwise needed to provide physical separation of data [20]. When MMU is enabled, non-interference also provides an isolation between users in different processes. That is, the high privilege resource in our setting may refer to the resource of other user processes that the current user does not have access to. This is particularly important in our project since we are interested in verifying properties for a multi-core hypervisor. Traditionally, non-interference for a deterministic program states that when a low privilege user is working on the machine, it will execute in the same manner regardless of the change of high privilege data [26]. At the ISA level, this is similar to the non-infiltration property à la Khakpour et al. [20]. Here we first show that non-interference is preserved in single step executions.

```
theorem non_interference_step:
assumes "((ucast (get_S (cpu_reg_val PSR s1)))::word1) = 0
good_context s1 ∧ good_context s2 ∧ low_equal s1 s2 ∧
get_delayed_pool s1 = [] ∧ get_trap_set s1 = {} ∧
((ucast (get_S (cpu_reg_val PSR s2)))::word1) = 0 ∧
get_delayed_pool s2 = [] ∧ get_trap_set s2 = {}"
shows "∃ t1 t2. Some t1 = NEXT s1 ∧ Some t2 = NEXT s2 ∧
((ucast (get_S (cpu_reg_val PSR t1)))::word1) = 0 ∧
((ucast (get_S (cpu_reg_val PSR t2)))::word1) = 0 ∧
low_equal t1 t2"
```

We assume that the two pre-states `s1` and `s2` are both in user mode, they satisfy `good_context`, they have no delayed writes and traps. We further assume that `s1` and `s2` are equivalent on low privilege resources. We show that the next states `t1`, `t2` must exist, they are both in user mode, and they are still equivalent on low privilege resources. The predicate `low_equal` is defined as:

```
low_equal s1 s2 ≡
(cpu_reg s1) = (cpu_reg s2) ∧ (user_reg s1) = (user_reg s2) ∧
(sys_reg s1) = (sys_reg s2) ∧ (∀ va. (virt_to_phys va (mmu s1)
(mem s1)) = (virt_to_phys va (mmu s2) (mem s2))) ∧
(∀ pa. (user_accessible s1 pa) → mem_equal s1 s2 pa) ∧
(mmu s1) = (mmu s2) ∧ (state_var s1) = (state_var s2) ∧
(traps s1) = (traps s2) ∧ (undef s1) = (undef s2)
```

Similarly to Khakpour et al.'s definition, our low-equivalence assumes that the two user mode states agree on the resources that may influence the user mode execution, but we assume no knowledge about other resources. Here, `user_accessible` means that the physical address `pa` is accessible in state `s1`. Since we assume that `s1` and `s2` have the same MMU setup (including the virtual to physical address translation `virt_to_phys`), `pa` is also accessible in `s2`. `mem_equal` states that the block of addresses where `pa` belongs to have the same content in `s1` and `s2`. A memory block is a group of four continuous addresses in which the first address ends with two 0s.

From the Single Step Theorem, we obtain that the one step execution from s1 and s2 will not result in failure, that is, t1 and t2 must exist. From the Safety Privilege Theorem, we know that t1 and t2 must be in user mode. The reminder of the proof for the Non-interference Step Theorem is a case analysis for each instruction and we examine that after the execution the predicate low_equal holds for t1 and t2.

Finally, we show that for any sequence of user mode execution, if the initial states s1 and s2 are equivalent on low privilege resources, then the final states t1 and t2 are also equivalent on low privilege resources.

```
theorem non_interference: assumes
"((ucast (get_S (cpu_reg_val PSR s1)))::word1) = 0 ∧
good_context s1 ∧ good_context s2 ∧ low_equal s1 s2 ∧
get_delayed_pool s1 = [] ∧ get_trap_set s1 = {} ∧
((ucast (get_S (cpu_reg_val PSR s2)))::word1) = 0 ∧
get_delayed_pool s2 = [] ∧ get_trap_set s2 = {} ∧
user_seq_exe n s1 ∧ user_seq_exe n s2"
shows "(∃ t1 t2. Some t1 = SEQ n s1 ∧ Some t2 = SEQ n s2 ∧
  ((ucast (get_S (cpu_reg_val PSR t1)))::word1) = 0 ∧
  ((ucast (get_S (cpu_reg_val PSR t2)))::word1) = 0 ∧
  low_equal t1 t2)"
```

Here, user_seq_exe simply assumes that every intermediate state has no traps and no delayed write instructions; these are necessary to ensure that the sequence of execution is in user mode. This proof is a simple induction on n using the Non-interference Step Theorem. The proof script of the theorems in this section measures over 7500 lines due to the large number of cases to be considered. The main difficulty is in checking that the store instructions preserve low_equal. This section demonstrates that we can prove interesting and non-trivial properties for SPARCv8 and LEON3 using our formalisation.

7 Conclusion

This paper describes the first formal model of the SPARCv8 ISA. Our formalisation has over 5000 lines of Isabelle code, not including the proofs. The model can be specialised to any SPARCv8 processor, and it contains many features specific to the SPARCv8 architecture. Our model is carefully designed to take advantage of the Isabelle code export functionality, through which we obtain executable code from our formal model.

We have validated our model against an official LEON3 simulator on more than 100k random instruction instances as well as real life programs. We believe our formalisation provides a solid foundation for future verification problems. To illustrate the applicability of our model, we have shown a non-interference property for the LEON3 processor. This property guarantees that user mode execution is independent of high privilege resources which the user has no access to.

With regard to machine code verification using our formal model, there are two possible angles in future work. First, although the provided operational semantics and the single step execution allow us to verify properties using Isabelle/HOL, automated reasoning about properties of machine code requires much work. Obtaining a functional representation of the SPARCv8 machine code in Isabelle/HOL from the semantics introduced in this work, in a similar fashion to [17], would ease the verification. Second, the memory model in our SPARCv8 formalisation is a strong consistency model, which is not suitable for verifying concurrent execution in modern day multi-core processors. This requires a weaker memory model, e.g., TSO, as well as a proof system for concurrency, such as Rely-Guarantee [19].

References

1. ESA LEON processor. http://www.esa.int/Our_Activities/Space_Engineering_Technology/LEON_the_space_chip_that_Europe_built. Accessed 27 Jan 2016
2. K computer. http://www.top500.org/system/177232. Accessed 27 Jan 2016
3. L3 specification language for ISAs. http://www.cl.cam.ac.uk/~acjf3/l3/. Accessed 09 Dec 2015
4. LEON3 processor. http://www.gaisler.com/index.php/products/processors/leon3. Accessed 27 Oct 2015
5. RISC-V architecture. https://riscv.org/. Accessed 10 Aug 2016
6. Securify: micro-kernel verification. http://securify.scse.ntu.edu.sg/MicroVer/. Accessed 24 May 2016
7. The SPARC architecture manual version 8. http://gaisler.com/doc/sparcv8.pdf. Accessed 27 Oct 2015
8. Tianhe-2. http://top500.org/system/177999. Accessed 27 Jan 2016
9. Xtratum hypervisor. http://www.xtratum.org/. Accessed 29 Jan 2016
10. Atkey, R.: CoqJVM: an executable specification of the java virtual machine using dependent types. In: Miculan, M., Scagnetto, I., Honsell, F. (eds.) TYPES 2007. LNCS, vol. 4941, pp. 18–32. Springer, Heidelberg (2008). doi:10.1007/978-3-540-68103-8_2
11. Campbell, B., Stark, I.: Randomised testing of a microprocessor model using SMT-solver state generation. In: Lang, F., Flammini, F. (eds.) FMICS 2014. LNCS, vol. 8718, pp. 185–199. Springer, Heidelberg (2014). doi:10.1007/978-3-319-10702-8_13
12. Cock, D., Klein, G., Sewell, T.: Secure microkernels, state monads and scalable refinement. In: Mohamed, O.A., Muñoz, C., Tahar, S. (eds.) TPHOLs 2008. LNCS, vol. 5170, pp. 167–182. Springer, Heidelberg (2008). doi:10.1007/978-3-540-71067-7_16
13. El Kady, S., Khater, M., Alhafnawi, M.: MIPS, ARM and SPARC-an architecture comparison. In: Proceedings of the World Congress on Engineering, vol. 1 (2014)
14. Fox, A.: Formal specification and verification of ARM6. In: Basin, D., Wolff, B. (eds.) TPHOLs 2003. LNCS, vol. 2758, pp. 25–40. Springer, Heidelberg (2003). doi:10.1007/10930755_2
15. Fox, A.: Directions in ISA specification. In: Beringer, L., Felty, A. (eds.) ITP 2012. LNCS, vol. 7406, pp. 338–344. Springer, Heidelberg (2012). doi:10.1007/978-3-642-32347-8_23
16. Fox, A.: Improved tool support for machine-code decompilation in HOL4. In: Urban, C., Zhang, X. (eds.) ITP 2015. LNCS, vol. 9236, pp. 187–202. Springer, Heidelberg (2015). doi:10.1007/978-3-319-22102-1_12

17. Fox, A., Myreen, M.O.: A trustworthy monadic formalization of the ARMv7 instruction set architecture. In: Kaufmann, M., Paulson, L.C. (eds.) ITP 2010. LNCS, vol. 6172, pp. 243–258. Springer, Heidelberg (2010). doi:10.1007/978-3-642-14052-5_18
18. Goel, S., Hunt, W.A., Kaufmann, M.: Abstract stobjs and their application to ISA modeling. In: ACL2 2013, pp. 54–69 (2013)
19. Jones, C.B.: Specification and design of (parallel) programs. In: Proceedings of IFIP 1983, pp. 321–332. North-Holland (1983)
20. Khakpour, N., Schwarz, O., Dam, M.: Machine assisted proof of ARMv7 instruction level isolation properties. In: Gonthier, G., Norrish, M. (eds.) CPP 2013. LNCS, vol. 8307, pp. 276–291. Springer, Heidelberg (2013). doi:10.1007/978-3-319-03545-1_18
21. Leroy, X.: Formal certification of a compiler back-end, or: programming a compiler with a proof assistant. In: Proceedings of the 33rd ACM Symposium on Principles of Programming Languages (2006)
22. Leroy, X.: The CompCert C verified compiler (2015). http://compcert.inria.fr/man/manual.pdf. Accessed 29 Jan 2016
23. Liu, H., Moore, J.S.: Executable JVM model for analytical reasoning: a study. In: Proceedings of the 2003 Workshop on Interpreters, Virtual Machines and Emulators, pp. 15–23. ACM (2003)
24. Santoro, A., Park, W., Luckham, D.: SPARC-V9 architecture specification with Rapide. Technical report, Stanford, CA, USA (1995)
25. Sarkar, S., Sewell, P., Nardelli, F.Z., Owens, S., Ridge, T., Braibant, T., Myreen, M.O., Alglave, J.: The semantics of x86-CC multiprocessor machine code. In: Proceedings of the 36th Annual ACM Symposium on Principles of Programming Languages, pp. 379–391. ACM (2009)
26. Smith, G.: Principles of secure information flow analysis. In: Christodorescu, M., Jha, S., Maughan, D., Song, D., Wang, C. (eds.) Malware Detection. Advances in Information Security, vol. 27, pp. 291–307. Springer, Heidelberg (2007). doi:10.1007/978-0-387-44599-1_13
27. Zhao, Y., Sanán, D., Zhang, F., Liu, Y.: Reasoning about information flow security of separation Kernels with channel-based communication. In: Chechik, M., Raskin, J.-F. (eds.) TACAS 2016. LNCS, vol. 9636, pp. 791–810. Springer, Heidelberg (2016). doi:10.1007/978-3-662-49674-9_50

Hybrid Statistical Estimation of Mutual Information for Quantifying Information Flow

Yusuke Kawamoto[1(✉)], Fabrizio Biondi[2], and Axel Legay[2]

[1] AIST, Tsukuba, Japan
yusuke.kawamoto.aist@gmail.com
[2] Inria, Rennes, France

Abstract. Analysis of a probabilistic system often requires to learn the joint probability distribution of its random variables. The computation of the exact distribution is usually an exhaustive *precise analysis* on all executions of the system. To avoid the high computational cost of such an exhaustive search, *statistical analysis* has been studied to efficiently obtain approximate estimates by analyzing only a small but representative subset of the system's behavior. In this paper we propose a *hybrid statistical estimation method* that combines precise and statistical analyses to estimate mutual information and its confidence interval. We show how to combine the analyses on different components of the system with different precision to obtain an estimate for the whole system. The new method performs weighted statistical analysis with different sample sizes over different components and dynamically finds their optimal sample sizes. Moreover it can reduce sample sizes by using prior knowledge about systems and a new *abstraction-then-sampling* technique based on qualitative analysis. We show the new method outperforms the state of the art in quantifying information leakage.

1 Introduction

In modeling and analyzing software and hardware systems, the statistical approach is often useful to evaluate quantitative aspects of the behaviors of the systems. In particular, probabilistic systems with complicated internal structures can be approximately and efficiently modeled and analyzed. For instance, statistical model checking has widely been used to verify quantitative properties of many kinds of probabilistic systems [40].

The *statistical analysis* of a probabilistic system is usually considered as a black-box testing approach in which the analyst does not require prior knowledge of the internal structure of the system. The analyst runs the system many times and records the execution traces to construct an approximate model of the system. Even when the formal specification or precise model of the system

This work was supported by JSPS KAKENHI Grant Number JP15H06886, by the MSR-Inria Joint Research Center, by the Sensation European grant, and by région Bretagne.

J. Fitzgerald et al. (Eds.): FM 2016, LNCS 9995, pp. 406–425, 2016.
DOI: 10.1007/978-3-319-48989-6_25

is not provided to the analyst, statistical analysis can be directly applied to the system if the analyst can execute the black-box implementation. Due to this random sampling of the systems, statistical analysis provides only approximate estimates. However, it can evaluate the accuracy and error of the analysis for instance by providing the confidence intervals of the estimated values.

One of the important challenges in statistical analysis is to estimate entropy-based properties in probabilistic systems. For example, statistical methods [8,13,19–21] have been studied for *quantitative information flow analysis* [14,22,38], which estimates an entropy-based property to quantify the leakage of confidential information in a system. More specifically, the analysis estimates *mutual information* or other properties between two random variables on the secrets and on the observable outputs in the system to measure the amount of information that is inferable about the secret by observing the output. The main technical difficulties in the estimation of entropy-based properties are

1. to efficiently compute large matrices that represent probability distributions, and
2. to provide a statistical method for correcting the bias of the estimate and computing a confidence interval to evaluate the accuracy of the estimation.

To overcome these difficulties we propose a method for statistically estimating mutual information, one of the most popular entropy-based properties. The new method, called *hybrid statistical estimation method*, integrates black-box statistical analysis and white-box *precise analysis*, exploiting the advantages of both. More specifically, this method employs some prior knowledge on the system and performs precise analysis (e.g., static analysis of the source code or specification) on some components of the system. Since precise analysis computes the exact sub-probability distributions of the components, the hybrid method using precise analysis is more accurate than statistical analysis alone.

Moreover, the new method can combine multiple statistical analyses on different components of the system to improve the accuracy and efficiency of the estimation. This is based on our new theoretical results that extend and generalize previous work [9,13,43] on purely statistical estimation. As far as we know this is the first work on a hybrid method for estimating entropy-based properties and their confidence intervals.

To illustrate the method we propose, Fig. 1 presents an example of a joint probability distribution P_{XY} between two random variables X and Y, built up from 3 overlapping components S_1, S_2 and T. To estimate the full joint distribution P_{XY}, the analyst separately computes the joint sub-distribution for the component T by precise analysis, estimates those for S_1 and S_2 by

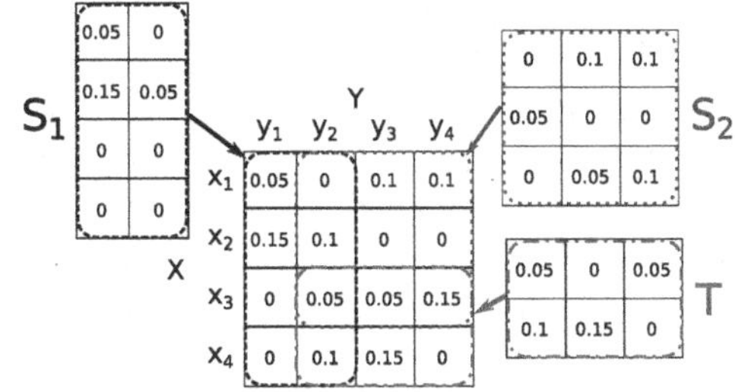

Fig. 1. Joint distribution composed of 3 components.

statistical analysis, and then combines these sub-distributions. Since the statistical analysis is based on the random sampling of execution traces, the empirical sub-distributions for S_1 and S_2 are different from the true ones, while the sub-distribution for T is exact. From these approximate and precise sub-distributions, the proposed method can estimate the mutual information for the entire system and evaluate its accuracy by providing a confidence interval. Owing to the combination of different kinds of analyses (with possibly different parameters such as sample sizes), the computation of the bias and confidence interval of the estimate is more complicated than the previous work on statistical analysis.

1.1 Contributions

The contributions of this paper are as follows:

- We propose a new method, called hybrid statistical estimation, that combines statistical and precise analyses on the estimation of mutual information (which can also be applied to Shannon entropy and conditional Shannon entropy). Specifically, we show theoretical results on compositionally computing the bias and confidence interval of the estimate from multiple statistical and precise analyses;
- We present a weighted statistical analysis method with different sample sizes over different components and a method for adaptively optimizing sample sizes for different components by evaluating the quality and cost of the analysis;
- We show how to reduce the sample sizes by using prior knowledge about systems, including an abstraction-then-sampling technique based on qualitative analysis;
- We show that the proposed method can be applied not only to composed systems but also to the source codes of a single system by decomposing it into components and determine the analysis method for each component;
- We evaluate the quality of the estimation in this method, showing that the estimates are more accurate than statistical analysis alone for the same sample size, and that the new method outperforms the state-of-the-art statistical analysis tool LeakWatch [20];
- We demonstrate the effectiveness of the hybrid method in case studies on the quantification of information leakage.

The rest of the paper is structured as follows. Section 2 introduces background in information theory and quantification of information. We compare precise analysis with statistical analysis for the estimation of mutual information. Section 3 describes the main results of this paper: the hybrid method for mutual information estimation, including the method for optimizing sample sizes for different components. Section 4 presents how to reduce sample sizes by using prior knowledge about systems, including the abstraction-then-sampling technique with qualitative analysis. Section 5 overviews how to decompose the source code of a system into components and to determine the analysis method for each component. Section 6 evaluates the proposed method and illustrates its effectiveness against the state of the art. Section 7 discusses related work and Sect. 8 concludes the paper. All proofs can be found in full version [35] of the paper.

2 Information Theory and Quantification of Information

In this section we introduce some background on information theory, which we use to quantify the amount of information in a system. We write X and Y to denote two random variables, and $\mathcal{X}$ and $\mathcal{Y}$ to denote the sets of all possible values of X and Y, respectively. We denote the number of elements of a set $\mathcal{S}$ by $\#\mathcal{S}$.

2.1 Channels

In information theory, a *channel* models the input-output relation of a system as a conditional probability distribution of outputs given inputs. This model has also been used to formalize information leakage in a system that processes confidential data: *inputs* and *outputs* of a channel are respectively regarded as *secrets* and *observables* in the system and the channel represents relationships between the secrets and observables.

A *discrete channel* is a triple $(\mathcal{X}, \mathcal{Y}, C)$ where $\mathcal{X}$ and $\mathcal{Y}$ are two finite sets of discrete input and output values respectively and C is an $\#\mathcal{X} \times \#\mathcal{Y}$ matrix where each element $C[x, y]$ represents the conditional probability of an output y given an input x; i.e., for each $x \in \mathcal{X}, \sum_{y \in \mathcal{Y}} C[x, y] = 1$ and $0 \leq C[x, y] \leq 1$ for all $y \in \mathcal{Y}$.

A *prior* is a probability distribution on input values $\mathcal{X}$. Given a prior P_X over $\mathcal{X}$ and a channel C from $\mathcal{X}$ to $\mathcal{Y}$, the *joint probability distribution* P_{XY} of X and Y is defined by: $P_{XY}[x, y] = P_X[x]C[x, y]$ for each $x \in \mathcal{X}$ and $y \in \mathcal{Y}$.

2.2 Mutual Information

The amount of information gained about a random variable X by knowing a random variable Y is defined as the difference between the uncertainty about X before and after observing Y. The *mutual information* $I(X; Y)$ between X and Y is one of the most popular measures to quantify the amount of information on X gained/leaked by Y:

$$I(X; Y) = \sum_{x \in \mathcal{X}, y \in \mathcal{Y}} P_{XY}[x, y] \log_2 \left(\frac{P_{XY}[x, y]}{P_X[x] P_Y[y]} \right)$$

where P_Y is the marginal probability distribution defined as $P_Y[y] = \sum_{x \in \mathcal{X}} P_{XY}[x, y]$.

In the security scenario, information-theoretical measures quantify the amount of secret information leaked against some particular attacker: the mutual information between two random variables X on the secrets and Y on the observables in a system measures the information that is inferable about the secret by knowing the observable. In this scenario mutual information, or Shannon leakage, assumes an attacker that can ask binary questions on the secret's value after observing the system while min-entropy leakage [47] considers an attacker that has only one attempt to guess the secret's value.

Mutual information has been employed in many other applications including Bayesian networks [33], telecommunications [31], pattern recognition [28], machine learning [41], quantum physics [49], and biology [1]. In this work we focus on mutual information for the above security scenario.

2.3 Precise Analysis vs. Statistical Analysis

The calculation of the mutual information $I(X;Y)$ between input X and output Y in a probabilistic system requires the computation of the joint probability distribution P_{XY} of X and Y. The joint distribution can be computed precisely or estimated statistically.

Precise Analysis. To obtain the exact joint probability $P_{XY}[x, y]$ for each $x \in \mathcal{X}$ and $y \in \mathcal{Y}$, we sum the probabilities of all execution traces of the system that have input x and output y. This means the computation time depends on the number of traces in the system. If the system has a very large number of traces, it is intractable for analysts to precisely compute the joint distribution and consequently the mutual information.

In [50] the calculation of mutual information is shown to be computationally expensive. This computational difficulty comes from the fact that entropy-based properties are hyperproperties [25] that are defined using all execution traces of the system and therefore cannot be verified on each single trace. For example, when we investigate the leakage of confidential information in a system, it is insufficient to check the information leakage separately for each component of the system, because the attacker may derive sensitive information by combining the outputs of different components. More generally, the computation of entropy-based properties (such as the amount of leaked information) is not compositional in the sense that an entropy-based property of a system is not the (weighted) sum of those of the components.

For this reason it is inherently difficult to naïvely combine analyses of different components of a system to compute entropy-based properties. In fact, previous studies on the compositional approach in quantitative information flow analysis have faced certain difficulties in obtaining useful bounds on information leakage [4,29,36,37].

Statistical Analysis. Due to the complexity of precise analysis, some previous studies have focused on computing approximate values of entropy-based measures. One of the common approaches is the *statistical analysis* based on Monte Carlo methods, in which approximate values are computed from repeated random sampling. Previous work on quantitative information flow has used statistical analysis to mutual information [9,13,43], channel capacity [8,13] and min-entropy leakage [16,20].

In the statistical estimation of mutual information between two random variables X and Y in a probabilistic system, analysts execute the system many times and collect the execution traces each recording a pair of values $(x, y) \in \mathcal{X} \times \mathcal{Y}$.

This set of execution traces is used to estimate the empirical joint distribution $\hat{P}_{XY}$ of X and Y and then to compute the mutual information $I(X;Y)$.

Note that the empirical distribution $\hat{P}_{XY}$ is different from the true distribution P_{XY} and thus the estimated mutual information is different from the true value. In fact, it is known that entropy-based measures such as mutual information and min-entropy leakage have some bias and error that depends on the number of collected traces, the matrix size and other factors. However, results on statistics allow us to correct the bias of the estimate and to compute its 95 % confidence interval. This way we can guarantee the quality of the estimation, which differentiates our approach from *testing*.

Comparing the Two Analysis Methods. The cost of the statistical analysis is proportional to the size $\#\mathcal{X} \times \#\mathcal{Y}$ of the joint distribution matrix (strictly speaking, to the number of non-zero elements in the matrix). Therefore, this method is significantly more efficient than precise analysis if the matrix is relatively small and the number of all traces is very large (for instance because the system's internal variables have a large range). On the other hand, if the matrix is very large, the number of executions needs to be very large to obtain a reliable and small confidence interval. In particular, for a small sample size, statistical analysis does not detect rare events, i.e., traces with a low probability that affect the result.

Table 1. Comparison of the two analysis methods.

	Precise	Statistical
Type	White box	Black/gray box
Analyzes	Source code	Implementation
Impractical for	Large number of traces	Large matrices
Produces	Exact value	Estimate & confidence

Main differences between precise and statistical analysis are summarized in Table 1.

3 Hybrid Statistical Estimation of Mutual Information

To overcome the above limitations on the previous approaches we introduce a new method, called *hybrid statistical estimation method*, that integrates both precise and statistical analyses. In this section we present the method for estimating the mutual information between two random variables X (over the inputs $\mathcal{X}$) and Y (over the outputs $\mathcal{Y}$) in a probabilistic system S, and for providing a confidence interval of this estimate. In the method we perform different types of analysis (with different parameters) on different components of a system.

- If a component is deterministic, we perform a precise analysis on it.
- If a component S_i has a joint sub-distribution matrix over *small* subsets of $\mathcal{X}$ and $\mathcal{Y}$ (relatively to the number of all traces), then we perform a statistical analysis on S_i.
- If a component T_j has a *large* matrix (relatively to the number of all traces), we perform a precise analysis on T_j.

- By combining the analysis results on all components we compute the mutual information estimate and its confidence interval. See the rest of Sect. 3 for details.
- By *qualitative* information flow analysis, the analyst may obtain partial knowledge on components and reduce the sample sizes. See Sect. 4 for details.

One of the main advantages of the new method is that we guarantee the quality of the outcome by providing its confidence interval even though different kinds of analyses with different parameters are combined together, such as multiple statistical analyses with different sample sizes.

Another advantage is the compositionality in estimating bias and confidence intervals. The random sampling of execution traces is performed independently for each component. Thanks to this we obtain that the bias and confidence interval of mutual information can be computed in a compositional way. This compositionality enables us to find optimal sample sizes for the different components that maximize the accuracy of the estimation (i.e., minimize the confidence interval size) given a fixed total sample size for the entire system. On the other hand, the computation of mutual information itself is not compositional; It requires calculating the *full* joint probability distribution of the system by summing the joint sub-distributions of all components of the system.

Note that these results can be applied to the estimation of Shannon entropy and conditional Shannon entropy as special cases. See the full version for the details.

3.1 Computation of Probability Distributions

We consider a probabilistic system S that consists of $(m + k)$ components S_1, S_2, ..., S_m and T_1, T_2, ..., T_k each executed with probabilities θ_1, θ_2, ..., θ_m and ξ_1, ξ_2, ..., ξ_k; i.e., when S is executed, it yields S_i with the probability θ_i and T_j with the probability ξ_j. We assume S does not have non-deterministic transitions. Let $\mathcal{I} = \{1, 2, \ldots, m\}$ and $\mathcal{J} = \{1, 2, \ldots, k\}$, one of which can be empty. We assume the analyst can run the component S_i for each $i \in \mathcal{I}$ to record its execution traces, and precisely analyze the components T_j for $j \in \mathcal{J}$, e.g., by static analysis of the source code or specification.

In the estimation of mutual information between two random variables X and Y in the system S, we need to estimate the joint distribution P_{XY} of X and Y. In our approach this is obtained by combining the joint *sub-probability distributions* of X and Y for all the components S_i's and T_j's. More specifically, let R_i and Q_j be the joint sub-distributions of X and Y for the components S_i's and T_j's respectively. Then the joint (full) distribution P_{XY} for the whole system S is defined by:

$$P_{XY}[x, y] \stackrel{\text{def}}{=} \sum_{i \in \mathcal{I}} R_i[x, y] + \sum_{j \in \mathcal{J}} Q_j[x, y]$$

for $x \in \mathcal{X}$ and $y \in \mathcal{Y}$. Note that for each $i \in \mathcal{I}$ and $j \in \mathcal{J}$, the sums of all probabilities in R_i and Q_j equal the probabilities θ_i and ξ_j of executing S_i and T_j respectively.

To estimate the joint distribution P_{XY} the analyst computes

- for each $i \in \mathcal{I}$, the *empirical* sub-distribution $\hat{R}_i$ for the component S_i from a set of traces obtained by executing S_i, and
- for each $j \in \mathcal{J}$, the *exact* sub-distribution Q_j for T_j by a precise analysis on T_j.

The empirical sub-distribution $\hat{R}_i$ is constructed as follows. Let n_i be the number of S_i's executions. For each $x \in \mathcal{X}$ and $y \in \mathcal{Y}$, let K_{ixy} be the number of S_i's traces that have input x and output y. Then $n_i = \sum_{x\in\mathcal{X},y\in\mathcal{Y}} K_{ixy}$. From these we compute the empirical joint (full) distribution $\hat{D}_i$ of X and Y by $\hat{D}_i[x,y] \stackrel{\text{def}}{=} \frac{K_{ixy}}{n_i}$. Since S_i is executed with probability θ_i, $\hat{R}_i$ is given by $\hat{R}_i[x,y] \stackrel{\text{def}}{=} \theta_i \hat{D}_i[x,y] = \frac{\theta_i K_{ixy}}{n_i}$.

3.2 Estimation of Mutual Information and Its Confidence Interval

In this section we present our new method for estimating mutual information and its confidence interval. For each component S_i let D_i be the joint (full) distribution of X and Y obtained by normalizing R_i: $D_i[x,y] = \frac{R_i[x,y]}{\theta_i}$. Let $D_{Xi}[x] = \sum_{y\in\mathcal{Y}} D_i[x,y]$, $D_{Yi}[y] = \sum_{x\in\mathcal{X}} D_i[x,y]$ and $\mathcal{D} = \{(x,y) \in \mathcal{X}\times\mathcal{Y} : P_{XY}[x,y] \neq 0\}$.

Using the estimated $\hat{P}_{XY}$ we can compute the mutual information estimate $\hat{I}(X;Y)$. Note that the mutual information of the whole system is smaller than (or equals) the weighted sum of those of the components, because of its convexity w.r.t. the channel matrix. Therefore it cannot be computed compositionally from those of the components; i.e., it requires to compute the joint distribution matrix $\hat{P}_{XY}$ for the whole system.

Since $\hat{I}(X;Y)$ is obtained from a limited number of traces, it is different from the true value $I(X;Y)$. The following theorem quantifies the bias $E(\hat{I}(X;Y)) - I(X;Y)$.

Theorem 1. *The expectation $E(\hat{I}(X;Y))$ of the mutual information is given by:*

$$I(X;Y) + \sum_{i\in\mathcal{I}} \frac{\theta_i^2}{2n_i}\Bigg(\sum_{(x,y)\in\mathcal{D}} \varphi_{ixy} - \sum_{x\in\mathcal{X}^+} \varphi_{ix} - \sum_{y\in\mathcal{Y}^+} \varphi_{iy}\Bigg) + \mathcal{O}(n_i^{-2})$$

where $\varphi_{ixy} = \frac{D_i[x,y]-D_i[x,y]^2}{P_{XY}[x,y]}$, $\varphi_{ix} = \frac{D_{Xi}[x]-D_{Xi}[x]^2}{P_X[x]}$ *and* $\varphi_{iy} = \frac{D_{Yi}[y]-D_{Yi}[y]^2}{P_Y[y]}$.

The proof is based on the Taylor expansion w.r.t. multiple dependent variables and can be found in the full version. Since the higher-order terms in the formula are negligible when the sample sizes n_i are large enough, we use the following as the *point estimate*:

$$pe = \hat{I}(X;Y) - \sum_{i\in\mathcal{I}} \frac{\theta_i^2}{2n_i}\Bigg(\sum_{(x,y)\in\mathcal{D}} \widehat{\varphi}_{ixy} - \sum_{x\in\mathcal{X}^+} \widehat{\varphi}_{ix} - \sum_{y\in\mathcal{Y}^+} \widehat{\varphi}_{iy}\Bigg)$$

where $\widehat{\varphi}_{ixy}$, $\widehat{\varphi}_{ix}$ and $\widehat{\varphi}_{iy}$ are empirical values of φ_{ixy}, φ_{ix} and φ_{iy} respectively (that are computed from traces). Then the bias is closer to 0 when the sample sizes n_i are larger.

The quality of the estimate depends on the sample sizes n_i and other factors. The sampling distribution of the estimate $\hat{I}(X;Y)$ tends to follow the normal distribution when n_i's are large enough. The following gives the variance of the distribution.

Theorem 2. *The variance $V(\hat{I}(X;Y))$ of the mutual information is given by*

$$\sum_{i\in\mathcal{I}} \frac{\theta_i^2}{n_i}\Bigg(\sum_{(x,y)\in\mathcal{D}} D_i[x,y]\Big(1+\log\frac{P_X[x]P_Y[y]}{P_{XY}[x,y]}\Big)^2 - \Big(\sum_{(x,y)\in\mathcal{D}} D_i[x,y]\Big(1+\log\frac{P_X[x]P_Y[y]}{P_{XY}[x,y]}\Big)\Big)^2\Bigg) + \mathcal{O}(n_i^{-2})$$

The confidence interval of the estimate of mutual information is useful to know how accurate the estimate is. When the interval is smaller, we learn the estimate is more accurate. The confidence interval is calculated using the variance v obtained by Theorem 2. Given a significance level α, we denote by $z_{\alpha/2}$ the *z-score* for the $100(1-\frac{\alpha}{2})$ percentile point. Then *the* $(1-\alpha)$ *confidence interval* of the estimate is given by:

$$[\max(0, pe - z_{\alpha/2}\sqrt{v}),\ pe + z_{\alpha/2}\sqrt{v}\,] \,.$$

For example, we use the z-score $z_{0.0025} = 1.96$ to compute the 95 % confidence interval. To ignore the higher order terms the sample size $\sum_{i\in\mathcal{I}} n_i$ needs to be at least $4\cdot\#\mathcal{X}\cdot\#\mathcal{Y}$.

By Theorems 1 and 3, the bias and confidence interval for the whole system can be computed compositionally from those for the components, unlike the mutual information itself. This allows us to adaptively optimize the sample sizes for the components.

3.3 Adaptive Optimization of Sample Sizes

The computational cost of the statistical analysis of each component S_i generally depends on the sample size n_i and the cost of each execution of S_i. When we choose n_i we take into account the trade-off between quality and cost of the analysis: a larger sample size provides a smaller confidence interval, while the cost increases proportionally to n_i.

In this section we present a method for deciding how many times we should run each component S_i to collect a sufficient number of traces to estimate mutual information. More specifically, we show how to compute optimal sample sizes n_i that achieves the smallest confidence interval size within the budget of the total sample size $n = \sum_{i\in\mathcal{I}} n_i$.

To compute the optimal sample sizes, we first run each component to collect a smaller number (for instance dozens) of execution traces. Then we calculate certain intermediate values in computing the variance to determine sample sizes for further executions. Formally, let v_i be the following intermediate value of the variance for S_i:

$$v_i = \theta_i^2 \left(\sum_{(x,y)\in\mathcal{D}} \hat{D}_i[x,y] \left(1 + \log \frac{\hat{P}_X[x]\hat{P}_Y[y]}{\hat{P}_{XY}[x,y]}\right)^2 - \left(\sum_{(x,y)\in\mathcal{D}} \hat{D}_i[x,y] \left(1 + \log \frac{\hat{P}_X[x]\hat{P}_Y[y]}{\hat{P}_{XY}[x,y]}\right)\right)^2 \right)$$

Then we find n_i's that minimize the variance $v = \sum_{i\in\mathcal{I}} \frac{v_i}{n_i}$ of the mutual information.

Theorem 3. *Given the total sample size n and the above intermediate variance v_i of the component S_i for each $i \in \mathcal{I}$, the variance of the mutual information estimate is minimized if, for all $i \in \mathcal{I}$, the sample size n_i for S_i satisfies $n_i = \frac{\sqrt{v_i}n}{\sum_{j=1}^{m}\sqrt{v_j}}$.*

By this result the estimation of a confidence interval size is useful to optimally assign sample sizes to components even when the analyst is not interested in the interval itself. We show experimentally the effectiveness of this optimization in the full version.

4 Estimation Using Prior Knowledge About Systems

In this section we show how to use prior knowledge about systems to improve the estimation, i.e., to make the size of the confidence intervals smaller and reduce the required sample sizes.

4.1 Approximate Estimation Using Knowledge of Prior Distributions

Our hybrid statistical estimation method integrates both precise and statistical analysis, and it can be seen as a generalization and extension of previous work [9, 13, 43].

For example, Chatzikokolakis et al. [13] present a method for estimating mutual information between two random variables X (over secret values $\mathcal{X}$) and Y (over observable values $\mathcal{Y}$) when the analyst knows the (prior) distribution P_X of X. In the estimation they collect execution traces by running a system for each secret value $x \in \mathcal{X}$. Thanks to the precise knowledge of P_X, they have more accurate estimates than the other previous work [9, 43] that also estimates P_X from execution traces.

Estimation using the precise knowledge of P_X is an instance of our result if a system is partitioned into the component S_x for each secret $x \in \mathcal{X} = \mathcal{I}$. If we assume all joint probabilities are non-zero, the approximate result in [13] follows from Theorem 1.

Corollary 1. *The expectation $E(\hat{I}(X;Y))$ of the mutual information is given by*

$$I(X;Y) + \frac{(\#\mathcal{X}-1)(\#\mathcal{Y}-1)}{2n} + \mathcal{O}(n^{-2}).$$

In this result from [13] the bias $\frac{(\#\mathcal{X}-1)(\#\mathcal{Y}-1)}{2n}$ depends only on the size of the joint distribution matrix. However, the bias can be strongly influenced by zeroes or very small probabilities in the distribution, therefore their approximate results can be correct only when all joint probabilities are non-zero and large enough, which is a strong restriction in practice. The tool LeakWatch [20] implicitly assumes that all probabilities are large enough, and consequently miscalculates bias and gives an estimate far from the true value in the presence of very small probabilities.

4.2 Our Estimation Using Knowledge of Prior Distributions

To overcome these issues we present more general results in the case the analyst knows the prior distribution P_X. We assume that a system S is partitioned into the disjoint component S_{ix} for each index $i \in \mathcal{I}$ and secret $x \in \mathcal{X}$, and that each S_{ix} is executed with probability θ_{ix} in the system S. Let $\Theta = \{\theta_{ix} : i \in \mathcal{I}, x \in \mathcal{X}\}$.

In the estimation of mutual information we run each component S_{ix} separately many times to collect execution traces. Unlike the previous work we may change the number of executions $n_i P_X[x]$ to $n_i \lambda_i[x]$ where $\lambda_i[x]$ is an *importance prior* that decides how the sample size n_i is allocated for each component S_{ix}. Let $\Lambda = \{\lambda_i : i \in \mathcal{I}\}$.

Given the number K_{ixy} of S_{ix}'s traces with output y, we define the conditional distribution D_i of output given input: $D_i[y|x] \stackrel{\text{def}}{=} \frac{K_{ixy}}{n_i \lambda_i[x]}$. Let $M_{ixy} = \frac{\theta_{ix}^2}{\lambda_i[x]} D_i[y|x]\,(1 - D_i[y|x])$. Then the following is the expectation and variance of the mutual information $\hat{I}_{\Theta,\Lambda}(X;Y)$ calculated using $\hat{D}_i$, Θ, Λ.

Proposition 1. *The expectation $E(\hat{I}_{\Theta,\Lambda}(X;Y))$ of the mutual information is given by*

$$I(X;Y) + \sum_{i\in\mathcal{I}} \frac{1}{2n_i} \sum_{y\in\mathcal{Y}^+} \left(\sum_{x\in\mathcal{D}_y} \frac{M_{ixy}}{P_{XY}[x,y]} - \frac{\sum_{x\in\mathcal{D}_y} M_{ixy}}{P_Y[y]} \right) + \mathcal{O}(n_i^{-2})$$

Proposition 2. *The variance $V(\hat{I}_{\Theta,\Lambda}(X;Y))$ of the mutual information is given by*

$$\sum_{i\in\mathcal{I}} \sum_{x\in\mathcal{X}^+} \frac{\theta_{ix}^2}{n_i \lambda_i[x]} \left(\sum_{y\in\mathcal{D}_x} D_i[y|x] \left(\log \frac{P_Y[y]}{P_{XY}[x,y]} \right)^2 - \left(\sum_{y\in\mathcal{D}_x} D_i[y|x] \left(\log \frac{P_Y[y]}{P_{XY}[x,y]} \right) \right)^2 \right) + \mathcal{O}(n_i^{-2})$$

By applying Theorem 3, the sample sizes n_i and the importance priors λ_i can be adaptively optimized.

4.3 Abstraction-Then-Sampling Using Partial Knowledge of Components

In this section we extend our estimation method to consider the case in which the analyst has partial knowledge of components (e.g. by static analysis of the source code or specification) before sampling. Such prior knowledge may help us abstract components into simpler ones and thus reduce the sample size for the statistical analysis.

For instance, let us consider an analyst who knows two pairs (x, y) and (x', y') of inputs and outputs have the same probability in a component S_i: $D_i[x, y] = D_i[x', y']$. Then, when we construct the empirical distribution $\hat{D}_i$ from a set of traces, we can count the number $K_{i\{(x,y),(x',y')\}}$ of traces having either (x, y) or (x', y'), and divide it by two: $K_{ixy} = K_{ix'y'} = \frac{K_{i\{(x,y),(x',y')\}}}{2}$. Then the sample size required for a certain accuracy is smaller than when we do not use the prior knowledge on the equality $K_{ixy} = K_{ix'y'}$.

In the following we generalize this idea to deal with more knowledge of components. Let us consider a (probabilistic) system in which some components leak no information on inputs and the analyst can learn this by *qualitative* information analysis (for verifying non-interference). Then such a component S_i has a sub-channel matrix where all non-zero rows have an identical conditional distribution of outputs given inputs [26]. Consequently, when we estimate the $\#\mathcal{X}_i \times \#\mathcal{Y}_i$ matrix of S_i it suffices to estimate one of the rows, hence the number of executions is proportional to $\#\mathcal{Y}_i$ instead of $\#\mathcal{X}_i \times \#\mathcal{Y}_i$. Note that even when some components leak no information, computing the mutual information for the whole system requires constructing the matrix of the system, hence the matrices of all components.

The following results show that the bias and confidence interval are narrower than when not using the prior knowledge of components. Let $\mathcal{I}^\star$ be the set of indices of components that have channel matrices whose non-zero rows consist of the same distribution. For each $i \in \mathcal{I}^\star$, we define $\pi_i[x]$ as the probability of having an input x in the component S_i. Then the expectation and variance of the mutual information are as follows.

Theorem 4. *The expectation $E(\hat{I}_{\mathcal{I}^\star}(X;Y))$ of the mutual information is given by*

$$I(X;Y) + \sum_{i \in \mathcal{I} \setminus \mathcal{I}^\star} \frac{\theta_i^2}{2n_i} \Big(\sum_{(x,y) \in \mathcal{D}} \varphi_{ixy} - \sum_{x \in \mathcal{X}^+} \varphi_{ix} - \sum_{y \in \mathcal{Y}^+} \varphi_{iy} \Big) + \sum_{i \in \mathcal{I}^\star} \frac{\theta_i^2}{2n_i} \Big(\sum_{(x,y) \in \mathcal{D}} \psi_{ixy} - \sum_{y \in \mathcal{Y}^+} \varphi_{iy} \Big) + \mathcal{O}(n_i^{-2})$$

where $\psi_{ixy} \stackrel{\text{def}}{=} \frac{D_i[x,y]\pi_i[x] - D_i[x,y]^2}{P_{XY}[x,y]}$.

Theorem 5. *The variance $V(\hat{I}_{\mathcal{I}^\star}(X;Y))$ of the mutual information is given by*

$$\sum_{i \in \mathcal{I} \setminus \mathcal{I}^\star} \frac{\theta_i^2}{n_i} \Bigg(\sum_{(x,y) \in \mathcal{D}} D_i[x,y] \Big(1 + \log \frac{P_X[x] P_Y[y]}{P_{XY}[x,y]}\Big)^2 - \Big(\sum_{(x,y) \in \mathcal{D}} D_i[x,y] \Big(1 + \log \frac{P_X[x] P_Y[y]}{P_{XY}[x,y]}\Big)\Big)^2 \Bigg)$$

$$+\sum_{i\in\mathcal{I}^\star}\frac{\theta_i^2}{n_i}\Bigg(\sum_{y\in\mathcal{Y}^+} D_{Y^i}[y]\Big(\log P_Y[y]-\sum_{x\in\mathcal{X}}\pi_i[x]\log P_{XY}[x,y]\Big)^2 - \Big(\sum_{y\in\mathcal{Y}^+} D_{Y^i}[y]\Big(\log P_Y[y]-\sum_{x\in\mathcal{X}}\pi_i[x]\log P_{XY}[x,y]\Big)\Big)^2\Bigg)+\mathcal{O}(n_i^{-2})\,.$$

5 Estimation via Program Decomposition

The hybrid statistical estimation presented in the previous sections is designed to analyze a system composed of subsystems (for instance, a distributed system over different software or hardware, potentially geographically separated). However, it can also be applied to the source code of a system by decomposing it into disjoint components. In this section we show how to decompose a code into components and determine for each component which analysis method to use and the method's parameters.

The principles to decompose a system's source code in components are as follows:

- The code may be decomposed only at conditional branching. Moreover, each component must be a terminal in the control flow graph, hence no component is executed afterwards. This is because the estimation method requires that the channel matrix for the system is the weighted sum of those for its components, and that the weight of a component is the probability of executing it.
- The analysis method and its parameters for each component S_i are decided by estimating the computational cost of analyzing S_i. Let $\mathcal{Z}_i$ be the set of all *internal randomness* (i.e., the variables whose values are assigned according to probability distributions) in S_i. Then the cost of the statistical analysis is proportional to S_i's matrix size $\#\mathcal{X}_i \times \#\mathcal{Y}_i$, while the cost of the precise

1. Build the control flow graph of the system.
2. Mark all possible components based on each conditional branching. Each possible component must be a terminal as explained in Section 5.
3. For each possible component S_i, check whether it is deterministic or not (by syntactically checking an occurrence of a probabilistic assignment or a probabilistic function call). If it is, mark the component for precise analysis.
4. For each possible component S_i, check whether S_i's output variables are independent of its input variables inside S_i (by *qualitative* information flow). If so, mark that the abstraction-then-sampling technique in Section 4.3 is to be used on the component.
5. For each S_i, estimate an approximate range size of its internal and observable variables.
6. Looking from the leaves to the root of the graph, decide the decomposition into components. Estimate the cost of statistical and precise analyses and mark the component for analysis by the cheapest of the two.
7. Join together adjacent components if they are marked for precise analysis, or if they are marked for statistical analysis and have the same input and output ranges.
8. For each component, perform precise analysis or statistical analysis as marked.

Fig. 2. Procedure for decomposing a system given its source code.

analysis is proportional to the number of all traces in S_i's control flow graph (in the worst case proportional to $\#\mathcal{X}_i \times \#\mathcal{Z}_i$). Hence the cost estimation is reduced to counting $\#\mathcal{Y}_i$ and $\#\mathcal{Z}_i$.

The procedure for decomposition is shown in Fig. 2. Since this is heuristic, it is not guaranteed to produce an optimal decomposition. While the procedure is automated, for usability the choice of analysis can be controlled by user's annotations on the code.

6 Evaluation

We evaluate experimentally the effectiveness of our hybrid method compared to the state of the art. We first discuss the cost and quality of the estimation, then test the hybrid method against fully precise/fully statistical analyses on Shannon leakage benchmarks.

6.1 On the Tradeoff Between the Cost and Quality of Estimation

In the hybrid statistical estimation, the estimate takes different values probabilistically, because it is computed from a set of traces that are generated by executing a probabilistic system. Figure 3 shows the sampling distribution of the mutual information estimate of the joint distribution in Fig. 1 in Sect. 1. The graph shows the frequency (on the y axis) of the mutual information estimates (on the x axis) when performing the estimation 1000 times. In each estimation we perform precise analysis on the component T and statistical analysis on S_1 and S_2 (with a sample size of 5000). As shown in Fig. 3 the estimate after the correction of bias by Theorem 1 is closer to the true value. The estimate is roughly between the lower and upper bounds of the 95 % confidence interval calculated using Theorem 2.

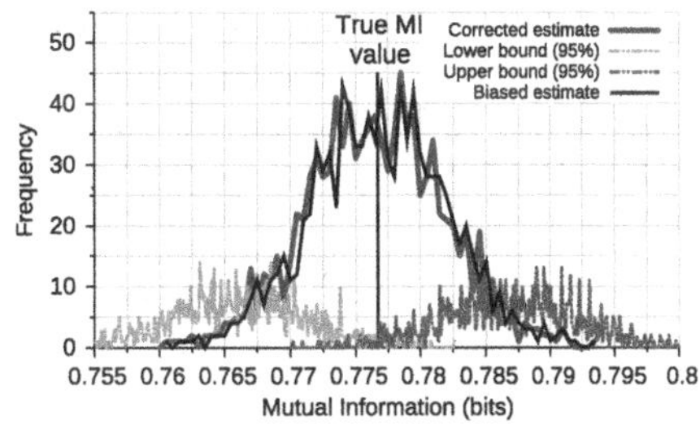

Fig. 3. Distribution of mutual information estimate and its confidence interval.

The interval size depends on the sample size in statistical analysis as shown in Fig. 4a. When the sample size is k times larger, the confidence interval is $\sqrt{k}$ times narrower. The interval size also depends on the amount of precise analysis as shown in Fig. 4b. If we perform precise analysis on larger components, then the sampling distribution becomes more centered (with shorter tails) and the confidence interval becomes narrower.

The hybrid approach produces better estimates than the state of the art in statistical analysis. Due to the combination with precise analysis, the confidence interval estimated by our approach is smaller than LeakWatch [20] for the same sample size.

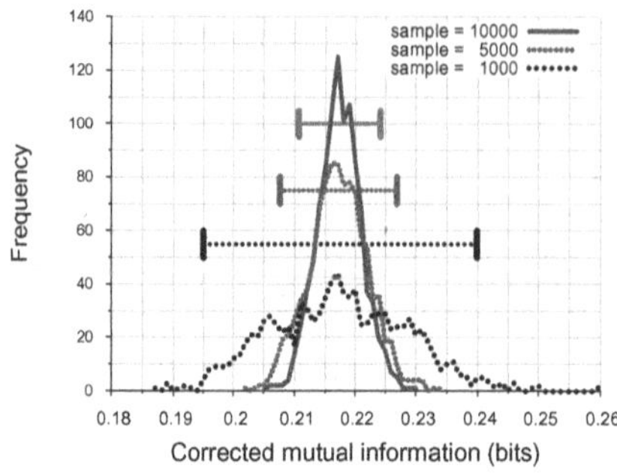

(a) Estimates and sample sizes.

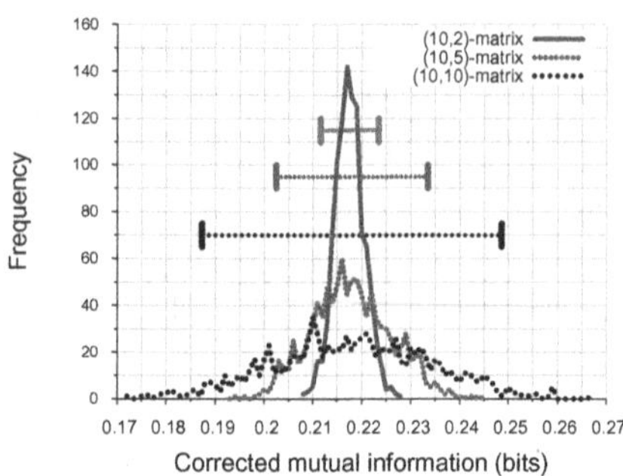

(b) Estimates and the ratio of precise analysis.

Fig. 4. Smaller intervals when increasing the sample size or the ratio of precise analysis.

6.2 Shannon Leakage Benchmarks

We compare the performance of our hybrid method with fully precise/statistical analysis on Shannon leakage benchmarks. Our implementations of precise and statistical analyses are variants of the state-of-the art tools QUAIL [6,7] and LeakWatch [17,20] respectively. They are fully automated except for human-provided annotations to determine the analysis method for each component. All experiments are performed on an Intel i7-4960HQ 2.6 GHz quad-core machine with 8 GB of RAM running Ubuntu 16.04.

```
secret array bit[N] s;
observable array bit[K] r;
for i=0..K-1 do r[i]=s[i] ;
for i=K..N-1 do
    j = uniform(0..i);
    if j<K then r[j]=s[i];
end
```

Fig. 5. Reservoir sampling.

Reservoir Sampling. The reservoir sampling problem [48] consists of selecting K elements randomly from a pool of $N > K$ elements. We quantify the information flow of the commonly-used *Algorithm R* [48], presented in Fig. 5, for various values of N and $K = N/2$. In the algorithm, the first K elements are chosen as the sample, then each other element has a probability to replace one element in the sample.

```
secret int h = [0, N];
observable array bit[N] decl;
int lie = uniform(1..N);
randomly generated array bit[N] coin;
for c in coin do c = uniform(0..1) ;
for i=0..N-1 do
    decl[i]=coin[i] xor coin[(i+1)%N];
    if h==i+1 then decl[i]=!decl[i];
    if i==lie then decl[i]=!decl[i];
end
```

Fig. 6. Lying cryptographers.

Multiple Lying Cryptographers Protocol. We test our hybrid method to compute the Shannon leakage of a distributed version of the lying cryptographers protocol. The lying cryptographers protocol is a variant of the dining cryptographer multi-party computation protocol [15] in which a randomly-chosen cryptographer declares the opposite of what they would normally declare, i.e. they lie if they are not the payer, and do not lie if they are the payer. We consider three simultaneous lying cryptographers implementation in which 8 cryptographers run the protocol on three separate overlapping tables A, B and C with 4 cryptographers each. Table A hosts cryptographers 1 to 4, Table B hosts cryptographers 3 to 6, and Table C hosts cryptographers 5 to 8. The identity of the payer is the same in all tables (Fig. 6).

```
secret int sec = [0,N-1];
observable int obs;
int S = uniform(0,N-W-1);
int ws = uniform(1,W);
int O = uniform(0,N-W-1);
int wo = uniform(1,W);
if S ≤ sec ≤ S+ws then
  | obs = uniform(O,O+wo);
else
  | obs = uniform(0,N-1);
end
```

Fig. 7. Shifting window.

Shifting Window. In the shifting window example the secret has N possible values, and a contiguous sequence of this values (the "window") of random size from 1 to W is chosen. We assume for simplicity that $N = 2W$. If the secret is inside the window then another random window is chosen in the same way and a random value from the new window is printed. Otherwise, a random value from 0 to $N - 1$ is printed (Fig. 7).

Results. In Table 2 we show the results of the benchmarks using fully precise, fully statistical and hybrid analyses, for a sample size of 100000 executions. Timeout is set at 10 min. On the reservoir benchmark the precise analysis is faster for small instances but does not scale, timing out on larger values of N. The hybrid method is consistently faster than the fully statistical analysis and often has a smaller error. On the other benchmarks the hybrid method usually outperforms the others and produces better approximations than the statistical analysis.

Table 2. Shannon leakage benchmark results.

		Reservoir				Lying crypt	Window		
		N=6	N=8	N=10	N=12		N=20	N=22	N=24
Precise	**Time(s)**	0.7	11.4	timeout	timeout	506.4	10.0	16.0	28.3
	Error	0	0	-	-	0	0	0	0
Statistical	**Time(s)**	21.6	35.2	60.7	91.5	254.3	7.5	7.7	7.1
	Error	10^{-3}	10^{-3}	-	-	10^{-3}	10^{-3}	10^{-3}	10^{-4}
Hybrid	**Time(s)**	13.4	22.5	34.6	58.4	240.1	6.6	7.1	7.1
	Error	10^{-4}	10^{-3}	-	-	10^{-3}	10^{-7}	10^{-4}	10^{-4}

The results in Table 2 show the superiority of our hybrid approach compared to the state of the art. The hybrid analysis scales better than the precise analysis, since it does not need to analyze every trace of the system. Compared to fully statistical analysis, our hybrid analysis exploits precise analysis on components of the system where statistical estimation would be more expensive than precise analysis. This allows the hybrid analysis to focus the statistical estimation on components of the system where it converges faster, thus obtaining a smaller confidence interval in a shorter time.

7 Related Work

The information-theoretical approach to program security dates back to the work of Denning [27] and Gray [32]. Clark et al. [22,23] presented techniques to automatically compute mutual information of an imperative language with loops. For a deterministic program, leakage can be computed from the equivalence relations on the secret induced by the possible outputs, and such relations can be automatically quantified [2]. Under- and over-approximation of leakage based on the observation of some traces have been studied for deterministic programs [42,44]. The combination of static and statistical approaches to quantitative information flow is proposed in [39] while our paper is general enough to deal with probabilistic systems under various prior information conditions.

The statistical approach to quantifying information leakage has been studied since the seminal work by Chatzikokolakis et al. [13]. Chothia et al. have developed this approach in tools leakiEst [18,19] and LeakWatch [17,20]. The hybrid statistical method in this paper can be considered as their extension with the inclusion of component weighting and adaptive priors inspired by the importance sampling in statistical model checking [3,24]. To the best of our knowledge, no prior work has applied weighted statistical analysis to the estimation of mutual information or any other leakage measures.

Fremont and Seshia [30] have presented a polynomial time algorithm to approximate the weight of traces of deterministic programs with possible application to quantitative information leakage. Progress in statistical program analysis includes a scalable algorithm for uniform generation of sample from a distribution defined as constraints [11,12], with applications to constrained-random program verification.

The algorithms for precise computation of information leakage used in this paper are based on trace analysis [5], implemented in the QUAIL tool [6,7]. Phan et al. [45,46] developed tools to compute channel capacity of deterministic programs written in the C or Java languages. McCamant et al. [34] developed tools implementing dynamic quantitative taint analysis techniques for security. The recent tool Moped-QLeak [10] is able to efficiently compute information leakage of programs as long as it can produce a complete symbolic representation of the program.

8 Conclusions and Future Work

We have proposed a method for estimating mutual information by combining precise and statistical analyses and for compositionally computing the bias and confidence interval of the estimate. The results are also used to adaptively find the optimal sample sizes for different components in the statistical analysis.

Moreover, we have shown how to reduce sample sizes by using prior knowledge about systems, including the abstraction-then-sampling technique with qualitative analysis. To apply our new method to the source codes of systems we have shown how to decompose the codes into components and determine the analysis method for each component. We have shown both theoretical and experimental results to demonstrate that the proposed approach outperforms the state of the art. To obtain better results we are developing theory and tools that integrate symbolic abstraction techniques in program analysis into our estimation method.

References

1. Adami, C.: Information theory in molecular biology. Phys. Life Rev. **1**(1), 3–22 (2004)
2. Backes, M., Köpf, B., Rybalchenko, A.: Automatic discovery and quantification of information leaks. In: 30th IEEE Symposium on Security and Privacy (S&P 2009), 17–20 May 2009, Oakland, California, USA, pp. 141–153. IEEE Computer Society (2009)
3. Barbot, B., Haddad, S., Picaronny, C.: Coupling and importance sampling for statistical model checking. In: Flanagan, C., König, B. (eds.) TACAS 2012. LNCS, vol. 7214, pp. 331–346. Springer, Heidelberg (2012). doi:10.1007/978-3-642-28756-5_23
4. Barthe, G., Köpf, B.: Information-theoretic bounds for differentially private mechanisms. In: Proceedings of CSF, pp. 191–204. IEEE (2011)
5. Biondi, F., Legay, A., Malacaria, P., Wasowski, A.: Quantifying information leakage of randomized protocols. Theor. Comput. Sci. **597**, 62–87 (2015)
6. Biondi, F., Legay, A., Traonouez, L.M., Wasowski, A.: QUAIL. https://project.inria.fr/quail/
7. Biondi, F., Legay, A., Traonouez, L.-M., Wąsowski, A.: QUAIL: a quantitative security analyzer for imperative code. In: Sharygina, N., Veith, H. (eds.) CAV 2013. LNCS, vol. 8044, pp. 702–707. Springer, Heidelberg (2013). doi:10.1007/978-3-642-39799-8_49
8. Boreale, M., Paolini, M.: On formally bounding information leakage by statistical estimation. In: Chow, S.S.M., Camenisch, J., Hui, L.C.K., Yiu, S.M. (eds.) ISC 2014. LNCS, vol. 8783, pp. 216–236. Springer, Heidelberg (2014). doi:10.1007/978-3-319-13257-0_13
9. Brillinger, D.R.: Some data analysis using mutual information. Braz. J. Probab. Stat. **18**(6), 163–183 (2004)
10. Chadha, R., Mathur, U., Schwoon, S.: Computing information flow using symbolic model-checking. In: Raman, V., Suresh, S.P. (eds.) FSTTCS 2014. Proceedings. LIPIcs, vol. 29, pp. 505–516. Schloss Dagstuhl - Leibniz-Zentrum fuer Informatik (2014)
11. Chakraborty, S., Fremont, D.J., Meel, K.S., Seshia, S.A., Vardi, M.Y.: On parallel scalable uniform SAT witness generation. In: Baier, C., Tinelli, C. (eds.) TACAS 2015. LNCS, vol. 9035, pp. 304–319. Springer, Heidelberg (2015). doi:10.1007/978-3-662-46681-0_25
12. Chakraborty, S., Meel, K.S., Vardi, M.Y.: A scalable approximate model counter. In: Schulte, C. (ed.) CP 2013. LNCS, vol. 8124, pp. 200–216. Springer, Heidelberg (2013). doi:10.1007/978-3-642-40627-0_18

13. Chatzikokolakis, K., Chothia, T., Guha, A.: Statistical measurement of information leakage. In: Esparza, J., Majumdar, R. (eds.) TACAS 2010. LNCS, vol. 6015, pp. 390–404. Springer, Heidelberg (2010). doi:10.1007/978-3-642-12002-2_33
14. Chatzikokolakis, K., Palamidessi, C., Panangaden, P.: Anonymity protocols as noisy channels. Inf. Comp. **206**(2–4), 378–401 (2008)
15. Chaum, D.: The dining cryptographers problem: unconditional sender and recipient untraceability. J. Cryptol. **1**, 65–75 (1988)
16. Chothia, T., Kawamoto, Y.: Statistical estimation of min-entropy leakage, April 2004. http://www.cs.bham.ac.uk/research/projects/infotools/. (Manuscript)
17. Chothia, T., Kawamoto, Y., Novakovic, C.: LeakWatch. http://www.cs.bham.ac.uk/research/projects/infotools/leakwatch/
18. Chothia, T., Kawamoto, Y., Novakovic, C.: LeakiEst. http://www.cs.bham.ac.uk/research/projects/infotools/leakiest/
19. Chothia, T., Kawamoto, Y., Novakovic, C.: A Tool for Estimating Information Leakage. In: Sharygina, N., Veith, H. (eds.) CAV 2013. LNCS, vol. 8044, pp. 690–695. Springer, Heidelberg (2013). doi:10.1007/978-3-642-39799-8_47
20. Chothia, T., Kawamoto, Y., Novakovic, C.: LeakWatch: estimating information leakage from java programs. In: Kutyłowski, M., Vaidya, J. (eds.) ESORICS 2014. LNCS, vol. 8713, pp. 219–236. Springer, Heidelberg (2014). doi:10.1007/978-3-319-11212-1_13
21. Chothia, T., Kawamoto, Y., Novakovic, C., Parker, D.: Probabilistic point-to-point information leakage. In: Proceedings of CSF 2013, pp. 193–205. IEEE (2013)
22. Clark, D., Hunt, S., Malacaria, P.: Quantitative analysis of the leakage of confidential data. Electr. Notes Theor. Comput. Sci. **59**(3), 238–251 (2001)
23. Clark, D., Hunt, S., Malacaria, P.: A static analysis for quantifying information flow in a simple imperative language. J. Comput. Secur. **15**(3), 321–371 (2007)
24. Clarke, E.M., Zuliani, P.: Statistical model checking for cyber-physical systems. In: Bultan, T., Hsiung, P.-A. (eds.) ATVA 2011. LNCS, vol. 6996, pp. 1–12. Springer, Heidelberg (2011). doi:10.1007/978-3-642-24372-1_1
25. Clarkson, M.R., Schneider, F.B.: Hyperproperties. J. Comput. Secur. **18**(6), 1157–1210 (2010)
26. Cover, T.M., Thomas, J.A.: Elements of Information Theory, 2nd edn. A Wiley-Interscience publication, Wiley, New York (2006)
27. Denning, D.E.: A lattice model of secure information flow. Commun. ACM **19**(5), 236–243 (1976)
28. Escolano, F., Suau, P., Bonev, B.: Information Theory in Computer Vision and Pattern Recognition. Springer, London (2009). http://opac.inria.fr/record=b1130015
29. Espinoza, B., Smith, G.: Min-entropy as a resource. Inf. Comput. **226**, 57–75 (2013)
30. Fremont, D.J., Seshia, S.A.: Speeding up SMT-based quantitative program analysis. In: Rümmer, P., Wintersteiger, C.M. (eds.) SMT 2014. Proceedings. CEUR Workshop Proceedings, vol. 1163, pp. 3–13. CEUR-WS.org (2014)
31. Gallager, R.G.: Information Theory and Reliable Communication. Wiley, New York (1968)
32. Gray, J.W.: Toward a mathematical foundation for information flow security. In: IEEE Symposium on Security and Privacy, pp. 21–35 (1991)
33. Jensen, F.V.: Introduction to Bayesian Networks, 1st edn. Springer, Secaucus (1996)
34. Kang, M.G., McCamant, S., Poosankam, P., Song, D.: DTA++: dynamic taint analysis with targeted control-flow propagation. In: Proceedings of NDSS 2011. The Internet Society (2011)

35. Kawamoto, Y., Biondi, F., Legay, A.: Hybrid statistical estimation of mutual information for quantifying information flow. Research report, INRIA (2016). https://hal.inria.fr/hal-01241360
36. Kawamoto, Y., Chatzikokolakis, K., Palamidessi, C.: Compositionality results for quantitative information flow. In: Norman, G., Sanders, W. (eds.) QEST 2014. LNCS, vol. 8657, pp. 368–383. Springer, Heidelberg (2014). doi:10.1007/978-3-319-10696-0_28
37. Kawamoto, Y., Given-Wilson, T.: Quantitative information flow for scheduler-dependent systems. In: Proceedings of QAPL 2015, vol. 194, pp. 48–62 (2015)
38. Köpf, B., Basin, D.A.: An information-theoretic model for adaptive side-channel attacks. In: Proceedings of CCS, pp. 286–296. ACM (2007)
39. Köpf, B., Rybalchenko, A.: Approximation and randomization for quantitative information-flow analysis. In: Proceedings CSF 2010, pp. 3–14. IEEE Computer Society (2010)
40. Legay, A., Delahaye, B., Bensalem, S.: Statistical model checking: an overview. In: Barringer, H., Falcone, Y., Finkbeiner, B., Havelund, K., Lee, I., Pace, G., Roşu, G., Sokolsky, O., Tillmann, N. (eds.) RV 2010. LNCS, vol. 6418, pp. 122–135. Springer, Heidelberg (2010). doi:10.1007/978-3-642-16612-9_11
41. MacKay, D.J.C.: Information Theory, Inference & Learning Algorithms. Cambridge University Press, New York (2002)
42. McCamant, S., Ernst, M.D.: Quantitative information flow as network flow capacity. In: Gupta, R., Amarasinghe, S.P. (eds.) Proceedings of the ACM SIGPLAN 2008 Conference on Programming Language Design and Implementation, Tucson, AZ, USA, 7–13 June 2008, pp. 193–205. ACM (2008)
43. Moddemeijer, R.: On estimation of entropy and mutual information of continuous distributions. Sig. Process. **16**, 233–248 (1989)
44. Newsome, J., McCamant, S., Song, D.: Measuring channel capacity to distinguish undue influence. In: Chong, S., Naumann, D.A. (eds.) Proceedings of the 2009 Workshop on Programming Languages and Analysis for Security, PLAS 2009, Dublin, Ireland, 15–21 June 2009, pp. 73–85. ACM (2009)
45. Phan, Q., Malacaria, P.: Abstract model counting: a novel approach for quantification of information leaks. In: Moriai, S., Jaeger, T., Sakurai, K. (eds.) Proceedings of AsiaCCS 2014, pp. 283–292. ACM (2014)
46. Phan, Q., Malacaria, P., Pasareanu, C.S., d'Amorim, M.: Quantifying information leaks using reliability analysis. In: Rungta, N., Tkachuk, O. (eds.) Proceedings of SPIN 2014, pp. 105–108. ACM (2014)
47. Smith, G.: On the foundations of quantitative information flow. In: Alfaro, L. (ed.) FoSSaCS 2009. LNCS, vol. 5504, pp. 288–302. Springer, Heidelberg (2009). doi:10.1007/978-3-642-00596-1_21
48. Vitter, J.S.: Random sampling with a reservoir. ACM Trans. Math. Softw. **11**(1), 37–57 (1985). http://doi.acm.org/10.1145/3147.3165
49. Wilde, M.M.: Quantum Information Theory, 1st edn. Cambridge University Press, New York (2013)
50. Yasuoka, H., Terauchi, T.: Quantitative information flow as safety and liveness hyperproperties. Theor. Comput. Sci. **538**, 167–182 (2014)

A Generic Logic for Proving Linearizability

Artem Khyzha[1(✉)], Alexey Gotsman[1], and Matthew Parkinson[2]

[1] IMDEA Software Institute, Madrid, Spain
artem.khyzha@imdea.org
[2] Microsoft Research Cambridge, Cambridge, UK

Abstract. Linearizability is a commonly accepted notion of correctness for libraries of concurrent algorithms, and recent years have seen a number of proposals of program logics for proving it. Although these logics differ in technical details, they embody similar reasoning principles. To explicate these principles, we propose a logic for proving linearizability that is generic: it can be instantiated with different means of compositional reasoning about concurrency, such as separation logic or rely-guarantee. To this end, we generalise the Views framework for reasoning about concurrency to handle relations between programs, required for proving linearizability. We present sample instantiations of our generic logic and show that it is powerful enough to handle concurrent algorithms with challenging features, such as helping.

1 Introduction

To manage the complexity of constructing concurrent software, programmers package often-used functionality into *libraries* of concurrent algorithms. These encapsulate data structures, such as queues and lists, and provide clients with a set of methods that can be called concurrently to operate on these (e.g., java.util.concurrent). To maximise performance, concurrent libraries may use sophisticated non-blocking techniques, allowing multiple threads to operate on the data structure with minimum synchronisation. Despite this, each library method is usually expected to behave as though it executes atomically. This requirement is formalised by the standard notion of correctness for concurrent libraries, *linearizability* [14], which establishes a form of a simulation between the original *concrete* library and another *abstract* library, where each method is implemented atomically.

A common approach to proving linearizability is to find a *linearization point* for every method of the concrete library at which it can be thought of taking effect.[1] Given an execution of a concrete library, the matching execution of the abstract library, required to show the simulation, is constructed by executing the atomic abstract method at the linearization point of the concrete method. A difficulty in this approach is that linearization points are often not determined

[1] Some algorithms cannot be reasoned about using linearization points, which we discuss in Sect. 7.

J. Fitzgerald et al. (Eds.): FM 2016, LNCS 9995, pp. 426–443, 2016.
DOI: 10.1007/978-3-319-48989-6_26

by a statically chosen point in the method code. For example, in concurrent algorithms with *helping* [13], a method may execute an operation originally requested by another method, called in a different thread; then the linearization point of the latter method is determined by an action of the former.

Recent years have seen a number of program logics for proving linearizability (see [6] for a survey). To avoid reasoning about the high number of possible interleavings between concurrently executing threads, these logics often use *thread-modular* reasoning. They establish protocols that threads should follow when operating on the shared data structure and reason separately about every thread, assuming that the rest follow the protocols. The logics for proving linearizability, such as [18,26], usually borrow thread-modular reasoning rules from logics originally designed for proving non-relational properties of concurrent programs, such as rely-guarantee [15], separation logic [21] or combinations thereof [7,26]. Although this leads the logics to differ in technical details, they use similar methods for reasoning about linearizability, usually based on linearization points. Despite this similarity, designing a logic for proving linearizability that uses a particular thread-modular reasoning method currently requires finding the proof rules and proving their soundness afresh.

To consolidate this design space of linearization-point-based reasoning, we propose a logic for linearizability that is *generic*, i.e., can be instantiated with different means of thread-modular reasoning about concurrency, such as separation logic [21] or rely-guarantee [15]. To this end, we build on the recently-proposed Views framework [3], which unifies thread-modular logics for concurrency, such as the above-mentioned ones. Our contribution is to generalise the framework to reason about relations between programs, required for proving linearizability. In more detail, assertions in our logic are interpreted over a monoid of *relational views*, which describe relationships between the states of the concrete and the abstract libraries and the protocol that threads should follow in operating on these. The operation of the monoid, similar to the separating conjunction in separation logic [21], combines the assertions in different threads while ensuring that they agree on the protocols of access to the state. The choice of a particular relational view monoid thus determines the thread-modular reasoning method used by our logic.

To reason about linearization points, relational views additionally describe a set of special *tokens* (as in [2,18,26]), each denoting a one-time permission to execute a given atomic command on the state of the abstract library. The place where this permission is used in the proof of a concrete library method determines its linearization point, with the abstract command recorded by the token giving its specification. Crucially, reasoning about the tokens is subject to the protocols established by the underlying thread-modular reasoning method; in particular, their *ownership* can be transferred between different threads, which allows us to deal with helping.

We prove the soundness of our generic logic under certain conditions on its instantiations (Definition 2, Sect. 3). These conditions represent our key technical contribution, as they capture the essential requirements for soundly

$$\longrightarrow\ \subseteq \mathsf{Com} \times \mathsf{PCom} \times \mathsf{Com}$$

$$\frac{C_1 \xrightarrow{\alpha} C_1'}{C_1 \ ; C_2 \xrightarrow{\alpha} C_1' \ ; C_2} \quad \frac{}{C^\star \xrightarrow{\mathsf{id}} C; C^\star} \quad \frac{}{\alpha \xrightarrow{\alpha} \mathsf{skip}}$$

$$\frac{i \in \{1,2\}}{C_1 + C_2 \xrightarrow{\mathsf{id}} C_i} \quad \frac{}{\mathsf{skip} \ ; C \xrightarrow{\mathsf{id}} C} \quad \frac{}{C^\star \xrightarrow{\mathsf{id}} \mathsf{skip}}$$

$$\twoheadrightarrow\ \subseteq (\mathsf{Com} \times \mathsf{State}) \times (\mathsf{ThreadID} \times \mathsf{PCom}) \times (\mathsf{Com} \times \mathsf{State})$$

$$\frac{\sigma' \in [\![\alpha]\!]_t(\sigma) \quad C \xrightarrow{\alpha} C'}{\langle C, \sigma\rangle \xrightarrow{t,\alpha}\!\!\!\!\twoheadrightarrow \langle C', \sigma'\rangle}$$

Fig. 1. The operational semantics of sequential commands

combining a given thread-modular method for reasoning about concurrency with the linearization-point method for reasoning about linearizability.

To illustrate the use of our logic, we present its example instantiations where thread-modular reasoning is done using disjoint concurrent separation logic [20] and a combination of separation logic and rely-guarantee [26]. We then apply the latter instantiation to prove the correctness of a sample concurrent algorithm with helping. We expect that our results will make it possible to systematically design logics using the plethora of other methods for thread-modular reasoning that have been shown to be expressible in the Views framework [1,4,20].

2 Methods Syntax and Sequential Semantics

We consider concurrent programs that consist of two components, which we call *libraries* and *clients*. Libraries provide clients with a set of methods, and clients call them concurrently. We distinguish *concrete* and *abstract* libraries, as the latter serve as specification for the former due to its methods being executed atomically.

Syntax. Concrete methods are implemented as *sequential commands* having the syntax:

$$C \in \mathsf{Com} ::= \alpha \mid C \ ; C \mid C + C \mid C^\star \mid \mathsf{skip}, \quad \text{where } \alpha \in \mathsf{PCom}$$

The grammar includes *primitive commands* α from a set PCom, sequential composition $C \ ; C$, non-deterministic choice $C + C$ and a finite iteration $C^\star$ (we are interested only in terminating executions) and a termination marker skip. We use $+$ and $(\cdot)^\star$ instead of conditionals and while loops for theoretical simplicity: as we show at the end of this section, given appropriate primitive commands the conditionals and loops can be encoded. We also assume a set APCom of *abstract primitive commands*, ranged over by A, with which we represent methods of an abstract library.

Semantics. We assume a set State of concrete states of the memory, ranged over by σ, and abstract states AState, ranged over by Σ. The memory is shared among N threads with thread identifiers $\mathsf{ThreadID} = \{1, 2, \ldots, N\}$, ranged over by t.

We assume that semantics of each primitive command α is given by a non-deterministic *state transformer* $[\![\alpha]\!]_t : \mathsf{State} \to \mathcal{P}(\mathsf{State})$, where $t \in \mathsf{ThreadID}$. For a state σ, the set of states $[\![\alpha]\!]_t(\sigma)$ is the set of possible resulting states for α executed atomically in a state σ and a thread t. State transformers may have different semantics depending on a thread identifier, which we use to introduce thread-local memory cells later in the technical development. Analogously, we assume semantics of abstract primitive commands with state transformers $[\![\mathrm{A}]\!]_t : \mathsf{AState} \to \mathcal{P}(\mathsf{AState})$, all of which update abstract states atomically. We also assume a primitive command $\mathsf{id} \in \mathsf{PCom}$ with the interpretation $[\![\mathsf{id}]\!]_t(\sigma) \triangleq \{\sigma\}$, and its abstract counterpart $\mathsf{id} \in \mathsf{APCom}$.

The sets of primitive commands PCom and APCom as well as corresponding state transformers are parameters of our framework. In Fig. 1 we give rules of operational semantics of sequential commands, which are parametrised by semantics of primitive commands. That is, we define a transition relation $\twoheadrightarrow \subseteq (\mathsf{Com} \times \mathsf{State}) \times (\mathsf{ThreadID} \times \mathsf{PCom}) \times (\mathsf{Com} \times \mathsf{State})$, so that $\langle C, \sigma\rangle \xrightarrow{t,\alpha}\!\!\!\!\twoheadrightarrow \langle C', \sigma'\rangle$ indicates a transition from C to C' updating the state from σ to σ' with a primitive command α in a thread t. The rules of the operational semantics are standard.

Let us show how to define traditional control flow primitives, such as an if-statement and a while-loop, in our programming language. Assuming a language for arithmetic expressions, ranged over by E, and a function $[\![E]\!]_\sigma$ that evaluates expressions in a given state σ, we define a primitive command $\mathtt{assume}(E)$ that acts as a filter on states, choosing only those where E evaluates to non-zero values.

$$[\![\mathtt{assume}(E)]\!]_t(\sigma) \triangleq \text{ if } [\![E]\!]_\sigma \neq 0 \text{ then } \{\sigma\} \text{ else } \emptyset.$$

Using $\mathtt{assume}(E)$ and the C-style negation $!E$ in expressions, a conditional and a while-loop can be implemented as the following commands:

$$\mathtt{if}\ E\ \mathtt{then}\ C_1\ \mathtt{else}\ C_2 \triangleq (\mathtt{assume}(E); C_1) + (\mathtt{assume}(!E); C_2)$$
$$\mathtt{while}\ E\ \mathtt{do}\ C \triangleq (\mathtt{assume}(E); C)^\star; \mathtt{assume}(!E)$$

3 The Generic Logic

In this section, we present our framework for designing program logics for linearizability proofs. Given a concrete method and a corresponding abstract method, we aim to demonstrate that the former has a linearization point either within its code or in the code of another thread. The idea behind such proofs is to establish simulation between concrete and abstract methods using linearization points to determine when the abstract method has to make a transition to match a given execution of the concrete method. To facilitate such simulation-based proofs, we design our relational logic so that formulas in it denote relations between concrete states, abstract states and special *tokens*.

Tokens are our tool for reasoning about linearization points. At the beginning of its execution in a thread t, each concrete method m is given a token $\mathsf{todo}(\mathrm{A}_m)$ of the corresponding abstract primitive command A_m. The token represents a one-time permission for the method to take effect, i.e. to perform a primitive command A_m on an abstract machine. When the permission is used, a token $\mathsf{todo}(\mathrm{A}_m)$ in a thread t is irreversibly replaced with $\mathsf{done}(\mathrm{A}_m)$. Thus, by requiring that a method start its execution in a thread t with a token $\mathsf{todo}(\mathrm{A}_m)$ and ends with $\mathsf{done}(\mathrm{A}_m)$, we ensure that it has in its code a linearization point. The tokens of all threads are described by $\Delta \in \mathsf{Tokens}$:

$$\mathsf{Tokens} = \mathsf{ThreadID} \rightharpoonup (\{\mathsf{todo}(\mathrm{A}) \mid \mathrm{A} \in \mathsf{APCom}\} \cup \{\mathsf{done}(\mathrm{A}) \mid \mathrm{A} \in \mathsf{APCom}\})$$

Reasoning about states and tokens in the framework is done with the help of relational *views*. We assume a set Views, ranged over by p, q and r, as well as a reification function $\lfloor\ \rfloor : \mathsf{Views} \to \mathcal{P}(\mathsf{State} \times \mathsf{AState} \times \mathsf{Tokens})$ that interprets views as ternary relations on concrete states, abstract states and indexed sets of tokens.

Definition 1. *A relational view monoid is a commutative monoid* $(\mathsf{Views}, *, u)$, *where* Views *is an underlying set of relational views,* $*$ *is a monoid operation and* u *is a unit.*

The monoid structure of relational views allows treating them as restrictions on the environment of threads. Intuitively, each thread uses views to declare a protocol that other threads should follow while operating with concrete states, abstract states and tokens. Similarly to the separating conjunction from separation logic, the monoid operation $*$ (view composition) applied to a pair of views combines protocols of access to the state and ensures that they do not contradict each other.

Disjoint Concurrent Separation Logic. To give an example of a view monoid, we demonstrate the structure inspired by Disjoint Concurrent Separation logic (DCSL). A distinctive feature of DCSL is that its assertions enforce a protocol, according to which threads operate on disjoint pieces of memory. We assume a set of values Val, of which a subset $\mathsf{Loc} \subseteq \mathsf{Val}$ represents heap addresses. By letting $\mathsf{State} = \mathsf{AState} = (\mathsf{Loc} \rightharpoonup_{\mathrm{fin}} \mathsf{Val}) \cup \{\lightning\}$ we represent a state as either a finite partial function from locations to values or an exceptional faulting state $\lightning$, which denotes the result of an invalid memory access. We define an operation $\bullet$ on states, which results in $\lightning$ if either of the operands is $\lightning$, or the union of partial functions if their domains are disjoint. Finally, we assume that the set PCom consists of standard heap-manipulating commands with usual semantics [3,21].

We consider the view monoid $(\mathcal{P}((\mathsf{State} \setminus \{\lightning\}) \times (\mathsf{AState} \setminus \{\lightning\}) \times \mathsf{Tokens}), *_{\mathsf{SL}}, ([\ ], [\ ], [\ ]))$: the unit is a triple of nowhere defined functions $[\ ]$, and the view composition defined as follows:

$$p *_{\mathsf{SL}} p' \triangleq \{(\sigma \bullet \sigma', \Sigma \bullet \Sigma', \Delta \uplus \Delta') \mid (\sigma, \Sigma, \Delta) \in p \wedge (\sigma', \Sigma', \Delta') \in p'\}.$$

In this monoid, the composition enforces a protocol of exclusive ownership of parts of the heap: a pair of views can be composed only if they do not simultaneously describe the content of the same heap cell or a token. Since tokens are exclusively owned in DCSL, they cannot be accessed by other threads, which makes it impossible to express a helping mechanism with the DCSL views. In Sect. 5, we present another instance of our framework and reason about helping in it.

Reasoning about linearization points. We now introduce *action judgements*, which formalise linearization-points-based approach to proving linearizability within our framework.

Let us assume that α is executed in a concrete state σ with an abstract state Σ and a set of tokens Δ satisfying a precondition p. According to the action judgement $\alpha \Vdash_t \{p\}\{q\}$, for every update $\sigma' \in [\![\alpha]\!]_t(\sigma)$ of the concrete state, the abstract state may be changed to $\Sigma' \in [\![\mathrm{A}]\!]_{t'}(\Sigma)$ in order to satisfy the postcondition q, provided that there is a token $\mathsf{todo}(\mathrm{A})$ in a thread t'. When the abstract state Σ is changed and the token $\mathsf{todo}(\mathrm{A})$ of a thread t' is used, the concrete state update corresponds to a linearization point, or to a regular transition otherwise.

$$\begin{array}{ccc} \sigma & \xrightarrow{\lfloor p*r \rfloor} & \Sigma \\ \downarrow {\scriptstyle [\![\alpha]\!]} & & \downarrow {\scriptstyle [\![\mathrm{A}]\!]} \\ \sigma' & \dashrightarrow_{\lfloor q*r \rfloor} & \Sigma' \end{array}$$

Definition 2. *The action judgement* $\alpha \Vdash_t \{p\}\{q\}$ *holds, iff the following is true:*

$$\forall r, \sigma, \sigma', \Sigma, \Delta.\, (\sigma, \Sigma, \Delta) \in \lfloor p * r \rfloor \wedge \sigma' \in [\![\alpha]\!]_t(\sigma) \implies \exists \Sigma', \Delta'.\, \mathsf{LP}^*(\Sigma, \Delta, \Sigma', \Delta') \wedge (\sigma', \Sigma', \Delta') \in \lfloor q * r \rfloor,$$

where LP^* *is the transitive closure of the following relation:*

$$\mathsf{LP}(\Sigma, \Delta, \Sigma', \Delta') \triangleq \exists t', \mathrm{A}.\, \Sigma' \in [\![\mathrm{A}]\!]_{t'}(\Sigma) \wedge \Delta(t') = \mathsf{todo}(\mathrm{A}) \wedge \Delta' = \Delta[t' : \mathsf{done}(\mathrm{A})],$$

and $f[x : a]$ *denotes the function such that* $f[x : a](x) = a$ *and for any* $y \neq x$, $f[x : a](y) = f(y)$.

Note that depending on pre- and postconditions p and q, $\alpha \Vdash_t \{p\}\{q\}$ may encode a regular transition, a conditional or a standard linearization point. It is easy to see that the latter is the case only when in all sets of tokens Δ from $\lfloor p \rfloor$ some thread t' has a todo-token, and in all Δ' from $\lfloor q \rfloor$ it has a done-token. Additionally, the action judgement may represent a conditional linearization point of another thread, as the LP relation allows using tokens of other threads.

Action judgements have a closure property that is important for thread-modular reasoning: when $\alpha \Vdash_t \{p\}\{q\}$ holds, so does $\alpha \Vdash_t \{p * r\}\{q * r\}$ for

$$[\![\mathcal{P} * \mathcal{Q}]\!]_{\mathbf{i}} = [\![\mathcal{P}]\!]_{\mathbf{i}} * [\![\mathcal{Q}]\!]_{\mathbf{i}} \qquad [\![\mathcal{P} \Rrightarrow \mathcal{Q}]\!]_{\mathbf{i}} = [\![\mathcal{P}]\!]_{\mathbf{i}} \Rrightarrow [\![\mathcal{Q}]\!]_{\mathbf{i}}$$
$$[\![\mathcal{P} \vee \mathcal{Q}]\!]_{\mathbf{i}} = [\![\mathcal{P}]\!]_{\mathbf{i}} \vee [\![\mathcal{Q}]\!]_{\mathbf{i}} \qquad [\![\exists X.\, \mathcal{P}]\!]_{\mathbf{i}} = \bigvee_{n \in \mathsf{Val}} [\![\mathcal{P}]\!]_{\mathbf{i}[X:n]}$$

Fig. 2. Satisfaction relation for the assertion language Assn

every view r. That is, execution of α and a corresponding linearization point preserves every view r that p can be composed with. Consequently, when in every thread action judgements hold of primitive commands and thread's views, all threads together mutually agree on each other's protocols of the access to the shared memory encoded in their views. This enables reasoning about every thread in isolation with the assumption that its environment follows its protocol. Thus, the action judgements formalise the requirements that instances of our framework need to satisfy in order to be sound. In this regard action judgements are inspired by semantic judgements of the Views Framework [3]. Our technical contribution is in formulating the essential requirements for thread-modular reasoning about linearizability of concurrent libraries with the linearization-point method and in extending the semantic judgement with them.

We let a *repartitioning implication* of views p and q, written $p \Rrightarrow q$, denote $\forall r.\, \lfloor p * r \rfloor \subseteq \lfloor q * r \rfloor$. A repartitioning implication $p \Rrightarrow q$ ensures that states satisfying p also satisfy q and additionally requires this property to preserve any view r.

Program logic. We are now in a position to present our generic logic for linearizability proofs via the linearization-point method. Assuming a view monoid and reification function as parameters, we define a minimal language Assn for assertions $\mathcal{P}$ and $\mathcal{Q}$ denoting sets of views:

$$\mathcal{P}, \mathcal{Q} \in \mathsf{Assn} ::= \rho \mid \mathcal{P} * \mathcal{Q} \mid \mathcal{P} \vee \mathcal{Q} \mid \mathcal{P} \Rrightarrow \mathcal{Q} \mid \exists X.\, \mathcal{P} \mid \ldots$$

The grammar includes view assertions ρ, a syntax VAssn of which is a parameter of the framework. Formulas of Assn may contain the standard connectives from separation logic, the repartitioning implication and the existential quantification over logical variables X, ranging over a set LVar.

Let us assume an interpretation of logical variables $\mathbf{i} \in \mathsf{Int} = \mathsf{LVar} \to \mathsf{Val}$ that maps logical variables from LVar to values from a finite set Val. In Fig. 2, we define a function $[\![\cdot]\!]_{.} : \mathsf{Assn} \times \mathsf{Int} \to \mathsf{Views}$ that we use to interpret assertions. Interpretation of assertions is parametrised by $[\![\cdot]\!]_{.} : \mathsf{VAssn} \times \mathsf{Int} \to \mathsf{Views}$. In order to interpret disjunction, we introduce a corresponding operation on views and require the following properties from it:

$$\lfloor p \vee q \rfloor = \lfloor p \rfloor \cup \lfloor q \rfloor \qquad (p \vee q) * r = (p * r) \vee (q * r) \tag{1}$$

The judgements of the program logic take the form $\vdash_t \{\mathcal{P}\}\ C\ \{\mathcal{Q}\}$. In Fig. 3, we present the proof rules, which are mostly standard. Among them, the Prim rule is noteworthy, since it encorporates the simulation-based approach to reasoning about linearization points introduced by action judgements. The Frame

$$\text{(PRIM)}\ \frac{\forall \mathrm{i}.\ \alpha \Vdash_t \{[\![\mathcal{P}]\!]_{\mathrm{i}}\}\{[\![\mathcal{Q}]\!]_{\mathrm{i}}\}}{\vdash_t \{\mathcal{P}\}\ \alpha\ \{\mathcal{Q}\}} \qquad \text{(SEQ)}\ \frac{\vdash_t \{\mathcal{P}\}\ C_1\ \{\mathcal{P}'\} \quad \vdash_t \{\mathcal{P}'\}\ C_2\ \{\mathcal{Q}\}}{\vdash_t \{\mathcal{P}\}\ C_1\ ;\ C_2\ \{\mathcal{Q}\}}$$

$$\text{(FRAME)}\ \frac{\vdash_t \{\mathcal{P}\}\ C\ \{\mathcal{Q}\}}{\vdash_t \{\mathcal{P} * \mathcal{R}\}\ C\ \{\mathcal{Q} * \mathcal{R}\}} \qquad \text{(DISJ)}\ \frac{\vdash_t \{\mathcal{P}_1\}\ C\ \{\mathcal{Q}_1\} \quad \vdash_t \{\mathcal{P}_2\}\ C\ \{\mathcal{Q}_2\}}{\vdash_t \{\mathcal{P}_1 \vee \mathcal{P}_2\}\ C\ \{\mathcal{Q}_1 \vee \mathcal{Q}_2\}}$$

$$\text{(EX)}\ \frac{\vdash_t \{\mathcal{P}\}\ C\ \{\mathcal{Q}\}}{\vdash_t \{\exists X.\mathcal{P}\}\ C\ \{\exists X.\mathcal{Q}\}} \qquad \text{(CHOICE)}\ \frac{\vdash_t \{\mathcal{P}\}\ C_1\ \{\mathcal{Q}\} \quad \vdash_t \{\mathcal{P}\}\ C_2\ \{\mathcal{Q}\}}{\vdash_t \{\mathcal{P}\}\ C_1 + C_2\ \{\mathcal{Q}\}}$$

$$\text{(ITER)}\ \frac{\vdash_t \{\mathcal{P}\}\ C\ \{\mathcal{P}\}}{\vdash_t \{\mathcal{P}\}\ C^\star\ \{\mathcal{P}\}} \qquad \text{(CONSEQ)}\ \frac{\mathcal{P}' \Rrightarrow \mathcal{P} \quad \vdash_t \{\mathcal{P}\}\ C\ \{\mathcal{Q}\} \quad \mathcal{Q} \Rrightarrow \mathcal{Q}'}{\vdash_t \{\mathcal{P}'\}\ C\ \{\mathcal{Q}'\}}$$

Fig. 3. Proof rules

rule applies the idea of local reasoning from separation logic [21] to views. The CONSEQ enables weakening a precondition or a postcondition in a proof judgement and uses repartitioning implications to ensure the thread-modularity of the weakened proof judgement.

Semantics of proof judgements. We give semantics to judgements of the program logic by lifting the requirements of action judgements to sequential commands.

Definition 3 (Safety Judgement). *We define* safe_t *as the greatest relation such that the following holds whenever* $\mathsf{safe}_t(p, C, q)$ *does:*

- *if* $C \neq \mathsf{skip}$, *then* $\forall C', \alpha.\ C \xrightarrow{\alpha} C' \implies \exists p'.\ \alpha \Vdash_t \{p\}\{p'\} \wedge \mathsf{safe}_t(p', C', q)$,
- *if* $C = \mathsf{skip}$, *then* $p \Rrightarrow q$.

Lemma 4. $\forall t, \mathcal{P}, C, \mathcal{Q}.\ \vdash_t \{\mathcal{P}\}\ C\ \{\mathcal{Q}\} \implies \forall \mathrm{i}.\ \mathsf{safe}_t([\![\mathcal{P}]\!]_{\mathrm{i}}, C, [\![\mathcal{Q}]\!]_{\mathrm{i}})$.

We can understand the safety judgement $\mathsf{safe}_t([\![\mathcal{P}]\!]_{\mathrm{i}}, C, [\![\mathcal{Q}]\!]_{\mathrm{i}})$ as an obligation to create a sequence of views $[\![\mathcal{P}]\!]_{\mathrm{i}} = p_1, p_2, \ldots, p_{n+1} = [\![\mathcal{Q}]\!]_{\mathrm{i}}$ for each finite trace $\alpha_1, \alpha_2, \ldots, \alpha_n$ of C to justify each transition with action judgements $\alpha_1 \Vdash_t \{p_1\}\{p_2\}, \ldots,\ \alpha_n \Vdash_t \{p_n\}\{p_{n+1}\}$. Thus, when $\mathsf{safe}_t([\![\mathcal{P}]\!]_{\mathrm{i}}, C, [\![\mathcal{Q}]\!]_{\mathrm{i}})$ holds, it ensures that every step of the machine correctly preserves a correspondence between a concrete and abstract execution. Intuitively, the safety judgement lifts the simulation between concrete and abstract primitive commands established with action judgements to the implementation and specification of a method.

In Lemma 4, we establish that the proof judgements of the logic imply the safety judgements. As a part of the proof, we show that each of the proof rules of the logic holds of safety judgements. Due to space constraints, this and other proofs are given in the extended version of the paper [17].

4 Soundness

In this section, we formulate linearizability for libraries. We also formulate the soundness theorem, in which we state proof obligations that are necessary to conclude linearizability.

Libraries. We assume a set of method names Method, ranged over by m, and consider *a concrete library* $\ell : \mathsf{Method} \rightharpoonup ((\mathsf{Val} \times \mathsf{Val}) \to \mathsf{Com})$ that maps method names to commands from Com, which are parametrised by a pair of values from Val. For a given method name $m \in \mathsf{dom}(\ell)$ and values $a, v \in \mathsf{Val}$, a command $\ell(m, a, v)$ is an implementation of m, which accepts a as a method argument and either returns v or does not terminate. Such an unusual way of specifying method's arguments and return values significantly simplifies further development, since it does not require modelling a call stack.

Along with the library ℓ we consider its specification in the form of an abstract library $\mathcal{L} \in \mathsf{Method} \rightharpoonup ((\mathsf{Val} \times \mathsf{Val}) \to \mathsf{APCom})$ implementing a set of methods $\mathsf{dom}(\mathcal{L})$ atomically as abstract primitive commands $\{\mathcal{L}(m, a, v) \mid m \in \mathsf{dom}(\mathcal{L})\}$ parametrised by an argument a and a return value v. Given a method $m \in \mathsf{Method}$, we assume that a parametrised abstract primitive command $\mathcal{L}(m)$ is intended as a specification for $\ell(m)$.

Linearizability. The linearizability assumes a complete isolation between a library and its client, with interactions limited to passing values of a given data type as parameters or return values of library methods. Consequently, we are not interested in internal steps recorded in library computations, but only in the interactions of the library with its client. We record such interactions using *histories*, which are traces including only events $\mathsf{call}\ m(a)$ and $\mathsf{ret}\ m(v)$ that indicate an invocation of a method m with a parameter a and returning from m with a return value v, or formally:

$$h ::= \varepsilon \mid (t, \mathsf{call}\ m(a)) :: h \mid (t, \mathsf{ret}\ m(v)) :: h.$$

Given a library ℓ, we generate all finite histories of ℓ by considering N threads repeatedly invoking library methods in any order and with any possible arguments. The execution of methods is described by semantics of commands from Sect. 2.

We define a *thread pool* $\tau : \mathsf{ThreadID} \to (\mathsf{idle} \uplus (\mathsf{Com} \times \mathsf{Val}))$ to characterise progress of methods execution in each thread. The case of $\tau(t) = \mathsf{idle}$ corresponds to no method running in a thread t. When $\tau(t) = (C, v)$, to finish some method returning v it remains to execute C.

Definition 5. *We let* $\mathcal{H}[\![\ell, \sigma]\!] = \bigcup_{n \geq 0} \mathcal{H}_n[\![\ell, (\lambda t.\, \mathsf{idle}), \sigma]\!]$ *denote the set of all possible histories of a library* ℓ *that start from a state* σ*, where for a given thread pool* τ*,* $\mathcal{H}_n[\![\ell, \tau, \sigma]\!]$ *is defined as a set of histories such that* $\mathcal{H}_0[\![\ell, \tau, \sigma]\!] \triangleq \{\varepsilon\}$ *and:*

$$\begin{aligned}
\mathcal{H}_n[\![\ell, \tau, \sigma]\!] \triangleq\ & \{((t, \mathsf{call}\ m(a)) :: h) \mid a \in \mathsf{Val} \wedge m \in \mathsf{dom}(\ell) \wedge \tau(t) = \mathsf{idle} \wedge \\
& \qquad \exists v.\, h \in \mathcal{H}_{n-1}[\![\ell, \tau[t : (\ell(m, a, v), v)], \sigma]\!]\} \\
& \cup \{h \mid \exists t, \alpha, C, C', \sigma', v.\, \tau(t) = (C, v) \wedge \langle C, \sigma \rangle \xrightarrow{t,\alpha} \langle C', \sigma' \rangle \wedge \\
& \qquad h \in \mathcal{H}_{n-1}[\![\ell, \tau[t : (C', v)], \sigma']\!]\} \\
& \cup \{((t, \mathsf{ret}\ m(v)) :: h) \mid m \in \mathsf{dom}(\ell) \wedge \tau(t) = (\mathsf{skip}, v) \wedge \\
& \qquad h \in \mathcal{H}_{n-1}[\![\ell, \tau[t : \mathsf{idle}], \sigma]\!]\}
\end{aligned}$$

Thus, we construct the set of all finite histories inductively with all threads initially idling. At each step of generation, in any idling thread t any method

$m \in \mathsf{dom}(\ell)$ may be called with any argument a and an expected return value v, which leads to adding a command $\ell(m, a, v)$ to the thread pool of a thread t. Also, any thread t, in which $\tau(t) = (C, v)$, may do a transition $\langle C, \sigma\rangle \xrightarrow{t,\alpha} \langle C', \sigma'\rangle$ changing a command in the thread pool and the concrete state. Finally, any thread that has finished execution of a method's command ($\tau(t) = (\mathsf{skip}, v)$) may become idle by letting $\tau(t) = \mathsf{idle}$.

We define $\mathcal{H}_n[\![\mathcal{L}, \mathcal{T}, \Sigma]\!]$ analogously and let the set of all histories of an abstract library $\mathcal{L}$ starting from the initial state Σ be $\mathcal{H}[\![\mathcal{L}, \Sigma]\!] = \bigcup_{n\geq 0} \mathcal{H}_n[\![\mathcal{L}, (\lambda t.\, \mathsf{idle}), \Sigma]\!]$.

Definition 6. *For libraries ℓ and $\mathcal{L}$ such that $\mathsf{dom}(\ell) = \mathsf{dom}(\mathcal{L})$, we say that $\mathcal{L}$* ***linearizes*** *ℓ in the states σ and Σ, written $(\ell, \sigma) \sqsubseteq (\mathcal{L}, \Sigma)$, if $\mathcal{H}[\![\ell, \sigma]\!] \subseteq \mathcal{H}[\![\mathcal{L}, \Sigma]\!]$.*

That is, an abstract library $\mathcal{L}$ linearizes ℓ in the states σ and Σ, if every history of ℓ can be reproduced by $\mathcal{L}$. The definition is different from the standard one [14]: we use the result obtained by Gotsman and Yang [10] stating that the plain subset inclusion on the sets of histories produced by concrete and abstract libraries is equivalent to the original definition of linearizability.

Soundness w.r.t. linearizability. We now explain proof obligations that we need to show for every method m of a concrete library ℓ to conclude its linearizability. Particularly, for every thread t, argument a, return value v, and a command $\ell(m, a, v)$ we require that there exist assertions $\mathcal{P}(t, \mathcal{L}(m, a, v))$ and $\mathcal{Q}(t, \mathcal{L}(m, a, v))$, for which the following Hoare-style specification holds:

$$\vdash_t \{\mathcal{P}(t, \mathcal{L}(m, a, v))\}\ \ell(m, a, v)\ \{\mathcal{Q}(t, \mathcal{L}(m, a, v))\} \tag{2}$$

In the specification of $\ell(m, a, v)$, $\mathcal{P}(t, \mathcal{L}(m, a, v))$ and $\mathcal{Q}(t, \mathcal{L}(m, a, v))$ are assertions parametrised by a thread t and an abstract command $\mathcal{L}(m, a, v)$. We require that in a thread t of all states satisfying $\mathcal{P}(t, \mathcal{L}(m, a, v))$ and $\mathcal{Q}(t, \mathcal{L}(m, a, v))$ there be only tokens $\mathsf{todo}(\mathcal{L}(m, a, v))$ and $\mathsf{done}(\mathcal{L}(m, a, v))$ respectively:

$$\begin{aligned} &\forall \mathbf{i}, t, \sigma, \Sigma, \Delta, r. \\ &\quad ((\sigma, \Sigma, \Delta) \in \lfloor [\![\mathcal{P}(t, \mathcal{L}(m, a, v))]\!]_{\mathbf{i}} * r \rfloor \implies \Delta(t) = \mathsf{todo}(\mathcal{L}(m, a, v))) \\ &\quad \wedge ((\sigma, \Sigma, \Delta) \in \lfloor [\![\mathcal{Q}(t, \mathcal{L}(m, a, v))]\!]_{\mathbf{i}} * r \rfloor \implies \Delta(t) = \mathsf{done}(\mathcal{L}(m, a, v))) \end{aligned} \tag{3}$$

Together, (2) and (3) impose a requirement that a concrete and an abstract method return the same return value v. We also require that the states satisfying the assertions only differ by a token of a thread t:

$$\begin{aligned} \forall \mathbf{i}, t, \mathrm{A}, \mathrm{A}', r, \Delta.\, &(\sigma, \Sigma, \Delta[t : \mathsf{done}(\mathrm{A})]) \in \lfloor [\![\mathcal{Q}(t, \mathrm{A})]\!]_{\mathbf{i}} * r \rfloor \iff \\ &(\sigma, \Sigma, \Delta[t : \mathsf{todo}(\mathrm{A}')]) \in \lfloor [\![\mathcal{P}(t, \mathrm{A}')]\!]_{\mathbf{i}} * r \rfloor. \end{aligned} \tag{4}$$

Theorem 7. *For given libraries ℓ and $\mathcal{L}$ together with states σ and Σ, $(\ell, \sigma) \sqsubseteq (\mathcal{L}, \Sigma)$ holds, if $\mathsf{dom}(\ell) = \mathsf{dom}(\mathcal{L})$ and (2), (3) and (4) hold for every method m, thread t and values a and v.*

5 The RGSep-Based Logic

In this section, we demonstrate an instance of the generic proof system that is capable of handling algorithms with helping. This instance is based on RGSep [26], which combines rely-guarantee reasoning [15] with separation logic [21].

The main idea of the logic is to partition the state into several thread-local parts (which can only be accessed by corresponding threads) and the shared part (which can be accessed by all threads). The partitioning is defined by proofs in the logic: an assertion in the code of a thread restricts its local state and the shared state. In addition, the partitioning is dynamic, meaning that resources, such as a part of a heap or a token, can be moved from the local state of a thread into the shared state and vice versa. By transferring a token to the shared state, a thread gives to its environment a permission to change the abstract state. This allows us to reason about environment helping that thread.

The RGSep-based view monoid. Similarly to DCSL, we assume that states represent heaps, i.e. that $\mathsf{State} = \mathsf{AState} = \mathsf{Loc} \rightharpoonup_{\mathrm{fin}} \mathsf{Val} \uplus \{\lightning\}$, and we denote all states but a faulting one with $\mathsf{State_H} = \mathsf{AState_H} = \mathsf{Loc} \rightharpoonup_{\mathrm{fin}} \mathsf{Val}$. We also assume a standard set of heap-manipulating primitive commands with usual semantics.

We define views as triples consisting of three components: a predicate P and binary relations R and G. A predicate $P \in \mathcal{P}((\mathsf{State_H} \times \mathsf{AState_H} \times \mathsf{Tokens})^2)$ is a set of pairs (l, s) of local and shared parts of the state, where each part consists of concrete state, abstract state and tokens. *Guarantee* G and *rely* R are relations from $\mathcal{P}((\mathsf{State} \times \mathsf{AState} \times \mathsf{Tokens})^2)$, which summarise how individual primitive commands executed by the method's thread (in case of G) and the environment (in case of R) may change the shared state. Together guarantee and rely establish a protocol that views of the method and its environment respectively must agree on each other's transitions, which allows us to reason about every thread separately without considering local state of other threads, assuming that they follow the protocol. The agreement is expressed with the help of a well-formedness condition on views of the RGSep-based monoid that their predicates must be *stable* under rely, meaning that their predicates take into account whatever changes their environment can make:

$$\mathsf{stable}(P, R) \triangleq \forall l, s, s'.\, (l, s) \in P \land (s, s') \in R \implies (l, s') \in P.$$

A predicate that is stable under rely cannot be invalidated by any state transition from rely. Stable predicates with rely and guarantee relations form the view monoid with the underlying set of views $\mathsf{Views_{RGsep}} = \{(P, R, G) \mid \mathsf{stable}(P, R)\} \cup \{\bot\}$, where $\bot$ denotes a special *inconsistent* view with the empty reification. The reification of other views simply joins shared and local parts of the state:

$$\lfloor (P, R, G) \rfloor = \{(\sigma_l \bullet \sigma_s, \Sigma_l \bullet \Sigma_s, \Delta_l \uplus \Delta_s) \mid ((\sigma_l, \Sigma_l, \Delta_l), (\sigma_s, \Sigma_s, \Delta_s)) \in P\}.$$

Let an operation $\cdot$ be defined on states analogously to DCSL. Given predicates P and P', we let $P * P'$ be a predicate denoting the pairs of local and shared states in which the local state can be divided into two substates such that one

$\models$: (State × AState × Tokens) × (State × AState × Tokens) × Int × Assn

$$
\begin{array}{ll}
((\sigma_l, \Sigma_l, \Delta_l), (\sigma_s, \Sigma_s, \Delta_s), \mathbf{i}) \models E \mapsto F, & \text{iff } \sigma_l = [[\![E]\!]_{\mathbf{i}} : [\![F]\!]_{\mathbf{i}}], \Sigma_l = [\,], \text{ and } \Delta_l = [\,] \\
((\sigma_l, \Sigma_l, \Delta_l), (\sigma_s, \Sigma_s, \Delta_s), \mathbf{i}) \models E \Mapsto F, & \text{iff } \sigma_l = [\,], \Sigma_l = [[\![E]\!]_{\mathbf{i}} : [\![F]\!]_{\mathbf{i}}], \text{ and } \Delta_l = [\,] \\
((\sigma_l, \Sigma_l, \Delta_l), (\sigma_s, \Sigma_s, \Delta_s), \mathbf{i}) \models [\mathsf{todo}(\mathrm{A})]_t, & \text{iff } \sigma_l = [\,], \Sigma_l = [\,], \text{ and } \Delta_l = [t : \mathsf{todo}(\mathrm{A})] \\
((\sigma_l, \Sigma_l, \Delta_l), (\sigma_s, \Sigma_s, \Delta_s), \mathbf{i}) \models [\mathsf{done}(\mathrm{A})]_t, & \text{iff } \sigma_l = [\,], \Sigma_l = [\,], \text{ and } \Delta_l = [t : \mathsf{done}(\mathrm{A})] \\
((\sigma_l, \Sigma_l, \Delta_l), (\sigma_s, \Sigma_s, \Delta_s), \mathbf{i}) \models \boxed{\pi}, & \text{iff } \sigma_l = [\,], \Sigma_l = [\,], \Delta_l = [\,], \text{ and} \\
& \quad ((\sigma_s, \Sigma_s, \Delta_s), ([\,], [\,], [\,]), \mathbf{i}) \models \pi \\
((\sigma_l, \Sigma_l, \Delta_l), (\sigma_s, \Sigma_s, \Delta_s), \mathbf{i}) \models \pi * \pi', & \text{iff there exist } \sigma_l', \sigma_l'', \Sigma_l', \Sigma_l'', \Delta_l', \Delta_l'' \text{ such that} \\
& \sigma_l = \sigma_l' \bullet \sigma_l'', \Sigma_l = \Sigma_l' \bullet \Sigma_l'', \Delta_l = \Delta_l' \uplus \Delta_l'', \\
& ((\sigma_l', \Sigma_l', \Delta_l'), (\sigma_s, \Sigma_s, \Delta_s), \mathbf{i}) \models \pi, \text{ and} \\
& ((\sigma_l'', \Sigma_l'', \Delta_l''), (\sigma_s, \Sigma_s, \Delta_s), \mathbf{i}) \models \pi'
\end{array}
$$

Fig. 4. Satisfaction relation for a fragment of the assertion language VAssn

of them together with the shared state satisfies P and the other together with the shared state satisfies P':

$$P * P' \triangleq \{((\sigma_l \bullet \sigma_l', \Sigma_l \bullet \Sigma_l', \Delta_l \uplus \Delta_l'), s) \mid ((\sigma_l, \Sigma_l, \Delta_l), s) \in P \wedge ((\sigma_l', \Sigma_l', \Delta_l'), s) \in P'\}$$

We now define the monoid operation $*$, which we use to compose views of different threads. When composing views (P, R, G) and (P', R', G') of the parallel threads, we require predicates of both to be immune to interference by all other threads and each other. Otherwise, the result is inconsistent:

$$(P, R, G) * (P', R', G') \triangleq \text{if } G \subseteq R' \wedge G' \subseteq R \text{ then } (P * P', R \cap R', G \cup G') \text{ else } \bot.$$

That is, we let the composition of views be consistently defined when the state transitions allowed in a guarantee of one thread are treated as environment transitions in the other thread, i.e. $G \subseteq R'$ and $G' \subseteq R$. The rely of the composition is $R \cap R'$, since the predicate $P * P'$ is guaranteed to be stable only under environment transitions described by both R and R'. The guarantee of the composition is $G \cup G'$, since other views need to take into account all state transitions either from G or from G'.

The RGSep-based program logic. We define the view assertion language VAssn that is a parameter of the proof system. Each view assertion ρ takes form of a triple $(\pi, \mathcal{R}, \mathcal{G})$, and the syntax for π is:

$$
\begin{array}{l}
E ::= a \mid X \mid E + E \mid \ldots, \quad \text{where } X \in \mathsf{LVar}, a \in \mathsf{Val} \\
\pi ::= E = E \mid E \mapsto E \mid E \Mapsto E \mid [\mathsf{todo}(\mathrm{A})]_t \mid [\mathsf{done}(\mathrm{A})]_t \mid \boxed{\pi} \mid \pi * \pi \mid \neg \pi \mid \ldots
\end{array}
$$

Formula π denotes a predicate of a view as defined by a satisfaction relation $\models$ in Fig. 4. There $E \mapsto E$ and $E \Mapsto E$ denote a concrete and an abstract state describing singleton heaps. A non-boxed formula π denotes the view with the local state satisfying π and shared state unrestricted; $\boxed{\pi}$ denotes the view with the empty local state and the shared state satisfying π; $\pi * \pi'$ the composition of predicates corresponding to π and π'. The semantics of the rest of connectives

```
int L = 0, k = 0, arg[N], res[N]; \\ initially all res[i] ≠ nil

ℓ(inc, a, r):
  { global ∗ M(t) ∗ [todo(ℒ(inc, a, r))]_t }
  arg[mytid()] := a;
  res[mytid()] := nil;
  { global ∗ [true ∗ (task_todo(t, a, r) ∨ task_done(t, a, r))] }
  while (res[mytid()] = nil):
    if (CAS(&L, 0, mytid())):
      { [&L ↦ t ∗ ⊛_{j∈ThreadID} tinv(j)] ∗ [true ∗ (task_todo(t, a, r) ∨ task_done(t, a, r))] ∗ kinv(_) }
      for (i := 1; i ≤ N; ++i):
        { [&L ↦ t ∗ ⊛_{j∈ThreadID} tinv(j)] ∗ kinv(_) ∗ LI(i, t, a, r) }
        if (res[i] = nil):
          { ∃V, A, R. kinv(V) ∗ LI(i, t, a, r) ∗
            [&L ↦ t ∗ ⊛_{j∈ThreadID} tinv(j)] ∗ [true ∗ task_todo(i, A, R)] }
          k := k + arg[i];
          { ∃V, A, R. &k ↦ V + A ∗ &K ⤇ V ∗ LI(i, t, a, r) ∗
            [&L ↦ t ∗ ⊛_{j∈ThreadID} tinv(j)] ∗ [true ∗ task_todo(i, A, R)] }
          res[i]  := k;
          { ∃V, A, R. kinv(V + A) ∗ LI(i + 1, t, a, r) ∗
            [&L ↦ t ∗ ⊛_{j∈ThreadID} tinv(j)] ∗ [true ∗ task_done(i, A, R)] }
      { [&L ↦ t ∗ ⊛_{j∈ThreadID} tinv(j)] ∗ [true ∗ task_done(t, a, r)] ∗ kinv(_) }
      L = 0;
  assume(res[mytid()] = r);
  { global ∗ M(t) ∗ [done(ℒ(inc, a, r))]_t }
```

Fig. 5. Proof outline for a flat combiner of a concurrent increment. Indentation is used for grouping commands.

is standard. Additionally, for simplicity of presentation of the syntax, we require that boxed assertions $\boxed{\pi}$ be not nested (as opposed to preventing that in the definition).

The other components $\mathcal{R}$ and $\mathcal{G}$ of a view assertion are sets of *rely/guarantee actions* $\mathcal{A}$ with the syntax: $\mathcal{A} ::= \pi \rightsquigarrow \pi'$. An action $\pi \rightsquigarrow \pi'$ denotes a change of a part of the shared state that satisfies π into one that satisfies π', while leaving the rest of the shared state unchanged. We associate with an action $\pi \rightsquigarrow \pi'$ all state transitions from the following set:

$$\begin{aligned}\llbracket \pi \rightsquigarrow \pi' \rrbracket = \{&((\sigma_s \bullet \sigma''_s, \Sigma_s \bullet \Sigma''_s, \Delta_s \uplus \Delta''_s), (\sigma'_s \bullet \sigma''_s, \Sigma'_s \bullet \Sigma''_s, \Delta'_s \uplus \Delta''_s)) \mid \\ &\exists \mathbf{i}. (([\,],[\,],[\,]), (\sigma_s, \Sigma_s, \Delta_s), \mathbf{i}) \models \boxed{\pi} \wedge (([\,],[\,],[\,]), (\sigma'_s, \Sigma'_s, \Delta'_s), \mathbf{i}) \models \boxed{\pi'}\}\end{aligned}$$

We give semantics to view assertions with the function $\llbracket \cdot \rrbracket_{.}$ that is defined as follows:

$$\llbracket (\pi, \mathcal{R}, \mathcal{G}) \rrbracket_{\mathbf{i}} \triangleq (\{(l, s) \mid (l, s, \mathbf{i}) \models \pi\}, \bigcup_{\mathcal{A} \in \mathcal{R}} \llbracket \mathcal{A} \rrbracket, \bigcup_{\mathcal{A} \in \mathcal{G}} \llbracket \mathcal{A} \rrbracket).$$

$$
\begin{array}{ll}
X \not\mapsto Y & \triangleq \exists Y'.\, X \mapsto Y' * Y \neq Y' \\
M(t) & \triangleq \boxed{\mathsf{true} * (\&\mathtt{arg}[t] \mapsto \_ * \&\mathtt{res}[t] \not\mapsto \mathtt{nil})} \\
\mathsf{task}_{\mathsf{todo}}(t,a,r) & \triangleq \&\mathtt{arg}[t] \mapsto a * \&\mathtt{res}[t] \mapsto \mathtt{nil} * [\mathsf{todo}(\mathcal{L}(\mathsf{inc},a,r))]_t\,; \\
\mathsf{task}_{\mathsf{done}}(t,a,r) & \triangleq \&\mathtt{arg}[t] \mapsto a * \&\mathtt{res}[t] \mapsto r * r \neq \mathtt{nil} * [\mathsf{done}(\mathcal{L}(\mathsf{inc},a,r))]_t\,; \\
\mathsf{kinv}(V) & \triangleq \&\mathtt{k} \mapsto V * \&\mathtt{K} \Mapsto V \\
\mathsf{LI}(i,t,a,r) & \triangleq \boxed{\begin{array}{l}\mathsf{true} * ((t < i \wedge \mathsf{task}_{\mathsf{done}}(t,a,r)) \vee \\ (t \geq i \wedge (\mathsf{task}_{\mathsf{todo}}(t,a,r) \vee \mathsf{task}_{\mathsf{done}}(t,a,r))))\end{array}} \\
\mathsf{tinv}(i) & \triangleq \&\mathtt{arg}[i] \mapsto \_ * \&\mathtt{res}[i] \Mapsto \_ \vee \mathsf{task}_{\mathsf{todo}}(i,\_,\_) \vee \mathsf{task}_{\mathsf{done}}(i,\_,\_) \\
\mathsf{global} & \triangleq \boxed{(\&\mathtt{L} \mapsto 0 * \mathsf{kinv}(\_) \vee \&\mathtt{L} \not\mapsto 0) * \circledast_{j \in \mathsf{ThreadID}} \mathsf{tinv}(j)},
\end{array}
$$

Fig. 6. Auxiliary predicates. $\circledast_{j \in \mathsf{ThreadID}} \mathsf{tinv}(j)$ denotes $\mathsf{tinv}(1) * \mathsf{tinv}(2) * \cdot * \mathsf{tinv}(N)$

6 Example

In this section, we demonstrate how to reason about algorithms with helping using relational views. We choose a simple library ℓ implementing a concurrent increment and prove its linearizability with the RGSep-based logic.

The concrete library ℓ has one method inc, which increments the value of a shared counter `k` by the argument of the method. The specification of ℓ is given by an abstract library $\mathcal{L}$. The abstract command, provided by $\mathcal{L}$ as an implementation of inc, operates with an abstract counter `K` as follows (assuming that `K` is initialised by zero):

```
L(inc, a, r):    < __kabs := __kabs + a; assume(__kabs == r); >
```

That is, $\mathcal{L}(\mathsf{inc}, a, r)$ atomically increments a counter and a command $\mathtt{assume}(\mathtt{K} == r)$, which terminates only if the return value r chosen at the invocation equals to the resulting value of `K`. This corresponds to how we specify methods' return values in Sect. 4.

In Fig. 5, we show the pseudo-code of the implementation of a method inc in a C-style language along with a proof outline. The method $\ell(\mathsf{inc}, a, r)$ takes one argument, increments a shared counter `k` by it and returns the increased value of the counter. Since `k` is shared among threads, they follow a protocol regulating the access to the counter. This protocol is based on flat combining [11], which is a synchronisation technique enabling a parallel execution of sequential operations.

The protocol is the following. When a thread t executes $\ell(\mathsf{inc}, a, r)$, it first makes the argument of the method visible to other threads by storing it in an array `arg`, and lets $\mathtt{res}[t] = \mathtt{nil}$ to signal to other threads its intention to execute an increment with that argument. It then spins in the loop on line 8, trying to write its thread identifier into a variable `L` with a compare-and-swap (CAS). Out of all threads spinning in the loop, the one that succeeds in writing into `L` becomes a *combiner*: it performs the increments requested by all threads with arguments stored in `arg` and writes the results into corresponding cells of the array `res`. The other threads keep spinning and periodically checking the value of their cells in `res` until a non-`nil` value appears in it, meaning that a combiner has performed the operation requested and marked it as finished. The protocol relies on the assumption that `nil` is a value that is never returned by the method. Similarly to the specification of the increment method, the implementation in Fig. 5 ends with a command $\texttt{assume}(\texttt{res}[\texttt{mytid}()] = r)$.

The proof outline features auxiliary assertions defined in Fig. 6. In the assertions we let $\_$ denote a value or a logical variable whose name is irrelevant. We assume that each program variable `var` has a unique location in the heap and denote it with &`var`. Values a, r and t are used in the formulas and the code as constants.

We prove the following specification for $\ell(\mathsf{inc}, a, r)$:

$$\mathcal{R}_t, \mathcal{G}_t \vdash_t \left\{ \begin{array}{c} \mathsf{global} * M(t) * \\ [\mathsf{todo}(\mathcal{L}(\mathsf{inc}, a, r))]_t \end{array} \right\} \ell(\mathsf{inc}, a, r) \left\{ \begin{array}{c} \mathsf{global} * M(t) * \\ [\mathsf{done}(\mathcal{L}(\mathsf{inc}, a, r))]_t \end{array} \right\}$$

In the specification, $M(t)$ asserts the presence of $\texttt{arg}[t]$ and $\texttt{res}[t]$ in the shared state, and global is an assertion describing the shared state of all the threads. Thus, the pre- and postcondition of the specification differ only by the kind of token given to t.

The main idea of the proof is in allowing a thread t to share the ownership of its token $[\mathsf{todo}(\mathcal{L}(\mathsf{inc}, a, r))]_t$ with the other threads. This enables two possibilities for t. Firstly, t may become a combiner. Then t has a linearization point on line 17 (when the loop index i equals to t). In this case t also *helps* other concurrent threads by performing their linearization points on line 17 (when $i \neq t$). The alternative possibility is that some other thread becomes a combiner and does a linearization point of t. Thus, the method has a non-fixed linearization point, as it may occur in the code of a different thread.

We further explain how the tokens are transferred. On line 6 the method performs the assignment `res[mytid()] := nil`, signalling to other threads about a task this thread is performing. At this step, the method transfers its token $[\mathsf{todo}(\mathcal{L}(\mathsf{inc}, a, r))]_t$ to the shared state, as represented by the assertion $\boxed{\mathsf{true} * \mathsf{task}_{\mathsf{todo}}(t, a, r)}$. In order to take into consideration other threads interfering with t and possibly helping it, here and further we stabilise the assertion by adding a disjunct $\mathsf{task}_{\mathsf{done}}(t, a, r)$.

If a thread t gets help from other threads, then $\mathsf{task}_{\mathsf{done}}(t, a, r)$ holds, which implies that $\texttt{res}[t] \neq \texttt{nil}$ and t cannot enter the loop on line 8. Otherwise, if t becomes a combiner, it transfers $\mathsf{kinv}(\_)$ from the shared state to the local state of t to take over the ownership of the counters `k` and `K` and thus ensure that the access to the counter is governed by the mutual exclusion protocol. At each iteration i of the forall loop, `res[i] = nil` implies that $\mathsf{task}_{\mathsf{todo}}(i, \_, \_)$ holds, meaning that there is a token of a thread i in the shared state. Consequently, on line 17 a thread t may use it to perform a linearization point of i.

The actions defining the guarantee relation $\mathcal{G}_t$ of a thread t' are the following:

1. $\&\texttt{arg}[t] \mapsto \_ * \&\texttt{res}[t] \not\mapsto \texttt{nil} \rightsquigarrow \&\texttt{arg}[t] \mapsto a * \&\texttt{res}[t] \not\mapsto \texttt{nil}$;
2. $\&\texttt{arg}[t] \mapsto a * \&\texttt{res}[t] \not\mapsto \texttt{nil} \rightsquigarrow \mathsf{task}_{\mathsf{todo}}(t, a, r)$;

3. $\&\mathsf{L} \mapsto 0 * \mathsf{kinv}(\_) \rightsquigarrow \&\mathsf{L} \mapsto t$;
4. $\&\mathsf{L} \mapsto t * \mathsf{task}_{\mathsf{todo}}(T, A, R) \rightsquigarrow \&\mathsf{L} \mapsto t * \mathsf{task}_{\mathsf{done}}(T, A, R)$
5. $\&\mathsf{L} \mapsto t \rightsquigarrow \&\mathsf{L} \mapsto 0 * \mathsf{kinv}(\_)$
6. $\mathsf{task}_{\mathsf{done}}(t, a, r) \rightsquigarrow \&\mathtt{arg}[t] \mapsto a * \&\mathtt{res}[t] \mapsto r$

Out of them, conditions 2 and 6 specify transfering the token of a thread t to and from the shared state, and condition 4 describes using the shared token of a thread T. The rely relation of a thread t is then defined as the union of all actions from guarantee relations of other threads and an additional action for each thread $t' \in \mathsf{ThreadID} \setminus \{t\}$ allowing the client to prepare a thread t' for a new method call by giving it a new token: $[\mathsf{done}(\mathcal{L}(\mathsf{inc}, A, R))]_{t'} \rightsquigarrow [\mathsf{todo}(\mathcal{L}(\mathsf{inc}, A', R'))]_{t'}$.

7 Related Work

There has been a significant amount of research on methods for proving linearizability. Due to space constraints, we do not attempt a comprehensive survey here (see [6]) and only describe the most closely related work.

The existing logics for linearizability that use linearization points differ in the thread-modular reasoning method used and, hence, in the range of concurrent algorithms that they can handle. Our goal in this paper was to propose a uniform basis for designing such logics and to formalise the method they use for reasoning about linearizability in a way independent of the particular thread-modular reasoning method used. We have only shown instantiations of our logic based on disjoint concurrent separation logic [20] and RGSep [26]. However, we expect that our logic can also be instantiated with more complex thread-modular reasoning methods, such as those based on concurrent abstract predicates [4] or islands and protocols [25].

Our notion of tokens is based on the idea of treating method specifications as resources when proving atomicity, which has appeared in various guises in several logics [2,18,26]. Our contribution is to formalise this method of handling linearization points independently from the underlying thread-modular reasoning method and to formulate the conditions for soundly combining the two (Definition 2, Sect. 3).

We have presented a logic that unifies the various logics based on linearization points with helping. However, much work still remains as this reasoning method cannot handle all algorithms. Some logics have introduced *speculative* linearization points to increase their applicability [18,25]; our approach to helping is closely related to this, and we hope could be extended to speculation. But there are still examples beyond this form of reasoning: for instance there are no proofs of the Herlihy-Wing queue [14] using linearization points (with helping and/or speculation). This algorithm can be shown linearizable using forwards/backwards simulation [14] and more recently has been shown to only require a backwards simulation [22]. But integrating this form of simulation with the more intrincate notions of interference expressible in the Views framework remains an open problem.

Another approach to proving linearizability is the aspect-oriented method. This gives a series of properties of a queue [12] (or a stack [5]) implementation which imply that the implementation is linearizable. This method been applied to algorithms that cannot be handled with standard linearization-point-based methods. However, the aspect-oriented approach requires a custom theorem per data structure, which limits its applicability.

In this paper we concentrated on linearizability in its original form [14], which considers only finite computations and, hence, specifies only safety properties of the library. Linearizability has since been generalised to also specify liveness properties [9]. Another direction of future work is to generalise our logic to handle liveness, possibly building on ideas from [19].

When a library is linearizable, one can use its atomic specification instead of the actual implementation to reason about its clients [8]. Some logics achieve the same effect without using linearizability, by expressing library specifications as judgements in the logic rather than as the code of an abstract library [16,23,24]. It is an interesting direction of future work to determine a precise relationship between this method of specification and linearizability, and to propose a generic logic unifying the two.

8 Conclusion

We have presented a logic for proving the linearizability of concurrent libraries that can be instantiated with different methods for thread-modular reasoning. To this end, we have extended the Views framework [3] to reason about relations between programs. Our main technical contribution in this regard was to propose the requirement for axiom soundness (Definition 2, Sect. 3) that ensures a correct interaction between the treatment of linearization points and the underlying thread-modular reasoning. We have shown that our logic is powerful enough to handle concurrent algorithms with challenging features, such as helping. More generally, our work marks the first step towards unifying the logics for proving relational properties of concurrent programs.

References

1. Bornat, R., Calcagno, C., O'Hearn, P.W., Parkinson, M.J.: Permission accounting in separation logic. In: POPL (2005)
2. Rocha Pinto, P., Dinsdale-Young, T., Gardner, P.: TaDA: a logic for time and data abstraction. In: Jones, R. (ed.) ECOOP 2014. LNCS, vol. 8586, pp. 207–231. Springer, Heidelberg (2014). doi:10.1007/978-3-662-44202-9_9
3. Dinsdale-Young, T., Birkedal, L., Gardner, P., Parkinson, M.J., Yang, H.: Views: compositional reasoning for concurrent programs. In: POPL (2013)
4. Dinsdale-Young, T., Dodds, M., Gardner, P., Parkinson, M.J., Vafeiadis, V.: Concurrent abstract predicates. In: D'Hondt, T. (ed.) ECOOP 2010. LNCS, vol. 6183, pp. 504–528. Springer, Heidelberg (2010). doi:10.1007/978-3-642-14107-2_24
5. Dodds, M., Haas, A., Kirsch, C.M.: A scalable, correct time-stamped stack. In: POPL, New York, NY, USA (2015)

6. Dongol, B., Derrick, J.: Verifying linearizability: a comparative survey. arXiv CoRR, 1410.6268 (2014)
7. Feng, X.: Local rely-guarantee reasoning. In: POPL (2009)
8. Filipovic, I., O'Hearn, P.W., Rinetzky, N., Yang, H.: Abstraction for concurrent objects. Theor. Comput. Sci. **411**, 4379 (2010)
9. Gotsman, A., Yang, H.: Liveness-preserving atomicity abstraction. In: Aceto, L., Henzinger, M., Sgall, J. (eds.) ICALP 2011. LNCS, vol. 6756, pp. 453–465. Springer, Heidelberg (2011). doi:10.1007/978-3-642-22012-8_36
10. Gotsman, A., Yang, H.: Linearizability with ownership transfer. In: Koutny, M., Ulidowski, I. (eds.) CONCUR 2012. LNCS, vol. 7454, pp. 256–271. Springer, Heidelberg (2012). doi:10.1007/978-3-642-32940-1_19
11. Hendler, D., Incze, I., Shavit, N., Tzafrir, M.: Flat combining and the synchronization-parallelism tradeoff. In: SPAA (2010)
12. Henzinger, T.A., Sezgin, A., Vafeiadis, V.: Aspect-oriented linearizability proofs. In: D'Argenio, P.R., Melgratti, H. (eds.) CONCUR 2013. LNCS, vol. 8052, pp. 242–256. Springer, Heidelberg (2013). doi:10.1007/978-3-642-40184-8_18
13. Herlihy, M., Shavit, N.: The Art of Multiprocessor Programming (2008)
14. Herlihy, M., Wing, J.M.: Linearizability: a correctness condition for concurrent objects. ACM TOPLAS **12**, 463 (1990)
15. Jones, C.B.: Specification and design of (parallel) programs. In: IFIP Congress (1983)
16. Jung, R., Swasey, D., Sieczkowski, F., Svendsen, K., Turon, A., Birkedal, L., Dreyer, D.: Iris: monoids and invariants as an orthogonal basis for concurrent reasoning. In: POPL (2015)
17. Khyzha, A., Gotsman, A., Parkinson, M.: A generic logic for proving linearizability (extended version). arXiv CoRR, 1609.01171, 2016
18. Liang, H., Feng, X.: Modular verification of linearizability with non-fixed linearization points. In: PLDI (2013)
19. Liang, H., Feng, X., Shao, Z.: Compositional verification of termination-preserving refinement of concurrent programs. In: LICS (2014)
20. O'Hearn, P.W.: Resources, concurrency, and local reasoning. Theor. Comput. Sci. **375**, 271 (2007)
21. O'Hearn, P., Reynolds, J.C., Yang, H.: Local reasoning about programs that alter data structures. In: Fribourg, L. (ed.) CSL 2001. LNCS, vol. 2142, pp. 1–19. Springer, Heidelberg (2001). doi:10.1007/3-540-44802-0_1
22. Schellhorn, G., Wehrheim, H., Derrick, J.: How to prove algorithms linearisable. In: Madhusudan, P., Seshia, S.A. (eds.) CAV 2012. LNCS, vol. 7358, pp. 243–259. Springer, Heidelberg (2012). doi:10.1007/978-3-642-31424-7_21
23. Sergey, I., Nanevski, A., Banerjee, A.: Specifying and verifying concurrent algorithms with histories and subjectivity. In: Vitek, J. (ed.) ESOP 2015. LNCS, vol. 9032, pp. 333–358. Springer, Heidelberg (2015). doi:10.1007/978-3-662-46669-8_14
24. Svendsen, K., Birkedal, L.: Impredicative concurrent abstract predicates. In: Shao, Z. (ed.) ESOP 2014. LNCS, vol. 8410, pp. 149–168. Springer, Heidelberg (2014). doi:10.1007/978-3-642-54833-8_9
25. Turon, A.J., Thamsborg, J., Ahmed, A., Birkedal, L., Dreyer, D.: Logical relations for fine-grained concurrency. In: POPL (2013)
26. Vafeiadis, V.: Modular fine-grained concurrency verification: Ph.D. Thesis. Technical report UCAM-CL-TR-726, University of Cambridge (2008)

Refactoring Refinement Structure of Event-B Machines

Tsutomu Kobayashi[1(✉)], Fuyuki Ishikawa[2], and Shinichi Honiden[1,2]

[1] The University of Tokyo, Tokyo, Japan
{t-kobayashi,honiden}@nii.ac.jp
[2] National Institute of Informatics, Tokyo, Japan
f-ishikawa@nii.ac.jp

Abstract. Refinement in formal specifications has received significant attention as a method to gradually construct a rigorous model. Although refactoring methods for formal specifications have been proposed, there are no methods for refactoring of refinement structures in formal specifications. In this paper, we describe a method to restructure refinements in specifications of Event-B, a formal specification method with supports for refinement. The core of our method is decomposition of refinements. Namely, when an abstract Event-B machine A, a concrete machine C refining A, and a slicing strategy are provided, our method constructs a consistent intermediate machine B, which refines A and is refined by C. We show effectiveness of our methods through two case studies on representative usages of our method: decomposition of large-scale refinements and extraction of reusable parts of specifications.

Keywords: Event-B · Refinement · Abstraction · Refactoring · Interpolation

1 Introduction

Formal specification methods with refinement mechanisms have been gaining much interest, because they help developers to do rigorous modeling while lessening the burden of modeling and verification. In particular, Event-B [1], which has a flexible refinement mechanism including support for *horizontal refinement*, mitigates the complexity of modeling and verification by distributing it amidst multiple steps, which form a refinement chain. In modeling in Event-B, developers construct specifications with a set of *machines*. After constructing an abstract machine, they introduce more aspects of the target system by constructing a new machine with more details and verifying the consistency between the new machine and the abstract one.

The refinement mechanism of Event-B enables developers to design structures composed of refinements. In other words, developers can decide aspects of the target system that are considered in each refinement step. Thus, the design is impor-

This work is partially supported by JSPS KAKENHI Grant Number 26700005.

J. Fitzgerald et al. (Eds.): FM 2016, LNCS 9995, pp. 444–459, 2016.
DOI: 10.1007/978-3-319-48989-6_27

tant for understandability, ease of verification, maintainability, and reusability. However, refinement structures have not been a target of refactoring.

In this paper, as a foundation to support refinement restructuring, we propose a method for decomposing refinements. In particular, for given consistent (i.e. proved) machines M_{A} and M_{C} such that M_{C} refines M_{A}, our method helps users to construct an *intermediate* machine M_{B} such that M_{C} refines M_{B} and M_{B} refines M_{A}. This enables users to decompose a refinement step into several substeps. The decomposition method can be combined with merging of refinements, which is simpler than decomposition, to restructure refinements.

We show the usefulness of refinement restructuring through two case studies. The first shows how decomposing large-scale refinements can improve the maintainability of existing machines. The second shows how to extract parts of existing machines and reuse them for constructing new machines of another system that is different from the original system at the first glance.

The remainder of this paper is organized as follows. First, we provide background on Event-B in Sect. 2. We then describe our proposal for decomposing (and merging) refinement in Sect. 3. Next, we show two case studies in Sect. 4. In Sects. 5 and 6, we discuss application of our method and related work, respectively. Finally, we conclude this study in Sect. 7.

2 Background

A model in Event-B is composed of contexts and machines. The static properties of the target system are specified in contexts, whereas its dynamic properties are specified in machines as predicates of invariants and events. Machines can refer to specifications in contexts. The main part of a specification of events consists of guards and actions. Guards are predicates of necessary conditions for executing the state transitions of an event. Actions describe the state transitions of an event with *before-after predicates* (BAPs), which are relationships between the before and after states of variables.

For example, a machine `ma` (Fig. 1) has specifications of variables a and b, invariant `typ_a`, and events `initialisation` and `evt_a`. An action is composed of the variables that are changed by the action and a BAP. In BAPs, the after states of variables are expressed using variables with primes, such as a'. In the figure, event `evt_a` increases the values of a and b by 1 and 2, respectively, and it can be executed if $0 \leq a$.

In modeling in Event-B, new aspects and details are gradually introduced to a machine through a refinement mechanism. A machine M_{C} can be defined as a refinement of another machine M_{A}. Here, M_{C} and M_{A} are called a concrete machine and an abstract machine, respectively.

We use the symbols V_{A} and V_{C} to denote M_{A}'s variables and M_{C}'s variables, respectively. The invariants in a concrete machine M_{C} can refer to V_{A} in addition to V_{C}. Those that refer to both variables in V_{A} and those in V_{C} are called *gluing invariants*, because they connect the state spaces of two machines.

```
variables: a, b
```

```
Event evt_a
  when
    grd_a1: 0 ≤ a
  then
    act_a1: a :| a' = a + 1
    act_a2: b :| b' = b + 2
  end
```

```
typ_a: {a, b} ⊂ ℕ
```

```
Event initialisation
  begin
    init_a1: a :| a' = 0
    init_a2: b :| b' = 0
  end
```

Fig. 1. Abstract machine ma

V_C does not need to be a superset of V_A. If $V_A \not\subseteq V_C$, some of the variables in V_A are *replaced* with some of the variables in V_C. In such a replacement, developers also need to provide gluing invariants that refer to the replaced variables (in V_A) and replacing variables (in V_C), in order to prove consistency between an abstract machine and a concrete machine.

Moreover, events in M_C may refine events in M_A. Concrete events, which refine events in the abstract machine (abstract events), need to have guards that are stronger than the guards of abstract events. Also, the actions of concrete events should simulate the actions of their abstract events.

For instance, suppose that machine mc (Fig. 2)[1] is defined as a refinement of ma (Fig. 1). In mc, a variable a is inherited from ma, variables c, d, e, and f are newly introduced, and a variable b, which is specified in ma, has disappeared. The gluing invariant gluinv_c1 describes the relationship among b, c, and d. Event evt_c is defined as a concrete event of evt_a of ma.

```
variables: a, c, d, e, f
```

```
Event evt_c
  refines evt_a
  when
    grd_c1: 0 ≤ a ∧ 0 ≤ c
    grd_c2: mod2(a + f) = 0
  then
    act_c1: a :| a' = a + 1
    act_c3: c :| c' = c + 1
    act_c4: d :| d' = d + 1
    act_c5: e :| e' = f + 2
    act_c6: f :| f' = f + 3
  end
```

```
typ_c: {a, c, d, e, f} ⊂ ℕ
gluinv_c1: b = c + d
inv_c1: mod2(a + e) = 0 ⇒ a < 1
inv_c2: mod2(e + f) = 1
```

```
Event initialisation
  begin
    init_c1: a :| a' = 0
    init_c3: c :| c' = 0
    init_c4: d :| d' = 0
    init_c5: e :| e' = 1
    init_c6: f :| f' = 2
  end
```

Fig. 2. Concrete machine mc

The refinement mechanism enables two styles of refinement, namely, gradual addition of concrete elements (*horizontal refinement*) and transformation of expressions to make them closer to the implementation (*vertical refinement*).

[1] Assume that a function mod2(n) that returns n modulo 2 is defined in a context.

The consistency of the specified machine is represented in the form of sequents, called *proof obligations* (POs), generated from the specification. POs include sequents of the machine's self-consistency and its consistency with the abstract machine. Developers confirm consistency by discharging all POs. When POs cannot be discharged, developers need to modify the specification.

For instance, one of the primary PO types is *invariant preservation* (written as $evt/inv/\mathrm{INV}$), which means an invariant inv holds after an event evt occurs.

The rule of PO $evt/inv/\mathrm{INV}$ is as follows:[2] $I, J, H(evt), T(evt) \vdash inv'$, where I and J are invariants of an abstract machine and a concrete machine, respectively, $H(evt)$ and $T(evt)$ are respectively the guards and BAPs of event evt in the concrete machine, and inv' is inv with the before-state variables replaced by after-state variables.

For example, the PO mc/evt_c/inv_c1/INV is as shown in Fig. 3.

grd_c2 BAP of act_c1 BAP of act_c5 ... $\vdash$ Modified inv_c1	$\mathrm{mod2}(a+f)=0$ $a'=a+1$ $e'=f+2$ ... $\vdash$ $\mathrm{mod2}(a'+e')=0 \Rightarrow a'<1$

Fig. 3. Invariant preservation of inv_c1 by evt_c in mc (provable)

3 Approach

3.1 Method Overview

We assume that we have given consistent (proved) machines M_A and M_C such that M_C refines M_A. The goal of our decomposition method is to construct an intermediate machine M_B such that M_C refines M_B and M_B refines M_A by using as much of the original specifications as possible. For this purpose, users give a slicing criterion as a set of variables $V_{\mathrm{B}0}$, which actually may be given by selecting variables in V_C. The first step is to use this criterion for syntactic slicing from M_A and M_C to construct the initial base $M_{\mathrm{B}0}$. The actual criterion for slicing V_B is extended from $V_{\mathrm{B}0}$ because of consistency constraints. In general, the result of this first step $M_{\mathrm{B}0}$ may have POs that are not provable. Thus, the second step adds complementary predicates to $M_{\mathrm{B}0}$ to make a consistent intermediate machine M_B. By handling replacement of variables through refinement and proof obligations, our decomposition method deals with both horizontal refinement and vertical refinement. Combined with merging of refinements, the decomposition method is extended as a restructuring method (Sect. 3.4).

[2] Actually static predicates (axioms) and predicates of event parameters are also included in POs. We will omit them for the sake of simplicity.

3.2 Step 1 of Decomposing Refinement: Slicing

Finding Additional Variables. If $M_{\rm C}$ refines $M_{\rm A}$, then $M_{\rm C}$ inherits variables $V_{\rm A} \cap V_{\rm C}$ from $M_{\rm A}$. The remaining variables of $M_{\rm A}$, that is, $V_{\rm A} \setminus V_{\rm C}$, are replaced with some of variables in $V_{\rm C} \setminus V_{\rm A}$, as described in Sect. 2.

As shown on the left side of Fig. 4, if $V_{\rm A} \cap V_{\rm C} \not\subseteq V_{\rm B}$, then the variables in $(V_{\rm A} \cap V_{\rm C}) \setminus V_{\rm B}$ $(= V_{\rm A\overline{B}C})$, which is a subset of $V_{\rm A} \setminus V_{\rm B}$, is specified in $M_{\rm C}$. The variables in $V_{\rm A} \setminus V_{\rm B}$ are, however, replaced with other variables in $M_{\rm B}$. Thus, selecting such a $V_{\rm B}$ makes the refinement "$M_{\rm C}$ refines $M_{\rm B}$" inconsistent. Therefore, $V_{\rm B}$ must satisfy $V_{\rm A} \cap V_{\rm C} \subseteq V_{\rm B}$. In addition, to take advantage of predicates in existing machines to construct $M_{\rm B}$, $V_{\rm B}$ should satisfy $V_{\rm B} \subseteq V_{\rm A} \cup V_{\rm C}$; otherwise, a user needs to design new variables $(V_{\rm B} \setminus (V_{\rm A} \cup V_{\rm C}))(= V_{\rm \overline{A}B\overline{C}})$ and predicates of them. Thus, $V_{\rm B}$ should be as depicted on the right side of Fig. 4. Hereinafter, we will use the symbols $V_{\rm A\overline{BC}}$, $V_{\rm AB\overline{C}}$, $V_{\rm ABC}$, $V_{\rm \overline{A}BC}$, and $V_{\rm \overline{AB}C}$ to represent $V_{\rm A} \setminus V_{\rm B}$, $V_{\rm B} \setminus V_{\rm C}$, $V_{\rm A} \cap V_{\rm C}$, $V_{\rm B} \setminus V_{\rm A}$, and $V_{\rm C} \setminus V_{\rm B}$, respectively.

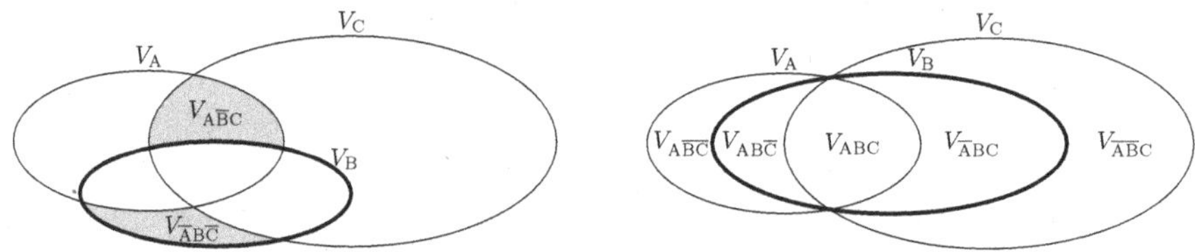

Fig. 4. Variables of $M_{\rm B}$: invalid case (left) and valid case (right)

This method assumes that $V_{\rm B0} = V_{\rm ABC} \cup V_{\rm \overline{A}BC}$, which is a subset of $V_{\rm C}$, is given as an input. This is because it is easy for a user to select the criterion from $V_{\rm C}$, without considering which variables in $V_{\rm A}$ must be replaced. To construct $M_{\rm B}$, the remaining variables $V_{\rm B} \setminus V_{\rm B0} (= V_{\rm AB\overline{C}})$ need to be identified. The remainder of this section describes a heuristic for automatically finding $V_{\rm AB\overline{C}}$.

To replace abstract variables with concrete ones in a refining machine, a user needs to provide gluing invariants about the relationships between the two sets of variables. In the case of constructing $M_{\rm B}$ as a machine that refines $M_{\rm A}$, the set of newly introduced variables $V_{\rm \overline{A}BC}$ is a subset of $V_{\rm C} \setminus V_{\rm A}$. Therefore, some of the gluing invariants in $M_{\rm C}$ may not be specified in $M_{\rm B}$. $M_{\rm B}$'s gluing invariants can describe the relationship between $V_{\rm A\overline{BC}}$ and $V_{\rm \overline{A}BC}$, but cannot describe the relationship between $V_{\rm AB\overline{C}}$ and $V_{\rm \overline{A}BC}$. Hence, $V_{\rm AB\overline{C}}$ can be obtained as $V_{\rm AB\overline{C}} = \{v \in V_{\rm A} \setminus V_{\rm C} | \exists i \in \mathrm{ginv}(M_{\rm C}).v \in (\mathrm{var}(i) \cap V_{\rm A}) \wedge (\mathrm{var}(i) \cap V_{\rm C}) \subseteq V_{\rm \overline{AB}C}\}$, where $\mathrm{ginv}(M)$ represents the gluing invariants in a machine M and $\mathrm{var}(p)$ represents the variables that occur in predicate p.

For example, let us assume that a and e are selected to be specified in `mb` $(V_{\rm B0} = V_{\rm B} \cap V_{\rm C} = \{a, e\})$. In `mc`, a gluing invariant `gluinv1:` $b = c + d$ describes replacement of b (of `ma`) with c and d (of `mc`). By contrast, in `mb`, `gluinv1` cannot describe replacement of b, since neither c nor d is selected to be specified in `mb`. Therefore, $V_{\rm AB\overline{C}} = \{b\}$; namely `mb` should specify b in addition to a and e.

Finding Certain Specifications through Slicing. For a predicate p and a set of variables V, we say p is *expressible* by V if and only if $\text{var}(p) \subseteq V$.

Predicates in M_{A} and M_{C} that are expressible by V_{B} are necessary (but not always sufficient, as described later) in M_{B}, because they certainly express the properties of V_{B}, which should be consistent with M_{A} and M_{C}. Therefore, in this step, invariants, guards, and BAPs in M_{A} and M_{C} that are expressible by V_{B} are specified in M_{B}.[3] For example, mb0 (Fig. 5) is constructed by collecting predicates that are expressible by $V_{\text{B}} = \{a, b, e\}$ from ma and mc.

```
variables: a, b, e
```

```
typ_b:  {a, b, e} ⊂ ℕ
inv_c1: mod2(a + e) = 0 ⇒ a < 1
```

```
Event evt_b
  refines evt_a
  begin
    act_c1: a :| a' = a + 1
    act_a2: b :| b' = b + 2
  end
```

```
Event initialisation
  begin
    init_c1: a :| a' = 0
    init_a2: b :| b' = 0
    init_c5: e :| e' = 1
  end
```

Fig. 5. Sliced machine mb0

Note that an action mc/evt_c/act_c5, which assigns a value to $e (\in V_{\text{B}})$, is not specified in mb0, because $f (\in V_{\overline{\text{ABC}}})$ occurs in its BAP.

We implemented this step as a plugin tool of Event-B's IDE, named SLICE-ANDMERGE[4]. Users of the tool can select V_{B0} with checkboxes and obtain a sliced machine M_{B0}. The tool also supports analysis of dependencies between invariants and variables, and merging of refinements (described in Sect. 3.4).

3.3 Step 2 of Decomposing Refinement: Complementing

Possible Lack of Consistency in M_{B0}. Although all POs of M_{A} and M_{C} are discharged, M_{B0}, which is constructed from fragments of the machines, is not ensured to be consistent. For example, some invariants in M_{B0} (from M_{A} and M_{C}) may not be preserved by events in M_{B0}, because the specification of M_{B0}'s events may be only part of the specification of M_{A} and M_{C}'s events.

For instance, the PO shown in Fig. 3 (mc/evt_c/inv_c1/INV), which has a succedent specified with the after-states of a and e, is provable because predicates including grd_c2 and act_c5 are in the antecedent.

Although the preservation of the same invariant inv_c1 by the event evt_b in mb0 (mb0/evt_b/inv_c1/INV) should also hold, this is not provable because predicates grd_c2 and act_c5, which are essential for proving that inv_c1 is preserved, are not included in the antecedent (Fig. 6), as they are predicates about variable f $(\in V_{\overline{\text{ABC}}})$.

[3] BAPs that are expressible by $V_{\text{B}} \cup V'_{\text{B}}$ are also specified, where V'_{B} represents the set of after-state variables of V_{B}.

[4] Available at http://tkoba.jp/software/slice_and_merge/.

BAP of `act_c1`	$a' = a + 1$
...	...
$\vdash$	$\vdash$
Modified `inv_c1`	$\mathrm{mod2}(a' + e') = 0 \Rightarrow a' < 1$

Fig. 6. Invariant preservation of `inv_c1` by `evt_b` in `mb0` (unprovable)

Complementary Predicates for Consistency. Since M_A and M_C are consistent, they have predicates that are essential for the consistency.

When such predicates are expressible by V_B, the consistency of M_B can be guaranteed by including them in M_B. Obviously in simple cases, this can be realized by slicing (Sect. 3.2).

However, as described above, sometimes M_B0 is inconsistent because M_B0, which is obtained by a syntactic predicate-level slicing, sometimes lacks some of these predicates. In such cases, predicates that are essential for discharging POs need to be added to M_B0, so that the resulting M_B is consistent. Moreover, such predicates need to be expressible by V_B. We call such additional predicates *complementary predicates* (CPs). Predicates that are essential for the consistency of original machines can be found from the specifications or the proof of consistency of M_A and M_C, and they can be "translated" into V_B as CPs. Some CPs may work as gluing invariants. We discuss how often CPs are required and how hard finding them is in Sect. 5. The rest of this section describes ways to do this.

Finding CPs Using Rule-based Analysis. In some cases, part of a predicate is expressible by V_B but the remainder of it is not; thus, the predicate cannot be obtained through predicate-level slicing. Simple heuristics can be used to find parts of such predicates that are expressible by V_B. For instance, a predicate $0 \leq a$ can be found by extracting a part that is expressible by V_B from `mc/evt_c/grd_c1` ($0 \leq a \land 0 \leq c$). A possible implementation of this is to convert predicates into CNF and extract clauses that are expressible by V_B.

Finding CPs from Existing Proofs. The essence of the consistency of M_A and M_C can be found by examining the proof of consistency and making an inference.

For example, the proof of `mc/evt_c/inv_c1`/INV can be summarized in terms of goals (succedents) as shown on the left side of Fig. 7. The initial goal GLc0: $\mathrm{mod2}(a' + e') = 0 \Rightarrow a' < 1$ can be derived because GLc1: $\mathrm{mod2}(a' + e') \neq 0$ can be derived from hypotheses including a guard `grd_c2`.

A proof with the same root goal is possible using the vocabulary of `mb` if the goal GLb1: $\mathrm{mod2}(a' + e') \neq 0$ can be derived from an event-local predicate (guard or BAP) p that is expressible by V_B. GLb1 can be transformed into GLb3: $\mathrm{mod2}(a + e') = 0$ by `act_c1`. We need to find p such that GLb3 can be derived from p, because there is no predicate about e' in `mb0`. A solution is to view GLb3 itself as p and add an action such as `act_NEW` : e :| $\mathrm{mod2}(a + e') = 0$ to `mb0` (the right side of Fig. 7).

GLc0: $mod2(a' + e')=0 \Rightarrow a' < 1$ (modified `inv_c1`)
- GLc1: $mod2(a' + e') \neq 0$
  - GLc2: $mod2((a + 1) + (f + 2)) \neq 0$ (by `act_c{1,5}`)
    - GLc3: $mod2(a + f + 1) \neq 0$
      - GLc4: $mod2(a + f)=0$
        - GLc5: $\top$ (by `grd_c2`)

GLb0: $mod2(a' + e')=0 \Rightarrow a' < 1$ (modified `inv_c1`)
- GLb1: $mod2(a' + e') \neq 0$
  - GLb2: $mod2((a + 1) + e') \neq 0$ (by `act_c1`)
    - GLb3: $mod2(a + e')=0$
      - GLb4: $\top$ (by `act_NEW`)

Fig. 7. Proof of `mc/evt_c/inv_c1`/INV (left) and `mb/evt_b/inv_c1`/INV (right)

Finding CPs as Craig Interpolant. The essence of consistency of M_A and M_C as expressed by V_B can often be found as a Craig interpolant of the proof of consistency.

Let ϕ_C: $\mathbf{Ant_C} \vdash \mathbf{Suc_C}$ be a sequent of the proof of consistency in M_C. A sequent ϕ'_C: $\mathbf{Ant'_C} \vdash \mathbf{Suc'_{BC}}$ such that $\mathcal{V}(\mathbf{Suc'_{BC}}) \subseteq V_B$ can be inferred by using inference rules for sequent calculus such as negation rules, where $\mathcal{V}(\mathbf{X})$ denotes the set of variables in $\mathbf{X}$.

An interpolant of ϕ'_C $\mathcal{I}$ can be obtained. According to the Craig's interpolation theorem, $\mathcal{I} \vdash \mathbf{Suc'_{BC}}$ is provable. Moreover, $\mathcal{V}(\mathcal{I}) \subseteq \mathcal{V}(\mathbf{Ant'_C}) \cap \mathcal{V}(\mathbf{Suc'_{BC}}) \subseteq V_B$. Thus, $\mathcal{I}'$ corresponds to an embodiment of the essence of ϕ'_C in V_B.

Let ϕ_{B0}: $\mathbf{Ant_{B0}} \vdash \mathbf{Suc_{B0}}$ be a (unprovable) sequent of consistency in M_{B0}. If another sequent ϕ'_{B0}: $\mathbf{Ant'_{B0}} \vdash \mathbf{Suc'_{BC}}$ can be inferred from ϕ_{B0} by using inference rules, then ϕ_{B0} becomes provable by adding a predicate $\mathcal{I}$ to M_{B0}, because $(\mathcal{I} \wedge \mathbf{Ant'_{B0}}) \vdash \mathbf{Suc'_{BC}}$.

For example, the sequent shown in Fig. 8 can be inferred from the sequent of `mc/evt_c/inv_c1`/INV (Fig. 3). Variables that occur in the succedent of the sequent are $\{a, a', e'\} \subset V_B \cup V'_B$. The predicate $\text{mod2}(a+e') = 0$ is an interpolant of the sequent, and it is expressible by V_B.

By adding the predicate to `mb0` as an action `act_NEW` : e :| $\text{mod2}(a+e') = 0$, the sequent `mb/evt_b/inv_c1`/INV becomes provable, as shown in Fig. 9 (because (BAP of `act_c1`) $\wedge$ (BAP of `act_NEW`) $\Rightarrow$ Modified `inv_c1`).

Note that if an action is obtained from the sequent of `mc/evt_c/inv_c1`/INV (Fig. 3) (i.e. action is obtained without applying inference rules), it becomes `act_NEW_nondet` : a, e :| $\text{mod2}(a' + e') \neq 0$, which is more non-deterministic than necessary (`act_NEW`).

grd_c2 BAP of act_c5 ... $\vdash$ Modified inv_c1 ¬ (BAP of act_c1)	$\text{mod2}(a + f) = 0$ $e' = f + 2$ ... $\vdash$ $\text{mod2}(a' + e') = 0 \Rightarrow a' < 1$ $\neg(a' = a + 1)$

Fig. 8. A sequent inferred from `mc/evt_c/inv_c1`/INV

BAP of `act_c1` BAP of `act_NEW` ... ⊢ Modified `inv_c1`	$a' = a + 1$ $\text{mod2}(a + e') = 0$ ... ⊢ $\text{mod2}(a' + e') = 0 \Rightarrow a' < 1$

Fig. 9. Invariant preservation of `inv1` by `evt_b` in `mb0` with interpolant (provable)

3.4 Restructuring Refinement

We call a sequence of machines $[M_n, M_{n+1}, \ldots M_{m-1}, M_m]$ *refinement chain (RC)* if M_{i+1} refines M_i for every natural number i such that $n \le i < m$.

In addition to decomposing, we can *merge* refinements as follows: When there is a RC $[M_0, M_1, M_2]$, merging M_1 and M_2 construct a new machine M_{12} such that M_{12} refines M_0. M_{12}'s variables, invariants, and events are composed of the unions of the variables, invariants, and events of M_1 and M_2.

Refinements can be restructured by merging and decomposing refinements. Suppose that a RC $[M_n, \cdots, M_m]$ is given. First, machines $(M_i)_{i=n+1}^{m}$ are merged as M'_m, which directly refines M_n. Then, a RC $[M_n, M'_m]$ is decomposed by constructing new machines $(\tilde{M}_i)_{i=k+1}^{l}$ that reflect the user's preference of aspects in terms of V_{B0}. As a result, the refinement is restructured into a RC $[M_n = \tilde{M}_k, \tilde{M}_{k+1}, \ldots, \tilde{M}_{l-1}, \tilde{M}_l = M'_m]$. As a result of restructuring refinements, the understandability of a specification increases because the meaning of each refinement step can be changed as the user likes. In Sect. 4.2, we describe an application of restructuring method to extract parts of an existing model for reuse.

4 Case Studies

4.1 Case Study 1: Decomposing Large Refinement Steps

This case study tried to determine whether we can improve maintainability of existing machines by decomposing refinements. One of the authors of this paper decomposed refinements in a large-scale Event-B model with several intermediate machines by following our method and verified their consistency. The target model was a specification about an autonomous satellite flight formation system [12], and it was constructed by a computer scientist who had over four years of experience in modeling in Event-B. The target system was a controller for two spacecraft (leader and follower), which run autonomously while maintaining two-layered communication, namely a higher-layer mode communication and a lower-layer phase communication.

The model has a RC of five steps $[\mathtt{m0}, \mathtt{m1}, \ldots, \mathtt{m5}]$. The second refinement ($[\mathtt{m1}, \mathtt{m2}]$) and the third refinement ($[\mathtt{m2}, \mathtt{m3}]$) were selected to be decomposed, because they were larger than the other steps. The row of `m2` in Table 1a and the row of `m3` in Table 1b show statistics of `m2` and `m3`, respectively. The N_V

and N_{I}[5] in Table 1 respectively list the numbers of variables and invariants of the models. In m2, seven variables and 46 invariants were introduced to specify mode transitions and communications in the spacecraft. In m3, two variables have disappeared, ten variables were introduced (N_{V} is "−2+10"), and 72 invariants were introduced to specify the phase transitions in modes of spacecraft.

Table 1. Results of case study 1

(a) Decomposition of second refinement

	N_{V}	N_{I}	N_{CP}	N_{UCP}	N_{PO}	N_{MPO}
m2	+7	46	–	–	454	53
m2_1	+4	12	21	5	112	12
m2_2	+1	9	10	6	87	0
m2_3	+1	8	12	6	80	5
m2_4	+1	17	0	0	218	33
Sum of m2_*	+7	46	43	17	497	50

(b) Decomposition of third refinement

	N_{V}	N_{I}	N_{CP}	N_{UCP}	N_{PO}	N_{MPO}
m3	-2+10	72	–	–	1127	175
m3_1	-1+3	7	17	4	112	6
m3_2	-1+3	17	17	8	261	30
m3_3	+2	14	3	2	202	30
m3_4	+2	34	0	0	584	81
Sum of m3_*	-2+10	72	37	14	1159	147

We selected slicing criteria V_{B0} to obtain the sliced machines. After that, we found CPs with the approach described in Sect. 3.3. Both of the refinements decomposed with four intermediate machines (m2_1, ..., m2_4, m3_1, ..., and m3_4). Thus, the machines form a RC [m1, m2_1, ..., m2_4, m3_1, ..., m3_4]. The most concrete intermediate machines m2_4 and m3_4 were semantically the same[6] as the corresponding original machines m2 and m3. We selected slicing criteria so that the slicing would distribute aspects in the original machines into small and meaningful sets of concepts. For example, the properties and behavior regarding communication failures, the follower's incoming buffer for mode messages, the leader's outgoing buffer, and the acknowledgement message were specified and verified in m2_1, m2_2, m2_3, and m2_4, respectively.

The results of decomposition are as shown in Table 1. The number of introduced invariants was reduced significantly through the decomposition, and the intermediate machines were more comprehensible than the originals. The replacement of the variables in m3 was also split into two steps. In both m3_1 and m3_2, one variable has disappeared (N_{V} of both machines is "−1+3").

We needed to add CPs to the intermediate machines except the most concrete ones. The N_{CP} in the Table 1 list the numbers of added CPs. Similar events in M_{B0}, such as the events of entering phase 1, phase 2, and phase 3, often had the same kind of inconsistency and thus required the same kind of CPs. The numbers of unique CPs (N_{UCP}) show the actual burden of finding CPs.

[5] For the sake of simplicity we did not count invariants for typing.

[6] There were differences in the actual specifications, because several invariants were moved in order to abstract the intermediate machines and the refinement structures of the events were changed.

The N_{PO} and N_{MPO} in Table 1 respectively list the numbers of all POs and the numbers of POs that were manually discharged, including those of POs related to CPs. Most of POs are usually discharged by automatic provers of the IDE for Event-B. Thus the number of manually discharged POs (N_{MPO} in Table 1) corresponds to the actual amount of effort for verification. The results show that our method decreased the labor of verification. For example, rows of `m3` and "sum of `m3_*`" in Table 1b show that the number of manually discharged POs decreased from 175 to 147 through decomposition, despite that the number of all POs increased from 1127 to 1159. This appears to be because direct inclusion of CPs added lemmas to the set of hypotheses. Our future work includes a detailed analysis of this effect.

4.2 Case Study 2: Extracting Reusable Parts of Machines

This case study[7] tried to determine whether we can extract reusable parts of existing machines by using restructuring (Sect. 3.4).

We used a model of a "location access controller" (from [1, Chap. 16]) as the original model $\mathbf{M_O}$ with a RC $[M_{\mathrm{O1}}, \ldots, M_{\mathrm{O5}}]$ (Fig. 10). The model is about a controller of doors between locations according to persons' permission to enter.

Step 1 (M_{O1}): <u>Persons</u> somehow *move* between <u>locations</u> according to the *authorization of persons to locations.*
Step 2 (M_{O2}): *Physical connections* between <u>locations</u> are introduced. Persons *move* between physically connected locations.
Step 3 (M_{O3}): *Doors* with <u>red</u>/*green* lights are introduced. Doors somehow <u>authenticate</u> persons.
Step 4 (M_{O4}): <u>ID cards</u> are introduced. *Doors* read cards and <u>communicate</u> with a controller by <u>messages</u> to <u>authenticate</u>.
Step 5 (M_{O5}): Physical movements of *doors*, *persons*, and <u>lights</u> are considered. <u>Communication</u> is a reaction to a physical event.

Fig. 10. Aspects introduced in each step of original model $\mathbf{M_O}$(Aspects that should be extracted from $\mathbf{M_O}$ to construct $\mathbf{M_N}$ are <u>underlined</u> and those that should be omitted from $\mathbf{M_O}$ are *slanted.*)

We constructed a new model $\mathbf{M_N}$ by reusing parts of $\mathbf{M_O}$. Aspects shown in Fig. 11 are specified in $\mathbf{M_N}$.

First, we constructed a machine M_{mrg} by merging all the machines of $\mathbf{M_O}$. Next, by slicing M_{mrg}, we extracted aspects that were common to $\mathbf{M_O}$ and $\mathbf{M_N}$. Thus, we extracted specifications related to authentication using communication between card readers and a controller (from M_{O4} and M_{O5}), persons (from M_{O1}), locations (from M_{O1}), and red lights (from M_{O3} and M_{O5}). In other words, we omitted aspects that would not be included in $\mathbf{M_N}$; i.e., we omitted authorization of persons to locations (from M_{O1}), physical connection of locations (from

[7] Models of this case study are at http://tkoba.jp/publications/fm2016/

- Persons are in locations but do not move to other locations.
- Locations have monitors and consoles with card readers.
- Authenticated persons log in to the server by inserting their ID card in a reader.
- A red light indicates an authentication failure.
- The controller tries to find an unoccupied monitor in the room.
- Consoles communicate with a controller by sending messages.

Fig. 11. Aspects of new model $\mathbf{M_N}$(Aspects that should be extracted from $\mathbf{M_O}$ to construct $\mathbf{M_N}$ are underlined and those that should be omitted from $\mathbf{M_O}$ are *slanted.*)

$M_{\mathrm{O}2}$), doors (from $M_{\mathrm{O}3}$), and green lights (from $M_{\mathrm{O}3}$ and $M_{\mathrm{O}5}$), in addition to movement of persons (from $M_{\mathrm{O}1}$), which is the primary aspect of $\mathbf{M_O}$.

As a result, we succeeded in automatically extracting the reusable parts from M_{mrg}. In other words, we did not need to add CPs to make the reusable parts consistent. After that, we successfully augmented the reusable parts with specifications that were unique to $\mathbf{M_N}$. We also succeeded in discharging all POs.

Note that not only omitted aspects in $\mathbf{M_O}$ but also extracted aspects were scattered over several refinement steps in the original specification. Therefore, simply copying a single step such as $M_{\mathrm{O}3}$ and modifying it is not an effective way of reusing such aspects. In contrast, we succeeded in extracting aspects in a cross-refinement manner by slicing after merging refinement steps.

5 Discussion

5.1 Discussion on Methods

Deriving CPs. All POs originate from specifications. Hypotheses essential to discharge POs are also inferred from specifications. We call predicates that raise a PO ϕ *raisers* of ϕ and predicates that provide hypotheses for discharging ϕ *hypothesis providers* of ϕ.

Suppose that ϕ is a PO in a concrete machine. If the raisers of ϕ are expressible by V_{B}, the hypotheses required to discharge ϕ should also be expressible by V_{B}. However, hypotheses providers are not always specified with vocabulary of V_{B}. Sometimes, a PO ϕ that is expressible by V_{B} is discharged with hypotheses including a hypothesis h that is expressible by V_{B}, and h is implied by hypotheses providers P that are expressible by V_{C} but not expressible by V_{B}. In other words, h is not directly specified in the machine but rather implicitly specified by P in this case. In such cases, ϕ is raised but cannot be discharged in the intermediate machine since the intermediate machine lacks some of hypotheses providers for ϕ. Thus, users need to add CPs that are expressible by V_{B} and able to imply hypothesis h.

However, developers tend to directly specify hypotheses in practice, because hypotheses raisers for POs are usually important properties of a target system; thus, directly specifying hypotheses to discharge the POs is usually a meaningful way of describing the system. Therefore, users do not need to add CPs frequently.

For instance, we did not need to add CPs in the second case study (Sect. 4.2), because all of the hypotheses providers were specified in V_B for all of the POs that were expressible by V_B.

Specifying a hypothesis provider in the form $h \wedge predicate$ to imply hypothesis h is another common case. Although users need to add CPs, they can be found with simple rules. In other cases, CPs can be found by reviewing the proofs for the original machines, as described in Sect. 3.3. This task is easy for users who are familiar with Event-B.

Therefore, we conclude that finding CPs is neither frequently required nor difficult. As a primary part of our future work, however, we are planning to construct systematic and complete methods for deriving CPs so that developers can easily derive consistent intermediate machines. We will investigate relationships between CPs and Craig interpolation of the completed proof further.

Selecting Slicing Criteria. Users of our decomposition method can select a slicing criterion, namely variables that are specified in the intermediate machine. Users may consider aspects of the intermediate machine and select some of the variables of the concrete machine, or they may consider properties that should be verified in the intermediate machine and select some of the invariants of the concrete machine. In the latter case, the slicing criterion is a set of variables that are required to specify selected invariants. Users can select an arbitrary V_{B0} so long as $V_A \cap V_C \subseteq V_B \subseteq V_A \cup V_C$.

Adding New Concepts of Abstraction. A user can add new concepts of abstraction to the machines, by decomposing refinement after adding new specifications for abstraction to the concrete machine.

One way is adding new variables. For example in Fig. 2, by creating an intermediate machine that have $\{g\}$ as V_{B0} after adding a variable g and an invariant $g = a + e$ and other predicates, a user can construct an intermediate machine for specification of variables b and g instead of variables b, a and e.

The other way is adding new events. Assume that a concrete machine has several events E that have common guards and actions. By selecting variables that occur in common predicates in E as V_{B0}, a user can construct an intermediate machine with an abstract event, which is refined by all events of E.

These appear to be useful for restructuring refinement of existing models.

5.2 Discussion on Applications

Improvement of Maintainability by Decomposition. In our first case study (Sect. 4.1), we decomposed large refinements into smaller ones. The primary benefit of reducing size of specifications is the support of maintaining machines. According to a study conducted in industries [11], activities for formal specifications' maintenance include impact analysis, refactoring identification, and validation. Our decomposition method makes such activities easier because it shrinks the size of the state space and the number of predicates and reveals implicit properties of concrete machines as CPs. In particular, reducing size of specifications can significantly reduce the cost of verification [9] in maintenance. Thus, our decomposition method improves maintainability of each single refinement step. Our future work includes evaluation of trade-off between this and the maintainability of the whole model.

Large Refinement Steps. Large refinement steps such as ones used in our first case study (Sect. 4.1) are common. Developers design refinements on the basis of properties that should be verified or subjects that should be considered in each step. Usually, such properties or subjects are about multiple aspects of the target system. Therefore, including many aspects in one refinement step may seem natural for developers when they construct machines and are in fact common, despite that smaller refinements are easier to comprehend. Thus, we believe our decomposition method is effective for most existing Event-B machines.

Effectiveness of Systematic Extraction of Reusable Parts. In our second case study (Sect. 4.2), we automatically extracted reusable parts of an existing model. Manually extracting such parts is not impossible, namely developers can extract such parts by examining several machines of the original model and copy-and-pasting. However, the number of predicates that should be examined is large. In addition, such predicates are usually scattered over several machines. Therefore, manual examination is tedious and error-prone. Our method makes this process more systematic (and sometimes automatic).

Feasibility of Automatic Extraction of Reusable Parts. In our second case study (Sect. 4.2), we extracted aspects of "authentication using communication between card readers and a controller" as reusable parts of the original machines. In the original machines, these aspects were introduced through several refinement steps and it seemed that they were dependent on other parts. However, they were actually independent of other parts, and we succeeded in extracting them in an automatic manner. We often see this kind of independence of parts embedded in machines. Our method is an automatic extraction of such parts. Although users sometimes need to add CPs, most of the predicates can be found with rules as we described in this section.

6 Related Work

Decomposition of Event-B machines (in "shared variable" style [2] and "shared event" style [3]) is one of primary mechanisms to deal with complexity of modeling in Event-B. The aim of these methods is decomposing a large single machine into several components. Conversely, our goal is decomposing and merging **refinement structure** of multiple machines.

There have been many studies on refactoring software models for the purpose of organizing and understanding of them. Refactoring rules for UML/OCL [5,8], ASM [14], Alloy [7], and Object-Z [10,11] have been proposed. Most of these rules are similar to popular refactoring rules such as move and modification, as well as rules for parameterization of expressions and introduction of inheritance and polymorphism. The goal of our work is similar to theirs, but we take a different approach based on refinement, namely by manipulating refinement structures according to criteria of the vocabulary of a machine.

From the point of view of refactoring of verifications, study by Whiteside [13] has a similar goal to ours. Their study manipulates proofs in proof assistants by providing a proof script framework that handles proof trees in a hierarchical way. One of their primary contributions is refactoring of proof scripts, including manipulating expressions of proof scripts, changing styles of proof, and generalizing tactics. Our approach, namely refinement refactoring considering the vocabulary of a module, is different from theirs.

A number of significant studies on formal methods have used Craig interpolation of logic formulas, which we found to be important for finding CPs. One of the primary applications of interpolation is counterexample-guided abstraction refinement [4] in model checking, which constructs a series of interpolants from the spurious behaviors of an abstract model and uses them to refine the model. One study [6] used interpolation to automatically construct a behavior model of a system from its goal model. The approach described therein updates a behavior model by using interpolants of counterexamples and goals. We believe we can use Craig interpolation in a similar way to systematically find CPs in future.

7 Conclusion and Future Work

We proposed a method to restructure the refinements of Event-B machines according to refactoring criterion in terms of the vocabulary of a new machine. Our method finds necessary variables and predicates from the original machines and helps to find complementary predicates to make the new machine consistent. It helps users to construct an abstraction of an existing machine that focuses on certain aspects of the original machine. By using our method, we split up refinements in large-scale Event-B machines and succeeded in constructing small and consistent machines. Moreover, our methods automatically extracted reusable parts of an existing model. We conclude that our method can help users to do refactoring of refinements in Event-B. Our primary future work will be a trial to enhance our method for finding complementary predicates to guarantee that generated intermediate machine is consistent with original machines.

References

1. Abrial, J.R.: Modeling in Event-B: System and Software Engineering. Cambridge University Press, New York (2010)
2. Abrial, J.R., Hallerstede, S.: Refinement, decomposition, and instantiation of discrete models: application to Event-B. Fundamenta Informaticae **77**(1–2), 1–28 (2007)
3. Butler, M.: Decomposition structures for Event-B. In: Leuschel, M., Wehrheim, H. (eds.) IFM 2009. LNCS, vol. 5423, pp. 20–38. Springer, Heidelberg (2009). doi:10.1007/978-3-642-00255-7_2

4. Clarke, E., Grumberg, O., Jha, S., Lu, Y., Veith, H.: Counterexample-guided abstraction refinement. In: Emerson, E.A., Sistla, A.P. (eds.) CAV 2000. LNCS, vol. 1855, pp. 154–169. Springer, Heidelberg (2000). doi:10.1007/10722167_15
5. Correa, A., Werner, C., Barros, M.: An empirical study of the impact of OCL smells and refactorings on the understandability of OCL specifications. In: Engels, G., Opdyke, B., Schmidt, D.C., Weil, F. (eds.) MODELS 2007. LNCS, vol. 4735, pp. 76–90. Springer, Heidelberg (2007). doi:10.1007/978-3-540-75209-7_6
6. Degiovanni, R., Alrajeh, D., Aguirre, N., Uchitel, S.: Automated goal operationalisation based on interpolation and SAT solving. In: Proceedings of the 36th International Conference on Software Engineering, pp. 129–139. ACM, New York (2014)
7. Gheyi, R., Borba, P.: Refactoring alloy specifications. Electron. Notes Theoret. Comput. Sci. **95**, 227–243 (2004)
8. Marković, S., Baar, T.: Refactoring OCL annotated UML class diagrams. In: Briand, L., Williams, C. (eds.) MODELS 2005. LNCS, vol. 3713, pp. 280–294. Springer, Heidelberg (2005). doi:10.1007/11557432_21
9. Matichuk, D., Murray, T., Andronick, J., Jeffery, R., Klein, G., Staples, M.: Empirical Study Towards a Leading Indicator for Cost of Formal Software Verification. In: Proceedings of the 37th International Conference on Software Engineering. pp. 722–732. ACM, New York (2015)
10. McComb, T., Smith, G.: A minimal set of refactoring rules for object-Z. In: Barthe, G., Boer, F.S. (eds.) FMOODS 2008. LNCS, vol. 5051, pp. 170–184. Springer, Heidelberg (2008). doi:10.1007/978-3-540-68863-1_11
11. Stepney, S., Polack, F., Toyn, I.: Refactoring in maintenance and development of Z specifications and proofs. ENTCS **70**(3), 50–69 (2002)
12. Tarasyuk, A., Pereverzeva, I., Troubitsyna, E., Latvala, T.: The formal derivation of mode logic for autonomous satellite flight formation. In: Koornneef, F., Gulijk, C. (eds.) SAFECOMP 2015. LNCS, vol. 9337, pp. 29–43. Springer, Heidelberg (2015). doi:10.1007/978-3-319-24255-2_4
13. Whiteside, I.J.: Refactoring Proofs. Ph.D. thesis, The University of Edinburgh (2013)
14. Yaghoubi Shahir, H., Farahbod, R., Glässer, U.: Refactoring abstract state machine models. In: Derrick, J., Fitzgerald, J., Gnesi, S., Khurshid, S., Leuschel, M., Reeves, S., Riccobene, E. (eds.) ABZ 2012. LNCS, vol. 7316, pp. 345–348. Springer, Heidelberg (2012). doi:10.1007/978-3-642-30885-7_28

Towards Concolic Testing for Hybrid Systems

Pingfan Kong[1(✉)], Yi Li[2], Xiaohong Chen[1,3], Jun Sun[1(✉)], Meng Sun[2], and Jingyi Wang[1]

[1] Singapore University of Technology and Design, Singapore, Singapore
{pingfan_kong,sunjun}@sutd.edu.sg
[2] LMAM & DI, School of Mathematical Sciences, Peking University, Beijing, China
[3] University of Illinois at Urbana-Champaign, Champaign, USA

Abstract. Hybrid systems exhibit both continuous and discrete behavior. Analyzing hybrid systems is known to be hard. Inspired by the idea of concolic testing (of programs), we investigate whether we can combine random sampling and symbolic execution in order to effectively verify hybrid systems. We identify a sufficient condition under which such a combination is more effective than random sampling. Furthermore, we analyze different strategies of combining random sampling and symbolic execution and propose an algorithm which allows us to dynamically switch between them so as to reduce the overall cost. Our method has been implemented as a web-based checker named HyChecker. HyChecker has been evaluated with benchmark hybrid systems and a water treatment system in order to test its effectiveness.

1 Introduction

Hybrid systems are ever more relevant these days with the rapid development of the so-called cyber-physical systems and Internet of Things. Like traditional software, hybrid systems rely on carefully crafted software to operate correctly. Unlike traditional software, the control software in hybrid systems must interact with a continuous environment through sensing and actuating. Analyzing hybrid systems automatically is highly nontrivial. With a reasonably precise model of the entire system (e.g., in the form of a hybrid automaton), analyzing its behaviors (e.g., answering the question whether the system would satisfy a safety property) is challenging due to multiple reasons. Firstly, the dynamics of the environment, often composed of ordinary differential equations (ODE), is hard to reason about. For instance, there may not be closed form mathematical solutions for certain ODE. Secondly, unlike in the setting of traditional model checking problems, the variables in the hybrid models are often of real type and the (mode) transitions are often guarded with propositional formulas over real variables. There have been theoretical studies on the complexity of analyzing hybrid systems. For instance, it has been proved that non-trivial verification and control problems on non-trivial nonlinear hybrid systems are undecidable [19,22]. As a result, researchers have proposed to either work on approximate models of hybrid systems [18,23], or adopt approximate methods and tools on the hybrid system models [5,6,17].

J. Fitzgerald et al. (Eds.): FM 2016, LNCS 9995, pp. 460–478, 2016.
DOI: 10.1007/978-3-319-48989-6_28

One line of research (which we believe is relevant) is on analyzing the behaviors of hybrid systems through *controlled* sampling. One example of those sampling-based methods is [17]. The idea is to approximate the behavior of a hybrid system probabilistically in the form of *discrete time Markov chains* (DTMC). The complex dynamics in hybrid automata model is approximated using numeric differential equations solvers, and the mode transitions are approximated by probabilistic transition distributions in Markov chains. Afterwards, methods like hypothesis testing can be applied to the Markov chain to verify, probabilistically, properties against the original hybrid model.

While sampling-based methods like [17] are typically more scalable, there are limitations. Arguably, the most important one is that random sampling does not work well when the system contains *rare events*, i.e., events which by definition are unlikely to occur through random sampling. When systems get complicated, every event becomes rarer in a way. Existing remedies for this problem include importance sampling [6] and importance splitting [25], which work by essentially increasing the probability of the rare events. Both approaches are however useful only in certain limited circumstances.

One potential remedy for the problem is concolic testing, which is a technique proposed for analyzing programs [15,36]. The idea is: if random sampling fails to fire certain transitions in certain state (i.e., a potential rare event), we apply symbolic execution to generate the specific inputs which would trigger the transition or to show that the transition is infeasible. In this work, we investigate the possibility of applying concolic testing to hybrid systems. In particular, we study two fundamental questions. One is under what condition combining random sampling and symbolic execution is beneficial, i.e., given a property, is it guaranteed to find a counterexample with a smaller number of samples? The other is, among different strategies of combining random sampling and symbolic execution (i.e., when and how to apply symbolic execution), how do we define and identify the more effective strategies? We remark that the latter question is particularly relevant to the analysis of hybrid systems as symbolic execution for hybrid automata is often very time consuming and thus a good strategy should perhaps be: applying symbolic execution as minimum as possible. Based on the answers, we then design an algorithm which adopts a strategy to dynamically switch between random sampling and symbolic execution. Intuitively, it works by continuously estimating whether certain transition is rare or not and applying symbolic execution only if the transition is estimated to be rarer than certain threshold. Furthermore, the threshold is calculated according to a cost model which estimates the cost of symbolic execution using certain constraint solver. Our method has been implemented as a self-contained web-based checker named HyChecker and evaluated with benchmark hybrid systems as well as a water treatment system in order to test its effectiveness.

The remainders of the paper are organized as follows. In Sect. 2, we define a DTMC interpretation of hybrid system models. In Sect. 3, we view symbolic execution as a form of importance sampling and establish a sufficient condition for importance sampling to be beneficial. In Sect. 4, we discuss strategies on combining random sampling and symbolic execution. In Sect. 5, we present our implementation and evaluate its effectiveness. In Sect. 6, we conclude and review related work.

2 A Probabilistic View

In this section, we present a probabilistic interpretation of hybrid system models, which provides the foundation for defining and comparing the effectiveness of random sampling, symbolic execution or their combinations. In this work, we assume that hybrid systems are modelled as hybrid automata [20]. The basic idea of hybrid automata is to model different discrete states in a hybrid system as different *modes* and use differential equations to describe how variables in the system evolve through time in the modes. For simplicity, we assume the differential equations are in the form of ordinary differential equations (ODEs).

Definition 1. *A* hybrid automaton *is a tuple* $\mathcal{H} = (Q, V, q_0, I, \{f_q\}_{q \in Q}, \{g_{(q,p)}\}_{\{q,p\} \subseteq Q})$ *such that* Q *is a finite set of modes;* V *is a finite set of state variables;* $q_0 \in Q$ *is the initial mode;* $I \subseteq \mathbb{R}^n$ *is a set of initial values of the state variables;* f_q *for any* $q \in Q$ *is an ODE describing how variables in* V *evolve through time at mode* q*; and* $g_{(q,p)}$ *for any* $q, p \in Q$ *is a guard condition on transiting from mode* q *to mode* p.

For simplicity, we often write $q \xrightarrow{g} p$ to denote $g_{(q,p)}$. For example, the hybrid automaton shown on the left of Fig. 1 models an underdamped oscillatory system [16], such as a spring-mass or a simple pendulum with a detector that raises an alarm whenever the displacement x exceeds the threshold a. The initial displacement $x(0) = 0$, while its tendency to deviate from the equilibrium $x'(0) \in [0, 2\pi]$. An alarm is raised when the system enters mode q_e, which is reachable only through the transition $q_0 \xrightarrow{x>a} q_e$.

Next, we define the semantics of a hybrid automaton in the form of an infinite-state labeled transition system (LTS).

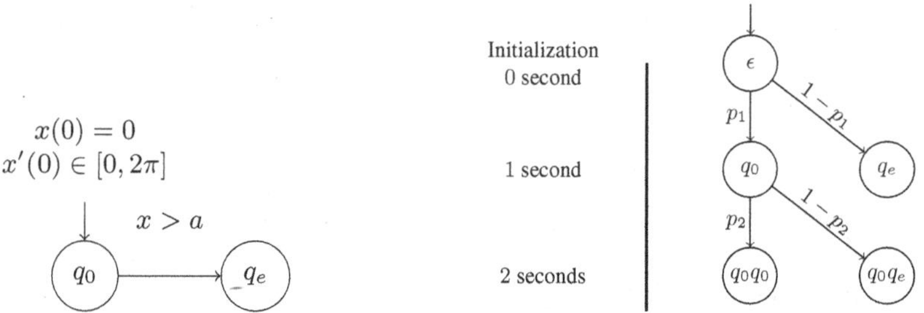

Fig. 1. An oscillatory system: the ODE at q_0 is $x'' + x' + 4\pi^2 x = 0$ and the one at q_e is $x' = 0$

Definition 2. *Let* $\mathcal{H} = (Q, V, q_0, I, \{f_q\}_{q \in Q}, \{g_{(p,q)}\}_{\{p,q\} \subseteq Q})$ *be a hybrid automaton. The semantics of* $\mathcal{H}$*, written as* $sem(\mathcal{H})$*, is an LTS* $(S, S_0, T, \rightarrow)$*, where* $S = \{(q, v) \mid q \in Q \text{ and } v \colon V \rightarrow \mathbb{R}^n\}$ *is the set of all (concrete) states;* $S_0 = \{(q_0, v) \mid v \in I\}$ *is the set of initial states;* $T = \mathbb{R}_+ \cup \{\epsilon\}$ *is the set of transition labels, where* ϵ *is a label for all discrete jumps; and* $\rightarrow \subseteq S \times T \times S$ *contains two sets of transitions. One is time transitions, i.e.,* $(q, v) \xrightarrow{t} (q, u)$ *if there exists a solution* ξ *to the differential equation* $\mathrm{d}V/\mathrm{dt} = f_q(V)$ *such that* $\xi(0) = v$ *and* $\xi(t) = u$*. The other is jumps, i.e.,* $(q, v) \xrightarrow{\epsilon} (p, v)$ *where there exists a transition* $q \xrightarrow{g} p$ *in* $\mathcal{H}$ *such that* v *satisfies* g*.*

A finite *run* ρ of $\mathcal{H}$ is a finite sequence of transitions of $sem(\mathcal{H})$. Since we are investigating random sampling and symbolic execution (both of which are limited to finite runs), we focus on runs of *bounded* length. For simplicity, we assume that all finite runs can be extended to an infinite non-Zeno run (such that time elapses unboundedly [20]). It is straightforward to see that there always exists a time unit $\Delta t > 0$ such that at most one jump (i.e., ϵ-transition) occurs with Δt time units. In the following, we simply assume that Δt is defined as one time unit. As a result, by observing the system mode at the end of every time unit, we can obtain a *trace* of $\mathcal{H}$ as $\pi = q_0 q_1 \ldots q_k$, i.e., the sequence of modes observed during the run. We remark that if there is no jump during the time unit, the same mode is observed.

In the following, we focus on reachability analysis of certain modes [17], i.e., certain modes in $\mathcal{H}$ are considered negative and we would like to check if any of them is reachable. We remark that the verification problem of properties expressed in BLTL formula [27] can be reduced to reachability analysis [17]. For instance, in the example shown in Fig. 1, the safety property is reduced to whether the negative mode q_e is reachable or not (within certain time). A trace is positive if it contains no negative mode. It is negative (a.k.a. a counterexample) if it contains at least one negative mode.

Next, we introduce a Markov chain interpretation of $\mathcal{H}$, adopted from [17]. Without loss of generality, we assume a uniform probability distribution on all initial states. This uniform distribution naturally induces a probability distribution over the traces of the system. Recall that a transition $q \xrightarrow{g} p$ of $\mathcal{H}$ can be fired only when g is satisfied. Suppose the system is in the state (q, v) initially and becomes (q, v_t) after a time transition of t. If v_t satisfies g, the transition is enabled. We denote the set of all points in time within $(0, 1)$ when the mode transition $q \xrightarrow{g} p$ is enabled as

$$T_q(v, g) = \{t \in (0, 1) \mid \theta_q(v, t) \text{ satisfies } g\}, \tag{1}$$

where $\theta_q(v, \cdot)$ is the solution of the ODE at mode q with the initial value v. If the transition is fired at some time point $t \in T_q(v, g)$, the following state is observed after 1 time unit: $(p, \theta_p(v_t, 1 - t)) = (p, \theta_p(\theta_q(v, t), 1 - t))$. That is, the new mode is p and the variables evolve according to the ODE at mode q for t time unit and then according to the ODE at mode p for $1 - t$ time unit. For simplicity, we write $v_{q,p}(v, t)$ to denote the variable state reached from state

(q, v) by firing transition $q \xrightarrow{g} p$ at time t, i.e., $v_{q,p}(v,t) = \theta_p(\theta_q(v,t), 1-t)$. Furthermore, we write $v_{q,p}(v)$ to denote the set of all variable states reached from state (q, v) by firing transition $q \xrightarrow{g} p$ at any time the transition is enabled, i.e., $v_{q,p}(v) = \{v_{q,p}(v,t) \mid t \in T_q(v,g)\}$.

By our assumption on the uniform random sampling, there is a uniform distribution over $T_q(v,g)$. This uniform distribution, denoted as $\mathbf{U}(T_q(v,g))$, naturally induces the following probability distribution over $v_{q,p}(v)$

$$\mathbf{P}(Y) = \int_{t \in T_q(v,g)} \frac{[v_{q,p}(v,t) \in Y]}{\|T_q(v,g)\|} \mathrm{d}t \tag{2}$$

for any $Y \subseteq v_{q,p}(v)$, where $[\,\cdot\,]$ is the Iverson bracket [24] and $\|\cdot\|$ is the Lebesgue measure [29]. Intuitively, if initially the system is in the state (q, v), we obtain a probability distribution over all possible states after taking the transition.

Next, we generalize the result so as to compare the probability of taking different transitions from different initial states. We assume a probability space $(X, \mathbf{P})$ where $X \subseteq \mathbb{R}^n$, and the automaton $\mathcal{H}$ starts from a state (q, v) with $v \sim \mathbf{P}$. Let $q \xrightarrow{g_i} p_i$ where $i \in \{1, \ldots, m\}$ be the transitions from q. Given an initial state (q, v), the time window in which the transition to p_i is enabled is $T_q(v, g_i)$. We assume that the system does not favor certain transitions and the probability of taking a transition is proportional to the size of the time window in which that transition is enabled. In other words, the probability of taking the transition $q \xrightarrow{g_i} p_i$ from state (q, v) is defined as $p_{q,p_i}(v) = \|T_q(v,g_i)\| / \sum_{j=1}^{m} \|T_q(v,g_j)\|$. According to the law of total probability, we have

$$p_{q,p_i} = \int_{v \in X} \frac{\|T_q(v,g_i)\|}{\sum_{j=1}^{m} \|T_q(v,g_j)\|} \mathrm{d}\mathbf{P}(v). \tag{3}$$

Furthermore, assume the transition $q \xrightarrow{g_i} p_i$ is fired. Given the condition that v is a fixed v_0, we know the conditional probability distribution over $v_{q,p}(v_0)$, for any $Y \subseteq v_{q,p}(v_0)$, is defined as:

$$\mathbf{P}(Y \mid v = v_0) = \int_{t \in T_q(v_0,g)} \frac{[v_{q,p}(v_0,t) \in Y]}{\|T_q(v_0,g)\|} \mathrm{d}t.$$

By the law of total probability, for any $Y \subseteq v_{q,p}(X)$, we have

$$\begin{aligned}
\mathbf{P}(Y) &= \int_{v \in X} \mathbf{P}(Y \mid v) \mathrm{d}\mathbf{P}(v) \\
&= \int_{v \in X} \int_{t \in T_q(v,g)} \frac{[v_{q,p}(v,t) \in Y]}{\|T_q(v,g)\|} \mathrm{d}t \mathrm{d}\mathbf{P}(v) \\
&= \int_{v \in X} \int_0^1 \frac{[t \in T_q(v,g) \wedge v_{q,p}(v,t) \in Y]}{\|T_q(v,g)\|} \mathrm{d}t \mathrm{d}\mathbf{P}(v).
\end{aligned} \tag{4}$$

Equations (3) and (4) effectively identify a discrete-time Markov chain (DTMC).

Definition 3. *Let* $\mathcal{H} = (Q, V, q_0, I, \{f_q\}_{q \in Q}, \{g_{(p,q)}\}_{\{p,q\} \subseteq Q})$ *be a hybrid automaton, and* K *be a bound of trace length. The DTMC associated with* $\mathcal{H}$ *is a tuple* $\mathcal{M}_{\mathcal{H}} = (S, u_0, Pr)$ *where a node in* S *is of the form* $(q, X, \mathbf{P}_X)$ *where* $q \in Q$ *is a mode,* X *is the set of values for* V *and* $\mathbf{P}_X$ *is a probability distribution of the values in* X*; the root* $u_0 = (q_0, I, \mathbf{U}_I)$ *where* $\mathbf{U}_I$ *is the uniform distribution over* I*; and for any* $(q, X, \mathbf{P}_X) \in S$*, the transition probability* $Pr((q, X, \mathbf{P}_X), (p, v_{q,p_i}(X), \mathbf{P}_i))$*, where the probability distribution* $\mathbf{P}_i$ *is defined as in Eq.* (4).

We remark that $\mathcal{M}_{\mathcal{H}}$ abstracts away the complicated ODE in $\mathcal{H}$ and replaces the guarded transitions with probabilistic transitions. A *path* of $\mathcal{M}_{\mathcal{H}}$ with non-zero probability always corresponds to a trace of $\mathcal{H}$ [17]. The partition of positive and negative traces in $\mathcal{H}$ naturally induces a partition of positive and negative paths in $\mathcal{M}_{\mathcal{H}}$. Notice that $\mathcal{M}_{\mathcal{H}}$ is by construction in the form of a tree. The degree of the tree is bounded by the number of modes in $\mathcal{H}$, and its depth is bounded by K, i.e., the bound on trace length.

For instance, following the above discussion, we can construct the DTMC of the oscillatory system shown on the right of Fig. 1. The root node is $s_0 = (q_0, I, \mathbf{U}_I)$ where $I = \{0\} \times [0, 2\pi]$ and $\mathbf{U}_I$ is the uniform distribution over I. There is one outgoing transition $q_0 \rightarrow q_e$ at mode q_0. Thus s_0 has two children nodes s_1 and s_2, where s_1 represents automaton taking the transition $q_0 \rightarrow q_e$ in the first second, and s_2 represents automaton staying in mode q_0. For this simple example, we can analytically compute the transition probability, e.g., p_1 and p_2 shown in Fig. 1. In general it is difficult.

3 Symbolic Execution as a Form of Importance Sampling

In this section, we analyze the effectiveness of random sampling and symbolic execution based on the DTMC interpretation of $\mathcal{H}$ developed in the previous section. In particular, we review symbolic execution as a form of importance sampling [39], which intuitively speaking alters the probability distribution of $\mathcal{M}_{\mathcal{H}}$ in certain way so that a negative path is more likely to be sampled. In the following, we first define a way of measuring the effectiveness of random sampling, symbolic execution and possibly other sampling methods.

3.1 Bayesian Inference

Recall that traces of $\mathcal{H}$ are partitioned into either positive trace, denoted as Π^+, or negative traces, denoted as Π^-. The probability of the system exhibiting a negative trace is called the *error probability* and is denoted as $\theta = \mathbf{P}(\Pi^-)$. Intuitively, after observing some sample traces (obtained either through random sampling or symbolic execution), we gain certain information on θ. Formally, we investigate the following questions: (1) how do we claim that the error probability θ is bounded by certain tolerance level δ and (2) how do we measure the confidence of the claim?

We answer the questions based on statistical inference. Intuitively, if we see many negative trace samples, we conclude *with certain confidence* that the system is likely to have an error probability that is larger than the tolerance level δ. If we identify few or even no negative traces, we conclude *with certain confidence* that the system is likely to have an error probability within the tolerance level δ. Formally, let random variable X denote whether a sample trace is positive or negative, i.e., $\mathbf{P}(X = 1)$ is the error probability θ. Let $B(N, \theta)$ denote the binomial distribution with parameters $N \in \mathbb{N}$ and $\theta \in [0, 1]$. We have $X \sim B(1, \theta)$. Given N independent and identically distributed sample traces, the number of negative traces is: $m = X_1 + X_2 + \ldots X_N \sim B(N, \theta)$. Initially, before witnessing any sample trace, we may only estimate the value of θ based on historical data. We thus assume a *prior knowledge* of θ in the form of a *prior distribution* $f(\theta)$. If no historical data are available, we set the prior distribution to be a non-informative one. In the following, for simplicity, we adopt the non-informative prior distribution $f(\theta) \equiv 1$ where $\theta \in [0, 1]$.

According to the Bayesian law, the *post distribution* of θ after witnessing m negative samples and $n = N - m$ positive samples is defined as follows.

$$f(\theta \mid n, m) = \frac{f(\theta) f(n, m \mid \theta)}{\displaystyle\int_0^1 f(\theta) f(n, m \mid \theta) \mathrm{d}\theta} = \frac{\theta^m (1-\theta)^n}{\mathrm{B}(m+1, n+1)}$$

where $\mathrm{B}(\,\cdot\,,\,\cdot\,)$ is the Beta function [3]. The *confidence* we have about the claim that $\theta < \delta$, denoted as $c(n, m, \delta)$, can be defined naturally as the probability of $\theta < \delta$ conditioned on observing the negative and positive samples. Formally,

$$c(n, m, \delta) = \int_0^\delta f(\theta \mid n, m) \mathrm{d}\theta = \frac{\mathrm{B}(\delta; m+1, n+1)}{\mathrm{B}(m+1, n+1)}$$

where $\mathrm{B}(\delta\,;\,\cdot\,,\,\cdot\,)$ is the incomplete Beta function [3].

The following proposition shows that our definition of confidence is consistent with our intuition, i.e., the more positive samples we observe, the more confidence we have.

Proposition 1. *For any tolerance* $0 < \delta < 1$, $c(n, 0, \delta) \to 1$ *as* $n \to \infty$*; and for any* $m > 0$, $c(n, m, \delta) \to 1$ *as* $n/m \to \infty$.

Thus, if we have dominantly sufficient positive samples, we would always be able to reach a target confidence level. In practice, however, we are always limited in the budget or time, we thus would like to reach a certain confidence level at a low cost. For instance, instead of random sampling, we can apply idea like importance sampling [39] so as to increase the probability of sampling a negative sample and hope to gain the same confidence level with fewer samples. Recall that we can view symbolic execution as a particular way of importance sampling. Compared with random sampling, it essentially alters the probabilistic distribution of the traces so that more probability is associated with those traces following a given path. In the following, we investigate the idea of importance sampling in our setting and establish a condition which must be satisfied so that importance sampling (including symbolic execution) must satisfy in order to be more effective in achieving the same confidence level.

3.2 Importance Sampling

Importance sampling is a widely-used technique in Monte Carlo method in order to approximate the expectation of a probability distribution. The intuition is after observing many positive samples, we should have more confidence in the system's correctness, *if the samples are generated by a method that is more likely to sample a negative one.* We remark that the notion of importance sampling we adopt here has nothing to do with the expectation approximation [39], but rather shares the same idea with the importance sampling in the Monte Carlo method.

Recall that θ is the error probability. The probability of a specific sampling method finding a negative trace is a function of θ, denoted as $\varphi(\theta)$. We refer to $\varphi(\theta)$ as the *effectiveness function* of the sampling method. Furthermore, $\varphi(\theta)$ is assumed to be continuous and strictly increasing on $[0, 1]$ with $\varphi(0) = 0$ and $\varphi(1) = 1$. Given a specific sampling method (e.g., random sampling or symbolic execution), we may be able to approximate its effectiveness through empirical study. In certain special cases, we might identify a closed form of the effectiveness function for a specific sampling method. For instance, in the case of random sampling, the effectiveness function $\varphi(\theta) = \theta$. A sampling method with effectiveness $\varphi(\theta)$ is said to be *more effective* than another with effectiveness $\phi(\theta)$, if $\varphi(\theta) > \phi(\theta)$ for all θ. Two sampling methods are called incomparable if no one is more effective than the other.

In the following, we show that a more effective sampling method leads to a higher confidence level. Without loss of generality, we focus on effectiveness functions which can be expressed in the form of a power function $\varphi(\theta) = \theta^\alpha$ where $\theta \in [0, 1]$ for $0 < \alpha \leq 1$. The reason for the assumption is that effectiveness functions in this form can be compared easily.

Following the discussion in Sect. 3.1, suppose that the effectiveness of a testing method is $\varphi(\theta) = \theta^\alpha$ and we have witnessed m negative samples and $n = N - m$ positive samples. The post distribution can be calculated as follows.

$$f(\theta \mid n, m) = \frac{\theta^{\alpha m}(1 - \theta^\alpha)^n}{\int_0^1 \theta^{\alpha m}(1 - \theta^\alpha)^n \mathrm{d}\theta} \tag{5}$$

Accordingly, the confidence is defined as follows.

$$c_\varphi(n, m, \delta) = \int_0^\delta f(\theta \mid n, m)\mathrm{d}\theta = \frac{\int_0^\delta \theta^{\alpha m}(1 - \theta^\alpha)^n \mathrm{d}\theta}{\int_0^1 \theta^{\alpha m}(1 - \theta^\alpha)^n \mathrm{d}\theta}. \tag{6}$$

The following theorem then establishes that a *more effective* sampling method would always result in more confidence.

Theorem 1. *Let* $\varphi(\theta) = \theta^\alpha$ *and* $\psi(\theta) = \theta^\beta$ *be the effectiveness function of two testing methods. If* $1 \geq \alpha > \beta > 0$*, then* $\varphi(\theta) \leq \psi(\theta)$ *for all* $\theta \in [0, 1]$*, and* $c_\varphi(n, m, \delta) \leq c_\psi(n, m, \delta)$ *for all* $n, m \in \mathbb{N}$ *and* $\delta \in (0, 1)$. □

The (rather involved) proof is presented in [28]. This theorem endorses our intuition that we should have more confidence in the systems' correctness when observing many positive samples, if the samples are generated by a method like symbolic execution (with a bias on negative samples). In general we cannot compare the confidence of two incomparable sampling methods. We remark that this result has not been formally proved before and it serves the foundation for the approach we propose next.

Based on the theorem, in order to apply symbolic execution to achieve better confidence than applying random sampling, we should apply it such that it is more likely to sample a negative trace. There are multiple different strategies on how/when to apply symbolic execution. For instance, we could symbolically execute a path which ends with a negative mode, or a part of the path (e.g., we solve for input values which are required to trigger the first few transitions of a path leading to a negative mode, if we have reasons to believe that only those transitions are unlikely to be fired through random sampling), or even simply symbolically execute a path which has not been visited before if all existing samples are positive. In the next section, we discuss how to compare these different strategies based on cost and propose a cost-effect algorithm.

4 Sampling Strategies

Recall that our objective is to check whether there is a trace which visits a negative mode. Theorem 1 certainly does not imply we should abandon random sampling. The simple reason is that it ignores the issue of time cost. In general, the cost of obtaining a negative trace through sampling (either random sampling or symbolic execution) is: c/pr where c is the cost of obtaining one sample and pr is the probability of the sample being a negative trace. In the case of random sampling, c is often low and pr is also likely low, especially so if the negative traces all contain certain rare event. In the case of symbolic execution, c is likely high since we need to solve a path condition to obtain a sample, whereas pr is likely high. Thus, in order to choose between random sampling and symbolic execution, we would like to know their time cost, i.e., c and pr. While knowing the cost of obtaining one sample through random sampling is relatively straightforward, knowing the cost c of symbolic execution is highly non-trivial. In this section, we assume there is a way of estimating that and propose an algorithm based on the assumption. In Sect. 5, we estimate c empirically and show that even a rough estimation serves a good basis for choosing the right strategy. We can calculate pr based on $\mathcal{M}_\mathcal{H}$. However, constructing $\mathcal{M}_\mathcal{H}$ is infeasible and thus we propose to approximate $\mathcal{M}_\mathcal{H}$ at runtime.

4.1 Probability Estimation

Initially, since we have no idea on the probability of obtaining a negative trace, we apply wishful thinking and start with random sampling, hoping that a negative trace will be sampled. If a negative trace is indeed sampled, we are done. Otherwise, the traces that have been sampled effectively identify a subgraph of $\mathcal{M}_{\mathcal{H}}$, denoted as $\mathcal{M}_{sub}$, which contains only modes and transitions visited by the sample traces. Without any clue on the transition probability between modes not in $\mathcal{M}_{sub}$, it is infeasible for us to estimate pr (i.e., the probability of reaching a negative mode). It is clear however that in order to reach a negative mode, we must sample in a way such that $\mathcal{M}_{sub}$ is expanded with unvisited modes. Thus, in the following, we focus on finding a strategy which is cost-effective in discovering new modes instead.

For each mode u in $\mathcal{M}_{sub}$ where there is an unvisited child mode v, we have the choice of either trying to reach v from u through more random sampling or through symbolic execution (i.e., solving the path condition). In theory, the choice is to be resolved as follows: random sampling if $c_t/q(u) < c_s$ and symbolic execution if $c_t/q(u) \geq c_s$, where c_t is the cost of generating a random sample; c_s is the cost of applying symbolic execution to generate a sample visiting an unvisited child of u in $\mathcal{M}_{sub}$; and $q(u)$ is the probability of finding a new mode from u, i.e., $q(u) = \sum_{v \in V \setminus V_0} p_{uv}$. Intuitively, for random sampling, the expected number of samples to find a new mode is $1/q(u)$ and thus the expected cost of using random sampling to discover a new mode is $c_t/q(u)$. Unfortunately, knowing $q(u)$ and $\mathcal{M}_{sub}$ exactly is expensive. The former is the subject of recent research on model counting and probabilistic symbolic execution [9,11,12,32], and the latter has been studied in [4]. Thus, in this work, we develop techniques to estimate their values.

In our approach, we actively estimate the probability of $q(u)$ (for each u in $\mathcal{M}_{sub}$) from historical observation through Bayesian inference, by recording how many times we sampled u. Assume $q = q(u)$ has a prior distribution $f(q)$. Let A denote the event that an unvisited child v remains unvisited after one sampling, and $\bar{A}$ denote the event that v becomes visited afterwards. Then,

$$f(q \mid A) = \frac{f(q)f(A \mid q)}{\displaystyle\int_0^1 f(q)f(A \mid q)\mathrm{d}q} = \frac{qf(q)}{\displaystyle\int_0^1 qf(q)\mathrm{d}q} \propto qf(q),$$

and similarly: $f(q \mid \bar{A}) \propto (1-q)f(q)$.

Suppose that mode u has been sampled for N times and for m out of N times, we end up with a child which has been visited previously. As a result, $n = N - m$ is the number of times we ended up with an unvisited child. We can compute the post distribution $f(q) \propto (1-q)^m q^n$ and the expectation as follows.

$$E(q) = \frac{\displaystyle\int_0^1 q(1-q)^m q^n \mathrm{d}q}{\displaystyle\int_0^1 (1-q)^m q^n \mathrm{d}q} = \frac{n+1}{m+n+2}.$$

Thus, we estimate $q(u)$ as $(n+1)/(m+n+2)$. Intuitively, the bigger m is, the less likely that an unvisited mode is going to be sampled through random sampling.

Next, we discuss how to apply symbolic execution in this setting. There are multiple strategies on how to apply symbolic execution to construct a sample for visiting v. For instance, we could solve a path condition from an initial mode to v so that it will surely result in a trace visiting v (if the path condition is satisfiable). Alternatively, we could take a sample trace which visits u and apply symbolic execution to see whether the trace can be altered to visit v after visiting u by letting a different amount of time elapsing at mode u. That is, assume that (u, X) is a concrete state of $sem(\mathcal{H})$ visited by a sample trace, where X is a valuation of V. We take the state (u, X) as the starting point and apply symbolic execution to solve a one-step path condition so that v is visited from state (u, X). This is meaningful for hybrid automata because, for every step, by letting a different amount of time elapsing, we may result in firing a different transition and therefore reaching a different mode. We remark that if solving the one-step path condition has no solution, it does not necessarily mean that v is unreachable from u. Nonetheless, we argue that this strategy is justified as, according to Theorem 1, such a sampling strategy would be more effective than random sampling. To distinguish these two strategies, we refer to the former as *global concolic sampling* and the latter *local concolic sampling*. The choice of strategy depends on c_s. We estimate c_s for particular solvers and systems in Sect. 5 and choose the right strategy accordingly.

4.2 Concolic Sampling

Based on the theoretical discussion presented above, we then present our sampling algorithm, which we call concolic sampling. The details are shown in Algorithm 1. The input is a hybrid automaton modeling a hybrid system, where some modes are identified as negative ones. The aim is to identify a trace which visits a negative mode or otherwise report that there is certain probabilistic guarantee on their absence. We remark that we skip the part on how the probabilistic guarantee is computed and refer the readers to [17] for details. We rather focus on our contribution on combining random sampling and symbolic execution for better counterexample identification in the following.

We maintain the set of sample traces as Π in the algorithm. Based on Π, we can construct the above-mentioned subgraph $\mathcal{M}_{sub}$ of $\mathcal{M}_{\mathcal{H}}$ systematically. Next, for each node u in $\mathcal{M}_{sub}$ which potentially has unvisited children, we maintain two numbers m and n as discussed above, in order to estimate the probability of $q(u)$. If according to our strategy, there is still some u such that it might be cheaper to discover a new child mode through random sampling, we proceed by generating a random sample using the algorithm presented in [17], which is shown as Algorithm 2.

We briefly introduce how Algorithm 2 works in the following. In a nutshell, the algorithm is designed to sample a run π according to an approximation of the probability distribution of $\mathcal{M}_{\mathcal{H}}$. The main idea is to use the Monte Carlo method to approximate the measure of time windows $\|T_q(v, g)\|$. Recall that

Algorithm 1. Concolic Sampling

Let Π be the set of sampled runs, initialized to the empty set;
Let $\mathcal{M}_{sub}$ be the subgraph of $\mathcal{M}$, initialized to the root node;
repeat
  Set $u = \arg\min_u \min(c_t/E(q(u)), c_s)$;
  if $c_t/q(u) < c_s$ **then**
    Invoke Random Sampling to generate a run π;
  else
    Apply symbolic execution to obtain a sample π visiting a new child of u;
  if π *visits a negative mode* **then**
    Present π as a counterexample and terminate;
  if π *visits an undiscovered mode* **then**
    $n_u := n_u + 1$;
  else
    $m_u := m_u + 1$;
  Add π into Π and add u to $\mathcal{M}_{sub}$;
until *time out*;

Algorithm 2. Random Sampling

Input: A hybrid automaton $\mathcal{H}$ and a state $\langle q, v\rangle$
Result: A successive state $\langle p, u\rangle$
1 Sample time points $t_1, \cdots, t_J$ uniformly from $[0, 1]$;
2 **foreach** *outgoing transition* $q \xrightarrow{g_i} q_i$ **do**
3   Set $T_i := \{t_j \mid \Phi_q(t_j, v) \models g_i\}$,
4 Choose a transition $q \xrightarrow{g_i} q_i$ with probability $\|T_i\|/\sum_i \|T_i\|$;
5 Sample a time point t uniformly from T_i;
6 Set $u := \Phi_{q_i}(1 - t, \Phi_q(t, v))$ and $p := q_i$;
7 Return $\langle p, u\rangle$;

$T_q(v, g) = \{t \in (0, 1) \mid \theta_q(v, t) \text{ satisfies } g\}$. Therefore the measure $\|T_q(v, g)\|$ is the mean of $[\theta_q(v, \tau) \models g]$, where the random variable $\tau \sim \mathbf{U}(0, 1)$. According to the law of large numbers [30], the sample mean almost surely converges to the expectation. Thus we have

$$\frac{\sum_{i=1}^{n} [\theta_q(v, \tau_i) \models g]}{n} \xrightarrow{a.s.} \|T_q(v, g_j)\| \quad \text{as} \quad n \to \infty,$$

where $\tau_1, \tau_2, \ldots, \tau_n \overset{i.i.d.}{\sim} \tau$. To generate a K-step run, Algorithm 2 works by generating one random step at a time. In particular, after each time unit, at line 4, firstly a set of time points are uniformly generated. By testing how often each transition from the current mode is enabled at these time points, we estimate the transition probability in $\mathcal{M}_{\mathcal{H}}$. At line 7, we sample a transition according to the estimated probability and generate a step. This procedure finishes when a run which spans K time units is generated.

If random sampling is unlikely to be cost-effective in discovering a new mode according to our strategy, symbolic execution is employed at line 7 in Algorithm 1 to generate a sample to cover a new node in $\mathcal{M}_{\mathcal{H}}$. Among all the nodes in $\mathcal{M}_{sub}$, we identify the one which would require the minimum cost to discover a new child according to our estimation c_s, encode the corresponding path condition and apply an existing constraint solver that supports ODE (i.e., dReal [14]) to generate a corresponding run. Once we obtain a new run π at line 8, we check whether it is a counterexample. If it is, we report and terminate at line 10. Otherwise, we repeat the same procedure until it times out.

5 Evaluation

We implemented our approach in a self-contained toolkit called HyChecker, available online at [2]. HyChecker is implemented with 1575 lines of Python codes (excluding external libraries we used) and is built with a web interface. HyChecker relies on the dReal constraint solver [14] for symbolic execution. In the following, we evaluate HyChecker in order to answer the following research question: does our strategy on combining random sampling and symbolic execution (resulting from our theoretical analysis) allow us to identify rare counterexamples more efficiently?

Our test subjects include three benchmark hybrid systems which we gather from previous publications as well as a simplified real-world water treatment system.

- *Thermodynamic system.* We first test our method on a room heating system from [10]. The system has n rooms and $m \leq n$ heaters which are used to tune the rooms' temperature. The temperature of a room is affected by the environment temperature and also by whether a heater is warming the room. The system therefore aims to maintain the rooms' temperature within certain comfortable range by moving around and turning on and off the heaters. We consider in the experiment such a system with three rooms and two heaters. We verify the same property as in [17], i.e., whether the two heaters will be moved to other rooms in the first five days.
- *Navigation system.* Our second test subject is the navigation system from [10]. This system contains a grid of cells, where each cell is associated with some particular velocity. Whenever a floating object moves from one cell to the other, it changes its acceleration rate according to the velocity in that cell. If the object leaves the grid, the velocity is the one of the closest cell. We check whether an object in the grid will leave its initial cell and will not enter a dangerous cell, within six minutes.
- *Traffic system.* Our third model is from the long standing research on modeling traffic and examining causes of traffic jams and car crashes. We use the ODE in [34] to describe the dynamics of a vehicle. We consider in the experiment a circular road with $n = 5$ cars on it. We are interested whether there could be

a potential traffic accident in the closed system, and whether there could be a potential traffic jam.
- *SWaT system.* Lastly, we tested our method on a simplified real-world system model. The Secure Water Testbed (SWaT) is a raw water purification laboratory located at SUTD [38]. SWaT is a complicated system involving a series of water treatments like ultrafiltration, chemical dosing, dechlorination through an ultraviolet system. We build a hybrid automaton model of SWaT based on the control program in the programmable logic control (PLC) in the system. The modes are defined based on the discrete states of the actuators (e.g., motorized valves and motorized pumps). These actuators are controlled by the PLC. There are in total 23 actuators, which results in many modes. By focusing on the hydraulic process in the system only, we build a hybrid automaton with 2721 modes. We skip the details of the model due to the limited space here. The readers are referred to [1] for details. The property we verify is that the water level in the backwash tank must not be too high or too low (otherwise, the system needs to be shut down), with some extreme initial setting (e.g., the water level in the tank is close to be too low) to analyze the system safety.

Estimating Cost of Symbolic Execution. In order to apply Algorithm 1 with the right strategy, we need to estimate c_s. The underlying question is how efficient a constraint solver can check the satisfiability of a given path condition. We remark that it is a challenging research problem and perhaps deserves a separate research project by itself. There are a dozen of various factors that determines how a solver performs in solving a given constraint, including the number of variables, the number of operators, the number of differential equations, the length of witnesses (if there is any), etc. Even on the same problem, different solvers have different performance due to different search strategies, ways of pruning and reducing state space, etc. [26,31]. All these facts make a precise estimation of efficiency of symbolic solvers extremely difficult.

In this work, following previous work on this topic [4], we estimate c_s as follows. First, we construct a sequence of increasingly more complicated random constraints (composed of constraints on ODE as well as ordinary constraints, which we obtain from examples in dReal). We then measure the time needed to solve them using dReal one-by-one. Based on the results, we observe that the dominant factor is the length of the formula and thus heuristically decide c_s to be a function of the length of constraints. Next, we apply a function fitting method to obtain a function for predicting c_s. The function we obtained is $\exp(1.73l - 1.65) - 1$ where l is the length of the formula, which suggests that the solving time is exponential in the length of the formula. It implies that dReal has problem solving path conditions containing two or more steps, which in turn means that our choice of strategy should be the *local concolic sampling*. We remark that this is unlikely a precise estimation. Nonetheless, as we show below, even a rough estimation would be useful in guiding when and how to do symbolic execution.

Table 1. Experiments results

		Random		Dynamic	Global	Local (our strategy)
Thermodynamic system	result	ct-eg found	pass	pass	pass	ct-eg found
	time(s)	340.4	600	600	600	41.25
	#samples	13K	22K	n/a	134	551
Navigation system	result	ct-eg found		pass	pass	ct-eg found
	time(s)	91.7		600	600	4.33
	#samples	354		n/a	4	5
Traffic system	result	pass		pass	pass	ct-eg found
	time(s)	600		600	600	28.86
	#samples	1240		n/a	2	2
SWaT system	result	ct-eg found		pass	pass	ct-eg found
	time(s)	102.4		600	600	64.6
	#samples	169		n/a	24	68

Experiment Results. Table 1 shows the experiment results. All experiment results are obtained in Ubuntu Linux 14.04 on a machine with an Intel(R) Core(TM) i5-4950, running with one 3.30 GHz CPU core (no parallel optimization), 6M cache and 12 GB RAM. We set a timeout of 10 min for each experiment, i.e., if no counterexample is identified after 10 min, the property has passed the test. Each experiment is repeated for 10 times and we report the average time. All details on the experiments are at [1].

We compare four approaches in order to show the effectiveness of our chosen strategy. The first is the random sampling approach proposed in [17]. The results are shown in column **random**. Note that there are two results for the thermodynamic system. This is because due to the randomness in the approach, the results are not always consistent (e.g., in one experiment, a counterexample is found, whereas none is found in another). The second approach is the concolic testing approach in [36] (i.e., applying random testing once and applying symbolic execution to visit the alternative path in the last branch and so on). The results are shown in column **dynamic**. The last two columns report the result of applying **global** concolic sampling and **local** concolic sampling respectively.

We have the following observations based on the results. First, among the four approaches, local concolic testing is able to spot counterexamples more efficiently in all cases. Compared with random sampling, the number of samples explored by local concolic sampling is significantly smaller. This confirms the result of the theoretical analysis in previous sections. Second, symbolic execution for hybrid systems are clearly constrained by the limited capability of existing hybrid constraint solvers like dReal. For all four cases, both concolic testing and global concolic sampling time out whilst waiting for dReal to solve the first path condition. This is because the path condition (composed of constraints from multiple steps) is complex and dReal takes a lot of time trying to solve it. The only difference is that while concolic testing got stuck after the first sample, global concolic sampling got stuck after it has randomly sampled a few traces and switched to symbolic execution. On the contrary, local concolic sampling uses dReal to solve a one-step path condition each time and is able to smartly switch between random sampling and symbolic execution, and eventually found a counterexample. Third, the experiment results suggest that the formula that we applied for estimating c_s turned out to be an under-approximation, i.e., the actual time cost is often much larger. If we modify the function to return a much larger cost for solving a path composed of two or more steps, global concolic sampling would be equivalent to random sampling as symbolic execution would never be selected due to its high cost.

6 Conclusion and Related Works

In this work, we investigated the effectiveness of different sampling methods (i.e., random sampling and symbolic execution) for hybrid systems. We established theoretical results on comparing their effectiveness and we developed an approach for combining random sampling and symbolic executions in a way which is provably cost-effective.

In the following, we discuss the related work, in addition to those discussed already. This work is inspired by [7], which initialized the discussion on the efficiency of random testing. Our work aims to combine random sampling and symbolic execution to identify rare counterexamples efficiently. It is thus closely related to work on handling rare events in the setting of statistical model checking [5,6,25]. In [5], the authors set up a theoretical framework using coupling theory and developed an efficient sampling method that guarantees a variance reduction and provides a confidence interval. In [6] the authors proposed the first importance sampling method for CTMC to provide a true confidence interval. In [25] the authors motivated the use of importance splitting to estimate the probability of a rare property. Our work is different as we complement sampling with symbolic execution to identify rare events efficiently.

This work borrows idea from work on combining program testing with symbolic execution (a.k.a. dynamic symbolic execution or concolic testing). In [15], the authors proposed a way of combining program testing with symbolic execution to achieve better test coverage. Random testing is first applied to explore program behaviors, after which symbolic execution is used to direct the test towards different program branches. Similar ideas later have been developed in [8,33,36,37]. Our work is different in two ways. One is that we target hybrid systems in work, which has different characteristics from ordinary programs. One of them is that symbolic execution of hybrid automata is considerable more expensive, which motivated us to find ways of justifying the use of symbolic execution. The other is that, based on the probabilistic abstraction of hybrid models, we are able to formally compare the cost of random sampling against symbolic execution to develop cost-effective sampling strategies. We remark that the same idea can be applied to concolic testing of programs as well.

HyChecker is a tool for analyzing hybrid systems and thus it is related to tools/systems on analyzing hybrid systems. In [35], the authors developed a theorem prover for hybrid systems. Users are required to use differential dynamic logic to model hybrid systems. Afterwards, the prover can be used interactively to find a sound and complete proof of certain properties of the system. It has been shown that the prover works for safety critical systems like aircrafts [35]. HyChecker is different as it is fully automatic. *dReach* [13] is a recent tool developed for verifying hybrid systems. It is based on the SMT solver *dReal* [14] developed by the same authors. *dReach* focuses on bounded δ-complete reachability analysis. It provides a relatively easy-to-use interface for modeling hybrid systems and verifies whether a system is δ-safe under given safety demands. We observe since *dReach* attempts to solve every path in a hybrid automaton, its performance suffers when the system becomes more complicated. HyChecker relies on *dReal* and tries to improve *dReach* by combining random sampling to avoid solving many of the paths. HyTech [21] is one of the earliest tools on verifying hybrid systems. It is limited to linear hybrid automata.

Acknowledgement. The project is supported by the NRF project IGDSi1305012 in SUTD and by the National Natural Science Foundation of China under grant no. 61532019, 61202069 and 61272160.

References

1. http://sav.sutd.edu.sg/?page_id=2803
2. http://sav.sutd.edu.sg/SMC/
3. Abramowitz, M.: Handbook of Mathematical Functions, With Formulas, Graphs, and Mathematical Tables. Dover Publications, New York (1974). Incorporated
4. Aziz, M.A., Wassal, A.G., Darwish, N.M.: A machine learning technique for hardness estimation of QFBV SMT problems. In: 10th International Workshop on Satisfiability Modulo Theories (SMT), pp. 57–66 (2012)
5. Barbot, B., Haddad, S., Picaronny, C.: Coupling and importance sampling for statistical model checking. In: Flanagan, C., König, B. (eds.) TACAS 2012. LNCS, vol. 7214, pp. 331–346. Springer, Heidelberg (2012). doi:10.1007/978-3-642-28756-5_23
6. Barbot, B., Haddad, S., Picaronny, C., et al.: Importance sampling for model checking of continuous time markov chains. In: SIMUL, pp. 30–35 (2012)
7. Böhme, M., Paul, S.: On the efficiency of automated testing. In: 22nd ACM SIGSOFT International Symposium on Foundations of Software Engineering (FSE-22), pp. 632–642 (2014)
8. Cadar, C., Dunbar, D., Engler, D.R.: KLEE: unassisted and automatic generation of high-coverage tests for complex systems programs. In: 8th USENIX Symposium on Operating Systems Design and Implementation (OSDI), pp. 209–224 (2008)
9. Chistikov, D., Dimitrova, R., Majumdar, R.: Approximate counting in SMT and value estimation for probabilistic programs. In: Baier, C., Tinelli, C. (eds.) TACAS 2015. LNCS, vol. 9035, pp. 320–334. Springer, Heidelberg (2015). doi:10.1007/978-3-662-46681-0_26
10. Fehnker, A., Ivančić, F.: Benchmarks for hybrid systems verification. In: Alur, R., Pappas, G.J. (eds.) HSCC 2004. LNCS, vol. 2993, pp. 326–341. Springer, Heidelberg (2004). doi:10.1007/978-3-540-24743-2_22
11. Filieri, A., Frias, M.F., Păsăreanu, C.S., Visser, W.: Model counting for complex data structures. In: Fischer, B., Geldenhuys, J. (eds.) SPIN 2015. LNCS, vol. 9232, pp. 222–241. Springer, Heidelberg (2015). doi:10.1007/978-3-319-23404-5_15

12. Filieri, A., Pasareanu, C.S., Visser, W., Geldenhuys, J.: Statistical symbolic execution with informed sampling. In: 22nd ACM SIGSOFT International Symposium on Foundations of Software Engineering (FSE-22), pp. 437–448 (2014)
13. Gao, S., Kong, S., Chen, W., Clarke, E.: Delta-complete analysis for bounded reachability of hybrid systems. arXiv preprint arXiv:1404.7171 (2014)
14. Gao, S., Kong, S., Clarke, E.M.: dReal: an SMT solver for nonlinear theories over the reals. In: Bonacina, M.P. (ed.) CADE 2013. LNCS (LNAI), vol. 7898, pp. 208–214. Springer, Heidelberg (2013). doi:10.1007/978-3-642-38574-2_14
15. Godefroid, P., Klarlund, N., Sen, K.: Dart: directed automated random testing. SIGPLAN Not. **40**(6), 213–223 (2005)
16. Gordon, J., Serway, R., McGrew, R.: Physics for Scientists and Engineers, vol. 2. Cengage Learning, Boston (2007)
17. Gyori, B.M., Liu, B., Paul, S., Ramanathan, R., Thiagarajan, P.S.: Approximate probabilistic verification of hybrid systems. In: Abate, A., Šafránek, D. (eds.) HSB 2015. LNCS (LNBI), vol. 9271, pp. 96–116. Springer, Heidelberg (2015). doi:10.1007/978-3-319-26916-0_6
18. Hahn, E.M., Hartmanns, A., Hermanns, H., Katoen, J.: A compositional modelling and analysis framework for stochastic hybrid systems. Formal Methods Syst. Des. **43**(2), 191–232 (2013)
19. Henzinger, T.A.: The theory of hybrid automata. In: 11th Annual IEEE Symposium on Logic in Computer Science (LICS), pp. 278–292 (1996)
20. Henzinger, T.A.: The theory of hybrid automata. In: Inan, M.K., Kurshan, R.P. (eds.) Verification of Digital and Hybrid Systems. NATO ASI Series, vol. 170, pp. 265–292. Springer, Heidelberg (2000)
21. Henzinger, T.A., Ho, P.-H., Wong-Toi, H.: HyTech: a model checker for hybrid systems. In: Grumberg, O. (ed.) CAV 1997. LNCS, vol. 1254, pp. 460–463. Springer, Heidelberg (1997). doi:10.1007/3-540-63166-6_48
22. Henzinger, T.A., Kopke, P.W., Puri, A., Varaiya, P.: What's decidable about hybrid automata? J. Comput. Syst. Sci. **57**(1), 94–124 (1998)
23. Henzinger, T.A., Majumdar, R.: Symbolic model checking for rectangular hybrid systems. In: Graf, S., Schwartzbach, M. (eds.) TACAS 2000. LNCS, vol. 1785, pp. 142–156. Springer, Heidelberg (2000). doi:10.1007/3-540-46419-0_11
24. Iverson, K.E.: A Programming Language. Wiley, New York (1962)
25. Jegourel, C., Legay, A., Sedwards, S.: Importance splitting for statistical model checking rare properties. In: Sharygina, N., Veith, H. (eds.) CAV 2013. LNCS, vol. 8044, pp. 576–591. Springer, Heidelberg (2013). doi:10.1007/978-3-642-39799-8_38
26. Jha, S., Limaye, R., Seshia, S.A.: Beaver: engineering an efficient SMT solver for bit-vector arithmetic. In: Bouajjani, A., Maler, O. (eds.) CAV 2009. LNCS, vol. 5643, pp. 668–674. Springer, Heidelberg (2009). doi:10.1007/978-3-642-02658-4_53
27. Kamide, N.: Bounded linear-time temporal logic: a proof-theoretic investigation. Ann. Pure Appl. Logic **163**(4), 439–466 (2012)
28. Kong, P., Li, Y., Chen, X., Sun, J., Sun, M., Wang, J.: Towards concolic testing for hybrid systems. In: Fitzgerald, J., et al. (eds.) FM 2016, LNCS 9995, pp. X–XY. Springer, Heidelberg (2016)
29. Lebesgue, H.: Intégrale, longueur, aire. Annali di Matematica Pura ed Applicata **7**(1), 231–359 (1902)
30. Leon-Garcia, A.: Probability and Random Processes For EE's, 3rd edn. Prentice-Hall Inc., Upper Saddle River (2007)
31. Lu, F., Iyer, M.K., Parthasarathy, G., Wang, L.-C., Cheng, K.-T., Chen, K.C.: An efficient sequential sat solver with improved search strategies. In: The Conference on Design, Automation and Test in Europe (DATE), 2005, pp. 1102–1107 (2005)

32. Luckow, K.S., Pasareanu, C.S., Dwyer, M.B., Filieri, A., Visser, W.: Exact and approximate probabilistic symbolic execution for nondeterministic programs. In: ACM/IEEE International Conference on Automated Software Engineering (ASE), pp. 575–586 (2014)
33. Majumdar, R., Sen, K.: Hybrid concolic testing. In: 29th International Conference on Software Engineering (ICSE 2007), pp. 416–426. IEEE (2007)
34. Orosz, G., Wilson, R.E., Szalai, R., Stépán, G.: Exciting traffic jams: nonlinear phenomena behind traffic jam formation on highways. Phys. Rev. E. **80**, 046205 (2009)
35. Platzer, A.: Logical Analysis of Hybrid Systems: Proving Theorems for Complex Dynamics. Springer, Heidelberg (2010). Incorporated
36. Sen, K.: Concolic testing. In: 22nd IEEE/ACM International Conference on Automated Software Engineering (ASE), pp. 571–572. ACM (2007)
37. Sen, K., Agha, G.: CUTE and jCUTE: concolic unit testing and explicit path model-checking tools. In: Ball, T., Jones, R.B. (eds.) CAV 2006. LNCS, vol. 4144, pp. 419–423. Springer, Heidelberg (2006). doi:10.1007/11817963_38
38. Swat, S.: A test bed for secure water treatment (2015). http://academics.sutd.edu.sg/news-events/event/news/media-release-swat-a-test-bed-for-secure-water-treatment-swat/
39. Veach, E., Guibas, L.J.: Optimally combining sampling techniques for monte carlo rendering. In: 22nd Annual Conference on Computer Graphics and Interactive Techniques (SIGGRAPH), pp. 419–428 (1995)

Explaining Relaxed Memory Models with Program Transformations

Ori Lahav(✉) and Viktor Vafeiadis

Max Planck Institute for Software Systems (MPI-SWS),
Kaiserslautern and Saarbrücken, Germany
orilahav@mpi-sws.org

Abstract. Weak memory models determine the behavior of concurrent programs. While they are often understood in terms of reorderings that the hardware or the compiler may perform, their formal definitions are typically given in a very different style—either axiomatic or operational. In this paper, we investigate to what extent weak behaviors of existing memory models can be fully explained in terms of reorderings and other program transformations. We prove that TSO is equivalent to a set of two local transformations over sequential consistency, but that non-multi-copy-atomic models (such as C11, Power and ARM) cannot be explained in terms of local transformations over sequential consistency. We then show that transformations over a basic non-multi-copy-atomic model account for the relaxed behaviors of (a large fragment of) Power, but that ARM's relaxed behaviors cannot be explained in a similar way. Our positive results may be used to simplify correctness of compilation proofs from a high-level language to TSO or Power.

1 Introduction

In a uniprocessor machine with a non-optimizing compiler, the semantics of a concurrent program is given by the set of interleavings of the memory accesses of its constituent threads (also known as *sequential consistency*). In multiprocessor machines and/or with optimizing compilers, however, more behaviors are possible; they are formally described by what is known as a *weak memory model*. Typical examples of such "weak" behaviors are in the SB (store buffering) and LB (load buffering) programs below:

$x := 1;$ $a := y;$ *// 0*	$y := 1;$ $b := x;$ *// 0*		$a := x;$ *// 1* $y := 1;$	$b := y;$ *// 1* $x := 1;$

Assuming all variables are 0 initially, the weak behaviors in question are the ones in which a and b have the values mentioned in the program comments. In the SB program on the left this behavior is allowed by all existing weak memory models, and can be easily explained in terms of reordering: the hardware may execute the independent store to x and load from y in reverse order. Similarly, the behavior in the LB program on the right, which is allowed by some models, can be explained by reordering the load from x and the subsequent store to y.

J. Fitzgerald et al. (Eds.): FM 2016, LNCS 9995, pp. 479–495, 2016.
DOI: 10.1007/978-3-319-48989-6_29

This explanation remains the same whether the hardware itself performs out-of-order execution, or the compiler, as a part of its optimization passes, performs these transformations, and the hardware actually runs a reordered program.

Formal memory models, however, choose a somewhat more complex explanation. Specifically, axiomatic memory model definitions construct a graph of memory access events for each program execution and impose various constraints on which store each load can read from. Similarly, operational definitions introduce concepts such as buffers, where the stores reside for some time before being propagated to other processors.

In this paper, we try to reconcile the formal model definitions with the more intuitive explanations in terms of program transformations. We consider the mainstream implemented memory models of TSO [16], C11's Release/Acquire fragment [7], Power [4], and ARM [12], and investigate whether their weak behaviors can be fully accounted for in terms of program transformations that are allowed in these models. In this endeavor, we have both positive and negative results to report on.

First, in Sect. 3, we show that the TSO memory model of the x86 and SPARC architectures can be precisely characterized in terms of two transformations over sequential consistency: write-read reordering and read-after-write elimination.

Second, in Sect. 4, we present examples showing that C11's Release/Acquire memory model cannot be defined in terms of a set of transformations over sequential consistency. This, in fact, holds for any memory model that allows non-multi-copy-atomic behaviors (where two different threads may observe a store of a third thread at different times), such as the full C11, Power, ARM, and Itanium models. Here, besides local instruction reorderings and eliminations we also consider the sequentialization transformation, that explains some non-multi-copy-atomic behaviors, but fails to account for all of them.

Next, in Sect. 5, we consider the Power memory model of Alglave et al. [4]. We show that the weak behaviors of this model, restricted to its fragment without "control fences" (Power's `isync` instructions), can be fully explained in terms of local reorderings over a stronger model that does not allow cycles in the entire program order together with the reads-from relation. In Sect. 6, we show that this is not possible for the ARM model: it allows some weak behaviors that cannot be explained in terms of local transformations over such stronger model.

Finally, in Sect. 7, we outline a possible application of the positive results of this paper, namely to simplify correctness of compilation proofs from a high-level language to either TSO or Power.

The proofs of this paper have also been formulated in Coq and are available at: http://plv.mpi-sws.org/trns/.

1.1 Related Work

Previous papers studied soundness of program transformations under different memory models (see, e.g., [15,18]), while we are interested in the "completeness" direction, namely whether program transformations completely characterize a memory model.

Concerning TSO, it has been assumed that it can be defined in terms of the two transformations mentioned above (e.g., in [2,9]), but to our knowledge a formal equivalence to the specification in [16] has not been established before. In the broader context of proposing a fixed memory model for Java, Demange et al. [10] prove a very close result, relating a TSO-like machine and local transformations of executions. Nevertheless, one of the transformations of [10] does not correspond to a local program transformation (as it depends on the write that was read by each read). We also note that the proofs in [10] are based on an operational model, while we utilize an equivalent axiomatic presentation of TSO, that allows us to have simpler arguments.

Alglave et al. [3] provide a method for reducing verification under a weak memory model to a verification problem under sequential consistency. This approach follows a global program transformation of a completely different nature than ours, that uses additional data structures to simulate the threads' buffers.

Finally, assuming a sequentially consistent hardware, Ševčík [19] proves that a large class of compiler transformations respect the DRF guarantee (no weak behaviors for programs with no data races) and a basic non-thin-air guarantee (all read values are mentioned in some statement of the program). The results of the current paper allow the application of Ševčík's theorems for TSO, as it is fully explained by transformations that are already covered as compiler optimizations. For the other models, however, our negative results show that the DRF and non-thin-air guarantees do not follow immediately from Ševčík's theorems.

2 Preliminaries: Axiomatic Memory Model Definitions

In this section, we present the basic axiomatic way of defining memory models.

Basic Notations. Given a binary relation R, $R^?$, R^+, and R^* respectively denote its reflexive, transitive, and reflexive-transitive closures. The inverse relation is denoted by R^{-1}. We denote by $R_1; R_2$ the left composition of two relations R_1, R_2. A relation R is called *acyclic* if R^+ is irreflexive. When R is a strict partial order, $R|_{\mathsf{imm}}$ denotes the relation consisting of all *immediate R-edges*, i.e., pairs $\langle a, b\rangle \in R$ such that for every c, $\langle c, b\rangle \in R$ implies $\langle c, a\rangle \in R^?$, and $\langle a, c\rangle \in R$ implies $\langle b, c\rangle \in R^?$. Finally, we denote by $[A]$ the identity relation on a set A. In particular, $[A]; R; [B] = R \cap (A \times B)$.

We assume finite sets Tid, Loc, and Val of thread identifiers, locations, and values. We use i as a metavariable for thread identifiers, x, y, z for locations, and v for values. Axiomatic memory models associate a set of graphs (called *executions*) to every program. The nodes of these graphs are called *events*, and they are related by different kinds of edges.

Events. An *event* consists of an identifier (natural number), a thread identifier (or 0 for initialization events), and a *type*, that can be R ("read"), W ("write"), U ("atomic update"), or F ("fence"). For memory accesses (R, W, U) the event also contains the accessed location, as well as the read and/or written value. Events in each specific memory model may contain additional information (e.g., fence type or C11-style access ordering). We use $a, b, \ldots$ as metavariables for events. The functions *tid*, *typ*, *loc*, val_r and val_w respectively return (when applicable) the thread identifier, type, location, read value, and written value of an event.

Notation 1. Given a relation R on events, $R|_x$ denotes the restriction of R to events accessing location x, and $R|_{loc}$ denotes the restriction of R to events accessing the same location (i.e., $R|_x = \{\langle a, b\rangle \in R \mid loc(a) = loc(b) = x\}$ and $R|_{loc} = \bigcup_{x \in loc} R|_x$).

Executions. An *execution* G consists of:[1]

1. a finite set $G.\mathtt{E}$ of events with distinct identifiers. This set always contains a set $G.\mathtt{E}_0$ of initialization events, consisting of one write event assigning the initial value for every location. We assume that all initial values are 0.
2. a binary relation $G.\mathtt{po}$, called *program order*, which is a disjoint union of relations $\{G.\mathtt{po}_i\}_{i \in \{0\} \cup \mathsf{Tid}}$, such that $G.\mathtt{po}_0 = G.\mathtt{E}_0 \times (G.\mathtt{E} \setminus G.\mathtt{E}_0)$, and for every $i \in \mathsf{Tid}$, the relation $G.\mathtt{po}_i$ is a strict total order on $\{a \in G.\mathtt{E} \mid tid(a) = i\}$.
3. a binary relation $G.\mathtt{rf}$, called *reads-from*, which is a set of reads-from edges. These are pairs $\langle a, b\rangle \in G.\mathtt{E} \times G.\mathtt{E}$ satisfying $a \neq b$, $typ(a) \in \{\mathtt{W}, \mathtt{U}\}$, $typ(b) \in \{\mathtt{R}, \mathtt{U}\}$, $loc(a) = loc(b)$, and $val_w(a) = val_r(b)$. It is required that an event cannot read from two different events (i.e., if $\langle a_1, b\rangle, \langle a_2, b\rangle \in G.\mathtt{rf}$ then $a_1 = a_2$).
4. a binary relation $G.\mathtt{mo}$, called *modification order*, whose properties vary from one model to another.

We identify an execution G with a set of tagged elements with the tags $\mathtt{E}$, $\mathtt{po}$, $\mathtt{rf}$, and $\mathtt{mo}$. For example, $\{\mathtt{E} : a, \mathtt{E} : b, \mathtt{po} : \langle a, b\rangle\}$ (where a and b are events) denotes an execution with $G.\mathtt{E} = \{a, b\}$, $G.\mathtt{po} = \{\langle a, b\rangle\}$, and $G.\mathtt{rf} = G.\mathtt{mo} = \emptyset$. Further, for a set E of events, $\{\mathtt{E} : E\}$ denotes the set $\{\mathtt{E} : e \mid e \in E\}$. A similar notation is used for the other tags, and it is particularly useful when writing expressions like $G \cup \{\mathtt{rf} : rf\}$ (that stand for the extension of an execution G with a set rf of reads-from edges). In addition, we denote by $G.\mathtt{T}$ ($\mathtt{T} \in \{\mathtt{R}, \mathtt{W}, \mathtt{U}, \mathtt{F}\}$) the set $\{e \in G.\mathtt{E} \mid typ(e) = \mathtt{T}\}$. We may also concatenate the event sets notations, and use a subscript to denote the accessed location (e.g., $G.\mathtt{RW} = G.\mathtt{R} \cup G.\mathtt{W}$ and $G.\mathtt{W}_x$ denotes all events $a \in G.\mathtt{W}$ with $loc(a) = x$). We omit the prefix "G." when it is clear from the context.

The exact definition of the set of executions associated with a given program depends on the particular programming language and the memory model. Figure 1 provides an example. Note that in this initial stage the read values are not restricted whatsoever, and the reads-from relation $\mathtt{rf}$ and the modification order $\mathtt{mo}$ are still empty. We refer to such executions as *plain executions*.

[1] Different models may include some additional relations (e.g., a dependency relation between events is used for Power, see Sect. 5).

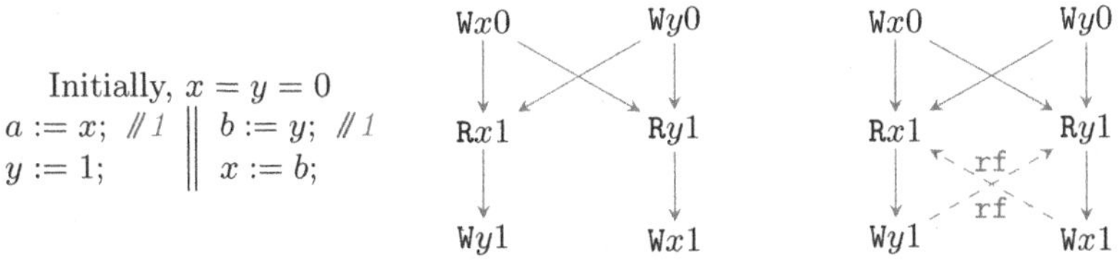

Fig. 1. A program together with one of its plain executions, and a complete execution extending the plain one. Solid arrows denote the transitive reduction of po (i.e., omitting edges implied by transitivity). The variables a, b are local registers, and these are not mentioned in executions.

Now, the main part of a memory model is the specification of which of the executions of a program P are allowed. The first requirement, agreed by all memory models, is that every read should be justified by some write. Such executions will be called *complete* (formally, G is complete if for every $b \in \mathtt{RU}$, we have $\langle a, b\rangle \in \mathtt{rf}$ for some event a). To filter out disallowed executions among the complete ones, each memory model M defines a notion of when an execution G is M-*coherent*, which is typically defined with the help of a few *derived relations*, and places several restrictions on the rf and mo relations. Then, we say that a plain execution G is M-*consistent* if there exist relations *rf* and *mo* such that $G \cup \{\mathtt{rf} : \mathit{rf}\} \cup \{\mathtt{mo} : \mathit{mo}\}$ is a complete and M-coherent execution. The semantics of a program under M is taken to be the set of its M-consistent executions.

2.1 Sequential Consistency

As a simple instance of this framework, we define sequential consistency (SC). There are multiple equivalent axiomatic presentations of SC. Here, we choose one that is specifically tailored for studying the relation to TSO in Sect. 3.

Definition 1. An execution G is SC-*coherent* if the following hold:

1. mo is a strict total order on WUF.
2. **hb** is irreflexive.
3. mo; **hb** is irreflexive.
4. **rb**; **hb** is irreflexive.
5. **rb**; mo is irreflexive.
6. **rb**; mo; **hb** is irreflexive.

where:

- $\mathbf{hb} = (\mathtt{po} \cup \mathtt{rf})^+$ (*happens-before*)
- $\mathbf{rb} = (\mathtt{rf}^{-1}; \mathtt{mo}|_{loc}) \setminus [\mathtt{E}]$ (*reads-before*)

Intuitively speaking, mo denotes the order in which stores happen in the memory, **hb** represents a causality order between events, and **rb** says that a read is before a write to the same location if it reads from a prior write in modification order. Figure 2 depicts the conditions for SC-coherence. It can be easily seen that the weak behavior of the SB program in the introduction is disallowed under SC due to condition 6 (together with conditions 1 and 3), while the one of the LB program is disallowed under SC due to condition 2.

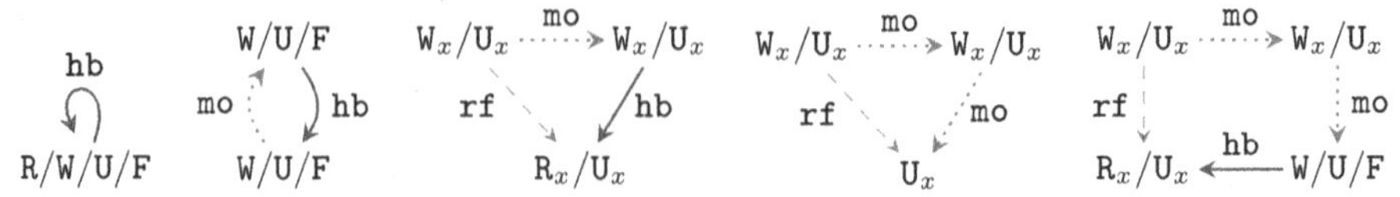

Fig. 2. Illustration of SC's irreflexivity conditions.

Proposition 1. *Our notion of* SC*-consistency defines sequential consistency [14].*

Proof (Outline). The SC-coherence definition above guarantees that $(\mathtt{po} \cup \mathtt{rf} \cup \mathtt{mo} \cup \mathtt{rb})^+$ is a partial order. Following [17], any total order extending this partial order defines an interleaving of the memory accesses, which agrees with po and ensures that every read/update obtains its value from the last previous write/update to the same location. For the converse, one can take mo to be the restriction of the interleaving order to WUF. □

3 TSO

In this section, we study the TSO (*total store ordering*) memory model provided by the x86 and SPARC architectures. Its common presentation is operational: on top of usual interleaving semantics, each hardware thread has a queue of pending memory writes (called *store buffer*), that non-deterministically propagate (in order) to a main memory [16]. When a thread reads from a location x, it obtains the value of the last write to x that appears in its buffer, or the value of x in the memory if no such write exists. Fence instructions flush the whole buffer into the main memory, and atomic updates perform flush, read, write, and flush again in one atomic step.

To simplify our formal development, we use an *axiomatic* definition of TSO from [13]. By [16, Theorem 3] and [13, Theorem 5], this definition is equivalent to the operational one.[2]

Definition 2. An execution G is TSO-*coherent* if the following hold:

1. mo is a strict total order on WUF.
2. hb is irreflexive.
3. mo; hb is irreflexive.
4. rb; hb is irreflexive.
5. rb; mo is irreflexive.
6. rb; mo; rfe; po is irreflexive.
7. rb; mo; [UF]; po is irreflexive.

where hb and rb are defined as in Definition 1, and:

– $\mathtt{rfe} = \mathtt{rf} \setminus \mathtt{po}$ (*external reads-from*)

[2] Lahav et al. [13] treat fence instructions as syntactic sugar for atomic updates of a distinguished location. Here, we have fences as primitive instructions that induce fence events in the program executions.

The first five conditions of the TSO-coherence definition are the same as those of SC-coherence. Conditions 6 and 7 are relaxations of condition 6 in the SC-coherence definition (depicted in Fig. 3). Intuitively speaking, mo is the order in which the writes propagate to the main memory of the TSO-machine, and the two conditions ensure that a read from the main memory can only read from the last write (to the same location) that was propagated.

$a : \mathtt{W}_x/\mathtt{U}_x \xrightarrow{\mathtt{mo}} b : \mathtt{W}_x/\mathtt{U}_x \xrightarrow{\mathtt{mo}} c : \mathtt{W}/\mathtt{U}$; $a \xrightarrow{\mathtt{rf}} d$; $c \xrightarrow{\mathtt{rf}\setminus\mathtt{po}} e$; $d : \mathtt{R}_x/\mathtt{U}_x \xleftarrow{\mathtt{po}} e : \mathtt{R}_y/\mathtt{U}_y$

$a : \mathtt{W}_x/\mathtt{U}_x \xrightarrow{\mathtt{mo}} b : \mathtt{W}_x/\mathtt{U}_x$; $a \xrightarrow{\mathtt{rf}} d$; $b \xrightarrow{\mathtt{mo}} c$; $d : \mathtt{R}_x/\mathtt{U}_x \xleftarrow{\mathtt{po}} c : \mathtt{U}/\mathtt{F}$

Fig. 3. Illustration of the alternative irreflexivity conditions of TSO. Requiring an external reads-from edge or an update/fence (that flush the store buffer) immediately after the second mo-edge ensures that events a, b and c are in main memory at the point d is executed and therefore the rf-edge $\langle a, d\rangle$ corresponds to reading from the main memory, rather than from the local buffer.

Next, we present the key lemma that identifies more precisely the difference between TSO and SC.

Lemma 1. *Irreflexivity of the following relation suffices to guarantee that a* TSO*-coherent complete execution G is also* SC*-coherent:*

$$\mathtt{rb}; \mathtt{mo}; [\mathtt{W}]; (po' \cup rfi); [\mathtt{R}]; \mathtt{po}^?$$

where $po' = \mathtt{po}|_{imm} \setminus (\mathtt{po}|_{loc} \cup (\mathtt{mo}; \mathtt{rf}))$*, and* $rfi = \mathtt{po}|_{imm} \cap \mathtt{rf}$.

Now, we turn to our first main positive result, showing that TSO is precisely characterized by write-read reordering and read-after-write elimination over sequential consistency. First, we define write-read reordering.

Definition 3 (Write-Read Reordering). For an execution G and events a and b, $\mathsf{ReorderWR}(G, a, b)$ is the execution G' obtained from G by inverting the program order from a to b, i.e., it is given by: $G'.\mathtt{po} = (G.\mathtt{po} \setminus \{\langle a, b\rangle\}) \cup \{\langle b, a\rangle\}$, and $G'.\mathsf{C} = G.\mathsf{C}$ for every other component C. $\mathsf{ReorderWR}(G, a, b)$ is defined only when $\langle a, b\rangle \in [\mathtt{W}]; \mathtt{po}|_{\mathrm{imm}}; [\mathtt{R}]$ and $loc(a) \neq loc(b)$.

The condition $\langle a, b\rangle \in \mathtt{po}|_{\mathrm{imm}}$ guarantees that only adjacent accesses are reordered. This transformation does not inspect the rf and mo components of G, and thus also applies to plain executions. This fact ensures that it corresponds to a program transformation. Note that additional rewriting are sometimes needed in order to make two adjacent accesses in the program's execution to be adjacent instructions in the program. For example, to reorder the store $x := 1$ and load $a := y$ in the following program, one can first rewrite the program as follows:

$x := 1;$		$x := 1;$		**if** b **then** $a := y;$
if b **then** $a := y;$	$\rightsquigarrow$	**if** b **then** $a := y;$	$\rightsquigarrow$	$x := 1;$
else $y := 2;$		**if** $\neg b$ **then** $y := 2;$		**if** $\neg b$ **then** $y := 2;$

Similarly, reordering of local register assignments and unfolding of loops may be necessary. To relate reorderings on plain executions to reorderings on (non-straightline) programs, one should assume that these transformations may be freely applied.

Remark 1. Demange et al. [10, Definition 5.3] introduce a related *write-read-read* reordering, which allows to reorder a read before a write and a sequence of subsequent reads *reading from that write*. This reordering does not correspond to a local program transformation, as it inspects the reads-from relation, that is not available in plain executions, and cannot be inferred from the program code.

The second transformation we use, called *WR-elimination*, replaces a read from some location directly after a write to that location by the value written by the write (e.g., $x := 1; a := x \rightsquigarrow x := 1; a := 1$). Again, we place conditions to ensure that the execution transformation corresponds to a program one.

Definition 4 (Read-After-Write Elimination). For an execution G and events a and b, $\mathsf{RemoveWR}(G, a, b)$ is the execution G' obtained by removing b from G, i.e., G' is given by: $G'.\mathtt{E} = G.\mathtt{E} \setminus \{b\}$, and $G'.\mathtt{C} = G.\mathtt{C} \cap (G'.\mathtt{E} \times G'.\mathtt{E})$ for every other component $\mathtt{C}$. $\mathsf{RemoveWR}(G, a, b)$ is defined only when $\langle a, b \rangle \in [\mathtt{W}]; \mathtt{po}|_{\mathrm{imm}}; [\mathtt{R}]$, $loc(a) = loc(b)$, and $val_w(a) = val_r(b)$.

Note that WR-reordering is unsound under SC (the reordered program may exhibit behaviors that are not possible in the original program). WR-elimination, however, is sound under SC. Nevertheless, WR-elimination is needed below, since, by removing a read access, it may create new opportunities for WR-reordering.

We can now state the main theorem of this section. We write $G \rightsquigarrow_{\mathsf{TSO}} G'$ if $G' = \mathsf{ReorderWR}(G, a, b)$ or $G' = \mathsf{RemoveWR}(G, a, b)$ for some a, b.

Theorem 1. *A plain execution G is TSO-consistent iff $G \rightsquigarrow^*_{\mathsf{TSO}} G'$ for some* SC*-consistent execution G'.*

The rest of this section is devoted to the proof of Theorem 1. First, the soundness of the two transformations under TSO is well-known.

Proposition 2. *If $G \rightsquigarrow_{\mathsf{TSO}} G'$ and G' is* TSO*-consistent, then so is G.*

The converse is not generally true. It does (trivially) hold for eliminations:

Proposition 3. *Let G be a complete and* TSO*-coherent execution. Then,* $\mathsf{RemoveWR}(G, a, b)$*, if defined, is complete and* TSO*-coherent.*

Proof. Removing a read event from an execution reduces all relations mentioned in Definition 2, and hence preserves their irreflexivity. □

Proposition 4. *Let G be a complete and* TSO*-coherent execution. Let a, b such that* $\mathsf{ReorderWR}(G, a, b)$ *is defined. If $\langle a, b \rangle \notin \mathtt{mo}; \mathtt{rf}$, then* $\mathsf{ReorderWR}(G, a, b)$ *is complete and* TSO*-coherent.*

Proposition 5. *Suppose that* G *is complete and* TSO*-coherent but not* SC*-coherent. Then,* $G \leadsto_{\mathsf{TSO}} G'$ *for some* TSO*-coherent complete execution* G'.

Proof. By Lemma 1, there must exist events $a \in \mathtt{W}$ and $b \in \mathtt{R}$, such that $\langle a, b\rangle \in po' \cup rfi$, (where po' and rfi are the relations defined in Lemma 1). Now, if $\langle a, b\rangle \in po'$, we can apply WR-reordering, and take $G' = \mathsf{ReorderWR}(G, a, b)$. By Proposition 4, G' is complete and TSO-coherent. Otherwise, $\langle a, b\rangle \in rfi$. In this case, we can apply WR-elimination, and take $G' = \mathsf{RemoveWR}(G, a, b)$. By Proposition 3, G' is complete and TSO-coherent. □

We can now prove the main theorem.

Proof (of Theorem 1). The right-to-left direction is easily proven using Proposition 2, by induction on the number of transformations in the sequence deriving G' from G (note that the base case trivially holds as SC-consistency implies TSO-consistency). We prove the converse. Given two plain executions G and G', we write $G' < G$ if either $G'.\mathtt{E} \subset G.\mathtt{E}$ or ($G'.\mathtt{E} = G.\mathtt{E}$ and $[\mathtt{W}]; G'.\mathtt{po}; [\mathtt{R}] \subset G.\mathtt{po}$). Clearly, $<$ is a well-founded partial order. We prove the claim by induction on G (using $<$ on the set of all executions). Let G be an execution, and assume that the claim holds for all $G' < G$. Suppose that G is TSO-consistent. If G is SC-consistent, then we are done. Otherwise, by Proposition 5, $G \leadsto_{\mathsf{TSO}} G'$ for some TSO-consistent execution G'. It is easy to see that we have $G' < G$. By the induction hypothesis, $G' \leadsto^*_{\mathsf{TSO}} G''$ for some SC-consistent execution G''. Then, we also have $G \leadsto^*_{\mathsf{TSO}} G''$. □

4 Release-Acquire

Next, we turn to the *non-multi-copy-atomic* memory model (i.e., two different threads may detect a store by a third thread at different times) of C11's Release/Acquire. By RA we refer to the memory model of C11, as defined in [7], restricted only to programs in which all reads are acquire reads, writes are release writes, and atomic updates are acquire-release read-modify-writes (RMWs). We further assume that this model has no fence events. Fence instructions under RA, as proposed in [13], can be implemented using atomic updates to an otherwise unused distinguished location.

Definition 5. An execution G is RA*-coherent* if the following hold:

1. $\mathtt{mo}$ is a disjoint union of relations $\{\mathtt{mo}_x\}_{x \in \mathsf{Loc}}$, such that each relation $\mathtt{mo}_x$ is a strict total order on $\mathtt{W}_x\mathtt{U}_x$.
2. $\mathtt{hb}$ is irreflexive.
3. $\mathtt{mo}; \mathtt{hb}$ is irreflexive.
4. $\mathtt{rb}; \mathtt{hb}$ is irreflexive.
5. $\mathtt{rb}; \mathtt{mo}$ is irreflexive.

where $\mathtt{hb}$ and $\mathtt{rb}$ are defined as in Definition 1.

Note that unlike SC and TSO, the relation mo in the RA-coherence definition relates only events accessing the same location. The following IRIW (independent reads, independent writes) program shows that RA is more than local program transformations over SC.

$$\begin{array}{l} a := x; \; \textit{// 1} \\ b := y; \; \textit{// 0} \end{array} \;\Bigg\|\; x := 1; \;\Bigg\|\; y := 1; \;\Bigg\|\; \begin{array}{l} c := y; \; \textit{// 1} \\ d := x; \; \textit{// 0} \end{array}$$

The behavior in question is allowed under RA, although RA forbids any reorderings and eliminations in this program. In particular, reordering of reads is unsound under RA (because RA supports message passing). One may observe that this behavior can be explained if we add *sequentialization* to the set of program transformations, to allow transformations of the form $C_1 \parallel C_2 \rightsquigarrow C_1; C_2$ and $C_1; C_1' \parallel C_2 \rightsquigarrow C_1; C_2; C_1'$. By sequentializing the $x := 1$ store instruction to be before its corresponding load we obtain the program on the left:

$$\begin{array}{l} x := 1; \\ a := x; \; \textit{// 1} \\ b := y; \; \textit{// 0} \end{array} \;\Bigg\|\; y := 1; \;\Bigg\|\; \begin{array}{l} c := y; \; \textit{// 1} \\ d := x; \; \textit{// 0} \end{array} \rightsquigarrow \begin{array}{l} b := y; \; \textit{// 0} \\ x := 1; \\ a := 1; \; \textit{// 1} \end{array} \;\Bigg\|\; y := 1; \;\Bigg\|\; \begin{array}{l} c := y; \; \textit{// 1} \\ d := x; \; \textit{// 0} \end{array}$$

Now, this behavior is allowed under SC after applying a WR-elimination followed by a WR-reordering in the first thread (obtaining the program on the right). At the execution level, sequentialization increases its po component, and it is sound under RA, simply because it may only increase all the relations mentioned in Definition 5. Note that, unlike RA and SC, sequentialization is unsound under TSO: while the weak behavior of the IRIW program is forbidden under TSO, it is allowed after applying sequentialization. Other examples show that sequentialization is unsound under Power and ARM as well [1].

Even with sequentialization, however, we cannot reduce RA to SC, as the following program demonstrates.

$$\begin{array}{l} y := 1; \\ x := 1; \\ a := x; \; \textit{// 3} \\ b := z; \; \textit{// 0} \end{array} \;\Bigg\|\; x := 3; \;\Bigg\|\; \begin{array}{l} z := 1; \\ x := 2; \\ c := x; \; \textit{// 3} \\ d := y; \; \textit{// 0} \end{array}$$

The behavior in question is allowed by RA (by putting the write of 3 to x after the two other writes to x in mo). In this program, no sound reorderings or eliminations can explain the weak behavior, and, moreover, any possible sequentialization will forbid this behavior.

In fact, the above example applies also to SRA, the stronger version of RA studied in [13], obtained by requiring that mo is a total order on WU (as in TSO), instead of condition 1 in Definition 5 (but still excluding irreflexivity of rb; mo; **hb** that is required for SC-coherence). As RA, SRA forbids thread-local transformations in this program, but allows its weak behavior.

5 Power

In this section, we study the model provided by the Power architecture, using the recent axiomatic model by Alglave et al. [4]. Here, our positive result is somewhat limited:

1. Like RA, the Power model is non-multi-copy-atomic, and thus, it cannot be explained using transformations over SC. Instead, we explain Power's weak behaviors starting from a stronger non-multi-copy-atomic model, that, we believe, is easier to understand and reason about, than the Power model.
2. Power's control fence (`isync`) is used to enforce a stronger ordering on memory reads. Its special effect cannot be accounted for by program transformations (see example in [1]). Hence, we only consider here a restricted fragment of the Power model, that has two types of fence events: `sync` ("strong fence") and `lwsync` ("lightweight fence"). $G.\mathtt{F}_{\mathtt{sync}}$ and $G.\mathtt{F}_{\mathtt{lwsync}}$ respectively denote the set of events $a \in G.\mathtt{E}$ with $typ(a)$ being `sync` and `lwsync`.

The Power architecture performs out-of-order and speculative execution, but respects dependencies between instructions. Accordingly, Power's axiomatic executions keep track of additional relations for data, address and control dependency between events, that are derived directly from the program syntax. For example, in all executions of $a := x;\ y := a$, we will have a data dependency edge from the read event to the write event, since the load and store use the same register a. Here, we include all sort of dependencies in one relation between events, denoted by **deps**. Note that we always have $\mathtt{deps} \subseteq \mathsf{po}$, and that only read and update events may have outgoing dependency edges.

Based on **deps**, the Power model employs a relation called *preserved program order*, denoted ppo, which is a subset of po that is guaranteed to be preserved. The exact definition of ppo is somewhat intricate (we refer the reader to [4] for details). For our purposes, it suffices to use the following properties of ppo:

$$[\mathtt{RU}]; (\mathtt{deps} \cup \mathsf{po}|_{loc})^+; [\mathtt{WU}] \subseteq \mathsf{ppo} \qquad \text{(ppo-lower-bound)}$$

$$\mathsf{ppo} \cap \mathsf{po}|_{\mathsf{imm}} \subseteq (\mathtt{deps} \cup \mathsf{po}|_{loc})^+ \qquad \text{(ppo-upper-bound)}$$

Remark 2. Atomic updates are not considered in the text of [4]. In the accompanying herd simulator, they are modeled using pairs of a read and a write events related by an atomicity relation. Here we follow a different approach, model atomic updates using a single update event, and adapt herd's model accordingly. Thus we are only considering Power programs in which `lwarx` and `stwcx` appear in separate adjacent pairs. These instructions are used to implement locks and compare-and-swap commands, and they indeed appear only in such pairs when following the intended mapping of programs to Power [6].

Using the preserved program order, Power-coherence is defined as follows (the reader is referred to [4] for further explanations and details).

Definition 6. An execution G is Power-*coherent* if the following hold:

1. $\mathtt{mo}$ is a disjoint union of relations $\{\mathtt{mo}_x\}_{x\in\mathsf{Loc}}$, such that each relation $\mathtt{mo}_x$ is a strict total order on $\mathtt{W}_x\mathtt{U}_x$.
2. $\mathtt{hb}$ is acyclic. *(no-thin-air)*
3. $\mathtt{po}|_x \cup \mathtt{rf} \cup \mathtt{rb} \cup \mathtt{mo}$ is acyclic for every $x \in \mathsf{Loc}$. *(SC-per-loc)*
4. $\mathtt{rbe}; \mathtt{prop}; \mathtt{hb}^*$ is irreflexive. *(observation)*
5. $\mathtt{mo} \cup \mathtt{prop}$ is acyclic. *(propagation)*
6. $\mathtt{rb}; \mathtt{mo}$ is irreflexive. *(atomicity)*
7. $\mathtt{mo}; [\mathtt{U}]; \mathtt{po}; [\mathtt{U}]$ is acyclic.

where $\mathtt{rb}$ is defined as in Definition 1, and:

- $\mathtt{sync} = \mathtt{po}; [\mathtt{F_{sync}}]; \mathtt{po}$ and $\mathtt{lwsync} = \mathtt{po}; [\mathtt{F_{lwsync}}]; \mathtt{po}$
- $\mathtt{fence} = \mathtt{sync} \cup ([\mathtt{RU}]; \mathtt{lwsync}; [\mathtt{RWU}] \cup ([\mathtt{W}]; \mathtt{lwsync}; [\mathtt{WU}]))$ *(fence order)*
- $\mathtt{rfe} = \mathtt{rf} \setminus \mathtt{po}$ and $\mathtt{rbe} = \mathtt{rb} \setminus \mathtt{po}$ *(external reads-from and reads-before)*
- $\mathtt{hb} = \mathtt{ppo} \cup \mathtt{fence} \cup \mathtt{rfe}$ *(happens-before)*
- $\mathtt{prop}_1 = [\mathtt{WU}]; \mathtt{rfe}^?; \mathtt{fence}; \mathtt{hb}^*; [\mathtt{WU}]$
- $\mathtt{prop}_2 = ((\mathtt{mo} \cup \mathtt{rb}) \setminus \mathtt{po})^?; \mathtt{rfe}^?; (\mathtt{fence}; \mathtt{hb}^*)^?; \mathtt{sync}; \mathtt{hb}^*$
- $\mathtt{prop} = \mathtt{prop}_1 \cup \mathtt{prop}_2$ *(propagation relation)*

In particular, Power allows the weak behavior in the LB program presented in the introduction. Indeed, unlike the other models discussed above, the Power model does not generally forbid ($\mathtt{po} \cup \mathtt{rf}$)-cycles. Thus, Power-consistent executions are not "prefix-closed"— it may happen that G is Power-consistent, but some $\mathtt{po}$-prefix of G is not. This makes reasoning about the Power model extremely difficult, because it precludes the understanding a program in terms of its partial executions, and forbids proofs by induction on $\mathtt{po}$-prefixes of an execution. In the following we show that all weak behaviors of Power can be explained by starting from a stronger prefix-closed model, and applying various reorderings of independent adjacent memory accesses to different locations. First, we define the stronger model.

Definition 7. An execution G is SPower-*coherent* if it is Power-coherent and $\mathtt{po} \cup \mathtt{rf}$ is acyclic.

Note that this additional acyclicity condition is a strengthening of the *"no-thin-air"* condition in Definition 6. A similar strengthening for the C11 memory model was suggested in [8], as a straightforward solution to the "out-of-thin-air" problem (see also [5]). In addition, the same acyclicity condition was assumed for proving soundness of FSL [11] (a program logic for C11's relaxed accesses).

Next, we turn to relate Power and SPower using general reorderings of adjacent memory accesses.

Definition 8 (Reordering). For an execution G and events a and b, $\mathsf{Reorder}(G, a, b)$ is the execution G' obtained from G by inverting the program order from a to b, i.e., it is given by: $G'.\mathtt{po} = (G.\mathtt{po} \setminus \{\langle a, b\rangle\}) \cup \{\langle b, a\rangle\}$, and $G'.\mathtt{C} = G.\mathtt{C}$ for every other component $\mathtt{C}$. $\mathsf{Reorder}(G, a, b)$ is defined only when $a, b \notin \mathtt{F}$ and $\langle a, b\rangle \in \mathtt{po}|_{\mathrm{imm}} \setminus \mathtt{deps}$, and $loc(a) \neq loc(b)$.

We write $G \rightsquigarrow_{\mathsf{Power}} G'$ if $G' = \mathsf{Reorder}(G, a, b)$ for some a, b.

Proposition 6. *Suppose that* $G \rightsquigarrow_{\mathsf{Power}} G'$. *Then,* G *is* Power*-coherent iff* G' *is* Power*-coherent.*

The following observation is useful in the proof below.

Proposition 7. *The following relation is acyclic in* Power*-coherent executions:*

$$\mathtt{deps} \cup \mathtt{po}|_{loc} \cup (\mathtt{po}; [\mathtt{F}]) \cup ([\mathtt{F}]; \mathtt{po}) \cup \mathtt{rfe}$$

Theorem 2. *A plain execution* G *is* Power*-consistent iff* $G \rightsquigarrow^{*}_{\mathsf{Power}} G'$ *for some* SPower*-consistent execution* G'.

Proof. The right-to-left direction is proven by induction using Proposition 6. We prove the converse. Let G be a Power-consistent plain execution, and let rf and mo be relations such that $G_0 = G \cup \{\mathtt{rf} : rf\} \cup \{\mathtt{mo} : mo\}$ is complete and Power-coherent. Let S be a total strict order on $\mathtt{E}$ extending the relation R given in Proposition 7. Let G' be the execution given by $G'.\mathtt{po} = \bigcup_{i \in \mathsf{Tid}} \{\langle a, b \rangle \in S \mid tid(a) = tid(b) = i\} \cup (\mathtt{E}_0 \times \mathtt{E})$ (where $\mathtt{E}_0$ is the set of initialization events in G), while all other components of G' are as in G. It is easy to see that $G \rightsquigarrow^{*}_{\mathsf{Power}} G'$. Indeed, recall that a list L of elements totally ordered by $<$ can be sorted by repeatedly swapping adjacent unordered elements $l_i > l_{i+1}$ (as done in "bubble sort"). Since $R \subseteq S$, no reordering step from G to G' will reorder dependent events, events accessing the same location, or fence events. Now, Proposition 6 ensures that $G'_0 = G' \cup \{\mathtt{rf} : rf\} \cup \{\mathtt{mo} : mo\}$ is complete and Power-coherent. To see that it is also SPower-coherent, note that $(\mathtt{E} \backslash \mathtt{E}_0); (G'_0.\mathtt{po} \cup G'_0.\mathtt{rf}) \subseteq S$. □

Remark 3. Note that the reordering operation does not affect the dependency relation. To allow this, and still understand reordering on the program level, we actually consider a slightly weaker model of Power than the one in [4], that do not carry control dependencies across branches. For instance, in a program like $a := y; (\mathtt{if}\, a\, \mathtt{then}\, z := 1); x := 1$, which can be a result of reordering of the stores to x and z in $a := y; x := 1; (\mathtt{if}\, a\, \mathtt{then}\, z := 1)$, we will not have a control dependency between the load of y and the store to x.

6 ARM

We now turn to the ARM architecture and show that it cannot be modeled by any sequence of sound reorderings and eliminations over a basic model satisfying $(\mathtt{po} \cup \mathtt{rf})$-acyclicity.

Consider the program in Fig. 4. Note that no reorderings or eliminations can be applied to this program. In the second and the third threads, reordering is forbidden because of the dependency between the load and the subsequent store. On the first thread, there is no dependency, but since the load and the store access the same location, their reordering is generally unsound, as it allows the load to read from the (originally subsequent) store. Moreover, this program

Initially, $x = y = 0$

$$a := x; \ /\!/1 \quad x := 1; \quad \Big\| \quad y := x; \quad \Big\| \quad x := y;$$

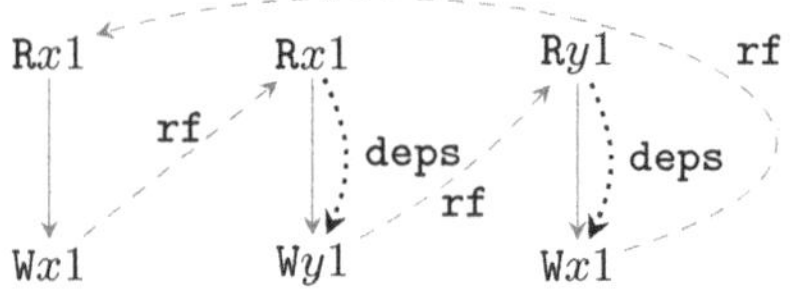

Fig. 4. A weak behavior of ARM, that is not explained by program transformations.

cannot return $a = 1$ under a (po ∪ rf)-acyclic model, because the only instance of the constant 1 in the program occurs after the load of x in the first thread. Nevertheless, this behavior is allowed under both the axiomatic ARMv7 model of Alglave et al. [4] and the ARMv8 Flowing and POP models of Flur et al. [12].

The axiomatic ARMv7 model [4] is the same as the Power model presented in Sect. 5, with the only difference being the definition of ppo (preserved program order). In particular, this model does not satisfy (ppo-lower-bound) because $[\mathtt{RU}]; \mathrm{po}|_{loc}; [\mathtt{WU}] \not\subseteq \mathrm{ppo}$. Hence, the first thread's program order in the example above is not included in ppo, and there is no happens-before cycle. For the same reason, our proof for Power does not carry over to ARM.

In the ARMv8 Flowing model [12], consider the topology where the first two threads share a queue and the third thread is separate. The following execution is possible: (1) the first thread issues a load request from x and immediately commits the $x := 1$ store; (2) the second thread then issues a load request from x, which gets satisfied by the $x := 1$ store, and then (3) issues a store to $y := 1$; (4) the store to y gets reordered with the x-accesses, and flows to the third thread; (5) the third thread then loads $y = 1$, and also issues a store $x := 1$, which flows to the memory; (6) the load of x flows to the next level and gets satisfied by the $x := 1$ store of the third thread; and (7) finally the $x := 1$ store of the first thread also flows to the next level. The POP model is strictly weaker than the Flowing model, and thus also allows this outcome.

7 Application: Correctness of Compilation

Our theorems can be useful to prove correctness of compilation of a programming language with some memory model (such as C11) for the TSO and Power architectures. We outline this idea in a more abstract setting.

Let $[\![P]\!]_{\mathsf{M}}$ denote the possible behaviors of a program P under memory model M. A formal definition of a behavior can be given using a distinguished *world* location, whose values are inspected by an external observer. Assume some compilation scheme from a source language C to a target language A (i.e., a mapping of C instructions to sequences of A ones), and let $\mathtt{compile}(P_C)$ denote the program P_A obtained by applying this scheme on a program P_C. Further, assume memory models M_C and M_A (we do not assume that M_C has an axiomatic presentation; an operational one would work out the same). Correct compilation is expressed by:

$$\forall P_C.\ [\![\mathtt{compile}(P_C)]\!]_{\mathsf{M}_A} \subseteq [\![P_C]\!]_{\mathsf{M}_C}.$$

Applied on the program level, the $(2 \Rightarrow 1)$ directions of Theorems 1 and 2 provide us with the following:

$$\forall P_C.\ [\![\texttt{compile}(P_C)]\!]_{\mathsf{M}_A} \subseteq \bigcup\{[\![P'_A]\!]_{\mathsf{SM}_A} \mid P'_A \ s.t.\ \texttt{compile}(P_C) \rightsquigarrow^*_{\mathsf{M}_A} P'_A\},$$

where SM_A is a stronger model than M_A (SC for TSO and SPower for Power). Then, correctness of compilation easily follows from the following two conditions. First, compilation should be correct for the strong model SM_A:

$$\forall P_C.\ [\![\texttt{compile}(P_C)]\!]_{\mathsf{SM}_A} \subseteq [\![P_C]\!]_{\mathsf{M}_C}.$$

Second, there should exist a set of source program transformations, described by $\rightsquigarrow_{\mathsf{M}_C}$, that (i) is sound for M_C, i.e.,

$$\forall P_C, P'_C.\ P_C \rightsquigarrow_{\mathsf{M}_C} P'_C \implies [\![P'_C]\!]_{\mathsf{M}_C} \subseteq [\![P_C]\!]_{\mathsf{M}_C};$$

and (ii) captures all target transformations from a compiled program:

$$\forall P_C, P'_A.\ \texttt{compile}(P_C) \rightsquigarrow_{\mathsf{M}_A} P'_A \implies \exists P'_C.\ \texttt{compile}(P'_C) = P'_A \wedge P_C \rightsquigarrow^*_{\mathsf{M}_C} P'_C.$$

For TSO meeting the first condition is trivial, because sequential consistency is the strongest model. In the case of Power, proving this property for SPower is easier than for Power. Roughly speaking, to show that behaviors of SPower are allowed by a model M_C would require less "features" of M_C, and can be done by induction on $(\texttt{po} \cup \texttt{rf})^+$ in SPower-coherent executions.

Fulfilling the second requirement is typically easy, because the source language, its memory model, and the mapping of its statements to processors are often explicitly designed to enable such transformations. In fact, when one aims to validate an *optimizing* compiler, the first part of the second requirement should be anyway established. For example, consider the compilation of C11 to TSO. Here, we need to show that WR-reordering and WR-elimination on compiled code could be done by C11-sound transformations on corresponding instructions of the source. Indeed, the mapping of C11 accesses to TSO instructions (see [7]) ensures that any adjacent WR-pair results from adjacent C11 accesses with access ordering strictly weaker than `sc` (sequential consistent accesses). Reordering and eliminations in this case is known to be sound under the C11 memory model [18].

8 Conclusion

In this paper, we have shown that the TSO memory model and (a substantial fragment of) the Power memory model can be defined by a set of reorderings and eliminations starting from a stronger and simpler memory model. Nevertheless, the counterexamples in Sects. 4 and 6 suggest that there is more to weak memory consistency than just instruction reorderings and eliminations.

We further sketched a possible application of the alternative characterizations of TSO and Power: proofs of compilation correctness can be simplified by using the soundness of local transformations in the source language. To follow this approach in a formal proof of correctness of a compiler, however, further work is required to formulate precisely the syntactic transformations in the target programming language. In the future, we also plan to investigate the application of these characterizations for proving soundness of program logics with respect to TSO and Power.

Acknowledgments. We would like to thank the FM'16 reviewers for their feedback. This research was supported by an ERC Consolidator Grant for the project "RustBelt", funded under Horizon 2020 grant agreement no. 683289.

References

1. Coq development for this paper and further supplementary material. http://plv.mpi-sws.org/trns/
2. Adve, S.V., Gharachorloo, K.: Shared memory consistency models: a tutorial. Computer **29**(12), 66–76 (1996)
3. Alglave, J., Kroening, D., Nimal, V., Tautschnig, M.: Software verification for weak memory via program transformation. In: Felleisen, M., Gardner, P. (eds.) ESOP 2013. LNCS, vol. 7792, pp. 512–532. Springer, Heidelberg (2013). doi:10.1007/978-3-642-37036-6_28
4. Alglave, J., Maranget, L., Tautschnig, M.: Herding cats: modelling, simulation, testing, and data mining for weak memory. ACM Trans. Program. Lang. Syst. **36**(2), 7:1–7:74 (2014)
5. Batty, M., Memarian, K., Nienhuis, K., Pichon-Pharabod, J., Sewell, P.: The problem of programming language concurrency semantics. In: Vitek, J. (ed.) ESOP 2015. LNCS, vol. 9032, pp. 283–307. Springer, Heidelberg (2015). doi:10.1007/978-3-662-46669-8_12
6. Batty, M., Memarian, K., Owens, S., Sarkar, S., Sewell, P.: Clarifying and compiling C/C++ concurrency: from C++11 to POWER. In: Proceedings of the 39th Annual ACM SIGPLAN-SIGACT Symposium on Principles of Programming Languages, POPL 2012, pp. 509–520. ACM, New York (2012)
7. Batty, M., Owens, S., Sarkar, S., Sewell, P., Weber, T.: Mathematizing C++ concurrency. In: Proceedings of the 38th Annual ACM SIGPLAN-SIGACT Symposium on Principles of Programming Languages. POPL 2011, pp. 55–66. ACM, New York (2011)
8. Boehm, H.J., Demsky, B.: Outlawing ghosts: avoiding out-of-thin-air results. In: Proceedings of the Workshop on Memory Systems Performance and Correctness. MSPC 2014, pp. 7:1–7:6. ACM, New York (2014)
9. Burckhardt, S., Musuvathi, M., Singh, V.: Verifying local transformations on relaxed memory models. In: Gupta, R. (ed.) CC 2010. LNCS, vol. 6011, pp. 104–123. Springer, Heidelberg (2010). doi:10.1007/978-3-642-11970-5_7
10. Demange, D., Laporte, V., Zhao, L., Jagannathan, S., Pichardie, D., Vitek, J.: Plan B: a buffered memory model for Java. In: Proceedings of the 40th Annual ACM SIGPLAN-SIGACT Symposium on Principles of Programming Languages. POPL 2013, pp. 329–342. ACM, New York (2013)
11. Doko, M., Vafeiadis, V.: A program logic for C11 memory fences. In: Jobstmann, B., Leino, K.R.M. (eds.) VMCAI 2016. LNCS, vol. 9583, pp. 413–430. Springer, Heidelberg (2016). doi:10.1007/978-3-662-49122-5_20

12. Flur, S., Gray, K.E., Pulte, C., Sarkar, S., Sezgin, A., Maranget, L., Deacon, W., Sewell, P.: Modelling the ARMv8 architecture, operationally: concurrency and ISA. In: Proceedings of the 43rd Annual ACM SIGPLAN-SIGACT Symposium on Principles of Programming Languages. POPL 2016, pp. 608–621. ACM, New York (2016)
13. Lahav, O., Giannarakis, N., Vafeiadis, V.: Taming release-acquire consistency. In: Proceedings of the 43rd Annual ACM SIGPLAN-SIGACT Symposium on Principles of Programming Languages. POPL 2016, pp. 649–662. ACM, New York (2016)
14. Lamport, L.: How to make a multiprocessor computer that correctly executes multiprocess programs. IEEE Trans. Comput. **28**(9), 690–691 (1979)
15. Morisset, R., Pawan, P., Zappa Nardelli, F.: Compiler testing via a theory of sound optimisations in the C11/C++11 memory model. In: Proceedings of the 34th ACM SIGPLAN Conference on Programming Language Design and Implementation. PLDI 2013, pp. 187–196. ACM, New York (2013)
16. Owens, S., Sarkar, S., Sewell, P.: A better x86 memory model: x86-TSO. In: Berghofer, S., Nipkow, T., Urban, C., Wenzel, M. (eds.) TPHOLs 2009. LNCS, vol. 5674, pp. 391–407. Springer, Heidelberg (2009). doi:10.1007/978-3-642-03359-9_27
17. Shasha, D., Snir, M.: Efficient and correct execution of parallel programs that share memory. ACM Trans. Program. Lang. Syst. **10**(2), 282–312 (1988)
18. Vafeiadis, V., Balabonski, T., Chakraborty, S., Morisset, R., Zappa Nardelli, F.: Common compiler optimisations are invalid in the C11 memory model and what we can do about it. In: Proceedings of the 42nd Annual ACM SIGPLAN-SIGACT Symposium on Principles of Programming Languages. POPL 2015, pp. 209–220. ACM, New York (2015)
19. Ševčík, J.: Safe optimisations for shared-memory concurrent programs. In: Proceedings of the 32nd ACM SIGPLAN Conference on Programming Language Design and Implementation. PLDI 2011, pp. 306–316. ACM, New York (2011)

SpecCert: Specifying and Verifying Hardware-Based Security Enforcement

Thomas Letan[1,2(✉)], Pierre Chifflier[1], Guillaume Hiet[2], Pierre Néron[1], and Benjamin Morin[1]

[1] French Network Information Security Agency (ANSSI), Paris, France
thomas.letan@ssi.gouv.fr

[2] CIDRE – Inria, IRISA, CentraleSupélec, Rennes, France

Abstract. Over time, hardware designs have constantly grown in complexity and modern platforms involve multiple interconnected hardware components. During the last decade, several vulnerability disclosures have proven that trust in hardware can be misplaced. In this article, we give a formal definition of *Hardware-based Security Enforcement* (HSE) mechanisms, a class of security enforcement mechanisms such that a software component relies on the underlying hardware platform to enforce a security policy. We then model a subset of a x86-based hardware platform specifications and we prove the soundness of a realistic HSE mechanism within this model using Coq, a proof assistant system.

Modern hardware architectures have grown in complexity. They now are made of numerous devices which expose multiple programmable functions. In this article, we identify a class of security enforcement mechanisms we call Hardware-based Security Enforcement (HSE) such that a set of software components configures the hardware in a way which prevents the other software components to break a security policy. For instance, when an operating system uses the ring levels and memory paging features of x86 microprocessors to isolate the userland applications, it implements a HSE mechanism. A HSE mechanism is sound when it succeeds in enforcing a security policy. It requires (1) the hardware functions to provide the expected properties and (2) the software components to make a correct use of these hardware functions. In practice, both requirements are hard to meet.

First, hardware architectures comprise multiple interconnected devices which interact together. From a security perspective, it implies considering the devices both individually and as a whole. Hardware functions are not immune to security vulnerabilities. For instance, early versions of the `sinit` instruction implementation of the Intel TXT technology [13] allowed an attacker to perform a privilege escalation [22]. The legitimate use of a hardware mechanism can also break the security promised by another. For instance, until 2008, the x86 cache allowed to circumvent an access control mechanism exposed by the memory controller [18, 23]. Secondly, hardware architectures have grown in complexity and, as a consequence, HSE mechanisms too. To take the example of the x86 architecture, each generation of CPU brings its own new security hardware mechanisms

J. Fitzgerald et al. (Eds.): FM 2016, LNCS 9995, pp. 496–512, 2016.
DOI: 10.1007/978-3-319-48989-6_30

(from the ring levels and the MMU to the new SGX technology). There are many examples of security vulnerabilities which are the consequence of an incorrect HSE mechanism implementation [5,9,27].

In this paper, we introduce SpecCert, a framework for specifying and verifying HSE mechanisms against hardware architecture models. SpecCert relies on a three-step methodology. First, we model the hardware architecture specifications. Then, we specify the software requirements that must be satisfied by the trusted software components which implement the HSE mechanism. Finally, we prove that the HSE mechanism is sound under the assumption that the software components complies to the specified requirements. This implies the hardware involved in the HSE mechanism indeed provides the security properties they promise. We believe this approach to be beneficial to both hardware designers and software developers. The former can verify their hardware mechanism assumptions and the latter can get a formal specification to implement the HSE mechanism.

In Sect. 1, we give a formal definition of the SpecCert formalism. In Sect. 2, we define a model of x86-based hardware architectures to verify HSE mechanisms targeting software isolation policies using publicly available Intel specifications. In Sect. 3, we verify the soundness of the HSE mechanism implemented in many x86 computer firmware codes to isolate the code executed while the CPU is in System Management Mode (SMM), a highly privileged execution mode of x86 microprocessors. Our model and proofs have been implemented using Coq, a proof assistant system and have been released as an open source software[1]. We discuss our results in Sect. 4, some related works in Sect. 5 and conclude in Sect. 6.

1 The SpecCert Formalism

In SpecCert, we model the hardware architecture and its features with a set of states $\mathcal{H}$, a set of events $\mathcal{E}$ and a Computing Platform Σ which defines a semantics of events as state-transformers. Hence, the execution of a set of software components by a hardware architecture is a sequence of state-transformations (denoted $h \xrightarrow[\Sigma]{ev} h'$) in this model. In this paper, we consider exclusively Execution Monitoring (EM) enforceable security policies [4,25] that are security policies which can be enforced by monitoring the software execution. As a consequence, we model a security policy with a predicate P on sequences of state-transformations. Finally, we model a HSE mechanism Δ with a set of requirements on states to characterize safe hardware configurations and a set of requirements on state-transformations for trusted software components to preserve the state requirements through software execution. A HSE mechanism is sound when every sequence of state-transformations which satisfies these requirements also satisfies the security policy predicate.

[1] Which can be found at: https://github.com/lethom/speccert.

1.1 Computing Platforms

We now dive more deeply into the SpecCert formalism and give a formal definition of the Computing Platform. We model a hardware architecture which executes several software components using states, events and a semantics of events as state-transformers.

The state of a hardware architecture models the configuration of its devices at a given time. This configuration may change over time with respect to the hardware specifications and comprises any relevant data such as registers values, inner memory contents, etc. A hardware architecture state update is triggered by some events. We distinguish two classes of events: the software events which are direct and forseeable side-effects of the execution of an instruction and the hardware events which are not. The execution of an instruction can be broken down into a sequence of software events.

For instance, to execute the x86 instruction[2] `mov (%ecx),%eax`, a x86 CPU:

- reads the content of the register `ecx` as an address
- reads the main memory at this address
- writes this content into the register `eax`
- updates the register `eip` with the address of the next instruction to execute.

We model this sequence of actions as four software events which trigger four state updates. Note that if the content of the `ecx` register is not a valid address, the scenario is different. In such a case, the read access to the main memory fails and an interrupt is raised. This second scenario is modeled with another sequence of events which involved a hardware event *i.e.* the interrupt.

The semantics of events as state-transformers is specified using preconditions and postconditions. Preconditions specify the state requirements which are necessary for an event to be observed. Postconditions specify the consequences of an event on the hardware architecture state.

Definition 1 (Computing System). Given $\mathcal{H}$ a set of hardware architecture states and $\mathcal{E}$ a set of events, a Computing Platform Σ is a pair of (*precondition*, *postcondition*) where *precondition* is a predicate on $\mathcal{H} \times \mathcal{E}$ and *postcondition* is a predicate on $\mathcal{H} \times \mathcal{E} \times \mathcal{H}$. Σ defines a semantics of events as state-transformers such as

$$\frac{precondition(h, ev) \qquad postcondition(h, ev, h')}{h \xrightarrow[\Sigma]{ev} h'}$$

$h \xrightarrow[\Sigma]{ev} h'$ is called a state-transformation of Σ.

[2] Written in AT&T syntax here.

1.2 Security Policies

Given $\mathcal{H}$ a set of states of a hardware architecture, $\mathcal{E}$ a set of events, Σ a Computing Platform and $\mathcal{S}$ a set of software components being executed by the hardware architecture, a particular execution of a set of software components is modeled with a sequence of state-transformations we call a run of Σ.

Definition 2 (Run). A run of the Computing Platform Σ is a sequence of state-transformations of Σ such that for two consecutive transformations, the resulting state of the first is the initial state of the next. We denote $\mathcal{R}(\Sigma)$ the set of runs of the Computing Platform Σ and $init(\rho)$ the initial state of a run ρ.

We consider EM-enforceable security policies [4,25] specified with predicates on runs. A run is said to be secure according to a security policy when it satisfies the predicate specifying this policy.

In this paper, we focus on a class of security policies we call software execution isolation policies. Such a policy prevents a set of untrusted software components to tamper with the execution of another set of so-called trusted software components. We consider that a software component tampers with the execution of another when it is able to make the latter execute an instruction of its choice.

In practice, a subset of states of the hardware architecture is dedicated to each software component. For instance, the x86 CPU has a feature called protection rings where each ring can be seen as an execution mode dedicated to a software component. Hence, the ring 0 is dedicated to the operating system whereas the userland applications are executed when the CPU is in ring 3. In SpecCert, we take advantage of this CPU state mapping to infer which software component is currently executed from a hardware architecture state. For the following definitions, we assume the hardware architecture contains only one CPU.

Definition 3 (Hardware-Software Mapping). A hardware-software mapping $context : \mathcal{H} \rightarrow \mathcal{S}$ is a function which takes a hardware state and returns the software component currently executed.

Dealing with multi-core architectures would require additional efforts and notations. One possible solution could be to define an identifier per core and to use this identifier in addition to the current hardware state to deduce the software component currently executed by the corresponding core. However, this is out of the scope of this article.

We now introduce the concept of *memory location ownership*. A memory location within a hardware architecture is a container which is able to store data used by a software component *e.g.* a general-purpose register of a CPU, a DRAM memory cell, etc. We say that a Computing Platform tracks the memory location ownership if the hardware architecture states maps each memory location with a software component called its *owner*, and the Computing Platform semantics updates this mapping through state-transformations. A software component becomes the new owner of a memory location when it overrides its content during a state-transformation. By extension, we say a software component owns some data when it owns the memory location in which these data are stored.

With this mapping, it becomes possible to determine the owner of an instruction fetched by the CPU in order to be decoded and executed.

Definition 4 (Event-Software Mapping). An event-software mapping $fetched : \mathcal{H} \times \mathcal{E} \rightarrow \mathcal{P}(\mathcal{S})$ is a function which takes an initial hardware state and an event and returns the set of the fetched instructions owners during this state-transformation.

Hence, $s \in fetched(h, ev)$ means that an instruction owned by a software component s was fetched during a state-transformation triggered by an event ev from a state h. With a hardware-software mapping and an event-software mapping, we give a formal definition of a *software execution tampering.*

Definition 5 (Software Execution Tampering). Given h the initial state of a state-transformation triggered by an event ev, $context$ a hardware-software mapping, $fetched$ an event-software mapping and $x, y \in \mathcal{S}$ two software components, the software component y tampers with the execution of another software component x if the CPU fetches an instruction owned by y in a state dedicated to x.

$$software\_tampering(context, fetched, h, ev, x, y) \triangleq \\ context(h) = x \wedge y \in fetched(h, ev)$$

Given $\mathcal{T} \subseteq \mathcal{S}$ a set of trusted software components, the software execution isolation policy prevents the untrusted components from tampering with the execution of the trusted components. Such a policy is enforced during a run if no untrusted component is able to tamper with the execution of a trusted component.

Definition 6 (Software Execution Isolation). Given $context$ a hardware-software mapping, $fetched$ an event-software mapping and ρ a run of Σ,

$$software\_execution\_isolation(context, fetched, \rho, \mathcal{T}) \triangleq \\ \forall h \xrightarrow[\Sigma]{ev} h' \in \rho, \forall t \in \mathcal{T}, \forall u \notin \mathcal{T}, \\ \neg software\_tampering(context, fetched, h, ev, t, u)$$

In this definition, t is a trusted software component and u is an untrusted —potentially malicious or hijacked— one.

1.3 Hardware-Based Security Enforcement Mechanism

A HSE mechanism is a set of requirements on states to characterize safe hardware configurations and a set of requirements on state-transformations to preserve the state requirements through software execution. The software components which implement a HSE mechanism form the Trusted Computing Base (TCB).

Definition 7 (HSE Mechanism). Given $\mathcal{H}$ a set of states of a hardware architecture, $\mathcal{E}$ a set of events and Σ a Computing Platform, we model a HSE mechanism Δ with a tuple $(inv, behavior, \mathcal{T}, context)$ such as

- inv is a predicate on $\mathcal{H}$ to distinguish between safe hardware configurations and potentially vulnerable ones
- $behavior$ is a predicate on $\mathcal{H} \times \mathcal{E}_{Soft}$ to distinguish between safe software state-transformations and potentially harmful ones
- $\mathcal{T} \subseteq S$ is the set of software components which form the TCB of the HSE mechanism
- $context$ is a hardware-software mapping to determine when the TCB is executed

For instance, in x86-based hardware architectures, the SPI Flash contents (the code and configuration of the firmware) is protected as follows:

1. By default, the SPI Flash is locked and its content cannot be overriden until it has been unlocked
2. Some software components can unlock the SPI Flash
3. When they do so, the CPU is forced to start the execution of a special-purpose software component
4. This software component has to lock the SPI Flash before the end of its execution

In this example, the special-purpose software component is the TCB. A safe hardware state (modeled with inv) is either a state wherein the special-purpose software component is executed or a state wherein the SPI Flash is locked. This requirement on hardware architecture states is preserved by preventing the special-purpose software component to end its execution before it has locked the SPI Flash (modeled with $behavior$).

For a HSE mechanism to be correctly defined, it must obey a few axioms, together called the HSE Laws. The first law says that the state requirements specified by inv are preserved through state-transformations if the software transformations which do not satisfy $behavior$ are discarded. The second law says that the $behavior$ predicate specifies state-transformations restrictions for the TCB only. The software components which are not part of the TCB are considered untrusted and we make no assumption on their behavior.

Definition 8 (HSE Laws). A HSE mechanism $\Delta = (inv, behavior, \mathcal{T}, context)$ has to satisfy the following properties:

1. $behavior$ preserves inv: $\forall h \xrightarrow[\Sigma]{ev} h'$,

$$inv(h) \Rightarrow (ev \in \mathcal{E}_{Soft} \Rightarrow behavior(h, ev)) \Rightarrow inv(h')$$

2. $behavior$ only restricts the TCB: $\forall x \notin \mathcal{T}, \forall h \in \mathcal{H}, \forall ev \in \mathcal{E}_{Soft}$,

$$context(h) = x \Rightarrow behavior(h, ev)$$

A run complies to a HSE mechanism definition if its initial state satisfies the state requirements and each state-transformation of the run satisfies the state-transformations requirements. The set of the runs which comply with Δ is denoted by $\mathcal{C}(\Delta)$.

Definition 9 (Compliant Runs). Given $\rho \in \mathcal{R}(\Sigma)$,

$$\rho \in \mathcal{C}(\Delta) \triangleq inv(init(\rho)) \land \forall h \xrightarrow[\Sigma]{ev} h', ev \in \mathcal{E}_{Soft} \Rightarrow behavior(h, ev)$$

Eventually, we aim to prove that a HSE mechanism is sound —it succeeds to enforce a security policy— under the assumption that software components of the TCB always behave according to the HSE mechanism specification.

Definition 10 (Sound HSE Mechanism). A HSE mechanism Δ succeeds in enforcing a security policy P when each compliant run of Δ is secure. In such a case, Δ is said to be sound.

$$sound(\Delta, P) \triangleq \forall \rho \in \mathcal{C}(\Delta), P(\rho)$$

2 Minx86: A x86 Model

The SpecCert formalism is the foundation of the SpecCert framework. It comprises a set of high-level definitions to specify a HSE mechanism against a hardware architecture model. In its current state, the SpecCert framework contains a model of x86 called MINX86. MINX86 is intended to be a minimal model for single core x86-based machines and we have used publicly available Intel documents [10–12] to define it.

2.1 Model Scope

The hardware architecture we are modeling with MINX86 contains a CPU, a cache, a memory controller, a DRAM controller and a VGA controller[3] which both expose some memory to the CPU.

MINX86 is meant to be a proof of concept of the SpecCert formalism and thus is not exhaustive. In its current state of implementation, its scope focuses on the System Management Mode (SMM) feature of x86 microprocessors.

Hardware Specifications. We consider the CPU can be either in System Management Mode (SMM) or in an unprivileged mode. The SMM is "a special-purpose operating mode provided for handling system-wide functions like power management, system hardware control, or proprietary OEM-designed code" [12]. It is the most privileged execution mode of x86 processors. When a CPU receives a special hardware interrupt called System Management Interrupt (SMI), it halts

[3] A VGA controller is a hardware device which on we can connect a screen. It exposes some memory to the CPU for communication purposes.

its current execution and reconfigures itself to a specified state from which it executes the code stored in memory at the address $SMBASE + \texttt{0x8000}$. In practice, the SMBASE value points to the base of a memory region called the SMRAM. Leaving the SMM is done by executing a special purpose instruction called `rsm` (for *resume*).

The CPU relies on a cache to reduce the Input/Output (I/O, that is a read or write access to the memory) latency. We model one level of cache which stores both data and instructions and we consider two cache strategies: uncacheable (UC) and writeback (WB). With the UC cache strategy, the cache is not used and all I/O-s are forwarded to the memory controller, whereas with the WB strategy, the cache is used as much as possible[4]. To determine which cache strategy to use, the CPU relies on several configuration registers and mechanisms. One of them is a pair of registers called the System Management Range Registers (SMRR) which can only be configured when the CPU is in SMM. They are used to tell the CPU where the SMRAM is and which cache strategy to use for I/O targeting the SMRAM when the CPU is in SMM. When it is not in SMM, the CPU always uses the UC strategy for I/O targeting the SMRAM. SMRR have been introduced as a countermeasure of the SMRAM cache poisoning attack [18,23] which allowed an untrusted code to tamper with the copy of the SMRAM stored in the cache. The memory controller [11] receives all the CPU I/O-s which are not handled by the cache and dispatches them to the DRAM controller or to the VGA controller. It exposes a unified view (the memory map) of the system memory to the CPU. The CPU manipulates this memory map with a set of addresses called the physical addresses. The memory controller dedicates a special range of physical addresses to form the SMRAM. The SMRAM is dedicated to store the code intended to be executed when the CPU is in SMM.

Tracking the Memory Ownership. The MINX86 definition is parameterized with an hardware-software mapping (see Definition 3). The memory locations of MINX86 Computing Platforms are either cache lines or memory cells exposed by the DRAM controller or the VGA controller. The memory ownership is updated through state-transformations according to three rules:

1. When a cache line gets a copy of a DRAM or VGA cell content, the owner of this cell becomes the new owner of this cache line.
2. When the content of this cache line is written back to a memory cell, the new owner of this memory cell is the owner of this cache line.
3. When a state-transformation implies the content of a memory location to be overriden with a new value, the software currently executed becomes its new owner.

Given $\mathcal{S}$ a set of software components, the set of states of MINX86 Computing Platform hardware architecture is denoted by $\texttt{Archi}_{\mathcal{S}}$ and the set of MINX86 Computing Platform events is denoted by `Event`.

[4] These cache strategies are explained in [12], Volume 3A, Chap. 11, Sect. 11.3 (page 2316–2317).

2.2 Hardware Architecture State

$\texttt{Archi}_S$ is defined as the Cartesian product of the set of states of the CPU, the CPU's cache, the memory controller and the hardware memories exposed by both the DRAM controller and the VGA controller. Each of these sets is defined in order to model the hardware features we have previously described. We define $\texttt{PhysAddr} \triangleq \{\texttt{pa}_i \mid i \leq \texttt{max\_addr}\}$ the set of physical addresses the CPU uses to perform I/O. The maximal address offset (denoted by `max_addr` here) is specific to the CPU and may vary in time according to its addressing mode (real mode, long mode, etc.), therefore we left its value as a parameter of our model. An in-depth definition of $\texttt{Archi}_S$ is given in the Appendix A.1 of [16].

We model the projection of the SMRAM in the memory map such that $\texttt{pSmram} \triangleq \{\texttt{pa}_i \mid \texttt{smram\_base} \leq i \leq \texttt{smram\_end}\}$. The values of `smram_base` and `smram_end` are specified in the memory controller specifications. It is the software responsability to set the SMRR accordingly. We assume $\texttt{smram\_end} - \texttt{smram\_base} > \texttt{0x8000}$. This way, when the SMBASE contains the address of the beginning of the SMRAM, the SMM entry point (that is $SMBASE + \texttt{0x8000}$) is in SMRAM.

The hardware architecture states are implemented in the *SpecCert.x86.Architecture* module (about 1 500 lines of code).

2.3 Events as State-Transformers

The set of events which trigger the state-transformations is denoted by `Event`. As we said in Sect. 1.1, we distinguish hardware events denoted by $\texttt{Event}_{Hard}$ and software events denoted by $\texttt{Event}_{Soft}$.

Table 1. List of software events

Event	Parameters	Description
$Write$	$pa \in \texttt{PhysAddr}$	CPU writes at physical address pa
$Read$	$pa \in \texttt{PhysAddr}$	CPU reads at physical address pa
$SetCacheStrat$	$pa \in \texttt{PhysAddr}$ $strat \in \{\texttt{UC}, \texttt{WB}\}$	Change the cache strategy for pa to $strat$ (`WB`: write-back, `UC`: uncacheable)
$UpdateSmrr$	$smrr \in \texttt{Smrr}$	Set the SMRR content to $smrr$
Rsm	–	CPU leaves SMM
$OpenBitFlip$	–	Flip the *d_open* bit
$LockSmramc$	–	Set the *d_lock* bit to 1
$NextInstruction$	$pa \in \texttt{PhysAddr}$	Set the program counter register to pa

Table 1 lists the software events we consider in the MINX86 Computing Platforms. We model the CPU I/O-s with *Read(pa)* and *Write(pa)*, the configuration of the memory controller with *OpenBitFlip* and *LockSmramc*, the configuration of the cache strategy with $SetCacheStrat(pa, strat)$, the configuration of

Table 2. List of hardware events

Event	Description
Fetch	A CPU I/O to fetch the instruction stored at the physical address contained in the program counter register
ReceiveSmi	A SMI is raised and the CPU handles it

the SMRR with $UpdateSmrr(smrr)$ the exit of the SMM with Rsm and the update of the CPU program counter register with $NextInstruction(pa)$.

The other causes of state-transformations are modeled using hardware events. Table 2 lists the hardware events we consider in the MINX86 Computing Platforms. $Fetch$ models the I/O to fetch the instruction pointed by the program counter register. *ReceiveSmi* models a System Management Interrupt being risen and handled by the CPU.

We define $minx86\_fetched$ an event-software mapping for MINX86 Computing Platforms (see Definition 4). The $minx86\_fetched$ function maps a state-transformation to the set of software components which own an instruction fetched during this state-transformation. In the case of MINX86, there is only one event which implies fetching instructions: $Fetch$. Let o be the owner of the instruction pointed by the program counter register in the formula

$$minx86\_fetched(h, ev) \triangleq \begin{cases} \{o\} & \text{if } ev = Fetch \\ \emptyset & \text{otherwise} \end{cases}$$

We can determine o because MINX86 tracks the memory location ownership.

Given $context$ a hardware-software mapping (see Definition 3), we denote the Computing Platform MINX86 parameterized with $context$ such that

$$\text{MINX86}(context) \triangleq (minx86\_pre, minx86\_post(context))$$

We give an informal description of the $minx86\_pre$ and $minx86\_post(context)$ for each event. These definitions have been implemented in Coq in the module *SpecCert.x86.Transition.*

We first give the semantics of software events as state-transformers. A software component can always read and write at any physical address. As a consequence, the precondition for $Read(pa)$ and $Write(pa)$ always holds true. The postcondition for $Read(pa)$ and $Write(pa)$ requires the memory ownership to be updated according to the memories and cache state updates. The memory controller enforces a simple access control to protect the SMRAM content in the DRAM memory by forwarding the related I/O to the VGA controller when the CPU is not in SMM. To determine the owner of the memory location which sees its content overriden during a state transformation, the postcondition uses the hardware-software mapping used to define the Computing Platform.

A software component can always update the cache strategy used for an I/O. The postcondition for $SetCacheStrat(pa, strat)$ requires only the cache strategy setting for this physical address *pa* to change. The precondition for *UpdateSmrr* requires the CPU to be in SMM. The postcondition requires the SMRR of the CPU to be updated with the correct value, the rest of the hardware architecture state being left unchanged.

A software component can jump to any physical address, hence the postcondition for *NextInstruction(pa)* always holds true. The postcondition for *NextInstruction(pa)* requires the program counter register to be updated with *pa*. The *OpenBitFlip* precondition requires the SMRAMC register to be unlocked. The postcondition requires the `d_open` bit to be updated. The *LockSmramc* precondition requires the `d_lock` bit to be unset. The postcondition requires the `d_open` bit to be unset and the *d_lock* bit to be unset.

We now describe the semantics of hardware events as state-transformers. *Fetch* models the fetching of an instruction by the CPU. The definition of its precondition and postcondition are the same as *Read(pa)* with *pa* being the program register value. *ReceiveSmi* precondition requires the CPU not to be in SMM because SMM is non-reentrant. The postcondition of *ReceiveSmi* requires the program counter to be set with the $smbase + \texttt{0x8000}$ (where *smbase* is the value of the SMBASE register of the CPU) and the CPU is in SMM.

3 System Management Mode HSE

In [12], Intel states "the main benefit of SMM is that it offers a distinct and easily isolated processor environment that operates transparently to the operating system or executive and software applications". For the SMM processor environment to be isolated, the code executed when the CPU is in SMM needs to implement a HSE mechanism. In this section, we formalize and verify this mechanism against the model we have previously introduced.

3.1 Computing Platform and Security Policy

We consider three software components: the boot sequence code, the SMM code and the OS code. During the boot sequence, only the boot sequence code is executed and it loads both the OS code and the SMM code into memory. At the end of the boot sequence, the OS kernel is executed. This OS kernel will schedule different applications. Because applications are less privileged than the OS kernel, we will not distinguish them from the kernel code. Thus, in the following, OS code refers to both OS kernel and application codes.

At runtime, both the OS code and the SMM code can be executed. Our objective is to evaluate the security provided by the hardware to isolate SMM code from OS code. Thus, we define

$$\mathcal{S} \triangleq \{\texttt{smm}, \texttt{os}\}$$

We assume the SMM is dedicated to the SMM code. Let cpu_in_smm : $\texttt{Archi}_{\mathcal{S}} \rightarrow \{\texttt{true}, \texttt{false}\}$ be the function which returns `true` if the CPU is in

SMM and `false` otherwise. We define *smm_context* a hardware-software mapping such that

$$smm\_context(h) \triangleq \begin{cases} \texttt{smm} & \text{if } cpu\_in\_smm(h) = \texttt{true} \\ \texttt{os} & \text{otherwise} \end{cases}$$

Let SMMX86 be the Computing Platform such as

$$\text{SMMX86} \triangleq \text{MINX86}(smm\_context)$$

We assume that both the OS code and the SMM code have been loaded in distinct memory regions. In particular, all the SMM code has been loaded in SMRAM. Our objective is to enforce a security policy which prevents the OS code to tamper with the SMM code execution. This way, the SMM (which is the most privileged execution mode of the CPU) cannot be used to perform an escalation privilege. We define *smm_security* a predicate to model this security policy such as given $\rho \in \text{SMMX86}$,

$$\begin{aligned} &smm\_security(\rho) \triangleq \\ &\quad software\_execution\_isolation(smm\_context, minx86\_execute, \rho, \{\texttt{smm}\}) \end{aligned}$$

3.2 HSE Definition

We define Δ_{Smm} to model the HSE mechanism applied by the SMM code such that $\Delta_{Smm} = (inv_{Smm}, behavior_{Smm}, \{\,\texttt{smm}\,\}, smm\_context)$ (see Definition 7).

In order to enforce the SMM security policy, we have identified six requirements on states.

- When the CPU executes the SMM code, the program counter register value needs to be an address in SMRAM.
- The SMBASE register was correctly set during the boot sequence to point to the base of the SMRAM.
- The SMRAM contains only SMM code.
- For a physical address in SMRAM, in case of cache hit, the related cache line content must be owned by the SMM code.
- In order to protect the content of the SMRAM inside the DRAM memory, the boot sequence code has locked the SMRAMC controller. This ensures that an OS cannot set the `d_open` bit any longer and only a CPU in SMM can modify the content of the SMRAM.
- The range of memory declared with the SMRR needs to overlap with the SMRAM.

The Appendix A.2 of [16] gives the formal definitions of each requirements and of inv_{Smm}. We now define $behavior_{Smm}$. We only define two restrictions. First, we force the SMM code execution to remain confined within the SMRAM. The reason is simple: the OS code can tamper with the memory outside the SMRAM. As a consequence, jumping outside the SMRAM is the best way to fail the security policy. Secondly, we prevent the SMM code to update the SMRR registers as it is the responsability of the boot sequence code to correctly set them.

$$behavior_{Smm}(h, ev) \triangleq \begin{array}{l} smm\_context(h) = \texttt{smm} \\ \Rightarrow ((e = NextInstruction(pa) \Rightarrow pa \in \texttt{pSmram}) \\ \quad \wedge (e \neq UpdateSmrr(smrr))) \end{array}$$

For Δ_{Smm} to be a HSE mechanism, we need to prove the two HSE Laws (see Definition 8). The first law states the state requirements modeled with inv_{Smm} are preserved through state-transformations if the transformations which do not satisfy $behavior_{Smm}$ are discarded. We prove this by enumeration of $ev \in \texttt{Event}$ and $h \in \texttt{Archi}_{Smm}$, we check that each requirement described previously is preserved by Δ_{Smm}. We use those intermediary results to conclude. The second law states that the $behavior_{Smm}$ predicate specifies state-transformation requirements for the TCB only. In this use case, it means $behavior_{Smm}$ should always hold true when the OS code is executed by the hardware architecture. By definition of $behavior_{Smm}$, $smm\_context(h) = \texttt{smm}$ is an antecedent of the conditional.

Let $smm\_secure\_transformation$ be a predicate which holds true when a state-transformation does not imply the OS code to tamper with the execution of SMM code.

$$\begin{array}{l} smm\_secure\_transformation(h, ev) \triangleq \\ \quad \neg software\_tampering(smm\_context, minx86\_execute, h, ev, \texttt{os}, \texttt{smm}) \end{array}$$

We prove that this predicate holds true for a state-transformation with respect to the HSE mechanism. With this result, we can prove the HSE mechanism is sound (see Definition 10).

Lemma 1 (Invariants Enforce Security). $\forall h \xrightarrow[\text{SMMX86}(ctx)]{ev} h'$,

$$\begin{array}{l} inv_{Smm}(h) \\ \quad \Rightarrow (ev \in \textbf{Event}_{Soft} \Rightarrow behavior_{Smm}(h, ev) \\ \qquad \Rightarrow smm\_secure\_transformation(h, ev) \end{array}$$

Proof. By enumeration of $ev \in \texttt{Event}$ and $h \in \texttt{Archi}_S$.

Theorem 1 (Δ_{Smm} is Sound).

$$sound(\Delta_{Smm}, smm\_security)$$

Proof. The "Invariants Enforce Security" lemma applies for one transition and the first HSE law allows to reason by induction on runs.

4 Discussion

Our effort has been originally motivated by the disclosure of several vulnerabilities targeting multiple x86 HSE mechanisms for the past few years [6,14,18,23,24]. These attacks do not benefit from a software implementation error but rather from a flaw in the hardware specifications themselves. The result of our work is a three-steps methodology for formally specifying and verifying HSE mechanisms against a hardware architecture model. We believe each aspect is important.

First, the hardware architecture model can be used as a formal specification. The main benefit of a formal specification is to avoid any ambiguity such as the one we have found in [11]. One can read at Sect. 3.8.3.8, page 102 that "the OPEN bit must be reset before the LOCK bit is set". At the same page, in the description of the LOCK bit, one can also read that "when [LOCK] is set to 1 then [OPEN] is reset to 0". We had modeled the second statement as the behavior of the memory controller is not specified if the first statement is true[5] Minx86 as a formal specification does not suffer from the same flaw. Minx86 is not complete, as it focuses on SMM-related mechanisms. Therefore, it would require some effort to use it in another context, but a potential user of SpecCert would not have to start its x86 hardware model from scratch.

Secondly, a formal specification of a HSE mechanism will help software developers when the time comes to implement it. For instance, the Chap. 34, Volume 3C of [12] about SMM is about 30 pages long, it gives many details on how the SMM actually works, yet no section is actually dedicated to security. On the contrary, our HSE mechanism definition gathers six requirements on hardware configurations and two requirements on software executions to enforce a well-defined security property. Even if the proofs only apply to an abstract model, we believe it is a valuable improvement.

Lastly, the verification process of a HSE mechanism specification against a hardware architecture model may help to highlight hidden flaws in the hardware specifications assumptions. We take the example of the SMRAM cache poisoning attack [18,23], which has motivated the introduction of the SMRR. If an attacker can set the proper cache strategy (WB) for the SMRAM physical addresses, then the code inside the SMRAM is loaded into the cache as soon as the CPU in SMM is executing it. From this point forward —because the access control is enforced at the memory controller level— nothing prevents the attacker to tamper with it. The next time the CPU enters in SMM, it executes the code stored in the cache. With a SMRR-less version of Minx86, we were not able to conclude our HSE mechanism was sound: such a scenario draws attention of the SpecCert user who is forced to investigate.

From our point of view, the clear separation between the hardware model, the security properties and the HSE mechanisms to enforce those properties are

[5] If we had to actually implement the HSE mechanism, we would have to assume the first was the correct one.

the main advantage of our approach. This separation minimizes the required amount of effort to study a new use case against the same hardware model.

5 Related Works

Several formal models of x86 architectures have been defined. For instance, Greg Morrisett *et al.* have developed RockSalt [21], a sandboxing policy checker, upon such a model. Peter Sewell *et al.* have proposed a model for x86 multiprocessors [26] which aims at replacing informal Intel and AMD specifications. Andrew Kennedy *et al.* have developed an assembler in Coq [15] which allows a developer to verify the correctness of a specification for an assembly code. These three projects have modeled (a subset of) the x86 instruction set against an idealized hardware. Our approach is different: we model the instructions' side effects on a hardware architecture model as close as possible to its specifications.

Our work is inspired by the efforts by Gilles Barthe *et al.* to formally verify an idealized model of virtualization [1–3]. In this work, the authors have developed a model of a hypervisor and have verified that the latter correctly enforces several security properties among which the guest OSes isolation. From the SpecCert perspective, a hypervisor relies on HSE mechanisms which could be specified and verified using SpecCert and a more complete version of the MINX86 model.

To the best of our knowledge, the closest related research project is the work of Lie *et al.* They have used a model checker (Murφ) to model and verify the eXecute Only Memory (XOM) architecture [17]. The XOM architecture allows an application to run in a secure compartment wherein its data are protected against other applications and even a malicious operating system. The main difference with our approach is that the XOM security properties are enforced as-is by a secure microprocessor without the need for a software component to configure anything. On the contrary, we intend to specify ways to use sets of hardware functions to enforce security policies.

From our point of view, the main limitation of the research previously described, including SpecCert, is the gap between the model and the concrete machine. The recent efforts around the Proof Carrying Hardware (PCH) [8,19, 20], inspired by the Proof Carrying Code (PCC), is promising. The main idea behind PCH is to derive a model from a hardware device implementation written in a Hardware Description Language (HDL). One of our objective is to investigate the possibility to adapt the SpecCert formalism to the PCH models.

6 Conclusion

In this paper, we have focused on a class of security enforcement mechanism we called Hardware-based Security Enforcement (HSE). The contribution of this article is threefold. First, we have proposed a formalism to specify and verify HSE mechanisms against hardware architecture models. Then, we have defined a minimalist x86 model called MINX86. Finally, we have specified and verified the HSE mechanism dedicated to enforce the SMM code execution isolation against this model. Our model and proofs have been implemented in Coq[6]. The project is about 4 500 Lines of Code (LoC) including 190 definitions and 150 proofs (theorems and lemmas).

For now, our proofs are built against an abstract model of the hardware architecture. One of the future work we aim to address is improving the scope of MINX86 in order to provide to potential SpecCert users a more complete model to use for verifying and specifying their x86-based HSE mechanisms. Ultimately, we aim to extend these proofs to a physical hardware platform. Therefore, the equivalence between the model and the implementation has to be established. In this perspective, the Proof Carrying Hardware framework [7,8,19,20] is particularly interesting and we intend to investigate in this direction.

References

1. Barthe, G., Betarte, G., Campo, J.D., Luna, C.: Formally verifying isolation and availability in an idealized model of virtualization. In: Butler, M., Schulte, W. (eds.) FM 2011. LNCS, vol. 6664, pp. 231–245. Springer, Heidelberg (2011). doi:10.1007/978-3-642-21437-0_19
2. Barthe, G., Betarte, G., Campo, J.D., Luna, C.: Cache-leakage resilient OS isolation in an idealized model of virtualization. In: 2012 IEEE 25th Computer Security Foundations Symposium (CSF), pp. 186–197. IEEE (2012)
3. Barthe, G., Betarte, G., Campo, J.D., Luna, C., Pichardie, D.: System-level non-interference for constant-time cryptography. In: Proceedings of the 2014 ACM SIGSAC Conference on Computer and Communications Security, pp. 1267–1279. ACM (2014)
4. Basin, D., Jugé, V., Klaedtke, F., Zălinescu, E.: Enforceable security policies revisited. ACM Trans. Inf. Syst. Secur. (TISSEC) **16**(1), 3 (2013)
5. Kallenberg, C., Cornwell, S., Kovah, X., Butterworth, J.: Setup for failure: defeating secure boot. In: The Symposium on Security for Asia Network (SyScan) (April 2014)
6. Domas, C.: The memory sinkhole. In: BlackHat USA, July 2015
7. Drzevitzky, S.: Proof-carrying hardware: runtime formal verification for secure dynamic reconfiguration. In: 2010 International Conference on Field Programmable Logic and Applications (FPL), pp. 255–258. IEEE (2010)
8. Guo, X., Dutta, R.G., Mishra, P., Jin, Y.: Scalable SoC trust verification using integrated theorem proving and model checking. In: IEEE Symposium on Hardware Oriented Security and Trust, pp. 124–129 (2016)
9. Intel: CHIPSEC: Platform Security Assessment Framework. http://github.com/chipsec/chipsec
10. Intel: Desktop 4th Generation Intel Core Processor Family, Desktop Intel Pentium Processor Family, and Desktop Intel Celeron Processor Family
11. Intel: Intel 5100 Memory Controller Hub Chipset
12. Intel: Intel 64 and IA32 Architectures Software Developer Manual
13. Intel: Intel Trusted Execution Technology (Intel TXT), July 2015
14. Kallenberg, C., Wojtczuk, R.: Speed racer: exploiting an Intel flash protection race condition, 6 January 2015

[6] Our implementation is available here: https://github.com/lethom/speccert.

15. Kennedy, A., Benton, N., Jensen, J.B., Dagand, P.E.: Coq: the world's best macro assembler? In: Proceedings of the 15th Symposium on Principles and Practice of Declarative Programming, pp. 13–24. ACM (2013)
16. Letan, T., Hiet, G., Chifflier, P., Néron, P., Morin, B.: SpecCert: specifying and verifying hardware-based security enforcement. Technical report, CentraleSupélec; Agence Nationale de Sécurité des Systèmes d'Information (2016). https://hal.inria.fr/hal-01356690
17. Lie, D., Mitchell, J., Thekkath, C., Horowitz, M., et al.: Specifying and verifying hardware for tamper-resistant software. In: Proceedings of 2003 Symposium on Security and Privacy, 2003, pp. 166–177. IEEE (2003)
18. Duflot, L., Levillain, O., Morin, B., Grumelard, O.: Getting into the SMRAM: SMM reloaded CanSecWest (March 2009)
19. Love, E., Jin, Y., Makris, Y.: Proof-carrying hardware intellectual property: a pathway to trusted module acquisition. IEEE Trans. Inf. Forensics Secur. **7**(1), 25–40 (2012)
20. Makris, Y.: Trusted module acquisition through proof-carrying hardware intellectual property. Technical report (2015)
21. Morrisett, G., Tan, G., Tassarotti, J., Tristan, J.B., Gan, E.: Rocksalt: better, faster, stronger SFI for the x86. ACM SIGPLAN Not. **47**, 395–404 (2012). ACM
22. Wojtczuk, R., Rutkowska, J.: Attacking intel TXT via SINIT code execution hijacking. In: Black Hat DC Conference (February 2009)
23. Wojtczuk, R., Rutkowska, J.: Attacking SMM memory via intel CPU cache poisoning (March 2009)
24. Rutkowska, J., Wojtczuk, R.: Preventing and detecting Xen hypervisor subversions. In: Blackhat Briefings USA (2008)
25. Schneider, F.B.: Enforceable security policies. ACM Trans. Inf. Syst. Secur. (TISSEC) **3**(1), 30–50 (2000)
26. Sewell, P., Sarkar, S., Owens, S., Nardelli, F.Z., Myreen, M.O.: x86-tso: a rigorous and usable programmer's model for x86 multiprocessors. Commun. ACM **53**(7), 89–97 (2010)
27. Bulygin, Y., Loucaides, J., Furtak, A., Bazhaniuk, O., Matrosov, A.: Summary of Attacks Against BIOS and Secure Boot, def Con 22 (August 2014)

Automated Verification of Timed Security Protocols with Clock Drift

Li Li[1(✉)], Jun Sun[1], and Jin Song Dong[2]

[1] Singapore University of Technology and Design, Singapore, Singapore
li_li@sutd.edu.sg
[2] National University of Singapore, Singapore, Singapore

Abstract. Time is frequently used in security protocols to provide better security. For instance, critical credentials often have limited lifetime which improves the security against brute-force attacks. However, it is challenging to correctly use time in protocol design, due to the existence of clock drift in practice. In this work, we develop a systematic method to formally specify as well as automatically verify timed security protocols with clock drift. We first extend the previously proposed *timed applied* π*-calculus* as a formal specification language for timed protocols with clock drift. Then, we define its formal semantics based on *timed logic rules*, which facilitates efficient verification against various security properties. Clock drift is encoded as parameters in the rules. The verification result shows the constraints associated with clock drift that are required for the security of the protocol, e.g., the maximum drift should be less than some constant. We evaluate our method with multiple timed security protocols. We find a time-related security threat in the TESLA protocol, a complex time-related broadcast protocol for lossy channels, when the clocks used by different protocol participants do not share the same clock rate.

1 Introduction

Time is essential in cyber-security, e.g., message transmissions and user authentications are often required to be finished in a timely manner. In order to check the relevant timing requirements, *timestamps* are constructed from *clocks*, sent through networks and checked by participants in security protocols. For example, in order to deliver a message m timely, the sender first attaches its current clock reading t_s to m and sends them in a secure way. Then, when the receiver obtains t_s and m, it checks t_s against its own clock reading t_r with $t_r - t_s \leq p$ to ensure that m is received within a certain timing threshold p. In the above example, the untimed security (m is not tampered, replayed nor disclosed) and the timed security (m is delivered in time) are equally important. Given a timed protocol, existing literatures [12,16] focus on checking its security when the clocks of different protocol participants are fully synchronized. However, in practice,

J. Sun—The project is supported by the NRF Project IGDSi1305012 in SUTD.

J. Fitzgerald et al. (Eds.): FM 2016, LNCS 9995, pp. 513–530, 2016.
DOI: 10.1007/978-3-319-48989-6_31

timestamps are often generated and checked based on different local clocks without perfect synchronization, which could compromise the security proved based on the assumption of perfect clock synchronization. Hence, this work studies the security of timed protocols with the present of the clock drift.

Clock drift commonly exists in practice. For instance, in sensor networks, cheap sensors usually do not have enough resources to maintain accurate clock rate and precise clock reading. Hence, small clock drift should be expected and considered in their applications. Even though the local clocks can be synchronized at runtime over the network, various unavoidable factors, e.g., network delay, traffic congestion, can lead to a certain level of inaccuracy. Furthermore, when attackers are present in the network, they may attack the clock synchronization protocol [23]. In such a case, the local clocks under the attack may have large clock drift. As a result, when the security depends on the clock reading, the protocol should provide counter-measures for the clock drift.

Clock drift can cause insecurity of timed protocols because the protocol participants rely on local clocks in practice, whereas the security protocol is designed based on the global clock. For instance, in the above message transmission example, let t'_s and t'_r be the readings of the global clock when t_s and t_r are read from the local clocks respectively. The receiver deems the message as timely by checking $t_r - t_s \leq p$. However, the security property requires $t'_r - t'_s \leq p$ to ensure a timely message transmission. In order to capture the inconsistency between local clocks and the (fictional) global clock, we first extend *timed applied π-calculus* [16] to formally specify clock drift in protocol models. Then, we define the semantics of the local clocks in Sect. 4, which captures their relationship to the global clock. By using this semantics, we can answer the following two security questions. First, our work can check whether a protocol is secure with the presence of clock drift. More importantly, our work can find out how much clock drift can be tolerated in a timed security protocol. We extend SPA, a verification tool we developed in [15,16], with the new calculus and semantics for clock drift. In this work, we use a corrected version [12] of Wide Mouthed Frog [7] as a running example to illustrate our specification and verification method. We apply our method to a number of timed security protocols and successfully find a security threat in TESLA [21,22] in Sect. 5.2, a complex time-related broadcast protocol for lossy channels, when the clocks used by different protocol participants do not share the same clock rate.

2 Specification

In this section, we first introduce CWMF [12], a *corrected* version of Wide Mouthed Frog [7] protocol, as a running example. When the local clocks of the protocol participants in CWMF are assumed to be perfectly synchronized, CWMF can be verified as secure [12,14] The verification proves that a secret session key can be established among its participants within a certain time. However, it is unclear whether clock drift, which is unavoidable in practice, would compromise the security of CWMF. In the following, we first present CWMF in details and then demonstrate how *timed applied π-calculus*, extended with local clocks, can be used to model such protocols.

2.1 Corrected Wide Mouthed Frog

CWMF is designed to establish a timely fresh session key k from an initiator A to a responder B through a server S. In CWMF, whenever a message is received, the receiver checks the message freshness before accepting it. To be general, we use a parameter p_m to represent the maximum message lifetime. Additionally, we consider the minimal network delay as a parameter p_n. Since p_n is a timing parameter related to the network environment, it is not directly used in the protocol specification. Instead, it is a compulsory delay that applies to all of the network transmissions.

CWMF is a key exchange protocol that involves three participants: an initiator A, a responder B and a server S. By assumption, A and B have registered their secret long-term keys at the server respectively. The registered key of a user u is written as $key(u)$, which is used to encrypt all network communications between the user and the server. Whenever a message m is transmitted between a user u and the server S, the message m is encrypted by the symmetric encryption function enc_s written as $enc_s(m, key(u))$. CWMF then can be described as the following three steps.

(1) A generates a random session key k at its local time t_a
$A \rightarrow S \quad : \langle A, enc_s(\langle t_a, B, k, tag_1 \rangle, key(A)) \rangle$
(2) S receives the request from A at its local time t_s
S checks : $t_s - t_a \leq p_m$
$S \rightarrow B \quad : enc_s(\langle t_s, A, k, tag_2 \rangle, key(B))$
(3) B receives the message from S at its local time t_b
B checks : $t_b - t_s \leq p_m$
B accepts the session key k

First, A generates a fresh key k at its local time t_a and initiates the CWMF protocol with B by sending its name A and the request $\langle t_a, B, k, tag_1 \rangle$ encrypted by $key(A)$ to S. Second, after receiving the request from A at S's local time t_s, S ensures the message freshness by checking $t_s - t_a \leq p_m$. Then, S accepts A's request by forwarding the request $\langle t_s, A, k, tag_2 \rangle$ encrypted by $key(B)$ to B. It informs B that S receives a request from A at its local time t_s to communicate with B using the key k. tag_1 and tag_2 are two constants that are used to distinguish these two messages. CWMF uses them to prevent the reflection attack [18] in the original Wide Mouthed Frog protocol [7]. Third, B checks the message freshness again and accepts the request from A if the message is received in a timely fashion. All of the transmitted messages are encrypted under the users' long-term keys that are pre-registered at S.

2.2 Timed Applied π-calculus

Timed applied π-calculus works as a specification language for timed protocols. It is essentially the calculus proposed in [2,16] with the extensions of local clocks and clock drift. Table 1 presents its syntax with the extensions highlighted in the **bold** font.

Table 1. Syntax of timed applied π-calculus

Type	Expression	
Message (m)	$f(m_1, m_2, ..., m_n)$	(function)
	A, B, C	(name)
	n, k	(nonce)
	t, t_1, t_i, t_n	(timestamp)
	x, y, z	(variable)
Parameter (p)	p, p_1, p_j, p_m	(parameter)
Clock (c)	c, c_1, c_k, c_s	**(clock)**
Constraint (B)	$\mathcal{CS}(t_1, t_2, \ldots, t_n, p_1, p_2, \ldots, p_m)$	(timing constraint)
Configuration (L)	$\mathcal{CS}(p_1, p_2, \ldots, p_m)$	(parameter relation)
Process (P, Q)	0	(null process)
	$P \mid Q$	(parallel)
	$!P$	(replication)
	$\nu n.P$	(nonce generation)
	$\mu t.P$	(global clock reading)
	$\mu t : c.P$	**(local clock reading)**
	if $m_1 = m_2$ then P [else Q][a]	(untimed condition)
	if B then P [else Q]	(timed condition)
	wait μt until B then P	(global timing delay)
	wait $\mu t : c$ until B then P	**(local timing delay)**
	let $x = f(m_1, \ldots)$ then P	(function application)
	$in(x).P$	(channel input)
	$\overline{out}(m).P$	(channel output)
	check m in db as unique then P	(replay checking)
	$init(m)@t.P$	(initialization claim)
	$join(m)@t.P$	(participation claim)
	$accept(m)@t.P$	(acceptance claim)

[a]The expression with the brackets '[E]' means that E can be omitted.

In *timed applied π-calculus*, we compose *messages* using *functions*, *names*, *nonces*, *variables* and *timestamps*. Functions are generally defined as $f(m_1, m_2, \ldots, m_n) \Rightarrow m$ @ D, where f is the function name, $m_1, m_2, \ldots, m_n$ are the input messages, m is the output message and D is the consumed timing range. When m is exactly the same as $f(m_1, m_2, \ldots, m_n)$, we call the function a *constructor*; otherwise, it is a *destructor*. For simplicity, we add some syntactic sugar as follows: (1) when $D = [0, \infty)$ which is the largest timing range of functions, we omit '@ D' in the function definition; (2) for constructors, we omit '$\Rightarrow m$' in the definition. For instance, the symmetric encryption function is defined as $enc_s(m, k)$, and its decryption function is defined as $dec_s(enc_s(m, k), k) \Rightarrow m$. Names are globally shared strings. Nonces are fresh random numbers. Variables are memory locations for holding messages. Timestamps are clock readings. Additionally, *parameters* are configurable constants (e.g., the maximum message lifetime p_m) and persistent settings (e.g., the minimal network latency p_n).

In this work, we extend [16] with local clocks. That is, timestamps can be read from these local clocks rather than the shared global clock. For instance, in CWMF, the local clocks of A, S and B can be declared as c_a, c_s and c_b respectively. The constraint set $B = \mathcal{CS}(t_1, \ldots, t_n, p_1, \ldots, p_m)$ represents a set of linear constraints over timestamps and parameters, which can acts as protocol checking conditions and environment assumptions in the protocol. For instance, given the minimal network latency p_n, when a message sent at t is received at t', we have $t' - t \geq p_n$. Additionally, the configuration $L = \mathcal{CS}(p_1, \ldots, p_m)$ is a set of linear constraints over only parameters that should be satisfied globally. For example, the configuration $p_n > 0$ should be satisfied because the message transmission delay should stay positive.

As shown in Table 1, processes are defined as follows. '0' is a null process that does nothing. '$P|Q$' is a parallel composition of processes P and Q. The replication '$!P$' stands for an infinite parallel composition of process P, which captures an unbounded number of protocol sessions running in parallel. The nonce generation process '$\nu n.P$' represents that a fresh nonce n is generated and bound to process P. The global clock reading process '$\mu t.P$' means that a timestamp t is read from the global clock and bound to process P. The local clock reading process '$\mu t : c.P$' similarly means that a timestamp t is read from a local clock c and bound to process P. The checking condition *cond* in the 'if *cond* then P else Q' process has two forms: (1) the untimed condition $m_1 = m_2$ is a symbolic equivalence checking between two messages; (2) the timed condition $\mathcal{CS}(t_1, t_2, \ldots, t_n, p_1, p_2, \ldots, p_m)$ is a constraint over timestamps and parameters. When *cond* evaluates to true, process P is executed; otherwise, Q is executed. The global timing delay process 'wait μt until B then P' means that P is executed until the reading t from the global clock satisfies the timing condition B. Similarly, the local timing delay process 'wait $\mu t : c$ until B then P' means that P is executed until the reading t from a local clock c satisfies the timing condition B. The function application 'let $x = f(m_1, \ldots, m_n)$ then P' means if the function f is applicable to a sequence of messages $m_1, \ldots, m_n$, its result is bound to the variable x in process P. The channel input '$in(x).P$' means that a message, bound to the variable x, should be received before executing P. The channel output '$\overline{out}(m).P$' describes that the message m shall be sent out before executing process P. The uniqueness checking expression 'check m in *db* as unique then P' ensures that (1) the value of m does not exist in a database *db* before this expression, and (2) m is inserted into *db* after this expression. The uniqueness checking is particularly useful for preventing replay attacks in practice.

Additionally, the *init*, *join* and *accept* events are introduced to specify the security properties. They represent the initialization, participation and acceptance of the protocol participants respectively according to their roles, which are elaborated in Sect. 3.

Notations and Definitions. For simplicity, $tuple_n(m_1, m_2, \ldots, m_n)$ is simply written as $\langle m_1, m_2, \ldots, m_n \rangle$. A variable x is bound to a process P when x is constructed by the function application process 'let $x = f(m_1, \ldots)$ then P else Q' or the channel input process '$c(x).P$' as shown in Table 1. When a variable x appears in a process P while it is not bound to P, it is a free variable in P. A process is *closed* when it does not have any free variable. Notice that all of the processes considered in this work are closed. When x is a tuple in the function application process or the channel input process above, we simply write x as $\langle x_1, x_2, \dots, x_n \rangle$. When we only want to check that a variable x_i equals to a constant C, we can replace 'x_i' with '$=C$' in the above tuple.

Remarks. We do not need special syntax to specify private channels in *timed applied π-calculus*. Private channels can be constructed with public channels and unbreakable encryptions. For instance, in order to model a message m transmitted in a private channel, we first introduce a secret key k_s. Then, we can model a private channel as $\overline{out}(enc_s(m, k_s)).P | in(x).\text{let } m' = dec_s(x, k_s) \text{ then } Q$.

2.3 CWMF Model

In order to verify CWMF in a hostile environment, we make the following assumptions. (1) The adversary can ask any protocol participant to join the protocol, including A, S and B. (2) The adversary controls the protocol participation time, e.g., the initialization time of A in CWMF. (3) S provides its session key exchange service to all of its registered users. (4) The adversary can register as any user at the server, except for A and B. The precise attacker model employed in our work is discussed in Sect. 3. In CWMF, because we are interested in the protocol acceptance between legitimate users, we assume that B only accepts requests from A. Additionally, a public channel controlled by the adversary is used in CWMF for network communication.

Before the protocol starts, all of its participants need to register a secret long-term key at the server. We assume that A and B have already registered at the server using their names. Hence, the server can generate new keys for any other user (possibly personated by the adversary), which can be modeled as the process P_r below.

$$P_r \triangleq in(u).if\ u \neq A \wedge u \neq B\ then\ \overline{out}(key(u)).0$$

In CWMF, A takes a role of the initiator as specified by P_a below. It first starts the protocol by receiving a responder's name r from c, assuming that r is specified by the adversary. Then, A generates a session key k and reads t_a from its local clock c_a. Then, A emits an *init* event to indicate the protocol initialization with the arguments A, r, k at t_a. Finally, the message $\langle A, enc_s(\langle t_a, r, k, tag_1 \rangle, key(A)) \rangle$ is sent from A to S.

$$P_a \triangleq in(r).\nu k.\mu t_a : c_a.init(A, r, k)@t_a.\overline{out}(\langle A, enc_s(\langle t_a, r, k, tag_1 \rangle, key(A)) \rangle).0$$

As specified by the process P_s, after S receives a user's request as a tuple $\langle i, x \rangle$, it records its local time from c_s as t_s and decrypts x using $key(i)$. If the decryption is successful, it obtains the initialization time t_i, the responder's name r and the session key k. When the freshness checking $t_s - t_i \leq p_m$ is passed, S

then believes that it is participating in a protocol run at time t_s and engages the *join* event. Later, a new message encrypted by the responder's key, written as $enc_s(\langle t_s, i, k, tag_2\rangle, key(r))$, is sent to the responder over the public channel.

$$P_s \triangleq in(\langle i, x\rangle).\mu t_s : c_s.let\ \langle t_i, r, k, =tag_1\rangle = dec_s(x, key(i))\ then$$
$$if\ t_s - t_i \leq p_m\ then\ join(i, r, k)@t_s.\overline{out}(enc_s(\langle t_s, i, k, tag_2\rangle, key(r))).0$$

Additionally, as shown in the process P_b, when B receives the message from S, B records its local time as t_b and tries to decrypt request as a tuple of the server's processing time t_s, the initiator's id i and the session key k. If $i = A$ and the freshness checking $t_b - t_s \leq p_m$ is passed, B then believes that the request is sent from A within $2 * p_m$ and engages the accept event at time t_b.

$$P_b \triangleq c(x).\mu t_b : c_b.let\ \langle t_s, =A, k, =tag_2\rangle = dec_s(x, key(B))\ then$$
$$if\ t_b - t_s \leq p_m\ then\ check\ k\ in\ db\ as\ unique\ then\ accept(A, B, k)@t_b.0$$

Finally, we have a process $P_p \triangleq \overline{c}(A).\overline{c}(B).0$ that broadcasts the names A and B. The overall process $P \triangleq (!P_r)|(!P_a)|(!P_s)|(!P_b)|(!P_p)$ is a parallel composition of the infinite replications of the five processes described above.

3 Timed Security Properties

In this section, we define the timed security properties. Notice that the properties are defined based on the global clocks, whereas the participants in the protocols rely on local clocks in practice. In this work, we focus on the authentication properties, as they can be largely affected by clock drift. We first introduce the adversary model as follows.

Adversary Model. We assume that an active attacker exists in the network, whose capabilities are extended from the Dolev-Yao model [13]. The attacker can intercept all communications, compute new messages, generate new nonces and send the messages he obtained. Additionally, he can use all the publicly available functions, e.g., encryption, decryption, concatenation. He can also ask the genuine protocol participants to take part in the protocol at any time. Comparing our attack model with the Dolev-Yao model, reading timestamps from various clocks, attacking weak cryptographic functions and compromising legitimate protocol participants are allowed additionally. A formal definition of the adversary model is defined as follows.

Definition 1 ***Adversary Process.*** *The adversary is defined as an arbitrary* closed *timed applied π-calculus process K which does not emit the* init, join *and* accept *events.*

Timed Authentication. In a protocol, we often have an initiator who starts the protocol and a responder who accepts the protocol. For instance, in CWMF, A is the initiator and B is the responder. Additionally, other entities called partners, e.g., S in CWMF, can be involved during the protocol execution. In general, the protocol authentication aims at establishing common knowledge among the protocol participants when the protocol successfully ends. Specifically, for timed protocols, the common knowledge contains the information on the participants' time.

Since different participants take different roles in the protocol, we introduce the *init*, *accept* and *join* events for the initiator, the responder and the partners respectively. Whenever a protocol participant believes that it is participating in a protocol as a certain role, it engages the corresponding event with the protocol parameters and the correct time. For instance, in CWMF, A engages $init(A, r, k)@t_a$; S engages $join(i, r, k)@t_s$; and B engages $accept(i, B, k)@t_b$. We remark that t_a, t_s and t_b in above events should be the correct readings from the global clock, which could be different from the values used for constructing messages in the protocol.

Based on the *init*, *join* and *accept* events, the protocol authentication properties then can be formally specified as event correspondences. The timed non-injective authentication is satisfied if and only if for every acceptance of the protocol responder, the protocol initiator indeed initiates the protocol and the protocol partners indeed join in the protocol, agreeing on the protocol arguments and timing requirements. We formally define the non-injective timed authentication as follows.

Definition 2 ***Non-injective Timed Authentication.*** *The non-injective timed authentication, denoted as* $Q_n = accept \leftarrow\!\!\![\ B\ ]\!\!\!- init, join_1, \ldots, join_n$, *is satisfied by a closed process* P, *if and only if, given the adversary process* K, *for every occurrence of an accept event in* $P|K$, *the corresponding init event and join events in* Q_n *have occurred before in* $P|K$, *agreeing on the arguments and the timing constraints* B.

In CWMF, the non-injective timed authentication can be written as

$$Q_n = accept(i, r, k)@t_r \leftarrow\!\!\![\ t_s - t_i \leq \S p_m \\ \wedge t_r - t_s \leq \S p_m\ ]\!\!\!- init(i, r, k)@t_i, join(i, r, k)@t_s.$$

The injective timed authentication additionally requires an injective correspondence between the protocol initialization and acceptance comparing with the non-injective timed authentication. Hence, the injective timed authentication, which ensures the infeasibility of replay attack, is strictly stronger than the non-injective one.

Definition 3 ***Injective Timed Authentication.*** *The injective timed authentication, denoted as* $Q_i = accept \leftarrow\!\!\![\ B\ ]\!\!\!\rightarrow init, join_1, \ldots, join_n$, *is satisfied by a closed process* P, *if and only if, (1) the non-injective timed authentication* $Q_n = accept \leftarrow\!\!\![\ B\ ]\!\!\!- init, join_1, \ldots, join_n$, *is satisfied by* P; *(2) given the adversary process* K, *for every init event of* Q_i *occurred in* $P|K$, *at most one accept event can occur in* $P|K$, *agreeing on the arguments in the events and the constraints* B *in global time.*

For simplicity, given a non-injective authentication property $Q_n = accept \leftarrow\!\!\{ B \} \vdash H$ and its injective version $Q_i = accept \leftarrow\!\!\{ B \} \mapsto H$, we define two functions such that $inj(Q_n) = Q_i$ and $non\_inj(Q_i) = Q_n$. Hence, we can write injective timed authentication of CWMF as $Q_i = inj(Q_n)$.

4 Semantics of Clock Drift

In this section, we first briefly introduce the *timed logic rules* [16] which are used to capture the semantics of the *timed applied* π*-calculus*. We use CWMF to demonstrate how *timed logic rules* can be used to capture the semantics of *timed applied* π*-calculus*. Particularly, we capture the semantics of reading timestamps from local clocks based on two different ways of modeling clock drift. We use these two different semantics to show that our method can be adopted to handle different scenarios in practice. We have implemented these two different clock drift semantics in SPA [16].

Table 2. Syntax of Timed Logic Rules

Type	Expression	
Message (m)	$f(m_1, m_2, ..., m_n)$	(function)
	$a[], b[], c[], A[], B[], C[]$	(name)
	$[n], [k], [N], [K]$	(nonce)
	$\mathfrak{t}, \mathfrak{t}_1, \mathfrak{t}_i, \mathfrak{t}_n$	(timestamp)
	x, y, z, X, Y, Z	(variable)
Parameter (p)	$\S p$	(parameter)
Constraint (B)	$\mathcal{C}(\mathfrak{t}_1, \mathfrak{t}_2, \ldots, \mathfrak{t}_n, \S p_1, \S p_2, \ldots, \S p_m)$	(timing relation)
Configuration (L)	$\mathcal{C}(\S p_1, \S p_2, \ldots, \S p_m)$	(parameter config)
Event (e)	$init(\star[d], m, \mathfrak{t})$	(initialization)
	$join(\star[d], m, \mathfrak{t})$	(participation)
	$accept(\star[d], m, \mathfrak{t})$	(acceptance)
	$know(\star m, \mathfrak{t})$	(knowledge)
	$new(\star[n], l[])$	(generation)
	$unique(\star u, \star l[], m)$	(uniqueness)
Rule (R)	$[\ G\ ]\ e_1, \ldots, e_n \dashv\!\{ B \} \mapsto e$	(rule)

4.1 Timed Logic Rules

In [16], we proposed the *timed logic rules* to define the semantics of the *timed applied* π*-calculus* in terms of the adversary capabilities, so timed security protocols can be verified efficiently. In this work, we show how to use them to capture clock drift. When the semantics of calculus processes are represented by logic rules, we need additional notations to differentiate the data types of names, nonces, timestamps, variables and parameters as shown in Table 2.

(1) The syntax of variables and functions are unchanged. (2) Names are appended with a pair of square brackets from A to $A[]$. (3) Nonces are put inside of a pair of square brackets from n to $[n]$. (4) Timestamps are written with a blackboard bold font from t to $\mathbb{t}$. (5) Parameters are prefixed from p to $\S p$.

Generally, each timed logic rule specifies a capability of the adversary in the form of $[\, G \,]\; e_1, e_2, \ldots, e_n \dashv\!\!\{\, B \,\}\!\!\mapsto e$. G is a set of untimed guards, $\{e_1, e_2, \ldots, e_n\}$ is a set of premise events, B is a set of timing constraints and e is a conclusion event. It means that if the untimed guard condition G, the premise events $\{e_1, e_2, \ldots, e_n\}$ and the timing constraints B are satisfied, the conclusion event e is ready to occur. When G is empty, we simply omit '$[G]$' in the rule.

The events represent the things that can occur in the protocol. In this work, six types of events are essential to the timed protocols with clock drift. Similar to the *timed applied π-calculus*, we have event *init*, *join* and *accept* that signal the authentication claims made by the legitimate protocol participants. In particular, the *init*, *join* events appear in the premise part whereas the *accept* events appear in the conclusion part. We amend the events from $init(m)@t$, $join(m)@t$ and $accept(m)@t$ to $init([d], m, \mathbb{t})$, $join([d], m, \mathbb{t})$ and $accept([d], m, \mathbb{t})$ respectively. The additional nonce $[d]$ represents the session id, which is specifically introduced to check the authentication properties.

Additionally, $know(m, \mathbb{t})$ means that the adversary obtains message m at time $\mathbb{t}$. Because the adversary intercepts all communications over the public channel, for every network input $in(x)$ at time t, we add $know(x, \mathbb{t}')$ satisfying $\mathbb{t}' \leq \mathbb{t}$ to the rule premises, meaning that the adversary need to know x before time t so as to send it at t; for every network output $\overline{out}(m)$ at time t, we construct a rule that concludes $know(m, \mathbb{t}')$ and satisfies $\mathbb{t}' - \mathbb{t} \geq \S p_n$, representing m can be intercepted by the adversary after the network delay $\S p_n$. Furthermore, given a nonce generated in $\nu n.P$, we add $new([n], l[])$ to the rule premises, denoting the generation of nonce $[n]$ at the process location $l[]$ (we use unique labels to represent different locations in the process). Lastly, $unique(u, db[], m)$ means that the message u should have a unique value in a database $db[]$ (any constant can be a database name). Given the above unique event constructed in a process, m is an ordered tuple of messages that can be identified by $\langle u, db[] \rangle$, consisting of the network inputs, generated nonces and read timestamps in the chronological order until the process ends or its sub-process is an infinite replication process. Unique events and new events are constructed in the following two cases: (1) when 'check u in db as unique then P' is present in the process, $unique(u, db[], m)$ is added; (2) given '$\nu n.P$' in the process at the location l, $new(n, l[])$ and $unique(n, l[], m)$ are added. The location names are generated by a special function $loc()$, which returns a unique name to represent the current process location. The semantics of *timed applied π-calculus* is presented in the full paper version [1].

Since we assume that different nonces must have different values, every rule can have at most one *new* event for every single nonce. When two *new* events have the same nonce in a rule, we merge them into a single event. Similarly, we need to merge other events in the following scenarios: *know* events of the same message; *unique* events with the same unique value and database; *init*, *join* or *accept* events with the same session id. In general, each event is associated with a signature and premise events with the same signatures in a rule should be merged. As shown in Table 2, event signature can be constructed by concatenating its event name with a sequence of messages prefixed by '$\star$'. For instance, in the event $unique(\star u, \star l[], m)$, the unique value u and the location $l[]$ is prefixed by $\star$, so its signature is '$unique.u.l[]$', where '.' concatenates the strings.

To provide a better understanding of the timed logic rules, we show three examples without clock drift. Later, we compare them with those rules with clock drift.

Example 1. Given that the symmetric encryption function enc_s is public, the adversary can use it to encrypt messages. In order to use this function, the adversary first needs to know a message m and a key k. Then, the encryption function returns the encrypted message $enc_s(m, k)$. Hence, the encryption can be represented as the following rule.

$$know(m, \mathbb{t}_1), know(k, \mathbb{t}_2) \dashv\!\![\, \mathbb{t}_1 \leq \mathbb{t} \wedge \mathbb{t}_2 \leq \mathbb{t} \,]\!\!\mapsto know(enc_s(m, k), \mathbb{t}) \quad (1)$$

Notice that the timing constraints means that $enc_s(m, k)$ can only be known to the adversary after m and k are known, following the chronological order. □

Example 2. In CWMF, the server provides its key registration service to the public as P_s. This service can be captured as follows.

$$[\ u \neq A[] \wedge u \neq B[]\ ]\ know(u, \mathbb{t}_1) \dashv\!\![\, \mathbb{t} - \mathbb{t}_1 \geq \S p_n \,]\!\!\mapsto know(key(u), \mathbb{t})$$

It means that anyone can register at the server using any name except A and B. □

Example 3. In this example, we demonstrate the *timed logic rule* for P_b in CWMF, when B reads the timestamps from the global clock rather than its local clock. B receives a message $enc_s(\langle t_s, A, k, tag_2\rangle, key(B))$ from S, records its current time as t_b and claims acceptance if $t_b - t_s \leq p_m$. Since the adversary can start the protocol at anytime, we assume that t_b is specified by the adversary. Then, the *timed logic rule* of P_b is written as the following rule, where $m_b = \langle enc_s(\langle \mathbb{t}_s, A[], k, tag_2[]\rangle, key(B[])), \mathbb{t}_b\rangle$.

$$\begin{aligned} &unique(k, db[], m_b), new([n_b], l_b[]), unique([n_b], l_b[], m_b), \\ &\quad know(\mathbb{t}_b, \mathbb{t}_b), know(enc_s(\langle \mathbb{t}_s, A[], k, tag_2[]\rangle, key(B[])), \mathbb{t}_1) \\ &\qquad \dashv\!\![\, \mathbb{t}_1 \leq \mathbb{t}_b \wedge \mathbb{t}_b - \mathbb{t}_s \leq \S p_m \,]\!\!\mapsto accept([n_b], \langle A[], B[], k\rangle, \mathbb{t}_b) \end{aligned} \quad (2)$$

In Sect. 4.2, we will compare it with the rules explicitly modeling the clock drift. □

4.2 Semantics of Local Clocks

In this work, we additionally introduce the operation $\mu t : c$ that reads a timestamp t from a local clock c. This operation is applicable to the local clock reading process and the local timing delay process shown in Table 1. In order to capture the semantics of timestamps constructed with $\mu t : c$ in the calculus, we need to record two timestamps $\mathbb{t}$ and $\mathbb{t}_g$ from the local clock c and the global clock respectively. The semantics of regular operations in protocol execution, e.g., message constructions and guard conditions, is defined based on the local time $\mathbb{t}$ because they use the real values read from local clocks. However, the semantics of the security claims, i.e., *init*, *join* and *accept* events, should be defined based on the global time $\mathbb{t}_g$ to indicate the correct timing of event engagement. In this way, we can correctly specify and distinguish two different types of timestamps that are (1) used in the protocol execution and (2) captured by the security properties. Hence, the remaining task is to establish the relation between $\mathbb{t}$ and $\mathbb{t}_g$ based on the assumptions of the clock drift. In the following, we show two different ways of modeling clock drift. Notice that, when all of the timestamps are read from the global clock, the *timed logic rules* remain the same as those in [16]. For instance, the *timed logic rules* in Examples 1 and 2 remain the same, while the *timed logic rule* in Example 3 shall be updated to take clock drift into account. In this work, we consider two different scenarios of clock drift: (**VR**) different clocks have different clock rates but concern their maximum drift bounds; (**SR**) different clocks share the same clock rate but have different readings. The differences between VR and SR in the following *time logic rules* are highlighted in the red font.

Variable Clock Rate (VR). In VR, we assume that the local clock rate can vary during the protocol execution. That is, local clocks can run faster or slower than the global clock from time to time. Additionally, we assume that their maximum clock drift are bounded, resulting in the following two properties. First, the timestamps read from the same local clock should always be monotonic. For example, given a process $\mu t_1 : c.\mu t_2 : c.0$, we have $t_1 \leq t_2$. However, if t_1 and t_2 are read from two different local clocks, e.g., $\mu t_1 : c_1.\mu t_2 : c_2.0$, t_2 could be smaller than t_1. Second, the differences between a local clock and the global clock are always bounded by a maximum drift parameter associated with that local clock. For instance, given a timestamp t read from c at global time t', we have $|t - t'| \leq p_c$, where p_c is the maximum drift of c, satisfying $p_c > 0$. If VR is assumed, the *timed logic rule* of P_b can be written as the following rule, where $m'_b = \langle enc_s(\langle \mathbb{t}_s, A[], k, tag_2[]\rangle, key(B[])), \langle \mathbb{t}_b, \mathbb{t}'_b\rangle\rangle$.

$$\begin{aligned} & unique(k, db[], m'_b), new([n_b], l_b[]), unique([n_b], l_b[], m'_b), \\ & \quad know(\mathbb{t}_b, \mathbb{t}'_b), know(enc_s(\langle \mathbb{t}_s, A[], k, tag_2[]\rangle, key(B[])), \mathbb{t}_1) \\ & \qquad \dashv \mathbb{t}_1 \leq \mathbb{t}'_b \wedge \mathbb{t}_b - \mathbb{t}_s \leq \S p_m \wedge |\mathbb{t}'_b - \mathbb{t}_b| \leq \S p_b \vdash\!\!\!\to accept([n_b], \langle A[], B[], k\rangle, \mathbb{t}'_b) \end{aligned}$$

Shared Clock Rate (SR). When the local clocks share the same clock rate of the (correct) global clock, the differences of the readings from different clocks are always the same. In this case, we introduce a clock drift parameter d_c for each clock c. Whenever a timestamp t is read from c at the global time t', we have $t = t' + d_c$. Hence, in this case, given the two timestamps extracted from the same local clock, their difference reflects the exact duration of that time period.

For instance, the *timed logic rule* of P_b can be written the following rule, where d_b is the clock drift of c_b and m_b' is the same as above.

$$\begin{aligned}&unique(k, db[], m_b'), new([n_b], l_b[]), unique([n_b], l_b[], m_b'),\\&\quad know(\mathbb{t}_b, \mathbb{t}_b'), know(enc_s(\langle \mathbb{t}_s, A[], k, tag_2[]\rangle, key(B[])), \mathbb{t}_1)\\&\qquad \dashv\!\{\, \mathbb{t}_1 \leq \mathbb{t}_b' \wedge \mathbb{t}_b - \mathbb{t}_s \leq \S p_m \wedge \mathbb{t}_b - \mathbb{t}_b' = \S d_b \,\}\!\!\rightarrow accept([n_b], \langle A[], B[], k\rangle, \mathbb{t}_b')\end{aligned}$$

Comparing VR and SR. The difference between VR and SR can be illustrated with the calculation of the round-trip delay (RTD) in the Network Time Protocol (NTP). NTP is designed to synchronize the clocks between a client A and a server B. In NTP, A first reads its clock c_a as t_a and then sends an authenticated signal to B. Once B receives the signal, it reads its clock c_b as t_b. After B verifies the signal successfully, B reads its clock c_b as t_b' and replies another authenticated signal back to A. Once A receives the reply signal, it reads its clock c_a as t_a'. If the reply signal is correctly verified, A calculates the RTD as $\delta = (t_a' - t_a) - (t_b' - t_b)$. When SR is assumed, the calculation of δ is accurate even if clock drift exists. However, when VR is assumed, δ is *not* accurate because the distance of clock drift can vary during the protocol execution.

4.3 Verification Overview

After obtaining the initial *timed logic rules* from the *timed applied π-calculus* as shown above, the security properties then can be verified using the method proposed in [16]. We briefly introduce the method in the following and refer the readers to [16] for details.

In general, the verification method works by composing all of the existing timed logic rules into new rules, by unifying the conclusion of one rule with the premises of other rules. For instance, we can compose Rule (1) to Rule (2) as the following rule.

$$\begin{aligned}&unique(k, db[], m_b'), new([n_b], l_b[]), unique([n_b], l_b[], m_b'),\\&\quad know(\mathbb{t}_b, \mathbb{t}_b), know(\langle \mathbb{t}_s, A[], k, tag_2[]\rangle, \mathbb{t}_1), know(key(B[]), \mathbb{t}_2)\\&\qquad \dashv\!\{\, \mathbb{t}_1 \leq \mathbb{t}_b \wedge \mathbb{t}_2 \leq \mathbb{t}_b \wedge \mathbb{t}_b - \mathbb{t}_s \leq \S p_m \,\}\!\!\rightarrow accept([n_b], \langle A[], B[], k\rangle, \mathbb{t}_b)\end{aligned}$$

We repeatedly generate new rules until no new rule can be generated. Then, we use the set of all rules to check the authentication properties, ensuring that no violating rule exists and every authentication property is satisfied. When the above two criteria can be met, the result of the verification is a set of configurations (each configuration is a set of constraints over the parameters). We prove that the protocol is guaranteed to satisfy the security property if its parameters choose values from the configurations. Due to the limitation of space, we demonstrate the full verification process of CWMF in the full paper version [1]. Notice that the verification process is not guaranteed to terminate in general. However, it has been shown that it often terminates for practical protocols [5,14,15]. After obtaining the secure configurations, we need to additionally ensure that clock

Table 3. Experiment results

Protocol	$\sharp\mathcal{R}$	No clock drift		Shared clock rate		Variable clock rate	
		Result	Time	Result	Time	Result	Time
Corrected WMF [7,16,18]	80	Secure	47.51 ms	Threat	112.75 ms	Attack	150.09 ms
TESLA [21,22]	343	Secure	3.17 s	Threat	3.55 s	Threat	4.37 s
Auth Range [6,8]	53	Secure	38.58 ms	Secure	60.73 ms	Attack	46.47 ms
CCITT X.509 (1c) [3]	135	Secure	162.69 ms	Secure	231.86 ms	Secure	224.00 ms
CCITT X.509 (3) BAN [7]	198	Secure	791.00 ms	Secure	1058.05 ms	Secure	969.97 ms
NS PK Time [10,17,20]	173	Secure	170.00 ms	Threat	205.93 ms	Threat	353.20 ms

drift parameters are not constrained by other protocol parameters. If any clock drift parameter is constrained by other protocol parameters, we believe that the protocol has security **threat** under the clock drift as those constraints must be checked at runtime in the real application. For instance, given the network latency p_n and the maximum drift p_c for a local clock c, if $p_c < p_n$ is required for security but it cannot be satisfied in the real application scenario, the protocol is vulnerable.

5 Evaluations

Our method has been integrated into the tool named Security Protocol Analyzer (SPA). SPA relies on PPL [4] to check the satisfaction of timing constraints, i.e., to tell whether a set of timing constraints is empty or not. We use SPA to check multiple timed protocols as shown in Table 3. All the experiments are conducted using a Mac OS X 10.10.5 with 2.3 GHz Intel Core i5 and 16G 1333 MHz DDR3. In order to clearly demonstrate how clock drift can affect the security of protocols, all of the protocols evaluated in this section are correct under perfect synchronization. The evaluated protocols are *corrected* WMF [7,12], TESLA [21, 22], a distance bounding protocol [6,8], *corrected* CCITT [3,7,9]. and a timing commitment version [10,15] of Needham-Schroeder [17,20]. All of the protocols can be verified or falsified for an unbounded number of protocol sessions. SPA and the protocol models are available at [1]. Notice that the security (secure constraints over parameters) is proved based on the satisfaction of all of the queries, so we do not show the results for different queries separately in the table. Particularly, we have found a new clock drift related security threat in TESLA. In the following, we illustrate how SPA works with our running example first and then other protocols.

5.1 CWMF Protocol

Based on the specification of CWMF in Sect. 2.3, WMF is checked in three different scenarios of clock drift. Let d_a, d_s and d_b be the drift distances of c_a, c_s and c_b respectively.

- When all clocks are perfectly synchronized, in order to finish CWMF, SPA returns that the minimum network latency p_n should be smaller than the maximum message lifetime p_m.
- (SR) When the local clocks share the same clock rate, CWMF is correct if and only if the following constraints are met: (1) $0 \leq d_s - d_a$; (2) $0 \leq d_b - d_s$; (3) $d_s - d_a \leq p_m - p_n$; (4) $d_b - d_s \leq p_m - p_n$. Constraint (1) and (2) ensure that the injective authentication is finished within p_m. Constraint (3) and (4) are required to finish the protocol. Since d_a, d_s and d_b exist in the constraints, which might not be satisfied in practice, the verification result presents a security threat of CWMF.
- (VR) When different local clocks have different clock rates, the constraint returned by SPA is *false*. It means that SPA cannot find the right parameter values to make CWMF secure in the case of VR. Intuitively, the authentication property requires CWMF to be finished within $2 \times p_m$, whereas the protocol itself can only achieve the timing threshold $2 \times p_m + p_a + p_b$. In order to ensure $2 \times p_m + p_a + p_b \leq 2 \times p_m$, we have $p_a + p_b \leq 0$. Since p_a and p_b are positives, SPA cannot find any suitable constraint for these parameters.

5.2 TESLA Protocol

TESLA [21,22] is short for Timed, Efficient, Streaming, Loss-tolerant Authentication protocol. It can provide efficient authenticated broadcast over lossy channels. Generally, it consists of many resource constrained receivers and a relatively powerful sender.

Protocol Description. The security goal of TESLA is to transfer a set of messages $\{M_j \mid j \in [0 \dots n]\}$ from a sender S to a receiver R in an authenticated manner, i.e., every message M_j accepted by R is sent by S previously. Since R have limited computing power, S cannot adopt signature for authentication purpose because of the large computing overhead. As a result, S computes hash values for messages with hash keys and uses these keys for authentication. Specifically, S divides the message transmission time into several continuous intervals. Each interval has the same length of p_d ($p_d > 0$). Then, S sends the messages with their hash values in different time intervals and reveals the corresponding hash keys in later time intervals. For example, S sends $\langle M_j, mac(M_j, k_i)\rangle$ in the i-th time interval and reveals the key k_i in the next interval. Since only S knows k_i before k_i is revealed, when k_i is check to be a hash key from S, $\langle M_j, mac(M_j, k_i)\rangle$ should be sent from S. In order to check the authenticity of the hash keys, TESLA requires these keys to form a chain such that k_i can be computed by k_{i+1} with a one-way function. Hence, when S can authenticate the first key k_0 to R, R can use k_0 to authenticate newly received hash keys. Additionally, using this method, even if some hash key k_i is lost, once k_{i+x} ($x > 0$) is received by R, k_i can be computed from k_{i+x} for authentication. In order to provide sound security, S in TESLA does not send the hash keys directly. Instead, it sends the hash key generators $\{k'_i\}$ and uses the generators to compute the actual hash keys $\{k_i\}$.

Unlike WMF and many other protocols, TESLA does not assume perfect clock synchronization. It rather requires loose time synchronization between S and R, where R knows the upper-bound of the local clock drift δ between S and R. In order to obtain the upper-bound, TESLA adopts the following two-step protocol. Firstly, R reads its current time as t_r, generates a nonce (a random number) n and sends n to S. Secondly, S reads its current time as t_s, sign t_s and n with its private signing key sk_s and sends the signature back to R. When R receives the signature from S, R can be sure that δ has an upper-bound of $t_s - t_r$. Thereafter, when R receives a message from S at its local time t'_r, he can claim that the current time of S is upper-bounded by $t'_r + t_s - t_r$. Due to the limited space, the modeling details of TESLA are available in the full paper version [1].

Verification Results. When TESLA is checked with *SR* or no clock drift, it is verified as correct with the requirement $2 \times p_n < p_d$, i.e., the length of every interval p_d should be larger than twice of the minimal network latency p_n. To the best of our knowledge, this configuration requirement, justified in the following, has not be reported in any other literature before. According to the verification result from SPA, this protocol configuration requirement is necessary because of the over-approximation of S's clock at R's side in TESLA. When a payload is sent by S at t'_s and received by R at t'_r based on their local clocks respectively, the *clock synchronization* ensures that $t'_s < t_s^{bound} = t'_r + t_s - t_r$. Additionally, in order to receive and check the payload successfully, t'_s and t_s^{bound} should belong to the same interval. Hence, given an initial time t_0 and an interval index i, we have $t_0 + i \times p_d \leq t'_s < t'_r + t_s - t_r < t_0 + (i+1) \times p_d$, which implies that p_d should be larger than $(t'_r - t_r) - (t'_s - t_s)$. That is, $2 \times p_n < p_d$.

When TESLA is checked with *VR*, SPA automatically reports a new security requirement such that $p_r + p_s \leq p_n$, where p_r and p_s are the maximum clock drift of R and S respectively. This configuration requirement is necessary because the *clock synchronization* alone fails to guarantee the bounding $t'_s < t'_r + t_s - t_r$[1]. Hence, in order to prevent the adversary from using the published keys to construct legal payloads, the sum of the clock drift values from R and S should be smaller than the network latency. This new configuration largely limits the application of TESLA protocol when *VR* is assumed, which is also unreported in existing literatures.

6 Related Works and Conclusions

This work builds on our previous works [14,15]. In this work, we extend the *timed applied π-calculus* with local clocks and clock drift. In order to verify the protocols specified in *timed applied π-calculus*, we define its semantics based on the *timed logic rules* [14,15]. We introduce two clock drift scenarios based on whether the clock rate is shared or not. During the evaluation, we show that our framework is able to verify timed security protocols with clock drift

[1] $2 \times p_n < p_d$ in SR has been updated to $2 \times p_n < p_d + 2 \times (p_s + p_r)$ in VR.

automatically, which is unique comparing with other existing works. The analyzing framework closest to ours was proposed by Delzanno and Ganty [12] which applies $MSR(\mathcal{L})$ to specify unbounded crypto protocols by combining first order multiset rewriting rules and linear constraints. According to [12], the protocol specification is modified by explicitly encoding an additional timestamp, representing the initialization time, into some messages. Thus the attack can be found by comparing the original timestamps with the new one in the messages. However, it is unclear how to verify timed protocol in general using their approach. Our method can be applied to verify protocols without any protocol modification. Many tools [5,11,19] for verifying *untimed* security protocols are related.

In this work, we develop a systematic method to formally specify as well as automatically verify timed security protocols with clock drift. We have integrated our method into SPA and used it to analyze several timed protocols. In the experiments, we have found new security threats related to clock drift in TESLA. Since the problem of verifying security protocols is undecidable in general, we cannot guarantee the termination of our method. However, similar to existing works on verifying security protocols [5,14,15], it has been shown that it often terminates for practical protocols.

References

1. Full paper, SPA tool and experiment models. http://lilissun.github.io/r/drift.html
2. Abadi, M., Fournet, C.: Mobile values, new names, and secure communication. In: POPL, pp. 104–115 (2001)
3. Abadi, M., Needham, R.M.: Prudent engineering practice for cryptographic protocols. IEEE Trans. Softw. Eng. **22**(1), 6–15 (1996)
4. Bagnara, R., Ricci, E., Zaffanella, E., Hill, P.M.: Possibly not closed convex polyhedra and the parma polyhedra library. In: Hermenegildo, M.V., Puebla, G. (eds.) SAS 2002. LNCS, vol. 2477, pp. 213–229. Springer, Heidelberg (2002). doi:10.1007/3-540-45789-5_17
5. Blanchet, B.: An efficient cryptographic protocol verifier based on Prolog rules. In: CSFW, pp. 82–96. IEEE CS (2001)
6. Brands, S., Chaum, D.: Distance-Bounding Protocols. In: Helleseth, T. (ed.) EUROCRYPT 1993. LNCS, vol. 765, pp. 344–359. Springer, Heidelberg (1994). doi:10.1007/3-540-48285-7_30
7. Burrows, M., Abadi, M., Needham, R.M.: A logic of authentication. ACM Trans. Comput. Syst. **8**(1), 18–36 (1990)
8. Capkun, S., Hubaux, J.-P.: Secure positioning in wireless networks. IEEE J. Sel. Areas Commun. **24**(2), 221–232 (2006)
9. CCITT. The directory authentication framework - Version 7, 1987. Draft Recommendation X.509
10. Chothia, T., Smyth, B., Staite, C.: Automatically checking commitment protocols in proverif without false attacks. In: Focardi, R., Myers, A. (eds.) POST 2015. LNCS, vol. 9036, pp. 137–155. Springer, Heidelberg (2015). doi:10.1007/978-3-662-46666-7_8
11. Cremers, C.J.F.: The Scyther tool: verification, falsification, and analysis of security protocols. In: Gupta, A., Malik, S. (eds.) CAV 2008. LNCS, vol. 5123, pp. 414–418. Springer, Heidelberg (2008). doi:10.1007/978-3-540-70545-1_38

12. Delzanno, G., Ganty, P.: Automatic verification of time sensitive cryptographic protocols. In: Jensen, K., Podelski, A. (eds.) TACAS 2004. LNCS, vol. 2988, pp. 342–356. Springer, Heidelberg (2004). doi:10.1007/978-3-540-24730-2_27
13. Dolev, D., Yao, A.C.-C.: On the security of public key protocols. IEEE Trans. Inf. Theory **29**(2), 198–207 (1983)
14. Li, L., Sun, J., Liu, Y., Dong, J.S.: TAuth: verifying timed security protocols. In: Merz, S., Pang, J. (eds.) ICFEM 2014. LNCS, vol. 8829, pp. 300–315. Springer, Heidelberg (2014). doi:10.1007/978-3-319-11737-9_20
15. Li, L., Sun, J., Liu, Y., Dong, J.S.: Verifying parameterized timed security protocols. In: Bjørner, N., de Boer, F. (eds.) FM 2015. LNCS, vol. 9109, pp. 342–359. Springer, Heidelberg (2015). doi:10.1007/978-3-319-19249-9_22
16. Li, L., Sun, J., Liu, Y., Sun, M., Dong, J.S.: A formal specification and verification framework for timed security protocols. Technical report, Singapore University of Technology and Design (2016)
17. Lowe, G.: An attack on the Needham-Schroeder public-key authentication protocol. Inf. Proces. Lett. **56**, 131–133 (1995)
18. Lowe, G.: A family of attacks upon authentication protocols. Technical report, Department of Mathematics and Computer Science, University of Leicester (1997)
19. Meier, S., Schmidt, B., Cremers, C., Basin, D.: The TAMARIN prover for the symbolic analysis of security protocols. In: Sharygina, N., Veith, H. (eds.) CAV 2013. LNCS, vol. 8044, pp. 696–701. Springer, Heidelberg (2013). doi:10.1007/978-3-642-39799-8_48
20. Needham, R.M., Schroeder, M.D.: Using encryption for authentication in large networks of computers. Commun. ACM **21**(12), 993–999 (1978)
21. Perrig, A., Canetti, R., Song, D.X., Tygar, J.D.: Efficient and secure source authentication for multicast. In: NDSS (2001)
22. Perrig, A., Canetti, R., Tygar, J.D., Song, D.X.: Efficient authentication and signing of multicast streams over lossy channels. In: S&P, pp. 56–73 (2000)
23. Sun, K., Ning, P., Wang, C.: Secure and resilient clock synchronization in wireless sensor networks. IEEE J. Sel. Areas Commun. **24**(2), 395–408 (2006)

Dealing with Incompleteness in Automata-Based Model Checking

Claudio Menghi[1(✉)], Paola Spoletini[2], and Carlo Ghezzi[1]

[1] DEIB, Politecnico di Milano, Milano, Italy
{claudio.menghi,carlo.ghezzi}@polimi.it
[2] Kennesaw State University, Marietta, USA
pspoleti@kennesaw.edu

Abstract. A software specification is often the result of an iterative process that transforms an initial incomplete model through refinement decisions. A model is incomplete because the implementation of certain functionalities is postponed to a later development step or is delegated to third parties. An unspecified functionality may be later replaced by alternative solutions, which may be evaluated to analyze tradeoffs. Model checking has been proposed as a technique to verify that a model of the system under development is compliant with a formal specification of its requirements. However, most classical model checking approaches assume that a complete model of the system is given: they do not support incompleteness. A verification-driven design process would instead benefit from the ability to apply formal verification at any stage, hence also to incomplete models. After any change, it is desirable that only the portion affected by the change, called replacement, is analyzed. To achieve this goal, this paper extends the classical automata-based model checking procedure to deal with incompleteness. The proposed model checking approach is able not only to evaluate whether a property definitely holds, possibly holds or does not hold in an incomplete model but, when the satisfaction of the specification depends on the incomplete parts, to compute the constraints that must be satisfied by their future replacements. Constraints are properties on the unspecified components that, if satisfied by the replacement, guarantee the satisfaction of the original specification in the refined model. Each constraint is verified in isolation on the corresponding replacement.

1 Introduction

The development process of any complex system can be viewed as a sequence of decisions that make the system *evolve* from an initial, high-level model into a fully detailed and verified implementation. Typically, this process is performed by iteratively decomposing the model of the system into smaller functionalities. At each stage, the model may be deliberately incomplete, either because development of certain functionalities is postponed or because the implementation will be provided by a third party, as in the case of a component-based or a service-based system. In the case of a postponed functionality, an implementation is usually provided at some later stage of the development process, possibly after exploring alternative solutions to evaluate their tradeoffs. There are also

J. Fitzgerald et al. (Eds.): FM 2016, LNCS 9995, pp. 531–550, 2016.
DOI: 10.1007/978-3-319-48989-6_32

cases in which the postponed functionality may become available at run time, as in the case of dynamically adaptive systems.

The verification community developed several techniques to check if a model of the system under development satisfies its requirements. In particular, model checking [3,10,11] has matured to a stage where practical use is now often possible. *Model checking* exhaustively analyzes the behavior of the system's model to ensure that all its executions satisfy the properties of interest. These techniques return *yes* if the model of the system satisfies its requirements, *no* and a *counterexample* in the opposite case. Mainstream model checking techniques assume that the model of the system and the properties against which it should be verified are completely defined when the verification takes place. This assumption is not always valid during the software development since, as we discussed earlier, models are often incomplete.

To support continuous verification, we should be able to *verify incomplete models* against given properties. This would allow even initial, incomplete, and high-level descriptions of the system to be verified against given properties, supporting early error detection. This is exactly the motivation of our work, which extends traditional *automata-based model checking* to verify if a model of the system $\mathcal{M}$ satisfies its properties, even when $\mathcal{M}$ is incomplete. The technique we develop assumes that $\mathcal{M}$ can contain one or more unspecified states, called *black box states*, that represent unspecified functionalities. To describe black box states, we introduce *Incomplete Büchi Automata* (IBAs), which extend the well known Büchi automata (BAs) and support the designer in the iterative, top-down refinement of a *sequential* system. Black box states can be (recursively) refined into other (I)BAs. Due to the presence of black box states, the model checking procedure is modified to produce three values: *yes* if the model of the system definitely satisfies its properties, *no* plus a counterexample if it does not, or *unknown* when the property is possibly satisfied, i.e., its satisfaction depends on the future refinement of the black box states. In this last case, a *constraint* per each black-box is synthesized, i.e., a property that must eventually be satisfied by the automata (replacement) that will replace the black box state in the refinement process. If, once refined, the replacements satisfy the synthesized constraints, then $\mathcal{M}$ fulfills its properties.

The paper is organized as follows. Section 2 introduces IBAs. Section 3 describes the advantages of using this new formalism on a small example. Section 4 shows how the classical verification procedure of BAs is modified to manage incompleteness in the model of the system. Section 5 describes how the constraint for the unspecified components is computed and used to verify the replacement of the corresponding black box state. Section 6 provides an experimental assessment of scalability of the approach. Section 7 presents related work and discusses its relation with our approach. Finally, Sect. 8 concludes the paper.

2 Modeling Formalisms

This section defines an extension of Büchi Automata [6] (BAs), called Incomplete Büchi Automata (IBAs), which support incomplete specifications, i.e., they contain some parts left as black boxes that will be later defined. It also describes how IBAs are refined by replacing the unspecified components.

BAs are widely used models of computation that describe systems through a finite set of states and transitions. *States* are snapshots of the system configurations and *transitions* describe how the state of the system changes over time. They are labeled with *atomic propositions*, i.e., statements that are true when the transitions are performed. IBAs extend BAs by partitioning states into *regular* and *black box*. A black box state, in the following often abbreviated as (black) box, is a placeholder for a functionality that is currently left unspecified and will be later refined by another automaton.

Definition 1. *Given a set of propositions AP, an* incomplete Büchi automaton *$\mathcal{M}$ is a tuple $\langle \Sigma, R, B, Q, \Delta, Q^0, F\rangle$, where (a) $\Sigma = 2^{AP}$ is a finite alphabet; (b) Q is a finite set of states, partitioned into R (the set of* regular *states) and B (the set of* black box *states), such that $Q = B \cup R$ and $B \cap R = \emptyset$; (c) $\Delta \subseteq Q \times \Sigma \times Q$ is a transition relation; (d) $Q^0 \subseteq Q$ is a set of initial states; (e) $F \subseteq Q$ is a set of accepting states.*

Graphically, boxes are filled with black, initial states are marked by an incoming arrow, and accepting states are double circled.

As BAs, IBAs use their accepting states to recognize infinite words (also called *ω-words*), as formally defined in the following. A run of an IBA is defined as follows:

Definition 2. *Given an IBA defined over AP, a set of atomic propositions AP', such that $AP \subseteq AP'$, and the alphabet $\Sigma^\omega = 2^{AP'}$, a* run *$\rho : \{0, 1, 2, \ldots\} \rightarrow Q$ over $v \in \Sigma^\omega$ is defined as follows: (a) $\rho(0) \in Q^0$; (b) for all $i \geq 0$, $(\rho(i), v_i, \rho(i+1)) \in \Delta \vee ((\rho(i) \in B) \wedge (\rho(i) = \rho(i+1)))$.*

Informally, a character v_i of the word v can be recognized by a transition of the IBA, changing the state of the automaton from $\rho(i)$ to $\rho(i+1)$, or can be recognized by a transition of the IBA that will replace the box $\rho(i) \in B$. In the latter case, the state $\rho(i+1)$ corresponds to $\rho(i)$, since the corresponding transition is fired inside the automaton that will replace $\rho(i)$. Note that characters in $AP' \setminus AP$, since they are not part of the already specified alphabet of the IBA, need to be recognized inside boxes.

Let $inf(\rho)$ be the states that appear infinitely often in the run ρ. A run ρ of an IBA $\mathcal{M}$ is *(a) definitely accepting* iff $(inf(\rho) \cap F \neq \emptyset) \wedge (\forall i \geq 0, \rho(i) \in R)$, i.e., some accepting states appear infinitely often in ρ and all of its states are regular; *(b) possibly accepting* iff $(inf(\rho) \cap F \neq \emptyset) \wedge (\exists i \geq 0 \mid \rho(i) \in B)$, i.e., some accepting states appear infinitely often in ρ and at least one of its states is a box; *(c) not accepting* otherwise.

An IBA $\mathcal{M}$ *definitely accepts* a word v iff there exists a definitely accepting run for v. Definitely accepted words describe behaviors the system is going to exhibit. $\mathcal{M}$ *possibly accepts* v iff it does not definitely accept v and there exists a possibly accepting run for v. Possibly accepted words describe possible behaviors. Finally, $\mathcal{M}$ *does not accept* v iff it does not contain any accepting or possibly accepting run for v. A word is not accepted if it is neither a definitely accepted nor a possibly accepted behavior. The language $\mathcal{L}(\mathcal{M}) \in \Sigma^\omega$ ($\mathcal{L}_p(\mathcal{M}) \in \Sigma^\omega$) of $\mathcal{M}$, consists of all the words definitely accepted (possibly accepted) by $\mathcal{M}$. $\mathcal{L}(\mathcal{M})$ can be defined by considering the BA $\mathcal{M}_c$, called *completion*, obtained from $\mathcal{M}$ by removing its boxes and their incoming and outgoing transitions.

The refinement relation $\preceq$ allows the iterative elaboration of the model of the system by replacing boxes with other IBAs, called *replacements.* The idea behind the refinement relation is that every behavior of $\mathcal{M}$ *must be preserved* in its refinement $\mathcal{N}$, and every behavior of $\mathcal{N}$ must correspond to a behavior of $\mathcal{M}$. The final BA is obtained by substituting all the boxes with the corresponding replacements. A BA $\mathcal{N}$ is an *implementation* of an IBA $\mathcal{M}$ if and only if $\mathcal{M} \preceq \mathcal{N}$. The formal definition of refinement, further definitions, lemmas and theorems together with all the proofs of theorems and lemmas that support this work can be found in [25].

The refinement relation is both reflexive and transitive, and preserves the language containment, i.e., a possibly accepted word of $\mathcal{M}$ can be definitely accepted, possibly accepted or not accepted in the refinement $\mathcal{N}$, but every definitely accepted and not accepted word remains definitely accepted or not accepted in $\mathcal{N}$.

Consider an IBA $\mathcal{M}$. A refinement step consists of replacing a box with an (I)BA. Intuitively, a replacement defines an automaton $\mathcal{T}$ that refines the box b and the incoming Δ^{inR} and outgoing transitions Δ^{outR} which describe how $\mathcal{T}$ is connected with $\mathcal{M}$. Formally, it is defined as follows:

Definition 3. *Given an IBA* $\mathcal{M} = \langle \Sigma_\mathcal{M}, R_\mathcal{M}, B_\mathcal{M}, Q_\mathcal{M}, \Delta_\mathcal{M}, Q^0_\mathcal{M}, F_\mathcal{M} \rangle$, *a replacement* $\mathcal{R}$ *of a box* $b \in B_\mathcal{M}$ *is a triple* $\langle \mathcal{T}, \Delta^{inR}, \Delta^{outR} \rangle$. $\mathcal{T} = \langle \Sigma_\mathcal{T}, R_\mathcal{T}, B_\mathcal{T}, Q_\mathcal{T}, \Delta_\mathcal{T}, Q^0_\mathcal{T}, F_\mathcal{T} \rangle$ *is an IBA.* $\Delta^{inR} \subseteq \{(q', a, q) \mid (q', a, b) \in \Delta_\mathcal{M}$ *and* $q \in Q_\mathcal{T}\}$ *and* $\Delta^{outR} \subseteq \{(q, a, q') \mid (b, a, q') \in \Delta_\mathcal{M}$ *and* $q \in Q_\mathcal{T}\}$ *are its incoming and outgoing transitions, respectively.* $\mathcal{R}$ *must satisfy the following:*

1. *if* $b \notin Q^0_\mathcal{M}$ *then* $Q^0_\mathcal{T} = \emptyset$;
2. *if* $b \notin F_\mathcal{M}$ *then* $F_\mathcal{T} = \emptyset$;
3. *if* $(q', a, b) \in \Delta_\mathcal{M}$ *then, there exists* $(q', a, q) \in \Delta^{inR}$ *such that* $q \in Q_\mathcal{T}$;
4. *if* $(b, a, q') \in \Delta_\mathcal{M}$ *then, there exists* $(q, a, q') \in \Delta^{outR}$ *such that* $q \in Q_\mathcal{M}$;
5. *if* $(b, a, b) \in \Delta_\mathcal{M}$ *then, there exists* $(q', a, q) \in \Delta_\mathcal{T}$.

Condition 1 (2) forces the replacement of a non-initial (non-accepting) box to not contain initial (accepting) states. Condition 3 (4) forces each incoming (outgoing) transition of b to be associated with at least an incoming (outgoing) transition of the replacement. Finally, Condition 5 states that if there exist a self-loop over the box b labeled with a, there exist at least a transition labeled with a in the replacement $\mathcal{R}$. Note that this transition could be not reachable in the replacement.

Additional definitions, theorems and proofs can be found in [25].

3 Motivating Example

To describe how IBAs support iterative refinement, we consider a simple system in charge of sending messages, described in [2]. An initial, high level and incomplete model of the system $\mathcal{M}$ is shown in Fig. 1. When the system starts, it moves from q_1 to $send_1$. The state $send_1$ represents a function performing the first attempt to send the message. If the attempt succeeds, the success state q_3 is reached. Otherwise, the function $send_2$, which performs a second attempt, is activated. If the attempt succeeds, the success state q_3 is entered, otherwise the system enters the abort state q_2.

The model $\mathcal{M}$ is defined over the alphabet $\Sigma_{\mathcal{M}}$ $=\{start,\ ok,\ fail,\ success,\ abort\}$. The *ω-word* v $=\{start\}.\{ok\}.\{success\}^\omega$ corresponds to two runs, ρ_1 and ρ_2. ρ_1 is a possibly accepting run such that $\rho_1(0) = q_1$, $\rho_1(1) = send_1$, and $\forall i \geq 2, \rho_1(i) = q_3$. ρ_2 is a not accepting run such that $\rho_2(0) = q_1$ and $\forall i \geq 1, \rho_2(i) = send_1$. Since there exists a possibly accepting run and no definitely accepting runs are present, $\mathcal{M}$ possibly accepts v. The word v $=\{start\}.\{success\}^\omega$ is instead not accepted since the only run associated with v is $\rho_3(0) = q_1$ and $\forall i \geq 1, \rho_3(i) = send_1$ which is neither definitely accepting nor possibly accepting. The language $\mathcal{L}(\mathcal{M})$ of behaviors associated with $\mathcal{M}$ is empty since there are no words accepted by $\mathcal{M}_c$. $\mathcal{M}_c$ is obtained by removing $send_1$ and $send_2$ and their incoming and outgoing transitions.

Figure 2 presents a BA $\mathcal{N}$ which is a refinement of the IBA $\mathcal{M}$. The boxes $send_1$ and $send_2$ are replaced with two instances of the same functionality $\mathcal{R}$, depicted inside two dashed-dotted frames. $\mathcal{R}$ *sends* a message and *waits* for an answer. If a *timeout* occurs, the sending procedure fails. If an *acknowledgement* is received, the procedure *succeeds* or *fails* depending on the type of

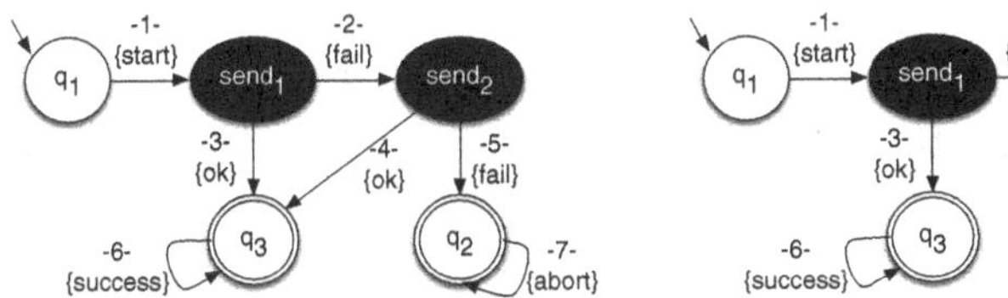

Fig. 1. The model $\mathcal{M}$.

Fig. 3. A refinement $\mathcal{N}'$ of $\mathcal{M}$.

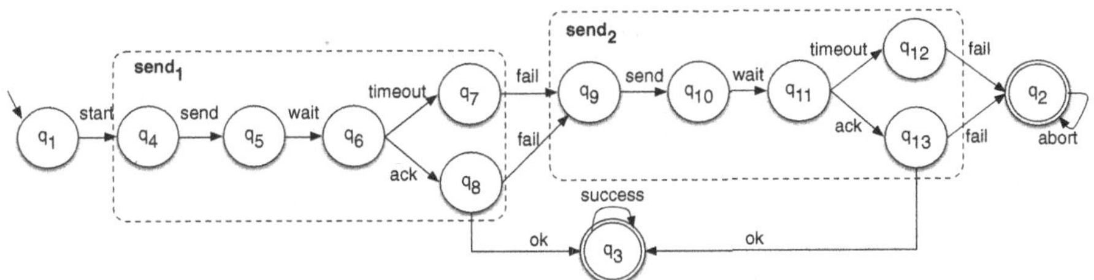

Fig. 2. A refinement $\mathcal{N}$ of $\mathcal{M}$.

acknowledgement. When the sending performed by $send_1$ fails, another attempt is performed by $send_2$, whose failure leads entering state q_2.

Figure 3 shows a hypothetical alternative refinement, which will be used later to explain our approach, where box $send_2$ is replaced by a component that always fails.

4 Automata-Based Checking

Given a model $\mathcal{M}$ and a property ϕ, model checking is used to verify whether $\mathcal{M}$ satisfies ϕ. When incomplete models are considered, the model checking algorithm may return three possible values depending on whether the property is *definitely satisfied* (T), *possibly satisfied* (?) or *not satisfied* (F).

The inductive (three-valued) semantic function $\|\mathcal{M}^{\phi}\|$ associates to $\mathcal{M}$ and ϕ one of the true values true (T), false (F) and unknown (?)

Definition 4. *Given an IBA $\mathcal{M}$ and an LTL formula ϕ:*

1. $\|\mathcal{M}^{\phi}\| = T \Leftrightarrow (\forall v \in (\mathcal{L}^{\omega}(\mathcal{M}) \cup \mathcal{L}^{\omega}_{p}(\mathcal{M})),\ v \models \phi)$;
2. $\|\mathcal{M}^{\phi}\| = F \Leftrightarrow (\exists v \in \mathcal{L}^{\omega}(\mathcal{M}) \mid v \not\models \phi)$;
3. $\|\mathcal{M}^{\phi}\| = ? \Leftrightarrow ((\forall v \in \mathcal{L}^{\omega}(\mathcal{M}),\ v \models \phi) \wedge (\exists u \in \mathcal{L}^{\omega}_{p}(\mathcal{M}) \mid u \not\models \phi))$.

Case 1 specifies that ϕ is true in $\mathcal{M}$ iff every word v that is in the language definitely or possibly accepted by $\mathcal{M}$ satisfies ϕ. Case 2 specifies that ϕ is false in $\mathcal{M}$ iff a word v that is in the language definitely accepted by the IBA exists and v does not satisfy ϕ. Case 3 specifies that ϕ is possibly satisfied in $\mathcal{M}$ iff there exists a word u that is in the language possibly accepted by the IBA that does not satisfy ϕ and all the words v in the language definitely accepted by $\mathcal{M}$ satisfy ϕ. For example, the property $\phi = G(send \rightarrow F(success))$ is possibly satisfied by the model described in Fig. 1 since there exists a word $\{start\}.\{send\}.\{fail\}.\{fail\}.\{abort\}^{\omega}$ in the possibly accepted language which does not satisfy ϕ and there are no words in the definitely accepted language. It is possible to specify the satisfaction of an LTL formula ϕ with respect to $\mathcal{M}$ using the BA $\mathcal{A}_{\phi}$ equivalent to ϕ.

Definition 5. *Given an IBA $\mathcal{M}$ and a BA $\mathcal{A}_{\phi}$,*

1. $\|\mathcal{M}^{\mathcal{A}_{\phi}}\| = T \Leftrightarrow (\mathcal{L}^{\omega}(\mathcal{M}) \cup \mathcal{L}^{\omega}_{p}(\mathcal{M}) \subseteq \mathcal{L}(\mathcal{A}_{\phi}))$;
2. $\|\mathcal{M}^{\mathcal{A}_{\phi}}\| = F \Leftrightarrow (\mathcal{L}^{\omega}(\mathcal{M}) \not\subseteq \mathcal{L}^{\omega}(\mathcal{A}_{\phi}))$;
3. $\|\mathcal{M}^{\mathcal{A}_{\phi}}\| = ? \Leftrightarrow ((\mathcal{L}^{\omega}(\mathcal{M}) \subseteq \mathcal{L}^{\omega}(\mathcal{A}_{\phi})) \wedge (\mathcal{L}^{\omega}_{p}(\mathcal{M}) \not\subseteq \mathcal{L}^{\omega}(\mathcal{A}_{\phi})))$.

Based on Definition 5 the automata-based model checking procedure is composed by the following six steps.

(1) *Create the automaton $\mathcal{A}_{\neg\phi}$*: as in the classical approach, first we build the BA that contains the set of behaviors forbidden by property ϕ. The complexity of this step is $\mathcal{O}(2^{(|\neg\phi|)})$. The BA corresponding to $\neg\phi$ is presented in Fig. 4.

(2) *Extract the completion automaton* $\mathcal{M}_c$ which contains the definitely accepting behaviors of $\mathcal{M}$. Computing $\mathcal{M}_c$ has in the worst case complexity $\mathcal{O}(|Q_\mathcal{M}|+|\Delta_\mathcal{M}|)$ since it is sufficient to visit all the states of the automaton, and, for each box s, remove its incoming and outgoing transitions and the state s itself. In the example, the BA $\mathcal{M}_c$, associated with $\mathcal{M}$ contains the states q_1, q_2 and q_3 and the transitions 6 and 7.

(3) *Build the intersection automaton* $\mathcal{I}_c = \mathcal{M}_c \cap \mathcal{A}_{\neg\phi}$: $\mathcal{I}_c$ contains in the worst case $3 \cdot |R_\mathcal{M}| \cdot |Q_{\mathcal{A}_{\neg\phi}}|$ states and describes the behaviors of $\mathcal{M}_c$ that violate the property. The intersection between $\mathcal{M}_c$ associated with the model $\mathcal{M}$ described in Fig. 1 and the automaton $\mathcal{A}_{\neg\phi}$ described in Fig. 4 contains all the behaviors of the sending message system that violate the property.

(4) *Check the emptiness of the intersection automaton* $\mathcal{I}_c$: if $\mathcal{I}_c$ is not empty, the condition $\mathcal{L}(\mathcal{M}) \cap \mathcal{L}(\mathcal{A}_{\neg\phi}) \neq \emptyset$ holds, i.e., the property is not satisfied and every infinite word in the intersection automaton is a counterexample. If, instead, $\mathcal{I}_c$ is empty, $\mathcal{M}$ possibly satisfies or definitely satisfies ϕ depending on the results of the next steps of the algorithm. The intersection automaton $\mathcal{I}_c$ of the motivating example is empty. Indeed, both q_2 and q_3, accepting states of $\mathcal{M}_c$, are never reachable from q_1. Thus, $\mathcal{M}$ definitely satisfies or possibly satisfies ϕ depending on the next steps of the algorithm.

(5) *Compute the intersection* $\mathcal{I} = \mathcal{M} \cap \mathcal{A}_{\neg\phi}$ *of the incomplete model* $\mathcal{M}$ and the automaton $\mathcal{A}_{\neg\phi}$ associated with the property ϕ: to check whether $\mathcal{M}$ definitely satisfies or possibly satisfies ϕ, it is necessary to verify whether $(\mathcal{L}(\mathcal{M}) \cup \mathcal{L}_p(\mathcal{M})) \cap \mathcal{L}(\mathcal{A}_{\neg\phi}) = \emptyset$. We propose a new algorithm to compute $\mathcal{I} = \mathcal{M} \cap \mathcal{A}_{\neg\phi}$ when $\mathcal{M}$ is incomplete. The intersection automaton $\mathcal{I} = \mathcal{M} \cap \mathcal{A}_{\neg\phi}$ between an IBA $\mathcal{M}$ and a BA $\mathcal{A}_{\neg\phi}$ is a BA $\langle \Sigma_\mathcal{I}, Q_\mathcal{I}, \Delta_\mathcal{I}, Q^0_\mathcal{I}, F_\mathcal{I} \rangle$ defined as follows:
   - $\Sigma_\mathcal{I} = \Sigma_\mathcal{M} \cup \Sigma_{\mathcal{A}_{\neg\phi}}$ is the alphabet of $\mathcal{I}$;
   - $Q_\mathcal{I} = ((R_\mathcal{M} \times R_{\mathcal{A}_{\neg\phi}}) \cup (B_\mathcal{M} \times R_{\mathcal{A}_{\neg\phi}})) \times \{0,\ 1,\ 2\}$ is the set of states;
   - $\Delta_\mathcal{I} = \Delta^c_\mathcal{I} \cup \Delta^p_\mathcal{I}$. $\Delta^c_\mathcal{I}$ is the set of transitions $(\langle q_i, q'_j, x\rangle, a, \langle q_m, q'_n, y\rangle)$ where $(q_i, a, q_m) \in \Delta_\mathcal{M}$ and $(q'_j, a, q'_n) \in \Delta_{\mathcal{A}_{\neg\phi}}$. $\Delta^p_\mathcal{I}$ corresponds to the set of transitions $(\langle q_i, q'_j, x\rangle, a, \langle q_m, q'_n, y\rangle)$ where $q_i = q_m$ and $q_i \in B_\mathcal{M}$ and $(q'_j, a, q'_n) \in \Delta_{\mathcal{A}_{\neg\phi}}$. Moreover, each transition in $\Delta_\mathcal{I}$ must satisfy the following conditions:
     - if $x = 0$ and $q_m \in F_\mathcal{M}$, then $y = 1$.
     - if $x = 1$ and $q'_n \in F_{\mathcal{A}_{\neg\phi}}$, then $y = 2$.
     - if $x = 2$ then $y = 0$.
     - otherwise, $y = x$;
   - $Q^0_\mathcal{I} = Q^0_\mathcal{M} \times Q^0_{\mathcal{A}_{\neg\phi}} \times \{0\}$ is the set of initial states;
   - $F_\mathcal{I} = F_\mathcal{M} \times F_{\mathcal{A}_{\neg\phi}} \times \{2\}$ is the set of accepting states.

   The intersection $\mathcal{I}$ between the model $\mathcal{M}$ depicted in Fig. 1 and the BA $\mathcal{A}_{\neg\phi}$ of Fig. 4 that corresponds to the negation of the property is the BA described in Fig. 5. The set of states $Q_\mathcal{I}$ is composed by states obtained by combining states of the automaton associated with the negation of the property $\mathcal{A}_{\neg\phi}$ with regular states and boxes of the model $\mathcal{M}$. We define $M_\mathcal{I} = B_\mathcal{M} \times R_{\mathcal{A}_{\neg\phi}} \times \{0,\ 1,\ 2\}$ as the set of *mixed* states (indicated in Fig. 5 with a stipple border). The portion of the state space that contains mixed states associated with the states of the model $send_1$ and $send_2$ are surrounded by a dashed-dotted frame. $PR_{\mathcal{I}} = R_{\mathcal{M}} \times R_{\mathcal{A}_{\neg\phi}} \times \{0, 1, 2\}$ is the set of *purely regular* states. For example, state ① is obtained by combining states q_1 of $\mathcal{M}$ and p_1 of $\mathcal{A}_{\neg\phi}$. This state is initial and purely regular since both q_1 and p_1 are initial and regular. State ② is mixed since it is obtained by combining the box $send_1$ of $\mathcal{M}$ and the state p_1 of $\mathcal{A}_{\neg\phi}$. As for classical intersection of BAs [11], labels 0, 1 and 2 indicate that no accepting state is entered, at least one accepting state of $\mathcal{M}$ is entered, and at least one accepting state of $\mathcal{M}$ and one accepting state of $\mathcal{A}_{\neg\phi}$ are entered, respectively.

The transitions in $\Delta^c_{\mathcal{I}}$ are obtained by the synchronous execution of transitions of $\mathcal{M}$ and $\mathcal{A}_{\neg\phi}$. For example, the transition from ② to ③ is obtained combining the transitions -2- of $\mathcal{M}$ and -1- of $\mathcal{A}_{\neg\phi}$. The transitions in $\Delta^p_{\mathcal{I}}$, graphically indicated through dashed lines in Fig. 5, are obtained when a transition of $\mathcal{A}_{\neg\phi}$ synchronizes with a transition in the replacement of a box of $\mathcal{M}$. For example, the transition from ② to ⑥ is generated when $\mathcal{A}_{\neg\phi}$ and $\mathcal{M}$ perform the transition -2- and a transition inside the box $send_1$, respectively.

The intersection $\mathcal{I}$ contains in the worst case $3 \cdot |Q_{\mathcal{M}}| \cdot |Q_{\mathcal{A}_{\neg\phi}}|$ states.

(6) *Check the emptiness of the intersection automaton* $\mathcal{I} = \mathcal{M} \cap \mathcal{A}_{\neg\phi}$: by checking the emptiness of the automaton $\mathcal{I}$ we verify whether the property ϕ is definitely satisfied or possibly satisfied by $\mathcal{M}$. Since we have already checked that $\mathcal{L}(\mathcal{M}) \subseteq \mathcal{L}(\mathcal{A}_{\neg\phi})$, two cases are possible: if $\mathcal{I}$ is empty, $\mathcal{L}_p(\mathcal{M}) \subseteq \mathcal{L}(\mathcal{A}_{\neg\phi})$ and the property is definitely satisfied whatever refinement is proposed for the boxes of $\mathcal{M}$, otherwise, $\mathcal{L}_p(\mathcal{M}) \not\subseteq \mathcal{L}(\mathcal{A}_{\neg\phi})$, meaning that there exists some refinement of $\mathcal{M}$ that violates the property. For example, the run $start.(send) \wedge (!success).fail.fail.abort^{\omega}$, which is a possible run of $\mathcal{M}$, violates ϕ since there exists a path where a *send* is not followed by a *success*. This behavior can be generated by replacing boxes $send_1$ and $send_2$ with a component that allows paths where a message is *sent* and no *success* is obtained, and an empty component that neither tries to *send* the message again nor waits for a *success*, respectively.

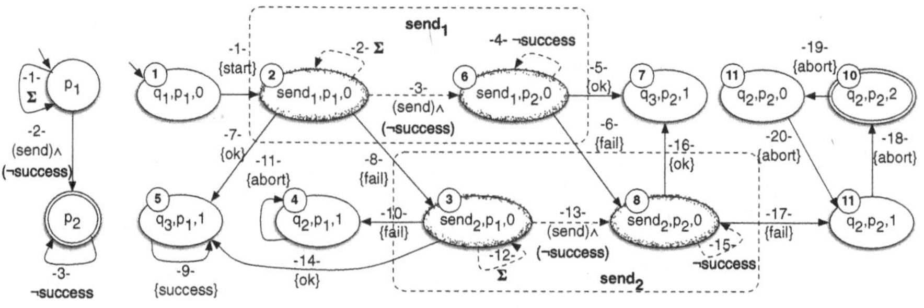

Fig. 4. $\mathcal{A}_{\neg\phi}$.

Fig. 5. $\mathcal{I} = \mathcal{M} \cap \mathcal{A}_{\neg\phi}$.

5 Constraint Computation and Replacement Checking

When a property ϕ is possibly satisfied, each word v that is recognized by the intersection automaton $\mathcal{I}$ corresponds to a behavior $\mathcal{B}$ the system may exhibit that violates ϕ. To satisfy ϕ, the developer must design the replacements of the boxes to forbid $\mathcal{B}$ from occurring. This section shows how to decompose the global information described by $\mathcal{B}$ into local constraints for boxes that become proof obligations for their replacements. For clarity and reasons of space, the section will give an informal, but precise, description of the process; all the formal details can be found in the report published at [25].

A local constraint C for a box b is a pair $\langle S, S_p \rangle$, where S and S_p are two *sub-properties* encoding the replacements of b that make ϕ not satisfied or possibly satisfied, respectively. Hereafter we will first assume that a box constraint only includes a sub-property S that specifies all behaviors that would lead to violating ϕ. This happens, for example, in the case where $\mathcal{M}$ contains *only one box*. Intuitively the reason is that when there are more boxes, the violating behavior may be caused by the "collaboration" of multiple boxes of the model. We will briefly describe the case with multiple boxes at the end of the section.

To compute the constraint C for the box b we need to identify the behaviors described by $\mathcal{I}$ that are recognized by the automaton and traverse the box. To do that, we first perform a cleaning step that eliminates all states from which an accepting state that can be entered infinitely many often is not reachable. This is done with a procedure similar to [7,19]. The resulting automaton will be $\mathcal{I}_{cl}$.

The sub-property S can be computed by first extracting from $\mathcal{I}_{cl}$ the fragment (called $\mathcal{P}$) where states are in the form $\langle b, -, - \rangle$ and then decorating the fragment with additional information, namely:

1. the set Δ^{inS} of incoming transitions that lead to $\mathcal{P}$ from the other states of $\mathcal{I}_{cl}$;
2. the set Δ^{outS} of outgoing transitions that lead from $\mathcal{P}$ to the other states of $\mathcal{I}_{cl}$;
3. the subset G of the source states of Δ^{inS} that are reachable in $\mathcal{I}_{cl}$ from one of its initial states without traversing any other state in the form $\langle b, -, - \rangle$;
4. the subset R of target states of transitions in Δ^{outS} such that an accepting state of $\mathcal{I}_{cl}$ can be reached without traversing any other state in the form $\langle b, -, - \rangle$;
5. a relation K between the target states of Δ^{outS} and the source states of Δ^{inS}. A pair $\langle s_1, s_2 \rangle$ exists in K iff state s_2 is reachable from s_1 by a path of $\mathcal{I}_{cl}$ that does not traverse any state in the form $\langle b, -, - \rangle$.

For example, the sub-property described in Fig. 7 is derived from the clean intersection automaton of Fig. 6 resulting from the model in Fig. 3 and the property in Fig. 4. The automaton $\mathcal{P}$ in Fig. 7 contains the states ② and ⑥ and the transitions -2-, -3- and -4. The transition -1- (-6-) is the incoming (outgoing) transition of $\mathcal{S}$ and its source (target) state is also contained in the set G (R). Because the source and destination states of the incoming and outgoing

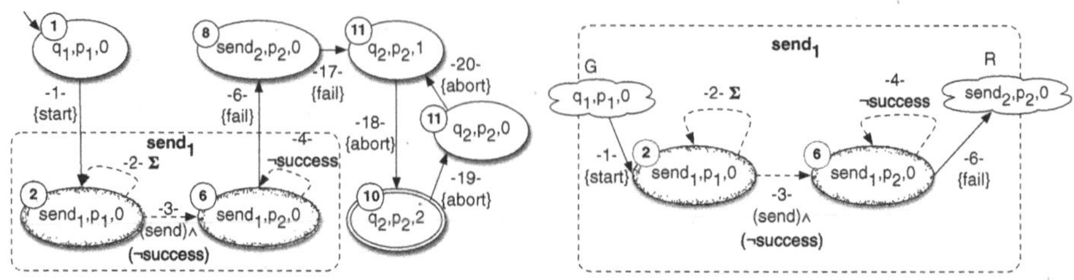

Fig. 6. The intersection $\mathcal{I}_{cl}$.

Fig. 7. The sub-property S.

transitions are states of $\mathcal{I}_{cl}$ that do not belong to $\mathcal{P}$, we graphically represent them with a cloud shape on the outer frame that encloses $\mathcal{P}$ (see Fig. 7, where the source state of -1- is indicated with the triple $\langle q_1, p_1, 0 \rangle$). Cloud states are also marked G or R if they belong to G or R, respectively. Cloud states on the frame that encloses a replacement are also used to indicate how the replacement is connected to the states of the embedding IBA (see Fig. 8). Intuitively, every path of that connects a G-marked cloud state with a R-marked cloud state of the sub-property is a behavior the replacement of the box $send_1$ should not exhibit. Such behavior would enable a violation of the original property. In our example K is empty, since there is no path from ⑧ to ①.

Suppose now that the designer proceeds in the top-down decomposition producing a replacement $\mathcal{R}$ for a box b and wants to check if ϕ is satisfied by the new design, e.g., she/he proposes the replacement of Fig. 8. One possible option would be *refinement checking*. The refinement checking procedure generates the refinement $\mathcal{N}$ of $\mathcal{M}$ by replacing b with $\mathcal{R}$ and checks $\mathcal{N}$ against ϕ. By following this approach, the entire model would be verified at each refinement round. This also implies that the verification needs to be performed by a party which knows the whole system and cannot be delegated to a third party which a partial view of the system. The reason for computing a constraint C for box b has instead the goal of enabling *replacement checking*, in which the verification is applied only on the replacement $\mathcal{R}$ (a small fragment of the model) by checking it against the previously generated constraint C.

To check whether a replacement *violates* a constraint, we build the intersection $\mathcal{U}$ of the automaton $\mathcal{T}$ (of the replacement) and $\mathcal{P}$ (of the sub-property). In doing so we ignore incoming and outgoing transitions. Because we are computing violating behaviors, boxes and their incoming and outgoing transitions are removed from $\mathcal{T}$. If the replacement contains boxes, the same procedure we describe is repeated without removing boxes to find possibly violating behaviors. The intersection $\mathcal{U}$ is shown in Fig. 10.

An additional initial state g and an additional accepting state r, with a self loop, are added to $\mathcal{U}$. States g and r are connected to states of $\mathcal{U}$ as follows. If there is an incoming (outgoing) transition $\langle q, l, q' \rangle$ ($\langle q'', l, q''' \rangle$) to (of) the replacement and an incoming (outgoing) transition $\langle \langle q, p, - \rangle, l, \langle b, p', - \rangle \rangle$ ($\langle \langle b, p'', - \rangle, l, \langle q''', p''', - \rangle \rangle$) to (of) the sub-property originating in a state in G (R), then a transition labeled l is added to $\mathcal{U}$ to connect state g

$(\langle q'', \langle b, p'', -\rangle, -\rangle)$ to each of the states labeled $\langle q', \langle b, p', -\rangle, 0\rangle$ (r). In our example, transition -10- is added to $\mathcal{U}$ since incoming transitions -1- and -7- are both labeled *start*, the source of -1- is in G and it is obtained from the state q_1. Transition -13- is added to $\mathcal{U}$ since both outgoing transitions of the replacement and of the sub-property are labeled *fail*, the destination of the transition -6- is in R and it is obtained from the state $send_2$ of the model.

In general, $\mathcal{U}$ must be further enriched by relation K to include all the paths in the intersection automaton which allow reaching the source of an incoming transition of the constraint from the destination of an outgoing transition. This does not happen for our example, because the relation is empty. If a tuple exists in K, a violating run recognized by $\mathcal{I}_{cl}$ exits a target state of one of its outgoing transitions and enters the source state of one of its incoming transitions.

Once the automaton $\mathcal{U}$ has been built, we can check whether the replacement violates the constraint by checking emptiness. If $\mathcal{U}$ is not empty, the constraint, and therefore also the property of interest, is violated. If the constraint is not violated, the same procedure can check possibly violating behaviors by considering $\mathcal{T}$ without removing boxes. If neither violating nor possibly violating behaviors are present, the property is definitely satisfied.

When an IBA $\mathcal{M}$ has to satisfy the property ϕ and contains multiple boxes, the constraint C computed for the box b may have both components: S and S_p. S specifies the behaviors rendered by $\mathcal{R}$ that would violate ϕ, and S_p specifies the possibly violating behaviors. S is computed as explained above, but, since there are multiple boxes, in the computation of G, R and K it is necessary to not traverse *any* state in the form $\langle b_i, -, -\rangle$, where b_i is a box of $\mathcal{M}$. In fact, when *violating* behaviors are considered, only states of the intersection automata which are not obtained from boxes can be traversed. For example, when the model of Fig. 1 and the property ϕ of Fig. 4 are evaluated, the sub-property S associated with $send_1$ (extracted from the intersection $\mathcal{I}$ presented in Fig. 5) does not contain any outgoing transition in R. Furthermore, the automaton $\mathcal{P}$ does not contain any accepting state. For this reason, no violating behaviors can be exhibited by the replacement. Thus, the replacement either definitely satisfies or possibly satisfies the constraint.

S_p is obtained similarly to S. However, possibly violating behaviors may also traverse states in the form $\langle b_i, -, -\rangle$, where b_i is a box of $\mathcal{M}$ different from b. Figure 9 shows the sub-property S_p for $send_1$ associated with the model of Fig. 1 –which contains multiple boxes– and the property ϕ of Fig. 4. S_p is extracted from the intersection automaton $\mathcal{I}$ presented in Fig. 5. Two types of possibly accepting runs are present: the ones that cross the component and leave S_p through the outgoing transition -8-, and behaviors in which a sending activity is performed and no *success* is obtained and the component is left by firing -6-. In the first case, there is no assurance the replacement of $send_2$ will guarantee a success after any send. In the second case, since the component is left after the execution of a sending activity, $send_2$ must wait for a success.

The replacement checker detects possibly violating behaviors by considering the replacement $\mathcal{R}$ against the sub-property S_p. In computing the intersection

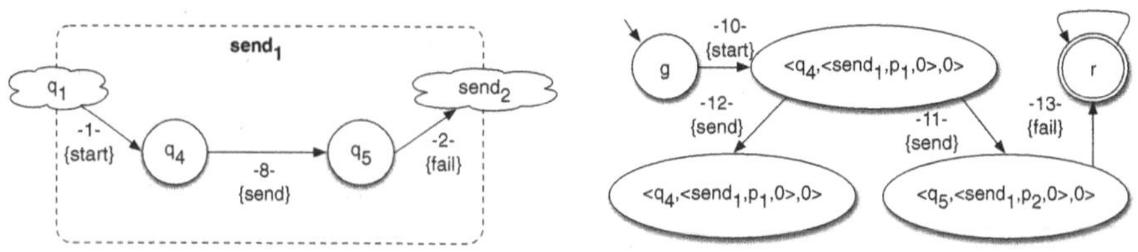

Fig. 8. Replacement $\mathcal{R}$.

Fig. 10. Intersection $\mathcal{U}$.

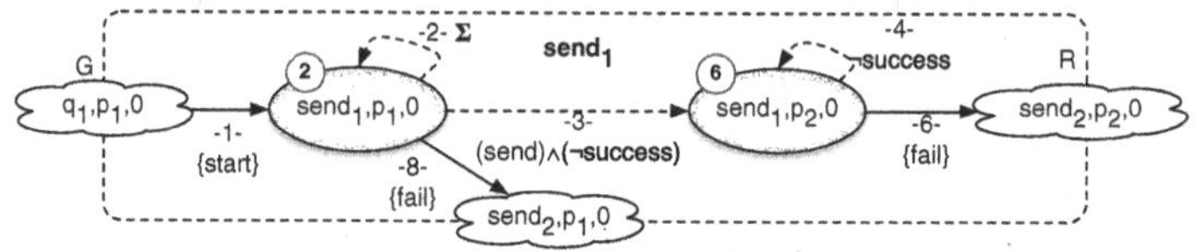

Fig. 9. Sub-property S_p.

automaton, the boxes of the automaton $\mathcal{T}$ of $\mathcal{R}$ are also considered (if present). For example, the intersection between the sub-property S_p of Fig. 9 and the replacement shown in Fig. 8, is presented in Fig. 10. Since the language accepted by the automaton is not empty, the replacement possibly satisfies the property. Note that, when multiple boxes are present, a possibly violating behavior may exist over which the box b has no control (this situation can be verified during the constraint computation). In this case, even if the intersection between the replacement and the property is empty, ϕ is possibly violated. If the sub-property S_p has no incoming transitions in G and there exists a possibly violating behavior of the system over which the box b has no control, the replacement checking procedure returns that the property is possibly satisfied in constant time.

Theorem 1. *The constraint computation procedure has a* $\mathcal{O}(|Q_{\mathcal{I}}|^3|)$ *temporal complexity. The replacement checking complexity is* $\mathcal{O}(|Q_{\mathcal{T}}| \cdot |Q_{\mathcal{P}}| + |\Delta_{\mathcal{T}}| \cdot |\Delta_{\mathcal{P}}| + |\Delta^{inR}| \cdot |\Delta^{inS}| + |\Delta^{outR}| \cdot |\Delta^{outS}| + (|\Delta^{outS}| \cdot |\Delta^{inS}|) \cdot (|\Delta^{outR}| \cdot |\Delta^{inR}|))$

The time complexity of computing constraints is due to the complexity of calculating the relation K, which requires computing the reachability relation between all the pairs of states in the automaton. In the replacement checking complexity the first part concerns the computation of the intersection of the replacement $\mathcal{T}$ and $\mathcal{P}$ (associated with the sub-property), the term $|\Delta^{inR}| \cdot |\Delta^{inS}| + |\Delta^{outR}| \cdot |\Delta^{outS}|$ concerns the computation of the transitions in the intersection automaton generated analyzing the incoming and outgoing transitions of the replacement and the sub-property, and the last part is due to the use of K in the replacement checking.

6 Evaluation

The proposed approach is evaluated through an empirical study that aims to assess its feasibility and scalability, by answering the following questions:

RQ1: How **feasible** is reasoning with IBAs with respect to BAs?
RQ2: How **effective** is replacement checking with respect to refinement checking?

To answer RQ1 and RQ2, we set up experiments based on random model generation, as done in [16,33,34,38]. We considered four tasks:

T1: we check fully refined, complete BAs $\mathcal{N}$ against selected LTL properties;
T2: for each BA $\mathcal{N}$ of task T1, we generate an IBA $\mathcal{M}$ of which it is a refinement. IBAs are verified against the same LTL properties;
T3: for all IBAs and LTL properties, we consider the IBAs that possibly satisfy one of the properties. For each IBA $\mathcal{M}$, we consider the replacement $\mathcal{R}$ of the box b that was abstracted into the box b by task T2. We refine $\mathcal{M}$ by expanding box b with the replacement $\mathcal{R}$ and verify the resulting IBA against ϕ;
T4: we evaluate replacements against their (previously computed) constraints.

To answer RQ1, we conducted two experiments: **(E1)** compares performance and results of T1 and T2; **(E2)** given a $\mathcal{M}$ obtained from $\mathcal{N}$ that possibly satisfies ϕ, considers performance and results of T2 and T3. To answer RQ2, we conducted one experiment: **(E3)** given a $\mathcal{M}$ that possibly satisfies ϕ and the replacement $\mathcal{R}$ of its box b, compares performance and results of T3 and T4.

The evaluation is based on the `CHIA` (CHecker for Incomplete Automata) prototype tool[1], a Java 7 stand-alone application. CHIA has been developed as a proof of concept and does not aim at competing with state of the art model checking tools.

Experimental inputs. The random generation of IBAs is based on the procedure presented in [34] (also used in [33,38]). BAs are generated over an alphabet of two propositions. For each proposition, a directed graph with a single initial state and k transitions is randomly created. The "hardness" of the problem is changed by controlling: 1. the number of states; ($|Q|$); 2. the density of the transitions, i.e., the ratio between the number of transitions per proposition p and the number of states; 3. the density of accepting states, i.e., the ratio between the accepting and total state number. To avoid trivial automata, the initial state is associated with an outgoing transition for each proposition of the alphabet. The BAs that are generated as explained above are also used to further generate the IBAs and replacements needed by tasks T2, T3 and T4. This is done by randomly abstracting fragments of the BAs into boxes. The automata fragments and the corresponding incoming and outgoing transitions are used as replacements associated with the boxes. The box density is used to compute the number of boxes to be injected in the IBA. The replacement density specifies the number of states of the BA to be encapsulated into these boxes. Table 1 presents the values of the parameters used in the scalability assessment.

The reported experiments used three properties randomly selected from the Büchi Store [36]: $\phi_1 = F(a \rightarrow Fb)$, $\phi_2 = G(a \rightarrow F(a \wedge Fb))$ and $\phi_3 = F(a \wedge X(a \wedge Xa)) \wedge F(b \wedge X(b \wedge Xb))$ which have one, three and six temporal operators and correspond to a BA of size 10, 28 and 41, respectively.

[1] https://github.com/claudiomenghi/CHIA.

Table 1. Parameters values.

Parameter	N of states	Transition density	Accepting density	Box density	Replacement density
Initial	100	1.0	0.1	0.1	0.1
Increment	100	1.0	0.2	0.2	0.2
Final	1000	3.0	0.5	0.5	0.5

Table 2. E1 and E2 verification results.

	E1					E2			
	T1	T2	ϕ_1	ϕ_2	ϕ_3	T3	ϕ_1	ϕ_2	ϕ_3
C1	T	T	42,7	42,8	48,0	T	0	1,8	1,9
C2	T	?	57,3	57,2	52,0	?	100	98,2	98,1
C3	F	F	55,5	55,9	55,6	F	2	1,8	1,8
C4	F	?	44,5	44,1	44,4	?	98	98,2	98,2

Table 3. $E3$ and $E3$b verification result.

			$E3$			$E3$b		
	T3	T4	ϕ_1	ϕ_2	ϕ_3	ϕ_1	ϕ_2	ϕ_3
C1	T	T	0,1	0	0,1	1,7	1,9	1,8
C2	?	?	96,3	96,3	96,3	-	-	-
C3	F	F	3,6	3,7	3,6	98,3	98,1	98,2

Each experiment is composed by a set of tests, which randomly generate a model, select a property, and perform the corresponding verification. The tests are performed 20 times to reduce biases due to the random generation.

Results. *E1.* Table 2 reports the results. Lines 1 and 2 (3 and 4) report data in which T1 returns T (F). The first line shows that both BAs (Column $T1$) and IBAs (Columns $T2$) return T 42,7 %, 42,8 % and 48,0 % of the cases for properties ϕ_1, ϕ_2 and ϕ_3, respectively. Likewise, line 3 shows that both BAs and IBAs return a value F in 55,5 %, 55,9 % and 55,6 % of the cases for ϕ_1, ϕ_2 and ϕ_3, respectively. Thus, in almost half of the cases the developer does not need to wait until the end of the development process to know if the property is definitely satisfied or violated.

Figure 11a shows the average ratio T_r between the verification time of BAs (computed by task $T1$) and the verification time of the corresponding IBAs (computed by task $T2$) with respect to the size of the automaton. As expected, IBA verification performs better when properties are violated both by the BA and the IBA, and worse in the case that the property is verified by the BA, while the result is unknown for the corresponding IBA. Performance results are similar for the other cases.

E2. Table 2 reports the results. Given that $T1$ has returned T, $T3$ returns T in 0 %, 1,8 % and 1,9 % of the cases for ϕ_1, ϕ_2 and ϕ_3, respectively. In this case the developer does not need to proceed with the refinement to infer that the property is satisfied. Likewise, when verification for the BA returns F. Task T3 returns F in 2 %, 1,8 % and 1,8 % of the cases for the properties ϕ_1, ϕ_2 and ϕ_3, respectively. In these cases, the developer has to fix her/his current design before proceeding in the refinement.

Figure 11b shows the average ratio T_r between the verification time of the BAs (computed by task $T1$) and the verification time of IBAs obtained by task $T3$ with respect to the size of the automaton. As expected, verification is faster

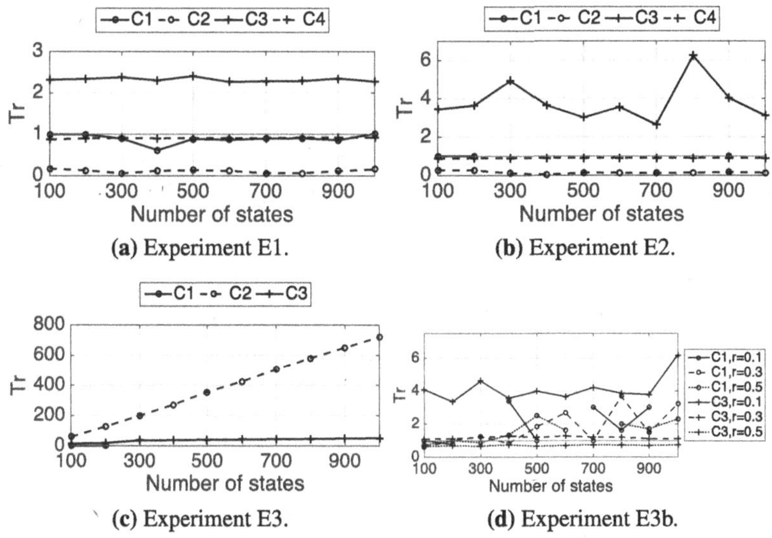

Fig. 11. Experiments results

for IBAs in case C3, and it is slower in case C2. Performance results are similar otherwise.

E3. As showed in Table 3, in all the considered cases, T3 and T4 return the same values, confirming correctness of the approach. The percentage of cases in which the verification result is unknown is high because the replacement is only applied to one box out of many others that may still be present in the refinement.

Figure 11c shows the average ratio T_r between the verification of the IBA after replacement and verification of the replacement against the constraint with respect to the number of the states of the IBA. In case $C2$ the ratio grows linearly, thus indicating that checking the replacement against the constraint is better that checking the refined IBA. Indeed, as the number of boxes increases, there is a high chance that the box b whose replacement $\mathcal{R}$ is considered, is only reachable from the initial state by traversing another box, and there exists another possibly accepting run in the intersection not involving b. Thus, replacement verification is performed in constant time: whatever replacement the developer proposes for b the property remains possibly satisfied. However, this is a favorable situation. For this reason, we refine the experiment ($E3$b) to consider the case in which the starting IBA contains only one box and therefore the replacement refines it to a complete BA.

E3b. In this setting, after a replacement is plugged into the box properties are either satisfied or not, as shown in Table 3, which summarizes our results. Figure 11d compares the performance of T3 and T4 with respect to the states of $\mathcal{M}$. We plot the data for three different values of the replacement density r. As the number of states in the replacement gets smaller with respect to the total number of states, verifying the replacement against the constraint performs better than verifying the refinement.

Conclusions. *E1* and *E2* demonstrate the advantages of reasoning with IBAs. There are no remarkable performance differences between the verification of IBAs and BAs. Furthermore, even if in some cases reasoning with IBAs implies an overhead, the proposed model checking procedure provides considerable benefits, allowing an earlier detection of design flaws. *E3* and *E3b* show that the speedup of checking replacements against checking the flattened refinement is generally considerable. This is in particular true when several boxes remain in the refinement and when the replacement that makes the refinement complete is small in size with respect to the complete automaton.

Threats to Validity. The most important threat to validity concerns the random generation of experimental inputs (IBAs and replacements). There is no guarantee that either the random generation procedure or the values of the parameters chosen in the generation reflect real-life examples. Furthermore, there is no assurance about the significance of the formulae, randomly selected from the Büchi Store [36], over the generated automata. To compensate for these threats, we have complemented the assessment with an analysis of two real world applications reported in [24].

7 Related Work

Modeling incompleteness. Many modeling formalisms, such as MTSs [23], PKSs [4], $\mathcal{X}$KSs [9] and LTS$^{\uparrow}$ [19], support the specification of incompleteness. These formalisms can be used in a top-down, hierarchical development process, but they have not been explicitly proposed with this purpose. MTSs represent incompleteness/uncertainty using maybe transitions, i.e., transitions that can be present or not in the final design of the system, while LTS$^{\uparrow}$ express the behavior of systems that are executed in an unknown environment. Differently, IBAs represents unspecified parts by means of black box states, i.e., states that can be refined in other state machines. In this sense IBAs are similar to HSMs [2] which have been proposed to model sequential processes when a top-down development process is used. However, HSMs can only be analyzed at the end of the development process when a fully specified model of the system is produced. Other formalisms, such as [16–18], support uncertainty i.e., they associate incomplete parts with a set of possible replacements. Finally, models, such as Featured Transition Systems (FSTs) [13], used in variability modeling, are also related. In variability modeling the goal is to represent a large family of different systems efficiently. Differently from IBAs in variability models the replacements (or variants) are known upfront.

Checking incomplete models. The verification procedure discussed in Sect. 4 is similar to others proposed in literature in which properties are expressed as LTL formulae or automata. The procedure was designed considering the three value inductive semantics of LTL. In the three valued semantics, when the property is possibly satisfied, there is no assurance on the existence of two refinements such that the first satisfies and the second violates the formula. This differentiate our work from others that consider the thorough semantics, e.g. [5]. The three valued semantics has been considered in the context of PKSs [4], MTSs [20,21, 23,37] and $\mathcal{X}$KSs [9]. Differently from these works, our procedure supports the verification of automata when the behavior of the system inside a set of states (black boxes) is currently unknown. [19] describes how to verify LTSs ($\text{LTS}^{\uparrow}$) when they are executed in an unknown environment. [2] proposes a technique to check HSMs. However, the proposed technique can only be executed when the whole behavior of the system is specified. Verification of variability-intensive systems aims at checking whether all the products of a family satisfy a property of interest. It has been proposed for example in [12,35], where MTSs and FSTs are considered, respectively.

Constraint computation. The constraint computation problem is similar to other problems, such as synthesis and supervisory control. In program synthesis [15,28] the developer usually computes a model of the system that satisfies the properties of interest. Differently, our goal is to compute sub-properties for the unspecified parts. In this sense, the addressed problem is more similar to assumption generation [19]. In [19], the authors, given a model of the system $\mathcal{M}$ which contains a set of controllable actions, compute an assumption for its environment. If the environment satisfies the assumption, when it is executed in parallel with $\mathcal{M}$ guarantees the satisfaction of the property of interest. Differently, our approach tries to compute assumptions for the unknown components of the system. The constraint computation can be interpreted also as a supervisory control problem [7,26,29,30] in which each box is associated with a set of controllable actions. The problem is to synthesize a strategy the controller can employ to modify the behavior of the incomplete model $\mathcal{M}$ in its boxes to satisfy the properties of interest. In this sense, supervisory control is more similar to the assumption generation problem [19]. Finally, in [37], the authors propose a synthesis technique that constructs MTSs from a combination of safety properties and scenarios but without considering the problem of constraining unspecified parts.

Replacement checking. The replacement checking goal is to verify, after a change, the portion of the state space affected by the change. Thus, problems such as compositional reasoning, component substitutability and hierarchical model checking are related to our work. Compositional reasoning [14] reduces the verification effort by verifying properties on individual components and inferring the properties that hold in the global system without its explicit creation. For example, in the assume-guarantee paradigm [1,22,27], if M guarantees ϕ and M' guarantees ψ when it is located in an environment that satisfies ϕ, then, when M and M' are executed in parallel, they satisfy ψ. In this framework, our constraint can be interpreted as a post-condition that a component has to guarantee. The replacement checking can be considered as a procedure used to verify whether the component ensures its post-condition. Component substitutability [8,32] considers the verification of a system when a component is removed from the system and replaced by a new one. The checker verifies whether the new component preserves the behaviors provided by the old one. A constraint can be interpreted as the "most general" component that ensures the properties of interest. Incremental verification [31] is a technique to efficiently verify code by focusing on the differences between the current and the previous version. Differently from replacement checking, it requires the whole system to run and, hence, is not tailored for distributed design.

8 Conclusion and Future Work

This paper presented an automata-based model checking algorithm that verifies whether an incomplete model of the system definitely satisfies, possibly satisfies or does not satisfy its requirements. If the specification is possibly satisfied, a constraint on the unspecified parts is computed. Whenever an unspecified part is refined, i.e., a replacement is proposed, it is verified in isolation against the previously computed constraint. We provided the theoretical background behind our framework and evaluated its feasibility and effectiveness using a set of random generated models. The presented approach is a step toward the integration of formal verification in modern development processes.

Evaluating the approach on a realistic case study is one of our future goals. Moreover, we also plan to realize a solid, efficient tool designed upon existing symbolic model checkers, and integrate it in commonly used IDEs. Finally, we also aim to analyze the benefits of applying our approach in a distribute development environment, where the refinement of some boxes is delegated to third parties.

References

1. Alur, R., Henzinger, T.A.: Reactive modules. Formal Methods Syst. Des. **15**(1), 7–48 (1999)
2. Alur, R., Yannakakis, M.: Model checking of hierarchical state machines. ACM Trans. Program. Lang. Syst. **23**(3), 273–303 (2001)
3. Baier, C., Katoen, J.: Principles of Model Checking. MIT Press, Cambridge (2008)
4. Bruns, G., Godefroid, P.: Model checking partial state spaces with 3-valued temporal logics. In: Halbwachs, N., Peled, D. (eds.) CAV 1999. LNCS, vol. 1633, pp. 274–287. Springer, Heidelberg (1999). doi:10.1007/3-540-48683-6_25
5. Bruns, G., Godefroid, P.: Generalized model checking: reasoning about partial state spaces. In: Palamidessi, C. (ed.) CONCUR 2000. LNCS, vol. 1877, pp. 168–182. Springer, Heidelberg (2000). doi:10.1007/3-540-44618-4_14
6. Büchi, J.R.: Symposium on decision problems: On a decision method in restricted second order arithmetic. Stud. Logic Found. Math. **44**, 1–11 (1966)
7. Cassandras, C.G., Lafortune, S.: Introduction to Discrete Event Systems, 2nd edn. Springer, New York (2008)
8. Chaki, S., Sharygina, N., Sinha, N.: Verification of evolving software. In: Specification and Verification of Component-Based Systems, SAVCBS (2004)

9. Chechik, M., Devereux, B., Easterbrook, S., Gurfinkel, A.: Multi-valued symbolic model-checking. Trans. Softw. Eng. Methodol. (TOSEM) **12**(4), 371–408 (2003)
10. Clarke, E.M., Emerson, E.A., Sistla, A.P.: Automatic verification of finite-state concurrent systems using temporal logic specifications. Trans. Program. Lang. Syst. (TOPLAS) **8**(2), 244–263 (1986)
11. Clarke, E.M., Grumberg, O., Peled, D.: Model Checking. MIT Press, Cambridge (1999)
12. Classen, A., Cordy, M., Schobbens, P., Heymans, P., Legay, A., Raskin, J.: Featured transition systems: foundations for verifying variability-intensive systems and their application to LTL model checking. IEEE Trans. Softw. Eng. **39**(8), 1069–1089 (2013)
13. Classen, A., Heymans, P., Schobbens, P., Legay, A., Raskin, J.: Model checking lots of systems: efficient verification of temporal properties in software product lines. In: International Conference on Software Engineering, pp. 335–344. ACM (2010)
14. de Roever, W.-P., de Boer, F., Hanneman, U., Hooman, J., Lakhnech, Y., Poel, M., Zwiers, J., Verification, C.: Introduction to Compositional and Non-compositional Methods. Cambridge University Press, Cambridge (2012)
15. D'ippolito, N., Braberman, V., Piterman, N., Uchitel, S.: Synthesizing non-anomalous event-based controllers for liveness goals. Trans. Softw. Eng. Method. (TOSEM) **22**(1), 9:1–9:36 (2013). Article no. 9
16. Famelis, M., Salay, R., Chechik, M.: Partial models: towards modeling and reasoning with uncertainty. In: International Conference on Software Engineering, ICSE, pp. 573–583. IEEE Computer Society (2012)
17. Famelis, M., Salay, R., Chechik, M.: The semantics of partial model transformations. In: International Workshop on Modeling in Software Engineering, pp. 64–69. IEEE Computer Society (2012)
18. Famelis, M., Salay, R., Sandro, A., Chechik, M.: Transformation of models containing uncertainty. In: Moreira, A., Schätz, B., Gray, J., Vallecillo, A., Clarke, P. (eds.) MODELS 2013. LNCS, vol. 8107, pp. 673–689. Springer, Heidelberg (2013). doi:10.1007/978-3-642-41533-3_41
19. Giannakopoulou, D., Pasareanu, C.S., Barringer, H.: Assumption generation for software component verification. In: International Conference on Automated Software Engineering, ASE, pp. 3–12. IEEE Computer Society (2002)
20. Huth, M.: Model checking modal transition systems using Kripke structures. In: Cortesi, A. (ed.) VMCAI 2002. LNCS, vol. 2294, pp. 302–316. Springer, Heidelberg (2002). doi:10.1007/3-540-47813-2_21
21. Huth, M., Jagadeesan, R., Schmidt, D.: Modal transition systems: a foundation for three-valued program analysis. In: Sands, D. (ed.) ESOP 2001. LNCS, vol. 2028, pp. 155–169. Springer, Heidelberg (2001). doi:10.1007/3-540-45309-1_11
22. Jones, C.B.: Tentative steps toward a development method for interfering programs. Trans. Program. Lang. Syst. (TOPLAS) **5**(4), 596–619 (1983)
23. Larsen, K.G., Thomsen, B.: A modal process logic. In: Third Annual Symposium on Logic in Computer Science, LICS, pp. 203–210. IEEE Computer Society (1988)
24. Menghi, C.: Dealing with incompleteness in automata based model checking. Ph.D. thesis, Politecnico di Milano (2015). https://www.politesi.polimi.ithandle/10589/114509
25. Menghi, C., Spoletini, P., Ghezzi, C.: Modeling, refining and analyzing Incomplete Büchi Automata. ArXiv e-prints (2016). http://arxiv.org/abs/1609.00610
26. Miremadi, S., Lennartson, B., Åkesson, K.: BDD-based supervisory control on extended finite automata. In: Conference on Automation Science and Engineering, CASE, pp. 25–31. IEEE (2011)

27. Pnueli, A.: In transition from global to modular temporal reasoning about programs. In: Apt, K.R. (ed.) Logics and Models of Concurrent Systems. NATO ASI Series, vol. 13, pp. 123–144. Springer, Heidelberg (1985)
28. Pnueli, A., Rosner, R.: On the synthesis of a reactive module. In: Symposium on Principles of Programming Languages, pp. 179–190. ACM Press (1989)
29. Ramadge, P.J., Wonham, W.M.: Supervisory control of a class of discrete event processes. SIAM J. Control Optim. **25**(1), 206–230 (1987)
30. Ramadge, P.J., Wonham, W.M.: The control of discrete event systems. Proc. IEEE **77**(1), 81–98 (1989)
31. Sery, O., Fedyukovich, G., Sharygina, N.: FunFrog: bounded model checking with interpolation-based function summarization. In: Chakraborty, S., Mukund, M. (eds.) ATVA 2012. LNCS, vol. 7561, pp. 203–207. Springer, Heidelberg (2012). doi:10.1007/978-3-642-33386-6_17
32. Sharygina, N., Chaki, S., Clarke, E., Sinha, N.: Dynamic component substitutability analysis. In: Fitzgerald, J., Hayes, I.J., Tarlecki, A. (eds.) FM 2005. LNCS, vol. 3582, pp. 512–528. Springer, Heidelberg (2005). doi:10.1007/11526841_34
33. Tabakov, D., Vardi, M.Y.: Experimental evaluation of classical automata constructions. In: Sutcliffe, G., Voronkov, A. (eds.) LPAR 2005. LNCS (LNAI), vol. 3835, pp. 396–411. Springer, Heidelberg (2005). doi:10.1007/11591191_28
34. Tabakov, D., Vardi, M.Y.: Model checking Büchi specifications. In: International Conference on Language and Automata Theory and Applications, LATA, pp. 565–576. Research Group on Mathematical Linguistics, Universitat Rovira i Virgili, Tarragona (2007)
35. ter Beek, M.H., Fantechi, A., Gnesi, S., Mazzanti, F.: Modelling and analysing variability in product families: model checking of modal transition systems with variability constraints. J. Log. Algebr. Math. Program. **85**(2), 287–315 (2016)
36. Tsay, Y.-K., Tsai, M.-H., Chang, J.-S., Chang, Y.-W.: Büchi store: an open repository of Büchi automata. In: Abdulla, P.A., Leino, K.R.M. (eds.) TACAS 2011. LNCS, vol. 6605, pp. 262–266. Springer, Heidelberg (2011). doi:10.1007/978-3-642-19835-9_23
37. Uchitel, S., Brunet, G., Chechik, M.: Synthesis of partial behavior models from properties and scenarios. IEEE Trans. Softw. Eng. **35**(3), 384–406 (2009)
38. Wulf, M., Doyen, L., Henzinger, T.A., Raskin, J.-F.: Antichains: a new algorithm for checking universality of finite automata. In: Ball, T., Jones, R.B. (eds.) CAV 2006. LNCS, vol. 4144, pp. 17–30. Springer, Heidelberg (2006). doi:10.1007/11817963_5

Equivalence Checking of a Floating-Point Unit Against a High-Level C Model

Rajdeep Mukherjee[1(✉)], Saurabh Joshi[2], Andreas Griesmayer[3], Daniel Kroening[1], and Tom Melham[1]

[1] University of Oxford, Oxford, UK
{rajdeep.mukherjee,kroening,tom.melham}@cs.ox.ac.uk
[2] IIT Hyderabad, Telangana, India
sbjoshi@iith.ac.in
[3] ARM Limited, Cambridge, UK
andreas.griesmayer@arm.com

Abstract. Semiconductor companies have increasingly adopted a methodology that starts with a system-level design specification in C/C++/SystemC. This model is extensively simulated to ensure correct functionality and performance. Later, a Register Transfer Level (RTL) implementation is created in Verilog, either manually by a designer or automatically by a high-level synthesis tool. It is essential to check that the C and Verilog programs are consistent. In this paper, we present a two-step approach, embodied in two equivalence checking tools, VERIFOX and HW-CBMC, to validate designs at the software and RTL levels, respectively. VERIFOX is used for equivalence checking of an untimed software model in C against a high-level reference model in C. HW-CBMC verifies the equivalence of a Verilog RTL implementation against an untimed software model in C. To evaluate our tools, we applied them to a commercial floating-point arithmetic unit (FPU) from ARM and an open-source dual-path floating-point adder.

1 Introduction

One of the most important tasks in Electronic Design Automation (EDA) is to check whether the low-level implementation (RTL or gate-level) complies with the system-level specification. Figure 1 illustrates the role of equivalence checking (EC) in the design process. In this paper, we present a new EC tool, VERIFOX, that is used for equivalence checking of an untimed software (SW) model against a high-level reference model. Later, a Register Transfer Level (RTL) model is implemented, either manually by a hardware designer or automatically by a synthesis tool. To guarantee that the RTL is consistent with the SW model, we use an existing tool, HW-CBMC [15], to check the correctness of the synthesized hardware RTL against a SW model.

In this paper, we address the most general and thus most difficult variant of EC: the case where the high-level and the low-level design are substantially different. State-of-the-art tools, such as Hector [14] from Synopsys and SLEC

J. Fitzgerald et al. (Eds.): FM 2016, LNCS 9995, pp. 551–558, 2016.
DOI: 10.1007/978-3-319-48989-6_33

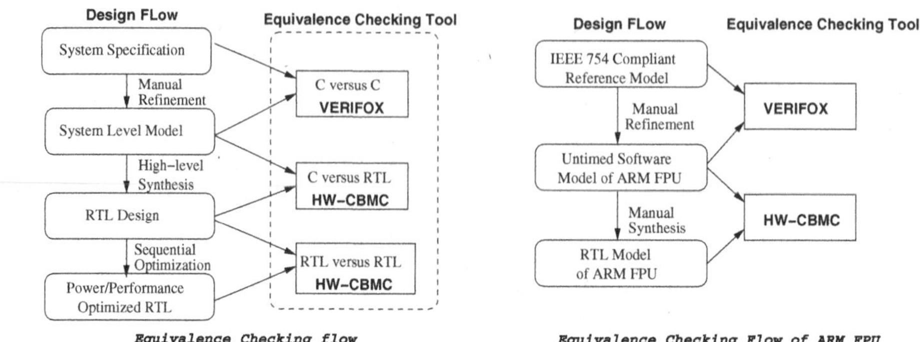

Fig. 1. Electronic design automation flow

from Calypto,[1] rely on *equivalence points* [18], and hence they are ineffective in this scenario. We present an approach based on bounded analysis, embodied in the tools VERIFOX and HW-CBMC, that can handle arbitrary designs.

EC is broadly classified into two separate categories: combinational equivalence checking (CEC) and sequential equivalence checking (SEC). CEC is used for a pair of models that are cycle accurate and have the same state-holding elements. SEC is used when the high-level model is not cycle accurate or has a substantially different set of state-holding elements [1,11]. It is well-known that EC of floating-point designs is difficult [12,19]. So there is a need for automatic tools that formally validate floating-point designs at various stages of the synthesis flow, as illustrated by right side flow of Fig. 1. An extended version of this paper, showing worked examples and giving further technical details, is available at [17].

2 VERIFOX: A Tool for Equivalence Checking of C Programs

VERIFOX is a path-based symbolic execution tool for equivalence checking of C programs. The tool architecture is shown on the left side of Fig. 2. VERIFOX supports the C89 and C99 standards. The key feature is symbolic reasoning about equivalence between FP operations. To this end, VERIFOX implements a model of the core IEEE 754 arithmetic operations—single- and double-precision addition, subtraction, multiplication, and division—which can be used as reference designs for equivalence checking. So VERIFOX does not require external reference models for equivalence checking of floating-point designs. This significantly simplifies the users effort to do equivalence checking at software level. The reference model in VERIFOX is equivalent to the Softfloat model.[2] VERIFOX also supports SAT and SMT backends for constraint solving.

[1] http://calypto.com/en/products/slec/.
[2] http://www.jhauser.us/arithmetic/SoftFloat.html.

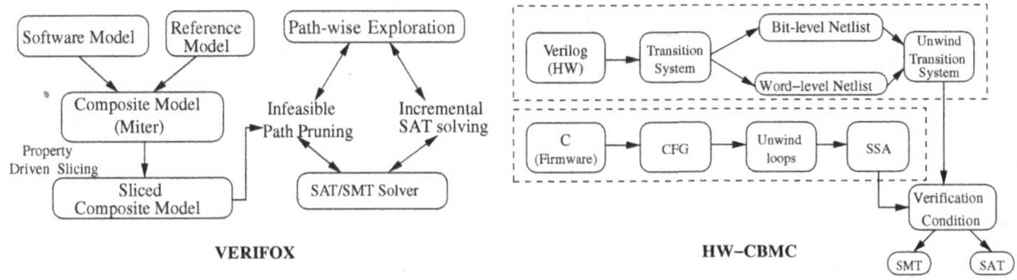

Fig. 2. VERIFOX and HW-CBMC tool architecture

Program	Path Constraint 1	Path Constraint 2	Path Constraint 3	Monolithic Path Constraint

`void top(){`
`if(reset) {`
`x=0;`
`y=0; }`
`else {`
`if(a > b)`
`x=a+b;`
`else`
`y=(a & 3)<<b; }}`
	$C_1 \equiv$
	$reset_1 \neq 0 \wedge$
	$x_2 = 0 \wedge$
	$y_2 = 0$
		$C_2 \equiv$
		$reset_1 = 0 \wedge$
		$b_1 \not\geq a_1 \wedge$
		$x_3 = a_1 + b_1$
			$C_3 \equiv$
			$reset_1 = 0 \wedge$
			$b_1 \geq a_1 \wedge$
			$y_3 = (a_1 \& 3)$
			$\ll b_1$
				$C \iff ((guard_1 = \neg(reset_1 = 0))\wedge$
				$(x_2 = 0) \wedge (y_2 = 0)\wedge$
				$(x_3 = x_1) \wedge (y_3 = y_1)\wedge$
				$(guard_2 = \neg(b_1 >= a_1))\wedge$
				$(x_4 = a_1 + b_1) \wedge (x_5 = x_3)\wedge$
				$(y_4 = (a_1 \& 3) \ll b_1)\wedge$
				$(x_6 = ite(guard_2, x_4, x_5))\wedge$
				$(y_5 = ite(guard_2, y_3, y_4))\wedge$
				$(x_7 = ite(guard_1, 0, x_6))\wedge$
				$(y_6 = ite(guard_1, 0, y_5)))$

Fig. 3. Single-path and monolithic symbolic execution

Given a reference model, an implementation model in C and a set of partition constraints, VERIFOX performs depth-first exploration of program paths with certain optimizations, such as eager infeasible path pruning and incremental constraint solving. This enables automatic decomposition of the verification state-space into subproblems, by input-space and/or state-space decomposition. The decomposition is done in tandem in both models, exploiting the structure present in the high-level model. The approach generates many but simpler SAT/SMT queries, similar to the technique followed in KLEE [4]. Figure 3 shows three feasible path constraints corresponding to the three paths in the program on the left. In contrast, the last column of Fig. 3 shows a monolithic path-constraint generated by HW-CBMC. VERIFOX is available at http://www.cprover.org/verifox.

***Incremental solving in* VERIFOX.** VERIFOX can be run in two different modes: partial incremental and full incremental. In partial incremental mode, only one solver instance is maintained while going down a single path. So when making a feasibility check from one branch b_1 to another branch b_2 along a single path, only the program segment from b_1 to b_2 is encoded as a constraint and added to the existing solver instance. Internal solver states and the information that the solver gathers during the search remain valid as long as all the queries that are posed to the solver in succession are monotonically stronger. If the solver solves a formula ϕ, then posing $\phi \wedge \psi$ as a query to the same solver instance allows one to reuse solver knowledge it has already acquired, because any assignment that falsifies ϕ also falsifies $\phi \wedge \psi$. Thus the solver need not revisit the assignments that it has already ruled out. This results in speeding up the feasibility check of the symbolic state at b_2, as the feasibility check at b_1 was *true*. A new solver instance is used to explore a different path, after the current path is detected as infeasible.

In full incremental mode, only one solver instance is maintained throughout the whole symbolic execution. Let $\phi_{b_1 b_2}$ denote the encoding of the path fragment from b_1 to b_2. It is added in the solver as $B_{b_1 b_2} \Rightarrow \phi_{b_1 b_2}$. Then, $B_{b_1 b_2}$ is added as a *blocking variable*[3] to enforce constraints specified by $\phi_{b_1 b_2}$. Blocking variables are treated specially inside the solvers: unlike regular variables or clauses, the blocking can be removed in subsequent queries without invalidating the solver instance. When one wants to back-track the symbolic execution, the blocking $B_{b_1 b_2}$ is removed and a unit clause $\neg B_{b_1 b_2}$ is added to the solver, thus effectively removing $\phi_{b_1 b_2}$.

3 HW-CBMC: A Tool for Equivalence Checking of C and RTL

HW-CBMC is used for bounded equivalence checking of C and Verilog RTL. The tool architecture is shown on the right side of Fig. 2. HW-CBMC supports IEEE 1364-2005 System Verilog standards and the C89, C99 standards. HW-CBMC maintains two separate flows for hardware and software. The top flow in Fig. 2 uses synthesis to obtain either a bit-level or a word-level netlist from Verilog RTL. The bottom flow illustrates the translation of the C program into static single assignment (SSA) form [9]. These two flows meet only at the solver. Thus, HW-CBMC generates a monolithic formula from the C and RTL description, which is then checked with SAT/SMT solvers. HW-CBMC provides specific handshake primitives such as *next_timeframe*() and *set_inputs*() that direct the tool to set the inputs to the hardware signals and advance the clock, respectively. The details of HW-CBMC are available online.[4]

4 Experimental Results

In this section, we report experimental results for equivalence checking of difficult floating-point designs. All our experiments were performed on an Intel® Xeon® machine with 3.07 GHz clock speed and 48 GB RAM. All times reported are in seconds. MiniSAT-2.2.0 [10] was used as underlying SAT solver with VERIFOX 0.1 and HW-CBMC 5.4. The timeout for all our experiments was set to 2 h.

Proprietary Floating-point Arithmetic Core: We verified parts of a floating-point arithmetic unit (FPU) of a next generation ARM® GPU. The FP core is primarily composed of single- and double-precision *ADD*, *SUB*, *FMA* and *TBL* functional units, the register files, and interface logic. The pipelined computation unit implements FP operations on a 128-bit data-path. In this paper,

[3] The SAT community uses the term *assumption variables* or *assumptions*, but we will use the term blocking variable to avoid ambiguity with assumptions in the program.

[4] http://www.cprover.org/hardware/sequential-equivalence/.

we verified the single-precision addition (*FP-ADD*), rounding (*FP-ROUND*), minimum (*FP-MIN*) and maximum (*FP-MAX*) operations. The FP-ADD unit can perform two operations in parallel by using two 64-bit adders over multiple pipeline stages. Each 64-bit unit can also perform operations with smaller bit widths. The FPU decodes the incoming instruction, applies the input modifiers and provides properly modified input data to the respective sub-unit. The implementation is around 38000 LOC, generating tens of thousands of gates. We obtained the SW model (in C) and the Verilog RTL model of the FPU core from ARM. (Due to proprietary nature of the FPU design, we can not share the commercial ARM IP.)

Open-source Dual-path Floating-point Adder: We have developed both a C and a Verilog implementation of an IEEE-754 32-bit single-precision dual-path floating point adder/subtractor. This floating-point design includes various modules for packing, unpacking, normalizing, rounding and handling of infinite, normal, subnormal, zero and NaN (Not-a-Number) cases. We distribute the C and RTL implementation of the dual-path FP adder at http://www.cprover.org/verifox.

Reference Model: The IEEE 754 compliant floating-point implementations in VERIFOX are used as the golden reference model for equivalence checking at the software level. For equivalence checking at the RTL phase, we used the untimed software model from ARM as the reference model, as shown on the right side of Fig. 1.

Miters for Equivalence Checking: A miter circuit [3] is built from two given circuits A and B as follows: identical inputs are fed into A and B, and the outputs of A and B are compared using a comparator. For equivalence checking at software level, one of the circuits is a SW program and the other is a high-level reference model. For the RTL phase, one of the circuits is a SW program treated as reference model and the other is an RTL implementation.

Case-splitting for Equivalence Checking: Case-splitting is a common practice to scale up formal verification [12,14,19] and is often performed by user-specified assumptions. The `CPROVER_assume(c)` statement instructs HW-CBMC and VERIFOX to restrict the analysis to only those paths satisfying a given condition `c`. For example, we can limit the analysis to those paths that are exercised by inputs where the rounding mode is nearest-even (RNE) and both input numbers are NaNs by adding the following line:

```
CPROVER_assume(roundingMode==RNE && uf_nan && ug_nan);
```

Discussion of Results: Table 1 reports the run times for equivalence checking of the ARM FPU and the dual-path FP adder. Column 1 gives the name of FP design and columns 2–6 show the runtimes for partition modes INF, ZERO, NaN, SUBNORMAL, and NORMAL respectively. For example, the partition constraint 'INF' means addition of two infinite numbers. Column 7 reports the total time for equivalence checking without any partitioning.

Table 1. Equivalence checking of ARM FPU and DUAL-PATH Adder (All time in seconds)

Design	Case-splitting					No-partition
	INF	ZERO	NaN	SUBNORMAL	NORMAL	Total
Equivalence Checking at Software Level (VERIFOX)						
FP-ADD	9.56	11.54	9.95	1124.18	77.74	1566.72
FP-ROUND	1.24	1.36	1.32	3.78	1.63	4.71
FP-MIN	9.76	9.85	9.78	28.67	9.86	48.70
FP-MAX	9.80	9.88	9.97	28.70	9.90	35.81
DUAL-PATH ADDER	3.15	3.11	2.14	88.12	55.28	497.67
Equivalence Checking at Register Transfer Level (HW-CBMC)						
FP-ADD	18.12	18.02	17.87	18.73	39.60	40.72
FP-ROUND	11.87	12.73	13.44	13.67	14.03	14.11
FP-MIN	13.72	13.62	ERROR	14.10	14.08	14.15
FP-MAX	13.70	13.58	ERROR	14.09	14.06	14.05
DUAL-PATH ADDER	0.88	0.87	0.99	169.49	22.42	668.61

VERIFOX successfully proved the equivalence of all FP operations in the SW implementation of ARM FPU against the built-in reference model. However, a bug in FP-MIN and FP-MAX (reported as ERROR in Table 1) is detected by HW-CBMC in the RTL implementation of ARM FPU when checked against the SW model of ARM FPU for the case when both the input numbers are NaN. This happens during manual translation of SW model to RTL. Further, we investigate the reason for higher verification times for subnormal numbers compared to normal, infinity, NaN's and zero's. This is attributed to higher number of paths in subnormal case compared to INF, NaN's and zero's. Closest to our floating-point symbolic execution technique in VERIFOX is the tool KLEE-FP [8]. We could not, however, run KLEE-FP on the software models because the front-end of KLEE-FP failed to parse the ARM models.

5 Related Work

The concept of symbolic execution [4,7,13] is prevalent in the software domain for automated test generation as well as bug finding. Tools such as Dart [13], Klee [4], EXE [5], Cloud9 [16] employ such a technique for efficient test case generation and bug finding. By contrast, we used path-wise symbolic execution for equivalence checking of software models against a reference model. A user-provided assumption specifies certain testability criteria that render majority of the design logic irrelevant [12,14,19], thus giving rise to large number of infeasible paths in the design. Conventional SAT-based bounded model checking [2,6,15] can not exploit this infeasibility because these techniques create a monolithic formula by unrolling the entire transition system up to a given bound, which is then passed to SAT/SMT solver. These tools perform case-splitting at the level of solver through the effect of constant propagation. Optimizations such as eager path pruning combined with incremental encoding enable VeriFOx to address this limitation.

6 Concluding Remarks

In this paper we presented VeriFOx, our path-based symbolic execution tool, which is used for equivalence checking of arbitrary software models in C. The key feature of VeriFOx is symbolic reasoning on the equivalence between floating-point operations. To this end, VeriFOx implements a model of the core IEEE 754 arithmetic operations, which can be used for reference models. Further, to validate the synthesis of RTL from software model, we used our existing tool, hw-cbmc, for equivalence checking of RTL designs against the software model used as reference. We successfully demonstrated the utility of our equivalence checking tool chain, VeriFOx and hw-cbmc, on a large commercial FPU core from ARM and a dual-path FP adder. Experience suggests that the synthesis of software models to RTL is often error prone—this emphasizes the need for automated equivalence checking tools at various stages of EDA flow. In the future, we plan to investigate various path exploration strategies and path-merging techniques in VeriFOx to further scale equivalence checking to complex data and control intensive designs.

Acknowledgements. Part of the presented work was conducted during an internship at ARM. The authors want to thank in particular Luka Dejanovic, Joe Tapply, and Ian Clifford for their help with setting up the experiments.

References

1. Baumgartner, J., Mony, H., Paruthi, V., Kanzelman, R., Janssen, G.: Scalable sequential equivalence checking across arbitrary design transformations. In: ICCD, pp. 259–266. IEEE (2006)
2. Biere, A., Cimatti, A., Clarke, E.M., Strichman, O., Zhu, Y.: Bounded model checking. Adv. Comput. **58**, 117–148 (2003)
3. Brand, D.: Verification of large synthesized designs. In: ICCAD, pp. 534–537 (1993)
4. Cadar, C., Dunbar, D., Engler, D.R.: KLEE: unassisted and automatic generation of high-coverage tests for complex systems programs. In: OSDI, pp. 209–224. USENIX (2008)
5. Cadar, C., Ganesh, V., Pawlowski, P.M., Dill, D.L., Engler, D.R.: EXE: automatically generating inputs of death. ACM Trans. Inf. Syst. Secur. **12**(2), 10:1–10:38 (2008). Article No.10
6. Clarke, E., Kroening, D.: Hardware verification using ANSI-C programs as a reference. In: Proceedings of the 2003 Asia and South Pacific Design Automation Conference, ASP-DAC, pp. 308–311. ACM (2003)
7. Clarke, L.A.: A system to generate test data and symbolically execute programs. IEEE Trans. Softw. Eng. **2**(3), 215–222 (1976)
8. Collingbourne, P., Cadar, C., Kelly, P.H.J.: Symbolic crosschecking of floating-point and SIMD code. In: EuroSys, pp. 315–328 (2011)

9. Cytron, R., Ferrante, J., Rosen, B.K., Wegman, M.N., Zadeck, F.K.: An efficient method of computing static single assignment form. In: POPL, pp. 25–35. ACM (1989)
10. Eén, N., Biere, A.: Effective preprocessing in SAT through variable and clause elimination. In: Bacchus, F., Walsh, T. (eds.) SAT 2005. LNCS, vol. 3569, pp. 61–75. Springer, Heidelberg (2005). doi:10.1007/11499107_5
11. van Eijk, C.A.J.: Sequential equivalence checking without state space traversal. In: DATE, pp. 618–623. IEEE (1998)
12. Fujita, M.: Verification of arithmetic circuits by comparing two similar circuits. In: Alur, R., Henzinger, T.A. (eds.) CAV 1996. LNCS, vol. 1102, pp. 159–168. Springer, Heidelberg (1996). doi:10.1007/3-540-61474-5_66
13. Godefroid, P., Klarlund, N., Sen, K.: DART: directed automated random testing. In: PLDI, pp. 213–223 (2005)
14. Kölbl, A., Jacoby, R., Jain, H., Pixley, C.: Solver technology for system-level to RTL equivalence checking. In: DATE, pp. 196–201. IEEE (2009)
15. Kroening, D., Clarke, E., Yorav, K.: Behavioral consistency of C and Verilog programs using bounded model checking. In: DAC, pp. 368–371 (2003)
16. Kuznetsov, V., Kinder, J., Bucur, S., Candea, G.: Efficient state merging in symbolic execution. In: PLDI, pp. 193–204 (2012)
17. Mukherjee, R., Joshi, S., Griesmayer, A., Kroening, D., Melham, T.: Equivalence checking a floating-point unit against a high-level C model: extended version. Computing Research Repository arXiv:1609.00169 [cs.SE], September 2016
18. Wu, W., Hsiao, M.S.: Mining global constraints for improving bounded sequential equivalence checking. In: DAC, pp. 743–748. ACM (2006)
19. Xue, B., Chatterjee, P., Shukla, S.K.: Simplification of C-RTL equivalent checking for fused multiply add unit using intermediate models. In: ASP-DAC, pp. 723–728. IEEE (2013)

Battery-Aware Scheduling in Low Orbit: The GomX–3 Case

Morten Bisgaard[1], David Gerhardt[1], Holger Hermanns[2], Jan Krčál[2], Gilles Nies[2(✉)], and Marvin Stenger[2]

[1] GomSpace ApS, Aalborg, Denmark
[2] Saarland University – Computer Science, Saarland Informatics Campus, Saarbrücken, Germany
nies@cs.uni-saarland.de

Abstract. When working with space systems the keyword is resources. For a satellite in orbit all resources are sparse and the most critical resource of all is power. It is therefore crucial to have detailed knowledge on how much power is available for an energy harvesting satellite in orbit at every time – especially when in eclipse, where it draws its power from onboard batteries. This paper addresses this problem by a two-step procedure to perform task scheduling for low-earth-orbit (LEO) satellites exploiting formal methods. It combines cost-optimal reachability analyses of priced timed automata networks with a realistic kinetic battery model capable of capturing capacity limits as well as stochastic fluctuations. The procedure is in use for the automatic and resource-optimal day-ahead scheduling of GomX–3, a power-hungry nanosatellite currently orbiting the earth. We explain how this approach has overcome existing problems, has led to improved designs, and has provided new insights.

1 Introduction

The GomX–3 CubeSat is a 3 kg nanosatellite designed, delivered, and operated by Danish sector leader GomSpace. GomX–3 is the first ever In-Orbit Demonstration (IOD) CubeSat commissioned by ESA. The GomX–3 system uses Commercial-off-the-shelf (COTS) base subsystems to reduce cost, enabling to focus on payload development and testing. GomX–3 was launched from Japan aboard the HTV–5 on August 19, 2015. It successfully berthed to the ISS a few days later. GomX–3 was deployed from the ISS on October 5, 2015. Figure 1 shows the satellite and its deployment.

Both GomSpace and ESA are interested in maximizing the functionality of their nanosatellite missions. As such, GomX–3 has been equipped with a variety of technical challenging payloads and components, among them: (*i*) 3-axis rotation and pointing with a precision of 2° or less, (*ii*) in-flight tracking of commercial aircrafts, (*iii*) monitoring signals from geostationary InmarSat satellites, and (*iv*) high-speed downlinking to stations in Toulouse (France) or Kourou (French Guiana).

J. Fitzgerald et al. (Eds.): FM 2016, LNCS 9995, pp. 559–576, 2016.
DOI: 10.1007/978-3-319-48989-6_34

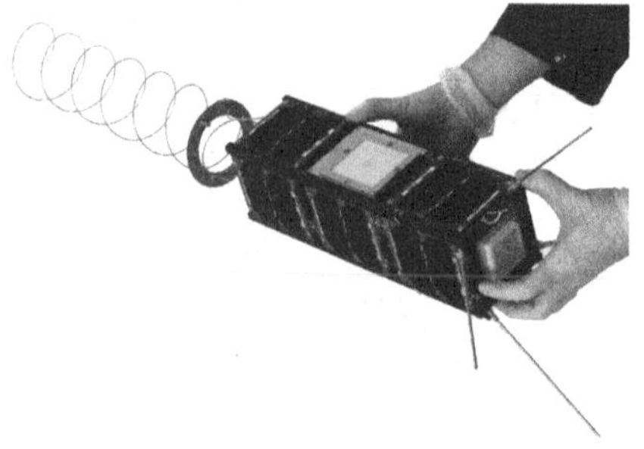
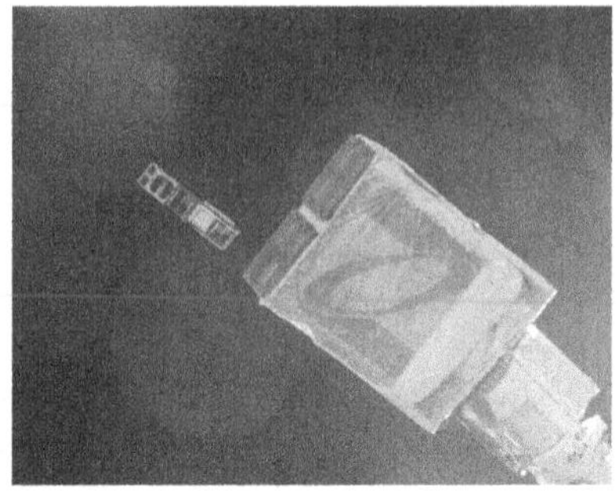

Fig. 1. The final GomX–3 nanosatellite (left) and its deployment from the ISS (right) together with AAUSAT5 (picture taken by Astronaut Scott Kelly).

For a satellite in orbit all resources are sparse and the most critical resources of all is power. Power is required to run the satellite, to communicate, to calculate, to perform experiments and all other operations. Detailed knowledge on the power budget is thus essential when operating a satellite in orbit. Furthermore, in a satellite not all power is used as it is generated. The satellite passes into eclipse each orbit and during those periods it must draw power from its batteries. This challenge is especially apparent for nanosatellites where not only the actual satellite but also the resources are very small. An operator of such a spacecraft is thus faced with a highly complex task when having to manually plan and command in-orbit operations constantly balancing power and data budgets.

In this paper we report on our joint activities, part of the EU-FP7 SENSATION project, to harvest formal modelling and verification technology, so as to provide support for commanding in-orbit operations while striving for an efficient utilization of spacecraft flight time. Concretely, we have developed a toolchain to automatically derive battery-aware schedules for in-orbit operation. The heterogeneous timing aspects and the experimental nature of the application domain make it impossible to use traditional scheduling approaches for periodic tasks.

The schedules we derive are tailored to maximize payload utilisation while minimizing the risk of battery depletion. The approach is flexible in the way it can express intentions of spacecraft engineers with respect to the finer optimisation goals. It comes as an automated two-step procedure, and provides quantifiable error bounds.

For the first step, we have developed a generic model of the GomX–3 problem characteristics in terms of a network of priced timed automata (PTA) [3]. This model is subjected to a sequence of analyses with respect to cost-optimal reachability (CORA) with dynamically changing cost and constraint assignments. We use Uppaal Cora for this step. The latter is a well understood and powerful tool to find cost optimal paths in PTA networks [4]. This first step takes the battery state into consideration by means of a linear battery representation (owed to the fact that nonlinearities are not supportable in CORA). As a result, any schedule generated in this step has a risk of not being safe when used in-orbit, running on a real battery and with real payload.

To account for this problem, a second step validates the generated schedule on a much more accurate model of the on-board battery, a model that includes nonlinearities and also accounts for the influence of stochastic perturbations of load or battery state. For this step, we employ a stochastic enhancement [5] of the kinetic battery model [10] (KiBaM) with capacity bounds. As a result it is possible to discriminate between schedules according to their quantified risk of depleting the battery. Low risk schedules are shipped to orbit and executed there. The satellite behaviour is tightly monitored and the results gained are used to improve the model as well as the overall procedure.

The entire toolchain has been developed, rolled out, experimented with, and tailored for in-the-loop use when operating the GomX–3 satellite. We report on experiences gained and lessons learned, and highlight the considerable prospect behind this work, in light of the future development in the space domain.

2 Prerequisites

Priced Timed Automata. The model of *Timed Automata* (TA) [2] has been established as a standard modelling formalism for real time systems. A timed automaton is an extension of finite state machines with non-negative real valued variables called *clocks* in order to capture timing constraints. Thus, a timed automaton is an annotated directed graph over a set of clocks C with vertex set (called *locations*) L and edge set E. Edges and locations are decorated with conjunctions of clock constraints of the form $c \bowtie k$ where $c \in C$, $k \in \mathbb{N}$ and $\bowtie \in \{<, \leq, =, \geq, >\}$. For edges such constraints are called *guards*, for locations they are called *invariants*. Edges are additionally decorated with *reset sets* of clocks. Intuitively, taking an edge causes an instantaneous change of location and a reset to 0 for each clock in the reset set. However an edge may only be taken if its guard and the target location's invariant evaluate to true. If this is not that case the current location remains active, if it's invariant permits, and clocks increase continuously with their assigned rates, thus modelling the passing of time.

In order to reason about resources, TAs are enriched with non-negative integer *costs* and non-negative *cost rates* in the form of annotations for edges and locations respectively [3]. The result are *priced timed automata* (PTA). The intuition is that cost accumulates continuously in a proportional manner to the sojourn time of locations and increases discretely upon taking an edge as specified by the respective annotations.

Definition 1 (Priced Timed Automata). *Let C be a set of clocks and $\mathbb{B}(C)$ be the set of all clock constraints as described above. A priced timed automaton is a tuple $\langle L, E, \ell_0, \mathsf{inv}, \mathsf{price}\rangle$ where L is a set of locations, $E \subseteq L \times \mathbb{B}(C) \times 2^C \times L$ is a set of edges, ℓ_0 is the initial location, $\mathsf{inv} : L \to \mathbb{B}(C)$ assigns invariants to locations, and $\mathsf{price} : L \cup E \to \mathbb{N}$ assigns costs and cost rates to edges and locations respectively.*

To meet space requirements we omit the formal semantics of PTA, and instead refer to [3] for a complete development.

A common problem to consider in the context of PTA is that of computating the minimum cost to reach a certain target location in a given PTA. This so-called *cost-optimal reachability analysis* (CORA) receives dedicated attention in the literature [4,8] and is well-known to the community. The CORA is implemented in a number of tools, most prominently UPPAAL CORA [1]. As input UPPAAL CORA accepts networks of PTAs extended by discrete variables, and thus allows for modular formalisation of individual components. The set of goal states is characterised by formulae over the variables in the network of PTAs.

Kinetic Battery Model. Batteries in-the-wild exhibit two non-linear effects widely considered to be the most important ones to capture: the *rate capacity effect* and the *recovery effect*. The former refers to the fact that if continuously discharged, a high discharge rate will cause the battery to provide less energy before depletion than a lower discharge rate. Thus a battery's effective capacity depends on the rate at which it is discharged. The latter effect describes the battery's ability to recover to some extent during periods of no or little discharge. We introduce the *kinetic battery model* (KiBaM) as the simplest model capturing these effects. It is known to provide a good approximation of the battery *state of charge* (SoC) across various battery types [5]. For a survey on battery models providing a context for the KiBaM we refer to [6,7].

The KiBaM divides the stored charge into two parts, the *available* charge and the *bound* charge. When the battery is strained only the available charge is consumed instantly, while the bound charge is slowly converted to available charge by diffusion. For this reason the KiBaM is often depicted by two wells holding liquid, interconnected by a pipe, as seen in Fig. 2.

The diffusion between available and bound charge can take place in either direction depending on the amount of both types of energy stored in the battery. Both non-linear effects are rooted in the relatively slow conversion of bound charge into available charge or vice versa. The KiBaM is characterized by two coupled differential equations:

$$\dot{a}(t) = -I(t) + p\left(\frac{b(t)}{1-c} - \frac{a(t)}{c}\right), \qquad \dot{b}(t) = p\left(\frac{a(t)}{c} - \frac{b(t)}{1-c}\right).$$

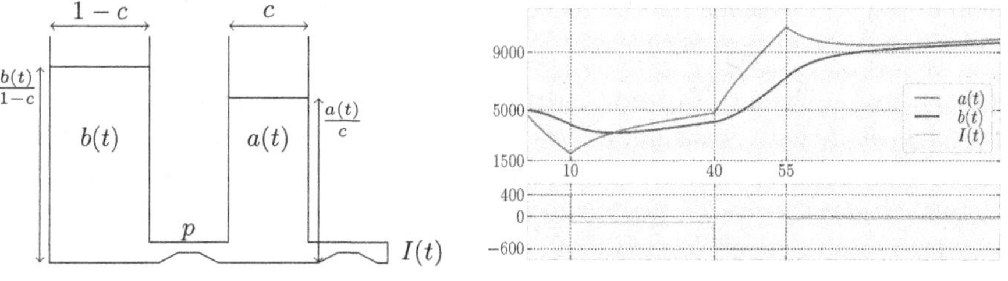

Fig. 2. The two-wells depiction of the KiBaM (left) and a SoC evolution trace over time under a piecewise constant load (right).

Here, the functions $a(t)$ and $b(t)$ describe the available and bound charge at time t respectively, $\dot{a}(t)$ and $\dot{b}(t)$ their time derivatives, and $I(t)$ is a *load* on the battery. We refer to the parameter p as the *diffusion rate* between both wells, while parameter $c \in [0,1]$ corresponds to the width of the available charge well, and $1-c$ is the width of the bound charge well. Intuitively, $a(t)/c$ and $b(t)/(1-c)$ are the level of the fluid stored in the available charge well and the bound charge well, respectively. Figure 2 shows a SoC trace of the KiBaM ODE system. We shall denote the KiBaM SoC at time t as $[a_t; b_t]$ and consider $I(t)$ to be piecewise constant.

Adding Randomness and Capacity Limits. The KiBaM model has been extended with capacity limits (say a_{max} for the available charge and b_{max} for the bound charge), as well as means to incorporate stochastic fluctuations in the SoC and the load imposed on the battery. Both extensions come with their own set of technical difficulties. For a complete technical development of this we refer to [5]. In this setting SoC distributions may not be absolutely continuous, because positive probability may accumulate in the areas $\{[0;b] \mid 0 < b < b_{\mathsf{max}}\}$ where the available charge is depleted and $\{[a_{\mathsf{max}};b] \mid 0 < b < b_{\mathsf{max}}\}$ where the available charge is full. Therefore, one works with representations of the *SoC distribution* in the form of triples $\langle f, \bar{f}, z\rangle$ where

- f is a joint density over $]0, a_{\mathsf{max}}[\times]0, b_{\mathsf{max}}[$, which represents the distribution of the SoC in the area within the limits,
- $\bar{f}$ is a density over $\{a_{\mathsf{max}}\} \times]0, b_{\mathsf{max}}[$ and captures the bound charge distribution while the available charge is at its limit a_{max},
- $z \in [0,1]$, the cumulative probability of depletion.

It is possible to analytically express an under-approximation of the SoC distribution $\langle f_T, \bar{f}_T, z_T\rangle$ after powering a task (T, g) when starting with the initial SoC distribution $\langle f_0, \bar{f}_0, z_0\rangle$, where T is a real time duration and g is the probability density function over loads. We omit the derivation of these expressions due to their lengthiness. Sequences of tasks can be handled iteratively, by considering the resulting SoC distribution after powering a task to be the initial SoC distribution for powering the next task.

Figure 3 displays the SoC distributions while powering an exemplary task sequence. Each distribution $\langle f, \bar{f}, z\rangle$ is visualized as three stacked plots: f is represented in the heatmap (middle), the curve of $\bar{f}$ in the small box (top), z in the small box as a colour-coded probability value representing the cumulative depletion risk (bottom).

3 Modelling the GomX–3 Nanosatellite

GomX–3 is a 3 L (30 × 10 × 10 cm, 3 kg) nanosatellite launched in October 2015 from the ISS. It's mission payloads are threefold: Tracking of ADS-B beacons emitted by commercial airplanes, testing a high-rate X-Band transmitter module for in-space adequacy, and monitoring spot-beams of geo-stationary satellites belonging to the InmarSat family, via an L-Band receiver. In addition,

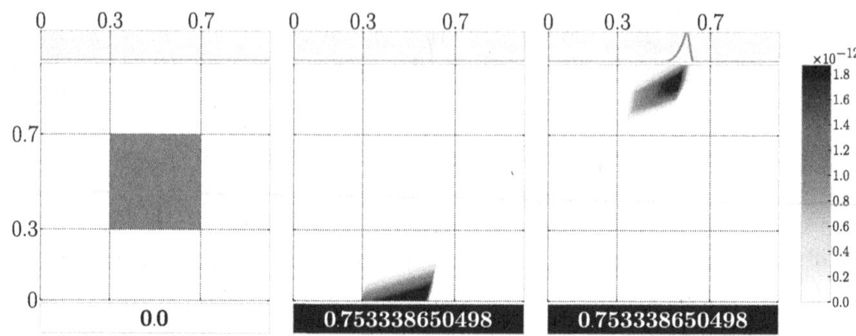

Fig. 3. An exemplary battery with $a_{\mathsf{max}} = b_{\mathsf{max}} = 5 \cdot 10^6$, $c = 0.5$, $p = 0.0003$ with an initially uniform SoC density over the area $[0.3, 0.7]\, a_{\mathsf{max}} \times [0.3, 0.7]\, b_{\mathsf{max}}$ (left), subjected to a task sequence $(500, \mathcal{U}[3000, 3600])$, $(600, \mathcal{U}[-3300, -3900])$ with $\mathcal{U}$ denoting uniform distribution. Roughly 75 % of the SoC density flows into the depletion area (negative available charge) after powering the first task and is thus accumulated in z (middle). The remaining 25 % are considered alive and transformed further. Some of it even reaches the capacity limit a_{max} of the available charge (right).

it features a UHF software defined radio module for downlinking collected data to – and uplinking new instructions from the GomSpace base station in Aalborg, Denmark. In the sequel, we refer to the operation of one of these payloads as a *job*. Each of these jobs comes with its own set of satellite attitude configurations, making an advanced 3-axis attitude control system indispensable. This attitude control uses gyroscopes and magnetorquers to enable the satellite to slew into any dedicated position with a precision of up to 2°. It is especially power-hungry.

As an earth-orbiting satellite, GomX–3 naturally enters eclipse. To continue operation, it draws the necessary power to sustain its operation from an onboard battery system. These batteries are, in turn, charged by excess energy harvested during insolation periods by solar panels that cover any non-occupied surface.

Since its launch, GomX's follows the roughly equatorial orbit of (and below) the ISS. Therefore, insolation periods as well as operation windows for the different jobs are well predictable over the time horizon of about a week ahead, yet they are highly irregular. Exploiting the pre-determined attitude configurations per mode of operation, the net power balance of every job can be predicted by the in-house GomSpace PowerSim tool. This information is the essence of the power-relevant behaviour of GomX–3. In order to understand their joint implications for the energy budget of GomX–3, it is important to accurately model these power-relevant aspects of the satellite components, and their interplay.

3.1 Objectives

In broad terms, the main mission goal of GomX–3 is to maximize the amount of jobs carried out without depleting the battery. The concrete objectives spelled out by GomSpace engineers changed several times along the mission. This meant that the models have to have the necessary flexibility needed to reflect the requirements once they are made formal.

GomX–3 switches to *Safe Mode* if the battery SoC falls below a given threshold. For GomX–3 this threshold is at 40 % of the battery's capacity. In Safe Mode, all non-essential hardware components are switched off, preventing of the satellite being productive. The primary objective is thus to avoid Safe Mode, while maximizing secondary objectives. Several such secondary objectives need to be taken into account.

- Whenever possible the UHF connection to the GomSpace base station must be scheduled and maintained throughout the entire operation window in order to enable monitoring the status of GomX–3 and to uplink new instructions if need be. This is crucial to maintain control over the satellite and thus considered vital for the success of the mission.
- Independent of the satellite attitude, the ADS-B helix antenna is able to receive ADS-B beacons. Thus this hardware module will be active at all times, thereby constantly collecting data of airplane whereabouts.
- The X-Band windows are small, as the downlink connection can only be established if the satellite is in line of sight and close enough to the receiving ground station. The corresponding downlink rate, however, is relatively high.
- L-Band jobs will have job windows as long as an orbit duration but vary a lot depending the time of the year, and will collect a lot of data if successful. The variations in window lengths can be observed in Sect. 5, where actual schedules are visualized.
- L-Band jobs are to become as balanced as possible across the available InmarSats.
- Jobs filling their entire job window are most valuable. Jobs that have been aborted early or started late are not considered interesting.
- L-Band and X-Band jobs are mutually exclusive, as they require different attitudes. UHF jobs may be scheduled regardless of the current attitude, even when L-Band or X-Band jobs are currently executed.
- Only downlinked data are useful, thus the time spent on data collection payloads (L-Band, ADS-B) and downlink opportunities (X-Band) needs to be balanced in such a way that only a minimal amount of data needs to be stored temporarily in the satellite's memory. This induces the need to weigh the data collection rate and the downlink speed against each other.

Based on these observations and the expertise of GomSpace engineers, it was deemed that two fully executed X-Band jobs are enough to downlink the data of one successful L-Band job together with the ADS-B data collected in the meanwhile.

3.2 PTA Modelling

As the central modelling formalism PTAs are employed when modelling the behaviour of GomX–3, with special emphasis being put on flexibility w.r.t. the optimization objective. In order to allow for easy extensibility, the modelling was purposely kept modular and generic. Notably, the TA formalism is not expressive enough for the nonlinearities of the kinetic battery model. Therefore we use a simple linear model (intuitively corresponding to a single well holding liquid) instead, and account for this discrepancy later. The component models belong to the following categories.

Background load comprises the energy consumption of modules that are always active, including the ADS-B module for tracking airplanes, the gyroscopes and magnetorquers (even though not at full power) for keeping the attitude invariant.

Jobs are dealt with in a generic way, so that only the common characteristics are modelled. A job has a finite time window of when it can be executed, it may be skipped, it may require an a priori *preheating* time (to ramp up the physical modules related to the job) as well as a specific attitude, it may need to activate a set of related modules inducing piecewise constant loads, its window may occur in a periodic pattern.

Battery represents a relatively simple linear battery which can support piecewise constant loads. It keeps track of its (one-dimensional) state of charge and updates that based on the (dis)charge rate and the time until the load changes again. Since the battery is modelled as an automaton, the system can monitor and take decisions based on the remaining battery charge.

Attitude represents the predetermined attitude requirements of each job and the worst case slewing time of 5 min.

Insolation is a simple two-state automaton (sun and eclipse) based upon the predicted insolation times, triggering a constant energy infeed due to the solar panels.

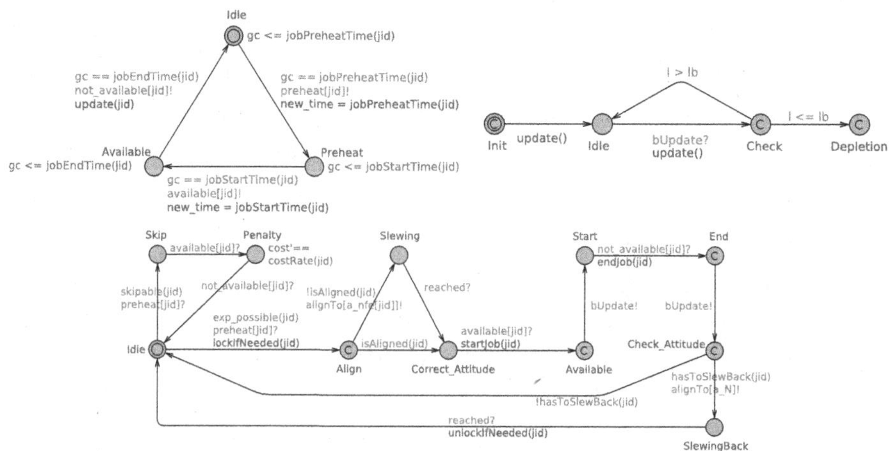

Fig. 4. The `JobProvider` automaton (top left), the `Job` instance automaton (bottom) and the `Battery` automaton (top right).

Among these components, the PTAs modelling the battery and the job aspects are the most interesting. They are depicted in Fig. 4 and explained in more detail below.

`JobProvider`: This automaton provides the interface between multiple arrays representing the job opportunities as well as their implied preheating times, and the actual `Job` automaton. It waits for a job window, discriminating whether the job needs preheating or not, and broadcasts signals triggering the actual decision making. In the Idle location, being initial, it waits for the global clock `gc` to hit a certain job preheat time event (stored in the array `jobPreheatTime`), sets the `time` variable to the current time, and notifies the `Job` automaton to start preheating over a the dedicated `preHeat[jid]` channel, where `jid` uniquely identifies a certain job type. Upon this notification it switches into the PreHeat location and waits for the actual job to start, i.e. the global time reaching the expected start time of the job identified by `jid`, consequently transitioning into location Available, where, in turn it waits for completion of the job (`gc` reaching `jobEndTime[jid]`), switching into location Idle yet again, all the while notifying its environment on the respective dedicated channels.

`Job`: This automaton represents the execution or skipping of a job. It starts in its Idle location, waiting to be notified of impending preheating duties. At this point the take-or-skip decision is taken, as witnessed by the two outgoing transitions into locations labelled Skip and Align. A job is either skipped because it is not optimal to take it, or because the attitude requirements don't match the current attitude of the satellite because of an already ongoing job. If the job is skipped, cost is accumulated with rate *costRate*(`jid`) over the duration of the job, effectively returning into location Idle. If it is taken, attitude requirements of the scheduled job are checked via the guard *isAligned*(`jid`), upon which the satellite starts slewing (location Slewing) to the correct attitude (location Correct_Attitude) if need be. Upon notification, the job is executed (Start → End → Check_Attitude) triggering the battery via channel `bUpdate` to update its SoC, and finally checks whether it has to change attitude to minimize atmospheric drag using guards *hasToSlewBack*(`jid`) to finally return eventually to location Idle.

`Battery`: This model represents a simple linear battery with capacity that can be (dis)charged with piecewise constant loads. It is notified of load changes via channel `bUpdate`, upon which it computes the length of a constant load interval via global integer variables `new_time` and `old_time`, and subtracts the result multiplied by `rate` from its internal SoC `l`, upon which it ends up in location Check. A check is performed whether the SoC fell below a threshold `lb`, upon which we either transition into (and stay in) the Depletion location or return to Idle to power another task.

3.3 Cost Model and Reachability Objectives

In the following we explain how the objectives derived by GomSpace engineers were turned into constraints and cost parameters of the PTA model.

The Safe Mode threshold is kept variable and must be set before scheduling. It appears as `lb` (for lower bound) in the automata models. Depending on the degree of aggressiveness of the intended schedule, it can either be set close to the real Safe Mode threshold of 40 % or it can be set higher, for example to 55 %, thereby adding an implicit safety margin.

UPPAAL CORA computes cost-minimal schedules. Therefore, we interpret the price annotations of PTA transitions as penalties for skipped jobs. Likewise cost rates in states accumulate penalty per time unit a job window is left unused. An optimal schedule will then have the property that the minimal portion of important jobs windows was left unexploited.

An immediate consequence of this setup is that UHF jobs have a high penalty if skipped, as they are supposed to be scheduled every time they are possible. For L-Band and X-Band jobs, the number of jobs scheduled should result in an average ratio of 1/2, according to the GomSpace directives. To arrive there, we proceed as follows. Let Δ_X and Δ_L denote the job windows length expectations of X-Band and L-Band jobs, respectively. Then the cost rate for skipping L-Band and X-Band window portions is set $2 \cdot \Delta_X$ and Δ_L, respectively. Likewise, the L-Band jobs on different INMARSAT are internally viewed as different jobs. Their cost rates for skipping should be set equal.

In order to generate an optimal schedule from the network of PTAs up to a certain time horizon (treated as an orbiting count), we need to define the goal set of states to be used in a reachability objective as supported by UPPAAL CORA. To this end, we simply introduce a small automaton that counts the orbits already scheduled for and manages this number globally, say in a variable $\mathtt{n}$. A query for a schedule of n orbits can then easily be formulated as $\exists\Diamond(\mathtt{n} = 20)$.

3.4 Model Quality Assurance

In light of the high overall significance of the GOMX–3 mission, it was from the start deemed important to assure the adequacy of the formal models used to represent and to eventually manoeuvre the satellite. For this reason, a series of dedicated workshops were organized in the context of the SENSATION project, comprising among others the authors of this paper. On these occasions, presentations of varying technical detail were delivered by both sides, so as to expose the formal approach, the set of concrete problems, as well as possible solutions thereof. In later stages, collaborative work was organised via Google docs and Skype, which indeed provided an effective way to communicate feedback in both directions. This altogether made it possible to effectively crossfertilize the domain expertise of the GomSpace engineers with the modelling and verification experience at Saarland University, so as to assure a high quality model. In the same vein, the design of the entire scheduling workflow (explained next) was a consensus decision.

4 The Scheduling Workflow

The scheduling workflow, depicted in Fig. 5, loops through a two-step procedure of schedule generation and schedule validation. The latter is needed to account for the inaccuracies of the simple linear battery model, which is used for schedule generation, relative to real battery kinetics. Therefore any generated schedule is validated along the stochastically enhanced KiBaM known to be sensitive to such effects. If the validation does not exhibit good enough guarantees, the current schedule is discarded and excluded from the generation step, and a new schedule is computed. Otherwise it will be accepted, upon which we break the loop and ship the schedule to orbit.

4.1 Schedule Generation

The mission times to be considered for automatic scheduling span between 24 and 72 h. Longer durations are not of interest since orbit predictions are highly accurate only for a time horizon of a handful of days, and because GomX–3 is as a whole an experimental satellite, requiring periods of manual intervention. However, even a 24 h schedule computation constitutes a challenge for plain CORA, since the number of states grows prohibitively large.

Heuristics. The state-space explosion can, to certain extend, be remedied by using heuristics, i.e. exclusion of certain schedules at the risk of losing optimality. Here is a brief overview of heuristics used:

1. **Take every job if battery is almost full.** Job opportunities will be taken if the battery is close to being full, since the battery cannot store more energy anyway. This minimizes the risk of not being able to harvest energy due to a full battery.
2. **Force discard of schedules on depletion.** This simple, yet effective heuristic forces the PTA network into a dedicated deadlock location (Depletion) whenever the battery automaton reaches a non positive SoC, resulting in the schedule to be dropped.

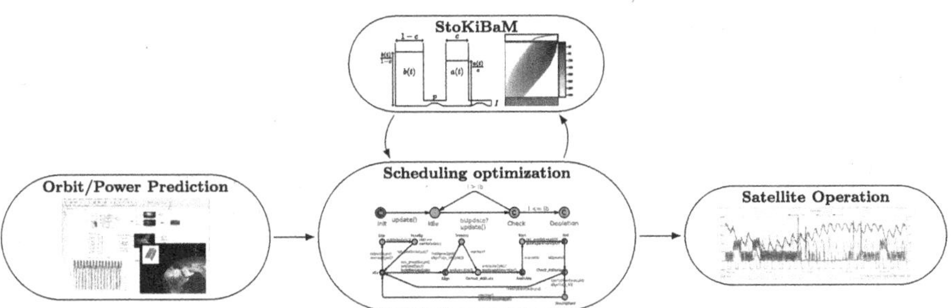

Fig. 5. Scheduling workflow.

The following heuristics are specific to objectives expressed by the engineers.

3. **An L-Band job precedes two X-Band jobs.** To avoid storage of large amounts of data on the satellite, we bound the ratio of data collection and downlink jobs. A ratio $\mathtt{r_X}/\mathtt{r_L}$ can be approximated greedily by adding a global variable $\mathtt{r}$ (initially 0) as well as guards to the `Job` automaton such that X-Band jobs are scheduled only if $\mathtt{r} \geq \mathtt{r_L}$ and L-Band jobs are scheduled only if $\mathtt{r} < (\mathtt{r_X} + \mathtt{r_L}) \cdot \mathtt{r_X}$. Upon scheduling an X-Band and L-Band job, we set $\mathtt{r} := \mathtt{r} - \mathtt{r_L}$ and $\mathtt{r} := \mathtt{r} + \mathtt{r_X}$ respectively. With $\mathtt{r_X} := 2$ and $\mathtt{r_y} := 1$ schedules never start with an X-Band job and in the long run, the ratio of X-Band and L-Band jobs stays between 1 and 2/1.
4. **Keep L-Band jobs in balance across InmarSats.** Similarly to the realization of the above heuristic we bound the difference among L-Band jobs on the relevant InmarSats to at most 2.
5. **Always schedule UHF jobs.** Instead of penalizing skipped UHF jobs by annotations of large costs (to enforce their scheduling), we enforce them on the automaton level, omitting any cost annotation.
6. **Impose upper bound on discharging loads.** This heuristic does what it says.

Especially heuristic 6 proves useful in several ways. First, the KiBaM used in the validation step yields less energy before depletion if subjected to high loads due to the rate-capacity effect (that is not captured by the linear battery model). Second, high loads are reached when UHF jobs are scheduled in addition to an L- or X-Band job. Such situations seem lucrative to Uppaal Cora, given that they don't accumulate much cost. Yet, they often result in schedules that leave the battery (almost) empty. Third, the bound can be chosen such that parallel experiments, and thus high loads, occurs only during insolation, but not in eclipse.

To give some insight into the effect of each heuristic on the computation with Uppaal Cora, we provide a comparison by means of an example, reported in the following table. In the example all the above mentioned heuristics were implemented (first row), except for the one mentioned.

Heuristics used	Total CORA time	States explored	Optimal value computed
All	2.6	172452	262792
All but 1	10.2	700429	262792
All but 2	80.7	5474775	262792
All but 3	8.9	592233	258081
All but 4	3.7	224517	262792
All but 5	2.7	175191	262792
All but 6	86.1	6029126	243269

It becomes apparent that heuristic 2 and 6 are the most effective. Most of the combinations studied induce the schedule depicted below, where job windows of a certain type, i.e. L-Band on different InmarSats (L_1, L_2), X-Band (X) and UHF, are displayed as black (grey) bars if they were indeed taken (skipped).

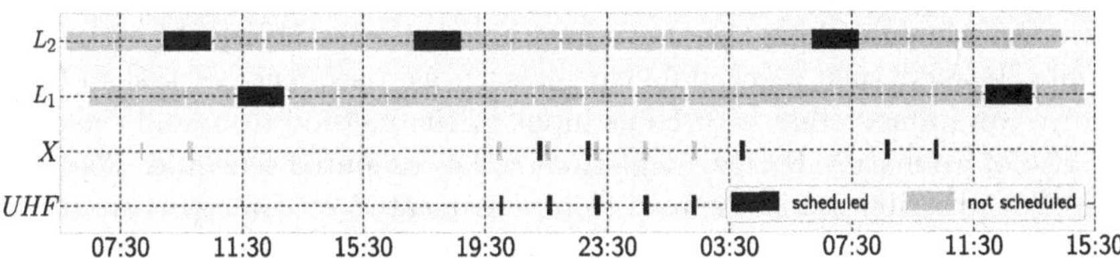

At first sight, dropping heuristics 3 or 6 lead to superior solutions. Without heuristic 3 one more X-Band job can indeed be scheduled, explaining why this schedule is cheaper in terms of accumulated penalty. It is however scheduled before the first L-Band job, rendering it useless because there is nothing to downlink. As expected, without heuristics 6 Uppaal Cora predominately schedules UHF jobs parallel to X- or L-Band jobs, thereby straining the battery. The large number of states explored indicates that the state space exploration in this case is often misguided into eventual battery depletion.

Dynamic Scheduling. Another issue is that Uppaal Cora's optimization criterion is static, i.e. the prices cannot be updated based on the schedule generated so far. This is contrasted by the GomSpace engineering intention of having a dynamic scheduling approach. We take care of this by viewing the PTA network as being *parameterized*, i.e. as templates that need to be instantiated by concrete values. This enables us to divide the scheduling interval into disjoint subintervals that can be scheduled individually, with distinct scheduling objectives and prices, all the while carrying over resulting quantities as initial values to the subsequent subinterval to be scheduled. Important quantities that need to be passed on are the resulting battery state, the number of individual jobs already scheduled and the state of the PTA network at the end of the previous subinterval. This information allows us to adjust the prices and scheduling objective at the end of each subinterval, depending on the requirements previously fixed. The subschedules are then conjoined to a schedule for the actual time interval. This line of action is a trade-off between optimality and being dynamic, as it implements a greedy heuristics.

Given the back-to-back nature of this approach, it is undesired to start with an almost empty battery after a scheduling interval. We require the battery to have a certain minimum charge at the end of the schedule. This requirement translates directly to a reachability query on the PTA network: $\exists\Diamond(\mathtt{n} = 20 \wedge \mathtt{l} \geq 75000000)$, where `l` is the global variable representing the battery SoC.

4.2 Schedule Validation

As mentioned, Uppaal Cora's expressiveness does not allow for direct modelling of the KiBaM as a PTA. Instead the schedule computed is based on the simple linear model, that is known to not capture important effects that can be observed from measurements of real batteries. In order to validate whether the computed schedule truly doesn't violate the constraints we imposed, we need to validate the schedule along the above mentioned stochastic KiBaM with capacity limits. In fact, such a schedule can be seen as a sequence of tasks (T_j, I_j), which we can immediately be used as input to the method to bound the cumulative risk of premature battery depletion of the computed schedule. The initial KiBaM SoC distribution is assumed to be a truncated 2D Gaussian around the initial battery state given to the PTA network and white noise is added to the loads of the tasks. If the validation step exhibits a low enough depletion risk, the computed schedule is accepted, otherwise the schedule is excluded and another schedule is computed.

4.3 Schedule Shipping

In order to uplink a schedule to GomX–3, several *comma separated files* (`.csv`) are generated. Each file contains a list of job opportunities of a certain type, for example L-Band (see below), given by two timestamps representing the start time and the end time of the job window respectively, the implied duration of the timestamps, as well as a flag that shows whether the opportunity should be taken. One such file could be read as follows:

Access	Start time (UTCG)	Stop time (UTCG)	Duration (sec)	Scheduled
1	17 Nov 2015 00:38:38.922	17 Nov 2015 01:09:42.642	1863.720	1
2	17 Nov 2015 02:16:24.134	17 Nov 2015 02:45:23.914	1739.781	0
⋮	⋮	⋮	⋮	⋮
15	17 Nov 2015 23:41:20.490	18 Nov 2015 00:12:38.983	1878.493	0

5 Results

A number of successful experiments have been carried out on GomX–3 in-orbit, so as to evaluate and refine our method, focussing on the determination of schedules to be followed for the days ahead. These in-orbit evaluations have successfully demonstrated the principal feasibility and adequacy of the approach, as we will discuss in this section.

In Figs. 6, 7 and 8 three representative in-orbit experiments are summarized. The schedules are visualised as three stacked plots of data against a common time line (left). The bottom ones are Gantt charts showing which jobs are scheduled (black bars) and which job windows are skipped (grey bars) respectively. The plots in the middle display the loads imposed by the jobs as predicted (purple) and as actually measured (green) on GomX–3. The top plots presents the

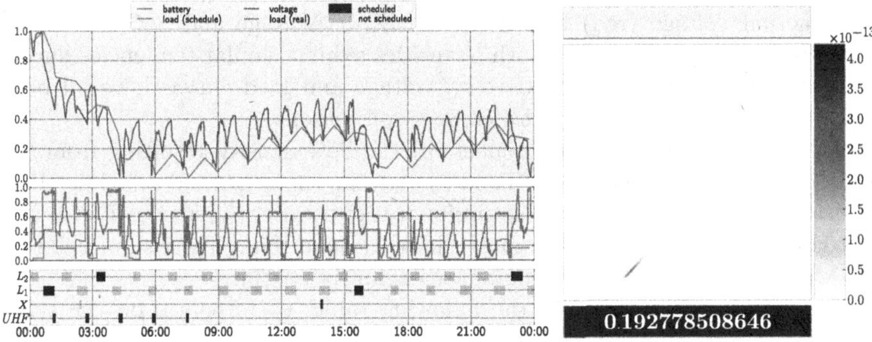

Fig. 6. Schedule November 17, 2015 midnight to November 18, 2015 midnight. (Color figure online)

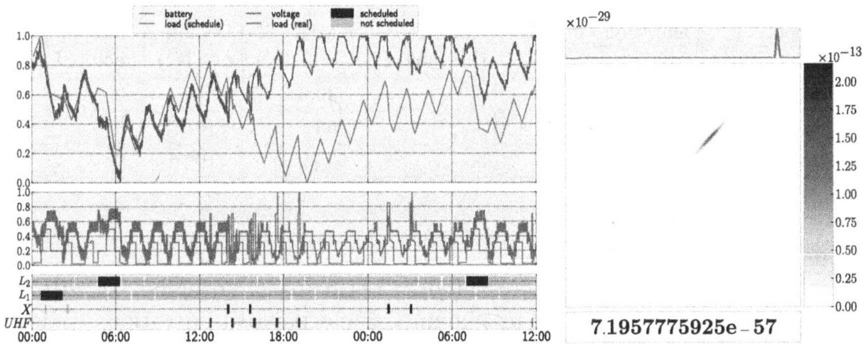

Fig. 7. Schedule February 14, 2016 midnight to February 15, 2016 noon. (Color figure online)

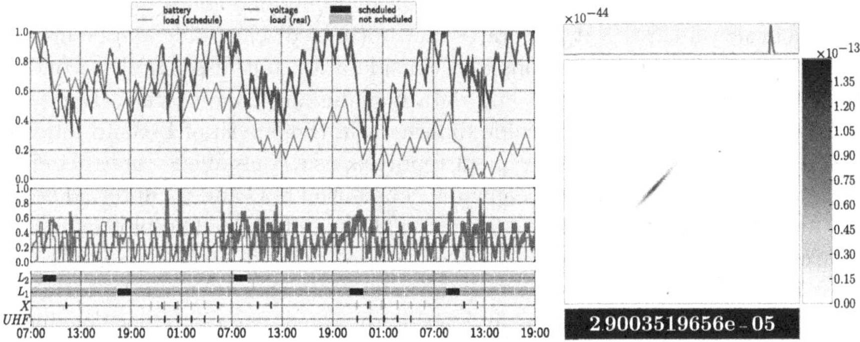

Fig. 8. Schedule March 20, 2016 7 AM to March 22, 2016 7 PM. (Color figure online)

battery SoC of the linear battery (blue) as predicted by Uppaal Cora as well as the actual voltage (red) logged by GomX–3. Voltage and SoC are generally not comparable. However, both quantities exhibit similar tendencies during the (dis)charging process. The battery, voltage and load curves have all been normalized to the interval $[0, 1]$ for comparison reasons.

On the right, the three components of the SoC density resulting from the validation step are displayed, obtained by running the generated schedule along the stochastic KiBaM with capacity limits. It is to be interpreted as in Fig. 3. The most crucial part is at the bottom of the plot, quantifying the risk of entering Safe Mode as specified by the GomSpace engineers (40 %).

The data is summarized in the following table, that reports on the value chosen as internal depletion threshold to the `battery` automaton, the initial SoC provided to Uppaal Cora, the minimal SoC along the schedule generated by Uppaal Cora, the depletion risk as calculated by the stochastic KiBaM validation step and how often GomX–3 actually entered Safe Mode.

Experiment *dd.mm.yy hh:mm*	Duration (h)	Initial SoC (%)	Depletion threshold (%)	Min. SoC (%)	Depletion risk (%)	Safe mode entered (*nr.*)
17.11.15 00:00	24	85	40	40.3	20	2
14.02.16 00:00	36	90	55	69	$<10^{-50}$	0
20.03.16 07:00	60	90	55	55.9	$<10^{-2}$	0

November 2015. The schedule presented in Fig. 6 spans November 17, 2015. It is a schedule that optimizes for maximum L-Band payload operations, yielding 4 L-Band operations and 1 X-Band operation together with the 5 UHF ground-station passes. The battery SoC and the measured battery voltage show a close correspondence. GomSpace reported that GomX–3 entered Safe Mode twice, if only for a short period of time.

February 2016. Figure 7 presents a schedule spanning one and a half day, starting on February 14, 2016. It illustrates how optimized scheduling can be utilized to not only take power limitations into consideration but also handle secondary constraints like data generation and data downlinking balance via L-Band and X-Band tasks. There is a noticeable difference in the length of L-Band job windows, relative to the earlier experiment reported, as a consequence of experiences gained by the engineers in the meanwhile. The initial SoC and the internal depletion threshold were communicated to us as 90 % and 55 %. The plot exhibits a drift between battery SoC and measured voltage around 3 PM of the first day, after initially showing a close correspondence, indicating that the battery is in a better state relative to our pessimistic predictions. The GomSpace engineers were able to track down this drift to a mismatch in the net power balance computed as input to the toolchain.

March 2016. The third schedule we present (Fig. 8) is the longest in duration, spanning from March 20 at 7 AM to March 22 at 7 PM. After initial close correspondence of SoC and voltage, around 18 h into the test run we observe a slight but continuous drift between predicted battery SoC and measured voltage, yet not as steep as in the February test run.

6 Discussion and Conclusion

This paper has presented a battery aware scheduling approach for low-earth orbiting nano satellites. The heterogeneous timing aspects and the experimental nature of this application domain pose great challenges, making it impossible to use traditional scheduling approaches for periodic tasks. Our approach harvests work on schedulability analysis with (priced) timed automata. It is distinguished by the following features: (*i*) The TA modelling approach is very flexible, adaptive to changing requirements, and particularly well-suited for discussion with space engineers, since easy-to-grasp. (*ii*) A dynamic approach to the use of cost decorations and constraints allows for a splitted scheduling approach optimising over intervals, at the (acceptable) price of potential sub-optimality of the resulting overall schedules. (*iii*) A linear battery model is employed while scheduling, but prior to shipping any computed schedule is subjected to a quantitative validation on the vastly more accurate Stochastic KiBaM, and possibly rejected. This last aspect is very close in spirit to the approach developed in [9], where a simulation-based analysis of computed schedules is used to validate or refute CORA schedules, under a model with stochastic breakdowns and repairs of production machinery. The stochastic KiBaM validation step is not based on simulation, but exact (or conservative) up to discretisation.

The GomX–3 in-orbit experiments have demonstrated an indeed great fit between the technology developed and the needs of the LEO satellite sector. The schedules generated are of unmatched quality: It became apparent that relative to a comparative manual scheduling approach, better quality schedules with respect to (*i*) number of experiments performed, (*ii*) avoidance of planning mistakes, (*iii*) scheduling workload, and (*iv*) battery depletion risk are provided. At the same time, the availability of scheduling tool support flexibilises the satellite design process considerably, since it allows the GomSpace engineers to obtain answers to what-if questions, in combination with their in-house PowerSim tool. This helps shortening development times and thus time-to-orbit.

State of the art technology and very rapid development cycles will continue to be a crucial part of the nanosatellite market. They are the roots of a steady stream of novel scientific challenges. In fact, GomSpace will launch a 2 spacecraft constellation (GomX–4 A and B) in 2017 and is actively pursuing several projects with much larger constellations. Deploying constellations of a large number of satellites (2 to 1000) brings a new level of complexity to the game, which in turn asks for a higher level of automation to be used than has previously been the case in the space industry. The technology investigated here is beneficial in terms of optimization and planning of satellite operations, so as to allow for more efficient utilization of spacecraft flight time. A spacecraft operator is faced with a highly complex task when having to plan and command in-orbit operations constantly balancing power and data budgets. This leads to the fact that for larger constellations tools for optimization, automation and validation are not only a benefit, but an absolutely necessity for proper operations.

Acknowledgements. This work has received support from the EU 7th Framework Programme project 318490 (SENSATION), by the European Space Agency under contract number RFP/NC/IPL-PTE/GLC/as/881.2014, by the ERC Advanced Investigators Grant 695614 (POWVER), and by the CDZ project 1023 (CAP). We are grateful to Boudewijn Haverkort and Marijn Jongerden (both from Universiteit Twente), Kim Larsen, Marius Mikučionis, Erik Ramsgaard Wognsen (all from Aalborg University), and all further participants of SENSATION as well as experts at GomSpace for very fruitful discussion and support.

References

1. Uppaal Cora (2005). http://people.cs.aau.dk/~adavid/cora/introduction.html
2. Alur, R., Dill, D.L.: A theory of timed automata. Theor. Comput. Sci. **126**, 183–235 (1994)
3. Behrmann, G., Fehnker, A., Hune, T., Larsen, K., Pettersson, P., Romijn, J., Vaandrager, F.: Minimum-cost reachability for priced time automata. In: Benedetto, M.D., Sangiovanni-Vincentelli, A. (eds.) HSCC 2001. LNCS, vol. 2034, pp. 147–161. Springer, Heidelberg (2001). doi:10.1007/3-540-45351-2_15
4. Behrmann, G., Larsen, K.G., Rasmussen, J.I.: Optimal scheduling using priced timed automata. ACM SIGMETRICS Perform. Eval. Rev. **32**(4), 34–40 (2005)
5. Hermanns, H., Krčál, J., Nies, G.: Recharging probably keeps batteries alive. In: Berger, C., Mousavi, M.R. (eds.) CyPhy 2015. LNCS, vol. 9361, pp. 83–98. Springer, Heidelberg (2015). doi:10.1007/978-3-319-25141-7_7
6. Jongerden, M.R., Haverkort, B.R.: Which battery model to use? IET Softw. **3**(6), 445–457 (2009). http://dx.doi.org/10.1049/iet-sen.2009.0001
7. Jongerden, M.R.: Model-based energy analysis of battery powered systems. Ph.D. thesis, Enschede. http://doc.utwente.nl/75079/
8. Larsen, K., Behrmann, G., Brinksma, E., Fehnker, A., Hune, T., Pettersson, P., Romijn, J.: As cheap as possible: effcient cost-optimal reachability for priced timed automata. In: Berry, G., Comon, H., Finkel, A. (eds.) CAV 2001. LNCS, vol. 2102, pp. 493–505. Springer, Heidelberg (2001). doi:10.1007/3-540-44585-4_47
9. Mader, A., Bohnenkamp, H., Usenko, Y.S., Jansen, D.N., Hurink, J., Hermanns, H.: Synthesis and stochastic assessment of cost-optimal schedules. Int. J. Softw. Tools Technol. Transf. **12**(5), 305–318 (2010)
10. Manwell, J.F., McGowan, J.G.: Lead acid battery storage model for hybrid energy systems. Solar Energy **50**(5), 399–405 (1993)

Discounted Duration Calculus

Heinrich Ody[1(✉)], Martin Fränzle[1], and Michael R. Hansen[2]

[1] Department of Computing Science, University of Oldenburg, Oldenburg, Germany
heinrich.ody@uni-oldenburg.de, fraenzle@informatik.uni-oldenburg.de
[2] DTU Compute, Technical University of Denmark, Kongens Lyngby, Denmark
mire@dtu.dk

Abstract. To formally reason about the temporal quality of systems discounting was introduced to CTL and LTL. However, these logic are discrete and they cannot express duration properties. In this work we introduce discounting for a variant of Duration Calculus. We prove decidability of model checking for a useful fragment of discounted Duration Calculus formulas on timed automata under mild assumptions. Further, we provide an extensive example to show the usefulness of the fragment.

Keywords: Duration calculus · Temporal logic · Model checking · Timed automata · Discounting

1 Introduction

In economics discounting represents that money earned soon can be reinvested earlier and hence yields more revenue than money earned later. Discounting has been introduced into temporal logics to represent that something happening earlier is more important than similar events happening later [14]. A typical example is a rail-road crossing. Consider the property "eventually the gates are open". While a controller leaving the gates closed an hour after the train has passed might be safe and alive, it is not useful. We can use discounting to express that the controller should not wait unnecessarily long before opening the gates. The discount here is a scalar defining the decrease rate of an exponential function assigning weights to events based on their (relative) time of occurrence. In [1,13,14] such weighted evaluation of temporal properties has been described as quantifying the temporal quality of a system.

Duration Calculus (DC) [12] was introduced to reason about *duration properties* of real time systems. In the prominent gas burner case study [24] the

An early version of this work was presented at the Nordic Workshop of Programming Theory 2015.

H. Ody—This Work is supported by the Deutsche Forschungsgemeinschaft (DFG) within the Research Training Group DFG GRK 1765 SCARE.

M. Fränzle—This Work was partially supported by Deutsche Forschungsgemeinschaft within the Transregional Collaborative Research Center SFB/TR 14 AVACS.

M.R. Hansen—This Work was partially supported by the Danish Research Foundation for Basic Research within the IDEA4CPS project.

J. Fitzgerald et al. (Eds.): FM 2016, LNCS 9995, pp. 577–592, 2016.
DOI: 10.1007/978-3-319-48989-6_35

following duration property was proven: "in any time interval of length ≥60 gas is leaking for at most 5 % of the time". The great expressiveness of DC however, makes automated reasoning in most cases undecidable [10,11,15].

So far discounting in logics only has been studied for discrete-time temporal logics (LTL, CTL*, μ-calculus) [1,13,14,20,21]. Here, we study discounting in the dense-time logic DC. Our interest in DC arises from its expressiveness, being able to express properties of accumulated durations instead of just temporal distances, and the consequential undecidability of most fragments over dense time. A primary objective of the work reported herein thus is to investigate the impact of discounting on effective approximability of model checking for DC formulas.

To this end we define *discounted Duration Calculus* (DDC), where the truth value is real-valued in the interval $[0, 1]$, instead of Boolean. A truth value closer to 1 means *higher temporal quality.* We point out that we use exponential discounting because this is the most common from of discounting. However, other discounting mechanisms are possible. With DDC we can express properties such as $\Diamond^d \phi$ (meaning "*soon* with *discount* d the system satisfies ϕ"), where ϕ is a DDC formula and $\Diamond$ is the *right neighbourhood* modality from [9]. To evaluate the truth value of $\Diamond^d \phi$ on the interval $[t_0, t_1]$ we search for a neighbouring interval $[t_1, t_2]$ such that the discounting factor $d^{t_2 - t_1}$ multiplied with the truth value of ϕ on $[t_1, t_2]$ is maximal.

Our main result is that for the fragment $\text{DDC}_{<1}$, which consists of all DDC formulas where all discounts are <1, model checking is approximable. This stems from the fact that the effect of the system behaviour on the satisfaction value becomes negligible as time advances. Hence, for approximation it suffices to only consider bounded prefixes of runs, which in turn enables us to use bounded model checking. Our model-checking method is extended to cope with modalities of the form $G_S \phi$ (meaning "whenever S happens ϕ holds thereon"). We provide an extensive example illustrating the usefulness of our approach.

Related Work. Discounting in temporal logics was first studied in [14] and later in [1,13,20,21]. However, in all of these works the logics are discrete and they cannot express duration properties. In [7] the authors introduce a method to perform model checking on weighted (or priced) timed automata with weighted versions of CTL and LTL. A cost in their work essentially corresponds to the duration of a state variable in our work. However, they do not consider discounting and in their case model checking becomes undecidable for automata with at least three clocks. For a fragment without duration properties called *test formulas*, which are used to express undesired behaviours, model checking has been shown decidable [22]. In [17] the authors define a model checking procedure for a fragment that allows duration properties, but disallows negation of the chop operator. In [16] the authors give a real-valued interpretation to DC and they provide an approximative procedure to check satisfiability. However, the authors do not consider model checking. Further, in none of the works on DC discounting is considered.

2 Discounted Duration Calculus (DDC)

We use an adapted version of Duration Calculus (DC), where the chop operator is replaced by a right neighbourhood modality. As atomic formulas, we allow comparison of linear combinations of durations with constants.

Definition 1 (Syntax of DDC). *Let $d, k_0, \ldots, k_n, c \in \mathbb{Q}$, where $d \in [0,1]$, $\gtrsim \in \{\geq, >\}$ and let $P \in AP$ denote arbitrary* atomic propositions *(or state variables or just variables). Then the formulas ϕ of* Discounted Duration Calculus *(abbreviated* DDC*) and* state expressions *S are defined by the grammar*

$$\phi ::= \Diamond^d \phi \mid \neg\phi \mid \phi \vee \phi \mid \Sigma_{i=0}^{n} k_i \textstyle\int S_i \gtrsim c\,,$$
$$S ::= P \mid \neg S \mid S \vee S\,.$$

We denote the fragment of DDC where all discounts are < 1 as $DDC_{<1}$.

Let AP be a finite set of atomic propositions. The semantics of DC is defined in terms of timed words. A *timed word* is a (possibly infinite) sequence

$$\tau = (\sigma_0, t_0)(\sigma_1, t_1) \cdots (\sigma_i, t_i) \cdots$$

where $\sigma_i \in 2^{AP}$ and $t_0 = 0$ and $t_i \in \mathbb{R}_{\geq 0}$. The sequence of time stamps $t_0, t_1, \ldots$ occurring in τ must be *weakly monotonically increasing*, that is $t_i \leq t_{i+1}$. Furthermore, we require *progress* in infinite timed words τ, that is, for every $t \in R_{\geq 0}$ there is an $i > 0$ such that $t_i > t$.

If τ is an infinite sequence, then we say that the *time span (or just span)* of τ comprises the non-negative reals and we write $\mathrm{span}(\tau) = \mathbb{R}_{\geq 0}$. If τ is a finite sequence having (σ_n, t_n) as its last element, the span of τ is the bounded (right-open) interval $[0, t_n)$ and we write $\mathrm{span}(\tau) = [0, t_n)$. We shall from now on restrict our attention to timed words having a non-empty time span.

For a timed word $\tau = (\sigma_0, t_0)(\sigma_1, t_1) \cdots (\sigma_i, t_i) \cdots$ and $\delta \in \mathrm{span}(\tau)$, where $\delta > 0$, we define the *time-bounded prefix* τ_δ of τ as the timed word:

$$\tau_\delta = (\sigma_0, t_0)(\sigma_1, t_1) \cdots (\sigma_i, t_i)(\sigma_i, \delta)$$

where i is given by $t_i \leq \delta < t_{i+1}$. Note that there is exactly one such i since $\delta \in \mathrm{span}(\tau)$.

A timed word $\tau = (\sigma_0, t_0)(\sigma_1, t_1) \cdots (\sigma_i, t_i) \cdots$ induces a function

$$\tau(P) : \mathrm{span}(\tau) \to \{0, 1\}$$

for every atomic proposition P, as follows:

$$\tau(P)(t) = \begin{cases} 1 & \text{if } P \in \sigma_i, \text{ for some } i \text{ where } t_i \leq t < t_{i+1}, \\ 0 & \text{otherwise}. \end{cases}$$

The function $\tau(P)$ is also called a *trajectory* for P. Trajectories are lifted to state expressions by a point-wise extension in a straightforward manner, for example,

$\tau(S_0 \vee S_1)(t) = \tau(S_0)(t) \vee \tau(S_1)(t)$. We use the abbreviation S_τ for $\tau(S)$. Notice that the progress requirement for infinite timed words guarantees that for every variable P, every finite part of P_τ has a finite number of discontinuity points, i.e. P_τ is of *finite variability*.

The *semantics of a DDC formula* ϕ on the basis of a timed word $\tau = (\sigma_0, t_0)(\sigma_1, t_1)\cdots(\sigma_i, t_i)\cdots$ is a function:

$$\tau(\phi) : \mathit{Intv} \to [0, 1]$$

where $\mathit{Intv} = \{[t, t'] \subseteq \mathrm{span}(\tau) \mid t \leq t'\}$ denotes the set of bounded and closed real intervals contained in $\mathrm{span}(\tau)$. The function assigns to $\tau(\phi)\,[a, b]$ a *satisfaction value* in the real interval $[0, 1]$, where closer to 1 means better.

Discounts d occur only in connection with the right neighbourhood modality $\Diamond^d \phi$, which expresses that an adjacent interval to the right of the current interval satisfies ϕ. The discount d is used to decrease the satisfaction value as the length of the adjacent interval necessary to find a satisfaction of ϕ increases. The modal formula $\Diamond^d \phi$ can be understood as "*soon* ϕ holds".

Definition 2 (Semantics of DDC). *The* semantics of a formula, *given a timed word* τ *and an interval* $[t_0, t_1]$*, is defined as*

$$\tau(\Diamond^d \phi)\,[t_0, t_1] = \sup\{d^{t_2 - t_1} \cdot \tau(\phi)\,[t_1, t_2] \mid t_2 \geq t_1 \wedge t_2 \in \mathrm{span}(\tau)\}$$

$$\tau(\Sigma_{i=0}^{n} k_i \textstyle\int S_i \gtrsim c)\,[t_0, t_1] = \begin{cases} 1 & \text{if } \Sigma_{i=0}^{n} k_i \int_{t=t_0}^{t_1} \tau(S_i)(t)\,\mathrm{d}t \gtrsim c \\ 0 & \text{otherwise} \end{cases}$$

$$\tau(\neg\phi)\,[t_0, t_1] = 1 - \tau(\phi)\,[t_0, t_1]$$

$$\tau(\phi_0 \vee \phi_1)\,[t_0, t_1] = \max\{\tau(\phi_0)\,[t_0, t_1], \tau(\phi_1)\,[t_0, t_1]\}$$

where $\gtrsim \in \{>, \geq\}$.

If we want to use the standard neighbourhood modalities without discounting then we use a discount of 1. In this case we do not explicitly write the discount.

We define as abbreviation a modality

$$\Box^d \phi = \neg \Diamond^d \neg \phi,$$

which can be understood as "ϕ holds for a *long* time". For some interval $[t_0, t_1]$ the semantics is

$$\tau(\Box^d \phi)\,[t_0, t_1] = 1 - \sup\{d^{t_2 - t_1} \cdot (1 - \tau(\phi)\,[t_1, t_2] \mid t_2 \geq t_1 \wedge t_2 \in \mathrm{span}(\tau))\}.$$

We point out that the supremum searches for a small $t_2 \geq t_1$ that makes the truth value of $\tau(\phi)$ on $[t_1, t_2]$ small. Further, the greater the interval $[t_1, t_2]$ is chosen, the greater the truth value of $\Box^d \phi$ becomes. Note that the truth value of $\Box^d \phi$ increases with the decrease of d, while the truth value of $\Diamond^d \phi$ decreases with the decrease of d.

To express that a state expression S holds throughout an interval, we use the abbreviation:

$$\lceil S \rceil = \int \neg S = 0 \wedge \ell > 0$$

where ℓ is an abbreviation of $\int (S' \vee \neg S')$ for an arbitrary state expression S'.

With $\Diamond \Diamond \phi$ we express that on some right interval, which may or may not be adjacent to the current interval, ϕ holds. We shall use the abbreviation $\mathrm{F}_S \phi$ to denote that there is some future point interval, say $[t, t]$, where S "happens" and ϕ holds, that is, ϕ holds on $[t, t]$ and S changes from 0 to 1 at t and keeps the value 1 for some nonzero time:

$$\mathrm{F}_S \phi = \Diamond \Diamond \left(\lceil \neg S \rceil \wedge \left(\begin{array}{c} \Diamond \lceil S \rceil \\ \wedge \Diamond (\ell = 0 \wedge \phi) \end{array} \right) \right)$$

Let $\mathrm{G}_S \phi = \neg \mathrm{F}_S \neg \phi$. The formula $\mathrm{G}_S \phi$ thus means that for all future time points t, if S happens at t, then ϕ holds on $[t, t]$.

Example 1. As an example we consider the three formulas:

$$\phi_0 = \Diamond^{0.8} (\int P \geq 3)$$
$$\phi_1 = \Diamond^{0.9} \Box^{0.8} (\int P - \int \neg P \leq 3)$$
$$\phi_2 = \mathrm{G}_Q \Diamond^{0.8} (\int P \geq 2)$$

and the two timed words:

- $\tau_0 = (\{P\}, 0)\ (\{\}, 2)\ (\{P\}, 3)\ (\{\}, 5)\ (\{P\}, 6)$
  $(\{\}, 8)\ (\{P\}, 9)\ (\{\}, 11)\ (\{P\}, 12)(\{\}, 14)$,
- $\tau_1 = (\{\}, 0)\ (\{Q\}, 1)\ (\{P\}, 2)\ (\{Q\}, 4)\ (\{P, Q\}, 5)$
  $(\{\}, 6)\ (\{P\}, 7)\ (\{\}, 8)\ (\{Q\}, 9)\ (\{\}, 10)$
  $(\{P\}, 11)\ (\{\}, 12)\ (\{P\}, 13)\ (\{\}, 14)$,

which induce the trajectories depicted in Fig. 1.

These above formulas can be explained as follows:

- ϕ_0 reads "soon P has held for at least 3 time units",
- ϕ_1 reads "soon P should hold no more than 3 time units more than $\neg P$, for a long time", and
- ϕ_2 reads "every time Q changes its value from 0 to 1, then soon P has held for 2 time units".

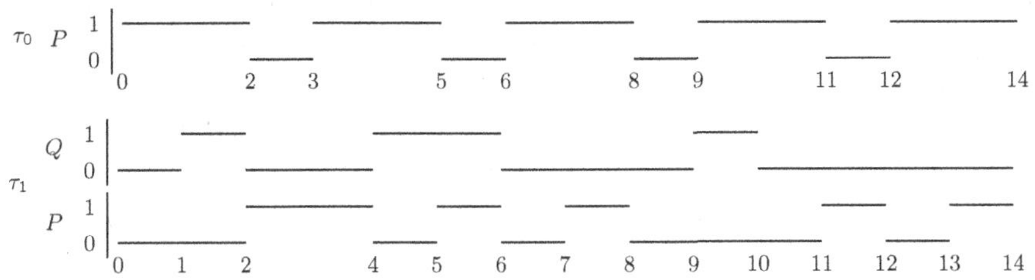

Fig. 1. Graphical representation of two timed words. The word τ_1 contains two atomic propositions P and Q. We assume that all values remain 0 after time point 14.

Evaluate ϕ_0 on τ_0: The earliest point when $\int P \geq 3$ is satisfied is at $t = 4$. We calculate:

$$\begin{aligned}&\tau_0(\Diamond^{0.8}(\textstyle\int P \geq 3))\,[0,0]\\&= \sup\{0.8^t \cdot \tau_0(\textstyle\int P \geq 3)\,[0,t] \mid t \in \operatorname{span}(\tau_0)\}\\&= 0.8^4 \approx 0.41\end{aligned}$$

Evaluate ϕ_1 on τ_0: In ϕ_1 the inner modality is given t_0 and chooses the smallest t_1 such that $\int P - \int \neg P \leq 3$ is violated. The outer modality chooses t_0 such that the product of its discount 0.9^{t_0} multiplied with the truth value archived by the inner modality becomes maximal. We calculate (assuming that $t_0, t_1 \in \operatorname{span}(\tau_0)$):

$$\begin{aligned}&\tau_0(\Diamond^{0.9}\,\Box^{0.8}(\textstyle\int P - \int \neg P \leq 3))\,[0,0]\\&= \sup_{t_0 \geq 0}\{0.9^{t_0} \cdot (1 - \sup_{t_1 \geq t_0}\{0.8^{t_1 - t_0} \cdot (1 - \tau_0(\textstyle\int P - \int \neg P \leq 3)\,[t_0,t_1])\})\}\\&= 0.9^2 \cdot (1 - 0.8^{12-2} \cdot (1 - \tau_0(\textstyle\int P - \int \neg P \leq 3)\,[t_0,t_1])\\&= 0.9^2 \cdot (1 - 0.8^{12-2} \cdot (1 - 0)) \approx 0.72\end{aligned}$$

Evaluate ϕ_2 on τ_1: We evaluate $\psi = \Diamond^{0.8}(\int P \geq 2)$ on all point intervals $[t,t]$, where Q changes its value from 0 to 1. For τ_1 these points are 1, 4 and 9. The truth value is $\min\{\tau_1(\psi)\,[1,1], \tau_1(\psi)\,[4,4], \tau_1(\psi)\,[9,9]\}$, which evaluates to $\min\{0.8^{4-1}, 0.8^{8-4}, 0.8^{14-9}\} \approx 0.33$.

3 Model Checking

In this section we prove that model checking for a relevent fragment of DDC is approximable, where the model is given as a timed automaton [2]. To this end we first show that for approximation it is sufficient to consider only bounded prefixes of runs. Then we give a reduction to quantified linear real arithmetic.

3.1 The Model

As model we use timed automata that have atomic propositions that hold in states (denoted by Λ) instead of events on edges. Additionally, our timed automata have a set of allowed initial clock valuations, where the initial value of a clock may be different from 0. Further, we assume that our timed automata are *strongly non-Zeno* [3]. This is the case, iff there is a non-zero constant $c \in \mathbb{R}_{>0}$ such that in every control cycle at least c units of time passes. Formally, for every path $l_0 \xrightarrow{e_0} \ldots \xrightarrow{e_{n-1}} l_n$ with $l_0 = l_n$ there is an edge that resets some clock x and an edge or a location with a constraint $x \geq c$. For ease of exposition we assume this constant to be a natural number greater than 0.

Definition 3 (Timed Automata). *Let $\mathcal{X}$ be a finite set of non-negative real-valued variables, called clocks and let $\mathbb{V}$ be the set of all clock valuations. Then $\mathbb{B}(\mathcal{X})$ is the set of all conjunctions of constraints of the form $x - y \bowtie c$ or $x \bowtie c$ with $x, y \in \mathcal{X}, c \in \mathbb{Q}, \bowtie \in \{<, >, \geq, \leq\}$. Further, let AP be a finite set of atomic propositions. A timed automaton is a tuple $A = (L, E, I, Inv, \Lambda, \mathcal{X})$, where L is* *the set of locations,* $E \subseteq L \times \mathbb{B}(\mathcal{X}) \times 2^{\mathcal{X}} \times L$ *is the set of edges,* $I \subseteq L \times \mathbb{V}$ *is the set of initial states,* $Inv : L \to \mathbb{B}(\mathcal{X})$ *are the invariants per location and* $\Lambda : L \to \mathbb{B}(AP)$ *assigns a set of atomic propositions which hold in a location.*

Note that commonly I is defined as $L' \times \{\mathbf{0}\}$, where $L' \subseteq L$ and $\mathbf{0} \in \mathbb{V}$ is the clock valuation where all clocks have value 0.

Let ν be a clock valuation, R a set of clocks and g a guard. We define $\nu + t$ is the clock valuation where the values of all clocks are increased by t. With $\nu[R \mapsto 0]$ we denote the clock valuation resulting from ν by setting all clock values in R to 0. And with $\nu \in g$ we denote that ν satisfies the constraints in g.

Definition 4 (Runs of Timed Automata). *Given a timed automaton* $A = (L, E, I, Inv, \Lambda, \mathcal{X})$ *and a possibly infinite timed word* $\tau = (\sigma_0, t_0) \dots (\sigma_i, t_i) \dots$ *let* $\Delta_i = t_{i+1} - t_i$ *and let* N *be the set of integers such that* $i \in N$ *iff there is an element* (σ_i, t_i) *in* τ. *This means that* $N = \mathbb{N}$ *if* τ *is infinite. A run of* A *on* τ *is a sequence*

$$\pi = (l_0, \nu_0) \dots (l_i, \nu_i) \dots$$

with $(l_0, \nu_0) \in I$, *for every* $j \in N$ *we have* $\sigma_j \implies \Lambda(l_j)$ *and for every* $j, j+1 \in N$ *there exists an edge* $(l_j, g_j, R_j, l_{j+1}) \in E$ *such that* $\forall t \in \mathbb{R}. 0 \leq t \leq \Delta_j \implies \nu_j + t \in Inv(l_j)$, $\nu_j + \Delta_j \in g$, $\nu_{j+1} \in Inv(l_{j+1})$ *and* $\nu_{j+1} = (\nu_j + \Delta_j)[R_j \mapsto 0]$.

With $L(A)$ *we denote the set of all timed words for which there exists a run on* A.

As we work with real-valued truth values, here model checking gives a value in the interval $[0, 1]$.

Definition 5 (Model Checking Timed Automata). *Let* A *be a timed automaton and* ϕ *be a DDC formula. We define* model checking *as computing*

$$\min_{\tau \in L(A)} \{\tau(\phi)\,[0, 0]\}.$$

When the timed automaton has upper bounds for the values of all clocks in all locations the set of reachable states is computable with a finite representation. The goal of this constraint is to avoid over approximation introduced by the *normalisation* step of reachability algorithms [5]. We use this to reduce computing the satisfaction value of $\mathrm{G}_S\phi$ by A to computing the satisfaction value of ϕ by a transformed automaton A'.

Lemma 1. *Let* ϕ *be a* $DDC_{<1}$ *formula,* $A = (L, E, I, Inv, \Lambda, \mathcal{X})$ *a timed automaton with* $\forall l \in L, x \in \mathcal{X}. \exists c \in \mathbb{Q}. x \lesssim c \in Inv(l), \lesssim \in \{<, \leq\}$, *and* S *a state expression. Then*

$$\min_{\tau \in L(A)} \{\tau(\mathrm{G}_S\phi)\,[0, 0]\} = \min_{\tau' \in L(A')} \{\tau'(\phi)\,[0, 0]\}$$

where $A' = (L, E, I', Inv, \Lambda, \mathcal{X})$ *is the timed automaton obtained from* A, *by letting the initial states* I' *be those where the state expression* S *just has become* *true. Let Reach be the set of reachable states in A, let L_S be the set of locations where S holds and define*

$$I' = \{(l, \nu) \mid l \in L_S \wedge (l', g, R, l) \in E \wedge (l', \nu') \in Reach \wedge \nu' \in g \wedge \nu \in Inv(l) \wedge \nu'[R \mapsto 0] = \nu \wedge l' \in L \setminus L_S\}.$$

Furthermore, I' is computable and has a finite representation using linear arithmetic [5].

We give our definition of approximate model checking.

Definition 6 (Approximate Model Checking). *Let A be a timed automaton, ϕ be a $DDC_{<1}$ formula and let $\epsilon \in (0, 1]$ be the desired precision. Then* approximate model checking *is to compute a truth value $v \in \mathbb{R}$ with $0 \leq v \leq 1$ such that*

$$v \in \min_{\tau \in L(A)} \{\tau(\phi)\,[0, 0]\} \pm \epsilon\,.$$

For this we compute the point in time $\delta = \log_d \epsilon$ such that the value of v is almost not affected by any suffix of the timed word starting at time δ. This is possible because all modalities in $\text{DDC}_{<1}$ are discounted by less than 1 and hence the effect of a timed word on the truth value becomes less and less as time advances. Note that for other discounting functions, e.g. $\frac{1}{1+d\cdot(t-t')}$ other computations are necessary. However, for any computable strictly monotonic discounting function with limit 0 such a point, after which the effect on the truth value is $\leq \epsilon$, is computable.

Lemma 2. *Given a $DDC_{<1}$ formula ϕ and an allowed error ϵ, let d_{m} be the largest discount constant occurring in ϕ such that for all other discounts d in ϕ we have $d \leq d_{\mathrm{m}}$ and let $\delta = \log_{d_{\mathrm{m}}} \epsilon$. Then for any timed word τ we have*

$$|\tau(\phi)\,[0, 0] - \tau_\delta(\phi)\,[0, 0]| \leq \epsilon\,.$$

We transform the approximate model checking problem for $\text{DDC}_{<1}$ to quantified linear real arithmetic, which we now define.

Definition 7 (Quantified Linear Real Arithmetic (QLRA)). *We define the syntax of* quantified linear real arithmetic *(QLRA) as*

$$\begin{aligned} \phi &::= \neg\phi \mid \phi \vee \phi \mid term \lesssim term \mid \exists x.\phi\,, \\ term &::= a \mid term + term \mid a \cdot term \mid x\,, \\ a &::\in \mathbb{Q} \end{aligned}$$

where $\lesssim \in \{<, \leq\}$ and x is a variable over $\mathbb{R}$.

With linear arithmetic *we denote the fragment of QLRA where all quantifiers are located under an even number of negations.*

To check to what extent a timed automaton satisfies a formula we use bounded reachability checking via linear arithmetic. The following lemma specifies which variables we use in the bounded reachability checking encoding. The construction can be found, e.g., in [4, 25].

Lemma 3 (Bounded Reachability, e.g. [4,25]). *Given a timed automaton A, an initial zone and a step bound l, we can encode the existence of a run of length $\leq l$, starting at any state in the initial zone, in linear arithmetic. We shall assume that this run is described using variables $\underline{t_i}, \underline{P_i}$, for $0 \leq i \leq l$, describing whether in the interval $[t_i, t_{i+1})$ the propositional variable P holds or not.*

3.2 Encoding of the Semantics for Formulas

We encode the semantics of DDC in QLRA. As the semantics of DDC uses exponentials we cannot encode the exact semantics. However, we can approximate the truth value with finite but arbitrary high precision. We use this encoding to prove that approximative model checking for strongly non-Zeno timed automata is computable.

Suppose that $F(\bar{y})$ is a formula of QLRA having $\bar{y}$ as free variables (and possibly others) and suppose that $e(\bar{y})$ is a linear term, then we can express

$$x = \text{lub}\{e(\bar{y}) \in \mathbb{R} \mid F(\bar{y})\}$$

in QLRA, using the abbreviations:

$$\begin{aligned}
\text{UB}(x, e(\bar{y}), F(\bar{y})) &= \forall \bar{y}.F(\bar{y}) \implies x \geq e(\bar{y}) \\
\text{LUB}(x, e(\bar{y}), F(\bar{y})) &= \text{UB}(x, e(\bar{y}), F(\bar{y})) \wedge \forall z.\text{UB}(z, e(\bar{y}), F(\bar{y})) \implies z \geq x
\end{aligned}$$

Furthermore, we shall use the following QLRA abbreviation to express that $x = \max(e_1, e_2)$:

$$\text{MAX}(x, e_1, e_2) = (e_1 < e_2 \implies x = e_2) \wedge (e_1 \geq e_2 \implies x = e_1)$$

When v, t, d range over a bounded domain we can approximate an exponential function $v \cdot d^t$ with an arbitrary precision using linear approximations. Below we will use the abbreviation x isApproxOf $v\ d\ t$ to denote that x is an approximation of $v \cdot d^t$.

The encoding of a formula ϕ in an interval $[t_0, t_1]$ is based on a symbolic first-order formula representation of a bounded model guaranteed by Lemma 3. We shall now show how the semantics of formulas on bounded runs are encoded in QLRA, by defining a QLRA formula x isSemOf^l $\phi\ t_0\ t_1$ denoting that x is (an approximation of) the semantics of ϕ in the interval $[t_0, t_1]$. This formula is defined by recursion over the structure of ϕ.

Encoding for $\tau(\Sigma_{j=0}^{n} k_j \int S_j \gtrsim c)\ [t_0, t_1]$

We show the encoding of $k \int S \gtrsim c$. The generalisation to linear combinations of durations is easily done in QLRA.

For every interval from $\underline{t_i}$ to $\underline{t_{i+1}}$ we introduce a variable x_i denoting the duration of S on this interval. To this end we introduce the following abbreviations:

z isOverlap$_i$ $t_0\ t_1$ denotes that z is the length of $[t_0, t_1] \cap [\underline{t_i}, \underline{t_{i+1}}]$ and
y isDur$_i$ $S\ t_0\ t_1$ denotes that y is the duration of S on $[t_0, t_1] \cap [\underline{t_i}, \underline{t_{i+1}}]$.

where the definitions are provided below.

For the formula x isSemOf^l $k\int S \gtrsim c\ t_0\ t_1$ we define that if the inequality $(k\int S \gtrsim c)$ holds $x = 1$, and otherwise $x = 0$:

$$((\exists y_0,\ldots,y_{l-1}.k \cdot \Sigma_{i=0}^{l-1} y_i \gtrsim c \wedge \bigwedge_{i=0}^{l-1}(y_i \text{ isDur}_i\ S\ t_0\ t_1)) \implies x = 1) \wedge$$
$$(\neg(\exists y_0,\ldots,y_{l-1}.k \cdot \Sigma_{i=0}^{l-1} y_i \gtrsim c \wedge \bigwedge_{i=0}^{l-1}(y_i \text{ isDur}_i\ S\ t_0\ t_1)) \implies x = 0)$$

It is easy to generalize this to cover linear sums of accumulated durations.

The abbreviation z isOverlap$_i$ $t_0\ t_1$ is as follows:

$$\begin{aligned}
&(t_0 \geq \underline{t_{i+1}} \vee t_1 \leq \underline{t_i} \implies z = 0)\\
&\wedge(t_0 \leq \underline{t_i} \wedge \underline{t_{i+1}} \leq t_1 \implies z = \underline{t_{i+1}} - \underline{t_i})\\
&\wedge(\underline{t_i} \leq t_0 \wedge \underline{t_{i+1}} \leq t_1 \implies z = \underline{t_{i+1}} - t_0)\\
&\wedge(t_0 \leq \underline{t_i} \wedge t_1 \leq \underline{t_{i+1}} \implies z = t_1 - \underline{t_i})\\
&\wedge(\underline{t_i} \leq t_0 \wedge t_1 \leq \underline{t_{i+1}} \implies z = t_1 - t_0)
\end{aligned}$$

and the abbreviation y isDur$_i$ $S\ t_0\ t_1$ is:

$$\begin{aligned}
&(\underline{S} \implies y \text{ isOverlap}_i\ t_0\ t_1)\\
\wedge\ &(\neg\underline{S} \implies y = 0)
\end{aligned}$$

where $\underline{S}$ is the formula obtained from S by replacing every occurrence of a state variable P with $\underline{P_i}$.

Encoding of $\tau(\phi_0 \vee \phi_1)\ [t_0, t_1]$

The formula x isSemOf^l $(\phi_0 \vee \phi_1)\ t_0\ t_1$ is defined by:

$$\exists y_0, y_1.(y_0 \text{ isSemOf}^l\ \phi_0\ t_0\ t_1) \wedge (y_1 \text{ isSemOf}^l\ \phi_1\ t_0\ t_1) \wedge \text{MAX}(x, y_0, y_1)$$

Encoding of $\tau(\neg\phi)\ [t_0, t_1]$

The formula x isSemOf^l $(\neg\phi)\ t_0\ t_1$ is defined by $\exists y.\ (y \text{ isSemOf}^l\ \phi\ t_0\ t_1) \wedge x = 1 - y$

Encoding of $\tau(\Diamond^d\phi)\ [t_0, t_1]$

The formula x isSemOf^l $(\Diamond^d\phi)\ t_0\ t_1$ is defined by $\exists t_2, r.\text{LUB}(x, e(y), F(t_2, y, r))$, where

$$\begin{aligned}
e(y) &= y\\
F(t_2, y, r) &= (r \text{ isSemOf}^l \phi\ t_1\ t_2) \wedge (y \text{ isApproxOf } r\ d\ (t_2 - t_1))\\
&\qquad \wedge t_2 \geq t_1 \wedge t_2 \leq \underline{t_l}
\end{aligned}$$

We use our approximation of the semantics in QLRA and the bounded model checking approach to prove that approximate model checking is computable.

Theorem 1 (Approximate Model Checking). *Given a strongly non-Zeno timed automaton A and a $DDC_{<1}$ formula ϕ and a desired precision $\epsilon \in \mathbb{R}_{>0}$, the approximate model-checking problem is effectively computable: There is a procedure computing $v \in [0,1]$ such that*

$$v \in \min_{\tau \in L(A)} \{\tau(\phi)\,[0,0]\} \pm \epsilon\,.$$

Proof. Let $\epsilon_1, \epsilon_2 > 0$ be such that $\epsilon_1 + \epsilon_2 = \epsilon$. According to Lemma 2, we can bound the time horizon of interest to $\delta = \log_{d_\mathrm{m}} \epsilon_1$ with d_m again being the largest discount constant occurring in ϕ, thereby obtaining

$$|\tau(\phi)\,[0,0] - \tau_\delta(\phi)\,[0,0]| \leq \epsilon_1\,. \tag{1}$$

As A is strongly non-Zeno, the number of transitions occurring in A within δ time units is bounded by a constant $l \in \mathbb{N}$, which can be computed as $\lceil M\delta \rceil$ with M being the length of the longest cycle in the transition graph of A.

Given this bound l on the length of the runs to be considered, we can easily obtain (Q)LRA encodings of both the runs of A of the appropriate length $\leq l$ and of the l-bounded DDC semantics: Let

$$R_j = F_A^j(\underline{t}, \underline{P})\,,$$

where $F_A^j(\underline{t}, \underline{P})$ is the LRA-encoding of the runs of A of length j according to Lemma 3, and let

$$Sem_j(y) = (y \text{ isSemOf}^j\ \phi\ 0\ 0)\,,$$

where y isSemOf^j ϕ 0 0 is the above encoding of the DDC semantics, with the look-up tables for approximating exponentials being developed to accuracy ϵ_2 over the argument range $[0, \delta]$.

We furthermore introduce an abbreviation GLB$(x, y, F(y))$ for a formula defining $x = \text{glb}\,\{y \mid F(y)\}$ just as we did for the least upper bound. Then the satisfying valuation of GLB$(x, y, \bigvee_{j=1}^{l}(R_j \wedge Sem_j(y)))$, which can be determined effectively by QLRA solving, satisfies

$$|x - \min_{\tau \in L(A)} \{\tau_\delta(\phi)\,[0,0]\}| \leq \epsilon_2$$

due to the accuracy of approximating the exponentials, which together with Eq. (1) in turn implies

$$|x - \min_{\tau \in L(A)} \{\tau(\phi)\,[0,0]\}| \leq \epsilon_2 + \epsilon_1 = \epsilon$$

$$\iff x \in \min_{\tau \in L(A)} \{\tau_\delta(\phi)\,[0,0]\} \pm \epsilon\,.$$

□

4 Example

To support our claims that we can reason about interesting problems with DDC we provide an example in this section.

4.1 Production Cell

We consider two drilling machines that generate heat while drilling. These machines independently of each other process work pieces of different sizes, and the drilling time needed to finish a work piece depends on the size of the piece. If a machine drills for a long time without interruption the machine becomes too hot. If the machine is too hot, it will gradually take damage. It is undesirable to always avoid that the machine becomes too hot, because then production will be too low. The desired property is that the machine soon cools down, after it became too hot.

Let $i \in \{0, 1\}$. We represent that machine i is too hot by a propositional variable H_i, that the machine is drilling by D_i and the durability of the machine by the discount (here 0.9, where closer to 1 means more durable). Further, there are coefficients (here 1, 2) representing how quickly the temperature changes over time in the respective locations and here 5 is the desired cooldown to achieve after the machine has become too hot. We formalise the desired property as

$$\mathrm{G}_{H_0}(\Diamond^{0.9}(\textstyle\int\neg D_0 - 2\int D_0 \geq 5)) \wedge \mathrm{G}_{H_1}(\Diamond^{0.9}(\int\neg D_1 - 2\int D_1 \geq 5)).$$

The controllers A_0 and A_1 of the machines are depicted on the left hand side of Fig. 2. On the right hand side of Fig. 2 we depict the automaton B that determines how quickly the working pieces may appear and that assigns the working pieces nondeterministically to the machines.

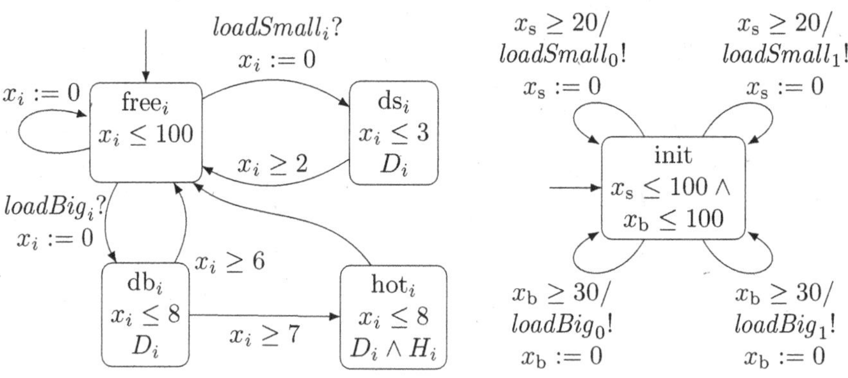

Fig. 2. On the left hand side we see the controller A_i with $i \in \{0, 1\}$ of a drilling machine. The upper bounds of 100, serve to make Lemma 1 applicable, the other upper bounds restrict the maximal drilling time needed for small and big working pieces. The self loop in free$_i$ serves to make the parallel composition $A_0 \parallel A_1 \parallel B$ deadlock free. On the right hand side we see B, which controls how quickly work pieces may appear.

4.2 Computing the Satisfaction Value

Here we focus on the satisfaction value of the subformula $\mathrm{G}_{H_0}(\Diamond^{0.9}(\int\neg D_0 - 2\int D_0 \geq 5))$. However, the satisfaction value for the other subformula is equal.

Let $C = (A_0 \parallel A_1 \parallel B) = (L, E, I, Inv, \Lambda, \mathcal{X})$ be the parallel composition of A_0, A_1 and B. To approximate the satisfaction value of $\mathrm{G}_{H_0}(\Diamond^{0.9}(\int\neg D_0 - 2\int D_0 \geq 5))$ by C we apply Lemma 1 for the first subformula and create $C' = (L, E, I', Inv, \Lambda, \mathcal{X})$ that has all states as initial states in which the edge from db_0 to hot_0 was just taken. The set I' is defined as[1]

$$\begin{aligned} I' =&\{((\mathrm{db}_0, \mathrm{free}_1, \mathrm{init}), \nu) \mid \nu \in (7 \leq x_0 \leq 8 \wedge x_0 = x_\mathrm{b} \wedge x_\mathrm{s} \leq 100 \wedge \\ &\quad ((x_1 - x_\mathrm{s} \leq -2 \wedge x_1 \leq x_\mathrm{b}) \vee (x_\mathrm{b} - x_\mathrm{s} \leq -2 \wedge x_1 \leq 100)))\} \cup \\ &\{((\mathrm{db}_0, \mathrm{ds}_1, \mathrm{init}), \nu) \mid \nu \in (7 \leq x_0 \leq 8 \wedge x_0 = x_\mathrm{b} \wedge x_\mathrm{s} \leq 3 \wedge x_1 = x_\mathrm{s})\}\,. \end{aligned}$$

Let the desired precision be $\epsilon = 0.1$. According to Lemma 2 we have $\delta = \log_{0.9}\epsilon$, which is less than 22. Let $\delta = 22$ and note that by choosing a larger δ than necessary we increase the precision of the computation. The approximation of the satisfaction value is

$$\min_{\tau \in L(C')} \{\sup\{0.9^t \cdot \tau_{22}(\textstyle\int\neg D_0 - 2\int D_0 \geq 5)\,[0,t] \mid 0 \leq t \leq 22\}\} \pm \epsilon\,.$$

Hence, we are looking for a run π in C', such that in the timed word induced by π the smallest t for which $\tau_{22}(\int\neg D_0 - 2\int D_0 \geq 5)\,[0,t]$ holds, is large.

A run that maximises the time t needed to satisfy $\int\neg D_0 - 2\int D_0 \geq 5$ is depicted below. The intuition of the run is that directly after the machine finished a big working piece, it has to work on a small working piece. The location of B always is init. Hence, the states in the run have the form $(l_0, l_1, \nu(x_0), \nu(x_1), \nu(x_\mathrm{s}), \nu(x_\mathrm{b}))$ where l_i is a location from A_i with $i \in \{0,1\}$ and $\nu(y)$ is the value of the clock y under the clock valuation ν:

$$\begin{aligned} \pi =&(\mathrm{hot}_0, \mathrm{free}_1, 7, 0, 19, 7)(\mathrm{hot}_0, \mathrm{free}_1, 8, 1, 20, 8)(\mathrm{free}_0, \mathrm{free}_1, 8, 1, 20, 8) \\ &(\mathrm{ds}_0, \mathrm{free}_1, 0, 1, 0, 8)(\mathrm{ds}_0, \mathrm{free}_1, 3, 4, 3, 11) \\ &(\mathrm{free}_0, \mathrm{free}_1, 3, 4, 3, 11)(\mathrm{free}_0, \mathrm{free}_1, 16, 17, 16, 24) \end{aligned}$$

The run spends 4 time units in locations where D_0 holds (hot_0, ds_0), and 13 time units in locations where $\neg D_0$ holds (free_0). Hence, it satisfies $\int\neg D_0 - 2\int D_0 \geq 5$ after $t = 17$ time units and we have

$$\min_{\tau \in L(C')} \{\tau(\Diamond^{0.9}(\textstyle\int\neg D_0 - 2\int D_0 \geq 5))\} \in\ 0.9^{17} \pm 0.1 \approx 0.17 \pm 0.1\,.$$

In general, by considering only bounded prefixes of all runs we introduce an error of at most ϵ. However, in our example the result 0.9^{17} is exact, because in C' all runs starting from I' satisfy $\int\neg D_0 - 2\int D_0 \geq 5$ in less than $\delta = 22$ time units.

[1] We computed the initial states with Uppaal Tiga [8] by computing a winning strategy for the property *control* : *A*[] *true* with the options `-c -w 2 -n 2`.

We see that the controllers of the drilling machines satisfy our cooldown property poorly. To fix this we could introduce a scheduler in between the controllers A_0, A_1 and the spawner of the working pieces B. This scheduler would then assign the working pieces to machines in a way that avoids assigning two successive working pieces to the same machine. As the model then would be quite big, we would need automation to compute the satisfaction value for the larger example. Fortunately, for strongly non-Zeno timed automata and properties of the form $\Diamond^d \Sigma_{i=0}^{n-1} k_i \int S_i \sim c$ and $\Box^d \Sigma_{i=0}^{n-1} k_i \int S_i \sim c$ we can compute the satisfaction value via optimisation modulo theories [6,23].

5 Conclusion

Discounting has been introduced to temporal logics to formalise reasoning about temporal quality of systems [1,13], where temporal quality quantifies how soon events of interest happen, rather than just answering the qualitative question whether they happen at all. We introduced discounting to Duration Calculus to be able to analyse the quality of real-time systems w.r.t. duration properties. Our main result is that, with the fragment $\text{DDC}_{<1}$ consisting of all formulas where the discounts are <1, we identified a fragment of DDC where model checking for timed automata is approximable under mild assumptions. While this only allows us to reason about bounded prefixes of runs, our reduction of approximating the satisfaction value for formulas $\text{G}_S\phi$ (read: "whenever S happens ϕ holds thereon") to model checking $\text{DDC}_{<1}$ enables us to also reason about infinite runs. At last, we provided an extensive example to demonstrate the usefulness of discounting in temporal logics in general and of discounting duration properties in particular.

For future work it is interesting to see how large the fragment of DDC is, for which model checking is approximable.

In Sect. 4 we mentioned that for properties of the form $\Diamond^d \Sigma_{i=0}^{n-1} k_i \int S_i \sim c$ and $\Box^d \Sigma_{i=0}^{n-1} k_i \int S_i \sim c$ with $d < 1$ the satisfaction value can be approximated efficiently via a reduction to optimisation modulo theories [6,23]. Naturally, it is desirable to find efficient algorithms for larger fragments of DDC.

Further, in [1,13] operators, such as taking the average of two formulas, that are not available in qualitative logics, were studied. To find or define such operators and evaluate their usefulness and their effect on computability is another interesting challenge. One such operator may be $\phi \to \psi = \min\{1, 1-u+v\}$ from Łukasiewicz logics [18], where u, v are the truth values of ϕ, ψ. This definition of implication allows for a closer connection between the truth values of ϕ and ψ than the definitions we used.

Durations in our setting correspond to costs in the setting of multi-priced timed automata (MPTA) [19]. In our work we discovered that often we are interested in the costs of handling a temporal event (as indicated by our use of $\text{G}_S\phi$). This could be modelled in MPTA by resetting the cost variable. As this reset action would not depend on the costs, but only on observable behaviour these enhanced MPTA might have interesting decidable problems.

Acknowledgement. We thank Peter Gjøl Jensen for advice on how to compute the set of reachable zones with UPPAAL TIGA.

References

1. Almagor, S., Boker, U., Kupferman, O.: Discounting in LTL. In: Ábrahám, E., Havelund, K. (eds.) TACAS 2014. LNCS, vol. 8413, pp. 424–439. Springer, Heidelberg (2014). doi:10.1007/978-3-642-54862-8_37
2. Alur, R., Dill, D.L.: A theory of timed automata. Theoret. Comput. Sci. **126**(2), 183–235 (1994)
3. Asarin, E., Maler, O., Pnueli, A., Sifakis, J.: Controller synthesis for timed automata. In: Symposium on System Structure and Control, pp. 469–474 (1998)
4. Badban, B., Lange, M.: Exact incremental analysis of timed automata with an SMT-Solver. In: Fahrenberg, U., Tripakis, S. (eds.) FORMATS 2011. LNCS, vol. 6919, pp. 177–192. Springer, Heidelberg (2011). doi:10.1007/978-3-642-24310-3_13
5. Bengtsson, J., Yi, W.: On clock difference constraints and termination in reachability analysis of timed automata. In: Dong, J.S., Woodcock, J. (eds.) ICFEM 2003. LNCS, vol. 2885, pp. 491–503. Springer, Heidelberg (2003). doi:10.1007/978-3-540-39893-6_28
6. Bjørner, N., Phan, A.-D., Fleckenstein, L.: νZ - an optimizing SMT solver. In: Baier, C., Tinelli, C. (eds.) TACAS 2015. LNCS, vol. 9035, pp. 194–199. Springer, Heidelberg (2015). doi:10.1007/978-3-662-46681-0_14
7. Bouyer, P., Larsen, K.G., Markey, N.: Model-checking one-clock priced timed automata. In: Seidl, H. (ed.) FoSSaCS 2007. LNCS, vol. 4423, pp. 108–122. Springer, Heidelberg (2007). doi:10.1007/978-3-540-71389-0_9
8. Cassez, F., David, A., Fleury, E., Larsen, K.G., Lime, D.: Efficient on-the-fly algorithms for the analysis of timed games. In: Abadi, M., Alfaro, L. (eds.) CONCUR 2005. LNCS, vol. 3653, pp. 66–80. Springer, Heidelberg (2005). doi:10.1007/11539452_9
9. Chaochen, Z., Hansen, M.R.: An adequate first order interval logic. In: Roever, W.-P., Langmaack, H., Pnueli, A. (eds.) COMPOS 1997. LNCS, vol. 1536, pp. 584–608. Springer, Heidelberg (1998). doi:10.1007/3-540-49213-5_23
10. Chaochen, Z., Hansen, M.R.: Duration Calculus - A Formal Approach to Real-Time Systems. Monographs in Theoretical Computer Science. An EATCS Series. Springer, Heidelberg (2004)
11. Chaochen, Z., Hansen, M.R., Sestoft, P.: Decidability and undecidability results for duration calculus. In: Enjalbert, P., Finkel, A., Wagner, K.W. (eds.) STACS 1993. LNCS, vol. 665, pp. 58–68. Springer, Heidelberg (1993). doi:10.1007/3-540-56503-5_8
12. Chaochen, Z., Hoare, C.A.R., Ravn, A.P.: A calculus of durations. Inf. Process. Lett. **40**(5), 269–276 (1991)
13. de Alfaro, L., Faella, M., Henzinger, T.A., Majumdar, R., Stoelinga, M.: Model checking discounted temporal properties. Theoret. Comput. Sci. **345**(1), 139–170 (2005)
14. de Alfaro, L., Henzinger, T.A., Majumdar, R.: Discounting the future in systems theory. In: Baeten, J.C.M., Lenstra, J.K., Parrow, J., Woeginger, G.J. (eds.) ICALP 2003. LNCS, vol. 2719, pp. 1022–1037. Springer, Heidelberg (2003). doi:10.1007/3-540-45061-0_79
15. Fränzle, M.: Model-checking dense-time duration calculus. Formal Aspects Comput. **16**(2), 121–139 (2004)

16. Fränzle, M., Hansen, M.R.: A robust interpretation of duration calculus. In: Hung, D., Wirsing, M. (eds.) ICTAC 2005. LNCS, vol. 3722, pp. 257–271. Springer, Heidelberg (2005). doi:10.1007/11560647_17
17. Fränzle, M., Hansen, M.R.: Deciding an interval logic with accumulated durations. In: Grumberg, O., Huth, M. (eds.) TACAS 2007. LNCS, vol. 4424, pp. 201–215. Springer, Heidelberg (2007). doi:10.1007/978-3-540-71209-1_17
18. Gottwald, S.: Many-valued logic. In: Zalta, E.N. (ed.) The Stanford Encyclopedia of Philosophy. The Metaphysics Research Lab of Stanford University (2015). http://plato.stanford.edu/archives/spr2015/entries/logic-manyvalued/
19. Larsen, K.G., Rasmussen, J.I.: Optimal reachability for multi-priced timed automata. Theoret. Comput. Sci. **390**(2–3), 197–213 (2008)
20. Mandrali, E.: Weighted LTL with discounting. In: Moreira, N., Reis, R. (eds.) CIAA 2012. LNCS, vol. 7381, pp. 353–360. Springer, Heidelberg (2012). doi:10.1007/978-3-642-31606-7_32
21. Mandrali, E., Rahonis, G.: On weighted first-order logics with discounting. Acta Informatica **51**(2), 61–106 (2014)
22. Meyer, R., Faber, J., Hoenicke, J., Rybalchenko, A.: Model checking duration calculus: a practical approach. Formal Aspects Comput. **20**(4–5), 481–505 (2008)
23. Nieuwenhuis, R., Oliveras, A.: On SAT modulo theories and optimization problems. In: Biere, A., Gomes, C.P. (eds.) SAT 2006. LNCS, vol. 4121, pp. 156–169. Springer, Heidelberg (2006). doi:10.1007/11814948_18
24. Ravn, A.P., Rischel, H., Hansen, K.M.: Specifying and verifying requirements of real-time systems. IEEE Trans. Softw. Eng. **19**(1), 41–55 (1993)
25. Torre, S., Mukhopadhyay, S., Murano, A.: Optimal-reachability and control for acyclic weighted timed automata. In: Baeza-Yates, R., Montanari, U., Santoro, N. (eds.) Foundations of Information Technology in the Era of Network and Mobile Computing. ITIFIP, vol. 96, pp. 485–497. Springer, Heidelberg (2002). doi:10.1007/978-0-387-35608-2_40

Sound and Complete Mutation-Based Program Repair

Bat-Chen Rothenberg and Orna Grumberg(✉)

CS Department, Technion, Haifa, Israel
{batg,orna}@cs.technion.ac.il

Abstract. This work presents a novel approach for automatically repairing an erroneous program with respect to a given set of assertions. Programs are repaired using a predefined set of mutations. We refer to a bounded notion of correctness, even though, for a large enough bound all returned programs are fully correct. To ensure no changes are made to the original program unless necessary, if a program can be repaired by applying a set of mutations Mut, then no superset of Mut is later considered. Programs are checked in increasing number of mutations, and every minimal repaired program is returned as soon as found.

We impose no assumptions on the number of erroneous locations in the program, yet we are able to guarantee soundness and completeness. That is, we assure that a program is returned iff it is minimal and bounded correct.

Searching the space of mutated programs is reduced to searching unsatisfiable sets of constraints, which is performed efficiently using a sophisticated cooperation between SAT and SMT solvers. Similarities between mutated programs are exploited in a new way, by using both the SAT and the SMT solvers incrementally.

We implemented a prototype of our algorithm, compared it with a state-of-the-art repair tool and got very encouraging results.

1 Introduction

In the process of software production and maintenance, much effort and many resources are invested in order to ensure that the product is as bug free as possible. Manual bug repair is time-consuming and requires close acquaintance with the checked program. Therefore, there is a great need for tools performing automated program repair. In recent years, there has been much progress in this field (e.g., [6,12,14,19,22,23]).

In previous work, the presented motivation for the development of program repair tools is to enable the automatic repair of real-world bugs found in large-scale software projects. As a result, existing tools for automated repair aim at being scalable and are targeted for the type of bugs found in deployed software.

We have designed our algorithm with a different goal in mind. In our opinion, automatic repair can be equally or even more useful when applied in the earlier stages of development, before any manual effort was invested in debugging at all.

J. Fitzgerald et al. (Eds.): FM 2016, LNCS 9995, pp. 593–611, 2016.
DOI: 10.1007/978-3-319-48989-6_36

This is because, in our view, it is precisely the initial debugging work that could benefit the most from this automation, since it involves relatively simple bugs being fixed manually by the programmer. For these early development stages, as well as for millions of independent programmers working on small pieces of code, even a non-scalable automatic repair method can help save a lot of time and avoid much frustration.

Our vision is to have a fast, easy-to-use program repair tool, which programmers can run routinely. Ideally, programmers will run the tool immediately after making changes to the program, before any manual effort was invested in debugging at all. Then, if the program contains an assertion violation, the chosen course of action will be determined by the tool's result. If the tool returns one or more possible repairs, those are guaranteed to suppress all assertion violations and thus may be safely applied to the program. If the tool does not return any possible repairs, the programmer can be sure that the problem can not be solved using changes within the search space of the tool. In the later case, though manual debugging will still be needed, knowing what will not solve the problem might give the programmer a head start.

In this work, we take a step forward towards accomplishing this vision, presenting a novel algorithm for automatically repairing a program with respect to a given set of assertions. We use a bounded notion of correctness. That is, for a given bound b, we consider only *bounded computations*, along which each loop in the program is performed at most b times and each recursive call is inlined at most b times. We say that a program is *repaired* if whenever a bounded computation reaches an assertion, the assertion is evaluated to true. Our repair method is *sound*, meaning that every returned program is repaired (i.e., no violation occurs in it up to the given bound). Just like Bounded Model Checking, this increases our confidence in the returned program.

Our programs are repaired using a predefined set of mutations, applied to expressions in conditionals and assignments (e.g. replacing a $+$ operator by a $-$), as was shown useful in previous work [4,5,27]. We impose no assumptions on the number of mutations needed to repair the program and are able to produce repairs involving multiple buggy locations, possibly co-dependent. To make sure that our suggested repairs are as close to the original program as possible, the repaired programs are examined and returned in increasing number of mutations. In addition, only *minimal* sets of mutations are taken into account. That is, if a program can be repaired by applying a set of mutations Mut, then no superset of Mut is later considered. Intuitively, this is our way to make sure all changes made to the program by a certain repair are indeed necessary. Our method is *complete* in the sense of returning *all* minimal sets of mutations that create a repaired program. Specifically, if no repair is found, one can conclude that the given set of mutations is not enough to repair the program. Furthermore, we show that for large enough bound, all returned programs are (unbounded) fully correct.

Note that, the choice to use mutations for repair makes the search space small enough to enable us to have completeness at an affordable cost, yet it is expressive enough to repair meaningful bugs (especially those present in earlier stages of development).

Our algorithm is based on the translation of the program into a set of SMT constraints which is satisfiable (i.e., the conjunction of constraints in it is satisfiable) iff the program contains an assertion violation. This was originally done for the purpose of bounded model checking in [1][1]. Our key observation is that mutating an expression in the program corresponds to replacing a constraint in the set of constraints encoding the program. Thus, searching the space of mutated programs is reduced to searching unsatisfiable sets of constraints. The latter can be performed efficiently using a sophisticated cooperation between SAT and SMT solvers, as was done in [16] for the purpose of finding minimal unsatisfiable cores.

The SAT solver is used to restrict the search space of mutated programs to only those obtained by a minimal mutation set and the SMT solver verifies whether a mutated program is indeed correct. Both the SAT solver and the SMT solver are used incrementally, which means that learned information is passed between successive calls, resulting in big savings in terms of resources used. Using an SMT solver incrementally constitutes a novel way to exploit information learned while checking the correctness of one program for the process of checking correctness of another program. Note, that if the programs are similar, their encoding as sets of SMT constraints will also be similar (due to our observation presented above), resulting in bigger savings when using incremental SMT. This is another important contribution of this paper.

We implemented a prototype of our algorithm for C programs, compared it with the methods of [11,12] and got very encouraging results.

To summarize, the main contributions of our work are:

- We propose a novel *sound and complete* algorithm which returns *all* minimal repaired programs.
- The returned programs are proved to be bounded correct. However, we show that for a large enough bound, all returned programs are fully correct and all minimal fully correct programs are returned.
- We develop an efficient implementation of the algorithm, based on sophisticated cooperation between SAT and SMT solvers, both used incrementally.

1.1 Related Work

Several repair methods follow a test-based "generate and validate" approach. They iteratively select a candidate from the repair search space and check its validity by running all tests in the test suite against it. Examples are GenProg [13,14], TrpAutoRepair [25], AE [31], RSRepair [26] and the more recent SPR [19]. PAR [9], Monperrus and Martinez [20] and Prophet [18] suggest to

[1] To be precise, [1] first translates the program into a bit-vector formula and then further translates it into a propositional formula. Here, we only use the first part of the translation.

use information learned from successful human repairs to extract and prioritize repair actions suitable for the suspected location of the error. Similarily, CodePhage [28] directly transfers pieces of code from correct donor applications to buggy recipient ones. AutoFix-E [30] and AutoFix [24] also use location based repair actions, but require programs to be equipped with contracts.

SemFix [23], DirectFix [21] and Angelix [22] use symbolic execution to infer a repair constraint and synthesize a repair based on it. Nopol [6] also uses synthesis, but only deals with buggy if conditions and missing pre conditions. [10] uses deductive synthesis and is based on pre and post conditions, rather than tests alone. [8,29] describe systems using automata and use LTL specifications for repair.

Mutation based program repair (where the term "mutation" has the same meaning as in this work) was previously done in [5,27]. Both use a test suite as the only specification and focus their efforts on efficient error localization. We, on the other hand, use a formal specification and have no use of localization, since we have to consider all locations in order to guarantee completeness. Also, we allow the repair of multiple expressions, whereas both methods assume a single fault ([5] mentions a possible extension to multiple faults, but this is not a part of the described method).

Finally, the methods of [11,12] are similar to ours in that they work on C programs equipped with assertions (or test suites) and assume faulty expressions. The differences are that they use program analysis based on a finite number of inputs each time, while we use incremental SMT solving that allows reuse of information. Also, they use templates (e.g. a linear combination of variables) for repair, while we use mutations and are able to guarantee completeness. We provide a comparison of performance results between our method and theirs in Sect. 6.

2 Preliminaries

Program Correctness. For our purposes, a *program* is a sequential program composed of standard commands: assignments, conditionals, loops and function calls. Each command is located at a certain *program location* l_i, and all commands are defined over the set of program variables X.

In addition to the standard commands, a program may contain assumptions and assertions, which are commands that help the user specify the desired behavior. *Assumptions* (resp., *assertions*) are commands of the form assume(e) (resp., assert(e)), where e is a boolean expression over X. An assertion assert(e) at location l_i, specifies that the user expects e to evaluate to true whenever control reaches l_i, in all program runs. If e evaluates to true every time control reaches l_i during a run r, we say the assertion *holds* for r. Otherwise, the assertion is *violated.* Once an assertion in the program is violated, the program terminates (this early termination indicates an error has occurred and is usually preceded by an error message explaining what went wrong). An assumption assume(e) at location l_i, specifies that every run reaching l_i with e evaluated to false is terminated. Unlike before, this early termination is not an indication that something went wrong, but simply that the user does not want to consider the rest of this run when checking correctness. For example, if a function f gets as input an integer n, but the user assumes it will only be called with $n \geq 2$, an assumption $assume(n \geq 2)$ can be inserted at the beginning of the function to make sure all runs in which this function is called inappropriately will be truncated.

Definition 1 (correct program). *A program is correct if all assertions in it hold in all runs.*

For a program P and an integer b, a *b-run* of P is a run of P that goes through each loop at most b times and has a recursion depth of at most b (i.e., the depth of the call stack is at most b during the entire run).

Definition 2 (b-correct program). *Let b be an integer. A program is b-correct if all assertions in it hold in all b-runs.*

Our repair method aims at finding programs which are b-correct, therefore we use the term *repaired program* as a notation for a b-correct program.

2.1 Incremental SAT and SMT Solving

A SAT solver is a decision procedure for deciding the satisfiability of a propositional formula. Formulas are usually in conjunction normal form (CNF) and can also be seen as a set of clauses. *Incremental SAT solving* is a general name for a set of techniques aimed at improving the SAT solver's performance when called repeatedly for similar formulas (i.e., similar sets of clauses). The basic principal behind these techniques is to save running time by retaining information learned by the SAT solver between calls.

An SMT solver (where SMT stands for satisfiability modulo theories), is another kind of decision procedure of much recent interest. It decides the satisfiability of a formula expressed in first order logic (FOL), where the interpretation of some symbols is constrained by a background theory (for more details see [3]). Examples of commonly used theories are the theory of linear arithmetic over integers and the theory of arrays. Just like a CNF formula can be seen as a set of clauses, an SMT formula can be seen as a set of constraints in the theory (referred to as *SMT constraints*).

Similarly to SAT solving, incremental techniques can be applied to SMT solving as well. For this to be useful, an SMT formula φ is usually instrumented with boolean variables called *guard variables*. The instrumentation of a formula φ is done as follows: each constraint $c_i \in \varphi$ is replaced by the constraint $x_i \rightarrow c_i$, where x_i is a fresh boolean variable. As a result, the new constraint can easily be satisfied by setting x_i to false. Guard variables are conjuncted with φ and are used as *assumptions*, passed to an incremental SMT solver. They have the effect of canceling out a subset of constraints. For example, if $\varphi = c_1 \wedge c_2$, after instrumentation we get the formula $\varphi' = (x_1 \rightarrow c_1) \wedge (x_2 \rightarrow c_2)$. Calling an incremental SMT solver on φ' with the set of assumptions $\{x_1\}$ causes the SMT solver to check the satisfiability of $\varphi' \wedge x_1$, which essentially disables the constraint c_2. That is, because nothing prevents x_2 from being set to false, and x_1 must be set to true, checking satisfiability of φ' is reduced to checking satisfiability of c_1.

Boolean Cardinality Constraints. Boolean cardinality constraints are constraints of the form $\sum_{i=1}^{n} l_i \leq k$, where l_i is a literal assigned the value 1 if true and 0 if false, and k is an integer constant. For readability, we will refer to these constraints using the notation AtMost$(\{l_1, .., l_n\}, k)$, also used in [17], in order to remind the reader of their intuitive meaning: require that at most k of these literals get the value true. Similarly, the notation AtLeast$(\{l_1, .., l_n\}, k)$, denotes the constraint $\sum_{i=1}^{n} l_i \geq k$. For our implementation we used Minicard [15], which is a SAT-solver designed to perform well on instances containing cardinality constraints.

3 Our Approach

In this section we fix a bound b and refer to repaired programs which are b-correct. Figure 1 presents an overview of our repair system. It is composed of three units: the translation unit, the mutation unit and the repair unit.

The initial processing is done in the translation unit. The translation unit translates the input program into two sets of SMT constraints: S_{hard}, encoding parts of the program which cannot be changed (e.g. assertions), and S_{soft}. Then, the mutation unit constructs for each constraint c_i in S_{soft} a set of alternative constraints S_i, by applying mutations to c_i. Finally, the repair unit searches for all sets of constraints encoding minimal repaired programs (where minimality will be defined with respect to the set of mutations used). In the rest of the section we explain in detail how each unit works.

3.1 The Translation Unit

The translation unit is the first step of the process. It gets an input program and an integer bound b and converts the input program into a set of SMT constraints s.t. the program is b-correct iff the set of constraints is unsatisfiable (i.e. the conjunction of all constraints in it is unsatisfiable).

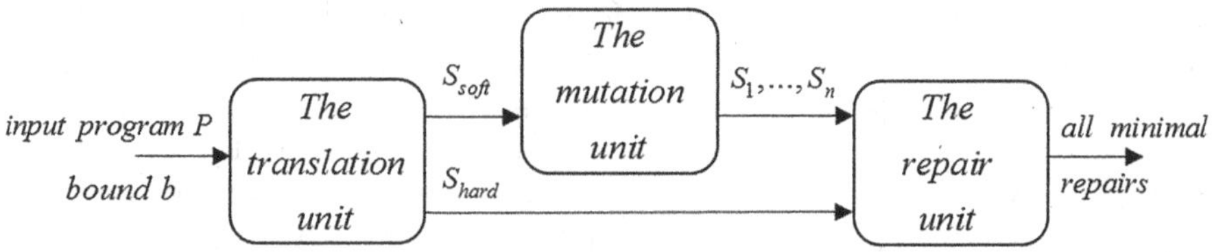

Fig. 1. Overview of the repair system

```
   int sum(int n){
1.     assume(n>=1);
2.     int sum = 0;
3.     for (i=0;i<n;i++){
4.         sum += i;
5.     }
6.     assert(sum=n*(n+1)/2);
7.     return sum;
   }
```

(a) Original program

```
    int sum(int n){
1.      assume(n>=1);
2.      int sum = 0;
3.      int i = 0;
4.      bool g = i<n;
5.      while (g){
6.          sum = sum+i;
7.          i = i+1;
8.          g = i<n;
9.      }
10.     assert(sum=n*(n+1)/2);
11.     return sum;
    }
```

(b) Program after simplification

```
    int sum(int n){
1.      assume(n>=1);
2.      int sum = 0;
3.      int i = 0;
4.      bool g = i<n;
5.      if (g){
6.          sum = sum+i;
7.          i = i+1;
8.          g = i<n;
9.          if (g){
10.             sum = sum+i;
11.             i = i+1;
12.             g = i<n;
13.             assume(!g)
14.         }
15.     }
16.     assert(sum=n*(n+1)/2);
17.     return sum;
    }
```

(c) Program after unwinding for $b = 2$

```
    int sum(int n_1){
1.      assume(n_1>=1);
2.      int sum_1 = 0;
3.      int i_1 = 0;
4.      bool g_1 = i_1<n_1;
5.      if (g_1){
6.          sum_2 = sum_1+i_1;
7.          i_2 = i_1+1;
8.          g_2 = i_2<n_1;
9.          if (g_2){
10.             sum_3 = sum_2+i_2;
11.             i_3 = i_2+1;
12.             g_3 = i_3<n_1;
13.             assume(!g_3)
14.         }
15.     }
16.     sum_4 = g_2 ? sum_3 : sum_2;
17.     sum_5 = g_1 ? sum4 : sum_1;
18.     assert(sum_5=n_1*(n_1+1)/2);
19.     return sum_5;
    }
```

(d) Program after conversion to SSA

Fig. 2. Example of program transformations during translation

Before the set of constraints is constructed, the program undergoes three transformations: simplification, unwinding, and conversion to static single assignment (SSA) form. This transformations are taken from [1], but we present them here because the details are important in order to understand our method.

To explain the different transformations we will use the example presented in Fig. 2. Figure 2a presents a C function named sum, which gets as input an integer n and is supposed to return $\sum_{1}^{n} i$. But, being used to 0-based counting, the programmer made a mistake in line 3, by initializing i to 0 instead of 1 and checking $i < n$ instead of $i <= n$. The assertion in line 6 specifies that the result should always be calculated according to the formula $\frac{n \cdot (n+1)}{2}$, which is the correct sum calculated using the formula for a sum of an arithmetic progression.

We will now go over each transformation and explain its role shortly, using the described example.

Simplification. Figure 2b shows the result of applying simplification to the program in Fig. 2a. Complex constructs are replaced with simpler ones (for example, the for loop was replaced with a while loop). More importantly, all conditions are assigned to auxiliary boolean variables (g in the example). Note that after this step, all original program expressions are right-hand-sides of assignments.

Unwinding. Figure 2c shows the result of applying unwinding for $b = 2$ to the program in Fig. 2b. The loop is unwound b times by duplicating the loop body b times, where each copy is guarded using an if statement that uses the same condition as the loop statement (lines 5–15). Inside the innermost copy, an assume statement is inserted with the negation of the condition (line 13), to specify we do not want to consider runs going through the loop more than b times.[2] Function calls are inlined, with recursive calls treated similarly to loops (inserted up to a depth of b).

Conversion to SSA form. The program is converted to SSA form (which means each variable is assigned only once). Figure 2d shows the result of converting the program in Fig. 2c to SSA form. All variables are replaced with indexed variables, and whenever a variable appears as the left-hand-side of an assignment, its index is increased by 1. If a variable x is assigned inside a conditional statement and is used after the statement, an assignment is inserted straight after the conditional statement to determine which copy of x should be used. For example, lines 16–17 determine the updated value of sum after the nested if statements, according to $g1$ and $g2$. We refer to this type of assignments as Φ-assignments.

After the above transformations, conversion to a set of SMT constraints S is straightforward. An assignment $x = e$ is converted to the constraint $x = e$, an $assume(e)$ is converted to the constraint e and an $assert(e)$ is converted to the constraint $\neg e$.[3] Shortly, we say that a constraint *encodes* a statement.

In the next step, the mutation unit will apply mutations independently to every constraint passed to it. The problem is that, due to unwinding, all statements which are part of a loop (as the loop condition or in the loop body) are encoded using more than one constraint in S. This is of course undesirable, because we do not want constraints encoding the same statement to be mutated using different mutations. To avoid this, if a statement s is encoded using the constraints $c_1, ..., c_t \in S$ (where $t > 1$), we remove $c_1, ..., c_t$ from S, and add instead one complex constraint, $\bigwedge_{i=1}^{t} c_i$. Note that this has no effect on the

[2] In [1] an assertion was inserted and not an assume. Since we fix the program with respect to all assertions in it, we need this to be an assume and not an assert, because we do not want to refer to unbounded runs as bugs.

[3] Assertions are negated because we want a satisfying assignment to the set of constraints to represent a violation of the assertion. If multiple assertions exist in the code, the disjunction of their negations is added as a constraint.

satisfiability of S (which is determined by the conjunction of all constraints in S anyway).

As a final step, the modified set S is partitioned into two sets: S_{soft}, containing all constraints encoding statements subject to repair (i.e. statements containing original program expressions), and S_{hard}, containing the rest (constraints encoding negated assertions, assumptions and Φ-assignments). Note that since we made sure all original program expressions are right-hand-sides of assignments using simplification, we can be sure all constraints in S_{soft} are of the form $(x = e)$ (where x is an SSA variable and e is an expression), or of the form $(c_1 \wedge c_2, ..., \wedge c_n)$ where each c_i is of the form $(x = e)$. Furthermore, we can be sure all program statements which are subject to repair are encoded using a single constraint and vice versa, and thus the size of S_{soft} will always be the same as the number of original program expressions (regardless of the bound b).

3.2 The Mutation Unit

We assume the program is incorrect because it contains one or more faulty expressions, and we try to repair it by applying mutations to program expressions. A *mutation* can be any function mapping a program expression to another program expression of the same type. Examples of mutations include replacing an operator by a similar one (e.g., $\leq$ by $<$) and applying constant manipulations (e.g., replacing a constant by 0). The mutation unit is the component in charge of applying the mutations. In fact, as described in Fig. 1, the mutations are not applied directly on the program, but on constraints encoding the program, received from the translation unit.

As explained in Sect. 3.1, the constraints in the input set, S_{soft}, can be single assignment constraints or multiple assignments constraints. Formally, given a mutation M, and a single assignment constraint $(x = e)$, $M(x = e)$ is the constraint $(x = M(e))$. For a multiple assignment constraint $c = (c_1 \wedge c_2 \wedge ... \wedge c_t)$, $M(c)$ is the constraint $(M(c_1) \wedge M(c_2) \wedge ... \wedge M(c_t))$.

The mutation unit maintains a fixed list of possible mutations, $M_1, M_2, ..., M_m$. For each $c_i \in S_{soft}$ $(1 \leq i \leq n)$ all the mutations are applied and the set $S_i = \{c_i, M_1(c_i), ..., M_m(c_i)\}$ is created.[4] Note that the set S_i contains the original constraint c_i, so leaving a statement intact is always an option. Finally, the sets $S_1, ..., S_n$ are passed on to the repair unit, which uses them to search for a repair.

3.3 The Repair Unit

Basic terms and definitions. The input to the repair unit is a set of "hard constraints", S_{hard}, encoding the parts of the program which can not be changed, and n disjoint sets of "soft constraints", $S_1, ..., S_n$, corresponding to n program

[4] This is a simplification made for ease of presentation. In practice, we might not be able to (or not want to) apply all mutations to all constraints. The choice of mutations to use may depend on the expression's type and/or its complexity.

locations where a possible fault may occur. Every set S_i contains one special constraint, c_o^i, encoding the original statement in line i, referred to as the *original constraint*. The rest of the constraints in S_i encode possible replacements for line i, obtained by applying mutations to the expression in the original statement.

Intuitively, the goal of the repair unit is to construct a repaired program by choosing one constraint from each S_i. Formally, we define a *selection vector* (**sv**) $[c_1, ..., c_n]$ as a vector of constraints where c_i is taken from S_i for all $1 \leq i \leq n$. Recall that constraints in S_i encode different statements for line i, therefore choosing a specific constraint from each S_i can be seen as choosing a statement to appear in each line, i.e. choosing a mutated program. Thus, each selection vector *encodes* a program. We are interested in selection vectors encoding repaired or correct programs. This leads to the following definitions.

Definition 3 (**Rsv**,**Csv**). *A selection vector is repaired, denoted* **Rsv**, *if it encodes a repaired program. A selection vector is correct, denoted* **Csv**, *if it encodes a correct program.*

Though (bounded) correctness is essential for repair, it is not enough. We would also like for the repair to be "minimal", in the sense that no changes are made unless necessary. For example, if a program can be repaired by applying a certain mutation to line number 2, we are not interested in a repair suggesting to additionally mutate line number 3, even if it makes the program repaired. To capture this intuition we define a partial order between constraints and between selection vectors.

Definition 4 ($\sqsubseteq$ partial order between constraints). *Let $c_i^1, c_i^2 \in S_i$. $c_i^1 \sqsubseteq c_i^2$ if $c_i^1 = c_o^i$ and $c_i^2 \neq c_o^i$ (i.e., only c_i^2 encodes a change to line i), or if $c_i^1 = c_i^2$ (i.e., both encode the same statement for line i).*

Definition 5 ($\sqsubseteq$ partial order between **sv**s). *Let $v_1 = [c_1^1, ..., c_n^1], v_2 = [c_1^2, ..., c_n^2]$ be selection vectors. $v_1 \sqsubseteq v_2$ if for all $1 \leq i \leq n$ $c_i^1 \sqsubseteq c_i^2$.*

Definition 6 (**mRsv**,**mCsv**). *A repaired selection vector v is minimal repaired, denoted* **mRsv**, *if there is no v' s.t. $v' \neq v$, v' is a repaired selection vector and $v' \sqsubseteq v$.*

A correct selection vector v is minimal correct, denoted **mCsv**, *if there is no v' s.t. $v' \neq v$, v' is a correct selection vector and $v' \sqsubseteq v$.*

Finally, it makes sense to prefer repairs involving as few statements as possible, because those are more likely to satisfy the user. For example, if the program can be repaired by mutating line 1 and also by mutating lines 2 and 3, the first repair is preferable. This intuition is formalized using the following definition:

Definition 7 (size). *Let v be a selection vector. The size of v, denoted size(v), is $|\{i | 1 \leq i \leq n, v[i] \neq c_o^i\}|$.*

In other words, size(v) is the number of mutated lines in the program encoded by v. Thus, the repair unit should only look for minimal repaired selection vectors, and amongst them prefer those with smaller size. In what follows, we present an algorithm that computes *all* minimal repaired selection vectors (**mRsv**s), and produces results in increasing size over time.

4 Algorithm AllRepair for the Repair Unit

4.1 Outline of the Algorithm

Figure 3 presents the general outline of our algorithm. Overall, the algorithm goes over the search space of all **sv**s, in increasing size order. This order is enforced using the variable k, which limits the allowed size of the searched **sv**s (k is initially 1 and grows over time)[5]. Once the search reaches an **sv** v, we say v has been *explored* (until then, v is *unexplored*). The algorithm is divided into two repeating phases:

Phase 1 is responsible for finding the next unexplored **sv**. First, it looks for an unexplored **sv** of size k. If one exists, it is passed on to Phase 2. Otherwise, it checks if there exist any unexplored **sv**s left at all. If not, the search is over and the procedure ends. Otherwise, k is repeatedly increased by one until an unexplored **sv** v of size k is found (v must be found for some k since we know an unexplored **sv** exists). Once found, v is passed on to Phase 2.

Phase 2 gets as input an unexplored **sv** v. First, it checks if v is repaired, that is, if v is b-correct. If it is, v is returned as a possible repair. In addition, if v is repaired, Phase 2 marks not only v as explored, but also every **sv** v' s.t. $v \sqsubseteq v'$. This is done in order to make sure that we will not waste time exploring v' in the future, since it is necessarily not minimal. If v is not repaired, then only v is marked as explored.

4.2 Algorithm AllRepair in Detail

The pseudo-code of algorithm **AllRepair** is presented in Fig. 4. This algorithm follows the general outline presented before, where an incremental SAT-solver with cardinality constraints is used for the implementation of Phase 1, and an incremental SMT-solver is used for the implementation of Phase 2. Note that, we are interested in the *satisfying assignments* returned by the SAT solver and

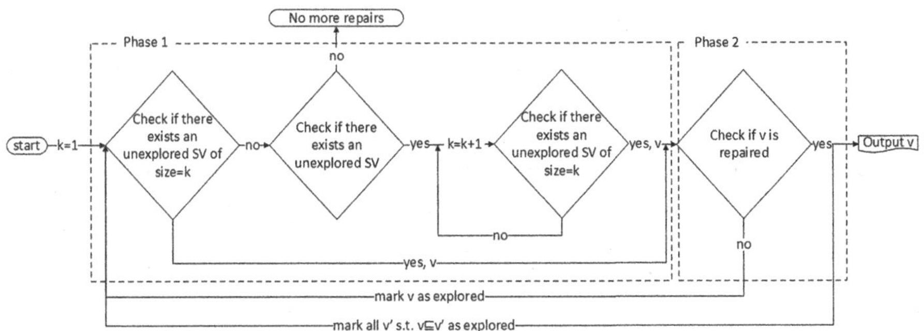

Fig. 3. Outline of algorithm **AllRepair**

[5] k is not to be confused with the unwinding bound b, which is fixed at this point.

```
1: function AllRepair(Input: S_hard, S_1, ..., S_n,  Output: All mRsvs)
2:     S'_1, ..., S'_n, V_1, ..., V_n ← AddSelVars(S_1, ..., S_n)
3:     τ ← true                                    ▷ initialization of SMT formula
4:     for c ∈ S_hard ∪ S'_1 ∪ ... ∪ S'_n do
5:         τ ← τ ∧ c
6:     end for
7:     φ ← true                                    ▷ initialization of boolean formula
8:     for 1 ≤ i ≤ n do
9:         φ ← φ∧AtMost(V_i,1)                     ▷ choose at most one statement per line
10:        φ ← φ∧(⋁_{v∈V_i} v)                     ▷ choose at least one statement per line
11:    end for
12:    V_o ← GetSelVarsOfOriginal(V_1, ..., V_n)
13:    k ← 1
14:    while true do
15:        φ_k ← φ ∧ AtLeast(V_o, n − k)
16:        satRes, V ← SAT(φ_k)
17:        if satRes is unsat then
18:            if ¬SAT(φ) then                     ▷ No more svs to explore
19:                return
20:            end if
21:            repeat
22:                k ← k + 1
23:                φ_k ← φ ∧ AtLeast(V_o, n − k)
24:                satRes, V ← SAT(φ_k)
25:            until satRes is sat
26:        end if
27:        smtRes ← IncrementalSMT(τ, V)           ▷ at this point V has been assigned
28:        if smtRes is SAT then
29:            φ_Block ← BlockUnrepairedsv(V)
30:        else
31:            output Getsv(V, S'_1, ..., S'_n)
32:            φ_Block ← BlockRepairedsv(V)
33:        end if
34:        φ ← φ ∧ φ_Block                         ▷ φ includes new blocking; k is not changed
35:    end while
36: end function
```

Fig. 4. Algorithm **AllRepair** for finding all **mRsvs**

in the *unsatisfiable instances* returned by the SMT solver. The former represent **svs** of desired sizes while the latter represent repaired programs.

The description below is strongly based on the background given in Sect. 2.1. The first step is to instrument all constraints in $S_1, \ldots, S_n$ with guard variables. This is done using a function call in line 2, and the results are the sets of instrumented constraints, $S'_1, \ldots, S'_n$ (where $S'_i = \{x_j \rightarrow c_j \mid \text{for every} c_j \in S_i\}$) and the sets of fresh guard variables used to guard the constraints in each set, $V_1, \ldots, V_n$ (where V_i contains the variables x_j used to guard constraints in S_i).

This instrumentation serves us in building both the SMT formula τ and the boolean formula φ (passed to the SAT-solver).

Next, in lines 3–6, τ is initialized to the conjunction of all constraints in S_{hard} and all the instrumented constraints. Notice that this will enable us to determine which of the soft constraints will be considered in each call to the SMT solver, by using their guard variables as assumptions (while hard constraints will be considered in all calls, regardless of the assumptions).

The boolean formula φ is initialized in lines 7–11. The boolean variables composing this formula are the guard variables $V_1, ..., V_n$, and therefore every satisfying assignment of it can be seen as a subset of guard variables (those assigned true by the assignment). We would like every satisfying assignment to be not just any subset of guard variables, but one consistent with the definition of an **sv**, i.e., a subset that contains exactly one selector variable from each V_i. Lines 9–10 add to φ the necessary constraints to enforce this. From now on, we will say that satisfying assignments returned by the SAT-solver *represent* **sv**s.

Next, we would like to be able to add an upper bound on the size of represented **sv**s. For this purpose, we define an additional formula, φ_k. In order to construct φ_k, we first need to identify which guard variables guard the original constraints. This is done in the function call in line 12, and the result is stored in V_o.

Lines 13–26 essentially implement Phase 1 of the outline in Fig. 3. k is initialized to 1 (line 13) and the iterative repetition of the two phases begins. First, φ_k is set to the conjunction of φ and the clause AtLeast$(V_o, n-k)$ (line 15). That is, in φ_k we additionally require that at least $n-k$ variables from V_o get the value true. This essentially means that every satisfying assignment to φ_k now represents an **sv** of size at most k.

Next, we check whether there exists an unexplored **sv** of size at most k by sending φ_k to the SAT solver (line 16). The satisfiability result (sat/unsat) is saved into *satRes*, and if the result is sat, V gets the set of all variables assigned true by the satisfying assignment. If the result is unsat, we check whether there exists an unexplored **sv** (without limitation on size) by sending φ to the SAT solver (line 18). If the result is unsat, the algorithm ends (line 19). Otherwise, we repeatedly increase k by one and resend φ_k to the SAT solver, until the result is sat (lines 21–25).

Phase 2 begins in line 27, by calling the function IncrementalSMT(τ, V), which checks the satisfiability of τ with all variables in V passed as assumptions. This is in fact equivalent to checking the satisfiabillity of the conjunction of all constraints in S_{hard} and all soft constraints guarded by variables in V (since all other constraints can be easily satisfied by setting their guard variables to false). Note that this formula is unsat iff the **sv** represented by V (i.e., the constraints guarded by variables in V) is an **Rsv**. Therefore, if the result is sat, we create a blocking clause φ_{Block} for the case in which V represents an **sv** that is not repaired (line 29). The blocking clause in this case is simply $\bigvee_{v \in V} \neg v$ (i.e. only V is blocked). If the result is unsat, we translate V into the represented **sv** and return it as a possible repair (line 31). The blocking clause we add in this case (line 32) is $\bigvee_{v \in V \setminus V_o} \neg v$, which requires that the same set of mutations will never appear as a subset of any future set of mutations. This way we block not only V but also every V' for which $v \sqsubseteq v'$ (where v, v' are the **sv**s represented by V, V', respectively).

5 Soundness and Completeness of Algorithm AllRepair

In this section we analyze our algorithm. We show that it is *sound*, that is, every returned **sv** is minimal repaired, and that it is *complete* in the sense that every minimal repaired **sv** is eventually returned.

Clearly, the algorithm returns all **mRsv**s, because we go over all **sv**s and only mark an **sv** as explored if it is returned (as repaired), if it is not repaired, or if it is not minimal. Also, all **sv**s returned by the algorithm are **mRsv**s, because every returned **sv** is repaired (it is explicitly checked), and is minimal repaired because otherwise it would have been marked as explored by another **sv** in a previous iteration. Thus, the following theorem holds:

Theorem 8 (Correctness of **AllRepair**). *Our algorithm is sound and complete. That is, every* **sv** *v returned by our algorithm is an* **mRsv** *and every* **mRsv** *v is returned by our algorithm at some point.*

5.1 Extension to Full Correctness

We now analyze the soundness and completeness of our algorithm with respect to full (unbounded) correctness. We show that there is a bound B for which the notion of B-correctness is equivalent to the notion of correctness.

We first notice that since the set of mutations we consider is finite, so is the set of mutated programs PG. For each $P \in PG$, if it is not correct then it has a b-run for some b, along which some assertion is violated. Let b_P be the smallest bound for which such a run exists for P. Then, by definition, P is not b-correct for any b greater than b_p. Let *max-bound* B be defined as follows. $B = 1 + max\{b_P \mid P \in PG$ and P is not correct. Clearly, for every program P in PG, P is B-correct iff P is correct. The following theorem describes this observation by means of the selection vectors encoding programs in PG.

Theorem 9 (Equivalence of B-correctness and Full correctness). *Let B be the max-bound defined above. Then v is an* **Rsv** *for bound B iff v is a* **Csv**. *Further, v is an* **mRsv** *for bound B iff v is an* **mCsv**.

Proof. The first part of the theorem is a direct consequence of the definition of B. The second part of the theorem is a direct consequence of the first part. This is because, by definition, v is an **mRsv** for bound B iff v is an **Rsv** for B and every v' s.t. $v' \sqsubseteq v$ and $v' \neq v$ is not an **Rsv** for B. By the first part, this happens iff v is a **Csv** and every v' s.t. $v' \sqsubseteq v$ and $v' \neq v$ is not a **Csv**, which means v is an **mCsv**. □

Theorem 9 implies that for a large enough bound, all returned programs are correct and all minimal correct programs are returned.

6 Experimental Results

We implemented a prototype of our algorithm on top of two existing tools. The translation unit and the mutation unit were implemented in C++, by modifying version 5.2 of the CBMC model checking tool [1]. The repair unit was implemented in Python, by modifying version 1.1 of the MARCO tool [16]. MARCO uses Z3 [2] as an SMT solver and Minicard [15] as a SAT solver.

Our current implementation works on C programs and uses a basic set of mutations, which is a subset of the set used in [27]. We define two *mutation levels*: level 2 contains all possible mutations and level 1 contains only a subset of them. Thus level 1 involves easier computation but may fail more often in finding a repaired program.

Table 1 shows the list of mutations used in every mutation level. For example, for the sub-category of arithmetic operator replacement, in mutation level 1, the table specifies two sets: $\{+, -\}$ and $\{*, /, \%\}$. This means that a + can be replaced with a −, and vice versa, and that the operators $*, /, \%$ can be replaced with each other. Constant manipulation mutations apply to a numeric constant and include increasing its value by 1 (C → C+1), decreasing it by 1 (C → C−1), setting it to 0 (C→0) and changing its sign (C → −C).

We have evaluated our algorithm on the TCAS benchmarks from the Siemens suite [7]. The TCAS program implements a traffic collision avoidance system for aircrafts. It has about 180 lines of code and it comes in 41 faulty versions, together with a reference implementation (a test suite is also included but we do not use it).

We compared our results to those obtained by Könighofer and Bloem [11,12]. The results are summarized in Table 2. Each row refers to a different faulty version of TCAS (we only include versions for which at least one method was able to produce a repair). The specification used (in both our work and their's) is an assertion requiring equivalence with the correct version[6]. For each method there are two columns: "Fixed?", which contains a + if the method was able to find a repair for that version, and "Time", which specifies the time (in seconds)

Table 1. Partition of mutations to levels

		Level 1	Level 2
Op. replacement	Arithmetic	$\{+, -\}, \{*, /, \%\}$	$\{+, -, *, /, \%\}$
	Relational	$\{>, >=\}, \{<, <=\}$	$\{>, >=, <, <=\}$, $\{==, !=\}$
	Logical	{‖,&&}	
	Bit-wise	{>>, <<},{&,|,^}	
Constant manipulation			C→C+1,C→C−1, C→ −C,C→0

[6] This is implemented by inlining the code of the correct version, saving the results of both versions to variables res1 and res2, and asserting that res1=res2. The code of the correct version is marked so that it will not be mutated (constraints encoding it are hard constraints).

Table 2. Performance results on TCAS versions

Ver.	Method of [11]		Method of [12]		Our method			
					Mutation level 1		Mutation level 2	
	Fixed?	Time[s]	Fixed?	Time[s]	Fixed?	Time[s]	Fixed?	Time[s]
1	+	65			+	1.392	+	8.879
2	+	26	+	12				
3					+	1.725	+	68.651
6	+	55	+	79	+	2.056	+	33.762
7	+	11	+	6				
8	+	17	+	38				
9	+	41	+	28	+	1.203	+	17.286
10					+	6.429	+	90.666
12					+	2.157	+	77.852
16	+	9	+	6			+	84.711
17	+	12	+	6			+	55.538
18	+	14	+	40				
19	+	18	+	37				
20	+	85	+	26	+	1.709	+	15.883
25	+	82	+	100	+	2.68	+	16.234
28	+	34	+	35			+	93.678
31					+	1.246	+	4.661
32					+	1.902	+	85.349
35	+	41	+	46			+	92.866
36	+	8	+	6			+	94.599
39	+	82	+	101	+	2.558	+	16.393
40							+	4.829
41							+	4.875
	16 (39%)	38	15 (36.6%)	38	11 (26.83%)	2.278	18 (43.9%)	48.151

it took to find a repair (if found). The bottom line specifies for each method the number of repaired versions along with their percentage from the total 41 faulty TCAS versions, and the average time it took to find a repair.

From Table 2 it is clear that there is a trade-off between repairability and runtime when deciding which mutations to use. When using mutation level 1, our method repairs less faulty versions than [11,12] (11 vs. 15,16), but is significantly faster (2.3 s vs. 38 s on average). When using mutation level 2, the number of faulty versions we fix increases to 18, which is better than [11,12], but the average time to repair increases to 48 s.

For all versions that we can not repair (including those that do not appear in the table), we are able to say that they can not be fixed using the given set of mutations. Using mutation level 1 it takes approximately 2 s on average to reach the conclusion that the program can not be fixed using mutation sets of size 1, and approximately 7 s to reach that conclusion for sets of size 2 (we did not collect information about larger sizes though it is possible). Using mutation level 2 these times increase significantly to 1.5 and 24 min, respectively.

Note that the runtime of mutation level 1 for version number 10 is exceptionally large. This is because this version requires applying two mutations in two different locations in order to be repaired. Since we inspect programs with increasing size of mutation sets, we have to first apply all mutation sets of size 1 before inspecting any mutation sets of size 2. Though our method takes longer to produce this multi-line repair, it succeeds while [11,12] fail.

Since the TCAS program does not contain any loops or recursive calls, all returned programs are guaranteed to be (fully) correct, and the unwinding bound is insignificant. Therefore, we also evaluated our algorithm on a set of programs with loops. This set contains implementations of commonly known algorithms (e.g., bubble-sort and max-sort) in which we inserted bugs to create different versions (a total of 10 faulty versions). All bugs can be fixed using mutation level 1, but some require multi-line repair (up to 3 mutations at a time). In all the above experiments a correct repair was found for a bound as small as 3. Furthermore, for a bound of 3, all returned programs were found to be correct (and not only bounded correct) by a manual inspection. These results suggest that though our algorithm only guarantees bounded correctness, in many cases the returned programs are correct, even when using a small bound and even in the presence of several bugs.

7 Conclusion and Future Work

This work presents a novel approach to program repair. Given an erroneous program, a set of assertions and a predefined set of mutations, our algorithm returns *all* minimal repairs to the program, in increasing number of changes.

Since the number of optional repairs might be huge, it is necessary to prune the search space whenever possible. Our technique does it by blocking all repairs that are not minimal: Whenever a successful repair is found, all repairs that use a superset of its mutations are blocked. Thus, a significant pruning of the search space is obtained.

Another promising direction is to block sets of mutations that are guaranteed *not* to succeed in repairing, based on previously seen unsuccessful once.

References

1. Clarke, E., Kroening, D., Lerda, F.: A tool for checking ANSI-C programs. In: Jensen, K., Podelski, A. (eds.) TACAS 2004. LNCS, vol. 2988, pp. 168–176. Springer, Heidelberg (2004). doi:10.1007/978-3-540-24730-2_15
2. Moura, L., Bjørner, N.: Z3: an efficient SMT solver. In: Ramakrishnan, C.R., Rehof, J. (eds.) TACAS 2008. LNCS, vol. 4963, pp. 337–340. Springer, Heidelberg (2008). doi:10.1007/978-3-540-78800-3_24
3. Moura, L., Bjørner, N.: Satisfiability modulo theories: an appetizer. In: Oliveira, M.V.M., Woodcock, J. (eds.) SBMF 2009. LNCS, vol. 5902, pp. 23–36. Springer, Heidelberg (2009). doi:10.1007/978-3-642-10452-7_3

4. Debroy, V., Wong, W.E.: Using mutation to automatically suggest fixes for faulty programs. In: Third International Conference on Software Testing, Verification and Validation (ICST), pp. 65–74. IEEE (2010)
5. Debroy, V., Wong, W.E.: Combining mutation and fault localization for automated program debugging. Jour. Sys. Soft. **90**, 45–60 (2014)
6. DeMarco, F., Xuan, J., Le Berre, D., Monperrus, M.: Automatic repair of buggy if conditions and missing preconditions with SMT. In: Proceedings of the 6th International Workshop on Constraints in Software Testing, Verification, and Analysis, pp. 30–39. ACM (2014)
7. Do, H., Elbaum, S., Rothermel, G.: Supporting controlled experimentation with testing techniques: an infrastructure and its potential impact. Empirical Softw. Eng. **10**(4), 405–435 (2005)
8. Jobstmann, B., Griesmayer, A., Bloem, R.: Program repair as a game. In: Etessami, K., Rajamani, S.K. (eds.) CAV 2005. LNCS, vol. 3576, pp. 226–238. Springer, Heidelberg (2005). doi:10.1007/11513988_23
9. Kim, D., Nam, J., Song, J., Kim, S.: Automatic patch generation learned from human-written patches. In: Proceedings of the International Conference on Software Engineering, pp. 802–811. IEEE Press (2013)
10. Kneuss, E., Koukoutos, M., Kuncak, V.: Deductive program repair. In: Kroening, D., Păsăreanu, C.S. (eds.) CAV 2015. LNCS, vol. 9207, pp. 217–233. Springer, Heidelberg (2015). doi:10.1007/978-3-319-21668-3_13
11. Könighofer, R., Bloem, R.: Automated error localization and correction for imperative programs. In: Proceedings of Formal Methods in Computer-Aided Design (FMCAD), pp. 91–100. IEEE(2011)
12. Könighofer, R., Bloem, R.: Repair with on-the-fly program analysis. In: Biere, A., Nahir, A., Vos, T. (eds.) HVC 2012. LNCS, vol. 7857, pp. 56–71. Springer, Heidelberg (2013). doi:10.1007/978-3-642-39611-3_11
13. Le Goues, C., Dewey-Vogt, M., Forrest, S., Weimer, W.: A systematic study of automated program repair: fixing 55 out of 105 bugs for 8 each. In: 34th International Conference on Software Engineering (ICSE), pp. 3–13. IEEE (2012)
14. Le Goues, C., Nguyen, T., Forrest, S., Weimer, W.: Genprog: a generic method for automatic software repair. IEEE Trans. Softw. Eng. **38**(1), 54–72 (2012)
15. Liffiton, M.H., Maglalang, J.C.: A cardinality solver: more expressive constraints for free. In: Cimatti, A., Sebastiani, R. (eds.) SAT 2012. LNCS, vol. 7317, pp. 485–486. Springer, Heidelberg (2012). doi:10.1007/978-3-642-31612-8_47
16. Liffiton, M.H., Previti, A., Malik, A., Marques-Silva, J.: Fast, flexible MUS enumeration. Constraints **21**, 1–28 (2015)
17. Liffiton, M.H., Sakallah, K.A.: Algorithms for computing minimal unsatisfiable subsets of constraints. J. Autom. Reasoning **40**(1), 1–33 (2008)
18. Long, F., Rinard, M.: Prophet: automatic patch generation via learning from successful patches (2015)
19. Long, F., Rinard, M.: Staged program repair with condition synthesis. In: Proceedings of the 10th Joint Meeting on Foundations of Software Engineering, pp. 166–178. ACM (2015)
20. Martinez, M., Monperrus, M.: Mining software repair models for reasoning on the search space of automated program fixing. Empirical Softw. Eng. **20**(1), 176–205 (2015)
21. Mechtaev, S., Yi, J., Roychoudhury, A.: Directfix: looking for simple program repairs. In: IEEE/ACM 37th IEEE International Conference on Software Engineering (ICSE), vol. 1, pp. 448–458. IEEE (2015)

22. Mechtaev, S., Yi, J., Roychoudhury, A.: Angelix: Scalable multiline program patch synthesis via symbolic analysis. ICSE (2016)
23. Nguyen, H.D.T., Qi, D., Roychoudhury, A., Chandra, S.: Semfix: program repair via semantic analysis. In: Proceedings of the International Conference on Software Engineering, pp. 772–781. IEEE Press (2013)
24. Pei, Y., Furia, C.A., Nordio, M., Wei, Y., Meyer, B., Zeller, A.: Automated fixing of programs with contracts. IEEE Trans. Softw. Eng. **40**(5), 427–449 (2014)
25. Qi, Y., Mao, X., Lei, Y.: Efficient automated program repair through fault-recorded testing prioritization. In: IEEE International Conference on Software Maintenance, pp. 180–189. IEEE (2013)
26. Qi, Y., Mao, X., Lei, Y., Dai, Z., Wang, C.: Does genetic programming work well on automated program repair? In: Fifth International Conference on Computational and Information Sciences (ICCIS), pp. 1875–1878. IEEE (2013)
27. Repinski, U., Hantson, H., Jenihhin, M., Raik, J., Ubar, R., Guglielmo, G.D., Pravadelli, G., Fummi, F.: Combining dynamic slicing and mutation operators for ESL correction. In: 17th IEEE European Test Symposium (ETS), pp. 1–6. IEEE (2012)
28. Sidiroglou-Douskos, S., Lahtinen, E., Long, F., Rinard, M.: Automatic error elimination by horizontal code transfer across multiple applications. In: Proceedings of the 36th ACM SIGPLAN Conference on Programming Language Design and Implementation, pp. 43–54. ACM (2015)
29. Von Essen, C., Jobstmann, B.: Program repair without regret. Formal Methods Syst. Des. **47**(1), 26–50 (2015)
30. Wei, Y., Pei, Y., Furia, C.A., Silva, L.S., Buchholz, S., Meyer, B., Zeller, A.: Automated fixing of programs with contracts. In: Proceedings of the 19th international symposium on Software testing and analysis, pp. 61–72. ACM (2010)
31. Weimer, W., Fry, Z.P., Forrest, S.: Leveraging program equivalence for adaptive program repair: Models and first results. In: IEEE/ACM 28th International Conference on Automated Software Engineering (ASE), pp. 356–366. IEEE (2013)

An Implementation of Deflate in Coq

Christoph-Simon Senjak(✉) and Martin Hofmann

Ludwig-Maximilians-Universität, Munich, Germany
{christoph.senjak,hofmann}@ifi.lmu.de

Abstract. The widely-used compression format "Deflate" is defined in RFC 1951 and is based on prefix-free codings and backreferences. There are unclear points about the way these codings are specified, and several sources for confusion in the standard. We tried to fix this problem by giving a rigorous mathematical specification, which we formalized in Coq. We produced a verified implementation in Coq which achieves competitive performance on inputs of several megabytes. In this paper we present the several parts of our implementation: a fully verified implementation of canonical prefix-free codings, which can be used in other compression formats as well, and an elegant formalism for specifying sophisticated formats, which we used to implement both a compression and decompression algorithm in Coq which we formally prove inverse to each other – the first time this has been achieved to our knowledge. The compatibility to other Deflate implementations can be shown empirically. We furthermore discuss some of the difficulties, specifically regarding memory and runtime requirements, and our approaches to overcome them.

Keywords: Formal verification · Program extraction · Compression · Coq

1 Introduction

It is more and more recognized that traditional methods for maintenance of software security reach their limits, and different approaches become inevitable [2]. At the same time, formal program verification has reached a state where it becomes realistic to prove correctness of low-level system components and combine them to prove the correctness of larger systems. A common pattern is to have a kernel that isolates parts of software by putting them in sandboxes. This way, one gets strong security guarantees, while being able to use unverified parts which might fail, but cannot access memory or resources outside their permissions. Examples are the L4 verified kernel [18] and the Quark browser [16].

This is an important step towards fully verified software, but it is also desirable to verify the low-level middleware. While for these components the adherence of access restrictions would be assured by an underlying sandbox, functional correctness becomes the main concern. The CompCert compiler is such a project, and as [19] points out, a compiler bug can invalidate all guarantees obtained by formal methods. The MiTLS [7] project implements TLS, and verifies cryptographic

J. Fitzgerald et al. (Eds.): FM 2016, LNCS 9995, pp. 612–627, 2016.
DOI: 10.1007/978-3-319-48989-6_37

security properties. We propose to add to this list a collection of compression formats; in this paper we look specifically at Deflate [10], which is a widely used standard for lossless general purpose compression. HTTP can make use of it [12], so does ZIP [22] and with it its several derived formats like Java Archives (JAR) and Android Application Packages (APK). Source-code-tarballs are usually compressed with GZip, which is a container around a Deflate stream [11]. Finally, TLS supports Deflate compression [14], though it is now discouraged due to the BREACH family of exploits [17]. Deflate compression can utilize Huffman codings and Backreferences as used in Lempel-Ziv-Compression (both defined later), but none of them are mandatory: The way a given file can be compressed is by no means unique, making it possible to use different compression algorithms. For example, the `gzip(1)` utility has flags `-1` through `-9`, where `-9` yields the strongest but slowest compression, while `-1` yields the weakest but fastest compression. Furthermore, there are alternative implementations like Zopfli [13], which gains even better compression at the cost of speed.

It is desirable to have some guarantees on data integrity, in the sense that the implementation itself will not produce corrupted output. A common complaint at this point is that you can get this guarantee by just re-defining your unverified implementations of compression, say c, and decompression, say d, by

$$c'x = \begin{cases} (\top, cx) & \text{for } d(cx) = x \\ (\bot, x) & \text{otherwise} \end{cases}$$

$$d'x = \begin{cases} dy & \text{for } x = (\top, y) \\ y & \text{for } x = (\bot, y) \end{cases}$$

This works well as long as one only has to work with one computer architecture. However, for secure long-term-archiving of important data, this is not sufficient: It is not clear that there will be working processors being able to run our d implementation in, say, 50 years; but a formal, mathematical, human-readable specification of the actual data format being used can mitigate against such digital obsolescence: The language of mathematics is universal. However, of course, this is a benchmark one should keep in mind. We are currently still far away from this performance level, but we are sure our work can lead to such a fast implementation, but not without lots of micro-optimization; for now the performance is acceptable but not fast enough yet, we are working on making it better.

Of course, one needs *some* specification. Besides having to rely on some hardware specification, as pointed out in [18], finding the right formal specification for software is not trivial. In MiTLS [7], an example about "alert fragmentation" is given, which might give an attacker the possibility to change error codes by injection of a byte. This is standard compliant, but obviously not intended. A rigorous formal specification of an informally stated standard must be carefully crafted, and we consider our mathematical specification of Deflate as a contribution in this direction.

1.1 Related Work

To our best knowledge, this is the first verified pair of compression and decompression algorithms, and it is practically usable, not just for toy examples. However, there have been several projects that are related. A formalization of Huffman's algorithm can be found in [8,23]. As we will point out in Sect. 3, the codings Deflate requires do not need to be Huffman codings, but they need to satisfy a canonicity condition. From the general topic of data compression, there is a formalization of Shannon's theorems in Coq [4].

There are two techniques in Coq that are commonly regarded as "program extraction": On the one hand, one can explicitly write functions with Coq, and prove properties about them, and the extract them to OCaml and Haskell. This is the method that is usually used. The complexity of the extracted algorithms can be estimated easily, but reasoning about the algorithms is disconnected from the algorithms themselves. On the other hand, it is possible to write constructive existence proofs and extract algorithms from these proofs directly. The advantage of this approach is that only a proof has to be given, which is usually about as long as a proof about an explicit algorithm, so the work only has to be done once. However, the disadvantage is that the complexity of the generated algorithm is not always obvious, especially in the presence of tactics. We think that this technique fits well especially for problems in which either the algorithm itself is complicated, because it usually has lots of invariants and proofs of such an algorithm require extensive use of the inner structure of the terms, or when the algorithm is trivial but the proofs are long. The case study [21], albeit on a different topic (Myhill-Nerode), is an interesting source of inspiration in that it distills general principles for improving efficiency of extracted programs which we have integrated where applicable. In particular, these were

- to use expensive statements non-computationally, which we have done in large parts of the code.
- to use existential quantifiers as memory, which we did, for example, in our proofs regarding strong decidability (see Sect. 5).
- to calculate values in advance, which we did, for example, for the value `fixed_lit_code`.
- to turn loop invariants into induction statements, which is not directly applicable because Coq does not have imperative loops, but corresponds to Coq's induction measures, which give a clue about the computational complexity.

We use both extraction techniques in our code. Besides the use of recursion operators instead of pattern matching, the extracted code is quite readable.

Our theory of parsers from Sect. 5 follows an idea similar to [6], trying to produce parsers directly from proofs, as opposed to other approaches, for example [9], which defines a formal semantic on parser combinators. Most of the algorithms involved in parsing are short, and therefore, as we already said, using the second kind of program extraction we mentioned was our method of choice for the largest part.

1.2 Overview

In summary, this paper provides a rigorous formal specification of Deflate and a reference implementation of both a compression and decompression algorithm which have been formally verified against this specification and tested against the ZLib.

This paper is organized as follows: In Sect. 2, we give a very brief overview over several aspects of the Deflate standard. In Sect. 3 we introduce concepts needed to understand the encoding mechanism of Deflate that is mostly used, namely *Deflate codings*, a special kind of prefix-free codings, and prove several theorems about them. In Sect. 4, we will introduce the concept of *backreferences* which is the second compression mechanism besides prefix-free codings that can be used with Deflate. Section 5 is about our mechanism of specifying and combining encoding relations, and how one can gain programs from these. Section 6 will introduce our current approach for a verified compression algorithm. Finally, Sect. 7 explains how our software can be obtained, compiled and tested. We published a version of this paper with an appendix containing an elaborate example of the Deflate compression standard, some benchmarks, and some explanatory tables, on Arxiv.

2 The Encoding Relation

The main problem when verifying an implementation of a standard is that a specification must be given, and this specification itself is axiomatic and cannot be formally verified. We address this problem in two ways. First, we try to put the complexity of the implementation into the proofs, and make the specification as simple as possible. The correctness of a specification should be "clear" by reading, or at least require only a minimal amount of thinking. This was not always possible, because the Deflate standard is intricate; in the cases when it was not possible, we tried to at least put the complexity into few definitions and reuse them as often as possible. In fact, most of our definitions in `EncodingRelation.v` should be easily understandable when knowing the standard. In addition to that, we give some plausibility checks in the form of little lemmas and examples which we formally prove. Secondly, we prove a decidability property for our encoding relation which yields—by program extraction—a reference implementation that we can apply to examples. This way, the implementation becomes empirically correct. However, even if there was a pathological example in which our specification is not compliant with other implementations, it would still describe a formally proved lossless compression format, and every file that was compressed with one of our verified compression algorithms could still be decompressed with every verified decompression algorithm.

On the toplevel, a stream compressed with Deflate is a sequence of blocks, each of which is a chunk of data compressed with a specific method. There are three possible types of blocks: uncompressed blocks, which save a small header and the clear text of the original, statically compressed blocks, which are compressed with codings defined in the standard, and dynamically compressed blocks, which have codings in their header. Their respective type is indicated by a two-bit header. Furthermore, a third bit indicates whether the block is the last block. The bit-level details of the format are not important for this paper, most of the relational definition can be found in the file `EncodingRelation.v`. For clarity, we give an informal illustration of the toplevel format:

```
Deflate            ::= ('0' Block)* '1' Block ( '0' | '1' )*
Block              ::= '00' UncompressedBlock |
                       '01' DynamicallyCompBl |
                       '10' StaticallyCompBl
UncompressedBlock  ::= length ~length bytes
StaticallyCompBl   ::= CompressedBlock(standard coding)
DynamicallyCompBl  ::= header coding CompressedBlock(coding)
CompressedBlock(c) ::= [^256]* 256 (encoded by c)
```

Compressed blocks can contain backreferences – instructions to copy already decompressed bytes to the front – which are allowed to point across the borders of blocks, see Sect. 4. A decompression algorithm for such blocks must, besides being able to resolve backreferences, be able to decompress the data according to two codings, where some of the codes have additional suffixes of a number of bits defined in a table. Additionally, for dynamically compressed blocks, the codings themselves, which are saved as sequences of numbers (see Sect. 3), are compressed by a third coding. This makes decompression of such blocks a lot harder than one would expect, and gives a broad vector for common bugs like off-by-one-errors or misinterpretations of the standard. For example, notice that while the first table from the first table in Sect. 3.2.5 from the standard [10] looks quite "continuous", the codepoint 284 can only encode 30 code lengths, which means that the suffixes 01111 and 11111 are illegal (this was actually a bug in an early version of our specification). Due to the space restrictions, we will not get deeply into the standard in this paper, and spare the readers the complicated parts as far as possible. For a deeper understanding, we give an elaborate example in the Arxiv-version of this paper and otherwise refer to [10].

3 Deflate Codings

Deflate codings are the heart of Deflate. Everything that is compressed in any way will be encoded by two Deflate codings, even if the coding itself is not used to save memory (this will usually be the case for statically compressed blocks which only utilize backreferences). In other literature, Deflate codings are also called **canonical prefix-free codings** – "canonical" because of the result shown in Theorem 1, "prefix-free" will be defined in Definition 1. Sometimes people talk about "codes" instead of "codings". However, in our terminology, a "code" is a sequence of bits from a coding, and a "coding" is a map from an alphabet into codes. Though we call them Deflate codings, they are also used in many other compression formats, like BZip2, and this part of our implementation can be reused.

It is well-known [15] that for every string $A \in \mathcal{A}^*$ over a finite alphabet $\mathcal{A}$, there is a **Huffman coding** $h : \mathcal{A} \to \{0,1\}^*$, which is a prefix-free coding such that the concatenation of the characters' images $\mathrm{foldl}(+\!\!+)[\,](\mathrm{map}\, hA)$ has minimal length. In fact, this has already been formally proved [8]. The standard [10] abuses terminology slightly by calling any not necessarily optimal prefix-free coding "Huffman coding". This makes sense because, especially for statically compressed blocks, fixed, not necessarily optimal encodings are used. On the other hand, the standard specifies canonical prefix-free codings which can be uniquely reconstructed from the respective code lengths for each encoded character. These canonical codings are referred to as Deflate codings. Therefore, instead of expensively saving a tree structure, it is sufficient to save the sequence of code lengths for the encoded characters. Optimal Deflate codings are also known as **canonical Huffman codings**.

In any practical case, there will be a canonical ordering on $\mathcal{A}$, so from now on, let us silently assume the alphabet $\mathcal{A} = \{0, \ldots, n-1\}$ for some $n \in \mathbb{N}$. We say a code a is a **prefix** of b and write $a \preccurlyeq b$, if there is a list $c \in \{0,1\}^*$ such that $a +\!\!+ c = b$. Notice that $\preccurlyeq$ is reflexive, transitive and decidable. We denote the standard **lexicographical ordering** on $\{0,1\}^*$ by $\sqsubseteq$. We have $[\,] \sqsubseteq a$ and $0 :: a \sqsubseteq 1 :: b$ for all a, b and $j :: a \sqsubseteq j :: b$ whenever $a \sqsubseteq b$. It is easy to show that this is a decidable total ordering relation. We can now make prefix-free codings unique. The code $[\,]$ is used to denote that the corresponding element of $\mathcal{A}$ does not occur. This is consistent with the standard that uses the code length 0 to denote this.

Definition 1. *A* **Deflate coding** *is a coding* $\lceil\cdot\rceil : \mathcal{A} \to \{0,1\}^*$ *which satisfies the following conditions:*

1. $\lceil\cdot\rceil$ *is prefix-free, except that there may be codes of length zero:*

$$\forall_{a,b}.(a \neq b \wedge \lceil a \rceil \neq [\,]) \to \lceil a \rceil \not\preccurlyeq \lceil b \rceil$$

2. *Shorter codes lexicographically precede longer codes:*

$$\forall_{a,b}.\, \mathrm{len}\lceil a \rceil < \mathrm{len}\lceil b \rceil \to \lceil a \rceil \sqsubseteq \lceil b \rceil$$

3. *Codes of the same length are ordered lexicographically according to the order of the characters they encode:*

$$\forall_{a,b}.(\mathrm{len}\lceil a \rceil = \mathrm{len}\lceil b \rceil \wedge a \leq b) \to \lceil a \rceil \sqsubseteq \lceil b \rceil$$

4. *For every code, all lexicographically smaller bit sequences of the same length are prefixed by some code:*

$$\forall_{a \in \mathcal{A}, l \in \{0,1\}^+}.(l \sqsubseteq \lceil a \rceil \wedge \mathrm{len}\, l = \mathrm{len}\lceil a \rceil) \to \exists_b.\lceil b \rceil \neq [\,] \wedge \lceil b \rceil \preccurlyeq l$$

These axioms are our proposed formalization of the informal specification in [10], which states: "The Huffman codes used for each alphabet in the 'deflate' format have two additional rules:

- All codes of a given bit length have lexicographically consecutive values, in the same order as the symbols they represent;
- Shorter codes lexicographically precede longer codes."

Notice that prefix-codes as given by their code lengths do not necessarily correspond to optimal, i.e. Huffman, codes. For example, the Deflate coding

$$0 \rightarrow [0], 1 \rightarrow [1,0,0], 2 \rightarrow [1,0,1], 3 \rightarrow [1,1,0]$$

is clearly not a Huffman coding, since for every case it would apply to, we could also use

$$0 \rightarrow [0], 1 \rightarrow [1,0], 2 \rightarrow [1,1,1], 3 \rightarrow [1,1,0]$$

which will always be better. Unique recoverability, however, holds true for all Deflate codings irrespective of optimality.

Axiom 3 is weaker than the first axiom from [10], as it does not postulate the consecutivity of the values, which is ensured by axiom 4: Assuming you have characters $a < b$ such that $\text{len}\lceil a \rceil = \text{len}\lceil b \rceil$, and there is a $l \in \{0,1\}^{\text{len}\lceil a \rceil}$ such that $\lceil a \rceil \sqsubseteq l \sqsubseteq \lceil b \rceil$, then by axiom 4 there is a d such that $\lceil d \rceil \preccurlyeq l$. Trivially, $\lceil a \rceil \sqsubseteq \lceil d \rceil$, therefore by axiom 2, it follows that $\lceil d \rceil = l$. That is, if there is a code of length $\text{len}\lceil a \rceil$ between $\lceil a \rceil$ and $\lceil b \rceil$, then it is the image of a character. Therefore, the values of codes of the same length are lexicographically consecutive.

Furthermore, consider our non-optimal coding from above: It has the lengths $0 \rightarrow 1, 1 \rightarrow 3, 2 \rightarrow 3, 3 \rightarrow 3$, and satisfies our axioms 1–3, and additionally, the codes of the same length have lexicographically consecutive values. But the same holds for the coding

$$0 \rightarrow [0], 1 \rightarrow [1,0,1], 2 \rightarrow [1,1,0], 3 \rightarrow [1,1,1]$$

However, in this coding, there is a "gap" between the codes of different lengths, namely between $[0]$ and $[1,0,1]$, and that is why it violates our axiom 4: The list $[1,0,0]$ is lexicographically smaller than $[1,0,1]$, but it has no prefix.

We can show that Deflate codings are uniquely determined by their code lengths:

Theorem 1 (uniqueness). *Let* $\lceil\cdot\rceil, \lfloor\cdot\rfloor : \mathcal{A} \rightarrow \{0,1\}^*$ *be two Deflate codings, such that* $\forall_{x\in\mathcal{A}}.\, \text{len}\lceil x \rceil = \text{len}\lfloor x \rfloor$. *Then* $\forall_{x\in\mathcal{A}}.\lceil x \rceil = \lfloor x \rfloor$.

Proof. Equality of codings is obviously decidable, therefore we can do a proof by contradiction, without using the law of excluded middle as an axiom. So assume there were two distinct deflate codings $\lceil\cdot\rceil$ and $\lfloor\cdot\rfloor$ with $\text{len}\lceil\cdot\rceil = \text{len}\lfloor\cdot\rfloor$. Then there must exist n, m such that $\lceil n \rceil = \min_{\sqsubseteq}\{\lceil x \rceil \mid \lceil x \rceil \neq \lfloor x \rfloor\}$ and $\lfloor m \rfloor = \min_{\sqsubseteq}\{\lfloor x \rfloor \mid \lceil x \rceil \neq \lfloor x \rfloor\}$. If $\text{len}\lceil n \rceil > \text{len}\lfloor m \rfloor$, then also $\text{len}\lceil n \rceil > \text{len}\lceil m \rceil$, and by our axiom 2, $\lceil m \rceil \sqsubseteq \lceil n \rceil$. But m was chosen minimally. Symmetric for $\text{len}\lceil n \rceil > \text{len}\lfloor m \rfloor$. Therefore, $\text{len}\lceil n \rceil = \text{len}\lfloor m \rfloor$. Also, $\lfloor m \rfloor \neq [\,]$, because otherwise $0 = \text{len}\lfloor m \rfloor = \text{len}\lceil n \rceil$, so $\lceil n \rceil = [\,]$, and so $\lceil m \rceil = \lfloor m \rfloor$, which contradicts our assumption on the choice of m. Analogous, $\lceil n \rceil \neq [\,]$. By totality of $\sqsubseteq$, we know that $\lceil n \rceil \sqsubseteq \lfloor m \rfloor \vee \lfloor m \rfloor \sqsubseteq \lceil n \rceil$. Both cases are symmetric, so without loss of generality assume $\lceil n \rceil \sqsubseteq \lfloor m \rfloor$. Now, by axiom 4, we know that some b exists, such that $\lfloor b \rfloor \preccurlyeq \lceil n \rceil$, therefore by axiom 2, $\lfloor b \rfloor \sqsubseteq \lfloor m \rfloor$, and thus, by the minimality of m, either $b = m$ or $\lfloor b \rfloor = \lceil b \rceil$. $b = m$ would imply $\lceil m \rceil = \lfloor m \rfloor$, which contradicts our choice of m. But $\lfloor b \rfloor = \lceil b \rceil$ would imply $\lceil b \rceil \preccurlyeq \lceil n \rceil$, which contradicts our axiom 1.

This theorem is proved as Lemma `uniqueness` in `DeflateCoding.v`. While uniqueness is a desirable property, it does not give us the guarantee that, for every configuration of lengths, there actually is a Deflate coding. And in fact, there isn't: Trivially, there is no Deflate coding that has three codes of length 1. It is desirable to have a simple criterion on the list of code lengths, that can be efficiently checked, before creating the actual coding.

Indeed, the well-known Kraft inequality [20] furnishes such a criterion. It asserts that a prefix-free coding with code lengths $k_0, \ldots, k_{N-1}$ exists iff

$$\sum_{i=0}^{N-1} 2^{-k_i} \leq 1$$

Deflate codings may, however, have $k_i = 0$ if the corresponding character does not occur. Moreover, we want to extract an algorithm from this proof, so we have to prove it constructively.

Theorem 2 (extended_kraft_ineq). *Let* $\lceil \cdot \rceil : \mathcal{A} \to \{0,1\}^*$ *be a Deflate coding. Then*

$$\sum_{\substack{i \in \mathcal{A} \\ \lceil i \rceil \neq []}} 2^{-\operatorname{len} \lceil i \rceil} \leq 1$$

Equality holds if and only if there is some $k \in \mathcal{A}$ *such that* $\lceil k \rceil \in \{1\}^+$.

This is formally proven as `extended_kraft_ineq` in `DeflateCoding.v`. The most important theorem regarding Deflate codings is:

Theorem 3 (existence). *Let* $l : \mathcal{A} \to \mathbb{N}$ *be such that*

$$\sum_{\substack{i \in \mathcal{A} \\ l(i) \neq 0}} 2^{-l(i)} \leq 1$$

Then there is a Deflate coding $\lceil \cdot \rceil : \mathcal{A} \to \{0,1\}^*$ *such that* $lx = \operatorname{len} \lceil x \rceil$.

For the proof, we introduce the notation $[n]^k := [\underbrace{n, \ldots, n}_{k\times}]$.

Proof. Let $\lesssim$ be the right-to-left lexicographical ordering relation on $\mathbb{N}$, defined by

$$\forall_{mqo}.q < o \to (q,m) \lesssim (o,m)$$

$$\forall_{m_1,m_2,n_1,n_2}.m_1 < m_2 \to (n_1,m_1) \lesssim (n_2,m_2)$$

Now let $R = L := \operatorname{sortBy}(\lesssim)(\operatorname{map}(\lambda_k(k, lk))[0, \ldots, n-1])$, $S = []$, $cx = []$. We will do a recursion on tuples (S, c, R), maintaining the following invariants:

1. If a pair is not in the list of already processed pairs S, then it is in the list of remaining pairs R, and the corresponding code is empty

$$\forall_q.(q, \mathrm{len}(c(q))) \notin S \to (c(q) = [\,] \wedge (q, l(q)) \in R)$$

2. L contains the elements of S and R

$$(\mathrm{rev}\ S) ++ R = L$$

3. Either S is empty, or the code corresponding to its first element is lexicographically larger than every code in the current coding

$$S = [\,] \vee \forall_q.c(q) \sqsubseteq c(\pi_1(\mathrm{first}\ S))$$

Furthermore, c will be a Deflate coding at every step. The decreasing element will be R, which will become shorter at every step. We first handle the simple cases:

- For the initial values $([\,], \lambda_x[\,], L)$, the invariants are easy to prove.
- For $R = [\,]$, we have $\mathrm{rev}\, S = L$ by 2 and therefore, either $c = \lambda_x[\,]$ if $L = [\,]$, or $\forall_q.(q, \mathrm{len}(c(q))) \in L$ by 1, and therefore, c is the desired coding.
- For $R = (q, 0) :: R'$, S can only contain elements of the form $(\_, 0)$. We proceed with $((q, 0) :: S, \lambda_x[\,], R')$. All invariants are trivially preserved.
- For $R = (q, 1+l) :: R'$ and $S = [\,]$ or $S = (r, 0) :: S'$, we set $c'(x) = [0]^{1+l}$ for $x = q$, and $c'(x) = [\,]$ otherwise. We proceed with $((q, 1+l) :: S, c', R')$. The invariants are easy to show. It is easy to show that c' is a Deflate coding.

The most general case is $R = (q, 1+l) :: R'$ and $S = (r, 1+m) :: S'$; let the intermediate Deflate coding c be given. We have

$$\sum_{\substack{i \in \mathcal{A} \\ c(i) \neq [\,]}} 2^{-\mathrm{len}(c(i))} < 2^{-l-1} + \sum_{\substack{i \in \mathcal{A} \\ c(i) \neq [\,]}} 2^{-\mathrm{len}(c(i))} \leq \sum_{\substack{i \in \mathcal{A} \\ li \neq 0}} 2^{-l(i)} \leq 1$$

By Theorem 2, $[1]^{1+m} \notin \mathrm{img}\, c$, and therefore, we can find a fresh code d' of length $1+m$. Let $d = d' ++ [0]^{l-m}$ and set

$$c'(x) := \begin{cases} d & \text{for } x = q \\ c(x) & \text{otherwise} \end{cases}$$

We have to show that c' is a Deflate coding. The axioms 2 and 3 are easy. For axiom 4, assume $x \neq [\,]$ and $x \sqsubseteq c'(q)$. If $x \sqsubseteq c'(r)$, the claim follows by axiom 4 for r. Otherwise, by totality $c'(r) \sqsubseteq x$. If $x \sqsubseteq d'$, by the minimality of d' follows $x = c'(r)$. If $d' \sqsubseteq x$, trivially, $d' \preccurlyeq c'(q)$. Axiom 4 holds. For axiom 2, it is sufficient to show that no other non-$[\,]$ code prefixes d. Consider a code $e \preccurlyeq d$. As all codes are shorter or of equal length than d', $e \preccurlyeq d'$. But then, either $e \preccurlyeq c(r)$, or $c(r) \sqsubseteq e$. Contradiction. Therefore, we can proceed with $((q, 1+l) :: S, c', r')$.

This is proved as Lemma `existence` in `DeflateCoding.v`. From this, we can extract an algorithm that calculates a coding from a sequence of lengths. For a better understanding of the algorithm proposed here, we consider the following length function as an example:

$$l : 0 \to 2; 1 \to 1; 2 \to 3; 3 \to 3; 4 \to 0$$

We first have to sort the graph of this function according to the $\lesssim$ ordering.

$$[(4, 0), (1, 1), (0, 2), (2, 3), (3, 3)]$$

Then, the following six steps are necessary to generate the coding.

Step	R	S	c(0)	c(1)	c(2)	c(3)	c(4)
0	[(4, 0), (1, 1), (0, 2), (2, 3), (3, 3)]	[]	[]	[]	[]	[]	[]
1	[(1, 1), (0, 2), (2, 3), (3, 3)]	[(4, 0)]	[]	[]	[]	[]	[]
2	[(0, 2), (2, 3), (3, 3)]	[(1, 1), (4, 0)]	[]	[0]	[]	[]	[]
3	[(2, 3), (3, 3)]	[(0, 2), (1, 1), (4, 0)]	[1,0]	[0]	[]	[]	[]
4	[(3, 3)]	[(2, 3), (0, 2), (1, 1), (4, 0)]	[1,0]	[0]	[1,1,0]	[]	[]
5	[]	[(3, 3), (2, 3), (0, 2), (1, 1), (4, 0)]	[1,0]	[0]	[1,1,0]	[1,1,1]	[]

The final values of c are, in fact, a Deflate coding. The main difference to the algorithm in the standard [10] is that we sort the character/length pairs and then incrementally generate the coding, while their algorithm counts the occurrences of every non-zero code length first, determines their lexicographically smallest code, and then increases these codes by one for each occurring character. In our case, that means that it would first generate the function $a : 1 \to 1; 2 \to 1; 3 \to 2$ and 0 otherwise, which counts the lengths, and then define

$$b(m) = \sum_{j=0}^{m-1} 2^j a(j)$$

which gets the numerical value for the lexicographically smallest code of every length when viewed as binary number with the most significant bit being the leftmost bit. In our case, this is $1 \to 0; 2 \to 2; 3 \to 6$. Then

$$c(n) = b(l(n)) + |\{r < n \mid l(r) = l(n)\}|$$

meaning $c(0) = b(2) = 10_{(2)}$, $c(1) = b(1) = 0_{(2)}$, $c(2) = b(3) = 110_{(2)}$, $c(3) = b(3) + 1 = 111_{(2)}$ which is consistent with the algorithm presented here. The algorithm described in the standard [10] is more desirable for practical purposes, as it can make use of low-level machine instructions like bit shifting. On the other hand, notice that our algorithm is purely functional.

4 Backreferences

Files usually contain lots of repetitions. A canonical example are C files which contain lots of `#include` statements, or Java files which contain lots of `import` statements in the beginning. Deflate can remove these repetitions, as long as they are not more than 32 KiB[1] apart from each other. The mechanism uses backreferences, as found in Lempel-Ziv-compression. An extension of the backreference mechanism also allows for run length encoding (see below). A backreference is an instruction to copy parts of already decompressed data to the front, so duplicate strings have to be saved only once. They are represented as a pair $\langle l, d\rangle$ of a length l and a distance d. The length is the number of bytes to be copied, the distance is the number of bytes in the backbuffer that has to be skipped before copying. Similar mechanisms are used in other compression formats, so our implementation can probably be used for them, too.

The resolution (decompression) of such backreferences in an imperative context is trivial, but uses lots of invariants that make it hard to prove correct. In a purely functional context, it is non-trivial to find data structures that are fast enough. We decided to stick with purely functional algorithms, as they can be verified directly using Coq, and optimization of purely functional programs is interesting for its own sake. In our current verified implementation, this is the slowest part. We already have figured out an algorithm with better performance, but we are not yet done proving it formally correct; we will not get deeper into this algorithm in this paper.

Assuming we wanted to compress the string

$$\texttt{ananas\_banana\_batata} \tag{1}$$

we could shorten it with backreferences to

$$\texttt{ananas\_b}\langle 5, 8\rangle\langle 3, 7\rangle\texttt{tata} \tag{2}$$

An intuitive algorithm to resolve such a backreference uses a loop that decreases the length and copies one byte from the backbuffer to the front each time (the example is written in Java; notice that this algorithm, while intuitive, is not suitable for actual use in a decompression program, because you usually do not know the length of the output in advance, and hence cannot allocate an array of the proper length):

[1] Kibibyte: 2^{10} Byte.

```
int resolve (int l, int d, int index, byte[] output) {
    while (l > 0) {
      output[index] = output[index-d];
      index = index + 1; l = l - 1; }
    return index; }
```

This intuitive algorithm works when $l > d$, and results in a repetition of already written bytes – which is what run length encoding would do. Therefore, Deflate explicitly allows $l > d$, allowing us to shorten (2) even further:

$$\texttt{an}\langle 3,2\rangle\texttt{s\_b}\langle 5,8\rangle\langle 3,7\rangle\texttt{t}\langle 3,2\rangle \tag{3}$$

More directly, the string **aaaaaaargh!** can be compressed as a$\langle 7,1\rangle$**rgh!**, which essentially is run length encoding.

As already mentioned, the efficient resolution of backreferences in a purely functional manner was a lot harder than we expected. An imperative implementation can utilize the fact that the distances are limited by 32 KiB, and use a 32 KiB ringbuffer in form of an array that is periodically iterated and updated in parallel to the file-I/O. This uses stateful operations on an array, and has complicated invariants.

4.1 A Verified Backreference-Resolver

The obvious approach to do this in a purely functional way is using a map-like structure instead of an array as a ring buffer. The best possible approach we found uses an exponential list

```
Inductive ExpList (A : Set) : Set :=
| Enil : ExpList A
| Econs1 : A -> ExpList (A * A) -> ExpList A
| Econs2 : A -> A -> ExpList (A * A) -> ExpList A.
```

This takes into account that – in our experience – most backreferences tend to be "near", that is, have small distances, and such elements can be accessed faster. We could just save our whole history in one `ExpList` that we always pass around, without performance penalty. However, this will take a lot of memory which we do not need, as backreferences are limited to 32 KiB. We use another technique which we call **Queue of Doom**: We save two `ExpLists` and memorize how many elements are in them. The front `ExpList` is filled until it contains 32 KiB. If a backreference is resolved, and its distance is larger than the amount of bytes saved in the front `ExpList`, it is looked up in the back `ExpList`. Now, if the front `ExpList` is 32 KiB large, the front `ExpList` becomes the new back `ExpList`, a new empty front `ExpList` is allocated, and the former back `ExpList` will be doomed to be eaten by the garbage collector. The following is an illustration of filling such a queue of doom, the `ExpLists` are denoted as lists, and their size is – for illustration – only 3:

start	[]	[]	
push 1	[1]	[]	
push 2	[2; 1]	[]	
push 3	[3; 2; 1]	[]	
push 4	[4]	[3; 2; 1]	[] → ☠
push 5	[5; 4]	[3; 2; 1]	
push 6	[6; 5; 4]	[3; 2; 1]	
push 7	[7]	[6; 5; 4]	[3; 2; 1] → ☠

The advantage of this algorithm is that we have a fully verified implementation in `EfficientDecompress.v`. The disadvantage is that while it does not perform badly, it still does not have satisfactory performance, taking several minutes. We are currently working on better algorithms. One such algorithm which is purely functional can be found in the file `NoRBR/BackRefs.hs` in the software directory, see Sect. 7. Another such algorithm which utilizes diffarrays [1] aka Parray [24], and resembles an imperative resolution procedure, can be found in the file `NoRBR/BackRefWithDiffArray.hs`. Both perform well, and we are currently working on verifying them.

5 Strong Decidability and Strong Uniqueness

So far we showed how we implemented several aspects of the standard. However, this was a very high-level view: We still need to combine the parts we implemented in the way specified in [10]. This is a lot less trivial than it might sound: A compressed block is associated with two codings, a "literal/length" coding, and a "distance" coding. The "literal/length" coding contains codes for raw bytes, a code for the end of the block, and "length" codes, which initialize a backreference, and can have suffixes of several bits. Such length codes and their suffix must be followed by a "distance" code which can also have a suffix. Dynamically compressed blocks have an additional header with the code-length sequences for these two codings (which are sufficient for reconstruction of the codings, as proved in Sect. 3). However, these sequences are themselves compressed by yet another mechanism that – besides Huffman-coding – allows for run-length-encoding. Therefore, a third coding must be specified in the header, the "code-length coding". Uncompressed blocks, on the other hand, must start at a byte-boundary, which means that when specifying, we cannot even forget the underlying byte sequence and just work on a sequence of bits.

We could have written a decompression function as specification, but there are several possible algorithms to do so, which we would have to prove equivalent. We decided that a relational specification is clearer and easier to use, and probably also easier to port to other systems (Isabelle, Agda, Minlog) if desired. We defined two properties that such relations must have to be suitable for parsing, which we will define in this section.

While efficiency in runtime and memory are desirable properties, the most important property of a lossless compression format is the guarantee that for any given data d, decompress(compress d) $= d$, which is what our final implementation guarantees. While most container formats have some checksum or error correction code, Deflate itself does not have mechanisms to cope with data corruption due to hardware failures and transcription errors, therefore a formal discussion of these is outside the scope of this paper; research in this direction can be found for example in [3].

We will work with relations of the form `OutputType -> InputType -> Prop`. The final relation is called `DeflateEncodes`.

Left-Uniqueness ("injectivity") can be formalized as $\forall_{a,b,l}.R\,a\,l \rightarrow R\,b\,l \rightarrow a = b$. However, when reading from a stream, it must always be clear when to "stop" reading, which essentially means that given an input l such that $R\,a\,l$, it cannot be extended: $\forall_{a,b,l,l'}.R\,a\,l \rightarrow R\,b\,(l{+\!\!+}l') \rightarrow l' = [\,]$. We proved that these two properties together are equivalent to the following property, which we call *strong uniqueness*:

$$\text{StrongUnique}(R) :\Leftrightarrow$$
$$\forall_{a,b,l_a,l'_a,l_b,l'_b}.l_a{+\!\!+}l'_a = l_b{+\!\!+}l'_b \rightarrow Ral_a \rightarrow Rbl_b \rightarrow a = b \wedge l_a = l_b$$

This is formally proved as `StrongUniqueLemma` in `StrongDec.v`. While strong uniqueness gives us uniqueness of a prefix, provided that it exists, we need an additional property that states that it is actually decidable whether such a prefix exists, which we call *strong decidability*:

$$\text{StrongDec}(R) :\Leftrightarrow \forall l.(\lambda_X.X \vee \neg X)(\exists_{a,l',l''}.l = l'{+\!\!+}l'' \wedge Ral')$$

All existences are constructive: If a prefix exists, then we can calculate it. Therefore, proving strong decidability yields a parser for the respective relation. Conversely, if you can write and verify a parser for it, then existence follows.

Strong decidability and strong uniqueness reflect the obvious type of a verified decoder: If a relation satisfies both properties, it is well-suited for parsing. Indeed, for R being our formalization of the Deflate standard, we give a formal proof of StrongDec(R) which is such that the extracted decoding function constitutes a usable reference implementation in the sense that it can successfully decompress files of several megabytes. We can combine such relations in a way similar to parser monads, a bind-like combinator can be defined that first applies the first relation, and then the second relation:

$$Q \ggg\!=_c R := \mu_\xi(\forall_{b_q,b_r,a_q,a_r}.Q\,b_q\,a_q \rightarrow R\,b_q\,b_r\,a_r \rightarrow \xi\,(c\,b_q\,b_r)\,(a_q\,{+\!\!+}a_r))$$

This combinator preserves strong uniqueness and decidability. More complicated combinators can be built from it. This makes it is easy to replace parts of strong decidability proofs and optimize them, and makes the implementation modular. This way we could benchmark optimizations before verifying them (by using `admit`, for example), which made programming much easier.

The definitions can be found in `StrongDec.v`, most proofs for our encoding relation can be found in `EncodingRelationProperties.v`.

We think that our overall theory of such grammars and parsers is usable for many other data formats: It should be usable whenever parsing does not need to be interactive in the sense that it must produce answers to requests (like in many bidirectional network protocols). But despite this drawback, it should be applicable in many practical situations, and is very simple.

6 Compression

Compression is by no means unique, and depends on the desired trade off between speed and compression ratio. We implemented an algorithm that does not yet utilize optimal Huffman codings, but only searches for possible backreferences, and saves everything as statically compressed blocks. Especially for ASCII texts this is usually a disadvantage, and we plan to include this into the algorithm in the future to gain better compression results. The algorithm calculates a hashsum of every three read bytes and saves their position in a hash table which has queues of doom as buckets. This follows a recommendation from [11], adapted to the purely functional paradigm. The implementation can be found in `Compress.v`.

7 Conclusion

Our contribution is a complete mathematical formalization of Deflate. We formalized the proofs in Coq, such that an implementation of a decompression algorithm in Haskell can be extracted. We tested this implementation against some datasets, and observed that it is compatible with other implementations of Deflate. We implemented a simple compression algorithm and a decompression algorithm, both fully verified against the specification, with reasonable speed.

The project's source code can be found under http://www2.tcs.ifi.lmu.de/~senjak/fm2016/deflate.tar.gz. For build instructions, see `README.txt`. It works under Coq 8.4pl6, and GHC version 7.10.3, but most of the code should be portable across versions. We also plan to maintain our GitHub-repository at https://github.com/dasuxullebt/deflate in the future.

We gave a flexible, modular and simple way of specifying grammars and using these specifications to create stream parsers. Our project shows that program extraction from proofs and performance are not a contradiction. We already developed two not-yet verified faster algorithms to resolve backreferences, one of which is purely functional, which we will formally verify in the future. While we believe that there is still potential for optimization of our Coq code, we hope to use our specification to create a verified implementation in C, using the Verified Software Toolchain [5].

References

1. The diffarray package. https://hackage.haskell.org/package/diffarray
2. High assurance cyber military systems proposers' day presentation, February 2012. http://www.darpa.mil/WorkArea/DownloadAsset.aspx?id=2147484882

3. Affeldt, R., Garrigue, J.: Formalization of error-correcting codes: from hamming to modern coding theory. In: Urban, C., Zhang, X. (eds.) ITP 2015. LNCS, vol. 9236, pp. 17–33. Springer, Heidelberg (2015). doi:10.1007/978-3-319-22102-1_2
4. Affeldt, R., Hagiwara, M., Sénizergues, J.: Formalization of Shannon's theorems. J. Autom. Reasoning **53**(1), 63–103 (2014). doi:10.1007/s10817-013-9298-1
5. Appel, A.W.: Program Logics for Certified Compilers. Cambridge University Press, New York (2014)
6. Berger, U., Jones, A., Seisenberger, M.: Program extraction applied to monadic parsing. J. Log. Comput. exv078 (2015). doi:10.1093/logcom/exv078
7. Bhargavan, K., Fournet, C., Kohlweiss, M., Pironti, A., Strub, P.Y.: Implementing TLS with verified cryptographic security (2013). http://www.mitls.org/downloads/miTLS-report.pdf
8. Blanchette, J.C.: Proof pearl: mechanizing the textbook proof of Huffman's algorithm. J. Autom. Reasoning **43**(1), 1–18 (2009). doi:10.1007/s10817-009-9116-y
9. Danielsson, N.A.: Total parser combinators. ACM SIGPLAN Not. **45**, 285–296 (2010)
10. Deutsch, P.: DEFLATE Compressed Data Format Specification version 1.3. RFC 1951 (Informational), May 1996. http://www.ietf.org/rfc/rfc1951.txt
11. Deutsch, P.: GZIP file format specification version 4.3. RFC 1952 (Informational), May 1996. http://www.ietf.org/rfc/rfc1952.txt
12. Fielding, R., Gettys, J., Mogul, J., Frystyk, H., Masinter, L., Leach, P., Berners-Lee, T.: Hypertext Transfer Protocol - HTTP/1.1. RFC 2616 (Draft Standard), June 1999. http://www.ietf.org/rfc/rfc2616.txt, obsoleted by RFCs 7230, 7231, 7232, 7233, 7234, 7235, updated by RFCs 2817, 5785, 6266, 6585
13. Google Inc.: Zopfli compression algorithm. https://github.com/google/zopfli
14. Hollenbeck, S.: Transport Layer Security Protocol Compression Methods. RFC 3749 (Proposed Standard), May 2004. http://www.ietf.org/rfc/rfc3749.txt
15. Huffman, D.: A method for the construction of minimum-redundancy codes. Proc. IRE **40**(9), 1098–1101 (1952)
16. Jang, D., Tatlock, Z., Lerner, S.: Establishing browser security guarantees through formal shim verification. In: Proceedings of the 21st USENIX Conference on Security Symposium, p. 8. USENIX Association (2012)
17. Kelsey, J.: Compression and information leakage of plaintext. In: Daemen, J., Rijmen, V. (eds.) FSE 2002. LNCS, vol. 2365, pp. 263–276. Springer, Heidelberg (2002). doi:10.1007/3-540-45661-9_21
18. Klein, G., Andronick, J., Elphinstone, K., Murray, T., Sewell, T., Kolanski, R., Heiser, G.: Comprehensive formal verification of an OS microkernel. ACM Trans. Comput. Syst. **32**(1), 2:1–2:70 (2014)
19. Leroy, X.: Formal verification of a realistic compiler. Commun. ACM **52**(7), 107–115 (2009). http://gallium.inria.fr/~xleroy/publi/compcert-CACM.pdf
20. McMillan, B.: Two inequalities implied by unique decipherability. IRE Trans. Inf. Theory **2**(4), 115–116 (1956)
21. Nogin, A.: Writing constructive proofs yielding efficient extracted programs
22. PKWARE Inc.: ZIP File Format Specification, September 2012. https://www.pkware.com/documents/APPNOTE/APPNOTE-6.3.3.TXT
23. Thery, L.: Formalising human's algorithm. Technical report, Technical report TRCS 034, Dept. of Informatics, Univ. of L'Aquila (2004)
24. Vafeiadis, V.: Adjustable references. In: Blazy, S., Paulin-Mohring, C., Pichardie, D. (eds.) ITP 2013. LNCS, vol. 7998, pp. 328–337. Springer, Heidelberg (2013). doi:10.1007/978-3-642-39634-2_24

Decoupling Abstractions of Non-linear Ordinary Differential Equations

Andrew Sogokon[1(✉)], Khalil Ghorbal[2(✉)], and Taylor T. Johnson[3]

[1] Vanderbilt University, Nashville, TN, USA
andrew.sogokon@vanderbilt.edu
[2] Inria, Rennes, Brittany, France
khalil.ghorbal@inria.fr
[3] Vanderbilt University, Nashville, TN, USA
taylor.johnson@vanderbilt.edu

Abstract. We investigate decoupling abstractions, by which we seek to simulate (i.e. abstract) a given system of ordinary differential equations (ODEs) by another system that features completely independent (i.e. uncoupled) sub-systems, which can be considered as separate systems in their own right. Beyond a purely mathematical interest as a tool for the qualitative analysis of ODEs, decoupling can be applied to verification problems arising in the fields of control and hybrid systems. Existing verification technology often scales poorly with dimension. Thus, reducing a verification problem to a number of independent verification problems for systems of smaller dimension may enable one to prove properties that are otherwise seen as too difficult. We show an interesting correspondence between Darboux polynomials and decoupling simulating abstractions of systems of polynomial ODEs and give a constructive procedure for automatically computing the latter.

Keywords: Ordinary differential equations · Darboux polynomials · Simulation · Abstraction · Decoupling

1 Introduction

Simulation relations are an important concept in the study of both discrete and continuous dynamical systems. Informally speaking, a system simulates another system if it over-approximates its set of possible behaviours. In practice, when analyzing systems, one often wants to construct simulations of the original system that are in some sense "simpler" to analyze. Then, by demonstrating some property of interest in the simulation one may infer the property in the original system.

In [22] Sankaranarayanan investigated an interesting technique for constructing simulations of continuous systems by employing change of basis transformations. It was shown how *linearizing* change of basis transformations of non-linear

This work was supported by the Air Force Research Laboratory (AFRL) through contract number FA8750-15-1-0105 and the Air Force Office of Scientific Research (AFOSR) under contract numbers FA9550-15-1-0258 and FA9550-16-1-0246.

J. Fitzgerald et al. (Eds.): FM 2016, LNCS 9995, pp. 628–644, 2016.
DOI: 10.1007/978-3-319-48989-6_38

systems of ODEs can yield simulations in which the dynamics is given by a system of linear ODEs. The motivation for considering such transformations is clear, since linear systems cannot exhibit some of the rich dynamic phenomena found in their non-linear counterparts and are more amenable to analysis [12]. In this paper we consider simulations of non-linear ODEs of a different kind: instead of linear dynamics, we seek to construct simulations that are potentially non-linear, but whose analysis can be performed in a lower-dimensional space than that of the original system.

Although our focus in this paper is on analyzing purely continuous systems, the methods we present are motivated by the broader goal of aiding the task of automatic verification of *hybrid dynamical systems* whose continuous modes are governed by non-linear ODEs. Hybrid systems combine discrete and continuous behaviour; their formal modelling and verification is of increasing interest and importance to modern engineering, where discrete digital controllers are used to control continuously evolving physical plants. In recent years, verification technology for hybrid systems has seen significant advances and number of interesting case studies, e.g. verification of train control systems [20,29], aircraft collision avoidance protocols [1,14], descent guidance control software in a lunar lander [28] and satellite rendezvous manoeuvres [8], to give a few examples. However, non-linear ODEs appearing in hybrid system models often present a serious challenge to verification due to their inherent complexity. In this paper we seek to overcome some aspects of this hurdle by constructing simulations of non-linear ODEs with structure that more readily lends itself to analysis.

1.1 Contributions

In this paper we `(I)` define *decoupled simulating abstractions* of non-linear ODEs, discuss their utility and relationship to *first integrals* [11] and *constant-scale continuous consecutions* [23]. `(II)` We give an algorithm for checking whether a given set of polynomial *abstract basis functions* can be used to create a decoupled abstraction of a system of polynomial ODEs and then `(III)` employ the theory of *Darboux polynomials* [11] to give sufficient criteria for non-existence of polynomial abstract basis functions suitable for constructing decoupled polynomial abstractions. Lastly, `(IV)` we show how Darboux polynomials can be used to construct the abstract basis functions for decoupled abstractions whenever they exist. We conclude with a summary of our findings, an overview of related work and directions for future research.

1.2 Preliminaries

An autonomous n-dimensional system of ODEs has the following form:

$$\dot{x}_1 = f_1(x_1, x_2, \ldots, x_n),$$
$$\vdots$$
$$\dot{x}_n = f_n(x_1, x_2, \ldots, x_n),$$

where for $i \in \{1, \ldots, n\}$ each $f_i : \mathbb{R}^n \to \mathbb{R}$ is a real-valued function (typically C^1), and $\dot{x}_i$ denotes the time derivative of x_i, i.e. $\frac{d}{dt}x_i(t)$. In applications, constraints are often imposed on the states where the system is allowed to evolve, i.e. the system may only evolve inside some given set $H \subseteq \mathbb{R}^n$, which is known as the *evolution constraint*. We may write this more concisely using vector notation as $\dot{\boldsymbol{x}} = f(\boldsymbol{x})$, $\boldsymbol{x} \in H$. Here $\dot{\boldsymbol{x}} = (\dot{x}_1, \ldots, \dot{x}_n)$ and $f : \mathbb{R}^n \to \mathbb{R}^n$ is a *vector field* generated by the system, i.e. $f(\boldsymbol{x}) = (f_1(\boldsymbol{x}), \ldots, f_n(\boldsymbol{x}))$ for all $\boldsymbol{x} \in \mathbb{R}^n$. When no evolution constraint is specified, H is assumed to be $\mathbb{R}^n$.

A *solution* to the initial value problem for the system of ODEs $\dot{\boldsymbol{x}} = f(\boldsymbol{x})$ with initial value $\boldsymbol{x}_0 \in \mathbb{R}^n$ is a differentiable function $\varphi_t(\boldsymbol{x}_0) : (a, b) \to \mathbb{R}^n$ defined for all t within some non-empty extended real interval including zero, i.e. $t \in (a, b) \subseteq \mathbb{R} \cup \{\infty, -\infty\}$, where $a < 0 < b$, and such that $\frac{d}{dt}\varphi_t(\boldsymbol{x}_0) = f(\varphi_t(\boldsymbol{x}_0))$ for all $t \in (a, b)$. If the solution $\varphi_t(\boldsymbol{x}_0)$ is available in closed-form,[1] then one can answer questions about the temporal behaviour of the system (such as e.g. safety and liveness) by analyzing the closed-form expression. In practice, however, it has long been established that explicit closed-form solutions to non-linear ODEs are highly uncommon [12].

In this paper we will work with systems of ODEs whose right-hand sides are given by polynomials in the state variables $x_1, \ldots, x_n$. Formally, we say that $f_i \in \mathbb{R}[X_1, \ldots, X_n]$ for all $i \in \{1, \ldots, n\}$, where $\mathbb{R}[X_1, \ldots, X_n]$ denotes the ring of multivariate polynomials with real coefficients and indeterminates $X_1, \ldots, X_n$. We write $f_i(x_1, \ldots, x_n)$ when we wish to make it clear that the polynomial is treated as a function, with indeterminates replaced by the appropriate variables. Polynomial systems of ODEs are necessarily locally Lipschitz continuous, which guarantees existence of unique solutions on some non-trivial time interval for any initial value $\boldsymbol{x}_0 \in \mathbb{R}^n$ (by the Picard-Lindelöf theorem; see e.g. [27]).

1.3 Coupling

Given a system of ODEs $\dot{\boldsymbol{x}} = f(\boldsymbol{x})$, the *maximum coupling coefficient* (henceforth mcc) is the size of the largest sub-system with no independent sub-systems. To define rigorously, we construct a finite *coupling graph* $CG = (V, E)$, where the set of vertices is precisely the set of state variables, i.e. $V = \{x_1, \ldots, x_n\}$, and there is an edge from x_i to some other vertex x_j, i.e. $(x_i, x_j) \in E$ with $i \neq j$, if and only if $\frac{\partial f_i}{\partial x_j} \neq 0$. The *coupling coefficients* cc are a finite multiset of natural numbers corresponding to the orders (i.e. the numbers of vertices) of all the weakly connected components in CG. The coefficient mcc is defined to be the maximum order of the weakly connected components in CG, i.e. $\mathsf{mcc} \equiv \max \mathsf{cc}$.

Definition 1 (Uncoupled system). *A system of ODEs $\dot{\boldsymbol{x}} = f(\boldsymbol{x})$ is* uncoupled *if and only if its* $\mathsf{mcc} = 1$*, i.e. if the rate of change of each state variable is completely independent of the other variables.*

[1] By this we understand a *finite* expression in terms of polynomials and elementary functions such as $\sin, \cos, \exp, \ln$, etc.

Example 1. Consider the following two planar polynomial systems:

$$\dot{x}_1 = x_1^2 x_2 + 5x_1 - 1, \qquad \dot{x}_1 = x_1^3 + 5x_1 - 10,$$
$$\dot{x}_2 = 3x_2^3 + 2x_1 x_2 - x_1. \qquad \dot{x}_2 = 2x_2^2 + 3x_2 + 1.$$

The system on the left has $\mathsf{mcc} = 2$ because the vertices $\{x_1, x_2\}$ in the coupling graph have edges connecting them in both directions, since $\frac{\partial}{\partial x_2}(x_1^2 x_2 + 5x_1 - 1) = x_1^2 \neq 0$ and $\frac{\partial}{\partial x_1}(3x_2^3 + 2x_1 x_2 - x_1) = 2x_2 - 1 \neq 0$. On the other hand, the system on the right has $\mathsf{mcc} = 1$ (i.e. is uncoupled) because $\frac{\partial}{\partial x_2}(x_1^3 + 5x_1 - 10) = 0$ and $\frac{\partial}{\partial x_1}(2x_2^2 + 3x_2 + 1) = 0$ and therefore the vertices $\{x_1, x_2\}$ in the graph are disconnected.

Uncoupled systems are appealing first and foremost because their 1-dimensional sub-systems can be analyzed independently, following a standard technique for 1-dimensional flows (see e.g. [25, Chap. 2]). For instance, consider the 1-dimensional system $\dot{x} = x^3 + 5x^2 + x - 10$. This system evolves on the real line and has fixed points at the real roots of $x^3 + 5x^2 + x - 10$, of which there are three: $\{-2, \frac{1}{2}\left(-3 - \sqrt{29}\right), \frac{1}{2}\left(-3 + \sqrt{29}\right)\}$. The direction of the flow is to the right whenever the graph of $\dot{x}$ is above zero (i.e. the rate of change of x is positive) and to the left when it is below (the rate of change is negative), as shown in Fig. 1.

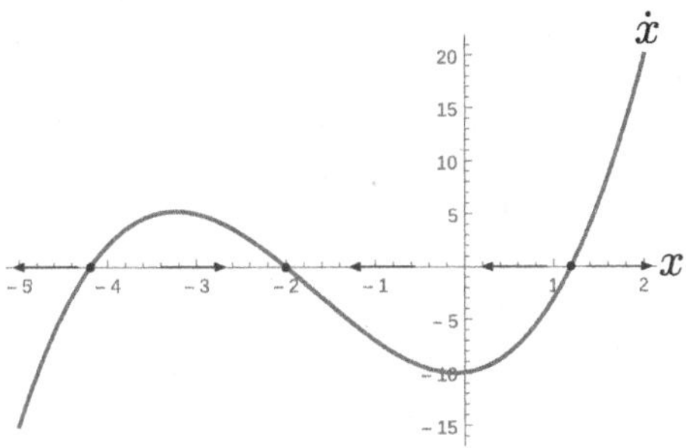

Fig. 1. Analysis of the 1-dimensional system $\dot{x} = x^3 + 5x^2 + x - 10$.

From inspecting the figure, one can readily see how one can construct the set of reachable states of any given initial point x_0 in a 1-dimensional polynomial system $\dot{x} = f(x)$: either the point is a root of the right-hand side, i.e. $f(x_0) = 0$, in which case x_0 remains invariant and the reachable set is simply $\{x_0\}$, or x_0 is not a root, i.e. $f(x) \neq 0$, in which case the reachable set is an interval of the form $[x_0, r)$ or $(r, x_0]$, where $r \in \mathbb{R} \cup \{\infty, -\infty\}$ is either a real root of f or it is ∞ or $-\infty$, respectively (if there are no real roots in the direction of motion). The reachable set from any initial point $\boldsymbol{x}_0 \in \mathbb{R}^n$ in a uncoupled system can thus also be bounded by combining the independent reachable sets in the 1-dimensional sub-systems.

Bounded-time reachable set computation using *verified integration* methods is also made easier because large systems of non-linear ODEs are typically expensive to integrate using methods that yield tight enclosures [16] (such as *Taylor models* [3,17]), whereas in an uncoupled system, no matter how large, each 1-dimensional sub-system can be integrated separately. An enclosure of the solution to the whole system at some time t can then be constructed directly from the enclosures of the solutions to the sub-systems at that time.

2 Decoupled Simulating Abstractions

In what follows, we will adopt the approach described by Sankaranarayanan in [22] to define *simulating abstractions* of non-linear ODEs using appropriate change of basis transformations.

Definition 2 (Simulating abstraction). *For a system* $\dot{\boldsymbol{x}} = f(\boldsymbol{x})$, $\boldsymbol{x} \in H$, *where* $f : \mathbb{R}^n \to \mathbb{R}^n$ *is locally Lipschitz continuous, equipped with an initial set of states* $X_0 \subseteq \mathbb{R}^n$, *a system* $\dot{\boldsymbol{\alpha}} = G(\boldsymbol{\alpha})$, $\boldsymbol{\alpha} \in \widehat{H}$, *where* $G : \mathbb{R}^m \to \mathbb{R}^m$ *is locally Lipschitz continuous and equipped with an initial set of states* $\widehat{X}_0 \subseteq \mathbb{R}^m$ *is a* simulating abstraction *if there exists a smooth (i.e.* C^∞*) mapping* $\boldsymbol{\alpha} : \mathbb{R}^n \to \mathbb{R}^m$ *such that: (i)* $\boldsymbol{\alpha}(X_0) \subseteq \widehat{X}_0$, *(ii)* $\boldsymbol{\alpha}(H) \subseteq \widehat{H}$, *and (iii) for any trajectory (i.e. solution in non-negative time)* $\varphi_T(\boldsymbol{x}_0) : [0, T) \to H$ *of the system* $\dot{\boldsymbol{x}} = f(\boldsymbol{x})$, $\boldsymbol{x} \in H$, *the trajectory* $\boldsymbol{\alpha} \circ \varphi_T(\boldsymbol{x}_0) : [0, T) \to \widehat{H}$ *is a trajectory of* $\dot{\boldsymbol{\alpha}} = G(\boldsymbol{\alpha})$, $\boldsymbol{\alpha} \in \widehat{H}$.

To ensure that the last condition in the above definition holds, it is sufficient to show that $G(\boldsymbol{\alpha}(\boldsymbol{x})) = J_{\boldsymbol{\alpha}} \cdot f(\boldsymbol{x})$, where $J_{\boldsymbol{\alpha}}$ is the Jacobian of the smooth mapping $\boldsymbol{\alpha}$ w.r.t. the state variables $x_1, \ldots, x_n$ (see [22, Theorem 2.1]), i.e.

$$G(\boldsymbol{\alpha}) = \begin{pmatrix} \frac{\partial \alpha_1}{\partial x_1} & \cdots & \frac{\partial \alpha_1}{\partial x_n} \\ \vdots & \ddots & \vdots \\ \frac{\partial \alpha_m}{\partial x_1} & \cdots & \frac{\partial \alpha_m}{\partial x_n} \end{pmatrix} \cdot \begin{pmatrix} f_1 \\ \vdots \\ f_n \end{pmatrix}.$$

Definition 3 (Lie derivative). *For a given system of ODEs* $\dot{\boldsymbol{x}} = f(\boldsymbol{x})$, *the* Lie derivative *of a smooth function* $p : \mathbb{R}^n \to \mathbb{R}$ *is given by*

$$\mathfrak{L}_f(p) = \nabla p \cdot f = \sum_{i=1}^{n} \frac{\partial p}{\partial x_i} \cdot f_i.$$

Note that since $f_i(\boldsymbol{x}) = \frac{dx_i}{dt}$, $\mathfrak{L}_f(p) = \left(\sum_{i=1}^n \frac{\partial p}{\partial x_i} \cdot \frac{dx_i}{dt}\right) = \frac{dp}{dt}$ *i.e. the total derivative of the function* p *with respect to time, which we denote by* $\dot{p}$.

Let us recall that the gradient ∇p gives the vector of all the partial derivatives of p, i.e. $\nabla p \equiv \left(\frac{\partial p}{\partial x_1}, \frac{\partial p}{\partial x_2}, \ldots, \frac{\partial p}{\partial x_n}\right)$, and thus the necessary condition for (iii) in Definition 2 to be satisfied may be equivalently stated as:

$$G(\boldsymbol{\alpha}) = \begin{pmatrix} \nabla \alpha_1 \\ \vdots \\ \nabla \alpha_m \end{pmatrix} \cdot f = \begin{pmatrix} \mathfrak{L}_f(\alpha_1) \\ \vdots \\ \mathfrak{L}_f(\alpha_m) \end{pmatrix}.$$

Remark 1. It is important to note that, following Definition 2, solutions to simulating abstractions are guaranteed to exist for at least as long as they do in the concrete system. This property is crucial to soundness of the abstraction. A rather different, but in a certain sense more general, concept was explored by Platzer, who introduced *differential ghosts* [19], where the original dynamics is augmented by introducing some fresh variables whose rate of change may feature the newly introduced variables themselves, but is not restricted in the same way as in Definition 2. However, extra care needs to be taken to ensure that the solutions of the newly defined dynamics exist for at least as long as the solutions to the original system (e.g. see [19, Proof of Theorem 38]).

Definition 4 (Decoupling simulating abstraction). *Given a system of ODEs $\dot{\boldsymbol{x}} = f(\boldsymbol{x})$, a simulating abstraction $\dot{\boldsymbol{\alpha}} = G(\boldsymbol{\alpha})$ is* decoupling *if and only if the equalities $\mathfrak{L}_f(\alpha_1) = G_1(\alpha_1), \ldots, \mathfrak{L}_f(\alpha_m) = G_m(\alpha_m)$ hold, where $(G_1, \ldots, G_m) = G$. Such an abstraction is thus uncoupled:*

$$\dot{\alpha}_1 = G_1(\alpha_1),$$
$$\vdots$$
$$\dot{\alpha}_m = G_m(\alpha_m).$$

In what follows, we will give some examples of how first integrals (see e.g. [11]) and constant-scale continuous consecutions [23] provide the abstract basis functions $\boldsymbol{\alpha}$ which lead to decoupling simulating abstractions.

Example 2 (Algebraically integrable system). The 3-dimensional system

$$\begin{aligned} \dot{x}_1 &= x_1(x_3 - x_2), \\ \dot{x}_2 &= x_2(x_1 - x_3), \\ \dot{x}_3 &= x_3(x_2 - x_1), \end{aligned}$$

has two independent polynomial conserved quantities, i.e. first integrals, given by $\alpha_1 = x_1x_2x_3$ and $\alpha_2 = x_1 + x_2 + x_3$ (see [9, Example 75]). If we let $\boldsymbol{\alpha} = (\alpha_1, \alpha_2)$, we obtain the decoupling simulating abstraction $\dot{\boldsymbol{\alpha}} = \mathbf{0}$, i.e. $\dot{\alpha}_1 = 0, \dot{\alpha}_2 = 0$.

Remark 2. A polynomial system $\dot{\boldsymbol{x}} = f(\boldsymbol{x})$ of size n is *algebraically integrable* if it possesses $n - 1$ independent polynomial conserved quantities (also known as first integrals; see [9,11]), i.e. polynomials $\{\alpha_1, \ldots, \alpha_{n-1}\}$, where for all $i = 1, \ldots, n-1$ one has $\mathfrak{L}_f(\alpha_i) \equiv \dot{\alpha}_i = 0$. Algebraic integrability is a very powerful property, since it allows one to construct tight approximations of the *orbit* $\gamma(\boldsymbol{x}_0)$, i.e. the reachable set from $\boldsymbol{x}_0 \in \mathbb{R}^n$ in positive as well as negative time. That is, for any given point $\boldsymbol{x}_0 \in \mathbb{R}^n$, if one evaluates each first integral $\alpha_1, \ldots, \alpha_{n-1}$ at $\boldsymbol{x}_0$, one obtains real constants $c_1, \ldots, c_{n-1}$. The orbit through $\boldsymbol{x}_0$ is guaranteed to satisfy the formula $\alpha_1 = c_1 \wedge \cdots \wedge \alpha_{n-1} = c_{n-1}$, which corresponds to a (real) algebraic subset of $\mathbb{R}^n$ given by the common real roots of the polynomials $\alpha_i - c_i$. Every point $\boldsymbol{\alpha}_0 \in \mathbb{R}^{n-1}$ in such an abstract system $\dot{\boldsymbol{\alpha}} = \mathbf{0}$ is invariant and corresponds to a real (and invariant) algebraic set containing the orbit of the system $\dot{\boldsymbol{x}} = f(\boldsymbol{x})$.

Polynomials p such that $\mathfrak{L}_f(p) = \lambda p$ for some $\lambda \in \mathbb{R}$ generalize polynomial first integrals[2] and were investigated by Sankaranarayanan et al. in [23], where they were used in *constant-scale continuous consecution* conditions. In general, if one can find polynomials $\alpha_1, \ldots, \alpha_m$ that satisfy $\mathfrak{L}_f(\alpha_i) = \lambda_i \alpha_i$, $\lambda_i \in \mathbb{R}$ for all $i \in \{1, \ldots, m\}$, then one obtains a decoupling abstraction of the form

$$\begin{aligned}\dot{\alpha}_1 &= \lambda_1 \alpha_1,\\ &\vdots\\ \dot{\alpha}_m &= \lambda_m \alpha_m.\end{aligned}$$

We generalize this idea to decoupling polynomial abstractions by considering polynomial functions $\alpha_i \in \mathbb{R}[X_1, \ldots, X_n]$ such that $\mathfrak{L}_f(\alpha_i) = G_i(\alpha)$, where $G_i \in \mathbb{R}[X]$, i.e. the derivative of α_i may be expressed as a polynomial in α_i with real coefficients.

Example 3 (Decoupling simulating abstraction). Consider the coupled system:

$$\begin{aligned}\dot{x}_1 &= \frac{1}{3}(1 - 3x_1 + 2x_1^2 - 6x_2 + 4x_1x_2 + 2x_2^2),\\ \dot{x}_2 &= \frac{1}{3}(-1 - 3x_1 + x_1^2 + 2x_1x_2 + x_2^2)\,.\end{aligned}$$

Let $\alpha_1 = x_1 + x_2 - 1$, $\alpha_2 = x_1 - 2x_2$. If we consider $\boldsymbol{\alpha} = (\alpha_1, \alpha_2)$, we arrive at the following system (left), which can be expressed as an uncoupled system in the new basis (right):

$$\begin{aligned}\dot{\alpha}_1 &= -2x_1 + x_1^2 - 2x_2 + 2x_1x_2 + x_2^2, & \dot{\alpha}_1 &= \alpha_1^2 - 1,\\ \dot{\alpha}_2 &= 1 + x_1 - 2x_2, & \dot{\alpha}_2 &= \alpha_2 + 1\,.\end{aligned}$$

3 Existence and Generation of Abstraction Polynomials

In what follows, we investigate the existence of polynomials that can be used to construct decoupling simulating abstractions of a given system. We show in Sect. 3.1 that their existence (to a given polynomial degree) is decidable and give a sufficient criterion for their non-existence (to a given degree) based on the existence of so-called *Darboux polynomials* (e.g. see [11]). We then explore the problems of *checking* and *generation.* The checking problem is concerned with determining whether a given candidate polynomial is suitable for constructing a decoupling simulating abstraction. In Sect. 3.2 we describe a procedure for solving the checking problem. In Sect. 3.3 we present a technique for generating all suitable polynomials for the decoupling abstract basis (up to a given polynomial degree).

[2] i.e. p is a first integral if $\mathfrak{L}_f(p) = \lambda p$ where $\lambda = 0$.

3.1 Decidability and Darboux Existence Criterion

For polynomial systems of ODEs $\dot{\boldsymbol{x}} = f(\boldsymbol{x})$, the problem of finding a non-constant polynomial in the state variables, $p \in \mathbb{R}[X_1, \ldots, X_n]$, for the decoupling abstract basis reduces to searching for those p such that $\mathfrak{L}_f(p) = G(p)$, where $G \in \mathbb{R}[X]$, i.e. G is a univariate polynomial with real coefficients. There may, however, be no such polynomial. Fortunately, it is decidable to check for existence of such a p.

Proposition 1 (Existence of decoupling abstract basis polynomials). *Given a positive integer d and a polynomial system $\dot{\boldsymbol{x}} = f(\boldsymbol{x})$, it is decidable to check whether there exists a polynomial $p \in \mathbb{R}[X_1, \ldots, X_n]$ of total degree d such that $\mathfrak{L}_f(p) = G(p)$, where $G \in \mathbb{R}[X]$ is a univariate polynomial with real coefficients.*

Proof. The problem can be stated as a sentence in the theory of real arithmetic which is decidable [26]. Let $\lambda_0, \ldots, \lambda_k$ denote the unknown coefficients of the generic polynomial template p of degree d, where $k := \binom{n+d}{d} - 1$ is the number of *non-constant* monomials of degree at most d in n variables. The Lie derivative $\mathfrak{L}_f(p)$ can therefore be symbolically computed (Definition 3). Let $\kappa_0, \ldots, \kappa_m$ denote the unknown coefficients of the polynomial $G \in \mathbb{R}[X]$ where $m := \lceil \deg(\mathfrak{L}_f(p))/d \rceil$. The decision problem stated in the proposition is therefore equivalent to deciding the truth of the following sentence:

$$\exists\ (\lambda_0, \ldots, \lambda_k) \in \mathbb{R}^{k+1}.\ \exists\ (\kappa_0, \ldots, \kappa_m) \in \mathbb{R}^{m+1}.$$
$$\forall (X_1, \ldots, X_n) \in \mathbb{R}^n.\ d > 0 \wedge \mathfrak{L}_f(p) - (\kappa_0 + \kappa_1 p + \cdots + \kappa_m p^m) = 0\,.$$

If λ_0 denotes the constant term of the generic polynomial template p, then the condition $d > 0$ is equivalent (over the reals) to the inequality $\sum_{0<i\leq k} \lambda_i^2 > 0$, ensuring that p is non-constant. □

In practice, there is currently no question of applying existing decision procedures to formulas constructed in the proof or Proposition 1. The complexity of the most popular procedure for real quantifier elimination (CAD, due to Collins [4]) is doubly exponential in the number of variables. In Sect. 3.3 we will pursue a more promising method of searching for decoupling abstract basis polynomials. First, we shall recall so-called *Darboux polynomials*, a well-known tool in the study integrability of dynamical systems (e.g. see [11]), and use them to give a non-existence criterion for decoupling abstract basis polynomials. We then explore an interesting relationship between the two concepts.

Definition 5 (Darboux polynomial). *A polynomial $q \in K[X_1, \ldots, X_n]$, where K is a field of characteristic zero (e.g. $\mathbb{C}, \mathbb{R}, \mathbb{Q}$), is a* Darboux polynomial[3] *for $\dot{\boldsymbol{x}} = f(\boldsymbol{x})$ iff $\mathfrak{L}_f(q) = \lambda q$, for some $\lambda \in K[X_1, \ldots, X_n]$.*

---

[3] When q is a constant, the Darboux polynomial is *trivial* [11, Definition 2.14]. In this paper we will generally be interested in the non-trivial case.

Proposition 2 (Criterion for non-existence of decoupled abstractions). *If a given system $\dot{\boldsymbol{x}} = f(\boldsymbol{x})$ does not admit any Darboux polynomials over $\mathbb{C}$ of degree d, then there is no polynomial $p \in \mathbb{R}[X_1, \ldots, X_n]$ of degree d such that $\mathfrak{L}_f(p) = G(p)$ for some* non-constant $G \in \mathbb{R}[X]$.

Proof. We prove the contrapositive. Suppose there exists a polynomial $p \in \mathbb{R}[X_1, \ldots, X_n]$ such that $\mathfrak{L}_f(p) = G(p)$, where $G \in \mathbb{R}[X]$ is non-constant. By the fundamental theorem of algebra, G must have at least one complex root $c \in \mathbb{C}$. Therefore $G = (X - c)H$, where $H \in \mathbb{C}[X]$. We see that $(p - c)$ is a Darboux polynomial for the system because

$$\mathfrak{L}_f(p - c) = \mathfrak{L}_f(p) - \mathfrak{L}_f(c) = \mathfrak{L}_f(p) = G(p) = (p - c)H(p).$$

The degree of the Darboux polynomial $p - c$ is equal to the degree of p. □

3.2 Checking Abstraction Polynomial Candidates

Before proceeding to methods for generating decoupling abstract basis polynomials for polynomial systems $\dot{\boldsymbol{x}} = f(\boldsymbol{x})$, we discuss the (easier) problem of checking if for a given $p \in \mathbb{R}[X_1, \ldots, X_n]$ one can write $\mathfrak{L}_f(p) = G(p)$, where $G \in \mathbb{R}[X]$.

In general, given any two polynomials $P, p \in \mathbb{R}[X_1, \ldots, X_n]$, if $\deg(P) \geq \deg(p)$, one may obtain a rewriting $P = G(p)$ by solving a system of linear equations. One proceeds by first defining the maximum degree of a possible G to be $d = \lceil \deg(P)/\deg(p) \rceil$. If an appropriate rewriting exists, then there is guaranteed to be a solution $(\lambda_0, \ldots, \lambda_d) \in \mathbb{R}^{d+1}$ to the equation $P = \lambda_0 + \lambda_1 p + \lambda_2 p^2 + \cdots + \lambda_d p^d$. By expanding and equating the monomial coefficients on both sides one arrives at a system of linear equations (of size no larger than the number of monomials of P) in the real variables $\lambda_0, \ldots, \lambda_d$. Thus, in the worst case, one has to solve a linear system with $d + 1$ variables and $\binom{n+\deg(P)}{\deg(P)}$ equational constraints. A solution may be computed using a linear solver and the rewriting polynomial constructed as $G = \lambda_0 + \lambda_1 X + \cdots + \lambda_d X^d$. In what follows, we will refer to the procedure for obtaining the rewriting as REWRITE, that is REWRITE(P, p) gives G whenever $P = G(p)$.

Remark 3. It is worth remarking that the procedure REWRITE can be implemented by performing successive *polynomial reductions*, rather than by solving a linear program. Polynomial reduction extends polynomial division for univariate polynomials to the multivariate case and in general requires the computation of *Gröbner bases.* This functionality is available in most modern computer algebra systems.

3.3 Automated Generation of Decoupling Abstractions

A highly efficient method for synthesizing polynomial first integrals for polynomial ODEs was reported by Matringe et al. in [15], where the synthesis problem is reduced to computing the null space of a matrix with real entries. In [7], the authors extended the work of Matringe et al. to generate real algebraic invariants of polynomial ODEs, giving a search procedure for the most general class of invariant sets that can be expressed using polynomial equations. The same procedure can be used to generate Darboux polynomials over the reals or over the complexes only by changing the underlying computational field. In general, there is no known bound for the degree of Darboux polynomials in a given system. However, the automatic generation procedure is guaranteed to find all the independent Darboux polynomials for the system up to a given degree.

In this section, we explore the relationship between polynomials in a decoupling abstract basis and Darboux polynomials. This relationship will enable us to exploit the efficient symbolic generation methods reported in [7,15]. We outline a procedure for constructing polynomials p such that $\mathfrak{L}_f(p) = G(p)$, where $G \in \mathbb{R}[X]$, from a list of automatically generated Darboux polynomials (up to some given degree). The procedure will require two lemmas given below.

We note first that whenever q is a Darboux polynomial, any constant multiple of q, i.e. aq for some $a \in \mathbb{R}$ or $\mathbb{C}$, is also Darboux. A similar property holds for the decoupling abstract basis functions in simulating abstractions.

Lemma 1. *If $p \in \mathbb{R}[X_1, \ldots, X_n]$ is such that $\mathfrak{L}_f(p) = G(p)$ where $G \in \mathbb{R}[X]$, then $s = ap + b$ for any real numbers a, b, is such that $\mathfrak{L}_f(s) = F(s)$, where $F \in \mathbb{R}[X]$.*

Proof. If $a = 0$ then $\mathfrak{L}_f(s) = \mathfrak{L}_f(b) = 0$ and F is simply the zero polynomial in $\mathbb{R}[X]$. If $a \neq 0$, by our hypothesis we have $\mathfrak{L}_f(p) = G(p)$. Let us write $p = \frac{s-b}{a}$ and note that

$$\mathfrak{L}_f(s) = \mathfrak{L}_f(ap + b) = a\mathfrak{L}_f(p) + \mathfrak{L}_f(b) = a\mathfrak{L}_f(p) = aG(p) = aG\left(\frac{s-b}{a}\right).$$

We see that $\mathfrak{L}_f(s) = aG\left(\frac{s-b}{a}\right)$ is a polynomial in s with real coefficients. □

One consequence of Lemma 1 is that whenever we assume the existence of a polynomial p such that $\mathfrak{L}_f(p) = G(p)$ for some $G \in \mathbb{R}[X]$, it always suffices to assume the existence of a decoupling abstract basis polynomial $p - r$ for any real number r.

In Proposition 2 we established that the existence of decoupling abstract basis polynomials p is related to the existence of a special Darboux polynomial $p - c$ for some complex number c. For any polynomial s, we denote by s^* the polynomial obtained by setting the constant term of s to zero. For instance, if $s = x + 1$ then, $s^* = x$. Thus, for the (Darboux) polynomial $p - c$, one has $(p - c)^* = p^*$ (by definition of the * operator) and therefore p^* is a decoupling abstract basis polynomial by Lemma 1, since it is an offset of the polynomial p by a real number (the constant term of p). Therefore, if one generates Darboux polynomials over the complex numbers and finds a Darboux polynomial q such that q^* is a polynomial over the reals (i.e. all the coefficients of q^* are real numbers), then q^* is potentially a decoupling abstract basis polynomial, which can be checked by solving a linear program, i.e. by running $\text{REWRITE}(\mathfrak{L}_f(q^*), q^*)$, as outlined in Sect. 3.2.

Nevertheless, generating Darboux polynomials over the complex numbers will not necessarily return Darboux polynomials q such that q^* is a polynomial over the reals even if the latter exist. For instance, if $q = x^2 + xy + c$ is a Darboux polynomial with some complex constant term c, then the procedure may return $\imath q$ instead of q ($\imath$ being the imaginary number satisfying $\imath^2 = -1$), although we are rather interested in looking for q. Enforcing such a constraint in the procedure for generating Darboux polynomials will require solving mixed non-linear equations where some variables are real and some are complex numbers. To avoid solving mixed problems, we can easily adapt the generation procedure to produce *monic* Darboux polynomials for any variable ordering, for instance the lexicographic order $X_1 > \cdots > X_n$. Recall that monic univariate polynomials are those polynomials where the leading coefficient (i.e. the coefficient of the leading monomial) is equal to 1. In the multivariate case, the notion of leading coefficient additionally requires a monomial ordering. For instance, for the order $X_1 > X_2$, the leading monomial of the polynomial $2X_1X_2 + X_1^2$ is X_1^2 and therefore the leading coefficient is 1, whereas the leading monomial in the reverse lexicographic ordering $X_2 > X_1$ is X_1X_2 and the leading coefficient is 2.

Lemma 2. *Given a polynomial $q \in \mathbb{C}[X_1, \ldots, X_n]$, let $p \in \mathbb{C}[X_1, \ldots, X_n]$ be the monic polynomial $\frac{q}{\mathsf{LC}(q)}$, where $\mathsf{LC}(q)$ is the* leading coefficient *of q with respect to some fixed monomial ordering. There exists a non-zero complex number z such that $(zq)^* \in \mathbb{R}[X_1, \ldots, X_n]$ if and only if $p^* \in \mathbb{R}[X_1, \ldots, X_n]$.*

Proof. Suppose there exists such a non-zero complex number z such that $(zq)^* \in \mathbb{R}[X_1, \ldots, X_n]$. Since $z\mathsf{LC}(q) = \mathsf{LC}(zq)$ we have that $\frac{zq}{\mathsf{LC}(zq)} = \frac{zq}{z\mathsf{LC}(q)} = \frac{q}{\mathsf{LC}(q)} = p$, therefore $\frac{1}{\mathsf{LC}(zq)}(zq) = p$ and $\frac{1}{\mathsf{LC}(zq)}(zq)^* = p^*$. Since $\mathsf{LC}(zq) \in \mathbb{R}$, we have $p^* \in \mathbb{R}[X_1, \ldots, X_n]$. Conversely, if $p^* \in \mathbb{R}[X_1, \ldots, X_n]$, take $z = \frac{1}{\mathsf{LC}(q)}$ so that $(zq)^* = p^*$. □

We now describe a procedure for generating decoupling abstract basis polynomials. Suppose we are given all the independent Darboux polynomials in $\mathbb{C}[X_1, \ldots, X_n]$ for the system $\dot{\boldsymbol{x}} = f(\boldsymbol{x})$ up to some degree $d > 0$. By Proposition 2, if there exists a polynomial $p \in \mathbb{R}[X_1, \ldots, X_n]$ of degree $d' \leq d$ such that $\mathfrak{L}_f(p) = G(p)$, where $G \in \mathbb{R}[X]$ is non-constant, then there necessarily exists a Darboux polynomial q of degree d' such that q^* is a polynomial over the reals, i.e. $q^* \in \mathbb{R}[X_1, \ldots, X_n]$. This fact suggests a simple search method. Below we describe the three main steps in the procedure.

1. For a fixed positive integer d, automatically generate all monic Darboux polynomials for the system up to degree d with coefficients in $\mathbb{C}$.
2. For each generated Darboux polynomial q check if $q^* \in \mathbb{R}[X_1, \ldots, X_n]$ and if so, store q^* as a candidate in a list L.
3. For all polynomials q^* in L, run REWRITE($\mathfrak{L}_f(q^*), q^*$). If q^* is a decoupling abstract basis polynomial, the rewriting procedure will return $G \in \mathbb{R}[X]$ s.t. $\mathfrak{L}_f(q^*) = G(q^*)$.

Example 4. Consider the following system

$$\dot{x}_1 = \frac{1}{3}(1 + x_1 - 2x_2 + 2(1 + (-1 + x_1 + x_2)^2))$$
$$\dot{x}_2 = \frac{1}{3}(-x_1 + 2x_2 + (-1 + x_1 + x_2)^2)$$

The automatic generation procedure for Darboux polynomials over $\mathbb{C}$ up to degree 1 gives us $(q_1, q_2, q_3) = (1+x_1-2x_2, (-1+\imath)+x_1+x_2, (-1-\imath)+x_1+x_2)$. In this case, q_1^*,q_2^* and q_3^* are all candidates for the short list L. Since $q_2^* = q_3^*$, $L = \{x_1 - 2x_2, x_1 + x_2\}$. Running REWRITE($\mathfrak{L}_f(q_1^*), q_1^*$) and REWRITE($\mathfrak{L}_f(q_2^*), q_2^*$) returns $2 - 2X + X^2$ and $1 + X$, respectively. Thus, letting $(\alpha_1, \alpha_2) = (q_1^*, q_2^*)$, we obtain the decoupled abstraction:

$$\dot{\alpha}_1 = 2 - 2\alpha_1 + \alpha_1^2,$$
$$\dot{\alpha}_2 = 1 + \alpha_2.$$

In general, a Darboux polynomial q, with $q^* \in \mathbb{R}[X_1, \ldots, X_n]$, is not necessarily a decoupling abstract basis polynomial. For instance, in the system $\dot{x}_1 = x_1x_2, \dot{x}_2 = x_2$, one has x_1 as a Darboux polynomial; however x_1 is not a decoupling abstract basis polynomial because $\mathfrak{L}_f(x_1) = x_1x_2$ cannot be rewritten as polynomial in x_1 only. The checking procedure REWRITE($\mathfrak{L}_f(x_1), x_1$) will thus fail to produce a solution.

It is natural to ask under what extra conditions is a Darboux polynomial q satisfying $q^* \in \mathbb{R}[X_1, \ldots, X_n]$ also a decoupling abstract basis polynomial. The following theorem explores this connection.

Theorem 1. *Given a system of polynomial ODEs $\dot{\boldsymbol{x}} = f(\boldsymbol{x})$, there exists a polynomial $p \in \mathbb{R}[X_1, \ldots, X_n]$ such that $\mathfrak{L}_f(p) = G(p)$, where $G \in \mathbb{R}[X]$ is of degree $d > 0$, if and only if the system has d Darboux polynomials $q_1, \ldots, q_d \in \mathbb{C}[X_1, \ldots, X_n]$ satisfying:*

(i) $q_1^* = q_2^* = \cdots = q_d^* \in \mathbb{R}[X_1, \ldots, X_n]$,
(ii) $\mathfrak{L}_f(q_1) = \mathfrak{L}_f(q_2) = \cdots = \mathfrak{L}_f(q_d) = rq_1q_2\cdots q_d$, $r \in \mathbb{R}$,
(iii) for all $i = 1, \ldots, d$, *either* $q_i^* - q_i \in \mathbb{R}$ *or there exists* $j \neq i$, $j = 1, \ldots, d$, *such that* $q_i = \bar{q}_j$.

Proof. Suppose there exists a $p \in \mathbb{R}[X_1, \ldots, X_n]$ such that $\mathfrak{L}_f(p) = G(p)$. When $G \in \mathbb{R}[X]$ is a non-constant polynomial of degree d, it can be factorized as $r(X - c_1)\cdots(X - c_d)$, where $r \in \mathbb{R}$ and the roots c_i are either real numbers, or complex numbers that come in conjugate pairs, i.e. if $c_i \in \mathbb{C}$ is a root of G, then its complex conjugate $\bar{c}_i$ is also a root. In the proof of Proposition 2 we have seen that for any such factor $(X - c_i)$ the polynomial $q_i = p - c_i$ is a Darboux polynomial for the system such that $\mathfrak{L}_f(q_i) = G(p)$. The properties (i), (ii) and (iii) follow immediately.

Conversely, let us assume that there are d Darboux polynomials $q_1, q_2, \ldots, q_d$ satisfying properties (i), (ii) and (iii). Then for any $r \in \mathbb{R}$ we have

$$rq_1q_2\cdots q_d = r(q_1^* - c_1)(q_2^* - c_2)\cdots(q_d^* - c_d),$$

where each $c_i = q_i^* - q_i$ is, by definition, a constant. By property (i) we have $q_1^* = q_2^* = \cdots = q_d^* \in \mathbb{R}[X_1, \ldots, X_n]$, so let us take $p = q_1^* = q_2^* = \cdots = q_d^*$ to obtain $r(q_1^* - c_1)(q_2^* - c_2) \cdots (q_d^* - c_d) = r(p - c_1)(p - c_2) \cdots (p - c_d)$. One can now write this as $r(p - c_1)(p - c_2) \cdots (p - c_d) = G(p)$, where $G \in \mathbb{R}[X]$ has degree d. The coefficients of G are real because by (iii) the roots c_i come in complex conjugate pairs. Since $q_i = q_i^* - (q_i^* - q_i) = p - c_i$, we have $\mathfrak{L}_f(q_i) = \mathfrak{L}_f(p - c_i) = \mathfrak{L}_f(p) - \mathfrak{L}_f(c_i) = \mathfrak{L}_f(p)$ and by (ii) $\mathfrak{L}_f(p) = r(p - c_1)(p - c_2) \cdots (p - c_d) = G(p)$. □

Notice that REWRITE does not require all of the d Darboux polynomials in order to construct G. If a family of Darboux polynomials $\{q_1, \ldots, q_d\}$ as stated in Theorem 1 exists, it suffices to supply only one element, say q_1^*, to REWRITE, which will then find a rewriting of $\mathfrak{L}_f(q_1^*)$ as $G(q_1^*)$, with $G \in \mathbb{R}[X]$. If however, the algorithm fails, then the polynomial supplied was not obtained from such a family of Darboux polynomials and therefore cannot be used to obtain a rewriting of its derivative in terms of itself.

Theorem 1 exposes the structure inherent in systems for which one can find decoupled simulating abstractions. The requirements (i)–(iii) are indeed quite strong. Observe that when G is a linear polynomial with a real coefficient λ, i.e. is of the form $G(X) = \lambda X$ and therefore necessarily has one real root, Theorem 1 reduces to the conditions for constant-scale consecution [23].

Remark 4. Theorem 1 relies on generating Darboux polynomials in order to compute a decoupling abstraction of a given system of polynomial ODEs. Nevertheless, polynomials having *constant* Lie derivatives (that is, those p s.t. $\mathfrak{L}_f(p) = G(p)$ where G has degree zero) can also be used for decoupling abstractions, but are not covered by Theorem 1, which requires the degree of G to be positive. The special case when G has degree zero is also related to Darboux polynomials as follows: (i) when G is the zero polynomial, then the system has a first integral which is a special Darboux polynomial as discussed in Sect. 2, (ii) when G is a non-zero constant, then the augmented system $(\dot{\boldsymbol{x}}, \dot{t}) = (f(\boldsymbol{x}), 1)$ obtained by appending the time derivative to the original system has a polynomial first integral. More precisely, when $p \in \mathbb{R}[X_1, \ldots, X_n]$ and the $\mathfrak{L}_f(p)$ is a real constant, say r, then in the augmented system $\mathfrak{L}_{(f,1)}(p - rt) = \mathfrak{L}_{(f,1)}(p) - r = \mathfrak{L}_f(p) - r = 0$ and $p - rt$ is thus a polynomial first integral of the augmented system. One may thus handle this case by computing first integrals (e.g. using the approach described in [15]) before searching for more sophisticated decoupling polynomials where G has a positive degree.

4 Outlook

Verification problems for systems of ODEs can be soundly translated to verification problems for their simulating abstractions. Below we sketch the case of a standard safety verification problem (S_x, f, F_x), where one wishes to prove that a given property, encoded as the region $F_x \subset \mathbb{R}^n$, is always satisfied if the system $\dot{\boldsymbol{x}} = f(\boldsymbol{x})$ is initialised in $\boldsymbol{x}_0 \in S_x \subset \mathbb{R}^n$. If a decoupling abstraction $\dot{\boldsymbol{\alpha}} = G(\boldsymbol{\alpha})$

exists, one can attempt to solve the simpler *abstract* safety verification problem (S_y, G, F_y) where $(y_1, \ldots, y_m) = (\alpha_1(\boldsymbol{x}), \ldots, \alpha_m(\boldsymbol{x}))$, denoted henceforth by $\boldsymbol{y} = \boldsymbol{\alpha}(\boldsymbol{x})$, i.e. $\dot{\boldsymbol{y}} = G(\boldsymbol{y})$ is a decoupled simulating abstraction. The initial set in the new abstract coordinates, $S_y \subset \mathbb{R}^m$ (resp. F_y), is computed as a projection of the semialgebraic set $S_x \wedge \boldsymbol{y} = \boldsymbol{\alpha}(\boldsymbol{x})$, which is a subset of $\mathbb{R}^{n+m}$ (resp. $F_x \wedge \boldsymbol{y} = \boldsymbol{\alpha}(\boldsymbol{x})$), onto $\mathbb{R}^m$. Such a projection can in principle be obtained by eliminating the existential quantifiers in the following sentence

$$\exists\, (x_1, \ldots, x_n) \in \mathbb{R}^n.\, S_x \;\wedge\; y_1 = \alpha_1(x_1, \ldots, x_n) \;\wedge\; \cdots \;\wedge\; y_m = \alpha_m(x_1, \ldots, x_n)\,.$$

The soundness of such an abstraction relies essentially on two facts: (i) the sets S_y and F_y are the exact images through $\boldsymbol{\alpha}$ of the sets S_x and F_x respectively (although using over-approximations of these sets is also sound) and (ii) the invariant regions of the decoupled abstract system, when expressed in terms of the old coordinates, define invariant regions of the original system (i.e. the abstraction is indeed *sound* [22, Theorem 2.2]). This means that if the safety problem holds true in the decoupled abstraction it also holds true in the original concrete system. If not, however, the abstraction may be too coarse.

Interesting directions for refining the abstraction include searching for more general simulating abstractions that are not necessarily completely decoupling. For instance, it is conceivable that a simulating abstraction may possess independent sub-systems that are of the form

$$\dot{\alpha}_i = G_i(\alpha_i, \alpha_j),$$
$$\dot{\alpha}_j = G_j(\alpha_i, \alpha_j),$$

where $G_i, G_j \in \mathbb{R}[X_1, X_2]$ and $\alpha_i, \alpha_j \in \mathbb{R}[X_1, \ldots, X_n]$ are the abstract basis functions. This idea is similar to the so-called algebraizing transformations, briefly discussed in [22, Definition 2.4]. The analysis of 2-dimensional (i.e. planar) polynomial ODEs is however vastly more difficult than the 1-dimensional case. Indeed, qualitative analysis of planar polynomial flows is an active area of mathematical research (e.g. see [5,6]). However, one hope is this greater generality would make simulating abstractions of this form more "common" in systems that one might encounter in applications.

Decoupling can help overcome some of the scalability issues in existing verification methodologies. For instance, in reachability analysis, *relational abstraction* [24] seeks to abstract the flow of a differential equation by an over-approximation of the reachability relation on the states of the system. Mathematically, a (timeless) relational abstraction of an autonomous system $\dot{\boldsymbol{x}} = f(\boldsymbol{x})$ is a relation $R \subseteq \mathbb{R}^n \times \mathbb{R}^n$ such that $(\boldsymbol{x}, \boldsymbol{y}) \in R$ if $\boldsymbol{y}$ is reachable from $\boldsymbol{x}$ in finite time by following the flow of the system [24, Definition 4], i.e. if $\exists t \geq 0.\ \varphi_t(\boldsymbol{x}) = \boldsymbol{y}$. Computing timeless relational abstractions for non-linear systems is difficult because it reduces to searching for positive invariants in the extended system of ODEs $\dot{\boldsymbol{y}} = f(\boldsymbol{y}), \dot{\boldsymbol{x}} = \mathbf{0}$ with dimension $2n$, i.e. with twice the number of state variables [24, Definition 5, Lemma 1]. When the system is uncoupled, one can instead work with n extended systems $\dot{y}_i = f_i(y_i), \dot{x}_i = 0$, $i = 1, \ldots, n$, each of dimension 2.

5 Related Work

Our work is closest in spirit to that of Sankaranarayanan [22], which studied simulating abstractions resulting from linearizing change of basis transformations. Our approach instead focused on simulating abstractions obtained via decoupling change of basis transformations.

Change of basis transformations are a standard technique for decoupling linear homogeneous systems of ODEs with constant coefficients, i.e. systems of the form $\dot{\boldsymbol{x}} = A\boldsymbol{x}$, where A is an $n \times n$ real matrix. A common technique applies when the matrix A has n real distinct eigenvalues and produces a decoupled linear homogeneous system $\dot{\boldsymbol{\alpha}} = B\boldsymbol{\alpha}$ of the *same dimension*, where $\boldsymbol{\alpha} = (\alpha_1, \dots, \alpha_n)$ is made up of *linear functions* $\alpha_i : \mathbb{R}^n \to \mathbb{R}$ in the state variables $x_1, \dots, x_n$ (see e.g. [21, Sects. 28.2 and 28.3]); in particular, such a decoupling is always possible when A is a real symmetric matrix. In our work, we consider more general polynomial systems of ODEs and a more general class of polynomials to act as the new basis; additionally, we do not require the dimension of the resulting decoupled system to match that of the original system of coupled ODEs. In short, our focus is not placed on solving the system, but rather on automatically discovering simulating abstractions that are more amenable to analysis.

Girard and Pappas explored *approximate bisimulation* of continuous systems in [10], and Pappas earlier developed (exact) bisimulations between continuous linear systems [18]. However, these works employ a different notion of simulation and do not seek to make the structure of the simulation easier to analyze in the way that we do with decoupling, and are in practice limited to linear ODEs due to reliance on solving linear matrix inequalities (LMIs). Han and Krogh have also explored sound order reduction techniques for verification with reachability analysis, but their approach is also limited to linear ODEs [13]. In contrast to all these existing works that employ different techniques as well as different formal development, our decoupled simulating abstractions are applicable to non-linear polynomial ODEs, and as such, are developed using significantly different methods.

6 Conclusion

In this paper we explored a technique for constructing decoupling simulating abstractions of non-linear polynomial ODEs, which can be more easily analyzed because their 1-dimensional sub-systems may be treated independently. We employed the theory of Darboux polynomials to give a sufficient criterion for non-existence of decoupled simulating abstractions (up to a some maximum degree of the abstract basis polynomials; see Proposition 2). Lastly, we described how automatically generated Darboux polynomials (up to some given polynomial degree) can be used to construct abstract basis polynomials that can yield decoupling simulating abstractions. The abstractions developed in this paper are in essence a form of model transformation, which can be integrated in source transformation and translation tools such as HyST [2]; we leave this for future work.

Acknowledgements. The authors would like to thank the anonymous reviewers for their careful reading and judicious critique and extend their thanks to Dr. André Platzer at Carnegie Mellon University for his technical questions and helpful insights into differential ghosts.

References

1. Abrial, J.-R., Su, W., Zhu, H.: Formalizing hybrid systems with Event-B. In: Derrick, J., Fitzgerald, J., Gnesi, S., Khurshid, S., Leuschel, M., Reeves, S., Riccobene, E. (eds.) ABZ 2012. LNCS, vol. 7316, pp. 178–193. Springer, Heidelberg (2012). doi:10.1007/978-3-642-30885-7_13
2. Bak, S., Bogomolov, S., Johnson, T.T.: HYST: a source transformation and translation tool for hybrid automaton models. In: HSCC, pp. 128–133. ACM (2015)
3. Berz, M., Makino, K.: Verified integration of ODEs and flows using differential algebraic methods on high-order Taylor models. Reliable Comput. **4**(4), 361–369 (1998)
4. Collins, G.E.: Quantifier elimination for real closed fields by cylindrical algebraic decompostion. In: Brakhage, H. (ed.) GI-Fachtagung 1975. LNCS, vol. 33, pp. 134–183. Springer, Heidelberg (1975). doi:10.1007/3-540-07407-4_17
5. Conti, R., Galeotti, M.: Totally bounded cubic systems in $\mathbb{R}^2$. In: Macki, J.W., Zecca, P. (eds.) Dynamical Systems. LNM, vol. 1822, pp. 103–171. Springer, Heidelberg (2003). doi:10.1007/978-3-540-45204-1_2
6. Dumortier, F., Llibre, J., Artés, J.C.: Qualitative Theory of Planar Differential Systems. Springer, Heidelberg (2006)
7. Ghorbal, K., Platzer, A.: Characterizing algebraic invariants by differential radical invariants. In: Ábrahám, E., Havelund, K. (eds.) TACAS 2014. LNCS, vol. 8413, pp. 279–294. Springer, Heidelberg (2014). doi:10.1007/978-3-642-54862-8_19
8. Giannakopoulou, D., Méry, D. (eds.): FM 2012. LNCS, vol. 7436. Springer, Heidelberg (2012)
9. Ginoux, J.M.: Differential Geometry Applied to Dynamical Systems. World Scientific Series on Nonlinear Science, vol. 66. World Scientific, Singapore (2009)
10. Girard, A., Pappas, G.J.: Approximate bisimulation: a bridge between computer science and control theory. Eur. J. Control **17**(5–6), 568–578 (2011)
11. Goriely, A.: Integrability and Nonintegrability of Dynamical Systems. Advanced Series in Nonlinear Dynamics. World Scientific, Singapore (2001)
12. Hale, J.K., LaSalle, J.P.: Differential equations: linearity vs. nonlinearity. SIAM Rev. **5**(3), 249–272 (1963)
13. Han, Z., Krogh, B.: Reachability analysis of hybrid control systems using reduced-order models. In: 2004 American Control Conference, Proceedings of the 2004, vol. 2, pp. 1183–1189, June 2004
14. Jeannin, J.-B., Ghorbal, K., Kouskoulas, Y., Gardner, R., Schmidt, A., Zawadzki, E., Platzer, A.: A formally verified hybrid system for the next-generation airborne collision avoidance system. In: Baier, C., Tinelli, C. (eds.) TACAS 2015. LNCS, vol. 9035, pp. 21–36. Springer, Heidelberg (2015). doi:10.1007/978-3-662-46681-0_2
15. Matringe, N., Moura, A.V., Rebiha, R.: Generating invariants for non-linear hybrid systems by linear algebraic methods. In: Cousot, R., Martel, M. (eds.) SAS 2010. LNCS, vol. 6337, pp. 373–389. Springer, Heidelberg (2010). doi:10.1007/978-3-642-15769-1_23

16. Nedialkov, N.S.: Interval tools for ODEs and DAEs. In: 12th GAMM - IMACS International Symposium on Scientific Computing, Computer Arithmetic and Validated Numerics (SCAN), p. 4, September 2006
17. Neher, M., Jackson, K.R., Nedialkov, N.S.: On Taylor model based integration of ODEs. SIAM J. Numer. Anal. **45**(1), 236–262 (2007)
18. Pappas, G.J.: Bisimilar linear systems. Automatica **39**(12), 2035–2047 (2003)
19. Platzer, A.: A complete uniform substitution calculus for differential dynamic logic. J. Autom. Reasoning, 1–47 (2016)
20. Platzer, A., Clarke, E.M.: Formal verification of curved flight collision avoidance maneuvers: a case study. In: Cavalcanti, A., Dams, D.R. (eds.) FM 2009. LNCS, vol. 5850, pp. 547–562. Springer, Heidelberg (2009). doi:10.1007/978-3-642-05089-3_35
21. Robinson, J.C.: An Introduction to Ordinary Differential Equations. Cambridge University Press, Cambridge (2004)
22. Sankaranarayanan, S.: Change-of-bases abstractions for non-linear hybrid systems. Nonlinear Anal. Hybrid Syst. **19**, 107–133 (2016)
23. Sankaranarayanan, S., Sipma, H.B., Manna, Z.: Constructing invariants for hybrid systems. Formal Methods Syst. Des. **32**(1), 25–55 (2008)
24. Sankaranarayanan, S., Tiwari, A.: Relational abstractions for continuous and hybrid systems. In: Gopalakrishnan, G., Qadeer, S. (eds.) CAV 2011. LNCS, vol. 6806, pp. 686–702. Springer, Heidelberg (2011). doi:10.1007/978-3-642-22110-1_56
25. Strogatz, S.H.: Nonlinear Dynamics and Chaos. Westview Press, New York (1994)
26. Tarski, A.: A decision method for elementary algebra and geometry. In: Bulletin of the American Mathematical Society, vol. 59 (1951)
27. Teschl, G.: Ordinary Differential Equations and Dynamical Systems. Graduate Studies in Mathematics, vol. 140. American Mathematical Society, Providence (2012)
28. Zhao, H., Yang, M., Zhan, N., Gu, B., Zou, L., Chen, Y.: Formal verification of a descent guidance control program of a lunar lander. In: Jones, C., Pihlajasaari, P., Sun, J. (eds.) FM 2014. LNCS, vol. 8442, pp. 733–748. Springer, Heidelberg (2014). doi:10.1007/978-3-319-06410-9_49
29. Zou, L., Lv, J., Wang, S., Zhan, N., Tang, T., Yuan, L., Liu, Y.: Verifying chinese train control system under a combined scenario by theorem proving. In: Cohen, E., Rybalchenko, A. (eds.) VSTTE 2013. LNCS, vol. 8164, pp. 262–280. Springer, Heidelberg (2014). doi:10.1007/978-3-642-54108-7_14

Regression Verification for Unbalanced Recursive Functions

Ofer Strichman[(✉)] and Maor Veitsman

Information Systems Engineering, IE, Technion, Haifa, Israel
ofers@ie.technion.ac.il, smaorus@gmail.com

Abstract. We address the problem of proving the equivalence of two recursive functions that have different base-cases and/or are not in lock-step. None of the existing software equivalence checkers (like RÊVE, RVT, SYMDIFF), or general unbounded software model-checkers (like SEAHORN, HSFC, AUTOMIZER) can prove such equivalences. We show a proof rule for the case of different base cases, based on separating the proof into two parts—inputs which result in the base case in at least one of the two compared functions, and all the rest. We also show how unbalanced unrolling of the functions can solve the case in which the functions are not in lock-step. In itself this type of unrolling may again introduce the problem of the different base cases, and we show a new proof rule for solving it. We implemented these rules in our regression-verification tool RVT. We conclude by comparing our approach to that of Felsig et al.'s counterexample-based refinement, which was implemented lately in their equivalence checker RÊVE.

1 Introduction

Given two similar programs P_1, P_2, a mapping map_f between their functions, and a definition of equivalence, Regression Verification [5] is the problem of identifying the pairs in map_f that are equivalent to one another. This undecidable problem can be thought of as a special case of *program equivalence*. Program equivalence has been discussed in the literature for over half a century (see, e.g., [10])—mostly in the ACL2 community—as a challenge and a use case for theorem proving (e.g., proving that quick-sort has the same output as merge-sort), but without exploiting the similarity between P_1 and P_2 that is assumed in the case of regression verification. This assumed similarity provides many opportunities for optimizations, and generally leads to a complexity which is dominated by the magnitude of change rather than by the magnitude of P_1 and P_2 themselves.

The classic use-case for regression verification is one in which P_1, P_2 are two consecutive versions of the same program, and the goal is to identify the impact of change. It can be used for checking that refactoring or a performance optimization has not changed the program in a nonintended way. It can also be used for verifying that a bug-fix or an added feature affects only the part intended by the programmer. In somewhat a different direction, it was recently

J. Fitzgerald et al. (Eds.): FM 2016, LNCS 9995, pp. 645–658, 2016.
DOI: 10.1007/978-3-319-48989-6_39

used for proving that the target code of two consecutive versions of a compiler are semantically the same [8]. In all these applications the typical definition of equivalence that is used is called *partial equivalence* [5]. It means that given the same inputs, the two functions return equal outputs, unless at least one of them does not terminate. By 'inputs' we mean the function parameters, global variables that it reads, and the heap; by 'outputs' we mean global variables to which the function writes, the heap and the return value.

There are several methods and tools for regression verification that are available in the public domain. MS-SymDiff [11,12] is a tool that reads two BPL (Boogie programming language) [13] files corresponding to P_1, P_2, and generates a verification condition in BPL for each pair of mapped functions. It uses Boogies's built-in access to Z3 [3] and the invariant generator Duality [14] to try and prove the equivalence of functions with loops and recursive calls. SymDiff supports user-defined specifications, which means that partial equivalence is just one possible equivalence criterion; the user can alternatively define any predicate over the inputs and outputs of the two compared functions as the proof obligation, e.g., that the output of f is always smaller or equal to the output of f', for $\langle f, f' \rangle \in map_f$.

The tool Rêve attempts to prove the equivalence of recursive functions (currently individual functions rather than whole programs), and is based on a direct translation to Z3's Horn-clause format. This gives them access to Z3's PDR engine [2], which attempts to prove the equivalence between the two functions by gradually detecting invariants.

The third tool is RVT [1,5]. Improving RVT's proof method is the focus of this article. RVT begins by turning all loops into separate recursive functions, and building a map map_f between the functions. This mapping does not have to be bijective. It then uses a bottom-up traversal of the call graphs of the two programs, each time attempting to prove the equivalence of a pair of functions from map_f. A pair of callees that were already proven to be equal are abstracted with the same uninterpreted function, and others—unless they are recursive—are inlined. If a callee is recursive and was not proven to be equal to a function on the other side, all the ancestors of this function are 'abandoned' by the algorithm, i.e., it does not attempt to prove their equivalence.

To prove the equivalence of two recursive functions RVT uses a proof rule that essentially applies induction: assume that the two functions are partially equivalent in the recursive calls, and try to prove that they are partially equivalent also in the current call. This is summarized by the following proof rule, for two simple recursive functions f and f':

$$\frac{\text{PARTIAL-EQUIV}(\texttt{call}f, \texttt{call}f') \vdash \text{PARTIAL-EQUIV}(f\ \texttt{body}, f'\ \texttt{body})}{\text{PARTIAL-EQUIV}(f, f')}\ (\text{PART-EQ}) \tag{1}$$

The more general case of mutually recursive functions is discussed in length in [5].

To check the premise, we need to replace the recursive calls in f and in f' with an over-approximation of f and f', respectively, that satisfies the predicate 'PARTIAL-EQUIV(`call`f, `call`f')'. This is easy to do (albeit not necessarily the best way in terms of the strength of the method) by replacing the recursive calls with the *same* uninterpreted function: by definition, two instances of the same uninterpreted function are partially equivalent. After the replacement we say that f and f' are *isolated*. The following example, taken from [5], demonstrates isolation.

Example 1. Consider the two functions in Fig. 1. Let U be the uninterpreted function such that calls to U replace the recursive calls to `gcd1` and `gcd2`. Figure 2 presents the isolated functions. These are now 'flat' functions, i.e., without loops and recursion, and hence their partial equivalence is decidable. If they are indeed partially equivalent, then (1) implies that the original functions are partially equivalent as well. □

RVT proves the equivalence of a pair of isolated functions f, f' by generating a program of the form appearing in Fig. 3, and invoking CBMC, a bounded model checker for C programs, to attempt to formally verify it. If it is successful, then f, f' are declared equivalent. The schema shown in the figure is for the simple case in which the two compared functions do not access the heap and global variables.

```
gcd1(int a, int b)
{ int g;
  if (!b) g = a;
  else {
    a = a%b;
    g = gcd1(b, a); }
  return g;
}
```

```
gcd2(int x, int y)
{ int z;
  z = x;

  if (y > 0)
    z = gcd2(y, z%y);
  return z;
}
```

Fig. 1. Two functions to calculate GCD of two nonnegative integers.

```
gcd1(int a, int b)
{ int g;
  if (!b) g = a;
  else {
    a = a%b;
    g = U(b, a); }
  return g;
}
```

```
gcd2(int x, int y)
{ int z;
  z = x;

  if (y > 0)
    z = U(y, z%y);
  return z;
}
```

Fig. 2. After isolation of the functions, i.e., replacing their function calls with calls to the same uninterpreted function U. By definition of uninterpreted functions U enforces partial equivalence of the recursive calls.

```
int main(){
  int n = non_det();
  int ret1,ret2;
  ret1 = f(n);
  ret2 = f'(n);
  assert(ret1 = ret2);
}
```

Fig. 3. RVT Generates such a main function for each pair of isolated functions $f, f' \in map_f$ that it attempts to prove partially-equivalent. If f, f' access global variables and the heap, then the construction is more involved.

The (PART-EQ) rule (1) is not, and cannot be, complete, owing to the undecidability of the problem. In this article we will focus on two specific reasons for the incompleteness of this rule: *different base-cases*, and *unbalanced recursion*. The former corresponds to a case in which for the same input, one of the functions returns on a base-case, and the other does not. The latter corresponds to a case in which the two recursive functions are not in *lock-step*. We will also consider the case in which both cases occur at the same time. The examples below demonstrates the weakness of (1) when it comes to such cases.

Example 2. The two programs in Fig. 4 are partially equivalent, but (1) fails to prove it. The reason is the different base cases. After isolating these two functions, namely replacing their recursive calls with the same uninterpreted function, say U, they may return *different* values when $n = 1$: `fact1` returns 1, whereas `fact2` returns $1 * U(0)$.

Now consider the two partially-equivalent functions in Fig. 5. Their base cases are in sync, but they are not in lock-step: `sum1` computes $\Sigma_{i=1..n} i$ in half the number of iterations comparing to `sum2`. After isolation, for equal input n such that $n > 1$, the uninterpreted functions are called with different values, which may lead these two functions to return different values. For example, for $n = 3$ `sum1` returns $3 + 2 + U(1)$, whereas `sum2` returns $3 + U(2)$. □

In the next section we will describe our solution strategy.

```
int fact1(int n){
  if (n <= 1) return 1;
  return n * fact1(n-1);
}
```

```
int fact2(int n){
  if (n <= 0) return 1;
  return n * fact2(n-1);
}
```

Fig. 4. The different base cases prevent (1) from proving the equivalence of these two functions. After isolation, when $n = 1$, `fact1` returns 1, whereas `fact2` returns $1*U(0)$, namely a nondeterministic value.

```
int sum1(int n){
  if (n <= 1) return n;
  return n + n-1 + sum1(n-2);
}
```

```
int sum2(int n){
  if (n <= 1) return n;
  return n + sum2(n-1);
}
```

Fig. 5. These two functions are not in lock-step, which prevents (1) from proving their partial equivalence. After isolation, for e.g., $n = 3$, `sum1` returns $3 + 2 + U(1)$ whereas `sum2` returns $3 + U(2)$, which are not necessarily equal terms.

2 Four Types of Unrolling

Given a recursive function f and a natural *unrolling factor* $i > 0$, we define four types of unrolling of f i times. Figure 6 illustrates the different unrolling types.

1. **Syntactic unrolling**: Create i copies of the original function: $f_1, f_2, .., f_i$, rename them, and rename accordingly their recursive calls. Replace the recursive call in the j-th copy, for $1 \leq j < i$ with a call to the $j + 1$ copy. The recursive call in the i-th copy remains unchanged. Let $unroll(f, i)$ denote the syntactically unrolled program.

```
int fact1(int n){
  if (n <= 0) return 1;
  return n * fact1(n-1);
}

int fact(int n){
  if (n <= 0) return 1;
  return n * fact1(n-1);
}
```

$\boldsymbol{Unroll(fact, 1)}$

```
int fact1(int n){
  assume(false);
}

int fact(int n){
  if (n <= 0) return 1;
  return n * fact1(n-1);
}
```

$\boldsymbol{Unroll\&Block(fact, 1)}$

```
int fact1(int n){
  assert(false);
}

int fact(int n){
  if (n <= 0) return 1;
  return n * fact1(n-1);
}
```

$\boldsymbol{Unroll\&check(fact, 1)}$

```
int fact1(int n){
  return uf_fact1(n-1);
}

int fact(int n){
  if (n <= 0) return 1;
  return n * fact1(n-1);
}
```

$\boldsymbol{Unroll\&UF(fact, 1)}$

Fig. 6. Four types of unrollings.

2. **Unroll and block**: The same as syntactic unrolling, but replace the body of the i-th copy f_i with a single call to assume($false$)[1]. The assume(exp) statement restricts program traces to those that satisfy the boolean parameter exp. Hence adding assume($false$) to our program 'blocks' traces that reach the location of that assertion. Let *unroll&block*(f, i) denote this variant of unrolling.
3. **Unroll and check**: The same as syntactic unrolling, but replace the body of the i-th copy f_i with a single call to assert($false$). This causes the model checker to fail the proof if there exists a program trace that reaches depth i in the recursion. Let *unroll&check*(f, i) denote this variant of unrolling.
4. **Unroll and UF**: The same as syntactic unrolling, but replace the body of the i-th copy of f with a single call statement to the an uninterpreted function U_f that is associated with f. We denote this action by *unroll&uf*(f, i).

Only the first of these four variants preserves the semantic of the original function f. *unroll&block*(f, i) underapproximates f, and *unroll&uf*(f, i) overapproximates it. *unroll&check*(f, i) is simply a way to check that i is high enough to capture all the traces of f.

We will use these unrollings variants in our proof rules below.

3 A Proof Rule Based on Domain Partitioning

Recall that when the base cases in recursive functions are not in sync, the proof rule (PART-EQ) (1) is not strong enough to prove partial equivalence. We suggest a new proof rule for this purpose, in which we break the premise into two separate parts:

$$\frac{\text{BASE-EQUIV}(f, f') \quad \text{STEP-EQUIV}(f, f')}{\text{PARTIAL-EQUIV}(f, f')}\,(\text{SEP-PART-EQ}) \tag{2}$$

Intuitively BASE-EQUIV(f, f') is true if f, f' are partially equivalent for any input that invokes the base case in at least one of f, f', and STEP-EQUIV(f, f') is true if f, f' are partially equivalent for all the other inputs.

More formally, let $in_B(f)$ denote the set of all inputs for which the resulting program traces do not reach a recursive call in function f, and $in_S(f)$ is the complement of $in_B(f)$. We note that for any f, f' with the same signature, $in_B(f) \cup in_B(f')$ and $in_S(f) \cap in_S(f')$ form a partition of the input domain.

We denote by PARTIAL-EQUIV$(f, f')|_s$ that f and f' are partially equivalent on the set of inputs s. Using this notation, we now define base-case equivalence:

$$\text{BASE-EQUIV}(f, f') \doteq \text{PARTIAL-EQUIV}(f, f')|_{in_B(f) \cup in_B(f')} \tag{3}$$

and similarly step-case equivalence:

$$\text{STEP-EQUIV}(f, f') \doteq \text{PARTIAL-EQUIV}(f, f')|_{in_S(f) \cap in_S(f')} \tag{4}$$

In the next section we will show how we use the various types of unrolling from Sect. 2 to prove the premise of (2) based on (3) and (4).

[1] Most software model checkers support assume statements.

```
for i = 1... {
  in=non_det();
  ret1=unroll&block(f,1)(in);
  ret2=unroll&check(f',i)(in);
  assert(ret1 = ret2);
}
```

Phase 1

```
for i = 1... {
  in=non_det();
  ret1=unroll&block(f',1)(in);
  ret2=unroll&check(f,i)(in);
  assert(ret1 = ret2);
}
```

Phase 2

Fig. 7. Pseudocode of the first and second step of the base-case proof. `i` is increased until there is no assertion failure in *unroll&check*.

3.1 Proving Base-Case Equivalence

According to (3), to prove the premise BASE-EQUIV(f, f'), we can create a check program, similar to the one in Fig. 3, but while limiting the inputs to those that invoke the base case in either one of f or f'. To that end, we divide our proof into two phases:

1. Prove equivalence for inputs that result in a base case in f.
2. Prove equivalence for inputs that result in a base case in f'.

The pseudocode in Fig. 7 exhibits the programs that we generate for these two phases. By performing *unroll&block* on f, we limit any program trace in the proof that may lead to a recursive call. Because input which results in a base case in function f may result in an unknown number of recursive iterations in function f', we must create a bound for the amount of possible recursive iterations in function f'. We do this by applying *unroll&check* on f', where the unrolling bound is increased up to the point that f' does not make another recursive call, or a time-out is reached.

3.2 Proving Step-Case Equivalence

To prove step-case equivalence we must limit our proof to program traces that result in a recursive call on **both** sides. To that end, we have to limit the inputs to $ins_S(f) \cap ins_S(f')$. Again, we use a program similar to the one in Fig. 3. However, we add a global variable *cnt* (initialized to 0), and increment it just before the call statement to the uninterpreted function (see `fact1` in *unroll&UF* in Fig. 6). We then change our assertion to **assert**$(cnt < 2 \;\; || \;\; ret1 = ret2)$, where as before $ret1$ and $ret2$ are the return values of the two functions. This way, we check equivalence only for inputs that invoked a recursive call both in f and in f'. Figure 8 illustrates the check program created for the step case.

4 A Generalization to Mutually Recursive Functions

We now generalize our proof rule to mutually recursive functions. Mutually recursive functions appear in the call graph as strongly connected components (SCCs)

```
in = non_det();
ret1 = unroll&uf(f,1)(in);
ret2 = unroll&uf(f',1)(in);
assert(cnt < 2 || ret1 = ret2);
```

Fig. 8. Pseudocode of the check program used to prove the step case.

of a size larger than one, and our focus is on maximal SCCs—MSCCs. For simplicity, we consider the case in which the two non-trivial MCSS's m, m' do not have edges outside the MSCC (i.e., functions in m, m' do not call functions outside of m, m') and that there is a bijective mapping between the functions in m, m', which we denote here by map_f. A proof rule for this case was given in [5] and repeated here:

$$\frac{\begin{array}{l}\forall (f, f') \in map_f.\\ ((\forall (g, g') \in map_f.\text{p-equiv}(\texttt{call}\, g, \texttt{call}\, g')) \vdash \text{p-equiv}(f \ \texttt{body}, f' \ \texttt{body}))\end{array}}{\forall (f, f') \in map_f.\text{p-equiv}(f, f')} \ (\text{PROC-P-EQ}) \quad (5)$$

This rule is more intuitive after seeing how its premise can be checked. For this, [5] defines

$$f^{UF} \doteq f[g \leftarrow UF(g) \mid g \text{ is called in } f]\ , \qquad (6)$$

or in words, f^{UF} replaces each function call to g in f, with a corresponding call to an uninterpreted function. Now (5) becomes

$$\frac{\forall (f, f') \in map_f.\ \text{PARTIAL-EQUIV}(f^{UF}, f'^{UF})}{\forall (f, f') \in map_f.\ \text{PARTIAL-EQUIV}(f, f')} \qquad (7)$$

In words, the premise we need to prove is that every pair in map_f has to be proven equivalent, while replacing the calls to other functions in m, m' with uninterpreted functions. We emphasize that the calls to mapped functions in map_f are replaced with the *same* uninterpreted function. A sample pair of size-2-MSCCs and the proof obligations according to (7) appear in Fig. 9.

Our generalization of (2) to mutual recursion, can be thought of as splitting the input domain in (5) to the base-case and step-case, similarly to what we have shown in Sect. 3:

$$\frac{\forall (f, f') \in map_f.\text{BASE-EQUIV}(f, f') \quad \forall (f, f') \in map_f.\text{STEP-EQUIV}(f, f')}{\forall (f, f') \in map_f.\text{PARTIAL-EQUIV}(f, f')} \qquad (8)$$

We now adjust the premise of (8) to support mutually recursive functions. First we generalize the definitions of $in_B(f)$ and $in_S(f)$. Let $in_B(f)$ denote the set of all inputs for which the resulting program traces do not reach a call to another function in the MSCC, and let $in_S(f)$ denote the complement of $in_B(f)$. To prove the base we use the inference rule:

$$\frac{\forall (f, f') \in map_f.\text{PARTIAL-EQUIV}(f, f')|_{in_B(f) \cup in_B(f')}}{\forall (f, f') \in map_f.\text{BASE-EQUIV}(f, f')}\ , \qquad (9)$$

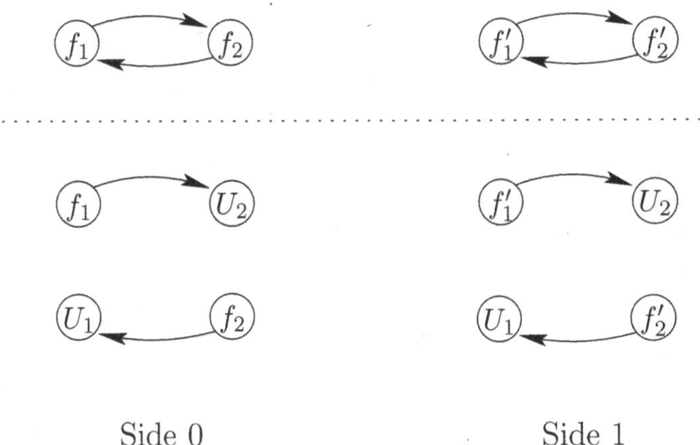

Fig. 9. To prove equivalence of mutually recursive functions (top) with (7), we check separately the equivalence of each pair of functions, while replacing the calls to other functions with calls to UFs (bottom).

and to prove the step, we use the rule:

$$\frac{\forall (f, f') \in map_f.\text{PARTIAL-EQUIV}(f, f')|_{ins(f) \cap ins(f')}}{\forall (f, f') \in map_f.\text{STEP-EQUIV}(f, f')} . \tag{10}$$

Since we are only partitioning the input domain in (7), whose correctness was already proven in [5], then correctness is implied.

5 Proving Equivalence of Functions Not in Lock-Step

Recall the two versions of the `sum` function in Fig. 5 which are not in lock-step and therefore cannot be proven partially equivalent by the rule (PART-EQ). To solve this, we unwind `sum2`: the result is visible in Fig. 10. We can now see that for $n = 3$ both `sum1` and `sum2` return $3 + 2 + U(1)$.

Now let us look at another example. For $n = 2$, `sum1` returns $2 + 1 + U(0)$ while the unrolled function `sum2` returns $2 + 1$. By performing un-balanced syntactic unrolling we created base cases that are not in sync. We solve this similarly by separating the premise of our proof rule into two parts, the base-case proof and the step-case proof as before. Our proof rule for functions f and f' with the respective unrolling factors of n and m is:

$$\frac{\text{BASE-EQUIV}_{n,m}(f, f') \quad \text{STEP-EQUIV}_{n,m}(f, f')}{\text{PARTIAL-EQUIV}(f, f')} (\text{SEP-PART-EQ}) \tag{11}$$

```
int sum2_1(int n){
 if (n <= 1){
   return n;
 }
 return n + sum2_1(n-1);
}

int sum2(int n){
 if (n <= 1){
   return n;
 }
 return n + sum2_1(n-1);
}
```

```
int sum1(int n){
 if (n <= 1){
   return n;
 }
 return n + n - 1 + sum1(n-1);
}
```

Fig. 10. The function `sum2` after being unrolled syntactically once.

The predicate BASE-EQUIV$_{n,m}(f, f')$ is true when f and f' are equivalent for each input that does not involve a recursive call in $unroll(f, n)$ or $unroll(f', m)$). More formally:

$$\text{BASE-EQUIV}_{n,m}(f, f') \doteq \\ \text{PARTIAL-EQUIV}(unroll(f, n), unroll(f', m))|_{in_B(unroll(f,n)) \cup in_B(unroll(f',m))} \quad (12)$$

The predicate STEP-EQUIV$_{n,m}(f, f')$ is true when f and f' are partially equivalent for all other inputs: those that involve a recursive call on **both** $unroll(f, n)$, and $unroll(f', m)$ sides, or, more formally:

$$\text{STEP-EQUIV}_{n,m}(f, f') \doteq \\ \text{PARTIAL-EQUIV}(unroll(f, n), unroll(f', m))|_{in_S(unroll(f,n)) \cap in_S(unroll(f',m))} \quad (13)$$

Next, we show how we verify that these predicates hold true, and thus prove the premise of 11.

Base Case: Since we limit our input to values in the union of $in_B(unroll(f, n))$ and $in_B(unroll(f', m))$, we prove the base case by separating the proof into two

```
for i = 1...{
  in=non_det();
  ret1=unroll&block(f,n)(in);
  ret2=unroll&check(f',i)(in);
  assert(ret1 = ret2);
}
```

Phase 1

```
for i = 1...{
  in=non_det();
  ret1=unroll&check(f',m)(in);
  ret2=unroll&block(f,i)(in);
  assert(ret1 = ret2);
}
```

Phase 2

Fig. 11. Pseudocode of the two phases of the base-case proof, for unbalanced recursive functions.

```
cnt = 0;
in = non_det();
ret1 = unroll&uf(f,n)(in);
ret2 = unroll&uf(f',m)(in);
assert(cnt < 2 || ret1 = ret2);
```

Fig. 12. Pseudocode of the check program used to prove the step case equivalence for unrolled functions.

phases, similarly to Sect. 3.1. These phases are illustrated by Fig. 11. Note that now, in the first step, we unroll and block f with an unrolling factor of n, in order to capture inputs that result in a program trace that reaches one of the base cases in one of the first n recursive iterations of f. Similarly, in the second phase we apply unroll and block m times on f'.

Step Case: According to (13), we need to limit the proof to program traces that result in a recursive call on both sides after being unrolled n and m times, respectively. Similar to the program in Fig. 8, we do this by utilizing the counter *cnt*. The program is given in Fig. 12.

This entire process is now automated in RVT via a flag `-unroll n m`, where the user only has to replace n and m with constants.

6 Related Work and Competing Tools

We have compared several leading unbounded model checkers that have scored high on recursive programs in the latest software verification competition. While they are not designed for program equivalence, Fig. 3 shows us that we can reduce this problem to a general verification problem over a single program. We have tested SEAHORN [7], HSF(C) [6] and AUTOMIZER [9] using the `factorial` and `sum` examples that we presented in previous sections. These model checkers were not able to prove equivalent the pair of functions in these examples.

RÊVE [4] is a program equivalence verifier. Specifically for the case of unbalanced base-cases, it uses a technique called *counterexample-based refinement*, by which counterexamples are checked individually by simulation and then blocked from the verification condition. For example, for our factorial example, the input triggering the base case not in sync is $n = 1$. After the proof failure RÊVE runs both programs with the given input to examine whether the counterexample in fact indicates an in-equivalence between the two programs. If it discovers that both outputs are equal for $n = 1$ then the program trace created by this input is blocked in the next iteration. Once this program input is disregarded then the proof succeeds. This process is unbounded, similarly to the iterative process in our base-case proof seen in Fig. 7.

Both tools may perform favourably in different scenarios. For example in programs where our inputs are from the integer domain and the expression applied on the parameter of the recursive call results in a series of inputs $\{n_1, n_2, ..\}$ which advances at a pace larger than one ($n_{i+1} - n_i > 1$) then our proof rule (SEP-PART-EQ) (2) may perform better. Generally speaking, (SEP-PART-EQ) may perform better when the expression applied on the parameters of the recursive call causes the series of input values of the recursive calls to be non-sequential over the input domain. Note how the recursion advances faster over the integer domain in the two programs in Fig. 13. These are two implementations of the factorial function, after applying loop unrolling. According to the proof method in Fig. 4 we prove equivalence for two domains of inputs:

1. For inputs that result in a base-case for `fact1` (when $n \in [1..4]$), the proof will be successful in the first iteration.
2. For inputs that result in a base for `fact2` (when $n \in [1..8]$), the proof will be successful in the second iteration.

On the other hand when using counterexample-based refinement, three counterexamples are created and blocked before the proof succeeds.

Counterexample-based refinement may perform better in other scenarios. In Fig. 14 we used two identical implementations of the factorial function and added a base condition for $n = 10$. In the second iteration, the program trace created by the input $n = 10$ will be blocked after one iteration using counterexample-based refinement and the proof succeeds. However if we try to prove this using our rule in Fig. 4, only after we apply *unroll&check* with a factor of 10 will the proof succeed. In other words, the counterexample-refinement method requires

```
int fact1(int n){
  if (n <= 1) return 1;
  if (n == 2) return 2;
  if (n == 3) return 6;
  if (n == 4) return 24;


  return n * (n-1) * (n-2)
       * (n-3) * fact1(n-4);
}
```

```
int fact2(int n){
  if (n <= 1) return 1;
  if (n == 2) return 2;
  if (n == 3) return 6;
  if (n == 4) return 24;
  ....
  if (n == 8) return 40320; //8!
  return n * (n-1) * (n-2)
       * (n-3) * fact1(n-4);
}
```

Fig. 13. Unrolled and optimized version of the factorial function.

```
int fact1(int n){
  if (n <= 1) return 1;
  return n * fact1(n-1);
}
```

```
int fact2(int n){
  if (n <= 1) return 1;
  if (n == 10)
     return 3628800; //10!
  return n * fact1(n-1);
}
```

Fig. 14. `fact2` contains a special condition.

fewer iterations with programs that have base-case conditions that are sporadic over the input domain.

7 Conclusions

We have presented techniques for proving the equivalence of two recursive functions that have different base-cases and/or are not in lock-step. As we have shown experimentally, none of the existing software equivalence checkers (like RÊVE, RVT, SYMDIFF), or general unbounded software model-checkers (like SEAHORN, HSFC, AUTOMIZER) can prove such equivalences. The proof rule that we presented for the case of different base cases is based on separating the proof into two parts—inputs which result in the base case in at least one of the two compared functions, and all the rest. To prove recursive functions that are not in lock-step, we showed that unbalanced unrolling does not solve in itself the problem, and requires a more elaborate solution that involves a variation of the first rule for different base cases. We implemented these rules in our regression-verification tool RVT, which now has a web-interface in [1] and is open-source.

References

1. RVT web-interface and sources. http://ie.technion.ac.il/~ofers/rvt/
2. Bjørner, N., Gurfinkel, A., McMillan, K., Rybalchenko, A.: Horn clause solvers for program verification. In: Beklemishev, L.D., Blass, A., Dershowitz, N., Finkbeiner, B., Schulte, W. (eds.) Fields of Logic and Computation II. LNCS, vol. 9300, pp. 24–51. Springer, Heidelberg (2015). doi:10.1007/978-3-319-23534-9_2
3. Moura, L., Bjørner, N.: Z3: an efficient SMT solver. In: Ramakrishnan, C.R., Rehof, J. (eds.) TACAS 2008. LNCS, vol. 4963, pp. 337–340. Springer, Heidelberg (2008). doi:10.1007/978-3-540-78800-3_24
4. Felsing, D., Grebing, S., Klebanov, V., Rmmer, P., Ulbrich, M.: Automating regression verification. In: International Conference on Automated Software Engineering (2014)
5. Godlin, B., Strichman, O.: Inference rules for proving the equivalence of recursive procedures. Acta Informatica **45**(6), 403–439 (2008)
6. Grebenshchikov, S., Gupta, A., Lopes, N.P., Popeea, C., Rybalchenko, A.: HSF(C): a software verifier based on horn clauses. In: Flanagan, C., König, B. (eds.) TACAS 2012. LNCS, vol. 7214, pp. 549–551. Springer, Heidelberg (2012). doi:10.1007/978-3-642-28756-5_46
7. Gurfinkel, A., Kahsai, T., Komuravelli, A., Navas, J.A.: The SeaHorn verification framework. In: Kroening, D., Păsăreanu, C.S. (eds.) CAV 2015. LNCS, vol. 9206, pp. 343–361. Springer, Heidelberg (2015). doi:10.1007/978-3-319-21690-4_20
8. Hawblitzel, C., Lahiri, S.K., Pawar, K., Hashmi, H., Gokbulut, S., Fernando, L., Detlefs, D., Wadsworth, S.: Will you still compile me tomorrow? Static cross-version compiler validation. In: Meyer, B., Baresi, L., Mezini, M. (eds.) Joint Meeting of the European Software Engineering Conference and the ACM SIGSOFT Symposium on the Foundations of Software Engineering, ESEC/FSE 2013, August 18–26 2013, Saint Petersburg, Russian Federation, pp. 191–201. ACM (2013)

9. Heizmann, M., Hoenicke, J., Podelski, A.: Software model checking for people who love automata. In: Sharygina, N., Veith, H. (eds.) CAV 2013. LNCS, vol. 8044, pp. 36–52. Springer, Heidelberg (2013). doi:10.1007/978-3-642-39799-8_2
10. Igarashi, S.: An axiomatic approach to equivalence problems of algorithms with applications. Ph.D. thesis, U. Tokyo, Rep. Compt. Centre, U. Tokyo 1968, pp. 1–101 (1964)
11. Lahiri, S.K., Hawblitzel, C., Kawaguchi, M., Rebêlo, H.: SYMDIFF: a language-agnostic semantic diff tool for imperative programs. In: Madhusudan, P., Seshia, S.A. (eds.) CAV 2012. LNCS, vol. 7358, pp. 712–717. Springer, Heidelberg (2012). doi:10.1007/978-3-642-31424-7_54
12. Lahiri, S.K., McMillan, K.L., Sharma, R., Hawblitzel, C.: Differential assertion checking. In: Meyer, B., Baresi, L., Mezini, M. (eds.) Joint Meeting of the European Software Engineering Conference and the ACM SIGSOFT Symposium on the Foundations of Software Engineering, ESEC/FSE 2013, 18–26 August 2013, Saint Petersburg, Russian Federation, pp. 345–355. ACM (2013)
13. Goues, C., Leino, K.R.M., Moskal, M.: The boogie verification debugger (tool paper). In: Barthe, G., Pardo, A., Schneider, G. (eds.) SEFM 2011. LNCS, vol. 7041, pp. 407–414. Springer, Heidelberg (2011). doi:10.1007/978-3-642-24690-6_28
14. McMillan, K.L.: Lazy annotation revisited. Technical report MSR-TR-2014-65, MSR (2014)

Automated Mutual Explicit Induction Proof in Separation Logic

Quang-Trung Ta[(✉)], Ton Chanh Le, Siau-Cheng Khoo, and Wei-Ngan Chin

School of Computing, National University of Singapore, Singapore, Singapore
{taqt,chanhle,khoosc,chinwn}@comp.nus.edu.sg

Abstract. We present a sequent-based deductive system for automatically proving entailments in separation logic by using mathematical induction. Our technique, called *mutual explicit induction proof*, is an instance of Noetherian induction. Specifically, we propose a novel induction principle on a well-founded relation of separation logic model, and follow the *explicit* induction methods to implement this principle as inference rules, so that it can be easily integrated into a deductive system. We also support *mutual* induction, a natural feature of implicit induction, where the goal entailment and other entailments derived during the proof search can be used as hypotheses to prove each other. We have implemented a prototype prover and evaluated it on a benchmark of handcrafted entailments as well as benchmarks from a separation logic competition.

1 Introduction

Separation logic (SL) [22,30] has been actively used recently to reason about imperative programs that alter data structures. For example, the static analysis tool Infer [15] of Facebook has been using SL to discover critical memory safety bugs in Android and iOS applications. One of the pivotal features making the success of SL is the *separating conjunction* operator ($*$), which is used to describe the separation of computer memory. In particular, the assertion $p * q$ denotes a memory portion which can be decomposed into two *disjoint* sub-portions held by p and q, respectively. In addition, SL is also equipped with the ability for users to define inductive heap predicates [4,16,29]. The combination of the separating conjunction and inductive heap predicates makes SL expressive enough to model various types of recursive data structures, such as linked lists and trees.

However, this powerful expressiveness also poses challenges in reasoning about SL entailments. Considerable researches have been conducted on the SL entailment proving problem, including the works [4,7,11] related to mathematical induction. In particular, Brotherston et al. [4,7] propose the *cyclic proof*, which allows proof trees to contain cycles, and can be perceived as infinite derivation trees. Furthermore, during the proof derivation, induction hypotheses are not explicitly identified via applications of induction rules; instead, they are implicitly obtained via the discovery of valid cycle proofs. Consequently, a

J. Fitzgerald et al. (Eds.): FM 2016, LNCS 9995, pp. 659–676, 2016.
DOI: 10.1007/978-3-319-48989-6_40

soundness condition needs to be checked globally on proof trees. On the other hand, Chu et al. [11] apply *structural induction* on inductive heap predicates for proving SL entailments. During proof search, this technique dynamically uses derived entailments as induction hypotheses. When applying induction hypotheses, it performs a local check to ensure that predicates in the target entailments are substructures of predicates in the entailments captured as hypotheses. This dynamicity in hypothesis generation enables multiple induction hypotheses within a single proof path to be exploited; however, it does not admit hypotheses obtained from different proof paths.

In this work, we develop a sequent-based deductive system for proving SL entailments by using mathematical induction. Our technique is an instance of Noetherian induction [8], where we propose a novel induction principle based on a well-founded relation of SL models. Generally, proof techniques based on Noetherian induction are often classified into two categories, i.e., *explicit* and *implicit* induction [8], and each of them presents advantages over the other. We follow the explicit induction methods to implement the induction principle as inference rules, so that it can be easily integrated into a deductive system, and the soundness condition can be checked locally in each application of inference rules. In addition, since the well-founded relation defined in our induction principle does not depend directly on the substructure relationship, induction hypotheses gathered in one proof path can be used for hypothesis applications at other proof paths of the entire proof tree. Thus, our induction principle also favors *mutual induction*, a natural feature of *implicit induction*, in which the goal entailment and other entailments derived during the proof search can be used as hypotheses to prove each other. Our proof technique, therefore, does not restrict induction hypotheses to be collected from only one proof path, but rather from all derived paths of the proof tree.

Related Work. The entailment proving problem in SL has been actively studied recently. Various sound and complete techniques have been introduced, but they deal with only *pre-defined* inductive heap predicates, whose definitions and semantics are given in advance [1–3,12,23–26]. Since these techniques are designated to only certain classes of pre-defined predicates, they are not suitable for handling general inductive heap predicates.

Iosif et al. [16,17] and Enea et al. [13] aim to prove entailments in more general SL fragments by translating SL assertions into tree automata. However, these approaches still have certain restrictions on inductive heap predicates, such as the predicates must have the *bounded tree width* property, or they are variants of linked list structures. Proof techniques proposed by Nguyen et al. [10,20,21] and by Madhusudan et al. [27] can prove SL entailments with *general* inductive heap predicates. Nonetheless, these techniques are semi-automated since users are required to provide supplementing lemmas to assist in handling those predicates. In [14], Enea et al. develop a mechanism to automatically synthesize these supporting lemmas, but solely limited to certain kinds of lemmas, i.e., *composition lemmas*, *completion lemmas* and *stronger lemmas*.

Cyclic proof [4,7] and induction proof in [11] are most closely related to our approach. We recall the aforementioned comments that cyclic proof requires soundness condition to be checked globally on proof trees, whereas proof technique in [11] restricts that induction hypotheses collected from one path of proof tree cannot be used to prove entailments in other paths. Our work differs from them as we not only allow soundness condition to be checked locally at inference rule level, but also support mutual induction where entailments from different proof paths can be used as hypotheses to prove each other.

Contribution. Our contributions in this work are summarized as follows:

- We define a well-founded relation on SL models and use it to construct a novel mutual induction principle for proving SL entailments.
- We develop a deductive system for proving SL entailments based on the proposed mutual induction principle, and prove soundness of the proof system.
- We implement a prototype prover, named Songbird, and experiment on it with benchmarks of handcrafted entailments as well as entailments collected from SL-COMP, an SL competition. Our prover is available for both online use and download at: http://loris-5.d2.comp.nus.edu.sg/songbird/.

2 Motivating Example

We consider the procedure `traverse` in Fig. 1, which traverses a linked list in an unusual way, by randomly jumping either one or two steps at a time. In order to verify memory safety of this program, automated verification tools such as [5,9,18] will first formulate the shape of the computer memory manipulated by `traverse`. Suppose the initially discovered shape is represented by an *inductive heap predicate* $\mathsf{tmp}(x)$ in SL, defined as:

$$\mathsf{tmp}(x) \triangleq \mathsf{emp} \vee \exists u.(x \mapsto u * \mathsf{tmp}(u)) \vee \exists u,v.(x \mapsto u * u \mapsto v * \mathsf{tmp}(v))$$

Intuitively, $\mathsf{tmp}(x)$ covers three possible cases of the shape, which can be an empty memory emp (when `x == NULL`), or be recursively expanded by a single data structure $x \mapsto u$ (when `traverse` jumps one step), or be recursively expanded by two structures $x \mapsto u$ and $u \mapsto v$ (when `traverse` jumps two steps). Note that $x \mapsto u$ and $u \mapsto v$ are SL predicates modeling the data structure `node`. Details about the SL syntax will be explained in Sect. 3.

```
struct node {struct node *next;}
void traverse(struct node *x){
   if (x == NULL) return;
   bool jump = random();
   if (jump && x→next != NULL)
      traverse(x→next→next);
   else traverse(x→next); }
```

Fig. 1. A linked-list traversal algorithm with random jump

Since the derived shape is anomalous, the verifiers or users may want to examine if it is actually a linked list segment, modeled by the following predicate:

$$\mathsf{ls}(x,y) \triangleq (\mathsf{emp} \wedge x = y) \vee \exists w.(x \mapsto w * \mathsf{ls}(w,y))$$

$$
\begin{array}{c l}
\hline
\mathit{true} \vdash \exists y, w.\, (u{=}w \wedge t{=}y) & (\vdash_{\text{pure}})\text{: Valid, proved by external provers, e.g. Z3.} \\
\hline
\mathsf{ls}(u,t) \vdash \exists y, w.\, (\mathsf{ls}(w,y) \wedge u{=}w) & (*\,\mathsf{P})\text{: Match and remove predicates } \mathsf{ls}(u,t) \text{ and } \mathsf{ls}(w,y). \\
\hline
x{\mapsto}u * \mathsf{ls}(u,t) \vdash \exists y, w.\, (x{\mapsto}w * \mathsf{ls}(w,y)) & (*\mapsto)\text{: Match and remove data nodes } x{\mapsto}u \text{ and } x{\mapsto}w. \\
\hline
(E_4)\ x{\mapsto}u * \mathsf{ls}(u,t) \vdash \exists y.\, \mathsf{ls}(x,y) & (\mathsf{PR})\text{: Unfold } \mathsf{ls}(x,y) \text{ by its inductive case.} \\
\hline
(E_2)\ x{\mapsto}u * \mathsf{tmp}(u) \vdash \exists y.\, \mathsf{ls}(x,y) & (\mathsf{AH})\text{: Apply IH } E \text{ with subst. } [u/x]\text{, rename } y \text{ to fresh } t.
\end{array}
$$

Fig. 2. Proof tree of E_2, using induction hypothesis E

This can be done by checking the validity of the following entailment:

$$E \triangleq \mathsf{tmp}(x) \vdash \exists y.\, \mathsf{ls}(x,y)$$

In the semantics of SL, the entailment E is said to be *valid*, if all memory models satisfying $\mathsf{tmp}(x)$ also satisfy $\exists y.\, \mathsf{ls}(x,y)$. To prove it by induction, E is firstly recorded as an induction hypothesis (IH), then the predicate $\mathsf{tmp}(x)$ is analyzed in each case of its definition, via a method called unfolding, to derive new entailments E_1, E_2, E_3 as follows.

$$E_1 \triangleq \mathsf{emp} \vdash \exists y.\, \mathsf{ls}(x,y) \qquad E_2 \triangleq x{\mapsto}u * \mathsf{tmp}(u) \vdash \exists y.\, \mathsf{ls}(x,y)$$
$$E_3 \triangleq x{\mapsto}u * u{\mapsto}v * \mathsf{tmp}(v) \vdash \exists y.\, \mathsf{ls}(x,y)$$

The entailment E_1 can be easily proved by unfolding the predicate $\mathsf{ls}(x,y)$ in the right side by its base case to obtain a valid entailment $\mathsf{emp} \vdash \exists y.(\mathsf{emp} \wedge x = y)$. On the contrary, the entailment E_2 can only be proved by using the induction hypothesis E. Its (simplified) proof tree can be depicted in Fig. 2.

We can also prove E_3 by the same method, i.e., applying the IH E, and its proof tree is shown in Fig. 3.

Using a different strategy, we observe that once E_2 is proved, entailments derived during its proof, i.e., E_2 and E_4, can be used as hypotheses to prove E_3. In this case, the new proof of E_3 is much simpler than the above original

$$
\begin{array}{c l}
\hline
\mathit{true} \vdash \exists y, z, w.\, (u{=}z \wedge v{=}w \wedge t{=}y) & (\vdash_{\text{pure}})\text{: Valid, proved by external prover, e.g. Z3.} \\
\hline
\mathsf{ls}(v,t) \vdash \exists y, z, w.\, (\mathsf{ls}(w,y) \wedge u{=}z \wedge v{=}w) & (*\,\mathsf{P})\text{: Remove predicates } \mathsf{ls}(v,t) \text{ and } \mathsf{ls}(w,y). \\
\hline
u{\mapsto}v * \mathsf{ls}(v,t) \vdash \exists y, z, w.\, (z{\mapsto}w * \mathsf{ls}(w,y) \wedge u{=}z) & (*\mapsto)\text{: Remove data nodes } u{\mapsto}v \text{ and } z{\mapsto}w. \\
\hline
u{\mapsto}v * \mathsf{ls}(v,t) \vdash \exists y, z.\, (\mathsf{ls}(z,y) \wedge u{=}z) & (\mathsf{PR})\text{: Unfolding } \mathsf{ls}(z,y) \text{ by inductive case.} \\
\hline
x{\mapsto}u * u{\mapsto}v * \mathsf{ls}(v,t) \vdash \exists y, z.\, (x{\mapsto}z * \mathsf{ls}(z,y)) & (*\mapsto)\text{: Remove data nodes } x{\mapsto}u \text{ and } x{\mapsto}z. \\
\hline
x{\mapsto}u * u{\mapsto}v * \mathsf{ls}(v,t) \vdash \exists y.\, \mathsf{ls}(x,y) & (\mathsf{PR})\text{: Unfold } \mathsf{ls}(x,y) \text{ by inductive case.} \\
\hline
(E_3)\ x{\mapsto}u * u{\mapsto}v * \mathsf{tmp}(v) \vdash \exists y.\, \mathsf{ls}(x,y) & (\mathsf{AH})\text{: Apply IH } E \text{ with substitution } [v/x]\text{, and rename } y \text{ to } t
\end{array}
$$

Fig. 3. Ordinary proof tree of E_3, using induction hypothesis E

$$\dfrac{\dfrac{\dfrac{\dfrac{}{true \vdash \exists y.\, y = z}\ (\vdash_{\text{pure}})}{\mathsf{ls}(x,z) \vdash \exists y.\, \mathsf{ls}(x,y)}\ (*\,\mathsf{P})}{x \mapsto u * \mathsf{ls}(u,r) \vdash \exists y.\, \mathsf{ls}(x,y)}\ (\mathsf{AH})}{(E_3)\ x \mapsto u * u \mapsto v * \mathsf{tmp}(v) \vdash \exists y.\, \mathsf{ls}(x,y)}\ (\mathsf{AH})$$

($\vdash_{\text{pure}}$): Valid, proved by external provers, e.g., Z3.

($*$ P): Remove predicates $\mathsf{ls}(x, z)$ and $\mathsf{ls}(x, y)$.

(AH): Apply E_4 with subst. $[r/t]$, and rename y to z.

(AH): Apply hypothesis E_2 with subst. $[u/x, v/u]$, and rename y to r.

Fig. 4. New proof tree of E_3, using hypotheses E_2 and E_4

induction proof, as demonstrated in Fig. 4; the proving process, therefore, is more efficient.

In the new proof tree, the entailment E_4 can be directly used as a hypothesis to prove other entailments since it is already proven *valid* (see Fig. 2). However, when E_2 is applied to prove E_3, thus prove E, it is not straightforward to conclude about E, since the validity of E_2 is still *unknown*. This is because the proof of E_2 in Fig. 2 also uses E as a hypothesis. Therefore, E and E_2 jointly form a *mutual induction* proof, in which they can be used to prove each other. The theoretical principle of this proof technique will be introduced in Sect. 4.

3 Theoretical Background

In this work, we consider the *symbolic-heap* fragment of separation logic with arbitrary user-defined inductive heap predicates. We denote this logic fragment as $\mathrm{SL_{ID}}$. It is similar to those introduced in [6,16], but extended with linear arithmetic (LA) to describe more expressive properties of the data structures, such as size or sortedness. The syntax and semantics of the $\mathrm{SL_{ID}}$ assertions and their entailments are introduced in this section.

3.1 Symbolic-Heap Separation Logic

Syntax. The syntax of our considered separation logic fragment $\mathrm{SL_{ID}}$ is described in Fig. 5. In particular, the predicate emp represents an *empty* memory. The *singleton* heap predicate $x \overset{\iota}{\mapsto} x_1,...,x_n$ models an n-field single data structure in memory where x points-to; its data type is represented by a unique *sort* ι[1] and values of its fields are captured by $x_1, ..., x_n$. The *inductive* heap predicate $\mathsf{P}(x_1,...,x_n)$ models a recursively defined data structure, which is formally defined in Definition 1. These three heap predicates, called *spatial atoms*, compose the *spatial* assertions Σ via the separating conjunction operator $*$. Π denotes *pure* assertions in linear arithmetic, which do not contain any spatial atoms.

Definition 1 (Inductive Heap Predicate). *A system of k inductive heap predicates P_i of arity n_i and parameters $x^i_1, ..., x^i_{n_i}$, with $i = 1, ..., k$, are syntac-*

[1] Note that for the simplicity of presenting the motivating example, we have removed the sort ι from the SL singleton heap predicate denoting the data structure `node`.

c, x, ι, P resp. denote constants, variables, data sorts, and predicate symbols.

$$
\begin{array}{llll}
e & ::= & c \mid x \mid -e \mid e_1{+}e_2 \mid e_1{-}e_2 & \text{Integer expressions} \\
a & ::= & \mathsf{nil} \mid x & \text{Spatial expressions} \\
\Pi & ::= & a_1 = a_2 \mid a_1 \neq a_2 \mid e_1 = e_2 \mid e_1 \neq e_2 \mid & \text{Pure assertions} \\
 & & e_1 > e_2 \mid e_1 \geq e_2 \mid e_1 < e_2 \mid e_1 \leq e_2 \mid & \\
 & & \neg\Pi \mid \Pi_1 \wedge \Pi_2 \mid \Pi_1 \vee \Pi_2 \mid \Pi_1 \Rightarrow \Pi_2 \mid \forall x.\Pi \mid \exists x.\Pi & \\
\Sigma & ::= & \mathsf{emp} \mid x \overset{\iota}{\mapsto} x_1,...,x_n \mid \mathsf{P}(x_1,...,x_n) \mid \Sigma_1 * \Sigma_2 & \text{Spatial assertions} \\
F & ::= & \Sigma \mid \Pi \mid \Sigma \wedge \Pi \mid \exists x.F & \text{SL}_{\text{ID}} \text{ assertions}
\end{array}
$$

Fig. 5. Syntax of assertions in SL_{ID}

tically defined as follows:

$$\left\{ \mathsf{P}_i(x^i_1, ..., x^i_{n_i}) \;\triangleq\; F^i_1(x^i_1, ..., x^i_{n_i}) \vee \cdots \vee F^i_{m_i}(x^i_1, ..., x^i_{n_i}) \right\}_{i=1}^{k}$$

where $F^i_j(x^i_1, ..., x^i_{n_i})$, *with* $1 \leq j \leq m_i$, *is a* definition case *of* $\mathsf{P}_i(x^i_1, ..., x^i_{n_i})$. *Moreover,* F^i_j *is a* base case *of* P_i, *if it does not contain any predicate symbol which is (mutually) recursively defined with* P_i; *otherwise, it is an* inductive case.

Definition 2 (Syntactic Equivalence). *The syntactical equivalence relation of two spatial assertions* Σ_1 *and* Σ_2, *denoted as* $\Sigma_1 \cong \Sigma_2$, *is recursively defined as follows:*

$-\mathsf{emp} \cong \mathsf{emp}$ $\quad -u \overset{\iota}{\mapsto} v_1,...,v_n \cong u \overset{\iota}{\mapsto} v_1,...,v_n$ $\quad -\mathsf{P}(u_1,...,u_n) \cong \mathsf{P}(u_1,...,u_n)$
$-$*If* $\Sigma_1 \cong \Sigma'_1$ *and* $\Sigma_2 \cong \Sigma'_2$, *then* $\Sigma_1 * \Sigma_2 \cong \Sigma'_1 * \Sigma'_2$ *and* $\Sigma_1 * \Sigma_2 \cong \Sigma'_2 * \Sigma'_1$

Semantics. The semantics of SL_{ID} assertions are given in Fig. 6. Given a set `Var` of variables, `Sort` of sorts, `Val` of values and `Loc` $\subset$ `Val` of memory addresses, a model of an assertion consists of:

- a *stack* model s, which is a function s: `Var` $\rightarrow$ `Val`. We write $[\![\Pi]\!]_s$ to denote valuation of a pure assertion Π under the stack model s. Note that the constant $\mathsf{nil} \in$ `Val`$\backslash$`Loc` denotes dangling memory address.
- a *heap* model h, which is a partial function h: `Loc` $\rightharpoonup_{\texttt{fin}}$ (`Sort` $\rightarrow$ (`Val list`)). $\text{dom}(h)$ denotes domain of h, and $|h|$ is cardinality of $\text{dom}(h)$. We follow Reynolds' semantics [28] to consider *finite* heap models, i.e., $|h| < \infty$. $h \# h'$ indicates that h and h' have disjoint domains, i.e., $\text{dom}(h) \cap \text{dom}(h') = \varnothing$, and $h \circ h'$ is the union of two disjoint heap models h, h', i.e., $h \# h'$.

3.2 Entailments in SL_{ID}

In this section, we formally define the SL_{ID} entailments and introduce a new concept of *model of entailments*, which will be used in the next section to construct the well-founded relation in our induction principle.

Definition 3 (Entailment). *An entailment between two assertions F and G, denoted as $F \vdash G$, is said to be* valid *(holds), iff $s, h \models F$ implies that $s, h \models G$, for all models s, h. Formally,*

$$F \vdash G \, is \, valid, \, iff \; \forall s, h.(s, h \models F \rightarrow s, \; h \models G)$$

Here, F and G are respectively called the *antecedent* and the *consequent* of the entailment. For simplicity, the entailment $F \vdash G$ can be denoted by just E, i.e., $E \triangleq F \vdash G$.

$s, h \models \Pi$	iff	$[\![\Pi]\!]_s = true$ and $\text{dom}(h) = \varnothing$
$s, h \models \mathsf{emp}$	iff	$\text{dom}(h) = \varnothing$
$s, h \models x \overset{\iota}{\mapsto} x_1,...,x_n$	iff	$s(x) \in \mathtt{Loc}$ and $\text{dom}(h) = \{s(x)\}$ and $h(s(x))\iota = (s(x_1), ..., s(x_n))$
$s, h \models \mathsf{P}(x_1,...,x_n)$	iff	$s, h \models R_i(x_1,...,x_n)$, with $R_i(x_1,...,x_n)$ is one of the definition cases of $\mathsf{P}(x_1,...,x_n)$
$s, h \models \Sigma_1 * \Sigma_2$	iff	there exist h_1, h_2 such that: $h_1 \# h_2$, $h_1 \circ h_2 = h$ and $s, h_1 \models \Sigma_1$ and $s, h_2 \models \Sigma_2$
$s, h \models \Sigma \wedge \Pi$	iff	$[\![\Pi]\!]_s = true$ and $s, h \models \Sigma$
$s, h \models \exists x.F$	iff	$\exists v \in \mathtt{Val} \, . \, [s \vert x{:}v], h \models F$

Fig. 6. Semantics of assertions in SL_{ID}. $[f \vert x{:}y]$ is a function like f except that it returns y for input x.

Definition 4 (Model and Counter-Model). *Given an entailment $E \triangleq F \vdash G$. An SL model s, h is called a* model *of E, iff $s, h \models F$ implies $s, h \models G$. On the contrary, s, h is called a* counter-model *of E, iff $s, h \models F$ and $s, h \not\models G$.*

We denote $s, h \models (F \vdash G)$, or $s, h \models E$, if s, h is a model of E. Similarly, we write $s, h \not\models (F \vdash G)$, or $s, h \not\models E$, if s, h is a counter-model of E. Given a list of n entailments $E_1, ..., E_n$, we write $s, h \models E_1, ..., E_n$ if s, h is a model of *all* $E_1, ..., E_n$, and $s, h \not\models E_1, ..., E_n$ if s, h is a counter-model of *some* $E_1, ..., E_n$.

4 Mutual Induction Proof for Separation Logic Entailment Using Model Order

In this section, we first introduce the general schema of *Noetherian induction, a.k.a. well-founded induction,* and then apply it in proving SL entailments.

Noetherian induction [8]. Given a conjecture $\mathcal{P}(\alpha)$, with α is a structure of type τ, the general schema of Noetherian induction on the structure α is

$$\frac{\forall \alpha : \tau.\ (\forall \beta : \tau.\ \beta \prec_\tau \alpha \rightarrow \mathcal{P}(\beta)) \rightarrow \mathcal{P}(\alpha))}{\forall \alpha : \tau.\ \mathcal{P}(\alpha)}$$

where $\prec_\tau$ is a well-founded relation on τ, i.e., there is no infinite descending chain, like $... \prec_\tau \alpha_n \prec_\tau ... \prec_\tau \alpha_2 \prec_\tau \alpha_1$. Noetherian induction can be applied for arbitrary type τ, such as data structures or control flow. However, success in proving a conjecture by induction is highly dependent on the choice of the induction variable α and the well-founded relation $\prec_\tau$.

Proving SL entailments using Noetherian induction. We observe that an SL entailment E is said to be *valid* if $s, h \models E$ for all model s, h, given that the heap domain is finite, i.e., $\forall h. |h| \in \mathbb{N}$, according to Reynolds' semantics [28]. This inspires us to define a well-founded relation among SL models, called *model order*, by comparing size of their heap domains. To prove an SL entailment by Noetherian induction based on this order, we will show that if all the smaller models satisfying the entailment implies that the bigger model also satisfies the entailment, then the entailment is satisfied by all models, thus it is valid. The model order and induction principle are formally described as follows.

Definition 5 (Model Order). *The* model order, *denoted by* $\prec$, *of SL models is a binary relation defined as:* $s_1, h_1 \prec s_2, h_2$, *if* $|h_1| < |h_2|$.

Theorem 1 (Well-Founded Relation). *The model order* $\prec$ *of SL models is a well-founded relation.*

Proof. By contradiction, suppose that $\prec$ were not well-founded, then there would exist an infinite descending chain: $... \prec s_n, h_n \prec ... \prec s_1, h_1$. It follows that there would exist an infinite descending chain: $... < |h_n| < ... < |h_1|$. This is impossible since domain size of heap model is finite, i.e., $|h_1|, ..., |h_n|, ... \in \mathbb{N}$. □

Theorem 2 (Induction Principle). *An entailment* E *is valid, if for all model* s, h, *the following holds:* $(\forall s', h'.\ s', h' \prec s, h \rightarrow s', h' \models E) \rightarrow s, h \models E$. *Formally:*

$$\frac{\forall s, h.\ (\forall s', h'.\ s', h' \prec s, h \rightarrow s', h' \models E) \rightarrow s, h \models E}{\forall s, h.\ s, h \models E}$$

Since our induction principle is constructed on the SL model order, an induction hypothesis can be used in the proof of any entailment whenever the decreasing condition on model order is satisfied. This flexibility allows us to extend the aforementioned principle to support *mutual induction*, in which multiple entailments can participate in an induction proof, and each of them can be used as a hypothesis to prove the other. In the following, we will introduce our *mutual induction principle.* Note that the induction principle in Theorem 2 is an instance of this principle, when only one entailment takes part in the induction proof.

Theorem 3 (Mutual Induction Principle). *Given* n *entailments* $E_1, ..., E_n$. *All of them are valid, if for all model* s, h, *the following holds:* $(\forall s', h'.\ s', h' \prec s, h \rightarrow s', h' \models E_1, ..., E_n) \rightarrow s, h \models E_1, ..., E_n$. *Formally:*

$$\frac{\forall s,h.\ (\forall s',h'.\ s',h' \prec s,h \rightarrow s',h' \models E_1,...,E_n) \rightarrow s,h \models E_1,...,E_n}{\forall s,h.\ s,h \models E_1,...,E_n}$$

Proof. By contradiction, assume that some of $E_1, ..., E_n$ were invalid. Then, there would exist some counter-models s, h such that $s, h \not\models E_1, ..., E_n$. Since $\prec$ is a well-founded relation, there would exist the *least* counter-model s_1, h_1 such that $s_1, h_1 \not\models E_1, ..., E_n$, and, $s_1', h_1' \models E_1, ..., E_n$ for all $s_1', h_1' \prec s_1, h_1$. Following the theorem's hypothesis $\forall s,h.\ (\forall s',h'.\ s',h' \prec s,h \rightarrow s',h' \models E_1,...,E_n) \rightarrow s,h \models E_1, ..., E_n$, we have $s_1, h_1 \models E_1, ..., E_n$. This contradicts with the assumption that s_1, h_1 is a counter-model. □

5 The Proof System

In this section, we introduce a sequent-based deductive system, which comprises a set of inference rules depicted in Fig. 7 (logical rules) and Fig. 8 (induction rules), and a proof search procedure in Fig. 10. Each inference rule has zero or more premises, a conclusion and possibly a side condition. A premise or a conclusion is described in the same form of $\mathcal{H},\ \rho,\ F_1 \vdash F_2$, where (i) $F_1 \vdash F_2$ is an entailment, (ii) $\mathcal{H}$ is a set of entailments with validity status, which are recorded during proof search and can be used as hypotheses to prove $F_1 \vdash F_2$, and (iii) ρ is a proof trace capturing a chronological list of inference rules applied by the proof search procedure to reach $F_1 \vdash F_2$.

In addition, the entailment in the conclusion of a rule is called the *goal entailment.* Rules with zero (empty) premise is called *axiom rules.* A proof trace ρ containing n rules $R_1, \ldots, R_n$, with $n \geq 0$, is represented by $[(R_1), \ldots, (R_n)]$, where the head (R_1) of ρ is the latest rule used by the proof search procedure. In addition, some operations over proof traces are (i) insertion: $(R) :: \rho$, (ii) membership checking: $(R) \in \rho$, and (iii) concatenation: $\rho_1 \mathbin{@} \rho_2$.

5.1 Logical Rules

Logical rules in Fig. 7 deal with the logical structure of SL entailments. For brevity, in these rules, we write the *complete* symbolic-heap assertion $\exists \vec{x}.(\Sigma \wedge \Pi)$ as a *standalone* F. We define the *conjoined* assertion $F * \Sigma' \triangleq \Sigma * \Sigma' \wedge \Pi$ and $F \wedge \Pi' \triangleq \Sigma \wedge \Pi \wedge \Pi'$, given that existential quantifiers does not occur in the outermost scope of F, i.e., $F \triangleq \Sigma \wedge \Pi$. The notation $\vec{u} = \vec{v}$ means $(u_1 = v_1) \wedge \ldots \wedge (u_n = v_n)$, given that $\vec{u} = u_1, \ldots, u_n$ and $\vec{v} = v_1, \ldots, v_n$ are two lists containing the same number of variables. We also write $\vec{x} \# \vec{y}$ to denote $\vec{x}$ and $\vec{y}$ are disjoint, i.e., $\nexists u.(u \in \vec{x} \wedge u \in \vec{y})$, and use $\mathtt{FV}(F)$ to denote the list of all free variables of an assertion F. Moreover, $F[e/x]$ is a formula obtained from F by substituting the expression e for all occurrences of the free variable x in F.

The set of logical rules are explained in details as follows:

- **Axiom rules.** The rule $\vdash_{\text{pure}}$ proves a pure entailment $\Pi_1 \vdash \Pi_2$ by invoking off-the-shelf provers such as Z3 [19] to check the pure implication $\Pi_1 \Rightarrow \Pi_2$

$$(\bot\mathsf{L}_1)\,\frac{}{\mathcal{H},\ \rho,\ F_1 \wedge u{\neq}u \vdash F_2} \qquad (\bot\mathsf{L}_2)\,\frac{}{\mathcal{H},\ \rho,\ F_1 * u \overset{\iota_1}{\mapsto} \vec{v} * u \overset{\iota_2}{\mapsto} \vec{w} \vdash F_2}$$

$$(\vdash_{\text{pure}})\,\frac{}{\mathcal{H},\ \rho,\ \Pi_1 \vdash \Pi_2}\ \Pi_1 \Rightarrow \Pi_2 \qquad (\mathsf{empL})\,\frac{\mathcal{H},\ \rho',\ F_1 \vdash F_2}{\mathcal{H},\ \rho,\ F_1 * \mathsf{emp} \vdash F_2}$$

$$(=\!\mathsf{L})\,\frac{\mathcal{H},\ \rho',\ F_1[u/v] \vdash F_2[u/v]}{\mathcal{H},\ \rho,\ F_1 \wedge u{=}v \vdash F_2} \qquad (\mathsf{empR})\,\frac{\mathcal{H},\ \rho',\ F_1 \vdash \exists\vec{x}.F_2}{\mathcal{H},\ \rho,\ F_1 \vdash \exists\vec{x}.(F_2 * \mathsf{emp})}$$

$$(=\!\mathsf{R})\,\frac{\mathcal{H},\ \rho',\ F_1 \vdash \exists\vec{x}.F_2}{\mathcal{H},\ \rho,\ F_1 \vdash \exists\vec{x}.(F_2 \wedge u{=}u)} \qquad (*\!\mapsto)\,\frac{\mathcal{H},\ \rho',\ F_1 \vdash \exists\vec{x}.(F_2 \wedge u{=}t \wedge \vec{v}{=}\vec{w})}{\mathcal{H},\ \rho,\ F_1 * u \overset{\iota}{\mapsto} \vec{v} \vdash \exists\vec{x}.(F_2 * t \overset{\iota}{\mapsto} \vec{w})}\ (u, \vec{v}) \# \vec{x}$$

$$(\exists\mathsf{L})\,\frac{\mathcal{H},\ \rho',\ F_1[u/x] \vdash F_2}{\mathcal{H},\ \rho,\ \exists x.F_1 \vdash F_2}\ u \notin \mathsf{FV}(F_2) \qquad (*\,\mathsf{P})\,\frac{\mathcal{H},\ \rho',\ F_1 \vdash \exists\vec{x}.(F_2 \wedge \vec{u}{=}\vec{v})}{\mathcal{H},\ \rho,\ F_1 * \mathsf{P}(\vec{u}) \vdash \exists\vec{x}.(F_2 * \mathsf{P}(\vec{v}))}\ \vec{u} \# \vec{x}$$

$$(\exists\mathsf{R})\,\frac{\mathcal{H},\ \rho',\ F_1 \vdash F_2[e/x]}{\mathcal{H},\ \rho,\ F_1 \vdash \exists x.F_2} \qquad (\mathsf{PR})\,\frac{\mathcal{H},\ \rho',\ F_1 \vdash \exists\vec{x}.(F_2 * F_i^{\mathsf{P}}(\vec{u}))}{\mathcal{H},\ \rho,\ F_1 \vdash \exists\vec{x}.(F_2 * \mathsf{P}(\vec{u}))}\ \begin{array}{l} F_i^{\mathsf{P}}(\vec{u}) \text{ is one of the} \\ \text{definition cases of } \mathsf{P}(\vec{u}) \end{array}$$

Fig. 7. Logical rules. Note that for a rule R with trace ρ in its conclusion, the trace in its premise is $\rho' \triangleq (R) :: \rho$.

in its side condition. The two rules $\bot\mathsf{L}_1$ and $\bot\mathsf{L}_2$ decide an entailment *vacuously* valid if its antecedent is unsatisfiable, i.e., the antecedent contains a contradiction ($u \neq u$) or overlaid data nodes ($u \overset{\iota_1}{\mapsto} \vec{v} * u \overset{\iota_2}{\mapsto} \vec{w}$).

- **Normalization rules.** These rules simplify their goal entailments by either eliminating existentially quantified variables ($\exists\mathsf{L}, \exists\mathsf{R}$), or removing equalities ($=\!\mathsf{L}, =\!\mathsf{R}$) or empty heap predicates ($\mathsf{empL}, \mathsf{empR}$) from antecedents (left side) or consequents (right side) of the entailments.
- **Frame rules.** The two rules $*\!\mapsto$ and $*\,\mathsf{P}$ applies the *frame property* of SL [28] to remove *identical* spatial atoms from two sides of entailments. Note that the identical condition is guaranteed by adding equality constraints of these spatial atoms' arguments into consequents of the derived entailments.
- **Unfolding rules.** The rule PR derives a new entailment by unfolding a heap predicate in the goal entailment's consequent by its inductive definition. Note that unfolding a heap predicate in the entailment's antecedent will be performed by the induction rule Ind, as discussed in the next section.

5.2 Induction Rules

Figure 8 presents inference rules implementing our mutual induction principle. The *induction* rule Ind firstly records its goal entailment as an induction hypothesis H, and unfolds an inductive heap predicate in the antecedent of H to derive new entailments. When H is inserted into the hypothesis vault $\mathcal{H}$, its status is initially assigned to **?** (*unknown*), indicating that its validity is not known at the moment. Later, the status of H will be updated to ✓ (*valid*) once the proof

$$(\mathsf{Ind})\ \frac{\mathcal{H}\cup\{(H,?)\},\ \rho',\ F_1 * F_1^{\mathsf{P}}(\vec{u}) \vdash F_2 \quad \ldots \quad \mathcal{H}\cup\{(H,?)\},\ \rho',\ F_1 * F_m^{\mathsf{P}}(\vec{u}) \vdash F_2}{\mathcal{H},\ \rho,\ F_1 * \mathsf{P}(\vec{u}) \vdash F_2}\ \dagger_{(\mathsf{Ind})}$$

Given $H \triangleq F_1 * \mathsf{P}(\vec{u}) \vdash F_2$, $\rho' = (\mathsf{Ind}) :: \rho$, and $\dagger_{(\mathsf{Ind})}$: $\mathsf{P}(\vec{u}) \triangleq F_1^{\mathsf{P}}(\vec{u}) \vee \ldots \vee F_m^{\mathsf{P}}(\vec{u})$

$$(\mathsf{AH})\ \frac{\mathcal{H}\cup\{(H, status)\},\ (\mathsf{AH}) :: \rho,\ F_4\theta * \Sigma' \wedge \Pi_1 \vdash F_2 \quad \exists\theta,\Sigma'.(\Sigma_1 {\cong} \Sigma_3\theta {*} \Sigma' \wedge \Pi_1 {\Rightarrow} \Pi_3\theta),}{\mathcal{H}\cup\{(H \triangleq \Sigma_3 \wedge \Pi_3 \vdash F_4, status)\},\ \rho,\ \Sigma_1 \wedge \Pi_1 \vdash F_2}\ \dagger_{(\mathsf{AH})}$$

with $\dagger_{(\mathsf{AH})}$: $(status{=}\checkmark) \vee \exists\iota, u, \vec{v}, \Sigma''.(\Sigma' \cong u \overset{\iota}{\mapsto} \vec{v} * \Sigma'')$
$\vee\ \exists\rho_1, \rho_2.(\rho = \rho_1@[(*\mapsto)]@\rho_2 \wedge (\mathsf{Ind}) \notin \rho_1 \wedge (\mathsf{Ind}) \in \rho_2)$.

Fig. 8. Induction rules

search procedure is able to prove it valid. Generally, given an entailment E and its proof tree $\mathcal{T}$, the proof search procedure concludes that E is valid if (i) every leaf of $\mathcal{T}$ is empty via applications of axiom rules, and (ii) all hypotheses used by the *apply hypothesis* rule AH must be derived in $\mathcal{T}$.

Rule AH is the key rule of our mutual induction principle, which applies an appropriate hypothesis $H \triangleq \Sigma_3 \wedge \Pi_3 \vdash F_4$ in proving its goal entailment $E \triangleq \Sigma_1 \wedge \Pi_1 \vdash F_2$. The rule firstly unifies the antecedents of H and E by a substitution θ, i.e., there exists a spatial assertion Σ' such that $\Sigma_1 \cong \Sigma_3\theta * \Sigma'$ and $\Pi_1 \Rightarrow \Pi_3\theta$. If such θ and Σ' exist, we can weaken the antecedent of E as follows $(\Sigma_1 \wedge \Pi_1) \vdash (\Sigma_3\theta * \Sigma' \wedge \Pi_3\theta \wedge \Pi_1) \vdash (F_4\theta * \Sigma' \wedge \Pi_1)$. Note that we use Reynolds's substitution law [28] to obtain $\Sigma_3\theta \wedge \Pi_3\theta \vdash F_4\theta$ from the hypothesis H. The proof system then derives the next goal entailment $F_4\theta * \Sigma' \wedge \Pi_1 \vdash F_2$ as shown in the premise of rule AH.

The side condition $\dagger_{(\mathsf{AH})}$ of rule AH ensures the decreasing condition of the mutual induction principle. In particular, suppose that the proof search procedure applies a hypothesis H in $\mathcal{H}$ to prove an entailment E via rule AH. If the status of H is $\checkmark$, denoted by the first condition in $\dagger_{(\mathsf{AH})}$, then H is already proved to be valid; thus it can be freely used to prove other entailments. Otherwise, the status of H is ?, and H may participate in a (mutual) induction proof with an entailment I in the proof path of E, as depicted in Fig. 9. Note that the entailment I has been recorded earlier as an induction hypothesis by an application of the induction rule Ind.

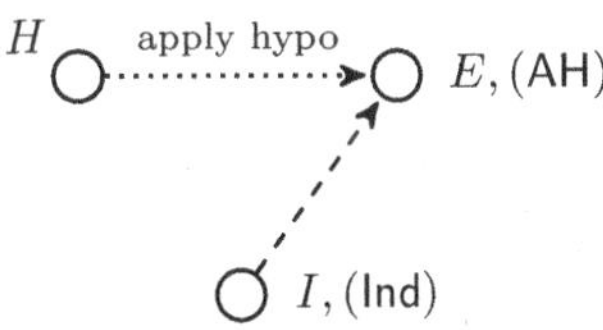

Fig. 9. Applying hypothesis

In the latter case, the induction principle requires the decrease of model size when applying the hypothesis H to prove entailment I. We then show that this decreasing condition holds if one of the following conditions of $\dagger_{(\mathsf{AH})}$ is satisfied.

(i) $\exists\iota, u, \vec{v}, \Sigma''.(\Sigma' {\cong} u \overset{\iota}{\mapsto} \vec{v} {*} \Sigma'')$ indicates that the left-over heap part Σ' after unifying antecedent of H into that of E contains at least one singleton heap predicate, or

(ii) $\exists \rho_1, \rho_2.(\rho = \rho_1 @[(* \mapsto)]@\rho_2 \wedge (\mathsf{Ind}) \notin \rho_1 \wedge (\mathsf{Ind}) \in \rho_2)$ requires that there is a removal step of a singleton heap predicate by the rule $* \mapsto$ applied between this hypothesis application AH and the most recent induction step Ind.

Consider an arbitrary model s, h satisfying I. During the derivation path from I to E, the model s, h is transformed into a corresponding model s_e, h_e of E. We always have $|h_e| \leq |h|$ as the applications of logical rules and rule Ind never increase heap model size of entailments. Moreover, when applying H to prove E, the model s', h' of H, which corresponds to s_e, h_e of E, satisfies $|h'| \leq |h_e|$, due to the unification step in rule AH. We consider two following cases. If condition (i) is satisfied, then heap model size of the left-over part Σ' is at least 1 since Σ' contains a singleton heap predicate. As a result, $|h'| < |h_e|$ and it follows that $|h'| < |h|$. If condition (ii) is satisfied, then $|h_e| < |h|$ since there is a singleton heap predicate, whose size of heap model is 1, is removed when deriving I to E. This implies that $|h'| < |h|$. In summary, we obtain that $|h'| < |h|$ for both cases; thus, $s', h' \prec s, h$. This concludes our explanation about the rule AH.

Procedure $\mathsf{Prove}(\mathcal{H}, \rho, F \vdash G)$

Input: $\mathcal{H}, F \vdash G$ and ρ are respectively a set of hypotheses, a goal entailment and its corresponding proof trace.
Output: Validity result (True or False), a set of derived entailments with their validity statuses, and a set of hypotheses used in proof of $F \vdash G$.

$\mathcal{S} \leftarrow \{ R_{inst} \mid R_{inst} = \mathsf{Unify}(R, (\mathcal{H}, \rho, F \vdash G)) \wedge R \in \mathcal{R} \}$
if $\mathcal{S} = \varnothing$ **then return** False, $\varnothing, \varnothing$ *// no rule is selected*
for each R_{inst} **in** $\mathcal{S}$ **do**
    if $\mathsf{GetName}(R_{inst}) \in \{\vdash_{\mathsf{pure}}, \bot \mathsf{L}_1, \bot \mathsf{L}_2\}$ **then** *// R is an axiom rule*
        return True, $\varnothing, \varnothing$
    $\mathcal{H}_{used} \leftarrow \varnothing$
    if $R_{inst} =$ AH with hypothesis E **then** $\mathcal{H}_{used} \leftarrow \mathcal{H}_{used} \cup \{E\}$
    $\mathcal{H}_{derived} \leftarrow \varnothing$
    $(\mathcal{H}_i, \rho_i, F_i \vdash G_i)_{i=1,\ldots,n} \leftarrow \mathsf{GetPremises}(R_{inst})$ *// all premises of R_{inst}*
    for i = 1 **to** n **do**
        $res, \mathcal{H}_{derived}, \mathcal{H}'_{used} \leftarrow \mathsf{Prove}(\mathcal{H}_i \oplus \mathcal{H}_{derived}, \rho_i, F_i \vdash G_i)$
        if $res =$ False **then return** False, $\varnothing, \varnothing$
        $\mathcal{H}_{used} \leftarrow \mathcal{H}_{used} \cup \mathcal{H}'_{used}$
    if $\mathcal{H}_{used} \subseteq (\mathsf{GetEntailments}(\mathcal{H}_{derived}) \cup \{F \vdash G\})$ **then**
        $\mathcal{H}_{derived} \leftarrow \mathcal{H}_{derived} \oplus \{(F \vdash G, \checkmark)\}$
    else $\mathcal{H}_{derived} \leftarrow \mathcal{H}_{derived} \oplus \{(F \vdash G, ?)\}$
    return True, $\mathcal{H}_{derived}, \mathcal{H}_{used}$ *// all derived premises are proved*
return False, $\varnothing, \varnothing$ *// all rules fail to prove $F \vdash G$*

Fig. 10. General proof search procedure, in which $\mathcal{R}$ is the set of inference rules given in Figs. 7 and 8.

5.3 Proof Search Procedure

Our proof search procedure Prove is designed in a self-recursive manner, as presented in Fig. 10. Its inputs consist of a set of hypotheses, a proof trace, and an entailment, which are components of an inference rule's conclusion. To prove a candidate entailment $F \vdash G$, initially the hypothesis set $\mathcal{H}$ and the proof trace are assigned to empty ($\varnothing$ and $[\,]$).

Firstly, the procedure Prove finds a set $\mathcal{S}$ of suitable rules, whose conclusion can be unified with the goal entailment $F \vdash G$, among all inference rules in $\mathcal{R}$ (line 1). If no suitable rule is found, the procedure immediately returns False, indicating that it is unable to prove the entailment (line 2). Otherwise, it subsequently processes each discovered rule R_{inst} in $\mathcal{S}$ by either (i) returning True to announce a valid result, if an axiom rule is selected (line 5), or (ii) recursively searching for proofs of the derived entailments in the premises of R_{inst} (lines 9–17). In the latter case, the procedure returns False if one of the derived entailments is not proved (line 12), or returns True if all of them are proved (line 17). Finally, it simply returns False when it cannot prove the goal entailment with all selected rules (line 18).

The procedure uses a local variable $\mathcal{H}_{used}$ to store all hypotheses used during the proof search. $\mathcal{H}_{used}$ is updated when the rule AH is applied (line 7) or after the procedure finishes proving a derived entailment (lines 11 and 13). We also use another variable $\mathcal{H}_{derived}$ to capture all generated entailments with their validity statuses. The condition at line 14 checks if all hypotheses used to prove the entailment $F \vdash G$ are only introduced during the entailment's proof. If this condition is satisfied, then $F \vdash G$ is updated with a *valid status* ✓ (line 15). Otherwise, the entailment may participate in a (mutual) induction proof, thus its status is assigned to *unknown* ? (line 16).

At line 11, the procedure uses not only the hypothesis set $\mathcal{H}_i$, introduced by the selected inference rule, but also the set $\mathcal{H}_{derived}$ containing entailments derived during proof search to prove a new goal entailment $F_i \vdash G_i$. This reflects our mutual induction principle which allows derived entailments to be used as hypotheses in other entailments' proofs. Note that the *union and update* operator $\oplus$ used in the algorithm will insert new entailments and their statuses into the set of hypotheses, or update the existing entailments with their new statuses. In addition, the auxiliary procedures used in our proof search procedure are named in a self-explanatory manner. In particular, Unify, GetName and GetPremises respectively unifies an inference rule with a goal entailment, or returns name and premises of an inference rule. Finally, GetEntailments returns all entailments stored in the set of derived entailments $\mathcal{H}_{derived}$.

Soundness. Soundness of our proof system is stated in Theorem 4. Due to page constraint, we present the detailed proof in the technical report [32].

Theorem 4 (Soundness). *Given an entailment E, if the proof search procedure returns* True *when proving E, then E is valid.*

6 Experiment

We have implemented the proposed induction proof technique into a prototype prover, named Songbird. The proof system and this paper's artifact are available for both online use and download at http://loris-5.d2.comp.nus.edu.sg/songbird/.

Category	Slide	Spen	Sleek	Cyclist	Songbird
singly-ll (64)	12	3	48	**63**	**63**
doubly-ll (37)	14	0	17	24	**26**
nested-ll (11)	0	**11**	5	6	**11**
skip-list (13)	0	**12**	4	5	7
tree (26)	12	1	14	18	**22**
Total (151)	38	27	88	116	**129**

(a)

	Songbird			
	$✓_{sb}✗_{o}$	$✗_{sb}✓_{o}$	$✓_{sb}✓_{o}$	$✗_{sb}✗_{o}$
Cyclist	13	0	116	22
Sleek	41	0	88	22
Spen	109	7	20	15
Slide	103	12	26	10

(b)

Fig. 11. Overall evaluation on the benchmark slrd_entl of SL-COMP

To evaluate our technique, we compared our system against state-of-the-art SL provers, including Slide [16,17], Spen [13], Sleek [10] and Cyclist [4,7], which had participated in the recent SL competition SL-COMP [31]. We are however unable to make direct comparison with the induction-based proof technique presented in [11] as their prover was not publicly available. Our evaluation was performed on an Ubuntu 14.04 machine with CPU Intel E5-2620 (2.4 GHz) and RAM 64 GB.

Firstly, we conduct the experiment on a set of *valid* entailments[2], collected from the benchmark slrd_entl[3] of SL-COMP. These entailments contain *general* inductive heap predicates denoting various data structures, such as singly linked lists (singly-ll), doubly linked lists (doubly-ll), nested lists (nested-ll), skip lists (skip-list) and trees (tree). We then categorize problems in this benchmark based on their predicate types. In Fig. 11(a), we report the number of entailments successfully proved by a prover in each category, with a timeout of 30 s for proving an entailment. For each category, the total number of problems is put in parentheses, and the maximum number of entailments that can be proved by the list of provers are highlighted in bold. As can be seen, Songbird can prove more entailments than all the other tools. In particular, we are the best in almost categories, except for skip-list. However, in this category, we are behind only Spen, which has been specialized for skip lists [13]. Our technique might require more effective generalization to handle the unproven skip-list examples.

In Fig. 11(b), we make a detailed comparison among Songbird and other provers. Specifically, the first column ($✓_{sb}✗_{o}$) shows the number of entailments

[2] We exclude the set of invalid entailments because some evaluated proof techniques, such as [4,10], aim to only prove validity of entailments.

[3] Available at https://github.com/mihasighi/smtcomp14-sl/tree/master/bench.

that Songbird can prove valid whereas the others cannot. The second column ($\text{✗}_{sb}\,\text{✓}_{o}$) reports the number of entailments that can be proved by other tools, but not by Songbird. The last two columns list the number of entailments that both Songbird and others can ($\text{✓}_{sb}\,\text{✓}_{o}$) or cannot ($\text{✗}_{sb}, \text{✗}_{o}$) prove. We would like to highlight that our prover efficiently proves *all* entailments proved by Cyclist (resp. Sleek) in *approximately half the time*, i.e., 20.92 vs 46.40 s for 116 entailments, in comparison with Cyclist (resp. 8.38 vs 15.50 s for 88 entailments, in comparison with Sleek). In addition, there are 13 (resp. 41) entailments that can be proved by our tool, but *not* by Cyclist (resp. Sleek). Furthermore, our Songbird outperforms Spen and Slide by more than 65 % of the total entailments, thanks to the proposed mutual induction proof technique.

Secondly, we would like to highlight the efficiency of *mutual induction* in our proof technique via a comparison between Songbird and its variant Songbird_{SI}, which exploits only induction hypotheses found within a *single* proof path. This mimics the structural induction technique which explores induction hypotheses in the same proof path. For this purpose, we designed a new entailment benchmark, namely slrd_ind, whose problems are more complex than those in the slrd_entl benchmark. For example, our handcrafted benchmark[4] contains an entailment $\mathsf{lsEven}(x, y) * y \mapsto z * \mathsf{lsEven}(z, t) \vdash \exists u.\, \mathsf{lsEven}(x, u) * u \mapsto t$ with the predicate $\mathsf{lsEven}(x, y)$ denoting list segments with even length. This entailment was inspired by the entailment $\mathsf{lsEven}(x, y) * \mathsf{lsEven}(y, z) \vdash \mathsf{lsEven}(x, z)$ in the problem 11.tst.smt2 of slrd_entl, contributed by team Cyclist. Note that entailments in our benchmark were constructed on the same set of linked list predicates provided in slrd_entl, comprised of regular singly linked lists (ll), linked lists with even or odd length (ll-even/odd) and linked list segments which are left- or right-recursively defined (ll-left/right). We also use a new ll2 list segment predicate whose structure is similar to the predicate tmp in our motivating example. In addition, problems in the misc. category involve all aforementioned linked list predicates.

As shown in Fig. 12, Songbird_{SI} is able to prove nearly 70 % of the total entailments, which is slightly better than Cyclist[5], whereas Songbird, with full capability of mutual induction, can prove the *whole* set of entailments. This result

Category		Cyclist	Songbird_{SI}	Songbird
ll/ll2	(24)	18	22	24
ll-even/odd	(20)	8	17	20
ll-left/right	(20)	12	10	20
misc.	(32)	17	16	32
Total	(96)	55	65	96

Fig. 12. Comparison on slrd_ind benchmark

[4] The full benchmark is available at http://loris-5.d2.comp.nus.edu.sg/songbird/.

[5] We do not list other provers in Fig. 12 as they cannot prove any problems in slrd_ind.

is encouraging as it shows the usefulness and essentials of our mutual explicit induction proof technique in proving SL entailments.

7 Conclusion

We have proposed a novel induction technique and developed a proof system for automatically proving entailments in a fragment of SL with general inductive predicates. In essence, we show that induction can be performed on the size of the heap models of SL entailments. The implication is that, during automatic proof construction, the goal entailment and entailments derived in the entire proof tree can be used as hypotheses to prove other derived entailments, and vice versa. This novel proposal has opened up the feasibility of mutual induction in automatic proof, leading to shorter proof trees being built. In future, we would like to develop a verification system on top of the prover Songbird, so that our *mutual explicit induction* technique can be effectively used for automated verification of memory safety in imperative programs.

Acknowledgement. We would like to thank the anonymous reviewers for their valuable and helpful feedback. The first author would like to thank Dr. James Brotherston for the useful discussion about the cyclic proof. This work has been supported by NUS Research Grant R-252-000-553-112. Ton Chanh and Wei-Ngan are partially supported by MoE Tier-2 grant MOE2013-T2-2-146.

References

1. Berdine, J., Calcagno, C., O'Hearn, P.W.: A decidable fragment of separation logic. In: Lodaya, K., Mahajan, M. (eds.) FSTTCS 2004. LNCS, vol. 3328, pp. 97–109. Springer, Heidelberg (2004). doi:10.1007/978-3-540-30538-5_9
2. Berdine, J., Calcagno, C., O'Hearn, P.W.: Symbolic execution with separation logic. In: Yi, K. (ed.) APLAS 2005. LNCS, vol. 3780, pp. 52–68. Springer, Heidelberg (2005). doi:10.1007/11575467_5
3. Bozga, M., Iosif, R., Perarnau, S.: Quantitative separation logic and programs with lists. J. Autom. Reason. **45**(2), 131–156 (2010)
4. Brotherston, J., Distefano, D., Petersen, R.L.: Automated cyclic entailment proofs in separation logic. In: Bjørner, N., Sofronie-Stokkermans, V. (eds.) CADE 2011. LNCS (LNAI), vol. 6803, pp. 131–146. Springer, Heidelberg (2011). doi:10.1007/978-3-642-22438-6_12
5. Brotherston, J., Gorogiannis, N.: Cyclic abduction of inductively defined safety and termination preconditions. In: Müller-Olm, M., Seidl, H. (eds.) SAS 2014. LNCS, vol. 8723, pp. 68–84. Springer, Heidelberg (2014). doi:10.1007/978-3-319-10936-7_5
6. Brotherston, J., Gorogiannis, N., Kanovich, M.I., Rowe, R.: Model checking for symbolic-heap separation logic with inductive predicates. In: Symposium on Principles of Programming Languages (POPL), pp. 84–96 (2016)
7. Brotherston, J., Gorogiannis, N., Petersen, R.L.: A generic cyclic theorem prover. In: Jhala, R., Igarashi, A. (eds.) APLAS 2012. LNCS, vol. 7705, pp. 350–367. Springer, Heidelberg (2012). doi:10.1007/978-3-642-35182-2_25

8. Bundy, A.: The automation of proof by mathematical induction. In: Handbook of Automated Reasoning, vol. 2, pp. 845–911 (2001)
9. Calcagno, C., Distefano, D., O'Hearn, P.W., Yang, H.: Compositional shape analysis by means of bi-abduction. In: Symposium on Principles of Programming Languages (POPL), pp. 289–300 (2009)
10. Chin, W., David, C., Nguyen, H.H., Qin, S.: Automated verification of shape, size and bag properties via user-defined predicates in separation logic. Sci. Comput. Program. (SCP) **77**(9), 1006–1036 (2012)
11. Chu, D., Jaffar, J., Trinh, M.: Automatic induction proofs of data-structures in imperative programs. In: Conference on Programming Language Design and Implementation (PLDI), pp. 457–466 (2015)
12. Cook, B., Haase, C., Ouaknine, J., Parkinson, M., Worrell, J.: Tractable reasoning in a fragment of separation logic. In: Katoen, J.-P., König, B. (eds.) CONCUR 2011. LNCS, vol. 6901, pp. 235–249. Springer, Heidelberg (2011). doi:10.1007/978-3-642-23217-6_16
13. Enea, C., Lengál, O., Sighireanu, M., Vojnar, T.: Compositional entailment checking for a fragment of separation logic. In: Garrigue, J. (ed.) APLAS 2014. LNCS, vol. 8858, pp. 314–333. Springer, Heidelberg (2014). doi:10.1007/978-3-319-12736-1_17
14. Enea, C., Sighireanu, M., Wu, Z.: On automated lemma generation for separation logic with inductive definitions. In: Finkbeiner, B., Pu, G., Zhang, L. (eds.) ATVA 2015. LNCS, vol. 9364, pp. 80–96. Springer, Heidelberg (2015). doi:10.1007/978-3-319-24953-7_7
15. Infer: A tool to detect bugs in Android and iOS apps before they ship. http://fbinfer.com/. Accessed 27 May 2016
16. Iosif, R., Rogalewicz, A., Simacek, J.: The tree width of separation logic with recursive definitions. In: Bonacina, M.P. (ed.) CADE 2013. LNCS (LNAI), vol. 7898, pp. 21–38. Springer, Heidelberg (2013). doi:10.1007/978-3-642-38574-2_2
17. Iosif, R., Rogalewicz, A., Vojnar, T.: Deciding entailments in inductive separation logic with tree automata. In: Cassez, F., Raskin, J.-F. (eds.) ATVA 2014. LNCS, vol. 8837, pp. 201–218. Springer, Heidelberg (2014). doi:10.1007/978-3-319-11936-6_15
18. Le, Q.L., Gherghina, C., Qin, S., Chin, W.-N.: Shape analysis via second-order bi-abduction. In: Biere, A., Bloem, R. (eds.) CAV 2014. LNCS, vol. 8559, pp. 52–68. Springer, Heidelberg (2014). doi:10.1007/978-3-319-08867-9_4
19. Moura, L., Bjørner, N.: Z3: an efficient SMT solver. In: Ramakrishnan, C.R., Rehof, J. (eds.) TACAS 2008. LNCS, vol. 4963, pp. 337–340. Springer, Heidelberg (2008). doi:10.1007/978-3-540-78800-3_24
20. Nguyen, H.H., Chin, W.-N.: Enhancing program verification with lemmas. In: Gupta, A., Malik, S. (eds.) CAV 2008. LNCS, vol. 5123, pp. 355–369. Springer, Heidelberg (2008). doi:10.1007/978-3-540-70545-1_34
21. Nguyen, H.H., David, C., Qin, S., Chin, W.-N.: Automated verification of shape and size properties via separation logic. In: Cook, B., Podelski, A. (eds.) VMCAI 2007. LNCS, vol. 4349, pp. 251–266. Springer, Heidelberg (2007). doi:10.1007/978-3-540-69738-1_18
22. O'Hearn, P., Reynolds, J., Yang, H.: Local reasoning about programs that alter data structures. In: Fribourg, L. (ed.) CSL 2001. LNCS, vol. 2142, pp. 1–19. Springer, Heidelberg (2001). doi:10.1007/3-540-44802-0_1
23. Pérez, J.A.N., Rybalchenko, A.: Separation logic + superposition calculus = heap theorem prover. In: Conference on Programming Language Design and Implementation (PLDI), pp. 556–566 (2011)

24. Navarro Pérez, J.A., Rybalchenko, A.: Separation logic modulo theories. In: Shan, C. (ed.) APLAS 2013. LNCS, vol. 8301, pp. 90–106. Springer, Heidelberg (2013). doi:10.1007/978-3-319-03542-0_7
25. Piskac, R., Wies, T., Zufferey, D.: Automating separation logic using SMT. In: Sharygina, N., Veith, H. (eds.) CAV 2013. LNCS, vol. 8044, pp. 773–789. Springer, Heidelberg (2013). doi:10.1007/978-3-642-39799-8_54
26. Piskac, R., Wies, T., Zufferey, D.: Automating separation logic with trees and data. In: Biere, A., Bloem, R. (eds.) CAV 2014. LNCS, vol. 8559, pp. 711–728. Springer, Heidelberg (2014). doi:10.1007/978-3-319-08867-9_47
27. Qiu, X., Garg, P., Stefanescu, A., Madhusudan, P.: Natural proofs for structure, data, and separation. In: Conference on Programming Language Design and Implementation (PLDI), pp. 231–242 (2013)
28. Reynolds, J.C.: An introduction to separation logic - Lecture Notes for the PhD Fall School on Logics and Semantics of State, Copenhagen (2008). http://www.cs.cmu.edu/jcr/copenhagen08.pdf. Accessed 20 Jan 2016
29. Reynolds, J.C.: Intuitionistic reasoning about shared mutable data structure. In: Millennial Perspectives in Computer Science, Palgrave, pp. 303–321 (2000)
30. Reynolds, J.C.: Separation Logic: A logic for shared mutable data structures. In: Symposium on Logic in Computer Science (LICS), pp. 55–74 (2002)
31. Sighireanu, M., Cok, D.R.: Report on SL-COMP 2014. J. Satisf. Boolean Model. Comput. **9**, 173–186 (2016)
32. Ta, Q.T., Le, T.C., Khoo, S.C., Chin, W.N.: Automated mutual explicit induction proof in separation logic. arXiv:1609.00919 (2016)

Finite Model Finding Using the Logic of Equality with Uninterpreted Functions

Amirhossein Vakili(✉) and Nancy A. Day

Cheriton School of Computer Science, University of Waterloo, Waterloo, Canada
{avakili,nday}@uwaterloo.ca

Abstract. The problem of finite model finding, finding a satisfying model for a set of first-order logic formulas for a finite scope, is an important step in many verification techniques. In MACE-style solvers, the problem is mapped directly to a SAT problem. We investigate an alternative solution of mapping the problem to the logic of equality with uninterpreted functions (EUF), a decidable logic with many well-supported tools (*e.g.,* SMT solvers). EUF reasoners take advantage of the typed functional structures found in the formulas to improve performance. The challenge is that EUF reasoning is not inherently finite scope. We present an algorithm for mapping a finite model finding problem to an equisatisfiable EUF problem. We present results that show our method has better overall performance than existing tools on a range of problems.

1 Introduction

Finite model finding is the problem of finding a satisfying model of a set of first-order logic (FOL) formulas for a finite scope. The utility of finite model finding in verification has been well-established with the popularity of the Alloy Analyzer [11], a tool for writing declarative models in relational algebra, and its Kodkod library for finding satisfying instances [22]. Finite scope analysis has been used in a range of applications, such as code analysis [21], test case generation [12], repairing invalid HTML code [19], temporal logic model checking [23], and counterexample generation for higher-order logic [6].

Approaches to finite model finding have followed two main styles: the MACE-style [14], which reduces the problem to SAT and uses a SAT solver; and the SEM-style [24], which develops an algorithm (usually a backtracking algorithm) for searching for a model explicitly. State-of-the-art tools for model finding are: Kodkod [22], Mace4 [16], and Paradox [8]. Kodkod is a MACE-style solver used in the Alloy Analyzer. Mace4 is used more in the mathematical community and is written in the SEM-style (unlike its predecessor Mace2, which is in the MACE-style). Paradox is a MACE-style solver.

The contribution of our work is the introduction of a new approach to finite model finding in the MACE-style, based on a reduction to the problem of satisfiability in the logic of equality with uninterpreted functions (EUF) [1], and the use of an SMT (satisfiability modulo theories) solver [4]. EUF is many-sorted (typed), quantifier-free first-order logic with equality. It is a decidable logic and

J. Fitzgerald et al. (Eds.): FM 2016, LNCS 9995, pp. 677–693, 2016.
DOI: 10.1007/978-3-319-48989-6_41

its complexity is NP-complete [1,13]. EUF has advanced solving implementations in many SMT solvers. SMT solvers are first-order logic reasoning tools with an integrated set of decision procedures that use the standard interpretations for various types. We use the SMT solver Z3 [17].

Reynolds *et al.* [18] wrote a SEM-style prover for finite model finding on top of the SMT solver CVC4 [2]. The goal of Reynolds' approach was to find finite satisfying solutions that the SMT solver deemed unsolvable. In our approach, we use the SMT solver directly to solve the whole problem (as in the MACE-style), in contrast to Reynolds approach, which creates a SEM-style solver integrated into the SMT architecture.

As pointed out by Kroening and Strichman [13], despite the fact that the complexity of EUF is the same as propositional logic, there are two reasons to use EUF rather than propositional logic: (1) convenience in modelling, and (2) performance. The larger vocabulary provided by EUF, *i.e.*, equality, uninterpreted functions and types, allows for more concise models. In the approaches that reduce the finite model finding problem to SAT, the structure of types and functions is not well preserved in propositional logic. Since we are reducing the problem to EUF, this structure is retained and exploited in the EUF solving process, which often results in better performance; moreover, translation to EUF eliminates some simplification steps such as term flattening.

The challenge, however, is that problems in EUF are not inherently finite, *i.e.*, the solver does not search only for finite models of a certain scope. To make our approach work, we add *range formulas* that force the solver to consider only instances of a certain finite scope. We re-use many of the techniques found in MACE-style provers, including symmetry breaking, to reduce the model space that must be searched.

The contributions of our work are:

1. Introduction of range formulas to force an EUF solver to search for solutions of an exact scope.
2. A Java library, called Fortress[1], for mapping typed FOL problems (including those specified in the input format TPTP) to SMT-LIB [3] (the standard input language for SMT solvers) for a finite scope.
3. Demonstration that on benchmark problems, overall, Fortress has better performance than Kodkod, Mace4, Paradox, and Reynolds. We show the most improvement on problems that include functions.
4. Demonstration that re-modelling some benchmark problems using the more convenient modelling approach with typed functions results in better performance in Fortress.
5. A comparison of the methods of all the tools to discuss in detail why using an SMT solver is preferable to mapping the problem directly to SAT.

In the next section, we provide some brief background on finite model finding. In Sect. 3, we show a simple example of how our approach works, and then we

[1] Available at: rebrand.ly/fortress.

define our translation in Sect. 4. Section 5 briefly overviews Fortress' implementation. Our results on benchmarks are presented in Sect. 6. Section 7 demonstrates the advantages of using typed functions, and it is followed by a detailed comparison to related work in Sect. 8. The conclusion and future work are presented in Sect. 9.

2 Background

In typed[2] first-order logic (FOL), a *signature* Σ is a pair $\langle \Theta, F \rangle$ where Θ is a set of types, and F is a set of typed functional symbols. Every signature contains the type `Bool`, which represents the Boolean type. A functional symbol $f \in F$ that takes as input n arguments of types $\theta_1, \ldots, \theta_n$ respectively and produces output type is θ is denoted as $f : \theta_1 \times \cdots \times \theta_n \rightarrow \theta$. A constant c of type θ, denoted by $c : \theta$, is a functional symbol that has no inputs. In FOL, predicate symbols are functional symbols whose output type is `Bool`. For example, a relational symbol $R : A \times A \rightarrow \texttt{Bool}$ denotes a binary relational symbol over type A. Figure 1 shows the rules for constructing the formulas and terms of FOL. The notation $t : \theta$ denotes that the type of the term t is θ. We use this notation only if the type of a term is not obvious from the context.

Formulas

$$\begin{aligned} \Phi &::= \top \mid \bot \mid p \\ &::= R(t_1 : \theta_1, \ldots, t_n : \theta_n) \\ &::= \neg\Phi \mid \Phi_1 \wedge \Phi_2 \mid \Phi_1 \vee \Phi_2 \mid \Phi_1 \Rightarrow \Phi_2 \mid \Phi_1 \Leftrightarrow \Phi_2 \\ &::= \exists v : \theta \bullet \Phi \mid \forall v : \theta \bullet \Phi \quad \text{where } v \in V \end{aligned}$$

Terms

$$\begin{aligned} t : \theta &::= v : \theta \quad \text{where } v \in V \\ &::= c : \theta \\ &::= f(t_1 : \theta_n, \ldots, t_n : \theta_n) \end{aligned}$$

Fig. 1. Syntax of FOL over signature $\Sigma = \langle \Theta, F \rangle$ and set of typed variables V, where $c : \theta$, $p : \texttt{Bool}$, $R : \theta_1 \times \cdots \times \theta_n \rightarrow \texttt{Bool}$, and $f : \theta_1 \times \cdots \times \theta_n \rightarrow \theta$ are in F.

A *structure* (also called a *model* or an *instance*) M over a signature $\Sigma = \langle \Theta, F \rangle$ is a pair $\langle \mathcal{U}, .^M \rangle$, where $\mathcal{U}$, the universe of M, is a collection of mutually disjoint non-empty sets, and $.^M$ is a mapping with the following properties:

1. for each θ in Θ, $\theta^M \in \mathcal{U}$,
2. for each two distinct θ_1 and θ_2, $\theta_1^M \cap \theta_2^M = \emptyset$,
3. for each $p : \texttt{Bool}$ in F, $p^M \in \{\texttt{True}, \texttt{False}\}$,
4. for each $R : \theta_1 \times \cdots \times \theta_n \rightarrow \texttt{Bool}$, R^M is a subset of $\theta_1^M \times \cdots \times \theta_n^M$,
5. for each $c : \theta$ in F, $c^M \in \theta^M$,
6. for each $f : \theta_1 \times \cdots \times \theta_n \rightarrow \theta$, f^M is a total function from $\theta_1^M \times \cdots \times \theta_n^M$ to θ^M.

[2] We use "type" and "sort" interchangeably in this paper.

We assume the standard semantics for FOL, and use $M \models \Phi$ to denote that M is a structure that *satisfies* the formula Φ [10], meaning that Φ is true in structure M. We also use the notation $M \models \Gamma$, where Γ is a set of FOL formulas, to denote that M satisfies all the formulas in Γ.

Given a set of FOL formulas Γ over signature $\Sigma = \langle \Theta, F \rangle$, and a function `bounds` from Θ to natural numbers, the *finite model finding problem* means determining if Γ has a satisfying structure M in which for every θ in Θ, the size of the set assigned to θ by M is the finite number $\texttt{bounds}(\theta)$ (*i.e.*, $|\theta^M| = \texttt{bounds}(\theta)$). For each type θ, $\texttt{bounds}(\theta)$ is called the *size of the scope* or just the scope. M is finite because the types in M are each of a fixed, finite, known size. In untyped FOL, there is only one type and therefore only one scope is relevant.

The *logic of equality with uninterpreted functions*, EUF, is a subset of FOL without quantifiers and variables, that includes the equality predicate (usually written in infix form) with its standard interpretation. Checking whether a finite set of EUF formulas has a satisfying structure is decidable and its complexity is NP-complete [13].

3 Small Example

In this section, we present a small example to illustrate the challenge in mapping the finite model finding problem to EUF.

Suppose $\Sigma = \langle \{A, B\}, \{f : A \rightarrow B\} \rangle$ is a signature, and we are given the following formula:

$$\forall x, y : A \bullet \ f(x) = f(y) \ \Rightarrow \ x = y \tag{1}$$

The functional symbol f maps elements of A to B and the formula in Eq. 1 states that every element of A is mapped to a unique element of B; in other words, no two distinct elements of A are mapped to the same element of B. We are interested in checking if this formula has a model where the size of A is 3 and the size of B is 2. Equation 1 means that in every finite model, the size of B must be greater or equal to the size of A; therefore, there is no model with the scopes proposed. To reduce this problem to checking the satisfiability of a set of EUF formulas, we introduce three new constant symbols of type A, a_1, a_2, a_3, two new constant symbols of type B, b_1, b_2, and generate a set of constraints stating that these new constants are distinct:

$$\{a_1 \neq a_2, \ a_1 \neq a_3, \ a_2 \neq a_3, \ b_1 \neq b_2\} \tag{2}$$

Using the introduced constants, we expand each quantifier by substituting the new constants for the variables. This step generates a set of EUF formulas:

$$\{f(a_i) = f(a_j) \Rightarrow a_i = a_j \mid 1 \leq i, j \leq 3\} \tag{3}$$

If we pass the formulas in Eqs. 2 and 3 to an EUF solver, such as an SMT solver, and check for their satisfiability, the solver finds a satisfying model where B has three elements, rather than B having two elements as required. This example shows that expanding quantifiers is not sufficient to reduce the finite model finding problem to EUF satisfiability checking. One might think a remedy to this problem is by adding a formula that states the only members of B are b_1 and b_2:

$$\forall b : B \bullet\ b = b_1 \vee b = b_2$$

This formula has a quantifier, therefore it is not part of EUF and its universal quantifier needs to be expanded with b_1 and b_2:

$$b_1 = b_1 \vee b_1 = b_2, \quad b_2 = b_1 \vee b_2 = b_2$$

This formula is a tautology and therefore, adding it has no effect.

Our solution to this problem is as follows: instead of adding a constraint that ensures B has only two elements, we add constraints, which we call *range formulas*, that guarantee the "effect" of B having two elements. In this example, the effect of B having two elements is that for all $a : A$, $f(a)$ must be either b_1 or b_2:

$$\forall a : A \bullet\ f(a) = b_1 \vee f(a) = b_2 \tag{4}$$

Expanding this equation results in the following set of EUF formulas:

$$\{f(a_i) = b_1 \vee f(a_i) = b_2 \mid 1 \leq i \leq 3\}$$

An EUF solver shows that this set of formulas along with the constraints of Eqs. 2 and 3 are unsatisfiable.

A range formula for a functional symbol ensures that an EUF solver does not generate an instance that is outside the provided scope:

Definition 1. For a finite type $\theta = \{e_1, .., e_n\}$ and a functional symbol $f : T_1 \times .. \times T_m \rightarrow \theta$, the following is the range formula that we add to ensure that the values assigned to f by an EUF solver are within the specified scope of θ:

$$\forall v_1 : T_1, .., v_m : T_m \bullet\ f(v_1, .., v_m) = e_1 \vee .. \vee f(v_1, .., v_m) = e_n$$

4 Translation to EUF Logic

Suppose Γ is a set of FOL formulas over signature $\Sigma = \langle \Theta, F \rangle$, and bounds is a function from Θ to natural numbers. The finite model finding problem means determining if Γ has a finite model M where for each type θ in Θ, the size of θ^M is equal to $\mathsf{bounds}(\theta)$. Our translation to EUF consists of four steps:

1. Normalize each formula in Γ
2. Generate the universe
3. Add range formulas
4. Ground each normalized formula

Step (3) is the main novel contribution of our paper along with the idea of using EUF solvers in the MACE-style for the finite model finding problem. For the other steps leading up to EUF, we borrow the best practices from existing solvers and include their description here for completeness. Next, we explain each step in detail and illustrate the translation using the following example:

Example 1. Let $\Sigma = \langle\{A\}, \{f : A \rightarrow A\}\rangle$ be a signature. We want to check if the following two formulas have a model where the size of A ($\texttt{bounds}(A)$) is 3 by translating it to an equisatisfiable set of EUF formulas.

1. $\forall x, y : A \bullet\ f(x) = f(y) \ \Rightarrow\ x = y$
2. $\exists y : A \bullet\ \forall x : A \bullet\ f(x) \neq y$

The first constraint states that f is a one-to-one mapping from A to itself. The second constraint states that the range of f is a proper subset of A. These two formulas are only satisfiable by an infinite model since it is not possible to have a one-to-one mapping from a finite set to one of its proper subsets.

Step 1 - Normalize. The normalization step consists of the following transformations: (1) put each formula in prenex normal form, and (2) skolemize and remove existential quantifiers. Applying these transformations to the formulas of Example 1 results in the following two formulas:

1. $\forall x, y : A \bullet\ \neg(f(x) = f(y)) \vee x = y$
2. $\forall x : A \bullet\ f(x) \neq sk$

In the second formula, sk is a constant of type A that is introduced as the result of skolemization. After normalization, each formula is either quantifier-free or it is of the following form $\forall x_1 : \theta_1, \ldots, x_n : \theta_n \bullet\ \Psi$, where Ψ is quantifier-free. The complexity of this step is linear with respect to the size of the FOL formulas.

Step 2 - Generate Universe. In this step, for each type θ in Θ, we generate $\texttt{bounds}(\theta)$ constants of type θ, and we assert that these constants are mutually distinct. The generated constants at this step are fresh, do not appear anywhere in Γ, and constitute the universe. In Step 3 (adding range formulas), the fact that the introduced constants do not appear in Γ allows us to generate optimized range formulas based on symmetry breaking.

In Example 1, we declare constants a_1, a_2, a_3 of type A and add a constraint to ensure that these constants are mutually distinct. The complexity of this step is linear with respect to the size of the provided bounds[3].

Step 3 - Add Range Formulas: EUF solvers check for the satisfiability of a set of quantifier-free formulas without putting any restrictions on the number of elements assigned to each type. To ensure that the elements of a type θ in a model generated by an EUF solver are exactly the ones declared in Step 2, we add range formulas for constants and functional symbols stating that their values must be equal to the elements of the universe of that type. As mentioned in Sect. 3, the range formulas allow us to reduce the finite model finding problem to EUF solving. The complexity of adding range formulas is exponential with respect to the arity of the functional symbols.

In Example 1, the following are the range constraints:

$$sk = a_1 \vee sk = a_2 \vee sk = a_3, \quad f(a_1) = a_1 \vee f(a_1) = a_2 \vee f(a_1) = a_3,$$
$$f(a_2) = a_1 \vee f(a_2) = a_2 \vee f(a_2) = a_3, \quad f(a_3) = a_1 \vee f(a_3) = a_2 \vee f(a_3) = a_3$$

[3] In SMT-LIB, this constraint is written simply as: (distinct a_1 a_2 a_3).

We use Claessen and Sörensson's symmetry breaking technique [8] to reduce the number of range formulas needed. Since the values a_1, a_2, and a_3 do not appear in the original formulas, one can assume an ordering on them and reduce the range formulas to the following:

$$\begin{aligned} sk &= a_1, \\ f(a_1) &= a_1 \lor f(a_1) = a_2, \\ f(a_2) = a_1 \lor f(a_2) &= a_2 \lor f(a_2) = a_3, \\ f(a_3) = a_1 \lor f(a_3) &= a_2 \lor f(a_3) = a_3 \end{aligned}$$

where the first term is required to be a certain constant and the subsequent terms have gradually more freedom in their possible values. Using symmetry breaking to reduce the number of range formulas does not reduce the complexity of this step.

Step 4 - Ground Formulas. The last step of our translation is grounding: instantiating each universally quantified formula with the generated universe of Step 2. As we substitute different constants for variables that are universally quantified, we immediately simplify the generated formulas based on literals that are discovered and the fact that the elements of the universe are mutually distinct. For example, in the formula $\forall x, y : A \bullet \ f(x) \neq f(y) \lor x = y$, when x and y are substituted with a_1, the generated formula $f(a_1) \neq f(a_1) \lor a_1 = a_1$ is simplified to $\top$ and it is discarded. Also, when x is substituted with a_3 and y with a_2, the generated formula $f(a_3) \neq f(a_2) \lor a_3 = a_2$ is simplified to $f(a_3) \neq f(a_2)$ since we know that $a_2 \neq a_3$. Moreover, we have a syntactic ordering on formulas where $t = s$ is considered to be the same as $s = t$ for any two terms. This ordering allows us to remove some redundant formulas that are generated during the grounding step. The result of grounding Example 1 is the following set of formulas:

$$\begin{aligned} f(a_1) \neq f(a_2), \quad f(a_1) \neq f(a_3), \quad f(a_2) \neq f(a_3), \\ f(a_1) \neq sk, \quad f(a_2) \neq sk, \quad f(a_3) \neq sk \end{aligned}$$

The complexity of this step is exponential with respect to the number of nested universal quantifiers.

We omit the proof that checking the satisfiability of the generated EUF formulas from Steps 3 and 4 is equivalent to checking if the original FOL formulas have a finite model where the size of each type θ is $\texttt{bounds}(\theta)$ since it is quite straightforward.

5 Implementation

Fortress is a Java library for creating typed first-order logic formulas and producing finite model finding problems in SMT-LIB based on the translation of Sect. 4. Besides the API, we parse a subset of TPTP. In Fortress, formulas are represented as typed lambda calculus terms and all type checking is done at this level for generality. Once type checked, FOL terms are converted to a more compact representation suitable for FOL.

There are two types of simplifications/optimizations that can be applied: (1) simplifications on FOL terms not specific to finite model finding, such as positive and negative propagations [16], (2) optimizations specific to finite model finding, such as symmetry breaking constraints [8]. Since SMT solvers do an excellent job at type 1 above, these are not implemented in Fortress. However, since SMT solvers do not treat uninterpreted types as finite sets, optimizations of type 2 are implemented in Fortress. We have flags to enable symmetry breaking and our experiments have shown that SMT solvers cannot infer symmetries for finite scope analysis and therefore, they need to be explicitly implemented.

6 Results

We compared our approach to Kodkod (version 2.1 with Minisat), Alloy (version 4.2 with Minisat), Mace4, and Paradox (version 4). We used Z3 (version 4.4.2) as our backend EUF solver for Fortress. We compared the performance of the tools on a set of TPTP benchmarks [20] that were originally used by Torlak and Jackson in [22]. We tested on increased scopes for some benchmarks compared the results reported in [22]. Fortress accepts TPTP as input. Torlak and Jackson had manually translated TPTP examples to Kodkod and we used their translated versions when comparing to Kodkod. Paradox accepts TPTP as input, and Mace4 comes with a tool (tptp_to_ladr [15]) that translates TPTP to its input format. To compare with Alloy, we developed a simple translator from TPTP to Alloy. We included Alloy in this comparison because it is equivalent to using Kodkod without special support for partial instances (see Sect. 8).

All of these benchmarks are unsat: they do not have finite models with respect to the provided scope sizes. Unsatisfiable cases are better for the comparison of different tools because they are usually much harder than satisfiable ones. These benchmark problems are all untyped and some contain functions.

Table 1 presents the performance of all tools. For Fortress, the performance numbers include both the time for translation and the time for solving by Z3. All our experiments were run on an Intel®Core™i7-3667U machine running Ubuntu 14.04 64-bit with up to 7.5 GB of user memory. We used the solvers in their default mode, without any flags or a customized configuration. Entries marked by "–" indicate the analyses that did not finish within 1800 s (30 min). The shaded entries show the fastest solver for each benchmark (based on all scopes considered); where the difference was negligible we shaded the entries for multiple tools.

The last three rows of Table 1 summarize the performance of the solvers: Fortress produced the best results more often than any other tool. We also added up the performance time for all the benchmark problems. In this summation, we counted timeouts as 1800 s, which is preferential to all the other solvers since

Table 1. Benchmark problems (time in seconds)

	Scope Size	Fortress	Kodkod	Alloy	Mace4	Paradox
alg195	14	1	0	30	–	5
alg197	21	1	0	20	–	5
num378	21	2	0	–	0	6
infinity	5	0	1	1	0	0
	15	0	19	57	0	0
	25	0	704	–	0	0
alg212	6	0	5	3	0	0
	8	8	207	201	1	5
	10	563	–	–	6	81
com008	7	4	0	0	–	0
	9	48	0	0	–	0
	11	335	1	4	–	58
geo091	7	3	2	12	–	7
	9	9	29	33	–	279
	11	24	745	268	–	–
geo158	7	3	1	1	–	80
	9	9	28	17	–	–
	11	24	378	233	–	–
med009	7	2	0	0	19	0
	9	11	0	0	141	0
	11	31	0	0	139	0
num374	5	2	21	20	0	3
	6	38	262	358	6	147
	7	850	–	–	613	–
set943	7	1	4	66	–	55
	9	2	–	–	–	–
	11	2	–	–	–	–
set948	7	1	0	71	–	62
	9	2	0	–	–	–
	11	4	1	–	–	–
top020	7	2	1	2	0	0
	8	13	4	8	0	1
	9	509	13	16	0	17
Best out of 13		7	6	1	5	2
Total Time		2504	9637	15821	31525	15211
Total Time X		1X	3.85X	6.32X	12.59X	6.07X
		Fortress	Kodkod	Alloy	Mace4	Paradox

Fortress produced results without timing out on all benchmark problems. The total time for Fortress was 2504 s. The total times for Kodkod, Alloy, Mace4, and Paradox are respectively 3.85, 6.32, 12.59, and 6.07 times the total time of Fortress. This shows that, overall, Fortress is significantly better than the state-of-art solvers.

Table 2. Comparing SMT solvers (time in seconds)

	alg212	com008	geo091	med009	num374	top020
Scope Size	10	9	11	11	6	8
Z3	562	47	6	6	38	11
CVC4	—	69	45	53	—	3
MathSAT5	—	91	7	20	117	3

We also ran the benchmarks using the tool of Reynolds *et al.* [18], however since their tool solved only 2 of the 33 benchmark problems within the 30 min time threshold, its results are not presented in Table 1.

A closer look at the benchmarks show that Fortress excels at solving problems that have functional symbols, such as `geo091` and `set943`. Also, SMT solvers are capable of using terms with functions to simplify the reasoning steps by rewriting equalities, such as those found in `alg195` and `num378`. In some cases, this rewriting can solve the problem without performing any search.

Next, we compared the performance of multiple SMT solvers as backends for Fortress. We compared the performance of Z3, CVC4 (version 1.4), and MathSAT5 (version 5.3.10) [7] on six of the nontrivial benchmarks. Table 2 presents the time that it took for each SMT solver to check the satisfiability of the SMT-LIB models generated by Fortress. Our results show that Z3 is more effective in solving EUF formulas that are generated as the result of finite model finding than CVC4 and MathSAT5.

7 Exploiting Functions and Types

Functions vs. Relations. Functions and relations have the same expressive power: a total function $f : A \rightarrow B$ can be described as a relation $R_f : A \times B \rightarrow$ `Bool` with the following two constraints:

$$\forall a : A \bullet \exists b : B \bullet \; R_f(a, b), \tag{5}$$

$$\forall a : A, \; b, b' : B \bullet \; b = b' \vee \neg R_f(a, b) \vee \neg R_f(a, b') \tag{6}$$

where Constraint 5, a *totality definition*, states that every element of A is mapped to some element of B and Constraint 6, a *functional definition*, states that every element of A is not mapped to more than one element of B. Every relation is also a function: a relation maps every tuple to `True` or `False`, depending on if the tuple is in the relation or not. Kodkod and Paradox consider functions as relations accompanied by the totality and functional definitions. Since functions are built into EUF, Fortress does not need to add the totality and functional definitions, which simplifies the translation.

Another important benefit of functions is that they allow "true" skolemization. Skolemization is a technique to remove existential quantifiers by introducing

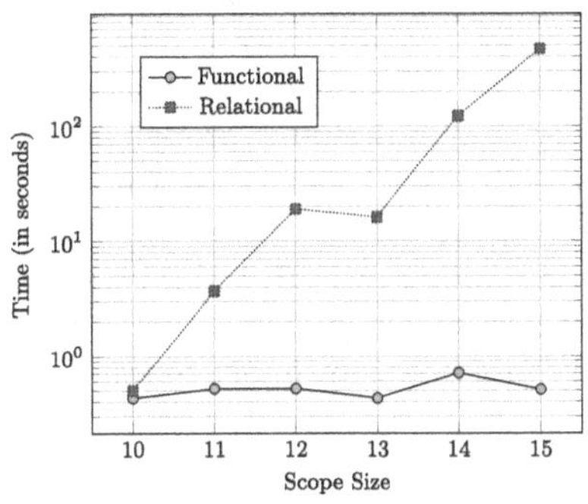

Fig. 2. Lists: Functions vs. relations

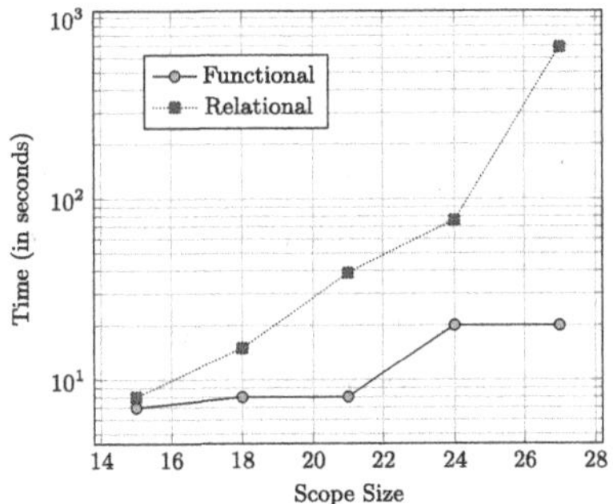

Fig. 3. MED009: Partitioning attributes

functions. For example, in the formula $\forall a : A, b : B \bullet \exists c : C \bullet P(a, b, c)$, skolemization results in the introduction of a functional symbol $sk : A \times B \to C$ and the formula $\forall a : A, b : B \bullet P(a, b, sk(a, b))$. In a language where functions are considered as relations, the skolem function sk needs to be accompanied by the totality definition $\forall a : A, b : B \bullet \exists c : C \bullet R_{sk}(a, b, c)$, which still has an existential quantifier.

To see the effect of using functions on the performance of the SMT solvers for finite model finding, in Fortress we modelled a simple theory of lists presented in [11] in both the functional and relational styles. Figure 2 compares the performance of Fortress for both approaches on different scopes. As depicted in this plot, functions improve the performance of Fortress. For the relational approach, the performance degrades rapidly as the scope size increases. For example, for the scope size 15, the relational approach takes over 7 min whereas in the functional approach the scope size of 30 is analyzed in less than 10 s (not shown on the plot).

Types. In an untyped system, all elements are in one set. For example, to model a database system for a university, `Person`, `Courses`, `IDs`, *etc.*, are entities that need to be modelled. In an untyped relational world, all these are in one set, and any mapping from one set to another, such as `id` : `Person` → `IDs`, becomes a relation that is only defined for people and needs totality and functional definitions. In typed systems, types *partition* the universe into subsets. These partitions have two benefits for finite model finding: (1) functions from one type to another can be defined succinctly, (2) in the grounding step (Step 4), a universal quantifier is only expanded for elements of the relevant type.

Together, functions and types can lead to concise modelling of some concepts. For example, in an untyped, relational language, to state that each `Person` in a university is either a `student`, `faculty`, or a `staff` member, three unary relations over the type `Person` must be declared. Four FOL constraints are required to express that these unary relations partition the set `Person`: every person belongs to one of the partitions, and three other constraints that ensure that no one belongs to more than one category. In a language with types and functions, the same concept can be modelled by introducing a new type `Role` with three elements `student`, `faculty`, `staff`, and introducing a function `attribute : Person` $\rightarrow$ `Role`. The totality and functional properties of `attribute` ensure that at least one role is assigned to each person and no one is assigned more than one role respectively. We call the values of the type `Role` *partitioning attributes*. In the relational style, the number of FOL formulas that are required to model partitioning attributes with N values is $\binom{N}{2} + 1$, which is quadratic with respect to the number of values. A functional approach eliminates the need for these constraints.

To evaluate the effect of using types and functions for partitioning, we manually translated a modified version of `med009` and compared the untyped, relational version to one with partitioning via types and functions, and compared the results. Figure 3 shows that performance of the functional approach is much better than the relational approach in Fortress.

8 Comparison with Related Work

In this section, we discuss the question of why our method of using EUF to solve FOL problems of finite scope has better overall performance than related solvers. First, we briefly present the method of each related solver and then present a number of points of comparison. Table 3 summarizes the options and methods supported by different finite model finders.

8.1 Related Solvers

Kodkod [22] is the MACE-style solver used in the Alloy Analyzer. Its Java API accepts untyped FOL formulas with relational constructs, such as join and transitive closure, as input. Functions must be transformed into relations having functional properties prior to using Kodkod. Once bounds are provided, Kodkod transforms transitive closure into a finite number of applications of join. Kodkod translates the finite model finding problem to SAT using the following steps: (1) detect symmetries in the model and compute symmetry breaking predicates, (2) allocate Boolean variables to represent relations, (3) expand quantified formulas

Table 3. Comparison of finite model finders

	Fortress	Kodkod	Paradox	Mace4	Reynolds
Solver	SMT	SAT	SAT	SEM	SEM/SMT
Input	TPTP, Java API	Java API	TPTP	LADR, TPTP	SMT-LIB
Types	YES	NO	NO	NO	YES
Functions	YES	NO	YES	YES	YES
Relational Ops	NO	YES	NO	NO	NO
Symmetry Breaking	Static	Static	Static	Dynamic	EUF
Partial Instances	NO	YES	NO	NO	NO

and make them into constraints over the allocated Boolean variables, and (4) transform the generated Boolean constraints to CNF form. Kodkod represents relations by sparse matrices of Boolean variables, and some of the relational operations become matrix operations. To simplify the translated formulas, Kodkod represents expanded quantified formulas as Compact Boolean Circuits (CBCs). This representation allows Kodkod to detect sharing structures in the grounded formulas and as a result, produce a more optimized CNF formula. Kodkod optimizes for explicitly provided partial instances by using this information during the translation to CNF step.

Paradox [8] is MACE-style prover, whose first step is to allocate a set of Boolean variables to represent each functional symbol. These Boolean variables encode each functional symbol as a relation. Then, every formula is "flattened": a process that removes nested function applications in a formula. For example, flattening the formula $\forall x \bullet f(g(x)) = x$ results in the formula $\forall x, t \bullet\ g(x) = t \Rightarrow f(t) = x$. At this point, the quantifiers of the given formulas are instantiated with all possible values from the universe resulting in a set of quantifier-free formulas. Each of these quantifier-free formulas are translated to propositional logic using the allocated Boolean variables. Since functional symbols are encoded as relations, Paradox adds "functional definition" constraints (every input is mapped to at most one value), and "totality definition" constraints (every input is mapped to some value). The result of this translation is a CNF formula that is passed to a SAT solver. To improve its performance, Paradox uses three techniques: (1) reduce the number of nested quantifiers by splitting disjunctions, (2) adding symmetry breaking constraints, and (3) inferring sorts (types) from the formulas to optimize the translation to SAT.

Mace4 [16] is a SEM-style finite model finder: it has its own backtracking search mechanism to try different assignments. To check if a set of FOL formulas has model of size n, Mace4 allocates "cells" that range from 0 to $n-1$ for each functional symbol. By skolemizing, every existential quantifier is removed. After skolemization, the universal quantifiers are expanded using the elements of $\{0, .., n-1\}$. The expanded formulas are now constraints over the allocated cells. The search mechanism assigns values to cells and checks if the assignment contradicts any of the expanded formulas. If a contradiction is detected, it backtracks; otherwise, the search goes on until either all cells are assigned or there is no possible assignment left. Mace4 uses the least number heuristic to detect some symmetries [25]. It also has a propagation mechanism that allows the search algorithm to prune its search tree.

Reynolds et al. [18] extended CVC4 with finite model finding capabilities so that for satisfiable instances of undecidable SMT logics a user could get a finite model and the SMT solver would not report "unknown". They combined finite model finding with decision procedures for built-in theories using the DPLL(T) architecture. Their approach does not introduce constants and can be classified as a SEM-style technique. According to our results, the method of Reynolds is not effective in finding finite models of a specific size when SMT theories are not used and the problem is unsatisfiable.

8.2 Comparison

Types. Since EUF is typed, in Fortress we benefit from types without requiring any special mechanism to infer sorts as is done in Paradox. In an untyped language, types can be mimicked by predicates and this is the approach used to translate problems in the typed Alloy language to Kodkod. Fortress' direct use of sorts can reduce the number of constraints generated in the quantifier expansion step because only elements of the correct sort are substituted into the formula for the quantified variable.

Functions. Kodkod does not support functions and assumes that functions have been converted to relations. In Fortress, we do not need to flatten the functional symbols or add the special functional definition and totality constraints required by Paradox since we are translating to a logic that includes functional symbols. As a result, there are fewer constraints in our representation in EUF and in that of Reynolds. Furthermore, the SMT solver can exploit the structure of these functions in its reasoning; in particular, terms that contain functional symbols are used for rewriting and simplification of the input problem. Examples of such techniques are *(near) assignment* and *(near) elimination* simplifications [16].

Relational Operators. The relational operators of Kodkod (e.g., join) do not increase its expressive power but they ease the modelling task. In FOL, the meaning of such operators can be represented through logical operations and quantifiers.

Symmetry Breaking Predicates. In most MACE-style finite model finders, such as Fortress, Kodkod, and Paradox, symmetry breaking is *static*: a set of constraints are added to the model to prevent the solver from exploring symmetric instances. Such constraints are called symmetry breaking predicates. Fortress uses the same symmetry breaking predicates as Paradox. In SEM-style finite model finding, the symmetry detection is built into the search algorithm and it is performed dynamically during the model finding stage [24].

Partial Instances. A partial instance for a set of FOL formulas is an explicit assignments of values to some variables. Kodkod supports explicitly provided partial instances. The first three case studies, `alg195`, `alg197`, and `num378` contain partial instances. Fortress and Kodkod outperform other tools on these case studies. Alloy uses Kodkod as its solver, and yet its performance on the first three case studies is not comparable to Kodkod because the partial instances are not explicitly given to Kodkod. In Fortress, we get good performance without any explicit support for partial instances. Partial instances in EUF are regular constraints that happen to be equalities of variables to values. SMT solvers have sophisticated mechanisms to propagate equalities and reduce the constraint solving time.

Exact Scopes. Currently, we only support analysis for a fixed scope, whereas in the Alloy Analyzer, a scope can be specified to include all instances of a certain size or smaller. Kodkod has this capability and it encodes the whole problem in one SAT formula. On the other hand, Mace4 has an iterative approach that solves each fixed scope separately.

Transitive Closure. Because the Alloy language includes the second-order transitive closure operator, Kodkod supports it and expands its definition using a brute force method (for a finite scope). Our method and the other solvers do not currently support transitive closure, but it would be straightforward to add a step to expand the transitive closure operator as is done in Kodkod.

8.3 Other Related Work

Baumgartner et al. reduce the finite model finding problem to function-free clause logic [5]. Similar to Kodkod, they represent functions as relations with functional constraints. As their results show, current function-free clause logic reasoners are not efficient enough. According to the authors, their results are "as good as" Paradox. We were not able to access their tool.

Elghazi and Taghdiri [9] translate Alloy to SMT-LIB to provide analysis of unbounded scopes. Alloy is translated to an undecidable logic, and SMT solvers are considered as FOL theorem provers that do not necessarily terminate.

9 Conclusion and Future Work

In this paper, we have shown that by reducing the finite model finding problem to the logic of equality with uninterpreted functions (EUF), we can use an SMT solver to find instances with better performance than existing approaches based on translations of the problem to SAT. In our translation, we add range formulas to force the SMT solver to search only for models of a finite scope. Our results show that maintaining the structure of problems (in this case, the types and function structure) can be beneficial in analysis procedures that need to explore exhaustively a model space (as opposed to flattening the problem before search). Our results also give credit to the excellent development of tools of the SMT-solver community.

With respect to modelling constructs, we would like to integrate with Alloy and extend our method to handle the transitive closure operator and a range of scopes. We are also considering taking SMT-LIB as input and the specification of scopes and creating SMT-LIB output. The challenge here is that we do not support all of SMT-LIB, *i.e.,* all of its built-in types (such as taking a finite scope for reals).

In the future, we plan to automate the inference of functional patterns, such as the partitioning attributes in Sect. 7, to improve the performance of Fortress. Also, our benchmarks show that despite the fact that our technique for finite model finding is superior to the state-of-the-art, there are some benchmarks that other tools solve faster than Fortress. We plan to explore a characterization of the problems that different methods are good at and create a *portfolio* solver for finite model finding.

References

1. Ackermann, W.: Solvable Cases of the Decision Problem. North Holland Publishing Company, Amsterdam (1954)
2. Barrett, C., Conway, C.L., Deters, M., Hadarean, L., Jovanović, D., King, T., Reynolds, A., Tinelli, C.: CVC4. In: Gopalakrishnan, G., Qadeer, S. (eds.) CAV 2011. LNCS, vol. 6806, pp. 171–177. Springer, Heidelberg (2011). doi:10.1007/978-3-642-22110-1_14
3. Barrett, C., Fontaine, P., Tinelli, C.: The SMT-LIB standard: Version 2.5. Technical report, Department of Computer Science, The University of Iowa (2015)
4. Barrett, C., Sebastiani, R., Seshia, S., Tinelli, C.: Satisfiability modulo theories, Frontiers. In: Artificial Intelligence and Applications, vol. 185, chap. 26, pp. 825–885. IOS Press, Amsterdam (2009)
5. Baumgartner, P., Fuchs, A., de Nivelle, H., Tinelli, C.: Computing finite models by reduction to function-free clause logic. J. Appl. Log. **7**(1), 58–74 (2009)
6. Blanchette, J.C., Nipkow, T.: Nitpick: a counterexample generator for higher-order logic based on a relational model finder. In: Kaufmann, M., Paulson, L.C. (eds.) ITP 2010. LNCS, vol. 6172, pp. 131–146. Springer, Heidelberg (2010). doi:10.1007/978-3-642-14052-5_11
7. Cimatti, A., Griggio, A., Schaafsma, B.J., Sebastiani, R.: The MathSAT5 SMT solver. In: Piterman, N., Smolka, S.A. (eds.) TACAS 2013. LNCS, vol. 7795, pp. 93–107. Springer, Heidelberg (2013). doi:10.1007/978-3-642-36742-7_7
8. Claessen, K., Sörensson, N.: New techniques that improve mace-style finite model finding. In: Proceedings of the CADE-19 Workshop: Model Computation - Principles, Algorithms, Applications (2003)
9. El Ghazi, A.A., Taghdiri, M.: Analyzing Alloy constraints using an SMT solver: a case study. In: International Workshop on Automated Formal Methods (2010)
10. Fitting, M.: First-Order Logic and Automated Theorem Proving. Springer, New York (1990)
11. Jackson, D.: Software Abstractions - Logic, Language, and Analysis. MIT Press, Cambridge (2012)
12. Khurshid, S., Marinov, D.: TestEra: specification-based testing of Java programs using SAT. Autom. Softw. Eng. **11**(4), 403–434 (2004)
13. Kroening, D., Strichman, O.: Decision Procedures: An Algorithmic Point of View. Springer, Heidelberg (2008)
14. McCune, W.: A Davis-Putnam program and its application to finite first-order model search: quasigroup existence problem. Technical report, Argonne National Laboratory (1994)
15. McCune, W.: Prover9 and Mace4 (2005–2010). http://www.cs.unm.edu/~mccune/prover9
16. McCune, W.: Mace4 reference manual and guide. CoRR cs.SC/0310055 (2003)
17. Moura, L., Bjørner, N.: Z3: an efficient SMT solver. In: Ramakrishnan, C.R., Rehof, J. (eds.) TACAS 2008. LNCS, vol. 4963, pp. 337–340. Springer, Heidelberg (2008). doi:10.1007/978-3-540-78800-3_24
18. Reynolds, A., Tinelli, C., Goel, A., Krstić, S.: Finite model finding in SMT. In: Sharygina, N., Veith, H. (eds.) CAV 2013. LNCS, vol. 8044, pp. 640–655. Springer, Heidelberg (2013). doi:10.1007/978-3-642-39799-8_42
19. Samimi, H.: Schfer, M., Artzi, S., Millstein, T., Tip, F., Hendren, L: Automated repair of HTML generation errors in PHP applications using string constraint solving. In: International Conference on Software Engineering (ICSE), pp. 277–287 (2012)

20. Sutcliffe, G.: The TPTP problem library and associated infrastructure: the FOF and CNF parts, v3.5.0. J. Autom. Reason. **43**(4), 337–362 (2009)
21. Taghdiri, M., Jackson, D.: Inferring specifications to detect errors in code. Autom. Softw. Eng. **14**(1), 87–121 (2007)
22. Torlak, E., Jackson, D.: Kodkod: a relational model finder. In: Grumberg, O., Huth, M. (eds.) TACAS 2007. LNCS, vol. 4424, pp. 632–647. Springer, Heidelberg (2007). doi:10.1007/978-3-540-71209-1_49
23. Vakili, A., Day, N.A.: Temporal logic model checking in alloy. In: Derrick, J., Fitzgerald, J., Gnesi, S., Khurshid, S., Leuschel, M., Reeves, S., Riccobene, E. (eds.) ABZ 2012. LNCS, vol. 7316, pp. 150–163. Springer, Heidelberg (2012). doi:10.1007/978-3-642-30885-7_11
24. Zhang, H., Zhang, J.: MACE4 and SEM: a comparison of finite model generators. In: Bonacina, M.P., Stickel, M.E. (eds.) Automated Reasoning and Mathematics. LNCS (LNAI), vol. 7788, pp. 101–130. Springer, Heidelberg (2013). doi:10.1007/978-3-642-36675-8_5
25. Zhang, J., Zhang, H.: Sem: A system for enumerating models. In: International Joint Conference on Artificial Intelligence (IJCAI)

GPUexplore 2.0: Unleashing GPU Explicit-State Model Checking

Anton Wijs[1], Thomas Neele[1,2(✉)], and Dragan Bošnački[1]

[1] Eindhoven University of Technology, Eindhoven, The Netherlands
{a.j.wijs,t.s.neele}@tue.nl
[2] University of Twente, Enschede, The Netherlands

Abstract. In earlier work, we were the first to investigate the potential of using graphics processing units (GPUs) to speed up explicit-state model checking. Back then, the conclusion was clearly that this potential exists, having measured speed-ups of around 10 times, compared to state-of-the-art single-core model checking. In this paper, we present a new version of our GPU model checker, GPUexplore. Since publication of our earlier work, we have identified and implemented several approaches to improve the performance of the model checker considerably. These include enhanced lock-less hashing of the states and improved thread synchronizations. We discuss experimental results that show the impact of both the progress in hardware in the last few years and our proposed optimisations. The new version of GPUexplore running on state-of-the-art hardware can be more than 100 times faster than a sequential implementation for large models and is on average eight times faster than the previous version of the tool running on the same hardware.

1 Introduction

Explicit-state model checking [1,8] is a push-button technique to formally verify the functional correctness of hardware and software models. It is performed by systematically exploring the state space implied by the model. The main drawback of model checking is the state space explosion problem: a linear growth of the model tends to lead to an exponential growth of the state space. Although traditionally, this meant that computer memory was the practical bottleneck, these days, with large amounts of memory at our disposal, scalability of the run time is often hindering our ability to reason about models in a reasonable amount of time.

One way to improve the run time of model checking is by exploiting the computing power of modern parallel architectures. Graphics processing units (GPUs) have a lot of potential in this respect: they can run thousands of threads in parallel and can offer a speed-up of several orders of magnitude. GPUs tend to have much less memory than modern computer systems, but the current trend is

A. Wijs—We gratefully acknowledge the support of NVIDIA Corporation with the donation of the GeForce Titan X used for this research.

J. Fitzgerald et al. (Eds.): FM 2016, LNCS 9995, pp. 694–701, 2016.
DOI: 10.1007/978-3-319-48989-6_42

that this amount doubles every few years. Hence, it is interesting to investigate to what extent model checking algorithms can be adapted to run on GPUs. In the last few years, GPUs have been successfully used for several model checking procedures [2–4, 7, 10, 16, 17].

Our tool GPUEXPLORE [14, 15] is the first to take an integrated approach: it runs a complete model checking algorithm on the GPU. Initial results were promising; speed ups of around 10 times were measured. However, at the time, two questions remained unanswered: (1) how does the approach scale over time as new hardware becomes available, and (2) are there still possibilities to further optimise GPUEXPLORE? In this paper, we present new insights concerning both these questions. For the same benchmark set of representative models as used in our previous work [14, 15], the new version of GPUEXPLORE executed on the latest GPU hardware achieves an average speed-up of 119 times. With this amount of speed-up, we can finally claim that the leash has truly been taken off GPU model checking.

2 Using the Tool

GPUEXPLORE[1] operates on networks of Labelled Transition Systems (LTSs) [12], which represent interacting parallel processes. An LTS is a directed graph in which the nodes represent states and the edges are transitions between the states. Each transition has an action label representing an event leading from one state to another. An example network can be found in Fig. 1, where the initial states are indicated by detached incoming arrows. One producer generates work and sends it to one of two consumers. This happens by means of synchronisation of the 'send' and 'rec' actions. The other actions can be executed independently. How the process LTSs should be combined using the relevant synchronisation rules is defined on the right in Fig. 1. The state space of this network consists of 8 states and 24 transitions. Networks are described in the EXP format and LTSs in the AUT format (both from CADP [11]).

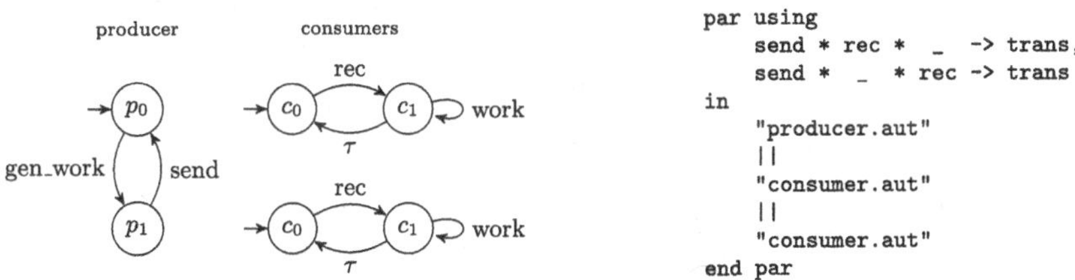

Fig. 1. Example of LTS network with one producer and two consumers.

Besides reachability analysis, GPUEXPLORE can also check functional properties on-the-fly. Currently, it can check for deadlocks and safety properties. Safety properties are expressed by an automaton included in the input network.

[1] Available at http://www.win.tue.nl/~awijs/GPUMC.

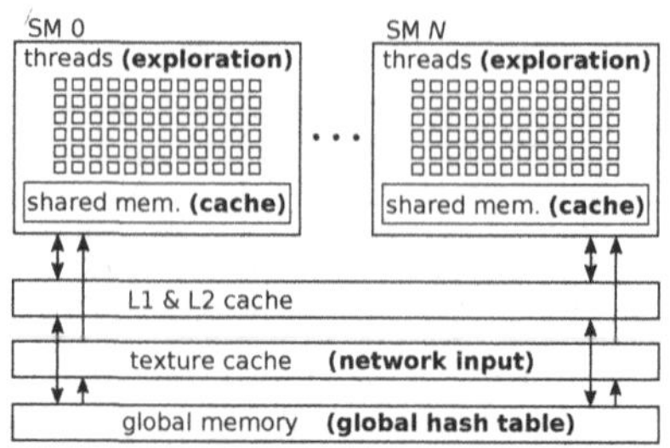

Fig. 2. Schematic overview of the GPU hardware architecture and GPUEXPLORE

3 How GPUexplore Operates

GPU Architecture. CUDA[2] is a programming interface developed by NVIDIA to enable general purpose programming on a GPU. It provides a unified view of the GPU ('device'), simplifying the process of developing for multiple devices. Code to be run on the device ('kernel') can be programmed using a subset of C++.

On the hardware level, a GPU has several *streaming multiprocessors* (SM) that contain hundreds of cores. On the programmer side, threads are grouped into *blocks*. The GPU schedules thread blocks on the SMs. One SM can run multiple blocks at the same time, but one block is assigned to a single SM. Internally, blocks are executed as one or more *warps*. A warp is a group of 32 threads that move in lock-step through the program instructions. A *half-warp* is either the first or second half of a warp.

Another important aspect of the GPU architecture is the memory hierarchy. Firstly, each block is allocated *shared memory* that is shared between its threads. The shared memory is placed on-chip, therefore it has a low latency. Secondly, there is the *global memory* that can be accessed by all the threads. It has a high bandwidth, but also a high latency. The amount of global memory is typically multiple gigabytes. There are three caches in between: the L1, L2 and the texture cache. Data in the global memory that is marked as read-only (a 'texture') may be placed in the texture cache. The global memory can be accessed by the CPU ('host'), thus it also serves as an interface between the host and the device. Figure 2 gives a schematic overview of the architecture.

The bandwidth between the SMs and the global memory is used optimally when a continuous block of 32 integers is fetched by a warp. In that case, those 32 memory transactions are performed in parallel. This is called *coalesced* access.

GPUexplore. Model checking tends to require many uncoalesced memory accesses, as it requires combining the behaviour of the processes in the network, and accessing and storing state vectors of the system state space in the

[2] https://developer.nvidia.com/cuda-zone.

global memory. In GPUEXPLORE, this is mitigated by combining relevant network information as much as possible in 32-bit integers, and storing these as textures, thereby using the texture cache to speed up random accesses.

State vectors are stored in a number of 32-bit integers. Their total size depends on the number of bits needed for each process in the LTS network. In the global memory, a hash table is used to store state vectors (Fig. 2). The hash table has been designed to optimise accesses of entire warps: the space is partitioned into buckets consisting of 32 integers, precisely enough for one warp to fetch a bucket with one combined memory access. State vectors are hashed to buckets, and placed within a bucket in an available slot. If the bucket is full, another hash function is used to find a new bucket.

To each state vector with n process states, a group of n threads (a *vector group*) is assigned to construct its successors using fine-grained parallelism. Each thread collects the relevant transitions of one specific process LTS. Since access to the global memory is slow, each block uses a dedicated state cache (Fig. 2). It serves to collect newly produced state vectors, that are subsequently stored in the global hash table in batches. With the cache, block-local duplicates can be detected. The approach allows to work with vectors that require any number of integers smaller than 32 to be stored.

GPUEXPLORE does not maintain a queue of states that need to be explored. Instead, it stores all states in the main hash table, and marks unexplored states. Additionally, a small amount of memory is allocated for each block to store unexplored states. We call this the *work tile*. Whenever a block has no unexplored states in its work tile, it linearly scans through its own slice of the hash table to gather new states for the work tile. Since each block only gathers work from its own slice, an unexplored state cannot be gathered more than once. Although this approach may result in an unbalanced distribution of work during the early and final stages of exploration, experimental evaluation showed that this does not impact runtime significantly.

Recently, we added support for partial-order reduction (POR), based on cluster-based POR [5,6]. This can greatly reduce the amount of memory needed.

4 Improvements

In our initial publications on GPUEXPLORE [14,15], we noted that the mechanism to insert state vectors in the global hash table was prone to producing duplicate entries, leading to additional exploration work and an incorrect report of the number of reachable states. In GPUEXPLORE 2.0, this problem is fixed. Also, since the initial publications, we have identified several performance bottlenecks. In this section, we both explain how the hashing mechanism now works, and discuss those improvements that had the highest impact on the performance.

Improving the Hash Table. For correct, lock-less hashing, it is important that element insertion can be done atomically. CUDA provides a number of atomic operations, such as *compare-and-swap*, but only for reading and writing

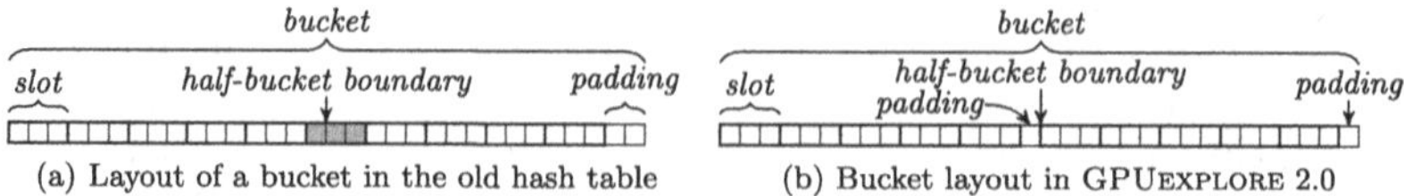

Fig. 3. Example of the layout of a bucket for a state vector length of three integers. Inconsistencies in the old hash table can occur when a slot crosses the half-bucket boundary (marked in orange). In the new situation, the padding is positioned in such a way that no element slot crosses the half-bucket boundary. (Color figure online)

individual integers (either 32-bit or 64-bit). This is problematic for GPUEXPLORE in those cases where state vectors require more than 64 bits. This is the main cause for the inaccuracy of the hash table as reported earlier [14, 15].

However, we have experimentally determined that whenever a warp is instructed to perform atomic operations on a continuous part of the memory, the GPU scheduler tends to schedule these memory requests in half-warps. For GPUEXPLORE, this means that if two warps execute atomic operations on the same bucket, the memory transactions will never be interleaved on a finer level than half-warps. Therefore, we can avoid data races by preventing state slots from spanning more than one half-bucket. The difference in layout of a bucket for a state vector length of three integers is displayed in Fig. 3. As an alternative, we considered the use of spin-locks, but a solution without any form of locking is always more desirable.

Performance Optimisations. Since the work scanning approach can incur significant overhead when the hash table is sparsely filled with unexplored states [15], we have implemented several optimisations in this area:

- The original version of GPUEXPLORE already implemented a technique called *work claiming*: once a work tile has been completely processed, i.e. all states in the tile have been explored, new states are copied directly from the cache to the work tile, which both reside in shared memory. This reduces the amount of scanning that needs to be performed. However, once a kernel execution terminates, the contents of the shared memory are lost. To mitigate this, GPUEXPLORE 2.0 temporarily stores the tile in global memory between kernel launches.
- We observed that the work scanning approach is especially inefficient whenever the hash table slice belonging to some block B contains no work. In that case, B would completely scan its slice at the beginning of every search iteration, thereby wasting a lot of time. GPUEXPLORE 2.0 prevents this by keeping track of the presence of unexplored states in each slice. When some block A places an unexplored state in the slice belonging to B, A sets B's work flag to **true**. Once B has gathered all the work in its slice, it sets its own flag to **false**.
- After a block has completed gathering work from some part of its hash table slice, it is not likely that this part will contain much new work once the next

work scanning is started. Therefore, in GPUEXPLORE 2.0, blocks keep track of which part of their hash table slice they last scanned. The next scan can then continue from the position where the previous one finished.

We also performed several optimisations concerning thread synchronisation. We modified the thread hierarchy so that vector groups never span more than one warp. This allows the threads in a group to share information through warp instructions for register swapping. With these changes, we were able to remove all calls to the `__syncthreads` CUDA function from the main loop of the kernel. This greatly improved the speed of successor generation, since now, warps spend less time waiting for each other.

5 Experimental Results

To show the improvements in runtime of GPUEXPLORE 2.0 (without applying partial-order reduction), we performed several experiments. We compared GPUEXPLORE 2.0 with the original version of GPUEXPLORE and with CADP [11]. The sequential experiments were executed on an Intel Xeon E5520 and 1TB of RAM. We used two different GPUs for running GPUEXPLORE: an NVIDIA K20m (13 SMs, 5 GB of global memory) and an NVIDIA Titan X (24 SMs, 12 GB of global memory). For the original version of GPUEXPLORE, we ran the kernel on 3,120 blocks of 512 threads each, and performed ten iterations, consisting of scanning for work and exploring the states in the resulting work tile, per kernel launch. For GPUEXPLORE 2.0, we ran 6,144 blocks of 512 threads each, and performed only one iteration per kernel launch. The optimal parameters for each version of our tool differ slightly due to the changes we made in the work scanning algorithm.

As benchmarks, we used models from different origins: `odp`, `transit` and `asyn3` are models from the CADP toolkit. The `1394`, `acs` and `wafer stepper` models originate from mCRL2 [9]. The `lamport`, `lann`, `peterson` and `szymanski` models come from the BEEM database[3]. All models are encoded in the EXP format. The models with a.1-suffix are enlarged versions of the original models [15].

For each model and tool, we measured the total runtime (initialisation and state space exploration). For the GPU experiments, we took the average of five runs. The CPU experiments were run a single time. The results can be found in Table 1. The two columns under 'speed-up' indicate the speed-up of GPUEXPLORE 2.0 over CADP and GPUEXPLORE on the Titan X, respectively. GPUEXPLORE 2.0 achieves an average speed-up of 70 times over CADP. It is worth noting that GPUEXPLORE 2.0 can offer more than two orders of magnitude speed-up for larger models, when the parallel potential of the GPU is fully used.

On average, the Titan X, released in 2015, yields a speed-up of 5.5 times compared to the K20m from 2012. The speed-up gained by our optimisations is

[3] http://paradise.fi.muni.cz/beem.

Table 1. Runtimes for CADP, the original GPUEXPLORE and GPUEXPLORE 2.0.

			CADP	GPUEXPLORE		GPUEXPLORE 2.0	Speed-up	
Model	#states	#transitions	CPU	K20m	Titan X	Titan X	Seq.	Orig
acs	4,764	14,760	2.25	10.51	2.26	0.33	6.9	6.9
odp	91,394	641,226	2.03	8.63	2.19	0.34	5.9	6.4
1394	198,692	355,338	2.10	23.10	3.85	0.51	4.1	7.6
acs.1	200,317	895,004	3.58	15.06	2.77	0.46	7.8	6.0
transit	3,763,192	39,925,524	37.79	26.20	4.54	1.21	31.3	3.8
wafer_stepper.1	3,772,753	19,028,708	22.25	47.25	7.33	1.42	15.7	5.2
odp.1	7,699,456	31,091,554	76.73	29.78	5.78	1.84	41.8	3.1
1394.1	10,138,812	96,553,318	66.33	61.40	8.44	1.90	34.8	4.4
asyn3	15,688,570	86,458,183	352.56	273.41	37.97	3.87	91.2	9.8
lamport8	62,669,317	304,202,665	944.80	221.80	41.30	6.91	136.7	6.0
des	64,498,297	518,438,860	468.51	107.22	25.42	18.64	25.1	1.4
szymanski5	79,518,740	922,428,824	1393.35	512.13	86.17	8.93	156.0	9.6
peterson7	142,471,098	626,952,200	3463.06	4337.41	1004.07	36.42	95.1	27.6
lann6	144,151,629	648,779,852	2377.73	492.70	94.85	12.52	189.9	7.6
lann7	160,025,986	944,322,648	3035.55	877.74	164.90	19.83	153.1	8.3
asyn3.1	190,208,728	876,008,628	4360.00	2703.61	421.87	36.61	119.1	11.5
Average							69.7	7.8

7.8 times. This results in a combined speed-up (hardware and software improvements) of 42.6 times relative to our last publication [15]. We remark that the speed-up measurement for the smaller models are skewed in favour of the original version of GPUEXPLORE, since GPUEXPLORE 2.0 spends most of the time on initialization when the state space is small. When measuring only the time required for exploration, our optimisations result in an average speed-up of 11.5 times.

6 Conclusions

We have presented a new version of the GPU explicit-state model checker GPUEXPLORE, which has been further optimised and supports partial-order reduction. Furthermore, we discussed the impact of both the optimisations and the recent improvements in hardware on the average runtime. For future work, we plan to add support for liveness properties. Recently, this has been investigated [13], but those findings are still to be added to the current stable version.

References

1. Baier, C., Katoen, J.P.: Principles of Model Checking. MIT Press, Cambridge (2008)
2. Barnat, J., Bauch, P., Brim, L., Češka, M.: Designing fast LTL model checking algorithms for many-core GPUs. J. Parallel Distrib. Comput. **72**(9), 1083–1097 (2012)

3. Barnat, J., Brim, L., Češka, M., Lamr, T.: CUDA accelerated LTL model checking. In: 15th International Conference on Parallel and Distributed Systems, pp. 34–41. IEEE (2009)
4. Bartocci, E., Defrancisco, R., Smolka, S.A.: Towards a GPGPU-parallel SPIN model checker. In: SPIN, pp. 87–96. ACM (2014)
5. Basten, T., Bošnački, D.: Enhancing Partial-Order Reduction via Process Clustering. In: 16th IEEE International Conference on Automated Software Engineering. pp. 245–253 (2001)
6. Basten, T., Bošnački, D., Geilen, M.: Cluster-based partial-order reduction. ASE **11**(4), 365–402 (2004)
7. Bošnački, D., Edelkamp, S., Sulewski, D., Wijs, A.: Parallel probabilistic model checking on general purpose graphics processors. STTT **13**(1), 21–35 (2010)
8. Clarke, E.M., Grumberg, O., Peled, D.: Model Checking. MIT Press, Cambridge (2001)
9. Cranen, S., Groote, J.F., Keiren, J.J.A., Stappers, F.P.M., Vink, E.P., Wesselink, W., Willemse, T.A.C.: An overview of the mCRL2 toolset and its recent advances. In: Piterman, N., Smolka, S.A. (eds.) TACAS 2013. LNCS, vol. 7795, pp. 199–213. Springer, Heidelberg (2013). doi:10.1007/978-3-642-36742-7_15
10. Edelkamp, S., Sulewski, D.: Efficient explicit-state model checking on general purpose graphics processors. In: Pol, J., Weber, M. (eds.) SPIN 2010. LNCS, vol. 6349, pp. 106–123. Springer, Heidelberg (2010). doi:10.1007/978-3-642-16164-3_8
11. Garavel, H., Lang, F., Mateescu, R., Serwe, W.: CADP 2011: a toolbox for the construction and analysis of distributed processes. STTT **15**(2), 89–107 (2013)
12. Lang, F.: Refined interfaces for compositional verification. In: Najm, E., Pradat-Peyre, J.-F., Donzeau-Gouge, V.V. (eds.) FORTE 2006. LNCS, vol. 4229, pp. 159–174. Springer, Heidelberg (2006). doi:10.1007/11888116_13
13. Wijs, A.: BFS-based model checking of linear-time properties with an application on GPUs. In: Chaudhuri, S., Farzan, A. (eds.) CAV 2016. LNCS, vol. 9780, pp. 472–493. Springer, Heidelberg (2016). doi:10.1007/978-3-319-41540-6_26
14. Wijs, A., Bošnački, D.: GPUexplore: many-core on-the-fly state space exploration using GPUs. In: Ábrahám, E., Havelund, K. (eds.) TACAS 2014. LNCS, vol. 8413, pp. 233–247. Springer, Heidelberg (2014). doi:10.1007/978-3-642-54862-8_16
15. Wijs, A., Bošnački, D.: Many-core on-the-fly model checking of safety properties using GPUs. STTT **18**(2), 1–17 (2015)
16. Wu, Z., Liu, Y., Liang, Y., Sun, J.: GPU accelerated counterexample generation in LTL model checking. In: Merz, S., Pang, J. (eds.) ICFEM 2014. LNCS, vol. 8829, pp. 413–429. Springer, Heidelberg (2014). doi:10.1007/978-3-319-11737-9_27
17. Wu, Z., Liu, Y., Sun, J., Shi, J., Qin, S.: GPU accelerated on-the-fly reachability checking. In: 20th International Conference on Engineering of Complex Computer Systems, pp. 100–109. IEEE (2015)

Approximate Bisimulation and Discretization of Hybrid CSP

Gaogao Yan, Li Jiao, Yangjia Li, Shuling Wang(✉), and Naijun Zhan(✉)

State Key Laboratory of Computer Science, Institute of Software,
Chinese Academy of Sciences, Beijing, China
{yangg,ljiao,yangjia,wangsl,znj}@ios.ac.cn

Abstract. Hybrid Communicating Sequential Processes (HCSP) is a powerful formal modeling language for hybrid systems, which is an extension of CSP by introducing differential equations for modeling continuous evolution and interrupts for modeling interaction between continuous and discrete dynamics. In this paper, we investigate the semantic foundation for HCSP from an operational point of view by proposing the notion of approximate bisimulation, which provides an appropriate criterion to characterize the equivalence between HCSP processes with continuous and discrete behaviour. We give an algorithm to determine whether two HCSP processes are approximately bisimilar. In addition, based on which, we propose an approach on how to discretize HCSP, i.e., given an HCSP process A, we construct another HCSP process B which does not contain any continuous dynamics such that A and B are approximately bisimilar with given precisions. This provides a rigorous way to transform a verified control model to a correct program model, which fills the gap in the design of embedded systems.

Keywords: HCSP · Approximately bisimilar · Hybrid systems · Discretization

1 Introduction

Embedded Systems (ESs) make use of computer units to control physical processes so that the behavior of the controlled processes meets expected requirements. They have become ubiquitous in our daily life, e.g., automotive, aerospace, consumer electronics, communications, medical, manufacturing and so on. ESs are used to carry out highly complex and often critical functions such as to monitor and control industrial plants, complex transportation equipments, communication infrastructure, etc. The development process of ESs is widely recognized as a highly complex and challenging task. Model-Based Engineering

This work is supported partly by "973 Program" under grant No. 2014CB340701, by NSFC under grants 91418204 and 61502467, by CDZ project CAP (GZ 1023), and by the CAS/SAFEA International Partnership Program for Creative Research Teams.

J. Fitzgerald et al. (Eds.): FM 2016, LNCS 9995, pp. 702–720, 2016.
DOI: 10.1007/978-3-319-48989-6_43

(MBE) is considered as an effective way of developing correct complex ESs, and has been successfully applied in industry [16,21]. In the framework of MBE, a model of the system to be developed is defined at the beginning; then extensive analysis and verification are conducted based on the model so that errors can be detected and corrected at early stages of design of the system. Afterwards, model transformation techniques are applied to transform abstract formal models into more concrete models, even into source code.

To improve the efficiency and reliability of MBE, it is absolutely necessary to automate the system design process as much as possible. This requires that all models at different abstraction levels have a precise mathematical semantics. Transformation between models at different abstraction levels should preserve semantics, which can be done automatically with tool support.

Thus, the first challenge in model-based formal design of ESs is to have a powerful modelling language which can model all kinds of features of ESs such as communication, synchronization, concurrency, continuous and discrete dynamics and their interaction, real-time, and so on, in an easy way. To address this issue, Hybrid Communicating Sequential Processes (HCSP) was proposed in [14,36], which is an extension of CSP by introducing differential equations for modeling continuous evolutions and interrupts for modeling interaction between continuous and discrete dynamics. Comparing with other formalisms, e.g., hybrid automata [17], hybrid programs [24], etc., HCSP is more expressive and much easier to be used, as it provides a rich set of constructors. Through which a complicated ES with different behaviours can be easily modeled in a compositional way. The semantic foundation of HCSP has been investigated in the literature, e.g., in He's original work on HCSP [14], an algebraic semantics of HCSP was given by defining a set of algebraic laws for the constructors of HCSP. Subsequently, a DC-based semantics for HCSP was presented in [36] due to Zhou *et al.* These two original formal semantics of HCSP are very restrictive and incomplete, for example, it is unclear whether the set of algebraic rules defined in [14] is complete, and super-dense computation and recursion are not well handled in [36]. In [8,13,22,33,35], the axiomatic, operational, and the DC-based and UTP-based denotational semantics for HCSP are proposed, and the relations among them are discussed. However, regarding operational semantics, just a set of transition rules was proposed in [35]. It is unclear in what sense two HCSP processes are equivalent from an operational point of view, which is the cornerstone of operational semantics, also the basis of refinement theory for a process algebra. So, it absolutely deserves to investigate the semantic foundation of HCSP from an operational point of view.

Another challenge in the model-based formal design of ESs is how to transform higher level abstract models (control models) to lower level program models (algorithm models), even to C code, seamlessly in a rigorous way. Although huge volume of model-based development approaches targeting embedded systems has been proposed and used in industry and academia, e.g., Simulink/Stateflow [1,2], SCADE [9], Modelica [31], SysML [3], MARTE [28], Ptolemy [10], hybrid automata [17], CHARON [5], HCSP [14,36], Differential Dynamic Logic [24], and Hybrid Hoare Logic [22], the gap between higher-level control models and lower-level algorithm models still remains.

Approximate bisimulation [12] is a popular method for analyzing and verifying complex hybrid systems. Instead of requiring observational behaviors of two systems to be exactly identical, it allows errors but requires the "distance" between two systems remain bounded by some precisions. In [11], with the use of simulation functions, a characterization of approximate simulation relations between hybrid systems is developed. A new approximate bisimulation relation with two parameters as precisions, which is very similar to the notion defined in this paper, is introduced in [18]. For control systems with inputs, the method for constructing a symbolic model which is approximately bisimilar with the original continuous system is studied in [26]. Moreover, [23] discusses the problem for building an approximately bisimilar symbolic model of a digital control system. Also, there are some works on building symbolic models for networks of control systems [27]. But for all the above works, either discrete dynamics is not considered, or it is assumed to be atomic actions independent of the continuous variables. In [15,20,32], the abstraction of hybrid automata is considered, but it is only guaranteed that the abstract system is an approximate simulation of the original system. In [25], a discretization of hybrid programs is presented for a proof-theoretical purpose, i.e., it aims to have a sound and complete axiomatization relative to properties of discrete programs. Differently from all the above works, we aim to have a discretization of HCSP, for which discrete and continuous dynamics, communications, and so on, are entangled with each other tightly, to guarantee that the discretized process has the approximate equivalence with the original process.

The main contributions of this paper include:

- First of all, we propose the notion of approximate bisimulation, which provides a criterion to characterize in what sense two HCSP processes with differential kinds of behaviours are equivalent from an operational point of view. Based on which, a refinement theory for HCSP could be developed.
- Then, we show that whether two HCSP processes are approximately bisimilar or not is decidable if all ordinary differential equations (ODEs) occurring in them satisfy globally asymptotical stability (GAS) condition (the definition will be given later). This is achieved by proposing an algorithm to compute an approximate bisimulation relation for the two HCSP processes.
- Most importantly, we present how to discretize an HCSP process (a control model) by a discrete HCSP process (an algorithm model), and prove they are approximately bisimilar, if the original HCSP process satisfies the GAS condition and is robustly safe with respect to some given precisions.

The rest of this paper is organized as follows: In Sect. 2, we introduce some preliminary notions on dynamical systems. Sect. 3 defines transition systems and the approximate bisimulation relation between transition systems. The syntax and the transition semantics of HCSP, and the approximately bisimilar of HCSP processes are presented in Sect. 4. The discretization of HCSP is presented in Sect. 5. Throughout the paper, and in Sect. 6, a case study on the water tank system [4] is shown to illustrate our method. At the end, Sect. 7 concludes the paper and discusses the future work. For space limitation, the proofs for all the lemmas and theorems are omitted, but can be found in [34].

2 Preliminary

In this section, we briefly review some notions in dynamical systems, that can be found at [19,29]. In what follows, $\mathbb{N}$, $\mathbb{R}$, $\mathbb{R}^+$, $\mathbb{R}_0^+$ denote the natural, real, positive and nonnegative real numbers, respectively. Given a vector $\mathbf{x} \in \mathbb{R}^n$, $\|\mathbf{x}\|$ denotes the infinity norm of $\mathbf{x} \in \mathbb{R}^n$, i.e., $\|\mathbf{x}\| \doteq \max\{|x_1|, |x_2|, ..., |x_n|\}$. A continuous function $\gamma : \mathbb{R}_0^+ \rightarrow \mathbb{R}_0^+$, is said in class $\mathcal{K}$ if it is strictly increasing and $\gamma(0) = 0$; γ is said in class $\mathcal{K}_\infty$ if $\gamma \in \mathcal{K}$ and $\gamma(r) \rightarrow \infty$ as $r \rightarrow \infty$. A continuous function $\beta : \mathbb{R}_0^+ \times \mathbb{R}_0^+ \rightarrow \mathbb{R}_0^+$ is said in class $\mathcal{KL}$ if for each fixed s, the map $\beta(r, s) \in \mathcal{K}_\infty$ with respect to r and, for each fixed r, $\beta(r, s)$ is decreasing with respect to s and $\beta(r, s) \rightarrow 0$ as $s \rightarrow \infty$.

A dynamical system is of the following form

$$\dot{\mathbf{x}} = \mathbf{f}(\mathbf{x}), \qquad \mathbf{x}(t_0) = \mathbf{x}_0 \tag{1}$$

where $\mathbf{x} \in \mathbb{R}^n$ is the state and $\mathbf{x}(t_0) = \mathbf{x}_0$ is the *initial condition.*

Suppose $a < t_0 < b$. A function $X(.) : (a, b) \rightarrow \mathbb{R}^n$ is said to be a *trajectory* (solution) of (1) on (a, b), if $X(t_0) = \mathbf{x}_0$ and $\dot{X}(t) = \mathbf{f}(X(t))$ for all $t \geq t_0$. In order to ensure the existence and uniqueness of trajectories, we assume $\mathbf{f}$ satisfying the local Lipschitz condition, i.e., for every compact set $S \subset \mathbb{R}^n$, there exists a constant $L > 0$ s.t. $\|\mathbf{f}(\mathbf{x}) - \mathbf{f}(\mathbf{y})\| \leq L\|\mathbf{x} - \mathbf{y}\|$, for all $\mathbf{x}, \mathbf{y} \in S$. Then, we write $X(t, \mathbf{x}_0)$ to denote the point reached at time $t \in (a, b)$ from initial condition $\mathbf{x}_0$, which should be uniquely determined. In addition, we assume (1) is *forward complete* [7], i.e., it is solvable on an open interval $(a, +\infty)$. An equilibrium point of (1) is a point $\bar{\mathbf{x}} \in \mathbb{R}^n$ s.t. $\mathbf{f}(\bar{\mathbf{x}}) = 0$.

Definition 1. *A dynamical system of form (1) is said to be* globally asymptotically stable (GAS) *if there exists a point* $\mathbf{x}_0$ *and a function* β *of class* $\mathcal{KL}$ *s.t.*

$$\forall \mathbf{x} \in \mathbb{R}^n\ \forall t \geq 0. \|X(t, \mathbf{x}) - \mathbf{x}_0\| \leq \beta(\|\mathbf{x} - \mathbf{x}_0\|, t).$$

It is easy to see that the point $\mathbf{x}_0$ is actually the unique equilibrium point of the system. When this point is previously known or can be easily computed, one can prove the system to be GAS by constructing a corresponding Lyapunov function. However, $\mathbf{x}_0$ cannot be found sometimes, for example, when the dynamics $\mathbf{f}$ of the system depends on external inputs and thus is not completely known. The concept of δ-GAS would be useful in this case.

Definition 2. *A dynamical system of (1) is said to be incrementally globally asymptotically stable (δ-GAS) if it is forward complete and there is a* $\mathcal{KL}$ *function* β *s.t.*

$$\forall \mathbf{x} \in \mathbb{R}^n\ \forall \mathbf{y} \in \mathbb{R}^n\ \forall t \geq 0. \|X(t, \mathbf{x}) - X(t, \mathbf{y})\| \leq \beta(\|\mathbf{x} - \mathbf{y}\|, t).$$

In [6], the relationship between GAS and δ-GAS was established, restated by the following proposition.

Proposition 1. – *If (1) is* δ-GAS*, then it is* GAS.
– *If there exist two strictly positive reals M and ε, and a differentiable function $V(\mathbf{x}, \mathbf{y})$ with $\alpha_1(\|\mathbf{x}-\mathbf{y}\|) \le V(\mathbf{x}, \mathbf{y}) \le \alpha_2(\|\mathbf{x}-\mathbf{y}\|)$ for some α_1, α_2 and ρ of class $\mathcal{K}_\infty$, s.t.*

$$\forall \mathbf{x}, \mathbf{y} \in \mathbb{R}^n. \begin{pmatrix} \|\mathbf{x}-\mathbf{y}\| \le \varepsilon \wedge \|\mathbf{x}\| \ge M \wedge \|\mathbf{y}\| \ge M \\ \Rightarrow \frac{\partial V}{\partial \mathbf{x}}\mathbf{f}(\mathbf{x}) + \frac{\partial V}{\partial \mathbf{y}}\mathbf{f}(\mathbf{y}) \le -\rho(\|\mathbf{x}-\mathbf{y}\|) \end{pmatrix},$$

then the system (1) is δ-GAS.

A function $V(\mathbf{x}, \mathbf{y})$ satisfying the condition in Proposition 1 is called a δ-GAS *Lyapunov function* of (1). Proposition 1 tells us that (1) is δ-GAS if and only if it admits a δ-GAS Lyapunov function. In general, checking the inequality in Definition 2 is difficult, one may construct δ-GAS Lyapunov functions as an alternative.

3 Transition Systems and Approximate Bisimulation

In the following, the set of actions, denoted by *Act*, is assumed to consist of a set of discrete actions which take no time (written as $\mathcal{E}$), $\mathbb{R}_0^+$ the set of delay actions which just take time delay, and a special internal action τ. Actions are ranged over $l_1, \ldots, l_n, \ldots$.

Definition 3 (Transition system). *A labeled transition system with observations is a tuple $T = \langle Q, L, \rightarrow, Q^0, Y, H\rangle$, where Q is a set of states, $L \subseteq Act$ is a set of labels, $Q^0 \subseteq Q$ is a set of initial states, Y is a set of observations, and H is an observation function $H : Q \rightarrow Y$, $\rightarrow \subseteq Q \times L \times Q$ is a transition relation, satisfying*

1, ***identity:*** *$q \xrightarrow{0} q$ always holds;*
2, ***delay determinism:*** *if $q \xrightarrow{d} q'$ and $q \xrightarrow{d} q''$, then $q' = q''$; and*
3, ***delay additivity:*** *if $q \xrightarrow{d_1} q'$ and $q' \xrightarrow{d_2} q''$ then $q \xrightarrow{d_1+d_2} q''$, where $d, d_1, d_2 \in \mathbb{R}_0^+$.*

A transition system T is said to be *symbolic* if Q and $L \cap \mathcal{E}$ are finite, and $L \cap \mathbb{R}_0^+$ is bounded, and *metric* if the output set Y is equipped with a metric $\mathbf{d} : Y \times Y \rightarrow \mathbb{R}_0^+$. In this paper, we regard Y as being equipped with the metric $\mathbf{d}(\mathbf{y}_1, \mathbf{y}_2) = \|\mathbf{y}_1 - \mathbf{y}_2\|$.

A *state trajectory* of a transition system T is a (possibly infinite) sequence of transitions $\mathbf{q}^0 \xrightarrow{l^0} \mathbf{q}^1 \xrightarrow{l^1} \cdots \xrightarrow{l^{i-1}} \mathbf{q}^i \xrightarrow{l^i} \cdots$, denoted by $\{\mathbf{q}^i \xrightarrow{l^i} \mathbf{q}^{i+1}\}_{i\in\mathbb{N}}$, s.t. $\mathbf{q}^0 \in Q^0$ and for any i, $\mathbf{q}^i \xrightarrow{l^i} \mathbf{q}^{i+1}$. An *observation trajectory* is a (possibly infinite) sequence $\mathbf{y}^0 \xrightarrow{l^0} \mathbf{y}^1 \xrightarrow{l^1} \cdots \xrightarrow{l^{i-1}} \mathbf{y}^i \xrightarrow{l^i} \cdots$, denoted by $\{\mathbf{y}^i \xrightarrow{l^i} \mathbf{y}^{i+1}\}_{i\in\mathbb{N}}$, and it is accepted by T if there exists a corresponding state trajectory of T s.t. $\mathbf{y}^i = H(\mathbf{q}^i)$ for any $i \in \mathbb{N}$. The set of observation trajectories accepted by T is called the *language* of T, and is denoted by $L(T)$. The reachable set of T is a subset of Y defined by

$$Reach(T) = \{\mathbf{y} \in Y | \exists \{\mathbf{y}^i \xrightarrow{l^i} \mathbf{y}^{i+1}\}_{i\in\mathbb{N}} \in L(T), \exists j \in \mathbb{N}, \mathbf{y}^j = \mathbf{y}\}.$$

We can verify the safety property of T by computing $Reach(T) \cap Y_U$, in which $Y_U \subseteq Y$ is the set of unsafe observations. If it is empty, then T is *safe*, otherwise, *unsafe*.

For a maximum sequence of τ actions $\mathbf{q}^i \xrightarrow{\tau} \mathbf{q}^{i+1} \xrightarrow{\tau} \cdots \xrightarrow{\tau} \mathbf{q}^{i+k}$, we remove the intermediate states and define the τ-*compressed* transition $\mathbf{q}^i \overset{\tau}{\twoheadrightarrow} \mathbf{q}^{i+k}$ instead. For unification, for a non-τ transition $\mathbf{q}^i \xrightarrow{l^i} \mathbf{q}^{i+1}$ where $l^i \neq \tau$, we define $\mathbf{q}^i \overset{l^i}{\twoheadrightarrow} \mathbf{q}^{i+1}$. In what follows, we will denote $\langle Q, L, \twoheadrightarrow, Q^0, Y, H\rangle$ the resulting labeled transition system from $\langle Q, L, \rightarrow, Q^0, Y, H\rangle$ by replacing each label transition with its τ-compressed version. As a common convention in process algebra, we use $\mathbf{p} \overset{l}{\Longrightarrow} \mathbf{p}'$ to denote the closure of τ transitions, i.e., $\mathbf{p}(\overset{\tau}{\twoheadrightarrow})^{\{0,1\}} \overset{l}{\twoheadrightarrow} (\overset{\tau}{\twoheadrightarrow})^{\{0,1\}}\mathbf{p}'$, for any $l \in L$ in the sequel.

Given $l_1, l_2 \in L \cup \{\tau\}$, we define the *distance* $dis(l_1, l_2)$ between them as follows:

$$dis(l_1, l_2) \overset{\text{def}}{=} \begin{cases} 0 & \text{if both } l_1 \text{ and } l_2 \text{ are in } \mathcal{E} \text{ or are } \tau \\ |d - d'| & \text{if } l_1 = d \text{ and } l_2 = d' \text{ are both delay actions, i.e., } d, d' \in \mathbb{R}_0^+ \\ \infty & \text{Otherwise} \end{cases}$$

Definition 4 (Approximate bisimulation). *Let $T_i = \langle Q_i, L_i, \twoheadrightarrow_i, Q_i^0, Y_i, H_i\rangle$, $(i = 1, 2)$ be two metric transition systems with the same output set Y and metric $\mathbf{d}$. Let h and ε be the time and value precision respectively. A relation $\mathcal{B}_{h,\varepsilon} \subseteq Q_1 \times Q_2$ is called a (h, ε)-approximate bisimulation relation between T_1 and T_2, if for all $(\mathbf{q}_1, \mathbf{q}_2) \in \mathcal{B}_{h,\varepsilon}$,*

1. $\mathbf{d}(H_1(\mathbf{q}_1), H_2(\mathbf{q}_2)) \leq \varepsilon$,
2. $\forall \mathbf{q}_1 \overset{l}{\twoheadrightarrow}_1 \mathbf{q}_1'$, $\exists \mathbf{q}_2 \overset{l'}{\Longrightarrow}_2 \mathbf{q}_2'$ *s.t.* $dis(l, l') \leq h$ *and* $(\mathbf{q}_1', \mathbf{q}_2') \in \mathcal{B}_{h,\varepsilon}$, *for* $l \in L_1$ *and* $l' \in L_2$
3. $\forall \mathbf{q}_2 \overset{l}{\twoheadrightarrow}_2 \mathbf{q}_2'$, $\exists \mathbf{q}_1 \overset{l'}{\Longrightarrow}_1 \mathbf{q}_1'$ *s.t.* $dis(l, l') \leq h$ *and* $(\mathbf{q}_1', \mathbf{q}_2') \in \mathcal{B}_{h,\varepsilon}$, *for* $l \in L_2$ *and* $l' \in L_1$.

Definition 5. *T_1 and T_2 are approximately bisimilar with the precision h and ε (denoted $T_1 \cong_{h,\varepsilon} T_2$), if there exists a (h, ε)-approximate bisimulation relation $\mathcal{B}_{h,\varepsilon}$ between T_1 and T_2 s.t. for all $\mathbf{q}_1 \in Q_1^0$, there exists $\mathbf{q}_2 \in Q_2^0$ s.t. $(\mathbf{q}_1, \mathbf{q}_2) \in \mathcal{B}_{h,\varepsilon}$, and vice versa.*

The following result ensures that the set of (h,ε)-approximate bisimulation relations has a maximal element.

Lemma 1. *Let* $\{\mathcal{B}^i_{h,\varepsilon}\}_{i\in I}$ *be a family of* (h,ε)*-approximate bisimulation relations between* T_1 *and* T_2*. Then,* $\bigcup_{i\in I}\mathcal{B}^i_{h,\varepsilon}$ *is a* (h,ε)*-approximate bisimulation relation between* T_1 *and* T_2*.*

By Lemma 1, given the precision parameters h and ε, let $\{\mathcal{B}^i_{h,\varepsilon}\}_{i\in I}$ be the set of all (h,ε)-approximate bisimulation relations between T_1 and T_2, then the maximal (h,ε)-approximate bisimulation relation between T_1 and T_2 is defined by $\mathcal{B}^{max}_{h,\varepsilon} = \bigcup\limits_{i\in I}\mathcal{B}^i_{h,\varepsilon}$. For two transition systems that are approximately bisimilar, the reachable sets have the following relationship:

Theorem 1. *If* $T_1 \cong_{h,\varepsilon} T_2$*, then* $Reach(T_1) \subseteq N(Reach(T_2),\varepsilon)$*, where* $N(Y,\varepsilon)$ *denotes the* ε *neighborhood of* Y*, i.e.* $\{x \mid \exists y.y \in Y \wedge \|x-y\| < \varepsilon\}$*.*

Thus, if the distance between $Reach(T_2)$ and the unsafe set Y_U is greater than ε, then the intersection of $Reach(T_1)$ and Y_U is empty and hence T_1 is safe, whenever $T_1 \cong_{h,\varepsilon} T_2$.

4 Hybrid CSP (HCSP)

In this section, we present a brief introduction to HCSP and define the transition system of HCSP from an operational point of view. An example is given for better understanding. Finally, we investigate the approximate bisimilarity for HCSP processes.

4.1 HCSP

Hybrid Communicating Sequential Process (HCSP) is a formal language for describing hybrid systems, which extends CSP by introducing differential equations for modelling continuous evolutions and interrupts for modeling the arbitrary interaction between continuous evolutions and discrete jumps. The syntax of HCSP can be described as follows:

$$
\begin{aligned}
P ::=&\,\text{skip} \mid x := e \mid \text{wait } d \mid ch?x \mid ch!e \mid P;Q \mid B \rightarrow P \mid P \sqcap Q \mid P^* \\
&\mid [\!]_{i\in I} io_i \rightarrow P_i \mid \langle F(\dot{\mathbf{s}},\mathbf{s}) = 0 \& B\rangle \mid \langle F(\dot{\mathbf{s}},\mathbf{s}) = 0 \& B\rangle \trianglerighteq [\!]_{i\in I}(io_i \rightarrow Q_i) \\
S ::=&\,P \mid S\|S
\end{aligned}
$$

where $x, \mathbf{s}$ for variables and vectors of variables, respectively, B and e are boolean and arithmetic expressions, d is a non-negative real constant, ch is the channel name, io_i stands for a communication event, i.e., either $ch_i?x$ or $ch_i!e$, P, Q, Q_i are sequential process terms, and S stands for an HCSP process term. Given an HCSP process S, we define $Var(S)$ for the set of variables in S, and $\Sigma(S)$ the set of channels occurring in S, respectively. The informal meanings of the individual constructors are as follows:

- skip, $x := e$, wait d, $ch?x$, $ch!e$, $P;Q$, $P \sqcap Q$, and $[]_{i \in I} io_i \to P_i$ are defined as usual. $B \to P$ behaves as P if B is true, otherwise terminates.
- For repetition P^*, P executes for an arbitrary finite number of times. We assume an oracle num, s.t. for a given P^* in the context process S, $num(P^*, S)$ returns the upper bound of the number of times that P is repeated in the context.
- $\langle F(\dot{\mathbf{s}}, \mathbf{s}) = 0 \& B \rangle$ is the continuous evolution statement. It forces the vector $\mathbf{s}$ of real variables to obey the differential equations F as long as B, which defines the domain of $\mathbf{s}$, holds, and terminates when B turns false. Without loss of generality, we assume that the set of B is open, thus the escaping point will be at the boundary of B. The communication interrupt $\langle F(\dot{\mathbf{s}}, \mathbf{s}) = 0 \& B \rangle \trianglerighteq []_{i \in I}(io_i \to Q_i)$ behaves like $\langle F(\dot{\mathbf{s}}, \mathbf{s}) = 0 \& B \rangle$, except that the continuous evolution is preempted as soon as one of the communications io_i takes place, which is followed by the respective Q_i. These two statements are the main extension of HCSP for describing continuous behavior.
- $S_1 \| S_2$ behaves as if S_1 and S_2 run independently except that all communications along the common channels connecting S_1 and S_2 are to be synchronized. S_1 and S_2 in parallel can neither share variables, nor input or output channels.

For better understanding of the HCSP syntax, we model the water tank system [4], for which two components *Watertank* and *Controller*, are composed in parallel. The HCSP model of the system is given by *WTS* as follows:

$$\begin{aligned}
WTS &\stackrel{\text{def}}{=} Watertank \| Controller \\
Watertank &\stackrel{\text{def}}{=} v := v_0; d := d_0; \\
&\quad (v = 1 \to \langle \dot{d} = Q_{max} - \pi r^2 \sqrt{2gd} \rangle \trianglerighteq (wl!d \to cv?v); \\
&\quad v = 0 \to \langle \dot{d} = -\pi r^2 \sqrt{2gd} \rangle \trianglerighteq (wl!d \to cv?v))^* \\
Controller &\stackrel{\text{def}}{=} y := v_0; x := d_0; (\text{wait } p; wl?x; x \geq ub \to y := 0; \\
&\quad x \leq lb \to y := 1; cv!y)^*
\end{aligned}$$

where Q_{max}, π, r and g are system parameters, v is the control variable which takes 1 or 0, depending on whether the valve is open or not, d is the water level of the *Watertank* and its dynamics depends on the value of v. v_0 and d_0 are the initial values of controller variable and water level, respectively. Two channels, wl and cv, are used to transfer the water level (d in *Watertank*) and control variable (y in *Controller*) between *Watertank* and *Controller*, respectively. The control value is computed by the *Controller* with a period of p. When the water level is less than or equal to lb, the control value is assigned to 1, and when the water level is greater than or equal to ub, the control value is assigned to 0, otherwise, it keeps unchanged. Basically, based on the current value of v, *Watertank* and *Controller* run independently for p time, then *Watertank* sends the current water level to *Controller*, according to which a new value of the control variable is generated and sent back to *Watertank*, after that, a new period repeats.

4.2 Transition System of HCSP

Given an HCSP process S, we can derive a transition system $T(S) = \langle Q, L, \rightarrow, Q^0, Y, H\rangle$ from S by the following procedure:

- the set of states $Q = (subp(S) \cup \{\epsilon\}) \times V(S)$, where $subp(S)$ is the set of sub-processes of S, e.g., $subp(S) = \{S, \text{wait } d, B \rightarrow P\} \cup subp(P)$ for S::=wait d; $B \rightarrow P$, ϵ is introduced to represent the terminal process, meaning that the process has terminated, and $V(S) = \{v | v \in Var(S) \rightarrow Val\}$ is the set of evaluations of the variables in S, with Val representing the value space of variables. Without confusion in the context, we often call an evaluation v a (process) state. Given a state $q \in Q$, we will use $fst(q)$ and $snd(q)$ to return the first and second component of q, respectively.
- The label set L corresponds to the actions of HCSP, defined as $L = \mathbb{R}_0^+ \cup \Sigma(S) \centerdot \{?, !\} \centerdot \mathbb{R} \cup \{\tau\}$, where $d \in \mathbb{R}_0^+$ stands for the time progress, $ch?c, ch!c \in \Sigma(S) \centerdot \{?, !\} \centerdot \mathbb{R}$ means that an input along channel ch with value c being received, an output along ch with value c being sent, respectively. Besides, the silent action τ represents a discrete non-communication action of HCSP, such as assignment, evaluation of boolean expressions, and so on.
- $Q^0 = \{(S, v) | v \in V(S)\}$, representing that S has not started to execute, and v is the initial process state of S.
- $Y = \overline{Val}$, represents the set of value vectors corresponding to $Var(S)$.
- Given $q \in Q$, $H(q) = vec(snd(q))$, where function vec returns the value vector corresponding to the process state of q.
- $\rightarrow$ is the transition relation of S, which is given next.

Sequential Processes. A transition relation of a sequential HCSP process takes the form $(P, v) \xrightarrow{l} (P', v')$, indicating that starting from state v, P executes to P' by performing action l, with the resulting state v'. Here we present the transition rules for continuous evolution as an illustration. Readers are referred to [35] for the full details of the transition semantics, for both sequential and parallel HCSP processes.

$$\frac{\begin{array}{c}\forall d > 0. \exists S(.) : [0, d] \rightarrow \mathbb{R}^n.(S(0) = v(\mathbf{s}) \wedge (\forall p \in [0, d).(F(\dot{S}(p), S(p)) = 0 \\ \wedge v[\mathbf{s} \mapsto S(p)](B) = true)))\end{array}}{(\langle F(\dot{\mathbf{s}}, \mathbf{s}) = 0 \& B\rangle, v) \xrightarrow{d} (\langle F(\dot{\mathbf{s}}, \mathbf{s}) = 0 \& B\rangle, v[\mathbf{s} \mapsto S(d)])}$$

$$\frac{v(B) = false}{(\langle F(\dot{\mathbf{s}}, \mathbf{s}) = 0 \& B\rangle, v) \xrightarrow{\tau} (\epsilon, v)}$$

For $\langle F(\dot{\mathbf{s}}, \mathbf{s}) = 0 \& B\rangle$, for any $d \geq 0$, it evolves for d time units according to F if B evaluates to true within this period (the right end exclusive). In the rule, $S(\cdot) : [0, d] \rightarrow \mathbb{R}^n$ defines the trajectory of the ODE F with initial value $v(\mathbf{s})$. Otherwise, by performing a τ action, the continuous evolution terminates if B evaluates to false.

Parallel Composition. Given two sequential processes P_1, P_2 and their transition systems $T(P_1) = \langle Q_1, L_1, \to_1, Q_1^0, Y_1, H_1\rangle$ and $T(P_2) = \langle Q_2, L_2, \to_2, Q_2^0, Y_2, H_2\rangle$, we can define the transition system of $P_1\|P_2$ as $T(P_1\|P_2) = \langle Q, L, \to, Q, Y, H\rangle$, where:

- $Q = ((subp(P_1) \cup \{\epsilon\})\|(subp(P_2) \cup \{\epsilon\})) \times \{v_1 \uplus v_2 | v_1 \in V(P_1), v_2 \in V(P_2)\}$, where given two sets of processes PS_1 and PS_2, $PS_1\|PS_2$ is defined as $\{\alpha\|\beta | \alpha \in PS_1 \wedge \beta \in PS_2\}$; $v_1 \uplus v_2$ represents the disjoint union, i.e. $v_1 \uplus v_2(x)$ is $v_1(x)$ if $x \in Var(P_1)$, otherwise $v_2(x)$.
- $L = L_1 \cup L_2$.
- $Q^0 = \{(P_1\|P_2, v_1^0 \uplus v_2^0) | (P_i, v_i^0) \in Q_i^0 \text{ for } i = 1, 2\}$.
- $Y = Y_1 \times Y_2$, the observation space of the parallel composition is obviously the Cartesian product of Y_1 and Y_2.
- $H(q) = H_1(q) \times H_2(q)$, the observation function is the Cartesian product of the two component observation functions correspondingly.
- $\to$ is defined based on the parallel composition of transitions of L_1 and L_2.

Suppose two transitions $(P_1, u) \xrightarrow{\alpha} (P_1', u')$ and $(P_2, v) \xrightarrow{\beta} (P_2', v')$ occur for P_1 and P_2, respectively. The rule for synchronization is given below:

$$\frac{\alpha = ch_i?c \wedge \beta = ch_i!e \wedge c = e}{(P_1\|P_2, u \uplus v) \xrightarrow{\tau} (P_1'\|P_2', u' \uplus v')}$$

4.3 Approximate Bisimulation Between HCSP Processes

Let P_1 and P_2 be two HCSP processes, and h, ε the time and value precisions. Let v_0 be an arbitrary initial state. P_1 and P_2 are (h,ε)-*approximately bisimilar*, denoted by $P_1 \cong_{h,\varepsilon} P_2$, if $T(P_1) \cong_{h,\varepsilon} T(P_2)$, in which $T(P_1)$ and $T(P_2)$ are the τ-compressed transition systems of P_1 and P_2 with the same initial state v_0, respectively.

In Algorithm 1, we consider the (h,ε)-approximate bisimilation between P_1 and P_2 for which all the ODEs occurring in P_1 and P_2 are GAS. Suppose the set of ODEs occurring in P_i is $\{F_1^i, \cdots, F_{ki}^i\}$, and the equilibrium points for them are $x_1^i, \cdots, x_{ki}^i$ for $i = 1, 2$ respectively. As a result, for each ODE, there must exist a sufficiently large time, called *equilibrium time*, s.t. after the time, the distance between the trajectory and the equilibrium point is less than ε. We denote the equilibrium time for each F_j^i for $j = 1, \cdots, ki$ by T_j^i, respectively. Furthermore, in order to record the execution time of ODEs, for each ODE F_j^i, we introduce an auxiliary time variable t_j^i and add $t_j^i := 0; \dot{t}_j^i = 1$ to F_j^i correspondingly.

Algorithm 1 decides whether P_1 and P_2 are (h,ε)-approximately bisimilar. When $P_1 \cong_{h,\varepsilon} P_2$, it returns **true**, otherwise, it returns **false**. Let d be the discretized time step. The algorithm is then taken in two steps. The first step (lines 1–6) constructs the transition systems for P_1 and P_2 with time step d. For $m = 1, 2$, $T(P_m).Q$ and $T(P_m).T$ represent the reachable set of states and transitions of P_m, respectively, which are initialized as empty sets and then constructed iteratively. At each step i, a new transition can be a d time progress,

Algorithm 1. Deciding approximately bisimilar between two HCSP processes

Input: Processes P_1, P_2, the initial state v_0, the time step d, and precisions h and ε;
Initialization:
$T(P_m).Q^0 = \{(P_m, v_0)\}, T(P_m).T^0 = \emptyset$ for $m = 1, 2$; $i = 0$;
1: **repeat**
2: $T(P_m).T^{i+1} = T(P_m).T^i \cup \{q \overset{l}{\twoheadrightarrow} q' | \forall q \in T(P_m).Q^i$, if $(\exists l \in \{d, \tau\} \cup \Sigma(P_m) \cdot \{?, !\} \cdot \mathbb{R}.q \overset{l}{\twoheadrightarrow} q')$ or $(\exists l = d'.l < d \wedge q \overset{l}{\twoheadrightarrow} q' \wedge$ not $(q \overset{d''}{\twoheadrightarrow}$ $)$ for any d'' in $(d', d])$ and $snd(q')(t_j^m) < T_j^m\}$;
3: $T(P_m).Q^{i+1} = T(P_m).Q^i \cup postState(T(P_m).T^{i+1})$;
4: $i \leftarrow i + 1$;
5: **until** $T(P_m).T^i = T(P_m).T^{i-1}$
6: $T(P_m).Q = T(P_m).Q^i; T(P_m).T = T(P_m).T^i$;
7: $\mathcal{B}^0_{h,\varepsilon} = \{(q_1, q_2) \in T(P_1).Q \times T(P_2).Q | \mathbf{d}(H_1(q_1), H_2(q_2)) \leq \varepsilon\}$; $i = 0$;
8: **repeat**
9: $\mathcal{B}^{i+1}_{h,\varepsilon} \leftarrow \{(q_1, q_2) \in B^i_{h,\varepsilon} | \forall q_1 \overset{l}{\twoheadrightarrow}_1 q_1' \in T(P_1).T, \exists q_2 \overset{l'}{\Longrightarrow}_2 q_2' \in T(P_2).T$ s.t. $(q_1', q_2') \in \mathcal{B}^i_{h,\varepsilon}$ and $dis(l, l') \leq h$, and $\forall q_2 \overset{l}{\twoheadrightarrow}_2 q_2' \in T(P_2).T, \exists q_1 \overset{l'}{\Longrightarrow}_1 q_1' \in T(P_1).T$ s.t. $(q_1', q_2') \in \mathcal{B}^i_{h,\varepsilon}$ and $dis(l, l') \leq h\}$;
10: $i \leftarrow i + 1$;
11: **until** $\mathcal{B}^i_{h,\varepsilon} = \mathcal{B}^{i-1}_{h,\varepsilon}$
12: $\mathcal{B}_{h,\varepsilon} = \mathcal{B}^i_{h,\varepsilon}$;
13: **if** $((P_1, v_0), (P_2, v_0)) \in \mathcal{B}_{h,\varepsilon}$ **then**
14: return **true**;
15: **else**
16: return **false**;
17: **end if**

a τ event, or a communication event. Besides, a transition can be a time progress less than d, which might be caused by the occurrence of a boundary interrupt or a communication interrupt during a continuous evolution. The new transition will be added only when the running time for each ODE F_j^m, denoted by t_j^m, is less than the corresponding equilibrium time. Therefore, for either process P_m, whenever some ODE runs beyond its equilibrium time, the set of reachable transitions reaches a fixpoint by allowing precision ε and will not be extended any more. The set of reachable states can be obtained by collecting the post states of reachable transitions. Based on Definition 4, the second step (lines 7–17) decides whether the transition systems for P_1 and P_2 are approximately bisimilar with the given precisions.

The first part (lines 1–6) of the algorithm computes the transitions of processes. For each process P_m, its complexity is $O(|T(P_m).T|)$, which is $O(\lceil \frac{T_m}{d} \rceil + N_m)$, where T_m represents the execution time of P_m till termination or reaching the equilibrium time of some ODE, and N_m the number of atomic statements of P_m. The second part (lines 7–17) checks for P_1 and P_2 each pair of the states whose distance is within ε by traversing the outgoing transitions, to see if they are truly approximate bisimilar, till the fixpoint $\mathcal{B}_{h,\varepsilon}$ is reached.

We can compute the time complexity to be $O(Q_1^2 Q_2^2 T_1 T_2)$, where Q_m and T_m represent $O(|T(P_m).Q|)$ and $O(|T(P_m).T|)$ for $m = 1, 2$ respectively.

Theorem 2 (Correctness). *Algorithm 1 terminates, and for any* v_0, $P_1 \cong_{h,\varepsilon} P_2$ *iff* $((P_1, v_0), (P_2, v_0)) \in \mathcal{B}_{h,\varepsilon}$.

5 Discretization of HCSP

In this section, we consider the discretization of HCSP processes, by which the continuous dynamics is represented by discrete approximation. Let P be an HCSP process and (h, ε) be the precisions, our goal is to construct a discrete process D from P, s.t. P is (h, ε)-bisimilar with D, i.e., $P \cong_{h,\varepsilon} D$ holds.

5.1 Discretization of Continuous Dynamics

Since most differential equations do not have explicit solutions, the discretization of the dynamics is normally given by discrete approximation. Consider the ODE $\dot{\mathbf{x}} = \mathbf{f}(\mathbf{x})$ with the initial value $\widetilde{\mathbf{x}}_0 \in \mathbb{R}^n$, and assume $X(t, \widetilde{\mathbf{x}}_0)$ is the trajectory of the initial value problem along the time interval $[t_0, \infty)$. In the following discretization, assume h and ξ represent the time step size and the precision of the discretization, respectively. Our strategy is as follows:

- First, from the fact that $\dot{\mathbf{x}} = \mathbf{f}(\mathbf{x})$ is GAS, there must exist a sufficiently large T s.t. $\|X(t, \widetilde{\mathbf{x}}_0) - \bar{\mathbf{x}}\| < \xi$ holds when $t > T$, where $\bar{\mathbf{x}}$ is an equilibrium point. As a result, after time T, the value of $\mathbf{x}$ can be approximated by the equilibrium point $\bar{\mathbf{x}}$ and the distance between the actual value of $\mathbf{x}$ and $\bar{\mathbf{x}}$ is always within ξ.
- Then, for the bounded time interval $[t_0, T]$, we apply Euler method to discretize the continuous dynamics.

There are a range of different discretization methods for ODEs [30] and the Euler method is an effective one among them. According to the Euler method, the ODE $\dot{\mathbf{x}} = \mathbf{f}(\mathbf{x})$ is discretized as

$$(\mathbf{x} := \mathbf{x} + h\mathbf{f}(\mathbf{x}); \text{wait } h)^N$$

A sequence of approximate solutions $\{\mathbf{x}_i\}$ at time stamps $\{h_i\}$ for $i = 1, 2, \cdots, N$ with $N = \lceil \frac{T - t_0}{h} \rceil$ are obtained, satisfying (define $\mathbf{x}_0 = \widetilde{\mathbf{x}}_0$):

$$h_i = t_0 + i * h \quad \mathbf{x}_i = \mathbf{x}_{i-1} + h\mathbf{f}(\mathbf{x}_{i-1}).$$

$\|X(h_i, \widetilde{\mathbf{x}}_0) - \mathbf{x}_i\|$ represents the discretization error at time h_i. To estimate the global error of the approximation, by Theorem **3** in [25], we can prove the following theorem:

Theorem 3 (Global error with an initial error). *Let $X(t, \widetilde{\mathbf{x}}_0)$ be a solution on $[t_0, T]$ of the initial value problem $\dot{\mathbf{x}} = \mathbf{f}(\mathbf{x}), \mathbf{x}(t_0) = \widetilde{\mathbf{x}}_0$, and L the Lipschitz constant s.t. for any compact set S of $\mathbb{R}^n$, $\|\mathbf{f}(\mathbf{y}_1) - \mathbf{f}(\mathbf{y}_2)\| \leq L\|\mathbf{y}_1 - \mathbf{y}_2\|$ for all $\mathbf{y}_1, \mathbf{y}_2 \in S$. Let $\mathbf{x}_0 \in \mathbb{R}^n$ satisfy $\|\mathbf{x}_0 - \widetilde{\mathbf{x}}_0\| \leq \xi_1$. Then there exists an $h_0 > 0$, s.t. for all h satisfying $0 < h \leq h_0$, and for all n satisfying $nh \leq (T - t_0)$, the sequence $\mathbf{x}_n = \mathbf{x}_{n-1} + h\mathbf{f}(\mathbf{x}_{n-1})$ satisfies:*

$$\|X(nh, \widetilde{\mathbf{x}}_0) - \mathbf{x}_n\| \leq e^{(T-t_0)L}\xi_1 + \frac{h}{2} \max_{\zeta \in [t_0, T]} \|X''(\zeta, \widetilde{\mathbf{x}}_0)\| \frac{e^{L(T-t_0)} - 1}{L}$$

By Theorem 3 and the property of GAS, we can prove the following main theorem.

Theorem 4 (Approximation of an ODE). *Let $X(t, \widetilde{\mathbf{x}}_0)$ be a solution on $[t_0, \infty]$ of the initial value problem $\dot{\mathbf{x}} = \mathbf{f}(\mathbf{x}), \mathbf{x}(t_0) = \widetilde{\mathbf{x}}_0$, and L the Lipschitz constant. Assume $\dot{\mathbf{x}} = \mathbf{f}(\mathbf{x})$ is GAS with the equilibrium point $\bar{\mathbf{x}}$. Then for any precision $\xi > 0$, there exist $h > 0, T > 0$ and $\xi_1 > 0$ s.t. $\dot{\mathbf{x}} = \mathbf{f}(\mathbf{x}), \mathbf{x}(t_0) = \widetilde{\mathbf{x}}_0$ and $\mathbf{x} := \mathbf{x}_0; (\mathbf{x} := \mathbf{x} + h\mathbf{f}(\mathbf{x}); \textit{wait } h)^N; \mathbf{x} := \bar{\mathbf{x}};$ **stop** with $N = \lceil \frac{T-t_0}{h} \rceil$ are (h, ξ)-approximately bisimilar, in which $\|\mathbf{x}_0 - \widetilde{\mathbf{x}}_0\| < \xi_1$ holds, i.e., there is an error between the initial values.*

5.2 Discretization of HCSP

We continue to consider the discretization of HCSP processes, among which any arbitrary number of ODEs, the discrete dynamics, and communications are involved. Below, given an HCSP process P, we use $D_{h,\varepsilon}(P)$ to represent the discretized process of P, with parameters h and ε to denote the step size and the precision (i.e. the maximal "distance" between states in P and $D_{h,\varepsilon}(P)$), respectively.

Before giving the discretization of HCSP processes, we need to introduce the notion of readiness variables. In order to express the readiness information of communication events, for each channel ch, we introduce two boolean variables $ch?$ and $ch!$, to represent whether the input and output events along ch are ready to occur. We will see that in the discretization, the readiness information of partner events is necessary to specify the behavior of communication interrupt.

Table 1 lists the definition of $D_{h,\varepsilon}(P)$. For each rule, the original process is listed above the line, while the discretized process is defined below the line. For skip, $x := e$ and wait d, they are kept unchanged in the discretization. For input $ch?x$, it is discretized as itself, and furthermore, before $ch?x$ occurs, $ch?$ is assigned to 1 to represent that $ch?x$ becomes ready, and in contrary, after $ch?x$ occurs, $ch?$ is reset to 0. The output $ch!e$ is handled similarly. The compound constructs, $P;Q$, $P \sqcap Q$, P^* and $P\|Q$ are discretized inductively according to their structure. For $B \rightarrow P$, B is still approximated to B and P is discretized inductively. For external choice $[]_{i \in I} io_i \rightarrow P_i$, the readiness variables io_i for all $i \in I$ are set to 1 at first, and after the choice is taken, all of them are reset to 0

Table 1. The rules for discretization of HCSP

$$\frac{\text{skip}}{\text{skip}} \quad \frac{x := e}{x := e} \quad \frac{\text{wait } d}{\text{wait } d}$$

$$\frac{ch?x}{ch? := 1; ch?x; ch? := 0} \quad \frac{ch!e}{ch! := 1; ch!e; ch! := 0}$$

$$\frac{P; Q}{D_{h,\varepsilon}(P); D_{h,\varepsilon}(Q)} \quad \frac{B \to P}{B \to D_{h,\varepsilon}(P)} \quad \frac{P \sqcap Q}{D_{h,\varepsilon}(P) \sqcap D_{h,\varepsilon}(Q)}$$

$$\frac{[\!]_{i \in I} io_i \to P_i}{\forall i \in I.io_i := 1; [\!]_{i \in I} io_i \to (\forall i \in I.io_i := 0; D_{h,\varepsilon}(P_i))}$$

$$\frac{\langle \dot{\mathbf{x}} = \mathbf{f}(\mathbf{x}) \& B \rangle}{(N(B,\varepsilon) \to (\mathbf{x} := \mathbf{x} + h\mathbf{f}(\mathbf{x}); \text{wait } h))^{\lceil \frac{T}{h} \rceil}; N(B,\varepsilon) \to (\mathbf{x} := \bar{\mathbf{x}}; \mathbf{stop})}$$

$$\frac{\langle \dot{\mathbf{x}} = \mathbf{f}(\mathbf{x}) \& B \rangle \trianglerighteq [\!]_{i \in I}(io_i \to Q_i)}{\begin{array}{c}\forall i \in I.io_i := 1; (N(B,\varepsilon) \to \forall i \in I.io_i \wedge \neg \overline{io_i} \to (\mathbf{x} := \mathbf{x} + h\mathbf{f}(\mathbf{x}); \text{wait } h))^{\lceil \frac{T}{h} \rceil}; \\ \neg N(B,\varepsilon) \wedge \forall i \in I.io_i \wedge \neg \overline{io_i} \to \forall i \in I.io_i := 0; \\ \exists i.io_i \wedge \overline{io_i} \to ([\!]_{i \in I} io_i \to (\forall i \in I.io_i := 0; D_{h,\varepsilon}(Q_i))); \\ (N(B,\varepsilon) \wedge \forall i \in I.io_i \wedge \neg \overline{io_i}) \to (\mathbf{x} := \bar{\mathbf{x}}; \mathbf{stop});\end{array}}$$

$$\frac{P^*}{(D_{h,\varepsilon}(P))^*} \quad \frac{P \| Q}{D_{h,\varepsilon}(P) \| D_{h,\varepsilon}(Q)}$$

and the corresponding process is discretized. Notice that because I is finite, the $\forall$ operator is defined as an abbreviation of the conjunction over I.

Given a boolean expression B and a precision ε, we define $N(B,\varepsilon)$ to be a boolean expression which holds in the ε-neighbourhood of B. For instance, if B is $x > 2$, then $N(B,\varepsilon)$ is $x > 2 - \varepsilon$. For a continuous evolution $\langle \dot{\mathbf{x}} = \mathbf{f}(\mathbf{x}) \& B \rangle$, under the premise that $\dot{\mathbf{x}} = \mathbf{f}(\mathbf{x})$ is GAS, there must exists time T such that when the time is larger than T, the distance between the actual state of $\mathbf{x}$ and the equilibrium point, denoted by $\bar{\mathbf{x}}$, is less than ε. Then according to Theorem 3, $\langle \dot{\mathbf{x}} = \mathbf{f}(\mathbf{x}) \& B \rangle$ is discretized as follows: First, it is a repetition of the assignment to $\mathbf{x}$ according to the Euler method for at most $\lceil \frac{T}{h} \rceil$ number of times, and then followed by the assignment of $\mathbf{x}$ to the equilibrium point and stop forever. Both of them are guarded by the condition $N(B,\varepsilon)$. For a communication interrupt $\langle \dot{\mathbf{x}} = \mathbf{f}(\mathbf{x}) \& B \rangle \trianglerighteq [\!]_{i \in I}(io_i \to Q_i)$, suppose T is sufficiently large s.t. when the time is larger than T, the distance between the actual state of $\mathbf{x}$ and the equilibrium point, denoted by $\bar{\mathbf{x}}$, is less than ε, and furthermore, if the interruption occurs, it must occur before T, and let $\overline{ch*}$ be the dual of $ch*$, e.g., if $ch* = ch?$, then $\overline{ch*} = ch!$ and vice versa. After all the readiness variables corresponding to $\{io_i\}_I$ are set to 1 at the beginning, the discretization is taken by the following steps: first, if $N(B,\varepsilon)$ holds and no communication among $\{io_i\}_{i \in I}$ is ready, it executes following the discretization of continuous evolution, for at most $\lceil \frac{T}{h} \rceil$ number of steps; then if $N(B,\varepsilon)$ turns false without any communication occurring, the whole process terminates and meanwhile the readiness variables are reset to 0; otherwise if some communications get ready, an external choice between these ready communications is taken, and then, the readiness variables are reset to 0 and the corresponding Q_i is followed; finally, if the communications never occur and the continuous evolution never terminates, the continuous variable is assigned to the equilibrium point and the time progresses forever. It should be noticed that, the readiness variables of the partner processes will be used to decide whether a communication is able to occur. They are shared between parallel processes, but will always be written by one side.

Consider the water tank system introduced in Sect. 4, by using the rules in Table 1, a discretized system $WTS_{h,\varepsilon}$ is obtained as follows:

$$
\begin{aligned}
WTS_{h,\varepsilon} &\stackrel{\text{def}}{=} Watertank_{h,\varepsilon} \| Controller_{h,\varepsilon} \\
Watertank_{h,\varepsilon} &\stackrel{\text{def}}{=} v := v_0; d := d_0; (v = 1 \rightarrow (wl! := 1; \\
&\quad (wl! \wedge \neg wl? \rightarrow (d = d + h(Q_{max} - \pi r^2 \sqrt{2gd}); wait\ h;))^{\lceil \frac{T_1}{h} \rceil}; \\
&\quad wl! \wedge wl? \rightarrow (wl!d; wl! := 0; cv? := 1; cv?v; cv? := 0); \\
&\quad wl! \wedge \neg wl? \rightarrow (d = Q_{max}^2 / 2g\pi^2 r^4; \mathbf{stop})); \\
&\quad v = 0 \rightarrow (wl! := 1; \\
&\quad (wl! \wedge \neg wl? \rightarrow (d = d + h(-\pi r^2 \sqrt{2gd}); wait\ h;))^{\lceil \frac{T_2}{h} \rceil}; \\
&\quad wl! \wedge wl? \rightarrow (wl!d; wl! := 0; cv? := 1; cv?v; cv? := 0); \\
&\quad wl! \wedge \neg wl? \rightarrow (d = 0; \mathbf{stop})))^* \\
Controller_{h,\varepsilon} &\stackrel{\text{def}}{=} y := v_0; x := d_0; (wait\ p; wl? := 1; wl?x; wl? := 0; \\
&\quad x \geq ub \rightarrow y := 0; x \leq lb \rightarrow y := 1; cv! := 1; cv!y; cv! := 0)^*
\end{aligned}
$$

5.3 Properties

Before giving the main theorem, we introduce some notations. In order to keep the consistency between the behavior of an HCSP process and its discretized process, we introduce the notion of (δ, ϵ)-robustly safe. First, let ϕ denote a formula and ϵ a precision, define $N(\phi, -\epsilon)$ as the set $\{\mathbf{x} | \mathbf{x} \in \phi \wedge \forall \mathbf{y} \in \neg\phi. \|\mathbf{x} - \mathbf{y}\| > \epsilon\}$. Intuitively, when $\mathbf{x} \in N(\phi, -\epsilon)$, then $\mathbf{x}$ is inside ϕ and moreover the distance between it and the boundary of ϕ is greater than ϵ.

Definition 6 (**(δ, ϵ)-robustly safe**). *An HCSP process P is (δ, ϵ)-robustly safe, for a given initial state v_0, a time precision $\delta > 0$ and a value precision $\epsilon > 0$, if the following two conditions hold:*

- *for every continuous evolution $\langle \dot{\mathbf{x}} = \mathbf{f}(\mathbf{x}) \& B \rangle$ occurring in P, when P executes up to $\langle \dot{\mathbf{x}} = \mathbf{f}(\mathbf{x}) \& B \rangle$ at time t with state v, if $v(B) = false$, then there exists $\widehat{t} > t$ with $\widehat{t} - t < \delta$ s.t. for any σ satisfying $\mathbf{d}(\sigma, v[\mathbf{x} \mapsto X(\widehat{t}, \widetilde{\mathbf{x}}_0)]) < \epsilon$, $\sigma \in N(\neg B, -\epsilon)$, where $X(t, \widetilde{\mathbf{x}}_0)])$ is the solution of $\dot{\mathbf{x}} = \mathbf{f}(\mathbf{x})$ with initial value $\widetilde{\mathbf{x}}_0 = v_0(\mathbf{x})$;*
- *for every alternative process $B \rightarrow P$ occurring in S, if B depends on continuous variables of P, then when P executes up to $B \rightarrow P$ at state v, $v \in N(B, -\epsilon)$ or $v \in N(\neg B, -\epsilon)$.*

As a result, when P is discretized with a time error less than δ and a value error less than ϵ, then P and its discretized process have the same control flow. The main theorem is given below.

Theorem 5. *Let P be an HCSP process and v_0 is the initial state. Assume P is (δ, ϵ)-robustly safe with respect to v_0. Let $0 < \varepsilon < \epsilon$ be a precision. If for any ODE $\dot{\mathbf{x}} = \mathbf{f}(\mathbf{x})$ occurring in P, $\mathbf{f}$ is Lipschitz continuous and $\dot{\mathbf{x}} = \mathbf{f}(\mathbf{x})$ is GAS with $\mathbf{f}(\bar{\mathbf{x}}) = 0$ for some $\bar{\mathbf{x}}$, then there exist $h > 0$ and the equilibrium time for each ODE F in P, $T_F > 0$, s.t. $P \cong_{h,\varepsilon} D_{h,\varepsilon}(P)$.*

We can compute that, the relation $\mathcal{L}\delta + Mh \leq \varepsilon$ holds for some constants $\mathcal{L}$ and M. Especially, $\mathcal{L}$ is the maximum value of the first derivative of $\mathbf{x}$ with respect to t. More details can be found in [34].

6 Case Study

In this section, we illustrate our method through the safety verification of the water tank system, *WTS*, that is introduced in Sect. 4. The safety property is to maintain the value of d within $[low, high]$, which needs to compute the reachable set of *WTS*. However, it is usually difficult because of the complexity of the system. Fortunately, the reachable set of the discretized $WTS_{h,\varepsilon}$ in Sect. 5 could be easily obtained. Therefore, we can verify the original system *WTS* through the discretized one, $WTS_{h,\varepsilon}$, as follows.

Table 2. The reachable set for different precisions

ε	h	$Reach(WTS_{h,\varepsilon})$	$Reach(WTS)$
0.2	0.2	[3.41, 6.5]	[3.21, 6.7]
0.1	0.05	[3.42, 6.47]	[3.32, 6.57]
0.05	0.01	[3.43, 6.46]	[3.38, 6.51]

In order to analyze the system, first of all, we set the values of parameters to $Q_{max} = 2.0$, $\pi = 3.14$, $r = 0.18$, $g = 9.8$, $p = 1$, $lb = 4.1$, $ub = 5.9$, $low = 3.3$, $high = 6.6$, $v_0 = 1$, and $d_0 = 4.5$ (units are omitted here). Then, by simulation, we compute the values of δ and ϵ as 0.5 and 0.24, s.t. *WTS* is (δ, ϵ)-robustly safe. By Theorem 5, for a given ε with $0 < \varepsilon < \epsilon$, since $\dot{d}$ and d are monotonic for both ODEs, we can compute a $h > 0$ s.t. $WTS \cong_{h,\varepsilon} WTS_{h,\varepsilon}$. For different values of ε and h, $Reach(WTS_{h,\varepsilon})$ could be computed, and then based on Theorem 1, we can obtain $Reach(WTS)$. Table 2 shows the results for different choices of ε and h. As seen from the results, when the values of precisions become smaller, $Reach(WTS_{h,\varepsilon})$ and $Reach(WTS)$ get closer and tighter. For the smaller precisions, i.e., $(\varepsilon = 0.1, h = 0.05)$ and $(\varepsilon = 0.05, h = 0.01)$, the safety property of the system is proved to be true. However, for $(\varepsilon = 0.2, h = 0.2)$, the safety property of the system can not be promised.

7 Conclusion

Approximate bisimulation is a useful notion for analyzing complex dynamic systems via simpler abstract systems. In this paper, we define the approximate bisimulation of hybrid systems modelled by HCSP, and present an algorithm for deciding whether two HCSP processes are approximately bisimilar. We have proved that if all the ODEs are GAS, then the algorithm terminates in a finite number of steps. Furthermore, we define the discretization of HCSP processes, by representing the continuous dynamics by Euler approximation. We have proved for an HCSP process that, if the process is robustly safe, and if each ODE occurring in the process is Lipschitz continuous and GAS, then there must exist a discretization of the original HCSP process such that they are approximate bisimilar with the given precisions. Thus, the results of analysis performed on the discrete system can be carried over into the original dynamic system, and vice versa. At the end, we illustrate our method by presenting the discretization of a water tank example. Note that GAS and robust safety are very restrictive from a theoretical point of view, but most of real applications satisfy these conditions in practice.

Regarding future work, we will focus on the implementation, in particular, the transformation from HCSP to ANSI-C. Moreover, it could be interesting to investigate approximate bisimularity with time bounds so that the assumptions of GAS and robust safety can be dropped. In addition, it deserves to investigate richer refinement theories for HCSP based on the notion of approximately bisimulation, although itself can be seen as a refinement relation as discussed in process algebra.

References

1. Simulink User's Guide (2013). http://www.mathworks.com/help/pdf_doc/simulink/sl_using.pdf
2. Stateflow User's Guide (2013). http://www.mathworks.com/help/pdf_doc/stateflow/sf_using.pdf
3. SysML V 1.4 Beta Specification (2013). http://www.omg.org/spec/SysML
4. Ahmad, E., Dong, Y., Wang, S., Zhan, N., Zou, L.: Adding formal meanings to AADL with hybrid annex. In: Lanese, I., Madelaine, E. (eds.) FACS 2014. LNCS, vol. 8997, pp. 228–247. Springer, Heidelberg (2015). doi:10.1007/978-3-319-15317-9_15
5. Alur, R., Dang, T., Esposito, J., Hur, Y., Ivancic, F., Kumar, V., Mishra, P., Pappas, G., Sokolsky, O.: Hierarchical modeling and analysis of embedded systems. Proc. IEEE **91**(1), 11–28 (2003)
6. Angeli, D., et al.: A Lyapunov approach to incremental stability properties. IEEE Trans. Autom. Control **47**(3), 410–421 (2002)
7. Angeli, D., Sontag, E.: Forward completeness, unboundedness observability, and their Lyapunov characterizations. Syst. Control Lett. **38**(4), 209–217 (1999)
8. Chen, M., Ravn, A., Wang, S., Yang, M., Zhan, N.: A two-way path between formal and informal design of embedded systems. In: UTP 2016. LNCS (2016)

9. Dormoy, F.: Scade 6: a model based solution for safety critical software development. ERTS **08**, 1–9 (2008)
10. Eker, J., Janneck, J., et al.: Taming heterogeneity - the Ptolemy approach. Proc. IEEE **91**(1), 127–144 (2003)
11. Girard, A., Julius, A., Pappas, G.: Approximate simulation relations for hybrid systems. Discrete Event Dyn. Syst. **18**(2), 163–179 (2008)
12. Girard, A., Pappas, G.: Approximation metrics for discrete and continuous systems. IEEE Trans. Autom. Control **52**(5), 782–798 (2007)
13. Guelev, D., Wang, S., Zhan, N.: Hoare-style reasoning about hybrid CSP in the duration calculus. Technical report ISCAS-SKLCS-13-01, Institute of Software, Chinese Academy of Sciences (2013)
14. He, J.: From CSP to hybrid systems. In: A Classical Mind, Essays in Honour of C.A.R. Hoare, pp. 171–189. Prentice Hall International (UK) Ltd. (1994)
15. Henzinger, T., Ho, P., Wong-Toi, H.: Algorithmic analysis of nonlinear hybrid systems. IEEE Trans. Autom. Control **43**(4), 540–554 (1998)
16. Henzinger, T.A., Sifakis, J.: The embedded systems design challenge. In: Misra, J., Nipkow, T., Sekerinski, E. (eds.) FM 2006. LNCS, vol. 4085, pp. 1–15. Springer, Heidelberg (2006). doi:10.1007/11813040_1
17. Henzinger, T.A.: The theory of hybrid automata. In: LICS 1996, pp. 278–292 (1996)
18. Julius, A., D'Innocenzo, A., Di Benedetto, M., Pappas, G.: Approximate equivalence and synchronization of metric transition systems. Syst. Control Lett. **58**(2), 94–101 (2009)
19. Khalil, H.K., Grizzle, J.W.: Nonlinear Systems, vol. 3. Prentice Hall, New Jersey (1996)
20. Lanotte, R., Tini, S.: Taylor approximation for hybrid systems. In: Morari, M., Thiele, L. (eds.) HSCC 2005. LNCS, vol. 3414, pp. 402–416. Springer, Heidelberg (2005). doi:10.1007/978-3-540-31954-2_26
21. Lee, E.A.: What's ahead for embedded software? Computer **33**(9), 18–26 (2000)
22. Liu, J., Lv, J., Quan, Z., Zhan, N., Zhao, H., Zhou, C., Zou, L.: A calculus for hybrid CSP. In: Ueda, K. (ed.) APLAS 2010. LNCS, vol. 6461, pp. 1–15. Springer, Heidelberg (2010). doi:10.1007/978-3-642-17164-2_1
23. Majumdar, R., Zamani, M.: Approximately bisimilar symbolic models for digital control systems. In: Madhusudan, P., Seshia, S.A. (eds.) CAV 2012. LNCS, vol. 7358, pp. 362–377. Springer, Heidelberg (2012). doi:10.1007/978-3-642-31424-7_28
24. Platzer, A.: Differential-algebraic dynamic logic for differential-algebraic programs. J. Logic Comput. **20**(1), 309–352 (2010)
25. Platzer, A.: The complete proof theory of hybrid systems. In: LICS, pp. 541–550. IEEE (2012)
26. Pola, G., Girard, A., Tabuada, P.: Approximately bisimilar symbolic models for nonlinear control systems. Automatica **44**(10), 2508–2516 (2008)
27. Pola, G., Pepe, P., Di Benedetto, M.: Symbolic models for networks of discrete-time nonlinear control systems. In: ACC, pp. 1787–1792. IEEE (2014)
28. Selic, B., Gérard, S.: Modeling and Analysis of Real-Time and Embedded Systems with UML and MARTE: Developing Cyber-Physical Systems. Elsevier, Amsterdam (2013)
29. Sontag, E.D.: Mathematical Control Theory: Deterministic Finite Dimensional Systems, vol. 6. Springer, Heidelberg (2013)
30. Stoer, J., Bulirsch, R.: Introduction to Numerical Analysis, vol. 12. Springer, Heidelberg (2013)
31. Tiller, M.: Introduction to Physical Modeling with Modelica, vol. 615. Springer, Heidelberg (2012)

32. Tiwari, A.: Abstractions for hybrid systems. Formal Methods Syst. Des. **32**(1), 57–83 (2008)
33. Wang, S., Zhan, N., Guelev, D.: An assume/guarantee based compositional calculus for hybrid CSP. In: Agrawal, M., Cooper, S.B., Li, A. (eds.) TAMC 2012. LNCS, vol. 7287, pp. 72–83. Springer, Heidelberg (2012). doi:10.1007/978-3-642-29952-0_13
34. Yan, G., Jiao, L., Li, Y., Wang, S., Zhan, N.: Approximate Bisimulation and Discretization of Hybrid CSP. CoRR, abs/1609.00091, August 2016
35. Zhan, N., Wang, S., Zhao, H.: Formal modelling, analysis and verification of hybrid systems. In: Liu, Z., Woodcock, J., Zhu, H. (eds.) Unifying Theories of Programming and Formal Engineering Methods. LNCS, vol. 8050, pp. 207–281. Springer, Heidelberg (2013). doi:10.1007/978-3-642-39721-9_5
36. Chaochen, Z., Ji, W., Ravn, A.P.: A formal description of hybrid systems. In: Alur, R., Henzinger, T.A., Sontag, E.D. (eds.) HS 1995. LNCS, vol. 1066, pp. 511–530. Springer, Heidelberg (1996). doi:10.1007/BFb0020972

A Linear Programming Relaxation Based Approach for Generating Barrier Certificates of Hybrid Systems

Zhengfeng Yang[1], Chao Huang[2], Xin Chen[2], Wang Lin[3(✉)], and Zhiming Liu[4]

[1] Shanghai Key Lab of Trustworthy Computing, East China Normal University, Shanghai, China
zfyang@sei.ecnu.edu.cn

[2] State Key Lab for Novel Software Technology, Nanjing University, Nanjing, China
{huangchao,chenxin}@nju.edu.cn

[3] Key Lab of Mathematics Mechanization, AMSS, CAS, Beijing, China
linwang@wzu.edu.cn

[4] Center for Research and Innovation in Software Engineering, Southwest University, Chongqing, China
zhimingliu88@swu.edu.cn

Abstract. This paper presents a linear programming (LP) relaxation based approach for generating polynomial barrier certificates for safety verification of semi-algebraic hybrid systems. The key idea is to introduce an LP relaxation to encode the set of nonnegativity constraints derived from the conditions of the associated barrier certificates and then resort to LP solvers to find the solutions. The most important benefit of the LP relaxation based approach is that it possesses a much lower computational complexity and hence can be solved very efficiently, which is demonstrated by the theoretical analysis on complexity as well as the experiment on a set of examples gathered from the literature. As far as we know, it is the first method that enables LP relaxation based polynomial barrier certificate generation.

Keywords: Formal verification · Hybrid systems · Barrier certificates · Linear programming relaxation

1 Introduction

Safety verification of hybrid systems has attracted much research attention in recent years [2]. This is mainly due to the requirement of ensuring the safety of embedded systems whose complex behaviors can be exhibited by hybrid systems via interacting discrete and continuous dynamics [3,12]. In principle, safety verification aims to decide that starting from an initial set, whether a system can evolve to some unsafe region in the state space. A successful verification can give more confidence in the verified systems.

Barrier certificate based methods are developed to handle the safety verification problem [13,16,17,27]. A barrier certificate is a function of state that

J. Fitzgerald et al. (Eds.): FM 2016, LNCS 9995, pp. 721–738, 2016.
DOI: 10.1007/978-3-319-48989-6_44

divides the state space into two parts. All system trajectories starting from a given set of initial conditions fall into one side while the unsafe region locates on the other. Thus, the problem of safety verification is converted to the problem of barrier certificate generation. Compared with reachable set computation, when encountering nonlinear systems, a barrier function is much easier to compute. It also gives more exact result when the safety property refers to infinite horizon [17].

Barrier certificate generation is a computationally intensive task. Usually, a function of a specific form with unknown coefficients is given as the template, and then computational methods based on different principles are used to determine the value of those unknown coefficients so that the conditions of the desired barrier certificate are satisfied. For barrier certificate based verification, its effectiveness and practicality are decided to a large extent by the efficiency of the computational methods, therefore the method for effective computation becomes a key point.

There have been many barrier certificates of different types proposed for hybrid systems with different features [13,15,21,27,31]. Among them, polynomial barrier certificates for semi-algebraic hybrid systems (i.e. those systems whose vector fields are polynomials and whose set descriptions are polynomial equalities or inequalities) receive most attention, as they are more universal. For barrier certificates generation, methods based on sums of squares (SOS) relaxation are quite popular, as the associated semidefinite programming (SDP) has a much lower computational complexity and there are many efficient solvers available.

The paper focuses on introducing linear programming (LP) relaxation to generating polynomial barrier certificates with convex condition for semi-algebraic hybrid systems. Compared with SOS relaxation based approaches, our LP relaxation based method offers three main advantages: First, LP has a much lower computational complexity than SDP does, thus it can be solved more quickly. Second, LP provides a much higher numerical stability and hence can treat many cases where SDP generates invalid polynomials due to numerical errors [15,21]. At last, LP gives a new encoding of polynomial positivity quite different from SDP, and thus has the potential to generate polynomials that SDP is unable to produce. It is a necessary complement to relaxation based methods as it can generate barrier certificates uncovered by existing methods.

The proposed method considers a polynomial barrier certificate whose coefficients must satisfy a set of nonnegativity constraints of multivariate polynomials over semi-algebraic sets. It employs the theory of Krivine-Vasilescu-Handelman's (KVH) Positivstellensatz [14] to construct an LP relaxation of the constraint set and then relies on LP solvers to find the solution for the coefficients of the barrier certificate. The theoretical analysis demonstrates that for a hybrid system, the complexity of finding the solution based on the LP solver is approximately $O(n^{2d+D})$ while that based on the SDP solver is approximately $O(n^{4D})$, where n is the number of system variables, d and D are the degree bounds of the barrier certificate and its nonnegative representation derived from LP relaxation and SOS relaxation, respectively. Our LP relaxation based method is compared with the SOS relaxation based approach over a set of benchmarks gathered from the literature, which shows that our method provides much better efficiency. To the best of our knowledge, it is the first study that enables LP relaxation based polynomial barrier certificate generation.

We start by defining continuous systems and hybrid systems in Sect. 2. We then present our approach and give a complexity analysis on both our LP relaxation based method and the SOS relaxation based method in Sect. 3. We present how to use our approach to generate barrier certificate for several nontrivial examples and compare the efficiency of our method with SOS relaxation based method over a set of benchmarks in Sect. 4. We compare with related works in Sect. 5 before concluding.

2 Continuous and Hybrid Systems

Notations. Let $\mathbb{R}$ and $\mathbb{N}$ be the field of real number and natural number, respectively; $\mathbb{R}[\mathbf{x}]$ denotes the polynomial ring with coefficients in $\mathbb{R}$ over $\mathbf{x} = [x_1, x_2, \cdots, x_n]^T$, and $\mathbb{R}[\mathbf{x}]^n$ denotes the n-dimensional polynomial ring vector.

A continuous dynamical system is modeled by a finite number of first-order ordinary differential equations

$$\dot{\mathbf{x}} = \mathbf{f}(\mathbf{x}), \tag{1}$$

where $\dot{\mathbf{x}}$ denotes the derivative of $\mathbf{x}$ with respect to the time variable t, and $\mathbf{f}(\mathbf{x})$ is called vector field $\mathbf{f}(\mathbf{x}) = [f_1(\mathbf{x}), \cdots, f_n(\mathbf{x})]^T$ defined on an open set $\Psi \subseteq \mathbb{R}^n$. We assume that $\mathbf{f}$ satisfies the local Lipschitz condition, which ensures that given $\mathbf{x}(0) = \mathbf{x}_0$, there exists a time $T > 0$ and a unique function $\tau : [0, T) \mapsto \mathbb{R}^n$ such that $\tau(t) = \mathbf{x}(t)$. And $\mathbf{x}(t)$ is called a solution of (1) that starts at a certain initial state $\mathbf{x}_0$. Namely, $\mathbf{x}(t)$ is also called a trajectory of (1) from $\mathbf{x}_0$.

Definition 1 (Continuous System). *A continuous system over* $\mathbf{x}$ *consists of a tuple* $\mathbf{S} : \langle \Theta, \mathbf{f}, \Psi \rangle$*, wherein* $\Theta \subseteq \mathbb{R}^n$ *is a set of initial states,* $\mathbf{f}$ *is a vector field over the domain* $\Psi \subseteq \mathbb{R}^n$.

Hybrid systems involve both continuous dynamics as well as discrete transitions. To model hybrid systems, we use the notion of hybrid automata [3].

Definition 2 (Hybrid Automata). *A* hybrid automaton *is a system* $\mathbf{H} : \langle L, X, F, \Psi, E, G, R, \Theta, \ell_0 \rangle$*, where*

- L*, a finite set of locations (or models);*
- $X \subseteq \mathbb{R}^n$ *is the continuous state space. The hybrid state space of the system is defined by* $\mathcal{X} = L \times X$ *and a state is defined by* $(\ell, \mathbf{x}) \in \mathcal{X}$*;*
- $F : L \to (\mathbb{R}^n \to \mathbb{R}^n)$*, assigns to each location* $\ell \in L$ *a locally Lipschitz continuous vector field* $\mathbf{f}_\ell$*;*
- Ψ *assigns to each location* $\ell \in L$ *a* location condition (location invariant) $\Psi(\ell) \subseteq \mathbb{R}^n$*;*

- $E \subseteq L \times L$ *is a finite set of discrete transitions;*
- G *assigns to each transition* $e \in E$ *a switching guard* $G_e \subseteq \mathbb{R}^n$*;*
- R *assigns to each transition* $e \in E$ *a reset function* $R_e : \mathbb{R}^n \rightarrow \mathbb{R}^n$*;*
- $\Theta \subseteq \mathbb{R}^n$*, an initial continuous state set;*
- $\ell_0 \in L$*, the initial location. The initial state space of the system is defined by* $\ell_0 \times \Theta$.

A trajectory [31] of $\mathbf{H}$ is an infinite sequence of states

$$(l_0, \mathbf{x}_0),\ (l_1, \mathbf{x}_1), \cdots, (l_i, \mathbf{x}_i),\ (l_{i+1}, \mathbf{x}_{i+1}), \cdots$$

such that

- **[Initiation]** $(l_0, \mathbf{x}_0) \in \ell_0 \times \Theta$;
  Furthermore, for each consecutive pair $(l_i, \mathbf{x}_i), (l_{i+1}, \mathbf{x}_{i+1})$, one of the two *consecution* conditions holds:
- **[Discrete Consecution]** $e = (l_i, l_{i+1}) \in E$, $\mathbf{x}_i \in G_e$ and $x_{i+1} = R_e(\mathbf{x}_i)$; or
- **[Continuous Consecution]** $l_i = l_{i+1} = \ell$, and there exists a time interval $[0, \delta]$ such that the solution $\mathbf{x}(\mathbf{x}_i; t)$ to $\dot{\mathbf{x}} = \mathbf{f}_\ell$ evolves from $\mathbf{x}_i$ to $\mathbf{x}_{i+1}$, while satisfying the location invariant $\Psi(\ell)$. Formally,
  - $\mathbf{x}(\mathbf{x}_i, \delta) = \mathbf{x}_{i+1}$ and
  - $\forall t \in [0, \delta], \mathbf{x}(\mathbf{x}_i, t) \in \Psi(\ell)$.

A state $(\ell, \mathbf{x})$ is called a *reachable state* of a hybrid system $\mathbf{H}$ from the initial state set $\ell_0 \times \Theta$ if it appears in some trajectory of $\mathbf{H}$. During a continuous flow, the discrete location ℓ_i is maintained and the continuous state variables $\mathbf{x}$ evolve according to the differential equations $\dot{\mathbf{x}} = \mathbf{f}_{\ell_i}(\mathbf{x})$, with $\mathbf{x}$ satisfying the location invariant $\Psi(\ell_i)$. At the state $(\ell_i, \mathbf{x})$, if there is a discrete transition $e = (\ell_i, \ell_j) \in E$ such that $\mathbf{x} \in G_e$, the system may undergo a transition to location ℓ_j, and $\mathbf{x}$ will take the new value $\mathbf{x}'$, which is determined by the reset function R_e.

In this paper, we focus on continuous systems and hybrid systems whose elements are represented as polynomial relations (equalities and inequalities) over the system variables. In what follows, the definition of semi-algebraic hybrid system is provided. The definition of semi-algebraic continuous system is similar.

Definition 3 *(Semi-algebraic Hybrid System). A semi-algebraic hybrid system is a hybrid system:* $\mathbf{H} : \langle L,\ X,\ F,\ \Psi, E, G, R, \Theta, \ell_0 \rangle$*, where*

- *the continuous vector field* $F(\ell)$ *for each* $\ell \in L$ *is of the form* $\dot{\mathbf{x}} = \mathbf{f}_\ell(\mathbf{x})$*, where* $\mathbf{f}_\ell(\mathbf{x}) \in \mathbb{R}[\mathbf{x}]^n$*;*
- *the initial condition* Θ*, the location invariant* $\Psi(\ell)$ *for each* $\ell \in L$*, and the guard condition* G_e *for each* $e \in E$ *are semi-algebraic sets defined by polynomial inequalities with variables* $\mathbf{x}$*;* $R_e \in \mathbb{R}[\mathbf{x}]^n$ *is the reset function for each* $e \in E$.

For ease of presentation, the semi-algebraic sets Θ, $\Psi(\ell)$ and G_e in Definition 3 are represented as follows:

$$\begin{aligned}\Theta :&= \{\mathbf{x} \in \mathbb{R}^n \mid \theta_1(\mathbf{x}) \geq 0, \ldots, \theta_q(\mathbf{x}) \geq 0\},\\ \Psi(\ell) :&= \{\mathbf{x} \in \mathbb{R}^n \mid \psi_{\ell,1}(\mathbf{x}) \geq 0, \ldots, \psi_{\ell,r}(\mathbf{x}) \geq 0\},\\ G_e :&= \{\mathbf{x} \in \mathbb{R}^n \mid g_{e,1}(\mathbf{x}) \geq 0, \ldots, g_{e,s}(\mathbf{x}) \geq 0\},\end{aligned}$$

where $\ell \in L$, $e \in E$, and $\theta_i(\mathbf{x})$, $\psi_{\ell,j}(\mathbf{x})$, $g_{e,k}(\mathbf{x})$ are polynomials. In addition, hereafter we assume that the above semi-algebraic sets are compact.

Given a semi-algebraic hybrid system $\mathbf{H}$ with prespecified unsafe state set $\mathcal{X}_u = \ell \times X_u$, we say that the system $\mathbf{H}$ is *safe* if all trajectories of $\mathbf{H}$ starting from the initial state set $\ell_0 \times \Theta$, can not evolve to any state specified by $\mathcal{X}_u$. Given a semi-algebraic hybrid system $\mathbf{H}$, the problem of verifying the safety property is to decide that whether $\mathbf{H}$ is safe, or, any state specified by $\mathcal{X}_u$ is not reachable. Here we also assume that $\mathcal{X}_u$ is a compact semi-algebraic set, defined by

$$X_u(\ell) := \{\mathbf{x} \in \mathbb{R}^n \mid \zeta_{\ell,1}(\mathbf{x}) \geq 0, \ldots, \zeta_{\ell,p}(\mathbf{x}) \geq 0, \},$$

where $\zeta_{\ell,i} \in \mathbb{R}[\mathbf{x}], 1 \leq i \leq p$.

3 Computational Method for Barrier Certificates

For safety verification of (continuous or hybrid) dynamical systems, the notion of barrier certificates [16] plays an important role. A barrier certificate maps all the states in the reachable set to non-negative reals and all the states in the unsafe set to negative reals, thus can be employed to prove safety of dynamical systems. Utilizing barrier certificates has the benefit of avoiding explicit computation of the exact reachable set which is usually not tractable for nonlinear continuous and hybrid systems. In other words, a barrier certificate can be regarded as the over-approximation of the reachable set, and most importantly, is a boundary between the reachable set and the given unsafe state set. In the sequel, we propose a new computational method for generating the barrier certificates for safety verification of dynamical systems.

3.1 Barriers Certificates

As stated in [13], the key point in generating barrier certificates is how to establish verification conditions that are as less conservative as possible and how to efficiently compute the barrier certificates satisfying these verification conditions. Taking them into account, the idea that introduces auxiliary polynomials to offer relaxed verification conditions for barrier certificates of continuous and hybrid systems can be applied.

Theorem 1. *Let* $\mathbf{S} : \langle \Theta, \mathbf{f}, \Psi \rangle$ *be a semi-algebraic continuous system, and* X_u *be the given unsafe state set. Let* $\lambda(\mathbf{x})$ *be a given polynomial. If there exists a polynomial* $B(\mathbf{x}) \in \mathbb{R}[\mathbf{x}]$, *which satisfies the following conditions:*

(i) $B(\mathbf{x}) \geq 0 \, \forall \mathbf{x} \in \Theta$,
(ii) $\dot{B}(\mathbf{x}) - \lambda(\mathbf{x})B(\mathbf{x}) > 0 \, \forall \mathbf{x} \in \Psi$, *here* $\dot{B}(\mathbf{x})$ *denotes the Lie-derivative of* $B(\mathbf{x})$ *along the vector field* $\mathbf{f}$, *i.e.,* $\dot{B}(\mathbf{x}) = \sum_{i=1}^{n} \frac{\partial B}{\partial x_i} \cdot f_i(\mathbf{x})$,
(iii) $B(\mathbf{x}) < 0 \, \forall \mathbf{x} \in X_u$,

then $B(\mathbf{x})$ *is a barrier certificate of system* $\mathbf{S}$, *and the safety of* $\mathbf{S}$ *is guaranteed.*

Proof. Condition (ii) indicates that $\dot{B}(\mathbf{x}) > 0$ if $B(\mathbf{x}) = 0$. Therefore, by condition (i) and (ii), $B(\mathbf{x})$ cannot become negative during the continuous evolution of $\mathbf{S}$. Condition (iii) implies that all trajectories starting from Θ can not enter X_u. We can conclude $B(\mathbf{x})$ is a barrier certificate of $\mathbf{S}$, which can guarantee the safety of the system. □

Clearly, the existence of such a barrier certificate in Theorem 1 suffices to guarantee the safety property of the given semi-algebraic continuous system. Likewise, Theorem 1 can be generalized to attack safety verification of semi-algebraic hybrid systems.

Theorem 2. *Let* $\mathbf{H} : \langle L, X, F, \Psi, E, G, R, \Theta, \ell_0 \rangle$ *be a semi-algebraic hybrid system,* $\mathcal{X}_u$ *be the unsafe assertion. Let* $\lambda_\ell(\mathbf{x})$ *be given polynomials for all* $\ell \in L$, *and* $\gamma_e(\mathbf{x})$ *be given nonnegative polynomials for all* $e \in E$. *If there exists a polynomial* $B_\ell(\mathbf{x}) \in \mathbb{R}[\mathbf{x}]$ *for each location* $\ell \in L$, *which satisfies the following conditions:*

(i) $B_{\ell_0}(\mathbf{x}) \geq 0 \, \forall \mathbf{x} \in \Theta$,
(ii) $\dot{B}_\ell(\mathbf{x}) - \lambda_\ell(\mathbf{x})B_\ell(\mathbf{x}) > 0 \, \forall \mathbf{x} \in \Psi(\ell)$, *here* $\dot{B}_\ell(\mathbf{x})$ *denotes the Lie-derivative of* $B_\ell(\mathbf{x})$ *along the vector field* $\mathbf{f}_\ell$, *i.e.,* $\dot{B}_\ell(\mathbf{x}) = \sum_{i=1}^{n} \frac{\partial B_\ell}{\partial x_i} \cdot f_{\ell,i}(\mathbf{x})$,
(iii) $B_{\ell'}(\mathbf{x}') - \gamma_e(\mathbf{x})B_\ell(\mathbf{x}) \geq 0 \, \forall \mathbf{x}' = R_e(\mathbf{x}) \;\; \forall \mathbf{x} \in G_e, \, \forall e = (\ell, \ell') \in E$,
(iv) $B_\ell(\mathbf{x}) < 0 \, \forall \mathbf{x} \in X_u(\ell)$,

then $B_\ell(\mathbf{x})$ *is a barrier certificate at the location* ℓ, *and the safety of the system* $\mathbf{H}$ *is guaranteed.*

Proof. By condition (i), $B_{\ell_0}(\mathbf{x})$ is nonnegative on Θ. Condition (ii) indicates that $\dot{B}_\ell(\mathbf{x}) > 0$ if $B_\ell(\mathbf{x}) > 0$, thus yielding that $B_\ell(\mathbf{x})$ is always nonnegative during the continuous flow. Since γ_e is nonnegative, condition (iii) guarantees that $B_\ell(\mathbf{x})$ cannot become negative during every discrete transition. Moreover, condition (iv) shows that all reachable states of $\mathbf{H}$ cannot intersect with the unsafe region X_u. □

Remark 1. Our verification conditions of barrier certificates in Theorems 1 and 2 are also called as the polynomial-scale consecution of the inductive invariants defined in [23], which is less conservative than the constant-scale consecution given in [13].

3.2 Computation of Barrier Certificates

In this section, we consider how to construct barrier certificates given in Theorems 1 and 2 for semi-algebraic dynamical systems. Investigating Theorems 1 and 2, it turns out that all verification conditions can be encoded as nonnegativity constraints for polynomials over the corresponding semi-algebraic sets. For the given degree bound, one may construct the template of the barrier polynomial $B_\ell(\mathbf{x})$ whose coefficients are parameters. In this case, our objective is to find real-valued coefficients of $B_\ell(\mathbf{x})$, satisfying the verification conditions, which is a typical quantifier elimination with polynomial equalities and inequalities constraints. Some symbolic methods, such as QEPCAD [7] and REDLOG [10] are available to offer mathematical proofs of the existence of the barrier certificate, at the cost of high computational complexity. To alleviate this computational intractability, we can apply SOS relaxation based approach [16] to compute $B_\ell(\mathbf{x})$, which starts with sufficient verification conditions by means of SOS representations, proceeds by dealing with SDP. Remark that SDP primarily relies on numerical interior-point SDP solvers running in fixed precision.

These limits may prevent the SOS relaxation based method from yielding valid $B_\ell(\mathbf{x})$. This paper follows another route: rather than applying SOS representations, we offer an alternative one for the nonnegativity of polynomials over compact semi-algebraic sets, and take advantage of this representation to propose new sufficient verification conditions for building the barrier certificates of dynamical systems. Notably, benefited from the above strategy, safety verification of dynamical systems can be converted into a tractable linear programming.

Let $\mathbb{K}$ be a compact semi-algebraic set defined by:

$$\mathbb{K} = \{\mathbf{x} \in \mathbb{R}^n \mid g_1(\mathbf{x}) \geq 0, \ldots, g_m(\mathbf{x}) \geq 0\}, \tag{2}$$

where $g_j(\mathbf{x}) \in \mathbb{R}[\mathbf{x}]$ for $j = 1, \cdots, m$. Since $\mathbb{K}$ is compact, one may compute $g^* := \max_{\mathbf{x} \in \mathbb{K}} g_j(\mathbf{x})$ for every $j = 1, \ldots, m$. Let $\tilde{g}_j(\mathbf{x})$ be the normalized polynomial of $g_j(\mathbf{x})$ with respect to $\mathbb{K}$, namely,

$$\tilde{g}_j(\mathbf{x}) = \begin{cases} g_j(\mathbf{x})/g^*, & \text{if} \quad g^* > 0, \\ g_j(\mathbf{x}), & \text{if} \quad g^* = 0. \end{cases} \tag{3}$$

For convenience, we introduce the following polynomial vector notation. Given a compact semi-algebraic set (2) with polynomials $g_1, \ldots, g_m$, denote by $\tilde{\boldsymbol{g}}$ the polynomial vector:

$$\tilde{\boldsymbol{g}} = [\tilde{g}_1, \ldots, \tilde{g}_m, 1 - \tilde{g}_1, \ldots, 1 - \tilde{g}_m]^T, \tag{4}$$

and $\tilde{\boldsymbol{g}}^\alpha$ stands for the polynomial product of the form:

$$\tilde{\boldsymbol{g}}^\alpha = \prod_{j=1}^{m} \tilde{g}_j^{\alpha_j} (1 - \tilde{g}_j)^{\alpha_{m+j}}, \tag{5}$$

where $\alpha \in \mathbb{N}^{2m}$.

Now we recap an alternative representation of a nonnegative polynomial on the compact semi-algebraic set.

Theorem 3 *(Krivine-Vasilescu-Handelman's(KVH) Positivstellensatz)[14]. Let $\mathbb{K}$ be a compact semi-algebraic set as in (2), and let $\tilde{g}_j(\mathbf{x})$ be the normalized polynomial $g_j(\mathbf{x})$ as in (3) for each j. Suppose the family $\{g_j, (1-g_j)\}_{j=0}^m$ generate $\mathbb{R}[\mathbf{x}]$ where $g_0 \equiv 1$. If $f(\mathbf{x}) \in \mathbb{R}[\mathbf{x}]$ is strictly positive on $\mathbb{K}$, then $f(\mathbf{x})$ can be represented as*

$$f(\mathbf{x}) = \sum_{\alpha \in \mathbb{N}^{2m}} c_\alpha \tilde{\boldsymbol{g}}^\alpha \tag{6}$$

where $c_\alpha \in \mathbb{R}_{\geq 0}$.

Remark 2. Following [14], if the polynomials $\{g_j, 1-g_j\}_{j=0}^m$ cannot generate $\mathbb{R}[\mathbf{x}]$, one can augment some linear functions such that the updated set of polynomials can generate $\mathbb{R}[\mathbf{x}]$. To be more precise, let $\underline{x}_k \leq \min\{x_k | \mathbf{x} \in \mathbb{K}\}$ for all $k = 1, \cdots, n$. Then, with $\mathbf{x} \mapsto g_{m+k}(\mathbf{x}) := x_k - \underline{x}_k$, the updated $\mathbb{K}$ can generate $\mathbb{R}[\mathbf{x}]$ by plugging the (redundant) constraints $g_{m+k} \geq 0$, $k = 1, \cdots, n$. Consider $\mathbb{K}$ is compact, lower bounds $\{\underline{x}_k\}$ on x_k can be obtained or are known. For more details, the reader refers to [14].

Assumption 1. *For every compact semi-algebraic set $\mathbb{K}$ in this paper, the polynomials $\{g_j\}_{j=0}^m$ can generate $\mathbb{R}[\mathbf{x}]$, where $g_1 \geq 0, \ldots, g_m \geq 0$ are the inequalities of $\mathbb{K}$ as in (2).*

From Theorem 3, the existence of the representation as in (6) provides a sufficient and necessary condition for the strict positiveness of $f(\mathbf{x})$ on the compact set $\mathbb{K}$. However, the number of the polynomial products in (6) is infinite, which means that generating its representation is computationally hard. To illustrate the computational applicability, we turn to selecting partial polynomial products in the representation (6) by fixing a priori (much smaller) degree bound D, in the following way. For the given positive integer $D \in \mathbb{Z}_{>0}$, we pick $\alpha \in \mathbb{N}^{2m}$ such that $\deg(\tilde{g}^\alpha) \leq D$. This strategy gives a sufficient condition for the nonnegativity of the given polynomial on the compact semi-algebraic set.

Theorem 4. *Let $\mathbb{K}$ be a compact semi-algebraic set as in (2), and let D be a positive integer. Let $\tilde{g}_j(\mathbf{x})$ be the normalized polynomial $g_j(\mathbf{x})$ as in (3) for each j. If $f(\mathbf{x}) \in \mathbb{R}[\mathbf{x}]$ can be written as*

$$f(\mathbf{x}) = \sum_{\deg(\tilde{\boldsymbol{g}}^\alpha) \leq D} c_\alpha \tilde{\boldsymbol{g}}^\alpha \text{ with } c_\alpha \geq 0, \tag{7}$$

then $f(\mathbf{x})$ is nonnegative on $\mathbb{K}$.

Proof. $\tilde{g}_j(\mathbf{x})$ is the normalized polynomial with respect to $\mathbb{K}$, which follows that $\tilde{g}_j(\mathbf{x})$ and $1 - \tilde{g}_j(\mathbf{x})$ are nonnegative on $\mathbb{K}$ for each j. The desired result can be easily obtained from $c_\alpha \geq 0$. □

The representation (7) ensures that $f(\mathbf{x})$ is nonnegative on $\mathbb{K}$. Observing the verification conditions in Theorems 1 and 2, we can see that all conditions can be rewritten as a unified type, namely, the nonnegativity of polynomials on the compact semi-algebraic set. From Theorem 4, the original verification conditions can be relaxed as more tractable ones by the representations as (7). Let us now demonstrate by an example on how to convert the verification condition into the associated nonnegative representation.

Example 1. Consider the first verification condition in Theorem 1, $B(\mathbf{x}) \geq 0 \, \forall \mathbf{x} \in \Theta$. Let $\tilde{\theta}_j(\mathbf{x})$ be the normalized polynomial of $\theta_j(\mathbf{x})$ with respect to Θ for each $j, 1 \leq j \leq q$. Let $\tilde{\boldsymbol{\theta}}$ be the normalized polynomial vector

$$\tilde{\boldsymbol{\theta}} = [\tilde{\theta}_1, \cdots, \tilde{\theta}_q, 1 - \tilde{\theta}_1, \ldots, 1 - \tilde{\theta}_q]^T.$$

Following Theorem 4, $B(\mathbf{x}) \geq 0 \, \forall \mathbf{x} \in \Theta$ can be converted into the conservative one with the given degree bound $D \in \mathbb{Z}_{>0}$, namely,

$$B(\mathbf{x}) = \sum_{\deg(\tilde{\boldsymbol{\theta}}^{\alpha}) \leq D} c_{\alpha} \tilde{\boldsymbol{\theta}}^{\alpha}, \; c_{\alpha} \in \mathbb{R}_{\geq 0} \quad \Longrightarrow \quad B(\mathbf{x}) \geq 0 \, \forall \mathbf{x} \in \Theta. \qquad \square$$

As demonstrated in Example 1, we next provide a more tractable verification condition for the barrier certificates of continuous systems and hybrid systems. For notational convenience, throughout the rest of this paper, we will use $\tilde{\boldsymbol{\theta}}$, $\tilde{\boldsymbol{\psi}}$, $\tilde{\boldsymbol{\zeta}}$ to denote the normalized polynomial vectors with respect to Θ, Ψ and X_u, respectively.

Theorem 5. *Let* $\mathbf{S} : \langle \Theta, \mathbf{f}, \Psi \rangle$ *be a semi-algebraic continuous system, and* X_u *be the given unsafe state set. Let* D *be a positive integer. If there exist* $B(\mathbf{x}), \lambda(\mathbf{x}) \in \mathbb{R}[\mathbf{x}]$*, which satisfy the following conditions:*

1. $B(\mathbf{x}) = \sum_{\deg(\tilde{\boldsymbol{\theta}}^{\alpha}) \leq D} c_{\alpha} \tilde{\boldsymbol{\theta}}^{\alpha}, \; c_{\alpha} \geq 0,$
2. $\dot{B}(\mathbf{x}) - \lambda(\mathbf{x}) B(\mathbf{x}) - \epsilon_1 = \sum_{\deg(\tilde{\boldsymbol{\psi}}^{\beta}) \leq D} c_{\beta} \tilde{\boldsymbol{\psi}}^{\beta}, \; c_{\beta} \geq 0, \; \epsilon_1 > 0,$
3. $-B(\mathbf{x}) - \epsilon_2 = \sum_{\deg(\tilde{\boldsymbol{\zeta}}^{\omega}) \leq D} c_{\omega} \tilde{\boldsymbol{\zeta}}^{\omega}, \; c_{\omega} \geq 0, \; \epsilon_2 > 0,$

then the safety of the system $\mathbf{S}$ *is guaranteed.*

Proof. Theorem 4 indicates that the conditions (1–3) can imply the conditions (i–iii) in Theorem 1, respectively. Thus, the safety of the system $\mathbf{S}$ is proved. $\square$

Theorem 6. *Let* $\mathbf{H} : \langle L, X, F, \Psi, E, G, R, \Theta, \ell_0 \rangle$ *be a semi-algebraic hybrid system,* $\mathcal{X}_u$ *be the unsafe assertion. Let* D *be a positive integer. If there exist* $B_{\ell}(\mathbf{x}), \lambda_{\ell}(\mathbf{x}) \in \mathbb{R}[\mathbf{x}]$ *for each* $\ell \in L$*, and nonnegative polynomial* $\gamma_e(\mathbf{x}) \in \mathbb{R}[\mathbf{x}]$ *for each* $e \in E$*, which satisfy*

1. $B_{\ell_0}(\mathbf{x}) = \sum_{\deg(\tilde{\boldsymbol{\theta}}^{\alpha_{\ell_0}}) \leq D} c_{\alpha_{\ell_0}} \tilde{\boldsymbol{\theta}}^{\alpha_{\ell_0}}, \; c_{\alpha_{\ell_0}} \geq 0 \,,$
2. $\dot{B}_{\ell}(\mathbf{x}) - \lambda_{\ell}(\mathbf{x}) B_{\ell}(\mathbf{x}) - \epsilon_{\ell,1} = \sum_{\deg(\tilde{\boldsymbol{\psi}}^{\beta_{\ell}}) \leq D} c_{\beta_{\ell}} \tilde{\boldsymbol{\psi}}_{\ell}^{\beta_{\ell}}, \; c_{\beta_{\ell}} \geq 0, \; \epsilon_{\ell,1} > 0,$

3. $B_{\ell'}(R_e(\mathbf{x})) - \gamma_e(\mathbf{x})B_\ell(\mathbf{x}) = \sum_{\deg(\tilde{\boldsymbol{g}}^{\mu_e})\le D} c_{\mu_e}\tilde{\boldsymbol{g}}_e^{\mu_e},\ c_{\mu_e}\ge 0,$

4. $-B_\ell(\mathbf{x}) - \epsilon_{\ell,2} = \sum_{\deg(\tilde{\boldsymbol{\zeta}}^{\omega_\ell})\le D} c_{\omega_\ell}\tilde{\boldsymbol{\zeta}}_\ell^{\omega_\ell},\ c_{\omega_\ell}\ge 0,\ \epsilon_{\ell,2}>0,$

then the safety of the system **H** *is guaranteed.*

Proof. Simiar to the proof of Theorem 5. □

Theorems 5 and 6 produce the sufficient conditions for generating the barrier certificates of continuous and hybrid systems, respectively. With unknown multipliers $\lambda(\mathbf{x})$, $\lambda_\ell(\mathbf{x})$, $\gamma_e(\mathbf{x})$ and unknown barrier certificates $B(\mathbf{x})$, $B_\ell(\mathbf{x})$, some nonlinear terms that are products of the coefficients of unknown polynomials will occur in the constraints in Theorems 5 and 6, which yields a non-convex bilinear matrix inequalities (BMI) problem. To alleviate this computational intractability, provided that the multipliers $\lambda_\ell(\mathbf{x})$ and $\gamma_e(\mathbf{x})$ are given in advance, the problem of generating the above barrier certificates can be transformed into the linear programming problem. To keep it concise, we only sketch the case of continuous systems, but the transformation procedure extends to the case of hybrid systems without much difficulty.

To start with, a key step is to parameterize $B(\mathbf{x})$ and the power products associated to each expression in the conditions (1–3) of Theorem 5. For the given degree d of $B(\mathbf{x})$, we first predetermine a template of $B(\mathbf{x})$ by setting its coefficients as parameters, i.e., $B(\mathbf{x}) = \sum_\alpha b_\iota \mathbf{x}^\iota$, where $\mathbf{x}^\iota = x_1^{\iota_1}\cdots x_n^{\iota_n}$, $\iota = (\iota_1,\ldots,\iota_n)\in\mathbb{Z}_{\ge 0}^n$ with $\sum_{i=1}^n \iota_i \le d$, and b_ι's are unknown coefficients. Let $\mathbf{b}$ be the coefficient vector of $B(\mathbf{x})$. In the sequel, we write $B(\mathbf{x})$ as $B(\mathbf{x},\mathbf{b})$ for clarity. Denote by $\mathbf{c}_\alpha, \mathbf{c}_\beta, \mathbf{c}_\omega$ the parameter vectors appearing in the conditions (1-3) of Theorem 5, respectively, and let $\mathbf{c} = [\mathbf{c}_\alpha^T, \mathbf{c}_\beta^T, \mathbf{c}_\omega^T]^T$. For the given degree bound D, it follows from Theorem 5 that generating a barrier certificate can be transformed into the following optimization problem:

$$\left.\begin{array}{ll}\text{find} & \mathbf{b}\\ \text{s.t.} & B(\mathbf{x},\mathbf{b}) = \sum_{\deg(\tilde{\boldsymbol{\theta}}^\alpha)\le D} c_\alpha\tilde{\boldsymbol{\theta}}^\alpha,\\ & \dot{B}(\mathbf{x},\mathbf{b}) - \lambda(\mathbf{x})B(\mathbf{x},\mathbf{b}) - \epsilon_1 = \sum_{\deg(\tilde{\boldsymbol{\psi}}^\beta)\le D} c_\beta\tilde{\boldsymbol{\psi}}^\beta,\\ & -B(\mathbf{x},\mathbf{b}) - \epsilon_2 = \sum_{\deg(\tilde{\boldsymbol{\zeta}}^\omega)\le D} c_\omega\tilde{\boldsymbol{\zeta}}^\omega,\\ & c_\alpha, c_\beta, c_\omega \ge 0,\end{array}\right\} \tag{8}$$

where $\lambda(\mathbf{x})$ is a prespecified polynomial, and $\epsilon_1,\epsilon_2\in\mathbb{R}_{>0}$ are prespecified small positive numbers. We can rewrite the equality constraints in (8) as a linear system with the variables $\mathbf{b},\mathbf{c}$ by sorting the coefficients with respect to the variables $\mathbf{x}$. By doing so, (8) is equivalent to the following linear programming problem:

$$\left.\begin{array}{r}\text{find}\ \mathbf{y}\\ \text{s.t.}\ A\cdot\mathbf{y}\ge 0,\end{array}\right\} \tag{9}$$

where $\mathbf{y} = (\mathbf{b}^T, \mathbf{c}^T)^T$ and A is a numerical matrix. Problem (9) can be solved by using conventional algorithms such as the interior-point method [6]. If (9) is feasible, the result yields a barrier certificate $B(\mathbf{x})$, which suffices to verify the safety of the continuous system $\mathbf{S}$. Our LP relaxation is based on the predetermined degree bound D. Once (9) is infeasible, one may improve the relaxation precision and then increase the possibility to find the barrier certificate by increasing the degree bound D. Detailed procedures are summarized in Algorithm 1.

Remark 3. Theorem 6 guarantees that λ_ℓ can be any constants or polynomials, and γ_e can be any nonnegative constants or polynomials. To ease computation, one prefers to set them as simple as possible. Here we choose λ_ℓ from $0, \pm 1, \pm(1+x_1^2+\cdots+x_n^2)$, and γ_e from $0, 1, 1+x_1^2+\cdots+x_n^2$, respectively. Like computing the fractional SOS representations of nonnegative polynomials, one may also choose the denominator as $(1+x_1^2+\cdots+x_n^2)^k$ for some integer exponent k.

Algorithm 1. Search for polynomial barrier certificates

Input: Semi-algebraic continuous system $\mathbf{S}$, or hybrid system $\mathbf{H}$; the degree bound d of the barrier certificate; the degree bound D of the representation (7).

Output: The barrier certificate $\{B_\ell(\mathbf{x})\}$.

forall the $\ell \in L$ **do**

    Parameterized $B_\ell(\mathbf{x})$ by polynomials of degree d

Construct the power-products with degree D of the polynomials defining the semi-algebraic sets in Theorem 2.

Set up the linear programming of the form (9) and apply an LP solver to compute its solutions.

if *the problem (9) is feasible* **then**

    return $\{B_\ell(\mathbf{x})\}$.

else

    return *"we cannot find the barrier certificates with the degree bound d."*

Remark 4. Like SOS relaxation method, our method cannot guarantee that the polynomial barrier certificates will always be found due to the limitation on presetting the degree bounds d and D. It is also difficult to predetermine whether such polynomial barrier certificates exist. Therefore, if our algorithm fails to yield any barrier certificate, it does not mean that the given hybrid system has no polynomial barrier certificates with the given degree bound, or that the given system is unsafe.

3.3 Complexity Analysis

In the section, we analyze the complexity of Algorithm 1, and further compare it with SOS relaxation method. Let n, $|L|$ and $|E|$ be the numbers of system variables, locations and discrete transitions in the given hybrid system $\mathbf{H}$, respectively. And let $d_{\mathfrak{f}}$ be the maximal degree of the polynomial vector fields of $\mathbf{H}$, and let d_v be the maximal degree among the polynomial lists, which are used to define the compact semi-algebraic sets appearing in $\mathbf{H}$. The linear programming problem (9) implies the predetermined degree bound D must satisfy $D \geq d + d_{\mathfrak{f}}$. Suppose that the numbers of the polynomials defining the compact semi-algebraic sets in $\mathbf{H}$ are bounded by s_p. Therefore, the number of the decision variables, denoted by $\mathcal{V}_l$, of the linear programming problem (9) is

$$\mathcal{V}_l = \binom{n+d}{d} + (1 + 2|L| + |E|)\binom{2s_p + D}{D}, \tag{10}$$

where the first term is the number of coefficients $\mathbf{b}$, and the second one is the number of coefficients $\mathbf{c}$. Meanwhile, the number of constraints, denoted by $\mathcal{C}_l$, in (9) is

$$\mathcal{C}_l = \binom{n+D}{D} + (1 + 2|L| + |E|)\binom{2s_p + D}{D}, \tag{11}$$

where the first term is the number of equality constraints associated with coefficients $\mathbf{b}$ and $\mathbf{c}$, and the second one is the number of nonnegative constraints of coefficients $\mathbf{c}$.

As is well known, the complexity of an LP using interior-point algorithms is approximately $O(\mathcal{V}_l^2 \mathcal{C}_l)$ [6]. Taking this together with (10) and (11), we get the complexity of Algorithm 1 based on the LP solver is approximately $O(n^{2d+D})$.

We also called the SOS relaxation (cf. (36)–(39) in [16]) to search for the barrier certificate of the hybrid system $\mathbf{H}$. Similarly, let D be the predetermined degree bound for all involved SOS polynomial multipliers. Then, the number of decision variables, denoted by $\mathcal{V}_s$, in the SDP associated with the SOS relaxation is

$$\mathcal{V}_s = (s_p + 1)\,(1 + 2|L| + |E|)\,\frac{N(N+1)}{2}, \tag{12}$$

where $N = \binom{n+D/2}{D/2}$ is the number of monomials in a polynomial of degree $D/2$. Meanwhile, the number of constraints, denoted by $\mathcal{C}s$, in the SDP associated with the SOS relaxation is

$$\mathcal{C}_s = (1 + 2|L| + |E|)\binom{n+D}{D}. \tag{13}$$

It is known that the complexity of SDP-solving via interior-point algorithms is approximately $O(\mathcal{C}_s^3 + \mathcal{V}_s^3\mathcal{C}_s + \mathcal{C}_s^2\mathcal{V}_s^2)$ [6]. From (12) and (13), we get the complexity of calling the SDP solver to search for a barrier certificate is approximately $O(n^{4D})$.

4 Experiments

In this section, we first demonstrate the application of our methods by two examples and then compare our LP relaxation method with the SOS relaxation method with respect to ability and efficiency on 10 examples. We used examples of high computational complexity from related works in the experiments [4,5,8, 16–19,22,24].

Example 2. Consider the following nonlinear continuous system [22]

$$\begin{bmatrix} \dot{x_1} \\ \dot{x_2} \\ \dot{x_3} \\ \dot{x_4} \end{bmatrix} = \begin{bmatrix} -x_1 + x_2^3 - 3x_3x_4 \\ -x_1 - x_2^3 \\ x_1x_4 - x_3 \\ x_1x_3 - x_4^3 \end{bmatrix},$$

with the location invariant $\Psi = \{\mathbf{x} \in \mathbb{R}^4 : -1 \le x_1, x_2, x_3, x_4 \le 1\}$. We will verify that all trajectories of the system starting from the initial set $\Theta = \{\mathbf{x} \in \mathbb{R}^4 : 0 \le x_1, x_2, x_3, x_4 \le 0.5\}$. will never enter the unsafe set $X_u = \{\mathbf{x} \in \mathbb{R}^4 : -1 \le x_1, x_2, x_3, x_4 \le -0.5\}$.

Let the degree bound D of the representation (7) be 8, and $\lambda(\mathbf{x})$ in Theorem 5 be 1, respectively. Our algorithm succeeds to yield the barrier certificate

$$B(\mathbf{x}) = \underbrace{-12.9713x_1^4 - 16.6808x_2^4 - 93.4687x_3^4 - 0.5426x_4^4 + \ldots + 779.0477}_{70 \ \ terms}.$$

Therefore, the safety of the above system is verified. □

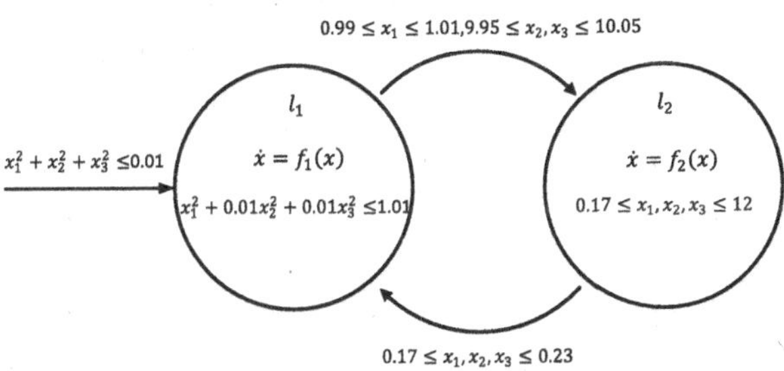

Fig. 1. The hybrid automata of the system in Example 3

Example 3. Consider the hybrid automata of the system depicted in Fig. 1, where

$$\mathbf{f}_1(\mathbf{x}) = \begin{bmatrix} -x_2 \\ -x_1 + x_3 \\ x_1 + (2x_2 + 3x_3)(1 + x_3^2) \end{bmatrix}, \quad \mathbf{f}_2(\mathbf{x}) = \begin{bmatrix} -x_2 \\ -x_1 + x_3 \\ -x_1 - 2x_2 - 3x_3 \end{bmatrix}.$$

Our task is to verify that the system will never enter the unsafe set

$$X_u(\ell_2) = \{\mathbf{x} \in \mathbb{R}^3 : x_1 \ge 5\}.$$

Let the degree bound D of the representation (7) be 6, and $\lambda_{\ell_1} = -0.2$, $\lambda_{\ell_2} = 0$, and $\gamma_{(\ell_1,\ell_2)} = \gamma_{(\ell_2,\ell_1)} = 1$. Applying Algorithm 1, we obtain the polynomial barrier certificate with degree 2:

$$B_{\ell_1}(\mathbf{x}) = \underbrace{-48.0832x_1^2 - 0.6225x_2^2 - 0.0005x_3^2 + \cdots + 1075.8714}_{10\ \ terms},$$

$$B_{\ell_2}(\mathbf{x}) = \underbrace{-0.8002{x_1}^2 + 0.4692{x_2}^2 + 0.5978x_3^2 + \cdots + 423.7896}_{10\ \ terms}.$$

Meanwhile, we apply the SOS relaxation based method to compute a barrier certificate with degree < 4. However, the SDP solver cannot return any barrier certificate. As discussed above, our LP relaxation based approach can find the barrier certificate that the SOS relaxation based method cannot yield. □

We compared our LP relaxation based method with the SOS relaxation based one over a set of benchmarks gathered from the related works. Table 1 shows the result. Here, the LP problems were settled by the *linprog* command in Matlab while the SDP problems were solved by the Matlab toolbox *SeDuMi* [29]. The experiments were performed on Intel(R) Core(TM) at 2.60 GHz with 8 GB of memory under Windows 8.

In Table 1, n and $|L|$ denote the number of the system variables and the number of the locations; $d_{\mathbf{f}}$ denotes the maximal degree of the polynomials in the vector fields; $d_l(B)$ and $d_s(B)$ denote the degrees of the barrier certificates obtained from LP and SDP solvers, respectively; D_l and D_s are the degree bounds of the nonnegative representation derived from the LP relaxation and SOS relaxation, respectively; $\mathcal{V}_l$ and $\mathcal{V}_c$ denote the numbers of the decision variables of the LP and SDP, respectively; T_l and T_s represent the entire computation times in seconds spent by LP and SDP solvers, respectively.

Table 1. Algorithm performance on benchmarks

Examples	n	$\|L\|$	$d_{\mathbf{f}}$	LP				SDP			
				$d_l(B)$	D_l	$\mathcal{V}_l$	$T_l(s)$	$d_s(B)$	D_s	$\mathcal{V}_s$	$T_s(s)$
Ex.1 from [18]	2	1	2	3	6	164	0.0221	3	6	292	0.1870
Ex.2 from [16]	2	1	3	4	6	328	0.0782	4	8	597	0.1179
Ex.3 from [8]	2	1	3	2	4	91	0.0140	2	6	299	0.1129
Ex.4 from [18]	2	1	1	3	4	129	0.0053	4	6	287	0.1193
Ex.5 from [18]	2	1	2	2	4	56	0.0073	2	4	95	0.1358
Ex.6 from [24]	3	1	2	4	6	917	0.1051	4	6	942	0.2187
Ex.7 from [19]	3	1	3	4	6	1379	0.1444	4	8	2977	0.2421
Ex.8 from [5]	3	1	2	4	6	890	0.0966	1	4	225	0.1815
Ex.9 from [4]	2	3	1	2	2	156	0.0941	2	2	278	0.1820
Ex.10 from [17]	3	2	3	2	4	370	0.0331	4	8	5952	0.8481

For 7 of the examples, both LP relaxation and SOS relaxation can successfully find the barrier certificates of polynomial forms with the same degree. However, as discussed in the Sect. 3.3, the number of decision variables in LP relaxation is much smaller than that in SOS relaxation. Plus the more efficiency LP solvers provide, our LP relaxation based method is much more efficient than the SOS relaxation method. For Ex.4 and Ex.10, SOS relaxation based method cannot find polynomial barrier certificates whose degrees are less than 4, whereas our LP relaxation method can yield two barrier certificates with the degrees 3 and 2, respectively. Ex.8 displays the opposite case where SOS relaxation performs better.

In fact, LP relaxation and SOS relaxation use different sufficient conditions for polynomial positivity and give different encodings of barrier certificate generation. Theoretically, for the given degree bound of the polynomial, there are cases where the SOS relaxation can find a barrier certificate, however, the LP relaxation cannot, and vice versa. Even for the cases that can be solved by both of them, there is no theoretical result predicting which method will produce barrier certificates of lower-degree. Thus, our LP relaxation based method and the SOS relaxation based method complement each other.

5 Related Work

A barrier certificate is a special kind of inductive invariant, thus research on safety verification using inductive invariants is related to our work. Sankaranarayanan et al. presented methods adopting the ideal theory over polynomial rings and quantifier elimination to automatically generate algebraic invariants for algebraic hybrid systems [21,23]. Sturm and Tiwari presented the application of quantifier elimination to formal verification and synthesis of continuous and switched dynamical systems [30]. Based on Gröbner basis manipulations, Rodríguez-Carbonell constructed polynomial invariants (a set of polynomial equations) for linear hybrid systems [20]. Platzer et al. adopted iterative fixedpoint calculations to find differential invariants, a boolean combination of multiple polynomial inequalities, to verify semi-algebraic hybrid systems [15]. Gulwani et al. defined a similar invariant with a different inductive condition and used the Farkas's theory and SMT solvers to solve it [11]. Sogokon et al. combined semi-algebraic abstractions with deductive verification method to generate semi-algebraic invariants for polynomial continuous systems [28].

For barrier certificates with convex conditions, the technique of sum-of-squares decomposition of semidefinite polynomials provides much better efficiency and thus is quite popular. Prajna et al. generated barrier certificates for semi-algebraic hybrid systems [16,17]. Kong et al. proposed a method to generate a barrier certificate defined over an exponential condition for semi-algebraic hybrid systems by SDP [13]. Dai et al. utilized different weaker conditions flexibly to synthesize different kinds of barrier certificates with more expressiveness efficiently using SDP [9]. Yang et al. presented a hybrid symbolic-numeric method to compute the exact inequality invariants of polynomial hybrid systems via

SOS relaxation [31]. Sloth et al. proposed compositional conditions for barrier certificates to verify the safety property of a group of interconnected hybrid systems [27].

LP relaxation based techniques have been successfully applied in stability analysis of nonlinear systems. Ahmadi et al. introduced two different positive representations: DSOS and SDSOS to take the place of SOS, and combined linear programming and second order cone programming to solve them [1]. Sankaranarayanan et al. investigated the stability of continuous systems with polyhedral domains. They used the Handelman positive representation to synthesize Lyapunov functions [22,25]. Ben Sassi et al. used polyhedra templates to analyse the reachability of polynomial systems. They reduced the problem of reachability analysis to a set of optimization problems involving polynomials over bounded polyhedra, then adopted the Bernstein expansions of polynomials to build LP relaxations [26]. In the paper, we treat the more general semi-algebraic hybrid systems and generate barrier certificates using KVH positivstellensatz. It is the first attempt to use LP relaxation for computing barrier certificates.

6 Conclusion

We have presented a linear programming (LP) relaxation based approach for generating barrier certificates of semi-algebraic hybrid systems. The main feature of this approach is that it uses an LP relaxation to encode the set of nonnegativity constraints associated with the barrier certificates. Thanks to the low computational complexity and the high numerical stability of LP, our approach is more efficient than the popular SOS relaxation based methods when treating barrier certificates with convex conditions. The conclusion is supported by a theoretical analysis on complexity and the experiments taken on a set of benchmarks gathered from the literature.

Acknowledgments. This material is supported in part by Key Basic Research Program of China (Grant No. 2014CB340703), the National Natural Science Foundation of China (Grant Nos. 61321064, 61361136002, 11471209, 11571350, 61672435, 61561146394, 91318301 and 61602348), the Innovation Program of Shanghai Municipal Education Commission (Grant No. 14ZZ046), the project on the Integration of Industry, Education and Research of Jiangsu Province (Grant No. BY2014126-03), the project SWU116007 funded by Southwest University. We would like to thank anonymous reviewers for their very valuable comments.

References

1. Ahmadi, A.A., Majumdar, A.: Dsos and sdsos optimization: Lp and socp-based alternatives to sum of squares optimization. In: 2014 48th Annual Conference on Information Sciences and Systems (CISS), pp. 1–5. IEEE (2014)
2. Alur, R.: Formal verification of hybrid systems. In: Proceedings of the International Conference on Embedded Software (EMSOFT), pp. 273–278. IEEE (2011)

3. Alur, R., Courcoubetis, C., Halbwachs, N., Henzinger, T.A., Ho, P.H., Nicollin, X., Olivero, A., Sifakis, J., Yovine, S.: The algorithmic analysis of hybrid systems. Theor. Comput. Sci. **138**(1), 3–34 (1995)
4. Alur, R., Dang, T., Ivančić, F.: Predicate abstraction for reachability analysis of hybrid systems. ACM Trans. Embed. Comput. Syst. (TECS) **5**(1), 152–199 (2006)
5. Bouissou, O., Chapoutot, A., Djaballah, A., Kieffer, M.: Computation of parametric barrier functions for dynamical systems using interval analysis. In: 2014 IEEE 53rd Annual Conference on Decision and Control (CDC), pp. 753–758. IEEE (2014)
6. Boyd, S., Vandenberghe, L.: Convex Optimization. Cambridge University Press, Cambridge (2004)
7. Brown, C.W.: QEPCAD B: a program for computing with semi-algebraic sets using CADs. ACM SIGSAM Bull. **37**(4), 97–108 (2003)
8. Chen, X., Abraham, E., Sankaranarayanan, S.: Taylor model flowpipe construction for non-linear hybrid systems. In: Proceedings of the 2012 IEEE 33rd Real-Time Systems Symposium (RTSS), pp. 183–192. IEEE (2012)
9. Dai, L., Gan, T., Xia, B., Zhan, N.: Barrier certificates revisited. To appear J. Symbolic Comput. (2016)
10. Dolzmann, A., Sturm, T.: Redlog: computer algebra meets computer logic. ACM Sigsam Bull. **31**(2), 2–9 (1997)
11. Gulwani, S., Tiwari, A.: Constraint-based approach for analysis of hybrid systems. In: Proceedings of the 20th International Conference on Computer Aided Verification (CAV), pp. 190–203 (2008)
12. Henzinger, T.A.: The theory of hybrid automata. In: Proceedings of the 11th Annual IEEE Symposium on Logic in Computer Science, pp. 278–292. IEEE Computer Society (1996)
13. Kong, H., He, F., Song, X., Hung, W.N.N., Gu, M.: Exponential-condition-based barrier certificate generation for safety verification of hybrid systems. In: Sharygina, N., Veith, H. (eds.) CAV 2013. LNCS, vol. 8044, pp. 242–257. Springer, Heidelberg (2013). doi:10.1007/978-3-642-39799-8_17
14. Lasserre, J.B.: Polynomial programming: Lp-relaxations also converge. SIAM J. Optim. **15**(2), 383–393 (2005)
15. Platzer, A., Clarke, E.M.: Computing differential invariants of hybrid systems as fixedpoints. Form. Methods Syst. Des. **35**(1), 98–120 (2009)
16. Prajna, S., Jadbabaie, A., Pappas, G.: A framework for worst-case and stochastic safety verification using barrier certificates. IEEE Trans. Autom. Control **52**(8), 1415–1429 (2007)
17. Prajna, S., Jadbabaie, A.: Safety verification of hybrid systems using barrier certificates. In: Alur, R., Pappas, G.J. (eds.) HSCC 2004. LNCS, vol. 2993, pp. 477–492. Springer, Heidelberg (2004). doi:10.1007/978-3-540-24743-2_32
18. Ratschan, S., She, Z.: Safety verification of hybrid systems by constraint propagation-based abstraction refinement. ACM Trans. Embed. Comput. Syst. **6**(1), 573–589 (2007)
19. Ratschan, S., She, Z.: Providing a basin of attraction to a target region of polynomial systems by computation of lyapunov-like functions. SIAM J. Control Optim. **48**(7), 4377–4394 (2010)
20. Rodríguez-Carbonell, E., Tiwari, A.: Generating polynomial invariants for hybrid systems. In: Proceedings of the 8th ACM International Conference on Hybrid Systems: Computation and Control, pp. 590–605 (2005)
21. Sankaranarayanan, S.: Automatic invariant generation for hybrid systems using ideal fixed points. In: Proceedings of the 13th ACM International Conference on Hybrid Systems: Computation and Control, pp. 221–230. ACM (2010)

22. Sankaranarayanan, S., Chen, X., Abrahám, E.: Lyapunov function synthesis using handelman representations. In: The 9th IFAC Symposium on Nonlinear Control Systems, pp. 576–581 (2013)
23. Sankaranarayanan, S., Sipma, H., Manna, Z.: Constructing invariants for hybrid systems. Formal Methods Syst. Des. **32**, 25–55 (2008)
24. Sassi, M.A.B., Sankaranarayanan, S.: Stabilization of polynomial dynamical systems using linear programming based on bernstein polynomials. arXiv preprint arXiv:1501.04578 (2015)
25. Sassi, M.A.B., Sankaranarayanan, S., Chen, X., Ábrahám, E.: Linear relaxations of polynomial positivity for polynomial lyapunov function synthesis. IMA J. Math. Control Inform., 1–34 (2015). doi:10.1093/imamci/dnv003
26. Sassi, M.A.B., Testylier, R., Dang, T., Girard, A.: Reachability analysis of polynomial systems using linear programming relaxations. In: Chakraborty, S., Mukund, M. (eds.) ATVA 2012. LNCS, vol. 7561, pp. 137–151. Springer, Heidelberg (2012)
27. Sloth, C., Pappas, G.J., Wisniewski, R.: Compositional safety analysis using barrier certificates. In: Proceedings of the 15th ACM International Conference on Hybrid Systems: Computation and Control, pp. 15–24. ACM (2012)
28. Sogokon, A., Ghorbal, K., Jackson, P.B., Platzer, A.: A method for invariant generation for polynomial continuous systems. In: Jobstmann, B., Leino, K.R.M. (eds.) VMCAI 2016. LNCS, vol. 9583, pp. 268–288. Springer, Heidelberg (2016). doi:10.1007/978-3-662-49122-5_13
29. Sturm, J.F.: Using SeDuMi 1.02, a MATLAB toolbox for optimization over symmetric cones. Optim. Methods Softw. **11**(12), 625–653 (1999)
30. Sturm, T., Tiwari, A.: Verification and synthesis using real quantifier elimination. In: Proceedings of the International Symposium on Symbolic and Algebraic Computation, ISSAC, pp. 329–336. ACM Press (2011)
31. Yang, Z., Wu, M., Lin, W.: Exact verification of hybrid systems based on bilinear SOS representation. ACM Trans. Embed. Comput. Syst. **14**(1), 1–19 (2015)

Industry Track

Model-Based Design of an Energy-System Embedded Controller Using TASTE

Roberto Cavada(✉), Alessandro Cimatti, Luigi Crema, Mattia Roccabruna, and Stefano Tonetta

Fondazione Bruno Kessler (FBK), Trento, Italy
{cavada,cimatti,crema,roccabruna,tonettas}@fbk.eu

Abstract. Model-based design has become a standard practice in the development of control systems. Many solutions provide simulation, code generation, and other functionalities to minimize the design time and optimize the resulting control system implementation.

In this paper, we report on the experience of using TASTE as the design environment for the controller of an energy system comprising a parabolic dish collector and a Stirling engine. Besides standard advantages of model-based design, an appealing feature of TASTE is the possibility of specifying the design model with a formal language such as SDL. The complexity of the designed system stressed the tool's performances and usability. Nevertheless, the functionalities provided by TASTE were essential to manage such complexity.

1 Introduction

Model-based design has become a standard practice in the design of embedded systems. It provides huge benefits in terms of cost and time savings, but also in high error reductions and higher maturity level of the developed systems. Tools supporting model-based design typically offer graphical interfaces with different views, early analysis and validation capabilities, and finally code generation for the desired target platform.

In this paper, we report on the experience of using TASTE [6], a tool set developed within the European Space Agency (ESA), to apply the model-based approach in the domain of Energy Systems. The activity has been conducted in the scope of *Contest*, aiming at building an efficient Combined Heat and Power (CHP) system, based on a large solar dish focusing energy on a Stirling engine.

Although there are numerous attempts to produce and validate models of such complex physical systems [5,9], they are ruled by multiple non-linear dimensions, and have many variables (e.g. the dynamic mechanical distortion of a moving heavy structures, the complexity of the involved thermal phenomena) that can dramatically change the response needed by the control system.

In this paper, we focus on the design and implementation of the control system, detailing aspects such as the tight integration of heterogeneous hardware and software subsystems, real time operating systems and a clearly characterized

J. Fitzgerald et al. (Eds.): FM 2016, LNCS 9995, pp. 741–747, 2016.
DOI: 10.1007/978-3-319-48989-6_45

execution model. In such conditions, model-based design supported by automatic code generation is mandatory to keep complexity still manageable.

To the best of our knowledge, this is the most complex system managed by TASTE reported in the literature. Differently from similar case studies, the controlled system is a real-life complex energy system, and it is released open source.

The paper is structured as follows: Sect. 2 gives an overview of the plant, Sect. 3 describes the adopted tool and modeling languages, Sect. 4 gives the details of the case study, Sect. 5 summarizes the lessons learnt, and Sect. 6 draws some conclusions and directions for future work.

2 The Plant

Stirling Engine. A Stirling [8] is an external-combustion engine that operates in cyclic compression and expansion of a fluid (typically air, helium or hydrogen), with a (reversible) conversion of thermal to mechanical energy. Rotation can be used to generate electricity, and exceeding heat can be used e.g. to warm cold water for domestic or industrial usage. We use an *Alpha* type Stirling engine able to supply 10 KW through an electrical motor, which serves both as starting engine and alternator. When consuming, the motors rotates at constant RPM, but, if heated enough, it will push RPM further, producing energy with self-stabilizing phase and frequency. Regulation is done by increasing and decreasing helium pressure. Higher efficiency is gained with higher pressure, but this causes an higher drop of temperature while the engine must operate at high temperature. The most important safety requirement concerns the low temperature of the hot side, which may be reached in a few seconds if not supplied with thermal energy: the engine may freeze and irreparably get wrecked.

Solar Dish. With a concentration factor of 3 k, the most important safety hazard is the high temperature reachable on the focusing area when tracking the Sun, as it can easily burn the Stirling ceramic shield and melt the supporting steal body. Related critical requirements concern the speed of entering and exiting from the hot zone, and possible dangerous reflections (Fig. 1).

Fig. 1. CAD of the Dish with the Stirling mounted on it

Controller Interface. Overall, we have the following data for sensing and control:

Inputs: 23 thermocouples, 2 pressure sensors, 2 flow meters, 2 sensors for incident radiation, 2 frequency readers, 2 absolute 15 bit encoders, 1 wind direction sensor, 1 wind speed sensor, about 24 bits for scalar and boolean values, 1 DCF77 receiver module, 1 electrical power sensor, 1 accelerometer for adjustment of inclination errors.

Outputs: 10 bits for sending actuation to the plant, and some additional bytes for their numeric parameters.

3 TASTE

3.1 Language Subset

TASTE [6] is an open-source tool chain for the development of embedded controllers using a model-based approach. The modeling language provides a mixture of languages used for different purposes: AADL [10] for the system-level view of the architecture; ASN.1 [3] for the data abstraction and implementation; different languages can be used for the behavior specification; in this case study, we used SDL [2] and C for utilities.

AADL is a language to describe the system architecture in terms of component types and implementations. Component types define the input/output ports, while implementations define the internal structure in terms of subcomponents and connections. Component implementations also contain the deployment details, specifically the hardware subcomponents (processors, networks, ...) and their binding with the functional components. TASTE provides a graphical interface to specify both the functional architectural decomposition and the deployment details.

ASN.1 is a standardized notation to specify data types. ASN.1 data types are automatically converted into data types of the specific languages. Data are associated with encoding rules that define the concrete representation of the data values.

SDL is a formal specification language to describe real-time distributed systems. In TASTE, behaviors of AADL components are described with SDL, as finite-state machines extended with ASN.1 data and timers. Processes run asynchronously and communicate through channels that carry messages/signals. The signals are queued and consumed in FIFO order. Each process is executed without interrupts, in a run-to-completion fashion, until it stops waiting for a signal or a real-time delay. TASTE restricts the language to ensure compatibility with embedded systems, mainly to avoid the usage of the heap and to meet real-time requirements. Moreover, the queues for the communication channels are bounded.

3.2 Code Generation

TASTE generates the code from the model, putting together drivers and communication means to ensure the specified real-time constraints. The AADL and ASN.1 specifications are used to create tasks, threads, and glue around the Ada code generated from SDL models, all layering over Ocarina middleware [4]. TASTE produces the binaries for different targets.

4 The Control System

4.1 Architecture

The system is made of three main blocks: the Hardware Interface (HWI), the Controller, and the UI & Logging system. Furthermore, a vertical separation makes the Stirling and the Dish controllers and devices independent. The HWIs and the UI were developed not using TASTE, which was used for the Controller only. The HWI are implemented with PLCs communicating with sensors and actuators via EtherCAT industrial RT protocol and hardware. The PLCs can filter or preprocess data and implement basic safety procedures in case the connection gets lost. Also, the PLC dedicated to the Dish controls the motor movements and implements the Solar Position Algorithm [7] and wind tracking. Both the PLCs receive and send data from/to the respective controllers, using the EtherCAT protocol (Fig. 2).

4.2 Controller Details

The Controller is decomposed in 12 SDL blocks: 4 for the Stirling, 3 for the Dish, and 5 to handle system-level functionalities. Five additional C blocks are for I/O with drivers, utilities, and data logging. The FSMs overall contain 86 locations and 175 transitions (not counting self-loops), and use 12 distinct timers (Fig. 3). All models are available at https://gitlab.fbk.eu/ITC4Energy/contest.

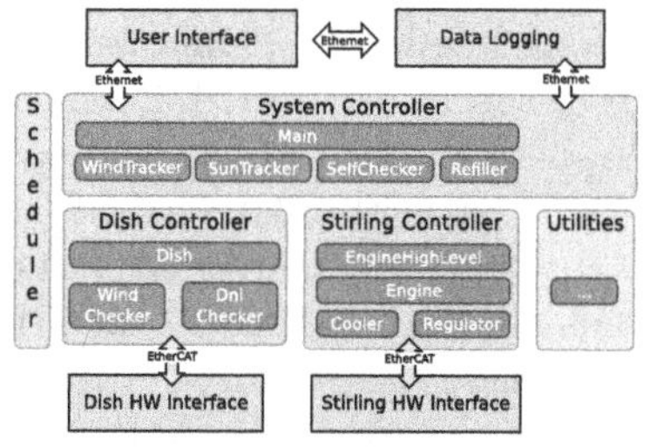

Fig. 2. Architecture of the controller

Most of the blocks are *on/off* type, in particular all high level blocks take decisions based on information available from the lower levels. The Stirling engine controller implements *proportional/derivative* control. The current absence of real experimental data does not allow to predict if some *integral* action will be needed to obtain better performances. The parts handling Sun tracking use *proportional* control to adjust the Sun position error due to the atmospheric refraction. A large source of complexity is in the management of faulty conditions which may happen at plant level.

The SDL models react to both inputs and continuous signals. For better performances we preferred the former, and when possible, we used single events carrying data instead of using multiple events (e.g. for sending commands). This reduced the number of threads generated by TASTE, which turned out to be critical under the target platform (see Sect. 4.3). We made a limited use of *all states* symbols, as when overused they break any readability of models, and for the same reason *labels* and corresponding *gotos* were used only locally to each state. In TASTE, multiple fan-out of a signal is not allowed. This limitation makes models more complex to read and maintain in same cases.

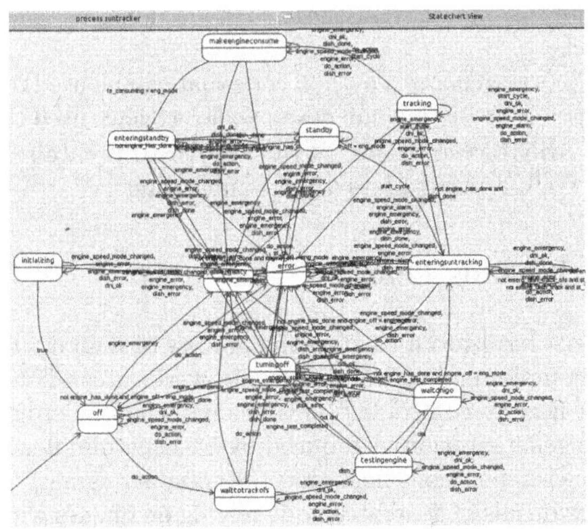

Fig. 3. FSM of SunTracker block, as shown in TASTE

About sampling times, PLCs implement different periods depending on the sensors involved, but at high level the sampling period is 50 ms, chosen as it is the maximum safe period for detecting Stirling engine RPM changes while maintaining needed control response time, and still being divisor of the minimum period for timers as imposed by TASTE, which is 100 ms.

In embedded systems the control loop is typically made of buffered sensing of inputs (I), control of the actuations (C), and output of the buffered actuations (O). To execute O with a constant frequency, the three phases are often carried out as an O/I/C sequence each cycle. In TASTE there is no explicit notion of delta cycle loop, so we added a block for enforcing it, by sending event *start_cycle* to each part of O/I/C in a sequence. Since the Controller is made of multiple asynchronous FSMs, we needed to assure that C runs to completion each cycle. This is theoretically assured if discrete transitions are instantaneous, there are no loops and eventually each FSM stops waiting either for event *start_cycle*, external events or a timer expiration, whose time can only be a multiple of the delta cycle period. Preliminary empirical data show that the cycle time ends within 2 ms, so a period of 50 ms should be largely safe, but a formal schedulability analysis is needed to prove it.

4.3 Generated Code

The executable of the Controller and HWIs runs in a single node and partition, so native encoding was used to communicate among them. The GUI runs in a different partition, and ACN is used for communication. The hosting platform is a x86 industrial PC, with Xenomai RTOS [1] in co-kernel configuration with Linux Debian.

TASTE generates 76 threads for the Controller, and performances meet the expectations with a load of CPU $< 2\,\%$ and about 14 MB of memory usage (when executing on Linux 32 bit). Once familiar with it, generated code is very readable, although generality introduces many function hops that could be optimized for local processes. As for correctness, validation and formal verification have not yet been done. Preliminary tests have found some bugs both in generated code and middleware (under Xenomai), which were promptly tracked and fixed. Some improvements of robustness shall be done, as some function calls miss sanity checks.

TASTE generates python code that can be used to ease the integration of other parts, or for writing unit tests. So far we have used this feature to cyclically dump the ASN.1 vector state of the system to a database and to communicate with the GUI, a python-based web application.

5 Lessons Learnt

TASTE has proven to fit in the process of design and implement control systems for complex embedded systems. However it can hardly be applied to RT systems that need to control fast phenomena, where micro or nano seconds are involved. The generalization introduced by Ocarina middleware introduces non-negligible latencies, functions hops that the compiler cannot optimize, and communication mechanisms in generated code relying on queues with limited performances. Targeting mid-slow system is also visible in TASTE from already mentioned 100 ms granularity of timers, and time expressed in integer milliseconds. However, even not considering fast systems a granularity of at least 100 µs would be highly desirable.

Using SDL for modeling the behavior can be very effective, but requires the designer to rely on good practices and rigorous method, as it is very easy to mess up the models and break model readability.

As most parts of TASTE are open source, we could extend it to make it generate code for automatic logging of traversed states, with no need to touch the model. These extensions should be properly integrated.

The size of the Controller's model can be considered middle/large for TASTE, as performances of the editor and the compiler show some difficulties when dealing with it. In particular, the system editor shows some usage limitations, that make difficult to work with large models. Since TASTE targets embedded systems, it would be very useful to have a native support for enforcing the delta loop cycle. Furthermore, the building system needs a speed-up, as it should not recompile parts uselessly: recompiling without any change takes 2 s less than scratch compilation, which overall takes about 6' 20" on a 2.4 Ghz Intel i7 CPU.

6 Conclusion and Future Directions

In this paper, we reported on the experience of a real implementation of the controller for an innovative complex energy system. Due to the complexity of the plant, implementing manually the controller's code for the target platform would have been impossible for us. TASTE provided a powerful model-based solution to ensure the real-time constraints of the controller. On the other hand, the case study provided a challenging benchmark that stressed the tool capabilities. To the best of our knowledge, it is the most complex system managed by TASTE reported in the literature.

We ran successfully the Stirling engine attached to the Controller, but not with the Dish as the plant is still under construction. Validation of a controller being designed and implemented with limited support from the real plant was faced by developing a simulator and its drivers. As simulator's and real plant's drivers offer an identical interface to the IO blocks of the Controller, the simulator can be removed to connect the controller to the real plant when available, and even a mixed solution is possible.

In the future, we want to exploit the python generated code for a structured validation through unit testing, and to exploit the formal specification of the model to apply formal techniques such as model checking, compositional reasoning, and failure analysis. Moreover, we would like to explore the usage of other techniques provided by the TASTE tool chain such as schedulability analysis and model interactive simulation at SDL level. Finally, after collecting real data coming from the field, we would like to formalize the regulation function of the Stirling engine to optimize it, as it represents the hearth of the energetic efficiency of the system.

References

1. Linux/Xenomai RTOS. https://xenomai.org/
2. ITU-T: Specification and description language (SDL). ITU-T Recommendation Z.100 (1999)
3. ITU-T: Information technology Abstract Syntax Notation One (ASN.1): Specification of basic notation. ITU-T Recommendation X.680 (2002)
4. Lasnier, G., Zalila, B., Pautet, L., Hugues, J.: OCARINA: an environment for AADL models analysis and automatic code generation for high integrity applications. In: Kordon, F., Kermarrec, Y. (eds.) Ada-Europe 2009. LNCS, vol. 5570, pp. 237–250. Springer, Heidelberg (2009). doi:10.1007/978-3-642-01924-1_17
5. McFarlane, P., Semperlotti, F., Sen, M.: Mathematical model of an air-filled alpha stirling refrigerator. J. Appl. Phys. **114**(14), 144508–144508 (2013)
6. Perrotin, M., Conquet, E., Delange, J., Schiele, A., Tsiodras, T.: TASTE: a real-time software engineering tool-chain overview, status, and future. In: Ober, I., Ober, I. (eds.) SDL 2011. LNCS, vol. 7083, pp. 26–37. Springer, Heidelberg (2011). doi:10.1007/978-3-642-25264-8_4
7. Reda, I., Andreas, A.: Solar position algorithm for solar radiation applications. Sol. Energy **76**(5), 577–589 (2008)
8. Ross, A.: Stirling cycle engines. Sol. Engines (1977)
9. Ruelas, J., Velzquez, N., Cerezo, J.: A mathematical model to develop a scheffler-type solar concentrator coupled with a stirling engine. Appl. Energy **101**, 253–260 (2013)
10. SAE Standards: Architecture Analysis & Design Language (AADL). n^o AS5506B, September 2012

Simulink to UPPAAL Statistical Model Checker: Analyzing Automotive Industrial Systems

Predrag Filipovikj[1(✉)], Nesredin Mahmud[1], Raluca Marinescu[1], Cristina Seceleanu[1], Oscar Ljungkrantz[2], and Henrik Lönn[2]

[1] Mälardalen University, Västerås, Sweden
{predrag.filipovikj,nesredin.mahmud,raluca.marinescu, cristina.seceleanu}@mdh.se

[2] Volvo Group Trucks Technology, Gothenburg, Sweden
{oscar.ljungkrantz,henrik.lonn}@volvo.com

Abstract. The advanced technology used for developing modern automotive systems increases their complexity, making their correctness assurance very tedious. To enable analysis by simulation, but also enhance understanding and communication, engineers use MATLAB/Simulink modeling during system development. In this paper, we provide further analysis means to industrial Simulink models by proposing a pattern-based, execution-order preserving transformation of Simulink blocks into the input language of UPPAAL Statistical Model checker, that is, timed (or hybrid) automata with stochastic semantics. The approach leads to being able to analyze complex Simulink models of automotive systems, and we report our experience with two vehicular systems, the Brake-by-Wire and the Adjustable Speed Limiter.

1 Introduction

Features for automating driving tasks, such as the Adjustable Speed Limiter (ASL) that enables drivers to set a maximum speed in order to reduce the risk of over speeding, as well as trends like the *drive-by-wire* technology, in which standard vehicle operations such as braking are carried out by electronic components rather than mechanical ones, make the assurance of a modern vehicle's correct operation extremely challenging.

Model-based design enables industry to create executable specifications in the form of MATLAB/Simulink [1] models that can be simulated and formally analyzed [2] to detect hidden design errors and requirements violations.

In this paper, we introduce a pattern-based approach (Sect. 3) that captures formally the behaviors of a large set of Simulink blocks, as networks of stochastic timed/hybrid automata, and report our experience with analyzing two industrial systems from Volvo Group Trucks Technology, the *Brake-by-Wire* (BBW) prototype and the operational *Adjustable Speed Limiter* (ASL), with UPPAAL SMC (Statistical Model Checker) [3] (Sect. 4). The crux of our method is twofold:

The original version of this chapter was revised: Figure 1a and 1b was corrected. The erratum to this chapter is available at DOI: 10.1007/978-3-319-48989-6_51

J. Fitzgerald et al. (Eds.): FM 2016, LNCS 9995, pp. 748–756, 2016.
DOI: 10.1007/978-3-319-48989-6_46

(i) using patterns in the transformation, which eases the modeling process while preserving the execution semantics of Simulink blocks, and (ii) verifying the encodings of the Simulink blocks behaviors as C routines in UPPAAL, with the program verifier Dafny [4].

Our endeavor is justified by the industrial needs of ensuring correctness with respect to both functional and timing behaviors of automotive embedded systems. Moreover, an initial investigation of verifying ASL's Simulink models with the Simulink Design Verifier (SDV) shows limitations in terms of verifying large models, and that a substantial part of the requirements cannot be directly concluded due to, for instance, translation problems and boundaries not being defined. The application of our approach to BBW and ASL (specifically ASL's Engine Manager) shows improved scalability in the sense of being able to functionally analyze via statistical model checking the complete transformed Simulink models, but it also reveals limitations in tackling timing requirements, due to using only information from Simulink models.

Related work. Several works have already tackled the formal analysis of Simulink models. Barnat et al. [5] and Meenakshi et al. [6] propose transformations that target only Simulink blocks with discrete-time behavior. The work of Agrawal et al. [7] focuses on the transformation of Simulink into networks of automata, without providing concrete means for formal verification. Miller [8] investigates how translating Simulink to Lustre enables formal verification with a constellation of model checkers and provers. Manamcheri et al. [9] and Jiang et al. [10] propose transformation frameworks for Stateflow diagrams, into timed and hybrid automata, respectively, yet not considering other types of Simulink blocks. Compared to these frameworks, our approach covers both continuous- and discrete-time blocks, and we show how our transformation leads to the formal analysis of industrial automotive systems models, against a wide set of requirements. This is an endeavor not really carried out before. One other solution is the use of PLASMA Lab [2], a tool that is able to take as input different Simulink simulations and provide statistical model checking results. Compared to this approach, we generate a formal model that can be extended further (e.g., with extra-functional information) to provide additional verification results.

2 Preliminaries

In this section, we present the tools used in our framework: (i) Simulink, which is used to model the automotive systems, and (ii) UPPAAL SMC, which is used to analyze the models.

Simulink. Simulink [1] is a graphical programming environment for modeling, simulation and code generation targeting multi-domain dynamic systems. The tool provides a set of libraries with predefined *blocks* that can be combined to create hierarchical diagrams of systems. A block represents an *atomic* dynamic module that computes an equation or another modeling concept to produce an output, either continuously (*continuous-time* block), or at specific points in time (*discrete-time* block). Besides these atomic blocks, Simulink supports the definition of custom blocks via Stateflow diagrams or user-defined functions called

S-Functions written in MATLAB, C, C++, or Fortran. A hierarchical diagram is achieved through the implementation of *subsystem* blocks, each containing sets of atomic blocks and possibly other subsystem blocks. Such subsystems can be *virtual* (blocks are evaluated according to the overall model), or *non virtual* (blocks are executed as a single unit, respectively). A non-virtual subsystem can also be conditionally executed based on a predefined triggering function. During simulation, Simulink determines the order in which to invoke the blocks. This block invocation order is done based on a predefined *sorted order*. In Simulink, the dynamic models can be simulated and the results can be displayed as simulation runs.

UPPAAL SMC. The UPPAAL SMC [11] tool provides statistical model checking for stochastic hybrid systems. A *hybrid automaton* (HA) is defined as a tuple:

$$HA = \langle L, l_0, X, \Sigma, E, F, I \rangle \tag{1}$$

where L is a finite set of locations, $l_0 \in L$ is the initial location, X is a finite set of continuous variables, $\Sigma = \Sigma_i \uplus \Sigma_o$ is a finite set of actions partitioned into inputs (Σ_i) and outputs (Σ_0), E is a finite set of edges of the form (l, g, a, φ, l'), where l and l' are locations, g is a predicate on $\mathbb{R}^X$, $a \in \Sigma$ is an action label, and φ is a binary relation on $\mathbb{R}^X$, $F(l)$ a delay function for the location $l \in L$, and I assigns an invariant predicate $I(l)$ to any location l. With this definition, UPPAAL SMC extends the timed automata (TA) tuple used by UPPAAL [12] with the delay function F that allows the continuous variables to evolve according to ordinary differential equations. In UPPAAL SMC, the automata have a stochastic interpretation based on: (i) the probabilistic choices between multiple enabled transitions, and (ii) the non-deterministic time delays that can be refined based on probability distributions, either uniform distributions for time-bounded delays or user-defined exponential distributions for unbounded delays.

A model in UPPAAL SMC consists of a network of interacting stochastic HA that communicate through broadcast channels and shared variables. In the network, the automata repeatedly race against each other, that is, they independently and stochastically decide how much to delay before delivering the output, and what output to broadcast at that moment, with the "winner" being the component that chooses the minimum delay.

UPPAAL SMC uses an extension of *weighted metric temporal logic* (WMTL) [13] to provide probability evaluation ($Pr(*_{x \leq C} \phi)$), where the symbol $*$ stands for $\Diamond$(*eventually*) or $\Box$(*always*), which calculates the probability that ϕ is satisfied within cost $x \leq C$, but also hypothesis testing and probability comparison.

3 Simulink to UPPAAL SMC: Transformation Approach

There are two major aspects of transforming Simulink models into networks of stochastic timed/hybrid automata: (1) transforming the individual blocks, and (2) synchronizing their execution to preserve the behavior of the model. In this section we present how we transform Simulink models into networks of TA with stochastic semantics, suitable for statistical model checking with UPPAAL SMC.

A discrete-time block executes its computational routine at a predefined observable time interval called *sample time*, whereas a continuous-time one executes the routine over infinitely small time intervals. The same classification applies for the *S-Functions* that are masked, preserving only the specification of their input-output relation. For a subsystem block, the transformation is reduced to a *flattening* procedure that eliminates the subsystem block from the model and replaces it with its inner content, with preserved atomicity of execution. The details and algorithm for flattening are given later in the section. The flattening procedure, however, does not apply for the *Referenced models* that are given as executables only, as in these cases no Simulink models are available. Such blocks are treated as atomic, and our transformation relies on their documentation.

In the following, we propose a formal definition of a Simulink block, as a tuple, as well as *patterns* for transforming both discrete- and continuous-time blocks into TA with stochastic semantics.

Any atomic Simulink block can be formally defined as a tuple:

$$B = \langle V_{in}, V_{out}, V_D, t_s, Init, blockRoutine \rangle \tag{2}$$

where: V_{in}, V_{out} and V_D denote the set of input, output, and data variables, respectively, t_s denotes the sample time, $Init$ is the initialization function, whereas the *blockRoutine* is a function that maps inputs and state variables onto output values. Our transformation is basically a semantic anchoring of tuple B of Eq. (2) onto the HA tuple given by Eq. (1).

The automata patterns corresponding to the discrete and continuous categories are given in Fig. 1a and b, respectively. Each of them has three locations, namely *Start*, *Offset* and *Operate*, with *Start* being the initial one. The *Offset* location is used to model the delay of the block execution. The last location is *Operate*, in which the automaton produces output either at predefined time intervals, or continuously. A local clock t is used to model the delay of the execution in both cases, and also to trigger the periodic behavior of the discrete blocks, whereas the continuous behavior is modeled via assigning *exponential rates* on the *Operate* location. The exponential rate is a mechanism used to specify the probability of the automaton to leave a location, according to an exponential distribution [3]. Simulation time is represented via the global clock *gtime*, which is used as part of the synchronization mechanism. The input parameters relevant for the pattern and its instantiation on a particular Simulink block are passed as the array called *param*. The start time of the automaton is calculated as a

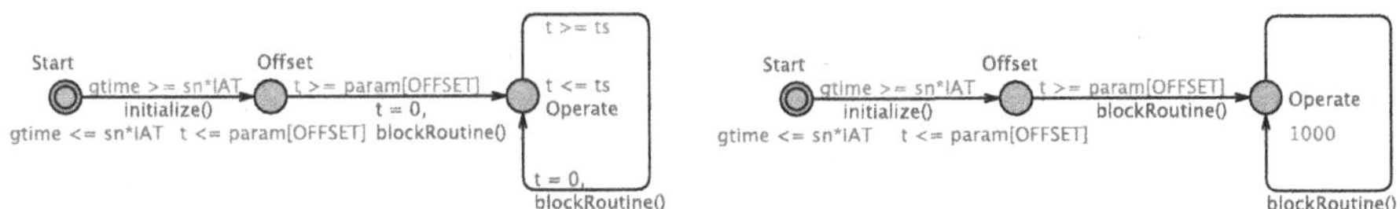

(a) Pattern for discrete blocks

(b) Pattern for continuous blocks

Fig. 1. Our used TA patterns

Algorithm 1. Flattening algorithm for slist.

```
function flatten(String currentBlockId, String currentBlockOrderNo, String parentBlockOrderNo)
    orderedList ← emptyList                                  ▷ Ordered list containing blocks IDs.
    if isAtomicBlock(currentBlockId) then                    ▷ The current block is atomic.
        orderedList.append(parentBlockOrderNo.concat(currentBlockOrderNo))
    else                                                     ▷ The current block is a subsystem.
        currentChildren ← getChildren(currentBlockId)
        concatenatedParentId ← parentBlockOrderNo.concat(currentBlockOrderNo)
        for all child in currentChildren do
            orderedList.append(flatten(child.id, child.orderNo, concatenatedParentId))
    return orderedList
```

combination of the block's execution order (*sn*), and the inter-arrival time of the block's input signal (*IAT*).

Preserving Block Execution Order. The execution order (sorted order) of the Simulink model blocks is generated by calling the *"slist"* function, while Simulink is in debug mode. Simulink uses the assigned execution order to invoke blocks during simulation, with a smaller execution order number denoting higher priority. We perform the flattening of the sorted order automatically, using Algorithm 1, which parses the *"slist"* output and assigns execution order numbers to atomic blocks that are nested at an arbitrary depth, inside a subsystem.

We use this execution order to release the discrete and continuous time blocks during initialization in the UPPAAL model, and to arbiter their execution at times when two or more blocks are ready to execute. Also, to ensure data integrity and predictability in the model, we also provide transformations for the *RateTransition* blocks that connect faster- to slower-rate blocks, and vice-versa.

Verifying UPPAAL Simulink Block Routines With Dafny. We use Dafny [4], a language and program verifier, to prove the functional correctness of the block routines that we encode as C functions in UPPAAL. Below we present an example that shows the verification of a simple block routine using Dafny.

Rounding is one of the fundamental operations in Simulink, with several variants including rounding to floor, ceiling, fix, etc. In this example, we consider the floor variation of the function for non-negative real numbers. Due to space limitation, we omit the encoding of the function and present only the assertions that are used for proving the correctness. By using Dafny, we establish the correctness of the function by checking the following pre- and postconditions, denoted as *requires* and *ensures* claims, respectively: "requires input $\geq$ 0.0", "ensures 0.0$\leq$ (input - output) $<$ 1.0", where output $\in \mathbb{Z}_{\geq 0}$. We use the same approach to verify the correctness of all Simulink block behaviors that we encode as C functions in UPPAAL.

4 Application on Industrial Use Cases: Results

The proposed transformation has been validated on two industrial use cases, namely the Brake-by-Wire (BBW) prototype, and the Engine Manager of the

Adjustable Speed Limiter operational system. In this section, we provide a brief overview of our results.

The BBW Use Case. The BBW system is a braking system equipped with an ABS function, and without any mechanical connection between the brake pedal and the brake actuators. A sensor reads the pedal's position, which is used to compute the desired brake torque. At each wheel, the ABS algorithm decides whether to apply the brake torque based on the slip rate. When the slip rate increases above 0.2 (this can actually be a model parameter), the friction coefficient of the wheel starts decreasing. For this reason, if the slip rate is greater than 0.2 the brake actuator is released and no brake is applied, otherwise the requested brake torque is used. The BBW system has a set of 13 functional and 4 timing requirements that need to be analyzed. Here, we present two such requirements, in natural language:

R1$_{\mathbf{BBW}}$(End-to-end deadline): The time needed for a brake request to propagate from the brake pedal sensor to the wheel actuator should not exceed 200 ms.

R2$_{\mathbf{BBW}}$(Functional requirement): If the slip rate exceeds 0.2, then the applied brake torque shall be set to 0.

Transformation. The hierarchical Simulink model for the BBW system consists of 320 blocks, out of which only 174 are computational blocks. The remaining 146 blocks define the structure of the model (e.g., Subsystem, Inport, Outport, From, Goto, Reference) and they are removed during the flattening. Consequently, the transformation provides a network of 174 TA. In this network, only 10 automata have continuous-time behavior; the rest compute their output only at sample times.

Verification. In order to verify the system properties mentioned above, we have implemented a *Monitor* automaton that follows the propagation of data throughout the system, from sensors to actuators. It relies on the definition of an array of broadcast channels trigg[N], with N $\in$ [1, 174]. Each TA in the network broadcasts the message trigg[own_id]! when it performs a new computation blockRutine(), and the Monitor receives these messages in a predefined order. For own_id we have used the predefined sorted number, since it is unique for each TA. Figure 2 presents an excerpt of the *Monitor* implemented for requirements **R1$_{\mathbf{BBW}}$** and **R2$_{\mathbf{BBW}}$**.

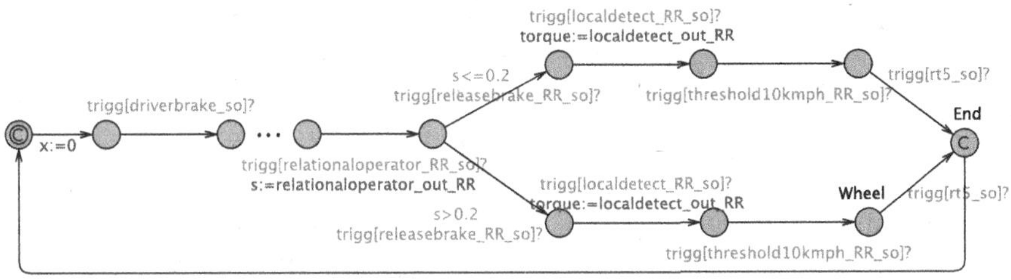

Fig. 2. BBW's monitor automaton.

Table 1. Overall results of statistical model checking.

Req.	Query	Result	Runs
$\mathbf{R1_{BBW}}$	$Pr[Monitor.x <= 200](<> Monitor.End)$	Probability $\in$ [0.902606, 1] with confidence 0.95	36
$\mathbf{R2_{BBW}}$	$Pr[Monitor.x <= 200]([]\ Monitor.Wheel$ $and\ Monitor.slipRate > 0.2\ and$ $Monitor.torque == 0)$	Probability $\in$ [0.900924, 1] with confidence 0.975	42

For the BBW system we have statistically verified all functional and timing requirements. In Table 1, we provide concrete SMC results for requirements $\mathbf{R1_{BBW}}$ and $\mathbf{R2_{BBW}}$.

The ASL Use Case. ASL is used to limit the truck speed to not exceed a maximum speed set by the driver. The driver normally enables and disables the function using control buttons located on the dashboard, and the freewheel. However, ASL can also be disabled when the accelerator pedal is pressed beyond a hard point, or the truck is subjected to overspeed, for instance, in downhill, or becomes faulty during operation. ASL implements around 300 requirements, and is modeled using 4845 Simulink blocks, of which 2835 are non-virtual blocks. We limit our analysis to the ASL Engine Manager (ASL-EM), which is a logical component, and an interface to the power train of the truck's engine. It enables several functions of the truck, e.g., engine start and stop, climate control, fuel economy strategy, and road speed limitation. In our case study, we have transformed 94 non-virtual Simulink blocks, and analyzed all their functional and timing requirements. Examples of ASL-EM requirements are: (i) $\mathbf{R1_{ASL}}$(Min. speed limit): The ASL-EM controller shall be able to handle road speed limit requests down to 5 km/h, (ii) $\mathbf{R2_{ASL}}$(Lowest speed limit): When several road speed limit sources are active at the same time, ASL-EM shall use the lowest speed limit value, (iii) $\mathbf{R3_{ASL}}$(Max. latency): The maximum latency of the ASL-EM block shall be 20 ms.

5 Discussion and Conclusions

In this paper, we have introduced a pattern-based transformation of discrete- and continuous-time Simulink blocks into networks of stochastic timed automata. The approach is motivated by the industry's need of increasing the assurance of vehicular systems developed using Simulink, and the possibly limited requirements coverage obtained by employing the SDV for verification. Applying our approach on the BBW and ASL-EM systems has provided improved scalability for verification, that is, we have analyzed statistically their complete Simulink models, at the expense of concrete challenges and limitations:

1. The formal model needs to obey the same execution order as the Simulink one. For this, we have enforced the *sorted order* as generated by Simulink, which is usually respected during execution, except for block methods (blocks operating at the same rate and in the same task). These exceptions need to also be taken into account during the transformation.

2. Simulink allows for the integration of code in the model by using *S-function*. In our transformation, we do not provide direct means to verify this code. We view such components as "black boxes", modeled based on their defined mask and not the code itself.
3. Simulink lacks the possibility of modeling the timing behavior of the system (beyond the sample time), thus limiting the formal verification of extra-functional requirements. By pairing the Simulink model with an architectural model that allows for the representation of a wide set of extra-functional properties (such as timing and possibly resource usage), the transformation and the verification could provide a deeper insight to the engineers. Moreover, in the current version of our transformation, we have not exploited the full power of UPPAAL SMC. We have used TA with stochastic behavior, rather than stochastic HA. This is due to the fact that for more complex blocks (e.g., Derivative, Integrator) we have chosen to use the numerical approximation performed by Simulink, instead of implementing the function directly in UPPAAL SMC. This modeling decision will be further investigated.

Acknowledgement. This work has been funded by the Swedish Governmental Agency for Innovation Systems (VINNOVA) under the VeriSpec project 2013-01299.

References

1. Dabney, J.B., Harman, T.L.: Mastering Simulink. Pearson/Prentice Hall, Upper Saddle River (2004)
2. Legay, A., Traonouez, L.-M.: Statistical model checking of Simulink models with Plasma Lab. In: Artho, C., Ölveczky, P.C. (eds.) FTSCS 2015. CCIS, vol. 596, pp. 259–264. Springer, Heidelberg (2016). doi:10.1007/978-3-319-29510-7_15
3. David, A., Larsen, K.G., Legay, A., Mikučionis, M., Poulsen, D.B.: UPPAAL SMC tutorial. STTT J. **17**(4), 397–415 (2015)
4. Leino, K.R.M.: Dafny: an automatic program verifier for functional correctness. In: Clarke, E.M., Voronkov, A. (eds.) LPAR 2010. LNCS (LNAI), vol. 6355, pp. 348–370. Springer, Heidelberg (2010). doi:10.1007/978-3-642-17511-4_20
5. Barnat, J., Beran, J., Brim, L., Kratochvíla, T., Ročkai, P.: Tool chain to support automated formal verification of avionics Simulink designs. In: Stoelinga, M., Pinger, R. (eds.) FMICS 2012. LNCS, vol. 7437, pp. 78–92. Springer, Heidelberg (2012). doi:10.1007/978-3-642-32469-7_6
6. Meenakshi, B., Bhatnagar, A., Roy, S.: Tool for translating Simulink models into input language of a model checker. In: Liu, Z., He, J. (eds.) ICFEM 2006. LNCS, vol. 4260, pp. 606–620. Springer, Heidelberg (2006). doi:10.1007/11901433_33
7. Agrawal, A., Simon, G., Karsai, G.: Semantic translation of Simulink/Stateflow models to hybrid automata using graph transformations. ENTCS J. **109**, 43–56 (2004)
8. Miller, S.P.: Bridging the gap between model-based development and model checking. In: Kowalewski, S., Philippou, A. (eds.) TACAS 2009. LNCS, vol. 5505, pp. 443–453. Springer, Heidelberg (2009). doi:10.1007/978-3-642-00768-2_36
9. Manamcheri, K., Mitra, S., Bak, S., Caccamo, M.: A step towards verification and synthesis from Simulink/Stateflow models. In: HSCC 2011, pp. 317–318. ACM (2011)
10. Jiang, Y., Yang, Y., Liu, H., Kong, H., Gu, M., Sun, J., Sha, L.: From Stateflow simulation to verified implementation: a verification approach and a real-time train controller design. In: RTAS 2016, pp. 1–11, April 2016

11. David, A., Du, D., Larsen, K.G., Legay, A., Mikučionis, M., Poulsen, D.B., Sedwards, S.: Statistical model checking for stochastic hybrid systems. arXiv preprint arXiv:1208.3856 (2012)
12. Larsen, K.G., Pettersson, P., Yi, W.: UPPAAL in a nutshell. STTT J. **1**(1), 134–152 (1997)
13. Bulychev, P., David, A., Larsen, K.G., Legay, A., Li, G., Poulsen, D.B.: Rewrite-based statistical model checking of WMTL. In: Qadeer, S., Tasiran, S. (eds.) RV 2012. LNCS, vol. 7687, pp. 260–275. Springer, Heidelberg (2013). doi:10.1007/978-3-642-35632-2_25

Safety-Assured Formal Model-Driven Design of the Multifunction Vehicle Bus Controller

Yu Jiang[1(✉)], Han Liu[1], Houbing Song[2], Hui Kong[3], Ming Gu[1], Jiaguang Sun[1], and Lui Sha[4]

[1] TNLIST, KLISS, School of Software, Tsinghua University, Beijing, China
jiangyu198964@gmail.com
[2] Department of Electrical and Computer Engineering, West Virginia University, Morgantown, USA
[3] Institute of Science and Technology Austria, Klosterneuburg, Austria
[4] Department of Computer Science, UIUC, Champaign, USA

Abstract. In this paper, we present a formal model-driven engineering approach to establishing a safety-assured implementation of Multifunction vehicle bus controller (MVBC) based on the generic reference models and requirements described in the International Electrotechnical Commission (IEC) standard IEC-61375. First, the generic models described in IEC-61375 are translated into a network of timed automata, and some safety requirements tested in IEC-61375 are formalized as timed computation tree logic (TCTL) formulas. With the help of Uppaal, we check and debug whether the timed automata satisfy the formulas or not. Within this step, several logic inconsistencies in the original standard are detected and corrected. Then, we apply the tool Times to generate C code from the verified model, which was later synthesized into a real MVBC chip. Finally, the runtime verification tool RMOR is applied to verify some safety requirements at the implementation level. We set up a real platform with worldwide mostly used MVBC D113, and verify the correctness and the scalability of the synthesized MVBC chip more comprehensively. The errors in the standard has been confirmed and the resulted MVBC has been deployed in real train communication network.

1 Introduction

The train communication network (TCN) enabling secure and fast data transmission in the entire rail vehicle has been standardized by the international railroad union and the International Electrical Commission, as presented in the international standard IEC-61375 [3]. Within the network, the multifunction vehicle bus controller (MVBC) is defined as a typical embedded software used mostly for the control of data transmission among the equipment (the traction control unit, air brake electronic control unit and door control unit etc.) onboard of each individual vehicle. Detail functions of the MVBC are based on the real-time protocol (RTP), which defines the rules (master-slave communication principle, data frame format and timing requirements, etc.) for process data and message data transmission.

J. Fitzgerald et al. (Eds.): FM 2016, LNCS 9995, pp. 757–763, 2016.
DOI: 10.1007/978-3-319-48989-6_47

Traditionally, from the perspective of industrial practice, most companies such as Siemens and Duagon develop their MVBCs by directly writing underlying C and VHDL code manually according tò the description of IEC-61375, accompanied with the complex system and physical testing to avoid defects. Increasingly developed modern railroad vehicles increased the functional complexity, and are more difficult to ensure the correctness through testing. For example, even the most widely used D113 MVBC of Duagon company contains some dead logic in the C code for process data communication. From the perspective of academia, there are many existing works for the design of MVBC, but mainly focusing on the novel implementation hardware architecture [5]. In [5], they propose to use materialization of slave nodes for MVBC in a single chip by using reconfigurable logic. In [11], they propose to use BeagleBone and some existing tools such as Simulink to implement the MVBC, which is starting from model construction and ending in programming according to the validated model. Most of them focus on the functional implementation and do not pay attention on safety assurance under dynamic physical environment. Besides, there are also some works about verifying the real time communication protocol of TCN [6], they do not cope with the implementation issue neither, they focus on the logic correctness of train communication protocol only. Little research has been conducted to address the safety issue of MVBC, and some failures of the communication function have been reported to result in the accidents of the railway and trains [12], and some cases with serious injuries of human.

In this paper, we collaborate with the researchers from China Railway Rolling Stock Corporation (CRRC), and use formal model-driven development approach to establishing a safety-assured implementation of an MVBC prototype based on

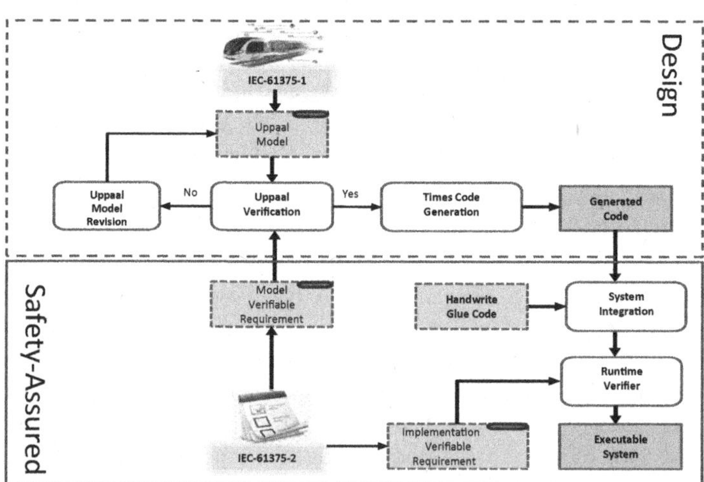

Fig. 1. Safety-assured design of MVBC. We may also replace these tools with similar functional tools such as SPIN and RV-Monitor. If we use SPIN to replace Uppaal, we need to build the SPIN Promela model instead of Uppaal timed automata model.

the standard IEC-61375, which consists of two parts: IEC-61375-1 describing the architecture and functional behaviors of MVBC, and IEC-61375-2 describing the conformance testing requirements. The overall procedure is presented in Fig. 1, where we leverage the formal modeling and verification technique as follows (1) the generic models and requirements in the standard are formalized as Uppaal timed automata and TCTL expressions [2] respectively, (2) formally verify the requirements and debug the models with Uppaal until the timed automata satisfies the TCTL expressions, (3) generate C code from the verified model with Times [1], which can be compiled and synthesized into a real MVBC chip with some auxiliary code developed to interface with hardware, and (4) use runtime verification to formally verify some implementation level safety requirements and test the consistency between the execution of the integrated system and the simulation of the verified model with RMOR [4]. Then, we set up a real platform, connecting the synthesized MVBC prototype for safety assured communication demonstration. During the practice, the errors detected in the standard has been confirmed and the synthesized prototype has been in productization and deployed in real train system control.

2 Safety-Assured Approach

Model construction and verification: First, we build a network of timed automata for the MVBC according to the architecture and functional description, such as the generic automata model, the function and action table, and the SDL (Specification and Description Language) diagram of IEC-611375-1. All these heterogeneous information are unified translated and encoded into the network of timed automata manually. Currently, it is not easy to automatically abstract the timed automata model from the text-based standard, and the whole construction procedure is manually accomplished and validated with the help of engineers from CRRC with the following modeling guidance rules.

Let us see the translation of generic automata and the accompanied function table. Each state in the generic automata is mapped to an ordinary location in Uppaal with the same name. For the packets of sending and receiving events with actual parameters specified for the control fields, we use the synchronous channel of Uppaal timed automata to simulate the communication. Because there are lots of none interrupt actions and packets associated with a single generic state while only one synchronous action is allowed to be attached in a single transition of Uppaal timed automata, we need to create a set of committed locations, where none interrupt actions are sequentially encoded into the transitions among those committed locations. Then, the attached actions described in the function table of the standard, they are translated into the accompanied actions of the Uppaal timed automata transition.

For the translation of SDL diagram, each state in the diagram is mapped to an ordinary location of Uppaal. Some plain C codes in the diagram are translated into the action attached on the transition of two locations. The event signal of SDL diagram is modeled by the synchronous channel of timed automata, where receiving an event is denoted as *Rcv_Channel_Name*? and sending an event is denoted as *Send_Channel_Name*!. In case of situations with more than two signals between two states, we need to add some intermediate locations of timed automata. Note that, for the clock signal, it is issued by itself. Hence, we do not need to translate it into a synchronous channel.

Safety Requirements Formalization: The MVBC safety requirements are mainly derived from the descriptions of the MVBC conformance testing requirement of IEC-61375-2. We divide the testing requirement into two groups: *model verifiable safety requirement* and *implementation verifiable safety requirement.*

Those requirements that are related to general functions of control logic and independent of platform are categorized as *model verifiable safety requirements.* We formalize them as timed computation tree logic formulas defined on the formal timed automata, and verify them in Uppaal. For example, the requirement that there is at most one regular master MVBC contained in the train communication network, is a typical *model verifiable safety requirements*, and can be formalized as $A[\ ]not(MVBC(1).Regular\_Master \&\& MVBC(2).Regular\_Master)$.

Those requirements related with dynamic runtime situation and uncertain environment are categorized as *implementation verifiable safety requirements.* They are not easy to be defined in the abstract timed automata level, because it is not easy to model dynamic transmission delay of data on MVBC bus and dynamic processing delay of hardware platform, even with a preliminary channel model and clock variable in Uppaal timed automata. We formalize these safety requirements as the runtime verification property of RMOR. We define some events based on the variables of the generated C code of Times, which are configured to I/O pins of the real hardware platform and will be continuously loaded by accompanied C functions. Then, the property and the accompanied C functions are transformed and input to RMOR to get the instrumented code, which can be made as an integral part of the target generated system, verifying and guiding its execution within the dynamic environment. For example, the requirement that he suggested time constraint on a master MVBC between the finish of a master frame sending and the start of a response slave frame receiving should be less than 42.7us is a typical *implementation verifiable safety requirements*, and can be formalized as below:

```
DataCenter Monitor TimeConstraints(){ ......
   event TimeoutResponse =
    ((T_Master_Send - T_Slav_Receive)<42.7)
   event Trigger = TimeoutResponse;
   state safe{When Trigger -> error;}
}
```

Listing 1.1. Runtime Property Definition for the Time Interval.

Code synthesis and verifier integration: For the code synthesis, automatical code generation tools such as Times can be applied to reduce the hard work efforts of manual implementation, which is also more human error prone. For example, the engineers from the industrial sources (the Duagon company, the China CR corporation) report that their MVBC is developed by directly writing underlying C or VHDL code manually, where there are still some bugs such as dead logic or dead code. Besides, the automatical code generation also facilitate the traceability between the model and implementation, which results in better documentations and easier maintains.

Before applying the code generation algorithm, we need to do some changes on the formal model. More specifically, we construct and initialize the timed automata template for two or more MVBCs for comprehensive verification, and now need to isolate the timed automata of a single MVBC for code synthesis. One way for isolation is to build a general environment model, which is ready to receive any output synchronization action from the isolated MVBC and send input synchronization action to the isolated MVBC. Then, we can generate execution code for both MVBC and the general environment, and manually separate the generated code. Another way for isolation is to do some reverse engineering, where the synchronization channels denoting the packets of sending and receiving events are reversed to the general variable. For example, a synchronization channel rcv_connect_req? can be replaced by a declaration of boolean variable rcv_connect_req. Meanwhile, an evaluation expression rcv_connect_req == true should be added to the guard segment, and an assignment expression rcv_connect_req := true should be added to the action segment. We use the second way, because it can be automatically accomplished by parsing and updating the XML file of the timed automata model, and the second isolation way is more closed to the real operation scenario where the sending and receiving packets from the physical bus is asynchronous. Besides, because the generated code is tightly coupled, the manually separation is more error prone.

After that, we also need to add some glue code, which is mainly used for two functionalities, the interface between the software and hardware platform, and timing implementation of the generated code on the hardware platform. For interface, we just need to initialize some configure mapping files, mapping the variable of software to the GPIO of the hardware platform. Accompanied type conversion functions may be needed. For clocks, let sc be a global system clock. For each clock x in the timed automata, let x_{reset} be an integer variable holding the system time of the last clock reset. The value of the clock is then $(sc - x_{reset})$, and a reset can be performed as $x_{reset} := sc$.

Finally, based on the generated code and the handwriting glue code, we input the formalized implementation verifiable safety requirement and the integrated code to RMOR to generate the runtime verifier, and the system integration is instrumented with the verifier for the runtime verification. The integrated verifier keeps verifying the safety requirements on the running executable system. To improve the safety confidence, we can also formalize some model verifiable requirement into verifier, but will increasing the storage overhead of the system.

Table 1. Resource utilization C compilation for MVBC, and the verification efficiency.

C compilation	Safety-Assured	BeagleBone
Binary File Size KB	302	683
Bug in IEC Standard Detected	6(verification)	1(Simulink Design Verifier)
Injected Division by Zero Detected	10/10(verification)	4/10(Simulink Design Verifier)

3 Experiment Results

To evaluate the effectiveness of the proposed approach, we apply it to the design of MVBC and compare it with BeagleBone [11], which is the most recently available design framework for MVBC based on Simulink. More specifically, we formalize 92 critical model verifiable safety requirements and 29 critical implementation verifiable safety requirements. During the verification process of the proposed approach, 11 requirement violates in the model or the implementation level. After discussion with the engineers from CRRC, 5 requirements are violated because of the error brought by our modeling behavior, and 6 requirements are violated because of the error of the control logic described in the standard. While in the verification process of BeagleBone, only one violation is detected due to the limited specification and verification of Simulink Design Verifier. For the second type of violation, we need to revise the timed automata model as well as the back end IEC standard according to analysis results of counter examples. Besides, these violations are consistent to existing works [7–10] and have already been confirmed and would be revised in the new version of IEC standard 61375. After revision, both the model level verification and the runtime verification reports no violation (Table 1).

Then, the generated code according to the revised model and the integrated executable system with the eCos (Embedded Configurable Operation System) is synthesized. Then, the synthesized binary files for the integrated C code can be loaded and run on ARM7-STM32F407IGH6 processor. The binary file is 302 kb and 683 kb for the code generated by Times and BeagleBone respectively. The difference is mainly derived from the fact that BeagleBone use Simulink C code generator to generate many extra configuration files and introduces many libraries for scalability. To test the reliability of the system as well as some requirements that can not be formalized, we connect the widely-used industrial product MVBC card D113 with our synthesized MVBC for real-time communication. We use the application running on the industrial computer to monitor communication, and read the message data from memory. It shows that the communications confirm to the requirements defined in the part two of standard IEC 61375.

4 Conclusion

In this paper, we present a formal model-driven engineering approach to establishing a safety-assured implementation of MVBC based on the generic reference models and requirements described in the International Electrotechnical Commission (IEC) standard 61375. The design part mainly includes formal model construction, code generation and integration, and the safety-assured part mainly includes model level verification and implementation level verification. During the engineering practice, several logic inconsistencies in the original standard are detected and corrected.

Acknowledgements. This research is sponsored in part by NSFC Program (No. 91218302, No. 61527812), National Science and Technology Major Project (No. 2016ZX01038101), Tsinghua University Initiative Scientific Research Program (20131089331), MIIT IT funds (Research and application of TCN key technologies) of China, and the National Key Technology R&D Program (No. 2015BAG14B01-02), Austrian Science Fund (FWF) under grants S11402-N23 (RiSE/SHiNE) and Z211-N23.

References

1. Amnell, T., Fersman, E., Mokrushin, L., Pettersson, P., Yi, W.: TIMES b— A tool for modelling and implementation of embedded systems. In: Katoen, J.-P., Stevens, P. (eds.) TACAS 2002. LNCS, vol. 2280, pp. 460–464. Springer, Heidelberg (2002). doi:10.1007/3-540-46002-0_32
2. Behrmann, G., David, A., Larsen, K.G.: A tutorial on UPPAAL. In: Bernardo, M., Corradini, F. (eds.) SFM-RT 2004. LNCS, vol. 3185, pp. 200–236. Springer, Heidelberg (2004). doi:10.1007/978-3-540-30080-9_7
3. International Electrotechnical Commission et al.: IEC 61375-1, Train Communication Network (2011)
4. Havelund, K.: Runtime verification of C programs. In: Suzuki, K., Higashino, T., Ulrich, A., Hasegawa, T. (eds.) FATES/TestCom -2008. LNCS, vol. 5047, pp. 7–22. Springer, Heidelberg (2008). doi:10.1007/978-3-540-68524-1_3
5. Iturbe, X., Zuloaga, A., Jiménez, J., Lázaro, J., Martín, J.L.: A novel SoC architecture for a MVB slave node. In: IECON 2008. IEEE (2008)
6. Jiang, Y., Gu, M., Sun, J.: Verification and implementation of the protocol standard in train control system. In: IEEE 37th Annual Computer Software and Applications Conference (COMPSAC), pp. 549–558 (2014)
7. Song, H., et al.: Data-centered runtime verification of wireless medical cyber-physical system. IEEE Transactions on Industry Informatics (2016)
8. Yang, Y., et al.: From stateflow simulation to verified implementation: a verification approach and a real-time train controller design. In: 2016 IEEE Real-Time and Embedded Technology and Applications Symposium (RTAS) (2016)
9. Zhang, H., et al.: Design and optimization of multi-clocked embedded systems using formal technique. IEEE Trans. Ind. Electron. **62**(2), 1270–1278 (2014)
10. Jiang, Y., et al.: Design of mixed synchronous/asynchronous systems with multiple clocks. IEEE Trans. Parallel Distrib. Syst. **26**, 2220–2232 (2014)
11. Aarthipriya, R., Chitrapreyanka, S.: FPGA implementation of multifunction vehicle bus controller with class 2 interface and verification using Beaglebone Black (2015)
12. Yunxiao, F., Zhi, L., Jingjing, P., Hongyu, L., Jiang, S.: Applying systems thinking approach to accident analysis in China: case study of "7.23" Yong-Tai-Wen high-speed train accident. Saf. Sci. **76**, 190–201 (2015)

Taming Interrupts for Verifying Industrial Multifunction Vehicle Bus Controllers

Han Liu[1,2,3(✉)], Yu Jiang[1,2,3], Huafeng Zhang[1,2,3], Ming Gu[1,2,3,4], and Jiaguang Sun[1,2,3]

[1] Key Laboratory for Information System Security, Ministry of Education, Beijing, China
[2] Tsinghua National Laboratory for Information Science and Technology, Beijing, China
[3] School of Software, Tsinghua University, Beijing, China
liuhan0518@gmail.com
[4] China Railway Rolling Stock Corporation (CRRC), Beijing, China

Abstract. Multifunction Vehicle Bus controllers (MVBC) are safety-critical sub-systems in the industrial train communication network. As an interrupt-driven system, MVBC is practically hard to verify. The reasons are twofold. First, MVBC introduces the concurrency semantics of deferred interrupt handlers and communication via hardware registers, making existing formalism infeasible. Second, verifying MVBC requires considering the environmental features (*i.e.*, interrupt ordering), which is hard to model and reason. To overcome these limitations, we proposed a novel framework for formal verification on MVBC. First, we formalized the concurrency semantics of MVBC and described a *sequentialization* technique so that well-designed sequential analyses can be performed. Moreover, we introduced the *happen-before interrupt graph* to model interrupt dependency and further eliminate false alarms. The framework scaled well on an industrial MVBC product from `CRRC Inc.` and found 3 severe software bugs, which were all confirmed by engineers.

1 Introduction

Multifunction Vehicle Bus controllers (MVBC) are an essential sub-system in the industrial train communication network (TCN). Unfortunately, as an interrupt-driven system with software and hardware, MVBC is highly error-prone. Even worse, employing formal verification on MVBC is practically challenging. The reasons are twofold. First, MVBC incurs concurrency from random arrival of interrupts, asynchronous handlers and software-hardware communication via registers. Such concurrency is little clearly investigated and can fail existing analyses. Second, MVBC is reactive to environmental inputs (*i.e.*, interrupts), but their dependency, *i.e.*, in what order interrupts occur, is hard to reason.

Our Solution. We proposed a novel framework to verify MVBC in practice. We first formalized its concurrency semantics and described a *sequentialization* technique, considering asynchronous deferral and hardware register communication.

J. Fitzgerald et al. (Eds.): FM 2016, LNCS 9995, pp. 764–771, 2016.
DOI: 10.1007/978-3-319-48989-6_48

The sequentialized programs can be then verified using existing sequential verifiers. Second, we introduced the *happen-before interrupt graph* to model interrupt dependency and further prune false alarms.

Contribution. Main contributions are summarized below.

- We formalized the interrupt-driven concurrency model of MVBC-like systems.
- We proposed a sequentialization based framework to practically verify MVBC.
- We have applied the framework on a real-world industrial MVBC product and found 3 severe previously unknown bugs, which were all confirmed.

2 Multifunction Vehicle Bus Controller

MVBC is used to control the communication between the train bus and devices [5,6]. As an interrupt-driven concurrent system, MVBC consists of both software and hardware. While the classical concurrency semantics are widely discussed [3, 7,8], MVBC-like systems are relatively little studied. We first introduce two highly-relevant concurrency features.

Asynchronous Deferral. To service an interrupt request, an Interrupt Service Routine (ISR) will be invoked. ISR is prioritized and preemptive. It can asynchronously post a *deferral* into a global FIFO queue for delayed execution. Deferrals cannot preempt each other but can be preempted by other ISRs.

Hardware Registers. The communication between software and hardware of MVBC is realized via shared hardware registers. The code below defines 2 macros for register writing and reading. Particularly, strict memory consistency may be violated in this type of communication, *e.g.*, a HAL_IO_INPUT after HAL_IO_OUTPUT cannot guarantee to access the same value.

```
/* Write to hardware registers */             /* Load from hardware registers */
HAL_IO_OUTPUT(IO_RESET | __content);          HAL_IO_INPUT(__content);
```

Table 1. $\mathbb{T}$: types. $\mathbb{N}$: priority. Var: variables. i: input. r: return value. e: expression. b: basic statement. c: predicate. λ: empty rule. a: address for a register.

$$
\begin{aligned}
Prog &:= Var\ (ISR, DF)^* \quad ISR := \textbf{task}\ p\ (i:\mathbb{T}, r:\mathbb{T}, n:\mathbb{N})\ (Var\ stmt^*) \\
DF &:= \textbf{deferral}\ d\ (i:\mathbb{T}, r:\mathbb{T})\ (Var\ stmt^*) \\
stmt &:= \lambda \mid b \mid stmt; stmt \mid \textbf{while}\ c\ \textbf{do}\ stmt \mid \textbf{if}\ c\ \textbf{then}\ stmt\ \textbf{else}\ stmt \\
&\quad\ \textbf{return}\ e \mid \textbf{post}\ d \mid \textbf{mask}\ p^* \mid \textbf{unmask}\ p^* \mid \textbf{write}\ a \mid \textbf{read}\ a
\end{aligned}
$$

Formulation. First, we present an abstract language for MVBC as in Table 1. We consider a collection of ISRs and deferral with shared variables. Supported operations include basic control flow and **post** a deferral, **(un)mask** certain ISR, **write** to and **read** from hardware registers. Then, we formalize the concurrency semantics as transitions on configurations. Each configuration is $\langle P, M, R, S, Q\rangle$ where $P = ISR \cup DF$. $M \doteq P \mapsto \{Idle, Run, Pend\}$ denotes the handler state. $R = ISR \mapsto \{\mathtt{true}, \mathtt{false}\} \times \{\mathtt{true}, \mathtt{false}\}$ identifies the arrival and masking of interrupts. S is a stack for ISR with operations push, pop and get the top. Q is a queue for deferral with operations enqueue, dequeue and get the head.

The formal concurrency semantics is shown in Table 2. The DISPATCH rule models a preemption behavior of a ISR. MASK rule disables specific ISR. Without arrival of interrupts, we EXECUTE the top of the stack, or head of the queue. RETURN semantics differs in ISR and deferral. The former leads to a pop while the latter causes a dequeue. The POST of a deferral amounts to an enqueue.

Table 2. Semantics of MVBC. $i, m, n \in ISR$ $df \in DF$ $p \in P$. $\top$ is a wildcard.

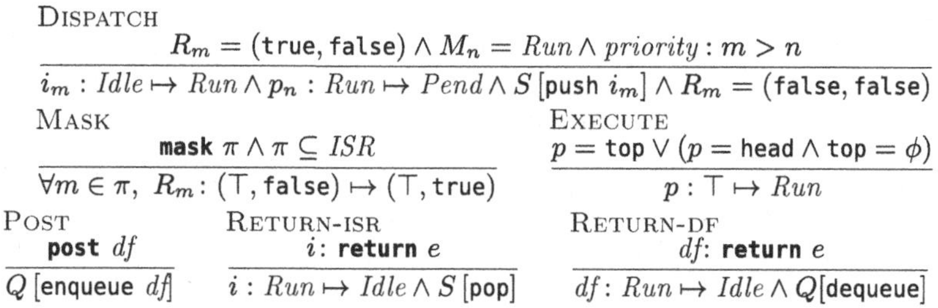

DISPATCH

$$\frac{R_m = (\mathtt{true}, \mathtt{false}) \wedge M_n = Run \wedge priority: m > n}{i_m : Idle \mapsto Run \wedge p_n : Run \mapsto Pend \wedge S\,[\mathtt{push}\ i_m] \wedge R_m = (\mathtt{false}, \mathtt{false})}$$

MASK

$$\frac{\mathtt{mask}\ \pi \wedge \pi \subseteq ISR}{\forall m \in \pi,\ R_m : (\top, \mathtt{false}) \mapsto (\top, \mathtt{true})}$$

EXECUTE

$$\frac{p = \mathtt{top} \vee (p = \mathtt{head} \wedge \mathtt{top} = \phi)}{p : \top \mapsto Run}$$

POST

$$\frac{\mathtt{post}\ df}{Q\,[\mathtt{enqueue}\ df]}$$

RETURN-ISR

$$\frac{i : \mathtt{return}\ e}{i : Run \mapsto Idle \wedge S\,[\mathtt{pop}]}$$

RETURN-DF

$$\frac{df : \mathtt{return}\ e}{df : Run \mapsto Idle \wedge Q[\mathtt{dequeue}]}$$

3 Approach

In this section, we describe a general framework for verifying MVBC. The workflow of the framework is shown in Fig. 1. Given the MVBC programs, we first employ a sequentialization via inserting *schedule functions* (Sect. 3.1). Then based on the IEC 61375 and specifications, we model the interrupt dependency using the *happen-before interrupt graph* (Sect. 3.2). The graph is leveraged to reduce the sequential programs. Next, we use an existing verifier (*e.g.*, CBMC [2]) to verify the reduced sequential programs on safety-critical properties of MVBC.

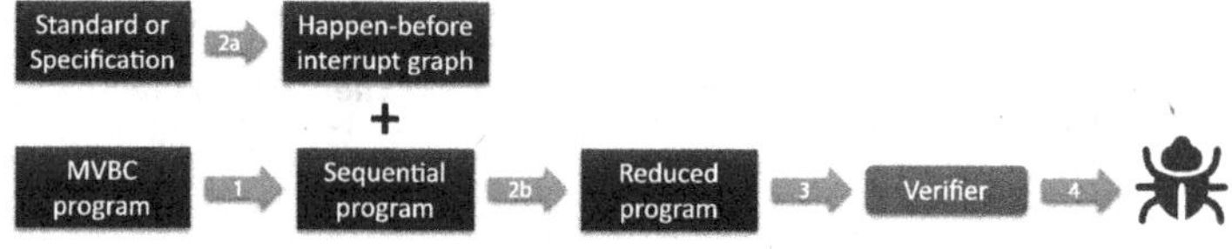

Fig. 1. The general framework for MVBC verification.

3.1 Sequentialization

The sequentialization of MVBC is realized via inserting the *schedule functions*, which can simulate the concurrency through non-deterministic function calls. For ISR, we adopt the similar sequentialization as [14] in left of Fig. 2. For deferral, we propose the `schedule_df` in right of Fig. 2 to run the FIFO queue. Furthermore, we use the `schedule_reg` below to sequentialize the communication via hardware registers. It non-deterministically modifies the register values.

```
void schedule_isr():
  int p = Prio;
  for(int i=1;i<=N;i++):
    if(prio[i]>=Prio && nondet()):
      Prio = prio[i]; ISR[i].entry();
  Prio = p;
```

```
/* Request the execution for deferral.
0 means fetching the head to run. */
void scheduler_df(int id):
  if(id != Queue->head.ID && id != 0)
    return;
  else Queue->head.entry();
```

Fig. 2. Schedule an ISR (**Left**) and a deferral (**Right**)

```
void scheduler_reg(int addr) { if(nondet()) update_reg(addr); }
```

```
1  /* A global variable x.
2  Interrupt 2 has higher
3  priority than 1. The
4  return value DF denotes
5  a post of deferral. */
6  int isr_1():
7    x = 0;
8    HAL_IO_OUTPUT(IO_RESET|x);
9    HAL_IO_INPUT(x);
10   return DONE;
11 int isr_2(){return DF;}
12 void df_2(){x=2;}
```

```
1  int isr_1():
2    x = 0; schedule_isr();
3    HAL_IO_OUTPUT(IO_RESET|x);
4    schedule_reg(ADDR);
5    HAL_IO_INPUT(x);
6    return DONE;
7  int isr_2():
8    enqueue(2); schedule_df(2);
9    return DF;
10 void df_2():
11   x=2; schedule_isr();
12   dequeue(); schedule_df(0);
```

Fig. 3. An example code before (**Left**) and after (**Right**) the sequentialization

Idea of Sequentialization. The insertion of `schedule_isr()` is described in [14]. `schedule_df()` is inserted when deferral is posted. `schedule_reg()` is inserted *after* a write and *before* a read of hardware registers. An example is shown in Fig. 3. In the right, `schedule_isr()` is inserted after an write to global variable in `isr_1()` (line 2) and `df_2()` (line 11). Because `isr_2()` has higher priority than `isr_1()`, no insertions are in `isr_2()`. `schedule_df()` is inserted at line 8 and 12 to run the deferral queue. `schedule_reg()` is inserted at line 4 to capture possible communication between line 8 and 9 in the left.

3.2 Happen-Before Interrupt Graph

Verification on MVBC requires reasoning the interrupt dependency. However, such dependency lacks formulation. For example, `IEC 61375` specifies that:

> *"After processing a main frame, a slave device will send a slave frame."*

We can conclude that no preemption occurs between interrupt handlers of main and slave frames. However, transferring this kind of knowledge into a practical use case is commonly time-consuming and error-prone. To mitigate this complexity, we proposed the *happen-before interrupt graph* (HBIG) to capture domain knowledge and automatically integrate with the verification.

The *happen-before* relation is denoted as $\prec \subseteq ISR \times ISR$. $a \prec b$ implies that `isr_a` is prior to and cannot be preempted by `isr_b`. A HBIG $\mathcal{G} = (\mathcal{V}, \mathcal{E})$, where $\mathcal{V}$ is a set of interrupts and $\mathcal{E}$ denotes a set of *happen-before* relations. HBIG can be considered as a directed graph. $a \prec b$ indicates a *path* from a to b in the graph. On the contrary, two interrupts are *unordered* if no path connects them. In the verification, a path suggests an infeasible interleaving between two interrupts. Taking the code in left of Fig. 3 as an example, if `isr_1` $\prec$ `isr_2`, the `schedule_isr` at line 2 of right of Fig. 3 can be reduced. To integrate HBIG with the sequentialization, we add the following code before line 4 in `schedule_isr` of Fig. 2 to filter out infeasible interleaving.

```
/* hb(a,b) checks the path existence between a and b. */
if(hb(id, i) || hb(i, id)) continue;
```

4 Evaluation

Target System. We selected TiMVB, an industrial MVBC product from `CRRC Inc.`, as shown in left of Fig. 4. The ARM processor runs C programs on the `eCos`[1] operating system, and communicates with an FPGA via general-purpose input output (GPIO) pins, which are hardware registers as in Sect. 2.

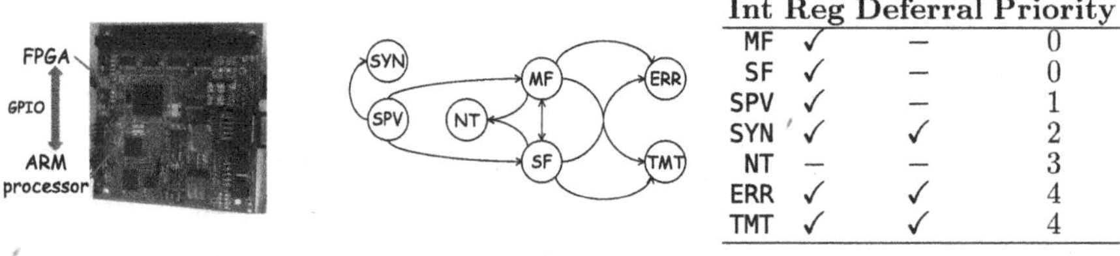

Int	Reg	Deferral	Priority
MF	✓	–	0
SF	✓	–	0
SPV	✓	–	1
SYN	✓	✓	2
NT	–	–	3
ERR	✓	✓	4
TMT	✓	✓	4

Fig. 4. TiMVB; HBIG; **Int**: interrupt, **Reg**: register communications.

TiMVB contains 4923 lines of C code and handles 7 types of interrupts, as in right of Fig. 4 Except NT, other interrupts all communicate with FPGA via

[1] http://ecos.sourceware.org/.

registers. 5 priorities are set (0 is the highest), indicating a large state space. Based on `IEC 61375` and discussions with domain experts, we developed an HBIG as in middle of Fig. 4. In specific, `SPV` *happen-before* all interrupts since it can reach any other nodes. `MF` and `SF` *happen-before* other less-prioritized interrupts except `SYN`, which implies that `SYN` interrupt can arrive in arbitrary orders.

Verification Results. In the verification, we focused on two kinds of safety-critical properties: (1) Data Validity (DV), Device state data must hold valid values. (2) Frame Consistency (FC), Frame data must match frame types.

The verification results are shown in Fig. 5. We have exposed 1 bug on data validity property (ID=2) and 2 bugs on frame consistency property (ID=6,7). We compared two verification strategies: with and without an HBIG. Based on Fig. 5, HBIG helped improve the time efficiency from 18.84 % to 67.35 %. In particular, it successfully scaled on a complex verification when non-HBIG strategy failed due to memory limitation (ID=4). Moreover, the non-HBIG strategy reported a false positive (ID=3) due to infeasible interleaving. HBIG based strategy, which sequentialized the programs with well-formalized concurrency semantics, generated no false alarms.

ID	Type	Time (Second)			Outcome	
		NoHB	HB	Improve	NoHB	HB
1	DV	639.20	488.17	23.63 %	TRUE	TRUE
2	DV	25.42	8.30	67.35 %	FALSE	FALSE
3	DV	37.68	211.75	−	FALSE	TRUE
4	DV	OOM	871.34	+∞	−	TRUE
5	DV	727.18	590.16	18.84 %	TRUE	TRUE
6	FC	23.41	10.06	57.03 %	FALSE	FALSE
7	FC	29.67	15.88	46.48 %	FALSE	FALSE

Fig. 5. Verification results. NoHB: without HBIG. HB: with HBIG. OOM: Out of memory. Framed cell: False alarm.

```
1  void syncprocess_handle():
2    if (sync_checkbit == HAL_IO_ENUM_SYNC_STATUS):
3      mvb_arm_receive_sync(mvb_device_status_16);
4      mvb_device_status = *((MVB_DEVICE_STATUS*) & mvb_device_status_16);
```

```
1  #define mvb_arm_send_main_frame(__content)
2      ba_mf = __content; HAL_IO_OUTPUT(IO_RESET | __content); \
3      HAL_IO_FRAME_WRITE_SIGNAL_PULSE; HAL_IO_SEND_MAIN_FRAME;
```

Two uncovered bugs are shown above (upper ID=2, lower ID=7). The upper bug occurs when the ISR of `SYN` interrupt is preempted by `MF` or `SF` between line 3 and 4. In that case, a *write-write-read* data race is triggered to taint the global variable `mvb_device_status_16`. As for the lower bug, content of a main frame is set (line 2) and then the frame type is set (line 3). A frame inconsistency manifests when the sending operation of the hardware is performed in between, causing a slave frame sent with the main frame content.

5 Lessons Learned

i. Software correctness is not system reliability. Verification of embedded software should reason their interactions with hardware, including the interaction semantics and how it is implemented. In our case, without considering hardware registers in TiMVB, the frame consistency bugs cannot be uncovered.

ii. "Interfaces" of formal methods are desired. One way to facilitate the practical application of formal methods is a convenient interface to the practice. In our case study, engineers used to hard-code the interrupt dependency, which is imprecise and error-prone. From this point, the HBIG is practically useful by encapsulating the implementation and offering high-level abstractions.

6 Related Work

Program Sequentialization. The original idea of sequentialization was to transform a program within bounded context switches [8,10]. Later attempts have considered balancing efficiency and accuracy [4,13], and handling asynchrony [3,7,14]. We extended the sequentialization by modeling deferral into a FIFO queue and leveraging HBIG for further reduction.

Analyses on Interrupts. Interrupt-driven software has been widely discussed [1,9,14]. Schwarz *et al.* provided static analyses on prioritized tasks under dynamical scheduling [12]. Schlich *et al.* proposed to reduce non-nested interrupts [11]. Our insight is to formalize and analyze more real-world interrupt semantics, including deferral and communication via hardware registers, which have long been ignored.

7 Conclusion

In this paper, we introduced a verification framework for MVBC systems. The framework is based on the formal semantics of MVBC to sequentialize interrupt handlers and model their dependency. On an industrial product TiMVB, the framework helped find two types of previously unknown defects, which were confirmed by engineers. Our future plan includes verifying extensive real-world systems and building industry-friendly tools.

Acknowledgement. This research is sponsored by NSFC Program (No.91218 302, No.61527812), National Science and Technology Major Project (N0.16ZX010 38101), MIIT IT funds (Research and application of TCN key technologies) of China, and National Key Technology R&D Program (No.2015BAG14B01-02).

References

1. Brylow, D., Damgaard, N., Palsberg, J.: Static checking of interrupt-driven software. In: ICSE 2001, pp. 47–56 (2001)
2. Clarke, E., Kroening, D., Lerda, F.: A tool for checking ANSI-C programs. In: Jensen, K., Podelski, A. (eds.) TACAS 2004. LNCS, vol. 2988, pp. 168–176. Springer, Heidelberg (2004)
3. Emmi, M., Lal, A., Qadeer, S.: Asynchronous programs with prioritized task-buffers. In: FSE 2012, pp. 48:1–48:11. ACM, New York (2012)
4. Inverso, O., Tomasco, E., Fischer, B., La Torre, S., Parlato, G.: Bounded model checking of multi-threaded C programs via lazy sequentialization. In: Biere, A., Bloem, R. (eds.) CAV 2014. LNCS, vol. 8559, pp. 585–602. Springer, Heidelberg (2014)
5. Jiang, Y., et al.: Design and optimization of multiclocked embedded systems using formal techniques. TIE **62**, 1270–1278 (2015)
6. Jiang, Y., et al.: Design of mixed synchronous/asynchronous systems with multiple clocks. TPDS **26**, 2220–2232 (2015)
7. Kidd, N., Jagannathan, S., Vitek, J.: One stack to run them all: reducing concurrent analysis to sequential analysis under priority scheduling. In: Pol, J., Weber, M. (eds.) SPIN 2010. LNCS, vol. 6349, pp. 245–261. Springer, Heidelberg (2010)
8. Lal, A., Reps, T.: Reducing concurrent analysis under a context bound to sequential analysis. FMSD **35**(1), 73–97 (2009)
9. Liu, H., et al.: idola: bridge modeling to verification and implementation of interrupt-driven systems. In: TASE, pp. 193–200 (2014)
10. Qadeer, S., Wu, D.: Kiss: keep it simple and sequential. In: PLDI 2004, pp. 14–24 (2004)
11. Schlich, B., Noll, T., Brauer, J., Brutschy, L.: Reduction of interrupt handler executions for model checking embedded software. In: Namjoshi, K., Zeller, A., Ziv, A. (eds.) HVC 2009. LNCS, vol. 6405, pp. 5–20. Springer, Heidelberg (2011). doi:10.1007/978-3-642-19237-1_5
12. Schwarz, D., et al.: Static analysis of interrupt-driven programs synchronized via the priority ceiling protocol. In: POPL, pp. 93–104 (2011)
13. Tomasco, E., Inverso, O., Fischer, B., Torre, S., Parlato, G.: Verifying concurrent programs by memory unwinding. In: Baier, C., Tinelli, C. (eds.) TACAS 2015. LNCS, vol. 9035, pp. 551–565. Springer, Heidelberg (2015). doi:10.1007/978-3-662-46681-0_52
14. Wu, X., Chen, L., Mine, A., Dong, W., Wang, J.: Numerical static analysis of interrupt-driven programs via sequentialization. In: EMSOFT 2015, pp. 55–64 (2015)

Rule-Based Incremental Verification Tools Applied to Railway Designs and Regulations

Bjørnar Luteberget[1(✉)], Christian Johansen[2], Claus Feyling[1], and Martin Steffen[2]

[1] RailComplete AS, Sandvika, Norway
{bjlut,clfey}@railcomplete.no
[2] Department of Informatics, University of Oslo, Oslo, Norway
{cristi,msteffen}@ifi.uio.no

Abstract. When designing railway infrastructure (tracks, signalling systems, etc.), railway engineers need to keep in mind numerous regulations for ensuring safety. Many of these regulations are simple, but demonstrably conforming with them often involves tedious manual work. We have worked on automating the verification of regulations against CAD designs, and integrated a verification tool and methodology into the tool chain of railway engineers. Automatically generating a model from the railway designs and running the verification tool on it is a valuable step forward, compared to manually reviewing the design for compliance and consistency. To seamlessly integrate the consistency checking into the CAD work-flow of the design engineers, however, requires a fast, on-the-fly mechanism, similar to real-time compilation done in standard programming tools.

In consequence, in this paper we turn to *incremental* verification and investigate existing rule-based tools, looking at various aspects relevant for engineering railway designs. We discuss existing state-of-the-art methods for incremental verification in the setting of rule-based modelling. We survey and compare relevant tools (ca. 30) and discuss if/how they could be integrated in a railway design environment, such as CAD software. We examine and compare four promising tools: XSB Prolog, a standard tool in the Datalog community, RDFox from the semantic web community, Dyna from the AI community, and LogicBlox, a proprietary solution.

1 Introduction

Verification of railway systems using formal methods often focuses on interlocking and dynamic safety of the implementation. Often overlooked, however, is the early-stage planning process for railway systems where the design decisions are made. The design process is concerned with producing a specification of the

Part of this research has been supported by the Norwegian Research Council project RailCons (Automated Methods and Tools for Ensuring Consistency of Railway Designs).

J. Fitzgerald et al. (Eds.): FM 2016, LNCS 9995, pp. 772–778, 2016.
DOI: 10.1007/978-3-319-48989-6_49

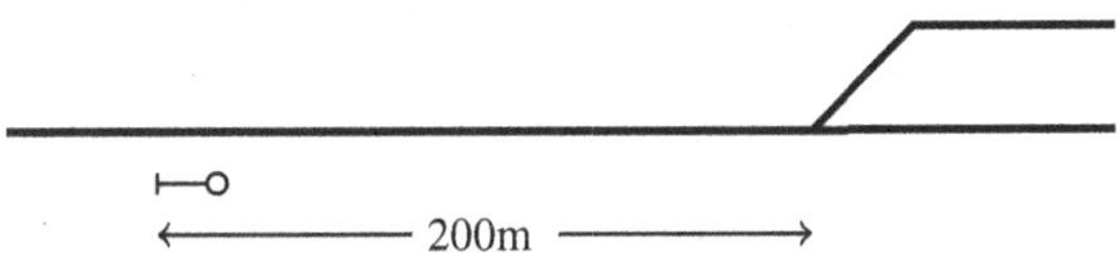

Fig. 1. Home signal layout rule example (Property 1).

railway infrastructure, which we call *the design*, with documented safety and performance requirements. During that phase, it is important to *efficiently handle changes* in track layouts, component capabilities, performance requirements, etc. Tool support for this process is practically unavailable. Such tools would be concerned with verification of the railway infrastructure w.r.t. technical regulations, typically expressing static properties concerned with object properties, topology, geometry, and interlocking specifications.

As an example of a regulation to be verified, we consider the *home signal* rule (Property 1 below, see also Fig. 1). Ensuring that a design is compliant with a large set such regulations could give significant productivity and quality gains, especially if the compliance information could be immediately available after making changes to the design.

Property 1 (Home Signal Layout Rule). *A* home main signal *shall be placed at least 200 m in front of the first controlled, facing switch in the entry train path.*

Section 2 shortly describes the current state of our tool for checking consistency of industrial railway designs, introducing the practical problem of on-the-fly verification. Sect. 3 then describes the *existing techniques for incremental verification* for rule-based modelling. We then survey in Sect. 4 existing tools related to Datalog and focus on those supporting incremental verification. We are particularly interested in industry-ready tools. We end in Sect. 5 by comparing efficiency gains due to incremental evaluation when applied to the industrial case study of the Arna station reconstruction, and suggesting how existing tools could be improved to help make our incremental verification production-ready.

2 Integrating Verification Tools into Railway Engineering Tools

In [8], we presented and demonstrated a verification tool for static infrastructure properties based on evaluation of Datalog rules. The tool is integrated into the RailCOMPLETE® software, a professional railway CAD program for producing and editing *railML* representations of railway infrastructure. The railML format [11] is an international standard for describing railway infrastructure, time tables, and rolling stock information. The railML description is transformed into a logical model for verification.

The modelling and verification has the following characteristics: it (1) uses Datalog (many properties depend on graph reachability encoded as transitive

```
%| rule: Home signal too close to first facing switch.
%| type: technical
%| severity: error
homeSignalBeforeFacingSwitchError(S,SW) :-
    firstFacingSwitch(B,SW,DIR),
    homeSignalBetween(S,B,SW),
    distance(S,SW,DIR,L), L < 200.
```

Fig. 2. Structured comments attached to a rule expressing violation of a regulation.

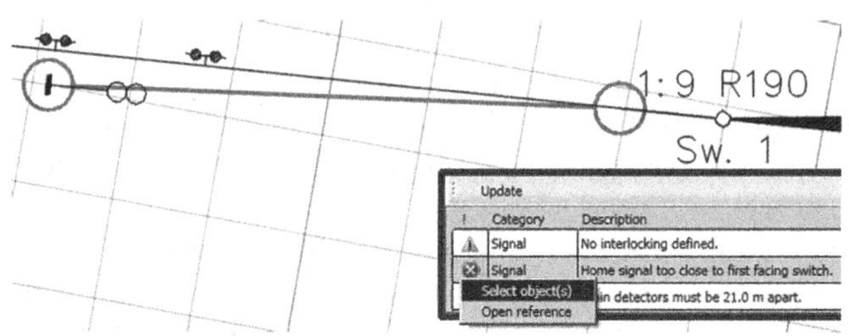

Fig. 3. Counter-example presentation within the RailCOMPLETE® CAD tool.

closures), and uses (2) negation with negation-as-failure semantics (stratified negation). Finally, and going beyond pure Datalog, it uses (3) arithmetic, to model aspects such as distances.

Our prototype implementation uses *XSB Prolog* which does conventional top-down Prolog search, combined with tabling of recursive predicates, ensuring the Datalog properties of termination and polynomial running time. Figure 2 shows an example rule input corresponding to a railway property, whereas Fig. 3 shows the graphical representation indicating to the engineer which regulation is violated. The tight integration into the CAD program and, as such, into the engineer's design process, creates the demand for fast re-evaluation of all conclusions upon small changes to the railway designs. The performance studies of [8] show that the current implementation is well acceptable for "one-shot" validation even for realistic designs with running times in the range of seconds (the tool is applied to a real train station currently under construction). However, it is not fast enough to *smoothly* and transparently be integrated such that it can automatically rerun the complete verification for each small change.

3 Incremental Verification for On-the-Fly Performance

An alternative approach that promises to be more efficient is *incremental verification*: instead of solving logic programs from scratch for each verification run, it tries to materialize all consequences of the base facts and then maintains this view under fact updates. The existing literature on incremental materialization of Datalog programs gives various strategies for doing this efficiently. We briefly survey methods for incremental evaluation of Datalog programs, also known in the deductive database literature as the *view maintenance* problem [5] [1, Chap. 22]. We also survey relevant tools and compare their features (e.g., availability, industry-quality, performance) in the context of our verification tool. A more thorough evaluation appears in a long version of this work [9].

Datalog systems use rules to derive a set of consequences (*intensional* facts), from a given set of base facts (*extensional* facts). Typically, Datalog systems use a *bottom-up* (or *forward-chaining*) evaluation strategy, where all possible consequences are materialized [15, Chap. 3] [1, Chap. 13]. This simplifies query answering to simply looking up values in the materialization tables. Any change to the base facts, however, will invalidate the materialization. Several approaches have been suggested to reduce the work required to find a new materialization after changing the base facts.

First, if considering only addition of facts to positive Datalog programs, i.e. without negation, then the standard *semi-naive* algorithm [15, Chap. 3] [1, Chap. 13] is already an efficient approach. The real challenge are non-monotonic changes, i.e., removing facts appearing positively in rules or adding facts appearing negatively in rules. Non-monotonicity is essential in our railway infrastructure verification rules. Graph reachability is prominent in many of the regulations for railway signalling, so efficiently maintaining rules involving transitivity is also essential. Some algorithms, such as truth maintenance systems [3], work by storing more information (in addition to the logical consequences) about the *supporting facts* for derived facts, so that removal of supporting facts may or may not remove a derived fact. This allows efficient removal of facts, at the cost of requiring more time and memory for normal derivations. Another class of algorithms, working *without* additional "bookkeeping", can be more efficient if the re-evaluation of sets of facts is relatively easy compared to re-materializing all facts. The Propagation-Filtering algorithm [7] works on each removed fact separately, propagating it through to all rules which depend on it. In contrast, the Delete-Rederive (DRed) algorithm [6] is rule-oriented and works on sets of facts, first over-approximating all possible deletions that may result from a change in base facts, then re-deriving any still-supported facts from the over-deleted state before finally continuing semi-naive materialization on newly added facts. Recently, the Forward/Backward/Forward (FBF) algorithm [10] used in RDFox improved the DRed algorithm in most cases by searching for alternative support (and caching the results) for each potentially deleted fact before proceeding to the next fact. Notably, this method performs better on rules involving *transitivity*, as deletions do not propagate further than necessary.

4 Datalog Tools for Incremental Verification

Our procedure uses rule-based modelling and verification techniques in the style of Datalog. In consequence, we perform a survey of Datalog-based and related tools. The logic programs for our verification make use of recursive predicates, stratified negation, and arithmetic. Therefore, we pay particular attention to tools that at least satisfy these needs. In addition, we are looking for high performance on relatively small (in-memory) data sets, so light-weight library-style logic engines are preferred. High-performance distributed "big data" type of tools have less value in this context.

XSB Prolog continuously developed since 1990, has constantly been pushing the state of the art in high-performance Prolog. XSB is especially known for its tabling support [14], which allows fast Datalog-like evaluation of logic programs without restricting ISO Prolog. The tabling support was extended to allow incremental evaluation [12], and these features have been under continued development and seem to have reached a mature state [13]. For some applications, however, the additional memory usage for incremental tabling can lead to a significant increase in the total memory needed.

RDFox is a multicore-scalable in-memory RDF triple store with Datalog reasoning. It reads semantic web formats (RDF/OWL) and stores RDF triples, but also includes a Datalog-like input language which can describe SWRL rules. This rule language has been extended to include stratified negation and arithmetic. The RDFox system also implements a new algorithm called FBF for incremental evaluation [10].
RDFox stores internally only triples as in RDF, which, in Datalog, corresponds to only using unary and binary predicates. A method of reifying the rules for higher-arity Datalog predicates into binary predicates allows RDFox to calculate any-arity Datalog programs. However, this requires separate rules for each component of the predicate, and when doing incremental evaluation, the FBF algorithm's backward chaining step then examines all combinations of components potentially involved. Because of this problem, using RDFox incrementally did not improve running times in our case study.

LogicBlox is a programming platform [2] for combining transactions with analytics in enterprise application areas including web-based retail planning and insurance. It uses a typed, Datalog-based custom language LogiQL and has a comprehensive development framework. It claims support for incremental verification, but we could not evaluate it on our railway example due to absence of freely downloadable distributions.

Dyna is a promising new Datalog-like language for modern statistical AI systems [4]. It has currently not matured sufficiently for our application, but its techniques are promising, and we hope to see it more fully developed in the future.

Many other Datalog tools are available (around 30), few of them supporting incremental evaluation. An overview and our brief evaluation of them can be found in the technical report [9]. We hope to include these findings also in the Wikipedia page for Datalog.[1]

5 Efficiency Gains, Shortcomings, and Possible Ways Forward

Table 1 compares the running time and memory usage for the verification on Arna station used as a reference station in RailCOMPLETE. The railway

[1] https://en.wikipedia.org/wiki/Datalog#Systems_implementing_Datalog.

Table 1. Case study size and running times on a standard laptop.

			Testing station	Arna phase *A*	Arna phase *B*
Relevant components			15	152	231
Interlocking routes			2	23	42
Datalog input facts			85	8283	9159
XSB:					
Non-incrementalverif.:	Running time	(s)	0.015	2.31	4.59
	Memory	(MB)	20	104	190
Incremental verif. baseline:	Running time	(s)	0.016	5.87	12.25
	Memory	(MB)	21	1110	2195
Incr. single object update:	Running time	(s)	0.014	0.54	**0.61**
	Memory	(MB)	22	1165	2267

signalling design project for this station is currently in progress by Norconsult AS. The extra bookkeeping required in XSB to prepare for incremental evaluation requires more time and memory than non-incremental evaluation, so we include both non-incremental and from-scratch incremental evaluation in the table for comparison. We show how updates can be calculated faster than from-scratch evaluation by moving a single object (an axle counter) in and out of a disallowed area near another object (regulations require at least 21.0 m separation between train detectors). Without using abstraction methods, the case study verification uses over 2 GB of memory. So, for any hope of handling larger stations on a standard laptop or workstation, this must be reduced. We were not able to reduce memory usage in this case study using the abstraction methods in XSB (version 3.6.0).

While currently none of the tools seem to satisfy all conditions we hoped for in our integration, notably efficiency, but also maturity and stability, it should also be noted that the need for incremental evaluation has been identified by the community not only as theoretically interesting, but also as of practical importance. The RDFox developers aim to support incremental updates of higher-arity predicates in a later version. The XSB project has made efforts to improve its abstraction mechanisms, so future versions might become feasible for our use. If reducing the memory usage would require adapting a Datalog algorithm (such as DRed), then XSB's unrestricted Prolog might be a challenge. A different approach would be to extend another efficient Datalog tool, such as Soufflé, to do incremental evaluation, which could require a significant effort.

References

1. Abiteboul, S., Hull, R., Vianu, V. (eds.): Foundations of Databases, 1st edn. Addison-Wesley Longman Publishing Co., Boston (1995)
2. Aref, M., ten Cate, B., Green, T.J., Kimelfeld, B., Olteanu, D., Pasalic, E., Veldhuizen, T.L., Washburn, G.: Design and implementation of the LogicBlox system. In: SIGMOD International Conference on Management of Data, pp. 1371–1382. ACM (2015)
3. Doyle, J.: A truth maintenance system. Artif. Intell. **12**(3), 231–272 (1979)
4. Eisner, J., Filardo, N.W.: Dyna: extending datalog for modern AI. In: Moor, O., Gottlob, G., Furche, T., Sellers, A. (eds.) Datalog 2.0 2010. LNCS, vol. 6702, pp. 181–220. Springer, Heidelberg (2011). doi:10.1007/978-3-642-24206-9_11
5. Gupta, A., Mumick, I.S., et al.: Maintenance of materialized views: problems, techniques, and applications. IEEE Data Eng. Bull. **18**(2), 3–18 (1995)
6. Gupta, A., Mumick, I.S., Subrahmanian, V.S.: Maintaining views incrementally. In: SIGMOD International Conference on Management of Data, pp. 157–166. ACM (1993)
7. Harrison, J.V., Dietrich, S.W.: Maintenance of materialized views in a deductive database: an update propagation approach. In: Workshop on Deductive Databases, pp. 56–65 (1992)
8. Luteberget, B., Johansen, C., Steffen, M.: Rule-based consistency checking of railway infrastructure designs. In: Ábrahám, E., Huisman, M. (eds.) IFM 2016. LNCS, vol. 9681, pp. 491–507. Springer, Heidelberg (2016). doi:10.1007/978-3-319-33693-0_31
9. Luteberget, B., Johansen, C., Steffen, M.: Rule-based consistency checking of railway infrastructure designs (long version). Technical report 450, University of Oslo (IFI) (2016)
10. Motik, B., Nenov, Y., Piro, R.E.F., Horrocks, I.: Incremental update of datalog materialisation: the backward/forward algorithm. In: Proceedings of AAAI 2015. AAAI Press (2015)
11. Nash, A., Huerlimann, D., Schütte, J., Krauss, V.P.: RailML – a standard data interface for railroad applications, pp. 233–240. WIT Press (2004)
12. Saha, D., Ramakrishnan, C.R.: Incremental evaluation of tabled logic programs. In: Palamidessi, C. (ed.) ICLP 2003. LNCS, vol. 2916, pp. 392–406. Springer, Heidelberg (2003). doi:10.1007/978-3-540-24599-5_27
13. Swift, T.: Incremental tabling in support of knowledge representation and reasoning. Theory Pract. Log. Program. **14**(4–5), 553–567 (2014)
14. Swift, T., Warren, D.S.: XSB: extending Prolog with tabled logic programming. Theory Pract. Log. Program. **12**(1–2), 157–187 (2012)
15. Ullman, J.D.: Principles of Database and Knowledge-base systems, vol. I & II. Computer Society Press (1988)

RIVER: A Binary Analysis Framework Using Symbolic Execution and Reversible x86 Instructions

Teodor Stoenescu[1], Alin Stefanescu[2(✉)], Sorina Predut[2], and Florentin Ipate[2]

[1] Bitdefender, Bucharest, Romania
[2] University of Bucharest, Bucharest, Romania
alin@fmi.unibuc.ro

Abstract. We present a binary analysis framework based on symbolic execution with the distinguishing capability to execute stepwise forward and also backward through the execution tree. It was developed internally at Bitdefender and code-named RIVER. The framework provides components such as a taint engine, a dynamic symbolic execution engine, and integration with Z3 for constraint solving.

1 Introduction

Given the nowadays extreme interconnectivity between multiple systems, networks and (big) data pools, the field of cybersecurity is a vitally important aspect, for which concentrated efforts and resources are invested. To mention only two recent examples in this direction, European Union just launched a new public-private partnership on cybersecurity which is expected to trigger a €1.8 billion of investment by 2020 [1] in advanced research and cooperation to improve the defence against the myriad of security attacks, and US currently organises, through DARPA, a cybersecurity grand challenge (CGC) [2], where successful teams compete to analyse and fix a benchmark of binary files using a combination of dynamic and static analysis, concolic, and fuzz testing.

Almost all the tools on the security market which aim to detect vulnerabilities of source or binary code employ static analysis or, more rarely, dynamic analysis through random values, a technique called fuzz testing. This may be more efficient than the alternative of symbolic execution that we explore here, but can miss many deeper or more insidious security issues. Symbolic execution is a promising approach whose foundational principles were laid thirty years ago [3], but which only recently started to regain attention from the research community due to advancement in constraint solving, various combinations of concrete and symbolic execution, and more computing power to fight the usual state explosion problem [4]. The basic idea of symbolic execution is to mark (some of) the program variables as symbolic rather than concrete and execute the program symbolically by accumulating constraints on those variables along the different paths explored in the execution tree.

J. Fitzgerald et al. (Eds.): FM 2016, LNCS 9995, pp. 779–785, 2016.
DOI: 10.1007/978-3-319-48989-6_50

Most of the symbolic execution tools work on source code or bytecode [5–7] rather than binary code [8–10]. However, binary code analysis is a very difficult task due to its complexity and lower level constructs. On the other hand, it is better to run the analysis directly at binary level, because this is the code which is executed by the operating system. Moreover, in cybersecurity, usually only the binary file is available, so recent research efforts are invested into dynamic analysis of binary files [2] with companies such as Bitdefender joining the trend.

Bitdefender is a Romanian software security company and the creator of one of the world's fastest and most effective lines of internationally certified security software and award-winning protection since 2001 [11]. Today, Bitdefender secures the digital experience of 500 million home and corporate users across the globe and, for that, Bitdefender is constantly performing research activities in the software security area. The RIVER framework is an example of such internal research effort with 2 person-years invested in the project until now.

Contributions: The main differentiator of RIVER is the design and implementation of a set of extended reversible x86 instructions, which allows an efficient control of the execution and their integration into a symbolic execution framework. For that, the following artifacts were created: RIVER intermediate representation, which adds necessary and sufficient information to the x86 set of instructions in order to efficiently "undo" the operations when needed or to track certain variables as tainted; dedicated taint analysis and symbolic execution engines based on the above; and, as a byproduct, a debugger at binary level with forward and backward step execution capabilities.

A technical report on RIVER is online at: http://tinyurl.com/river-tr-2016

2 Description of the Framework

This section details the overall design of the RIVER framework, which is shown in Fig. 1. RIVER (spelled backwards) stands for the *"REVersible Intermediate Representation"*. RIVER has a fixed length extended x86 instruction set and was designed to be efficiently translated to and from x86 normal ("forward") instructions. Its main novelty is the introduction of reverse ("backward") instructions. Also, specific tracking instructions were added to enable the taint analysis. This intermediate representation is depicted in the left hand side of Fig. 1. The RIVER code is obtained from an input as x86 native binary code (see bottom-left corner of Fig. 1) through the dynamic binary instrumentation component, by means of disassembly. Then, modified code is used by the components for on-the-fly reversible execution and taint analysis. All these are used by the symbolic execution engine which also uses a state-of-the-art SMT solver, Z3 [12], for dealing with the constraints for the symbolic variables (see top of Fig. 1) but also on-demand snapshots to save certain memory states. All these and various other aspects are discussed in this section.

RIVER Intermediate Language. Now we describe RIVER intermediate language (IL) by presenting a couple of design choices. More details and an example is given in the RIVER technical report mentioned above. First of all, RIVER

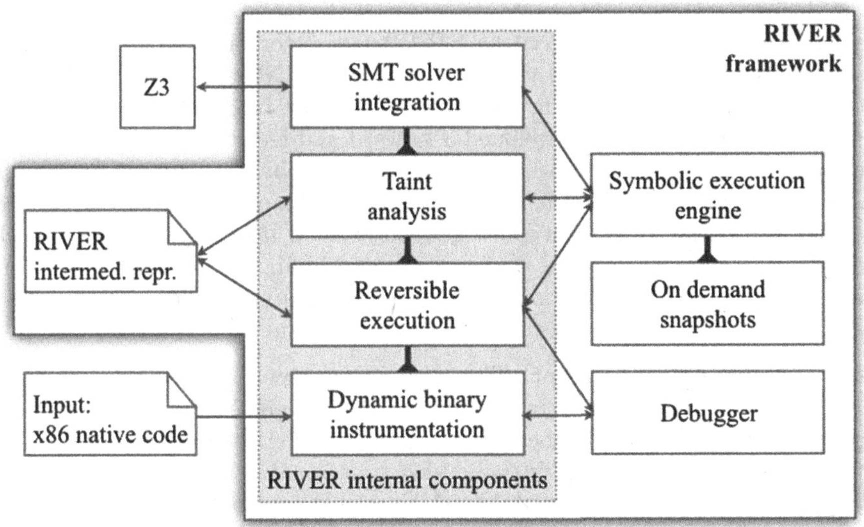

Fig. 1. RIVER architecture.

code is obtained automatically from the input native x86 through the dynamic binary instrumentation component (DBI) which is plugged in the reversible execution component (see bottom-left corner of Fig. 1). Thus, RIVER augments translated code in order to make it reversible. It uses a shadow stack in order to save instruction operands that are about to be destroyed. The original instructions are prefixed with operand saving ones. DBI also generates code for reversing the execution so that the destroyed values can be restored from the shadow stack. The RIVER instructions include modifiers, specifiers, operator codes and types as well as flags and a special field for the family of the instruction. These additional information is used to identify the prefixes and operand types and registers of the original instructions and help the data flow analysis.

RIVER DBI component also contains its own disassembler, which augments the code with the following properties: (a) implicit operands: some instructions implicitly modify registers and memory locations. These are added to the instruction as implicit operands; (b) register versioning: in order to simplify data flow analysis, the disassembler versions every register use; (c) meta operations: since the x86 instruction set is not orthogonal, some instructions may be split into several sub-operations, and (d) absolute jump addresses: relative jump operations are augmented with an additional operand containing the original instruction address. This makes it easier to compute the jump destination.

Reversible Execution Component. The reversible execution engine (see middle of Fig. 1) enables the forward and backward control of RIVER IL code that was translated from the native x86 code through the DBI component. It operates at the basic block level, i.e., a sequence of instructions terminated by a jump, by replacing the jump instruction in order to maintain the execution control. To implement reversibility, the RIVER translator inserts RIVER-specific instructions in the translated code. Then, the RIVER translator generates a second basic block for reversing the effects of the first block.

Based on the above, we developed a forward and backward binary debugger (see bottom-right of Fig. 1). We created it to be used by the software developers and security experts at Bitdefender, who need to examine dynamically certain behaviours of binary files with a fine-grained control. It operates at basic block level and it has a web front-end using JavaScript bindings for RIVER. Moreover, it offers the possibility to set breakpoints, but also so-called "waypoints", which are similar to breakpoints but referring to points in the past of the execution.

Taint Analysis Component. This component records the spread of taint through a program which uses tainted values. We implement classic taint spreading algorithms, but we adapt them to our RIVER IL to take into account also the reversibility feature. Technically, we added tracking instructions in RIVER IL which are used by DBI to enable determining locations (both memory and registers) that have been directly influenced by the input values. Initially all input locations are marked as tainted and everything else is untainted. At runtime, any instruction having a tainted operand produces tainted results (with some exceptions). There are two ways of tracking locations: using simple boolean values or binding custom values to memory locations (pointers to symbolic expressions). We use the former for simple taint analysis (if used as standalone) and the latter for symbolic execution.

Symbolic Execution Engine. In order to perform various types of analysis and testing using dynamic symbolic execution, the program has to exercise a large set of paths through its execution tree. The more paths are explored, the higher the coverage of examined behaviours. However, since the enumeration of paths is computationally expensive, several approaches have been proposed to minimize its footprint [4]. Our symbolic execution engine (see right of Fig. 1) aims to tackle the path explosion problem through its distinctive feature of reversibility. More precisely, instead of re-executing paths from the beginning each time, we generate them through backtracking (using, e.g., a depth first search strategy) and use the reversibility to keep the memory usage low for the backtracking steps. Moreover, we keep only the current path in memory rather than a whole set of paths and snapshots. Thus, we try to exploit the temporal and spatial data locality, since most execution paths have a lot of common subsequences. We do the above by keeping track of two things in parallel: a concrete stack for the current path plus, only when needed, snapshots. We optimise the latter during reverse execution using many implicit micro-snapshots as opposed to (expensive) macro-snapshots usually used by the current symbolic execution approaches. The micro-snapshots keep only the modified memory locations, so we can easily restore the previous snapshot at each program point.

It is a high priority for us to keep the snapshots at a minimum, and use it only on demand, i.e., when we cannot reverse the execution of specific instructions, such as system calls, processor exceptions, or interrupts (e.g., "`0x2e`").

The fact that they are quite uncommon also helps our performance. Furthermore, we try to avoid also the snapshots associated to system calls: we have started a detailed analysis of the reversibility of these problematic functions, by systematically examining Windows Native API (NTDLL) and implementing their inverse functions, whenever possible.

Regarding the symbolic execution engine, we do not implement "pure" symbolic execution, but use concolic execution, i.e., mixing concrete and symbolic execution at the binary level. Thus, instead of being only symbolic, the inputs have a concrete value which is a representative of the symbolic domain. Besides, the taint analysis component tracks the symbolic values.

Other Technical Aspects. RIVER framework is written in C++, having 14 KLOC in the current stable version, but is still under further development, with more components, optimisation and types of analyses to be added soon.

RIVER IL currently covers about 87 % of the integer x86 instruction set, which is the core of x86. This percentage is high enough to run most binary programs in RIVER reversible mode (including specific debugging) and for taint analysis. However, we cannot compare yet the performance of RIVER with other frameworks using symbolic execution on binaries, because the SMT solver integration does not have a high enough coverage to run on existing benchmarks.

Also, the symbolic execution engine implements only a straightforward depth-first exploration of paths using the C APIs of the RIVER components in the middle of Fig. 1, but we are now adapting several advanced features available in other state of the art symbolic execution frameworks [2,3,6,9,10,13,14]. There is great advancement in the dynamic symbolic execution research community, which was increasingly active over the last decade [3,4].

Moreover, we now develop an integration of our concolic execution with a parallel fuzz testing module, in order to increase the path coverage. We designed a distributed processing framework based on Apache Spark and Hadoop to apply fuzz testing on several parallel machines and obtain a first test suite with a good coverage. Then, we apply symbolic execution by tweaking certain paths to increase coverage, as done also by others [15,16]. This is still work in progress.

Also, RIVER IL increases sixfold the size of original x86 code. To lower this overhead, we are currently implementing some classic code optimisation methods such as instruction reordering. After first experiments, we estimate to reduce the size of RIVER code to only double the size of the original code, which should be an acceptable trade-off.

3 Conclusions

In this paper, we presented RIVER, a new binary analysis framework built from scratch with the idea of reversible basic block at its core. RIVER has all the components needed to perform dynamic symbolic execution, including: dynamic binary instrumentation and reversible execution, which enabled the construction of a dedicated debugger, and also, taint analysis and SMT solver integration, which enabled a lightweight symbolic execution engine with minimized footprint. This architecture was based on a novel intermediate representation, RIVER IL.

We plan to use RIVER internally at Bitdefender in order to both extensively test our commercial products, but also to find security vulnerabilities in external binary files, which is Bitdefender's core business. To reach this level, we need to implement several improvements mentioned before and then tune the framework for certain types of vulnerabilities. This will be our focus for the next months. Moreover, we want to experiment with idea cross-pollination between RIVER and related tools in both directions, i.e., to implement in RIVER heuristics that proved efficient in other frameworks, but also vice versa, to investigate if our concept of reversibility may improve the performance of existing tools (see how KLEE benefited from such a transfer of optimization ideas in [14]).

Acknowledgements. We thank Sorin Baltateanu and Traian Serbanuta for fruitful discussions and acknowledge partial support from MuVeT and MEASURE projects (PN-II-ID-PCE-2011-3-0688 and PN-III-P3-3.5-EUK-2016-0020).

References

1. European-Commission: Commission signs agreement with industry on cybersecurity and steps up efforts to tackle cyber-threats. http://europa.eu/rapid/press-release_IP-16-2321_en.htm. Accessed July 2016
2. DARPA-US: Cyber grand challenge (2016). http://cgc.darpa.mil
3. Cadar, C., Sen, K.: Symbolic execution for software testing: three decades later. Commun. ACM **56**(2), 82–90 (2013)
4. Pasareanu, C.S., Visser, W.: A survey of new trends in symbolic execution for software testing and analysis. STTT **11**(4), 339–353 (2009)
5. Sen, K., Marinov, D., Agha, G.: CUTE: a concolic unit testing engine for C. In: Proceedings of ESEC/FSE, pp. 263–272. ACM (2005)
6. Cadar, C., et al.: KLEE: unassisted and automatic generation of high-coverage tests for complex systems programs. In: Proceedings of OSDI, pp. 209–224. USENIX (2008)
7. Luckow, K.S., Pasareanu, C.S.: Symbolic PathFinder v7. ACM SIGSOFT Softw. Eng. Notes **39**(1), 1–5 (2014)
8. Song, D., et al.: BitBlaze: a new approach to computer security via binary analysis. In: Sekar, R., Pujari, A.K. (eds.) ICISS 2008. LNCS, vol. 5352, pp. 1–25. Springer, Heidelberg (2008). doi:10.1007/978-3-540-89862-7_1
9. Cha, S.K., Avgerinos, T., Rebert, A., Brumley, D.: Unleashing Mayhem on binary code. In: Proceedings of SP 2012, pp. 380–394. IEEE (2012)
10. Salwan, J., Saudel, F.: Triton: a dynamic symbolic execution framework. In: Proceedings of SSTIC, pp. 31–54 (2015). http://triton.quarkslab.com
11. Bitdefender (2016). http://www.bitdefender.com/business/awards.html
12. de Moura, L., Bjørner, N.: Z3: an efficient SMT solver. In: Ramakrishnan, C.R., Rehof, J. (eds.) TACAS 2008. LNCS, vol. 4963, pp. 337–340. Springer, Heidelberg (2008). doi:10.1007/978-3-540-78800-3_24
13. Chipounov, V., Kuznetsov, V., Candea, G.: The S2E platform: design, implementation, and applications. ACM Trans. Comput. Syst. **30**(1), 2 (2012)

14. Rizzi, E.F., et al.: On the techniques we create, the tools we build, and their misalignments: a study of KLEE. In: Proceedings of ICSE 2016, pp. 132–143. ACM (2016)
15. Ciortea, L., Zamfir, C., Bucur, S., Chipounov, V., Candea, G.: Cloud9: a software testing service. Oper. Syst. Rev. **43**(4), 5–10 (2009)
16. Stephens, N., et al.: Driller: augmenting fuzzing through selective symbolic execution. In: Proceedings of NDSS 2016, pp. 1–16. The Internet Society (2016)

Erratum to: Simulink to UPPAAL Statistical Model Checker: Analyzing Automotive Industrial Systems

Predrag Filipovikj[1(✉)], Nesredin Mahmud[1], Raluca Marinescu[1], Cristina Seceleanu[1], Oscar Ljungkrantz[2], and Henrik Lönn[2]

[1] Mälardalen University, Västerås, Sweden
{predrag.filipovikj, nesredin.mahmud, raluca.marinescu, cristina.seceleanu}@mdh.se
[2] Volvo Group Trucks Technology, Gothenburg, Sweden
{oscar.ljungkrantz, henrik.lonn}@volvo.com

Erratum to: Chapter "Simulink to UPPAAL Statistical Model Checker: Analyzing Automotive Industrial Systems" in: J. Fitzgerald et al. (Eds.): FM 2016: Formal Methods, LNCS, DOI: 10.1007/978-3-319-48989-6_46

The initially published version of Figure 1a and b is incorrect. This is the correct version.

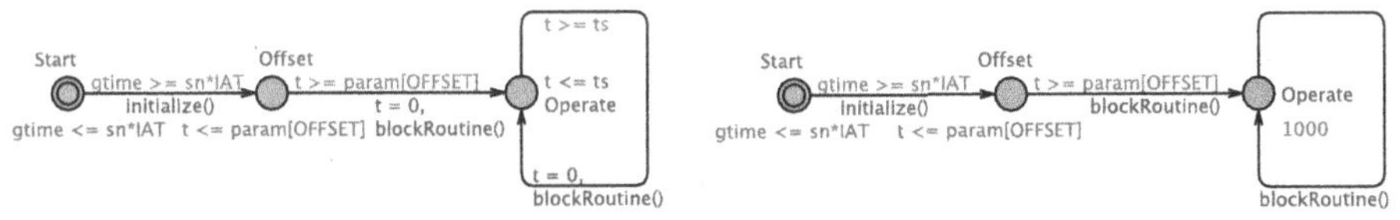

(a) Pattern for discrete blocks

(b) Pattern for continuous blocks

Fig. 1. Our used TA patterns

The updated original online version for this chapter can be found at DOI: 10.1007/978-3-319-48989-6_46

J. Fitzgerald et al. (Eds.): FM 2016, LNCS 9995, p. E1, 2016.
DOI: 10.1007/978-3-319-48989-6_51

Author Index